THE COMPLETE EUROPEAN FOOTBALL CHAMPIONSHIPS 1958-2000

Dirk Karsdorp

British Library Cataloguing in Publication Data
A catalogue record for this book is available from the British Library

ISBN: 978-1-86223-343-0

Copyright © 2017, SOCCER BOOKS LIMITED (01472 696226)
72 St. Peter's Avenue, Cleethorpes, N.E. Lincolnshire, DN35 8HU, England
Web site   www.soccer-books.co.uk
e-mail   info@soccer-books.co.uk

All rights are reserved. No part of this publication may be reproduced, stored in a retrieval system or transmitted, in any form or by any means, electronic, mechanical, photocopying, recording, or otherwise, without the prior written permission of Soccer Books Limited.

Printed in the UK by 4edge Ltd.

AN INTRODUCTION TO THE EUROPEAN FOOTBALL CHAMPIONSHIPS

ALTHOUGH the European Championship itself did not get underway until 5th April 1958, organised regional international tournaments were already well established throughout Europe.

Way back in 1883 England, Northern Ireland (then just Ireland), Scotland and Wales kicked-off the British Championship (known as the Home International Championship) followed, in 1924, by Denmark, Finland, Norway and Sweden with the Scandinavian Championship (the Nordic Cup). In 1927 Hugo Meisl, that great Austrian champion of the game, originated the Central European Championship between Austria, Czechoslovakia, Hungary, Italy and Switzerland. Indeed, although known as the Dr. Gero Cup from 1955, this tournament was variously called *The Nations Cup*, *The International Cup* and *The Europe Cup*!

Just as we have to thank a Frenchman, Jules Rimet, for the conception of the FIFA World Cup in 1930, we are indebted to another Frenchman, Henri Delaunay, for the European Championship. Monsieur Delaunay, the secretary of the French Football Federation, proposed the tournament in the mid-1950s but, sadly, died before the competition got under way, although the trophy still bears his name.

Originally known as *The European Nations' Cup*, the first tournament struggled to get off the ground and was poorly supported by the major footballing countries of Europe with just 17 entrants taking part.

However, following the success of the first series which ran between the years of 1958 and 1960, most eligible countries entered the second series running from 1962 to 1964 and now it would be unthinkable for any of the members of UEFA to boycott such an important event.

The official name of the competition was changed to *The European Football Championship* in 1966 and it is now considered to rank second only to the FIFA World Cup in order of importance in the world game.

The number of teams entering the competition has risen ever higher following the break up of the Soviet Union, the subsequent independence of nations from a number of other Eastern European countries and the recognition of smaller nations by UEFA. No fewer than 53 teams entered the qualification process for the Euro 2016 competition.

This book covers the European Football Championship from the start of the competition through to the finals tournament of Euro 2000 which was jointly hosted by Belgium and the Netherlands. Complete and comprehensive statistics are included for every game from the first game in the competition in 1958 through to the 2000 Final match itself.

A further publication containing newly-revised and collated statistics for the competition from the very first qualifier for Euro 2004 played in 2002 through to the Euro 2016 Final match is also available from Soccer Books Limited. Details of this and other statistical books which we publish are listed on the back cover.

1960 UEFA European Nations' Cup

PRELIMINARY ROUND

05-04-1959   Dalymount Park, Dublin: Republic of Ireland – Czechoslovakia   2-0 (2-0)
Republic of Ireland: James Anthony O'Neill, Brendan McNally, Noel Cantwell (C), Michael (Mick) McGrath, Charles (Charlie) Hurley, Patrick (Pat) Saward, Alfred (Alf) Ringstead, Thomas (Tommy) Hamilton, Christopher (Christy) Doyle, George Cummins, Liam Tuohy. (Coach: Committee).
Czechoslovakia: Imrich Stacho, Jirí Tichy, Ján Popluhár, Gustáv Mráz (23' Jirí Hildebrand), Svatopluk Pluskal (C), Titus Buberník, Jan Brumovsky, Anton Moravcik, Ladislav Kacáni, Pavol Molnár, Tadeás Kraus. (Coach: Rudolf Vytlacil (AUT)).
Goals: Republic of Ireland: 1-0 Liam Tuohy (22'), 2-0 Noel Cantwell (42' penalty).
Referee: Lucien Van Nuffel (BEL)   Attendance: 37.500

10-05-1959   Stadión Tehelné pole, Bratislava:
                      Czechoslovakia – Republic of Ireland   4-0 (1-0)
Czechoslovakia: Imrich Stacho, Jirí Tichy, Ján Popluhár, Ladislav Novák (C), Stefan Matlák, Titus Buberník, Ladislav Pavlovic, Adolf Scherer, Vlastimil Bubnik, Ladislav Kacáni, Milan Dolinsky. (Coach: Rudolf Vytlacil (AUT)).
Republic of Ireland: James Anthony O'Neill, Richard (Dick) Whittaker, Noel Cantwell (C), Francis (Frank) O'Farrell, Charles (Charlie) Hurley, Michael (Mick) McGrath, Alfred (Alf) Ringstead, Thomas (Tommy) Hamilton, Arthur Fitzsimons, George Cummins, Liam Tuohy. (Coach: Committee).
Goals: Czechoslovakia: 1-0 Imrich Stacho (3' penalty), 2-0 Titus Buberník (57'), 3-0 Ladislav Pavlovic (67'), 4-0 Milan Dolinsky (75').
Referee: Joseph Barbéran (FRA)   Attendance: 41.691

FIRST ROUND

28-09-1958   Central Lenin Stadium, Moscow: Soviet Union – Hungary   3-1 (3-0)
Soviet Union: Vladimir Belyaev, Vladimir Kesarev, Anatoli Maslenkin, Boris Kuznetsov, Yuri Voinov, Viktor Tsarev, Slava Metreveli, Valentin Ivanov, Nikita Simonyan (C), Alekper Mamedov, Anatoli Ilyin. (Coach: Gavril Kachalin (URS)).
Hungary: Béla Bakó, Béla Kárpáti, Ferenc Sipos, László Sárosi, Dezsö Bundzsák, Pál Berendi, László Budai (II) (C), János Göröcs, Lajos Csordás, Lajos Tichy, József Bencsics. (Coach: Lajos Baroti (HUN)).
Goals: Soviet Union: 1-0 Anatoli Ilyin (4'), 2-0 Slava Metreveli (20'), 3-0 Valentin Ivanov (32').
Hungary: 3-1 János Göröcs (84').
Referee: Alfred Grill (AUT)   Attendance: 100.572

5

01-10-1958   Parc des Princes, Paris: France – Greece   7-1 (3-0)
France: Dominique Colonna, Raymond Kaelbel, Maurice Lafont, André Lerond, Armand Penverne (C), Jean-Jacques Marcel, Yvon Douis, Just Fontaine, Raymond Kopa, Thadée Cisowski, Jean Vincent. (Coach: Albert Batteux (FRA)).
Greece: Savas Theodoridis, Takis Papoulidis, Kostas Linoxilakis (C), Mimis Stefanakos, Takis Loukanidis, Kostas Polychroniou, Lakis Emanouilidis, Dimitris Theofanis, Ilias Ifandis, Kostas Nestoridis, Giannis Cholevas. (Coach: Rino Martini (ITA)).
Goals: France: 1-0 Raymond Kopa (23'), 2-0 Just Fontaine (25'), 3-0 Thadée Cisowski (29'), 4-1 Jean Vincent (61'), 5-1 Thadée Cisowski (68'), 6-1 Just Fontaine (85'), 7-1 Jean Vincent (87').
Greece: 3-1 Ilias Ifandis (48').
Referee: Gottfried Dienst (SUI)   Attendance: 37.590

02-11-1958   Stadionul 23 August, Bucharest: Romania – Turkey   3-0 (0-0)
Romania: Costica Toma (C), Cornel Popa, Alexandru Karikas, Dumitru Macri, Vasile Alexandru, Ion Nunweiler, Nicolae Oaida, Gheorghe Constantin, Constantin Dinulescu, Haralambie Eftimie, Nicolae Tataru. (Coach: Augustin Botescu (ROM)).
Turkey: Turgay Seren (C), Ismail Kurt, Basri Dirimlili, Mustafa Ertan, Naci Erdem, Ahmet Berman, Hilmi Kiremitçi, Can Bartu, Metin Oktay, Kadri Aytaç, Lefter Küçükandonyadis. (Coach: Leandro Remondini (ITA)).
Goals: Romania: 1-0 Nicolae Oaida (62'), 2-0 Gheorghe Constantin (77'), 3-0 Constantin Dinulescu (81').
Referee: Gottfried Dienst (SUI)   Attendance: 67.200

03-12-1958   Apostolos Nikolaidis Stadium, Athens: Greece – France   1-1 (0-0)
Greece: Savas Theodoridis, Takis Papoulidis, Kostas Linoxilakis (C), Sotiris Angelopoulos, Kostas Polychroniou, Giannis Nembidis, Giorgos Sideris, Andreas Papaemanouil, Ilias Ifandis, Kostas Nestoridis, Stelios Psihos. (Coach: Andonis Miyakis (GRE)).
France: Claude Abbas, Raymond Kaelbel, Bruno Bollini, Roger Marche (C), René Ferrier, André Lerond, Maryan Wisnieski, Roland Guillas, Stéphane Bruey, Stanislas Dombeck, Léon Deladérière. (Coach: Albert Batteux (FRA)).
Goals: Greece: 1-1 Roger Marche (85' *own goal*).
France: 0-1 Stéphane Bruey (71').
Referee: Vincenzo Orlandini (ITA)   Attendance: 18.833

26-04-1959   Besiktas Inönü Stadi, Istanbul: Turkey – Romania   2-0 (1-0)
Turkey: Özcan Arkoç, Ismail Kurt, Basri Dirimlili, Mustafa Ertan, Naci Erdem, Ahmet Berman, Hilmi Kiremitçi, Can Bartu, Suat Mamat, Lefter Küçükandonyadis, Kadri Aytaç. (Coach: Leandro Remondini (ITA)).
Romania: Costica Toma, Cornel Popa, Alexandru Karikas, Valeriu Soare, Emeric Ienei, Ion Nunweiler, Nicolae Oaida, Vasile Alexandru, Ion Alexandrescu, Francisc Zavoda (I), Vasile Anghel. (Coach: Augustin Botescu (ROM)).
Goals: Turkey: 1-0 Lefter Küçükandonyadis (13'), 2-0 Lefter Küçükandonyadis (54' penalty).
Referee: Borce Nedelkovski (YUG)   Attendance: 23.567

20-05-1959   Ullevål, Oslo: Norway – Austria   0-1 (0-1)
Norway: Asbjorn Hansen, Arne Natland, Hans Jakob Mathisen, Roar Johansen, Thorbjorn Svenssen, Tore Halvorsen, Bjorn Borgen, Per Kristoffersen, Harald Hennum, Kjell Kristiansen, Rolf Birger Pedersen. (Coach: Kristian Henriksen (NOR)).
Austria: Kurt Schmied, Heinrich Büllwatsch, Erich Hasenkopf, Gerhard Hanappi, Karl Stotz, Karl Koller, Walter Horak, Adolf Knoll, Erich Hof, Josef Hamerl, Karl Skerlan. (Coach: Karl Decker (AUT)).
Goal: Austria: 0-1 Erich Hof (32').
Referee: Werner Bergmann (GDR)   Attendance: 27.566

31-05-1959   Stadion JNA, Belgrade: Yugoslavia – Bulgaria   2-0 (1-0)
Yugoslavia: Vladimir Beara, Bruno Belin, Tomislav Crnkovic, Dobroslav Krstic, Vasilije Sijakovic, Lazar Tasic, Dragoslav Sekularac, Aleksandar Petakovic, Branko Zebec, Milan Galic, Branislav Mihajlovic. (Coach: Ljubomir Lovric (YUG)).
Bulgaria: Georgi Naydenov, Ilya Kirchev, Ivan Dimitrov, Hristo Lazarov, Kiril Rakarov, Stoyan Kitov, Stefan Abadzhiev, Ivan Kolev, Panayot Panayotov (C), Bozhidar Mitkov, Aleksandar Vasilev. (Coach: Stoian Ormandjiev (BUL)).
Goals: Yugoslavia: 1-0 Milan Galic (1'), 2-0 Lazar Tasic (87').
Referee: Mihai Popa (ROM)   Attendance: 23.418

21-06-1959   Walter-Ulbricht-Stadion, Berlin: East Germany – Portugal   0-2 (0-1)
East Germany: Karl-Heinz Spickenagel, Bringfried Müller, Werner Heine, Konrad Wagner, Waldemar Mühlbächer, Manfred Kaiser, Horst Assmy, Günter Schröter (C), Gerhard Vogt, Lothar Meyer, Günther Wirth. (Coach: Fritz Gödicke (GDR)).
Portugal: ACÚRCIO Freire Alves CARRELO, VIRGÍLIO Marques Mendes (C), ÂNGELO Gaspar Martins, FERNANDO Mamede MENDES, Raúl António Leandro de FIGUEIREDO, VICENTE da Fonseca Lucas, CARLOS Domingos DUARTE, ANTÓNIO Dias TEIXEIRA, Sebastião Lucas da Fonseca "MATATEU", Mário Esteves COLUNA, Domiciano Barrocal Gomes CAVÉM. (Coach: Dr. José Maria ANTUNES Junior (POR)).
Goals: Portugal: 0-1 Sebastião Lucas da Fonseca "MATATEU" (12'), 0-2 Mário Esteves COLUNA (67').
Referee: Alojz Obtulovic (TCH)   Attendance: 25.000

28-06-1959   Estádio das Antas, Porto: Portugal – East Germany   3-2 (1-0)
Portugal: ACÚRCIO Freire Alves CARRELO, VIRGÍLIO Marques Mendes (C), ÂNGELO Gaspar Martins, FERNANDO Mamede MENDES, Raúl António Leandro de FIGUEIREDO, ALFREDO Saúl Abrantes de Abreu, CARLOS Domingos DUARTE, ANTÓNIO Dias TEIXEIRA, Sebastião Lucas da Fonseca "MATATEU", Mário Esteves COLUNA, Domiciano Barrocal Gomes CAVÉM. (Coach: Dr. José Maria ANTUNES Junior (POR)).
East Germany: Klaus Thiele, Bringfried Müller, Werner Heine, Konrad Wagner, Werner Unger, Siegfried Wolf, Roland Ducke, Günter Schröter (C), Gerhard Vogt, Dieter Erler, Horst Kohle. (Coach: Fritz Gödicke (GDR)).
Goals: Portugal: 1-0 Mário Esteves COLUNA (45'), 2-1 Mário Esteves COLUNA (62'), 3-1 Domiciano Barrocal Gomes CAVÉM (68').
East Germany: 1-1 Gerhard Vogt (47'), 3-2 Horst Kohle (72').
Referee: Juan Gardeazábal Garay (ESP)   Attendance: 19.124

28-06-1959   Stadion Slaski, Chorzów: Poland – Spain   2-4 (1-2)
Poland: Tomasz Stefaniszyn, Henryk Szczepanski, Roman Korynt, Jerzy Wozniak, Marceli Strzykalski, Edmund Zientara (C), Ernest Pohl, Lucjan Brychczy, Stanislaw Hachorek, Jan Liberda, Krzysztof Baszkiewicz. (Coach: Czeslaw Krug (POL)).
Spain: ANTONIO RAMALLETS Simón, Fernando OLIVELLA Pons, Jesús GARAY Vecino, Sigfrido GRÀCIA Royo, Joan SEGARRA Iracheta (C), Enrique GENSANA Merola, JUSTO TEJADA Martínez, Enrique MATEOS Mancebo, Alfredo Stéfano DI STÉFANO Laulhé, LUIS SUÁREZ Miramontes, Francisco GENTO López. (Coach: Helenio HERRERA Gavilán (ARG)).
Goals: Poland: 1-0 Ernest Pohl (34'), 2-3 Lucjan Brychczy (62').
Spain: 1-1 LUIS SUÁREZ Miramontes (40'), 1-2 Alfredo Stéfano DI STÉFANO Laulhé (41'), 1-3 LUIS SUÁREZ Miramontes (52'), 1-4 Alfredo Stéfano DI STÉFANO Laulhé (56').
Referee: Arthur Edward Ellis (ENG)   Attendance: 71.469

23-09-1959   Praterstadion, Vienna: Austria – Norway   5-2 (3-2)
Austria: Kurt Schmied, Rudolf Oslansky, Erich Hasenkopf, Gerhard Hanappi, Karl Stotz, Karl Koller, Paul Halla, Erich Hof, Horst Nemec, Wilhelm Huberts, Karl Skerlan. (Coach: Karl Decker (AUT)).
Norway: Sverre Andersen, Arne Bakker, Age Spydevold, Arne Natland, Thorbjorn Svenssen, Arnold Johannessen, Rolf Bjorn Backe, Age Sørensen, Harald Hennum, Ove Ødegaard, Finn Gundersen. (Coach: Kristian Henriksen (NOR)).
Goals: Austria: 1-0 Erich Hof (3'), 2-1 Horst Nemec (21'), 3-1 Erich Hof (25' penalty), 4-2 Karl Skerlan (59'), 5-2 Horst Nemec (67').
Norway: 1-1 Ove Ødegaard (19'), 3-2 Ove Ødegaard (35').
Referee: Dimosthemis Stathatos (GRE)   Attendance: 34.989

23-09-1959   Idrætsparken, Copenhagen: Denmark – Czechoslovakia   2-2 (2-2)
Denmark: Per Funch Jensen, Erling Linde Larsen, Poul Jensen, Bent Hansen, Hans Christian Nielsen, Erik Pondal Jensen, Poul Pedersen (C), John Danielsen, Harald Nielsen, Henning Enoksen, Jørn Sørensen. (Coach: Arne Sørensen (DEN)).
Czechoslovakia: Imrich Stacho, Jirí Tichy, Ján Popluhár, Ladislav Novák (C), Stefan Matlák, Titus Buberník, Ladislav Pavlovic, Adolf Scherer, Vlastimil Bubník, Ladislav Kacáni, Milan Dolinsky. (Coach: Rudolf Vytlacil (AUT)).
Goals: Denmark: 1-0 Poul Pedersen (18'), 2-0 Bent Hansen (20').
Czechoslovakia: 2-1 Ladislav Kacáni (30'), 2-2 Milan Dolinsky (43').
Referee: Johan (Jan) Bronkhorst (HOL)   Attendance: 34.200

27-09-1959   Népstadion, Budapest: Hungary – Soviet Union   0-1 (0-0)
Hungary: Gyula Grosics, Sándor Mátrai, Ferenc Sipos, László Sárosi, József Bozsik (C), Antal Kotász, Károly Sándor, János Göröcs, Flórián Albert, Lajos Tichy, Máté Fenyvesi. (Coach: Lajos Baroti (HUN)).
Soviet Union: Lev Yashin, Vladimir Kesarev, Anatoli Maslenkin, Boris Kuznetsov, Yuri Voinov, Igor Netto (C), Slava Metreveli, Anatoli Isayev, Valentin Ivanov, Valentin Bubukin, Mikheil Meskhi. (Coach: Mikhail Yakuschin (URS)).
Goal: Soviet Union: 0-1 Yuri Voinov (58').
Referee: József Kowal (POL)   Attendance: 78.481

14-10-1959   Estadio Santiago Bernabéu, Madrid: Spain – Poland   3-0 (1-0)
Spain: ANTONIO RAMALLETS Simón, Fernando OLIVELLA Pons, Jesús GARAY Vecino, Sigfrido GRÀCIA Royo, Joan SEGARRA Iracheta (C), Enrique GENSANA Merola, JUSTO TEJADA Martínez, László KUBALA Stecz, Alfredo Stéfano DI STÉFANO Laulhé, LUIS SUÁREZ Miramontes, Francisco GENTO López. (Coach: Helenio HERRERA Gavilán (ARG)).
Poland: Tomasz Stefaniszyn, Henryk Szczepanski, Roman Korynt, Fryderyk Monica, Witold Majewski, Henryk Grzybowski, Krzysztof Baszkiewicz, Ernest Pohl, Stanislaw Hachorek, Edmund Zientara (C), Zbigniew Szarzynski. (Coach: Czeslaw Krug (POL)).
Goals: Spain: 1-0 Alfredo Stéfano DI STÉFANO Laulhé (30'), 2-0 Enrique GENSANA Merola (69'), 3-0 Francisco GENTO López (85').
Referee: Karoly Balla (HUN)   Attendance: 62.070

18-10-1959   Stadion Za Luzánkami, Brno: Czechoslovakia – Denmark   5-1 (1-1)
Czechoslovakia: Viliam Schrojf, Jirí Tichy, Ján Popluhár, Ladislav Novák (C), Svatopluk Pluskal, Titus Buberník, Ladislav Pavlovic, Pavol Molnár, Anton Moravcík, Adolf Scherer, Milan Dolinsky. (Coach: Rudolf Vytlacil (AUT)).
Denmark: Erling Sørensen, Richard Møller Nielsen, Poul Jensen, Bent Hansen, Hans Christian Nielsen, Flemming Nielsen, Poul Pedersen (C), John Kramer, Henning Enoksen, John Danielsen, Jørn Sørensen. (Coach: Arne Sørensen (DEN)).
Goals: Czechoslovakia: 1-1 Titus Buberník (38'), 2-1 Adolf Scherer (49'), 3-1 Titus Buberník (56'), 4-1 Milan Dolinsky (63'), 5-1 Adolf Scherer (87').
Denmark: 0-1 John Kramer (35').
Referee: Helmut Köhler (GDR)   Attendance: 31.217

25-10-1959   Vasil Levski Stadium, Sofia: Bulgaria – Yugoslavia   1-1 (0-0)
Bulgaria: Georgi Naydenov, Kiril Rakarov, Manol Manolov (C), Ivan Dimitrov, Dimitar Largov, Nikola Kovachev, Todor Diev, Georgi Sokolov, Panayot Panayotov, Dimitar Yakimov, Ivan Kolev. (Coach: Stoian Ormandjiev (BUL)).
Yugoslavia: Blagoje Vidinic, Vladimir Djurkovic, Fahrudin Jusufi, Stevan Bena, Tomislav Crnkovic (C), Lazar Tasic, Luka Liposinovic, Dragoslav Sekularac, Muhamed Mujic, Borivoje Kostic, Branislav Mihajlovic. (Coach: Ljubomir Lovric (YUG)).
Goals: Bulgaria: 1-0 Todor Diev (50').
Yugoslavia: 1-1 Muhamed Mujic (56').
Referee: Kurt Tschenscher (FRG)   Attendance: 27.560
(Nikola Kovachev and Dragoslav Sekularac were both sent-off in the 63rd minute)

QUARTER-FINALS

13-12-1959   Stade Olympique de Colombes, Colombes: France – Austria   5-2 (3-1)
France: Georges Lamia, Jean Wendling, Robert Jonquet, Roger Marche (C), Armand Penverne, René Ferrier, François Heutte, Lucien Muller, Raymond Kopa, Just Fontaine, Jean Vincent. (Coach: Albert Batteux (FRA)).
Austria: Kurt Schmied, Paul Halla, Karl Nickerl, Gerhard Hanappi (C), Karl Stotz, Karl Koller, Walter Horak, Helmut Senekowitsch, Horst Nemec, Rudolf Pichler, Karl Höfer. (Coach: Karl Decker (AUT)).
Goals: France: 1-0 Just Fontaine (7'), 2-0 Just Fontaine (18'), 3-0 Jean Vincent (38'), 4-2 Just Fontaine (70'), 5-2 Jean Vincent (82').
Austria: 3-1 Walter Horak (40'), 3-2 Rudolf Pichler (65').
Referee: Manuel Martin Asensi (ESP)   Attendance: 43.775

27-03-1960   Praterstadion, Vienna: Austria – France   2-4 (1-0)
Austria: Rudolf Szanwald, Johann Windisch, Erich Hasenkopf, Gerhard Hanappi (C), Giose Koschier, Karl Koller, Walter Horak, Paul Kozlicek, Horst Nemec, Wilhelm Huberts, Erich Probst. (Coach: Karl Decker (AUT)).
France: Georges Lamia, Jean Wendling, Raymond Kaelbel, Bruno Rodzik, Jean-Jacques Marcel, René Ferrier, Pierre Grillet, Lucien Muller, Raymond Kopa (C), François Heutte, Bernard Rahis. (Coach: Albert Batteux (FRA)).
Goals: Austria: 1-0 Horst Nemec (26'), 2-2 Erich Probst (64').
France: 1-1 Jean-Jacques Marcel (46'), 1-2 Bernard Rahis (59'), 2-3 François Heutte (77'), 2-4 Raymond Kopa (83' penalty).
Referee: Leo Helge (DEN)   Attendance: 39.229

08-05-1960   Estádio Nacional, Lisbon: Portugal – Yugoslavia   2-1 (1-0)
Portugal: ACÚRCIO Freire Alves CARRELO, VIRGÍLIO Marques Mendes (C), ÂNGELO Gaspar Martins, FERNANDO Mamede MENDES, GERMANO Luiz de Figueiredo, David Abraão JÚLIO, HERNÂNI Ferreira Da Silva, Joaquim SANTANA Silva Guimarães, Sebastião Lucas da Fonseca "MATATEU", Mário Esteves COLUNA, Domiciano Barrocal Gomes CAVÉM. (Coach: Dr. José Maria ANTUNES Junior (POR)).
Yugoslavia: Milutin Soskic, Vladimir Djurkovic, Fahrudin Jusufi, Ante Zanetic, Tomislav Crnkovic (C), Zeljko Perusic, Dragoslav Sekularac, Muhamed Mujic, Branko Zebec, Milan Galic, Borivoje Kostic. (Coach: Ljubomir Lovric (YUG)).
Goals: Portugal: 1-0 Joaquim SANTANA Silva Guimarães (30'), 2-0 Sebastião Lucas da Fonseca "MATATEU" (70').
Yugoslavia: 2-1 Borivoje Kostic (81').
Referee: Joseph Barbéran (FRA)   Attendance: 39.978

22-05-1960   Stadion JNA, Belgrade: Yugoslavia – Portugal   5-1 (2-1)
Yugoslavia: Milutin Soskic, Vladimir Djurkovic, Fahrudin Jusufi, Ante Zanetic, Zarko Nikolic, Zeljko Perusic, Zvezdan Cebinac, Tomislav Knez, Milan Galic, Dragoslav Sekularac, Borivoje Kostic (C). (Coach: Ljubomir Lovric (YUG)).
Portugal: ACÚRCIO Freire Alves CARRELO, VIRGÍLIO Marques Mendes (C), MÁRIO JOÃO Sousa Alves, FERNANDO Mamede MENDES, GERMANO Luiz de Figueiredo, David Abraão JÚLIO, HERNÂNI Ferreira Da Silva, Joaquim SANTANA Silva Guimarães, Sebastião Lucas da Fonseca "MATATEU", Mário Esteves COLUNA, Domiciano Barrocal Gomes CAVÉM. (Coach: Dr. José Maria ANTUNES Junior (POR)).
Goals: Yugoslavia: 1-0 Dragoslav Sekularac (8'), 2-1 Zvezdan Cebinac (45'), 3-1 Borivoje Kostic (50'), 4-1 Milan Galic (79'), 5-1 Borivoje Kostic (88').
Portugal: 1-1 Domiciano Barrocal Gomes CAVÉM (29').
Referee: Josef Stoll (AUT)   Attendance: 43.000

22-05-1960   Stadionul 23 August, Bucharest: Romania – Czechoslovakia   0-2 (0-2)
Romania: Petre Mîndru, Cornel Popa, Alexandru Apolzan (C), Valeriu Soare, Emeric Ienei, Ion Nunweiler, Emanoil Hasoti, Gavril Raksi, Viorel Mateianu, Haralambie Eftimie, Nicolae Tataru. (Coach: Augustin Botescu (ROM)).
Czechoslovakia: Imrich Stacho, Jozef Bomba, Ján Popluhár, Ladislav Novák (C), Titus Buberník, Josef Masopust, Ladislav Pavlovic, Josef Vojta, Andrej Kvasnák, Vlastimil Bubník, Milan Dolinsky. (Coach: Rudolf Vytlacil (AUT)).
Goals: Czechoslovakia: 0-1 Josef Masopust (9'), 0-2 Vlastimil Bubník (45').
Referee: Andor Dorogi (HUN)   Attendance: 61.306

29-05-1960   Stadión Tehelné pole, Bratislava: Czechoslovakia – Romania   3-0 (3-0)
Czechoslovakia: Viliam Schrojf, Jozef Bomba, Ján Popluhár, Ladislav Novák (C), Titus Bubernik, Josef Masopust, Ladislav Pavlovic, Josef Vojta, Andrej Kvasnák, Vlastimil Bubnik, Milan Dolinsky. (Coach: Rudolf Vytlacil (AUT)).
Romania: Petre Mîndru, Cornel Popa, Alexandru Fronea, Valeriu Soare, Vasile Alexandru, Ion Nunweiler, Gheorghe Cacoveanu, Gheorghe Constantin, Constantin Dinulescu, Viorel Mateianu, Nicolae Tataru. (Coach: Augustin Botescu (ROM)).
Goals: Czechoslovakia: 1-0 Titus Bubernik (1'), 2-0 Titus Bubernik (15'), 3-0 Vlastimil Bubnik (18').
Referee: Leif Gulliksen (NOR)   Attendance: 31.057

29-05-1960   *Soviet Union – Spain* **cancelled**

09-06-1960   *Spain – Soviet Union* **cancelled**

Spain refused to travel to the Soviet Union for their quarter-final tie, so the Soviet Union was awarded a walkover victory.

FINAL TOURNAMENT IN FRANCE

SEMI-FINALS

06-07-1960   Parc des Princes, Paris: France – Yugoslavia   4-5 (2-1)
France: Georges Lamia, Jean Wendling, Robert Herbin, Bruno Rodzik, Jean-Jacques Marcel, René Ferrier, Michel Stievenard, Lucien Muller, Maryan Wisnieski (C), François Heutte, Jean Vincent. (Coach: Albert Batteux (FRA)).
Yugoslavia: Milutin Soskic, Vladimir Djurkovic, Fahrudin Jusufi, Ante Zanetic, Branko Zebec (C), Zeljko Perusic, Tomislav Knez, Drazan Jerkovic, Milan Galic, Dragoslav Sekularac, Borivoje Kostic. (Coach: Ljubomir Lovric (YUG)).
Goals: France: 1-1 Jean Vincent (12'), 2-1 François Heutte (43'), 3-1 Maryan Wisnieski (53'), 4-2 François Heutte (62').
Yugoslavia: 0-1 Milan Galic (11'), 3-2 Ante Zanetic (55'), 4-3 Tomislav Knez (75'), 4-4 Drazan Jerkovic (78'), 4-5 Drazan Jerkovic (79').
Referee: Gaston Grandain (BEL)   Attendance: 26.370

06-07-1960   Stade Vélodrome, Marseille: Czechoslvakia – Soviet Union   0-3 (0-1)
Czechoslovakia: Viliam Schrojf, Frantisek Safránek, Ján Popluhár, Ladislav Novák (C), Titus Bubernik, Josef Masopust, Josef Vojta, Anton Moravcík, Andrej Kvasnák, Vlastimil Bubnik, Milan Dolinsky. (Coach: Rudolf Vytlacil (AUT)).
Soviet Union: Lev Yashin, Givi Chokheli, Anatoli Maslenkin, Anatoli Krutikov, Yuri Voinov, Igor Netto (C), Slava Metreveli, Valentin Ivanov, Viktor Ponedelnik, Valentin Bubukin, Mikheil Meskhi. (Coach: Gavril Kachalin (URS)).
Goals: Soviet Union: 0-1 Valentin Ivanov (34'), 0-2 Valentin Ivanov (56'), 0-3 Viktor Ponedelnik (66').
Referee: Cesare Jonni (ITA)   Attendance: 25.184

THIRD PLACE PLAY-OFF

09-07-1960 Stade Vélodrome, Marseille: Czechoslovakia – France 2-0 (0-0)
Czechoslovakia: Viliam Schrojf, Frantisek Safránek, Ján Popluhár, Ladislav Novák (C), Titus Buberník, Josef Masopust, Ladislav Pavlovic, Josef Vojta, Pavol Molnár, Vlastimil Bubník, Milan Dolinsky. (Coach: Rudolf Vytlacil (AUT)).
France: Jean Taillandier, Bruno Rodzik, Robert Jonquet (C), André Chorda, Jean-Jacques Marcel, Robert Siatka, François Heutte, Yvon Douis, Maryan Wisnieski, Michel Stievenard, Jean Vincent. (Coach: Albert Batteux (FRA)).
Goals: Czechoslovakia: 1-0 Vlastimil Bubník (58'), 2-0 Ladislav Pavlovic (88').
Referee: Cesare Jonni (ITA)   Attendance: 9.438

FINAL

10-07-1960 Parc des Princes, Paris: Soviet Union – Yugoslavia 2-1 (0-1) (AET)
Soviet Union: Lev Yashin, Givi Chokheli, Anatoli Maslenkin, Anatoli Krutikov, Yuri Voinov, Igor Netto (C), Slava Metreveli, Valentin Ivanov, Viktor Ponedelnik, Valentin Bubukin, Mikheil Meskhi. (Coach: Gavril Kachalin (URS)).
Yugoslavia: Blagoje Vidinic, Vladimir Djurkovic, Fahrudin Jusufi, Ante Zanetic, Jovan Miladinovic, Zeljko Perusic, Dragoslav Sekularac, Drazan Jerkovic, Milan Galic, Zeljko Matus, Borivoje Kostic (C). (Coach: Ljubomir Lovric (YUG)).
Goals: Soviet Union: 1-1 Slava Metreveli (49'), 2-1 Viktor Ponedelnik (113').
Yugoslavia: 0-1 Milan Galic (43').
Referee: Arthur Edward Ellis (ENG)   Attendance: 17.966

*** Soviet Union were European Champions ***

GOALSCORERS TOURNAMENT 1958-1960:

Goals	Players
5	Just Fontaine (FRA), Jean Vincent (FRA), Titus Buberník (TCH)
4	Milan Galic (YUG)
3	Erich Hof (AUT), Horst Nemec (AUT), Alfredo Stéfano DI STÉFANO Laulhé (ESP), François Heutte (FRA), Mário Esteves COLUNA (POR), Vlasimil Bubník (TCH), Milan Dolinsky (TCH), Valentin Ivanov (URS), Bora Kostic (YUG)
2	LUIS SUÁREZ Miramontes (ESP), Thadée Cisowski (FRA), Raymond Kopa (FRA), Ove Ødegaard (NOR), Domiciano Barrocal Gomes CAVÉM (POR), Sebastião Lucas da Fonseca "MATATEU" (POR), Ladislav Pavlovic (TCH), Adolf Scherer (TCH), Lefter Küçükandonyadis (TUR), Slava Metreveli (URS), Viktor Ponedelnik (URS), Drazan Jerkovic (YUG)

1	Walter Horak (AUT), Rudolf Pichler (AUT), Erich Probst (AUT), Karl Skerlan (AUT), Todor Diev (BUL), Bent Hansen (DEN), John Kramer (DEN), Poul Pedersen (DEN), Enrique GENSANA Merola (ESP), Francisco GENTO López (ESP), Stéphane Bruey (FRA), Jean-Jacques Marcel (FRA), Bernard Rahis (FRA), Maryan Wisnieski (FRA), Horst Kohle (GDR), Gerhard Vogt (GDR), Elias Ifandis (GRE), János Göröcs (HUN), Noel Cantwell (IRL), Liam Tuohy (IRL), Lucjan Brychczy (POL), Ernest Pohl (POL), Joaquim SANTANA Silva Guimarães (POR), Gheorghe Constantin (ROM), Constantin Dinulescu (ROM), Nicolae Oaida (ROM), Ladislav Kacáni (TCH), Josef Masopust (TCH), Imrich Stacho (TCH), Anatoli Ilyin (URS), Yuri Voinov (URS), Zvezdan Cebinac (YUG), Tomislav Knez, Muhamed Mujic (YUG), Dragoslav Sekularac (YUG), Lazar Tasic (YUG), Ante Zanetic (YUG)
1 own goal	Roger Marche (FRA) for Greece

1964 UEFA European Nations' Cup

PRELIMINARY ROUND

Greece withdrew from the competition after they were drawn against Albania in the preliminary round.

Austria, Luxembourg and the Soviet Union all received byes to the first round.

21-06-1962   Ullevål, Oslo: Norway – Sweden   0-2 (0-2)
Norway: Sverre Andersen, Anders Svela, Ragnar Nikolay Larsen, Roar Johansen, Trygve Andersen, Olav Nilsen, Roald Jensen, Arne Pedersen, John Krogh, Erik Johansen, Olav Håkon Blengsli. (Coach: Wilhelm Kment (AUT)).
Sweden: Bengt Nyholm, Orvar Bergmark (C), Lennart Wing, Gösta Lundell, Åke Johansson, Prawitz Öberg, Bent Berndtsson, Ove Ohlsson, Örjan Martinsson, Harry Bild, Lennart Backman. (Coach: Lennart Nyman (SWE)).
Goals: Sweden: 0-1 Örjan Martinsson (10'), 0-2 Örjan Martinsson (40').
Referee: Gilbert Bowman (SCO)   Attendance: 28.249

21-06-1962   Greece – Albania   **cancelled**

28-06-1962   Idrætsparken, Copenhagen: Denmark – Malta   6-1 (3-0)
Denmark: Erik Gaardhøje, Kai Johansen, Poul Jensen (C), Bent Hansen, John Madsen, Jørgen Christian Thomdahl Olesen, Carl Bertelsen, Helge Jørgensen, Ole Madsen, Henning Enoksen, Eyvind Clausen. (Coach: Poul Eyvind Pedersen (DEN)).
Malta: Alfred Mizzi, John Privitera, Lolly Debattista, Frank Zammit, Joseph Cilia, Lino Falzon, Edward Theobald, Joseph Urpani, Tony Cauchi, Lolly Borg (C), Publius D'Emanuelle. (Coach: Carm Borg (MLT)).
Goals: Denmark: 1-0 Ole Madsen (9'), 2-0 Ole Madsen (14'), 3-0 Eyvind Clausen (22'), 4-0 Ole Madsen (49'), 5-1 Henning Enoksen (71'), 6-1 Carl Bertelsen (80').
Malta: 4-1 Edward Theobald (57').
Referee: Pieter Paulus (Piet) Roomer (HOL)   Attendance: 10.622

12-08-1962   Dalymount Park, Dublin: Republic of Ireland – Iceland   4-2 (2-1)
Republic of Ireland: Alan Kelly, Tony Dunne, Tommy Traynor, Pat Saward, Charlie Hurley, Mick Meagan, Alfie Hale, John Giles, Noel Cantwell, Amby Fogarty, Liam Tuohy. (Coach: John Carey (IRL)).
Iceland: Helgi Daníelsson, Arni Njálsson, Bjarni Felixson, Gardar Árnason, Hördur Felixson, Sveinn Jónsson, Skuli Ágústsson, Thorolfur Beck, Rikhardur Jónsson, Ellert B.Schram, Thordur Jónsson. (Coach: Karl Gudmundsson (ISL)).
Goals: Republic of Ireland: 1-0 Liam Tuohy (11'), 2-1 Amby Fogarty (41'), 3-1 Noel Cantwell (65'), 4-1 Noel Cantwell (76').
Iceland: 1-1 Rikhardur Jónsson (37'), 4-2 Rikhardur Jónsson (86').
Referee: Robert Ernest Smith (WAL)   Attendance: 19.848

02-09-1962   Laugardalsvöllur, Reykjavik: Iceland – Republic of Ireland   1-1 (0-1)
Iceland: Helgi Daníelsson, Arni Njálsson, Bjarni Felixson, Gardar Árnason, Jon Stefánsson, Sveinn Jónsson, Skuli Ágústsson, Thorolfur Beck, Rikhardur Jónsson, Ellert B.Schram, Sigurthor Jakobsson. (Coach: Karl Gudmundsson (ISL)).
Republic of Ireland: Alan Kelly, Brendan McNally, Tommy Traynor, Ronald Nolan, Charlie Hurley, Pat Saward, Dermot Curtis, Amby Fogarty, Noel Cantwell, Noel Peyton, Liam Tuohy. (Coach: John Carey (IRL)).
Goals: Iceland: 1-1 Gardar Árnason (59').
Republic of Ireland: 0-1 Liam Tuohy (38').
Referee: Birgir Nielsen (NOR)   Attendance: 9.014

03-10-1962   Hillsborough Stadium, Sheffield: England – France   1-1 (0-1)
England: Ron Springett, Jimmy Armfield (C), Ramon Wilson, Bobby Moore, Maurice Norman, Ron Flowers, Mike Hellawell, Chris Crowe, Ray Charnley, Jimmy Greaves, Alan Hinton. (Coach: Sir Walter Winterbottom (ENG)).
France: Pierre Bernard, Jean Wendling, André Lerond (C), André Chorda, Maryan Synakowski, René Ferrier, Laurent Robuschi, Joseph Bonnel, Raymond Kopa, Yvon Goujon, Paul Sauvage. (Coach: Henri Guérin (FRA)).
Goals: England: 1-1 Ron Flowers (57' penalty).
France: 0-1 Yvon Goujon (8').
Referee: Frede Hansen (DEN)   Attendance: 35.380

10-10-1962   Stadion Slaski, Chorzów: Poland – Northern Ireland   0-2 (0-1)
Poland: Edward Szymkowiak, Henryk Szczepanski, Slanislaw Oslizlo, Ryszard Budka, Bernard Blaut, Wladyslaw Kawula, Eugeniusz Faber, Jan Liberda, Norbert Gajda, Lucjan Brychczy, Roman Lentner. (Coach: Czeslaw Krug (POL)).
Northern Ireland: Robert Irvine, Eddie Magill, Alex Elder, Danny Blanchflower, Sammy Hatton, Jimmy Nicholson, Bill Humphries, Huber Barr, Derek Dougan, Jimmy McIlroy, Billy Bingham. (Coach: Robert Peacock (NIR)).
Goals: Northern Ireland: 1-0 Derek Dougan (17'), 0-2 Bill Humphries (54').
Referee: Bertil Wilhelm Lööw (SWE)   Attendance: 31.496

01-11-1962   Santiago Bernabéu Stadium, Madrid: Spain – Romania   6-0 (4-0)
Spain: José VICENTE Train, Enrique Pérez Diaz "PACHIN", Francisco Rodríguez García "RODRI", Isacio CALLEJA García, Francisco "PAQUITO" García Gómez, Jesús GLARÍA Jordán, Enrique COLLAR Monterrubio (C), ADELARDO Rodríguez Sánchez, José Luis Fidalgo VELOSO, Vicente GUILLOT Fabián, Francisco GENTO López. (Coach: JOSÉ VILLALONGA Llorente (ESP)).
Romania: Vasile Sfetcu, Mircea Georgescu, Ion Nunweiller, Dumitru Macri, Emil Petru, Constantin Koszka, Zoltan Ivansuc, Titus Ozon, Marin Voinea, Dumitru Popescu, Vasile Gergely. (Coach: Constantin Teasca (ROM)).
Goals: Spain: 1-0 Vicente GUILLOT Fabián (7'), 2-0 José Luis Fidalgo VELOSO (9'), 3-0 Enrique COLLAR Monterrubio (17'), 4-0 Vicente GUILLOT Fabián (27'), 5-0 Vicente GUILLOT Fabián (70'), 6-0 Ion Nunweiller (81' *own goal*).
Referee: Kevin Howley (ENG)   Attendance: 51.608

04-11-1962   Malmö Stadion, Malmö: Sweden – Norway   1-1 (0-0)
Sweden: Arne Arvidsson, Hans Mild, Lennart Wing, Yngve Brodd, Åke Johansson, Prawitz Öberg, Leif Eriksson, Ove Ohlsson, Örjan Martinsson, Leif Skiöld, Örjan Persson. (Coach: Lennart Nyman (SWE)).
Norway: Sverre Andersen, Edgar Stakset, Ragnar Nikolay Larsen, Roar Johansen, Trygve Andersen, Olav Nilsen, Roald Jensen, Arne Pedersen, John Krogh, Finn Thorsen, Oddvar Richardsen. (Coach: Ragnar Nikolay Larsen (NOR)).
Goals: Sweden: 1-0 Leif Eriksson (49').
Norway: 1-1 John Krogh (60').
Referee: Werner Bergmann (GDR)   Attendance: 8.726

04-11-1962   Stadion JNA, Belgrade: Yugoslavia – Belgium   3-2 (2-1)
Yugoslavia: Milutin Soskic, Slavko Svinjarevic, Fahrudin Jusufi, Petar Radakovic, Velibor Vasovic, Zeljko Perusic, Spasoje Samardzic, Vojislav Melic, Slaven Zambata, Milan Galic, Josip Skoblar. (Coach: Ljubomir Lovric (YUG)).
Belgium: Jean Nicolay, Yves Baré, Georges Heylens, Pierre Hanon, Lucien Spronck, Laurent Verbiest, Jef Jurion (C), Paul Van Himst, Jacques Stockman, Paul Vandenberg, Wilfried Puis. (Coaches: Arthur Ceuleers & Constant Vanden Stock (BEL)).
Goals: Yugoslavia: 1-0 Josip Skoblar (12'), 2-1 Josip Skoblar (32' penalty), 3-2 Velibor Vasovic (89').
Belgium: 1-1 Jacques Stockman (26'), 2-2 Jef Jurion (58').
Referee: Alojz Obtulovic (TCH)   Attendance: 25.430

07-11-1962   Vasil Levski Stadium, Sofia: Bulgaria – Portugal   3-1 (0-0)
Bulgaria: Georgi Naydenov (C), Vasil Metodiev, Dobromir Zhechev, Dimitar Dimov, Ivan Dimitrov, Nikola Kovachev, Todor Diev, Dimitar Yakimov, Georgi Asparuhov, Hristo Iliev, Ivan Kolev. (Coach: Georgi Patchedjiev (BUL)).
Portugal: Alberto da COSTA PEREIRA, ÂNGELO Gaspar Martins, Fernando da Conceição CRUZ, Domiciano Barrocal Gomes CAVÉM, RAÚL Martins MACHADO, JOSÉ CARLOS da Silva José, ANTÓNIO José SIMÕES da Costa, EUSÉBIO Ferreira da Silva, HERNÂNI Ferreira Da Silva (C), Mário Esteves COLUNA, Manuel SERAFIM Monteiro Pereira. (Coach: Dr. José Maria ANTUNES Juniór (POR)).
Goals: Bulgaria: 1-1 Georgi Asparuhov (65'), 2-1 Georgi Asparuhov (76'), 3-1 Todor Diev (84').
Portugal: 0-1 EUSÉBIO Ferreira da Silva (49').
Referee: Semih Zoroglu (TUR)   Attendance: 31.318

07-11-1962   Népstadion, Budapest: Hungary – Wales   3-1 (2-1)
Hungary: Antal Szentmihályi, Sándor Mátrai, Kálmán Mészöly, Kálmán Sóvári, Ernö Solymosi, Ferenc Sipos, Károly Sándor, János Göröcs, Flórián Albert, Lajos Tichy, Máté Fenyvesi. (Coach: Lajos Baróti (HUN)).
Wales: Tony Millington, Stuart Williams, Mel Hopkins, William Hennessy, Mel Nurse, Vic Crowe, Terry Medwin, Ivor Allchurch, Mel Charles, Roy Vernon, Barrie Jones. (Coach: Jimmy Murphy (WAL)).
Goals: Hungary: 1-0 Flórián Albert (5'), 2-1 Lajos Tichy (34'), 3-1 Károly Sándor (48').
Wales: 1-1 Terry Medwin (19').
Referee: Józef Kowal (POL)   Attendance: 30.412

11-11-1962   Olympisch stadion, Amsterdam: Netherlands – Switzerland   3-1 (1-1)
Netherlands: Peter van de Merwe, Guus Haak, Piet Ouderland, Fons van Wissen (C), Ton Pronk, Bennie Muller, Sjaak Swart, Henk Groot, Tonny van der Linden, Co Prins, Mick Clavan. (Coach: Elek Schwartz (FRA)).
Switzerland: Felix Ansermet, Heinz Schneiter, Ely Tacchella, André Grobéty, Jakob Kuhn, Paul Stehrenberger, Charles Hertig, Norbert Eschmann, Roger Vonlanthen, Philippe Pottier, Anton Allemann. (Coach: Karl Rappan (SUI)).
Goals: Netherlands: 1-0 Tonny van der Linden (11'), 2-1 Sjaak Swart (74'), 3-1 Henk Groot (76').
Switzerland: 1-1 Charles Hertig (42').
Referee: Joaquim Fernandes Campos (POR)   Attendance: 64.350

21-11-1962   Walter-Ulbricht-Stadion, East Berlin:
              East Germany – Czechoslovakia   2-1 (0-0)
East Germany: Horst Weigang, Klaus Urbanczyk, Werner Heine, Hans-Dieter Krampe, Manfred Kaiser, Kurt Liebrecht, Henning Frenzel, Dieter Erler, Peter Ducke, Günter Schröter (C), Roland Ducke. (Coach: Károly Sos (HUN)).
Czechoslovakia: Viliam Schrojf, Jan Lála, Svatopluk Pluskal, Jirí Tichy, Ladislav Novák (C), Andrej Kvasnák, Josef Masopust, Tomás Pospíchal, Josef Kadraba, Rudolf Kucera, Frantisek Valosek. (Coach: Rudolf Vytlacil (AUT)).
Goals: East Germany: 1-0 Dieter Erler (60'), 2-0 Kurt Liebrecht (80' penalty).
Czechoslovakia: 2-1 Rudolf Kucera (90').
Referee: Sergei Alimov (URS)   Attendance: 22.077

25-11-1962   Stadionul 23 August, Bucharest: Romania – Spain   3-1 (1-0)
Romania: Ion Voinescu, Cornel Popa, Ion Nunweiller, Dumitru Ivan, Emil Petru, Constantin Koszka, Ion Pîcalab, Gheorghe Constantin, Cicerone Manolache, Vasile Gergely, Nicolae Tataru. (Coach: Georghe Popescu (ROM)).
Spain: José VICENTE Train, Feliciano Muñoz RIVILLA, Francisco Rodríguez García "RODRI", Isacio CALLEJA García, Francisco "PAQUITO" García Gómez, Jesús GLARÍA Jordán, Enrique COLLAR Monterrubio (C), AMANCIO Amaro Varela, José Luis Fidalgo VELOSO, Vicente GUILLOT Fabián, Francisco GENTO López. (Coach: JOSÉ VILLALONGA Llorente (ESP)).
Goals: Romania: 1-0 Nicolae Tataru (2'), 2-0 Cicerone Manolache (8'), 3-0 Gheorghe Constantin (61').
Spain: 3-1 José Luis Fidalgo VELOSO (70').
Referee: Georgios Pelomis (GRE)   Attendance: 72.762

28-11-1962   Windsor Park, Belfast: Northern Ireland – Poland   2-0 (1-0)
Northern Ireland: Robert Irvine, Eddie Magill, Alex Elder, Danny Blanchflower, Terry Neill, Jimmy Nicholson, Billy Bingham, John Crossan, Derek Dougan, Jimmy McIlroy, Robert Braithwaite. (Coach: Robert Peacock (NIR)).
Poland: Edward Szymkowiak, Henryk Szczepanski, Slanislaw Oslizlo, Wlodzimierz Spiewak, Antoni Nieroba, Ryszard Grzegorczyk, Jozef Galeczka, Lucjan Brychczy, Erwin Wilczek, Roman Lentner, Eugeniusz Faber. (Coach: Czeslaw Krug (POL)).
Goals: Northern Ireland: 1-0 John Crossan (8'), 2-0 Billy Bingham (63').
Referee: Othmar Huber (SUI)   Attendance: 28.833

02-12-1962   Stadio Comunale, Bologna: Italy – Turkey   6-0 (4-0)
Italy: William Negri, Cesare Maldini (C), Enzo Robotti, Paride Tumburus, Francesco Janich, Romano Fogli, Alberto Orlando, Giacomo Bulgarelli, Angelo Sormani, Gianni Rivera, Ezio Pascutti. (Coach: Edmondo Fabbri (ITA).
Turkey: Özcan Arkoç, Candemir Berkman, Ahmet Berman, Suat Mamat, Naci Erdem (C), Mustafa Yürür, Tarik Kutver, Seref Has, Senol Birol, Metin Oktay, Kadri Aytaç. (Coach: Ljubisa Spajic (YUG)).
Goals: Italy: 1-0 Gianni Rivera (15'), 2-0 Alberto Orlando (22'), 3-0 Alberto Orlando (29'), 4-0 Alberto Orlando (35'), 5-0 Gianni Rivera (47'), 6-0 Alberto Orlando (85').
Referee: Lucien van Nuffel (BEL)   Attendance: 26.553

08-12-1962   Empire Stadium, Gzira: Malta – Denmark   1-3 (1-2)
Malta: Alfred Mizzi, John Privitera, Joseph Cilia, Joseph Cini, Emmanuel Attard, Louis Theobald, Lolly Borg (C), Edward Theobald, Joseph Urpani, Frank Zammit, Samuel Nicholl. (Coach: Carm Borg (MLT)).
Denmark: Erik Gaardhøje, Kai Johansen, Preben Emil Jensen, Egon Jensen, John Madsen, Jens Petersen, Carl Bertelsen, Carl Emil Christiansen, Ole Madsen (C), Tommy Brian Troelsen, Eyvind Clausen. (Coach: Poul Eyvind Pedersen (DEN)).
Goals: Malta: 1-1 Joseph Urpani (39').
Denmark: 0-1 Ole Madsen (14'), 1-2 Carl Emil Christiansen (42'), 1-3 Carl Bertelsen (47').
Referee: Raoul Righi (ITA)   Attendance: 6.987

16-12-1962   Estádio do Restelo, Lisbon: Portugal – Bulgaria   3-1 (2-0)
Portugal: Alberto da COSTA PEREIRA, ÂNGELO Gaspar Martins, Fernando da Conceição CRUZ, Mário Esteves COLUNA (C), RAÚL Martins MACHADO, JOSÉ CARLOS da Silva José, JOSÉ AUGUSTO Pinto de Almeida, EUSÉBIO Ferreira da Silva, AUGUSTO Francisco ROCHA, HERNÂNI Ferreira Da Silva, ANTÓNIO José SIMÕES da Costa. (Coach: Dr. José Maria ANTUNES Junióri (POR)).
Bulgaria: Georgi Naydenov (C), Vasil Metodiev, Ivan Vutsov, Dimitar Dimov, Ivan Dimitrov, Nikola Kovachev, Todor Diev, Stefan Abadzhiev, Georgi Asparuhov, Hristo Iliev, Ivan Kolev. (Coach: Georgi Patchedjiev (BUL)).
Goals: Portugal: 1-0 HERNÂNI Ferreira Da Silva (4'), 2-0 HERNÂNI Ferreira Da Silva (26'), 3-0 Mário Esteves COLUNA (53').
Bulgaria: 3-1 Hristo Iliev (83').
Referee: Henri Faucheux (FRA)   Attendance: 25.836

23-01-1963   Stadio Olimpico, Rome: Bulgaria – Portugal   1-0 (0-0)
Bulgaria: Yordan Yosifov, Vasil Metodiev, Ivan Vutsov, Petar Velichkov, Ivan Dimitrov, Nikola Kovachev (C), Todor Diev, Stefan Abadzhiev, Georgi Asparuhov, Hristo Iliev, Spiro Debarski. (Coach: Georgi Patchedjiev (BUL)).
Portugal: Alberto da COSTA PEREIRA, Alberto Augusto Antunes FESTA, Fernando da Conceição CRUZ, Mário Esteves COLUNA (C), Raúl MARTINS MACHADO, ANTÓNIO Manuel Louro PAULA, ANTÓNIO José SIMÕES da Costa, Joaquim SANTANA Silva Guimarães, JOSÉ Augusto Costa Sénica TORRES, AUGUSTO Francisco ROCHA, Manuel SERAFIM Monteiro Pereira. (Coach: Dr. José Maria ANTUNES Junióri (POR)).
Goal: Bulgaria: 1-0 Georgi Asparuhov (87').
Referee: Giuseppe Adami (ITA)   Attendance: 2.336
(The replay to determine the winner was played on a neutral ground)

27-02-1963   Parc des Princes, Paris: France – England   5-2 (3-0)
France: Pierre Bernard, Jean Wendling, André Lerond (C), Bruno Rodzik, Maryan Synakowski, Robert Herbin, Maryan Wisnieski, Joseph Bonnel, Yvon Goujon, Yvon Douis, Lucien Cossou. (Coach: Henri Guérin (FRA)).
England: Ron Springett, Jimmy Armfield (C), Ron Henry, Bobby Moore, Brian Labone, Ron Flowers, John Connelly, Bobby Tambling, Bobby Smith, Jimmy Greaves, Bobby Charlton. (Coach: Sir Alf Ramsey (ENG).
Goals: France: 1-0 Maryan Wisnieski (3'), 2-0 Yvon Douis (32'), 3-0 Lucien Cossou (43'), 4-2 Maryan Wisnieski (75'), 5-2 Lucien Cossou (82').
England: 3-1 Bobby Smith (57'), 3-2 Bobby Tambling (74').
Referee: Josef Kandlbinder (FRG)   Attendance: 23.986

27-03-1963   Mithat Pasa Stadium, Istanbul: Turkey – Italy   0-1 (0-0)
Turkey: Turgay Seren (C), Muzaffer Sipahi, Süreyya Özkefe, Özer Kanra, Güngör Tetik, Ismet Yurtsu, Ogün Altiparmak, Seref Has, Nedim Dogan, Suat Mamat, Ugur Köken. (Coach: Bülent Eken (TUR)).
Italy: Lido Vieri, Cesare Maldini (C), Giacinto Facchetti, Paride Tumburus, Alessandro Salvadore, Giovanni Trapattoni, Alberto Orlando, Giorgio Puia, Angelo Sormani, Mario Corso, Gianpaolo Menichelli. (Coach: Edmondo Fabbri (ITA).
Goal: Italy: 0-1 Angelo Sormani (86').
Referee: Dimitar Atanassov Roumentchev (BUL)   Attendance: 27.290

20-03-1963   Ninian Park, Cardiff: Wales – Hungary   1-1 (1-0)
Wales: Dave Hollins, Stuart Williams, Graham Wiliams, William Hennessy, Mike England, Alwyn Burton, Barrie Jones, Phil Woosnam, Graham Moore, Ivor Allchurch, Cliff Jones. (Coach: Jimmy Murphy (WAL)).
Hungary: Antal Szentmihályi, Sándor Mátrai, Kálmán Mészöly, László Sárosi, Ernö Solymosi, Ferenc Sipos, Károly Sándor, János Göröcs, Flórián Albert, Lajos Tichy, Máté Fenyvesi. (Coach: Lajos Baróti (HUN)).
Goals: Wales: 1-0 Cliff Jones (23' penalty).
Hungary: 1-1 Lajos Tichy (77' penalty).
Referee: John Spillane (IRL)   Attendance: 30.413

31-03-1963   Albania – Greece   **cancelled**

31-03-1963   Wankdorfstadion, Bern: Switzerland – Netherlands   1-1 (0-1)
Switzerland: Karl Elsener, Heinz Schneiter, Werner Leimgruber, André Grobéty, Hans Weber, Ely Tacchella, Bruno Brizzi, Rolf Wüthrich, Köbi Kuhn, Walter Heuri, Anton Allemann. (Coach: Karl Rappan (SUI)).
Netherlands: Eddy Pieters-Graafland, Guus Haak, Piet Ouderland, Fons van Wissen (C), Ton Pronk, Jan Klaassens, Sjaak Swart, Henk Groot, Piet Kruiver, Rinus Bennaars, Coen Moulijn. (Coach: Elek Schwartz (FRA)).
Goals: Switzerland: 1-1 Anton Allemann (75').
Netherlands: 0-1 Piet Kruiver (6').
Referee: Josef Kandlbinder (FRG)   Attendance: 31.794

31-03-1963   Strahov Stadium, Prague: Czechoslovakia – East Germany   1-1 (0-0)
Czechoslovakia: Vladimir Mokrohajsky, Jan Lála, Svatopluk Pluskal, Ján Popluhár, Ladislav Novák (C), Andrej Kvasnák, Josef Masopust, Tomás Pospíchal, Adolf Scherer, Rudolf Kucera, Václav Masek. (Coach: Rudolf Vytlacil (AUT)).
East Germany: Harald Fritzsche, Klaus Urbanczyk, Werner Heine (C), Hans-Dieter Krampe, Manfred Kaiser, Kurt Liebrecht, Henning Frenzel, Dieter Erler, Peter Ducke, Jürgen Nöldner, Roland Ducke. (Coach: Károly Sos (HUN)).
Goals: Czechoslovakia: 1-0 Václav Masek (66').
East Germany: 1-1 Peter Ducke (85').
Referee: Károly Balla (HUN)   Attendance: 19.504

31-03-1963   Stade du Heysel, Brussels: Belgium – Yugoslavia   0-1 (0-1)
Belgium: Jean Nicolay, Georges Heylens, Jean Cornelis, Pierre Hanon, Laurent Verbiest, Martin Lippens, Jacques Stockman, Paul Vandenberg, Paul Van Himst, Jef Jurion (C), Wilfried Puis. (Coaches: Arthur Ceuleers & Constant Vanden Stock (BEL)).
Yugoslavia: Milutin Soskic, Novak Tomic, Mirsad Fazlagic, Vladimir Popovic, Velibor Vasovic, Zeljko Perusic, Spasoje Samardzic, Djordje Pavlic, Milan Galic, Vojislav Melic, Josip Skoblar. (Coach: Ljubomir Lovric (YUG)).
Goal: Yugoslavia: 0-1 Milan Galic (21').
Referee: Vicente Antonio Caballero (ESP)   Attendance: 24.583

FIRST ROUND

30-05-1962   Estadio San Mamés, Bilbao: Spain – Northern Ireland   1-1 (0-0)
Spain: José VICENTE Train, Feliciano Muñoz RIVILLA, Luis María ECHEBERRÍA Igartua, Severino REIJA Vázquez, Francisco "PAQUITO" García Gómez, Enrique Pérez Diaz "PACHÍN", AMANCIO Amaro Varela, FÉLIX RUIZ Gabarri, Emilio MOROLLÓN Estébanez, ADELARDO Rodríguez Sánchez, Enrique COLLAR Monterrubio (C). (Coach: JOSÉ VILLALONGA Llorente (ESP)).
Northern Ireland: Robert Irvine, Eddie Magill, Alex Elder, Martin Harvey, Terry Neill, Billy McCullough, Billy Bingham, John Crossan, William Irvine, Bill Humphries, Robert Braithwaite. (Coach: Robert Peacock (NIR)).
Goals: Spain: 1-0 AMANCIO Amaro Varela (60').
Northern Ireland: 1-1 William Irvine (76').
Referee: Cesare Jonni (ITA)   Attendance: 27.960

19-06-1963   Stadion JNA, Belgrade: Yugoslavia – Sweden   0-0
Yugoslavia: Milutin Soskic, Novak Tomic, Fahrudin Jusufi, Zeljko Perusic, Velibor Vasovic, Vladimir Popovic, Spasoje Samardzic, Vladimir Kovacevic, Milan Galic, Drago Smailovic, Josip Skoblar. (Coach: Ljubomir Lovric (YUG)).
Sweden: Bengt Nyholm, Orvar Bergmark (C), Lennart Wing, Bengt Gustavsson, Åke Johansson, Hans Mild, Kurt Hamrin, Torbjörn Jonsson, Prawitz Öberg, Lennart Backman, Örjan Persson. (Coach: Lennart Nyman (SWE)).
Referee: Karl Kainer (AUT)   Attendance: 45.098

29-06-1963   Idrætsparken, Copenhagen: Denmark – Albania   4-0 (3-0)
Denmark: Erik Lykke Sørensen, Kai Johansen, Jens Jørgen Hansen, Bent Hansen, Birgir Larsen, Jens Petersen, Eyvind Clausen, Ole Sørensen, Ole Madsen (C), Palle Bruun, Henning Enoksen. (Coach: Poul Eyvind Pedersen (DEN)).
Albania: Sulejman Maliqati, Fatbardh Deliallisi, Skënder Halili, Fatmir Frashëri, Gëzim Kasmi, Lin Shllaku, Lorenc Vorfi, Mehdi Bushati, Pavllo Bukoviku, Panajot Pano, Fiqiri Thoma Duro. (Coach: Loro Boriçi (ALB)).
Goals: Denmark: 1-0 Jens Petersen (18' penalty), 2-0 Ole Madsen (25'), 3-0 Eyvind Clausen (36'), 4-0 Henning Enoksen (49').
Referee: Johan Einar Boström (SWE)   Attendance: 26.640

11-09-1963   Olympisch Stadion, Amsterdam: Netherlands – Luxembourg   1-1 (1-1)
Netherlands: Eddy Pieters-Graafland, Guus Haak, Piet Ouderland, Daan Schrijvers, Ton Pronk, Jan Klaassens (C), Sjaak Swart, Henk Groot, Klaas Nuninga, Tonny van der Linden, Coen Moulijn. (Coach: Elek Schwartz (FRA)).
Luxembourg: Nico Schmitt, Erny Brenner (C), Jean-Pierre Hoffstetter, Jean-Pierre Fiedler, Fernand Brosius, François Konter, Jean Klein, Adolphe Schmit, Louis Pilot, Paul May, Nicholas Hoffmann. (Coach: Robert Heinz (FGR)).
Goals: Netherlands: 1-0 Klaas Nuninga (5').
Luxembourg: 1-1 Paul May (33').
Referee: Arthur Blavier (BEL)   Attendance: 36.523

18-09-1963   Malmö Idrottsplats, Malmö: Sweden – Yugoslavia   3-2 (1-1)
Sweden: Bengt Nyholm, Hans Rosander, Lennart Wing, Orvar Bergmark, Åke Johansson, Hans Mild, Lennart Backman, Prawitz Öberg, Agne Simonsson, Harry Bild, Örjan Persson. (Coach: Lennart Nyman (SWE)).
Yugoslavia: Milutin Soskic, Fahrudin Jusufi, Mirko Braun, Zeljko Perusic, Velibor Vasovic, Vladimir Popovic, Spasoje Samardzic, Vojislav Melic, Slaven Zambata, Milan Galic, Josip Skoblar. (Coach: Ljubomir Lovric (YUG)).
Goals: Sweden: 1-1 Örjan Persson (30'), 2-1 Örjan Persson (60'), 3-2 Harry Mild (72').
Yugoslavia: 0-1 Slaven Zambata (21'), 2-2 Milan Galic (64').
Referee: John Keith (Jack) Taylor (ENG)   Attendance: 20.774

25-09-1963   Praterstadion, Vienna: Austria – Republic of Ireland   0-0
Austria: Gernot Fraydl, Peter Vargo, Erich Hasenkopf, Rudolf Oslansky, Walter Glechner, Karl Koller, Rudolf Flögel, Erich Hof, Horst Nemec, Ernst Fiala, Johann Hörmayer. (Coach: Karl Decker (AUT)).
Republic of Ireland: Alan Kelly, William Browne, Tommy Traynor, Raymond Brady, Charlie Hurley, Michael McGrath, John Giles, Ronald Whelan, Dermot Curtis, Amby Fogarty, Liam Tuohy. (Coach: John Carey (IRL)).
Referee: Gyula Gere (HUN)   Attendance: 26.741

29-09-1963   Vasil Levski Stadium, Sofia: Bulgaria – France   1-0 (1-0)
Bulgaria: Georgi Naydenov, Aleksandar Shalamanov, Ivan Vutsov, Dobromir Zhechev, Stoyan Kitov, Ivan Dimitrov, Petar Velichkov, Todor Diev, Georgi Asparuhov, Dimitar Yakimov, Ivan Kolev (C). (Coach: Béla Volentik (HUN)).
France: Pierre Bernard, Marcel Adamczyk, Pierre Michelin, Marcel Artelesa, André Chorda, Joseph Bonnel, Théodore Skudlapski, Laurent Robuschi, Yvon Douis (C), Lucien Cossou, Jean-Louis Buron. (Coaches: Henri Guérin (FRA) & Albert Batteux (FRA)).
Goal: Bulgaria: 1-0 Todor Diev (24').
Referee: Faruk Talu (TUR)   Attendance: 25.947

13-10-1963   Dalymount Park, Dublin: Republic of Ireland – Austria   3-2 (1-1)
Republic of Ireland: Alan Kelly, Tony Dunne, Tommy Traynor, Raymond Brady, Charlie Hurley, Michael McGrath, John Giles, Andy McEvoy, Noel Cantwell, Amby Fogarty, Joe Haverty. (Coach: John Carey (IRL)).
Austria: Gernot Fraydl, Peter Vargo, Erich Hasenkopf, Johann Frank, Walter Glechner, Karl Koller, Walter Koleznik, Johannes Jank, Johann Buzek, Horst Nemec, Rudolf Flögel. (Coach: Karl Decker (AUT)).
Goals: Republic of Ireland: 1-1 Noel Cantwell (45'), 2-1 Amby Fogarty (66'), 3-2 Noel Cantwell (89' penalty).
Austria: 0-1 Walter Koleznik (38'), 2-2 Rudolf Flögel (85').
Referee: Einar Poulsen (DEN)   Attendance: 39.963

13-10-1963   Central Lenin Stadium, Moscow: Soviet Union – Italy   2-0 (2-0)
Soviet Union: Ramaz Urushadze, Eduard Dubinskiy, Anatoli Krutikov, Albert Shesternev, Valeri Voronin (C), Valeri Korolenkov, Slava Metreveli, Igor Chislenko, Viktor Ponedelnik, Valentin Ivanov, Galimzyan Khusainov. (Coach: Konstantin Beskov (URS)).
Italy: William Negri, Cesare Maldini (C), Giacinto Facchetti, Aristide Guarneri, Alessandro Salvadore, Giovanni Trapattoni, Giacomo Bulgarelli, Mario Corso, Angelo Sormani, Gianni Rivera, Ezio Pascutti. (Coach: Edmondo Fabbri (ITA)).
Goals: Soviet Union: 1-0 Viktor Ponedelnik (22'), 2-0 Igor Chislenko (42').
Referee: Ryszard Banasiuk (POL)   Attendance: 102.358

19-10-1963   Walter-Ulbrich-Stadion, East Berlin: East Germany – Hungary   1-2 (0-1)
East Germany: Jürgen Heinsch, Martin Skaba, Werner Heine (C), Hans-Dieter Krampe, Manfred Kaiser, Kurt Liebrecht, Rainer Nachtigall, Dieter Erler, Peter Ducke, Jürgen Nöldner, Hermann Stöcker. (Coach: Károly Sos (HUN)).
Hungary: Antal Szentmihályi, Kálmán Ihász, Kálmán Mészöly, László Sárosi, István Nagy, Ernö Solymosi, Károly Sándor, Gyula Rákosi, Flórián Albert, Ferenc Bene, Máté Fenyvesi. (Coach: Lajos Baróti (HUN)).
Goals: East Germany: 1-1 Jürgen Nöldner (51').
Hungary: 0-1 Ferenc Bene (18'), 1-2 Gyula Rákosi (88').
Referee: Pyotr Andreyevich Belov (URS)   Attendance: 33.383

26-10-1963   Parc des Princes, Paris: France – Bulgaria   3-1 (1-0)
France: Pierre Bernard, Bruno Rodzik, Pierre Michelin, Marcel Artelesa, André Chorda, Robert Herbin, René Ferrier, Georges Lech, Yvon Goujon, Yvon Douis (C), Jean-Louis Buron. (Coaches: Henri Guérin (FRA) & Albert Batteux (FRA)).
Bulgaria: Georgi Naydenov, Vasil Metodiev, Ivan Dimitrov, Dobromir Zhechev, Ivan Vutsov, Petar Velichkov, Stoyan Kitov, Stefan Abadzhiev, Georgi Asparuhov, Dimitar Yakimov, Ivan Kolev (C). (Coach: Béla Volentik (HUN)).
Goals: France: 1-0 Yvon Goujon (44'), 2-1 Robert Herbin (78'), 3-1 Yvon Goujon (81').
Bulgaria: 1-1 Dimitar Yakimov (75').
Referee: José María Ortiz de Mendíbil (ESP)   Attendance: 32.233

30-10-1963   Windsor Park, Belfast: Northern Ireland – Spain   0-1 (0-0)
Northern Ireland: Victor Hunter, Eddie Magill, John Parke, Martin Harvey, Terry Neill, Billy McCullough, Billy Bingham, Bill Humphries, Sammy Wilson, John Crossan, James Hill. (Coach: Robert Peacock (NIR)).
Spain: José Casas "PEPÍN" Gris, Feliciano Muñoz RIVILLA, Fernando OLIVELLA Pons, Severino REIJA Vázquez, Ignacio ZOCO Esparza, FÉLIX RUIZ Gabarri, Jesús María PEREDA Ruiz de Temiño, LUIS DEL SOL Cascajares, José Antonio ZALDÚA Urdanavia, LUIS SUÁREZ Miramontes, Francisco GENTO López (C). (Coach: JOSÉ VILLALONGA Llorente (ESP)).
Goal: Spain: 0-1 Francisco GENTO López (66').
Referee: Andries van Leeuwen (HOL)   Attendance: 45.809

30-10-1963   Stadiumi Qemal Stafa, Tirana: Albania – Denmark   1-0 (1-0)
Albania: Shefqet Topi, Fatbardh Deliallisi, Skënder Halili, Fatmir Frashëri, Ali Mema, Lin Shllaku, Andon Zaho, Mehdi Bushati, Panajot Pano, Pavllo Bukoviku, Enver Ibërshimi. (Coach: Zyber Koni (ALB)).
Denmark: Erik Lykke Sørensen, Kai Johansen, Jens Jørgen Hansen, Bent Hansen, John Madsen, Jens Petersen, Carl Bertelsen, Kjeld Thorst, Ole Madsen (C), Ole Sørensen, John Danielsen. (Coach: Poul Eyvind Pedersen (DEN)).
Goal: Albania: 1-0 Panajot Pano (3').
Referee: Joseph M.Cassar Naudi (MLT)   Attendance: 27.765

30-10-1963   Stadion Feijenoord, Rotterdam: Luxembourg – Netherlands   2-1 (1-1)
Luxembourg: Nico Schmitt, Erny Brenner, Jean-Pierre Hoffstetter, Jean-Pierre Fiedler, Fernand Brosius, François Konter, Jean Klein, Adolphe Schmit, Camille Dimmer, Louis Pilot (C), Henri Klein. (Coach: Robert Heinz (FRG)).
Netherlands: Eddy Pieters-Graafland, Guus Haak, Cor Veldhoen, Fons van Wissen (C), Ton Pronk, Rinus Bennaars, Piet Giesen, Henk Groot, Piet Kruiver, Piet Keizer, Peet Petersen. (Coach: Elek Schwartz (FRA)).
Goals: Luxembourg: 1-0 Camille Dimmer (20'), 2-1 Camille Dimmer (67').
Netherlands: 1-1 Piet Kruiver (35').
Referee: Marcel Bois (FRA)   Attendance: 42.385

03-11-1963   Népstadion, Budapest: Hungary – East Germany   3-3 (2-2)
Hungary: Antal Szentmihályi, Sándor Mátrai, Kálmán Mészöly, Kálmán Ihász, István Nagy, Ernö Solymosi, Károly Sándor, Gyula Rákosi, Flórián Albert, Ferenc Bene, Máté Fenyvesi. (Coach: Lajos Baróti (HUN)).
East Germany: Jürgen Heinsch, Klaus Urbanczyk, Werner Heine (C), Hans-Dieter Krampe, Manfred Kaiser, Kurt Liebrecht, Rainer Nachtigall, Jürgen Nöldner, Peter Ducke, Dieter Erler, Roland Ducke. (Coach: Károly Sos (HUN)).
Goals: Hungary: 1-0 Ferenc Bene (7'), 2-1 Károly Sándor (17'), 3-2 Ernö Solymosi (51' penalty).
East Germany: 1-1 Werner Heine (12'), 2-2 Roland Ducke (26'), 3-3 Dieter Erler (81').
Referee: Borce Nedelkovski (YUG)   Attendance: 35.382

10-11-1963   Stadio Olimpico, Rome: Italy – Soviet Union   1-1 (0-1)
Italy: Giuliano Sarti, Tarcisio Burgnich, Giacinto Facchetti, Aristide Guarneri, Alessandro Salvadore (C), Giovanni Trapattoni, Angelo Domenghini, Giacomo Bulgarelli, Sandro Mazzola, Gianni Rivera, Gianpaolo Menichelli. (Coach: Edmondo Fabbri (ITA)).
Soviet Union: Lev Yashin, Eduard Mudrik, Albert Shesternev, Anatoli Krutikov, Valeri Voronin (C), Viktor Shustikov, Igor Chislenko, Valentin Ivanov, Gennadi Gusarov, Valeri Korolenkov, Galimzyan Khusainov. (Coach: Konstantin Beskov (URS)).
Goals: Italy: 1-1 Gianni Rivera (89').
Soviet Union: 0-1 Gennadi Gusarov (33').
Referee: Daniel Mellet (SUI)   Attendance: 69.567

QUARTER-FINALS

04-12-1963   Stade Municipal, Luxembourg: Luxembourg – Denmark   3-3 (2-2)
Luxembourg: Nico Schmitt, Erny Brenner, Jean-Pierre Hoffstetter, François Konter, Fernand Brosius, Adolphe Schmit, Jean Klein, Paul May, Johnny Léonard, Louis Pilot (C), Henri Klein. (Coach: Robert Heinz (FRG)).
Denmark: Erik Lykke Sørensen, Kai Johansen, Jens Jørgen Hansen, Bent Hansen, John Madsen, Jens Petersen, Carl Bertelsen, Kjeld Thorst, Ole Madsen (C), Ole Sørensen, John Danielsen. (Coach: Poul Eyvind Pedersen (DEN)).
Goals: Luxembourg: 1-0 Louis Pilot (1'), 2-1 Henri Klein (23'), 3-3 Henri Klein (51').
Denmark: 1-1 Ole Madsen (9'), 2-2 Ole Madsen (31'), 2-3 Ole Madsen (46').
Referee: Pierre Schwinté (FRA)   Attendance: 6.921

10-12-1963   Idrætsparken, Copenhagen: Denmark – Luxembourg   2-2 (1-1)
Denmark: Erik Lykke Sørensen, Kai Johansen, Jens Jørgen Hansen, Bent Hansen, John Madsen, Jens Petersen, Carl Bertelsen, John Danielsen, Ole Madsen (C), Ole Sørensen, Henning Enoksen. (Coach: Poul Eyvind Pedersen (DEN)).
Luxembourg: Nico Schmitt, Erny Brenner, Jean-Pierre Hoffstetter, François Konter (C), Fernand Brosius, Adolphe Schmit, Jean Klein, Paul May, Johnny Léonard, Louis Pilot, Henri Klein. (Coach: Robert Heinz (FRG)).
Goals: Denmark: 1-1 Ole Madsen (16'), 2-1 Ole Madsen (70').
Luxembourg: 0-1 Johnny Léonard (13'), 2-2 Adolphe Schmit (84').
Referee: Joseph Barbéran (FRA)   Attendance: 36.294

18-12-1963   Olympisch Stadion, Amsterdam: Denmark – Luxembourg   1-0 (1-0)
Denmark: Erik Lykke Sørensen, Kai Johansen, Jens Jørgen Hansen, Bent Hansen, John Madsen, Jens Petersen, Carl Bertelsen, Kjeld Thorst, Ole Madsen (C), Henning Enoksen, John Danielsen. (Coach: Poul Eyvind Pedersen (DEN)).
Luxembourg: Nico Schmitt, Erny Brenner, Jean-Pierre Hoffstetter, François Konter, Fernand Brosius, Adolphe Schmit (C), Jean Klein, Paul May, Johnny Léonard, Louis Pilot, Henri Klein. (Coach: Robert Heinz (FRG)).
Goal: Denmark: 1-0 Ole Madsen (41').
Referee: Pieter Paulus (Piet) Roomer (HOL)   Attendance: 5.700
(The replay to determine the winner was played on a neutral ground)

11-03-1964   Estadio Ramón Sánchez Pizjuán, Seville:
Spain – Republic of Ireland   5-1 (4-1)
Spain: José Ángel IRIBAR Cortajarena, Feliciano Muñoz RIVILLA, Fernando OLIVELLA Pons (C), Isacio CALLEJA García, Ignacio ZOCO Esparza, Josep María FUSTÉ Blanch, AMANCIO Amaro Varela, Jesús María PEREDA Ruiz de Temiño, MARCELINO Martínez Cao, Juan Manuel VILLA GUTIERREZ, Carlos LAPETRA Coarasa. (Coach: JOSÉ VILLALONGA Llorente (ESP)).
Republic of Ireland: Alan Kelly, Theobald Foley, Tommy Traynor, Raymond Brady, Charlie Hurley (C), Mick Meagan, John Giles, Andy McEvoy, Alfie Hale, Amby Fogarty, Joe Haverty. (Coach: John Carey (IRL)).
Goals: Spain: 1-0 AMANCIO Amaro Varela (12'), 2-0 Josep María FUSTÉ Blanch (15'), 3-1 AMANCIO Amaro Varela (29'), 4-1 MARCELINO Martínez Cao (33'), 5-1 MARCELINO Martínez Cao (89').
Republic of Ireland: 2-1 Andy McEvoy (22').
Referee: Lucien van Nuffel (BEL)   Attendance: 27.137

08-04-1964   Dalymount Park, Dublin: Republic of Ireland – Spain   0-2 (0-1)
Republic of Ireland: Alan Kelly, Tony Dunne, William Browne, Raymond Brady, Charlie Hurley, John Fullam, John Giles, Andy McEvoy, Noel Cantwell, Patrick Turner, Alfie Hale. (Coach: John Carey (IRL)).
Spain: José Ángel IRIBAR Cortajarena, Feliciano Muñoz RIVILLA, Fernando OLIVELLA Pons (C), Isacio CALLEJA García, Ignacio ZOCO Esparza, Josep María FUSTÉ Blanch, Pedro ZABALLA Barquín, Jesús María PEREDA Ruiz de Temiño, MARCELINO Martínez Cao, Juan Manuel VILLA GUTIERREZ, Carlos LAPETRA Coarasa. (Coach: JOSÉ VILLALONGA Llorente (ESP)).
Goals: Spain: 0-1 Pedro ZABALLA Barquín (25'), 0-2 Pedro ZABALLA Barquín (88').
Referee: Gérard Versyp (BEL)   Attendance: 38.027

25-04-1964   Stade Olympique, Colombes (Paris): France – Hungary   1-3 (0-2)
France: Pierre Bernard (C), Georges Casolari, Pierre Michelin, Marcel Artelesa, André Chorda, Joseph Bonnel, Lucien Muller, Georges Lech, Néstor Combin, Robert Herbin, Lucien Cossou. (Coach: Henri Guérin (FRA)).
Hungary: Antal Szentmihályi, Sándor Mátrai, Kálmán Mészöly, László Sárosi, István Nagy, Ferenc Sipos, János Göröcs, Gyula Rákosi, Flórián Albert, Lajos Tichy, Máté Fenyvesi. (Coach: Lajos Baróti (HUN)).
Goals: France: 1-3 Lucien Cossou (73').
Hungary: 0-1 Flórián Albert (15'), 0-2 Lajos Tichy (16'), 0-3 Lajos Tichy (70').
Referee: Cesare Jonni (ITA)   Attendance: 35.274

13-05-1964   Råsunda Stadion, Solna: Sweden – Soviet Union   1-1 (0-0)
Sweden: Arne Arvidsson, Hans Rosander, Lennart Wing, Orvar Bergmark, Åke Johansson, Hans Mild, Kurt Hamrin, Harry Bild, Agne Simonsson, Örjan Martinsson, Örjan Persson. (Coach: Lennart Nyman (SWE)).
Soviet Union: Lev Yashin, Eduard Mudrik, Albert Shesternev, Vladimir Glotov, Valeri Voronin, Aleksei Korneev, Igor Chislenko, Valentin Ivanov, Eduard Malofeev, Gennadi Gusarov, Valeri Korolenkov. (Coach: Konstantin Beskov (URS)).
Goals: Sweden: 1-1 Kurt Hamrin (88').
Soviet Union: 0-1 Valentin Ivanov (62').
Referee: James (Jim) Finney (ENG)   Attendance: 36.937

23-05-1964   Népstadion, Budapest: Hungary – France 2-1 (1-1)
Hungary: Antal Szentmihályi, Sándor Mátrai, Kálmán Mészöly, László Sárosi, István Nagy, Ferenc Sipos, Károly Sándor, Gyula Rákosi, Lajos Tichy, Ferenc Bene, Máté Fenyvesi. (Coach: Lajos Baróti (HUN)).
France: Pierre Bernard (C), Georges Casolari, Daniel Charles-Alfred, André Chorda, Marcel Artelesa, Edouard Stako, Georges Lech, Fleury Di Nallo, Néstor Combin, Joseph Bonnel, Angel Rambert. (Coach: Henri Guérin (FRA)).
Goals: Hungary: 1-1 Ferenc Sipos (24'), 2-1 Ferenc Bene (55').
France: 0-1 Néstor Combin (2').
Referee: Concetto Lo Bello (ITA)   Attendance: 70.120

27-05-1964   Central Lenin Stadium, Moscow: Soviet Union – Sweden 3-1 (1-0)
Soviet Union: Lev Yashin, Eduard Mudrik, Albert Shesternev, Vladimir Glotov, Valeri Voronin, Aleksei Korneev, Igor Chislenko, Valentin Ivanov, Viktor Ponedelnik, Gennadi Gusarov, Galimzyan Khusainov. (Coach: Konstantin Beskov (URS)).
Sweden: Arne Arvidsson, Hans Rosander, Lennart Wing, Orvar Bergmark, Hans Mild, Anders Svensson, Kurt Hamrin, Harry Bild, Agne Simonsson, Örjan Martinsson, Örjan Persson. (Coach: Lennart Nyman (SWE)).
Goals: Soviet Union: 1-0 Viktor Ponedelnik (32'), 2-0 Viktor Ponedelnik (56'), 3-1 Valeri Voronin (83').
Sweden: 2-1 Kurt Hamrin (78').
Referee: Arthur Holland (ENG)   Attendance: 99.609

FINAL TOURNAMENT IN SPAIN

SEMI-FINALS

17-06-1964   Santiago Bernabéu Stadium, Madrid: Spain – Hungary 2-1 (1-0) (AET)
Spain: José Ángel IRIBAR Cortajarena, Feliciano Muñoz RIVILLA, Fernando OLIVELLA Pons (C), Isacio CALLEJA García, Ignacio ZOCO Esparza, Josep María FUSTÉ Blanch, AMANCIO Amaro Varela, Jesús María PEREDA Ruiz de Temiño, MARCELINO Martínez Cao, LUIS SUÁREZ Miramontes, Carlos LAPETRA Coarasa. (Coach: JOSÉ VILLALONGA Llorente (ESP)).
Hungary: Antal Szentmihályi, Sándor Mátrai, Kálmán Mészöly, László Sárosi, István Nagy, Ferenc Sipos (C), Ferenc Bene, Imre Komora, Flórián Albert, Lajos Tichy, Máté Fenyvesi. (Coach: Lajos Baróti (HUN)).
Goals: Spain: 1-0 Jesús María PEREDA Ruiz de Temiño (35'), 2-1 AMANCIO Amaro Varela (112').
Hungary: 1-1 Ferenc Bene (84').
Referee: Arthur Blavier (BEL)   Attendance: 34.713

17-06-1964   Camp Nou, Barcelona: Denmark – Soviet Union 0-3 (0-2)
Denmark: Leif Nielsen, Jens Jørgen Hansen, Kaj Hansen, Bent Hansen, Birgir Larsen, Erling Nielsen, Carl Bertelsen, Ole Sørensen, Ole Madsen (C), Kjeld Thorst, John Danielsen. (Coach: Poul Eyvind Pedersen (DEN)).
Soviet Union: Lev Yashin, Viktor Shustikov, Albert Shesternev, Eduard Mudrik, Valeri Voronin, Viktor Anichkin, Igor Chislenko, Valentin Ivanov, Viktor Ponedelnik, Gennadi Gusarov, Galimzyan Khusainov. (Coach: Konstantin Beskov (URS)).
Goals: Soviet Union: 0-1 Valeri Voronin (19'), 0-2 Viktor Ponedelnik (40'), 0-3 Valentin Ivanov (87').
Referee: Concetto Lo Bello (ITA)   Attendance: 38.556

THIRD PLACE PLAY-OFF

20-06-1964   Camp Nou, Barcelona: Hungary – Denmark   3-1 (1-0) (AET)
Hungary: Antal Szentmihályi, Dezsö Novák, Kálmán Mészöly, Kálmán Ihász, Ernö Solymosi, Ferenc Sipos (C), János Farkas, Zoltán Varga, Flórián Albert, Ferenc Bene, Máté Fenyvesi. (Coach: Lajos Baróti (HUN)).
Denmark: Leif Nielsen, Bent Wolmar, Kaj Hansen, Bent Hansen, Birgir Larsen, Erling Nielsen, Carl Bertelsen, Ole Sørensen, Ole Madsen (C), Kjeld Thorst, John Danielsen. (Coach: Poul Eyvind Pedersen (DEN)).
Goals: Hungary: 1-0 Ferenc Bene (11'), 2-1 Dezsö Novák (107' penalty), 3-1 Dezsö Novák (110').
Denmark: 1-1 Carl Bertelsen (82').
Referee: Daniel Mellet (SUI)   Attendance: 3.869

FINAL

21-06-1964   Santiago Bernabéu Stadium, Madrid: Spain – Soviet Union   2-1 (1-1)
Spain: José Ángel IRIBAR Cortajarena, Feliciano Muñoz RIVILLA, Fernando OLIVELLA Pons (C), Isacio CALLEJA García, Ignacio ZOCO Esparza, Josep María FUSTÉ Blanch, AMANCIO Amaro Varela, Jesús María PEREDA Ruiz de Temiño, MARCELINO Martínez Cao, LUIS SUÁREZ Miramontes, Carlos LAPETRA Coarasa. (Coach: JOSÉ VILLALONGA Llorente (ESP)).
Soviet Union: Lev Yashin, Viktor Shustikov, Albert Shesternev, Eduard Mudrik, Valeri Voronin, Viktor Anichkin, Igor Chislenko, Valentin Ivanov (C), Viktor Ponedelnik, Aleksei Korneev, Galimzyan Khusainov. (Coach: Konstantin Beskov (URS)).
Goals: Spain: 1-0 Jesús María PEREDA Ruiz de Temiño (6'), 2-1 MARCELINO Martínez Cao (84').
Soviet Union: 1-1 Galimzyan Khusainov (8').
Referee: Arthur Holland (ENG)   Attendance: 79.115

*** Spain were European Champions ***

GOALSCORERS TOURNAMENT 1962-1964:

Goals	Players
11	Ole Madsen (DEN)
5	Ferenc Bene (HUN)
4	AMANCIO Amaro Varela (ESP), Lajos Tichy (HUN), Noal Cantwell (IRL), Alberto Orlando (ITA), Viktor Ponedelnik (URS)
3	Georgi Asparuhov (BUL), Carl Bertelsen (DEN), Vicente GUILLOT Fabián (ESP), MARCELINO Martínez Cao (ESP), Lucien Cossou (FRA), Yvon Goujon (FRA), Gianni Rivera (ITA)

2	Todor Diev (BUL), Eyvind Clausen (DEN), Henning Enoksen (DEN), Jesús María PEREDA Ruiz de Temiño (ESP), José Luis Fidalgo VELOSO (ESP), Pedro ZABALLA Barquín (ESP), Maryan Wisnieski (FRA), Dieter Erler (GDR), Piet Kruiver (HOL), Flórián Albert (HUN), Dezsö Novák (HUN), Károly Sándor (HUN), Amby Fogarty (IRL), Liam Tuohy (IRL), Ríkhardur Jónsson (ISL), Camille Dimmer (LUX), Henri Klein (LUX), HERNÂNI Ferreira da Silva (POR), Kurt Hamrin (SWE), Örjan Martinsson (SWE), Örjan Persson (SWE), Valentin Ivanov (URS), Valeri Voronin (URS), Milan Galic (YUG), Josip Skoblar (YUG)
1	Panajot Pano (ALB), Rudi Flögel (AUT), Walter Koleznik (AUT), Jef Jurion (BEL), Jacques Stockman (BEL), Hristo Iliev (BUL), Dimitar Yakimov (BUL), Carl Emil Christiansen (DEN), Jens Petersen (DEN), Ron Flowers (ENG), Bobby Smith (ENG), Bobby Tambling (ENG), Enrique COLLAR Monterrubio (ESP), Josep Maria FUSTÉ Blanch (ESP), Francisco GENTO López (ESP), Néstor Combin (FRA), Yvon Douis (FRA), Robert Herbin (FRA), Peter Ducke (GDR), Roland Ducke (GDR), Werner Heine (GDR), Kurt Liebrecht (GDR), Jürgen Nöldner (GDR), Henk Groot (HOL), Tonny van der Linden (HOL), Klaas Nuninga (HOL), Sjaak Swart (HOL), Gyula Rákosi (HUN), Ferenc Sipos (HUN), Ernö Solymosi (HUN), Andy McEvoy (IRL), Gardar Árnason (ISL), Angelo Sormani (ITA), Johnny Léonard (LUX), Paul May (LUX), Louis Pilot (LUX), Adolphe Schmit (LUX), Edward Theobald (MLT), Joseph Urpani (MLT), Billy Bingham (NIR), John Crossan (NIR), Derek Dougan (NIR), Bill Humphries (NIR), William Irvine (NIR), John Krogh (NOR), Mário Esteves COLUNA (POR), EUSÉBIO da Silva Ferreira (POR), Gheorghe Constantin (ROM), Cicerone Manolache (ROM), Nicolae Tataru (ROM), Anton Allemann (SUI), Charles Hertig (SUI), Harry Bild (SWE), Leif Eriksson (SWE), Rudolf Kucera (TCH), Václav Masek (TCH), Igor Chislenko (URS), Gennadi Gusarov (URS), Galimzyan Khusainov (URS), Cliff Jones (WAL), Terry Medwin (WAL), Velibor Vasovic (YUG), Slaven Zambata (YUG)
1 own goal	Ion Nunweiler (ROM) for Spain

1968 UEFA European Football Championship

QUALIFYING ROUND

GROUP 1

23-10-1966	Dublin	Republic of Ireland – Spain	0-0
16-11-1966	Dublin	Republic of Ireland – Turkey	2-1 (0-0)
07-12-1966	Valencia	Spain – Republic of Ireland	2-0 (2-0)
01-02-1967	Istanbul	Turkey – Spain	0-0
22-02-1967	Ankara	Turkey – Republic of Ireland	2-1 (1-0)
21-05-1967	Dublin	Republic of Ireland – Czechoslovakia	0-2 (0-1)
31-05-1967	Bilbao	Spain – Turkey	2-0 (0-0)
18-06-1967	Bratislava	Czechoslovokia – Turkey	3-0 (1-0)
01-10-1967	Prague	Czechoslovakia – Spain	1-0 (0-0)
22-10-1967	Madrid	Spain – Czechoslovakia	2-1 (1-0)
15-11-1967	Ankara	Turkey – Czechoslovakia	0-0
22-11-1967	Prague	Czechoslovakia – Republic of Ireland	1-2 (0-0)

FINAL STANDING

Pos	Team	Pld	W	D	L	GF	GA	GD	Pts
1	*Spain*	*6*	*3*	*2*	*1*	*6*	*2*	*+4*	*8*
2	Czechoslovakia	6	3	1	2	8	4	+4	7
3	Republic of Ireland	6	2	1	3	5	8	-3	5
4	Turkey	6	1	2	3	3	8	-5	4

Spain qualified for the Quarter-finals.

23-10-1966   Dalymount Park, Dublin: Republic of Ireland – Spain 0-0
Republic of Ireland: Alan Kelly, Noel Cantwell, Tony Dunne, Mick Meagan, Seamus Brennan, John Giles, Jimmy Conway, Francis O'Neill, Andy McEvoy, Ray Treacy, Anthony O'Connell. (Coach: John Carey (IRL)).
Spain: José Ángel IRIBAR Cortajarena, Severino Severino REIJA Vázquez, Manuel SANCHÍS Martínez, Francisco SANTAMARÍA Mirones, Jesús GLARÍA Jordán, Francisco "PAQUITO" García Gómez, José Luis VIOLETA Lajusticia, MARCIAL Pina Morales, Luciano "VAVÁ" Sánchez Rodríguez, José LUIS ARAGONÉS Suárez Martínez, Fernando ANSOLA San Martín. (Coach: Domènec BALMANYA Perera (ESP)).
Referee: Hans Carlsson (SWE)   Attendance: 38.877
(Domènec BALMANYA Perera also known as DOMINGO BALMAÑA)

16-11-1966   Dalymount Park, Dublin: Republic of Ireland – Turkey   2-1 (0-0)
Republic of Ireland: Pat Dunne, Charlie Hurley, Tony Dunne, Mick Meagan, Seamus Brennan, John Giles, Joe Haverty, Jimmy Conway, Francis O'Neill, Eamonn Dunphy, Andy McEvoy. (Coach: John Carey (IRL)).
Turkey: Ali Artuner, Talat Özkarsli, Yilmaz Sen, Ercan Aktuna, Seref Has (C), Nevzat Güzelirmak, Ogün Altiparmak, Fehmi Saginoglu, Ayhan Elmastasoglu, Fevzi Zemzem, Faruk Karadogan. (Coach: Adnan Süvari (TUR)).
Goals: Republic of Ireland: 1-0 Francis O'Neill (60'), 2-0 Andy McEvoy (74').
Turkey: 2-1 Ogün Altiparmak (88').
Referee: Tage Sørensen (DEN)   Attendance: 22.480

07-12-1966   Estadio de Mestalla, Valencia: Spain – Republic of Ireland   2-0 (2-0)
Spain: José Ángel IRIBAR Cortajarena, Severino Severino REIJA Vázquez, Manuel SANCHÍS Martínez, José LUIS ARAGONÉS Suárez Martínez, José Martínez Sánchez "PIRRI", Francisco Fernández Rodríguez "GALLEGO", Francisco "PAQUITO" García Gómez, José Luis VIOLETA Lajusticia, Fernando ANSOLA San Martín, Anastasio JARA Segovia, JOSÉ MARÍA García Lavilla. (Coach: Domènec BALMANYA Perera (ESP)).
Republic of Ireland: Alan Kelly, Charlie Hurley, Tony Dunne, Mick Meagan, Seamus Brennan, John Dempsey, Joe Haverty, Alfie Hale, Jimmy Conway, Francis O'Neill, Eamonn Dunphy. (Coach: John Carey (IRL)).
Goals: Spain: 1-0 JOSÉ MARÍA García Lavilla (21'), 2-0 José Martínez Sánchez "PIRRI" (35').
Referee: Pieter Paulus (Piet) Roomer (HOL)   Attendance: 9.810

01-02-1967   Ali Sami Yen Stadi, Istanbul: Turkey – Spain   0-0
Turkey: Ali Artuner, Talat Özkarsli, Yilmaz Sen, Ercan Aktuna, Seref Has (C), Nevzat Güzelirmak, Yusuf Tunaoglu, Ogün Altiparmak, Fehmi Saginoglu, Fevzi Zemzem, Faruk Karadogan. (Coach: Adnan Süvari (TUR)).
Spain: José Ángel IRIBAR Cortajarena, Severino Severino REIJA Vázquez, Manuel SANCHÍS Martínez, José Martínez Sánchez "PIRRI", Francisco Fernández Rodríguez "GALLEGO", Francisco "PAQUITO" García Gómez, José Luis VIOLETA Lajusticia, Manuel VELÁZQUEZ Villaverde, AMANCIO Amaro Varela, JOSÉ MARÍA García Lavilla, Ramón Moreno GROSSO. (Coach: Domènec BALMANYA Perera (ESP)).
Referee: Gyula Gere (HUN)   Attendance: 27.262

22-02-1967   19 Mayis Stadi, Ankara: Turkey – Republic of Ireland   2-1 (1-0)
Turkey: Ali Artuner, Talat Özkarsli, Ercan Aktuna, Sükrü Birant, Seref Has, Abdullah Çevrim, Ogün Altiparmak, Fehmi Saginoglu, Ayhan Elmastasoglu, Faruk Karadogan, Ergün Acuner. (Coach: Adnan Süvari (TUR)).
Republic of Ireland: Alan Kelly, Noel Cantwell, Charlie Hurley, Mick Meagan, Joe Kinnear, Michael McGrath, John Giles, Francis O'Neill, Eamonn Dunphy, Alphonsus Finucane, Charlie Gallagher. (Coach: John Carey (IRL)).
Goals: Turkey: 1-0 Ayhan Elmastasoglu (35'), 2-0 Ogün Altiparmak (78').
Republic of Ireland: 2-1 Noel Cantwell (89').
Referee: Dimitar Atanassov Roumentchev (BUL)   Attendance: 31.063

21-05-1967   Dalymount Park, Dublin: Republic of Ireland – Czechoslovakia   0-2 (0-1)
Republic of Ireland: Alan Kelly, Charlie Hurley (C), Theobald Foley, Mick Meagan, John Dempsey, Eamonn Dunphy, Alphonsus Finucane, Ollie Conmy, Andy McEvoy, Ray Treacy, Charlie Gallagher. (Coach: John Carey (IRL)).
Czechoslovakia: Ivo Viktor, Jan Lála, Ján Popluhár (C), Vladimír Táborsky, Kamil Majerník, Andrej Kvasnák, Ján Geleta, Juraj Szikora, Vojtech Masny, Dusan Kabát, Jozef Adamec. (Coach: Jozef Marko (TCH)).
Goals: Czechoslovakia: 0-1 Juraj Szikora (16'), 0-2 Vojtech Masny (47').
Referee: Robert Schaut (BEL)   Attendance: 6.257

31-05-1967   Estadio San Mamés, Bilbao: Spain – Turkey   2-0 (0-0)
Spain: José Ángel IRIBAR Cortajarena, Severino Severino REIJA Vázquez, Manuel SANCHÍS Martínez, Francisco GENTO López (C), Francisco Fernández Rodríguez "GALLEGO", Jesús GLARÍA Jordán, Francisco "PAQUITO" García Gómez, ADELARDO Rodríguez Sánchez, JOSÉ Armando UFARTE Ventoso, JOSÉ MARÍA García Lavilla, Ramón Moreno GROSSO. (Coach: Domènec BALMANYA Perera (ESP)).
Turkey: Ali Artuner, Talat Özkarsli, Yilmaz Sen, Sükrü Birant, Seref Has, Ogün Altiparmak, Fehmi Saginoglu, Ayhan Elmastasoglu, Fevzi Zemzem, Faruk Karadogan, Ergün Acuner. (Coach: Adnan Süvari (TUR)).
Goals: Spain: 1-0 Ramón Moreno GROSSO (63'), 2-0 Francisco GENTO López (81').
Referee: Othmar Huber (SUI)   Attendance: 27.336

18-06-1967   Stadión Tehelné pole, Bratislava: Czechoslovakia – Turkey   3-0 (1-0)
Czechoslovakia: Ivo Viktor, Jan Lála, Ján Popluhár (C), Vladimír Táborsky, Kamil Majerník, Andrej Kvasnák, Bohumil Vesely, Ján Geleta, Dusan Kabát, Jozef Adamec, Josef Jurkanin. (Coach: Jozef Marko (TCH)).
Turkey: Ali Artuner, Talat Özkarsli, Sükrü Birant, Hüseyin Yazici, Seref Has, Nevzat Güzelirmak, Abdullah Çevrim, Ogün Altiparmak, Fehmi Saginoglu, Fevzi Zemzem, Ergün Acuner. (Coach: Adnan Süvari (TUR)).
Goals: Czechoslovakia: 1-0 Jozef Adamec (25'), 2-0 Jozef Adamec (70'), 3-0 Josef Jurkanin (73').
Referee: Paul Schiller (AUT)   Attendance: 17.839

01-10-1967   Stadión dr.Vacka "Eden", Prague: Czechoslovakia – Spain   1-0 (0-0)
Czechoslovakia: Ivo Viktor, Jan Lála, Ján Popluhár (C), Alexander Horváth, Vladimír Táborsky, Ladislav Kuna, Bohumil Vesely, Ján Geleta, Juraj Szikora, Dusan Kabát, Jozef Adamec. (Coach: Jozef Marko (TCH)).
Spain: José Ángel IRIBAR Cortajarena, Severino Severino REIJA Vázquez, Manuel SANCHÍS Martínez, Antonio "TONONO" Alfonso Moreno, José Martínez Sánchez "PIRRI", Francisco Fernández Rodríguez "GALLEGO", ADELARDO Rodríguez Sánchez, AMANCIO Amaro Varela, MARCELINO Martínez Cao, JOSÉ MARÍA García Lavilla, Ramón Moreno GROSSO. (Coach: Domènec BALMANYA Perera (ESP)).
Goal: Czechoslovakia: 1-0 Alexander Horváth (47').
Referee: Gerhard Schulenburg (FRG)   Attendance: 20.354

22-10-1967   Estadio Santiago Bernabéu, Madrid: Spain – Czechoslovakia   2-1 (1-0)
Spain: José Ángel IRIBAR Cortajarena, Severino Severino REIJA Vázquez, Antonio
"TONONO" Alfonso Moreno, Manuel Fernández OSORIO, José Martínez Sánchez "PIRRI",
Francisco Fernández Rodríguez "GALLEGO", MARCIAL Pina Morales, AMANCIO Amaro
Varela, José LUIS ARAGONÉS Suárez Martínez, JOSÉ MARÍA García Lavilla, José Eulogio
GÁRATE Ormaechea. (Coach: Domènec BALMANYA Perera (ESP)).
Czechoslovakia: Ivo Viktor, Jan Lála, Ján Popluhár (C), Alexander Horváth, Vladimír
Táborsky, Jaroslav Boros, Ladislav Kuna, Bohumil Vesely, Ján Geleta, Juraj Szikora, Vojtech
Masny. (Coach: Jozef Marko (TCH)).
Goals: Spain: 1-0 José Martínez Sánchez "PIRRI" (32'), 2-0 José Eulogio GÁRATE
Ormaechea (61').
Chechoslovakia: 2-1 Ladislav Kuna (75').
Referee: Antonio Sbardella (ITA)   Attendance: 25.314

15-11-1967   19 Mayis Stadi, Ankara: Turkey – Czechoslovakia   0-0
Turkey: Ali Artuner, Talat Özkarsli, Yilmaz Sen, Ercan Aktuna, Nevzat Güzelirmak, Ogün
Altiparmak, Fehmi Saginoglu, Ayhan Elmastasoglu, Fevzi Zemzem, Faruk Karadogan, Sanli
Sarialioglu. (Coach: Adnan Süvari (TUR)).
Czechoslovakia: Ivo Viktor, Jan Lála, Ján Popluhár (C), Vladimír Táborsky, Andrej Kvasnák,
Ladislav Kuna, Ján Geleta, Juraj Szikora, Vojtech Masny, Dusan Kabát, Josef Jurkanin.
(Coach: Jozef Marko (TCH)).
Referee: Nicolae Mihailescu (ROM)   Attendance: 19.760

22-11-1967   Stadión dr.Vacka "Eden", Prague:
              Czechoslovakia – Republic of Ireland   1-2 (0-0)
Czechoslovakia: Antonín Kramerius, Jan Lála, Ján Popluhár, Alexander Horváth, Vladimír
Táborsky, Jozef Levicky, Ladislav Kuna, Ján Geleta, Juraj Szikora, Václav Vrána, Josef
Jurkanin. (Coach: Jozef Marko (TCH)).
Republic of Ireland: Alan Kelly, Charlie Hurley, Mick Meagan, John Dempsey, Joe Kinnear,
Jimmy Conway, Eamonn Dunphy, Ollie Conmy, Turlough O'Connor, Ray Treacy, Eamonn
Rogers. (Coach: John Carey (IRL)).
Goals: Czechoslovakia: 1-0 John Dempsey (58' *own goal*).
Republic of Ireland: 1-1 Ray Treacy (63'), 1-2 Turlough O'Connor (86' penalty).
Referee: Erwin Vetter (GDR)   Attendance: 7.615

GROUP 2

13-11-1966	Sofia	Bulgaria – Norway	4-2 (3-0)
13-11-1966	Oeiras	Portugal – Sweden	1-2 (1-1)
01-06-1967	Solna	Sweden – Portugal	1-1 (0-1)
08-06-1967	Oslo	Norway – Portugal	1-2 (1-1)
11-06-1967	Solna	Sweden – Bulgaria	0-2 (0-1)
29-06-1967	Oslo	Norway – Bulgaria	0-0
03-09-1967	Oslo	Norway – Sweden	3-1 (1-1)
05-11-1967	Solna	Sweden – Norway	5-2 (2-0)
12-11-1967	Oporto	Portugal – Norway	2-1 (1-1)
12-11-1967	Sofia	Bulgaria – Sweden	3-0 (2-0)
26-11-1967	Sofia	Bulgaria – Portugal	1-0 (0-0)
17-12-1967	Oeiras	Portugal – Bulgaria	0-0

FINAL STANDING

Pos	Team	Pld	W	D	L	GF	GA	GD	Pts
1	*Bulgaria*	*6*	*4*	*2*	*0*	*10*	*2*	*+8*	*10*
2	Portugal	6	2	2	2	6	6	0	6
3	Sweden	6	2	1	3	9	12	-3	5
4	Norway	6	1	1	4	9	14	-5	3

Bulgaria qualified for the Quarter-finals.

13-11-1966 Vasil Levski Stadium, Sofia: Bulgaria – Norway 4-2 (3-0)
Bulgaria: Simeon Simeonov, Dimitar Penev, Aleksandar Shalamanov, Boris Gaganelov (C), Dobromir Zhechev, Stoyan Aleksiev, Dinko Dermendzhiev, Ivan Davidov, Petar Zhekov, Aleksandar Vasilev, Nikola Zsanev. (Coach: Dobromir Tashkov (BUL)).
Norway: Kjell Kaspersen, Roar Johansen, Arne Pedersen (C), Arild Mathisen, Finn Thorsen, Bjorn Borgen, Olav Nilsen, Trygve Bornø, Harald Berg, Per Kristoffersen, Kjetil Hasund. (Coach: Ragnar Nikolay Larsen (NOR)).
Goals: Bulgaria: 1-0 Nikola Tsanev (18'), 2-0 Petar Zhekov (42'), 3-0 Nikola Tsanev (43'), 4-1 Petar Zhekov (85').
Norway: 3-1 Kjetil Hasund (59'), 4-2 Kjetil Hasund (86').
Referee: Muzaffer Sarvan (TUR) Attendance: 20.762

13-11-1966 Estádio Nacional, Oeiras: Portugal – Sweden 1-2 (1-1)
Portugal: José COSTA PEREIRA, HILÁRIO Rosario da Conceição, João Pedro MORAIS, José ALEXANDRE da Silva BAPTISTA, JACINTO José Martins Godinho SANTOS, OLIVEIRA António Oliveira DUARTE, Mário Esteves COLUNA, JAIME da Silva GRAÇA, JOSÉ AUGUSTO Pinto de Almeida, EUSÉBIO da Silva Ferreira, ANTÓNIO Da Silva MENDES. (Coaches: Manuel Da LUZ ALFONSO (POR) & OTTO Martins GLÓRIA (BRA)).
Sweden: Ronney Pettersson, Björn Nordqvist, Kurt Axelsson, Hans Selander, Rolf Björklund, Jim Nildén, Ingvar Svensson, Ulf Jansson, Tom Turesson, Agne Simonsson, Inge Danielsson. (Coach: Orvar Bergmark (SWE)).
Goals: Portugal: 1-0 JAIME da Silva GRAÇA (21').
Sweden: 1-1 Inge Danielsson (29'), 1-2 Inge Danielsson (87').
Referee: Jacques Colling (LUX) Attendance: 18.244

01-06-1967 Råsunda Stadion, Solna: Sweden – Portugal 1-1 (0-1)
Sweden: Ronney Pettersson, Björn Nordqvist, Kurt Axelsson, Hans Selander, Örjan Persson, Rolf Björklund, Jim Nildén, Ingvar Svensson, Roger Magnusson, Tom Turesson, Agne Simonsson. (Coach: Orvar Bergmark (SWE)).
Portugal: AMÉRICO Ferreira Lopes, HILÁRIO Rosario da Conceição, João Pedro MORAIS, JOSÉ CARLOS da Silva José, JAIME da Silva GRAÇA, Raúl MARTINS MACHADO, CUSTÓDIO João PINTO, JOSÉ AUGUSTO Pinto de Almeida, EUSÉBIO da Silva Ferreira, Manuel SERAFIM Monteiro Pereira, FERNANDO PERES da Silva. (Coach: José Gomes De Silva (POR)).
Goals: Sweden: 1-1 Ingvar Svensson (90').
Portugal: 0-1 CUSTÓDIO João PINTO (19').
Referee: Kevin Howley (ENG) Attendance: 49.689

08-06-1967   Ullevaal Stadion, Oslo: Norway – Portugal   1-2 (1-1)
Norway: Kjell Kaspersen, Roar Johansen, Arild Mathisen, Finn Thorsen, Nils Eggen, Olav Nilsen, Trygve Bornø, Harald Berg, Harald Sunde, Odd Iversen, Leif Eriksen. (Coach: Wilhelm Kment (AUT)).
Portugal: AMÉRICO Ferreira Lopes, HILÁRIO Rosario da Conceição, João Pedro MORAIS, JOSÉ CARLOS da Silva José, JAIME da Silva GRAÇA, Raúl MARTINS MACHADO, CUSTÓDIO João PINTO, JOSÉ MARÍA Júnior, ESTÊVÃO António do Espírito Santo MANSIDÃO, JOSÉ AUGUSTO Pinto de Almeida, EUSÉBIO da Silva Ferreira. (Coach: José Gomes De Silva (POR)).
Goals: Norway: 1-1 Odd Iversen (34').
Portugal: 0-1 EUSÉBIO da Silva Ferreira (15'), 1-2 EUSÉBIO da Silva Ferreira (61').
Referee: William Syme (SCO)   Attendance: 29.993

11-06-1967   Råsunda Stadion, Solna: Sweden – Bulgaria   0-2 (0-1)
Sweden: Ronney Pettersson, Björn Nordqvist, Kurt Axelsson, Hans Selander, Örjan Persson, Rolf Björklund, Jim Nildén, Ingvar Svensson, Tom Turesson, Agne Simonsson, Inge Danielsson. (Coach: Orvar Bergmark (SWE)).
Bulgaria: Simeon Simeonov, Dimitar Penev, Ivan Dimitrov, Aleksandar Shalamanov, Boris Gaganelov, Dobromir Zhechev, Hristo Bonev, Dimitar Yakimov, Dinko Dermendzhiev, Georgi Popov, Petar Zhekov. (Coach: Stefan Boshkov (BUL)).
Goals: Bulgaria: 0-1 Petar Zhekov (23'), 0-2 Dinko Dermendzhiev (82').
Referee: Leo Callaghan (WAL)   Attendance: 24.271

29-06-1967   Ullevaal Stadion, Oslo: Norway – Bulgaria   0-0
Norway: Kjell Kaspersen, Roar Johansen, Arild Mathisen, Finn Thorsen, Nils Eggen, Olav Nilsen, Trygve Bornø, Harald Berg, Harald Sunde, Kjetil Hasund, Odd Iversen. (Coach: Wilhelm Kment (AUT)).
Bulgaria: Simeon Simeonov, Dimitar Penev, Ivan Dimitrov, Aleksandar Shalamanov, Boris Gaganelov, Dobromir Zhechev, Hristo Bonev, Dimitar Yakimov, Dinko Dermendzhiev, Petar Zhekov, Vasil Mitkov. (Coach: Stefan Boshkov (BUL)).
Referee: John Adair (NIR)   Attendance: 25.545

03-09-1967   Ullevaal Stadion, Oslo: Norway – Sweden   3-1 (1-1)
Norway: Kjell Kaspersen, Roar Johansen, Finn Thorsen, Nils Eggen, Tore Børrehaug, Olav Nilsen, Trygve Bornø, Harald Berg, Harald Sunde, Odd Iversen, Sven Otto Birkeland. (Coach: Wilhelm Kment (AUT)).
Sweden: Ronney Pettersson, Hans Selander, Krister Kristensson, Tommy Svensson, Leif Eriksson, Thomas Nordahl, Rolf Björklund, Bertil Elmstedt, Sven Lindman, Harry Bild, Inge Danielsson. (Coach: Orvar Bergmark (SWE)).
Goals: Norway: 1-1 Harald Berg (24'), 2-1 Sven Otto Birkeland (46'), 3-1 Harald Sunde (79').
Sweden: 0-1 Thomas Nordahl (19').
Referee: Jan Pawlik (POL)   Attendance: 32.151

05-11-1967 Råsunda Stadion, Solna: Sweden – Norway 5-2 (2-0)
Sweden: Sven Gunnar Larsson, Björn Nordqvist, Sven Andersson, Stig Johansson, Leif Eriksson, Ulf Jansson, Bertil Elmstedt, Sven Lindman, Ingvar Svahn, Tom Turesson, Inge Danielsson. (Coach: Orvar Bergmark (SWE)).
Norway: Kjell Kaspersen, Arild Mathisen, Nils Eggen, Frank Olafsen, Per Pettersen, Olav Nilsen, Trygve Bornø, Harald Berg, Harald Sunde, Kjetil Hasund, Odd Iversen. (Coach: Wilhelm Kment (AUT)).
Goals: Sweden: 1-0 Tom Turesson (15'), 2-0 Inge Danielsson (40'), 3-0 Leif Eriksson (48'), 4-1 Leif Eriksson (85'), 5-1 Tom Turesson (89').
Norway: 3-1 Odd Iversen (57' penalty), 5-2 Olav Nilsen (90').
Referee: Rudolf (Rudi) Glöckner (GDR)   Attendance: 14.078

12-11-1967 Estádio das Antas, Oporto: Portugal – Norway 2-1 (1-1)
Portugal: AMÉRICO Ferreira Lopes, HILÁRIO Rosario da Conceição, JOSÉ CARLOS da Silva José, MANUEL de Sousa RODRIGUES, Mário Esteves COLUNA, JAIME da Silva GRAÇA, Raúl MARTINS MACHADO, JOSÉ AUGUSTO Pinto de Almeida, EUSÉBIO da Silva Ferreira, JOSÉ Augusto Costa Sénica TORRES, Francisco Lage Pereira de NÓBREGA. (Coach: José Gomes De Silva (POR)).
Norway: Kjell Kaspersen, Arild Mathisen, Nils Eggen, Per Pettersen, Tor Alsaker-Nøstdahl, Olav Nilsen, Trygve Bornø, Harald Berg, Harald Sunde, Kai Sjøberg, Odd Iversen. (Coach: Wilhelm Kment (AUT)).
Goals: Portugal: 1-0 JOSÉ Augusto Costa Sénica TORRES (29'), 2-1 JAIME da Silva GRAÇA (65').
Norway: 1-1 Olav Nilsen (40').
Referee: Michel Kitabdjian (FRA)   Attendance: 20.500

12-11-1967 Vasil Levski Stadium, Sofia: Bulgaria – Sweden 3-0 (2-0)
Bulgaria: Simeon Simeonov, Dimitar Penev, Aleksandar Shalamanov, Boris Gaganelov, Dobromir Zhechev, Hristo Bonev, Dinko Dermendzhiev, Todor Kolev, Vasil Mitkov, Nikola Kotkov, Georgi Asparuhov. (Coach: Stefan Boshkov (BUL)).
Sweden: Sven Gunnar Larsson, Björn Nordqvist (C), Sven Andersson, Leif Eriksson, Rolf Björklund, Ulf Jansson, Bertil Elmstedt, Sven Lindman, Ingvar Svahn, Tom Turesson, Inge Danielsson. (Coach: Orvar Bergmark (SWE)).
Goals: Bulgaria: 1-0 Nikola Kotkov (43'), 2-0 Vasil Mitkov (44'), 3-0 Georgi Asparuhov (75').
Referee: Dragomir Josip Horvath (YUG)   Attendance: 16.479

26-11-1967 Vasil Levski Stadium, Sofia: Bulgaria – Portugal 1-0 (0-0)
Bulgaria: Simeon Simeonov, Dimitar Penev, Aleksandar Shalamanov, Boris Gaganelov (C), Dobromir Zhechev, Hristo Bonev, Dinko Dermendzhiev, Ivan Davidov, Vasil Mitkov, Nikola Kotkov, Georgi Asparuhov. (Coach: Stefan Boshkov (BUL)).
Portugal: AMÉRICO Ferreira Lopes, HILÁRIO Rosario da Conceição, JOSÉ CARLOS da Silva José, MANUEL de Sousa RODRIGUES, RUI de Gouveia Pinto RODRIGUES, JAIME da Silva GRAÇA, José Maria de Freitas Pereira "PEDRAS", ANTÓNIO José SIMÕES da Costa, JOSÉ AUGUSTO Pinto de Almeida (C), EUSÉBIO da Silva Ferreira, JOSÉ Augusto Costa Sénica TORRES. (Coach: José Gomes De Silva (POR)).
Goal: Bulgaria: 1-0 Dinko Dermendzhiev (63').
Referee: Anvar Zverev (URS)   Attendance: 39.795

17-12-1967   Estádio Nacional, Oeiras: Portugal – Bulgaria   0-0
Portugal: AMÉRICO Ferreira Lopes, HILÁRIO Rosario da Conceição, JOSÉ CARLOS da Silva José, MANUEL de Sousa RODRIGUES, RUI de Gouveia Pinto RODRIGUES, JAIME da Silva GRAÇA, José Maria de Freitas Pereira "PEDRAS", ANTÓNIO José SIMÕES da Costa, JOSÉ AUGUSTO Pinto de Almeida (C), EUSÉBIO da Silva Ferreira, JOSÉ Augusto Costa Sénica TORRES. (Coach: José Gomes De Silva (POR)).
Bulgaria: Simeon Simeonov, Dimitar Penev, Ivan Dimitrov, Milko Gaydarski, Boris Gaganelov (C), Dobromir Zhechev, Hristo Bonev, Dimitar Yakimov, Dinko Dermendzhiev, Georgi Popov, Nikola Kotkov. (Coach: Stefan Boshkov (BUL)).
Referee: Antonio Sbardella (ITA)   Attendance: 13.408

GROUP 3

02-10-1966	Helsinki	Finland – Austria	0-0
16-10-1966	Salonika	Greece – Finland	2-1 (1-0)
10-05-1967	Helsinki	Finland – Greece	1-1 (1-1)
11-06-1967	Moscow	Soviet Union – Austria	4-3 (3-1)
16-07-1967	Tbilisi	Soviet Union – Greece	4-0 (0-0)
30-08-1967	Moscow	Soviet Union – Finland	2-0 (1-0)
06-09-1967	Turku	Finland – Soviet Union	2-5 (2-3)
24-09-1967	Vienna	Austria – Finland	2-1 (1-0)
04-10-1967	Piraeus	Greece – Austria	4-1 (2-0)
15-10-1967	Vienna	Austria – Soviet Union	1-0 (0-0)
31-10-1967	Piraeus	Greece – Soviet Union	0-1 (0-0)
05-11-1967	*Vienna*	*Austria – Greece*	*1-1 (1-0)*

FINAL STANDING

Pos	Team	Pld	W	D	L	GF	GA	GD	Pts
1	*Soviet Union*	*6*	*5*	*0*	*1*	*16*	*6*	*+10*	*10*
2	Greece	5	2	1	2	7	8	-1	5
3	Austria	5	2	1	2	7	9	-2	5
4	Finland	6	0	2	4	5	12	-7	2

The match Austria vs Greece, played on November 5, 1967, was abandoned at 1-1 and the result was declared void. The result is therefore not included in the final group standings.

Soviet Union qualified for the Quarter-finals.

02-10-1966   Olympiastadion, Helsinki: Finland – Austria   0-0
Finland: Lars Näsman, Timo Kautonen, Reijo Kanerva, Reima Nummila, Juhani Peltonen, Sino Syrjävaara, Matti Mäkelä (C), Pertti Mäkipää, Tommy Lindholm, Aulis Laine, Markku Hyvärinen. (Coach: Olavi Laaksonen (FIN)).
Austria: Roman Pichler, Robert Sara, Walter Glechner (C), Walter Gebhardt, Franz Viehböck, Horst Hirnschrodt, Heinz Binder, Rudolf Flögel, Anton Fritsch, Thomas Parits, Johann Hörmayer. (Coach: Eduard Frühwirth (AUT)).
Referee: Peter P.Coates (IRL)   Attendance: 10.070

16-10-1966   Kaftanzoglio Stadio, Salonika: Greece – Finland   2-1 (1-0)
Greece: Takis Ikonomopoulos, Tasos Vasiliou, Fotis Balopoulos, Stathis Chaitas, Mimis Domazos, Frangiskos Sourpis, Giorgos Skrekis, Stelios Skevofilax, Alekos Alexiadis, Mimis Papaloannou, Giorgos Dedes. (Coach: Panayotis Markovits (GRE)).
Finland: Lars Näsman, Timo Kautonen, Reijo Kanerva, Reima Nummila, Arto Tolsa, Juhani Peltonen, Sino Syrjävaara, Matti Mäkelä, Pertti Mäkipää, Aulis Laine, Markku Hyvärinen. (Coach: Olavi Laaksonen (FIN)).
Goals: Greece: 1-0 Alekos Alexiadis (39'), 2-1 Alekos Alexiadis (86').
Finland: 1-1 Pertti Mäkipää (57').
Referee: Zdenek Vales (TCH)   Attendance: 28.478

10-05-1967   Olympiastadion, Helsinki: Finland – Greece   1-1 (1-1)
Finland: Martti Halme, Rainer Aho, Timo Kautonen, Reijo Kanerva, Reima Nummila, Arto Tolsa, Juhani Peltonen, Matti Mäkelä, Pertti Mäkipää, Semi Nuoranen, Tommy Lindholm. (Coach: Olavi Laaksonen (FIN)).
Greece: Takis Ikonomopoulos, Kostas Polychroniou, Michalis Belis, Christos Zanderoglou, Takis Loukanidis, Alekos Sofianidis, Stathis Chaitas, Nikos Youtsos, Mimis Domazos, Mimis Papaloannou, Vasilis Botinos. (Coach: Lakis Petropoulos (GRE)).
Goals: Finland: 1-0 Juhani Peltonen (18').
Greece: 1-1 Stathis Chaitas (39).
Referee: Pieter Paulus (Piet) Roomer (HOL)   Attendance: 14.056

11-06-1967   Central Lenin Stadium, Moscow: Soviet Union – Austria   4-3 (3-1)
Soviet Union: Lev Yashin, Albert Shesternev, Valentin Afonin, Valeri Voronin, Anatoli Byshovets, Murtaz Khurtsilava, József Szabó, Aleksandr Lenev, Igor Chislenko, Eduard Malofeev, Eduard Streltsov. (Coach: Mikhail Yakuschin (URS)).
Austria: Roman Pichler, Walter Glechner, Helmut Wartusch, Erich Fak, Roland Eschlmüller, Gerhard Sturmberger, Rudolf Flögel, Erich Hof, Johann Hörmayer, Franz Wolny, Helmut Siber. (Coaches: Erwin Alge (AUT) & Johann (Hans) Pesser (AUT)).
Goals: Soviet Union: 1-0 Eduard Malofeev (25'), 2-0 Anatoli Byshovets (36'), 3-1 Igor Chislenko (43'), 4-3 Eduard Streltsov (90').
Austria: 2-1 Erich Hof (38'), 3-2 Franz Wolny (54'), 3-3 Helmut Siber (71').
Referee: Johan Einar Boström (SWE)   Attendance: 72.142
(Some sources report that the third Soviet goal was an own goal by Helmut Wartusch)

16-07-1967   Central Stadium Dynamo, Tbilisi: Soviet Union – Greece   4-0 (0-0)
Soviet Union: Lev Yashin, Albert Shesternev, Viktor Anichkin, Valeri Voronin, Anatoli Byshovets, Murtaz Khurtsilava, József Szabó, Aleksandr Lenev, Igor Chislenko, Anatoli Banishevski, Eduard Streltsov. (Coach: Mikhail Yakuschin (URS)).
Greece: Takis Ikonomopoulos, Kostas Polychroniou, Michalis Belis, Aristidis Kamaras, Takis Loukanidis, Stathis Chaitas, Mimis Domazos, Dimitris Plesas, Giorgos Sideris, Mimis Papaloannou, Vasilis Botinos. (Coach: Lakis Petropoulos (GRE)).
Goals: Soviet Union: 1-0 Anatoli Banishevski (50'), 2-0 József Szabó (72' penalty), 3-0 Banishevski (77'), 4-0 Igor Chislenko (83').
Referee: Birger Nielsen (NOR)   Attendance: 28.040

30-08-1967   Central Lenin Stadium, Moscow: Soviet Union – Finland   2-0 (1-0)
Soviet Union: Anzor Kavazashvili, Albert Shesternev, Valentin Afonin, Guram Tskhovrebov, Anatoli Byshovets, Murtaz Khurtsilava, József Szabó, Valeri Maslov, Igor Chislenko, Anatoli Banishevski, Eduard Malofeev. (Coach: Mikhail Yakuschin (URS)).
Finland: Lars Näsman, Timo Kautonen, Reima Nummila, Arto Tolsa, Seppo Kilponen, Juhani Peltonen, Simo Syrjävaara, Matti Mäkelä, Pertti Mäkipää, Kai Pahlman, Aulis Laine. (Coach: Olavi Laaksonen (FIN)).
Goals: Soviet Union: 1-0 Murtaz Khurtsilava (14'), 2-0 Igor Chislenko (80').
Referee: Muzaffer Sarvan (TUR)   Attendance: 20.597

06-09-1967   Kupittaan Stadion, Turku: Finland – Soviet Union   2-5 (2-3)
Finland: Lars Näsman, Timo Kautonen, Reima Nummila, Arto Tolsa, Seppo Kilponen, Juhani Peltonen, Simo Syrjävaara, Matti Pitko, Matti Mäkelä, Pertti Mäkipää, Aulis Laine. (Coach: Olavi Laaksonen (FIN)).
Soviet Union: Anzor Kavazashvili, Gennadi Logofet, Valentin Afonin, Viktor Anichkin, Anatoli Byshovets, Murtaz Khurtsilava, József Szabó, Valeri Maslov, Igor Chislenko, Anatoli Banishevski, Eduard Malofeev. (Coach: Mikhail Yakuschin (URS)).
Goals: Finland: 1-2 Juhani Peltonen (18' penalty), 2-2 Simo Syrjävaara (25').
Soviet Union: 0-1 József Szabó 2'), 1-2 Valeri Maslov (14'), 2-3 Anatoli Banishevski (35'), 2-4 József Szabó (56' penalty), 2-5 Eduard Malofeev (63').
Referee: Pavel Spoták (TCH)   Attendance: 7.793

24-09-1967   Praterstadion Vienna: Austria – Finland   2-1 (1-0)
Austria: Gerald Fuchsbichler, Walter Glechner, Gerhard Sturmberger, Walter Gebhardt, Karl Fröhlich, Johann Eigenstiller, Rudolf Flögel, Helmut Metzler, Franz Wolny, Leopold Grausam, Helmuth Redl. (Coaches: Erwin Alge (AUT) & Johann (Hans) Pesser (AUT)).
Finland: Lars Näsman, Timo Kautonen, Reima Nummila, Arto Tolsa, Seppo Kilponen, Juhani Peltonen, Simo Syrjävaara, Matti Pitko, Matti Mäkelä, Semi Nuoranen, Tommy Lindholm. (Coach: Olavi Laaksonen (FIN)).
Goals: Austria: 1-0 Rudolf Flögel (17'), 2-1 Leopold Grausam (81').
Finland: 1-1 Juhani Peltonen (57').
Referee: Milivoje Gugulovic (YUG)   Attendance: 25.231
(Timo Kautonen was sent off in the 79th minute)

04-10-1967   Stadio Karaiskaki, Piraeus: Greece – Austria   4-1 (2-0)
Greece: Takis Ikonomopoulos, Kostas Polychroniou, Christos Zanderoglou, Fotis Balopoulos, Takis Loukanidis, Nikos Youtsos, Mimis Domazos, Giannis Gaitatzis, Giorgos Sideris, Mimis Papaloannou, Vasilis Botinos. (Coach: Lakis Petropoulos (GRE)).
Austria: Gerald Fuchsbichler, Walter Glechner, Johann Frank, Walter Gebhardt, Karl Fröhlich, Johann Eigenstiller, Rudolf Flögel, Anton Fritsch, Helmut Siber, Leopold Grausam, Helmuth Redl. (Coaches: Erwin Alge (AUT) & Johann (Hans) Pesser (AUT)).
Goals: Greece: 1-0 Giorgos Sideris (27'), 2-0 Giorgos Sideris (34' penalty), 3-1 Giorgos Sideris (63'), 4-1 Mimis Papaloannou (75').
Austria: 2-1 Leopold Grausam (62').
Referee: Vasile Dumitrescu (ROM)   Attendance: 34.552

15-10-1967   Praterstadion, Vienna: Austria – Soviet Union   1-0 (0-0)
Austria: Wilhelm Harreither, Walter Glechner, Gerhard Sturmberger, Walter Gebhardt, Karl Fröhlich, Johann Eigenstiller, Walter Stamm, Rudolf Flögel, Walter Koleznik, Helmut Siber, Leopold Grausam. (Coaches: Erwin Alge (AUT) & Johann (Hans) Pesser (AUT)).
Soviet Union: Anzor Kavazashvili, Albert Shesternev, Valentin Afonin, Viktor Anichkin, Gurom Tskhovrebov, Anatoli Byshovets, Murtaz Khurtsilava, József Szabó, Valeri Maslov, Anatoli Banishevski, Eduard Streltsov. (Coach: Mikhail Yakuschin (URS)).
Goal: Austria: 1-0 Leopold Grausam (50').
Referee: Todor P.Betchirov (BUL)   Attendance: 37.400

31-10-1967   Stadio Karaiskaki, Piraeus: Greece – Soviet Union   0-1 (0-0)
Greece: Nikolas Christidis, Kostas Polychroniou, Christos Zanderoglou, Fotis Balopoulos, Takis Loukanidis, Stathis Chaitas, Nikos Youtsos, Mimis Domazos, Giannis Gaitatzis, Giorgos Sideris, Mimis Papaioannou. (Coach: Lakis Petropoulos (GRE)).
Soviet Union: Anzor Kavazashvili, Albert Shesternev, Valentin Afonin, Viktor Anichkin, Valeri Voronin, Murtaz Khurtsilava, József Szabó, Igor Chislenko, Anatoli Banishevski, Eduard Malofeev, Eduard Streltsov. (Coach: Mikhail Yakuschin (URS)).
Goal: Soviet Union: 0-1 Eduard Malofeev (50').
Referee: Gottfried Dienst (SUI)   Attendance: 33.588

05-11-1967   Praterstadion, Vienna: Austria – Greece   1-1 (1-0)
Austria: Wilhelm Harreither, Walter Glechner, Walter Gebhardt, Karl Fröhlich, Johann Eigenstiller, Walter Stamm, Walter Koleznik, Walter Skocik, Helmut Siber, Leopald Grausam, Helmut Redl. Coaches: Erwin Alge & Johann Pesser).
Greece: Nikolas Christidis, Kostas Polychroniou, Christos Zanderoglou, Aristidis Kamaras, Fotis Balopoulos, Giorgos Koudas, Takis Loukanidis, Mimis Domazos, Giannis Gaitatzis, Giorgos Sideris, Mimis Papaioannou. (Coach: Lakis Petropoulos (GRE)).
Goals: Austria: 1-0 Helmut Siber (31').
Greece: 1-1 Giorgos Sideris (71').
Referee: Gyula Gere (HUN)   Attendance: 31.996
(This match was abandoned in the 85th minute due to crowd trouble and the result is not included in the final group standings)

GROUP 4

08-04-1967	Dortmund	West Germany – Albania	6-0 (2-0)
03-05-1967	Belgrade	Yugoslavia – West Germany	1-0 (0-0)
14-05-1967	Tirana	Albania – Yugoslavia	0-2 (0-1)
07-10-1967	Hamburg	West Germany – Yugoslavia	3-1 (1-0)
12-11-1967	Belgrade	Yugoslavia – Albania	4-0 (1-0)
17-12-1967	Tirana	Albania – West Germany	0-0

FINAL STANDING

Pos	Team	Pld	W	D	L	GF	GA	GD	Pts
1	*Yugoslavia*	*4*	*3*	*0*	*1*	*8*	*3*	*+5*	*6*
2	West Germany	4	2	1	1	9	2	+7	5
3	Albania	4	0	1	3	0	12	-12	1

Yugoslavia qualified for the Quarter-finals.

08-04-1967   Stadion Rote Erde, Dortmund: West Germany – Albania 6-0 (2-0)
West Germany: Hans Tilkowski, Franz Beckenbauer, Horst-Dieter Höttges, Willi Schulz, Bernd Patzke, Wolfgang Weber, Wolfgang Overath, Bernd Dörfel, Gerd Müller, Johannes Löhr, Lothar Ulsaß. (Coach: Helmut Schön (FRG)).
Albania: Mikel Janku, Fatmir Frashëri, Ali Mema, Teodor Vaso, Bahri Ishka, Ramazan Rragami, Josif Kazanxhi, Niko Xhaçka, Panajot Pano, Skënder Hyka, Sabah Bizi. (Coach: Loro Boriçi (ALB)).
Goals: West Germany: 1-0 Gerd Müller (5'), 2-0 Gerd Müller (23'), 3-0 Gerd Müller (73'), 4-0 Johannes Löhr (77'), 5-0 Johannes Löhr (78'), 6-0 Gerd Müller (80' penalty).
Referee: Martti Hirviniemi (FIN)   Attendance: 27.674

03-05-1967   Stadion JNA, Belgrade: Yugoslavia – West Germany 1-0 (0-0)
Yugoslavia: Ilija Pantelic, Fahrudin Jusufi, Mirsad Fazlagic, Dragan Holcer, Marijan Brncic, Branko Rasovic, Radoslav Becejac, Dragan Dzajic, Josip Skoblar, Vojislav Melic, Mustafa Hasanagic. (Coach: Rajko Mitic (YUG)).
West Germany: Sepp Maier, Berti Vogts, Franz Beckenbauer, Willi Schulz (C), Klaus Fichtel, Bernd Patzke, Wolfgang Overath, Hans Küppers, Gerd Müller, Siegfried Held, Johannes Löhr. (Coach: Helmut Schön (FRG)).
Goal: Yugoslavia: 1-0 Josip Skoblar (67').
Referee: José María Ortiz de Mendíbil (ESP)   Attendance: 36.508

14-05-1967   Stadiumi Qemal Stafa, Tirana: Albania – Yugoslavia 0-2 (0-1)
Albania: Mikel Janku, Fatmir Frashëri, Ali Mema, Teodor Vaso, Ramazan Rragami, Josif Kazanxhi, Niko Xhaçka, Panajot Pano, Lorenc Vorfi, Medin Zhega, Lin Shilaku (C). (Coach: Loro Boriçi (ALB)).
Yugoslavia: Miodrag Knezevic, Mirsad Fazlagic, Dragan Holcer, Marijan Brncic, Branko Rasovic, Radoslav Becejac, Stjepan Lamza, Dragan Dzajic, Vojislav Melic (C), Slaven Zambata, Petar Nadoveza. (Coach: Rajko Mitic (YUG)).
Goals: Yugoslavia: 0-1 Slaven Zambata (22'), 0-2 Slaven Zambata (56').
Referee: Costas Xanthoulis (CYP)   Attendance: 18.573

07-10-1967   Volksparkstadion, Hamburg: West Germany – Yugolavia 3-1 (1-0)
West Germany: Sepp Maier, Horst-Dieter Höttges, Willi Schulz, Bernd Patzke, Wolfgang Weber, Wolfgang Overath, Hans Siemensmeyer, Franz Roth, Gerd Müller, Uwe Seeler (C), Johannes Löhr. (Coach: Helmut Schön (FRG)).
Yugoslavia: Ilija Pantelic, Mirsad Fazlagic, Dragan Holcer, Marijan Brncic, Branko Rasovic, Stevan Nesticki, Ivica Osim, Radoslav Becejac, Dragan Dzajic, Josip Skoblar, Slaven Zambata. (Coach: Rajko Mitic (YUG)).
Goals: West Germany: 1-0 Johannes Löhr (10'), 2-1 Gerd Müller (70'), 3-1 Uwe Seeler (86').
Yugoslavia: 1-1 Slaven Zambata (46').
Referee: Concetto Lo Bello (ITA)   Attendance: 70.573

12-11-1967   Stadion JNA, Belgrade: Yugoslavia – Albania 4-0 (1-0)
Yugoslavia: Radomir Vuksevic, Mirsad Fazlagic (C), Milan Damjanovic, Blagoje Paunovic, Dragan Holcer, Ivica Osim, Borivoje Djordjevic, Krasnodar Rora, Dragan Dzajic, Vojin Lazarevic, Edin Spreco. (Coach: Rajko Mitic (YUG)).
Albania: Jani Rama, Ali Mema, Teodor Vaso, Frederik Jorgaqi, Lin Shilaku (C), Ramazan Rragami, Gani Xhafa, Foto Andoni, Panajot Pano, Sabah Bizi, Medin Zhega. (Coach: Loro Boriçi (ALB)).
Goals: Yugoslavia: 1-0 Edin Spreco (44'), 2-0 Ivica Osim (48'), 3-0 Vojin Lazarevic (56'), 4-0 Ivica Osim (82').
Referee: Andrei Radulescu (ROM)   Attendance: 18.573

17-12-1967 Stadiumi Qemal Stafa, Tirana: Albania – West Germany 0-0
Albania: Koço Dinella, Ali Mema, Teodor Vaso, Frederik Jorgaqi, Frederik Gjinali, Lin Shilaku, Ramazan Rragami, Josif Kazanxhi, Panajot Pano, Sabah Bizi, Medin Zhega. (Coach: Loro Boriçi (ALB)).
West Germany: Horst Wolter, Horst-Dieter Höttges, Willi Schulz (C), Bernd Patzke, Wolfgang Weber, Wolfgang Overath, Günter Netzer, Hans Küppers, Siegfried Held, Johannes Löhr, Peter Meyer. (Coach: Helmut Schön (FRG)).
Referee: Ferdinand Marschall (AUT) Attendance: 21.889

GROUP 5

07-09-1966	Rotterdam	Netherlands – Hungary	2-2 (1-0)
21-09-1966	Budapest	Hungary – Denmark	6-0 (5-0)
30-11-1966	Rotterdam	Netherlands – Denmark	2-0 (0-0)
05-04-1967	Leipzig	East Germany – Netherlands	4-3 (0-2)
10-05-1067	Budapest	Hungary – Netherlands	2-1 (2-0)
24-05-1967	Copenhagen	Denmark – Hungary	0-2 (0-1)
04-06-1967	Copenhagen	Denmark – East Germany	1-1 (0-1)
13-09-1967	Amsterdam	Netherlands – East Germany	1-0 (1-0)
27-09-1967	Budapest	Hungary – East Germany	3-1 (1-0)
04-10-1967	Copenhagen	Denmark – Netherlands	3-2 (1-0)
11-10-1967	Leipzig	East Germany – Denmark	3-2 (1-2)
29-10-1967	Leipzig	East Germany – Hungary	1-0 (0-0)

FINAL STANDING

Pos	Team	Pld	W	D	L	GF	GA	GD	Pts
1	*Hungary*	*6*	*4*	*1*	*1*	*15*	*5*	*+10*	*9*
2	East Germany	6	3	1	2	10	10	0	7
3	Netherlands	6	2	1	3	11	11	0	5
4	Denmark	6	1	1	4	6	16	-10	3

Hungary qualified for the Quarter-finals.

07-09-1967 Stadion Feijenoord, Rotterdam: Netherlands – Hungary 2-2 (1-0)
Netherlands: Eddy Pieters-Graafland, Rinus Israël, Daan Schrijvers, Cor Veldhoen, Frits Flinkevleugel, Miel Pijs, Johan Cruijff, Bennie Muller, Piet Keizer, Sjaak Swart, Klaas Nuninga. (Coach: George Kessler (FRG)).
Hungary: Antal Szentmihályi, Benö Káposzta, Kálmán Mészöly, Kálmán Ihász, Zoltán Varga, Ferenc Sipos, Dezsö Molnár, Ferenc Bene, Flórián Albert, Gyula Rákosi, János Farkas. (Coach: Rudolf Illovszky (HUN)).
Goals: Netherlands: 1-0 Miel Pijs (35'), 2-0 Johan Cruijff (54').
Hungary: 2-1 Dezsö Molnár (70'), 2-2 Kálmán Mészöly (86').
Referee: Birger Nielsen (NOR) Attendance: 61.600

21-09-1966   Népstadion, Budapest: Hungary – Denmark   6-0 (5-0)
Hungary: Antal Szentmihályi, Sándor Mátrai (C), Kálmán Mészöly, Kálmán Ihász, Benö Káposzta, Imre Mathesz, Zoltán Varga, Flórián Albert, János Farkas, Ferenc Bene, Dezsö Molnár. (Coach: Rudolf Illovszky (HUN)).
Denmark: Leif Nielsen, Jens Jørgen Hansen, John Worbye, Henning Boel, Johnny Hansen, Niels-Erik Andersen (C), Bent Schmidt Hansen, Ulrik Le Fevre, Henning Enoksen, Niels Møller, René Møller. (Coach: Poul Eyvind Pedersen (DEN)).
Goals: Hungary: 1-0 Flórián Albert (1'), 2-0 Kálmán Mészöly (9' penalty), 3-0 Ferenc Bene (14'), 4-0 Flórián Albert (30'), 5-0 János Farkas (36'), 6-0 Zoltán Varga (83').
Referee: Petros Tzouvaras (GRE)   Attendance: 18.487

30-11-1966   Stadion Feijenoord, Rotterdam: Netherlands – Denmark   2-0 (0-0)
Netherlands: Eddy Pieters-Graafland, Wim Suurbier, Rinus Israël, Daan Schrijvers, Cor Veldhoen, Bennie Muller, Willy Dullens, Piet Keizer, Sjaak Swart, Klaas Nuninga, Willy van der Kuijlen. (Coach: George Kessler (FRG)).
Denmark: Leif Nielsen, John Worbye, Henning Boel, Johnny Hansen, Leif Hartwig, Henning Munk Jensen, Ulrik Le Fevre, John Steen Olsen, Kjeld Thorst, Finn Wiberg, Keld Bak. (Coach: Poul Eyvind Pedersen (DEN)).
Goals: Netherlands: 1-0 Sjaak Swart (58'), Willy van der Kuijlen (73').
Referee: Aníbal da Silva Oliveira (POR)   Attendance: 25.134

05-04-1967   Zentralstadion, Leipzig: East Germany – Netherlands   4-3 (0-2)
East Germany: Horst Weigang, Otto Fräßdorf, Manfred Geisler, Manfred Walter, Roland Ducke, Dieter Erler, Jürgen Nöldner, Herbert Pankau, Gerhard Körner, Eberhard Vogel, Henning Frenzel. (Coach: Karoly Sos (HUN)).
Netherlands: Tonny van Leeuwen, Wim Suurbier, Daan Schrijvers, Miel Pijs, Peter Kemper, Piet de Zoete, Piet Keizer, Sjaak Swart, Henk Groot, Klaas Nuninga, Jan Mulder. (Coach: George Kessler (FRG)).
Goals: East Germany: 1-2 Eberhard Vogel (50'), 2-2 Henning Frenzel (62'), 3-3 Henning Frenzel (78'), 4-3 Henning Frenzel (85').
Netherlands: 0-1 Jan Mulder (10'), 0-2 Piet Keizer (12'), 2-3 Piet Keizer (65').
Referee: Hannes Thorsteinn Sigurdsson (ISL)   Attendance: 30.207

10-05-1967   Népstadion, Budapest: Hungary – Netherlands   2-1 (2-0)
Hungary: Gyula Tamás, Sándor Mátrai, Kálmán Mészöly, Kálmán Ihász, Lajos Szücs, János Göröcs, Flórián Albert, Gyula Rákosi, János Farkas, Ferenc Bene, Dezsö Molnár. (Coach: Rudolf Illovszky (HUN)).
Netherlands: Tonny van Leeuwen (46' Pim Doesburg), Wim Suurbier, Rinus Israël, Cor Veldhoen, Bennie Muller, Hans Eijenbroek, Gerard Bergholtz, Piet Keizer, Henk Groot, Klaas Nuninga, Jan Mulder. (Coach: George Kessler (FRG)).
Goals: Hungary: 1-0 Kálmán Mészöly (8' penalty), 2-0 János Farkas (30').
Netherlands: 2-1 Wim Suurbier (63').
Referee: Friedrich (Franz) Mayer (AUT)   Attendance: 24.352

24-05-1967   Idrætsparken, Copenhagen: Denmark – Hungary   0-2 (0-1)
Denmark: Leif Nielsen, Jens Jørgen Hansen, John Worbye, Johnny Hansen, Bent Schmidt Hansen, Ulrik Le Fevre, Erik Sandvad, Kresten Bjerre, Finn Laudrup, René Møller, Tom Søndergaard. (Coach: Ernst Netuka (AUT)).
Hungary: Gyula Tamás, Sándor Mátrai, Kálmán Mészöly, Kálmán Ihász, Lajos Szücs, István Nagy, Flórián Albert (C), Gyula Rákosi, János Farkas, Ferenc Bene, Dezsö Molnár. (Coach: Rudolf Illovszky (HUN)).
Goals: Hungary: 0-1 Flórián Albert (30'), 0-2 Ferenc Bene (70').
Referee: William John Gow (WAL)   Attendance: 34.284

04-06-1967   Idrætsparken, Copenhagen: Denmark – East Germany   1-1 (0-1)
Denmark: Leif Nielsen, John Worbye (C), Henning Boel, Johnny Hansen, Bent Schmidt Hansen, Ulrik Le Fevre, Erik Sandvad, Kresten Bjerre, Finn Laudrup, René Møller, Tom Søndergaard. (Coach: Ernst Netuka (AUT)).
East Germany: Jürgen Croy, Bernd Bransch, Otto Fräßdorf, Manfred Geisler, Manfred Walter, Harald Irmscher, Roland Ducke, Jürgen Nöldner, Gerhard Körner, Wolfram Löwe, Henning Frenzel. (Coach: Karoly Sos (HUN)).
Goals: Denmark: 1-1 Kresten Bjerre (65' penalty).
East Germany: 0-1 Wolfram Löwe (5').
Referee: Joseph Hannet (BEL)   Attendance: 23.234

13-09-1967   Olympisch Stadion, Amsterdam: Netherlands – East Germany   1-0 (1-0)
Netherlands: Eddy Pieters-Graafland, Wim Suurbier, Rinus Israël, Cor Veldhoen, Hans Eijkenbroek, Bennie Muller, Johan Cruijff, Jan Klijnjan, Piet Keizer, Henk Groot, Klaas Nuninga. (Coach: George Kessler (FRG)).
East Germany: Wolfgang Blochwitz, Bernd Bransch, Otto Fräßdorf, Manfred Geisler, Wolfgang Wruck, Harald Irmscher, Roland Ducke, Dieter Erler, Herbert Pankau, Eberhard Vogel, Henning Frenzel. (Coach: Karoly Sos (HUN)).
Goals: Netherlands: 1-0 Johan Cruijff (2').
Referee: Thomas Wharton (SCO)   Attendance: 44.505

27-09-1967   Népstadion, Budapest: Hungary – East Germany   3-1 (1-0)
Hungary: Gyula Tamás, Sándor Mátrai, Kálmán Ihász, Lajos Szücs, Benö Káposzta, János Göröcs, Zoltán Varga, Flórián Albert, Gyula Rákosi, János Farkas, Ferenc Bene. (Coach: Rudolf Illovszky (HUN)).
East Germany: Jürgen Croy, Bernd Bransch, Otto Fräßdorf, Manfred Walter, Roland Ducke, Dieter Erler, Herbert Pankau, Gerhard Körner, Eberhard Vogel, Peter Ducke, Henning Frenzel. (Coach: Karoly Sos (HUN)).
Goals: Hungary: 1-0 János Farkas (9'), 2-0 János Farkas (48'), 3-0 János Farkas (50').
East Germany: 3-1 Henning Frenzel (58').
Referee: Tofiq Bakhramov (URS)   Attendance: 69.871

04-10-1967   Idrætsparken, Copenhagen: Denmark – Netherlands   3-2 (1-0)
Denmark: Leif Nielsen, John Worbye, Henning Boel, Johnny Hansen, Ulrik Le Fevre, John Steen Olsen, Erik Sandvad, Kresten Bjerre, Finn Laudrup, Tom Søndergaard, Erik Dyreborg. (Coach: Ernst Netuka (AUT)).
Netherlands: Eddy Pieters-Graafland, Wim Suurbier, Rinus Israël, Ton Pronk, Hans Eijkenbroek, Wim Jansen, Bennie Muller, Johan Cruijff, Piet Keizer, Henk Groot, Klaas Nuninga. (Coach: George Kessler (FRG)).
Goals: Denmark: 1-0 Kresten Bjerre (43' penalty), 2-0 Tom Søndergaard (54'), 3-0 Kresten Bjerre (74').
Netherlands: 3-1 Wim Suurbier (74'), 3-2 Rinus Israël (76').
Referee: Malcolm Hall Wright (NIR)   Attendance: 34.375

11-10-1967   Zentralstadion, Leipzig: East Germany – Denmark   3-2 (1-2)
East Germany: Wolfgang Blochwitz, Bernd Bransch, Klaus Urbanczyk, Manfred Walter, Roland Ducke, Jürgen Nöldner, Herbert Pankau, Gerhard Körner, Eberhard Vogel, Peter Ducke, Henning Frenzel. (Coach: Karoly Sos (HUN)).
Denmark: Leif Nielsen, John Worbye (C), Henning Boel, Johnny Hansen, Ulrik Le Fevre, John Steen Olsen, Erik Sandvad, Kresten Bjerre, Finn Laudrup, Tom Søndergaard, Erik Dyreborg. (Coach: Ernst Netuka (AUT)).
Goals: East Germany: 1-1 Gerhard Körner (35' penalty), 2-2 Herbert Pankau (59'), 3-2 Herbert Pankau (73').
Denmark: 0-1 Erik Dyreborg (25'), 1-2 Tom Søndergaard (38').
Referee: Ryszaard Banasiuk (POL)   Attendance: 18.519

29-10-1967   Zentralstadion, Leipzig: East Germany – Hungary   1-0 (0-0)
East Germany: Wolfgang Blochwitz, Bernd Bransch, Klaus Urbanczyk, Wolfgang Wruck, Harald Irmscher, Dieter Erler, Jürgen Nöldner, Herbert Pankau, Wolfram Löwe, Henning Frenzel, Günter Hoge. (Coach: Karoly Sos (HUN)).
Hungary: Gyula Tamás, Kálmán Ihász, Miklós Páncsics, Lajos Szücs, Benö Káposzta, Imre Mathesz, Zoltán Varga, Flórián Albert, Gyula Rákosi, János Farkas, Ferenc Bene. (Coach: Rudolf Illovszky (HUN)).
Goal: East Germany: 1-0 Henning Frenzel (51').
Referee: Robert Héliès (FRA)   Attendance: 48.872

GROUP 6

02-11-1966	Bucharest	Romania – Switzerland	4-2 (4-0)
26-11-1966	Naples	Italy – Romania	3-1 (2-1)
03-12-1966	Nicosia	Cyprus – Romania	1-5 (1-0)
22-03-1967	Nicosia	Cyprus – Italy	0-2 (0-0)
23-04-1967	Bucharest	Romania – Cyprus	7-0 (3-0)
24-05-1967	Zürich	Switzerland – Romania	7-1 (3-0)
25-06-1967	Bucharest	Romania – Italy	0-1 (0-0)
01-11-1967	Cosenza	Italy – Cyprus	5-0 (2-0)
08-11-1967	Lugano	Switzerland – Cyprus	5-0 (2-0)
18-11-1967	Bern	Switzerland – Italy	2-2 (1-0)
23-12-1967	Cagliari	Italy – Switzerland	4-0 (3-0)
17-02-1968	Nicosia	Cyprus – Switzerland	2-1 (1-1)

FINAL STANDING

Pos	Team	Pld	W	D	L	GF	GA	GD	Pts
1	*Italy*	*6*	*5*	*1*	*0*	*17*	*3*	*+14*	*11*
2	Romania	6	3	0	3	18	14	+4	6
3	Switzerland	6	2	1	3	17	13	+4	5
4	Cyprus	6	1	0	5	3	25	-22	2

Italy qualified for the Quarter-finals.

02-11-1966   Stadionul Republicii, Bucharest: Romania- Switzerland   4-2 (4-0)
Romania: Mihai Ionescu, Mihai Mocanu, Cornel Popa, Simion Surdan, Bujor Halmageanu, Dan Coe, Mircea Lucescu, Dumitru Popescu, Ion Pircalab, Constantin Fratila, Mircea Dridea. (Coach: Ilie Oana (ROM)).
Switzerland: Mario Prosperi, Hansruedi Fuhrer, Alex Matter, Georges Perroud, Richard Dürr, Heinz Bäni, Fritz Künzli, Karl Odermatt, Vittore Gottardi, René Pierre Quentin, Bruno Bernasconi. (Coach: Dr.Alfredo Foni (ITA)).
Goals: Romania: 1-0 Mircea Dridea (8'), 2-0 Constantin Fratila (11' penalty), 3-0 Constantin Fratila (25'), 4-0 Constantin Fratila (38' penalty).
Switzerland: 4-1 Fritz Künzli (53'), 4-2 Karl Odermatt (70').
Referee: James (Jim) Finney (ENG)   Attendance: 14.209

26-11-1966   Stadio San Paolo, Naples: Italy – Romania   3-1 (2-1)
Italy: Giuliano Sarti, Giacinto Facchetti (C), Aristide Guarneri, Spartaco Landini, Armando Picchi, Sandro Mazzola, Antonio Juliano, Mario Corso, Ottavio Bianchi, Angelo Domenghini, Virginio De Paoli. (Coach: Ferruccio Valcareggi (ITA)).
Romania: Ilie Datcu, Cornel Popa (C), Dan Coe, Ion Barbu, Augustin Pax Deleanu, Vasile Gergely, Mircea Lucescu, Nicolae Dobrin, Ion Pircalab, Constantin Fratila, Mircea Dridea. (Coach: Ilie Oana (ROM)).
Goals: Italy: 1-1 Sandro Mazzola (30'), 2-1 Virginio De Paoli (43'), 3-1 Sandro Mazzola (67'). Romania: 0-1 Nicolae Dobrin (7').
Referee: Gerhard Schulenburg (FRG)   Attendance: 68.145

03-12-1966   GSP Stadium, Nicosia: Cyprus – Romania   1-5 (1-0)
Cyprus: Nicos Eleftheriades (55' Varnavas Christofi), Costas Christou, Kostas Panagiotou (C), Kyriacos Koureas, Ploutis Pallas, Costakis Pierides, Nikos Kantzilieris, Christofis Christofi, Pambos Papadopoulos, Panicos Krystallis, Andreas Stylianou. (Coach: Argyris Gavalas (CYP)).
Romania: Mihai Ionescu, Cornel Popa, Ion Nunweiller, Dan Coe, Augustin Pax Deleanu, Vasile Gergely, Mircea Lucescu, Nicolae Dobrin, Ion Pircalab, Constantin Fratila, Mircea Dridea. (Coach: Ilie Oana (ROM)).
Goals: Cyprus: 1-0 Costakis Pierides (31').
Romania: 1-1 Mircea Dridea (49'), 1-2 Mircea Lucescu (51'), 1-3 Constantin Fratila (65'), 1-4 Constantin Fratila (74'), 1-5 Mircea Dridea (82').
Referee: Arthur Lentini (MLT)   Attendance: 4.823

22-03-1967   GSP Stadium, Nicosia: Cyprus – Italy   0-2 (0-0)
Cyprus: Varnavas Christofi, Costas Christou, Kostas Panagiotou (C), Ploutis Pallas, Panikos Iacovou, Costakis Pierides, Christofis Christofi, George Kettenis, Drosos Kalotheou, Panicos Krystallis, Andreas Stylianou. (Coach: Argyris Gavalas (CYP)).
Italy: Giuliano Sarti, Giacinto Facchetti (C), Tarcisio Burgnich, Aristide Guarneri, Armando Picchi, Gianni Rivera, Giovanni Lodetti, Antonio Juliano, Mario Corso, Angelo Domenghini, Renato Cappellini. (Coach: Ferruccio Valcareggi (ITA)).
Goals: Italy: 0-1 Angelo Domenghini (76'), 0-2 Giacinto Facchetti (88').
Referee: Atanas Stavrev Kiryakov (BUL)   Attendance: 5.380

23-04-1967   Stadionul 23. August, Bucharest: Romania – Cyprus   7-0 (3-0)
Romania: Mihai Ionescu, Mihai Mocanu, Cornel Popa, Ion Nunweiller, Dumitru Nicolae, Vasile Gergely, Mircea Lucescu, Nicolae Dobrin, Florea Martinovici, Emil Dumitriu, Ion Ionescu. (Coach: Ilie Oana (ROM)).
Cyprus: Varnavas Christofi, Costas Christou, Kostas Panagiotou (C), Ploutis Pallas, Panikos Iacovou, Costakis Pierides, Christofis Christofi, George Kettenis, Drosos Kalotheou, Panicos Krystallis, Andreas Stylianou. (Coach: Argyris Gavalas (CYP)).
Goals: Romania: 1-0 Mircea Lucescu (4'), 2-0 Florea Martinovici (15'), 3-0 Emil Dumitriu (24'), 4-0 Ion Ionescu (47'), 5-0 Emil Dumitriu (52'), 6-0 Emil Dumitriu (77'), 7-0 Ion Ionescu (86').
Referee: Milivoje Gugulovic (YUG)   Attendance: 9.412

24-05-1967   Hardturm Stadion, Zürich: Switzerland – Romania   7-1 (3-0)
Switzerland: Marcel Kunz, Ely Tacchella (C), Georges Perroud, Markus Pfirter, Bruno Michaud, Richard Dürr, Heinz Bäni, Fritz Künzli, Karl Odermatt, René Pierre Quentin, Rolf Blättler. (Coach: Erwin Ballabio (SUI)).
Romania: Mihai Ionescu (46' Ilie Datcu), Mihai Mocanu, Cornel Popa, Ion Nunweiller, Dumitru Nicolae, Vasile Gergely, Mircea Lucescu, Nicolae Dobrin, Ion Pircalab, Mircea Dridea, Ion Ionescu. (Coach: Ilie Oana (ROM)).
Goals: Switzerland: 1-0 Fritz Künzli (12'), 2-0 René Pierre Quentin (15'), 3-0 René Pierre Quentin (32'), 4-0 Rolf Blättler (47'), 5-0 Rolf Blättler (59'), 6-0 Karl Odermatt (63'), 7-0 Fritz Künzli (66').
Romania: 7-1 Nicolae Dobrin (70').
Referee: Robert Lacoste (FRA)   Attendance: 21.337

25-06-1967   Stadionul 23. August, Bucharest: Romania – Italy   0-1 (0-0)
Romania: Raducanu Necula, Nicolae Lupescu, Mihai Mocanu, Ion Nunweiller (C), Ion Barbu, Radu Nunweiller, Vasile Gergely, Mircea Lucescu, Iuliu Naftanaila, Emil Dumitriu, Ion Ionescu. (Coach: Angelo Niculescu (ROM)).
Italy: Enrico Albertosi, Giacinto Facchetti (C), Aristide Guarneri, Armando Picchi, Adolfo Gori, Gianni Rivera, Giacomo Bulgarelli, Mario Bertini, Antonio Juliano, Ezio Pascutti, Gianfranco Zigoni. (Coach: Ferruccio Valcareggi (ITA)).
Goal: Italy: 0-1 Mario Bertini (81').
Referee: Manuel Gómez Arribas (ESP)   Attendance: 54.371

01-11-1967   Stadio San Vito, Cosenza: Italy – Cyprus   5-0 (2-0)
Italy: Enrico Albertosi, Giacinto Facchetti (C), Tarcisio Burgnich, Giancarlo Bercellino, Armando Picchi, Sandro Mazzola, Giancarlo "Picchio" De Sisti, Romano Fogli, Antonio Juliano, Luigi Riva, Angelo Domenghini. (Coach: Ferruccio Valcareggi (ITA)).
Cyprus: Varnavas Christofi, Costas Christou, Kostas Panagiotou (C), Kyriacos Koureas, Ploutis Pallas, Nikos Kantzilleris, Christofis Christofi, Panais Nikolaou, Panicos Krystallis, Andreas Stylianou, Grigoris Filiastidis. (Coach: Argyris Gavalas (CYP)).
Goals: Italy: 1-0 Sandro Mazzola (12'), 2-0 Sandro Mazzola (22'), 3-0 Luigi Riva (46'), 4-0 Luigi Riva (55'), 5-0 Luigi Riva (59').
Referee: Antoine Queudeville (LUX)   Attendance: 22.059

08-11-1967   Stadio Comunale de Cornaredo, Lugano: Switzerland – Cyprus   5-0 (2-0)
Switzerland: Marcel Kunz, Ely Tacchella (C), Hansruedi Fuhrer, Georges Perroud, Markus Pfirter, Bruno Michaud, Richard Dürr, Fritz Künzli, Karl Odermatt, René Pierre Quentin, Rolf Blättler. (Coach: Alfredo Foni (ITA)).
Cyprus: Varnavas Christofi, Costas Christou, Kostas Panagiotou (C), Kyriacos Koureas, Ploutis Pallas, Nikos Kantzilleris, Pambos Papadopoulos, Panais Nikolaou, Panicos Krystallis, Andreas Stylianou, Grigoris Filiastidis. (Coach: Argyris Gavalas (CYP)).
Goals: Switzerland: 1-0 Rolf Blättler (30'), 2-0 Fritz Künzli (41'), 3-0 Rolf Blättler (55'), 4-0 Richard Dürr (56' penalty), 5-0 Karl Odermatt (72').
Referee: Robert Schaut (BEL)   Attendance: 3.737

18-11-1967   Wankdorfstadion, Bern: Switzerland – Italy   2-2 (1-0)
Switzerland: Marcel Kunz, Ely Tacchella (C), Hansruedi Fuhrer, Georges Perroud, Markus Pfirter, Bruno Michaud, Richard Dürr, Fritz Künzli, Karl Odermatt, René Pierre Quentin, Rolf Blättler. (Coach: Alfredo Foni (ITA)).
Italy: Enrico Albertosi, Giacinto Facchetti (C), Tarcisio Burgnich, Roberto Rosato, Giancarlo Bercellino, Armando Picchi, Giancarlo "Picchio" De Sisti, Antonio Juliano, Luigi Riva, Roberto Boninsegna, Angelo Domenghini. (Coach: Ferruccio Valcareggi (ITA)).
Goals: Switzerland: 1-0 René Pierre Quentin (34'), 2-1 Fritz Künzli (68').
Italy: 1-1 Luigi Riva (66'), 2-2 Luigi Riva (85' penalty).
Referee: István Zsolt (HUN)   Attendance: 53.137

23-12-1967   Stadio Amsicora, Cagliari: Italy – Switzerland   4-0 (3-0)
Italy: Enrico Albertosi, Giacinto Facchetti (C), Tarcisio Burgnich, Giancarlo Bercellino, Armando Picchi, Gianni Rivera, Sandro Mazzola, Giorgio Ferrini, Antonio Juliano, Luigi Riva, Angelo Domenghini. (Coach: Ferruccio Valcareggi (ITA)).
Switzerland: Marcel Kunz (82' Karl Grob), Ely Tacchella (C), Hansruedi Fuhrer, Georges Perroud, Markus Pfirter, Bruno Michaud, Richard Dürr, Fritz Künzli, Karl Odermatt, René Pierre Quentin, Bruno Bernasconi. (Coach: Alfredo Foni (ITA)).
Goals: Italy: 1-0 Sandro Mazzola (3'), 2-0 Luigi Riva (13'), 3-0 Angelo Domenghini (45'), 4-0 Angelo Domenghini (67').
Referee: Thomas (Tiny) Wharton (SCO)   Attendance: 24.743

17-02-1968   GSP Stadium, Nicosia: Cyprus – Switzerland   2-1 (1-1)
Cyprus: Andreas Filotas (46' Makis Alkiviades), Costas Christou, Kostas Panagiotou (C), Panikos Iacovou, Yoannis Xipolitas, Pambos Papadopoulos, Drosos Kalotheou, Andreas Pakkos, Panikos Efthymiades, Melis Asprou, Panicos Krystallis. (Coach: Pambos Avraamides (CYP)).
Switzerland: Marcel Kunz, Hansruedi Fuhrer, Markus Pfirter, Bruno Michaud, Paul Marti, Renzo Bionda, Richard Dürr, Fritz Künzli, Karl Odermatt (C), René Pierre Quentin, Rolf Blättler. (Coach: Alfredo Foni (ITA)).
Goals: Cyprus: 1-1 Melis Asprou (22'), 2-1 Pambos Papadopoulos (46').
Switzerland: 0-1 Kostas Panagiotou (9' *own goal*).
Referee: Pavel Spoták (TCH)   Attendance: 7.500

GROUP 7

02-10-1966	Szczecin	Poland – Luxembourg	4-0 (0-0)
22-10-1966	Paris	France – Poland	2-1 (1-0)
11-11-1966	Brussels	Belgium – France	2-1 (0-0)
26-11-1966	Luxembourg	Luxembourg – France	0-3 (0-3)
19-03-1967	Luxembourg	Luxembourg – Belgium	0-5 (0-3)
16-04-1967	Luxembourg	Luxembourg – Poland	0-0
21-05-1967	Chorzów	Poland – Belgium	3-1 (2-0)
17-09-1967	Warsaw	Poland – France	1-4 (1-2)
08-10-1967	Brussels	Belgium – Poland	2-4 (2-2)
28-10-1967	Nantes	France – Belgium	1-1 (0-1)
22-11-1967	Bruges	Belgium – Luxembourg	3-0 (0-0)
23-12-1967	Paris	France – Luxembourg	3-1 (1-0)

FINAL STANDING

Pos	Team	Pld	W	D	L	GF	GA	GD	Pts
1	*France*	6	4	1	1	14	6	+8	9
2	Belgium	6	3	1	2	14	9	+5	7
3	Poland	6	3	1	2	13	9	+4	7
4	Luxembourg	6	0	1	5	1	18	-17	1

France qualified for the Quarter-finals.

02-10-1966   Stadion Pogon, Szcecin: Poland – Luxembourg   4-0 (0-0)
Poland: Stanislaw Majcher, Roman Strzalkowski, Henryk Brejza, Zygmunt Anczok, Pawel Orzechowski, Ryszard Grzegorczyk, Zygmunt Szmidt, Jan Liberda (C), Jerzy Sadek, Andrzej Jarosik, Janusz Kowalik. (Coach: Antoni Brzezanczzyk (POL)).
Luxembourg: Théo Stendebach, Jean-Pierre Hoffstetter (C), Erwin Kuffer, Fernand Jeitz, Jean Hardt, François Konter, Jean Klein, Nicholas Hoffmann, René Schneider, Edouard Dublin, Johnny Leonard. (Coach: Robert Heinz (FRG)).
Goals: Poland: 1-0 Andrzej Jarosik (49'), 2-0 Jan Liberda (54'), 3-0 Ryszard Grzegorczyk (73'), 4-0 Jerzy Sadek (87').
Referee: Erwin Vetter (GDR)   Attendance: 10.840

22-10-1966 Parc des Princes, Paris: France – Poland 2-1 (1-0)
France: Georges Carnus, Robert Budzynski (C), Jean Djorkaeff, André Chorda, Claude Robin, Yves Herbet, Georges Lech, Jean-Claude Suaudeau, Jacques Simon, Fleury Di Nallo, Paul Courtin. (Coaches: José Arribas (FRA) & Jean Snella (FRG)).
Poland: Jan Gomola, Stanislaw Oslizlo, Roman Strzalkowski, Zygmunt Anczok, Jacek Gmoch, Ryszard Grzegorczyk, Piotr Suski, Wlodzimierz Lubanski, Jan Liberda, Jerzy Sadek, Andrzej Jarosik. (Coach: Alfred Nowakowski (POL)).
Goals: France; 1-0 Fleury Di Nallo (26'), 2-1 Georges Lech (85').
Poland: 1-1 Ryszard Grzegorczyk (61').
Referee: Gerhard Schulenburg (FRG)   Attendance: 23.524

11-11-1966   Stade du Heysel, Brussels: Belgium – France 2-1 (0-0)
Belgium: Jean Nicolay, Georges Heylens, Yves Baré, Pierre Hanon, Jean Plaskie, Wilfried Van Moer, Jozef Jurion (C), Paul Van Himst, Wilfried Puis, Raoul Lambert, Johny Thio. (Coaches: Raymond Goethals (BEL) & Constant Vanden Stock (BEL)).
France: Georges Carnus, Robert Budzynski, Jean Djorkaeff, André Chorda, Claude Robin, Georges Lech, Jean-Claude Suaudeau, Gérard Hausser, Jacques Simon, Hervé Revelli, Bernard Blanchet. (Coaches: José Arribas (FRA) & Jean Snella (FRG)).
Goals: Belgium: 1-0 Paul Van Himst (51'), 2-0 Paul Van Himst (54').
France: 2-1 Georges Lech (67').
Referee: John Keith (Jack) Taylor (ENG)   Attendance: 43.404

26-11-1967   Stade Municipal, Luxembourg: Luxembourg – France 0-3 (0-3)
Luxembourg: Théo Stendebach, Jean-Pierre Hoffstetter, Erwin Kuffer, Fernand Jeitz, Mathias Ewen, François Konter, Nicholas Hoffmann, Edouard Dublin, Adolphe Schmit (C), Johnny Leonard, Joseph Kirchens. (Coach: Robert Heinz (FRG)).
France: Georges Carnus, Bernard Bosquier, Jean Djorkaeff, André Chorda, Marcel Artelesa (C), Joseph Bonnel, Yves Herbet, Georges Lech, Michel Watteua, Laurent Robuschi, Hervé Revelli. (Coaches: José Arribas (FRA) & Jean Snella (FRG)).
Goals: France: 0-1 Yves Herbet (8'), 0-2 Hervé Revelli (40'), 0-3 Georges Lech (41').
Referee: Laurens van Ravens (HOL)   Attendance: 3.465

19-03-1967   Stade Municipal, Luxembourg: Luxembourg – Belgium 0-5 (0-3)
Luxembourg: Théo Stendebach, Jean-Pierre Hoffstetter, Erwin Kuffer, Fernand Jeitz, Mathias Ewen, François Konter, Louis Pilot, Nicholas Hoffmann, Henri Klein, Edouard Dublin, Johnny Leonard. (Coach: Robert Heinz (FRG)).
Belgium: Jean Nicolay, Georges Heylens, Pierre Hanon, Jean Plaskie, Florent Bohez, Wilfried Van Moer, Jozef Jurion, Paul Van Himst, Wilfried Puis, Johny Thio (C), Jacques Stockman, (Coaches: Raymond Goethals (BEL) & Constant Vanden Stock (BEL)).
Goals: Belgium: 0-1 Paul Van Himst (19'), 0-2 Jacques Stockman (30'), 0-3 Paul Van Himst (36'), 0-4 Jacques Stockman (59'), 0-5 Jacques Stockman (73').
Referee: Karl Göppel (SUI)   Attendance: 9.107

16-04-1967   Stade Municipal, Luxembourg: Luxembourg – Poland 0-0
Luxembourg: René Hoffmann, Jean-Pierre Hoffstetter, Erwin Kuffer, Fernand Jeitz, Mathias Ewen, François Konter, Jean Klein, Louis Pilot, Edouard Dublin, Adolphe Schmit, Johnny Leonard. (Coach: Robert Heinz (FRG)).
Poland: Konrad Kornek, Stanislaw Oslizlo, Roman Strzalkowski, Zygmunt Anczok, Jacek Gmoch, Zygmunt Szmidt, Zygfryd Szoltysik, Wlodzimierz Lubanski, Andrzej Jarosik, Krzysztof Hausner, Jerzy Musialek. (Coach: Michal Matyas (POL)).
Referee: Einar Poulsen (DEN)   Attendance: 7.229

21-05-1967   Stadion Slaski, Chorzów: Poland – Belgium   3-1 (2-0)
Poland: Konrad Kornek, Roman Strzalkowski, Zygmunt Anczok, Jacek Gmoch, Pawel Kowalski, Zygmunt Szmidt, Piotr Suski, Zygfryd Szoltysik, Wlodzimierz Lubanski, Jan Liberda, Jerzy Sadek. (Coach: Michal Matyas (POL)).
Belgium: Jean Nicolay, Georges Heylens, Jean Plaskie, Florent Bohez, Albert Sulon, Wilfried Van Moer (C), Jozef Jurion, Prudent Bettens, Paul Van Himst, Wilfried Puis, Jacques Stockman. (Coaches: Raymond Goethals (BEL) & Constant Vanden Stock (BEL)).
Goals: Poland: 1-0 Wlodzimierz Lubanski (28'), 2-0 Wlodzimierz Lubanski (41'), 3-1 Zygfryd Szoltysik (72').
Belgium: 2-1 Wilfried Puis (52').
Referee: Toimi Olkku (FIN)   Attendance: 57.050

17-09-1967   Stadion Dziesieciolecia, Warsaw: Poland – France   1-4 (1-2)
Poland: Hubert Kostka, Stanislaw Oslizlo, Zygmunt Anczok, Jacek Gmoch, Pawel Kowalski, Piotr Suski, Zygfryd Szoltysik, Robert Gadocha, Wlodzimierz Lubanski, Lucjan Brychczy (C), Eugeniusz Faber. (Coach: Michal Matyas (POL)).
France: Marcel Aubour, Bernard Bosquier, Jean Djorkaeff, Jean Baeza, Yves Herbet, Robert Herbin (C), Roland Mitoraj, Henri Michel, Fleury Di Nallo, Charly Loubet, André Guy. (Coach: Louis Dugauguez (FRA)).
Goals: Poland: 1-1 Lucjan Brychczy (26').
France: 0-1 Robert Herbin (13'), 1-2 Fleury Di Nallo (33'), 1-3 André Guy (63'), 1-4 Fleury Di Nallo (85').
Referee: Ferdinand Marschall (AUT)   Attendance: 51.010

08-10-1967   Stade du Heysel, Brussels: Belgium – Poland   2-4 (2-2)
Belgium: Jean Nicolay, Georges Heylens, Yves Baré, Pierre Hanon, Jean Plaskie, Paul Vandenberg, Alfons Haagdoren, Johan Devrindt, Paul Van Himst, Wilfried Puis, Johny Thio. (Coaches: Raymond Goethals (BEL) & Constant Vanden Stock (BEL)).
Poland: Hubert Kostka, Stanislaw Oslizlo, Henryk Brejza, Jacek Gmoch, Antoni Piechniczek, Stefan Szefer, Zygmunt Szmidt, Wlodzimierz Lubanski, Lucjan Brychczy, Eugeniusz Faber, Janusz Zmijewski. (Coach: Michal Matyas (POL)).
Goals: Belgium: 1-0 Johan Devrindt (15'), 2-1 Johan Devrindt (35').
Poland: 1-1 Janusz Zmijewski (26'), 2-2 Lucjan Brychczy (45'), 2-3 Janusz Zmijewski (51'), 2-4 Janusz Zmijewski (70').
Referee: Juan Gardeazábal Garay (ESP)   Attendance: 35.897

28-10-1967   Stade Marcel Saupin, Nantes: France – Belgium   1-1 (0-1)
France: Marcel Aubour, Bernard Bosquier, Jean Djorkaeff, Claude Quittet, Jean Baeza, Henri Michel, Yves Herbet, Robert Herbin (C), Fleury Di Nallo, Charly Loubet, Hervé Revelli. (Coach: Louis Dugauguez (FRG)).
Belgium: Fernand Boone, Georges Heylens, Nicolas Dewalque, Pierre Hanon (C), Jean Cornelis, Jean Plaskie, André Stassart, Johan Devrindt, Wilfried Puis, Raoul Lambert, Roger Claessen. (Coaches: Raymond Goethals (BEL) & Constant Vanden Stock (BEL)).
Goals: France: 1-1 Robert Herbin (84').
Belgium: 0-1 Roger Claessen (37').
Referee: Francesco Francescon (ITA)   Attendance: 14.591

22-11-1967   Stade Klokke, Bruges: Belgium – Luxembourg   3-0 (0-0)
Belgium: Fernand Boone, Georges Heylens, Pierre Hanon (C), Jean Cornelis, Jean Plaskie, Alfons Peeters, Jean Dockx, Johan Devrindt, Wilfried Puis, Johny Thio, Roger Claessen.
(Coaches: Raymond Goethals (BEL) & Constant Vanden Stock (BEL)).
Luxembourg: René Hoffmann, Jean-Pierre Hoffstetter, Erwin Kuffer, Fernand Jeitz, Mathias Ewen, Jean Klein, Louis Pilot (C), Nicholas Hoffmann, Edouard Dublin, Adolphe Schmit, Johnny Leonard. (Coach: Robert Heinz (FRG)).
Goals: Belgium: 1-0 Johny Thio (62'), 2-0 Roger Claessen (66'), 3-0 Johny Thio (76').
Referee: William Augustine O'Neill (IRL)   Attendance: 6.745

23-12-1967   Parc des Princes, Paris: France – Luxembourg   3-1 (1-0)
France: Marcel Aubour, Bernard Bosquier, Jean Djorkaeff, Claude Quittet, Jean Baeza, Henri Michel, Georges Bereta, Robert Szczepaniak, Richard Krawczyk, Charly Loubet, Didier Couécou. (Coach: Louis Dugauguez (FRG)).
Luxembourg: René Hoffmann, Jean-Pierre Hoffstetter, Erwin Kuffer, Fernand Jeitz, Mathias Ewen, François Konter, Jean Klein, Louis Pilot (C), Edouard Dublin, Adolphe Schmit, Johnny Leonard. (Coach: Robert Heinz (FRG)).
Goals: France: 1-0 Charly Loubet (42'), 2-0 Charly Loubet (47'), 3-0 Charly Loubet (53').
Luxembourg: 3-1 Jean Klein (85').
Referee: Salvador Heliodoro Garcia (POR)   Attendance: 7.320

GROUP 8

22-10-1966	Cardiff	Wales – Scotland	1-1 (0-0)
22-10-1966	Belfast	Northern Ireland – England	0-2 (0-1)
16-11-1966	Glasgow	Scotland – Northern Ireland	2-1 (2-1)
16-11-1966	London	England – Wales	5-1 (3-1)
12-04-1967	Belfast	Northern Ireland – Wales	0-0
15-04-1967	London	England – Scotland	2-3 (0-1)
21-10-1967	Cardiff	Wales – England	0-3 (0-1)
21-10-1967	Belfast	Northern Ireland – Scotland	1-0 (0-0)
22-11-1967	Glasgow	Scotland – Wales	3-2 (1-1)
22-11-1967	London	England – Northern Ireland	2-0 (1-0)
24-02-1968	Glasgow	Scotland – England	1-1 (1-1)
28-02-1968	Wrexham	Wales – Northern Ireland	2-0 (0-0)

FINAL STANDING

Pos	Team	Pld	W	D	L	GF	GA	GD	Pts
1	England	6	4	1	1	15	5	+10	9
2	Scotland	6	3	2	1	10	8	+2	8
3	Wales	6	1	2	3	6	12	-6	4
4	Northern Ireland	6	1	1	4	2	8	-6	3

The results of this group were formed by combining the results of the 1967 and 1968 British Home Championships.

England qualified for the Quarter-finals.

22-10-1966   Ninian Park, Cardiff: Wales – Scotland   1-1 (0-0)
Wales: Gary Sprake, Terry Hennessy, Graham Williams, Mike England (C), Peter Rodrigues, Barrington Hole, Gil Reece, Alan Jarvis, Cliff Jones, Ronald Wyn Davies, Ronald Tudor Davies. (Coach: David Bowen (WAL)).
Scotland: Bobby Ferguson, Tommy Gemmell, Ronnie McKinnon, Billy Bremner, John Greig, John Clark, Jimmy Johnstone, Jim Baxter, Willie Henderson, Denis Law, Joe McBride. (Coach: Malcolm MacDonald (SCO)).
Goals: Wales: 1-0 Ronald Tudor Davies (76').
Scotland: 1-1 Denis Law (86').
Referee: Kenneth (Ken) Dagnall (ENG)   Attendance: 33.269

22-10-1966   Windsor Park, Belfast: Northern Ireland – England   0-2 (0-1)
Northern Ireland: Pat Jennings (46' Willie McFaul), Alex Elder (C), Martin Harvey, Billy McCullough, John Parke, Sammy Todd, Derek Dougan, John Crossan, William Irvine, William Ferguson, George Best. (Coach: Robert Peacock (NIR)).
England: Gordon Banks, Ramon Wilson, Bobby Moore (C), George Cohen, Jack Charlton, Alan Ball, Martin Peters, Nobby Stiles, Bobby Charlton, Geoff Hurst, Roger Hunt. (Coach: Alf Ramsey (ENG)).
Goals: England: 0-1 Roger Hunt (40'), 0-2 Martin Peters (60').
Referee: Robert Holley Davidson (SCO)   Attendance: 47.897

16-11-1966   Hampden Park, Glasgow: Scotland – Northern Ireland   2-1 (2-1)
Scotland: Bobby Ferguson, Tommy Gemmell, Ronnie McKinnon, Billy Bremner, John Greig, John Clark, Willie Henderson, Bobby Murdoch, Joe McBride, Stephen Chalmers, Bobby Lennox. (Coach: Malcolm (Malky) MacDonald (SCO)).
Northern Ireland: Pat Jennings, Alex Elder, Martin Harvey, Terry Neill, John Parke, Jimmy Nicholson, David Clements, Derek Dougan, John Crossan, William Irvine, Sammy Wilson. (Coach: Robert Peacock (NIR)).
Goals: Scotland: 1-1 Bobby Lennox (35'), 2-1 Bobby Murdoch (40').
Northern Ireland: 0-1 Jimmy Nicholson (9').
Referee: John Keith (Jack) Taylor (ENG)   Attendance: 45.281

16-11-1966   Wembley Stadium, London: England – Wales   5-1 (3-1)
England: Gordon Banks, Ramon Wilson, Bobby Moore (C), George Cohen, Jack Charlton, Alan Ball, Martin Peters, Nobby Stiles, Bobby Charlton, Geoff Hurst, Roger Hunt. (Coach: Alf Ramsey (ENG)).
Wales: Tony Millington, Terry Hennessy, Graham Williams, Mike England (C), Colin Green, Barrington Hole, Alan Jarvis, Ronnie Rees, Cliff Jones, Ronald Wyn Davies, Ronald Tudor Davies. (Coach: David Bowen (WAL)).
Goals: England: 1-0 Geoff Hurst (30'), 2-0 Geoff Hurst (34'), 3-1 Bobby Charlton (43'), 4-1 Terry Hennessy (65' *own goal*), 5-1 Jack Charlton (84').
Wales: 2-1 Ronald Wyn Davies (36').
Referee: Thomas (Tiny) Wharton (SCO)   Attendance: 75.380

12-04-1967   Windsor Park, Belfast: Northern Ireland – Wales   0-0
Northern Ireland: Roderick McKenzie, Alex Elder, Terry Neill, David Craig, Arthur Stewart, Jimmy Nicholson, David Clements, Walter Bruce, Derek Dougan, Eric Welsh, Daniel Trainor. (Coach: Robert Peacock (NIR)).
Wales: Tony Millington, Graham Williams, Rod Thomas, Edward James, Barrington Hole, Alan Jarvis, Ronnie Rees, Alan Durban, Keith Pring, Roy Vernon, Ronald Tudor Davies. (Coach: David Bowen (WAL)).
Referee: Kevin Howley (ENG)   Attendance: 17.643

15-04-1967   Wembley Stadium, London: England – Scotland   2-3 (0-1)
England: Gordon Banks, Ramon Wilson, Bobby Moore (C), George Cohen, Jack Charlton, Alan Ball, Martin Peters, Nobby Stiles, Bobby Charlton, Jimmy Greaves, Geoff Hurst. (Coach: Alf Ramsey (ENG)).
Scotland: Ronnie Simpson, Tommy Gemmell, Ronnie McKinnon, Eddie McCreadie, Billy Bremner, John Greig (C), Jim Baxter, Jim McCalliog, Denis Law, Bobby Lennox, Willie Wallace. (Coach: Robert (Bobby) Brown (SCO)).
Goals: England: 1-2 Jack Charlton (84'), 2-3 Geoff Hurst (88').
Scotland: 0-1 Denis Law (27'), 0-2 Bobby Lennox (78'), 2-3 Jim McCalliog (87').
Referee: Gerhard Schulenburg (FRG)   Attendance: 99.063

21-10-1967   Ninian Park, Cardiff: Wales – England   0-3 (0-1)
Wales: Gary Sprake, Terry Hennessy, Mike Holland (C), Peter Rodrigues, Colin Green, Barrington Hole, Ronnie Rees, Alan Durban, John Mahoney, Cliff Jones, Roy Vernon. (Coach: David Bowen (WAL)).
England: Gordon Banks, Bobby Moore (C), Keith Newton, George Cohen, Jack Charlton, Alan Mullery, Alan Ball, Martin Peters, Bobby Charlton, Geoff Hurst, Roger Hunt. (Coach: Alf Ramsey (ENG)).
Goals: England: 0-1 Martin Peters (34'), 0-2 Bobby Charlton (87'), 0-3 Alan Ball (90' penalty).
Referee: John Robertson Proudfoot Gordon (SCO)   Attendance: 44.960

21-10-1967   Windsor Park, Belfast: Northern Ireland – Scotland   1-0 (0-0)
Northern Ireland: Pat Jennings, Terry Neill, John Parke, Arthur Stewart, William McKeag, Jimmy Nicholson, David Clements, William Campbell, Derek Dougan, John Crossan, George Best. (Coach: William Laurence (Billy) Bingham (NIR)).
Scotland: Ronnie Simpson, Tommy Gemmell, Ronnie McKinnon, Eddie McCreadie, John Ure, John Greig, Bobby Murdoch, Jim McCalliog, Denis Law, Willie Morgan, Willie Wallace. (Coach: Robert (Bobby) Brown (SCO)).
Goal: Northern Ireland: 1-0 David Clements (69').
Referee: James (Jim) Finney (ENG)   Attendance: 47.359

22-11-1967   Hampden Park, Glasgow: Scotland – Wales   3-2 (1-1)
Scotland: Bobby Clark, Ronnie McKinnon, Eddie McCreadie, Jim Craig, Billy Bremner, John Greig, Jimmy Johnstone, Jim Baxter, Willie Johnston, Bobby Lennox, Alan Gilzean. (Coach: Robert (Bobby) Brown (SCO)).
Wales: Gary Sprake, Terry Hennessy, Peter Rodrigues, Colin Green, Edward James, Barrington Hole, Ronnie Rees, Alan Durban, Cliff Jones, Ronald Wyn Davies, Ronald Tudor Davies. (Coach: David Bowen (WAL)).
Goals: Scotland: 1-0 Alan Gilzean (16'), 2-2 Alan Gilzean (65'), 3-2 Ronnie McKinnon (78').
Wales: 1-1 Ronald Tudor Davies (18'), 1-2 Alan Durban (57').
Referee: James (Jim) Finney (ENG)   Attendance: 57.472

22-11-1967   Wembley Stadium, London: England – Northern Ireland   2-0 (1-0)
England: Gordon Banks, Ramon Wilson, Bobby Moore (C), George Cohen, David Sadler, Alan Mullery, Martin Peters, Peter Thompson, Bobby Charlton, Geoff Hurst, Roger Hunt. (Coach: Alf Ramsey (ENG)).
Northern Ireland: Pat Jennings, Alex Elder, Martin Harvey, Terry Neill (C), John Parke, Arthur Stewart, Jimmy Nicholson, David Clements, William Campbell, William Irvine, Sammy Wilson. (Coach: William Laurence (Billy) Bingham (NIR)).
Goals: England: 1-0 Geoff Hurst (43'), 2-0 Bobby Charlton (62').
Referee: Leo Callaghan (WAL)   Attendance: 83.969

24-02-1968   Hampden Park, Glasgow: Scotland – England   1-1 (1-1)
Scotland: Ronnie Simpson, Tommy Gemmell, Ronnie McKinnon, Eddie McCreadie, Billy McNeill, Billy Bremner, John Greig (C), Charlie Cooke, Willie Johnston, Bobby Lennox, John Hughes. (Coach: Robert (Bobby) Brown (SCO)).
England: Gordon Banks, Ramon Wilson, Bobby Moore (C), Keith Newton, Brian Labone, Alan Mullery, Alan Ball, Martin Peters, Mike Summerbee, Bobby Charlton, Geoff Hurst. (Coach: Alf Ramsey (ENG)).
Goals: Scotland: 1-1 John Hughes (39').
England: 0-1 Martin Peters (19').
Referee: Laurens van Ravens (HOL)   Attendance: 134.461

28-02-1968   The Racecourse Ground, Wrexham: Wales – Northern Ireland   2-0 (0-0)
Wales: Tony Millington, Terry Hennessy, Graham Williams, Mike England (C), Peter Rodrigues, Colin Green, Barrington Hole, Ronnie Rees, Alan Durban, Ronald Wyn Davies, Ronald Tudor Davies. (Coach: David Bowen (WAL)).
Northern Ireland: Pat Jennings, Alex Elder, Martin Harvey (C), Sammy Todd, David Craig, Arthur Stewart, William McKeag, Jimmy Nicholson, Derek Dougan, William Irvine, Terry Harkin. (Coach: William Laurence (Billy) Bingham (NIR)).
Goals: Wales: 1-0 Ronnie Rees (75'), 2-0 Ronald Wyn Davies (84').
Referee: Robert Holley Davidson (SCO)   Attendance: 17.548

QUARTER-FINALS

03-04-1968   Wembley Stadium, London: England – Spain   1-0 (0-0)
England: Gordon Banks, Ramon Wilson, Bobby Moore (C), Jack Charlton, Cyril Knowles, Alan Mullery, Alan Ball, Martin Peters, Mike Summerbee, Bobby Charlton, Roger Hunt. (Coach: Alf Ramsey (ENG)).
Spain: Salvador SADURNÍ Urpi, José Ignacio "IÑAKI" SÁEZ Ruiz, Juan Manuel CANÓS Ferrer, José Martínez Sánchez "PIRRI", Ignacio ZOCO Esparza, Francisco Fernández Rodríguez "GALLEGO", Manuel Polinario "POLI" Muñoz, José CLARAMUNT Torres, AMANCIO Amaro Varela, Fernando ANSOLA San Martín, Ramón Moreno GROSSO. (Coach: Domènec BALMANYA Perera (ESP)).
Goal: England: 1-0 Bobby Charlton (84').
Referee: Gilbert Droz (SUI)   Attemdance: 94.586

54

06-04-1968   Lasil Levski Stadium, Sofia: Bulgaria – Italy   3-2 (1-0)
Bulgaria: Stancho Bonchev, Dimitar Penev, Aleksandar Shalamanov, Boris Gaganelov (C), Dobromir Zhechev, Dimitar Yakimov, Dinko Dermendzhiev, Georgi Popov, Petar Zhekov, Nikola Kotkov, Georgi Asparuhov. (Coach: Stefan Boshkov (BUL)).
Italy: Enrico Albertosi (66' Lido Vieri), Giacinto Facchetti (C), Tarcisio Burgnich, Giancarlo Bercellino, Armando Picchi, Gianni Rivera, Sandro Mazzola, Mario Bertini, Antonio Juliano, Angelo Domenghini, Piero Prati. (Coach: Ferruccio Valcareggi (ITA)).
Goals: Bulgaria: 1-0 Nikola Kotkov (11' penalty), 2-1 Dinko Dermendzhiev (66'), 3-1 Petar Zhekov (73').
Italy: 1-1 Dimitar Penev (60' *own goal*), 3-2 Piero Prati (83').
Referee: Gerhard Schulenburg (FRG)   Attendance: 57.689

06-04-1968   Stade Vélodrome, Marseille: France – Yugoslavia   1-1 (0-0)
France: Marcel Aubour, Bernard Bosquier (C), Jean Djorkaeff, Claude Quittet, Jean Baeza, Robert Herbin, Georges Bereta, Néstor Combin, Jacques Simon, Fleury Di Nallo, Charly Loubet. (Coach: Louis Dugauguez (FRA)).
Yugoslavia: Ilija Pantelic, Mirsad Fazlagic, Blagoje Paunovic, Dragan Holcer, Dobrivoje Trivic, Ljubomir Mihajlovic, Ivica Osim, Dragan Dzajic, Vahidin Musemic, Borivoje Djordjevic, Dzemaludin Musomic. (Coach: Rajko Mitic (YUG)).
Goals: France: 1-1 Fleury Di Nallo (78').
Yugoslavia: 0-1 Vahidin Musemic (66').
Referee: Erwin Vetter (GDR)   Attendance: 35.423

20-04-1968   Stadio San Paolo, Naples: Italy – Bulgaria   2-0 (1-0)
Italy: Dino Zoff, Giacinto Facchetti (C), Tarcisio Burgnich, Aristide Guarneri, Ernesto Castano, Gianni Rivera, Sandro Mazzola, Giorgio Ferrini, Antonio Juliano, Angelo Domenghini, Piero Prati. (Coach: Ferruccio Valcareggi (ITA)).
Bulgaria: Simeon Simeonov, Dimitar Penev, Ivan Dimitrov, Aleksandar Shalamanov, Boris Gaganelov (C), Dobromir Zhechev, Hristo Bonev, Dimitar Yakimov, Dinko Dermendzhiev, Georgi Popov, Georgi Asparuhov. (Coach: Stefan Boshkov (BUL)).
Goals: Italy: 1-0 Piero Prati (14'), 2-0 Angelo Domenghini (55').
Referee: Gottfried Dienst (SUI)   Attendance: 83,830

24-04-1968   Crvena Zvezda Stadium, Belgrade: Yugoslavia – France   5-1 (4-1)
Yugoslavia: Ilija Pantelic, Mirsad Fazlagic (C), Dragan Holcer, Dobrivoje Trivic, Ljubomir Mihajlovic, Mladen Ramljak, Ilija Petkovic, Ivica Osim, Rudolf Belin, Dragan Dzajic, Vahidin Musemic. (Coach: Rajko Mitic (YUG)).
France: Marcel Aubour, Bernard Bosquier (C), Jean Djorkaeff, Claude Quittet, Jean Baeza, Vincent Estève, Yves Herbet, Robert Szczepaniak, Fleury Di Nallo, Charly Loubet, André Guy. (Coach: Louis Dugauguez (FRA)).
Goals: Yugoslavia: 1-0 Ilija Petkovic (2'), 2-0 Vahidin Musemic (13'), 3-0 Dragan Dzajic (14'), 4-0 Ilija Petkovic (32'), 5-1 Vahidin Musemic (79').
France: 4-1 Fleury Di Nallo (33').
Referee: Paul Schiller (AUT)   Attendance: 47.747

04-05-1968   Népstadion, Budapest: Hungary – Soviet Union   2-0 (1-0)
Hungary: Karoly Fatér, Kálmán Mészöly, Dezsö Novák, Kálmán Ihász, Lajos Szücs, Ernö Solymosi, János Göröcs, Zoltán Varga, László Fazekas, Gyula Rákosi, János Farkas. (Coach: Karoly Sos (HUN)).
Soviet Union: Anzor Kavazashvili, Volodymyr Kaplychniy, Albert Shesternev, Viktor Anichkin, Yuri Istomin, Valeri Voronin, Murtaz Khurtsilava, Igor Chislenko, Anatoli Banishevski, Eduard Malofeev, Eduard Streltsov. (Coach: Mikhail Yakuschin (URS)).
Goals: Hungary: 1-0 János Farkas (21'), 2-0 János Göröcs (85').
Referee: Laurens van Ravens (HOL)   Attendance: 71.556

08-05-1968   Estadio Santiago Bernabéu, Madrid: Spain – England   1-2 (0-0)
Spain: Salvador SADURNÍ Urpi, José Ignacio "IÑAKI" SÁEZ Ruiz, Juan Manuel CANÓS Ferrer, Francisco GENTO López (C), José Martínez Sánchez "PIRRI", Ignacio ZOCO Esparza, Francisco Fernández Rodríguez "GALLEGO", Manuel VELÁZQUEZ Villaverde, Joaquín RIFÉ Climent, AMANCIO Amaro Varela, Ramón Moreno GROSSO. (Coach: Domènec BALMANYA Perera (ESP)).
England: Peter Bonetti, Ramon Wilson, Bobby Moore (C), Keith Newton, Brian Labone, Norman Hunter, Alan Mullery, Alan Ball, Martin Peters, Bobby Charlton, Roger Hunt. (Coach: Alf Ramsey (ENG)).
Goals: Spain: 1-0 AMANCIO Amaro Varela (47').
England: 1-1 Martin Peters (54'), 1-2 Norman Hunter (81').
Referee: Josef Krnávek (TCH)   Attendance: 66.994

11-05-1968   Central Lenin Stadium, Moscow: Soviet Union – Hungary   3-0 (1-0)
Soviet Union: Yuri Pshenichnikov, Volodymyr Kaplychniy, Albert Shesternev, Valentin Afonin, Viktor Anichkin, Valeri Voronin, Gennadi Evryuzhikhin, Anatoli Byshovets, Murtaz Khurtsilava, Igor Chislenko, Anatoli Banishevski. (Coach: Mikhail Yakuschin (URS)).
Hungary: Gyula Tamás, Kálmán Mészöly, Dezsö Novák, Kálmán Ihász, Lajos Szücs, Ernö Solymosi, Zoltán Varga, Imre Komora, Flórián Albert, Gyula Rákosi, János Farkas. (Coach: Karoly Sos (HUN)).
Goals: Soviet Union: 1-0 Ernö Solymosi (22' *own goal*), 2-0 Murtaz Khurtsilava (59'), 3-0 Anatoli Byshovets (73').
Referee: Kurt Tschenscher (FRG)   Attendance: 91.129

FINAL TOURNAMENT IN ITALY

SEMI-FINALS

05-06-1968   Stadio San Paolo, Naples: Italy – Soviet Union   0-0 (AET)
Italy: Dino Zoff, Giacinto Facchetti (C), Tarcisio Burgnich, Giancarlo Bercellino, Ernesto Castano, Gianni Rivera, Sandro Mazzola, Giorgio Ferrini, Antonio Juliano, Angelo Domenghini, Piero Prati. (Coach: Ferruccio Valcareggi (ITA)).
Soviet Union: Yuri Pshenichnikov, Volodymyr Kaplychniy, Gennadi Logofet, Albert Shesternev (C), Valentin Afonin, Yuri Istomin, Gennadi Evryuzhikhin, Anatoli Byshovets, Aleksandr Lenev, Anatoli Banishevski, Eduard Malofeev. (Coach: Mikhail Yakuschin (URS)).
Referee: Kurt Tschenscher (FRG)   Attendance: 68.582

The result was decided by the toss of coin: Italian captain Giacinto Facchetti called correctly and Italy progressed to the final.

05-06-1968   Stadio Comunale, Florence: Yugoslavia – England   1-0 (0-0)
Yugoslavia: Ilija Pantelic, Miroslav Pavlovic, Mirsad Fazlagic (C), Milan Damjanovic, Blagoje Paunovic, Dragan Holcer, Dobrivoje Trivic, Ilija Petkovic, Ivica Osim, Dragan Dzajic, Vahidin Musemic. (Coach: Rajko Mitic (YUG)).
England: Gordon Banks, Ramon Wilson, Bobby Moore (C), Keith Newton, Brian Labone, Norman Hunter, Alan Mullery, Alan Ball, Martin Peters, Bobby Charlton, Roger Hunt. (Coach: Alf Ramsey (ENG)).
Goal: Yugoslavia: 1-0 Dragan Dzajic (87').
Referee: José María Ortiz de Mendíbil (ESP)   Attendance: 21.834
(Alan Mullery was sent-off in the 89th minute)

THIRD PLACE PLAY-OFF

08-06-1968   Stadio Olimpico, Rome: England – Soviet Union   2-0 (1-0)
England: Gordon Banks, Ramon Wilson, Bobby Moore (C), Brian Labone, Tommy Wright, Norman Hunter, Martin Peters, Nobby Stiles, Bobby Charlton, Geoff Hurst, Roger Hunt. (Coach: Alf Ramsey (ENG)).
Soviet Union: Yuri Pshenichnikov, Volodymyr Kaplychniy, Gennadi Logofet, Albert Shesternev (C), Valentin Afonin, Yuri Istomin, Gennadi Evryuzhikhin, Anatoli Byshovets, Aleksandr Lenev, Anatoli Banishevski, Eduard Malofeev. (Coach: Mikhail Yakuschin (URS)).
Goals: England: 1-0 Bobby Charlton (39'), 2-0 Geoff Hurst (63').
Referee: István Zsolt (HUN)   Attendance: 68.817

FINAL

08-06-1968   Stadio Olimpico, Rome: Italy – Yugoslavia   1-1 (0-1, 1-1) (AET)
Italy: Dino Zoff, Giacinto Facchetti (C), Tarcisio Burgnich, Aristide Guarneri, Ernesto Castano, Giorgio Ferrini, Giovanni Lodetti, Antonio Juliano, Pietro Anastasi, Angelo Domenghini, Piero Prati. (Coach: Ferruccio Valcareggi (ITA)).
Yugoslavia: Ilija Pantelic, Miroslav Pavlovic, Mirsad Fazlagic (C), Milan Damjanovic, Blagoje Paunovic, Dragan Holcer, Dobrivoje Trivic, Jovan Acimovic, Ilija Petkovic, Dragan Dzajic, Vahidin Musemic. (Coach: Rajko Mitic (YUG)).
Goals: Italy: 1-1 Angelo Domenghini (80').
Yugoslavia: 0-1 Dragan Dzajic (39').
Referee: Gottfried Dienst (SUI)   Attendance: 68.817

The match ended in a draw and was a replay was required to determine the winner.

FINAL REPLAY

10-06-1968   Stadio Olimpico, Rome: Italy – Yugoslavia   2-0 (2-0)
Italy: Dino Zoff, Giacinto Facchetti (C), Tarcisio Burgnich, Alessandro Salvadore, Roberto Rosato, Aristide Guarneri, Sandro Mazzola, Giancarlo "Picchio" De Sisti, Luigi Riva, Pietro Anastasi, Angelo Domenghini. (Coach: Ferruccio Valcareggi (ITA)).
Yugoslavia: Ilija Pantelic, Miroslav Pavlovic, Mirsad Fazlagic, Milan Damjanovic, Blagoje Paunovic, Dragan Holcer, Dobrivoje Trivic, Jovan Acimovic, Dragan Dzajic (C), Vahidin Musemic, Idriz Hosic. (Coach: Rajko Mitic (YUG)).
Goals: Italy: 1-0 Luigi Riva (12'), 2-0 Pietro Anastasi (31').
Referee: José María Ortiz de Mendíbil (ESP)   Attendance: 32.866

*** **Italy were European Champions** ***

GOALSCORERS TOURNAMENT 1966-1968:

Goals	Players
7	Luigi Riva (ITA)
6	János Farkas (HUN)
5	Bobby Charlton (ENG), Geoff Hurst (ENG), Fleury Di Nallo (FRA), Gerd Müller (FRG), Henning Frenzel (GDR), Angelo Domenghini (ITA), Sandro Mazzola (ITA), Constantin Fratila (ROM), Fritz Künzli (SUI)
4	Paul Van Himst (BEL), Petar Zhekov (BUL), Martin Peters (ENG), Rolf Blättler (SUI)
3	Leopold Grausam (AUT), Jacques Stockman (BEL), Dinko Dermendzhiev (BUL), Kresten Bjerre (DEN), Juhani Peltonen (FIN), Georges Lech (FRA), Charly Loubet (FRA), Johannes Löhr (FRG), Giorgos Sideris (GRE), Flórián Albert (HUN), Kálmán Mészöly (HUN), Odd Iversen (NOR), Janusz Zmijewski (POL), Mircea Dridea (ROM), Emil Dumitriu (ROM), Karl Odermatt (SUI), René Pierre Quentin (SUI), Inge Danielsson (SWE), Anatoli Banishevski (URS), Igor Chislenko (URS), Eduard Malofeev (URS), József Szabó (URS), Dragan Dzajic (YUG), Vahidin Musemic (YUG), Slaven Zambata (YUG)
2	Roger Claessen (BEL), Johan Devrindt (BEL), Johny Thio (BEL), Nikola Kotkov (BUL), Nikola Tsanev (BUL), Tom Søndergaard (DEN), Jack Charlton (ENG), José Martínez Sánchez "PIRRI" (ESP), Robert Herbin (FRA), Herbert Pankau (GDR), Alekos Alexiadis (GRE), Johan Cruijff (HOL), Piet Keizer (HOL), Wim Suurbier (HOL), Ferenc Bene (HUN), Piero Prati (ITA), Kjetil Hasund (NOR), Lucjan Brychczy (POL), Ryszard Grzegorczyk (POL), Wlodzimierz Lubanski (POL), EUSÉBIO da Silva Ferreira (POR), JAIME da Silva GRAÇA (POR), Nicolae Dobrin (ROM), Ion Ionescu (ROM), Mircea Lucescu (ROM), Alan Gilzean (SCO), Denis Law (SCO), Bobby Lennox (SCO), Leif Eriksson (SWE), Tom Turesson (SWE), Jozef Adamec (TCH), Ogün Altiparmak (TUR), Anatoli Byshovets (URS), Murtaz Khurtsilava (URS), Ronald Tudor Davies (WAL), Ronald Wyn Davies (WAL), Ivica Osim (YUG), Ilija Petkovic (YUG)
1	Rudolf Flögel (AUT), Erich Hof (AUT), Helmut Siber (AUT), Franz Wolny (AUT), Wilfried Puis (BEL), Georgi Asparuhov (BUL), Vasil Mitkov (BUL), Melis Asprou (CYP), Pambos Papadopoulos (CYP), Costakis Pierides (CYP), Erik Dyreborg (DEN), Alan Ball (ENG), Roger Hunt (ENG), Norman Hunter (ENG), AMANCIO Amaro Veral (ESP), José Eulogio GÁRATE Ormaechea (ESP), Francisco GENTO López (ESP), Ramón Moreno GROSSO (ESP), JOSÉ MARÍA García Lavilla (ESP), Pertti Mäkipää (FIN), Simo Syrjävaara (FIN), André Guy (FRA), Yves Herbet (FRA), Hervé Revelli (FRA), Uwe Seeler (FRG), Gerhard Körner (GDR), Wolfram Löwe (GDR), Eberhard Vogel (GDR), Stathis Chaitas (GRE), Mimis Papaloannou (GRE), Rinus Israël (HOL), Willy van der Kuijlen (HOL), Jan Mulder (HOL), Miel Pijs (HOL), Sjaak Swart (HOL), János Göröcs (HUN), Dezsö Molnár (HUN), Zoltán Varga (HUN), Noel Cantwell (IRL), Andy McEvoy (IRL), Turlough O'Connor (IRL), Francis O'Neill (IRL), Ray Treacy (IRL), Pietro Anastasi (ITA), Mario Bertini (ITA), Virginio De Paoli (ITA), Giacinto Facchetti (ITA), Jean Klein (LUX), David Clements (NIR), Jimmy Nicholson (NIR), Haral Berg (NOR), Sven Otto Birkeland (NOR), Olav Nilsen (NOR), Harald Sunde

	(NOR), Andrzej Jarosik (POL), Jan Liberda (POL), Jerzy Sadek (POL), Zygfryd Szoltysik (POL), CUSTÓDIO João PINTO (POR), JOSÉ Augusto Costa Sénica TORRES (POR), Florea Martinovici (ROM), John Hughes (SCO), Jim McCalliog (SCO), Ronnie McKinnon (SCO), Bobby Murdoch (SCO), Richard Dürr (SUI), Thomas Nordahl (SWE), Ingvar Svensson (SWE), Alexander Horváth (TCH), Josef Jurkanin (TCH), Ladislav Kuna (TCH), Juraj Szikora (TCH), Vojtech Masny (TCH), Ayhan Elmastasoglu (TUR), Valeri Maslov (URS), Eduard Streltsov (URS), Alan Durban (WAL), Ronnie Rees (WAL), Vojin Lazarevic (YUG), Josip Skoblar (YUG), Edin Spreco (YUG)
1 own goal	Dimitar Penev (BUL) for Italy, Kostas Panagiotou (CYP) for Switzerland, Ernö Solymosi (HUN) for Soviet Union, John Demspsey (IRL) for Czechoslovakia, Terry Hennessy (WAL) for England

1972 UEFA European Football Championship

QUALIFYING ROUND

GROUP 1

07-10-1970	Prague	Czechoslavakia – Finland	1-1 (1-1)
11-10-1970	Bucharest	Romania – Finland	3-0 (2-0)
11-11-1970	Cardiff	Wales – Romania	0-0
21-04-1971	Swansea	Wales – Czechoslovakia	1-3 (0-0)
16-05-1971	Bratislava	Czechoslovakia – Romania	1-0 (0-0)
26-05-1971	Helsinki	Finland – Wales	0-1 (0-0)
16-06-1971	Helsinki	Finland – Czechoslovakia	0-4 (0-2)
22-09-1971	Helsinki	Finland – Romania	0-4 (0-2)
13-10-1971	Swansea	Wales – Finland	3-0 (1-0)
27-10-1971	Prague	Czechoslovakia – Wales	1-0 (0-0)
14-11-1971	Bucharest	Romania – Czechoslovakia	2-1 (1-0)
24-11-1971	Bucharest	Romania – Wales	2-0 (1-0)

FINAL STANDING

Pos	Team	Pld	W	D	L	GF	GA	GD	Pts
1	*Romania*	*6*	*4*	*1*	*1*	*11*	*2*	*+9*	*9*
2	Czechoslovakia	6	4	1	1	11	4	+7	9
3	Wales	6	2	1	3	5	6	-1	5
4	Finland	6	0	1	5	1	16	-15	1

Romania qualified for the Quarter-finals.

07-10-1970   Letensky stadion, Prague: Czechoslovakia – Finland 1-1 (1-1)
Czechoslovakia: Frantisek Schmucker, Jozef Bomba (C), Jirí Vecerek, Jozef Desiatnik (77' Oldrich Urban), Peter Mutkovic, Vladimír Mojzís, Alexander Nagy, Dusan Bartovic (YC), Stanislav Strunc (71' Frantisek Hoholko), Pavel Stratil, Milan Albrecht. (Coach: Antonín Rygr (TCH)).
Finland: Paavo Heinonen, Timo Kautonen, Seppo Kilponen, Vilho Rajantie, Jouko Suomalainen, Raimo Toivanen, Pentti Toivola (YC), Pekka Heikkilä, Pertti Mäkipää (C), Olavi Litmanen (YC), Matti Paatelainen (71' Seppo Mäkelä). (Coach: Olavi Laaksonen (FIN)).
Goals: Czechoslovakia: 1-0 Milan Albrecht (30').
Finland: 1-1 Matti Paatelainen (41').
Referee: William Augustine O'Neill (IRL)   Attendance: 5.549

11-10-1970 Stadionul 23. August, Bucharest: Romania – Finland 3-0 (2-0)
Romania: Raducanu Necula, Lajos Satmareanu, Nicolae Lupescu (C), Cornel Dinu, Iosif Vigu, Radu Nunweiller, Ion Dumitru, Nicolae Dobrin, Florea Dumitrache, Alexandru Neagu (46' Gheorghe Tataru (II)), Florian Dumitrescu. (Coach: Angelo Niculescu (ROM)).
Finland: Paavo Heinonen, Timo Kautonen, Seppo Kilponen, Vilho Rajantie, Jouko Suomalainen (55' Seppo Mäkelä), Raimo Toivanen, Pentti Toivola, Pekka Heikkilä, Pertti Mäkipää (C), Raimo Saviomaa (65' Olavi Litmanen), Matti Paatelainen. (Coach: Olavi Laaksonen (FIN)).
Goals: Romania: 1-0 Florea Dumitrache (28'), 2-0 Florea Dumitrache (42'), 3-0 Radu Nunweiller (77').
Referee: Léonidas Vamvakopoulos (GRE)   Attendance: 36.584
(Raducanu Necula is also known as Rica Raducanu)

11-11-1970 Ninian Park, Cardiff: Wales – Romania 0-0
Wales: Gary Sprake, Mike England (C), Peter Rodrigues, Rod Thomas, David Powell, Graham Moore, Barrington Hole, Ronnie Rees, Alan Durban, Ronald Tudor Davies, Richard Krzywicki. (Coach: David Bowen (WAL)).
Romania: Raducanu Necula, Lajos Satmareanu, Nicolae Lupescu, Mihai Mocanu, Cornel Dinu (46' Bujor Halmageanu), Radu Nunweiller, Ion Dumitru, Nicolae Dobrin (76' Flavius Domide), Florea Dumitrache, Alexandru Neagu, Florian Dumitrescu. (Coach: Angelo Niculescu (ROM)).
Referee: Arie van Gemert (HOL)   Attendance: 19.882

21-04-1971 Vetch Field, Swansea: Wales – Czechoslovakia 1-3 (0-0)
Wales: Tony Millington, Peter Rodrigues, Rod Thomas, Edward James, Leighton Phillips, John Walley, Ronnie Rees, Alan Durban, John Mahoney (46' Arfon Griffiths), Ronald Wyn Davies, Ronald Tudor Davies. (Coach: David Bowen (WAL)).
Czechoslovakia: Ivo Viktor, Karol Dobias, Vladimír Hrivnák, Vladimír Táborsky, Jozef Desiatnik, Ladislav Kuna, Frantisek Vesely, Jaroslav Pollák, Jozef Adamec (C), Ján Capkovic, Pavel Stratil. (Coach: Ladislav Novák (TCH)).
Goals: Wales: 1-0 Ronald Tudor Davies (49' penalty).
Czechoslovakia: 1-1 Ján Capkovic (80'), 1-2 Vladimír Táborsky (81'), 1-3 Ján Capkovic (83').
Referee: Johan Einar Boström (SWE)   Attendance: 12.767

16-05-1971 Stadión Tehelné pole, Bratislava: Czechoslovakia – Romania 1-0 (0-0)
Czechoslovakia: Ivo Viktor, Karol Dobias, Vladimír Hrivnák, Vladimír Táborsky, Jozef Desiatnik, Ladislav Kuna, Frantisek Vesely, Jaroslav Pollák, Jozef Adamec (C), Ján Capkovic (76' Dusan Kabát), Pavel Stratil (72' Karol Jokl). (Coach: Ladislav Novák (TCH)).
Romania: Raducanu Necula, Lajos Satmareanu, Mihai Mocanu, Cornel Dinu, Dan Coe, Emerich Dembrovschi, Ion Dumitru, Mircea Lucescu, Dan Emil Anca, Florea Dumitrache, Alexandru Neagu (61' Radu Nunweiller). (Coach: Angelo Niculescu (ROM)).
Goal: Czechoslovakia: 1-0 Frantisek Vesely (88').
Referee: Fernando Nunes dos Santos Leite (POR)   Attendance: 38.207

26-05-1971   Olympiastadion, Helsinki: Finland – Wales   0-1 (0-0)
Finland: Lars Näsman, Timo Kautonen (C), Arto Tolsa (YC), Timo Nummelin, Vilho Rajantie, Jouko Suomalainen, Raimo Toivanen (YC) (46' Jarmo Flink), Pekka Heikkilä, Tommy Lindholm, Raimo Saviomaa, Matti Paatelainen. (Coach: Olavi Laaksonen (FIN)).
Wales: Tony Millington, Malcolm Page, Steve Derrett, Ray Mielczarek (YC), John Roberts, Gil Reece, Ronnie Rees, Alan Durban (C), Wayne Jones, Richard Krzywicki, John Toshack (YC). (Coach: David Bowen (WAL)).
Goal: Wales: 0-1 John Toshack (54').
Referee: Günter Männig (GDR)   Attendance: 5.410

16-06-1971   Olympiastadion, Helsinki: Finland – Czechoslovakia   0-4 (0-2)
Finland: Lars Näsman, Timo Kautonen, Arto Tolsa, Seppo Kilponen (C), Timo Nummelin, Jarmo Flink, Vilho Rajantie, Jouko Suomalainen, Raimo Toivanen (65' Tommy Lindholm), Pekka Heikkilä (46' Matti Paatelainen), Olavi Rissanen. (Coach: Olavi Laaksonen (FIN)).
Czechoslovakia: Ivo Viktor, Karol Dobias, Vladimír Hrivnák, Vladimír Táborsky, Jozef Desiatnik, Ladislav Kuna, Frantisek Vesely (76' Frantisek Karkó), Jaroslav Pollák, Jozef Adamec (76' Ivan Hrdlicka), Ján Capkovic, Pavel Stratil. (Coach: Ladislav Novák (TCH)).
Goals: Czechoslovakia: 0-1 Ján Capkovic (10'), 0-2 Jaroslav Pollák (16'), 0-3 Frantisek Karkó (83'), 0-4 Frantisek Karkó (89').
Referee: Marian Srodecki (POL)   Attendance: 4.658

22-09-1971   Olympiastadion, Helsinki: Finland – Romania   0-4 (0-2)
Finland: Lars Näsman (46' Paavo Heinonen), Ari Mäkynen, Esko Ranta, Jouko Suomalainen, Raimo Toivanen (C) (65' Timo Nummelin), Pekka Heikkilä, Miikka Toivola, Tommy Lindholm, Raimo Saviomaa, Timo Rahja, Antero Nikkanen. (Coach: Olavi Laaksonen (FIN)).
Romania: Raducanu Necula, Lajos Satmareanu, Nicolae Lupescu, Mihai Mocanu, Cornel Dinu, Emerich Dembrovschi, Radu Nunweiller, Ion Dumitru, Mircea Lucescu (C), Alexandru Neagu, Anghel Iordanescu (46' Gheorghe Tataru (II)). (Coach: Angelo Niculescu (ROM)).
Goals: Romania: 0-1 Anghel Iordanescu (25'), 0-2 Nicolae Lupescu (37'), 0-3 Emerich Dembrovschi (55'), 0-4 Mircea Lucescu (64' penalty).
Referee: Pius Kamber (SUI)   Attendance: 2.084

13-10-1971   Vetch Field, Swansea: Wales – Finland   3-0 (1-0)
Wales: Gary Sprake (46' Tony Millington), Terry Hennessey (C), Mike England, Peter Rodrigues, Rod Thomas, John Roberts, Gil Reece, Alan Durban, Brian Evans, Trevor Hockey, John Toshack. (Coach: David Bowen (WAL)).
Finland: Lars Näsman, Seppo Kilponen, Jarmo Flink, Ari Mäkynen, Pekka Kosonen, Raimo Elo, Pekka Heikkilä, Miikka Toivola, Heikki Suhonen (22' Henry Bergström), Tommy Lindholm, Raimo Saviomaa. (Coach: Olavi Laaksonen (FIN)).
Goals: Wales: 1-0 Alan Durban (10'), 2-0 John Toshack (53'), 3-0 Gil Reece (89').
Referee: Kaj Bernhard Rasmussen (DEN)   Attendance: 10.301

27-10-1971   Letensky stadion, Prague: Czechoslovakia – Wales   1-0 (0-0)
Czechoslovakia: Ivo Viktor, Karol Dobias (C), Vladimír Hrivnák, Vladimír Táborsky, Ludovít Zlocha, Ladislav Kuna, Bohumil Vesely (88' Znedek Nehoda), Jaroslav Pollák, Dusan Kabát, Karol Jokl (65' Ondrej Danko), Pavel Stratil. (Coach: Ladislav Novák (TCH)).
Wales: Tony Millington, Terry Hennessey (C) (57' Ronnie Rees), Alwyn Burton, Peter Rodrigues, Rod Thomas, Leighton Phillips, Alan Durban, Brian Evans (78' Richard Krzywicki), Terry Yorath, Mick Hill, Leighton James. (Coach: David Bowen (WAL)).
Goal: Czechoslovakia: 1-0 Ladislav Kuna (60').
Referee: Mariano Medina Iglésias (ESP)   Attendance: 20.051

14-11-1971   Stadionul 23. August, Bucharest: Romania – Czechoslovakia 2-1 (1-0)
Romania: Raducanu Necula, Lajos Satmareanu, Nicolae Lupescu, Cornel Dinu, Augustin Pax Deleanu, Emerich Dembrovschi (72' Flavius Domide), Radu Nunweiller, Mircea Lucescu (C), Nicolae Dobrin, Dan Emil Anca, Anghel Iordanescu. (Coach: Angelo Niculescu (ROM)).
Czechoslovakia: Ivo Viktor, Karol Dobias (C), Vladimír Hrivnák, Vladimír Táborsky, Vladimír Hagara, Ladislav Kuna, Ivan Hrdlicka, Bohumil Vesely (72' Znedek Nehoda), Jaroslav Pollák, Ján Capkovic, Pavel Stratil. (Coach: Ladislav Novák (TCH)).
Goals: Romania: 1-0 Emerich Dembrovschi (26'), 2-1 Nicolae Dobrin (52').
Czechoslovakia: 1-1 Ján Capkovic (50').
Referee: Milivoje Gugulovic (YUG)   Attendance: 63.583

24-11-1971   Stadionul 23. August, Bucharest: Romania – Wales 2-0 (1-0)
Romania: Raducanu Necula, Lajos Satmareanu, Nicolae Lupescu, Cornel Dinu, Augustin Pax Deleanu, Emerich Dembrovschi, Radu Nunweiller, Mircea Lucescu (C), Nicolae Dobrin, Anghel Iordanescu. (Coach: Angelo Niculescu (ROM)).
Wales: Tony Millington, Peter Rodrigues, Rod Thomas, Leighton Phillips, Gil Reece, Ronnie Rees, Trevor Hockey, Ronald Tudor Davies, Mick Hill (46' Cyril Davies), Leighton James, Herbie Williams. (Coach: David Bowen (WAL)).
Goals: Romania: 1-0 Nicolae Lupescu (9'), 2-0 Mircea Lucescu (74').
Referee: Alfred (Fred) Delcourt (BEL)   Attendance: 35.251

GROUP 2

07-10-1970	Oslo	Norway – Hungary	1-3 (0-2)
11-11-1970	Lyon	France – Norway	3-1 (1-0)
15-11-1970	Sofia	Bulgaria – Norway	1-1 (1-0)
24-04-1971	Budapest	Hungary – France	1-1 (0-0)
19-05-1971	Sofia	Bulgaria – Hungary	3-0 (1-0)
09-06-1971	Oslo	Norway – Bulgaria	1-4 (0-4)
08-09-1971	Oslo	Norway – France	1-3 (0-2)
25-09-1971	Budapest	Hungary – Bulgaria	2-0 (0-0)
09-10-1971	Colombes	France – Hungary	0-2 (0-2)
27-10-1971	Budapest	Hungary – Norway	4-0 (3-0)
10-11-1971	Nantes	France – Bulgaria	2-1 (0-0)
04-12-1971	Sofia	Bulgaria – France	2-1 (0-0)

FINAL STANDING

Pos	Team	Pld	W	D	L	GF	GA	GD	Pts
1	*Hungary*	*6*	*4*	*1*	*1*	*12*	*5*	*+7*	*9*
2	Bulgaria	6	3	1	2	11	7	+4	7
3	France	6	3	1	2	10	8	+2	7
4	Norway	6	0	1	5	5	18	-13	1

Hungary qualified for the Quarter-finals.

07-10-1970   Ullevaal Stadion, Oslo: Norway – Hungary   1-3 (0-2)
Norway: Geir Karlsen, Thor Spydevold, Finn Thorsen, Per Pettersen, Sigbjorn Slinning, Svein Kvia, Olav Nilsen, Trygve Bornø, Egil Roger Olsen, Tor Fuglset (46' Finn Seemann), Odd Iversen (85' Kjetil Hasund). (Coach: Øivind Johannesen (NOR)).
Hungary: Ádám Rothermel, Kálmán Mészöly, Miklós Páncsics, Ernö Noskó (YC), Sándor Müller, László Nagy, Lajos Kocsis, Zoltán Halmosi, Csaba Vidáts, László Fazekas, Ferenc Bene (C). (Coach: József Hoffer (HUN)).
Goals: Norway: 1-2 Odd Iversen (50').
Hungary: 0-1 Ferenc Bene (6'), 0-2 László Nagy (23'), 1-3 Geir Karlsen (69' *own goal*).
Referee: Adrianus (Ad) Boogaerts (HOL)   Attendance: 16.090

11-11-1970   Stade de Gerland, Lyon: France – Norway   3-1 (1-0)
France: Georges Carnus, Bernard Bosquier, Jean Djorkaeff (C), Jacky Novi, Jean-Paul Rostagni, Georges Lech, Jean-Noël Huck, Henri Michel, Michel Mézy, Charly Loubet, Louis Floch. (Coach: Georges Boulogne (FRA)).
Norway: Per Haftorsen, Thor Spydevold, Finn Thorsen, Per Pettersen, Arild Hetløen, Sigbjorn Slinning, Olav Nilsen, Trygve Bornø (C), Egil Roger Olsen, Harry Hestad, Finn Seemann. (Coach: Øivind Johannesen (NOR)).
Goals: France: 1-0 Louis Floch (30'), 2-0 Georges Lech (55'), 3-0 Michel Mézy (63').
Norway: 3-1 Olav Nilsen (79').
Referee: António Saldanha Ribeiro (POR)   Attendance: 10.357

15-11-1970   Vasil Levski Stadium, Sofia: Bulgaria – Norway   1-1 (1-0)
Bulgaria: Yordan Filipov, Asparuh Donev Nikodimov, Stefan Aladzhov, Dobromir Zhechev (C), Ivan Zafirov, Bozhil Kolev, Hristo Bonev, Tsvetan Atanasov (82' Dinko Dermendzhiev), Georgi Denev, Atanas Mihaylov (46' Kiril Raykov), Vasil Mitkov. (Coach: Vasil Spasov (BUL)).
Norway: Per Haftorsen, Thor Spydevold, Finn Thorsen, Per Pettersen, Arild Hetløen, Sigbjorn Slinning, Olav Nilsen, Trygve Bornø (C), Egil Roger Olsen (82' Arnfinn Espeseth), Tor Fuglset, Kjetil Hasund. (Coach: Øivind Johannesen (NOR)).
Goals: Bulgaria: 1-0 Tsvetan Atanasov (29').
Norway: 1-1 Tor Fuglset (83').
Referee: Michalakis Kyriakides (CYP)   Attendance: 21.465

24-04-1971   Népstadion, Budapest: Hungary – France   1-1 (0-0)
Hungary: Ádám Rothermel, Miklós Páncsics, Péter Juhász, Lajos Szücs, Ernö Noskó, Lajos Kocsis, Sándor Zámbó, Mihály Kozma (65' László Karsay), László Fazekas, Flórián Albert, Ferenc Bene. (Coach: József Hoffer (HUN)).
France: Georges Carnus, Bernard Bosquier, Jean Djorkaeff (C), Jacky Novi, Roger Lemerre, Francis Camerini, Georges Lech, Henri Michel, Georges Bereta, Fleury Di Nallo (46' Charly Loubet), Hervé Revelli. (Coach: Georges Boulogne (FRA)).
Goals: Hungary: 1-1 Lajos Kocsis (70' penalty).
France: 0-1 Hervé Revelli (64').
Referee: Joaquim Fernandes dos Campos (POR)   Attendance: 45.867

19-05-1971   Vasil Levski Stadium, Sofia: Bulgaria – Hungary   3-0 (1-0)
Bulgaria: Stoyan Yordanov, Dimitar Penev (C), Milko Gaydarski, Dobromir Zhechev, Bozhil Kolev, Hristo Bonev, Stefan Velichkov, Atanas Mihaylov (46' Petko Petkov), Mladen Vasilev, Petar Zhekov, Georgi Vasilev. (Coach: Vasil Spasov (BUL)).
Hungary: Ádám Rothermel, Tibor Fábián, Miklós Páncsics, Péter Juhász, Lajos Kocsis, Sándor Zámbó, Mihály Kozma (YC), Csaba Vidáts, Ede Dunai, László Fazekas (70' László Karsay), Flórián Albert. (Coach: József Hoffer (HUN)).
Goals: Bulgaria: 1-0 Bozhil Kolev (38'), 2-0 Petko Petkov (48'), 3-0 Stefan Velichkov (72').
Referee: Tofiq Bakhramov (URS)   Attendance: 28.342

09-06-1971   Ullevaal Stadion, Olso: Norway – Bulgaria   1-4 (0-4)
Norway: Kjell Kaspersen, Finn Thorsen (C), Frank Olafsen (80' Arild Hetløen), Per Pettersen, Robert Nilsson, Sigbjorn Slinning, Olav Nilsen, Tor Egil Johansen (75' Harald Sunde), Odd Iversen, Jan Fuglset, Thomas Lund. (Coach: Øivind Johannesen (NOR)).
Bulgaria: Stoyan Yordanov (60' Stefan Aladzhov), Dimitar Penev (C), Milko Gaydarski, Dobromir Zhechev, Bozhil Kolev, Hristo Bonev, Stefan Velichkov, Georgi Vasilev (70' Georgi Georgiev), Petar Zhekov, Mladen Vasilev, Petko Petkov. (Coach: Vasil Spasov (BUL)).
Goals: Norway: 1-4 Odd Iversen (80').
Bulgaria: 0-1 Hristo Bonev (26'), 0-2 Petar Zhekov (29'), 0-3 Mladen Vasilev (37'), 0-4 Hristo Bonev (42' penalty).
Referee: William John Gow (WAL)   Attendance: 22.041

08-09-1971   Ullevaal Stadion, Olso: Norway – France   1-3 (0-2)
Norway: Geir Karlsen (83' Svein Bjorn Olsen), Thor Spydevold, Tore Børrehaug, Sigbjorn Slinning, Anbjorn Ekeland, Egil Roger Olsen, Jan Christiansen (C), Tom Jacobsen, Kjetil Hasund, Jan Fuglset, Thomas Lund (75' Ola Dybwad-Olsen). (Coach: Øivind Johannesen (NOR)).
France: Georges Carnus, Bernard Bosquier, Jean Djorkaeff (C), Jacky Novi, Jean-Paul Rostagni, Georges Bereta, Henri Michel, Michel Mézy, Charly Loubet, Bernard Blanchet (76' Georges Lech), Jacky Vergnes. (Coach: Georges Boulogne (FRA)).
Goals: Norway: 1-3 Ola Dybwad-Olsen (80').
France: 0-1 Jacky Vergnes (33'), 0-2 Bernard Blanchet (34'), 0-3 Charly Loubet (46').
Referee: John Wright Paterson (SCO)   Attendance: 16.544

25-09-1971   Népstadion, Budapest: Hungary – Bulgaria   2-0 (0-0)
Hungary: István Géczi, Tibor Fábián, Miklós Páncsics, Péter Juhász (79' Ernö Noskó), Lajos Szücs, István Szöke, Sándor Zámbó (76' István Juhasz), Csaba Vidáts, László Fazekas, Ferenc Bene (C), Antal Dunai (II). (Coach: Rudolf Illovszky (HUN)).
Bulgaria: Biser Mihaylov, Dimitar Penev (C), Milko Gaydarski, Dobromir Zhechev, Bozhil Kolev, Hristo Bonev, Dinko Dermendzhiev, Stefan Velichkov, Mladen Vasilev, Petar Zhekov (59' Georgi Vasilev), Petko Petkov. (Coach: Vasil Spasov (BUL)).
Goals: Hungary: 1-0 Péter Juhász (51'), 2-0 Csaba Vidáts (52').
Referee: Robert Holley (Bobby) Davidson (SCO)   Attendance: 67.740

09-10-1971   Stade Olympique, Colombes: France – Hungary   0-2 (0-2)
France: Georges Carnus, Bernard Bosquier, Jean Djorkaeff (C), Jacky Novi, Jean-Paul Rostagni, Georges Lech, Georges Bereta, Henri Michel, Michel Mézy, Charly Loubet (46' Gilbert Gress (YC64)), Hervé Revelli. (Coach: Georges Boulogne (FRA)).
Hungary: István Géczi, Miklós Páncsics, Péter Juhász (YC28), Lajos Szücs, Ernö Noskó, Sándor Zámbó, István Juhasz (YC28), Csaba Vidáts, László Fazekas, Ferenc Bene (C), Antal Dunai (II). (Coach: Rudolf Illovszky (HUN)).
Goals: Hungary: 0-1 Ferenc Bene (35'), 0-2 Jacky Novi (43' *own goal*).
Referee: Gaspar Pintado Viu (ESP)   Attendance: 21.756

27-10-1971   Népstadion, Budapest: Hungary – Norway   4-0 (3-0)
Hungary: István Géczi, Miklós Páncsics, Péter Juhász (YC82), Lajos Szücs, Ernö Noskó, Sándor Zámbó (YC70), István Juhasz, Csaba Vidáts, László Fazekas, Ferenc Bene (C), Antal Dunai (II). (Coach: Rudolf Illovszky (HUN)).
Norway: Geir Karlsen, Thor Spydevold, Tore Børrehaug, Frank Olafsen, Per Pettersen (C), Thor Alsaker-Nøstdahl, Sigbjorn Slinning, Roald Jensen, Tom Jacobsen, Kjetil Hasund, Jan Fuglset (79' Egil Roger Olsen). (Coach: Øivind Johannesen (NOR)).
Goals: Hungary: 1-0 Ferenc Bene (22'), 2-0 Antal Dunai (II) (24'), 3-0 Ferenc Bene (43'), 4-0 Lajos Szücs (63').
Referee: Dogan Babacan (TUR)   Attendance: 29.253

10-11-1971   Stade Marcel Saupin, Nantes: France – Bulgaria   2-1 (0-0)
France: Georges Carnus, Jean Djorkaeff (C), Claude Quittet, Jacky Novi, Francis Camerini, Georges Lech, Henri Michel, Michel Mézy, Charly Loubet, Hervé Revelli (80' Louis Floch), Bernard Blanchet. (Coach: Georges Boulogne (FRA)).
Bulgaria: Yordan Filipov, Dimitar Penev (C), Dobromir Zhechev, Ivan Zafirov, Bozhil Kolev, Hristo Bonev (YC50), Dinko Dermendzhiev, Stefan Velichkov, Georgi Denev, Mladen Vasilev (82' Georgi Tsvetkov), Petko Petkov. (Coach: Vasil Spasov (BUL)).
Goals: France: 1-1 Georges Lech (64'), 2-1 Charly Loubet (84').
Bulgaria: 0-1 Hristo Bonev (54' penalty).
Referee: John Keith (Jack) Taylor (ENG)   Attendance: 9.405

04-12-1971   Vasil Levski Stadium, Sofia: Bulgaria – France   2-1 (0-0)
Bulgaria: Rumyancho Goranov (54' Yordan Filipov), Dimitar Penev (C), Milko Gaydarski, Dobromir Zhechev (YC), Bozhil Kolev, Hristo Bonev, Dinko Dermendzhiev, Stefan Velichkov (46' Viktor Yonov), Atanas Mihaylov, Mladen Vasilev, Petar Zhekov (YC). (Coach: Vasil Spasov (BUL)).
France: Georges Carnus, Marius Trésor, Bernard Bosquier (YC), Jean Djorkaeff (C) (YC), Jacky Novi, Georges Lech, Michel Mézy, Henri Michel (74' Georges Bereta) , Charly Loubet, Hervé Revelli (58' Louis Floch) , Bernard Blanchet. (Coach: Georges Boulogne (FRA)).
Goals: Bulgaria: 1-0 Petar Zhekov (47'), 2-0 Atanas Mihaylov (82').
France: 2-1 Bernard Blanchet (84').
Referee: Kurt Tschenscher (FRG)   Attendance: 18.057

GROUP 3

11-10-1970	Gzira	Malta – Greece	1-1 (0-0)
16-12-1970	Piraeus	Greece – Switzerland	0-1 (0-0)
20-12-1970	Gzira	Malta – Switzerland	1-2 (0-0)
03-02-1971	Gzira	Malta – England	0-1 (0-1)
21-04-1971	Lucerne	Switzerland – Malta	5-0 (5-0)
21-04-1971	London	England – Greece	3-0 (1-0)
12-05-1971	London	England – Malta	5-0 (2-0)
12-05-1971	Bern	Switzerland – Greece	1-0 (0-0)
18-06-1971	Piraeus	Greece – Malta	2-0 (0-0)
13-10-1971	Basle	Switzerland – England	2-3 (2-2)
10-11-1971	London	England – Switzerland	1-1 (1-1)
01-12-1971	Piraeus	Greece – England	0-2 (0-0)

FINAL STANDING

Pos	Team	Pld	W	D	L	GF	GA	GD	Pts
1	*England*	*6*	*5*	*1*	*0*	*15*	*3*	*+12*	*11*
2	Switzerland	6	4	1	1	12	5	+7	9
3	Greece	6	1	1	4	3	8	-5	3
4	Malta	6	0	1	5	2	16	-14	1

England qualified for the Quarter-finals.

11-10-1970   Empire Stadium, Gzira: Malta – Greece   1-1 (0-0)
Malta: Alfred Mizzi, Joseph Grima, Anthony Camilleri, Alfred Mallia (C) (78' John Privitera), Emmanuel Micallef, Edward Theobald, Ronald Cocks, William Vassallo, John Bonett (70' Charles Micallef (I)), Edward Vella, Louis Arpa. (Coach: Karm Borg (MLT)).
Greece: Takis Ikonomopoulos, Aristidis Kamaras, Apostolos Toskas, Kostas Eleftherakis, Nikos Stathopoulos (C), Giorgos Koudas (68' Michalis Kritikopoulos), Stathis Chaitas, Nikos Youtsos (68' Antonis Antoniadis), Mimis Domazos (YC75), Giorgos Skrekis, Mimis Papaioannou. (Coach: Lakis Petropoulos (GRE)).
Goals: Malta: 1-0 William Vassallo (66').
Greece: 1-1 Michalis Kritikopoulos (80').
Referee: Concetto Lo Bello (ITA)   Attendance: 8.689

16-12-1970   Stadio Karaiskaki, Piraeus: Greece – Switzerland   0-1 (0-0)
Greece: Nikolas Christidis, Aristidis Kamaras, Kostas Eleftherakis (75' Michalis Kritikopoulos), Nikos Stathopoulos, Giorgos Koudas, Stathis Chaitas, Nikos Youtsos, Mimis Domazos (C), Giorgos Skrekis, Angelos Spiridon, Mimis Papaioannou. (Coach: Lakis Petropoulos (GRE)).
Switzerland: Mario Prosperi, Georges Perroud, Peter Ramseier, Anton Weibel, Jakob (Köbi) Kuhn, Marc Berset, Peter Wenger, Fritz Künzli (75' Marcel Kunz *goalkeeper*), Karl Odermatt (C), Rolf Blättler (46' Walter Balmer) , Kurt Müller. (Coach: Louis Maurer (SUI)).
Goal: Switzerland: 0-1 Kurt Müller (85').
Referee: Milivoje Gugulovic (YUG)   Attendance: 30.699

20-12-1970   Empire Stadium, Gzira: Malta – Switzerland   1-2 (0-0)
Malta: Alfred Mizzi, John Privitera, Joseph Grima, Anthony Camilleri, Emmanuel Micallef, Alfred Delia, Edward Theobald (75' Edward Vella), Ronald Cocks, William Vassallo, John Bonett, Charles Micallef (I). (Coach: Karm Borg (MLT)).
Switzerland: Marcel Kunz, Georges Perroud, Peter Ramseier, Anton Weibel, Jakob (Köbi) Kuhn, Marc Berset, Peter Wenger (46' René Pierre Quentin), Fritz Künzli (65' Walter Balmer), Karl Odermatt (C), Rolf Blättler, Kurt Müller. (Coach: Louis Maurer (SUI)).
Goals: Malta: 1-1 Edward Theobald (55' penalty).
Switzerland: 0-1 René Pierre Quentin (49'), 1-2 Fritz Künzli (57').
Referee: Gocho Rusev (BUL)   Attendance: 4.739

03-02-1971   Empire Stadium, Gzira: Malta – England   0-1 (0-1)
Malta: Alfred Mizzi, Joseph Grima, Anthony Camilleri, Edward Darmanin, Alfred Mallia, Emmanuel Micallef, Edward Theobald, Joseph Cini (C), Ronald Cocks, William Vassallo, Louis Arpa. (Coach: Karm Borg (MLT)).
England: Gordon Banks, Norman Hunter, Paul Reaney, Roy McFarland, Alan Mullery (C), Alan Ball, Martin Peters, Emlyn Hughes, Colin Harvey, Martin Chivers, Joe Royle. (Coach: Alf Ramsey (ENG)).
Goal: England: 0-1 Martin Peters (35').
Referee: Ferdinand Marschall (AUT)   Attendance: 29.751

21-04-1971   Allmend Stadion, Lucerne: Switzerland – Malta   5-0 (5-0)
Switzerland: Mario Prosperi, Jean-Pierre Boffi, Peter Ramseier (46' Anton Weibel), Pierre-Albert Chapuisat, Roland Citherlet, Jakob (Köbi) Kuhn, Fritz Künzli, Karl Odermatt (C), René Pierre Quentin, Rolf Blättler, Kurt Müller. (Coach: Louis Maurer (SUI)).
Malta: Alfred Mizzi (29' Vincent Borg Bonaci), Joseph Grima, Anthony Camilleri, Edward Darmanin, Alfred Mallia, Emmanuel Micallef, Joseph Cini (C), Ronald Cocks, William Vassallo, John Bonett, Louis Arpa (YC) (84' Alfred Delia). (Coach: Karm Borg (MLT)).
Goals: Switzerland: 1-0 Rolf Blättler (14'), 2-0 Fritz Künzli (17'), 3-0 René Pierre Quentin (26'), 4-0 Roland Citherlet (28'), 5-0 Kurt Müller (30').
Referee: Gunnar Michaelsen (DEN)   Attendance: 16.470

21-04-1971   Wembley Stadium, London: England – Greece   3-0 (1-0)
England: Gordon Banks, Bobby Moore (C), Roy McFarland, Peter Storey, Alan Mullery, Alan Ball (80' Ralph Coates), Martin Peters, Emlyn Hughes, Francis Lee, Geoff Hurst, Martin Chivers. (Coach: Alf Ramsey (ENG)).
Greece: Nikolas Christidis, Apostolos Toskas, Nikos Stathopoulos (57' Stathis Chaitas), Dimitrios Synetopoulos, Giorgos Koudas (72' Kostas Aidiniou), Giannis Gaitatzis, Michalis Kritikopoulos, Angelos Spiridon, Dinos Kambas, Mimis Papaioannou (C), Giorgos Dedes. (Coach: Lakis Petropoulos (GRE)).
Goals: England: 1-0 Martin Chivers (23'), 2-0 Geoff Hurst (68'), 3-0 Francis Lee (87').
Referee: Martti Hirviniemi (FIN)   Attendance: 55.123

12-05-1971   Wembley Stadium, London: England – Malta   5-0 (2-0)
England: Gordon Banks, Bobby Moore (C), Terry Cooper, Roy McFarland, Chris Lawler, Martin Peters, Emlyn Hughes, Ralph Coates, Francis Lee, Allan Clarke (62' Alan Ball), Martin Chivers. (Coach: Alf Ramsey (ENG)).
Malta: Vincent Borg Bonaci (62' Alfred Mizzi), Louis Pace, Joseph Grima, Anthony Camilleri, Edward Darmanin, Alfred Delia, Edward Theobald, Ronald Cocks (C), William Vassallo, John Bonett, Louis Arpa. (Coach: Karm Borg (MLT)).
Goals: England: 1-0 Martin Chivers (1'), 2-0 Francis Lee (41'), 3-0 Allan Clarke (46' penalty), 4-0 Martin Chivers (47'), 5-0 Chris Lawler (74').
Referee: Einar Røad (NOR)   Attendance: 41.534

12-05-1971   Wankdorfstadion, Bern: Switzerland – Greece   1-0 (0-0)
Switzerland: Mario Prosperi, Georges Perroud, Peter Ramseier, Anton Weibel, Pierre-Albert Chapuisat, Jakob (Köbi) Kuhn, Walter Balmer, Daniel Jeandupeux, Fritz Künzli, Karl Odermatt (C), Rolf Blättler. (Coach: Louis Maurer (SUI)).
Greece: Nikolas Christidis, Apostolos Toskas, Apostolos Glezos, Nikos Stathopoulos, Dimitrios Synetopoulos, Giannis Gaitatzis (YC), Dinos Kambas, Takis Chatziioanoglou (74' Michalis Kritikopoulos), Mimis Papaioannou (C), Giorgos Dedes (YC), Thanasis Intzoglou (77' Giorgos Karafeskos). (Coach: Lakis Petropoulos (GRE)).
Goal: Switzerland: 1-0 Karl Odermatt (73').
Referee: Iorwerth Price Jones (WAL)   Attendance: 32.770
(Referee Iorwerth Price Jones was injured in the 29th minute and replaced by Thomas Henry Charles Reynolds (WAL)).

18-06-1971   Stadio Karaiskaki, Piraues: Greece – Malta   2-0 (0-0)
Greece: Lefteris Poupakis, Giannis Gounaris, Vasilis Siokos (85' Apostolos Toskas), Apostolos Glezos (YC) (70' Giorgos Karafeskos), Takis Eleftheriadis, Tasos Pappas, Michalis Kritikopoulos (C), Babis Stavropoulos, Kostas Aidiniou, Stavros Sarafis, Kostas Davourlis. (Coach: Lakis Petropoulos (GRE)).
Malta: Vincent Borg Bonaci, Louis Pace, Joseph Grima, Anthony Camilleri, Edward Darmanin (68' Charles Micallef (I)), Edward Theobald, Joseph Cini (C), Ronald Cocks, William Vassallo, John Bonett, Joseph Farrugia (46' Louis Arpa). (Coach: Anthony Formosa (MLT)).
Goals: Geece: 1-0 Kostas Davourlis (60'), 2-0 Kostas Aidiniou (80').
Referee: István Zsolt (HUN)   Attendance: 9.561

13-10-1971   St. Jakob Stadium, Basle: Switzerland – England   2-3 (2-2)
Switzerland: Marcel Kunz, Peter Ramseier, Anton Weibel, Pierre-Albert Chapuisat (81' Kurt Müller), Pirmin Stierli, Jakob (Köbi) Kuhn, Walter Balmer, Daniel Jeandupeux, Fritz Künzli, Karl Odermatt (C), Rolf Blättler (74' Georges Perroud). (Coach: Louis Maurer (SUI)).
England: Gordon Banks, Bobby Moore (C), Terry Cooper, Roy McFarland, Chris Lawler, Alan Mullery, Martin Peters, Paul Madeley, Francis Lee, Geoff Hurst (84' John Radford), Martin Chivers. (Coach: Alf Ramsey (ENG)).
Goals: Switzerland: 1-1 Daniel Jeandupeux (10'), 2-2 Fritz Künzli (44').
England: 0-1 Geoff Hurst (1'), 1-2 Martin Chivers (12'), 2-3 Anton Weibel (77' *own goal*).
Referee: Vital Georges Gilbert Loraux (BEL)   Attendance: 47.877

10-11-1971   Wembley Stadium, London: England – Switzerland 1-1 (1-1)
England: Peter Shilton, Bobby Moore (C), Terry Cooper, Peter Storey, Larry Lloyd, Alan Ball, Mike Summerbee (YC) (60' Martin Chivers), Emlyn Hughes, Paul Madeley, Francis Lee (YC) (83' Rodney Marsh), Geoff Hurst. (Coach: Alf Ramsey (ENG)).
Switzerland: Mario Prosperi, Georges Perroud, Peter Ramseier, Pierre-Albert Chapuisat, Pirmin Stierli, Jakob (Köbi) Kuhn, Walter Balmer, Daniel Jeandupeux (63' Peter Meier), Fritz Künzli, Karl Odermatt, Rolf Blättler. (Coach: Louis Maurer (SUI)).
Goals: England: 1-0 Mike Summerbee (9').
Switzerland: 1-1 Karl Odermatt (26').
Referee: Constantin Barbulescu (ROM)   Attendance: 90.423

01-12-1971   Stadio Karaiskaki, Piraeus: Greece – England 0-2 (0-0)
Greece: Nikolas Christidis, Anthimos Kapsis, Apostolos Toskas, Kostas Eleftherakis, Thodoros Palas, Thanasis Angelis, Giorgos Koudas (59' Michalis Kritikopoulos), Mimis Domazos, Mimis Papaioannou, Antonis Antoniadis, Kostas Nikolaidis (71' Kostas Davourlis). (Coach: William Laurence (Billy) Bingham (NIR)).
England: Gordon Banks, Bobby Moore (C), Roy McFarland, Alan Ball, Martin Peters, Colin Bell, Emlyn Hughes, Paul Madeley, Francis Lee, Geoff Hurst, Martin Chivers. (Coach: Alf Ramsey (ENG)).
Goals: England: 0-1 Geoff Hurst (57'), 0-2 Martin Chivers (90').
Referee: José María Ortiz de Mendíbil (ESP)   Attendance: 34.014

GROUP 4

11-11-1970	Seville	Spain – Northern Ireland	3-0 (1-0)
15-11-1970	Nicosia	Cyprus – Soviet Union	1-3 (1-2)
03-02-1971	Nicosia	Cyprus – Northern Ireland	0-3 (0-0)
21-04-1971	Belfast	Northern Ireland – Cyprus	5-0 (2-0)
09-05-1971	Nicosia	Cyprus – Spain	0-2 (0-1)
30-05-1971	Moscow	Soviet Union – Spain	2-1 (0-0)
07-06-1971	Moscow	Soviet Union – Cyprus	6-1 (3-0)
22-09-1971	Moscow	Soviet Union – Northern Ireland	1-0 (1-0)
13-10-1971	Belfast	Northern Ireland – Soviet Union	1-1 (1-1)
27-10-1971	Seville	Spain – Soviet Union	0-0
24-11-1971	Granada	Spain – Cyprus	7-0 (3-0)
16-02-1972	Kingston upon Hull	Northern Ireland – Spain	1-1 (0-1)

FINAL STANDING

Pos	Team	Pld	W	D	L	GF	GA	GD	Pts
1	Soviet Union	6	4	2	0	13	4	+9	10
2	Spain	6	3	2	1	14	3	+11	8
3	Northern Ireland	6	2	2	2	10	6	+4	6
4	Cyprus	6	0	0	6	2	26	-24	0

Soviet Union qualified for the Quarter-finals.

11-11-1970   Estadio Ramón Sánchez Pizjuán, Seville: Spain – Northern Ireland 3-0 (1-0)
Spain: José Ángel IRIBAR Cortajarena, JUAN Cruz SOL Oria (46' Juan López HITA), Enrique Álvarez COSTAS, José Martínez Sánchez "PIRRI", Carlos REXACH Cerda, Francisco Fernández Rodríguez "GALLEGO", José Luis VIOLETA Lajusticia, Joaquín RIFÉ Climent, Enrique Castro González "QUINI" (46' Enrique LORA Millán), José LUIS ARAGONÉS Suárez Martínez (C), Antonio ARIETA Araunabeña Piedra. (Coach: László "LADISLAO" KUBALA Stecz (ESP)).
Northern Ireland: Willie McFaul, Sammy Nelson, Terry Neill (C), David Craig, Liam O'Kane, David Clements, Tommy Jackson, Derek Dougan (20' Sammy Todd), George Best, Terry Harkin, David Sloan. (Coach: William Laurence (Billy) Bingham (NIR)).
Goals: Spain: 1-0 Carlos REXACH Cerda (39'), 2-0 José Martínez Sánchez "PIRRI" (60'), 3-0 José LUIS ARAGONÉS Suárez Martínez (75').
Referee: Gyula Emsberger (HUN)   Attendance: 26.215

15-11-1970   GSP Stadium, Nicosia: Cyprus – Soviet Union 1-3 (1-2)
Cyprus: Michalis Akliviades, Kostas Christou, Kyriacos Koureas, Paschalis Fokis, Demos Kavazis, Pambos Papadopoulos, Pavlos Vasiliou, Michalakis Theodorou (75' Marios Markou), Tassos Constantinou (83' Marios Kythreotis), Nikos Charalambous, Andreas Stylianou. (Coach: Raymond Ernest (Ray) Wood (ENG)).
Soviet Union: Viktor Bannikov, Volodymyr Kaplychniy, Albert Shesternev, Yuri Istomin, Evgeni Lovchev, Volodymyr Muntyan, Gennadi Evryuzhikhin, Viktor Kolotov, Boris Kopeykin (70' Givi Nodia), Vladimir Fedotov, Vitali Shevchenko. (Coach: Valentin Aleksandrovich Nikolayev (URS)).
Goals: Cyprus: 1-2 Nikos Charalambous (42').
Soviet Union: 0-1 Viktor Kolotov (10'), 0-2 Gennadi Evryuzhikhin (16'), 1-3 Vitali Shevchenko (50').
Referee: Petar Kostovki (YUG)   Attendance: 8.980

03-02-1971   GSP Stadium, Nicosia: Cyprus – Northern Ireland 0-3 (0-0)
Cyprus: Erodotos Koupanos, Kostas Christou (73' Michalakis Theodorou), Kyriacos Koureas (YC63), Paschalis Fokis, Demos Kavazis, Stephanis Michael, Pambos Papadopoulos, Pavlos Vasiliou, Nikos Charalambous, Kallis Constantinou, Andreas Stylianou. (Coach: Raymond Ernest (Ray) Wood (ENG)).
Northern Ireland: Pat Jennings, Sammy Nelson, Terry Neill, Sammy Todd, David Craig, Allan Hunter, Jimmy Nicholson, Bryan Hamilton, Eric McMordie, Derek Dougan, George Best. (Coach: William Laurence (Billy) Bingham (NIR)).
Goals: Northern Ireland: 0-1 Jimmy Nicholson (53'), 0-2 Derek Dougan (55'), 0-3 George Best (86' penalty).
Referee: Francesco Francescon (ITA)   Attendance: 9.119

21-04-1971   Windsor Park, Belfast: Northern Ireland – Cyrpus 5-0 (2-0)
Northern Ireland: Pat Jennings, Martin Harvey, Sammy Todd (88' Peter Watson), David Craig, Allan Hunter, Jimmy Nicholson, David Clements, Bryan Hamilton, Eric McMordie, Derek Dougan (C), George Best. (Coach: William Laurence (Billy) Bingham (NIR)).
Cyprus: Erodotos Koupanos, Kyriacos Koureas, Paschalis Fokis, Demos Kavazis, Stephanis Michael, Michalakis Michael (54' Michalakis Theodorou), Pambos Papadopoulos, Pavlos Vasiliou, Tasso Constantinou (65' Takis Papettas), Kallis Constantinou, Andreas Stylianou. (Coach: Raymond Ernest (Ray) Wood (ENG)).
Goals: Northern Ireland: 1-0 Derek Dougan (2'), 2-0 George Best (44'), 3-0 George Best (47'), 4-0 George Best (56'), 5-0 Jimmy Nicholson (85').
Referee: Jacques Colling (LUX)   Attendance: 19.153

09-05-1971   GSP Stadium, Nicosia: Cyprus – Spain   0-2 (0-1)
Cyprus: Dimos Eleftheriades, Paschalis Fokis, Demos Kavazis, Stephanis Michael, Takis Papettas, Haris Kantzilieris, George "Kokos" Antoniou, Kostas Alexandrou, Pambos Papadopoulos, Pavlos Vasiliou (66' Michalakis Theodorou), Andreas Stylianou. (Coach: Raymond Ernest (Ray) Wood (ENG)).
Spain: Miguel REINA Santos, Antonio "TONONO" Alfonso Moreno, Gregorio BENITO Rubio, Antonio Manuel Martínez Morales "ANTÓN", José Martínez Sánchez "PIRRI", José Luis VIOLETA Lajusticia, José CLARAMUNT Torres, Fidel URIARTE Macho (46' Enrique LORA Millán), Enrique Castro González "QUINI", AMANCIO Amaro Varela (C), José Ignacio CHURRUCA Sistiaga (55' Carlos REXACH Cerda). (Coach: László "LADISLAO" KUBALA Stecz (ESP)).
Goals: Spain: 0-1 José Martínez Sánchez "PIRRI" (3'), 0-2 José Luis VIOLETA Lajusticia (86').
Referee: Constantin Barbulescu (ROM)   Attendance: 5.818

30-05-1971   Central Lenin Stadium, Moscow: Soviet Union – Spain   2-1 (0-0)
Soviet Union: Evgeni Rudakov, Volodymyr Kaplychniy, Albert Shesternev, Revaz Dzodzuashvili, Valeri Zykov, Volodymyr Muntyan (76' Givi Nodia), Gennadi Evryuzhikhin, József Szabó, Viktor Kolotov, Anatoli Banishevski (80' Vladimir Fedotov), Vitali Shevchenko. (Coach: Valentin Aleksandrovich Nikolayev (URS)).
Spain: José Ángel IRIBAR Cortajarena, Antonio "TONONO" Alfonso Moreno, JUAN Cruz SOL Oria (65' Antonio Manuel Martínez Morales "ANTÓN"), Gregorio BENITO Rubio, Carlos REXACH Cerda, Francisco Fernández Rodríguez "GALLEGO", José Luis VIOLETA Lajusticia (60' Enrique LORA Millán), José CLARAMUNT Torres, Fidel URIARTE Macho, AMANCIO Amaro Varela (C), José Ignacio CHURRUCA Sistiaga. (Coach: László "LADISLAO" KUBALA Stecz (ESP)).
Goals: Soviet Union: 1-0 Viktor Kolotov (79'), 2-0 Vitali Shevchenko (83').
Spain: 2-1 Carlos REXACH Cerda (88').
Referee: Ferdinand Biwersi (FRG)   Attendance: 81.700

07-06-1971   Central Lenin Stadium, Moscow: Soviet Union – Cyprus   6-1 (3-0)
Soviet Union: Viktor Bannikov (46' Evgeni Rudakov), Volodymyr Kaplychniy, Albert Shesternev, Yuri Istomin, Valeri Zykov, Volodymyr Muntyan, Gennadi Evryuzhikhin (68' Vitaliy Khmelnitskiy), Viktor Kolotov, Vladimir Fedotov, Anatoli Banishevski, Vitali Shevchenko. (Coach: Valentin Aleksandrovich Nikolayev (URS)).
Cyprus: Varnavas Christofi, Paschalis Fokis, Demos Kavazis, Stephanis Michael, Michalakis Michael, Haris Kantzilieris (79' Takis Papettas), Pavlos Vasiliou, Marios Markou, Kallis Constantinou, Andreas Constantinou (YC77), Andreas Stylianou (52' Michalakis Theodorou). (Coach: Raymond Ernest (Ray) Wood (ENG)).
Goals: Soviet Union: 1-0 Vladimir Fedotov (4'), 2-0 Gennadi Evryuzhikhin (23'), 3-0 Gennadi Evryuzhikhin (38'), 4-0 Viktor Kolotov (59'), 5-1 Anatoli Banishevski (85'), 6-1 Vladimir Fedotov (86').
Cyprus: 4-1 Stephanis Michael (75').
Referee: Erik Beijar (FIN)   Attendance: 21.159

22-09-1971   Central Lenin Stadium, Moscow: Soviet Union – Northern Ireland   1-0 (1-0)
Soviet Union: Evgeni Rudakov, Albert Shesternev, Revaz Dzodzuashvili, Valeri Zykov, Volodymyr Muntyan, Gennadi Evryuzhikhin, Murtaz Khurtsilava, Viktor Kolotov, Oleg Dolmatov, Vladimir Fedotov, Vitali Shevchenko (74' Yuri Istomin). (Coach: Valentin Aleksandrovich Nikolayev (URS)).
Northern Ireland: Willie McFaul, Sammy Nelson, Terry Neill, David Craig (70' Bryan Hamilton), Liam O'Kane, Allan Hunter, Jimmy Nicholson, David Clements, Daniel Hegan, Derek Dougan, George Best. (Coach: William John Terence (Terry) Neill (NIR)).
Goal: Soviet Union: 1-0 Volodymyr Muntyan (43' penalty).
Referee: Ove Dahlberg (SWE)   Attendance: 51.186

13-10-1971   Windsor Park, Belfast: Northern Ireland – Soviet Union   1-1 (1-1)
Northern Ireland: Pat Jennings, Sammy Nelson, Terry Neill, Liam O'Kane, Allan Hunter, Pat Rice, Jimmy Nicholson, David Clements, Bryan Hamilton (73' Thomas Cassidy) , Eric McMordie, Derek Dougan (C) (46' Martin O'Neill). (Coach: William John Terence (Terry) Neill (NIR)).
Soviet Union: Evgeni Rudakov, Albert Shesternev, Revaz Dzodzuashvili, Evgeni Lovchev (YC43), Anatoli Byshovets, Murtaz Khurtsilava, Mykola Kiselev, Viktor Kolotov, Anatoliy Konkov, Oleg Dolmatov, Vitali Shevchenko (73' Levon Ishtoyan). (Coach: Valentin Aleksandrovich Nikolayev (URS)).
Goals: Northern Ireland: 1-0 Jimmy Nicholson (13').
Soviet Union: 1-1 Anatoli Byshovets (32').
Referee: Rolf Nyhus (NOR)   Attendance: 16.573

27-10-1971   Estadio Ramón Sánchez Pizjuán, Seville: Spain – Soviet Union   0-0
Spain: Miguel REINA Santos, Antonio "TONONO" Alfonso Moreno, JUAN Cruz SOL Oria, Antonio Manuel Martínez Morales "ANTÓN" (78' MARCIAL Pina Morales), Francisco Fernández Rodríguez "GALLEGO" (YC32), José CLARAMUNT Torres, Enrique LORA Millán, Enrique Castro González "QUINI", AMANCIO Amaro Varela (C), José Ignacio CHURRUCA Sistiaga, Joaquín Sierra Vallejo "QUINO". (Coach: László "LADISLAO" KUBALA Stecz (ESP)).
Soviet Union: Evgeni Rudakov, Albert Shesternev (C), Yuri Istomin, Revaz Dzodzuashvili, Volodymyr Muntyan, Anatoli Byshovets, Murtaz Khurtsilava, Viktor Kolotov, Oleg Dolmatov, Vladimir Fedotov (83' Mykola Kiselev), Levon Ishtoyan (63' Vitali Shevchenko). (Coach: Valentin Aleksandrovich Nikolayev (URS)).
Referee: Norman Charles H.Burtenshaw (ENG)   Attendance: 40.169

24-11-1971   Estadio Los Cármenes, Granada: Spain – Cyprus   7-0 (3-0)
Spain: José Ángel IRIBAR Cortajarena, Antonio "TONONO" Alfonso Moreno, JUAN Cruz SOL Oria, Juan López HITA, José Martínez Sánchez "PIRRI", Francisco Fernández Rodríguez "GALLEGO", José CLARAMUNT Torres, Enrique LORA Millán (53' José Agustín Aranzábal Ascariba "GAZTELU"), AMANCIO Amaro Varela (C) (46' Francisco Javier AGUILAR García), José Francisco "CHECHU" ROJO Arroita (I), Joaquín Sierra Vallejo "QUINO". (Coach: László "LADISLAO" KUBALA Stecz (ESP)).
Cyprus: Erodotos Koupanos, Demos Kavazis (YC), Stephanis Michael, George "Kokos" Antoniou (48' Michalakis Michael), Ioannis Mertakas, Charalambos Partassides, Pavlos Vasiliou, Tassos Constantinou, Kallis Constantinou (71' Michalakis Theodorou), Michael Athinadorou, Andreas Stylianou (C) (YC). (Coach: Raymond Ernest (Ray) Wood (ENG)).
Goals: Spain: 1-0 José Martínez Sánchez "PIRRI" (9'), 2-0 Joaquín Sierra Vallejo "QUINO" (15'), 3-0 Joaquín Sierra Vallejo "QUINO" (22'), 4-0 José Martínez Sánchez "PIRRI" (47' penalty), 5-0 Francisco Javier AGUILAR García (63'), 6-0 Enrique LORA Millán (66'), 7-0 José Francisco "CHECHU" ROJO Arroita (I) (75').
Referee: Joseph M.Cassar Naudi (MLT)   Attendance: 19.176

16-02-1972   Boothferry Park, Kingston upon Hull: Northern Ireland – Spain   1-1 (0-1)
Northern Ireland: Pat Jennings, Sammy Nelson, Terry Neill, Allan Hunter, Pat Rice, Sammy McIlroy, David Clements, Bryan Hamilton (C) (46' Martin O'Neill), Eric McMordie, George Best, Sammy Morgan. (Coach: William John Terence (Terry) Neill (NIR)).
Spain: José Ángel IRIBAR Cortajarena, Antonio "TONONO" Alfonso Moreno, JUAN Cruz SOL Oria (YC41), Gregorio BENITO Rubio (YC67), Enrique Álvarez COSTAS, Francisco Fernández Rodríguez "GALLEGO", Enrique LORA Millán (60' Miguel Ramos Vargas "MIGUELI"), Enrique Castro González "QUINI" (14' Manuel Ríos Quintanilla "MANOLETE"), José Francisco "CHECHU" ROJO Arroita (I), Joaquín Sierra Vallejo "QUINO", Francisco Javier AGUILAR García. (Coach: László "LADISLAO" KUBALA Stecz (ESP)).
Goals: Northern Ireland: 1-1 Sammy Morgan (71').
Spain: 0-1 José Francisco "CHECHU" ROJO Arroita (I) (41').
Referee: John Keith (Jack) Taylor (ENG)   Attendance: 19.925

GROUP 5

14-10-1970	Copenhagen	Denmark – Portugal	0-1 (0-1)
11-11-1970	Glasgow	Scotland – Denmark	1-0 (1-0)
25-11-1970	Bruges	Belgium – Denmark	2-0 (2-0)
03-02-1971	Liège	Belgium – Scotland	3-0 (1-0)
17-02-1971	Anderlecht	Belgium – Portugal	3-0 (1-0)
21-04-1971	Lisbon	Portugal – Scotland	2-0 (1-0)
12-05-1971	Oporto	Portugal – Denmark	5-0 (2-0)
26-05-1971	Copenhagen	Denmark – Belgium	1-2 (0-0)
09-06-1971	Copenhagen	Denmark – Scotland	1-0 (1-0)
13-10-1971	Glasgow	Scotland – Portugal	2-1 (1-0)
10-11-1971	Aberdeen	Scotland – Belgium	1-0 (1-0)
21-11-1971	Lisbon	Portugal – Belgium	1-1 (0-0)

FINAL STANDING

Pos	Team	Pld	W	D	L	GF	GA	GD	Pts
1	*Belgium*	*6*	*4*	*1*	*1*	*11*	*3*	*+8*	*9*
2	Portugal	6	3	1	2	10	6	+4	7
3	Scotland	6	3	0	3	4	7	-3	6
4	Denmark	6	1	0	5	2	11	-9	2

Belgium qualified for the Quarter-finals.

14-10-1970   Idrætsparken, Copenhagen: Denmark – Portugal   0-1 (0-1)
Denmark: Kaj Paulsen, Jens Jørgen Hansen (C), Poul Henning Frederiksen, Torben Nielsen, Flemming Pedersen, Erik Sandvad, Bent Outzen, Kurt Præst (YC), Jan Andersen (YC) (85' Per Madsen (YC)), Jørgen Markussen, Keld Pedersen (60' Poul-Erik Thygesen). (Coach: Rudolf (Rudi) Strittich (AUT)).
Portugal: Vítor Manuel Alfonso de Oliveira "DAMAS", HILÁRIO Rosario da Conceição, JOSÉ CARLOS da Silva José (C), Manuel PEDRO GOMES, HUMBERTO Manuel de Jesus COELHO, JOSÉ MARÍA Júnior (62' Augusto Matine), JACINTO JOÃO, ANTÓNIO José SIMÕES da Costa (53' JAIME da Silva GRAÇA), EUSÉBIO da Silva Ferreira, FERNANDO PERES da Silva, ARTUR JORGE Braga Melo Teixeira. (Coach: José Gomes De Silva (POR)).
Goal: Portugal: 0-1 JACINTO JOÃO (40').
Referee: Leo Callaghan (WAL)   Attendance: 17.317

11-11-1970   Hampden Park, Glasgow: Scotland – Denmark   1-0 (1-0)
Scotland: Jim Cruickshank, Ronnie McKinnon, Bobby Moncur (C), David Hay (46' Sandy Jardine), John Greig, Jimmy Johnstone, Pat Stanton, Willie Carr, Willie Johnston, Colin Stein, John O'Hare (70' Peter Cormack). (Coach: Robert (Bobby) Brown (SCO)).
Denmark: Kaj Paulsen, Morten Olsen (46' Poul-Erik Thygesen), Jens Jørgen Hansen (C), Poul Henning Frederiksen, Torben Nielsen, Flemming Pedersen, Erik Sandvad, Bent Outzen, Keld Pedersen, Kristen Nygaard, Benny Nielsen. (Coach: Rudolf (Rudi) Strittich (AUT)).
Goal: Scotland: 1-0 John O'Hare (13').
Referee: Erich Linemayr (AUT)   Attendance: 24.618

25-11-1970   Stade Klokke, Bruges: Belgium – Denmark   2-0 (2-0)
Belgium: Christian Piot, Georges Heylens (C), Jean Thissen, Nicolas Dewalque, Léon Jeck, Erwin Vandendaele, Wilfried Van Moer (59' Jan Verheyen), Pierre Carteus, Johan Devrindt, Raoul Lambert, Johny Thio. (Coach: Raymond Goethals (BEL)).
Denmark: Kaj Paulsen (YC), Morten Olsen (59' Poul-Erik Thygesen (YC)), Jens Jørgen Hansen (C), Poul Henning Frederiksen, Torben Nielsen, Flemming Pedersen, Erik Sandvad, Bent Outzen, Keld Pedersen, Kristen Nygaard, Benny Nielsen (60' Mogens Haastrup (YC)). (Coach: Rudolf (Rudi) Strittich (AUT)).
Goals: Belgium: 1-0 Johan Devrindt (17'), 2-0 Johan Devrindt (37').
Referee: John Carpenter (IRL)   Attendance: 9.697

03-02-1971   Stade Sclessin, Liège: Belgium – Scotland   3-0 (1-0)
Belgium: Christian Piot, Georges Heylens, Jean Thissen, Nicolas Dewalque, Erwin Vandendaele, Jean Plaskie, Wilfried Van Moer, Léon Semmeling, Henri Depireux (YC70), Paul Van Himst (C), André De Nul. (Coach: Raymond Goethals (BEL)).
Scotland: Jim Cruickshank, Tommy Gemmell, Ronnie McKinnon, Bobby Moncur (C), David Hay (YC70), Archie Gemmill, John Greig, Charlie Cooke, Pat Stanton (46' Tony Green), Colin Stein (46' Jim Forrest), John O'Hare. (Coach: Robert (Bobby) Brown (SCO)).
Goals: Belgium: 1-0 Ronnie McKinnon (39' *own goal*), 2-0 Paul Van Himst (57'), 3-0 Paul Van Himst (85' penalty).
Referee: Antonio Sbardella (ITA)   Attendance: 13.931

17-02-1971   Stade Émile Versé, Anderlecht: Belgium – Portugal   3-0 (1-0)
Belgium: Christian Piot, Georges Heylens, Jean Thissen, Nicolas Dewalque, Erwin Vandendaele, Jean Plaskie, Wilfried Van Moer, Léon Semmeling (46' Johny Thio), Paul Van Himst (C), Raoul Lambert, André De Nul. (Coach: Raymond Goethals (BEL)).
Portugal: Vítor Manuel Alfonso de Oliveira "DAMAS", HILÁRIO Rosario da Conceição (C), RUI de Gouveia Pinto RODRIGUES, HUMBERTO Manuel de Jesus COELHO, Amandio José MALTA DA SILVA (46' FRANCISCO Moreira Silva REBELO), José ROLANDO Andrade Gonçalves (YC), Fernando Pascoal Das Neves "PAVÃO", VÍTOR Manuel Ferreira BAPTISTA, ANTÓNIO José SIMÕES da Costa, EUSÉBIO da Silva Ferreira, FERNANDO PERES da Silva (65' FÉLIX Marques GUERREIRO). (Coach: José Gomes De Silva (POR)).
Goals: Belgium: 1-0 Raoul Lambert (14'), 2-0 Raoul Lambert (64' penalty), 3-0 André De Nul (75').
Referee: Gaspar Pintado Viu (ESP)   Attendance: 26.921

21-04-1971   Estádio da Luz, Lisbon: Portugal – Scotland   2-0 (1-0)
Portugal: Vítor Manuel Alfonso de Oliveira "DAMAS", JOSÉ CARLOS da Silva José (C), RUI de Gouveia Pinto RODRIGUES, HUMBERTO Manuel de Jesus COELHO, Amandio José MALTA DA SILVA, ADOLFO António da Luz CALISTO, VÍTOR Manuel Ferreira BAPTISTA (75' ARTUR JORGE Braga Melo Teixeira), ANTÓNIO José SIMÕES da Costa, EUSÉBIO da Silva Ferreira, Tamagnini Manuel Gomes Batista "NENÉ" (86' Fernando Pascoal Das Neves "PAVÃO"), FERNANDO PERES da Silva. (Coach: José Gomes De Silva (POR)).
Scotland: Bobby Clark, Ronnie McKinnon, Bobby Moncur (C), Jim Brogan, David Hay, Willie Henderson, Jim McCalliog (62' Drew Jarvie), Pat Stanton (74' Tony Green), Alan Gilzean, Peter Cormack, Davie Robb. (Coach: Robert (Bobby) Brown (SCO)).
Goals: Portugal: 1-0 Pat Stanton (22' *own goal*), 2-0 EUSÉBIO da Silva Ferreira (83').
Referee: Michel Kitabdjian (FRA)   Attendance: 35.463

12-05-1971   Estádio das Antas, Oporto: Portugal – Denmark   5-0 (2-0)
Portugal: Vítor Manuel Alfonso de Oliveira "DAMAS", JOSÉ CARLOS da Silva José (C), RUI de Gouveia Pinto RODRIGUES, HUMBERTO Manuel de Jesus COELHO, Amandio José MALTA DA SILVA (78' FRANCISCO Moreira Silva REBELO), ADOLFO António da Luz CALISTO, VÍTOR Manuel Ferreira BAPTISTA (85' ARTUR JORGE Braga Melo Teixeira), ANTÓNIO José SIMÕES da Costa, EUSÉBIO da Silva Ferreira, Tamagnini Manuel Gomes Batista "NENÉ", FERNANDO PERES da Silva. (Coach: José Gomes De Silva (POR)).
Denmark: Erik Sørensen, Morten Olsen, Henning Boel, Mogens Berg (34' Erik Nielsen (YC)), Jørgen Rasmussen, Erik Sandvad, Kresten Bjerre (C), Finn Laudrup, Preben Arentoft, Ole Bjørnmose, Benny Nielsen. (Coach: Rudolf (Rudi) Strittich (AUT)).
Goals: Portugal: 1-0 RUI de Gouveia Pinto RODRIGUES (17'), 2-0 EUSÉBIO da Silva Ferreira (42'), 3-0 VÍTOR Manuel Ferreira BAPTISTA (47'), 4-0 VÍTOR Manuel Ferreira BAPTISTA (51'), 5-0 Erik Sandvad (87' *own goal*).
Referee: Malcolm Hall Wright (NIR)   Attendance: 16.391

26-05-1971   Idrætsparken, Copenhagen: Denmark – Belgium   1-2 (0-0)
Denmark: Erik Sørensen, Henning Boel (YC), Torben Nielsen, Mogens Berg, John Steen Olsen (72' Keld Pedersen), Erik Sandvad, Kresten Bjerre (C), Finn Laudrup, Preben Arentoft, Ole Bjørnmose, Benny Nielsen (82' Birger Pedersen). (Coach: Rudolf (Rudi) Strittich (AUT)).
Belgium: Christian Piot, Georges Heylens, Jean Thissen, Erwin Vandendaele, Jean Plaskie, Léon Semmeling, Jan Verheyen, Jean Dockx, Johan Devrindt, Paul Van Himst (C), Wilfried Puis. (Coach: Raymond Goethals (BEL)).
Goals: Denmark: 1-2 Kresten Bjerre (76').
Belgium: 0-1 Johan Devrindt (65'), 0-2 Johan Devrindt (75').
Referee: Kåre Sirevaag (NOR)   Attendance: 27.266

09-06-1971   Idrætsparken, Copenhagen: Denmark – Scotland   1-0 (1-0)
Denmark: Erik Sørensen, Torben Nielsen, Mogens Berg, Jørgen Rasmussen, Ulrik Le Fevre, Kresten Bjerre (C), Finn Laudrup (75' Flemming Pedersen), Preben Arentoft, Ole Bjørnmose, Benny Nielsen (62' Bent Outzen (YC)), Jørgen Kristensen. (Coach: Rudolf (Rudi) Strittich (AUT)).
Scotland: Bobby Clark, Tom Forsyth (46' Davie Robb), Ronnie McKinnon, Bobby Moncur (C), Frank Munro (YC), Billy Dickson, Pat Stanton, Tommy McLean, Colin Stein, Jim Forrest (70' John Scott), Hugh Curran. (Coach: Robert (Bobby) Brown (SCO)).
Goal: Denmark: 1-0 Finn Laudrup (43').
Referee: Wolfgang Riedel (GDR)   Attendance: 37.682

13-10-1971   Hampden Park, Glasgow: Scotland – Portugal   2-1 (1-0)
Scotland: Bob Wilson, Sandy Jardine, Eddie Colquhoun, Billy Bremner (C), David Hay, Archie Gemmill, Jimmy Johnstone (83' Tony Green), Pat Stanton, Alex Cropley, George Graham, John O'Hare. (Coach: Thomas Hendersen (Tommy) Docherty (SCO)).
Portugal: Vítor Manuel Alfonso de Oliveira "DAMAS", RUI de Gouveia Pinto RODRIGUES, Amandio José MALTA DA SILVA, ADOLFO António da Luz CALISTO, FRANCISCO António Galinho CALÓ (YC35), JAIME da Silva GRAÇA (YC58) (77' FERNANDO PERES da Silva), José ROLANDO Andrade Gonçalves, VÍTOR Manuel Ferreira BAPTISTA, ANTÓNIO José SIMÕES da Costa, EUSÉBIO da Silva Ferreira (C) (46' ARTUR JORGE Braga Melo Teixeira), Tamagnini Manuel Gomes Batista "NENÉ". (Coach: José Gomes De Silva (POR)).
Goals: Scotland: 1-0 John O'Hare (22'), 2-1 Archie Gemmill (58').
Portugal: 1-1 RUI de Gouveia Pinto RODRIGUES (56').
Referee: Bruno Piotrowicz (POL)   Attendance: 58.612

10-11-1971   Pittodrie Stadium, Aberdeen: Scotland – Belgium   1-0 (1-0)
Scotland: Bobby Clark, Sandy Jardine, Martin Buchan, Billy Bremner (C), David Hay, Jimmy Johnstone (82' John Hansen), Pat Stanton, Alex Cropley (47' Kenny Dalglish), Steve Murray, John O'Hare, Eddie Gray. (Coach: Thomas Hendersen (Tommy) Docherty (SCO)).
Belgium: Christian Piot, Georges Heylens, Nicolas Dewalque, Léon Dolmans, Erwin Vandendaele, André Stassart, Wilfried Van Moer (61' Maurice Martens), Léon Semmeling, Johan Devrindt, Paul Van Himst (C), Wilfried Puis (68' Raoul Lambert). (Coach: Raymond Goethals (BEL)).
Goal: Scotland: 1-0 John O'Hare (6').
Referee: Johan Einar Boström (SWE)   Attendance: 36.500

21-11-1971   Estádio da Luz, Lisbon: Portugal – Belgium   1-1 (0-0)
Portugal: Vítor Manuel Alfonso de Oliveira "DAMAS", RUI de Gouveia Pinto RODRIGUES, HUMBERTO Manuel de Jesus COELHO (YC81), Amandio José MALTA DA SILVA (46' OCTÁVIO Joaquim Coelho MACHADO), JOSÉ de Jesus MENDES, JAIME da Silva GRAÇA, ANTÓNIO José SIMÕES da Costa, EUSÉBIO da Silva Ferreira (C) , JOSÉ Augusto da Costa Séneca TORRES, Tamagnini Manuel Gomes Batista "NENÉ" (58' ARTUR JORGE Braga Melo Teixeira) , FERNANDO PERES da Silva. (Coach: José Gomes De Silva (POR)).
Belgium: Christian Piot, Georges Heylens, Nicolas Dewalque (YC38), Léon Dolmans (YC9), Erwin Vandendaele, Maurice Martens (72' Wilfried Puis), André Stassart, Léon Semmeling, Jean Dockx, Paul Van Himst (C), Raoul Lambert. (Coach: Raymond Goethals (BEL)).
Goals: Portugal: 1-1 FERNANDO PERES da Silva (90' penalty).
Belgium: 0-1 Raoul Lambert (61').
Referee: Kenneth Howard Burns (ENG)   Attendance: 53.577

GROUP 6

14-10-1970	Dublin	Republic of Ireland – Sweden	1-1 (1-0)
28-10-1970	Solna	Sweden – Republic of Ireland	1-0 (0-0)
31-10-1970	Vienna	Austria – Italy	1-2 (1-2)
08-12-1970	Florence	Italy – Republic of Ireland	3-0 (2-0)
10-05-1971	Dublin	Republic of Ireland – Italy	1-2 (1-1)
26-05-1971	Solna	Sweden – Austria	1-0 (0-0)
30-05-1971	Dublin	Republic of Ireland – Austria	1-4 (0-3)
09-06-1971	Solna	Sweden – Italy	0-0
04-09-1971	Vienna	Austria – Sweden	1-0 (1-0)
09-10-1971	Milan	Italy – Sweden	3-0 (2-0)
10-10-1971	Linz	Austria – Republic or Ireland	6-0 (3-0)
20-11-1971	Rome	Italy – Austria	2-2 (1-1)

FINAL STANDING

Pos	Team	Pld	W	D	L	GF	GA	GD	Pts
1	*Italy*	6	4	2	0	12	4	+8	*10*
2	Austria	6	3	1	2	14	6	+8	7
3	Sweden	6	2	2	2	3	5	-2	6
4	Republic of Ireland	6	0	1	5	3	17	-14	1

Italy qualified for the Quarter-finals.

14-10-1970   Dalymount Park, Dublin: Republic of Ireland – Sweden   1-1 (1-0)
Republic of Ireland: Alan Kelly, Tony Dunne (C), John Dempsey, Thomas Carroll (70' Joe Kinnear), Paddy Mulligan, Tony Byrne, Eamonn Dunphy, Michael Lawlor, Steve Heighway, Daniel Givens (YC60) (83' Ray Treacy) , Terry Conroy. (Coach: Michael Meagan (IRL)).
Sweden: Sven Gunnar Larsson, Björn Nordqvist (C) (YC70), Roland Grip, Hans Selander, Krister Kristensson, Jan Olsson, Tommy Svensson, Leif Eriksson, Ove Grahn, Bo Larsson, Inge Danielsen (46' Dan Brzokoupil). (Coach: Orvar Bergmark (SWE)).
Goals: Republic of Ireland: 1-0 Thomas Carroll (44' penalty).
Sweden: 1-1 Dan Brzokoupil (61').
Referee: Robert Héliès (FRA)   Attendance: 28.194

28-10-1970   Råsunda Stadion, Solna: Sweden – Republic of Ireland   1-0 (0-0)
Sweden: Ronnie Hellström, Björn Nordqvist (C), Roland Grip (65' Claes Cronqvist), Hans Selander, Krister Kristensson, Jan Olsson, Tommy Svensson, Leif Eriksson, Ove Grahn, Bo Larsson, Dan Brzokoupil (61' Tom Turesson). (Coach: Orvar Bergmark (SWE)).
Republic of Ireland: Alan Kelly, Seamus Brennan, John Dempsey, Tony Byrne, Patrick Dunning, Eamonn Dunphy, Alphonsus Finucane, Michael Lawlor, Steve Heighway, Ray Treacy, Terry Conroy. (Coach: Michael Meagan (IRL)).
Goal: Sweden: 1-0 Tom Turesson (74').
Referee: Pavel Nyikolajevics Kazakov (URS)   Attendance: 11.922

31-10-1970   Praterstadion, Vienna: Austria – Italy   1-2 (1-2)
Austria: Friedrich Koncilia (46' Herbert Rettensteiner), Gerhard Sturmberger (C), Johann Schmidradner, Norbert Hof, Peter Pumm, Josef Hickersberger, Thomas Parits, August Starek, Hans Ettmayer, Wilhelm Kreuz, Helmuth Redl. (Coach: Leopold Stastny (TCH)).
Italy: Enrico Albertosi, Giacinto Facchetti (C), Tarcisio Burgnich, Pierluigi Cera, Roberto Rosato, Gianni Rivera, Sandro Mazzola, Mario Bertini, Giancarlo "Picchio" De Sisti, Luigi Riva (YC) (77' Sergio Gori) , Angelo Domenghini. (Coach: Ferruccio Valcareggi (ITA)).
Goals: Austria: 1-1 Thomas Parits (29').
Italy: 0-1 Giancarlo "Picchio" De Sisti (27'), 1-2 Sandro Mazzola (34').
Referee: Laurens van Ravens (HOL)   Attendance: 54.953

08-12-1970   Stadio Comunale, Florence: Italy – Republic of Ireland   3-0 (2-0)
Italy: Enrico Albertosi, Giacinto Facchetti (C), Tarcisio Burgnich, Pierluigi Cera, Roberto Rosato, Sandro Mazzola, Mario Bertini, Giancarlo "Picchio" De Sisti, Roberto Boninsegna, Angelo Domenghini, Piero Prati. (Coach: Ferruccio Valcareggi (ITA)).
Republic of Ireland: Alan Kelly, Seamus Brennan (C), John Dempsey, Tony Byrne, Patrick Dunning, Eamonn Dunphy (36' Michael Lawlor), Alphonsus Finucane, Daniel Givens, Ray Treacy, Eamonn Rogers, Terry Conroy. (Coach: Michael Meagan (IRL)).
Goals: Italy: 1-0 Giancarlo "Picchio" De Sisti (22' penalty), 2-0 Roberto Boninsegna (42'), 3-0 Piero Prati (84').
Referee: Robert Schaut (BEL)   Attendance: 41.092

10-05-1971 Lansdowne Road, Dublin: Republic of Ireland – Italy 1-2 (1-1)
Republic of Ireland: Alan Kelly, Tony Dunne, Joe Kinnear, Paddy Mulligan, Tony Byrne, John Giles (C) (YC72), John Conway, Eamonn Dunphy, Steve Heighway, Daniel Givens, Eamonn Rogers (46' Alphonsus Finucane). (Coach: Michael Meagan (IRL)).
Italy: Dino Zoff, Giacinto Facchetti (C), Tarcisio Burgnich, Pierluigi Cera, Roberto Rosato, Sandro Mazzola, Mario Bertini, Giancarlo "Picchio" De Sisti, Mario Corso (YC), Roberto Boninsegna, Piero Prati. (Coach: Ferruccio Valcareggi (ITA)).
Goals: Republic of Ireland: 1-1 John Conway (23').
Italy: 0-1 Roberto Boninsegna (15'), 1-2 Piero Prati (59').
Referee: Gerhard Schulenburg (FRG)   Attendance: 22.613

26-05-1971 Råsunda Stadion, Solna: Sweden – Austria 1-0 (0-0)
Sweden: Ronnie Hellström, Björn Nordqvist (C), Roland Grip, Kurt Axelsson (46' Krister Kristensson), Hans Selander, Jan Olsson, Örjan Persson (88' Ove Eklund), Tommy Svensson, Bengt Johansson, Bo Larsson, Sten Pålsson. (Coach: Georg Vilhelm (Åby) Ericson (SWE)).
Austria: Herbert Rettensteiner, Gerhard Sturmberger, Johann Eigenstiller, Johann Schmidradner, Peter Pumm, Josef Hickersberger, August Starek (80' Werner Kriess), Hans Ettmayer, Wilhelm Kreuz, Karl Kodat, Alfred Gassner (62' Geza Gallos). (Coach: Leopold Stastny (TCH)).
Goal: Sweden: 1-0 Jan Olsson (62').
Referee: Stanislaw Ekstajn (POL)   Attendance: 5.416

30-05-1971 Dalymount Park, Dublin: Republic of Ireland – Austria 1-4 (0-3)
Republic of Ireland: Alan Kelly, Tony Dunne (C) (YC), Tony Byrne, James Dunne, Eoin Hand, John Conway, Eamonn Dunphy (46' Noel Campbell), Steve Heighway, Daniel Givens (74' Jimmy Holmes), Ray Treacy, Eamonn Rogers. (Coach: Michael Meagan (IRL)).
Austria: Herbert Rettensteiner, Gerhard Sturmberger, Johann Eigenstiller, Johann Schmidradner, Werner Kriess (78' Rainer Schlagbauer), Norbert Hof, Josef Hickersberger, August Starek, Hans Ettmayer, Wilhelm Kreuz, Karl Kodat (YC). (Coach: Leopold Stastny (TCH)).
Goals: Republic of Ireland: 1-3 Eamonn Rogers (46' penalty).
Austria: 0-1 Johann Schmidradner (4' penalty), 0-2 Karl Kodat (11'), 0-3 Tony Dunne (31' own goal), 1-4 August Starek (71').
Referee: Henry Verner Øberg (NOR)   Attendance: 14.674

09-06-1971 Råsunda Stadion, Solna: Sweden – Italy 0-0
Sweden: Ronnie Hellström, Björn Nordqvist (C), Roland Grip, Krister Kristensson, Christer Hult, Ove Kindvall (61' Jan Olsson), Örjan Persson (YC), Tommy Svensson, Leif Eriksson, Bengt Johansson (74' Claes Cronqvist), Bo Larsson. (Coach: Georg Vilhelm (Åby) Ericson (SWE)).
Italy: Dino Zoff, Giacinto Facchetti (C), Tarcisio Burgnich, Pierluigi Cera, Roberto Rosato (54' Luciano Spinosi), Sandro Mazzola, Mario Bertini (YC), Giancarlo "Picchio" De Sisti, Roberto Boninsegna, Angelo Domenghini, Piero Prati. (Coach: Ferruccio Valcareggi (ITA)).
Referee: Rudolf Scheurer (SUI)   Attendance: 36.528

04-09-1971   Praterstadion Vienna: Austria – Sweden   1-0 (1-0)
Austria: Herbert Rettensteiner, Gerhard Sturmberger (YC), Johann Eigenstiller, Johann Schmidradner, Norbert Hof, Peter Pumm, August Starek, Hans Ettmayer (70' Alois Jagodic), Josef Stering (58' Josef Hickersberger), Johann Pirkner, Karl Kodat. (Coach: Leopold Stastny (TCH)).
Sweden: Ronnie Hellström, Björn Nordqvist (C), Roland Grip, Kurt Axelsson, Krister Kristensson, Christer Hult, Jan Olsson (YC), Sven Lindman, Bo Larsson (YC), Roland Sandberg (73' Dan Brzokoupil), Sten Pålsson (58' Hans Selander). (Coach: Georg Vilhelm (Åby) Ericson (SWE)).
Goal: Austria: 1-0 Josef Stering (23').
Referee: Rudolf (Rudi) Glöckner (GDR)   Attendance: 38.274

09-10-1971   Stadio San Siro, Milan: Italy – Sweden   3-0 (2-0)
Italy: Dino Zoff (46' Enrico Albertosi), Giacinto Facchetti (C), Tarcisio Burgnich, Pierluigi Cera, Roberto Rosato, Romeo Benetti, Gianni Rivera, Sandro Mazzola (80' Mario Corso), Mario Bertini, Luigi Riva, Roberto Boninsegna. (Coach: Ferruccio Valcareggi (ITA)).
Sweden: Ronnie Hellström, Björn Nordqvist (C), Roland Grip, Krister Kristensson (65' Hans Nilsson), Christer Hult (60' Claes Cronqvist), Thomas Nordahl, Curt Olsberg, Ove Grahn (YC79), Bo Larsson, Roland Sandberg, Inge Danielsson. (Coach: Georg Vilhelm (Åby) Ericson (SWE)).
Goals: Italy: 1-0 Luigi Riva (3'), 2-0 Roberto Boninsegna (40'), 3-0 Luigi Riva (83').
Referee: Roger Machin (FRA)   Attendance: 65.582

10-10-1971   Linzer Stadion, Linz: Austria – Republic of Ireland   6-0 (3-0)
Austria: Adolf Antrich, Gerhard Sturmberger, Johann Eigenstiller, Johann Schmidradner, Norbert Hof, Peter Pumm, Rudolf Horvath, Kurt Jara, Thomas Parits, Hans Ettmayer, Johann Pirkner. (Coach: Leopold Stastny (TCH)).
Republic of Ireland: Paddy Roche, Paddy Mulligan, Mick Gannon, Tommy McConville, John Herrick, Francis O'Neill, Alphonsus Finucane (C), Turlough O'Connor, Mick Kearin (52' Alfie Hale (YC)), Michael Martin (65' Damian Richardson), Michael Leech. (Coach: Liam Tuohy (IRL)).
Goals: Austria: 1-0 Kurt Jara (12'), 2-0 Johann Pirkner (41' penalty), 3-0 Thomas Parits (45'), 4-0 Thomas Parits (51'), 5-0 Kurt Jara (85'), 6-0 Thomas Parits (89').
Referee: Karl Göppel (SUI)   Attendance: 15.050

20-11-1971   Stadio Olimpico, Rome: Italy – Austria   2-2 (1-1)
Italy: Dino Zoff, Giacinto Facchetti (C), Tazio Roversi, Aldo Bet, Sergio Santarini, Romeo Benetti (53' Claudio Sala), Mario Bertini (46' Gianfranco Bedin), Giancarlo "Picchio" De Sisti, Luigi Riva, Roberto Boninsegna, Piero Prati. (Coach: Ferruccio Valcareggi (ITA)).
Austria: Adolf Antrich, Robert Sara, Johann Eigenstiller, Johann Schmidradner, Norbert Hof, Peter Pumm, Rudolf Horvath, Kurt Jara, Hans Ettmayer (C), Johann Pirkner, Helmut Köglberger. (Coach: Leopold Stastny (TCH)).
Goals: Italy: 1-0 Piero Prati (10'), 2-2 Giancarlo "Picchio" De Sisti (75').
Austria: 1-1 Kurt Jara (36'), 1-2 Robert Sara (59').
Referee: Gyula Emsberger (HUN)   Attendance: 58.752

GROUP 7

11-10-1970	Rotterdam	Netherlands – Yugoslavia	1-1 (0-1)
14-10-1970	Luxembourg	Luxembourg – Yugoslavia	0-2 (0-1)
11-11-1970	Dresden	East Germany – Netherlands	1-0 (0-0)
15-11-1970	Luxembourg	Luxembourg – East Germany	0-5 (0-4)
24-02-1971	Rotterdam	Netherlands – Luxembourg	6-0 (1-0)
04-04-1971	Split	Yugoslavia – Netherlands	2-0 (1-0)
24-04-1971	Gera	East Germany – Luxembourg	2-1 (1-0)
09-05-1971	Leipzig	East Germany – Yugoslavia	1-2 (0-2)
10-10-1971	Rotterdam	Netherlands – East Germany	3-2 (1-1)
16-10-1971	Belgrade	Yugoslavia – East Germany	0-0
27-10-1971	Titograd	Yugoslavia – Luxembourg	0-0

FINAL STANDING

Pos	Team	Pld	W	D	L	GF	GA	GD	Pts
1	*Yugoslavia*	*6*	*3*	*3*	*0*	*7*	*2*	*+5*	*9*
2	Netherlands	6	3	1	2	18	6	+12	7
3	East Germany	6	3	1	2	11	6	+5	7
4	Luxembourg	6	0	1	5	1	23	-22	1

Yugoslavia qualified for the Quarter-finals.

11-10-1970   Stadion Feijenoord, Rotterdam: Netherlands – Yugoslavia   1-1 (0-1)
Netherlands: Jan van Beveren, Rinus Israël (C), Pleun Strik, Theo Laseroms, Theo van Duivenbode, Wim van Hanegem, Wim Jansen, Jan Klijnjan, Nico Rijnders (50' Wijtse Couperus), Wietse Veenstra, Willy van der Kuijlen (38' Henk Wery). (Coach: Frantsek Fadrhonc (TCH)).
Yugoslavia: Ivan Curkovic, Miroslav Pavlovic (25' Jovan Acimovic, 82' Branko Oblak), Blagoje Paunovic, Dragan Holcer, Andjelko Tesan, Dragoslav Stepanovic (YC), Jurica Jerkovic, Ilija Petkovic, Dragan Dzajic (C), Dusan Bajevic, Vahidin Musemic. (Coach: Rajko Mitic (YUG)).
Goals: Netherlands: 1-1 Rinus Israël (50' penalty).
Yugoslavia: 0-1 Dragan Dzajic (22').
Referee: William Joseph Mullan (SCO)   Attendance: 56.200

14-10-1970   Stade Municipal, Luxembourg: Luxembourg – Yugoslavia   0-2 (0-1)
Luxembourg: René Hoffmann, Erwin Kuffer (46' René Flenghi), Fernand Jeitz, Louis Pilot, John Hoffmann (C), Norbert Leszczynski, Paul Philipp, Adolphe Schmit, Johnny Leonard, Joseph Kirchens, Nico Braun. (Coach: Ernst Melchior (LUX)).
Yugoslavia: Dragomir Mutibaric, Blagoje Paunovic, Dragan Holcer, Andjelko Tesan, Dragoslav Stepanovic, Jurica Jerkovic, Ilija Petkovic, Dragan Dzajic, Dusan Bajevic, Borivoje Djordjevic, Josip Bukal. (Coach: Rajko Mitic (YUG)).
Goals: Yugoslavia: 0-1 Josip Bukal (44'), 0-2 Josip Bukal (62').
Referee: Vital Georges Gilbert Loraux (BEL)   Attendance: 5.163

11-11-1970   Rudolf-Harbig-Stadion, Dresden: East Germany – Netherlands   1-0 (0-0)
East Germany: Jürgen Croy, Lothar Kurbjuweit, Otto Fräßdorf (C), Klaus Sammer, Frank Ganzera (YC), Michael Strempel, Hans-Jürgen Kreische, Peter Rock, Eberhard Vogel, Peter Ducke (YC), Henning Frenzel (57' Harald Irmscher). (Coach: Georg Buschner (GDR)).
Netherlands: Jan van Beveren, Wim Suurbier, Rinus Israël (C), Pleun Strik, Epi Drost, Wim van Hanegem, Wim Jansen, Johan Neeskens, Jan Klijnjan, Nico Rijnders, Piet Keizer (YC) (69' Henk Wery (YC)). (Coach: Frantsek Fadrhonc (TCH)).
Goal: East Germany: 1-0 Peter Ducke (56').
Referee: Curt F.W.Liedberg (SWE)   Attendance: 30.089

15-11-1970   Stade Municipal, Luxembourg: Luxembourg – East Germany   0-5 (0-4)
Luxembourg: René Hoffmann (32' Jeannot Moes), Erwin Kuffer, Fernand Jeitz, Louis Pilot, John Hoffmann (C), Louis Trierweiler, Jeannot Krecké, Adolphe Schmit (46' Nico Braun), Johnny Leonard, Joseph Kirchens, René Flenghi. (Coach: Ernst Melchior (LUX)).
East Germany: Jürgen Croy, Lothar Kurbjuweit, Klaus Sammer, Frank Ganzera, Michael Strempel, Harald Irmscher, Hans-Jürgen Kreische, Peter Rock, Eberhard Vogel, Peter Ducke (72' Rainer Schlutter), Henning Frenzel (C) (59' Jürgen Sparwasser). (Coach: Georg Buschner (GDR)).
Goals: East Germany: 0-1 Eberhard Vogel (21'), 0-2 Hans-Jürgen Kreische (29'), 0-3 Hans-Jürgen Kreische (36'), 0-4 Hans-Jürgen Kreische (39'), 0-5 Hans-Jürgen Kreische (78').
Referee: Anton Bucheli (SUI)   Attendance: 3.795

24-02-1971   Stadion Feijenoord, Rotterdam: Netherlands – Luxembourg   6-0 (1-0)
Netherlands: Jan van Beveren, Wim Suurbier, Rinus Israël (C), Epi Drost, Wim van Hanegem (YC44), Wim Jansen, Johan Cruijff, Johan Neeskens, Theo Pahlplatz, Piet Keizer, Willy Lippens. (Coach: Frantsek Fadrhonc (TCH)).
Luxembourg: René Hoffmann, Fernand Jeitz, Léon Schmit, Louis Pilot, Nicholas Hoffmann, John Hoffmann (C), Paul Philipp, Joseph Kirchens, Gilbert Dussier, Nico Braun, René Flenghi. (Coach: Ernst Melchior (LUX)).
Goals: Netherlands: 1-0 Willy Lippens (26'), 2-0 Piet Keizer (53'), 3-0 Johan Cruijff (59'), 4-0 Johan Cruijff (69'), 5-0 Piet Keizer (80'), 6-0 Wim Suurbier (83').
Referee: Faik Bajrami (ALB)   Attendance: 38.117

04-04-1971   Stadion Stari plac, Split: Yugoslavia – Netherlands   2-0 (1-0)
Yugoslavia: Radomir Vukcevic, Miroslav Pavlovic, Blagoje Paunovic, Dragan Holcer, Zoran Antonijevic, Dragoslav Stepanovic (YC), Jovan Acimovic, Jurica Jerkovic, Ilija Petkovic (YC), Dragan Dzajic (C), Josip Bukal. (Coach: Vujadin Boskov (YUG)).
Netherlands: Jan van Beveren, Wim Suurbier, Pleun Strik (YC), Epi Drost (65' Jan Klijnjan), Wim van Hanegem (C), Wim Jansen, Johan Neeskens, Gerrie Mühren, Piet Keizer, Henk Wery, Eef Mulders. (Coach: Frantsek Fadrhonc (TCH)).
Goals: Yugoslavia: 1-0 Jurica Jerkovic (8'), 2-0 Dragan Dzajic (84').
Referee: Kurt Tschenscher (FRG)   Attendance: 15.563

24-04-1971   Stadion der Freundschaft, Gera: East Germany – Luxembourg   2-1 (1-0)
East Germany: Jürgen Croy, Bernd Bransch, Konrad Weise, Klaus Sammer, Frank Ganzera, Michael Strempel, Jürgen Sparwasser (85' Frank Richter), Hans-Jürgen Kreische, Helmut Stein (C), Rainer Schlutter, Henning Frenzel. (Coach: Georg Buschner (GDR)).
Luxembourg: René Hoffmann, Fernand Jeitz, Jean-Pierre Hoffmann, Nicholas Hoffmann (C), John Hoffmann, Louis Trierweiler, Joseph Kirchens, Gilbert Dussier, Nico Braun, René Flenghi, Dominique Di Genova. (Coach: Ernst Melchior (LUX)).
Goals: East Germany: 1-0 Hans-Jürgen Kreische (31'), 2-0 Henning Frenzel (88').
Luxembourg: 2-1 Gilbert Dussier (90').
Referee: Hugh Wilson (NIR)   Attendance: 11.276

09-05-1971   Zentralstadion, Leipzig: East Germany – Yugoslavia   1-2 (0-2)
East Germany: Jürgen Croy, Bernd Bransch, Konrad Weise, Klaus Sammer, Michael Strempel, Hans-Jürgen Kreische, Helmut Stein (C), Rainer Schlutter, Eberhard Vogel (66' Wolfram Löwe), Peter Ducke, Henning Frenzel (78' Harald Irmscher). (Coach: Georg Buschner (GDR)).
Yugoslavia: Radomir Vukcevic, Miroslav Pavlovic, Blagoje Paunovic, Dragan Holcer, Mladen Ramljak, Zoran Antonijevic (YC74), Branko Oblak (65' Vladislav Bogicevic), Jovan Acimovic, Ilija Petkovic (75' Nenad Bjekovic), Dragan Djzajic (C), Zoran Filipovic. (Coach: Vujadin Boskov (YUG)).
Goals: East Germany: 1-2 Wolfram Löwe (70').
Yugoslavia: 0-1 Zoran Filipovic (11'), 0-2 Dragan Djzajic (19').
Referee: Paul Schiller (AUT)   Attendance: 94.876

10-10-1971   Stadion Feijenoord, Rotterdam: Netherlands – East Germany   3-2 (1-1)
Netherlands: Jan van Beveren, Rinus Israël, Pleun Strik, Hans Venneker, Barry Hulshoff, Wim van Hanegem (C), Wim Jansen, Johan Cruijff, Piet Keizer, Henk Wery, Dick van Dijk (68' Jan Jeuring). (Coach: Frantsek Fadrhonc (TCH)).
East Germany: Jürgen Croy, Bernd Bransch (C), Konrad Weise, Gerd Kische, Klaus Sammer, Michael Strempel, Jürgen Sparwasser (82' Harald Irmscher), Hans-Jürgen Kreische, Joachim Streich, Eberhard Vogel, Peter Ducke (YC75) (78' Wolfram Löwe). (Coach: Georg Buschner (GDR)).
Goals: Netherlands: 1-1 Barry Hulshoff (25'), 2-1 Piet Keizer (52'), 3-1 Piet Keizer (63').
East Germany: 0-1 Eberhard Vogel (10'), 3-2 Eberhard Vogel (82').
Referee: Concetto Lo Bello (ITA)   Attendance: 48.037

16-10-1971   Stadion JNA, Belgrade: Yugoslavia – East Germany   0-0
Yugoslavia: Ratomir Dujkovic, Miroslav Pavlovic, Blagoje Paunovic, Dragan Holcer, Dragoslav Stepanovic, Ljubisa Rajkovic, Branko Oblak (62' Petar Nikezic), Jovan Acimovic, Ilija Petkovic, Dragan Djzajic (C), Josip Bukal (76' Zoran Filipovic). (Coach: Vujadin Boskov (YUG)).
East Germany: Jürgen Croy, Bernd Bransch (C), Konrad Weise, Gerd Kische, Klaus Sammer, Michael Strempel, Hans-Jürgen Kreische (70' Harald Irmscher), Helmut Stein (C) (80' Wolfram Löwe), Joachim Streich, Eberhard Vogel, Peter Ducke. (Coach: Georg Buschner (GDR)).
Referee: John Keith (Jack) Taylor (ENG)   Attendance: 2.340

27-10-1971   Stadion pod Goricom, Titograd: Yugoslavia – Luxembourg   0-0
Yugoslavia: Ratomir Dujkovic, Miroslav Pavlovic, Blagoje Paunovic, Dragan Holcer, Dragoslav Stepanovic, Ljubisa Rajkovic (60' Zoran Filipovic), Branko Oblak (33' Jurica Jerkovic), Jovan Acimovic, Ilija Petkovic, Josip Bukal, Nenad Bjekovic. (Coach: Vujadin Boskov (YUG)).
Luxembourg: Jeannot Moes, Jean-Pierre Hoffmann, René Kollwelter, Nicholas Hoffmann (C), John Hoffmann, Paul Philipp, Jeannot Krecké, Joseph Kirchens, Gilbert Dussier, Nico Braun, René Flenghi. (Coach: Ernst Melchior (LUX)).
Referee: Muzaffer Sarvan (TUR)   Attendance: 10.022

17-11-1971   Philips Stadion, Eindhoven: Luxembourg – Netherlands   0-8 (0-5)
Luxembourg: Jeannot Moes (46' Théo Stendebach), Jean-Pierre Hoffmann, René Kollwelter, Nicholas Hoffmann (C), John Hoffmann, Paul Philipp, Jeannot Krecké, Joseph Kirchens, Gilbert Dussier, Nico Braun, René Flenghi. (Coach: Ernst Melchior (LUX)).
Netherlands: Jan van Beveren, Rinus Israël, Ruud Krol, Hans Venneker, Barry Hulshoff, Wim Jansen, Johan Cruijff, Theo Pahlplatz, Gerrie Mühren, Piet Keizer (C), Oeki Hoekema. (Coach: Frantsek Fadrhonc (TCH)).
Goals: Netherlands: 0-1 Johan Cruijff (4'), 0-2 Piet Keizer (7'), 0-3 Theo Pahlplatz (12'), 0-4 Johan Cruijff (14'), 0-5 Barry Hulshoff (37'), 0-6 Oeki Hoekema (54'), 0-7 Johan Cruijff (60'), 0-8 Rinus Israël (82').
Referee: Michal Jursa (TCH)   Attendance: 12.561

GROUP 8

14-10-1970	Chorzów	Poland – Albania	3-0 (1-0)
17-10-1970	Cologne	West Germany – Turkey	1-1 (1-1)
13-12-1970	Istanbul	Turkey – Albania	2-1 (2-1)
17-02-1971	Tirana	Albania – West Germany	0-1 (0-1)
25-04-1971	Istanbul	Turkey – West Germany	0-3 (0-1)
12-05-1971	Tirana	Albania – Poland	1-1 (1-1)
12-06-1971	Karlsruhe	West Germany – Albania	2-0 (2-0)
22-09-1971	Kraków	Poland – Turkey	5-1 (1-0)
10-10-1971	Warsaw	Poland – West Germany	1-3 (1-1)
14-11-1971	Tirana	Albania – Turkey	3-0 (1-0)
17-11-1971	Hamburg	West Germany – Poland	0-0
05-12-1971	Izmir	Turkey – Poland	1-0 (0-0)

FINAL STANDING

Pos	Team	Pld	W	D	L	GF	GA	GD	Pts
1	*West Germany*	6	4	2	0	10	2	+8	*10*
2	Poland	6	2	2	2	10	6	+4	6
3	Turkey	6	2	1	3	5	13	-8	5
4	Albania	6	1	1	4	5	9	-4	3

West Germany qualified for the Quarter-finals.

14-10-1970 Stadion Slaski, Chorzów: Poland – Albania 3-0 (1-0)
Poland: Piotr Czaja, Jerzy Gorgon, Adam Musial, Wladyslaw Stachurski, Jerzy Wyrobek, Kazimierz Deyna, Zygfryd Szoltysik, Robert Gadocha, Wlodzimierz Lubanski (C), Bronislaw Bula, Joachim Marx. (Coach: Ryszard Tadeusz Koncewicz (POL)).
Albania: Koço Dinella, Fatmir Frashëri, Bujar Çani, Perikli Dhales, Gëzim Kasmi, Lin Shllaku (C), Ramazan Rragami, Iljaz Çeço, Panajot Pano, Sabah Bizi, Medin Zhega. (Coach: Loro Boriçi (ALB)).
Goals: Poland: 1-0 Robert Gadocha (19'), 2-0 Wlodzimierz Lubanski (83'), 3-0 Zygfryd Szoltysik (90').
Referee: Andreas Kouniaides (CYP)   Attendance: 8.507

17-10-1970 Müngersdorfer Stadion, Cologne: West Germany – Turkey 1-1 (1-1)
West Germany: Sepp Maier, Berti Vogts, Franz Beckenbauer, Horst-Dieter Höttges, Klaus Fichtel, Wolfgang Weber (YC), Klaus-Dieter Seiloff (72' Jupp Heynckes), Wolfgang Overath (C), Jürgen Grabowski, Gerd Müller, Reinhard Libuda. (Coach: Helmut Schön (FRG)).
Turkey: Ali Artuner (C), Muzaffer Sipahi, Ercan Aktuna, Alpaslan Eratli, Kamuran Yavuz, Metin Kurt, Ziya Sengül, Ergün Acuner (YC), Sanli Sarialioglu, Cemil Turan (YC) (46' Yasar Mumcuoglu), Ender Konca (YC). (Coach: Dogan Andaç (TUR)).
Goals: West Germany: 1-1 Gerd Müller (37' penalty).
Turkey: 0-1 Kamuran Yavuz (15').
Referee: Paul Bonett (MLT)   Attendance: 52.204

13-12-1970 Inönü Stadi, Istanbul: Turkey – Albania 2-1 (2-1)
Turkey: Ali Artuner (C), Muzaffer Sipahi, Ercan Aktuna, Alpaslan Eratli, Kamuran Yavuz, Metin Kurt (77' Yasar Mumcuoglu), Ziya Sengül, Ergün Acuner, Sanli Sarialioglu, Cemil Turan, Ender Konca. (Coach: Dogan Andaç (TUR)).
Albania: Koço Dinella (49' Jani Rama), Teodor Vaso, Safet Berisha, Bujar Çani, Perikli Dhales, Ramazan Rragami, Astrit Ziu, Iljaz Çeço, Panajot Pano (C), Sabah Bizi, Medin Zhega. (Coach: Loro Boriçi (ALB)).
Goals: Turkey: 1-0 Metin Kurt (4'), 2-1 Cemil Turan (43').
Albania: 1-1 Astrit Ziu (22').
Referee: János Biróczky (HUN)   Attendance: 39.000

17-02-1971 Stadiumi Qemal Stafa, Tirana: Albania – West Germany 0-1 (0-1)
Albania: Koço Dinella, Teodor Vaso, Mihal Gjika, Bujar Çani, Perikli Dhales, Gëzim Kasmi, Ramazan Rragami, Astrit Ziu, Iljaz Çeço, Panajot Pano (C), Sabah Bizi. (Coach: Loro Boriçi (ALB)).
West Germany: Sepp Maier, Berti Vogts, Franz Beckenbauer, Karl-Heinz Schnellinger, Bernd Patzke (67' Michael Bella), Wolfgang Weber, Wolfgang Overath (C), Günter Netzer, Jürgen Grabowski, Jupp Heynckes, Gerd Müller. (Coach: Helmut Schön (FRG)).
Goal: West Germany: 0-1 Gerd Müller (38').
Referee: Todor P.Betchirov (BUL)   Attendance: 18.082

25-04-1971   Inönü Stadi, Istanbul: Turkey – West Germany   0-3 (0-1)
Turkey: Ali Artuner (C), Muzaffer Sipahi, Ercan Aktuna, Alpaslan Eratli, Mehmet Isikal (58'
Zekeriya Alp), Mehmet Oguz, Kamuran Yavuz, Ziya Sengül, Sanli Sarialioglu (72' Fethi
Heper), Cemil Turan, Ender Konca. (Coach: Cihat Arman (TUR)).
West Germany: Sepp Maier, Berti Vogts, Franz Beckenbauer, Bernd Patzke, Wolfgang Weber,
Günter Netzer, Horst Köppel (75' Heinz Flohe), Jürgen Grabowski, Jupp Heynckes, Gerd
Müller, Herbert Wimmer. (Coach: Helmut Schön (FRG)).
Goals: West Germany: 0-1 Gerd Müller (43'), 0-2 Gerd Müller (47'), 0-3 Horst Köppel (73').
Referee: Karlo Kruashvili (URS)   Attendance: 38.097

12-05-1971   Stadiumi Qemal Stafa, Tirana: Albania – Poland   1-1 (1-1)
Albania: Koço Dinella, Teodor Vaso (46' Safet Berisha), Mihal Gjika, Bujar Çani, Perikli
Dhales, Gëzim Kasmi, Ramazan Rragami, Iljaz Çeço, Panajot Pano (C), Sabah Bizi, Medin
Zhega. (Coach: Loro Boriçi (ALB)).
Poland: Wladyslaw Grotynski, Zygmunt Anczok, Jerzy Wyrobek, Jan Wrazy, Walter Winkler,
Kazimierz Deyna (72' Leslaw Cmikiewicz), Bernard Blaut, Zygfryd Szoltysik, Jan Banas,
Robert Gadocha (46' Marian Kozerski), Wlodzimierz Lubanski. (Coach: Kazimierz Klaudiusz
Górski (POL)).
Goals: Albania: 1-1 Medin Zhega (31').
Poland: 0-1 Jan Banas (6').
Referee: Robert Héliès (FRA)   Attendance: 18.182

12-06-1971   Wildparkstadion, Karlsruhe: West Germany – Albania   2-0 (2-0)
West Germany: Sepp Maier, Berti Vogts (72' Hartwig Bleidick), Hans-Georg Schwarzenbeck,
Franz Beckenbauer, Klaus-Dieter Sieloff, Wolfgang Overath (C) (56' Siegfried Held), Günter
Netzer, Horst Köppel, Jürgen Grabowski, Jupp Heynckes, Herbert Wimmer. (Coach: Helmut
Schön (FRG)).
Albania: Bashkim Muhedini, Mihal Gjika, Safet Berisha (58' Teodor Vaso), Bujar Çani,
Vladimir Balluku, Ramazan Rragami, Astrit Ziu, Faruk Sejdini, Panajot Pano (C), Sabah Bizi,
Medin Zhega. (Coach: Loro Boriçi (ALB)).
Goals: West Germany: 1-0 Günter Netzer (17'), 2-0 Jürgen Grabowski (45').
Referee: Timoleon Latsios (GRE)   Attendance: 44.833

22-09-1971   Stadion Wisla, Kraków: Poland – Turkey   5-1 (1-0)
Poland: Jan Gomola, Jerzy Gorgon, Adam Musial, Zygmunt Anczok, Andrzej Zygmunt,
Kazimierz Deyna (46' Andrzej Jarosik), Zygfryd Szoltysik, Jan Banas, Robert Gadocha,
Wlodzimierz Lubanski (C), Bronislaw Bula. (Coach: Kazimierz Klaudiusz Górski (POL)).
Turkey: Ali Artuner (C), Muzaffer Sipahi, Ercan Aktuna (YC), Zekeriya Alp, Yusuf Tunaoglu
(78' Sanli Sarialioglu), Kamuran Yavuz, Metin Kurt, Abdurrahman Temel, Vahap Özbayer,
Fethi Heper, Cemil Turan (46' Nihat Yayöz). (Coach: Cihat Arman (TUR)).
Goals: Poland: 1-0 Bronislaw Bula (32'), 2-0 Wlodzimierz Lubanski (62'), 3-0 Robert
Gadocha (69'), 4-0 Wlodzimierz Lubanski (73'), 5-1 Wlodzimierz Lubanski (90').
Turkey: 4-1 Nihat Yayöz (83').
Referee: Antoine Queudeville (LUX)   Attendance: 20.241

10-10-1971   Stadion Dziesieciolecia, Warsaw: Poland – West Germany   1-3 (1-1)
Poland: Jan Tomaszewski, Jerzy Gorgon, Adam Musial, Stanislaw Oslizlo, Zygmunt Anczok, Zygmunt Maszczyk, Zygfryd Szoltysik, Jan Banas (60' Jerzy Sadek), Robert Gadocha, Wlodzimierz Lubanski, Bronislaw Bula (46' Antoni Kot). (Coach: Kazimierz Klaudiusz Górski (POL)).
West Germany: Sepp Maier, Hans-Georg Schwarzenbeck, Franz Beckenbauer (C), Klaus Fichtel, Paul Breitner, Günter Netzer, Horst Köppel, Jürgen Grabowski, Jupp Heynckes, Gerd Müller, Herbert Wimmer. (Coach: Helmut Schön (FRG)).
Goals: Poland: 1-0 Robert Gadocha (27').
West Germany: 1-1 Gerd Müller (29'), 1-2 Gerd Müller (64'), 1-3 Jürgen Grabowski (70').
Referee: Ferdinand Marschall (AUT)   Attendance: 63.300

14-11-1971   Stadiumi Qemal Stafa, Tirana: Albania – Turkey   3-0 (1-0)
Albania: Bashkim Muhedini (C), Mihal Gjika, Safet Berisha, Bujar Çani, Astrit Ziu, Faruk Sejdini, Iljaz Çeço, Panajot Pano (C), Sabah Bizi, Ilir Përnaska, Maksut Leshteni (81' Enver Ibërshimi). (Coach: Loro Boriçi (ALB)).
Turkey: Ali Artuner, Muzaffer Sipahi, Ercan Aktuna (YC60), Zekeriya Alp, Vahit Kolukisa (YC33) (67' Alpaslan Eratli), Mehmet Oguz, Kamuran Yavuz, Vedat Okyar, Metin Kurt, Necati Göçmen (C), Osman Arpacioglu. (Coach: Cihat Arman (TUR)).
Goals: Albania: 1-0 Ilir Përnaska (22'), 2-0 Ilir Përnaska (53'), 3-0 Panajot Pano (64').
Referee: Iván Plácek (TCH)   Attendance: 18.159

17-11-1971   Volksparkstadion, Hamburg: West Germany – Poland   0-0
West Germany: Sepp Maier, Hans-Georg Schwarzenbeck, Franz Beckenbauer (C), Horst-Dieter Höttges, Klaus Fichtel, Wolfgang Weber, Wolfgang Overath (C), Jürgen Grabowski, Gerd Müller, Herbert Wimmer (75' Horst Köppel), Reinhard Libuda. (Coach: Helmut Schön (FRG)).
Poland: Marian Szeja, Antoni Szymanowski, Jerzy Gorgon, Zygmunt Anczok (68' Jerzy Wyrobek), Marian Ostafinski, Grzegorz Lato (83' Bronislaw Bula), Kazimierz Deyna, Bernard Blaut (C), Zygfryd Szoltysik, Wlodzimierz Lubanski, Joachim Marx (YC74). (Coach: Kazimierz Klaudiusz Górski (POL)).
Referee: William Joseph Mullan (SCO)   Attendance: 60.448

05-12-1971   Atatürk Stadi, Izmir: Turkey – Poland   1-0 (0-0)
Turkey: Yasin Özdenak, Muzaffer Sipahi, Zekeriya Alp (83' Vahit Kolukisa), Ekrem Günalp, Özer Yurteri, Mehmet Oguz, Vedat Okyar, Metin Kurt, Ayfer Elmastasoglu, Cemil Turan, Ender Konca (30' Çetin Erdogan). (Coach: Nicolae Petrescu (ROM)).
Poland: Marian Szeja, Antoni Szymanowski, Jerzy Gorgon, Adam Musial, Marian Ostafinski, Grzegorz Lato, Kazimierz Deyna (70' Bronislaw Bula), Bernard Blaut, Zygfryd Szoltysik, Robert Gadocha (63' Andrzej Jarosik), Joachim Marx. (Coach: Kazimierz Klaudiusz Górski (POL)).
Goal: Turkey: 1-0 Cemil Turan (52').
Referee: Petar Hristov Nikolov (BUL)   Attendance: 57.794

QUARTER-FINALS

29-04-1972   Stadio San Siro, Milan: Italy – Belgium   0-0
Italy: Enrico Albertosi, Giacinto Facchetti (C), Tarcisio Burgnich, Pierluigi Cera, Roberto Rosato, Sandro Mazzola, Giancarlo "Picchio" De Sisti, Gianfranco Bedin, Luigi Riva, Pietro Anastasi, Angelo Domenghini (46' Franco Causio). (Coach: Ferruccio Valcareggi (ITA)).
Belgium: Christian Piot, Georges Heylens, Jean Thissen, Erwin Vandendaele, Maurice Martens (53' Léon Dolmans), Wilfried Van Moer (YC64), Léon Semmeling, Jan Verheyen, Jean Dockx, Paul Van Himst (C), Raoul Lambert. (Coach: Raymond Goethals (BEL)).
Referee: Petar Hristov Nikolov (BUL)   Attendance: 63.549

29-04-1972   Népstadion, Budapest: Hungary – Romania   1-1 (1-0)
Hungary: István Géczi, László Bálint, Tibor Fábián, Miklós Páncsics, Lajos Szücs (YC59), Péter Vépi, Lajos Kocsis (59' Ferenc Bene), Sándor Zámbó, László Fazekas, Antal Dunai (II), László Branikovits. (Coach: Rudolf Illovszky (HUN)).
Romania: Raducanu Necula, Lajos Satmareanu, Nicolae Lupescu, Cornel Dinu (YC45), Augustin Pax Deleanu, Emerich Dembrovschi, Radu Nunweiller (YC74), Ion Dumitru (YC17), Mircea Lucescu (C), Anghel Iordanescu, Flavius Domide. (Coach: Angelo Niculescu (ROM)).
Goals: Hungary: 1-0 László Branikovits (11').
Romania: 1-1 Lajos Satmareanu (56').
Referee: David William Smith (ENG)   Attendance: 68.585

29-04-1972   Wembley Stadium, London: England – West Germany   1-3 (0-1)
England: Gordon Banks, Bobby Moore (C), Norman Hunter, Alan Ball, Martin Peters, Colin Bell, Emlyn Hughes, Paul Madeley, Francis Lee, Geoff Hurst (60' Rodney Marsh), Martin Chivers. (Coach: Alf Ramsey (ENG)).
West Germany: Sepp Maier, Hans-Georg Schwarzenbeck, Franz Beckenbauer (C), Horst-Dieter Höttges, Paul Breitner, Uli Hoeneß, Günter Netzer, Jürgen Grabowski, Gerd Müller, Herbert Wimmer, Siegfried Held. (Coach: Helmut Schön (FRG)).
Goals: England: 1-1 Francis Lee (78').
West Germany: 0-1 Uli Hoeneß (27'), 1-2 Günter Netzer (84' penalty), 1-3 Gerd Müller (88').
Referee: Robert Héliès (FRA)   Attendance: 96.766

30-04-1972   Stadion Crvena zvezda, Belgrade: Yugoslavia – Soviet Union   0-0
Yugoslavia: Enver Maric, Miroslav Pavlovic, Blagoje Paunovic, Dragan Holcer, Mladen Ramljak, Dragoslav Stepanovic, Branko Oblak, Jovan Acimovic, Dragan Dzajic, Josip Bukal (84' Dusan Bajevic), Bozidar Jankovic. (Coach: Vujadin Boskov (YUG)).
Soviet Union: Evgeni Rudakov, Volodymyr Kaplychniy, Yuri Istomin, Revaz Dzodzuashvili, Aleksandr Makhovikov (YC10) (61' Volodymyr Troshkin), Murtaz Khurtsilava (C), Anatoliy Konkov, Oleg Dolmatov, Anatoli Banishevski, Anatoli Baidachny, Eduard Kozynkevych (78' Gennadi Evryuzhikhin). (Coach: Aleksandr Ponomarev (URS)).
Referee: Rudolf Scheurer (SUI)   Attendance: 58.312

13-05-1972   Central Lenin Stadium, Moscow: Soviet Union – Yugoslavia   3-0 (0-0)
Soviet Union: Evgeni Rudakov, Yuri Istomin, Revaz Dzodzuashvili, Volodymyr Troshkin, Nikolai Abramov, Gennadi Evryuzhikhin (46' Eduard Kozynkevych), Murtaz Khurtsilava (C), Viktor Kolotov, Anatoliy Konkov, Anatoli Banishevski, Anatoli Baidachny (65' Boris Kopeykin). (Coach: Aleksandr Ponomarev (URS)).
Yugoslavia: Enver Maric, Miroslav Pavlovic, Blagoje Paunovic, Dragan Holcer (57' Ilija Petkovic), Mladen Ramljak, Zoran Antonijevic, Dragoslav Stepanovic, Branko Oblak (71' Juric Jerkovic), Jovan Acimovic, Dragan Dzajic (C), Bozidar Jankovic. (Coach: Vujadin Boskov (YUG)).
Goals: Soviet Union: 1-0 Viktor Kolotov (53'), 2-0 Anatoli Banishevski (74'), 3-0 Eduard Kozynkevych (90').
Referee: Aurelio Angonese (ITA)   Attendance: 90.263

13-05-1972   Olympiastadion, West Berlin: Germany – England   0-0
West Germany: Sepp Maier, Hans Georg Schwarzenbeck, Franz Beckenbauer (C), Horst-Dieter Höttges, Paul Breitner, Uli Hoeneß (51' Jupp Heynckes), Heinz Flohe, Günter Netzer, Gerd Müller, Herbert Wimmer, Siegfried Held. (Coach: Helmut Schön (FRG)).
England: Gordon Banks, Bobby Moore (C), Norman Hunter (57' Malcolm MacDonald), Roy McFarland, Peter Storey, Alan Ball, Colin Bell, Emlyn Hughes, Paul Madeley, Martin Chivers, Rodney Marsh (20' Colin Todd). (Coach: Alf Ramsey (ENG)).
Referee: Milivoje Gugulovic (YUG)   Attendance: 76.122

13-05-1972   Stade Émile Versé, Brussels: Belgium – Italy   2-1 (1-0)
Belgium: Christian Piot (YC71), Georges Heylens, Jean Thissen, Léon Dolmans, Erwin Vandendaele, Wilfried Van Moer (46' Odilon Polleunis), Léon Semmeling, Jan Verheyen, Jean Dockx, Paul Van Himst (C), Raoul Lambert. (Coach: Raymond Goethals (BEL)).
Italy: Enrico Albertosi, Luciano Spinosi, Giacinto Facchetti (C), Tarcisio Burgnich, Pierluigi Cera, Romeo Benetti, Sandro Mazzola, Mario Bertini (46' Fabio Capello), Giancarlo "Picchio" De Sisti, Luigi Riva, Roberto Boninsegna (YC71). (Coach: Ferruccio Valcareggi (ITA)).
Goals: Belgium: 1-0 Wilfried Van Moer (23'), 2-0 Paul Van Himst (71').
Italy: 2-1 Luigi Riva (86' penalty).
Referee: Paul Schiller (AUT)   Attendance: 26.561

14-05-1972   Stadionul 23 August, Bucharest: Romania – Hungary   2-2 (1-2)
Romania: Raducanu Necula, Lajos Satmareanu, Nicolae Lupescu, Cornel Dinu, Augustin Pax Deleanu (69' Dan Emil Anca), Emerich Dembrovschi (75' Alexandru Neagu), Radu Nunweiller, Ion Dumitru, Nicolae Dobrin, Anghel Iordanescu, Flavius Domide. (Coach: Angelo Niculescu (ROM)).
Hungary: István Géczi, László Bálint, Tibor Fábián (YC81), Miklós Páncsics, Péter Juhász, Lajos Szücs, István Szöke (YC7), Lajos Kocsis (61' Antal Dunai (II), Sándor Zámbó (61' Lajos Kü), István Juhász, Ferenc Bene (C). (Coach: Rudolf Illovszky (HUN)).
Goals: Romania: 1-1 Nicolae Dobrin (14'), 2-2 Alexandru Neagu (81').
Hungary: 0-1 István Szöke (5'), 1-2 Lajos Kocsis (36').
Referee: Kurt Tschenscher (FRG)   Attendance: 60.254

17-05-1972   Stadion JNA, Belgrade: Hungary – Romania 2-1 (1-1)
Hungary: Ádám Rothermel, László Bálint, Tibor Fábián, Miklós Páncsics (YC), Péter Juhász, István Juhász, Lajos Kocsis, Sándor Zámbó, István Szöke, Ferenc Bene (C), Lajos Kü. (Coach: Rudolf Illovszky (HUN)).
Romania: Raducanu Necula, Lajos Satmareanu, Nicolae Lupescu, Cornel Dinu, Augustin Pax Deleanu (54' Bujor Halmageanu), Radu Nunweiller, Ion Dumitru, Alexandru Neagu, Nicolae Dobrin (YC22), Mircea Lucescu (C), Flavius Domide. (Coach: Angelo Niculescu (ROM)).
Goals: Hungary: 1-0 Lajos Kocsis (27'), 2-1 István Szöke (89').
Romania: 1-1 Alexandru Neagu (34').
Referee: Christos Michas (GRE)   Attendance: 32.130
(The replay to determine the winner was played on a neutral ground)

FINAL TOURNAMENT IN BELGIUM

SEMI-FINALS

14-06-1972   Bosuilstadion, Antwerp: Belgium – West Germany 1-2 (0-1)
Belgium: Christian Piot, Georges Heylens, Jean Thissen, Léon Dolmans, Erwin Vandendaele (YC17), Maurice Martens (70' Odilon Polleunis), Léon Semmeling, Jan Verheyen, Jean Dockx, Paul Van Himst (C), Raoul Lambert. (Coach: Raymond Goethals (BEL)).
West Germany: Sepp Maier, Hans-Georg Schwarzenbeck, Franz Beckenbauer (C), Horst-Dieter Höttges, Paul Breitner, Uli Hoeneß (59' Jürgen Grabowski), Günter Netzer, Jupp Heynckes, Gerd Müller, Herbert Wimmer, Erwin Kremers. (Coach: Helmut Schön (FRG)).
Goals: Belgium: 1-2 Odilon Polleunis (83').
West Germany: 0-1 Gerd Müller (24'), 0-2 Gerd Müller (71').
Referee: William Joseph Mullan (SCO)   Attendance: 55.669

14-06-1972   Stade Émile Versé, Brussels: Hungary – Soviet Union 0-1 (0-0)
Hungary: István Géczi, László Bálint (YC72), Tibor Fábián, Miklós Páncsics, Péter Juhász, István Szöke, Lajos Kocsis (60' Antal Dunai (II)), Sándor Zámbó, István Juhász, Ferenc Bene (C) (60' Flórián Albert), Lajos Kü. (Coach: Rudolf Illovszky (HUN)).
Soviet Union: Evgeni Rudakov, Volodymyr Kaplychniy, Yuri Istomin, Revaz Dzodzuashvili, Volodymyr Troshkin, Murtaz Khurtsilava (C) (YC84), Viktor Kolotov, Anatoliy Konkov, Anatoli Banishevski (70' Givi Nodia), Anatoli Baidachny, Volodymyr Onyshchenko. (Coach: Aleksandr Ponomarev (URS)).
Goal: Soviet Union: 0-1 Anatoliy Konkov (53').
Referee: Rudolf (Rudi) Glöckner (GDR)   Attendance: 16.590

THIRD PLACE PLAY-OFF

17-06-1972   Stade Maurice Dufrasne, Liège: Hungary – Belgium   1-2 (0-2)
Hungary: István Géczi, László Bálint, Tibor Fábián, Miklós Páncsics (C), Péter Juhász (YC60), Sándor Zámbó (46' Lajos Szücs), István Juhász, Mihály Kozma, Flórián Albert, Lajos Kü, Antal Dunai (II). (Coach: Rudolf Illovszky (HUN)).
Belgium: Christian Piot, Georges Heylens, Jean Thissen, Léon Dolmans (YC61), Erwin Vandendaele, Léon Semmeling, Jan Verheyen, Jean Dockx, Paul Van Himst (C), Raoul Lambert, Odilon Polleunis. (Coach: Raymond Goethals (BEL)).
Goals: Hungary: 1-2 Lajos Kü (53' penalty).
Belgium: 0-1 Raoul Lambert (24'), 0-2 Paul Van Himst (28').
Referee: Johan Einar Boström (SWE)   Attendance: 6.184

FINAL

18-06-1972   Stade du Heysel, Brussels: West Germany – Soviet Union   3-0 (1-0)
West Germany: Sepp Maier, Hans-Georg Schwarzenbeck, Franz Beckenbauer (C), Horst-Dieter Höttges, Paul Breitner, Uli Hoeneß, Günter Netzer, Jupp Heynckes, Gerd Müller, Herbert Wimmer, Erwin Kremers. (Coach: Helmut Schön (FRG)).
Soviet Union: Evgeni Rudakov, Volodymyr Kaplychniy (YC), Yuri Istomin, Revaz Dzodzuashvili, Volodymyr Troshkin, Murtaz Khurtsilava (C), Viktor Kolotov, Anatoliy Konkov, Anatoli Banishevski (46' Oleg Dolmatov), Anatoli Baidachny (66' Eduard Kozynkevych), Volodymyr Onyshchenko. (Coach: Aleksandr Ponomarev (URS)).
Goals: West Germany: 1-0 Gerd Müller (27'), 2-0 Herbert Wimmer (52'), 3-0 Gerd Müller (58').
Referee: Ferdinand Marschall (AUT)   Attendance: 43.437

*** **West Germany were European Champions** ***

GOALSCORERS TOURNAMENT 1970-1972:

Goals	Players
11	Gerd Müller (FRG)
5	Martin Chivers (ENG), Hans-Jürgen Kreische (GDR), Johan Cruijff (HOL), Piet Keizer (HOL)
4	Thomas Parits (AUT), Johan Devrindt (BEL), Paul Van Himst (BEL), Raoul Lambert (BEL), José Martínez Sánchez "PIRRI" (ESP), Ferenc Bene (HUN), George Best (NIR), Wlodzimierz Lubanski (POL), Ján Capkovic (TCH), Viktor Kolotov (URS)
3	Kurt Jara (AUT), Hristo Bonev (BUL), Geoff Hurst (ENG), Francis Lee (ENG), Eberhard Vogel (GDR), Lajos Kocsis (HUN), Roberto Boninsegna (ITA), Giancarlo "Picchio" De Sisti (ITA), Piero Prati (ITA), Luigi Riva (ITA), Jimmy Nicholson (NIR), Robert Gadocha (POL), John O'Hare (SCO), Fritz Künzli (SUI), Gennadi Evryuzhikhin (URS), Dragan Dzajic (YUG)
2	Ilir Përnaska (ALB), Petar Zhekov (BUL), José Francisco "CHECHU" ROJO Arroita (I) (ESP), Joaquín Sierra Vallejo "QUINO" (ESP), Carlos REXACH Cerda (ESP), Bernard Blanchet (FRA), Georges Lech (FRA),

	Charly Loubet (FRA), Jürgen Grabowski (FRG), Günter Netzer (FRG), Barry Hulshoff (HOL), Rinus Israël (HOL), István Szöke (HUN), Derek Dougan (NIR), Odd Iversen (NOR), EUSÉBIO da Silva Ferreira (POR), RUI de Gouveia Pinto RODRIGUES (POR), VÍTOR Manuel Ferreira BAPTISTA (POR), Emerich Dembrovschi (ROM), Nicolae Dobrin (ROM), Florea Dumitrache (ROM), Mircea Lucescu (ROM), Nicolae Lupescu (ROM), Alexandru Neagu (ROM), Kurt Müller (SUI), Karl Odermatt (SUI), René Pierre Quentin (SUI), Frantisek Karkó (TCH), Cemil Turan (TUR), Anatoli Banishevski (URS), Vladimir Fedotov (URS), Vitali Shevchenko (URS), John Toshack (WAL), Josip Bukal (YUG)
1	Panajot Pano (ALB), Medin Zhega (ALB), Astrit Ziu (ALB), Karl Kodat (AUT), Johann Pirkner (AUT), Robert Sara (AUT), Johann Schmidradner (AUT), August Starek (AUT), Josef Stering (AUT), Wilfried Van Moer (BEL), André De Nul (BEL), Odilon Polleunis (BEL), Tsvetan Atanasov (BUL), Bozhil Kolev (BUL), Atanas Mihaylov (BUL), Petko Petkov (BUL), Mladen Vasilev (BUL), Stefan Velichkov (BUL), Nikos Charalambous (CYP), Stephanis Michael (CYP), Kresten Bjerre (DEN), Finn Laudrup (DEN), Allan Clarke (ENG), Chris Lawler (ENG), Martin Peters (ENG), Mike Summerbee (ENG), Francisco Javier AGUILAR García (ESP), Enrique LORA Millán (ESP), José LUIS ARAGONÉS Suárez Martínez (ESP), José Luis VIOLETA Lajusticia (ESP), Matti Paatelainen (FIN), Louis Floch (FRA), Michel Mézy (FRA), Hervé Revelli (FRA), Jacky Vergnes (FRA), Uli Hoeneß (FRG), Horst Köppel (FRG), Herbert Wimmer (FRG), Peter Ducke (GDR), Henning Frenzel (GDR), Wolfram Löwe (GDR), Kostas Aidiniou (GRE), Kostas Davourlis (GRE), Michalis Kritikopoulos (GRE), Oeki Hoekema (HOL), Willy Lippens (HOL), Theo Pahlplatz (HOL), Wim Suurbier (HOL), László Branikovits (HUN), Antal Dunai (II) (HUN), Péter Juhász (HUN), Lajos Kü (HUN), László Nagy (HUN), Lajos Szücs (HUN), Csaba Vidáts (HUN), Thomas Carroll (IRL), John Conway (IRL), Eamonn Rogers (IRL), Sandro Mazzola (ITA), Gilbert Dussier (LUX), Edward Theobald (MLT), William Vassallo (MLT), Sammy Morgan (NIR), Ola Dybwad-Olsen (NOR), Tor Fuglset (NOR), Olav Nilsen (NOR), Jan Banas (POL), Bronislaw Bula (POL), Zygfryd Szoltysik (POL), FERNANDO PERES da Silva (POR), JACINTO JOÃO (POR), Anghel Iordanescu (ROM), Radu Nunweiller (ROM), Lajos Satmareanu (ROM), Archie Gemmill (SCO), Rolf Blättler (SUI), Roland Citherlet (SUI), Daniel Jeandupeux (SUI), Dan Brzokoupil (SWE), Jan Olsson (SWE), Tom Turesson (SWE), Milan Albrecht (TCH), Ladislav Kuna (TCH), Jaroslav Pollák (TCH), Vladimír Táborsky (TCH), Frantisek Vesely (TCH), Metin Kurt (TUR), Kamuran Yavuz (TUR), Nihat Yayöz (TUR), Anatoli Byshovets (URS), Anatoliy Konkov (URS), Eduard Kozynkevych (URS), Volodymyr Muntyan (URS), Ronald Tudor Davies (WAL), Alan Durban (WAL), Gil Reece (WAL), Zoran Filipovic (YUG), Jurica Jerkovic (YUG)
1 own goal	Erik Sandvad (DEN) for Portugal, Jacky Novi (FRA) for Hungary, Tony Dunne (IRL) for Austria, Geir Karlsen (NOR) for Hungary, Ronnie McKinnon (SCO) for Belgium, Pat Stanton (SCO) for Portugal, Anton Weibel (SUI) for England

1976 UEFA European Football Championship

QUALIFYING ROUND

GROUP 1

30-10-1974	London	England – Czechoslovakia	3-0 (0-0)
20-11-1974	London	England – Portugal	0-0
16-04-1975	London	England – Cyprus	5-0 (2-0)
20-04-1975	Prague	Czechoslovakia – Cyprus	4-0 (2-0)
30-04-1975	Prague	Czechoslovakia – Portugal	5-0 (3-0)
11-05-1975	Limassol	Cyprus – England	0-1 (0-1)
08-06-1975	Limassol	Cyprus – Portugal	0-2 (0-1)
30-10-1975	Bratislava	Czechoslovakia – England	2-1 (1-1)
12-11-1975	Porto	Portugal – Czechoslovakia	1-1 (1-1)
19-11-1975	Lisbon	Portugal – England	1-1 (1-1)
23-11-1975	Limassol	Cyprus – Czechoslovakia	0-3 (0-3)
03-12-1975	Setúbal	Portugal – Cyprus	1-0 (1-0)

FINAL STANDING

Pos	Team	Pld	W	D	L	GF	GA	GD	Pts
1	*Czechoslovakia*	6	4	1	1	15	5	+10	9
2	England	6	3	2	1	11	3	+8	8
3	Portugal	6	2	3	1	5	7	-2	7
4	Cyprus	6	0	0	6	0	16	-16	0

Czechoslovakia qualified for the Quarter-finals.

30-10-1974   Wembley Stadium, London: England – Czechoslavakia   3-0 (0-0)
England: Ray Clemence, Norman Hunter, Dave Watson, Colin Bell, Emlyn Hughes (C), Paul Madeley, John Dobson (62' Dave Thomas), Gerry Francis, Kevin Keegan, Mick Channon, Frank Worthington (62' Trevor Brooking). (Coach: Donald George (Don) Revie (ENG)).
Czechoslovakia: Ivo Viktor, Anton Ondrus, Ján Pivarník (C), Vojtech Varadín, Premysl Bicovsky (70' Ladislav Kuna), Jozef Capkovic (62' Rostislav Vojácek), Ivan Pekárik (YC), Marián Masny, Ján Svehlík, Miroslav Gajdusek, Pavel Stratil. (Coach: Vaclav Jezek (TCH)).
Goals: England: 1-0 Mick Channon (72'), 2-0 Colin Bell (80'), 3-0 Colin Bell (83').
Referee: Michel Kitabdjian (FRA)   Attendance: 83.858

20-11-1974 Wembley Stadium, London: England – Portugal 0-0
England: Ray Clemence, Terry Cooper (20' Frank Worthington), Dave Watson, Trevor Brooking, Colin Bell, Emlyn Hughes (C), Paul Madeley, Gerry Francis, Dave Thomas, Allan Clarke (65' Colin Todd), Mick Channon. (Coach: Donald George (Don) Revie (ENG)).
Portugal: Vítor Manuel Alfonso de Oliveira "DAMAS", HUMBERTO Manuel de Jesus COELHO, ARTUR Manuel Soares CORREIA (YC65), CARLOS Alexandre Frotes ALHINHO, Firmino Baleizão da Graça Sardinha "OSVALDINHO" (YC65), OCTÁVIO Joaquim Coelho MACHADO, ADELINO de Jesus TEIXEIRA, JOÃO António Ferreira Resende ALVES, VÍTOR Manuel Rosa MARTINS, Tamagnini Manuel Gomes Batista "NENÉ" (76' António José Conceição Oliveira "TONI"), Francisco Delfim Dias "CHICO" FARIA (76' ROMEU Fernando Fernandes da Silva). (Coach: JOSÉ MARIA Carvalho PEDROTO (POR)).
Referee: Anton Bucheli (SUI)   Attendance: 84.461

16-04-1975 Wembley Stadium, London: England – Cyprus 5-0 (2-0)
England: Peter Shilton, Dave Watson, Kevin Beattie, Colin Todd, Allan Ball (C), Colin Bell, Paul Madeley, Allan Hudson, Kevin Keegan, Malcolm MacDonald, Mick Channon (65' Dave Thomas). (Coach: Donald George (Don) Revie (ENG)).
Cyprus: Michalis Akliviades (60' Andreas Constantinou (II)), Kyriacos Koureas, Stephanis Michael, Christakis Kovis (YC25), Nikos Pantziaras, Marios Markou, Michalakis Theodorou, Nikos Charalambous (46' Andreas Konstantinou (I)), Dimitris Kyzas, Gregory Savva, Andreas Stylianou (C). (Coach: Pambos Avraamides (CYP)).
Goals: England: 1-0 Malcolm MacDonald (2'), 2-0 Malcolm MacDonald (32'), 3-0 Malcolm MacDonald (52'), 4-0 Malcolm MacDonald (56'), 5-0 Malcolm MacDonald (87').
Referee: Martti Hirviniemi (FIN)   Attendance: 68.245

20-04-1975 Letensky Stadion, Prague: Czechoslovakia – Cyprus 4-0 (2-0)
Czechoslovakia: Ivo Viktor, Anton Ondrus, Ján Pivarník (C), Zdenek Koubek, Antonín Panenka, Premysl Bicovsky, Jozef Capkovic (74' Ladislav Petrás), Zdenek Nehoda, Marián Masny, Ján Svehlík, Miroslav Gajdusek. (Coach: Vaclav Jezek (TCH)).
Cyprus: Fanos Stylianou, Stephanis Michael (75' Christakis Yiolitis), Christakis Kovis, Nikos Pantziaras, Stavros Stylianou, Melis Asprou (46' Panikos Efthymiades), Marios Markou, Nikos Charalambous, Dimitris Kyzas, Gregory Savva, Andreas Stylianou (C). (Coach: Pambos Avraamides (CYP)).
Goals: Czechoslovakia: 1-0 Antonín Panenka (10'), 2-0 Antonín Panenka (35' penalty), 3-0 Antonín Panenka (57'), 4-0 Marián Masny (78').
Referee: Heinz Einbeck (GDR)   Attendance: 4.994

30-04-1975   Letensky Stadion, Prague: Czechoslovakia – Portugal   5-0 (3-0)
Czechoslovakia: Ivo Viktor, Anton Ondrus, Ján Pivarník (C), Zdenek Koubek (76' Jindrich Svoboda), Premysl Bicovsky, Jozef Capkovic, Lubomír Knapp (80' Ján Medvid), Zdenek Nehoda, Marián Masny, Ladislav Petrás, Miroslav Gajdusek (YC14). (Coach: Vaclav Jezek (TCH)).
Portugal: Vítor Manuel Alfonso de Oliveira "DAMAS", HUMBERTO Manuel de Jesus COELHO (YC13), FRANCISCO Moreira Silva REBELO, CARLOS Alexandre Frotes ALHINHO, ANTÓNIO Monteiro Teixeira de BARROS, OCTÁVIO Joaquim Coelho MACHADO, JOÃO António Ferreira Resende ALVES, António José Conceição Oliveira "TONI" (49' MINERVINO José Lopes PIETRA), SAMUEL Ferreira FRAGUITO, Tamagnini Manuel Gomes Batista "NENÉ" (64' FERNANDO Mendes Soares GOMES), Mário Da Silva Mateus "MARINHO". (Coach: JOSÉ MARIA Carvalho PEDROTO (POR)).
Goals: Czechoslavakia: 1-0 Premysl Bicovsky (11'), 2-0 Premysl Bicovsky (22'), 3-0 Zdenek Nehoda (25'), 4-0 Zdenek Nehoda (46'), 5-0 Ladislav Petrás (52').
Referee: Ferdinand Biwersi (FRG)   Attendance: 12.034

11-05-1975   Tsirion Stadium, Limassol: Cyprus – England   0-1 (0-1)
Cyprus: Andreas Constantinou (II), Stephanis Michael, Christakis Kovis, Nikos Pantziaras, Stavros Stylianou, Tassos Konstantinou, Nikos Charalambous, Dimitris Kyzas, Gregory Savva, Andreas Miamiliotis (78' Takis Papettas), Demetrakis Panayiotou (57' George "Kokos" Antoniou). (Coach: Pambos Avraamides (CYP)).
England: Ray Clemence, Dave Watson, Kevin Beattie (41' Emlyn Hughes), Steve Whitworth, Colin Todd, Allan Ball (C), Colin Bell, Dave Thomas (72' Dennis Tueart), Kevin Keegan, Malcolm MacDonald, Mick Channon. (Coach: Donald George (Don) Revie (ENG)).
Goal: England: 0-1 Kevin Keegan (6').
Referee: Tzvetan Petrov Stanev (BUL)   Attendance: 15.708

08-06-1975   Tsirion Stadium, Limassol: Cyprus – Portugal   0-2 (0-1)
Cyprus: Fanos Stylianou, Stephanis Michael, Takis Papettas (72' Andreas Kanaris), Christakis Kovis, Nikos Pantziaras, Stavros Stylianou, Marios Markou, Nikos Charalambous (C) (65' Dimitrios Economou), Dimitris Kyzas, Gregory Savva, Andreas Savva. (Coach: Pambos Avraamides (CYP)).
Portugal: Vítor Manuel Alfonso de Oliveira "DAMAS", HUMBERTO Manuel de Jesus COELHO (C), ARTUR Manuel Soares CORREIA, ANTÓNIO Monteiro Teixeira de BARROS, FERNANDO José António FREITAS Alexandrino (YC38), OCTÁVIO Joaquim Coelho MACHADO, JOÃO António Ferreira Resende ALVES, António José Conceição Oliveira "TONI", VÍTOR Manuel da Cruz GODINHO, Tamagnini Manuel Gomes Batista "NENÉ" (55' MÁRIO Jorge MOÍNHOS Matos), Mário Da Silva Mateus "MARINHO" (80' FRANCISCO MÁRIO Pinto da Silva). (Coach: JOSÉ MARIA Carvalho PEDROTO (POR)).
Goals: Portugal: 0-1 Tamagnini Manuel Gomes Batista "NENÉ" (25'), 0-2 MÁRIO Jorge MOÍNHOS Matos (89').
Referee: Gherogre Limona (ROM)   Attendance: 8.615

30-10-1975 Stadión Tehelné pole, Bratislava: Czechoslovakia – England 2-1 (1-1)
Czechoslovakia: Ivo Viktor, Ladislav Jurkemik (YC35), Anton Ondrus, Ján Pivarník (C), Koloman Gögh (81' Karol Dobias), Premysl Bicovsky, Jaroslav Pollák, Lubomír Knapp, Zdenek Nehoda, Marián Masny, Dusan Galis. (Coach: Vaclav Jezek (TCH)). (Not used sub: Alexander Vencel (RC32)).
England: Ray Clemence, Roy McFarland (56' Dave Watson), Ian Gillard (YC19), Colin Todd, Colin Bell, Paul Madeley, Gerry Francis (C), Kevin Keegan, Allan Clarke, Malcolm MacDonald, Mick Channon (72' Dave Thomas). (Coach: Donald George (Don) Revie (ENG)).
Goals: Czechoslovakia: 1-1 Zdenek Nehoda (45'), 2-1 Dusan Galis (46').
England: 0-1 Mick Channon (27').
Referee: Alberto Michelotti (ITA) Attendance: 50.651
(The match was originally abandoned due to heavy fog after 17 minutes had been played on 29th October 1975. The score at the time of abandonment was 0-0.)

12-11-1975 Estádio das Antas, Porto: Portugal – Czechoslovakia 1-1 (1-1)
Portugal: Vítor Manuel Alfonso de Oliveira "DAMAS", HUMBERTO Manuel de Jesus COELHO (C) (YC65), FRANCISCO Moreira Silva REBELO, ARTUR Manuel Soares CORREIA, FERNANDO José António FREITAS Alexandrino, VÍTOR Manuel Ferreira BAPTISTA, OCTÁVIO Joaquim Coelho MACHADO, JOÃO António Ferreira Resende ALVES, António José Conceição Oliveira "TONI", Tamagnini Manuel Gomes Batista "NENÉ" (46' ANTÓNIO Luís Alves Ribeiro de OLIVEIRA, 75' Mário Da Silva Mateus "MARINHO"), MÁRIO Jorge MOÍNHOS Matos. (Coach: JOSÉ MARIA Carvalho PEDROTO (POR)).
Czechoslovakia: Ivo Viktor, Ladislav Jurkemik, Anton Ondrus, Ján Pivarník (C), Koloman Gögh, Premysl Bicovsky, Jaroslav Pollák, Jozef Móder, Zdenek Nehoda, Marián Masny (88' Karol Dobias), Dusan Galis (YC70) (78' Frantisek Vesely). (Coach: Vaclav Jezek (TCH)).
Goal: Portugal: 1-1 Tamagnini Manuel Gomes Batista "NENÉ" (7').
Czechoslovakia: 0-1 Anton Ondrus (6').
Referee: Charles George Reinier Corver (HOL) Attendance: 21.978

19-11-1975 Estádio José Alvalade, Lisbon: Portugal – England 1-1 (1-1)
Portugal: Vítor Manuel Alfonso de Oliveira "DAMAS", RUI de Gouveia Pinto RODRIGUES (50' Álvaro CAROLINO do Nascimento), FRANCISCO Moreira Silva REBELO (46' António José LIMA PEREIRA), ARTUR Manuel Soares CORREIA, FERNANDO José António FREITAS Alexandrino, VÍTOR Manuel Ferreira BAPTISTA, OCTÁVIO Joaquim Coelho MACHADO, JOÃO António Ferreira Resende ALVES, António José Conceição Oliveira "TONI" (C), Tamagnini Manuel Gomes Batista "NENÉ", MÁRIO Jorge MOÍNHOS Matos. (Coach: JOSÉ MARIA Carvalho PEDROTO (POR)).
England: Ray Clemence, Dave Watson, Kevin Beattie (YC40), Steve Whitworth, Colin Todd, Trevor Brooking, Paul Madeley (70' Allan Clarke), Gerry Francis (C), Kevin Keegan, Malcolm MacDonald (70' Dave Thomas), Mick Channon. (Coach: Donald George (Don) Revie (ENG)).
Goals: Portugal: 1-0 RUI de Gouveia Pinto RODRIGUES (16').
England: 1-1 Mick Channon (42').
Referee: Erich Linemayr (AUT) Attendance: 13.912

23-11-1975 Tsirion Stadium, Limassol: Cyprus – Czechoslovakia 0-3 (0-3)
Cyprus: Michalis Akliviades, Paschalis Fokis (66' Kallis Konstantinou), Stephanis Michael (C), Takis Papettas, Nikos Pantziaras, Stavros Stylianou, Ioannis Mertakas, Marios Markou, Gregory Savva, Andreas Kanaris, Soteris Kaiafas (35' Andreas Miamiliotis). (Coach: Pambos Avraamides (CYP)).
Czechoslovakia: Ivo Viktor, Ladislav Jurkemik, Anton Ondrus, Ján Pivarník (C), Koloman Gögh, Premysl Bicovsky, Jaroslav Pollák (66' Ján Medvid), Jozef Móder, Zdenek Nehoda, Marián Masny, Ján Svehlík (70' Frantisek Vesely). (Coach: Vaclav Jezek (TCH)).
Goals: Czechoslovakia: 0-1 Zdenek Nehoda (9'), 0-2 Premysl Bicovsky (27'), 0-3 Marián Masny (33').
Referee: Sándor Petri (HUN)   Attendance: 8.636

03-12-1975 Estádio do Bonfim, Setúbal: Portugal – Cyprus 1-0 (1-0)
Portugal: ANTÓNIO José da Silva BOTELHO, António José LIMA PEREIRA, JOSÉ de Jesus MENDES, ARTUR Manuel Soares CORREIA, FERNANDO José António FREITAS Alexandrino, VÍTOR Manuel Ferreira BAPTISTA, OCTÁVIO Joaquim Coelho MACHADO, JOÃO António Ferreira Resende ALVES, António José Conceição Oliveira "TONI" (C), ANTÓNIO Luís Alves Ribeiro de OLIVEIRA, MÁRIO Jorge MOÍNHOS Matos (46' MANUEL José Tavares FERNANDES). (Coach: JOSÉ MARIA Carvalho PEDROTO (POR)).
Cyprus: Fanos Stylianou, Stephanis Michael (C), Takis Papettas (YC33) (59' Panikos Efthymiades), Nikos Pantziaras, Stavros Stylianou, Ioannis Mertakas, Marios Markou, Kallis Konstantinou, Gregory Savva, Andreas Miamiliotis, Andreas Kanaris (75' Demetrakis Panayiotou). (Coach: Pambos Avraamides (CYP)).
Goal: Portugal: 1-0 JOÃO António Ferreira Resende ALVES (20').
Referee: Richard Casha (MLT)   Attendance: 4.994

GROUP 2

04-09-1974	Vienna	Austria – Wales	2-1 (0-1)
13-10-1974	Luxembourg	Luxembourg – Hungary	2-4 (2-2)
30-10-1974	Cardiff	Wales – Hungary	2-0 (0-0)
20-11-1974	Swansea	Wales – Luxembourg	5-0 (1-0)
16-03-1975	Luxembourg	Luxembourg – Austria	1-2 (1-0)
02-04-1975	Veinna	Austria – Hungary	0-0
16-04-1975	Budapest	Hungary – Wales	1-2 (0-1)
01-05-1975	Luxembourg	Luxembourg – Wales	1-3 (1-2)
24-09-1975	Budapest	Hungary – Austria	2-1 (2-1)
15-10-1975	Vienna	Austria – Luxembourg	6-2 (3-2)
19-10-1975	Szombathely	Hungary – Luxembourg	8-1 (4-0)
19-11-1975	Wrexham	Wales – Austria	1-0 (0-0)

FINAL STANDING

Pos	Team	Pld	W	D	L	GF	GA	GD	Pts
1	*Wales*	*6*	*5*	*0*	*1*	*14*	*4*	*+10*	*10*
2	Hungary	6	3	1	2	15	8	+7	7
3	Austria	6	3	1	2	11	7	+4	7
4	Luxembourg	6	0	0	6	7	28	-21	0

Wales qualified for the Quarter-finals.

04-09-1974   Praterstadion, Vienna: Austria – Wales   2-1 (0-1)
Austria: Herbert Rettensteiner, Eduard Krieger, Johann Eigenstiller (C), Werner Kriess, Johannes Winkelbauer, Werner Walzer, August Starek, Rainer Schlagbauer (61' Helmut Köglberger), Josef Stering, Hans Krankl, Wilhelm Kreuz. (Coach: Leopold Stastny (TCH)).
Wales: Gary Sprake, Leighton Phillips, John Roberts, Phil Roberts (YC41), David Roberts, Gil Reece, John Mahoney, Arfon Griffiths, John Toshack (YC52), Terry Yorath (C), Leighton James. (Coach: Michael John (Mike) Smith (ENG)).
Goals: Austria: 1-1 Wilhelm Kreuz (63'), 2-1 Hans Krankl (75').
Wales: 0-1 Arfon Griffiths (34').
Referee: Dogan Babacan (TUR)   Attendance: 30.795

13-10-1974   Stade Municipal, Luxembourg: Luxembourg – Hungary   2-4 (2-2)
Luxembourg: Jeannot Moes, Roger Fandel, Joé Hansen, Louis Trierweiler, Paul Philipp (C), Robert Da Grava, Jean Zuang, Gilbert Dussier, Nico Braun, René Flenghi, Pierrot Langers. (Coach: Gilbert Legrand (FRA)).
Hungary: Ferenc Mészáros, László Bálint, Péter Török, László Harsányi, Mihály Kántor, László Nagy, József Horváth (C), Tibor Kiss, László Fazekas, András Toth, Mihály Pénzes. (Coach: Ede Moór (HUN)).
Goals: Luxembourg: 1-0 Gilbert Dussier (14'), 2-2 Gilbert Dussier (43' penalty).
Hungary: 1-1 József Horváth (18'), 1-2 László Nagy (29'), 2-3 László Nagy (55'), 2-4 László Bálint (71').
Referee: Magnus V.Pétursson (ISL)   Attendance: 3.326

30-10-1974   Ninian Park, Cardiff: Wales – Hungary   2-0 (0-0)
Wales: Gary Sprake (84' John Phillips), Mike England (YC23), Rod Thomas, Leighton Phillips, Phil Roberts, Gil Reece, John Mahoney, Arfon Griffiths, John Toshack, Terry Yorath (C), Leighton James. (Coach: Michael John (Mike) Smith (ENG)).
Hungary: Ferenc Mészáros, László Bálint (C), Péter Török, Mihály Kántor (YC72), László Nagy, Zoltán Halmosi, Tibor Kiss, József Mucha (YC15), László Fazekas, András Toth (63' József Póczik), László Fekete. (Coach: Ede Moór (HUN)).
Goals: Wales: 1-0 Arfon Griffiths (57'), 2-0 John Toshack (87').
Referee: António José da Silva Garrido (POR)   Attendance: 8.445

20-11-1974   Vetch Field, Swansea: Wales – Luxembourg   5-0 (1-0)
Wales: Gary Sprake, Mike England, Rod Thomas, Leighton Phillips, Phil Roberts, Gil Reece, John Mahoney (70' Brian Flynn), Arfon Griffiths, John Toshack, Terry Yorath (C), Leighton James. (Coach: Michael John (Mike) Smith (ENG)).
Luxembourg: Lucien Thill, Roger Fandel (YC30), Joé Hansen, Louis Pilot (C), Louis Trierweiler, Paul Philipp, Robert Da Grava (YC54) (73' Henri Roemer), Jean Zuang, Gilbert Dussier, René Flenghi, Pierrot Langers (63' Jean-Paul Martin). (Coach: Gilbert Legrand (FRA)).
Goals: Wales: 1-0 John Toshack (34'), 2-0 Mike England (53'), 3-0 Phil Roberts (70'), 4-0 Arfon Griffiths (73'), 5-0 Terry Yorath (74').
Referee: Preben Christophersen (DEN)   Attendance: 10.539

16-03-1975   Stade Municipal, Luxembourg: Luxembourg – Austria   1-2 (1-0)
Luxembourg: Jeannot Moes, Roger Fandel, Joé Hansen, Jean-Louis Margue, Louis Pilot (C), Louis Trierweiler, Paul Philipp, Jean Zuang, Gilbert Dussier, Nico Braun, Gilbert Zender (80' Jean-Paul Goerres). (Coach: Gilbert Legrand (FRA)).
Austria: Friedrich Koncilia, Johann Eigenstiller (C), Norbert Hof, Roland Hattenberger, Herbert Prohaska, Josef Hickersberger, Josef Stering, Egon Pajenk (YC25), Manfred Gombasch, Hans Krankl, Kurt Welzl (46' Helmut Köglberger). (Coach: Leopold Stastny (TCH)).
Goals: Luxembourg: 1-0 Nico Braun (11').
Austria: 1-1 Helmut Köglberger (58'), 1-2 Hans Krankl (75').
Referee: Leonardus Wilhelmus (Leo) van der Kroft (HOL)   Attendance: 5.340

02-04-1975   Praterstadion, Vienna: Austria – Hungary   0-0
Austria: Friedrich Koncilia, Erich Obermayer, Heinrich Strasser, Johann Eigenstiller (C), Johannes Winkelbauer, Roland Hattenberger, Herbert Prohaska, Hans Krankl, Wilhelm Kreuz, Alfred Riedl, Helmut Köglberger (69' Johann Pirkner). (Coach: Leopold Stastny (TCH)).
Hungary: Ferenc Mészáros, László Bálint (C), József Tóth, Péter Török, János Nagy (III), Károly Csapó, Lajos Kocsis, József Horváth (C), András Toth (69' László Fekete), Ferenc Bene, László Branikovits (69' Sándor Pintér). (Coach: János Szöcs (HUN)).
Referee: John Keith (Jack) Taylor (ENG)   Attendance: 65.674

16-04-1975   Népstadion, Budapest: Hungary – Wales   1-2 (0-1)
Hungary: Ferenc Mészáros (YC46), László Bálint (C), József Tóth, Péter Török, János Nagy (III), Károly Csapó (55' Ferenc Bene), Lajos Kocsis, Mihály Kozma, József Horváth (C) (46' Sándor Pintér), László Branikovits, János Máté. (Coach: Lajos Baroti (HUN)).
Wales: Dai Davies, Rod Thomas, Leighton Phillips, Malcolm Page (YC39), John Roberts, Gil Reece (YC46) (83' Dave Smallman), John Mahoney, Arfon Griffiths, John Toshack, Terry Yorath (C), Leighton James (59' Brian Flynn). (Coach: Michael John (Mike) Smith (ENG)).
Goals: Hungary: 1-2 László Branikovits (77').
Wales: 0-1 John Toshack (44'), 0-2 John Mahoney (69').
Referee: Pablo Augusto Sánchez Ibáñez (ESP)   Attendance: 21.080

01-05-1975   Stade Municipal, Luxembourg: Luxembourg – Wales   1-3 (1-2)
Luxembourg: Jeannot Moes, Roger Fandel, Joé Hansen, Jean-Louis Margue, Louis Pilot (C), Louis Trierweiler, Paul Philipp, Jean Zuang, Nico Braun, Jean-Paul Martin (46' Jeannot Krecké, 77' Henri Roemer), Gilbert Zender. (Coach: Gilbert Legrand (FRA)).
Wales: Dai Davies, Rod Thomas, Leighton Phillips, Malcolm Page, David Roberts, Gil Reece, John Mahoney, Arfon Griffiths (58' Brian Flynn), John Toshack (YC79), Terry Yorath (C), Leighton James. (Coach: Michael John (Mike) Smith (ENG)).
Goals: Luxembourg: 1-2 Paul Philipp (39' penalty).
Wales: 0-1 Gil Reece (24'), 0-2 Leighton James (32'), 1-3 Leighton James (83').
Referee: Jan Peeters (BEL)   Attendance: 3.289

24-09-1975   Népstadion, Budapest: Hungary – Austria   2-1 (2-1)
Hungary: László Kovács, László Bálint, Tibor Rab, János Nagy (III), Sándor Lukács, Tibor Nyilasi (YC17), László Nagy (46' Béla Várady), Lajos Kocsis, László Fazekas (C), András Tóth (75' Sándor Pintér), László Pusztai. (Coach: Lajos Baroti (HUN)).
Austria: Friedrich Koncilia, Erich Obermayer (46' Johannes Winkelbauer), Bruno Pezzey, Robert Sara, Werner Kriess (C), Herbert Prohaska (46' Manfred Steiner (YC69)), Kurt Jara, Peter Koncilia (YC20), Günther Rinker, Hans Krankl, Kurt Welzl. (Coach: Leopold Stastny (TCH)).
Goals: Hungary: 1-0 Tibor Nyilasi (3'), 2-1 László Pusztai (33').
Austria: 1-1 Hans Krankl (17' penalty).
Referee: René Vigliani (FRA)   Attendance: 31.270

15-10-1975   Praterstadion, Vienna: Austria – Luxembourg   6-2 (3-2)
Austria: Friedrich Koncilia, Bruno Pezzey, Heinrich Strasser (YC30), Werner Kriess (C), Johannes Winkelbauer, Herbert Prohaska, Kurt Jara, Hans Ettmayer, Peter Koncilia, Hans Krankl, Kurt Welzl. (Coach: Branko Elsner (YUG)).
Luxembourg: René Hoffmann, Joé Hansen, Jean-Louis Margue (YC10), Emile Lahure, Louis Pilot (C), Louis Trierweiler, Paul Philipp, Jean Zuang, Gilbert Dussier (75' François Hauer), Nico Braun, Pierrot Langers (78' Jeannot Krecké). (Coach: Gilbert Legrand (FRA)).
Goals: Austria: 1-0 Kurt Welzl (1'), 2-2 Hans Krankl (38'), 3-2 Kurt Jara (41'), 4-2 Kurt Welzl (46'), 5-2 Hans Krankl (76' penalty), 6-2 Herbert Prohaska (80').
Luxembourg: 1-1 Nico Braun (5'), 1-2 Paul Philipp (32').
Referee: Miroslav Kopal (TCH)   Attendance: 14.499

19-10-1975   Stadion Rohonci Út, Szombathely: Hungary – Luxembourg   8-1 (4-0)
Hungary: Ádám Rothermel, László Bálint, Tibor Rab, József Kovács, János Nagy (III), Sándor Lukács, Tibor Nyilasi, Sándor Pintér (70' Tibor Wollek), László Nagy, László Fazekas (C), Béla Várady. (Coach: Lajos Baroti (HUN)).
Luxembourg: Raymond Zender, Léon Schmit, Joé Hansen, Emile Lahure, Louis Pilot (C), Louis Trierweiler (57' René Flenghi), Paul Philipp (YC38), Jean Zuang, Gilbert Dussier, Nico Braun, Pierrot Langers (75' Jeannot Krecké). (Coach: Gilbert Legrand (FRA)).
Goals: Hungary: 1-0 Sándor Pintér (13'), 2-0 Tibor Nyilasi (21'), 3-0 Tibor Nyilasi (32'), 4-0 Tibor Nyilasi (44'), 5-0 Tibor Nyilasi (57'), 6-0 Tibor Nyilasi (67'), 7-0 Tibor Wollek (78'), 8-1 Béla Várady (84').
Luxembourg: 7-1 Gilbert Dussier (83').
Referee: Nikola Milanov Doudine (BUL)   Attendance: 7.503

19-11-1975   The Racecourse Ground, Wrexham: Wales – Austria   1-0 (0-0)
Wales: Brian Lloyd, Rod Thomas, Leighton Phillips, Joey Jones, Ian Evans, John Mahoney, Arfon Griffiths, Brian Flynn, Terry Yorath (C) (YC75), Leighton James, Dave Smallman (YC51). (Coach: Michael John (Mike) Smith (ENG)).
Austria: Friedrich Koncilia, Bruno Pezzey (YC50), Robert Sara, Werner Kriess (C) (28' Heinrich Strasser), Johannes Winkelbauer, Manfred Steiner, Herbert Prohaska (YC37), Kurt Jara, Hans Ettmayer, Hans Krankl, Kurt Welzl (70' Josef Stering). (Coach: Branko Elsner (YUG)).
Goal: Wales: 1-0 Arfon Griffiths (69').
Referee: Sergio Gonella (ITA)   Attendance: 27.578

GROUP 3

04-09-1974	Oslo	Norway – Northern Ireland	2-1 (0-1)
30-10-1974	Belgrade	Yugoslavia – Norway	3-1 (1-1)
30-10-1974	Solna	Sweden – Northern Ireland	0-2 (0-2)
16-04-1975	Belfast	Northern Ireland – Yugoslavia	1-0 (1-0)
04-06-1975	Solna	Sweden – Yugoslavia	1-2 (1-1)
09-06-1975	Oslo	Norway – Yugoslavia	1-3 (0-3)
30-06-1975	Solna	Sweden – Norway	3-1 (1-0)
13-08-1975	Oslo	Norway – Sweden	0-2 (0-1)
03-09-1975	Belfast	Northern Ireland – Sweden	1-2 (1-1)
15-10-1975	Zagreb	Yugoslavia – Sweden	3-0 (1-0)
29-10-1975	Belfast	Northern Ireland – Norway	3-0 (2-0)
19-11-1975	Belgrade	Yugoslavia – Northern Ireland	1-0 (1-0)

FINAL STANDING

Pos	Team	Pld	W	D	L	GF	GA	GD	Pts
1	*Yugoslavia*	*6*	*5*	*0*	*1*	*12*	*4*	*+8*	*10*
2	Northern Ireland	6	3	0	3	8	5	+3	6
3	Sweden	6	3	0	3	8	9	-1	6
4	Norway	6	1	0	5	5	15	-10	2

Yugoslavia qualified for the Quarter-finals.

04-09-1974   Ullevaal Stadion, Oslo: Norway – Northern Ireland   2-1 (0-1)
Norway: Geir Karlsen, Svein Kvia (C), Reidar Goa, Jan Birkelund, Torkild Brakstad, Svein Grøndalen, Tor Egil Johansen, Harry Hestad, Egil Austbø, Jan Fuglset, Thomas Lund. (Coach: Kjell Schou Andreassen (NOR)).
Northern Ireland: Pat Jennings, David Craig (46' Hugh Dowd), Liam O'Kane, Allan Hunter, Pat Rice, Sammy McIlroy, Thomas Cassidy, David Clements (C), Bryan Hamilton, Tommy Finney, Chris McGrath (65' Tommy Jackson). (Coach: William John Terence Neill (NIR)).
Goals: Norway: 1-1 Thomas Lund (59'), 2-1 Thomas Lund (72').
Northern Ireland: 0-1 Tommy Finney (3').
Referee: Alfred (Fred) Delcourt (BEL)   Attendance: 7.192

30-10-1974   Stadion JNA, Belgrade: Yugoslavia – Norway   3-1 (1-1)
Yugoslavia: Ognjen Petrovic, Ivan Buljan, Josip Katalinski, Vilson Dzoni, Dzemal Hadziabdic, Jurica Jerkovic, Franjo Vladic (78' Ljubisa Rajkovic), Ivan Surjak, Dragan Dzajic (C), Slavisa Zungul, Momcilo Vukotic. (Coach: Ante Mladinic (YUG)).
Norway: Geir Karlsen, Svein Kvia (C) (72' Jan Fuglset), Jan Birkelund, Torkild Brakstad, Svein Grøndalen, Øystein Wormdahl, Tor Egil Johansen, Harry Hestad, Egil Austbø, Thomas Lund, Terje Olsen. (Coach: Kjell Schou Andreassen (NOR)).
Goals: Yugoslavia: 1-1 Momcilo Vukotic (43'), 2-1 Josip Katalinski (58'), 3-1 Josip Katalinski (72').
Norway: 0-1 Thomas Lund (36').
Referee: Antoine Queudeville (LUX)   Attendance: 9.910

30-10-1974 Råsunda Stadion, Solna: Sweden – Northern Ireland 0-2 (0-2)
Sweden: Ronnie Hellström, Kent Karlsson, Björn Andersson, Björn Nordqvist (C), Roland Andersson, Ove Kindvall (64' Thomas Nordahl), Staffan Tapper, Bo Larsson, Conny Torstensson (46' Jan Mattsson), Ralf Edström, Roland Sandberg. (Coach: George Ericsson (SWE)).
Northern Ireland: Pat Jennings, Chris Nicholl, Sammy Nelson (46' Ronald Blair), Liam O'Kane, Allan Hunter (C), Sammy McIlroy, Martin O'Neill, Tommy Jackson, Bryan Hamilton, Hugh Dowd, Sammy Morgan. (Coach: William John Terence Neill (NIR)).
Goals: Northern Ireland: 0-1 Chris Nicholl (7'), 0-2 Martin O'Neill (23').
Referee: Theodorus (Theo) Boosten (HOL)   Attendance: 18.131

16-04-1975 Windsor Park, Belfast: Northern Ireland – Yugoslavia 1-0 (1-0)
Northern Ireland: Pat Jennings, Chris Nicholl, Sammy Nelson, Allan Hunter, Pat Rice, Sammy McIlroy (YC72), Martin O'Neill, David Clements (C), Tommy Jackson, Bryan Hamilton, Derek Spence. (Coach: David (Dave) Clements (NIR)).
Yugoslavia: Ognjen Petrovic, Ivan Buljan (YC72), Drazen Muzinic, Josip Katalinski (C), Luka Peruzovic, Dzemal Hadziabdic, Branko Oblak, Jurica Jerkovic (75' Ivan Miljkovic), Slobodan Jankovic, Ivan Surjak, Momcilo Vukotic (46' Franjo Vladic). (Coach: Ante Mladinic (YUG)).
Goal: Northern Ireland: 1-0 Bryan Hamilton (22').
Referee: Robert Charles Paul Wurtz (FRA)   Attendance: 25.847

04-06-1975 Råsunda Stadion, Solna: Sweden – Yugoslavia 1-2 (1-1)
Sweden: Ronnie Hellström (46' Göran Hagberg), Kent Karlsson, Björn Nordqvist (C), Jörgen Augustsson, Roland Andersson, Thomas Sjöberg (65' Thomas Nordahl), Eine Fredriksson, Ove Grahn, Ralf Edström, Roland Sandberg, Benny Wendt. (Coach: Georg (Åby) Ericson (SWE)).
Yugoslavia: Ognjen Petrovic, Ivan Buljan, Drazen Muzinic, Josip Katalinski (C), Vladislav Bogicevic, Dzemal Hadziabdic, Branko Oblak, Danilo Popivoda, Franjo Vladic, Ivan Surjak, Dusan Savic (65' Zvonko Ivezic). (Coach: Ante Mladinic (YUG)).
Goals: Sweden: 1-1 Ralf Edström (17').
Yugoslavia: 1-1 Josip Katalinski (41'), 1-2 Zvonko Ivezic (77').
Referee: Vital Georges Gilbert Loraux (BEL)   Attendance: 25.712

09-06-1975 Ullavaal Stadion, Oslo: Norway – Yugoslavia 1-3 (0-3)
Norway: Erik Johannessen (74' Geir Karlsen), Svein Kvia, Reidar Goa (40' Trond Pedersen), Jan Birkelund, Svein Grøndalen, Erling Meirik, Tor Egil Johansen, Harry Hestad, Stein Thunberg, Thomas Lund, Gabriel Høyland. (Coach: Kjell Schou Andreassen (NOR)).
Yugoslavia: Ognjen Petrovic, Ivan Buljan, Drazen Muzinic, Josip Katalinski (C), Vladislav Bogicevic, Dzemal Hadziabdic, Branko Oblak, Danilo Popivoda, Franjo Vladic, Ivan Surjak, Dusan Savic (69' Zvonko Ivezic). (Coach: Ante Mladinic (YUG)).
Goals: Norway: 1-3 Stein Thunberg (65').
Yugoslavia: 0-1 Ivan Buljan (12'), 0-2 Vladislav Bogicevic (13'), 0-3 Ivan Surjak (25').
Referee: Edgar Pedersen (DEN)   Attendance: 21.843

30-06-1975   Råsunda Stadion, Solna: Sweden – Norway   3-1 (1-0)
Sweden: Ronnie Hellström, Kent Karlsson (C), Jörgen Augustsson, Roy Andersson, Roland Andersson, Thomas Nordahl, Anders Linderoth, Eine Fredriksson (60' Curt Olsberg), Ove Grahn, Roland Sandberg, Benny Wendt (65' Jan Mattsson). (Coach: Georg (Åby) Ericson (SWE)).
Norway: Erik Johannessen (80' Tore Antonsen), Svein Kvia (C), Svein Grøndalen, Erling Meirik, Trond Pedersen, Helge Karlsen, Tor Egil Johansen, Erik Just Olsen, Helge Skuseth, Gabriel Høyland, Frode Larsen (70' Stein Thunberg). (Coach: Kjell Schou Andreassen (NOR)).
Goals: Sweden: 1-0 Thomas Nordahl (33'), 2-1 Thomas Nordahl (56'), 3-1 Ove Grahn (65' penalty).
Norway: 1-1 Erik Just Olsen (54' penalty).
Referee: Rudolf (Rudi) Glöckner (GDR)   Attendance: 8.264

13-08-1975   Ullevaal Stadion, Oslo: Norway – Sweden   0-2 (0-1)
Norway: Tore Antonsen, Sigbjorn Slinning (YC51), Svein Kvia (C), Svein Grøndalen, Trond Pedersen, Helge Karlsen, Stein Thunberg (80' Tor Egil Johansen), Helge Skuseth, Jan Hansen, Gabriel Høyland (68' Svein Mathisen), Frode Larsen. (Coach: Kjell Schou Andreassen (NOR)).
Sweden: Ronnie Hellström, Kent Karlsson, Björn Nordqvist (C), Jörgen Augustsson, Roland Andersson, Anders Linderoth, Thomas Sjöberg, Ove Grahn, Ralf Edström (YC85), Roland Sandberg, Benny Wendt (72' Jan Mattsson). (Coach: Georg (Åby) Ericson (SWE)).
Goals: Sweden: 0-1 Roland Sandberg (29'), 0-2 Thomas Sjöberg (53').
Referee: Anders Mattsson (FIN)   Attendance: 18.011

03-09-1975   Windsor Park, Belfast: Northern Ireland – Sweden   1-2 (1-1)
Northern Ireland: Pat Jennings, Chris Nicholl, Sammy Nelson, Allan Hunter, Pat Rice, Sammy McIlroy, David Clements (C), Tommy Jackson, Bryan Hamilton (65' Sammy Morgan), Ronald Blair, Derek Spence. (Coach: David (Dave) Clements (NIR)).
Sweden: Ronnie Hellström, Kent Karlsson, Björn Nordqvist (C), Jörgen Augustsson (YC87), Roland Andersson, Anders Linderoth, Thomas Sjöberg, Curt Olsberg (46' Staffan Tapper), Eine Fredriksson, Conny Torstensson, Jan Mattsson. (Coach: Georg (Åby) Ericson (SWE)).
Goals: Northern Ireland: 1-0 Allan Hunter (32').
Sweden: 1-1 Thomas Sjöberg (44'), 1-2 Conny Torstensson (56').
Referee: Hans-Joachim Weyland (FRG)   Attendance: 14.622

15-10-1975   Stadion Maksimir, Zagreb: Yugoslavia – Sweden   3-0 (1-0)
Yugoslavia: Ognjen Petrovic, Ivan Buljan, Drazen Muzinic, Josip Katalinski, Dzemal Hadziabdic, Branko Oblak (C), Jurica Jerkovic, Franjo Vladic, Ivan Surjak, Dragan Dzajic, Drago Vabec. (Coach: Ante Mladinic (YUG)).
Sweden: Ronnie Hellström, Kent Karlsson, Björn Nordqvist (C), Jörgen Augustsson, Roland Andersson, Staffan Tapper, Anders Linderoth, Thomas Sjöberg (65' Jan Mattsson), Conny Torstensson, Ralf Edström, Roland Sandberg. (Coach: Georg (Åby) Ericson (SWE)).
Goals: Yugoslavia: 1-0 Branko Oblak (18'), 2-0 Franjo Vladic (50'), 3-0 Drago Vabec (83').
Referee: Walter Hungerbühler (SUI)   Attendance: 29.836

29-10-1975   Windsor Park, Belfast: Northern Ireland – Norway   3-0 (2-0)
Northern Ireland: Pat Jennings, Chris Nicholl, Sammy Nelson, Allan Hunter (C), Pat Rice, Sammy McIlroy, Tommy Jackson, Bryan Hamilton, Tommy Finney, John Jamison, Sammy Morgan (60' Terry Cochrane). (Coach: David (Dave) Clements (NIR)).
Norway: Geir Karlsen (64' Tom Rüsz Jacobsen), Sigbjorn Slinning, Svein Kvia (C), Svein Grøndalen (35' Borge Josefsen), Trond Pedersen, Helge Karlsen, Harry Hestad, Helge Skuseth, Jan Hansen, Gabriel Høyland, Pal Jacobsen. (Coach: Kjell Schou Andreassen (NOR)).
Goals: Northern Ireland: 1-0 Sammy Morgan (2'), 2-0 Sammy McIlroy (5'), 3-0 Bryan Hamilton (53').
Referee: Gudjón Finnbogason (ISL)   Attendance: 8.923

19-11-1975   Stadion JNA, Belgrade: Yugoslavia – Northern Ireland   1-0 (1-0)
Yugoslavia: Ognjen Petrovic, Ivan Buljan (C), Drazen Muzinic, Josip Katalinski, Dzemal Hadziabdic, Branko Oblak, Jurica Jerkovic, Franjo Vladic, Ivan Surjak, Dragan Dzajic, Momcilo Vukotic. (Coach: Ante Mladinic (YUG)).
Northern Ireland: Pat Jennings, Chris Nicholl, Allan Hunter, Pat Rice, Peter Scott, Sammy McIlroy (YC78), David Clements (C), Tommy Jackson (30' David McCreery), Bryan Hamilton, Tommy Finney, Sammy Morgan. (Coach: David (Dave) Clements (NIR)).
Goal: Yugoslavia: 1-0 Branko Oblak (21').
Referee: Antonio Camacho Jiménez (ESP)   Attendance: 21.545

GROUP 4

25-09-1974	Copenhagen	Denmark – Spain	1-2 (0-2)
18-10-1974	Copenhagen	Denmark – Romania	0-0
20-11-1974	Glasgow	Scotland – Spain	1-2 (1-1)
05-02-1975	Valencia	Spain – Scotland	1-1 (0-1)
17-04-1975	Madrid	Spain – Romania	1-1 (1-0)
11-05-1975	Bucharest	Romania – Denmark	6-1 (2-0)
01-06-1975	Bucharest	Romania – Scotland	1-1 (1-0)
03-09-1975	Copenhagen	Denmark – Scotland	0-1 (0-0)
12-10-1975	Barcelona	Spain – Denmark	2-0 (1-0)
29-10-1975	Glasgow	Scotland – Denmark	3-1 (0-1)
16-11-1975	Bucharest	Romania – Spain	2-2 (0-1)
17-12-1975	Glasgow	Scotland – Romania	1-1 (1-0)

FINAL STANDING

Pos	Team	Pld	W	D	L	GF	GA	GD	Pts
1	*Spain*	*6*	*3*	*3*	*0*	*10*	*6*	*+4*	*9*
2	Romania	6	1	5	0	11	6	+5	7
3	Scotland	6	2	3	1	8	6	+2	7
4	Denmark	6	0	1	5	3	14	-11	1

Spain qualified for the Quarter-finals.

25-09-1974   Idrætsparken, Copenhagen: Denmark – Spain   1-2 (0-2)
Denmark: Benno Larsen, Morten Olsen, Henning Munk Jensen (YC56), Jørgen Rasmussen, Flemming Mortensen, Kjell Seneca, Niels Sørensen (72' Jørgen Jørgensen), Allan Simonsen, Kristen Nygaard, Henning Jensen, Niels Christian Holmstrøm (C) (46' Ove Flindt Bjerg). (Coach: Rudolf (Rudi) Strittich (AUT)).
Spain: José Ángel IRIBAR Cortajarena, JUAN Cruz SOL Oria, Gregorio BENITO Rubio, JOSÉ Luis CAPÓN González, JESÚS MARTÍNEZ Rivadeneyra, Ángel CASTELLANOS Céspedes, Juan Manuel ASENSI Ripoll, MARCIAL Pina Morales, José CLARAMUNT Torres (C) (YC,YC70), Enrique Castro González "QUINI", Juan ROBERTO MARTÍNEZ Martínez (62' Juan Antonio GARCÍA SORIANO). (Coach: László "LADISLAO" KUBALA Stecz (ESP)).
Goals: Denmark: 1-2 Kristen Nygaard (48' penalty).
Spain: 0-1 José CLARAMUNT Torres (27' penalty), 0-2 Juan ROBERTO MARTÍNEZ Martínez (41').
Referee: John Carpenter (IRL)   Attendance: 27.300

13-10-1974   Idrætsparken, Copenhagen: Denmark – Romania   0-0
Denmark: Benno Larsen, Morten Olsen, Henning Munk Jensen, Jørgen Rasmussen, Flemming Mortensen, Steen Danielsen, Ulrik Le Fevre, Flemming Lund, Benny Nielsen, Niels Christian Holmstrøm (C), Jørgen Jørgensen. (Coach: Rudolf (Rudi) Strittich (AUT)).
Romania: Raducanu Necula, Cornel Dinu (C) (YC49), Florin Cheran, Dumitru Antonescu, Teodor Anghelini, Radu Nunweiller, Ion Dumitru, Mircea Lucescu (80' Radu Troi), Alexandru Satmareanu, Anghel Iordanescu, Attila Kun (II). (Coach: Valentin Stanescu (ROM)).
Referee: Ferdinand Biwersi (FRG)   Attendance: 15.700

20-11-1974   Hampden Park, Glasgow: Scotland – Spain   1-2 (1-1)
Scotland: David Harvey, Sandy Jardine, Kenny Burns, Alex Forsyth, Gordon McQueen, Graeme Souness, Billy Bremner (C), Jimmy Johnstone, Tommy Hutchison (65' Kenny Dalglish), John Deans (65' Peter Lorimer, Joe Jordan (YC72). (Coach: William Esplin (Willie) Ormond (SCO)).
Spain: José Ángel IRIBAR Cortajarena, Miguel Bernardo Bianquetti "MIGUELI" (YC19) (68' JUAN Cruz SOL Oria), Gregorio BENITO Rubio, Enrique Álvarez COSTAS, JOSÉ Luis CAPÓN González, Ángel CASTELLANOS Céspedes, Carles REXACH Cerdà (C) (YC88), Ángel María VILLAR Llona (YC14), Javier PLANAS Abad (II) (YC90), Enrique Castro González "QUINI", Juan ROBERTO MARTÍNEZ Martínez. (Coach: László "LADISLAO" KUBALA Stecz (ESP)).
Goals: Scotland: 1-0 Billy Bremner (11').
Spain: 1-1 Enrique Castro González "QUINI" (36'), 1-2 Enrique Castro González "QUINI" (61').
Referee: Erich Linemayr (AUT)   Attendance: 94.331

05-02-1975   Estadio Luis Casanova, Valencia: Spain – Scotland   1-1 (0-1)
Spain: José Ángel IRIBAR Cortajarena, JOSÉ Antonio CAMACHO Alfaro (YC77), JUAN Cruz SOL Oria, Gregorio BENITO Rubio, Enrique Álvarez COSTAS (68' Miguel Bernardo Bianquetti "MIGUELI"), Juan Manuel ASENSI Ripoll, Carles REXACH Cerdà, José CLARAMUNT Torres (C), Ángel María VILLAR Llona, Enrique Castro González "QUINI", José Eulogio GÁRATE Ormaechea (63' Alfredo MEGIDO Sánchez). (Coach: László "LADISLAO" KUBALA Stecz (ESP)).
Scotland: David Harvey, Danny McGrain, Sandy Jardine, Martin Buchan, Kenny Burns (78' Paul Wilson), Gordon McQueen, Billy Bremner (C), Charlie Cooke (YC59), Tommy Hutchison (YC77), Kenny Dalglish, Joe Jordan (63' Derek Parlane). (Coach: William Esplin (Willie) Ormond (SCO)).
Goals: Spain: 1-1 Alfredo MEGIDO Sánchez (67').
Scotland: 0-1 Joe Jordan (1').
Referee: Alfred (Fred) Delcourt (BEL)   Attendance: 40.952

17-04-1975   Estadio Santiago Bernadbéu, Madrid: Spain – Romania   1-1 (1-0)
Spain: José Ángel IRIBAR Cortajarena, JOSÉ Antonio CAMACHO Alfaro (YC77), Gregorio BENITO Rubio, JOSÉ Luis CAPÓN González, José Martinez Sanchez "PIRRI", Carles REXACH Cerdà, Vicente DEL BOSQUE, Manuel VELÁZQUEZ Villaverde (46' Javier "IRURETA" Iruretagoyena Amiano), Carlos Alonso González "SANTILLANA", José Eulogio GÁRATE Ormaechea, José Francisco José Francisco "CHECHU" ROJO Arroita (I). (Coach: László "LADISLAO" KUBALA Stecz (ESP)).
Romania: Raducanu Necula, Florin Cheran, Teodor Anghelini, Gabriel Sandu, Radu Nunweiller (41' Zoltan Crisan), Ion Dumitru, Mircea Lucescu (C), Ilie Balaci (YC62), Alexandru Satmareanu (YC81), Attila Kun (II) (41' Anghel Iordanescu), Dudu Georgescu. (Coach: Valentin Stanescu (ROM)).
Goals: Spain: 1-0 Manuel VELÁZQUEZ Villaverde (6').
Romania: 1-1 Zoltan Crisan (70').
Referee: Charles George Reinier Corver (HOL)   Attendance: 54.660

11-05-1975   Stadionul 23. August, Bucharest: Romania – Denmark   6-1 (2-0)
Romania: Raducanu Necula, Cornel Dinu (C), Florin Cheran, Teodor Anghelini, Gabriel Sandu, Ion Dumitru (80' Ilie Balaci), Mircea Lucescu, Nicolae Dobrin (80' Attila Kun (II)), Alexandru Satmareanu, Zoltan Crisan, Dudu Georgescu. (Coach: Valentin Stanescu (ROM)).
Denmark: Benno Larsen (21' Per Poulsen), Morten Olsen, Henning Munk Jensen, Jørgen Rasmussen (C), Flemming Mortensen, Niels Sørensen (62' Frank Nielsen), Lars Larsen, Jørgen Jørgensen, Birger Mauritzen, Peter Dahl, Eigil Nielsen. (Coach: Rudolf (Rudi) Strittich (AUT)).
Goals: Romania: 1-0 Dudu Georgescu (28'), 2-0 Zoltan Crisan (40'), 3-0 Zoltan Crisan (59'), 4-0 Dudu Georgescu (76'), 5-0 Mircea Lucescu (83'), 6-0 Cornel Dinu (85').
Denmark: 6-1 Peter Dahl (86').
Referee: Nikolaos Zlatanos (GRE)   Attendance: 37.773

01-06-1975   Stadionul 23. August, Bucharest: Romania – Scotland   1-1 (1-0)
Romania: Raducanu Necula, Cornel Dinu (C), Florin Cheran (YC), Teodor Anghelini, Gabriel Sandu, Ion Dumitru, Mircea Lucescu, Nicolae Dobrin (80' Attila Kun (II)), Alexandru Satmareanu, Zoltan Crisan, Dudu Georgescu (25' Ilie Balaci (YC)). (Coach: Valentin Stanescu (ROM)).
Scotland: Jim Brown, Danny McGrain (YC), Willie Miller, Frank Munro, Alex Forsyth (YC), Gordon McQueen (C) (YC), Bruce Rioch (YC) (65' Bobby Robinson), Lou Macari (75' Tommy Hutchison), Arthur Duncan, Kenny Dalglish, Derek Parlane. (Coach: William Esplin (Willie) Ormond (SCO)).
Goals: Romania: 1-0 Dudu Georgescu (21').
Scotland: 1-1 Gordon McQueen (89').
Referee: Ertugrul Dilek (TUR)   Attendance: 52.203

03-09-1975   Idrætsparken, Copenhagen: Denmark – Scotland   0-1 (0-0)
Denmark: Birger Jensen, Henning Munk Jensen, Flemming Mortensen, Niels Tune Hansen, Ulrik Le Fevre (C), Ole Bjørnmose, Ove Flindt Bjerg, Lars Larsen, Allan Simonsen, Benny Nielsen, Henning Jensen. (Coach: Rudolf (Rudi) Strittich (AUT)).
Scotland: David Harvey, Danny McGrain, Martin Buchan, Alex Forsyth (YC84), Gordon McQueen, Billy Bremner (C), Bruce Rioch, Joe Harper, Tommy Hutchison (70' Arthur Duncan), Kenny Dalglish, Peter Lorimer. (Coach: William Esplin (Willie) Ormond (SCO)).
Goal: Scotland: 0-1 Joe Harper (51').
Referee: Robert Schaut (BEL)   Attendance: 40.300

12-10-1975   Estadio Sarriá, Barcelona: Spain – Denmark   2-0 (1-0)
Spain: MIGUEL ÁNGEL González Suarez, Miguel Bernardo Bianquetti "MIGUELI", Gregorio BENITO Rubio, JOSÉ Luis CAPÓN González, José Antonio RAMOS Huete, José Martinez Sanchez "PIRRI" (C), Carles REXACH Cerdà (67' José Ignacio CHURRUCA Sistiaga), Vicente DEL BOSQUE (46' Juan Manuel ASENSI Ripoll), Marcial MARCIAL Pina Morales, Daniel SOLSONA Puig, Carlos Alonso González "SANTILLANA". (Coach: László "LADISLAO" KUBALA Stecz (ESP)).
Denmark: Birger Jensen, Johnny Hansen, Henning Munk Jensen (C) (YC59), John Andersen (YC21), Ole Rasmussen, Niels Sørensen (59' Carsten Nielsen), Ove Flindt Bjerg, Lars Larsen, Heino Hansen, Peter Dahl, Lars Bastrup. (Coach: Rudolf (Rudi) Strittich (AUT)).
Goals: Spain: 1-0 Carlos Alonso González "SANTILLANA" (40'), 2-0 JOSÉ Luis CAPÓN González (85').
Referee: Paul Bonett (MLT)   Attendance: 6.869

29-10-1975   Hampden Park, Glasgow: Scotland – Denmark   3-1 (0-1)
Scotland: David Harvey, Danny McGrain, Stewart Houston, Colin Jackson, Asa Hartford, Bruce Rioch, Archie Gemmill, John Greig (C), Kenny Dalglish (86' Derek Parlane), Peter Lorimer, Ted MacDougall. (Coach: William Esplin (Willie) Ormond (SCO)).
Denmark: Birger Jensen, Johnny Hansen, Henning Munk Jensen (C), John Andersen, Niels Tune Hansen, Niels Sørensen, Lars Larsen, Heino Hansen, Jens Kolding, Kristen Nygaard (59' Frank Nielsen), Lars Bastrup. (Coach: Rudolf (Rudi) Strittich (AUT)).
Goals: Scotland: 1-1 Kenny Dalglish (47'), 2-1 Bruce Rioch (53'), 3-1 Ted MacDougall (61').
Denmark: 0-1 Lars Bastrup (15').
Referee: Rolf Nyhus (NOR)   Attendance: 48.021

16-11-1975   Stadionul 23. August, Bucharest: Romania – Spain   2-2 (0-1)
Romania: Raducanu Necula, Cornel Dinu (C) (YC65), Teodor Anghelini, Gabriel Sandu, Teodor Lucuta, Mircea Lucescu, Nicolae Dobrin, Alexandru Satmareanu, Constantin Zamfir (61' Zoltan Crisan), Dudu Georgescu, Mircea Traian Sandu (46' Anghel Iordanescu). (Coach: Valentin Stanescu (ROM)).
Spain: MIGUEL ÁNGEL González Suarez, JOSÉ Antonio CAMACHO Alfaro (YC54), Miguel Bernardo Bianquetti "MIGUELI", JUAN Cruz SOL Oria, Gregorio BENITO Rubio, José Martinez Sanchez "PIRRI" (C), Vicente DEL BOSQUE, Ángel María VILLAR Llona, Enrique Castro González "QUINI" (88' Jesús María SATRÚSTEGUI Azpiroz), Carlos Alonso González "SANTILLANA", José Francisco "CHECHU" ROJO Arroita (I) (75' Francisco "PACO" FORTES Calvo). (Coach: László "LADISLAO" KUBALA Stecz (ESP)).
Goals: Romania: 1-2 Dudu Georgescu (72' penalty), 2-2 Anghel Iordanescu (80').
Spain: 0-1 Ángel María VILLAR Llona (38'), 0-2 Carlos Alonso González "SANTILLANA" (56').
Referee: Hans-Joachim Weyland (FRG)   Attendance: 45.381

17-12-1975   Hampden Park, Glasgow: Scotland – Romania   1-1 (1-0)
Scotland: Jim Cruickshank, Martin Buchan (C), Willie Donachie, Colin Jackson, John Brownlie, Asa Hartford, Bruce Rioch, Archie Gemmill, John Doyle (YC53) (73' Peter Lorimer), Kenny Dalglish (73' Ted MacDougall), Andy Gray. (Coach: William Esplin (Willie) Ormond (SCO)).
Romania: Raducanu Necula, Cornel Dinu (C) (YC53), Florin Cheran, Teodor Anghelini (YC61), Gabriel Sandu, Mircea Lucescu (63' Zoltan Crisan), Laszlo Bölöni, Alexandru Satmareanu, Mihai Romila (II), Anghel Iordanescu (YC33), Dudu Georgescu. (Coach: Cornel Dragusin (ROM)).
Goals: Scotland: 1-0 Bruce Rioch (39').
Romania: 1-1 Zoltan Crisan (73').
Referee: Adolf Prokop (GDR)   Attendance: 11.375

GROUP 5

01-09-1974	Helsinki	Finland – Poland	1-2 (1-1)
25-09-1974	Helsinki	Finland – Netherlands	1-3 (1-2)
09-10-1974	Poznan	Poland – Finland	3-0 (2-0)
20-11-1974	Rotterdam	Netherlands – Italy	3-1 (1-1)
19-04-1975	Rome	Italy – Poland	0-0
05-06-1975	Helsinki	Finland – Italy	0-1 (0-1)
03-09-1975	Nijmegen	Netherlands – Finland	4-1 (2-1)
10-09-1975	Chorzów	Poland – Netherlands	4-1 (2-0)
27-09-1975	Rome	Italy – Finland	0-0
15-10-1975	Amsterdam	Netherlands – Poland	3-0 (1-0)
26-10-1975	Warsaw	Poland – Italy	0-0
22-11-1975	Rome	Italy – Netherlands	1-0 (1-0)

FINAL STANDING

Pos	Team	Pld	W	D	L	GF	GA	GD	Pts
1	Netherlands	6	4	0	2	14	8	+6	8
2	Poland	6	3	2	1	9	5	+4	8
3	Italy	6	2	3	1	3	3	0	7
4	Finland	6	0	1	5	3	13	-10	1

Netherlands qualified for the Quarter-finals.

01-09-1974 Olympiastadion, Helsinki: Finland – Poland 1-2 (1-1)
Finland: Pertti Alaja, Arto Tolsa, Esko Ranta, Henry Forssell, Jouko Suomalainen (C), Miikka Toivola, Erkki Vihtilä, Aki Heiskainen (YC48), Juha-Pekka Laine, Matti Paatelainen (63' Jarmo Manninen), Timo Rahja (79' Antero Nikkanen). (Coach: Olavi Laaksonen (FIN)).
Poland: Jan Tomaszewski, Antoni Szymanowski, Jerzy Gorgon, Adam Musial, Miroslaw Bulzacki, Grzegorz Lato, Henry Kasperczak (76' Marek Kusto), Zygmunt Maszczyk, Leslaw Cmikiewicz (C), Andrzej Szarmach, Robert Gadocha. (Coach: Kazimierz Górski (POL)).
Goals: Finland: 1-0 Timo Rahja (4').
Poland: 1-1 Andrzej Szarmach (23'), 1-2 Grzegorz Lato (50').
Referee: John Wright Paterson (SCO)   Attendance: 18.759

25-09-1974 Olympiastadion, Helsinki: Finland – Netherlands 1-3 (1-2)
Finland: Harri Holli, Arto Tolsa (YC30), Esko Ranta, Raimo Saari, Jouko Suomalainen (C), Erkki Vihtilä, Aki Heiskainen (60' Olavi Rissanen), Juha-Pekka Laine, Raimo Hukka (55' Miikka Toivola), Timo Rahja, Rutger Pettersson. (Coach: Olavi Laaksonen (FIN)).
Netherlands: Jan Jongbloed, Ruud Krol, Kees van Ierssel, Wim van Hanegem (46' René Notten), Wim Jansen, Johan Cruijff (C) (YC68), Theo de Jong, Arie Haan, Johan Neeskens (YC53), Peter Ressel, Johnny Rep (65' Ruud Geels). (Coach: George Knobel (HOL)).
Goals: Finland: 1-0 Timo Rahja (16').
Netherlands: 1-1 Johan Cruijff (28'), 1-2 Johan Cruijff (40'), 1-3 Johan Neeskens (51' penalty).
Referee: Wolfgang Riedel (GDR)   Attendance: 20.449

09-10-1974 Stadion Warty, Poznan: Poland – Finland 3-0 (2-0)
Poland: Jan Tomaszewski, Antoni Szymanowski, Jerzy Wyrobek, Marian Ostafinski, Piotr Drzewiecki, Grzegorz Lato, Kazimierz Deyna (C), Henry Kasperczak (55' Roman Jakóbczak), Andrzej Szarmach (YC) (75' Joachim Marx), Robert Gadocha, Bronislaw Bula. (Coach: Kazimierz Górski (POL)).
Finland: Harri Holli, Arto Tolsa, Esko Ranta, Raimo Saari, Jouko Suomalainen (C), Miikka Toivola, Erkki Vihtilä, Aki Heiskainen (46' Juha-Pekka Laine), Matti Paatelainen (46' Rutger Pettersson), Olavi Rissanen, Timo Rahja. (Coach: Olavi Laaksonen (FIN)).
Goals: Poland: 1-0 Henry Kasperczak (13'), 2-0 Robert Gadocha (15' penalty), 3-0 Grzegorz Lato (53').
Referee: Dusan Aron Maksimovic (YUG)   Attendance: 38.724

20-11-1974   Stadion Feijenoord, Rotterdam: Netherlands – Italy 3-1 (1-1)
Netherlands: Jan Jongbloed, Wim Rijsbergen, Wim Suurbier, Ruud Krol, Wim van Hanegem (YC40), Johan Cruijff (C), Arie Haan, Johan Neeskens, Rob Rensenbrink, Johnny Rep (46' Willy van de Kerkhof), Willy van der Kuijlen. (Coach: George Knobel (HOL)).
Italy: Dino Zoff (C), Francesco Morini, Francesco Rocca, Moreno Roggi, Luciano Zecchini, Giancarlo Antognoni, Antonio Juliano, Andrea Orlandini, Franco Causio, Pietro Anastasi (YC43), Roberto Boninsegna. (Coach: Dr.Fulvio Bernardini (ITA)).
Goals: Netherlands: 1-1 Rob Rensenbrink (24'), 2-1 Johan Cruijff (64'), 3-1 Johan Cruijff (80').
Italy: 0-1 Roberto Boninsegna (5').
Referee: Pavel Nyikolajevics Kazakov (URS)   Attendance: 58.463

19-04-1975   Stadio Olimpico, Rome: Italy – Poland 0-0
Italy: Dino Zoff, Claudio Gentile, Giacinto Facchetti (C), Francesco Rocca, Giancarlo Antognoni, Mauro Bellugi, Franco Cordova, Giorgio Morini, Francesco Graziani, Giorgio Chinaglia, Paolo Pulici (YC). (Coach: Dr.Fulvio Bernardini (ITA)).
Poland: Jan Tomaszewski, Wladyslaw Zmuda, Antoni Szymanowski, Jerzy Gorgon, Henryk Wawrowski, Grzegorz Lato, Kazimierz Deyna (C), Henry Kasperczak (46' Leslaw Cmikiewicz), Zygmunt Maszczyk, Andrzej Szarmach (YC), Robert Gadocha. (Coach: Kazimierz Górski (POL)).
Referee: Robert Héliès (FRA)   Attendance: 66.048

05-06-1975   Olympiastadion, Helsinki: Finland – Italy 0-1 (0-1)
Finland: Göran Enckelman, Arto Tolsa (YC), Esko Ranta, Pauno Kymäläinen (46' Olavi Rissanen), Jouko Suomalainen, Miikka Toivola, Erkki Vihtilä, Aki Heiskainen, Juha-Pekka Laine (72' Kalle Nieminen), Matti Paatelainen (C), Jarmo Manninen. (Coach: Aulis Ryfkönen (FIN)).
Italy: Dino Zoff, Claudio Gentile, Giacinto Facchetti (C), Francesco Rocca, Giancarlo Antognoni, Mauro Bellugi, Fabio Capello, Franco Cordova (46' Andrea Orlandini), Francesco Graziani (YC), Giorgio Chinaglia, Roberto Bettega. (Coach: Dr.Fulvio Bernardini (ITA)).
Goal: Italy: 0-1 Giorgio Chinagli (26' penalty).
Referee: Walter Eschweiler (FRG)   Attendance: 17.732

03-09-1975   Stadion De Goffert, Nijmegen: Netherlands – Finland 4-1 (2-1)
Netherlands: Jan van Beveren, Wim Suurbier, Adrie van Kraay, Ruud Krol (C), Niels Overweg, Wim van Hanegem, Wim Jansen, Jan Peters, Harry Lubse, Willy van de Kerkhof, Willy van der Kuijlen. (Coach: George Knobel (HOL)).
Finland: Göran Enckelman, Ari Mäkynen, Esko Ranta, Henry Forssell, Jouko Suomalainen, Erkki Vihtilä, Aki Heiskainen (78' Pertti Jantunen), Hannu Hämäläinen (50' Juha-Pekka Laine), Matti Paatelainen (C), Olavi Rissanen, Eero Rissanen. (Coach: Aulis Ryfkönen (FIN)).
Goals: Netherlands: 1-1 Willy van der Kuijlen (29'), 2-1 Willy van der Kuijlen (35'), 3-1 Harry Lubse (48'), 4-1 Willy van der Kuijlen (55').
Finland: 0-1 Matti Paatelainen (9').
Referee: Eric Smyton (NIR)   Attendance: 19.189

10-09-1975   Stadion Slaski, Chorzów: Poland – Netherlands   4-1 (2-0)
Poland: Jan Tomaszewski, Wladyslaw Zmuda, Antoni Szymanowski, Miroslaw Bulzacki, Henryk Wawrowski, Grzegorz Lato, Kazimierz Deyna (C), Henry Kasperczak, Zygmunt Maszczyk, Andrzej Szarmach, Robert Gadocha. (Coach: Kazimierz Górski (POL)).
Netherlands: Jan van Beveren, Wim Suurbier, Adrie van Kraay, Ruud Krol, Niels Overweg, Wim van Hanegem (46' Ruud Geels), Wim Jansen, Johan Cruijff (C), Johan Neeskens, Willy van de Kerkhof, Willy van der Kuijlen. (Coach: George Knobel (HOL)).
Goals: Poland: 1-0 Grzegorz Lato (14'), 2-0 Robert Gadocha (44'), 3-0 Andrzej Szarmach (63'), 4-0 Andrzej Szarmach (77').
Netherlands: 4-1 Willy van de Kerkhof (80').
Referee: Patrick Partridge (ENG)   Attendance: 70.409

27-09-1975   Stadio Olimpico, Rome: Italy – Finland   0-0
Italy: Dino Zoff, Giacinto Facchetti (C), Francesco Rocca, Moreno Roggi (YC), Giancarlo Antognoni, Romeo Benetti, Mauro Bellugi, Giorgio Morini, Eraldo Pecci, Francesco Graziani, Giuseppe Savoldi. (Coach: Vincenzo Bearzot (ITA)).
Finland: Göran Enckelman, Arto Tolsa, Ari Mäkynen (34' Timo Kautonen), Esko Ranta, Jouko Suomalainen (YC), Miikka Toivola, Erkki Vihtilä, Aki Heiskainen, Pertti Jantunen, Matti Paatelainen (C), Olavi Rissanen (1' Hannu Hämäläinen). (Coach: Aulis Ryfkönen (FIN)).
Referee: Costas Xanthoulis (CYP)   Attendance: 29.203

15-10-1975   Olympisch Stadion, Amsterdam: Netherlands – Poland   3-0 (1-0)
Netherlands: Piet Schrijvers, Wim Suurbier, Adrie van Kraay, Ruud Krol, Kees Krijgh, Wim Jansen, Johan Cruijff (C) (YC33), Johan Neeskens, René van de Kerkhof, Frans Thijssen, Ruud Geels. (Coach: George Knobel (HOL)).
Poland: Jan Tomaszewski, Wladyslaw Zmuda, Antoni Szymanowski, Miroslaw Bulzacki, Henryk Wawrowski, Grzegorz Lato, Kazimierz Deyna (64' Bronislaw Bula), Henry Kasperczak, Zygmunt Maszczyk (C), Andrzej Szarmach, Robert Gadocha. (Coach: Kazimierz Górski (POL)).
Goals: Netherlands: 1-0 Johan Neeskens (16'), 2-0 Ruud Geels (47'), 3-0 Frans Thijssen (59').
Referee: Károly Palotai (HUN)   Attendance: 56.030

26-10-1975   Stadion Dziesieciolecia, Warsaw: Polen – Italy   0-0
Poland: Jan Tomaszewski, Wladyslaw Zmuda (YC74), Antoni Szymanowski (C), Marian Ostafinski, Henryk Wawrowski, Grzegorz Lato, Kazimierz Deyna, Henry Kasperczak, Andrzej Szarmach, Robert Gadocha (78' Kazimierz Kmiecik), Bronislaw Bula (59' Joachim Marx). (Coach: Kazimierz Górski (POL)).
Italy: Dino Zoff, Claudio Gentile (YC81), Giacinto Facchetti (C), Antonello Cuccureddu, Francesco Rocca, Giancarlo Antognoni (86' Renato Zaccarelli), Romeo Benetti, Mauro Bellugi, Franco Causio, Pietro Anastasi (66' Roberto Bettega), Paolo Pulici. (Coach: Vincenzo Bearzot (ITA)).
Referee: Paul Schiller (AUT)   Attendance: 59.773

22-11-1975   Stadio Olimpico, Rome: Italy – Netherlands 1-0 (1-0)
Italy: Dino Zoff, Claudio Gentile (YC81), Giacinto Facchetti (C), Francesco Rocca, Romeo Benetti, Mauro Bellugi, Franco Causio, Giancarlo Antognoni, Giuseppe Savoldi, Fabio Capello, Paolo Pulici. (Coach: Vincenzo Bearzot (ITA)).
Netherlands: Piet Schrijvers, Wim Suurbier, Adrie van Kraay, Ruud Krol (C), Kees Krijgh, Jan Peters, Wim Jansen, Willy van de Kerkhof (70' René Notten), Ruud Geels, Frans Thijssen, René van de Kerkhof. (Coach: George Knobel (HOL)).
Goal: Italy: 1-0 Fabio Capello (20').
Referee: Robert Schaut (BEL)   Attendance: 33.307

GROUP 6

30-10-1974	Dublin	Republic of Ireland – Soviet Union	3-0 (2-0)
20-11-1974	Izmir	Turkey – Republic of Ireland	1-1 (0-0)
01-12-1974	Izmir	Turkey – Switzerland	2-1 (1-1)
02-04-1975	Kiev	Soviet Union – Turkey	3-0 (1-0)
30-04-1975	Zürich	Switzerland – Turkey	1-1 (1-0)
10-05-1975	Dublin	Republic of Ireland – Switzerland	2-1 (2-0)
18-05-1975	Kiev	Soviet Union – Republic of Ireland	2-1 (2-0)
21-05-1975	Bern	Switzerland – Republic of Ireland	1-0 (0-0)
12-10-1975	Zürich	Switzerland – Soviet Union	0-1 (0-0)
29-10-1975	Dublin	Republic of Ireland – Turkey	4-0 (3-0)
12-11-1975	Kiev	Soviet Union – Switzerland	4-1 (2-1)
23-11-1975	Izmir	Turkey – Soviet Union	1-0 (1-0)

FINAL STANDING

Pos	Team	Pld	W	D	L	GF	GA	GD	Pts
1	*Soviet Union*	*6*	*4*	*0*	*2*	*10*	*6*	*+4*	*8*
2	Republic of Ireland	6	3	1	2	11	5	+6	7
3	Turkey	6	2	2	2	5	10	-5	6
4	Switzerland	6	1	1	4	5	10	-5	3

Soviet Union qualified for the Quarter-finals.

30-10-1974   Dalymount Park, Dublin: Republic of Ireland – Soviet Union 3-0 (2-0)
Republic of Ireland: Paddy Roche, Joe Kinnear, Paddy Mulligan, Jimmy Holmes, Terry Mancini (RC32), John Giles (C), Steve Heighway, Michael Martin, Liam Brady, Daniel Givens, Ray Treacy. (Player-coach: Michael John (Johnny) Giles (IRL)).
Soviet Union: Vladimir Pilguy, Volodymyr Kaplychniy (RC32), Viktor Matviyenko, Sergei Nikulin (YC), Sergei Olshanskiy (C), Evgeni Lovchev, Viktor Kolotov, Vladimir Fedotov (57' Vladimir Fyodorov), Volodymyr Veremeev, Oleh Blokhin, Volodymyr Onyshchenko. (Coach: Konstantin Ivanovich Beskov (URS)).
Goals: Republic of Ireland: 1-0 Daniel Givens (23'), 2-0 Daniel Givens (30'), 3-0 Daniel Givens (70').
Referee: Erik Axelryd (SWE)   Attendance: 31.758

20-11-1974 Atatürk Stadi, Izmir: Turkey – Republic of Ireland 1-1 (0-0)
Turkey: Yasin Özdenak, Alpaslan Eratli, Zekeriya Alp, Ismail Arca, Mehmet Oguz (YC24), Metin Kurt, Ziya Sengül (C), Selçuk Yalçintas, Engin Verel, Cemil Turan, Mehmet Türkkan (80' Osman Arpacioglu (YC80)). (Coach: Sabri Kiraz (TUR)).
Republic of Ireland: Paddy Roche, Tony Dunne, Joe Kinnear, Paddy Mulligan (YC52), Eoin Hand, John Giles (C), Steve Heighway, Michael Martin, Liam Brady, Daniel Givens, Terry Conroy (85' Miah Dennehy). (Player-coach: Michael John (Johnny) Giles (IRL)).
Goals: Turkey: 1-0 Tony Dunne (54' *own goal*).
Republic of Ireland: 1-1 Daniel Givens (61').
Referee: Marian Srodecki (POL)   Attendance: 69.999

01-12-1974 Atatürk Stadi, Izmir: Turkey – Switzerland 2-1 (1-1)
Turkey: Yasin Özdenak, Alpaslan Eratli (YC47), Zekeriya Alp, Ismail Arca, Metin Kurt, Ziya Sengül, Selçuk Yalçintas (46' Rasit Karasu), Engin Verel (C), Mehmet Özgül, Osman Arpacioglu (46' Mehmet Oguz), Cemil Turan. (Coach: Sabri Kiraz (TUR)).
Switzerland: Erich Burgener, Gilbert Guyot, Luciano Bizzini, Jakob (Köbi) Kuhn, Daniel Jeandupeux, René Hasler, Hanspeter Schild, René Botteron, Kurt Müller (YC18), Rudolf Schneeberger, Hans Jörg Pfister (C) (70' Ernst Rutschmann). (Coach: René Hüssy (SUI)).
Goals: Turkey: 1-1 Ismail Arca (21'), 2-1 Mehmet Oguz (85').
Switzerland: 0-1 Hanspeter Schild (18').
Referee: Milivoje Gugulovic (YUG)   Attendance: 51.410

02-04-1975 Kiev Central Stadium, Kiev: Soviet Union – Turkey 3-0 (1-0)
Soviet Union: Evgeni Rudakov, Volodymyr Troshkin, Viktor Matviyenko, Mykhailo Fomenko, Stefan Reshko, Volodymyr Muntyan, Viktor Kolotov (C), Anatoliy Konkov (72' Leonid Buryak), Volodymyr Veremeev, Oleh Blokhin, Volodymyr Onyshchenko (79' Vladimir Fyodorov). (Coach: Konstantin Ivanovich Beskov (URS)).
Turkey: Sabri Dino, Alpaslan Eratli, Ismail Arca, Kemal Batmaz, Metin Kurt (51' Tuncay Temeller), Ziya Sengül (C), Engin Verel, Rasit Karasu, Zafer Göncüler (YC60), Ali Denizci, Cemil Turan. (Coach: Sabri Kiraz (TUR)).
Goals: Soviet Union: 1-0 Viktor Kolotov (25' penalty), 2-0 Viktor Kolotov (56' penalty), 3-0 Oleh Blokhin (75').
Referee: Robert Holley (Bobby) Davidson (SCO)   Attendance: 74.223

30-04-1975 St.Jakob-Park, Basle: Switzerland – Turkey 1-1 (1-0)
Switzerland: Hans Küng, Gilbert Guyot, Luciano Bizzini, Max Heer, Pius Fischbach, Daniel Jeandupeux, René Hasler (90' Hanspeter Schild), René Botteron, Ernst Rutschmann (59' Hans Jörg Pfister), Kurt Müller, Karl Elsener. (Coach: René Hüssy (SUI)).
Turkey: Yasin Özdenak, Fatih Terim, Alpaslan Eratli, Zekeriya Alp, Ismail Arca, Niko Kovi, Ziya Sengül, Engin Verel, Ali Denizci (69' Aydin Çelik), Cemil Turan, Gökmen Özdenak. (Coach: Sabri Kiraz (TUR)).
Goals: Switzerland: 1-0 Kurt Müller (43').
Turkey: 1-1 Alpaslan Eratli (54').
Referee: Riccardo Lattanzi (ITA)   Attendance: 21.965
(Niko Kovi was also known as Nikos Kovis)

10-05-1975   Lansdowne Road, Dublin: Republic of Ireland – Switzerland   2-1 (2-0)
Republic of Ireland: Paddy Roche, Tony Dunne, Joe Kinnear (YC60), Paddy Mulligan, Eoin Hand, John Giles (C), Michael Martin, Liam Brady, Daniel Givens (C), Ray Treacy, Terry Conroy. (Player-coach: Michael John (Johnny) Giles (IRL)).
Switzerland: Erich Burgener, Gilbert Guyot, Luciano Bizzini, Max Heer, Jakob (Köbi) Kuhn (C), Daniel Jeandupeux, René Hasler, Hanspeter Schild, René Botteron, Ernst Rutschmann, Kurt Müller. (Coach: René Hüssy (SUI)).
Goals: Republic of Ireland: 1-0 Michael Martin (2'), 2-0 Ray Treacy (28').
Switzerland: 2-1 Kurt Müller (74').
Referee: Paul Schiller (AUT)   Attendance: 48.074

18-05-1975   Kiev Central Stadium, Kiev: Soviet Union – Republic of Ireland   2-1 (2-0)
Soviet Union: Evgeni Rudakov, Volodymyr Troshkin, Viktor Matviyenko, Mykhailo Fomenko, Volodymyr Muntyan (46' Stefan Reshko), Viktor Kolotov (C), Anatoliy Konkov, Volodymyr Veremeev (84' Vladimir Fyodorov), Leonid Buryak, Oleh Blokhin, Volodymyr Onyshchenko (YC80). (Coach: Konstantin Ivanovich Beskov (URS)).
Republic of Ireland: Paddy Roche, Tony Dunne, Joe Kinnear, Paddy Mulligan, Eoin Hand, John Giles (C), Steve Heighway, Michael Martin, Liam Brady, Daniel Givens, Terry Conroy. (Player-coach: Michael John (Johnny) Giles (IRL)).
Goals: Soviet Union: 1-0 Oleh Blokhin (13'), 2-0 Viktor Kolotov (29').
Republic of Ireland: 2-1 Eoin Hand (79').
Referee: René Vigliani (FRA)   Attendance: 84.480

21-05-1975   Wankdorfstadion, Bern: Switzerland – Republic of Ireland   1-0 (0-0)
Switzerland: Erich Burgener, Gilbert Guyot, Luciano Bizzini, Pius Fischbach, Serge Trinchero, Jakob (Köbi) Kuhn (C), Daniel Jeandupeux, René Hasler, René Botteron, Ernst Rutschmann (46' Hans Jörg Pfister), Kurt Müller (68' Rudolf Elsener). (Coach: René Hüssy (SUI)).
Republic of Ireland: Paddy Roche, Tony Dunne, Paddy Mulligan, Eoin Hand, Jimmy Holmes, John Giles (C) (80' Gerry Daly), Michael Martin, Liam Brady, Daniel Givens, Ray Treacy, Terry Conroy. (Player-coach: Michael John (Johnny) Giles (IRL)).
Goal: Switzerland: 1-0 Rudolf Elsener (75').
Referee: César da Luz Diaz Correia (POR)   Attendance: 12.793

12-10-1975   Hardturm Stadion, Zürich: Switzerland – Soviet Union   0-1 (0-0)
Switzerland: Erich Burgener, Gilbert Guyot, Luciano Bizzini, Pius Fischbach, Serge Trinchero (75' Alfred Scheiwiler), Jakob (Köbi) Kuhn (C), Daniel Jeandupeux, René Botteron (75' Rudolf Schneeberger), Kurt Müller, Hans Jörg Pfister, Peter Risi. (Coach: René Hüssy (SUI)).
Soviet Union: Evgeni Rudakov, Volodymyr Troshkin (YC24) (30' Stefan Reshko), Mykhailo Fomenko (C) (YC28), Viktor Zvyagintsev, Evgeni Lovchev, Volodymyr Muntyan, Anatoliy Konkov (54' Vladimir Sakharov), Volodymyr Veremeev, Leonid Buryak, Oleh Blokhin, Volodymyr Onyshchenko. (Coach: Konstantin Ivanovich Beskov (URS)).
Goal: Soviet Union: 0-1 Volodymyr Muntyan (78').
Referee: Leonardus Wilhelmus (Leo) van der Kroft (HOL)   Attendance: 17.887

29-10-1975   Lansdowne Road, Dublin: Republic of Ireland – Turkey   4-0 (3-0)
Republic of Ireland: Paddy Roche, Tony Dunne (74' Joe Kinnear), Paddy Mulligan, Eoin Hand, Jimmy Holmes, John Giles (C), Steve Heighway (46' Terry Conroy), Michael Martin (RC70), Liam Brady, Daniel Givens, Ray Treacy. (Player-coach: Michael John (Johnny) Giles (IRL)).
Turkey: Yasin Özdenak (38' Rasim Kara), Fatih Terim, Alpaslan Eratli (RC70), Ismail Arca (C) (34' Zafer Göncüler), Sabahattin Erboga, Kadir Özcan (YC10), Necati Özçaglayan, Engin Verel (YC43), Ali Denizci, Cemil Turan, Gökmen Özdenak. (Coach: Sabri Kiraz (TUR)).
Goals: Republic of Ireland: 1-0 Daniel Givens (26'), 2-0 Daniel Givens (33'), 3-0 Daniel Givens (38'), 4-0 Daniel Givens (89').
Referee: Ángel Franco Martínez (ESP)   Attendance: 23.000

12-11-1975   Kiev Central Stadium, Kiev: Soviet Union – Switzerland   4-1 (2-1)
Soviet Union: Evgeni Rudakov, Volodymyr Troshkin (YC59), Mykhailo Fomenko (C), Viktor Zvyagintsev, Evgeni Lovchev, Volodymyr Muntyan (64' Viktor Kolotov (YC76)), Anatoliy Konkov (87' Vladimir Sakharov), Volodymyr Veremeev, Leonid Buryak, Oleh Blokhin (YC83), Volodymyr Onyshchenko. (Coach: Konstantin Ivanovich Beskov (URS)).
Switzerland: Erich Burgener, Gilbert Guyot, Luciano Bizzini, Pius Fischbach, Serge Trinchero, Jakob (Köbi) Kuhn (C), Daniel Jeandupeux, René Botteron, Kurt Müller, Rudolf Schneeberger, Peter Risi. (Coach: René Hüssy (SUI)).
Goals: Soviet Union: 1-0 Anatoliy Konkov (13'), 2-0 Volodymyr Onyshchenko (14'), 3-1 Volodymyr Onyshchenko (68'), 4-1 Volodymyr Veremeev (81').
Switzerland: 2-1 Peter Risi (45').
Referee: Klaus Ohmsen (FRG)   Attendance: 24.581

23-11-1975   Atatürk Stadi, Izmir: Turkey – Soviet Union   1-0 (1-0)
Turkey: Rasim Kara, Fatih Terim, Ismail Arca (C), Sabahattin Erboga, Kadir Özcan, Turgay Semercioglu, Ali Yavas, Ali Denizci, Cemil Turan, Mehmet Türkkan (88' Hüseyin Nuri Tok), Gökmen Özdenak (89' Orhan Özselek). (Coach: Sabri Kiraz (TUR)).
Soviet Union: Evgeni Rudakov, Mykhailo Fomenko (C), Stefan Reshko, Viktor Zvyagintsev, Valeriy Zuyev, Volodymyr Muntyan (72' Leonid Buryak), Viktor Kolotov (C), Anatoliy Konkov, Volodymyr Veremeev, Oleh Blokhin, Volodymyr Onyshchenko. (Coach: Konstantin Ivanovich Beskov (URS)).
Goal: Turkey: 1-0 Cemil Turan (22').
Referee: Petar Hristov Nikolov (BUL)   Attendance: 21.325

GROUP 7

08-09-1974	Reykjavik	Iceland – Belgium	0-2 (0-1)
12-10-1974	Magdeburg	East Germany – Iceland	1-1 (1-1)
12-10-1974	Brussels	Belgium – France	2-1 (1-1)
16-11-1974	Paris	France – East Germany	2-2 (0-1)
07-12-1974	Leipzig	East Germany – Belgium	0-0
25-05-1975	Reykjavik	Iceland – France	0-0
05-06-1975	Reykjavik	Iceland – East Germany	2-1 (2-0)
03-09-1975	Nantes	France – Iceland	3-0 (1-0)
06-09-1975	Liège	Belgium – Iceland	1-0 (1-0)
27-09-1975	Anderlecht	Belgium – East Germany	1-2 (0-0)
12-10-1975	Leipzig	East Germany – France	2-1 (0-0)
15-11-1975	Paris	France – Belgium	0-0

FINAL STANDING

Pos	Team	Pld	W	D	L	GF	GA	GD	Pts
1	Belgium	6	3	2	1	6	3	+3	8
2	East Germany	6	2	3	1	8	7	+1	7
3	France	6	1	3	2	7	6	+1	5
4	Iceland	6	1	2	3	3	8	-5	4

Belgium qualified for the Quarter-finals.

08-09-1974   Laugardalsvöllur, Reykjavik: Iceland – Belgium   0-2 (0-1)
Iceland: Thorsteinn Olafsson, Gisli Torfason, Jon Pétursson, Marteinn Geirsson, Johannes Edvaldsson (C), Karl Hermannsson, Gudgeir Leifsson, Grétar Magnússon, Ásgeir Sigurvinsson, Ásgeir Elíasson (77' Matthias Hallgrímsson), Teitur Thordarson (YC). (Coach: Anthony (Tony) Knapp (ENG)).
Belgium: Christian Piot, Erwin Vandendaele, Gilbert Van Binst, Ludo Coeck (46' Julien Cools), Wilfried Van Moer, Hugo Broos, Jan Verheyen, Roger Henrotay, François Van Der Elst, Paul Van Himst, Jean Janssens (80' Jacques Teugels). (Coach: Raymond Goethals (BEL)).
Goals: Belgium: 0-1 Wilfried Van Moer (39' penalty), 0-2 Jacques Teugels (87' penalty).
Referee: Thomas Henry Charles Reynolds (WAL)   Attendance: 7.540

12-10-1974   Ernst-Grube-Stadion, Magdeburg: East Germany – Iceland   1-1 (1-1)
East Germany: Ulrich Schulze, Bernd Bransch (C), Konrad Weise, Siegmar Wätzlich (56' Hans-Jürgen Dörner), Martin Hoffmann, Lothar Kurbjuweit, Manfred Zapf (YC), Klaus Decker, Jürgen Pommerenke (70' Eberhard Vogel), Joachim Streich, Peter Ducke. (Coach: Georg Buschner (GDR)).
Iceland: Thorsteinn Olafsson, Gisli Torfason (69' Eirikur Thorsteinsson), Jon Pétursson (YC), Marteinn Geirsson, Johannes Edvaldsson (C), Gudgeir Leifsson, Grétar Magnússon, Ásgeir Sigurvinsson (YC), Ásgeir Elíasson, Teitur Thordarson (Atli Thor Hédinsson), Matthias Hallgrímsson. (Coach: Anthony (Tony) Knapp (ENG)).
Goals: East Germany: 1-0 Martin Hoffmann (7').
Iceland: 1-1 Matthias Hallgrímsson (25').
Referee: Svein Inge Thime (NOR)   Attendance: 8.410

12-10-1974   Stade du Heysel, Brussels: Belgium – France   2-1 (1-1)
Belgium: Christian Piot, Erwin Vandendaele, Maurice Martens (YC76), Gilbert Van Binst, Wilfried Van Moer, Hugo Broos, Jan Verheyen, François Van Der Elst, Paul Van Himst (C) (72' Jean Dockx), Raoul Lambert, Jacques Teugels. (Coach: Raymond Goethals (BEL)). Ludo Coeck (46' Julien Cools), Roger Henrotay, Jean Janssens (80'
France: Dominique Baratelli, Marius Trésor, François Bracci, Jean-François Jodar, Jean-Pierre Adams (YC57), Jean-Marc Guillou, Georges Bereta (C), Henri Michel, Jean-Noël Huck, Bernard Lacombe (YC58) (83' Jean Gallice), Christian Coste. (Coach: Stefan Kovács (ROM)).
Goals: Belgium: 1-0 Maurice Martens (12'), 2-1 François Van Der Elst (75').
France: 1-1 Christian Coste (16').
Referee: Kenneth Howard Burns (ENG)   Attendance: 32.108

117

16-11-1974   Parc des Prince, Paris: France – East Germany   2-2 (0-1)
France: Jean-Paul Bertrand-Demanes, Marius Trésor, François Bracci (YC61), Jean-François Jodar, Jean-Pierre Adams, Jean-Marc Guillou, Georges Bereta (C), Jean-Noël Huck, Henri Michel (68' Christian Synaeghel), Gérard Soler (RC86), Christian Coste (46' Jean Gallice).
(Coach: Stefan Kovács (ROM)).
East Germany: Jürgen Croy (YC65), Konrad Weise, Siegmar Wätzlich, Gerd Kische, Martin Hoffmann, Lothar Kurbjuweit, Hans-Jürgen Dörner, Jürgen Sparwasser (C), Hans-Jürgen Kreische (77' Wolfgang Seguin), Reinhard Lauck, Reinhard Häfner. (Coach: Georg Buschner (GDR)).
Goals: France: 1-2 Jean-Marc Guillou (79'), 2-2 Jean Gallice (88').
East Germany: 0-1 Jürgen Sparwasser (25'), 0-2 Hans-Jürgen Kreische (57').
Referee: Pablo Augusto Sánchez Ibáñez (ESP)   Attendance: 45.381

07-12-1974   Zentralstadion, Leipzig: East Germany – Belgium   0-0
East Germany: Jürgen Croy, Konrad Weise, Siegmar Wätzlich (70' Hans-Jürgen Kreische), Gerd Kische, Martin Hoffmann, Lothar Kurbjuweit, Hans-Jürgen Dörner, Reinhard Lauck, Reinhard Häfner, Joachim Streich (YC42), Eberhard Vogel (C). (Coach: Georg Buschner (GDR)).
Belgium: Christian Piot, Nicolas Dewalque (YC36), Erwin Vandendaele, Maurice Martens, Gilbert Van Binst (YC27), Hugo Broos, Jan Verheyen, Julien Cools, Paul Van Himst (C) (16' François Van Der Elst), Raoul Lambert, Jacques Teugels. (Coach: Raymond Goethals (BEL)).
Referee: Sergio Gonella (ITA)   Attendance: 20.557

25-05-1975   Laugardalsvöllur, Reykjavik: Iceland – France   0-0
Iceland: Sigurdur Dagsson, Gisli Torfason, Jon Pétursson, Marteinn Geirsson, Johannes Edvaldsson, Karl Hermannsson (77' Grétar Magnússon), Gudgeir Leifsson, Ásgeir Sigurvinsson, Ólafur Júliusson, Teitur Thordarson, Matthias Hallgrímsson (55' Elmar Geirsson). (Coach: Anthony (Tony) Knapp (ENG)).
France: Dominique Baratelli, Christian López, Marius Trésor, François Bracci, Jean-Pierre Adams, Jean-Marc Guillou, Georges Bereta (C), Henri Michel, Jean Gallice (75' Patrick Parizon), Jean-Michel Larqué, Marc Berdoll. (Coach: Stefan Kovács (ROM)).
Referee: Malcolm Hall Wright (NIR)   Attendance: 7.613

05-06-1975   Laugardalsvöllur, Reykjavik: Iceland – East Germany   2-1 (2-0)
Iceland: Sigurdur Dagsson, Gisli Torfason, Jon Pétursson, Marteinn Geirsson, Johannes Edvaldsson (C), Gudgeir Leifsson, Ásgeir Sigurvinsson, Ólafur Júliusson, Elmar Geirsson (87' Matthias Hallgrímsson), Hördur Hilmarsson (80' Karl Hermannsson), Teitur Thordarson. (Coach: Anthony (Tony) Knapp (ENG)).
East Germany: Jürgen Croy, Konrad Weise, Siegmar Wätzlich, Gerd Kische, Martin Hoffmann, Lothar Kurbjuweit, Rüdiger Schnuphase (56' Hans-Jürgen Dörner), Manfred Zapf (82' Hans-Jürgen Riediger), Jürgen Pommerenke, Joachim Streich, Eberhard Vogel (C). (Coach: Georg Buschner (GDR)).
Goals: Iceland: 1-0 Johannes Edvaldsson (12'), 2-0 Ásgeir Sigurvinsson (32').
East Germany: 2-1 Jürgen Pommerenke (48').
Referee: Ian M.D.Foote (SCO)   Attendance: 10.373

03-09-1975   Stade Marcel Saupin, Nantes: France – Iceland   3-0 (1-0)
France: Dominique Baratelli, Marius Trésor, François Bracci, Raymond Domenech, Jean-Pierre Adams, Jean-Marc Guillou, Jean-Noël Huck, Henri Michel (C), Marco Molitor (46' Marc Berdoll), Dominique Rocheteau, Albert Emon. (Coach: Stefan Kovács (ROM)).
Iceland: Árni Stefánsson, Gisli Torfason, Jon Pétursson, Marteinn Geirsson, Johannes Edvaldsson (C), Ólafur Sigurvinsson, Gudgeir Leifsson, Ásgeir Sigurvinsson, Hördur Hilmarsson (61' Karl Thordarsson), Teitur Thordarson, Matthias Hallgrímsson (76' Elmar Geirsson). (Coach: Anthony (Tony) Knapp (ENG)).
Goals: France: 1-0 Jean-Marc Guillou (20'), 2-0 Jean-Marc Guillou (74'), 3-0 Marc Berdoll (87').
Referee: Albert Victor (LUX)   Attendance: 25.418

06-09-1975   Stade Sclessin, Liège: Belgium – Iceland   1-0 (1-0)
Belgium: Christian Piot (C), Nicolas Dewalque, Maurice Martens, Gilbert Van Binst, Hugo Broos, Jan Verheyen (61' Ludo Coeck), Julien Cools, Johan Devrindt, Raoul Lambert, Odilon Polleunis, Jacques Teugels. (Coach: Raymond Goethals (BEL)).
Iceland: Árni Stefánsson, Gisli Torfason, Jon Pétursson, Marteinn Geirsson, Ólafur Sigurvinsson, Björn Lárusson, Gudgeir Leifsson, Ásgeir Sigurvinsson (YC53), Elmar Geirsson, Karl Thordarsson (75' Árni Sveinsson), Matthias Hallgrímsson. (Coach: Anthony (Tony) Knapp (ENG)).
Goal: Belgium: 1-0 Raoul Lambert (43').
Referee: Henning Lund-Sørensen (DEN)   Attendance: 9.371

27-09-1975   Stade Émile Versé, Anderlecht: Belgium – East Germany   1-2 (0-0)
Belgium: Christian Piot (C), Nicolas Dewalque, Eric Gerets, Erwin Vanderdaele, Maurice Martens, Ludo Coeck (YC35), Julien Cools, Johan Devrindt, Wilfried Puis, Odilon Polleunis (76' Jean Janssens), Jacques Teugels. (Coach: Raymond Goethals (BEL)).
East Germany: Jürgen Croy (85' Hans-Ulrich Grapenthin), Konrad Weise, Martin Hoffmann, Lothar Kurbjuweit, Hans-Jürgen Dörner (C), Joachim Fritsche, Reinhard Lauck, Reinhard Häfner, Gerd Weber (YC81), Peter Ducke, Hans-Jürgen Riediger. (Coach: Georg Buschner (GDR)).
Goals: Belgium: 1-1 Wilfried Puis (60').
East Germany: 0-1 Peter Ducke (50'), 1-2 Reinhard Häfner (71').
Referee: Nicolae Rainea (ROM)   Attendance: 17.281

12-10-1975   Zentralstadion, Leipzig: East Germany – France   2-1 (0-0)
East Germany: Jürgen Croy, Konrad Weise, Hans-Jürgen Dörner (C), Joachim Fritsche, Reinhard Lauck, Reinhard Häfner, Gerd Weber, Hartmut Schade, Joachim Streich (75' Martin Hoffmann), Eberhard Vogel, Peter Ducke. (Coach: Georg Buschner (GDR)).
France: Dominique Baratelli, Marius Trésor, Gérard Janvion, François Bracci, Jean-Pierre Adams (YC41), Jean-Marc Guillou, Dominique Bathenay (YC71), Henri Michel (C), Jean Gallice, Dominique Rocheteau, Albert Emon. (Coach: Stefan Kovács (ROM)).
Goals: East Germany: 1-1 Joachim Streich (55'), 2-1 Eberhard Vogel (77' penalty).
France: 0-1 Dominique Bathenay (50').
Referee: Erik Fredriksson (SWE)   Attendance: 28.544

119

15-11-1975 Parc des Princes, Paris: France – Belgium 0-0
France: Dominique Baratelli, Raymond Domenech, Marius Trésor, François Bracci, Charles Orlanducci, Jean-Marc Guillou, Jean-Noël Huck (46' Jean-Michel Larqué (RC65)), Dominique Rocheteau, Henri Michel, Christian Coste (82' Jean Gallice), Albert Emon. (Coach: Stefan Kovács (ROM)).
Belgium: Christian Piot (C), Gilbert Van Binst, Jean Dockx, Georges Leekens, Erwin Vanderdaele, Ludo Coeck, Julien Cools, Jan Verheyen, Roger Van Gool, Raoul Lambert, René Vandereycken (82' Jacques Teugels). (Coach: Raymond Goethals (BEL)).
Referee: Robert Holley Davidson (SCO) Attendance: 35.547

GROUP 8

13-10-1974	Sofia	Bulgaria – Greece	3-3 (3-1)
20-11-1974	Piraeus	Greece – West Germany	2-2 (1-0)
18-12-1974	Piraeus	Greece – Bulgaria	2-1 (2-0)
22-12-1974	Gzira	Malta – West Germany	0-1 (0-1)
23-02-1975	Gzira	Malta – Greece	2-0 (1-0)
27-04-1975	Sofia	Bulgaria – West Germany	1-1 (0-0)
04-06-1975	Salonika	Greece – Malta	4-0 (2-0)
11-06-1975	Sofia	Bulgaria – Malta	5-0 (3-0)
11-10-1975	Düsseldorf	West Germany – Greece	1-1 (0-0)
19-11-1975	Stuttgart	West Germany – Bulgaria	1-0 (0-0)
21-12-1975	Gzira	Malta – Bulgaria	0-2 (0-0)
28-02-1976	Dortmund	West Germany – Malta	8-0 (4-0)

FINAL STANDING

Pos	Team	Pld	W	D	L	GF	GA	GD	Pts
1	West Duitsland	6	3	3	0	14	4	+10	9
2	Greece	6	2	3	1	12	9	+3	7
3	Bulgaria	6	2	2	2	12	7	+5	6
4	Malta	6	1	0	5	2	20	-18	2

West Duitsland qualified for the Quarter-finals.

13-10-1974 Vasil Levski Stadium, Sofia: Bulgaria – Greece 3-3 (3-1)
Bulgaria: Stoyan Yordanov, Dimitar Penev (C), Ivan Zafirov, Borislav Dimitrov, Bozhil Kolev, Voin Voynov, Hristo Bonev, Traycho Sokolov (68' Pavel Panov), Georgi Denev, Krasimir Borisov, Chavdar Tsvetkov (60' Todor Barzov). (Coach: Dimitar Doichinov (BUL)).
Greece: Takis Ikonomopoulos, Kostas Iosifidis, Giogos Firos, Christos Terzanidis (YC32), Apostolos Glezos, Thodoros Palas, Giorgos Delikaris, Kostas Eleftherakis, Mimis Papaioannou, Stavros Sarafis (60' Kostas Papaioannou), Antonis Antoniadis (68' Lakis Nikolaou). (Coach: Alketas Panagoulias (GRE)). Not used sub: Lefteris Poupakis (YC86).
Goals: Bulgaria: 1-0 Hristo Bonev (2'), 2-0 Georgi Denev (27'), 3-1 Georgi Denev (29').
Greece: 2-1 Antonis Antoniadis (28'), 3-2 Mimis Papaioannou (86'), 3-3 Apostolos Glezos (88').
Referee: Alberto Michelotti (ITA) Attendance: 14.291

20-11-1974   Stadio Karaiskaki, Piraeus: Greece – West Germany   2-2 (1-0)
Greece: Takis Ikonomopoulos, Kostas Iosifidis, Christos Terzanidis, Vasilis Siokos (YC69), Apostolos Glezos (61' Giogos Firos), Giannis Kirastas, Mimis Domazos (C, Giorgos Delikaris, Kostas Eleftherakis, Mimis Papaioannou (70' Achileas Aslanidis), Stavros Sarafis. (Coach: Alketas Panagoulias (GRE)).
West Germany: Sepp Maier, Berti Vogts, Hans-Georg Schwarzenbeck, Franz Beckenbauer (C), Bernhard Cullmann (76' Hans-Josef Kapellmann), Uli Hoeneß, Helmut Kremers, Jupp Heynckes (78' Josef Pirrung), Bernd Hölzenbein, Herbert Wimmer, Rainer Geye. (Coach: Helmut Schön (FRG)).
Goals: Greece: 1-0 Giorgos Delikaris (12'), 2-1 Kostas Eleftherakis (70').
West Germany: 1-1 Bernhard Cullmann (51'), 2-2 Herbert Wimmer (83').
Referee: Nicolae Rainea (ROM)   Attendance: 11.425

18-12-1974   Stadio Karaiskaki, Piraeus: Greece – Bulgaria   2-1 (2-0)
Greece: Vasilis Konstantinou, Christos Terzanidis, Vasilis Siokos, Apostolos Glezos, Takis Eleftheriadis, Thodoros Palas, Kostas Eleftherakis (YC74), Mimis Papaioannou (C) (75' Giannis Kirastas), Stavros Sarafis, Antonis Antoniadis (YC32), Achileas Aslanidis. (Coach: Alketas Panagoulias (GRE)).
Bulgaria: Yordan Filipov, Tsonyo Vasilev (YC43), Kiril Ivkov (C), Stefan Aladzhov, Bozhil Kolev, Voin Voynov (46' Boris Angelov), Hristo Bonev, Kiril Stankov, Nikolas Hristov (70' Chavdar Tsvetkov), Nikolai Kurbanov, Georgi Denev. (Coach: Stoyan Ormandzhiev (BUL)).
Goals: Greece: 1-0 Stavros Sarafis (4'), 2-0 Antonis Antoniadis (40').
Bulgaria: 2-1 Bozhil Kolev (89').
Referee: Paul Schiller (AUT)   Attendance: 22.328

22-12-1974   Empire Stadium, Gzira: Malta – West Germany   0-1 (0-1)
Malta: Alfred Debono, Anthony Camilleri, Edward Darmanin, John Holland, Joseph Borg (I), Edward Aquilina (50' Richard Aquilina (YC80)), Vincent Magro, William Vassallo (C), Edward Vella, Raymond Xuereb, Carlo Seychell. (Coach: Terenzio Polvertini (MLT)).
West Germany: Norbert Nigbur, Berti Vogts (YC80), Franz Beckenbauer (C), Bernhard Cullmann (75' Rudolf Seliger), Bernhard Dietz, Karl-Heinz Körbel, Heinz Flohe, Rainer Bonhof, Josef Pirrung (46' Bernd Nickel), Bernd Hölzenbein, Erwin Kostedde. (Coach: Helmut Schön (FRG)).
Goal: West Germany: 0-1 Bernhard Cullmann (44').
Referee: Gyula Emsberger (HUN)   Attendance: 12.528

23-02-1975   Empire Stadium, Gzira: Malta – Greece   2-0 (1-0)
Malta: Robert Gatt, Anthony Camilleri, Edward Darmanin, George Ciantar, John Holland, Vincent Magro, David Azzopardi (58' Carlo Seychell), William Vassallo (C), Edward Vella, Richard Aquilina, Raymond Xuereb. (Coach: Terenzio Polvertini (MLT)).
Greece: Vasilis Konstantinou, Kostas Iosifidis, Giorgos Firos, Vasilis Siokos, Thodoros Palas, Mimis Domazos (C), Michalis Kritikopoulos, Dimitris Dimitriou (30' Dimitris Paridis, 75' Lakis Nikolaou), Mimis Papaioannou, Stavros Sarafis, Antonis Antoniadis (YC79). (Coach: Alketas Panagoulias (GRE)).
Goals: Malta: 1-0 Richard Aquilina (33'), 2-0 Vincent Magro (70').
Referee: Robert (Bob) Matthewson (ENG)   Attendance: 8.621

27-04-1975   Vasil Levski Stadium, Sofia: Bulgaria – West Germany   1-1 (0-0)
Bulgaria: Yordan Filipov, Ivan Zafirov (C), Borislav Dimitrov, Todor Marev, Milcho Evtimov, Angel Rangelov (YC), Andrey Zhelyaskov, Bozhil Kolev, Atanas Aleksandrov (58' Radoslav Zdravkov), Georgi Denev (YC), Pavel Panov. (Coach: Stoyan Ormandzhiev (BUL)).
West Germany: Sepp Maier, Berti Vogts, Hans-Georg Schwarzenbeck, Franz Beckenbauer (C), Paul Breitner, Uli Hoeneß (74' Karl-Heinz Körbel), Günther Netzer, Rainer Bonhof, Manfred Ritschel, Wolfgang Seel, Jupp Heynckes (34' Bernd Hölzenbein). (Coach: Helmut Schön (FRG)).
Goals: Bulgaria: 1-0 Bozhil Kolev (73' penalty).
West Germany: 1-1 Manfred Ritschel (75' penalty).
Referee: Jean Dubach (SUI)   Attendance: 47.200

04-06-1975   Stadio Toumbas, Thessaloniki: Greece – Malta   4-0 (2-0)
Greece: Stelios Papafloratos, Kostas Iosifidis, Giorgos Firos, Thodoros Palas, Filotas Pellios (80' Lakis Nikolaou), Angelos Anastasiadis, Thomas Mavros, Mimis Papaioannou, Antonis Antoniadis (75' Nikos Kalambakas), Achileas Aslanidis, Koulis Apostolidis. (Coach: Alketas Panagoulias (GRE)).
Malta: Robert Gatt (70' Alfred Debono), Edward Darmanin, Edwin Farrugia, John Holland, Joseph Borg (I), Vincent Magro (YC31), David Azzopardi, William Vassallo (C), Richard Aquilina, Raymond Xuereb (7' George Ciantar), Carlo Seychell. (Coach: Terenzio Polvertini (MLT)).
Goals: Greece: 1-0 Thomas Mavros (32'), 2-0 Antonis Antoniadis (34' penalty), 3-0 Kostas Iosifidis (47'), 4-0 Mimis Papaioannou (50').
Referee: Marijan Raus (YUG)   Attendance: 16.545

11-06-1975   Vasil Levski Stadium, Sofia: Bulgaria – Malta   5-0 (3-0)
Bulgaria: Yordan Filipov, Ivan Zafirov, Borislav Dimitrov, Todor Marev, Milcho Evtimov, Andrey Zhelyaskov, Hristo Bonev, Nikolai Kurbanov (46' Atanas Aleksandrov), Kostas Isakidis (59' Kiril Milanov), Georgi Denev, Pavel Panov. (Coach: Stoyan Ormandzhiev (BUL)).
Malta: Alfred Debono, Edward Darmanin, George Ciantar, Edwin Farrugia, John Holland, Joseph Borg (I), Edward Aquilina (68' Raymond Xuereb), Vincent Magro, William Vassallo (C), Edward Vella, Richard Aquilina. (Coach: Terenzio Polvertini (MLT)).
Goals: Bulgaria: 1-0 Borislav Dimitrov (2'), 2-0 Georgi Denev (22'), 3-0 Pavel Panov (25'), 4-0 Hristo Bonev (68' penalty), 5-0 Kiril Milanov (71').
Referee: Michal Jursa (TCH)   Attendance: 17.256

11-10-1975   Rheinstadion, Düsseldorf: West Germany – Greece   1-1 (0-0)
West Germany: Sepp Maier, Manfred Kaltz, Berti Vogts, Franz Beckenbauer (C), Karl-Heinz Körbel, Paul Breitner, Günther Netzer, Erich Beer, Jupp Heynckes, Bernd Hölzenbein, Erwin Kostedde. (Coach: Helmut Schön (FRG)).
Greece: Panagiotis Kelesidis, Giorgos Firos, Christos Terzanidis (YC60), Dimitrios Sinetopoulos (46' Koulis Apostolidis), Thodoros Palas, Giannis Kirastas, Giorgos Koudas (86' Achileas Aslanidis), Michalis Kritikopoulos, Giorgos Delikaris, Mimis Papaioannou, Stavros Sarafis. (Coach: Alketas Panagoulias (GRE)).
Goals: West Germany: 1-0 Jupp Heynckes (67').
Greece: 1-1 Giorgos Delikaris (79').
Referee: Clive Thomas (WAL)   Attendance: 61.252

19-11-1975   Neckarstadion, Stuttgart: West Germany – Bulgaria   1-0 (0-0)
West Germany: Sepp Maier, Berti Vogts, Hans-Georg Schwarzenbeck, Franz Beckenbauer (C), Bernhard Dietz, Uli Stieleke, Erich Beer, Dietmar Danner, Jupp Heynckes, Bernd Hölzenbein, Herbert Wimmer. (Coach: Helmut Schön (FRG)).
Bulgaria: Yordan Filipov, Tsonyo Vasilev, Kiril Ivkov, Ivan Zafirov, Angel Rangelov, Bozhil Kolev (72' Pavel Panov), Hristo Bonev (C), Boris Angelov, Atanas Aleksandrov (75' Voin Voynov), Chavdar Tsvetkov, Kiril Milanov. (Coach: Stoyan Ormandzhiev (BUL)).
Goal: West Germany: 1-0 Jupp Heynckes (64').
Referee: Alistair McKenzie (SCO)   Attendance: 68.819

21-12-1975   Empire Stadium, Gzira: Malta – Bulgaria   0-2 (0-0)
Malta: Alfred Debono, Edward Darmanin, Edwin Farrugia, Sunny Gouder (90' Edward Vella), John Holland, Edward Aquilina, Vincent Magro (46' Christopher Vella), David Azzopardi, William Vassallo (C), Richard Aquilina, Carlo Seychell. (Coach: Terenzio Polvertini (MLT)).
Bulgaria: Georgi Tihanov, Tsonyo Vasilev, Kiril Ivkov, Ivan Zafirov (46' Stoyan Yordanov), Angel Rangelov, Voin Voynov, Hristo Bonev (C), Boris Angelov, Pavel Panov, Chavdar Tsvetkov (65' Atanas Aleksandrov), Kiril Milanov. (Coach: Stoyan Ormandzhiev (BUL)).
Goals: Bulgaria: 0-1 Pavel Panov (69'), 0-2 Stoyan Yordanov (88').
Referee: Norbert Rolles (LUX)   Attendance: 7.174

28-02-1976   Westfalenstadion, Dortmund: West Germany – Malta   8-0 (4-0)
West Germany: Sepp Maier, Berti Vogts, Hans-Georg Schwarzenbeck, Franz Beckenbauer (C), Bernhard Dietz, Uli Stieleke (46' Bernhard Cullmann), Erich Beer, Jupp Heynckes, Bernd Hölzenbein, Herbert Wimmer (57' Hans Bongartz), Ronald Worm. (Coach: Helmut Schön (FRG)).
Malta: Charles Sciberras, Edwin Farrugia, Sunny Gouder, Oliver Losco, Dennis Fenech, John Holland, Vincent Magro (46' Carlo Seychell), Mario Loporto (28' Edward Aquilina), William Vassallo (C), Richard Aquilina, Raymond Xuereb. (Coach: Terenzio Polvertini (MLT)).
Goals: West Germany: 1-0 Ronald Worm (6'), 2-0 Ronald Worm (27'), 3-0 Jupp Heynckes (34'), 4-0 Erich Beer (41'), 5-0 Jupp Heynckes (58'), 6-0 Erich Beer (77' penalty), 7-0 Berti Vogts (82'), 8-0 Bernd Hölzenbein (87').
Referee: Marian Kuston (POL)   Attendance: 52.248

QUARTER-FINALS

24-04-1975   Stadion Maksimir, Zagreb: Yugoslavia – Wales   2-0 (1-0)
Yugoslavia: Ognjen Petrovic, Ivan Buljan (C), Dzemal Hadziabdic, Drazen Muzinic (YC57), Josip Katalinski, Branko Oblak, Jovan Acimovic, Danilo Popivoda, Ivan Surjak, Momcilo Vukotic (60' Jurica Jerkovic), Drago Vabec. (Coach: Ante Mladinic (YUG)).
Wales: Dai Davies, Rod Thomas, Leighton Phillips, Malcolm Page, Ian Evans, John Mahoney, Arfon Griffiths, Brian Flynn, John Toshack, Terry Yorath (C), Leighton James (83' Alan Curtis). (Coach: Michael John (Mike) Smith (ENG)).
Goals: Yugoslavia: 1-0 Momcilo Vukotic (1'), 2-0 Danilo Popivoda (54').
Referee: Paul Schiller (AUT)   Attendance: 36.917

24-04-1976   Stadión Tehelné pole, Bratislava: Czechoslovakia – Soviet Union   2-0 (1-0)
Czechoslovakia: Ivo Viktor, Karol Dobias, Anton Ondrus (C), Koloman Gögh, Antonín Panenka, Jaroslav Pollák, Jozef Capkovic, Jozef Móder (81' Lubomír Knapp), Zdenek Nehoda, Marián Masny, Ladislav Petrás (66' Karel Kroupa). (Coach: Vaclav Jezek (TCH)).
Soviet Union: Aleksandr Prokhorov, Volodymyr Troshkin, Viktor Matviyenko, Mykhailo Fomenko, Stefan Reshko, Viktor Zvyagintsev, Evgeni Lovchev (72' Volodymyr Veremeev), Viktor Kolotov (C), Anatoliy Konkov, Oleh Blokhin, Volodymyr Onyshchenko (78' Leonid Nazarenko). (Coach: Valeriy Vasylyovych Lobanovskiy (URS)).
Goals: Czechoslovakia: 1-0 Jozef Móder (34'), 2-0 Antonín Panenka (47').
Referee: Hilmi Ok (TUR)   Attendance: 47.621

24-04-1976   Estadio Vicente Calderón, Madrid: Spain – West Germany   1-1 (1-0)
Spain: José Ángel IRIBAR Cortajarena, JOSÉ Antonio CAMACHO Alfaro, Miguel Bernardo Bianquetti "MIGUELI" (81' Jesús María SATRÚSTEGUI Azpiroz), JUAN Cruz SOL Oria (C), Gregorio BENITO Rubio (YC83), JOSÉ Luis CAPÓN González, Vicente DEL BOSQUE, Ángel María VILLAR Llona, Enrique Castro González "QUINI" (81' Sebastián ALABANDA González), Carlos Alonso González "SANTILLANA", José Ignacio CHURRUCA Sistiaga. (Coach: László "LADISLAO" KUBALA Stecz (ESP)).
West Germany: Sepp Maier, Berti Vogts, Hans-Georg Schwarzenbeck (46' Bernhard Cullmann), Franz Beckenbauer (C), Bernhard Dietz (YC35) (81' Peter Reichel), Rainer Bonhof, Erich Beer, Dietmar Danner, Bernd Hölzenbein, Herbert Wimmer, Ronald Worm. (Coach: Helmut Schön (FRG)).
Goals: Spain: 1-0 Carlos Alonso González "SANTILLANA" (1').
West Germany: 1-1 Erich Beer (60').
Referee: John Keith (Jack) Taylor (ENG)   Attendance: 51.771

25-04-1976   Stadion Feijenoord, Rotterdam: Netherlands – Belgium   5-0 (2-0)
Netherlands: Piet Schrijvers, Wim Rijsbergen (YC65), Wim Suurbier, Adrie van Kraay, Ruud Krol, Wim Jansen, Johan Cruijff (C), Johan Neeskens (84' Jan Peters), Rob Rensenbrink, Johnny Rep, Willy van de Kerkhof. (Coach: George Knobel (HOL)).
Belgium: Christian Piot (C), Eric Gerets, Maurice Martens, Gilbert Van Binst, René Vandereycken, Ludo Coeck, Georges Leekens, Jan Verheyen (YC), Julien Cools (46' François Van Der Elst (YC)), Raoul Lambert (83' Jacques Teugels), Roger Van Gool. (Coach: Raymond Goethals (BEL)).
Goals: Netherlands: 1-0 Wim Rijsbergen (17'), 2-0 Rob Rensenbrink (27'), 3-0 Rob Rensenbrink (58'), 4-0 Johan Neeskens (79' penalty), 5-0 Rob Rensenbrink (85').
Referee: Jean Dubach (SUI)   Attendance: 48.706

22-05-1976   Ninian Park, Cardiff: Wales – Yugoslavia   1-1 (1-1)
Wales: Dai Davies, Leighton Phillips (YC), Malcolm Page, David Roberts, Ian Evans, John Mahoney, Arfon Griffiths (67' Alan Curtis), Brian Flynn (YC), John Toshack, Terry Yorath (C) (YC), Leighton James. (Coach: Michael John (Mike) Smith (ENG)).
Yugoslavia: Enver Maric, Ivan Buljan (C), Drazen Muzinic, Josip Katalinski, Dzemal Hadziabdic, Branko Oblak, Danilo Popivoda, Jurica Jerkovic (YC), Ivan Surjak, Borislav Djordjevic, Slavisa Zungul (61' Franjo Vladic). (Coach: Ante Mladinic (YUG)).
Goals: Wales: 1-1 Ian Evans (38').
Yugoslavia: 0-1 Josip Katalinski (19').
Referee: Rudolf (Rudi) Glöckner (GDR)   Attendance: 30.346

22-05-1976   Olympiastadion, Munich: West Germany – Spain   2-0 (2-0)
West Germany: Sepp Maier, Berti Vogts, Hans-Georg Schwarzenbeck, Franz Beckenbauer (C), Bernhard Dietz, Uli Hoeneß, Rainer Bonhof, Erich Beer, Bernd Hölzenbein, Herbert Wimmer, Klaus Toppmöller. (Coach: Helmut Schön (FRG)).
Spain: MIGUEL ÁNGEL González Suarez, JOSÉ Antonio CAMACHO Alfaro (YC51), JUAN Cruz SOL Oria (17' Ignacio CORTABARRÍA Abarrategui), JOSÉ Luis CAPÓN González, Juan Manuel ASENSI Ripoll, José Martinez Sanchez "PIRRI" (C) (YC44), Vicente DEL BOSQUE, Ángel María VILLAR Llona (46' José Antonio RAMOS Huete), Enrique Castro González "QUINI", Carlos Alonso González "SANTILLANA", José Ignacio CHURRUCA Sistiaga. (Coach: László "LADISLAO" KUBALA Stecz (ESP)).
Goals: West Germany: 1-0 Uli Hoeneß (17'), 2-0 Klaus Toppmöller (43').
Referee: Robert Charles Paul Wurtz (FRA)   Attendance: 77.673

22-05-1976   NSK Olimpiyskyi, Kiev: Soviet Union – Czechoslovakia   2-2 (0-1)
Soviet Union: Evgeni Rudakov, Volodymyr Troshkin (YC37), Mykhailo Fomenko (C), Viktor Zvyagintsev, Evgeni Lovchev, Volodymyr Muntyan (56' Aleksandr Minaev), Anatoliy Konkov, Volodymyr Veremeev, Leonid Buryak, Oleh Blokhin, Volodymyr Onyshchenko. (Coach: Valeriy Vasylyovych Lobanovskiy (URS)).
Czechoslovakia: Ivo Viktor, Karol Dobias, Anton Ondrus (C), Ján Pivarník, Koloman Gögh (80' Ladislav Jurkemik), Jaroslav Pollák, Jozef Capkovic, Jozef Móder (YC60), Zdenek Nehoda, Marián Masny, Dusan Galis (86' Ján Svehlík). (Coach: Vaclav Jezek (TCH)).
Goals: Soviet Union: 1-1 Leonid Buryak (53'), 2-2 Oleh Blokhin (87').
Czechoslovakia: 0-1 Jozef Móder (45'), 1-2 Jozef Móder (82').
Referee: Alistair McKenzie (SCO)   Attendance: 76.495

22-05-1976   Stade Roi Baudouin, Brussels: Belgium – Netherlands   1-2 (1-0)
Belgium: Jean-Marie Pfaff, Michel Renquin, Maurice Martens (C) (YC49), Gilbert Van Binst, René Vandereycken, Robert Dalving, René Verheyen, Julien Cools, Willy Wellens, François Van Der Elst, Roger Van Gool (65' Hervé Delesie (YC83)). (Coach: Guy Jean Léonard Thijs (BEL)).
Netherlands: Piet Schrijvers, Wim Rijsbergen, Wim Suurbier, Adrie van Kraay, Ruud Krol, Wim van Hanegem (80' Jan Peters), Johan Cruijff (C), Johan Neeskens, Rob Rensenbrink, Johnny Rep, Willy van de Kerkhof. (Coach: George Knobel (HOL)).
Goals: Belgium: 1-0 Roger Van Gool (27').
Netherlands: 1-1 Johnny Rep (62'), 1-2 Johan Cruijff (78').
Referee: Alberto Michelotti (ITA)   Attendance: 19.050

FINAL TOURNAMENT IN YUGOSLAVIA

SEMI-FINALS

16-06-1976   Maksimir Stadium, Zagreb:
Czechoslovakia – Netherlands   3-1 (1-0, 1-1) (AET)
Czechoslovakia: Ivo Viktor, Karol Dobias (YC102), Anton Ondrus (C), Ján Pivarník, Koloman Gögh, Antonín Panenka, Jaroslav Pollák (YC51,YC60), Jozef Capkovic (106' Ladislav Jurkemik), Jozef Móder (91' Frantisek Vesely), Zdenek Nehoda, Marián Masny. (Coach: Vaclav Jezek (TCH)).
Netherlands: Piet Schrijvers, Wim Rijsbergen (37' Wim van Hanegem (RC115)), Wim Suurbier, Adrie van Kraay, Ruud Krol, Wim Jansen, Johan Cruijff (C) (YC), Johan Neeskens (RC76), Rob Rensenbrink, Johnny Rep (65' Ruud Geels), Willy van de Kerkhof (YC57). (Coach: George Knobel (HOL)).
Goals: Czechoslovakia: 1-0 Anton Ondrus (19'), 2-1 Zdenek Nehoda (114'), 3-1 Frantisek Vesely (118').
Netherlands: 1-1 Anton Ondrus (73' *own goal*).
Referee: Clive Thomas (WAL)   Attendance: 17.969

17-06-1976   Crvena Zvezda Stadium, Belgrade:
Yugoslavia – West Germany   2-4 (2-0, 2-2) (AET)
Yugoslavia: Ognjen Petrovic, Ivan Buljan, Drazen Muzinic, Josip Katalinski, Branko Oblak (105' Franjo Vladic), Jovan Acimovic (C) (105' Luka Peruzovic), Danilo Popivoda, Jurica Jerkovic, Ivan Surjak, Dragan Dzajic, Slavisa Zungul. (Coach: Ante Mladinic (YUG)).
West Germany: Sepp Maier, Berti Vogts, Hans-Georg Schwarzenbeck, Franz Beckenbauer (C), Bernhard Dietz, Uli Hoeneß, Rainer Bonhof, Erich Beer, Dietmar Danner (46' Heinz Flohe), Bernd Hölzenbein, Herbert Wimmer (79' Dieter Müller). (Coach: Helmut Schön (FRG)).
Goals: Yugoslavia: 1-0 Danilo Popivoda (19'), 2-0 Dragan Dzajic (30').
West Duitsland: 2-1 Heinz Flohe (64'), 2-2 Dieter Müller (82'), 2-3 Dieter Müller (115'), 2-4 Dieter Müller (119').
Referee: Alfred (Fred) Delcourt (BEL)   Attendance: 50.562

THIRD PLACE PLAY-OFF

19-06-1976   Maksimir Stadium, Zagreb: Netherlands – Yugoslavia   3-2 (2-1, 2-2) (AET)
Netherlands: Piet Schrijvers, Wim Suurbier, Adrie van Kraay, Ruud Krol (C), Wim Jansen (46' Wim Meutstege), Peter Arntz (70' Kees Kist), Jan Peters, Rob Rensenbrink, René van de Kerkhof, Willy van de Kerkhof, Ruud Geels. (Coach: George Knobel (HOL)).
Yugoslavia: Ognjen Petrovic, Ivan Buljan, Drazen Muzinic, Josip Katalinski, Branko Oblak, Jovan Acimovic (C) (46' Franjo Vladic), Danilo Popivoda, Jurica Jerkovic, Ivan Surjak, Dragan Dzajic, Slavisa Zungul (46' Vahid Halilhodzic). (Coach: Ante Mladinic (YUG)).
Goals: Netherlands: 1-0 Ruud Geels (27'), 2-0 Willy van de Kerkhof (39'), 3-2 Ruud Geels (107').
Yugoslavia: 2-1 Josip Katalinski (43'), 2-2 Dragan Dzajic (82').
Referee: Walter Hungerbühler (SUI)   Attendance: 6.766

FINAL

29-06-1976 Crvena Zvezda Stadium, Belgrade:
Czechoslovakia – West Germany 2-2 (2-1, 2-2) (AET)
Czechoslovakia: Ivo Viktor, Karol Dobias (YC55) (109' Frantisek Vesely), Anton Ondrus (C), Ján Pivarník, Koloman Gögh, Antonín Panenka, Jozef Capkovic, Jozef Móder (YC59), Zdenek Nehoda, Marián Masny, Ján Svehlík (80' Ladislav Jurkemik). (Coach: Vaclav Jezek (TCH)).
West Germany: Sepp Maier, Berti Vogts, Hans-Georg Schwarzenbeck, Franz Beckenbauer (C), Bernhard Dietz, Uli Hoeneß, Rainer Bonhof, Erich Beer (80' Hans Bongartz), Bernd Hölzenbein, Herbert Wimmer (46' Heinz Flohe), Dieter Müller. (Coach: Helmut Schön (FRG)).
Goals: Czechoslovakia: 1-0 Ján Svehlík (8'), 2-0 Karol Dobias (25').
West Germany: 2-1 Dieter Müller (28'), 2-2 Bernd Hölzenbein (89').
Referee: Sergio Gonella (ITA)   Attendance: 30.790
Penalties: 1 Marián Masny   1 Rainer Bonhof
                2 Zdenek Nehoda   2 Heinz Flohe
                3 Anton Ondrus   3 Hans Bongartz
                4 Ladislav Jurkemik * Uli Hoeneß
                5 Antonín Panenka
(After extra time Czechoslovakia won 5-3 on penalties)

*** **Czechoslovakia were European Champions** ***

GOALSCORERS TOURNAMENT 1974-1976:

Goals	Players
8	Daniel Givens (IRL)
6	Tibor Nyilasi (HUN)
5	Hans Krankl (AUT), Malcolm MacDonald (ENG), Johan Cruijff (HOL), Zdenek Nehoda (TCH), Josip Katalinski (YUG)
4	Jupp Heynckes (FRG), Dieter Müller (FRG), Rob Rensenbrink (HOL), Zoltan Crisan (ROM), Dudu Georgescu (ROM), Antonín Panenka (TCH), Arfon Griffiths (URS)
3	Georgi Denev (BUL), Mick Channon (ENG), Carlos Alonso González "SANTILLANA" (ESP), Jean-Marc Guillou (FRA), Erich Beer (FRG), Antonis Antoniadis (GRE), Ruud Geels (HOL), Willy van der Kuijlen (HOL), Johan Neeskens (HOL), Gilbert Dussier (LUX), Thomas Lund (NOR), Grzegorz Lato (POL), Andrzej Szarmach (POL), Premysl Bicovsky (TCH), Jozef Móder (TCH), Oleh Blokhin (URS), Viktor Kolotov (URS), John Toshack (WAL)
2	Kurt Welzl (AUT), Hristo Bonev (BUL), Bozhil Kolev (BUL), Pavel Panov (BUL), Colin Bell (ENG), Enrique Castro González "QUINI" (ESP), Timo Rahja (FIN), Bernhard Cullmann (FRG), Bernd Hölzenbein (FRG), Ronald Worm (FRG), Giorgos Delikaris (GRE), Mimis Papaioannou (GRE), Willy van de Kerkhof (HOL), László Nagy (HUN), Nico Braun (LUX), Paul Philipp (LUX), Bryan Hamilton (NIR), Robert Gadocha (POL), Tamagnini

1	Manuel Gomes Batista "NENÉ" (POR), Bruce Rioch (SCO), Kurt Müller (SUI), Thomas Nordahl (SWE), Thomas Sjöberg (SWE), Marián Masny (TCH), Anton Ondrus (TCH), Volodymyr Onyshchenko (URS), Leighton James (WAL), Dragan Dzajic (YUG), Branko Oblak (YUG), Danilo Popivoda (YUG), Momcilo Vukotic (YUG)
	Kurt Jara (AUT), Helmut Köglberger (AUT), Wilhelm Kreuz (AUT), Herbert Prohaska (AUT), François Van Der Elst (BEL), Roger Van Gool (BEL), Raoul Lambert (BEL), Maurice Martens (BEL), Wilfried Van Moer (BEL), Wilfried Puis (BEL), Jacques Teugels (BEL), Borislav Dimitrov (BUL), Kiril Milanov (BUL), Stoyan Yordanov (BUL), Lars Bastrup (DEN), Peter Dahl (DEN), Kristen Nygaard (DEN), Kevin Keegan (ENG), José CLARAMUNT Torres (ESP), JOSÉ Luis CAPÓN González (ESP), Alfredo MEGIDO Sánchez (ESP), Juan ROBERTO MARTÍNEZ Martínez (ESP), Manuel VELÁZQUEZ Villaverde (ESP), Ángel María VILLAR Llona (ESP), Matti Paatelainen (FIN), Dominique Bathenay (FRA), Marc Berdoll (FRA), Christian Coste (FRA), Jean Gallice (FRA), Heinz Flohe (FRG), Uli Hoeneß (FRG), Manfred Ritschel (FRG), Klaus Toppmöller (FRG), Berti Vogts (FRG), Herbert Wimmer (FRG), Peter Ducke (GDR), Reinhard Häfner (GDR), Martin Hoffmann (GDR), Hans-Jürgen Kreische (GDR), Hans-Jürgen Kreische (GDR), Jürgen Sparwasser (GDR), Joachim Streich (GDR), Eberhard Vogel (GDR), Kostas Eleftherakis (GRE), Apostolos Glezos (GRE), Kostas Iosifidis (GRE), Thomas Mavros (GRE), Stavros Sarafis (GRE), Harry Lubse (HOL), Johnny Rep (HOL), Wim Rijsbergen (HOL), Frans Thijssen (HOL), László Bálint (HUN), László Branikovits (HUN), József Horváth (HUN), Sándor Pintér (HUN), László Pusztai (HUN), Béla Várady (HUN), Tibor Wollek (HUN), Eoin Hand (IRL), Michael Martin (IRL), Ray Treacy (IRL), Johannes Edvaldsson (ISL), Matthias Hallgrímsson (ISL), Ásgeir Sigurvinsson (ISL), Roberto Boninsegna (ITA), Fabio Capello (ITA), Giorgio Chinagli (ITA), Richard Aquilina (MLT), Vincent Magro (MLT), Tommy Finney (MLT), Allan Hunter (NIR), Sammy McIlroy (NIR), Sammy Morgan (NIR), Chris Nicholl (NIR), Martin O'Neill (NIR), Erik Just Olsen (NOR), Stein Thunberg (NOR), Henry Kasperczak (POL), JOÃO António Ferreira Resende ALVES (POR), MÁRIO Jorge MOÍNHOS Matos (POR), RUI de Gouveia Pinto RODRIGUES (POR), Cornel Dinu (ROM), Anghel Iordanescu (ROM), Mircea Lucescu (ROM), Billy Bremner (SCO), Kenny Dalglish (SCO), Joe Harper (SCO), Joe Jordan (SCO), Ted MacDougall (SCO), Gordon McQueen (SCO), Rudolf Elsener (SUI), Peter Risi (SUI), Hanspeter Schild (SUI), Ralf Edström (SWE), Ove Grahn (SWE), Roland Sandberg (SWE), Conny Torstensson (SWE), Karol Dobias (TCH), Dusan Galis (TCH), Ladislav Petrás (TCH), Ján Svehlík (TCH), Frantisek Vesely (TCH), Ismail Arca (TUR), Alpaslan Eratli (TUR), Mehmet Oguz (TUR), Cemil Turan (TUR), Leonid Buryak (URS), Anatoliy Konkov (URS), Volodymyr Muntyan (URS), Volodymyr Veremeev (URS), Mike England (WAL), Ian Evans (WAL), John Mahoney (WAL), Gil Reece (WAL), Phil Roberts (WAL), Terry Yorath (WAL), Vladislav Bogicevic (YUG), Ivan Buljan (YUG), Zvonko Ivezic (YUG), Ivan Surjak (YUG), Drago Vabec (YUG), Franjo Vladic (YUG)
1 own goal	Tony Dunne (IRL) for Turkey, Anton Ondrus for Netherlands

1980 UEFA European Football Championship

QUALIFYING ROUND

GROUP 1

24-05-1978	Copenhagen	Denmark – Republic of Ireland	3-3 (1-2)
20-09-1978	Dublin	Republic of Ireland – Norhtern Ireland	0-0
20-09-1978	Copenhagen	Denmark – England	3-4 (2-2)
11-10-1978	Copenhagen	Denmark – Bulgaria	2-2 (1-1)
25-10-1978	Dublin	Republic of Ireland – England	1-1 (1-1)
25-10-1978	Belfast	Northern Ireland – Denmark	2-1 (0-0)
29-11-1978	Sofia	Bulgaria – Northern Ireland	0-2 (0-1)
07-02-1979	London	England – Northern Ireland	4-0 (1-0)
02-05-1979	Dublin	Republic of Ireland – Denmark	2-0 (1-0)
02-05-1979	Belfast	Northern Ireland – Bulgaria	2-0 (2-0)
19-05-1979	Sofia	Bulgaria – Republic of Ireland	1-0 (0-0)
06-06-1979	Sofia	Bulgaria – England	0-3 (0-1)
06-06-1979	Copenhagen	Denmark – Northern Ireland	4-0 (2-0)
12-09-1979	London	England – Denmark	1-0 (1-0)
17-10-1979	Dublin	Republic of Ireland – Bulgaria	3-0 (1-0)
17-10-1979	Belfast	Northern Ireland – England	1-5 (0-2)
31-10-1979	Sofia	Bulgaria – Denmark	3-0 (1-0)
21-11-1979	Belfast	Northern Ireland – Republic of Ireland	1-0 (0-0)
22-11-1979	London	England – Bulgaria	2-0 (1-0)
06-02-1980	London	England – Republic of Ireland	2-0 (1-0)

FINAL STANDING

Pos	Team	Pld	W	D	L	GF	GA	GD	Pts
1	*England*	*8*	*7*	*1*	*0*	*22*	*5*	*+17*	*15*
2	Northern Ireland	8	4	1	3	8	14	-6	9
3	Republic of Ireland	8	2	3	3	9	8	+1	7
4	Bulgaria	8	2	1	5	6	14	-8	5
5	Denmark	8	1	2	5	13	17	-4	4

England qualified for the final tournament in Italy.

24-05-1978   Parken Stadium, Copenhagen: Denmark – Republic of Ireland   3-3 (1-2)
Denmark: Birger Jensen, Morten Olsen (75' Jan Højland), Johnny Hansen, Henning Munk Jensen, Per Røntved, Søren Lerby, Jan Sørensen, Kristen Nygaard (66' Frank Arnesen), Benny Nielsen, Jørgen Kristensen, Henning Jensen. (Coach: Kurt Børge Nikolaj Nielsen (DEN)).
Republic of Ireland: Mick Kearns, David O'Leary, Paddy Mulligan, Jimmy Holmes (52' Eamonn Gregg), Mark Lawrenson, John Giles, Steve Heighway, Gerry Daly, Tony Grealish, Frank Stapleton, Daniel Givens (46' Paul McGee). (Player-coach: Michael John (Johnny) Giles (IRL)).
Goals: Denmark: 1-2 Henning Munk Jensen (33'), 2-3 Benny Nielsen (79' penalty), 3-3 Søren Lerby (80').
Republic of Ireland: 0-1 Frank Stapleton (11'), 0-2 Tony Grealish (25'), 1-3 Gerry Daly (65').
Referee: Johannes Frederik (Jan) Beck (HOL)   Attendance: 28.900

20-09-1978   Lansdowne Road, Dublin: Republic of Ireland – Northern Ireland   0-0
Republic of Ireland: Mick Kearns, Jimmy Holmes, Mark Lawrenson, Noel Synnott, John Giles (C), Steve Heighway (63' Daniel Givens), Liam Brady, Gerry Daly, Tony Grealish, Frank Stapleton (54' Micky Walsh), Paul McGee. (Player-coach: Michael John (Johnny) Giles (IRL)).
Northern Ireland: Pat Jennings, Jimmy Nicholl, Chris Nicholl, Sammy Nelson, Allan Hunter (72' Bryan Hamilton), Pat Rice, David McCreery, Sammy McIlroy, Martin O'Neill, Gerry Armstrong, Derek Spence (69' Terry Cochrane). (Coach: Robert Dennis (Danny) Blanchflower (NIR)).
Goals: Francis Elisa Rion (BEL)   Attendance: 37.681

20-09-1978   Parken Stadium, Copenhagen: Denmark – England   3-4 (2-2)
Denmark: Birger Jensen, Henning Munk Jensen, Per Røntved, Flemming Nielsen, Frank Arnesen, Søren Lerby, Flemming Lund, Carsten Nielsen, Allan Simonsen, Benny Nielsen (46' Allan Hansen), Jørgen Kristensen. (Coach: Kurt Børge Nikolaj Nielsen (DEN)).
England: Ray Clemence, Mick Mills, Phil Neal, Dave Watson, Steve Coppell, Ray Wilkins, Trevor Brooking, Emlyn Hughes, Peter Barnes, Kevin Keegan, Bob Latchford. (Coach: Ronald (Ron) Greenwood (ENG)).
Goals: Denmark: 1-2 Allan Simonsen (23' penalty), 2-2 Frank Arnesen (28'), 3-3 Per Røntved (86').
England: 0-1 Kevin Keegan (17'), 0-2 Kevin Keegan (22'), 2-3 Bob Latchford (51'), 2-4 Phil Neal (84').
Referee: Adolf Prokop (GDR)   Attendance: 47.600

11-10-1978   Parken Stadium, Copenhagen: Denmark – Bulgaria   2-2 (1-1)
Denmark: Ole Kjær, Morten Olsen, Per Røntved, Flemming Nielsen, Frank Arnesen, Søren Lerby, Flemming Lund, Lars Larsen, Heino Hansen, Benny Nielsen (YC), Jørgen Kristensen. (Coach: Kurt Børge Nikolaj Nielsen (DEN)).
Bulgaria: Rumyancho Goranov, Radoslav Zdravkov, Plamen Nikolov, Petar Stankov, Georgi Bonev, Nikolai Grancharov (11' Ivan Iliev), Anguel Stankov, Stoicho Mladenov, Pavel Panov, Roussi Gochev, Gueorgui Slavkov (80' Alexandre Ivanov). (Coach: Zvetan Iltchev (BUL)).
Goals: Denmark: 1-0 Benny Nielsen (17'), 2-1 Søren Lerby (63').
Bulgaria: 1-1 Pavel Panov (34'), 2-2 Ivan Iliev (84').
Referee: Ángel Franco Martínez (ESP)   Attendance: 15.800

25-10-1978   Lansdowne Road, Dublin: Republic of Ireland – England   1-1 (1-1)
Republic of Ireland: Mick Kearns, David O'Leary (74' Eamonn Gregg), Paddy Mulligan, Jimmy Holmes, Mark Lawrenson, Liam Brady, Gerry Daly, Tony Grealish, Daniel Givens, Paul McGee (65' Frank Stapleton), Gerry Ryan. (Player-coach: Michael John (Johnny) Giles (IRL)).
England: Ray Clemence, Mick Mills, Phil Neal, Dave Watson (22' Phil Thompson), Steve Coppell, Ray Wilkins, Trevor Brooking, Emlyn Hughes, Peter Barnes (85' Tony Woodcock), Kevin Keegan, Bob Latchford. (Coach: Ronald (Ron) Greenwood (ENG)).
Goals: Republic of Ireland: 1-1 Gerry Daly (27').
England: 0-1 Bob Latchford (8').
Referee: Heinz Aldinger (FRG)   Attendance: 48.613

25-10-1978   Windsor Park, Belfast: Northern Ireland – Denmark   2-1 (0-0)
Northern Ireland: Pat Jennings, Jimmy Nicholl, Sammy Nelson, Allan Hunter, Pat Rice, David McCreery, Sammy McIlroy, Martin O'Neill, Gerry Armstrong, Sammy Morgan (61' Derek Spence, 67' Trevor Anderson), Terry Cochrane. (Coach: Robert Dennis (Danny) Blanchflower (NIR)).
Denmark: Ole Kjær, Henning Munk Jensen, John Andersen, Per Røntved, Flemming Nielsen, Ole Rasmussen, Ove Flindt Bjerg, Lars Larsen, Carsten Nielsen, Jørgen Kristensen, Henrik Agerbeck (53' Jan Sørensen). (Coach: Kurt Børge Nikolaj Nielsen (DEN)).
Goals: Northern Ireland: 1-1 Derek Spence (63'), 2-1 Trevor Anderson (85').
Denmark: 0-1 Henning Munk Jensen (51').
Referee: Rolf Haugen (NOR)   Attendance: 20.184

29-11-1978   Vasil Levski National Stadium, Sofia: Bulgaria – Northern Ireland   0-2 (0-1)
Bulgaria: Rumyancho Goranov, Gueorgui Dimitrov, Petar Stankov, Nikolai Grancharov, Roman Karakolev, Anguel Stankov (46' Chavdar Tsvetkov), Borislav Sredkov, Stoicho Mladenov (54' Spas Dzhevizov), Pavel Panov, Roussi Gochev, Gueorgui Slavkov. (Coach: Zvetan Iltchev (BUL)).
Northern Ireland: Pat Jennings, Jimmy Nicholl, Chris Nicholl, Sammy Nelson, David McCreery, Sammy McIlroy (66' Victor Moreland), Martin O'Neill, Bryan Hamilton, Gerry Armstrong, Terry Cochrane (63' Chris McGrath), Billy Caskey. (Coach: Robert Dennis (Danny) Blanchflower (NIR)).
Goals: Northern Ireland: 0-1 Gerry Armstrong (17'), 0-2 Billy Caskey (83').
Referee: Hilmi Ok (TUR)   Attendance: 11.048

07-02-1979   Wembley Stadium, London: England – Northern Ireland   4-0 (1-0)
England: Ray Clemence, Mick Mills, Phil Neal, Dave Watson, Steve Coppell, Trevor Brooking, Emlyn Hughes, Peter Barnes, Tony Currie, Kevin Keegan, Bob Latchford. (Coach: Ronald (Ron) Greenwood (ENG)).
Northern Ireland: Pat Jennings, Jimmy Nicholl, Chris Nicholl, Sammy Nelson, Pat Rice, David McCreery, Sammy McIlroy, Martin O'Neill, Gerry Armstrong, Terry Cochrane (82' Chris McGrath), Billy Caskey (54' Derek Spence). (Coach: Robert Dennis (Danny) Blanchflower (NIR)).
Goals: England: 1-0 Kevin Keegan (24'), 2-0 Bob Latchford (46'), 3-0 Dave Watson (46'), 4-0 Bob Latchford (63').
Referee: Ulf Johan Eriksson (SWE)   Attendance: 91.244

02-05-1979 Lansdowne Road, Dublin: Republic of Ireland – Denmark 2-0 (1-0)
Republic of Ireland: Gerry Peyton, Paddy Mulligan, Jimmy Holmes, Eamonn Gregg, John Giles, Michael Martin, Liam Brady, Gerry Daly, Austin Hayes (64' Michael Walsh), Frank Stapleton, Daniel Givens (74' Paul McGee). (Player-coach: Michael John (Johnny) Giles (IRL)).
Denmark: Ole Kjær, Morten Olsen, Per Røntved, Flemming Nielsen (YC), Frank Arnesen, Søren Lerby (YC), Flemming Lund, Lars Larsen, Preben Elkjær Larsen, Allan Simonsen, Benny Nielsen (YC) (70' Henrik Agerbeck). (Coach: Kurt Børge Nikolaj Nielsen (DEN)).
Goals: Republic of Ireland: 1-0 Gerry Daly (44'), 2-0 Daniel Givens (66').
Referee: Michel Vautrot (FRA)   Attendance: 37.260

02-05-1979 Windsor Park, Belfast: Northern Ireland – Bulgaria 2-0 (2-0)
Northern Ireland: Pat Jennings, Jimmy Nicholl (65' Victor Moreland), Chris Nicholl, Sammy Nelson, David McCreery, Sammy McIlroy, Martin O'Neill, Bryan Hamilton, Gerry Armstrong, Terry Cochrane, Billy Caskey (78' Derek Spence). (Coach: Robert Dennis (Danny) Blanchflower (NIR)).
Bulgaria: Stoyan Stoyanov, Radoslav Zdravkov (64' Ivan Iliev), Tsonyo Vasilev, Kiril Ivkov, Georgi Bonev, Ljuben Kolev, Borislav Sredkov, Aleksandre Rainov, Pavel Panov, Chavdar Tsvetkov, Spas Dzhevizov. (Coach: Yanko Dinkov (BUL)).
Goals: Northern Ireland: 1-0 Chris Nicholl (16'), 2-0 Gerry Armstrong (30').
Referee: Anders Mattsson (FIN)   Attendance: 15.540

19-05-1979 Vasil Levski National Stadium, Sofia: Bulgaria – Republic of Ireland 1-0 (0-0)
Bulgaria: Yordan Filipov, Radoslav Zdravkov, Tsonyo Vasilev, Kiril Ivkov, Nikolai Grancharov, Ivan Iliev, Andrey Zhelyaskov, Voin Voynov, Pavel Panov, Krasimir Borisov, Chavdar Tsvetkov. (Coach: Zvetan Iltchev (BUL)).
Republic of Ireland: Gerry Peyton, David O'Leary, Jimmy Holmes (55' Paddy Mulligan), Eamonn Gregg, John Giles, Steve Heighway, Michael Martin, Liam Brady, Gerry Daly, Daniel Givens, Michael Walsh (75' Paul McGee). (Player-coach: Michael John (Johnny) Giles (IRL)).
Goal: Bulgaria: 1-0 Chavdar Tsvetkov (81').
Referee: Josef Bucek (AUT)   Attendance: 10.896

06-06-1979 Vasil Levski National Stadium, Sofia: Bulgaria – England 0-3 (0-1)
Bulgaria: Yordan Filipov, Radoslav Zdravkov (60' Todor Barzov), Kiril Ivkov, Georgi Bonev, Nikolai Grancharov, Ivan Iliev, Andrey Zhelyaskov, Voin Voynov, Pavel Panov (46' Roussi Gochev), Pavel Panov, Krasimir Borisov, Chavdar Tsvetkov. (Coach: Zvetan Iltchev (BUL)).
England: Ray Clemence, Mick Mills, Phil Thompson, Phil Neal, Dave Watson, Steve Coppell, Ray Wilkins, Trevor Brooking, Peter Barnes (76' Tony Woodcock), Kevin Keegan, Bob Latchford (65' Trevor Francis). (Coach: Ronald (Ron) Greenwood (ENG)).
Goals: England: 0-1 Kevin Keegan (33'), 0-2 Dave Watson (53'), 0-3 Peter Barnes (54').
Referee: Ernst Dörflinger-Buser (SUI)   Attendance: 31.322

06-06-1979   Parken Stadium, Copenhagen: Denmark – Northern Ireland   4-0 (2-0)
Denmark: Ole Kjær, Søren Busk, Morten Olsen, John Andersen, Ole Højgaard (76' Peter Poulsen), Frank Arnesen, Søren Lerby, Sten Ziegler, Klaus Nørregaard (58' Per Røntved), Preben Elkjær Larsen, Allan Simonsen. (Coach: Kurt Børge Nikolaj Nielsen (DEN)).
Northern Ireland: Pat Jennings, Jimmy Nicholl, Sammy Nelson, Allan Hunter, Pat Rice, David McCreery, Sammy McIlroy, Martin O'Neill (67' Thomas Sloan), Bryan Hamilton, Gerry Armstrong (54' Billy Caskey), Derek Spence. (Coach: Robert Dennis (Danny) Blanchflower (NIR)).
Goals: Denmark: 1-0 Preben Elkjær Larsen (13'), 2-0 Preben Elkjær Larsen (33'), 3-0 Allan Simonsen (64'), 4-0 Preben Elkjær Larsen (83').
Referee: Rudolf Frickel (FRG)   Attendance: 16.800

12-09-1979   Wembley Stadium, London: England – Denmark   1-0 (1-0)
England: Ray Clemence, Mick Mills, Phil Thompson, Phil Neal, Dave Watson, Steve Coppell, Ray Wilkins, Trevor Brooking, Terry McDermott, Peter Barnes, Kevin Keegan. (Coach: Ronald (Ron) Greenwood (ENG)).
Denmark: Birger Jensen, Søren Busk, Morten Olsen, Ole Højgaard, Frank Arnesen, Søren Lerby, Sten Ziegler, Preben Elkjær Larsen (YC) (80' Ove Flindt Bjerg), Allan Simonsen, Benny Nielsen (67' Jens Jørn Bertelsen), Henning Munk Jensen. (Coach: Josef (Sepp) Piontek (FRG)).
Goal: England: 1-0 Kevin Keegan (17').
Referee: César Da Luz Dias Correia (POR)   Attendance: 88.660

17-10-1979   Lansdowne Road, Dublin: Republic of Ireland – Bulgaria   3-0 (1-0)
Republic of Ireland: Gerry Peyton, David O'Leary, Paddy Mulligan, Ashley Grimes, Pierce O'Leary, Steve Heighway, Michael Martin, Liam Brady, Tony Grealish, Frank Stapleton, Paul McGee. (Player-coach: Michael John (Johnny) Giles (IRL)).
Bulgaria: Rumyancho Goranov, Gueorgui Dimitrov, Tsonyo Vasilev, Georgi Bonev, Ivan Iliev, Vanio Kostov (46' Kostadin Kostadinov), Andrey Zhelyaskov, Todor Barzov, Plamen Markov, Boycho Velichkov, Chavdar Tsvetkov. (Coach: Zvetan Iltchev (BUL)).
Goals: Republic of Ireland: 1-0 Michael Martin (39'), 2-0 Tony Grealish (46'), 3-0 Frank Stapleton (83').
Referee: Heinz Einbeck (GDR)   Attendance: 18.909

17-10-1979   Windsor Park, Belfast: Northern Ireland – England   1-5 (0-2)
Northern Ireland: Pat Jennings, Jimmy Nicholl, Sammy Nelson, Allan Hunter (46' Peter Rafferty), Pat Rice, David McCreery, Sammy McIlroy, Thomas Cassidy, Gerry Armstrong, Tommy Finney (70' Billy Caskey), Victor Moreland. (Coach: Robert Dennis (Danny) Blanchflower (NIR)).
England: Peter Shilton, Mick Mills, Phil Thompson, Phil Neal, Dave Watson, Steve Coppell, Ray Wilkins, Trevor Brooking (85' Terry McDermott), Trevor Francis, Tony Woodcock, Kevin Keegan. (Coach: Ronald (Ron) Greenwood (ENG)).
Goals: Northern Ireland: 1-2 Victor Moreland (49' penalty).
England: 0-1 Trevor Francis (18'), 0-2 Tony Woodcock (34'), 1-3 Trevor Francis (62'), 1-4 Tony Woodcack (71'), 1-5 Jimmy Nicholl (74' *own goal*).
Referee: Alexis Ponnet (BEL)   Attendance: 17.755

31-10-1979   Vasil levski National Stadium, Sofia: Bulgaria – Denmark 3-0 (1-0)
Bulgaria: Hristo Hristov, Tsonyo Vasilev, Borislav Dimitrov, Georgi Bonev, Ivan Iliev, Andrey Zhelyaskov, Todor Barzov, Kostadin Kostadinov (70' Roussi Gochev), Plamen Markov, Boycho Velichkov, Chavdar Tsvetkov. (Coach: Zvetan Iltchev (BUL)).
Denmark: Ole Qvist, Søren Busk, Jens Jørn Bertelsen, Morten Olsen, Jens Steffensen, Frank Arnesen, Søren Lerby (YC), Sten Ziegler, Allan Simonsen, Kristen Nygaard (71' Carsten Nielsen), Henning Munk Jensen. (Coach: Josef (Sepp) Piontek (FRG)).
Goals: Bulgaria: 1-0 Andrey Zhelyaskov (21'), 2-0 Chavdar Tsvetkov (51'), 3-0 Chavdar Tsvetkov (88').
Referee: Sotos Afxentiou (CYP)   Attendance: 19.384

21-11-1979   Windsor Park, Belfast: Northern Ireland – Republic of Ireland 1-0 (0-0)
Northern Ireland: Pat Jennings, Jimmy Nicholl, Chris Nicholl, Sammy Nelson, Allan Hunter, David McCreery, Sammy McIlroy, Martin O'Neill (66' Thomas Cassidy), Victor Moreland, Gerry Armstrong, Derek Spence. (Coach: Robert Dennis (Danny) Blanchflower (NIR)).
Republic of Ireland: Mick Kearns, David O'Leary, Ashley Grimes, Pierce O'Leary, John Devine, Steve Heighway, Michael Martin, Gerry Daly (54' Joseph Waters), Tony Grealish, Frank Stapleton, Paul McGee (76' Daniel Givens). (Player-coach: Michael John (Johnny) Giles (IRL)).
Goal: Northern Ireland: 1-0 Gerry Armstrong (54').
Referee: André Daina (SUI)   Attendance: 13.215

22-11-1979   Wembley Stadium, London: England – Bulgaria 2-0 (1-0)
England: Ray Clemence, Kenny Sansom, Phil Thompson, Viv Anderson, Dave Watson, Ray Wilkins, Glenn Hoddle, Trevor Francis, Tony Woodcock, Ray Kennedy, Kevin Reeves. (Coach: Ronald (Ron) Greenwood (ENG)).
Bulgaria: Hristo Hristov, Gueorgiu Dimitrov, Borislav Dimitrov, Georgi Bonev, Ivan Iliev, Roman Karakolev, Andrey Zhelyaskov, Todor Barzov, Plamen Markov, Boycho Velichkov (87' Krassimir Manolov), Chavdar Tsvetkov (30' Kostadin Kostadinov). (Coach: Zvetan Iltchev (BUL)).
Goals: England: 1-0 Dave Watson (9'), 2-0 Glenn Hoddle (68').
Referee: Erik Fredriksson (SWE)   Attendance: 71.491

06-02-1980   Wembley Stadium, London: England – Republic of Ireland 2-0 (1-0)
England: Ray Clemence, Kenny Sansom, Phil Thompson, Dave Watson, Trevor Cherry, Bryan Robson, Terry McDermott, Tony Woodcock, Kevin Keegan, David Johnson (60' Steve Coppell), Laurie Cunningham. (Coach: Ronald (Ron) Greenwood (ENG)).
Republic of Ireland: Gerry Peyton (60' Ronald Healey), Chris Hughton, David O'Leary (69' Pierce O'Leary), Mark Lawrenson, Ashley Grimes, Steve Heighway, Liam Brady, Gerry Daly, Tony Grealish, Francis O'Brien, Frank Stapleton. (Player-coach: Michael John (Johnny) Giles (IRL)).
Goals: England: 1-0 Kevin Keegan (34'), Kevin Keegan (74').
Referee: Klaus Scheurell (GDR)   Attendance: 90.299

GROUP 2

30-08-1978	Oslo	Norway – Austria	0-2 (0-2)
20-09-1978	Vienna	Austria – Scotland	3-2 (1-0)
20-09-1978	Lokeren	Belgium – Norway	1-1 (0-1)
11-10-1978	Lisbon	Portugal – Belgium	1-1 (1-1)
25-10-1978	Glasgow	Scotland – Norway	3-2 (1-1)
15-11-1978	Vienna	Austria – Portugal	1-2 (0-1)
29-11-1978	Lisbon	Portugal – Scotland	1-0 (1-0)
28-03-1979	Brussels	Belgium – Austria	1-1 (1-0)
02-05-1979	Vienna	Austria – Belgium	0-0
09-05-1979	Oslo	Norway – Portugal	0-1 (0-1)
07-06-1979	Oslo	Norway – Scotland	0-4 (0-3)
29-08-1979	Vienna	Austria – Norway	4-0 (1-0)
12-09-1979	Oslo	Norway – Belgium	1-2 (1-1)
17-10-1979	Brussels	Belgium – Portugal	2-0 (0-0)
17-10-1979	Glasgow	Scotland – Austria	1-1 (0-1)
01-11-1979	Lisbon	Portugal – Norway	3-1 (1-1)
21-11-1979	Brussels	Belgium – Scotland	2-0 (1-0)
21-11-1979	Lisbon	Portugal – Austria	1-2 (1-1)
19-12-1979	Glasgow	Scotland – Belgium	1-3 (0-3)
26-03-1979	Glasgow	Scotland – Portugal	4-1 (2-0)

FINAL STANDING

Pos	Team	Pld	W	D	L	GF	GA	GD	Pts
1	Belgium	8	4	4	0	12	5	+7	12
2	Austria	8	4	3	1	14	7	+7	11
3	Portugal	8	4	1	3	10	11	-1	9
4	Scotland	8	3	1	4	15	13	+2	7
5	Norway	8	0	1	7	5	20	-15	1

Belgium qualified for the final tournament in Italy.

30-08-1978   Ullevaal Stadion, Oslo: Norway – Austria   0-2 (0-2)
Norway: Tom Risz Jacobsen, Jan Birkelund, Svein Grøndalen, Trond Pedersen, Helge Karlsen (22' Bjarne Berntsen), Einar Jan Aas, Tor Egil Johansen, Stein Thunberg, Svein Mathisen, Hallvar Thoresen, Odd Iversen (71' Arne Larsen Økland). (Coach: Tor Roste Fossen (NOR)).
Austria: Erwin Fuchsbichler, Erich Obermayer, Bruno Pezzey, Heribert Weber, Robert Sara, Heinrich Strasser, Herbert Prohaska, Kurt Jara (65' Reinhold Hintermaier), Walter Schachner, Hans Krankl, Wilhelm Kreuz. (Coach: Karl Stotz (AUT)).
Goals: Austria: 0-1 Bruno Pezzey (25'), 0-2 Hans Krankl (43').
Referee: Patrick Partridge (ENG)   Attendance: 13.075

20-09-1978   Prater Stadium, Vienna: Austria – Scotland   3-2 (1-0)
Austria: Erwin Fuchsbichler, Erich Obermayer, Bruno Pezzey, Heribert Weber, Robert Sara, Heinrich Strasser, Herbert Prohaska (87' Franz Oberacher), Kurt Jara, Walter Schachner, Hans Krankl, Wilhelm Kreuz. (Coach: Karl Stotz (AUT)).
Scotland: Alan Rough, Martin Buchan, Stewart Kennedy, Willie Donachie, Gordon McQueen, Graeme Souness, Asa Hartford, Archie Gemmill, Kenny Dalglish, Joe Jordan (61' Arthur Graham), Andy Gray. (Coach: John (Jock) Stein (SCO)).
Goals: Austria: 1-0 Bruno Pezzey (26'), 2-0 Walter Schachner (48'), 3-0 Wilhelm Kreuz (65').
Scotland: 3-1 Gordon McQueen (68'), 3-2 Andy Gray (78').
Referee: Alberto Michelotti (ITA)   Attendance: 62.281

20-09-1978   Daknam Stadium, Lokeren: Belgium – Norway   1-1 (0-1)
Belgium: Jean-Marie Pfaff, Walter Meeuws, Eric Gerets (46' François Van Der Elst), René Vandereycken, Ludo Coeck, René Verheyen, Georges Leekens, Julien Cools (C), Paul Courant (46' Willy Geurts), Eddy Voordeckers, Roger Van Gool. (Coach: Guy Jean Léonard Thijs (BEL)).
Norway: Tom Risz Jacobsen, Svein Grøndalen, Trond Pedersen, Einar Jan Aas, Bjarne Berntsen, Tore Kordahl, Tor Egil Johansen, Svein Mathisen (34' Stein Thunberg), Hallvar Thoresen, Roger Albertsen, Arne Larsen Økland (61' Pal Jacobsen). (Coach: Tor Roste Fossen (NOR)).
Goals: Belgium: 1-1 Julien Cools (65').
Norway: 0-1 Arne Larsen Økland (8').
Referee: Marijan Raus (YUG)   Attendance: 5.272

11-10-1978   Estádio da Luz, Lisbon: Portugal – Belgium   1-1 (1-1)
Portugal: Manuel Galrinho BENTO, EURICO Monteiro GOMES (46' ARTUR Manuel Soares CORREIA), HUMBERTO Manuel de Jesus COELHO, GABRIEL Azevedo MENDES, ADELINO de Jesus TEIXEIRA (YC20), JOÃO António Ferreira Resende ALVES, ANTÓNIO Luís Alves Ribeiro de OLIVEIRA, JOSÉ Alberto COSTA, SHÉU Han, FERNANDO Mendes Soares GOMES, MANUEL José Tavares FERNANDES (70' Tamagnini Manuel Gomes Batista "NENÉ"). (Coach: Mário Wilson (POR)).
Belgium: Jean-Marie Pfaff, Walter Meeuws, Eric Gerets, Michel Renquin, René Vandereycken, Ludo Coeck, Frank Vercauteren, Hugo Broos, Julien Cools, Guy Dardenne (67' François Van Der Elst), Eddy Voordeckers (60' Jean Ceulemans). (Coach: Guy Jean Léonard Thijs (BEL)).
Goals: Portugal: 1-0 FERNANDO Mendes Soares GOMES (31').
Belgium: 1-1 Frank Vercauteren (37').
Referee: Georges Konrath (FRA)   Attendance: 14.401

25-10-1978   Hampden Park, Glasgow: Scotland – Norway   3-2 (1-1)
Scotland: Jim Stewart, Frank Gray, Martin Buchan, Willie Donachie, Gordon McQueen, Graeme Souness, Asa Hartford, Archie Gemmill, Arthur Graham, Kenny Dalglish, Andy Gray. (Coach: John (Jock) Stein (SCO)).
Norway: Tom Risz Jacobsen, Jan Birkelund, Svein Grøndalen, Trond Pedersen (85' Jan Hansen), Einar Jan Aas, Tore Kordahl, Tor Egil Johansen, Tom Jacobsen (37' Helge Karlsen), Svein Mathisen, Hallvar Thoresen, Arne Larsen Økland. (Coach: Tor Roste Fossen (NOR)).
Goals: Scotland: 1-1 Kenny Dalglish (35'), 2-2 Kenny Dalglish (81'), 3-2 Archie Gemmill (87' penalty).
Norway: 0-1 Einar Jan Aas (3'), 1-2 Arne Larsen Økland (64').
Referee: Vojtech Christov (TCH)   Attendance: 65.372

15-11-1978   Prater Stadium, Vienna: Austria – Portugal   1-2 (0-1)
Austria: Friedrich Koncilia, Erich Obermayer, Bruno Pezzey, Robert Sara, Heinrich Strasser, Roland Hattenberger, Herbert Prohaska, Kurt Jara (75' Ernst Baumeister), Walter Schachner, Hans Krankl, Wilhelm Kreuz (84' Felix Gasselich). (Coach: Karl Stotz (AUT)).
Portugal: Manuel Galrinho BENTO, HUMBERTO Manuel de Jesus COELHO, ARTUR Manuel Soares CORREIA (YC34), CARLOS Alexandre Fortes ALHINHO, MINERVINO José Lopes PIETRA, ALBERTO Gomes FONSECA Júnior, ADELINO de Jesus TEIXEIRA, JOÃO António Ferreira Resende ALVES, ANTÓNIO Luís Alves Ribeiro de OLIVEIRA (87' SHÉU Han), JOSÉ Alberto COSTA, Tamagnini Manuel Gomes Batista "NENÉ" (88' FERNANDO Mendes Soares GOMES). (Coach: Mário Wilson (POR)).
Goals: Austria: 1-1 Walter Schachner (74').
Portugal: 0-1 Tamagnini Manuel Gomes Batista "NENÉ" (30'), 1-2 ALBERTO Gomes FONSECA Júnior (90').
Referee: Nicolae Rainea (ROM)   Attendance: 64.024

29-11-1978   Estádio da Luz, Lisbon: Portugal – Scotland   1-0 (1-0)
Portugal: Manuel Galrinho BENTO, HUMBERTO Manuel de Jesus COELHO, ARTUR Manuel Soares CORREIA, CARLOS Alexandre Fortes ALHINHO, MINERVINO José Lopes PIETRA, ALBERTO Gomes FONSECA Júnior, JOÃO António Ferreira Resende ALVES, ANTÓNIO Luís Alves Ribeiro de OLIVEIRA (78' EURICO Monteiro GOMES), JOSÉ Alberto COSTA (46' SHÉU Han), FERNANDO Mendes Soares GOMES, Tamagnini Manuel Gomes Batista "NENÉ". (Coach: Mário Wilson (POR)).
Scotland: Alan Rough, Frank Gray (65' Willie Donachie), David Narey, Martin Buchan, Stewart Kennedy, Gordon McQueen, John Robertson, Asa Hartford, Archie Gemmill, Kenny Dalglish, Joe Jordan (78' Ian Wallace). (Coach: John (Jock) Stein (SCO)).
Goal: Portugal: 1-0 ALBERTO Gomes FONSECA Júnior (28').
Referee: Ernst Dörflinger-Buser (SUI)   Attendance: 49.153

28-03-1979   Constant Vanden Stock Stadium, Brussels: Belgium – Austria   1-1 (1-0)
Belgium: Jean-Marie Pfaff, Walter Meeuws, Eric Gerets, Michel Renquin, René Vandereycken, Frank Vercauteren, Hugo Broos, Julien Cools (C) (70' Willy Geurts), Albert Cluytens, François Van Der Elst, Jean Janssens. (Coach: Guy Jean Léonard Thijs (BEL)).
Austria: Friedrich Koncilia, Erich Obermayer, Bruno Pezzey, Heribert Weber, Robert Sara, Dietmar Mirnegg, Roland Hattenberger, Ernst Baumeister, Walter Schachner, Hans Krankl, Wilhelm Kreuz. (Coach: Karl Stotz (AUT)).
Goals: Belgium: 1-0 René Vandereycken (21' penalty).
Austria: 1-1 Hans Krankl (61').
Referee: Ángel Franco Martínez (ESP)   Attendance: 6.264

02-05-1979   Prater Stadium, Vienna: Austria – Belgium   0-0
Austria: Friedrich Koncilia, Erich Obermayer, Bruno Pezzey, Robert Sara, Dietmar Mirnegg, Roland Hattenberger, Herbert Prohaska (74' Felix Gasselich), Ernst Baumeister, Walter Schachner, Hans Krankl, Wilhelm Kreuz (81' Reinhold Hintermaier). (Coach: Karl Stotz (AUT)).
Belgium: Michel Preud'homme, Walter Meeuws, Eric Gerets, Michel Renquin, René Vandereycken (YC), Frank Vercauteren, Hugo Broos, Julien Cools (C), François Van Der Elst (YC), Jean Janssens, Charles Jacobs (86' Guy Dardenne). (Coach: Guy Jean Léonard Thijs (BEL)).
Referee: Hilmi Ok (TUR)   Attendance: 42.903

09-05-1979   Ullevaal Stadion, Oslo: Norway – Portugal   0-1 (0-1)
Norway: Roy Amundsen, Svein Grøndalen, Trond Pedersen, Einar Jan Aas, Tore Kordahl, Tor Egil Johansen (70' Stein Thunberg), Jan Hansen, Svein Mathisen (55' Isak Arne Refvik), Roger Albertsen, Thomas Lund, Arne Larsen Økland. (Coach: Tor Roste Fossen (NOR)).
Portugal: Manuel Galrinho BENTO, EURICO Monteiro GOMES, HUMBERTO Manuel de Jesus COELHO, ARTUR Manuel Soares CORREIA, CARLOS Alexandre Fortes ALHINHO, MINERVINO José Lopes PIETRA, ALBERTO Gomes FONSECA Júnior, JOÃO António Ferreira Resende ALVES, ANTÓNIO Luís Alves Ribeiro de OLIVEIRA, JOSÉ Alberto COSTA (89' António José BASTOS LOPES), Tamagnini Manuel Gomes Batista "NENÉ" (80' FERNANDO Mendes Soares GOMES). (Coach: Mário Wilson (POR)).
Goal: Portugal: 0-1 JOÃO António Ferreira Resende ALVES (35').
Referee: Siegfried Kirschen (GDR)   Attendance: 9.876

07-06-1979   Ullevaal Stadion, Oslo: Norway – Scotland   0-4 (0-3)
Norway: Tom Risz Jacobsen, Svein Grøndalen, Trond Pedersen (60' Jan Hansen), Helge Karlsen, Einar Jan Aas, Tore Kordahl, Stein Thunberg (77' Torbjørn Svendsen), Svein Mathisen, Hallvar Thoresen, Roger Albertsen, Arne Larsen Økland. (Coach: Tor Roste Fossen (NOR)).
Scotland: Alan Rough, Gordon McQueen, George Burley (46' Paul Hegarty, 61' John Wark), Tommy Burns, John Robertson, Asa Hartford, Archie Gemmill, Arthur Graham, Iain Munro, Kenny Dalglish, Joe Jordan. (Coach: John (Jock) Stein (SCO)).
Goals: Scotland: 0-1 Joe Jordan (32'), 0-2 Kenny Dalglish (39'), 0-3 John Robertson (43'), 0-4 Gordon McQueen (54').
Referee: Ib Nielsen (DEN)   Attendance: 17.269

29-08-1979   Prater Stadium, Vienna: Austria – Norway   4-0 (1-0)
Austria: Friedrich Koncilia, Erich Obermayer, Bruno Pezzey, Robert Sara, Günther Pospischil, Roland Hattenberger, Herbert Prohaska (76' Heribert Weber), Kurt Jara, Walter Schachner, Hans Krankl, Wilhelm Kreuz. (Coach: Karl Stotz (AUT)).
Norway: Roy Amundsen, Svein Grøndalen, Trond Pedersen, Einar Jan Aas, Bjarne Berntsen, Morten Vinje, Tor Egil Johansen, Stein Thunberg (32' Rune Ottesen), Svein Mathisen (73' Torbjørn Svendsen), Pal Jacobsen, Arne Larsen Økland. (Coach: Tor Roste Fossen (NOR)).
Goals: Austria: 1-0 Kurt Jara (42'), 2-0 Herbert Prohaska (46' penalty), 3-0 Wilhelm Kreuz (75'), 4-0 Hans Krankl (86').
Referee: Jaromír Fausek (TCH)   Attendance: 30.991

12-09-1979   Ullevaal Stadion, Oslo: Norway – Belgium   1-2 (1-1)
Norway: Roy Amundsen, Svein Grøndalen, Trond Pedersen, Einar Jan Aas, Morten Vinje, Tor Egil Johansen (76' Rune Ottesen), Jan Hansen, Hallvar Thoresen (82' Svein Mathisen), Roger Albertsen, Odd Iversen, Pal Jacobsen. (Coach: Tor Roste Fossen (NOR)).
Belgium: Jean-Marie Pfaff, Luc Millecamps, Walter Meeuws, Eric Gerets, Michel Renquin, René Vandereycken, Frank Vercauteren (76' René Verheyen), Julien Cools (C), Albert Cluytens, François Van Der Elst, Jean Janssens (76' Jan Ceulemans). (Coach: Guy Jean Léonard Thijs (BEL)).
Goals: Norway: 1-0 Pal Jacobsen (7').
Belgium: 1-1 Jean Janssens (31'), 1-2 François Van Der Elst (75').
Referee: Alojzy Jarguz (POL)   Attendance: 11.255

17-10-1979   Stade du Heysel, Brussels: Belgium – Portugal   2-0 (0-0)
Belgium: Theo Custers, Luc Millecamps, Walter Meeuws, Eric Gerets, Michel Renquin (75'
Philippe Garot), René Vandereycken, Wilfried Van Moer (75' René Verheyen), Julien Cools
(C), François Van Der Elst, Jan Ceulemans, Eddy Voordeckers. (Coach: Guy Jean Léonard
Thijs (BEL)).
Portugal: Manuel Galrinho BENTO, EURICO Monteiro GOMES (52' ANTÓNIO Manuel
FRASCO Vieira), HUMBERTO Manuel de Jesus COELHO, ARTUR Manuel Soares
CORREIA, CARLOS Alexandre Fortes ALHINHO, MINERVINO José Lopes PIETRA (61'
Rui Manuel Trindade JORDÃO), ALBERTO Gomes FONSECA Júnior, ROMEU Fernando
Fernandes da Silva, ANTÓNIO Luís Alves Ribeiro de OLIVEIRA, FERNANDO Mendes
Soares GOMES, Tamagnini Manuel Gomes Batista "NENÉ". (Coach: Mário Wilson (POR)).
Goals: Belgium: 1-0 Wilfried Van Moer (46'), 2-0 François Van Der Elst (56').
Referee: Ulf Johan Eriksson (SWE)   Attendance: 8.799

17-10-1979   Hampden Park, Glasgow: Scotland – Austria   1-1 (0-1)
Scotland: Alan Rough, Sandy Jardine, Gordon McQueen, Tommy Burns, Graeme Souness,
John Wark, John Robertson, Archie Gemmill (YC), Arthur Graham (61' Davie Cooper), Iain
Munro, Kenny Dalglish. (Coach: John (Jock) Stein (SCO)).
Austria: Friedrich Koncilia, Bruno Pezzey, Heribert Weber, Robert Sara, Dietmar Mirnegg,
Roland Hattenberger, Herbert Prohaska, Kurt Jara, Walter Schachner (80' Gerhard
Steinkogler), Hans Krankl (88' Reinhold Hintermaier), Wilhelm Kreuz. (Coach: Karl Stotz
(AUT)).
Goals: Scotland: 1-1 Archie Gemmill (75').
Austria: 0-1 Hans Krankl (40').
Referee: Károly Palotai (HUN)   Attendance: 67.895

01-11-1979   Estádio da Luz, Lisbon: Portugal – Norway   3-1 (1-1)
Portugal: Manuel Galrinho BENTO, HUMBERTO Manuel de Jesus COELHO, ARTUR
Manuel Soares CORREIA, CARLOS António Fonseca SIMÕES, ALFREDO Manuel Ferreira
Silva MURÇA, ANTÓNIO Manuel FRASCO Vieira, JOSÉ Alberto COSTA, RODOLFO Dos
Reis Ferreira, FERNANDO Mendes Soares GOMES, Tamagnini Manuel Gomes Batista
"NENÉ", Mauricio Zacarias REINALDO Rodrigues Gomes. (Coach: Mário Wilson (POR)).
Norway: Roy Amundsen, Svein Grøndalen, Trond Pedersen, Bjarne Berntsen (69' Jan
Hansen), Morten Vinje, Georg Hammer, Tor Egil Johansen, Hallvar Thoresen (72' Svein
Mathisen), Roger Albertsen, Pal Jacobsen, Arne Larsen Økland. (Coach: Tor Roste Fossen
(NOR)).
Goals: Portugal: 1-1 ARTUR Manuel Soares CORREIA (37'), 2-1 Tamagnini Manuel Gomes
Batista "NENÉ" (59'), 3-1 Tamagnini Manuel Gomes Batista "NENÉ" (71').
Norway: 0-1 Georg Hammer (10').
Referee: Riccardo Lattanzi (ITA)   Attendance: 34.394

21-11-1979   Stade du Heysel, Brussels: Belgium – Scotland   2-0 (1-0)
Belgium: Theo Custers, Luc Millecamps, Walter Meeuws, Eric Gerets, Michel Renquin, René
Vandereycken, Wilfried Van Moer (74' René Verheyen), Julien Cools (C), François Van Der
Elst, Jan Ceulemans, Eddy Voordeckers. (Coach: Guy Jean Léonard Thijs (BEL)).
Scotland: Alan Rough, Alan Hansen, Willie Miller, Sandy Jardine, Graeme Souness, John
Wark, John Robertson, Asa Hartford, Iain Munro (60' Frank Gray), Kenny Dalglish, Joe
Jordan (60' Davie Provan). (Coach: John (Jock) Stein (SCO)).
Goals: Belgium: 1-0 François Van Der Elst (5'), 2-0 Eddy Voordeckers (47').
Referee: Eldar Azim-Zade (URS)   Attendance: 14.289

21-11-1979   Estádio da Luz, Lisbon: Portugal – Austria   1-2 (1-1)
Portugal: Manuel Galrinho BENTO, HUMBERTO Manuel de Jesus COELHO, ARTUR Manuel Soares CORREIA (78' SHÉU Han), ALBERTO Gomes FONSECA Júnior, CARLOS António Fonseca SIMÕES, ANTÓNIO Manuel FRASCO Vieira (66' Rui Manuel Trindade JORDÃO), JOSÉ Alberto COSTA, RODOLFO Dos Reis Ferreira, FERNANDO Mendes Soares GOMES, Tamagnini Manuel Gomes Batista "NENÉ", Mauricio Zacarias REINALDO Rodrigues Gomes. (Coach: Mário Wilson (POR)).
Austria: Friedrich Koncilia, Erich Obermayer, Bruno Pezzey, Robert Sara, Dietmar Mirnegg, Roland Hattenberger, Herbert Prohaska, Kurt Jara, Walter Schachner, Kurt Welzl (81' Hans Krankl), Wilhelm Kreuz. (Coach: Karl Stotz (AUT)).
Goals: Portugal: 1-1 Mauricio Zacarias REINALDO Rodrigues Gomes (42').
Austria: 0-1 Kurt Welzl (37'), 1-2 Walter Schachner (51').
Referee: Charles George Reinier Corver (HOL)   Attendance: 52.815

19-12-1979   Hampden Park, Glasgow: Scotland – Belgium   1-3 (0-3)
Scotland: Alan Rough, Danny McGrain, Sandy Jardine, Gordon McQueen, Tommy Burns (YC), Roy Aitken, John Wark, John Robertson, Eamonn Bannon (46' Davie Provan), Kenny Dalglish (YC), Derek Johnstone. (Coach: John (Jock) Stein (SCO)).
Belgium: Theo Custers, Luc Millecamps, Walter Meeuws, Eric Gerets, Maurice Martens, René Vandereycken, Wilfried Van Moer (50' Gerard Plessers), Julien Cools (C), Erwin Vandenbergh (73' Guy Dardenne), François Van Der Elst, Jan Ceulemans. (Coach: Guy Jean Léonard Thijs (BEL)).
Goals: Scotland: 1-3 John Robertson (55').
Belgium: 0-1 Erwin Vandenbergh (18'), 0-2 François Van Der Elst (23'), 0-3 François Van Der Elst (29').
Referee: Heinz Aldinger (FRG)   Attendance: 25.389

26-03-1980   Hampden Park, Glasgow: Scotland – Portugal   4-1 (2-0)
Scotland: Alan Rough, Danny McGrain, Alan Hansen, David Narey, Alex McLeish, George Burley, Graeme Souness, John Robertson (75' Steve Archibald), Archie Gemmill, Kenny Dalglish (48' Davie Provan), Andy Gray. (Coach: John (Jock) Stein (SCO)).
Portugal: Manuel Galrinho BENTO, EURICO Monteiro GOMES (34' SHÉU Han), HUMBERTO Manuel de Jesus COELHO, ALBERTO Gomes FONSECA Júnior, CARLOS António Fonseca SIMÕES, ANTÓNIO Manuel FRASCO Vieira (77' CARLOS MANUEL Correia dos Santos), ADELINO de Jesus TEIXEIRA, JOSÉ Alberto COSTA, FERNANDO Mendes Soares GOMES, Rui Manuel Trindade JORDÃO, Tamagnini Manuel Gomes Batista "NENÉ". (Coach: Mário Wilson (POR)).
Goals: Scotland: 1-0 Kenny Dalglish (5'), 2-0 Andy Gray (30'), 3-0 Steve Archibald (68'), 4-1 Archie Gemmill (84' penalty).
Portugal: 3-1 FERNANDO Mendes Soares GOMES (74').
Referee: Robert Charles Paul Wurtz (FRA)   Attendance: 20.233

GROUP 3

04-10-1978	Zagreb	Yugoslavia – Spain	1-2 (1-2)
25-10-1978	Bucharest	Romania – Yugoslavia	3-2 (0-1)
15-11-1978	Valencia	Spain – Romania	1-0 (1-0)
13-12-1978	Salamanca	Spain – Cyprus	5-0 (2-0)
01-04-1979	Nicosia	Cyprus – Yugoslavia	0-3 (0-1)
04-04-1979	Craiova	Romania – Spain	2-2 (0-0)
13-05-1979	Limassol	Cyprus – Romania	1-1 (1-1)
10-10-1979	Valencia	Spain – Yugoslavia	0-1 (0-1)
31-10-1979	Kosovska Mitrovica	Yugoslavia – Romania	2-1 (0-0)
14-11-1979	Novi Sad	Yugoslavia – Cyprus	5-0 (1-0)
18-11-1979	Bucharest	Romania – Cyprus	2-0 (1-0)
09-12-1979	Limassol	Cyprus – Spain	1-3 (0-2)

FINAL STANDING

Pos	Team	Pld	W	D	L	GF	GA	GD	Pts
1	Spain	6	4	1	1	13	5	+8	9
2	Yugoslavia	6	4	0	2	14	6	+8	8
3	Romania	6	2	2	2	9	8	+1	6
4	Cyprus	6	0	1	5	2	19	-17	1

Spain qualified for the final tournament in Italy.

04-10-1978   Maksimir Stadium, Zagreb: Yugoslavia – Spain 1-2 (1-2)
Yugoslavia: Zelimir Stincic, Velimir Zajec (67' Nikica Cukrov), Nenad Stojkovic, Drazen Muzinic, Vilson Dzoni, Vedran Rozic, Ivan Surjak (YC46), Safet Susic, Slavisa Zungul (67' Dusan Savic), Momcilo Vukotic, Vahid Haliljodzic. (Coach: Ante Mladinic (YUG)).
Spain: MIGUEL ÁNGEL González Suarez (YC72), Miguel Bernardo Bianquetti "MIGUELI", MARCELINO Pérez Ayllón, Francisco Javier Alvarez URÍA, Secundino Suárez Vázquez "CUNDI", Juan Manuel ASENSI Ripoll, Antonio OLMO Rodriguez (YC34), Vicente DEL BOSQUE, Ángel María VILLAR Llona, Juan Gómez Gónzalez "JUANITO" (86' José Vicente "TENTE" SÁNCHEZ Felip), Carlos Alonso González "SANTILLANA" (89' RUBÉN Andres CANO Martinez). (Coach: László "LADISLAO" KUBALA Stecz (ESP)).
Goals: Yugoslavia: 1-2 Vahid Halilhodzic (44').
Spain: 0-1 Juan Gómez Gónzalez "JUANITO" (19'), 0-2 Carlos Alonso González "SANTILLANA" (28').
Referee: Erich Linemayr (AUT)   Attendance: 41.539

25-10-1978   Ghencea Stadium, Bucharest: Romania – Yugoslavia 3-2 (0-1)
Romania: Raducanu Necula, Costica Stefanescu, Iosif Vigu, Teodor Anghelini, Stefan Sames, Laszlo Bölöni, Nicolae Dobrin, Zoltan Crisan, Mihai Romila (II), Anghel Iordanescu, Doru Nicolae (46' Aurel Radulescu). (Coach: Stefan Kovacs (ROM)).
Yugoslavia: Petar Borota, Nenad Stojkovic, Drazen Muzinic, Dzemal Hadziabdic, Vladimir Petrovic, Nikica Cukrov, Aleksandar Trifunovic (70' Vedran Rozic), Ivan Surjak, Safet Susic, Slavisa Zungul (70' Damir Desnica), Vahid Haliljodzic. (Coach: Ante Mladinic (YUG)).
Goals: Romania: 1-1 Stefan Sames (62'), 2-1 Stefan Sames (68'), 3-1 Anghel Iordanescu (75' penalty).
Yugoslavia: 0-1 Vladimir Petrovic (22' penalty), 3-2 Damir Desnica (90').
Referee: Riccardo Lattanzi (ITA)   Attendance: 24.090

15-11-1978   Estadio Mestalla, Valencia: Spain – Romania   1-0 (1-0)
Spain: MIGUEL ÁNGEL González Suarez, José Ramón ALEXANCO Ventosá, Miguel Bernardo Bianquetti "MIGUELI", MARCELINO Pérez Ayllón, José CARRETE de Julián, Juan Manuel ASENSI Ripoll, Vicente DEL BOSQUE, Ángel María VILLAR Llona, Juan Carlos HEREDIA Anaya (75' Enrique SAURA Gil), Carlos Alonso González "SANTILLANA", José Francisco "CHECHU" ROJO Arroita (I) (62' RUBÉN Andres CANO Martinez). (Coach: László "LADISLAO" KUBALA Stecz (ESP)).
Romania: Narcis Coman, Costica Stefanescu, Iosif Vigu, Stefan Sames, Mihai Zamfir, Laszlo Bölöni, Zoltan Crisan, Mihai Romila (II), Anghel Iordanescu, Dudu Georgescu, Aurel Radulescu. (Coach: Stefan Kovacs (ROM)).
Goal: Spain: 1-0 Juan Manuel ASENSI Ripoll (9').
Referee: Johannes Nicolaus Ignacius (Jan) Keizer (HOL)   Attendance: 46.000

13-12-1978   Estadio El Helmántico, Salamanca: Spain – Cyprus   5-0 (2-0)
Spain: MIGUEL ÁNGEL González Suarez, José Ramón ALEXANCO Ventosá, Miguel Bernardo Bianquetti "MIGUELI", MARCELINO Pérez Ayllón, Secundino Suárez Vázquez "CUNDI", Juan Manuel ASENSI Ripoll, Vicente DEL BOSQUE, Ángel María VILLAR Llona (46' Eugenio LEAL Vargas), Juan Carlos HEREDIA Anaya (46' RUBÉN Andres CANO Martinez), Estanislao ARGOTE Salaberría, Carlos Alonso González "SANTILLANA". (Coach: László "LADISLAO" KUBALA Stecz (ESP)).
Cyprus: George Pantziaras, Nikos Pantziaras, Stephanos Lysandrou, Stavros Papadopoulos (YC52), Dimitris Kyzas, Gregory Savva, Andreas Miamiliotis (64' Christakis Antoniou), Dimitrios Economou, Andreas Kanaris, Filippos Kalotheou, Fivos Vrahimis. (Coach: Costas Taliano (CYP)).
Goals: Spain: 1-0 Juan Manuel ASENSI Ripoll (8'), 2-0 Vicente DEL BOSQUE (10'), 3-0 Carlos Alonso González "SANTILLANA" (52'), 4-0 RUBÉN Andres CANO Martinez (65'), 5-0 Carlos Alonso González "SANTILLANA" (72').
Referee: Paul Bonett (MLT)   Attendance: 14.974

01-04-1979   Makario Stadium, Nicosia: Cyprus – Yugoslavia   0-3 (0-1)
Cyprus: Fanos Stylianou, Nikos Pantziaras (46' Andreas Papacostas), Stephanos Lysandrou, Vassas Violaris, Gregory Savva, Andreas Miamiliotis, Dimitrios Economou, Andreas Kanaris, Filippos Kalotheou, Antonis Kalimeras, Andreas Kissonergis. (Coach: Costas Taliano (CYP)).
Yugoslavia: Ratko Svilar, Nenad Stojkovic, Drazen Muzinic, Luka Peruzovic, Ismet Hadzic, Nenad Starovlah, Nikica Cukrov, Ante Mirocevic (83' Nikola Jovanovic), Zlatko Vujovic, Ivan Surjak, Dusan Savic (83' Miso Krsticevic). (Coach: Miljan Miljanic (YUG)).
Goals: Yugoslavia: 0-1 Zlatko Vujovic (40'), 0-2 Zlatko Vujovic (79'), 0-3 Ivan Surjak (87' penalty).
Referee: László Pádár (HUN)   Attendance: 3.376

04-04-1979   Ion Oblemenco Stadium, Craiova: Romania – Spain   2-2 (0-0)
Romania: Silviu Lung, Cornel Dinu, Teodor Lucuta, Stefan Sames, Mihai Zamfir, Ion Dumitru (80' Costica Stefanescu), Mircea Lucescu (51' Zoltan Crisan (RC59)), Laszlo Bölöni, Mihai Romila (II) (YC68), Dudu Georgescu, Dumitru Marcu. (Coach: Stefan Kovacs (ROM)).
Spain: Luis Miguel ARCONADA Echarri, José Ramón ALEXANCO Ventosá, MARCELINO Pérez Ayllón, Juan FELIPE Martín Martín, Juan Manuel ASENSI Ripoll, Isidoro SAN JOSÉ Pozo, Vicente DEL BOSQUE (60' Secundino Suárez Vázquez "CUNDI"), Ángel María VILLAR Llona, Enrique Castro González "QUINI" (87' Francisco José "LOBO" CARRASCO Hidalgo), Daniel Ruiz Bazan Justa "DANI", RUBÉN Andres CANO Martinez (YC73). (Coach: László "LADISLAO" KUBALA Stecz (ESP)).
Goals: Romania: 1-0 Dudu Georgescu (56' penalty), 2-1 Dudu Georgescu (64').
Spain: 1-1 Daniel Ruiz Bazan Justa "DANI" (59'), 2-2 Daniel Ruiz Bazan Justa "DANI" (70').
Referee: Marcel Van Langenhove (BEL)   Attendance: 47.000

13-05-1979   Tsirion Stadium, Limassol: Cyprus – Romania   1-1 (1-1)
Cyprus: George Pantziaras, Nikos Pantziaras, Stephanos Lysandrou, Stavros Papadopoulos, Nikos Patikis, Gregory Savva, Filippos Kalotheou, Andreas Kissonergis (73' Fivos Vrahimis), Loizos Mavroudis (80' George Aristidou), Marios Tsingis, Soteris Kaiafas. (Coach: Costas Talianos (CYP)).
Romania: Andrei Speriatu, Costica Stefanescu, Mihai Zamfir, Petre Ivan (II), Ilie Barbulescu, Constantin Carstea, Sevastian Iovanescu, Ionel Augustin, Doru Nicolae, Marin Radu (46' Doru Rodion Camataru), Contin Stan (67' Marcel Raducanu). (Coach: Stefan Kovacs (ROM)).
Goals: Cyprus: 1-1 Soteris Kaiafas (31').
Romania: 0-1 Ionel Augustin (30').
Referee: Dimitar Yordanov Parmakov (BUL)   Attendance: 6.488

10-10-1979   Estadio Mestalla, Valencia: Spain – Yugoslavia   0-1 (0-1)
Spain: Luis Miguel ARCONADA Echarri, José Ramón ALEXANCO Ventosá (YC36,YC80), Miguel Bernardo Manquetti "MIGUELI", Francisco Javier Alvarez URÍA, Juan Manuel ASENSI Ripoll, Isidoro SAN JOSÉ Pozo, Vicente DEL BOSQUE, Ángel María VILLAR Llona, Juan Carlos HEREDIA Anaya, Enrique Castro González "QUINI" (46' Carlos Alonso González "SANTILLANA"), Daniel Ruiz Bazan Justa "DANI". (Coach: László "LADISLAO" KUBALA Stecz (ESP)).
Yugoslavia: Dragan Pantelic, Velimir Zajec, Vedran Rozic, Miso Krsticevic (YC73,YC90), Zoran Vujovic, Boro Primorac, Blaz Sliskovic (YC82), Zlatko Vujovic, Ivan Surjak, Milos Sestic (75' Drazen Muzinic (YC77)), Safet Susic. (Coach: Miljan Miljanic (YUG)).
Goal: Yugoslavia: 0-1 Ivan Surjak (5').
Referee: Brian R.McGinlay (SCO)   Attendance: 28.078

31-10-1979   Stadion Trepca, Kosovska Mitrovica: Yugoslavia – Romania   2-1 (0-0)
Yugoslavia: Dragan Pantelic, Velimir Zajec, Ismet Hadzic, Nenad Starovlah, Boro Primorac, Vladimir Petrovic, Blaz Sliskovic (87' Nenad Stojkovic), Zlatko Vujovic, Ivan Surjak (82' Nikica Cukrov), Milos Sestic, Safet Susic. (Coach: Miljan Miljanic (YUG)).
Romania: Cristian Gheorghe, Cornel Dinu, Costica Stefanescu, Stefan Sames, Neculai Tilihoi, Ion Munteanu (II), Ilie Balaci (78' Ionel Augustin), Laszlo Bölöni, Zoltan Crisan, Gheorghe Multescu (87' Alexandru Nicolae), Marcel Raducanu. (Coach: Stefan Kovacs (ROM)).
Goals: Yugoslavia: 1-0 Zlatko Vujovic (48'), 2-0 Blaz Sliskovic (50').
Romania: 2-1 Marcel Raducanu (79').
Referee: Jan Redelfs (FRG)   Attendance: 24.397

143

14-11-1979   Gradski stadion, Novi Sad: Yugoslavia – Cyprus   5-0 (1-0)
Yugoslavia: Dragan Pantelic, Velimir Zajec, Nenad Stojkovic, Vedran Rozic, Vladimir
Petrovic, Nikica Cukrov, Blaz Sliskovic (10' Zlatko Kranjcar), Zlatko Vujovic (80' Dusan
Savic), Ivan Surjak, Milos Sestic, Safet Susic. (Coach: Miljan Miljanic (YUG)).
Cyprus: George Pantziaras, Nikos Pantziaras, Stephanos Lysandrou, Neophytos Neophytou,
Costas Constantinou, Andreas Kanaris, Filippos Kalotheou, Andreas Kissonergis (68' Petros
Theophanous), Loizos Mavroudis, Marios Tsingis, Soteris Kaiafas. (Coach: Costas Talianos
(CYP)).
Goals: Yugoslavia: 1-0 Zlatko Kranjcar (32'), 2-0 Zlatko Kranjcar (50'), 3-0 Zlatko Vujovic
(60'), 4-0 Vladimir Petrovic (75'), 5-0 Dusan Savic (87').
Referee: Yordan Zhezhov (BUL)   Attendance: 14.134

18-11-1979   Stadionul Dinamo, Bucharest: Romania – Cyprus   2-0 (1-0)
Romania: Cristian Gheorghe, Stefan Sames, Alexandru Nicolae, Neculai Tilihoi, Ion Munteanu
(II), Laszlo Bölöni, Zoltan Crisan (46' Sorin Cartu), Gheorghe Multescu, Marcel Raducanu,
Aurel Beldeanu (65' Ilie Balaci), Doru Rodion Camataru. (Coach: Stefan Kovacs (ROM)).
Cyprus: George Pantziaras, Nikos Pantziaras, Stephanos Lysandrou, Neophytos Neophytou,
Costas Constantinou, Pambos Papadopoulos, Andreas Kanaris, Filippos Kalotheou, Loizos
Mavroudis (85' Fivos Vrahimis), Marios Tsingis (46' Dimitrios Economou), Soteris Kaiafas.
(Coach: Costas Talianos (CYP)).
Goals: Romania: 1-0 Gheorghe Multescu (42'), 2-0 Marcel Raducanu (75').
Referee: Dusan Krchnák (TCH)   Attendance: 3.000

09-12-1979   Tsirion Stadium, Limassol: Cyprus – Spain   1-3 (0-2)
Cyprus: Erodotos Koupanos, Nikos Pantziaras, Stephanos Lysandrou, Stavros Papadopoulos,
Pambos Papadopoulos (67' Fivos Vrahimis), Dimitris Kyzas, Andreas Kanaris, Filippos
Kalotheou, Loizos Mavroudis, Marios Tsingis, Petros Theophanous (46' Andreas Papacostas).
(Coach: Costas Talianos (CYP)).
Spain: Luis Miguel ARCONADA Echarri, Miguel Bernardo Bianquetti "MIGUELI",
Francisco Javier Alvarez URÍA, Secundino Suárez Vázquez "CUNDI", Antonio OLMO
Rodriguez, Vicente DEL BOSQUE (78' Francisco José "LOBO" CARRASCO Hidalgo),
Ángel María VILLAR Llona (78' JESÚS María ZAMORA Ansorena), Enrique SAURA Gil,
Enrique Castro González "QUINI", Carlos Alonso González "SANTILLANA", Daniel Ruiz
Bazan Justa "DANI". (Coach: László "LADISLAO" KUBALA Stecz (ESP)).
Goals: Cyprus: 1-2 Fivos Vrahimis (69').
Spain: 0-1 Ángel María VILLAR Llona (5'), 0-2 Carlos Alonso González "SANTILLANA"
(41'), 1-3 Enrique SAURA Gil (89').
Referee: Josef Bucek (AUT)   Attendance: 9.128

GROUP 4

06-09-1978	Reykjavik	Iceland – Poland	0-2 (0-1)
20-09-1978	Nijmegen	Netherlands – Iceland	3-0 (1-0)
04-10-1978	Halle	East Germany – Iceland	3-1 (2-1)
11-10-1978	Bern	Switzerland – Netherlands	1-3 (1-1)
15-11-1978	Rotterdam	Netherlands – East Germany	3-0 (1-0)
15-11-1978	Wroclaw	Poland – Switzerland	2-0 (1-0)
28-03-1979	Eindhoven	Netherlands – Switzerland	3-0 (0-0)
18-04-1979	Leipzig	East Germany – Poland	2-1 (0-1)
02-05-1979	Chorzów	Poland – Netherlands	2-0 (1-0)
05-05-1979	St.Gallen	Switzerland – East Germany	0-2 (0-1)
22-05-1979	Bern	Switzerland – Iceland	2-0 (1-0)
09-06-1979	Reykjavik	Iceland – Switzerland	1-2 (0-0)
05-09-1979	Reykjavik	Iceland – Netherlands	0-4 (0-0)
12-09-1979	Reykjavik	Iceland – East Germany	0-3 (0-0)
12-09-1979	Lausanne	Switzerland – Poland	0-2 (0-1)
26-09-1979	Chorzów	Poland – East Germany	1-1 (0-0)
10-10-1979	Kraków	Poland – Iceland	2-0 (0-0)
13-10-1979	East Berlin	East Germany – Switzerland	5-2 (3-1)
17-10-1979	Amsterdam	Netherlands – Poland	1-1 (0-1)
21-11-1979	Leipzig	East Germany – Netherlands	2-3 (2-1)

FINAL STANDING

Pos	Team	Pld	W	D	L	GF	GA	GD	Pts
1	*Netherlands*	8	6	1	1	20	6	+14	13
2	Poland	8	5	2	1	13	4	+9	12
3	East Germany	8	5	1	2	18	11	+7	11
4	Switzerland	8	2	0	6	7	18	-11	4
5	Iceland	8	0	0	8	2	21	-19	0

Netherlands qualified for the final tournament in Italy.

06-09-1978   Laugardalsvöllur, Reykjavik: Iceland – Poland   0-2 (0-1)
Iceland: Árni Stefánsson, Atli Edvaldsson, Gisli Torfason, Jon Pétursson, Johannes Edvaldsson (C), Hördur Hilmarsson (46' Ingi Björn Albertsson), Karl Thordarsson, Árni Sveinsson, Janus Gudlaugsson, Pétur Pétursson, Gudmundur Thorbjörnsson. (Coach: Yury Ilitecev (URS)).
Poland: Zygmunt Kukla, Stefan Majewski, Antoni Szymanowski (C), Henryk Maculewicz, Wojciech Rudy, Grzegorz Lato, Leslaw Cmikiewicz, Bogdan Masztaler (YC65), Tadeusz Blachno, Zbigniew Boniek, Marek Kusto. (Coach: Jacek Gmoch (POL)).
Goals: Poland: 0-1 Marek Kusto (24'), 0-2 Grzegorz Lato (85').
Referee: Thomas Perry (NIR)   Attendance: 6.594

20-09-1978   De Goffert, Nijmegen: Netherlands – Iceland   3-0 (1-0)
Netherlands: Piet Schrijvers, Pieter Wildschut, Ernie Brandts, Ruud Krol, Wim Jansen, Dick Nanninga, Jan Poortvliet, Arie Haan, Rob Rensenbrink, Willy van de Kerkhof, Adrie Koster (75' Jan Peters). (Coach: Johannes Hermanus Hendrikus (Jan) Zwartkruis (HOL)).
Iceland: Thorsteinn Bjarnason, Atli Edvaldsson (YC63), Jon Pétursson, Johannes Edvaldsson, Ásgeir Sigurvinsson, Karl Thordarsson, Árni Sveinsson (YC42), Janus Gudlaugsson, Pétur Pétursson, Gudmundur Thorbjörnsson, Ingi Björn Albertsson (68' Dyri Gudmundsson). (Coach: Yury Ilitecev (URS)).
Goals: Netherlands: 1-0 Ruud Krol (31'), 2-0 Ernie Brandts (53'), 3-0 Rob Rensenbrink (63' penalty).
Referee: Anders Mattsson (FIN)   Attendance: 13.113

04-10-1978   Kurt-Wabbel-Stadion, Halle: East Germany – Iceland   3-1 (2-1)
East Germany: Jürgen Croy, Konrad Weise, Martin Hoffmann, Hans-Jürgen Dörner, Lothar Hause, Jürgen Pommerenke, Reinhard Häfner (35' Lutz Lindemann), Gerd Weber, Lutz Eigendorf, Hans-Jürgen Riediger, Werner Peter. (Coach: Georg Buschner (GDR)).
Iceland: Thorsteinn Bjarnason (46' Árni Stefánsson), Atli Edvaldsson, Jon Pétursson, Karl Thordarsson, Árni Sveinsson (80' Ingi Björn Albertsson), Janus Gudlaugsson, Sigurdur Björgvinsson, Stefan Orn Sigurdsson, Pétur Pétursson, Teitur Thordarsson, Gudmundur Thorbjörnsson. (Coach: Yury Ilitecev (URS)).
Goals: East Germany: 1-0 Werner Peter (6'), 2-1 Hans-Jürgen Riediger (29'), 3-1 Martin Hoffmann (72').
Iceland: 1-1 Pétur Pétursson (14' penalty).
Referee: Thomas Henry Charles Reynolds (WAL)   Attendance: 9.084

11-10-1978   Wankdorfstadion, Bern: Switzerland – Netherlands   1-3 (1-1)
Switzerland: Erich Burgener, Pierre-Albert Chapuisat, Luciano Bizzini, Jakob Brechbühl, Francis Montandon, René Botteron, Marc Schnyder (46' Raimondo Ponte), Karl Elsener, Markus Tanner (82' Roger Wehrli), Umberto Barberis, Claudio Sulser. (Coach: Roger Vonlanthen (SUI)).
Netherlands: Piet Schrijvers, Pieter Wildschut, Ernie Brandts, Ruud Krol (C), Hugo Hovenkamp (34' John Dusbaba), Dick Nanninga, Jan Poortvliet, Arie Haan, Rob Rensenbrink, Willy van de Kerkhof (34' Jan Peters), Ruud Geels. (Coach: Johannes Hermanus Hendrikus (Jan) Zwartkruis (HOL)).
Goals: Switzerland: 1-1 Markus Tanner (32').
Netherlands: 0-1 Pieter Wildschut (19'), 1-2 Ernie Brandts (67'), 1-3 Ruud Geels (90').
Referee: César da Luz Dias Correia (POR)   Attendance: 20.732

15-11-1978   Stadion Feijenoord, Rotterdam: Netherlands – East Germany   3-0 (1-0)
Netherlands: Piet Schrijvers, Pieter Wildschut, Ernie Brandts, Adrie van Kraay, Ruud Krol, Hugo Hovenkamp (78' Adrie Koster), Johan Neeskens (54' Johnny Metgod), Jan Peters, Rob Rensenbrink, Willy van de Kerkhof, Ruud Geels. (Coach: Johannes Hermanus Hendrikus (Jan) Zwartkruis (HOL)).
East Germany: Jürgen Croy, Gerd Kische, Martin Hoffmann, Rüdiger Schnuphase, Hans-Jürgen Dörner, Reinhard Häfner, Gerd Weber, Hartmut Schade (46' Werner Peter), Lutz Eigendorf, Lutz Lindemann (53' Wolf-Rüdiger Netz), Hans-Jürgen Riediger. (Coach: Georg Buschner (GDR)).
Goals: Netherlands: 1-0 Gerd Kische (18' *own goal*), 2-0 Ruud Geels (72' penalty), 3-0 Ruud Geels (88').
Referee: Ulf Johan Eriksson (SWE)   Attendance: 33.972

15-11-1978   Stadion Olimpijski, Wroclaw: Poland – Switzerland   2-0 (1-0)
Poland: Zygmunt Kukla, Wladyslaw Zmuda, Stefan Majewski (85' Wojciech Rudy), Antoni Szymanowski (C), Henryk Maculewicz, Grzegorz Lato, Leslaw Cmikiewicz, Adam Nawalka, Zbigniew Boniek, Roman Ogaza, Stanislaw Terlecki. (Coach: Ryszard Kulesza (POL)).
Switzerland: Karl Engel, Pierre-Albert Chapuisat, Luciano Bizzini (C), Jakob Brechbühl, Francis Montandon, René Botteron, Marc Schnyder, André Meyer (YC70), Karl Elsener (46' Raimondo Ponte), Umberto Barberis, Claudio Sulser. (Coach: Roger Vonlanthen (SUI)).
Goals: Poland: 1-0 Zbigniew Boniek (39'), 2-0 Roman Ogaza (58').
Referee: Franz Wöhrer (AUT)   Attendance: 27.576

28-03-1979   Philips Stadion, Eindhoven: Netherlands – Switzerland   3-0 (0-0)
Netherlands: Piet Schrijvers, Pieter Wildschut (84' Huub Stevens), Ernie Brandts, Wim Jansen (C) (YC34), Jan Poortvliet, Johan Neeskens, Jan Peters, Rob Rensenbrink, René van de Kerkhof, Willy van de Kerkhof (54' Johnny Metgod) , Kees Kist. (Coach: Johannes Hermanus Hendrikus (Jan) Zwartkruis (HOL)).
Switzerland: Erich Burgener, Pierre-Albert Chapuisat, Luciano Bizzini (C) (58' Roger Wehrli), Jakob Brechbühl (65' Raimondo Ponte), Francis Montandon, Heinz Hermann, René Botteron, Marc Schnyder, Karl Elsener, Umberto Barberis, Claudio Sulser. (Coach: Roger Vonlanthen (SUI)).
Goals: Netherlands: 1-0 Kees Kist (56'), 2-0 Johnny Metgod (84'), 3-0 Jan Peters (89').
Referee: John Hunting (ENG)   Attendance: 21.674

18-04-1979   Zentralstadion, Leipzig: East Germany – Poland   2-1 (0-1)
East Germany: Hans-Ulrich Grapenthin, Konrad Weise, Gerd Kische, Martin Hoffmann, Hans-Jürgen Dörner (C), Reinhard Häfner, Gerd Weber, Hartmut Schade (46' Jürgen Pommerenke), Lutz Lindemann, Joachim Streich, Hans-Jürgen Riediger. (Coach: Georg Buschner (GDR)).
Poland: Zygmunt Kukla, Pawel Janas, Wladyslaw Zmuda, Stefan Majewski (76' Michal Wrobel), Marek Dziuba (58' Wojciech Rudy), Antoni Szymanowski (C), Grzegorz Lato, Leslaw Cmikiewicz, Adam Nawalka, Zbigniew Boniek (YC1), Roman Ogaza. (Coach: Ryszard Kulesza (POL)).
Goals: East Germany: 1-1 Joachim Streich (50'), 2-1 Lutz Lindemann (63').
Poland: 0-1 Zbigniew Boniek (8').
Referee: Eldar Azim-Zade (URS)   Attendance: 45.254

02-05-1979   Stadion Slaski, Chorzów: Poland – Netherlands   2-0 (1-0)
Poland: Zygmunt Kukla, Wladyslaw Zmuda, Marek Dziuba, Antoni Szymanowski (C), Zbigniew Plaszewski, Grzegorz Lato, Adam Nawalka, Leszek Lipka, Zbigniew Boniek, Roman Ogaza, Stanislaw Terlecki (46' Wlodzimierz Mazur). (Coach: Ryszard Kulesza (POL)).
Netherlands: Piet Schrijvers, Huub Stevens, Ernie Brandts, Ruud Krol (C), Hugo Hovenkamp, Wim Jansen, Jan Peters, Rob Rensenbrink (73' Johnny Metgod), René van de Kerkhof (46' Ruud Geels), Willy van de Kerkhof, Kees Kist. (Coach: Johannes Hermanus Hendrikus (Jan) Zwartkruis (HOL)).
Goals: Poland: 1-0 Zbigniew Boniek (19'), 2-0 Wlodzimierz Mazur (64' penalty).
Referee: Robert Charles Paul Wurtz (FRA)   Attendance: 71.298

05-05-1979   Espenmoos Stadium, St.Gallen: Switzerland – East Germany   0-2 (0-1)
Switzerland: Roger Berbig, Luciano Bizzini (C), Roger Wehrli, Heinz Lüdi, Heinz Hermann, Erni Maissen, Raimondo Ponte, Markus Tanner, Umberto Barberis, Jean-Paul Brigger (46' René Botteron), Thomas Zwahlen (73' Herbert Hermann). (Coach: Léon Walker (SUI)).
East Germany: Hans-Ulrich Grapenthin, Konrad Weise, Gerd Kische, Martin Hoffmann, Hans-Jürgen Dörner (C), Jürgen Pommerenke, Reinhard Häfner, Gerd Weber, Lutz Lindemann, Joachim Streich, Hans-Jürgen Riediger. (Coach: Georg Buschner (GDR)).
Goals: East Germany: 0-1 Lutz Lindemann (45'), 0-2 Joachim Streich (90').
Referee: Augusto Lamo Castillo (ESP)   Attendance: 7.486

22-05-1979   Wankdorfstadion, Bern: Switzerland – Iceland   2-0 (1-0)
Switzerland: Walter Eichenberger, Jakob Brechbühl, Roger Wehrli (46' Markus Tanner), Heinz Lüdi, Gian Pietro Zappa, Heinz Hermann, René Botteron (C), Erni Maissen, Herbert Hermann, Raimondo Ponte (60' Marc Schnyder), Umberto Barberis. (Coach: Léon Walker (SUI)).
Iceland: Thorsteinn Olafsson, Atli Edvaldsson, Jon Pétursson, Marteinn Geirsson, Johannes Edvaldsson (C) (79' Otto Gudmundsson), Ásgeir Sigurvinsson, Árni Sveinsson, Janus Gudlaugsson, Arnor Gudjohnsen, Pétur Pétursson (60' Karl Thordarsson), Gudmundur Thorbjörnsson. (Coach: Yury Ilitecev (URS)).
Goals: Switzerland: 1-0 Herbert Hermann (27'), 2-0 Gian Pietro Zappa (53').
Referee: Albert Victor (LUX)   Attendance: 20.234

09-06-1979   Laugardalsvöllur, Reykjavik: Iceland – Switzerland   1-2 (0-0)
Iceland: Thorsteinn Olafsson, Atli Edvaldsson, Marteinn Geirsson, Johannes Edvaldsson, Trausli Haraldsson, Ásgeir Sigurvinsson, Janus Gudlaugsson, Arnor Gudjohnsen, Pétur Pétursson, Teitur Thordarsson (78' Karl Thordarsson), Gudmundur Thorbjörnsson (66' Árni Sveinsson). (Coach: Yury Ilitecev (URS)).
Switzerland: Roger Berbig, Jakob Brechbühl, Roger Wehrli, Heinz Lüdi, Gian Pietro Zappa, Heinz Hermann (71' Andy Egli), René Botteron (75' Markus Tanner), Herbert Hermann, Claude Andrey, Raimondo Ponte, Umberto Barberis. (Coach: Léon Walker (SUI)).
Goals: Iceland: 1-0 Janus Gudlaugsson (49').
Switzerland: 1-1 Raimondo Ponte (59'), 1-2 Heinz Hermann (61').
Referee: Eamonn A. Farrell (IRL)   Attendance: 10.469

05-09-1979   Laugardalsvöllur, Reykjavik: Iceland – Netherlands   0-4 (0-0)
Iceland: Thorsteinn Bjarnason, Atli Edvaldsson, Marteinn Geirsson, Johannes Edvaldsson (C), Dyri Gudmundsson, Trausli Haraldsson, Karl Thordarsson, Árni Sveinsson, Sigurlas Thorleifsson (65' Tomas Pálsson), Pétur Pétursson, Gudmundur Thorbjörnsson. (Coach: Yury Ilitecev (URS)).
Netherlands: Piet Schrijvers, Huub Stevens, Ernie Brandts, Ruud Krol (C), Hugo Hovenkamp, Dick Nanninga, Jan Poortvliet (YC58), Simon Tahamata, Tscheu La Ling (46' Johnny Metgod), René van de Kerkhof, Willy van de Kerkhof. (Coach: Johannes Hermanus Hendrikus (Jan) Zwartkruis (HOL)).
Goals: Netherlands: 0-1 Johnny Metgod (48'), 0-2 Willy van de Kerkhof (71'), 0-3 Dick Nanninga (73'), 0-4 Dick Nanninga (87').
Referee: Clive Thomas (WAL)   Attendance: 10.375

12-09-1979   Laugardalsvöllur, Reykjavik: Iceland – East Germany   0-3 (0-0)
Iceland: Thorsteinn Bjarnason, Atli Edvaldsson, Marteinn Geirsson, Johannes Edvaldsson (C), Örn Óskarsson, Gudgeir Leifsson (YC68), Ásgeir Sigurvinsson, Hördur Hilmarsson, Árni Sveinsson, Sigurlas Thorleifsson, Gudmundur Thorbjörnsson. (Coach: Yury Ilitecev (URS)).
East Germany: Hans-Ulrich Grapenthin, Konrad Weise (C), Gerd Kische, Martin Hoffmann, Rüdiger Schnuphase, Hans-Jürgen Dörner, Reinhard Häfner, Gerd Weber, Lutz Lindemann, Joachim Streich, Hans-Jürgen Riediger. (Coach: Georg Buschner (GDR)).
Goals: East Germany: 0-1 Gerd Weber (66' penalty), 0-2 Gerd Weber (73'), 0-3 Joachim Streich (80').
Referee: Svein Inge Thime (NOR)   Attendance: 9.162

12-09-1979   Stade Olympique de la Pontaise, Lausanne: Switzerland – Poland   0-2 (0-1)
Switzerland: Erich Burgener, Luciano Bizzini (C), Jakob Brechbühl, Heinz Lüdi, Gian Pietro Zappa, Marc Schnyder, Claude Andrey, Raimondo Ponte, Hans Jörg Pfister, Umberto Barberis, Claudio Sulser (70' Heinz Hermann). (Coach: Léon Walker (SUI)).
Poland: Zygmunt Kukla, Pawel Janas, Stefan Majewski (87' Antoni Szymanowski), Marek Dziuba, Wojciech Rudy, Grzegorz Lato (C), Adam Nawalka, Henryk Wieczorek, Zbigniew Boniek, Kazimierz Kmiecik (88' Wlodzimierz Mazur), Stanislaw Terlecki. (Coach: Ryszard Kulesza (POL)).
Goals: Poland: 0-1 Stanislaw Terlecki (34'), 0-2 Stanislaw Terlecki (63').
Referee: Otto Anderco (ROM)   Attendance: 22.363

26-09-1979   Stadion Slaski, Chorzów: Poland – East Germany   1-1 (0-0)
Poland: Zygmunt Kukla, Pawel Janas, Marek Dziuba (70' Wlodzimierz Mazur), Antoni Szymanowski (C), Wojciech Rudy, Grzegorz Lato, Adam Nawalka (74' Henryk Wieczorek), Leszek Lipka, Zbigniew Boniek (YC27), Roman Ogaza, Stanislaw Terlecki. (Coach: Ryszard Kulesza (POL)).
East Germany: Hans-Ulrich Grapenthin, Konrad Weise (YC36), Gerd Kische, Martin Hoffmann, Rüdiger Schnuphase, Hans-Jürgen Dörner (C), Gert Brauer (YC69), Reinhard Häfner, Gerd Weber, Lutz Lindemann, Hans-Jürgen Riediger. (Coach: Georg Buschner (GDR)).
Goals: Poland: 1-1 Henryk Wieczorek (77').
East Germany: 0-1 Reinhard Häfner (62').
Referee: Patrick Partridge (ENG)   Attendance: 63.938

10-10-1979   Stadion Miejski im. Henryka Reymana, Kraków: Poland – Iceland   2-0 (0-0)
Poland: Zygmunt Kukla, Pawel Janas, Antoni Szymanowski (C), Wojciech Rudy, Grzegorz Lato, Adam Nawalka, Leszek Lipka, Henryk Wieczorek, Zbigniew Boniek, Roman Ogaza, Stanislaw Terlecki (55' Janusz Sybis). (Coach: Ryszard Kulesza (POL)).
Iceland: Thorsteinn Bjarnason, Atli Edvaldsson, Marteinn Geirsson, Johannes Edvaldsson (C) (YC71), Dyri Gudmundsson, Trausti Haraldsson, Örn Óskarsson, Ásgeir Sigurvinsson, Árni Sveinsson, Pétur Pétursson (YC74), Teitur Thordarsson. (Coach: Yury Ilitecev (URS)).
Goals: Poland: 1-0 Roman Ogaza (55'), 2-0 Roman Ogaza (74' penalty).
Referee: Henning Lund-Sørensen (DEN)   Attendance: 13.352

13-10-1979   Stadion der Weltjugend, East Berlin: East Germany – Switzerland 5-2 (3-1)
East Germany: Hans-Ulrich Grapenthin, Gerd Kische, Martin Hoffmann, Rüdiger Schnuphase, Hans-Jürgen Dörner (C), Gert Brauer, Reinhard Häfner, Gerd Weber, Lutz Lindemann, Joachim Striech (66' Peter Kotte), Hans-Jürgen Riediger. (Coach: Georg Buschner (GDR)).
Switzerland: Erich Burgener, Luciano Bizzini (C), Jakob Brechbühl, Heinz Lüdi, Gian Pietro Zappa, Heinz Hermann, Marc Schnyder, Hans Jörg Pfister, Markus Tanner (46' Raimondo Ponte), Umberto Barberis, Claudio Sulser (57' Andy Egli). (Coach: Léon Walker (SUI)).
Goals: East Germany: 1-0 Gerd Weber (1'), 2-0 Martin Hoffmann (11'), 3-1 Rüdiger Schnuphase (26'), 4-2 Martin Hoffmann (75'), 5-2 Martin Hoffmann (80').
Switzerland: 2-1 Umberto Barberis (19'), 3-2 Hans Jörg Pfister (72').
Referee: Robert Charles Paul Wurtz (FRA)   Attendance: 32.406

17-10-1979   Olympisch Stadion, Amsterdam: Netherlands – Poland 1-1 (0-1)
Netherlands: Piet Schrijvers, Huub Stevens, Ernie Brandts (46' Tscheu La Ling), Ruud Krol (C), Ben Wijnstekers, Hugo Hovenkamp, Wim Jansen, Simon Tahamata, Johnny Rep, Willy van de Kerkhof, Kees Kist. (Coach: Johannes Hermanus Hendrikus (Jan) Zwartkruis (HOL)).
Poland: Zygmunt Kukla, Pawel Janas (YC50), Marek Dziuba, Antoni Szymanowski (C), Wojciech Rudy, Grzegorz Lato, Adam Nawalka, Leszek Lipka, Zbigniew Boniek, Stanislaw Terlecki, Janusz Sybis (70' Wlodzimierz Mazur). (Coach: Ryszard Kulesza (POL)).
Goals: Netherlands: 1-1 Huub Stevens (65').
Poland: 0-1 Wojciech Rudy (39').
Referee: Paolo Casarin (ITA)   Attendance: 45.049

21-11-1979   Zentralstadion, Leipzig: East Germany – Netherlands 2-3 (2-1)
East Germany: Hans-Ulrich Grapenthin, Konrad Weise (YC34,YC40), Gerd Kische, Martin Hoffmann, Rüdiger Schnuphase (60' Hartmut Schade), Hans-Jürgen Dörner (C), Gert Brauer, Reinhard Häfner, Gerd Weber (72' Jürgen Pommerenke), Joachim Streich, Peter Kotte. (Coach: Georg Buschner (GDR)).
Netherlands: Piet Schrijvers, Huub Stevens (69' Ernie Brandts), Ruud Krol (C), Michel van de Korput, Ben Wijnstekers, Hugo Hovenkamp (YC46) (46' Kees Kist (YC67)), Dick Schoenaker, Frans Thijssen, Simon Tahamata, Tscheu La Ling (RC40), Willy van de Kerkhof. (Coach: Johannes Hermanus Hendrikus (Jan) Zwartkruis (HOL)).
Goals: East Germany: 1-0 Rüdiger Schnuphase (17'), 2-0 Joachim Streich (33' penalty).
Netherlands: 2-1 Frans Thijssen (45'), 2-2 Kees Kist (50'), 2-3 Willy van de Kerkhof (67').
Referee: António José da Silva Garrido (POR)   Attendance: 89.297

GROUP 5

01-09-1978	Paris	France – Sweden	2-2 (0-0)
04-10-1978	Stockholm	Sweden – Czechoslovakia	1-3 (1-1)
07-10-1978	Luxembourg	Luxembourg – France	1-3 (0-1)
25-02-1979	Paris	France – Luxembourg	3-0 (1-0)
04-04-1979	Bratislava	Czechoslovakia – France	2-0 (0-0)
01-05-1979	Luxembourg	Luxembourg – Czechoslovakia	0-3 (0-1)
07-06-1979	Malmö	Sweden – Luxembourg	3-0 (2-0)
05-09-1979	Stockholm	Sweden – France	1-3 (1-1)
10-10-1979	Prague	Czechoslovakia – Sweden	4-1 (3-0)
23-10-1979	Esch-sur-Alzette	Luxembourg – Sweden	1-1 (1-0)
17-11-1979	Paris	France – Czechoslovakia	2-1 (0-0)
24-11-1979	Prague	Czechoslovakia – Luxembourg	4-0 (3-0)

FINAL STANDING

Pos	Team	Pld	W	D	L	GF	GA	GD	Pts
1	*Czechoslovakia*	*6*	*5*	*0*	*1*	*17*	*4*	*+13*	*10*
2	France	6	4	1	1	13	7	+6	9
3	Sweden	6	1	2	3	9	13	-4	4
4	Luxembourg	6	0	1	5	2	17	-15	1

Czechoslovakia qualified for the final tournament in Italy.

01-09-1978   Parc des Princes, Paris: France – Sweden   2-2 (0-0)
France: André Rey, Patrick Battiston, Max Bossis, Christian López, Patrice Rio, Dominique Bathenay, Roger Jouve, Henri Michel (C) (77' Alain Giresse), Didier Six, Olivier Rouyer, Albert Gemmrich (65' Marc Berdoll). (Coach: Michel Hidalgo (FRA)).
Sweden: Ronnie Hellström, Björn Nordqvist (C), Hasse Borg, Ronald Åhman, Håkan Arvidsson, Anders Linderoth, Lennart Larsson, Thomas Sjöberg (75' Tommy Berggren), Mats Nordgren, Benny Wendt, Anders Grönhagen. (Coach: Georg (Åby) Ericsson (SWE)).
Goals: France: 1-1 Marc Berdoll (72'), 2-1 Didier Six (83').
Sweden: 0-1 Mats Nordgren (54'), 2-2 Anders Grönhagen (90').
Referee: Károly Palotai (HUN)   Attendance: 44.703

04-10-1978   Råsunda Stadion, Solna: Sweden – Czechoslovakia   1-3 (1-1)
Sweden: Ronnie Hellström, Björn Nordqvist (C), Hasse Borg, Ronald Åhman, Håkan Arvidsson, Anders Linderoth, Lennart Larsson, Mats Nordgren, Tommy Berggren (70' Billy Ohlsson), Benny Wendt, Anders Grönhagen. (Coach: Georg (Åby) Ericsson (SWE)).
Czechoslovakia: Pavel Michalík, Jozef Barmos, Rostislav Vojácek, Anton Ondrus (C), Koloman Gögh, Frantisek Stambachr, Jaroslav Pollák, Zdenek Nehoda, Marián Masny, Miroslav Gajdusek, Karel Kroupa (80' Ján Kozák). (Coach: Jozef Venglos (TCH)).
Goals: Sweden: 1-0 Hasse Borg (14' penalty).
Czechoslovakia: 1-1 Marián Masny (18'), 1-2 Marián Masny (48'), 1-3 Zdenek Nehoda (85').
Referee: John Robertson Proudfoot Gordon (SCO)   Attendance: 11.985

07-10-1978   Stade Josy Barthel, Luxembourg: Luxembourg – France   1-3 (0-1)
Luxembourg: Jeannot Moes, Jean-Louis Margue (62' Aldo Catani), Hubert Meunier, Nico Rohmann, Gilbert Dresch, Romain Michaux, Fernand Raths (YC39) (43' Roger Fandel), Carlo Weis, Paul Philipp (C), Camille Neumann, Gilbert Dussier. (Coach: Louis Pilot (LUX)).
France: Dominique Dropsy, Patrick Battiston, Max Bossis, Christian López (YC41), Marius Trésor (C), Jean François Larios (63' Jean Petit), Roger Jouve, Francis Piasecki, Dominique Rocheteau (59' Albert Gemmrich), Didier Six (YC88), Bernard Lacombe. (Coach: Michel Hidalgo (FRA)).
Goals: Luxembourg: 1-2 Romain Michaux (74').
France: 0-1 Didier Six (15'), 0-2 Marius Trésor (63'), 1-3 Albert Gemmrich (79').
Referee: Hendrik (Henk) Weerink (HOL)   Attendance: 12.652

25-02-1979   Parc des Princes, Paris: France – Luxembourg   3-0 (1-0)
France: Dominique Dropsy, Patrick Battiston, Max Bossis, Marius Trésor, Léonard Specht, Henri Michel, Jean Petit, Francis Piasecki (61' Jean François Larios), Dominique Rocheteau, Marc Berdoll (65' Eric Pécout), Albert Emon. (Coach: Michel Hidalgo (FRA)).
Luxembourg: Jeannot Moes, Jean-Louis Margue, Hubert Meunier, Nico Rohmann, Gilbert Dresch, Romain Michaux, Fernand Raths, Carlo Weis (YC) (46' Jeannot Reiter), Paul Philipp, Nico Wagner (YC), André Zwally (74' Camille Neumann). (Coach: Louis Pilot (LUX)).
Goals: France: 1-0 Jean Petit (38'), 2-0 Albert Emon (62'), 3-0 Jean François Larios (78').
Referee: Ronald Bridges (WAL)   Attendance: 46.988

04-04-1979   Stadión Tehelné pole, Bratislava: Czechoslovakia – France   2-0 (0-0)
Czechoslovakia: Jaroslav Netolicka, Jozef Barmos, Rostislav Vojácek, Anton Ondrus (C), Koloman Gögh, Antonín Panenka, Frantisek Stambachr, Ján Kozák, Zdenek Nehoda (56' Ladislav Vízek), Marián Masny, Miroslav Gajdusek. (Coach: Jozef Venglos (TCH)).
France: Dominique Dropsy, Max Bossis, Christian López (C), Raymond Domenech, Léonard Specht, Jean François Larios, Jean Petit, Michel Platini, Löic Amisse, Marc Berdoll, Albert Emon. (Coach: Michel Hidalgo (FRA)).
Goals: Czechoslovakia: 1-0 Antonín Panenka (68' penalty), 2-0 Frantisek Stambachr (71').
Referee: Heinz Aldinger (FRG)   Attendance: 48.138

01-05-1979   Stade Josy Bathel, Luxembourg: Luxembourg – Czechoslovakia   0-3 (0-1)
Luxembourg: Jeannot Moes (C), Jean-Louis Margue, Hubert Meunier (82' Roger Fandel), Nico Rohmann, Gilbert Dresch, Romain Michaux, Carlo Weis, Nico Wagner, Léon Mond, Marcel Di Domenico, André Zwally (21' Camille Neumann). (Coach: Louis Pilot (LUX)).
Czechoslovakia: Jaroslav Netolicka, Jozef Barmos, Rostislav Vojácek, Anton Ondrus (C), Koloman Gögh, Antonín Panenka, Frantisek Stambachr (80' Karol Dobias), Ján Kozák, Marián Masny, Miroslav Gajdusek, Karel Kroupa (46' Ladislav Vízek). (Coach: Jozef Venglos (TCH)).
Goals: Czechoslovakia: 0-1 Marián Masny (22'), 0-2 Miroslav Gajdusek (67'), 0-3 Frantisek Stambachr (68').
Referee: Bruno Galler (SUI)   Attendance: 4.027

07-06-1979   Malmö Idrottsplats, Malmö: Sweden – Luxembourg   3-0 (2-0)
Sweden: Ronnie Hellström (C), Hasse Borg, Ronald Åhman, Håkan Arvidsson (70' Klas Johansson), Stig Fredriksson, Anders Linderoth, Olle Nordin, Mats Nordgren, Anders Grönhagen, Tore Cervin, Pär-Olof Ohlsson. (Coach: Georg (Åby) Ericsson (SWE)).
Luxembourg: Jeannot Moes, Jean-Louis Margue, Hubert Meunier, Francis Kremer, Nico Rohmann, Gilbert Dresch (85' William Bianchini), Romain Michaux, Carlo Weis, Paul Philipp (C) (YC70), Marcel Di Domenico, André Zwally. (Coach: Louis Pilot (LUX)).
Goals: Sweden: 1-0 Anders Grönhagen (15'), 2-0 Tore Cervin (28'), 3-0 Hasse Borg (53' penalty).
Referee: Aleksander Suchanek (POL)   Attendance: 7.298

05-09-1979   Råsunda Stadion, Solna: Sweden – France   1-3 (1-1)
Sweden: Ronnie Hellström, Hasse Borg, Ingemar Erlandsson, Kent Jönsson, Anders Linderoth, Olle Nordin, Mats Nordgren, Mikael Rönnberg (75' Jan Svensson), Anders Grönhagen, Rutger Backe, Sigvard Johansson. (Coach: Georg (Åby) Ericsson (SWE)).
France: Dominique Dropsy, Patrick Battiston, Max Bossis, Christian López (C), Léonard Specht, Dominique Bathenay, Alain Moizan, Michel Platini, Löic Amisse, Dominique Rocheteau (55' Jacques Zimako), Bernard Lacombe. (Coach: Michel Hidalgo (FRA)).
Goals: Sweden: 1-1 Rutger Backe (23').
France: 0-1 Bernard Lacombe (14'), 1-2 Michel Platini (54'), 1-3 Patrick Battiston (71').
Referee: Ángel Franco Martínez (ESP)   Attendance: 14.393

10-10-1979   Letná Stadium, Prague: Czechoslovakia – Sweden   4-1 (3-0)
Czechoslovakia: Zdenek Hruska, Jozef Barmos, Rostislav Vojácek (8' Ladislav Jurkemík), Anton Ondrus (C), Koloman Gögh, Antonín Panenka, Frantisek Stambachr, Ján Kozák, Ladislav Vízek, Zdenek Nehoda (52' Karel Kroupa), Miroslav Gajdusek. (Coach: Jozef Venglos (TCH)).
Sweden: Jan Möller, Hasse Borg, Ingemar Erlandsson, Kent Jönsson, Magnus Andersson, Anders Linderoth (C), Mats Nordgren, Jan Svensson, Peter Nilsson (YC75), Pär-Olof Ohlsson (67' Anders Grönhagen), Sigvard Johansson (11' Eine Fredriksson). (Coach: Georg (Åby) Ericsson (SWE)).
Goals: Czechoslovakia: 1-0 Zdenek Nehoda (20'), 2-0 Ján Kozák (34'), 3-0 Ladislav Vízek (41'), 4-1 Ladislav Vízek (78').
Sweden: 3-1 Jan Svensson (61').
Referee: Talat Tokat (TUR)   Attendance: 24.783

23-10-1979   Stade de la Frontière, Esch-sur-Alzette: Luxembourg – Sweden   1-1 (1-0)
Luxembourg: Lucien Thill, Jean-Louis Margue, Nico Rohmann, Gilbert Dresch (60' Nico Wagner), Romain Michaux (YC19), Carlo Weis, Paul Philipp (C), Juan Zuang, Nico Braun, Marcel Di Domenico (72' Camille Neumann), Jeannot Reiter. (Coach: Louis Pilot (LUX)).
Sweden: Thomas Wernersson, Hasse Borg, Klas Johansson, Ulf Lundberg, Thom Åhlund (70' Leif Lindén), Eine Fredriksson, Mats Nordgren, Jan Svensson (46' Anders Grönhagen), Peter Nilsson, Rutger Backe, Sigvard Johansson. (Coach: Georg (Åby) Ericsson (SWE)).
Goals: Luxembourg: 1-0 Nico Braun (4' penalty).
Sweden: 1-1 Anders Grönhagen (61').
Referee: Walter Horstmann (FRG)   Attendance: 2.123

17-11-1979   Parc des Princes, Paris: France – Czechoslovakia   2-1 (0-0)
France: Dominique Dropsy, Patrick Battiston, Max Bossis, Christian López (C), Léonard Specht, Alain Moizan, Jean Petit, Löic Amisse, Jacques Zimako, Patrick Rampillon, Bernard Lacombe (46' Eric Pécout). (Coach: Michel Hidalgo (FRA)).
Czechoslovakia: Zdenek Hruska, Ladislav Jurkemík, Jozef Barmos, Anton Ondrus (C) (YC55), Koloman Gögh, Antonín Panenka, Frantisek Stambachr, Ján Kozák, Ladislav Vízek, Miroslav Gajdusek, Karel Kroupa (73' Marián Masny). (Coach: Jozef Venglos (TCH)).
Goals: France: 1-0 Eric Pécout (67'), 2-0 Patrick Rampillon (76').
Czechoslovakia: 2-1 Ján Kozák (80').
Referee: Horst Brummeier (AUT)   Attendance: 39.973

24-11-1979   Stadion Evzena Rosického, Prague: Czechoslovakia – Luxembourg   4-0 (3-0)
Czechoslovakia: Zdenek Hruska, Ladislav Jurkemík (61' Rostislav Vojácek), Jozef Barmos, Anton Ondrus (C), Koloman Gögh, Antonín Panenka, Frantisek Stambachr, Ján Kozák, Ladislav Vízek, Marián Masny, Miroslav Gajdusek. (Coach: Jozef Venglos (TCH)).
Luxembourg: Jeannot Moes, Jean-Louis Margue, Nico Rohmann, Romain Michaux, Carlo Weis, Paul Philipp (C) (YC42), Juan Zuang, Nico Wagner, Nico Braun, Marcel Di Domenico (69' Gilbert Dresch), Jeannot Reiter. (Coach: Louis Pilot (LUX)).
Goals: Czechoslovakia: 1-0 Antonín Panenka (37'), 2-0 Marián Masny (39'), 3-0 Marián Masny (45'), 4-0 Ladislav Vízek (61').
Referee: Marcel Van Langenhove (BEL)   Attendance: 10.063

GROUP 6

24-05-1978	Helsinki	Finland – Greece	3-0 (1-0)
20-09-1978	Helsinki	Finland – Hungary	2-1 (1-0)
20-09-1978	Yerevan	Soviet Union – Greece	2-0 (1-0)
11-10-1979	Budapest	Hungary – Soviet Union	2-0 (1-0)
11-10-1978	Athens	Greece – Finland	8-1 (5-0)
29-10-1978	Thessaloniki	Greece – Hungary	4-1 (0-0)
02-05-1979	Budapest	Hungary – Greece	0-0
19-05-1979	Tbilisi	Soviet Union – Hungary	2-2 (1-1)
04-07-1979	Helsinki	Finland – Soviet Union	1-1 (0-1)
12-09-1979	Athens	Greece – Soviet Union	1-0 (1-0)
17-10-1979	Debrecen	Hungary – Finland	3-1 (2-0)
31-10-1979	Moscow	Soviet Union – Finland	2-2 (0-0)

FINAL STANDING

Pos	Team	Pld	W	D	L	GF	GA	GD	Pts
1	*Greece*	6	3	1	2	13	7	+6	7
2	Hungary	6	2	2	2	9	9	0	6
3	Finland	6	2	2	2	10	15	-5	6
4	Soviet Union	6	1	3	2	7	8	-1	5

Greece qualified for the final tournament in Italy.

24-05-1978   Olympiastadion, Helsinki: Finland – Greece   3-0 (1-0)
Finland: Pertti Alaja, Arto Tolsa, Ari Mäkynen, Esko Ranta, Miikka Toivola (YC1), Erkki Vihtilä, Aki Heiskanen (YC75), Pertti Jantunen, Leo Houtsonen (61' Olavi Rissanen), Jyrki Nieminen, Atik Ismail. (Coach: Aulis Rytkönen (FIN)).
Greece: Nikolas Christidis, Kostas Iosifidis, Giorgos Firos, Christos Terzanidis (YC2), Lakis Nikolaou, Thodoros Palas (79' Petros Karavitis), Mike Galakos, Giannis Damanakis, Christos Ardizoglou (46' Giorgos Semertzidis), Thomas Mavros, Mimis Papaioannou. (Coach: Alketas Panagoulias (GRE)).
Goals: Finland: 1-0 Atik Ismail (35'), 2-0 Jyrki Nieminen (80'), 3-0 Atik Ismail (82').
Referee: Heinz Einbeck (GDR)   Attendance: 7.740

20-09-1978   Olympiastadion, Helsinki: Finland – Hungary   2-1 (1-0)
Finland: Pertti Alaja, Arto Tolsa, Esko Ranta, Risto Salonen, Jouko Suomalainen (63' Juha Helin), Miikka Toivola (YC51), Erkki Vihtilä, Pertti Jantunen, Jyrki Nieminen, Atik Ismail (YC85), Seppo Pyykkö (82' Arto Uimonen). (Coach: Aulis Rytkönen (FIN)).
Hungary: Sándor Gujdar, László Bálint (YC32), Zoltán Kereki, József Kovács (57' László Szokolai), Sándor Lukács, Sándor Paróczai, Sándor Pintér, László Gyimesi, György Tatár, Emö Kardos, László Tieber. (Coach: Ferenc Kovács (HUN)).
Goals: Finland: 1-0 Atik Ismail (30'), 2-0 Seppo Pyykkö (53').
Hungary: 2-1 László Tieber (74').
Referee: Erik Fredriksson (SWE)   Attendance: 4.797

20-09-1978   Hrazdan Stadium, Yerevan: Soviet Union – Greece   2-0 (1-0)
Soviet Union: Yuri Degtiariev, Volodymyr Bezsonov, Vagiz Khidiyatullin (74' Mikhail An), Alexandre Bubnov, Vassili Zhupikov, Alexandre Berezhnoi, Sergei Prigoda, Anatoliy Konkov (C), Leonid Buryak, Oleh Blokhin, Yuri Chesnokov. (Coach: Nikita Simonjan (URS)).
Greece: Nikolas Christidis (C), Giorgos Firos, Christos Terzanidis (YC60,YC71), Petros Ravousis (YC70), Thodoros Palas, Anastasios Mitropoulos, Giannis Kirastas, Takis Nikoloudis, Giannis Damanakis (YC14), Giorgos Delikaris, Thomas Mavros. (Coach: Alketas Panagoulias (GRE)).
Goals: Soviet Union: 1-0 Yuri Chesnokov (20'), 2-0 Volodymyr Bezsonov (53').
Referee: John Carpenter (IRL)   Attendance: 26.913

11-10-1978   Népstadion, Budapest: Hungary – Soviet Union   2-0 (1-0)
Hungary: Béla Katzirz, Gyözö Martos, István Kocsis, Zoltán Kereki, Sándor Lukács, Sándor Pintér (C) (YC78), György Tatár (YC87), József Pál, Béla Várady, László Szokolai (86' László Gyimesi), István Kovács (69' László Fekete (YC75)). (Coach: Ferenc Kovács (HUN)).
Soviet Union: Yuri Degtiariev (43' Nikolai Gontar), Volodymyr Bezsonov (YC20), Vagiz Khidiyatullin (YC16), Alexandre Bubnov, Aleksandr Makhovikov, Vassili Zhupikov, Alexandre Berezhnoi, Anatoliy Konkov, Leonid Buryak (65' Georgi Yartsev), Oleh Blokhin, Vladimir Gutsaev. (Coach: Nikita Simonjan (URS)).
Goals: Hungary: 1-0 Béla Várady (26'), 2-0 László Szokolai (60').
Referee: Walter Eschweiler (FRG)   Attendance: 23.110

11-10-1978   Stadio Apóstolos Nikolaidis, Athens: Greece – Finland   8-1 (5-0)
Greece: Vasilis Konstantinou, Giorgos Firos, Petros Ravousis, Thodoros Palas, Anastasios Mitropoulos (68' Giorgos Semertzidis), Giannis Kirastas, Mike Galakos (84' Hristos Ziakos), Takis Nikoloudis, Giorgos Delikaris (C), Christos Ardizoglou, Thomas Mavros. (Coach: Alketas Panagoulias (GRE)).
Finland: Pertti Alaja, Arto Tolsa (YC), Esko Ranta, Risto Salonen, Jouko Suomalainen (74' Kalle Nieminen), Erkki Vihtilä (C), Aki Heiskanen, Pertti Jantunen, Jyrki Nieminen, Atik Ismail, Seppo Pyykkö (30' Arto Uimonen). (Coach: Aulis Rytkönen (FIN)).
Goals: Greece: 1-0 Takis Nikoloudis (15'), 2-0 Giorgos Delikaris (23'), 3-0 Takis Nikoloudis (25'), 4-0 Thomas Mavros (38'), 5-0 Thomas Mavros (44'), 6-0 Giorgos Delikaris (47'), 7-1 Thomas Mavros (75' penalty), 8-1 Mike Galakos (81').
Finland: 6-1 Aki Heiskanen (61').
Referee: Marcel Van Langenhove (BEL)   Attendance: 4.857

29-10-1978   Kaftanzoglio Stadium, Thessaloniki: Greece – Hungary   4-1 (0-0)
Greece: Vasilis Konstantinou, Kostas Iosifidis, Giorgos Firos, Babis Xanthopoulos, Petros Ravousis, Mike Galakos, Takis Nikoloudis, Giorgos Koudas, Giorgos Delikaris (76' Giannis Damanakis), Christos Ardizoglou (83' Anastasios Mitropoulos), Thomas Mavros. (Coach: Alketas Panagoulias (GRE)).
Hungary: Béla Katzirz, Györö Martos, István Kocsis, Zoltán Kereki, Sándor Lukács, Sándor Zombori, Sándor Pintér (C), György Tatár, József Pál, Béla Várady, László Szokolai (65' István Kovács). (Coach: Ferenc Kovács (HUN)).
Goals: Greece: 1-0 Mike Galakos (58'), 2-0 Mike Galakos (67'), 3-0 Christos Ardizoglou (71'), 4-0 Thomas Mavros (89').
Hungary: 4-1 Béla Várady (90').
Referee: Nikola Milanov Doudine (BUL)   Attendance: 13.460

02-05-1979   Népstadion, Budapest: Hungary – Greece   0-0
Hungary: Béla Katzirz, László Bálint, Péter Török, István Kocsis, László Kutasi, Sándor Zombori, Károly Csapó (32' István Magyar), Béla Kovács, László Fazekas (C), András Töröcsik, László Fekete (75' László Kuti). (Coach: Ferenc Kovács (HUN)).
Greece: Panagiotis Kelesidis, Kostas Iosifidis, Giorgos Firos, Anthimos Kapsis, Giannis Gounaris, Spiros Livathinos (YC67), Takis Nikoloudis (C), Giannis Damanakis (65' Evangelos Kousoulakis), Giorgos Kostikos, Christos Ardizoglou (78' Konstantinos Orfanos), Thomas Mavros. (Coach: Alketas Panagoulias (GRE)).
Referee: Bartley John Homewood (ENG)   Attendance: 15.028

19-05-1979   Lenin Dinamo Stadium, Tbilisi: Soviet Union – Hungary   2-2 (1-1)
Soviet Union: Nikolai Gontar, Alexandre Bubnov (YC45,YC80), Aleksandr Makhovikov, Alexandre Berezhnoi, Yuri Adzhem, Ramaz Shengelia, Vitali Darasselia, Manuchar Machaidze, Vakhtang Koridze (70' David Kipiani), Oleh Blokhin (C), Yuri Chesnokov (82' Vassili Zhupikov). (Coach: Konstantin Ivanovich Beskov (URS)).
Hungary: Zoltán Tóth, László Bálint, József Tóth, Péter Török (YC18) (23' Gyözö Martos), István Kocsis, Tibor Nyilasi (C), György Tatár, Béla Kovács (55' Tibor Rab), István Magyar, András Töröcsik, László Pusztai. (Coach: Ferenc Kovács (HUN)).
Goals: Soviet Union: 1-0 Yuri Chesnokov (23'), 2-2 Ramaz Shengelia (75').
Hungary: 1-1 György Tatár (33'), 1-2 László Pusztai (63').
Referee: Brian R.McGinlay (SCO)   Attendance: 75.174

04-07-1979   Olympiastadion, Helsinki: Finland – Soviet Union   1-1 (0-1)
Finland: Pertti Alaja, Arto Tolsa (C), Esko Ranta, Mikko Lampi, Petteri Kupiainen, Miikka Toivola (28' Reima Kokko), Leo Houtsonen, Jyrki Nieminen, Pasi Rautiainen, Atik Ismail, Seppo Pyykkö (77' Risto Salonen). (Coach: Esko Malm (FIN)).
Soviet Union: Yuri Romenski, Volodymyr Bezsonov, Vagiz Khidiyatullin, Alexandre Bubnov, Aleksandr Makhovikov (C) (YC69), Sergei Prigoda, Shota Khinchagashvili, Alexandre Khapsalis, Vitali Darasselia, David Kipiani (70' Ramaz Shengelia), Yuri Chesnokov. (Coach: Nikita Pavlovich Simonyan (URS)).
Goals: Finland: 1-1 Atik Ismail (55').
Soviet Union: 0-1 Alexandre Khapsalis (28').
Referee: Ole Amundsen (DEN)   Attendance: 13.119

12-09-1979   Stadio Apóstolos Nikolaidis, Athens: Greece – Soviet Union   1-0 (1-0)
Greece: Vasilis Konstantinou, Kostas Iosifidis, Giorgos Firos, Anthimos Kapsis, Giannis Gounaris (74' Giannis Kirastas), Spiros Livathinos, Mike Galakos, Takis Nikoloudis (YC43), Giannis Damanakis, Giorgos Delikaris (C), Christos Ardizoglou (64' Konstantinos Orfanos). (Coach: Alketas Panagoulias (GRE)).
Soviet Union: Rinat Dasayev, Vagiz Khidiyatullin, Alexandre Bubnov (YC53), Aleksandr Makhovikov, Sergei Nikulin (YC61), Sergei Prigoda (35' Sergei Shalvo), Ramaz Shengelia, Fyodor Cherenkov, Alexandre Maksimenkov, Yuri Gavrilov, David Kipiani (46' Stepan Yurchishin). (Coach: Konstantin Ivanovich Beskov (URS)).
Goal: Greece: 1-0 Takis Nikoloudis (25').
Referee: António José da Silva Garrido (POR)   Attendance: 25.537

17-10-1979   Oláh Gábor utcai stadion, Debrecen: Hungary – Finland   3-1 (1-0)
Hungary: Gábor Zsiborás, László Kutasi (69' János Kiss), Gábor Szántó, József Salamon (C), József Póczik, György Tatár, Mihaly Borostyán (46' Béla Bodonyi), László Kiss, László Fekete, László Kuti, István Weimper. (Coach: Dr.Károly Lakat (HUN)).
Finland: Seppo Sairanen, Arto Tolsa, Esko Ranta, Mikko Lampi, Miikka Toivola (C), Heikki Suhonen (57' Petteri Kupiainen), Leo Houtsonen, Pasi Rautiainen, Kai Haaskivi (YC80), Atik Ismail (67' Juha Helin), Seppo Pyykkö. (Coach: Esko Malm (FIN)).
Goals: Hungary: 1-0 László Fekete (22'), 2-0 László Fekete (42'), 3-1 György Tatár (49').
Finland: 2-1 Miikka Toivola (47').
Referee: Charles George Reinier Corver (HOL)   Attendance: 7.977

31-10-1979   Central Lenin Stadium, Moscow: Soviet Union – Finland   2-2 (0-0)
Soviet Union: Nikolai Gontar, Volodymyr Bezsonov, Vagiz Khidiyatullin, Alexandre Bubnov, Aleksandr Makhovikov, Alexandre Berezhnoi, Volodymyr Veremeev, Sergei Shalvo, Yuri Gavrilov, Sergei Andreev (64' Khoren Oganesyan (YC79)), Stepan Yurchishin. (Coach: Konstantin Ivanovich Beskov (URS)).
Finland: Seppo Sairanen, Arto Tolsa (YC65), Esko Ranta (YC79), Mikko Lampi, Erkki Vihtilä, Leo Houtsonen, Jyrki Nieminen (73' Tuomo Hakala), Kai Haaskivi (YC72), Atik Ismail, Seppo Pyykkö (44' Hannu Turunen), Juhani Himanka. (Coach: Esko Malm (FIN)).
Goals: Soviet Union: 1-0 Sergei Andreev (50'), 2-0 Yuri Gavrilov (67').
Finland: 2-1 Kai Haaskivi (76'), 2-2 Tuomo Hakala (82').
Referee: Aleksandar Nikic (YUG)   Attendance: 1.090

GROUP 7

25-10-1978	Wrexham	Wales – Malta	7-0 (3-0)
29-11-1978	Wrexham	Wales – Turkey	1-0 (0-0)
25-02-1979	Gzira	Malta – West Germany	0-0
18-03-1979	Izmir	Turkey – Malta	2-1 (1-0)
01-04-1979	Izmir	Turkey – West Germany	0-0
02-05-1979	Wrexham	Wales – West Germany	0-2 (0-1)
02-06-1979	Gzira	Malta – Wales	0-2 (0-1)
17-10-1979	Cologne	West Germany – Wales	5-1 (4-0)
28-10-1979	Gzira	Malta – Turkey	1-2 (0-2)
21-11-1979	Izmir	Turkey – Wales	1-0 (0-0)
22-12-1979	Gelsenkirchen	West Germany – Turkey	2-0 (1-0)
27-02-1980	Bremen	West Germany – Malta	8-0 (3-0)

FINAL STANDING

Pos	Team	Pld	W	D	L	GF	GA	GD	Pts
1	*West Germany*	*6*	*4*	*2*	*0*	*17*	*1*	*+16*	*10*
2	Turkey	6	3	1	2	5	5	0	7
3	Wales	6	3	0	3	11	8	+3	6
4	Malta	6	0	1	5	2	21	-19	1

West Germany qualified for the final tournament in Italy.

25-10-1978   Racecourse Ground, Wrexham: Wales – Malta   7-0 (3-0)
Wales: Dai Davies, Leighton Phillips (C), Malcolm Page, Joey Jones, Brian Flynn, Byron Stevenson, Mickey Thomas, Carl Harris, Robbie James, Ian Edwards, Les Cartwright (15' Peter O'Sullivan). (Coach: Michael John (Mike) Smith (ENG)).
Malta: Robert Gatt (YC80), George Ciantar, Edwin Farrugia (41' Costantino Consiglio), Simon Tortell, Mario Schembri, John Holland (C), Vincent Magro, George Xuereb, Richard Aquilina (74' Ernest Spiteri-Gonzi), Raymond Xuereb, Carlo Seychell. (Coach: Victor Scerri (MLT)).
Goals: Wales: 1-0 Peter O'Sullivan (18'), 2-0 Ian Edwards (20'), 3-0 Ian Edwards (45'), 4-0 Ian Edwards (48'), 5-0 Ian Edwards (51'), 6-0 Mickey Thomas (71'), 7-0 Brian Flynn (82').
Referee: Magnus V.Pétursson (ISL)   Attendance: 11.475

29-11-1978   Racecourse Ground, Wrexham: Wales – Turkey   1-0 (0-0)
Wales: Dai Davies, Leighton Phillips, Joey Jones, Phil Dwyer, Brian Flynn, Byron Stevenson, Mickey Thomas, Carl Harris, Terry Yorath (C), Leighton James, Nick Deacy. (Coach: Michael John (Mike) Smith (ENG)).
Turkey: Senol Günes, Fatih Terim (C), Necati Özçaglayan, Turgay Semercioglu, Erdogan Arica, Cem Pamiroglu, Ahmet Ceyland (78' Isa Ertürk), Mehmet Eksi, Sedat Özden, Önder Mustafaoglu, Necdet Ergün (YC81). (Coach: Sabri Kiraz (TUR)).
Goal: Wales: 1-0 Nick Deacy (70').
Referee: Alojzy Jarguz (POL)   Attendance: 11.794

25-02-1979   Empire Stadium, Gzira: Malta – West Germany   0-0
Malta: Charles Sciberras, Edwin Farrugia, David Buckingham, Norman Buttigieg (85' Carlo Seychell), Emanuel Farrugia, John Holland, Vincent Magro, George Xuereb, Raymond Xuereb, Ernest Spiteri-Gonzi, Joseph Xuereb. (Coach: Victor Scerri (MLT)).
West Germany: Sepp Maier (C), Karlheinz Förster, Manfred Kaltz, Bernhard Cullmann, Bernhard Dietz, Gerd Zewe (70' Klaus Allofs), Hansi Müller, Rainer Bonhof, Karl-Heinz Rummenigge (70' Klaus Toppmöller), Klaus Fischer, Rüdiger Abramczik. (Coach: Josef (Jupp) Derwall (FRG)).
Referee: Vojtech Christov (TCH)   Attendance: 8.450

18-03-1979   Folkart Altay Alsancak Stadium, Izmir: Turkey – Malta 2-1 (1-0)
Turkey: Senol Günes, Fatih Terim (C) (YC89), Necati Özçaglayan, Turgay Semercioglu, Cem Pamiroglu, Erhan Önal, Sedat Özden, Tuna Güneysu (90' Isa Ertürk), Mustafa Denizli, Necdet Ergün, Bahtiyar Yorulmaz (90' Erhan Aslan). (Coach: Sabri Kiraz (TUR)).
Malta: Charles Sciberras, George Ciantar (YC89), Edwin Farrugia (YC1) (67' David Buckingham), Norman Buttigieg, Emanuel Farrugia, John Holland (C), Vincent Magro, George Xuereb, Raymond Xuereb, Ernest Spiteri-Gonzi, Joseph Xuereb. (Coach: Victor Scerri (MLT)).
Goals: Turkey: 1-0 Sedat Özden (34'), 2-1 Fatih Terim (56').
Malta: 1-1 Ernest Spiteri-Gonzi (52').
Referee: Tome Manojlovski (YUG)   Attendance: 34.154

01-04-1979   Folkart Altay Alsancak Stadium, Izmir: Turkey – West Germany   0-0
Turkey: Senol Günes, Fatih Terim, Necati Özçaglayan, Turgay Semercioglu, Cem Pamiroglu, Erhan Önal, Engin Verel, Sedat Özden, Mustafa Denizli, Cemil Turan (C), Necdet Ergün (70' Tuna Güneysu). (Coach: Sabri Kiraz (TUR)).
West Germany: Dieter Burdenski, Manfred Kaltz, Bernhard Cullmann, Bernhard Dietz (C), Uli Stielike, Hansi Müller, Rainer Bonhof, Herbert Zimmermann (70' Karlheinz Förster), Ronald Borchers, Karl-Heinz Rummenigge (75' Walter Kelsch), Klaus Toppmöller. (Coach: Josef (Jupp) Derwall (FRG)).
Referee: Myroslav Ivanovych Stupar (URS)   Attendance: 69.800

02-05-1979   Racecourse Ground, Wrexham: Wales – West Germany   0-2 (0-1)
Wales: Dai Davies, Leighton Phillips, Malcolm Page, Joey Jones, George Berry, John Mahoney, Mickey Thomas, Carl Harris, Terry Yorath (C) (YC54) (73' Robbie James), Alan Curtis, Ian Edwards (63' John Toshack). (Coach: Michael John (Mike) Smith (ENG)).
West Germany: Sepp Maier (C), Karlheinz Förster, Manfred Kaltz (YC16), Bernhard Cullmann, Bernhard Dietz, Uli Stielike (89' Bernd Martin), Rainer Bonhof, Herbert Zimmermann, Karl-Heinz Rummenigge, Klaus Fischer, Klaus Allofs. (Coach: Josef (Jupp) Derwall (FRG)).
Goals: West Germany: 0-1 Herbert Zimmermann (30'), 0-2 Klaus Fischer (52').
Referee: Alberto Michelotti (ITA)   Attendance: 26.975

02-06-1979   Empire Stadium, Gzira: Malta – Wales   0-2 (0-1)
Malta: Charles Sciberras, Edwin Farrugia, David Buckingham, Norman Buttigieg, Emanuel Farrugia, John Holland (C), Vincent Magro, George Xuereb, Raymond Xuereb, Ernest Spiteri-Gonzi (46' Emanuel Fabri), Joseph Xuereb (78' John Joseph Aquilina). (Coach: Victor Scerri (MLT)).
Wales: Dai Davies, Leighton Phillips (C), Joey Jones, Peter Nicholas, John Mahoney (89' Phil Dwyer), Brian Flynn, Byron Stevenson, Carl Harris (65' Mickey Thomas), Robbie James, John Toshack, Alan Curtis. (Coach: Michael John (Mike) Smith (ENG)).
Goals: Wales: 0-1 Peter Nicholas (15'), 0-2 Brian Flynn (51').
Referee: Nikolaos Lagoyannis (GRE)   Attendance: 8.358

17-10-1979   Müngensdorfer Stadion, Cologne: West Germany – Wales   5-1 (4-0)
West Germany: Dieter Burdenski, Karlheinz Förster, Manfred Kaltz, Bernhard Cullmann, Bernhard Dietz, Hansi Müller, Rainer Bonhof, Bernd Schuster (73' Herbert Zimmermann), Karl-Heinz Rummenigge (77' Hans-Peter Briegel), Klaus Fischer, Klaus Allofs. (Coach: Josef (Jupp) Derwall (FRG)).
Wales: Dai Davies, Leighton Phillips (C), Joey Jones (14' George Berry), Phil Dwyer, Peter Nicholas, John Mahoney (YC50), Brian Flynn, Byron Stevenson, Robbie James, John Toshack (77' Mickey Thomas), Alan Curtis. (Coach: Michael John (Mike) Smith (ENG)).
Goals: West Germany: 1-0 Klaus Fischer (21'), 2-0 Manfred Kaltz (32'), 3-0 Klaus Fischer (38'), 4-0 Karl-Heinz Rummenigge (42'), 5-0 Karlheinz Förster (83').
Wales: 5-1 Alan Curtis (84').
Referee: Johannes Nicolaus Ignacius (Jan) Keizer (HOL)   Attendance: 53.390

28-10-1979   Empire Stadium, Gzira: Malta – Turkey   1-2 (0-2)
Malta: John Bonello, Edwin Farrugia, Dennis Fenech, David Buckingham, Norman Buttigieg, Emanuel Farrugia, John Holland (C), Vincent Magro, George Xuereb, Raymond Xuereb (90' Emanuel Fabri), Joseph Xuereb. (Coach: Victor Scerri (MLT)).
Turkey: Senol Günes, Fatih Terim (C), Turgay Semercioglu, Cem Pamiroglu, Erol Togay, Mehmet Eksi, Sedat Özden, Serdar Bali, Mustafa Denizli, Necdet Ergün, Isa Ertürk. (Coach: Sabri Kiraz (TUR)).
Goals: Malta: 1-2 Emanuel Farrugia (62').
Turkey: 0-1 Sedat Özden (20'), 0-2 Mustafa Denizli (25').
Referee: Gianfranco Menegali (ITA)   Attendance: 1.976

21-11-1979   Folkart Altay Alsancak Stadium, Izmir: Turkey – Wales   1-0 (0-0)
Turkey: Senol Günes, Fatih Terim (C), Turgay Semercioglu, Cem Pamiroglu, Erhan Önal, Erol Togay, Mehmet Eksi, Sedat Özden, Arif Güney, Mustafa Denizli (70' Mustafa Bülent Turgat), Isa Ertürk (46' Sadullah Acele). (Coach: Coskun Özari (TUR)).
Wales: Dai Davies, Leighton Phillips, Joey Jones, George Berry, Peter Nicholas, Byron Stevenson, Mickey Thomas, Terry Yorath, Alan Curtis, Gordon Davies (76' John Mahoney), Ian Walsh (65' Ian Edwards). (Coach: Michael John (Mike) Smith (ENG)).
Goal: Turkey: 1-0 Erhan Önal (80').
Referee: Constantin Ghita (ROM)   Attendance: 30.650

22-12-1979   Parkstadion, Gelsenkirchen: West Duitsland – Turkey   2-0 (1-0)
West Germany: Norbert Nigbur, Manfred Kaltz, Bernhard Cullmann, Bernd Förster, Bernhard Dietz (C), Uli Stielike (83' Herbert Zimmermann), Hansi Müller, Rainer Bonhof, Karl-Heinz Rummenigge, Klaus Fischer, Harald Nickel. (Coach: Josef (Jupp) Derwall (FRG)).
Turkey: Senol Günes, Fatih Terim (C), Turgay Semercioglu, Cem Pamiroglu, Erhan Önal, Güngör Tekin, Engin Verel, Mehmet Eksi, Sedat Özden (62' Arif Güney), Sadullah Acele (46' Mustafa Bülent Turgat), Resit Kaynak. (Coach: Sabri Kiraz (TUR)).
Goals: West Duitsland: 1-0 Klaus Fischer (15'), 2-0 Herbert Zimmermann (89').
Referee: Rudolf (Ruedi) Renggli (SUI)   Attendance: 68.270

27-02-1980   WeserStadion, Bremen: West Duitsland – Malta   8-0 (3-0)
West Germany: Dieter Burdenski, Karlheinz Förster, Manfred Kaltz, Bernhard Cullmann, Bernd Förster (60' Harald Nickel), Bernhard Dietz (C), Hansi Müller, Rainer Bonhof, Karl-Heinz Rummenigge, Klaus Fischer, Klaus Allofs (60' Walter Kelsch). (Coach: Josef (Jupp) Derwall (FRG)).
Malta: John Bonello, Edwin Farrugia, Dennis Fenech, Norman Buttigieg, Emanuel Farrugia, Gennaro Camilleri (44' David Buckingham), John Holland (C), George Xuereb, Emanuel Fabri, Joseph Xuereb, Eric Schembri. (Coach: Victor Scerri (MLT)).
Goals: West Duitsland: 1-0 Klaus Fischer (14'), 2-0 Rainer Bonhof (19' penalty), 3-0 Klaus Fischer (40'), 4-0 Klaus Allofs (55'), 5-0 John Holland (61' *own goal*), 6-0 Walter Kelsch (70'), 7-0 Karl-Heinz Rummenigge (74'), 8-0 Klaus Fischer (90').
Referee: Norbert Rolles (LUX)   Attendance: 33.278

FINALS TOURNAMENT IN ITALY

GROUP STAGE

GROUP 1

11-06-1980	Rome	Czechoslovakia – West Germany	0-1 (0-0)
11-06-1980	Naples	Netherlands – Greece	1-0 (0-0)
14-06-1980	Naples	West Germany – Netherlands	3-2 (1-0)
14-06-1980	Rome	Greece – Czechoslovakia	1-3 (1-2)
17-06-1980	Milan	Netherlands – Czechoslovakia	1-1 (0-1)
17-06-1980	Turin	Greece – West Germany	0-0

FINAL STANDING

Pos	Team	Pld	W	D	L	GF	GA	GD	Pts
1	*West Germany*	*3*	*2*	*1*	*0*	*4*	*2*	*+2*	*5*
2	*Czechoslovakia*	*3*	*1*	*1*	*1*	*4*	*3*	*+1*	*3*
3	Netherlands	3	1	1	1	4	4	0	3
4	Greece	3	0	1	2	1	4	-3	1

West Germany qualified for the Final and Czechoslovakia qualified for the Third place play-off.

11-06-1980 Stadio Olimpico, Rome: Czechoslovakia – West Germany 0-1 (0-0)
Czechoslovakia: Jaroslav Netolicka, Ladislav Jurkemík, Jozef Barmos, Anton Ondrus (C), Koloman Gögh, Antonín Panenka, Frantisek Stambachr, Ján Kozák, Ladislav Vízek, Zdenek Nehoda, Miroslav Gajdusek (66' Marián Masny). (Coach: Jozef Venglos (TCH)).
West Germany: Harald Schumacher, Hans-Peter Briegel, Karlheinz Förster, Manfred Kaltz, Bernhard Cullmann, Bernd Förster (60' Felix Magath), Bernhard Dietz (C) (YC), Uli Stielike, Hansi Müller, Karl-Heinz Rummenigge, Klaus Allofs (YC). (Coach: Josef (Jupp) Derwall (FRG)).
Goal: West Germany: 0-1 Karl-Heinz Rummenigge (57').
Referee: Alberto Michelotti (ITA)   Attendance: 11.059

11-06-1980 Stadio San Paolo, Naples: Netherlands – Greece 1-0 (0-0)
Netherlands: Piet Schrijvers (15' Pim Doesburg), Huub Stevens, Ruud Krol (C), Michel van de Korput, Ben Wijnstekers, Hugo Hovenkamp, Arie Haan, René van de Kerkhof, Willy van de Kerkhof (YC), Kees Kist, Martien Vreijsen (46' Dick Nanninga). (Coach: Johannes Hermanus Hendrikus (Jan) Zwartkruis (HOL)).
Greece: Vasilis Konstantinou, Kostas Iosifidis, Giorgos Firos, Christos Terzanidis, Anthimos Kapsis (C), Giannis Kirastas, Spiros Livathinos, Dinos Kouis, Giorgos Kostikos (78' Mike Galakos), Christos Ardizoglou (68' Nikos Anastopoulos), Thomas Mavros (YC). (Coach: Alketas Panagoulias (GRE)).
Goal: Netherlands: 1-0 Kees Kist (65' penalty).
Referee: Adolf Prokop (GDR)   Attendance: 14.990

14-06-1980 Stadio San Paolo, Naples: West Germany – Netherlands 3-2 (1-0)
West Germany: Harald Schumacher, Hans-Peter Briegel, Manfred Kaltz, Karlheinz Förster, Bernhard Dietz (C) (73' Lothar Matthäus), Uli Stielike, Bernd Schuster (YC), Hansi Müller (65' Felix Magath), Horst Hrubesch, Karl-Heinz Rummenigge, Klaus Allofs. (Coach: Josef (Jupp) Derwall (FRG)).
Netherlands: Piet Schrijvers, Huub Stevens (YC), Ruud Krol (C), Michel van de Korput, Ben Wijnstekers, Hugo Hovenkamp (46' Dick Nanninga), Arie Haan, Johnny Rep, René van de Kerkhof, Willy van de Kerkhof, Kees Kist (69' Frans Thijssen). (Coach: Johannes Hermanus Hendrikus (Jan) Zwartkruis (HOL)).
Goals: West Duitsland: 1-0 Klaus Allofs (20'), 2-0 Klaus Allofs (60'), 3-0 Klaus Allofs (65').
Netherlands: 3-1 Johnny Rep (79' penalty), 3-2 Willy van de Kerkhof (85').
Referee: Robert Charles Paul Wurtz (FRA)   Attendance: 26.546

14-06-1980 Stadio Olimpico, Rome: Greece – Czechoslovakia 1-3 (1-2)
Greece: Vasilis Konstantinou, Kostas Iosifidis, Giorgos Firos, Christos Terzanidis (46' Mike Galakos), Anthimos Kapsis (C), Giannis Kirastas, Spiros Livathinos, Dinos Kouis, Giorgos Kostikos (57' Babis Xanthopoulos), Nikos Anastopoulos, Thomas Mavros. (Coach: Alketas Panagoulias (GRE)).
Czechoslovakia: Stanislav Seman, Ladislav Jurkemík, Jozef Barmos, Anton Ondrus (C), Koloman Gögh, Antonín Panenka, Ján Berger (23' Werner Licka), Ján Kozák, Ladislav Vízek, Zdenek Nehoda (74' Miroslav Gajdusek), Marián Masny. (Coach: Jozef Venglos (TCH)).
Goals: Greece: 1-1 Nikos Anastopoulos (14').
Czechoslovakia: 0-1 Antonín Panenka (6'), 1-2 Ladislav Vízek (26'), 1-3 Zdenek Nehoda (63').
Referee: Patrick (Pat) Partridge (ENG)   Attendance: 4.726

17-07-1980   Stadio Giuseppe Meazza, Milan: Netherlands – Czechoslovakia   1-1 (0-1)
Netherlands: Piet Schrijvers, Ruud Krol (C), Michel van de Korput, Ben Wijnstekers, Hugo Hovenkamp, Dick Nanninga (46' Arie Haan (YC)), Jan Poortvliet, Frans Thijssen, Johnny Rep (YC), Willy van de Kerkhof, René van de Kerkhof (15' Kees Kist). (Coach: Johannes Hermanus Hendrikus (Jan) Zwartkruis (HOL)).
Czechoslovakia: Jaroslav Netolicka, Ladislav Jurkemík, Jozef Barmos, Rostislav Vojacek, Anton Ondrus (C), Koloman Gögh, Antonín Panenka (89' Frantisek Stambachr), Ján Kozák, Ladislav Vízek, Zdenek Nehoda, Marián Masny (66' Werner Licka). (Coach: Jozef Venglos (TCH)).
Goals: Netherlands: 1-1 Kees Kist (59').
Czechoslovakia: 0-1 Zdenek Nehoda (16').
Referee: Hilmi Ok (TUR)   Attendance: 11.889

17-06-1980   Stadio Comunale, Turin: Greece – West Germany   0-0
Greece: Lefteris Poupakis, Babis Xanthopoulos, Giannis Gounaris (YC), Lakis Nikolaou, Petros Ravousis, Spiros Livathinos, Dinos Kouis, Mike Galakos, Takis Nikoloudis (65' Giorgos Koudas), Christos Ardizoglou, Thomas Mavros (79' Giorgos Kostikos). (Coach: Alketas Panagoulias (GRE)).
West Germany: Harald Schumacher, Hans-Peter Briegel, Karlheinz Förster, Manfred Kaltz, Bernhard Cullmann (C), Bernd Förster (46' Miroslav Votava), Uli Stielike, Hansi Müller, Caspar Memering, Horst Hrubesch, Karl-Heinz Rummenigge (66' Calle Del'Haye). (Coach: Josef (Jupp) Derwall (FRG)).
Referee: Brian R.McGinlay (SCO)   Attendance: 13.901

GROUP 2

12-06-1980	Turin	Belgium – England	1-1 (1-1)
12-06-1980	Milan	Spain – Italy	0-0
15-06-1980	Milan	Belgium – Spain	2-1 (1-1)
15-06-1980	Turin	England – Italy	0-1 (0-0)
18-06-1980	Naples	Spain – England	1-2 (0-1)
18-06-1980	Rome	Italy – Belgium	0-0

FINAL STANDING

Pos	Team	Pld	W	D	L	GF	GA	GD	Pts
1	*Belgium*	*3*	*1*	*2*	*0*	*3*	*2*	*+1*	*4*
2	*Italy*	*3*	*1*	*2*	*0*	*1*	*0*	*+1*	*4*
3	England	3	1	1	1	3	3	0	3
4	Spain	3	0	1	2	2	4	-2	1

Belgium qualified for the Final and Italy qualified for the Third place play-off.

12-06-1980   Stadio Comunale, Turin: Belgium – England   1-1 (1-1)
Belgium: Jean-Marie Pfaff, Luc Millecamps, Walter Meeuws, Eric Gerets, Michel Renquin, René Vandereycken, Wilfried Van Moer (88' Raymond Mommens), Julien Cools (C), Erwin Vandenbergh, François Van Der Elst, Jan Ceulemans. (Coach: Guy Jean Léonard Thijs (BEL)).
England: Ray Clemence, Kenny Sansom, Phil Thompson, Phil Neal, Dave Watson, Steve Coppell (81' Terry McDermott), Ray Wilkins, Trevor Brooking, Tony Woodcock, Kevin Keegan, David Johnson (70' Ray Kennedy). (Coach: Ronald (Ron) Greenwood (ENG)).
Goals: Belgium: 1-1 Jan Ceulemans (29').
England: 0-1 Ray Wilkins (26').
Referee: Heinz Aldinger (FRG)   Attendance: 15.186

12-06-1980   Stadio Giuseppe Meazza, Milan: Spain – Italy   0-0
Spain: Luis Miguel ARCONADA Echarri, Miguel TENDILLO Belenguer, José Ramón ALEXANCO Ventosá, Rafael GORDILLO Vázquez, Miguel Bernardo Bianquetti "MIGUELI", JESÚS María ZAMORA Ansorena, Juan Manuel ASENSI Ripoll (C), Jesús María SATRÚSTEGUI Azpiroz (YC12), Enrique SAURA Gil, Enrique Castro González "QUINI", Daniel Ruiz Bazan Justa "DANI" (53' Juan Gómez Gónzalez "JUANITO"). (Coach: László "LADISLAO" KUBALA Stecz (ESP)).
Italy: Dino Zoff (C), Antonio Cabrini (56' Romeo Benetti), Fulvio Collovati, Claudio Gentile, Gaetano Scirea, Giancarlo Antognoni, Marco Tardelli, Gabriele Oriali, Francesco Graziani (YC43), Franco Causio, Roberto Bettega. (Coach: Vincenzo Bearzot (ITA)).
Referee: Károly Palotai (HUN)   Attendance: 46.816

15-06-1980   Stadio Giuseppe Meazza, Milan: Belgium – Spain   2-1 (1-1)
Belgium: Jean-Marie Pfaff, Luc Millecamps, Walter Meeuws, Eric Gerets, Michel Renquin, René Vandereycken, Wilfried Van Moer (80' Raymond Mommens), Julien Cools (C), Erwin Vandenbergh (81' René Verheyen), François Van Der Elst, Jan Ceulemans. (Coach: Guy Jean Léonard Thijs (BEL)).
Spain: Luis Miguel ARCONADA Echarri, Miguel TENDILLO Belenguer (79' Francisco José "LOBO" CARRASCO Hidalgo), José Ramón ALEXANCO Ventosá, Rafael GORDILLO Vázquez, Miguel Bernardo Bianquetti "MIGUELI" (YC29), JESÚS María ZAMORA Ansorena, Juan Manuel ASENSI Ripoll (C) (YC) (37' Vicente DEL BOSQUE), Juan Gómez Gónzalez "JUANITO", Jesús María SATRÚSTEGUI Azpiroz, Enrique SAURA Gil, Enrique Castro González "QUINI". (Coach: László "LADISLAO" KUBALA Stecz (ESP)).
Goals: Belgium: 1-0 Eric Gerets (17'), 2-1 Julien Cools (65').
Spain: 1-1 Enrique Castro González "QUINI" (36').
Referee: Charles George Reinier Corver (HOL)   Attendance: 11.430

15-06-1980   Stadio Comunale, Turin: England – Italy   0-1 (0-0)
England: Peter Shilton, Kenny Sansom, Phil Thompson, Phil Neal, Dave Watson, Steve Coppell, Ray Wilkins, Tony Woodcock, Kevin Keegan (C), Ray Kennedy, Garry Birtles (75' Paul Mariner). (Coach: Ronald (Ron) Greenwood (ENG)).
Italy: Dino Zoff (C), Fulvio Collovati, Claudio Gentile, Gaetano Scirea, Giancarlo Antognoni, Marco Tardelli (YC), Gabriele Oriali, Romeo Benetti (YC), Francesco Graziani, Franco Causio (88' Giuseppe Baresi), Roberto Bettega. (Coach: Vincenzo Bearzot (ITA)).
Goal: Italy: 0-1 Marco Tardelli (79').
Referee: Nicolae Rainea (ROM)   Attendance: 59.646

18-06-1980   Stadio San Paolo, Naples: Spain – England   1-2 (0-1)
Spain: Luis Miguel ARCONADA Echarri, José Ramón ALEXANCO Ventosá, Rafael
GORDILLO Vázquez, Francisco Javier Alvarez URÍA, Secundino Suárez Vázquez "CUNDI",
JESÚS María ZAMORA Ansorena, Julio CARDEÑOSA Rodriguez (46' Francisco José
"LOBO" CARRASCO Hidalgo (YC65)), Antonio OLMO Rodriguez, Juan Gómez Gónzalez
"JUANITO" (46' Daniel Ruiz Bazan Justa "DANI"), Enrique SAURA Gil, Carlos Alonso
González "SANTILLANA" (C). (Coach: László "LADISLAO" KUBALA Stecz (ESP)).
England: Ray Clemence, Mick Mills, Phil Thompson, Viv Anderson (86' Trevor Cherry),
Dave Watson, Ray Wilkins, Glenn Hoddle (77' Paul Mariner), Trevor Brooking, Terry
McDermott (YC65), Tony Woodcock, Kevin Keegan (C). (Coach: Ronald (Ron) Greenwood
(ENG)).
Goals: Spain: 1-1 Daniel Ruiz Bazan Justa "DANI" (48' penalty).
England: 0-1 Trevor Brooking (19'), 1-2 Tony Woodcock (61').
Referee: Erich Linemayr (AUT)   Attendance: 14.440

18-06-1980   Stadio Olimpico, Rome: Italy – Belgium   0-0
Italy: Dino Zoff (C), Fulvio Collovati, Claudio Gentile, Gaetano Scirea, Giancarlo Antognoni
(35' Giuseppe Baresi), Marco Tardelli, Gabriele Oriali (YC) (46' Alessandro Altobelli),
Romeo Benetti, Francesco Graziani, Franco Causio (YC), Roberto Bettega. (Coach: Vincenzo
Bearzot (ITA)).
Belgium: Jean-Marie Pfaff, Luc Millecamps, Walter Meeuws (YC), Eric Gerets, Michel
Renquin, René Vandereycken (YC), Wilfried Van Moer (48' René Verheyen), Raymond
Mommens (77' Erwin Vandenbergh), Julien Cools (C), François Van Der Elst (YC), Jan
Ceulemans. (Coach: Guy Jean Léonard Thijs (BEL)).
Referee: António José da Silva Garrido (POR)   Attendance: 42.318

THIRD PLACE PLAY-OFF

21-06-1980   Stadio San Paolo, Naples: Czechoslovakia – Italy   1-1 (0-0, 1-1) (AET)
Czechoslovakia: Jaroslav Netolicka, Ladislav Jurkemík (YC), Jozef Barmos, Rostislav
Vojacek, Anton Ondrus (C), Koloman Gögh, Antonín Panenka, Ján Kozák, Ladislav Vízek
(64' Miroslav Gajdusek), Zdenek Nehoda, Marián Masny. (Coach: Jozef Venglos (TCH)).
Italy: Dino Zoff (C), Giuseppe Baresi, Antonio Cabrini, Fulvio Collovati, Claudio Gentile,
Gaetano Scirea, Marco Tardelli, Francesco Graziani, Alessandro Altobelli, Franco Causio,
Roberto Bettega (83' Romeo Benetti). (Coach: Vincenzo Bearzot (ITA)).
Goals: Czechoslovakia: 1-0 Ladislav Jurkemík (54').
Italy: 1-1 Francesco Graziani (73').
Referee: Erich Linemayr (AUT)   Attendance: 24.652
Penalties: 1 Marián Masny   1 Franco Causio
               2 Zdenek Nehoda   2 Alessandro Altobelli
               3 Anton Ondrus   3 Giuseppe Baresi
               4 Ladislav Jurkemík   4 Antonio Cabrini
               5 Antonín Panenka   5 Romeo Benetti
               6 Koloman Gögh   6 Francesco Graziani
               7 Miroslav Gajdusek   7 Gaetano Scirea
               8 Ján Kozák   8 Marco Tardelli
               9 Jozef Barmos   * Fulvio Collovati

FINAL

22-06-1980   Stadio Olimpico, Rome: Belgium – West Germany   1-2 (0-1)
Belgium: Jean-Marie Pfaff, Luc Millecamps (YC35), Walter Meeuws, Eric Gerets, Michel Renquin, René Vandereycken (YC55), Wilfried Van Moer, Raymond Mommens, Julien Cools (C), François Van Der Elst (YC89), Jan Ceulemans. (Coach: Guy Jean Léonard Thijs (BEL)).
West Germany: Harald Schumacher, Hans-Peter Briegel (55' Bernhard Cullmann), Karlheinz Förster (YC59), Manfred Kaltz, Bernhard Dietz (C), Uli Stielike, Hansi Müller, Bernd Schuster, Horst Hrubesch, Karl-Heinz Rummenigge, Klaus Allofs. (Coach: Josef (Jupp) Derwall (FRG)).
Goals: Belgium: 1-1 René Vandereycken (75' penalty).
West Germany: 0-1 Horst Hrubesch (10'), 1-2 Horst Hrubesch (88').
Referee: Nocilae Rainea (ROM)   Attendance: 47.864

*** **West Germany were European Champions** ***

GOALSCORERS TOURNAMENT 1978-1980:

Goals	Players
7	Kevin Keegan (ENG)
6	Klaus Fischer (FRG)
5	François Van Der Elst (BEL), Klaus Allofs (FRG), Marián Masny (TCH)
4	Hans Krankl (AUT), Bob Latchford (ENG), Carlos Alonso González "SANTILLANA" (ESP), Atik Ismail (FIN), Martin Hoffmann (GDR), Joachim Streich (GDR), Thomas Mavros (GRE), Kees Kist (HOL), Kenny Dalglish (SCO), Zdenek Nehoda (TCH), Ladislav Vízek (TCH), Ian Edwards (WAL), Zlatko Vujovic (YUG)
3	Walter Schachner (AUT), Chavdar Tsvetkov (BUL), Preben Elkjær Larsen (DEN), Dave Watson (ENG), Tony Woodcock (ENG), Daniel Ruiz Bazan Justa "DANI" (ESP), Karl-Heinz Rummenigge (FRG), Gerd Weber (GDR), Mike Galakos (GRE), Takis Nikoloudis (GRE), Ruud Geels (HOL), Willy van de Kerkhof (HOL), Gerry Daly (IRL), Gerry Armstrong (NIR), Zbigniew Boniek (POL), Roman Ogaza (POL), Tamagnini Manuel Gomes Batista "NENÉ" (POR), Archie Gemmill (SCO), Anders Grönhagen (SWE), Antonín Panenka (TCH)
2	Wilhelm Kreuz (AUT), Bruno Pezzey (AUT), Julien Cools (BEL), René Vandereycken (BEL), Henning Munk Jensen (DEN), Søren Lerby (DEN), Benny Nielsen (DEN), Allan Simonsen (DEN), Trevor Francis (ENG), Juan Manuel ASENSI Ripoll (ESP), Didier Six (FRA), Horst Hrubesch (FRG), Herbert Zimmermann (FRG), Lutz Lindemann (GDR), Rüdiger Schnuphase (GDR), Giorgos Delikaris (GRE), Ernie Brandts (HOL), Johnny Metgod (HOL), Dick Nanninga (HOL), László Fekete (HUN), György Tatár (HUN), Béla Várady (HUN), Tony Grealish (IRL), Frank Stapleton (IRL), Arne Larsen Økland (NOR), Stanislaw Terlecki (POL), ALBERTO Gomes FONSECA Júnior (POR), FERNANDO Mendes Soares GOMES (POR), Dudu Georgescu (ROM), Marcel Raducanu (ROM), Stefan Sames (ROM), Andy Gray (SCO), Gordon McQueen (SCO), John Robertson (SCO), Hasse Borg (SWE), Ján Kozák (TCH), Frantisek Stambachr (TCH), Sedat Özden (TUR), Yuri Chesnokov (URS), Brian Flynn (WAL), Zlatko Kranjcar (YUG), Vladimir Petrovic (YUG), Ivan Surjak (YUG)

1	Kurt Jara (AUT), Herbert Prohaska (AUT), Kurt Welzl (AUT), Jan Ceulemans (BEL), Eric Gerets (BEL), Jean Janssens (BEL), Wilfried Van Moer (BEL), Erwin Vandenbergh (BEL), Frank Vercauteren (BEL), Eddy Voordeckers (BEL), Ivan Iliev (BUL), Pavel Panov (BUL), Andrey Zhelyaskov (BUL), Soteris Kaiafas (CYP), Fivos Vrahimis (CYP), Frank Arnesen (DEN), Per Røntved (DEN), Peter Barnes (ENG), Trevor Brooking (ENG), Glenn Hoddle (ENG), Phil Neal (ENG), Ray Wilkins (ENG), Vicente DEL BOSQUE (ESP), Juan Gómez Gónzalez "JUANITO" (ESP), Enrique Castro González "QUINI" (ESP), RUBÉN Andres CANO Martinez (ESP), Enrique SAURA Gil (ESP), Ángel María VILLAR Llona (ESP), Kai Haaskivi (FIN), Tuomo Hakala (FIN), Aki Heiskanen (FIN), Jyrki Nieminen (FIN), Seppo Pyykkö (FIN), Miikka Toivola (FIN), Patrick Battiston (FRA), Marc Berdoll (FRA), Albert Emon (FRA), Albert Gemmrich (FRA), Bernard Lacombe (FRA), Jean François Larios (FRA), Eric Pécout (FRA), Jean Petit (FRA), Michel Platini (FRA), Patrick Rampillon (FRA), Marius Trésor (FRA), Rainer Bonhof (FRG), Karlheinz Förster (FRG), Manfred Kaltz (FRG), Walter Kelsch (FRG), Reinhard Häfner (GDR), Werner Peter (GDR), Hans-Jürgen Riediger (GDR), Nikos Anastopoulos (GRE), Christos Ardizoglou (GRE), Ruud Krol (HOL), Jan Peters (HOL), Rob Rensenbrink (HOL), Johnny Rep (HOL), Huub Stevens (HOL), Frans Thijssen (HOL), Pieter Wildschut (HOL), László Pusztai (HUN), László Szokolai (HUN), László Tieber (HUN), Daniel Givens (IRL), Michael Martin (IRL), Janus Gudlaugsson (ISL), Pétur Pétursson (ISL), Francesco Graziani (ITA), Marco Tardelli (ITA), Nico Braun (LUX), Romain Michaux (LUX), Emanuel Farrugia (MLT), Ernest Spiteri-Gonzi (MLT), Trevor Anderson (NIR), Billy Caskey (NIR), Victor Moreland (NIR), Chris Nicholl (NIR), Derek Spence (NIR), Einar Jan Aas (NOR), Georg Hammer (NOR), Pal Jacobsen (NOR), Marek Kusto (POL), Grzegorz Lato (POL), Wlodzimierz Mazur (POL), Wojciech Rudy (POL), Henryk Wieczorek (POL), ARTUR Manuel Soares CORREIA (POR), JOÃO António Ferreira Resende ALVES (POR), Mauricio Zacarias REINALDO Rodrigues Gomes (POR), Ionel Augustin (ROM), Anghel Iordanescu (ROM), Gheorghe Multescu (ROM), Steve Archibald (SCO), Joe Jordan (SCO), Umberto Barberis (SUI), Heinz Hermann (SUI), Herbert Hermann (SUI), Hans Jörg Pfister (SUI), Raimondo Ponte (SUI), Markus Tanner (SUI), Gian Pietro Zappa (SUI), Rutger Backe (SWE), Tore Cervin (SWE), Mats Nordgren (SWE), Jan Svensson (SWE), Miroslav Gajdusek (TCH), Ladislav Jurkemík (TCH), Mustafa Denizli (TUR), Erhan Önal (TUR), Fatih Terim (TUR), Sergei Andreev (URS), Volodymyr Bezsonov (URS), Yuri Gavrilov (URS), Alexandre Khapsalis (URS), Ramaz Shengelia (URS), Alan Curtis (WAL), Nick Deacy (WAL), Peter Nicholas (WAL), Peter O'Sullivan (WAL), Mickey Thomas (WAL), Damir Desnica (YUG), Vahid Halilhodzic (YUG), Dusan Savic (YUG), Blaz Sliskovic (YUG)
1 own goal	Gerd Kische (GDR) for Netherlands, John Holland (MLT) for West Germany, Jimmy Nicholl (NIR) for England

1984 UEFA European Football Championship

QUALIFYING ROUND

GROUP 1

06-10-1982	Brussels	Belgium – Switzerland	3-0 (1-0)
13-10-1982	Glasgow	Scotland – East Germany	2-0 (0-0)
17-11-1982	Bern	Switzerland – Scotland	2-0 (0-0)
15-12-1982	Brussels	Belgium – Scotland	3-2 (2-2)
30-03-1983	Leipzig	East Germany – Belgium	1-2 (0-1)
30-03-1983	Glasgow	Scotland – Switzerland	2-2 (0-1)
27-04-1983	Brussels	Belgium – East Germany	2-1 (2-1)
14-05-1983	Bern	Switzerland – East Germany	0-0
12-10-1983	East Berlin	East Germany – Switzerland	3-0 (1-0)
12-10-1983	Glasgow	Scotland – Belgium	1-1 (0-1)
09-11-1983	Bern	Switzerland – Belgium	3-1 (1-0)
16-11-1983	Halle	East Germany – Scotland	2-1 (2-0)

FINAL STANDING

Pos	Team	Pld	W	D	L	GF	GA	GD	Pts
1	*Belgium*	6	4	1	1	12	8	+4	9
2	Switzerland	6	2	2	2	7	9	-2	6
3	East Germany	6	2	1	3	7	7	0	5
4	Scotland	6	1	2	3	8	10	-2	4

Belgium qualified for the final tournament in France.

06-10-1982 Stade du Heysel, Brussels: Belgium – Switzerland 3-0 (1-0)
Belgium: Jean-Marie Pfaff, Marc Baecke (YC63), Walter Meeuws, Eric Gerets (C), Ludo Coeck, Frank Vercauteren, Jos Daerden, Erwin Vandenbergh, Guy Vandersmissen, Alexandre Czerniatynski, Jan Ceulemans. (Coach: Guy Jean Léonard Thijs (BEL)).
Switzerland: Erich Burgener, Andy Egli, Roger Wehrli (56' Lucien Favre), Heinz Lüdi, Charly In-Albon (YC71), Heinz Hermann, René Botteron (C), Alfred Scheiwiler (YC35) (69' Emi Maissen), Karl Elsener, Umberto Barberis, Claudio Sulser. (Coach: Paul Wolfisberg (SUI)).
Goals: Belgium: 1-0 Heinz Lüdi (2' *own goal*), 2-0 Ludo Coeck (48'), 3-0 Erwin Vandenbergh (82').
Referee: Paolo Bergamo (ITA) Attendance: 16.808

13-10-1982 Hampden Park, Glasgow: Scotland – East Germany 2-0 (0-0)
Scotland: Jim Leighton, Frank Gray, Alan Hansen, David Narey, Willie Miller, Graeme Souness (C), Gordon Strachan, John Wark, John Robertson, Alan Brazil (71' Paul Sturrock), Steve Archibald. (Coach: John (Jock) Stein (SCO)).
East Germany: Bodo Rudwaleit, Rüdiger Schnuphase (C), Hans-Jürgen Dörner (72' Jürgen Pommerenke), Ronald Kreer (YC60), Dirk Stahmann, Frank Baum, Hans-Uwe Pilz, Reinhard Häfner (72' Matthias Liebers), Norbert Trieloff, Joachim Streich, Hans-Jürgen Riediger. (Coach: Dr.Rudolf Krause (GDR)).
Goals: Scotland: 1-0 John Wark (53'), 2-0 Paul Sturrock (75').
Referee: Georges Konrath (FRA)   Attendance: 40.335

17-11-1982 Wankdorfstadion, Bern: Switzerland – Scotland 2-0 (0-0)
Switzerland: Erich Burgener (C), Alain Geiger, Andy Egli, Roger Wehrli, Heinz Lüdi, Lucien Favre, Michel Decastel (61' Umberto Barberis), Heinz Hermann, Raimondo Ponte, Karl Elsener (84' Hans-Peter Zwicker), Claudio Sulser. (Coach: Paul Wolfisberg (SUI)).
Scotland: Jim Leighton, Frank Gray, Alan Hansen, David Narey, Willie Miller, Graeme Souness (C), Gordon Strachan, John Wark, John Robertson, Alan Brazil, Paul Sturrock (46' Steve Archibald). (Coach: John (Jock) Stein (SCO)).
Goals: 1-0 Claudio Sulser (49'), 2-0 Andy Egli (61').
Referee: Vojtech Christov (TCH)   Attendance: 22.198

15-12-1982 Stade du Heysel, Brussels: Belgium – Scotland 3-2 (2-2)
Belgium: Jean-Marie Pfaff, Marc Baecke, Walter Meeuws, Eric Gerets (C), Ludo Coeck, Frank Vercauteren (64' René Verheyen), Jos Daerden, Erwin Vandenbergh (87' Maurice de Schryver), Guy Vandersmissen, François Van Der Elst, Jan Ceulemans. (Coach: Guy Jean Léonard Thijs (BEL)).
Scotland: Jim Leighton, Frank Gray, Alan Hansen, David Narey, Alex McLeish, Roy Aitken (YC83), Jim Bett (77' Tommy Burns), Graeme Souness (C), Gordon Strachan (77' Paul Sturrock), Kenny Dalglish, Steve Archibald (YC9). (Coach: John (Jock) Stein (SCO)).
Goals: Belgium: 1-1 Erwin Vandenbergh (25'), 2-2 François Van Der Elst (39'), 3-2 François Van Der Elst (63').
Scotland: 0-1 Kenny Dalglish (13'), 1-2 Kenny Dalglish (35').
Referee: António José Da Silva Garrido (POR)   Attendance: 48.877

30-03-1983 Zentralstadion, Leipzig: East Germany – Belgium 1-2 (0-1)
East Germany: Bodo Rudwaleit, Rüdiger Schnuphase (C), Hans-Jürgen Dörner, Ronald Kreer, Dirk Stahmann, Norbert Trieloff, Matthias Liebers, Andreas Trautmann, Joachim Streich, Hans Richter (70' Martin Busse), Dieter Kühn (60' Jürgen Heun). (Coach: Dr.Rudolf Krause (GDR)).
Belgium: Jacques Munaron, Luc Millecamps, Walter Meeuws (YC32) (85' Lei Clijsters), Eric Gerets (C) (YC60), Michel de Groote (46' Marc Baecke), Ludo Coeck, Frank Vercauteren, Erwin Vandenbergh, Guy Vandersmissen, François Van Der Elst, Jan Ceulemans. (Coach: Guy Jean Léonard Thijs (BEL)).
Goals: East Germany: 1-2 Joachim Streich (82').
Belgium: 0-1 François Van Der Elst (35'), 0-2 Erwin Vandenbergh (70').
Referee: John Capenter (IRL)   Attendance: 70.188

30-03-1983   Hampden Park, Glasgow: Scotland – Switzerland   2-2 (0-1)
Scotland: Jim Leighton, Richard Gough, Frank Gray, Alan Hansen (46' Alex McLeish), Willie Miller, Graeme Souness (C), Gordon Strachan, John Walk, Peter Weir, Kenny Dalglish, Charlie Nicholas. (Coach: John (Jock) Stein (SCO)).
Switzerland: Erich Burgener (C), Alain Geiger, Andy Egli, Roger Wehrli, Heinz Lüdi, Lucien Favre, Michel Decastel, Heinz Hermann (69' Hans-Peter Zwicker), Raimondo Ponte, Karl Elsener, Claudio Sulser (YC14) (83' Charly In-Albon). (Coach: Paul Wolfisberg (SUI)).
Goals: Scotland: 1-2 John Walk (70'), 2-2 Charlie Nicholas (75').
Switzerland: 0-1 Andy Egli (14'), 0-2 Heinz Hermann (57').
Referee: Charles George Reinier Corver (HOL)   Attendance: 36.923

27-04-1983   Stade du Heysel, Brussels: Belgium – East Germany   2-1 (2-1)
Belgium: Jean-Marie Pfaff, Luc Millecamps, Walter Meeuws, Eric Gerets (C), Michel de Groote, Ludo Coeck, Frank Vercauteren, Erwin Vandenbergh, Guy Vandersmissen, François Van Der Elst, Jan Ceulemans. (Coach: Guy Jean Léonard Thijs (BEL)).
East Germany: Bodo Rudwaleit, Rüdiger Schnuphase (C), Ronald Kreer, Dirk Stahmann, Frank Baum, Hans-Uwe Pilz (70' Rainer Ernst), Rainer Troppa, Matthias Liebers, Martin Busse (61' Hans Richter (YC76)), Wolfgang Steinbach, Joachim Streich. (Coach: Dr.Rudolf Krause (GDR)).
Goals: Belgium: 1-1 Jan Ceulemans (18'), 2-1 Ludo Coeck (39').
East Germany: 0-1 Joachim Streich (9').
Referee: Emilio Carlos Gucuceta Muro (ESP)   Attendance: 43.894

14-05-1983   Wankdorfstadion, Bern: Switzerland – East Germany   0-0
Switzerland: Roger Berbig (C), Andy Egli, Roger Wehrli, Charly In-Albon (YC1), Beat Rietmann, Lucien Favre, Michel Decastel, Heinz Hermann, Karl Elsener (YC57) (58' Jean-Paul Brigger), Claudio Sulser, Manfred Braschler. (Coach: Paul Wolfisberg (SUI)).
East Germany: Bodo Rudwaleit, Rüdiger Schnuphase (C), Ronald Kreer, Dirk Stahmann, Frank Baum, Rainer Troppa, Matthias Liebers (73' Jürgen Heun), Wolfgang Steinbach (62' Hans-Uwe Pilz), Joachim Streich, Andreas Bielau, Ralf Minge (YC62). (Coach: Dr.Rudolf Krause (GDR)).
Referee: Rolf Ericsson (SWE)   Attendance: 29.738

12-10-1983   Friedrich-Ludwig-Jahn-Sportpark, East Berlin:
              East Germany – Switzerland   3-0 (1-0)
East Germany: Bodo Rudwaleit, Rüdiger Schnuphase (C), Ronald Kreer, Rainer Troppa, Uwe Zötzsche, Wolfgang Steinbach, Christian Backs (YC36), Jürgen Raab (71' Ralf Minge), Joachim Streich, Hans Richter, Rainer Ernst. (Coach: Bernd Stange (GDR)).
Switzerland: Roger Berbig (C), Alain Geiger, Andy Egli, Roger Wehrli, Beat Rietmann, Lucien Favre, Heinz Hermann, Raimondo Ponte (69' Beat Sutter), Umberto Barberis, Claudio Sulser (YC33) (69' Marcel Koller), Manfred Braschler. (Coach: Paul Wolfisberg (SUI)).
Goals: East Germany: 1-0 Hans Richter (45'), 2-0 Rainer Ernst (73'), 3-0 Joachim Streich (90').
Referee: Keith Stuart Hackett (ENG)   Attendance: 6.755

12-10-1983   Hampden Park, Glasgow: Scotland – Belgium   1-1 (0-1)
Scotland: Jim Leighton, Richard Gough, Willie Miller (C), Arthur Albiston, Alex McLeish, Paul McStay, Jim Bett, John Walk (80' Roy Aitken), John Robertson, Kenny Dalglish, Charlie Nicholas (74' Frank McGarvey). (Coach: John (Jock) Stein (SCO)).
Belgium: Jean-Marie Pfaff, Luc Millecamps, Walter Meeuws (78' Michel De Wolf), Eric Gerets (C), Michel Wintacq, Ludo Coeck, Frank Vercauteren, Nico Claesen, François Van Der Elst, Jan Ceulemans, Eddy Voordeckers. (Coach: Guy Jean Léonard Thijs (BEL)).
Goals: Scotland: 1-1 Charlie Nicholas (75').
Belgium: 0-1 Frank Vercauteren (4').
Referee: Enzo Barbaresco (ITA)   Attendance: 23.475

09-11-1983   Wankdorfstadion, Bern: Switzerland – Belgium   3-1 (1-0)
Switzerland: Roger Berbig (C), Alain Geiger, Andy Egli, Roger Wehrli, Heinz Lüdi, Charly In-Albon (YC49), Marco Schällibaum (74' André Ladner), Heinz Hermann, Beat Sutter (81' Marcel Koller), Raimondo Ponte, Jean-Paul Brigger. (Coach: Paul Wolfisberg (SUI)).
Belgium: Jean-Marie Pfaff, Luc Millecamps, Walter Meeuws, Eric Gerets (C) (YC60), Ludo Coeck (64' Nico Claesen), Raymond Mommens, Frank Vercauteren, Erwin Vandenbergh, François Van Der Elst (YC15) (46' Guy Vandersmissen), Jan Ceulemans, Eddy Voordeckers. (Coach: Guy Jean Léonard Thijs (BEL)).
Goals: Switzerland: 1-0 Marco Schällibaum (23'), 2-1 Jean-Paul Brigger (75'), 3-1 Alain Geiger (89').
Belgium: 1-1 Erwin Vandenbergh (63').
Referee: Volker Roth (FRG)   Attendance: 7.446

16-11-1983   Kurt-Wabbel Stadion, Halle: East Germany – Scotland   2-1 (2-0)
East Germany: Bodo Rudwaleit, Ronald Kreer, Dirk Stahmann, Hans-Uwe Pilz, Rainer Troppa, Uwe Zötzsche, Wolfgang Steinbach, Christian Backs, Joachim Streich (C), Hans Richter, Rainer Ernst (87' Jürgen Raab). (Coach: Bernd Stange (GDR)).
Scotland: Billy Thomson, Richard Gough, Willie Miller (C), Arthur Albiston, Alex McLeish, Paul McStay (60' Frank McGarvey), Gordon Strachan, John Walk, Eamonn Bannon, Kenny Dalglish, Steve Archibald. (Coach: John (Jock) Stein (SCO)).
Goals: East Germany: 1-0 Ronald Kreer (34'), 2-0 Joachim Streich (43').
Scotland: 2-1 Eamonn Bannon (77').
Referee: Franz Wöhrer (AUT)   Attendance: 14.729

GROUP 2

08-09-1982	Kuopio	Finland – Poland	2-3 (0-2)
22-09-1982	Helsinki	Finland – Portugal	0-2 (0-1)
10-10-1982	Lisbon	Portugal – Poland	2-1 (1-0)
13-10-1982	Moscow	Soviet Union – Finland	2-0 (1-0)
17-04-1983	Warsaw	Poland – Finland	1-1 (1-1)
27-04-1983	Moscow	Soviet Union – Portugal	5-0 (2-0)
22-05-1983	Chorzów	Poland – Soviet Union	1-1 (1-0)
01-06-1983	Helsinki	Finland – Soviet Union	0-1 (0-0)
21-09-1983	Lisbon	Portugal – Finland	5-0 (2-0)
09-10-1983	Moscow	Soviet Union – Poland	2-0 (1-0)
28-10-1983	Wroclaw	Poland – Portugal	0-1 (0-1)
13-11-1983	Lisbon	Portugal – Soviet Union	1-0 (1-0)

FINAL STANDING

Pos	Team	Pld	W	D	L	GF	GA	GD	Pts
1	Portugal	6	5	0	1	11	6	+5	10
2	Soviet Union	6	4	1	1	11	2	+9	9
3	Poland	6	1	2	3	6	9	-3	4
4	Finland	6	0	1	5	3	14	-11	1

Portugal qualified for the final tournament in France.

08-09-1982   Kuopion Keskuskenttä, Kuopio: Finland – Poland   2-3 (0-2)
Finland: Olavi Huttunen, Pauno Kymäläinen, Hannu Turunen, Aki Lahtinen, Mikael Granskog, Esa Pekonen, Ilkka Remes, Pasi Rautiainen, Jukka Ikäläinen (C), Atik Ismail (61' Ari Valvee), Juhani Himanka (72' Keijo Kousa). (Coach: Martti Kuusela (FIN)).
Poland: Jacek Kazimierski, Pawel Janas, Stefan Majewski, Tadeusz Dolny, Jan Jalocho, Andrzey Buncol, Janusz Kupcewicz, Wlodzimierz Ciolek, Wlodzimierz Smolarek (C), Zbigniew Boniek, Dariusz Dziekanowski (74' Wlodzimierz Mazur). (Coach: Antoni Piechniczek (POL)).
Goals: Finland: 1-3 Ari Valvee (83'), 2-3 Keijo Kousa (84').
Poland: 0-1 Wlodzimierz Smolarek (16' penalty), 0-2 Dariusz Dziekanowski (27'), 0-3 Janusz Kupcewicz (72').
Referee: Marcel Van Langenhove (BEL)   Attendance: 3.529

22-09-1982   Helsinki Olympic Stadium, Helsinki: Finland – Portugal   0-2 (0-1)
Finland: Olli Isoaho, Pauno Kymäläinen, Hannu Turunen, Aki Lahtinen (C), Esa Pekonen, Reijo Vaittinen, Ilkka Remes, Pasi Rautiainen (46' Ari Valvee), Jari Parikka, Atik Ismail, Juhani Himanka (79' Keijo Kousa). (Coach: Martti Kuusela (FIN)).
Portugal: Manuel Galrinho BENTO, Augusto Soares INÁCIO, ANTÓNIO Augusto da Silva VELOSO, António José BASTOS LOPES, HUMBERTO Manuel de Jesus COELHO (C), MINERVINO José Lopes PIETRA, JOÃO António Ferreira Resende ALVES, ANTÓNIO Luis Alves Ribeiro de OLIVEIRA, SHÉU Han, FERNANDO Mendes Soares GOMES (73' Luís Maria Cabral NORTON DE MATOS), Tamagnini Manuel Gomes Batista "NENÉ". (Coach: OTTO Martins GLÓRIA (BRA)).
Goals: Portugal: 0-1 Tamagnini Manuel Gomes Batista "NENÉ" (15'), 0-2 ANTÓNIO Luis Alves Ribeiro de OLIVEIRA (89').
Referee: Klaus Scheurell (GDR)   Attendance: 3.132

10-10-1982   Estádio da Luz, Lisbon: Portugal – Poland   2-1 (1-0)
Portugal: Manuel Galrinho BENTO, Augusto Soares INÁCIO, ANTÓNIO Augusto da Silva VELOSO, António José BASTOS LOPES, HUMBERTO Manuel de Jesus COELHO (C), MINERVINO José Lopes PIETRA, CARLOS MANUEL Correia dos Santos, JOÃO António Ferreira Resende ALVES (36' EURICO Monteiro GOMES), ANTÓNIO Luis Alves Ribeiro de OLIVEIRA (89' José Alberto COSTA), FERNANDO Mendes Soares GOMES, Tamagnini Manuel Gomes Batista "NENÉ" (YC86). (Coach: OTTO Martins GLÓRIA (BRA)).
Poland: Jacek Kazimierski, Pawel Janas (YC63), Stefan Majewski (C), Roman Wojcicki, Pawel Król, Jozef Adamiec, Jan Jalocho, Andrzey Buncol, Zbigniew Boniek, Dariusz Dziekanowski, Wlodzimierz Mazur (46' Marek Dziuba). (Coach: Antoni Piechniczek (POL)).
Goals: Portugal: 1-0 Tamagnini Manuel Gomes Batista "NENÉ" (2'), 2-0 FERNANDO Mendes Soares GOMES (82').
Poland: 2-1 Pawel Król (90').
Referee: Franz Wöhrer (AUT)   Attendance: 56.809

13-10-1982   Central Lenin Stadium, Moscow: Soviet Union – Finland   2-0 (1-0)
Soviet Union: Rinat Dasayev, Volodymyr Bezsonov, Anatoliy Demyanenko, Serhiy Baltacha, Alexandre Chivadze (C), Vladimir Lozinskiy, Ramaz Shengelia (30' Vadim Yevtushenko), Andrei Bal, Khoren Oganesyan (70' Sergei Borovskiy), Leonid Buryak, Sergei Andreev. (Coach: Valeriy Vasylyovych Lobanovskyi (URS)).
Finland: Olavi Huttunen, Pauno Kymäläinen, Hannu Turunen, Aki Lahtinen (C) (55' Atik Ismail), Mikael Granskog, Esa Pekonen, Ilkka Remes, Peter Utriainen, Juhani Himanka (75' Keijo Kousa), Ari Valvee, Vesa Mars. (Coach: Martti Kuusela (FIN)).
Goals: Soviet Union: 1-0 Serhiy Baltacha (2'), 2-0 Sergei Andreev (57').
Referee: Jakob Baumann (SUI)   Attendance: 18.086

17-04-1983   Stadion Dziesieciolecia, Warsaw: Poland – Finland   1-1 (1-1)
Poland: Jozef Mlynarczyk, Pawel Janas, Stefan Majewski (C), Roman Wojcicki (YC59), Jan Jalocho, Andrzey Buncol (YC62), Janusz Kupcewicz, Wlodzimierz Ciolek (65' Kazimierz Buda), Wlodimierz Smolarek (C), Zbigniew Boniek, Miroslaw Okonski. (Coach: Antoni Piechniczek (POL)).
Finland: Olli Isoaho, Pauno Kymäläinen (C), Hannu Turunen, Mikael Granskog, Esa Pekonen, Ilkka Remes (41' Aki Lahtinen (YC79)), Kari Ukkonen, Leo Houtsonen, Atik Ismail, Tuomo Hakala, Mika Lipponen (65' Ari Hjelm). (Coach: Martti Kuusela (FIN)).
Goals: Poland: 1-0 Wlodimierz Smolarek (2' penalty).
Finland: 1-1 Pawel Janas (5' *own goal*).
Referee: Reidar P.Bjørnestad (NOR)   Attendance: 63.000

27-04-1983   Central Lenin Stadium, Moscow: Soviet Union – Portugal   5-0 (2-0)
Soviet Union: Rinat Dasayev, Volodymyr Bezsonov, Anatoliy Demyanenko, Nikolai Larionov, Tengiz Sulakvelidze, Serhiy Baltacha, Alexandre Chivadze (C), Khoren Oganesyan (74' Leonid Buryak), Fyodor Cherenkov, Oleh Blokhin, Sergei Rodionov (76' Ramaz Shengelia). (Coach: Valeriy Vasylyovych Lobanovskyi (URS)).
Portugal: Manuel Galrinho BENTO, António José BASTOS LOPES, HUMBERTO Manuel de Jesus COELHO (C), MINERVINO José Lopes PIETRA, JOÃO Soares CARDOSO, CARLOS MANUEL Correia dos Santos, JAIME Moreira PACHECO, JOÃO António Ferreira Resende ALVES, FERNANDO António De Carvalho FESTAS (YC22) (46' José Alberto COSTA), FERNANDO Mendes Soares GOMES, Tamagnini Manuel Gomes Batista "NENÉ". (Coach: OTTO Martins GLÓRIA (BRA)).
Goals: Soviet Union: 1-0 Fyodor Cherenkov (16'), 2-0 Sergei Rodionov (40'), 3-0 Anatoliy Demyanenko (53'), 4-0 Fyodor Cherenkov (63'), 5-0 Nikolai Larionov (86').
Referee: John Hunting (ENG)   Attendance: 82.114

22-05-1983   Stadion Slaski, Chorzów: Poland – Soviet Union   1-1 (1-0)
Poland: Jozef Mlynarczyk, Pawel Janas, Stefan Majewski, Roman Wojcicki (YC59), Jan Jalocho, Andrzey Buncol, Janusz Kupcewicz (73' Andrzej Iwan), Jerzy Wijas, Adam Kensy, Wlodimierz Smolarek (C) (80' Dariusz Dziekanowski), Zbigniew Boniek. (Coach: Antoni Piechniczek (POL)).
Soviet Union: Rinat Dasayev, Volodymyr Bezsonov, Anatoliy Demyanenko, Nikolai Larionov, Tengiz Sulakvelidze, Serhiy Baltacha, Sergei Borovskiy, Alexandre Chivadze (C), Khoren Oganesyan (84' Andrei Bal), Fyodor Cherenkov, Oleh Blokhin (74' Sergei Andreev). (Coach: Valeriy Vasylyovych Lobanovskyi (URS)).
Goals: Poland: 1-0 Zbigniew Boniek (16').
Soviet Union: 1-1 Roman Wojcicki (62' *own goal*).
Referee: Luigi Agnolin (ITA)   Attendance: 69.044

01-06-1983   Helsinki Olympic Stadium, Helsinki: Finland – Soviet Union   0-1 (0-0)
Finland: Olavi Huttunen, Pauno Kymäläinen (C), Hannu Turunen, Aki Lahtinen, Mikael Granskog, Esa Pekonen, Kari Ukkonen, Leo Houtsonen, Pasi Rautiainen, Atik Ismail (65' Tuomo Hakala), Ari Valvee. (Coach: Martti Kuusela (FIN)).
Soviet Union: Rinat Dasayev, Anatoliy Demyanenko, Nikolai Larionov, Tengiz Sulakvelidze, Serhiy Baltacha (25' Andrei Bal), Alexandre Chivadze (C), Ramaz Shengelia (74' Sergei Andreev), Khoren Oganesyan, Leonid Buryak, Fyodor Cherenkov, Oleh Blokhin. (Coach: Valeriy Vasylyovych Lobanovskyi (URS)).
Goal: Soviet Union: 0-1 Oleh Blokhin (75').
Referee: Dusan Krchnák (TCH)   Attendance: 16.966

21-09-1983   Estádio José de Alvalade, Lisbon: Portugal – Finland   5-0 (2-0)
Portugal: Manuel Galrinho BENTO (C), Augusto Soares INÁCIO, António José LIMA PEREIRA, António José BASTOS LOPES, MINERVINO José Lopes PIETRA, CARLOS MANUEL Correia dos Santos, JAIME Moreira PACHECO (59' PAULO Jorge FUTRE dos Santos), ANTÓNIO Luis Alves Ribeiro de OLIVEIRA, JOSÉ LUIS Lopes da Costa e Silva, FERNANDO Mendes Soares GOMES, Rui Manuel Trindade JORDÃO (46' Tamagnini Manuel Gomes Batista "NENÉ"). (Coach: FERNANDO da Silva CABRITA (POR)).
Finland: Pertti Alaja, Erkka Petäjä, Hannu Turunen, Mikael Granskog, Esa Pekonen, Keijo Kousa, Kari Ukkonen, Leo Houtsonen, Jukka Ikäläinen (C), Kari Virtanen, Mika Lipponen. (Coach: Martti Kuusela (FIN)).
Goals: Portugal: 1-0 Rui Manuel Trindade JORDÃO (18'), 2-0 CARLOS MANUEL Correia dos Santos (23'), 3-0 Jukka Ikäläinen (47' *own goal*), 4-0 JOSÉ LUIS Lopes da Costa e Silva (83'), 5-0 ANTÓNIO Luis Alves Ribeiro de OLIVEIRA (86').
Referee: Karl-Heinz Tritschler (FRG)   Attendance: 15.136

09-10-1983   Central Lenin Stadium, Moscow: Soviet Union – Poland   2-0 (1-0)
Soviet Union: Rinat Dasayev, Anatoliy Demyanenko, Tengiz Sulakvelidze, Serhiy Baltacha (YC29), Alexandre Chivadze (C), Vadim Yevtushenko (46' Alexandre Tarkhanov), Andrei Bal, Khoren Oganesyan, Fyodor Cherenkov, Oleh Blokhin, Yuri Gavrilov (84' Leonid Buryak). (Coach: Valeriy Vasylyovych Lobanovskyi (URS)).
Poland: Jozef Mlynarczyk (C), Stefan Majewski, Roman Wojcicki, Pawel Król, Kazimierz Buda, Krzysztof Urbanowicz, Andrzey Buncol (23' Waldemar Prusik), Jerzy Wijas, Adam Kensy, Wlodimierz Smolarek (68' Dariusz Dziekanowski), Zbigniew Boniek. (Coach: Antoni Piechniczek (POL)).
Goals: Soviet Union: 1-0 Anatoliy Demyanenko (10'), 2-0 Oleh Blokhin (62').
Referee: Johannes Nicolaus Ignacius (Jan) Keizer (HOL)   Attendance: 72.504

28-10-1983   Olympic Stadium, Wroclaw: Poland – Portugal   0-1 (0-1)
Poland: Jozef Mlynarczyk (C), Stefan Majewski, Marek Ostrowski, Roman Wojcicki, Jan Jalocha, Andrzej Iwan, Waldemar Prusik, Wlodzimierz Ciolek (46' Miroslaw Okonski), Jerzy Wijas, Adam Kensy (65' Andrzej Palasz), Wlodimierz Smolarek. (Coach: Antoni Piechniczek (POL)).
Portugal: Manuel Galrinho BENTO, Augusto Soares INÁCIO, EURICO Monteiro GOMES, JOÃO Domingos da Silva PINTO, António José LIMA PEREIRA (YC71), CARLOS MANUEL Correia dos Santos, JAIME Moreira PACHECO, José Alberto COSTA (46' José Elben De Araujo Lobo Júnior "LITO"), JOSÉ LUIS Lopes da Costa e Silva (YC73), FERNANDO Mendes Soares GOMES, Tamagnini Manuel Gomes Batista "NENÉ" (C) (80' Manuel Fernandes Miranda DIAMANTINO). (Coach: FERNANDO da Silva CABRITA (POR)).
Goal: Portugal: 0-1 CARLOS MANUEL Correia dos Santos (32').
Referee: Ulf Johan Eriksson (SWE)   Attendance: 8.625

13-11-1983   Estádio da Luz, Lisbon: Portugal – Soviet Union   1-0 (1-0)
Portugal: Manuel Galrinho BENTO (C), Augusto Soares INÁCIO, EURICO Monteiro GOMES, JOÃO Domingos da Silva PINTO, António José LIMA PEREIRA, CARLOS MANUEL Correia dos Santos, JAIME Moreira PACHECO, Fernando Albino Sousa CHALANA (79' SHÉU Han), JOSÉ LUIS Lopes da Costa e Silva, FERNANDO Mendes Soares GOMES, Rui Manuel Trindade JORDÃO (75' Manuel Fernandes Miranda DIAMANTINO). (Coach: FERNANDO da Silva CABRITA (POR)).
Soviet Union: Rinat Dasayev, Anatoliy Demyanenko, Tengiz Sulakvelidze (YC61), Serhiy Baltacha, Sergei Borovskiy, Alexandre Chivadze (C), Andrei Bal, Fyodor Cherenkov, Oleh Blokhin, Sergei Rodionov (70' Vadim Yevtushenko), Yuri Gavrilov (60' Khoren Oganesyan). (Coach: Valeriy Vasylyovych Lobanovskyi (URS)).
Goal: Portugal: 1-0 Rui Manuel Trindade JORDÃO (44' penalty).
Referee: Georges Konrath (FRA)   Attendance: 32.243

GROUP 3

22-09-1982	Copenhagen	Denmark – England	2-2 (0-1)
09-10-1982	Luxembourg	Luxembourg – Greece	0-2 (0-2)
10-11-1982	Luxembourg	Luxembourg – Denmark	1-2 (0-1)
17-11-1982	Thessaloniki	Greece – England	0-3 (0-1)
15-12-1982	London	England – Luxembourg	9-0 (4-0)
27-03-1983	Luxembourg	Luxembourg – Hungary	2-6 (1-2)
30-03-1983	London	England – Greece	0-0
17-04-1983	Budapest	Hungary – Luxembourg	6-2 (3-0)
27-04-1983	Copenhagen	Denmark – Greece	1-0 (0-0)
27-04-1983	London	England – Hungary	2-0 (1-0)
15-05-1983	Budapest	Hungary – Greece	2-3 (1-2)
01-06-1983	Copenhagen	Denmark – Hungary	3-1 (1-1)
21-09-1983	London	England – Denmark	0-1 (0-1)
12-10-1983	Budapest	Hungary – England	0-3 (0-3)
12-10-1983	Copenhagen	Denmark – Luxembourg	6-0 (4-0)
26-10-1983	Budapest	Hungary – Denmark	1-0 (0-0)
16-11-1983	Athens	Greece – Denmark	0-2 (0-1)
16-11-1983	Luxembourg	Luxembourg – England	0-4 (0-2)
03-12-1983	Thessaloniki	Greece – Hungary	2-2 (1-2)
14-12-1983	Piraeus	Greece – Luxembourg	1-0 (1-0)

FINAL STANDING

Pos	Team	Pld	W	D	L	GF	GA	GD	Pts
1	*Denmark*	8	6	1	1	17	5	+12	13
2	England	8	5	2	1	23	3	+20	12
3	Greece	8	3	2	3	8	10	-2	8
4	Hungary	8	3	1	4	18	17	+1	7
5	Luxembourg	8	0	0	8	5	36	-31	0

Denmark qualified for the final tournament in France.

22-09-1982   Idrætsparken, Copenhagen: Denmark – England   2-2 (0-1)
Denmark: Troels Rasmussen, Søren Busk, Ivan Nielsen, Jens Jørn Bertelsen, Per Røntved, Søren Lerby (YC49), Jesper Olsen, Ole Rasmussen, Allan Hansen, Preben Elkjær Larsen, Lars Bastrup. (Coach: Josef Emmanuel Hubertus Piontek (FRG)).
England: Peter Shilton, Kenny Sansom, Phil Neal (YC4), Russell Osman, Graham Rix, Bryan Robson (YC80), Ray Wilkins (C), Terry Butcher, Tony Morley (83' Ricky Hill), Trevor Francis, Paul Mariner. (Coaches: Robert William (Bobby) Robson (ENG) & Ronald (Ron) Greenwood (ENG)).
Goals: Denmark: 1-1 Allan Hansen (68' penalty), 2-2 Jesper Olsen (89').
England: 0-1 Trevor Francis (8'), 1-2 Trevor Francis (82').
Referee: Charles George Reinier Corver (HOL)   Attendance: 44.300

09-10-1982   Stade Municipal, Luxembourg: Luxembourg – Greece   0-2 (0-2)
Luxembourg: Jeannot Moes (C), Hubert Meunier, Nico Rohmann, Gilbert Dresch, Michel Bechet (46' Romain Schreiner), Guy Hellers, Jean-Paul Girres (65' Marcel Di Domenico), Carlo Weis, John Clemens, Robert Langers, Jeannot Reiter. (Coach: Louis Pilot (LUX)).
Greece: Nikos Sarganis (YC82), Kostas Iosifidis, Giorgos Firos, Anthimos Kapsis (C), Giannis Gounaris (YC35), Spiros Livathinos, Dinos Kouis (86' Giorgos Kostikos), Petros Michos, Apostolakis Papaioanou (62' Savas Haralampo Kofidis), Nikos Anastopoulos, Hristos Dimopoulos. (Coach: Vasilis Archontidis (GRE)).
Goals: Greece: 0-1 Nikos Anastopoulos (7' penalty), 0-2 Nikos Anastopoulos (26').
Referee: Karl-Heinz Tritschler (FRG)   Attendance: 2.858

10-11-1982   Stade Municipal, Luxembourg: Luxembourg – Denmark   1-2 (0-1)
Luxembourg: Jeannot Moes (C), Hubert Meunier, Nico Rohmann, Gilbert Dresch, Guy Hellers, Jean-Paul Girres, Carlo Weis, John Clemens, Robert Langers (YC38), Marcel Di Domenico (73' Manou Scheitler), Jeannot Reiter (79' Romain Schreiner). (Coach: Louis Pilot (LUX)).
Denmark: Ole Qvist, Søren Busk, Ivan Nielsen, Morten Olsen, Per Røntved (C), Søren Lerby (YC68), Jesper Olsen (88' Morten Donnerup), Jan Mikkelsen Lauridsen, Ole Rasmussen, Preben Elkjær Larsen (46' Klaus Berggreen), Lars Bastrup. (Coach: Josef Emmanuel Hubertus Piontek (FRG)).
Goals: Luxembourg: 1-1 Marcel Di Domenico (54').
Denmark: 0-1 Søren Lerby (31' penalty), 1-2 Klaus Berggreen (67').
Referee: Gérard Biguet (FRA)   Attendance: 2.057

17-11-1982   Kaftanzoglio Stadium, Thessaloniki: Greece – England   0-3 (0-1)
Greece: Nikos Sarganis, Kostas Iosifidis, Giorgos Firos, Anthimos Kapsis (C), Giannis Gounaris, Anastasios Mitropoulos, Spiros Livathinos, Petros Michos, Christos Ardizoglou (41' Giorgos Kostikos), Nikos Anastopoulos, Thomas Mavros (78' Savas Haralampo Kofidis). (Coach: Vasilis Archontidis (GRE)).
England: Peter Shilton, Kenny Sansom, Phil Thompson, Phil Neal, Alvin Martin, Gary Mabbutt, Bryan Robson (C), Tony Morley, Sammy Lee, Paul Mariner, Tony Woodcock. (Coaches: Robert William (Bobby) Robson (ENG) & Ronald (Ron) Greenwood (ENG)).
Goals: England: 0-1 Tony Woodcock (1'), 0-2 Tony Woodcock (64'), 0-3 Sammy Lee (68').
Referee: Adolf Prokop (GDR)   Attendance: 41.534

15-12-1982   Wembley Stadium, London: England – Luxembourg   9-0 (4-0)
England: Ray Clemence, Kenny Sansom, Phil Neal, Alvin Martin, Gary Mabbutt (74' Glenn Hoddle), Steve Coppell (66' Mark Chamberlain), Bryan Robson (C), Terry Butcher, Sammy Lee, Tony Woodcock, Luther Blissett. (Coaches: Robert William (Bobby) Robson (ENG) & Ronald (Ron) Greenwood (ENG)).
Luxembourg: Jeannot Moes (C), Marcel Bossi, Hubert Meunier, Nico Rohmann, Gilbert Dresch, Guy Hellers, Jean-Paul Girres, Carlo Weis, John Clemens, Marcel Di Domenico (46' Alain Nurenberg), Jeannot Reiter. (Coach: Louis Pilot (LUX)).
Goals: England: 1-0 Marcel Bossi (18' *own goal*), 2-0 Steve Coppell (22'), 3-0 Tony Woodcock (34'), 4-0 Luther Blissett (44'), 5-0 Luther Blissett (62'), 6-0 Mark Chamberlain (71'), 7-0 Luther Blissett (86'), 8-0 Glenn Hoddle (87'), 9-0 Phil Neal (89').
Referee: Hreidar Jonsson (ISL)   Attendance: 33.977

27-03-1983   Stade Municipal, Luxembourg: Luxembourg – Hungary   2-6 (1-2)
Luxembourg: Jeannot Moes (C), Marcel Bossi, Hubert Meunier, Gilbert Dresch, Romain Michaux, Jean-Paul Girres, Carlo Weis, Romain Schreiner, Fred Schreiner (62' Alain Nurenberg), Robert Langers (YC44), Jeannot Reiter. (Coach: Louis Pilot (LUX)).
Hungary: Béla Katzirz (C), Zoltán Péter, József Tóth, Attila Kerekes (YC70), Imre Garaba (YC73), Tibor Nyilasi, Péter Hannich (YC34), József Póczik, László Fazekas (62' László Kiss), András Törőcsik (72' Gyula Hajszán), Gábor Pölöskei. (Coach: Kálmán Mészöly (HUN)).
Goals: Luxembourg: 1-0 Jeannot Reiter (4'), 2-3 Romain Schreiner (55').
Hungary: 1-1 József Póczik (30'), 1-2 Tibor Nyilasi (40'), 1-3 Gábor Pölöskei (50'), 2-4 Péter Hannich (56'), 2-5 József Póczik (59'), 2-6 József Póczik (69').
Referee: Gerardus Johannes Maria (Gerard) Geurts (HOL)   Attendance: 2.159

30-03-1983   Wembley Stadium, London: England – Greece   0-0
England: Peter Shilton (C), Kenny Sansom, Phil Neal, Alvin Martin, Gary Mabbutt, Steve Coppell, Terry Butcher, Sammy Lee, Alan Devonshire (73' Luther Blissett), Trevor Francis, Tony Woodcock (73' Graham Rix). (Coach: Robert William (Bobby) Robson (ENG)).
Greece: Nikos Sarganis (YC83), Babis Xanthopoulos (YC81), Giannis Gounaris (C), Ioannis Galitsios, Nikos Karoulias, Anastasios Mitropoulos (78' Giannis Dontas), Dinos Kouis, Evangelos Kousoulakis, Petros Michos, Giorgos Kostikos, Nikos Anastopoulos (87' Christos Ardizoglou). (Coach: Vasilis Archontidis (GRE)).
Referee: Dusan Krchnák (TCH)   Attendance: 44.051

17-04-1983   Népstadion, Budapest: Hungary – Luxembourg   6-2 (3-0)
Hungary: Béla Katzirz (C), Zoltán Péter, József Tóth, Attila Kerekes, Imre Garaba, Tibor Nyilasi, Péter Hannich, József Póczik (28' Győző Burcsa), Gyula Hajszán, Gábor Pölöskei (25' Lázár Szentes), László Kiss. (Coach: Kálmán Mészöly (HUN)).
Luxembourg: Jean-Paul Defrang, Théo Malget (65' Nico Wagner), Marcel Bossi (YC30), Hubert Meunier, Gilbert Dresch, Romain Michaux, Jean-Paul Girres (YC51), Carlo Weis, Romain Schreiner, Fred Schreiner (46' Alain Nurenberg), Jeannot Reiter (YC51). (Coach: Louis Pilot (LUX)).
Goals: Hungary: 1-0 Gyula Hajszán (21'), 2-0 Tibor Nyilasi (33'), 3-0 László Kiss (35'), 4-2 Lázár Szentes (61'), 5-2 Tibor Nyilasi (63'), 6-2 Győző Burcsa (65').
Luxembourg: 3-1 Jeannot Reiter (56'), 3-2 Théo Malget (57').
Referee: Edgar Azzopardi (MLT)   Attendance: 12.278

27-04-1983   Idrætsparken, Copenhagen: Denmark – Greece   1-0 (0-0)
Denmark: Ole Qvist, Søren Busk, Jens Jørn Bertelsen, Morten Olsen (C), Ole Madsen, Jesper Olsen (46' Lars Bastrup), Jan Mikkelsen Lauridsen, Ole Rasmussen, Klaus Berggreen, Preben Elkjær Larsen, Allan Simonsen (80' John Sivebæk). (Coach: Josef Emmanuel Hubertus Piontek (FRG)).
Greece: Georgios Plitsis, Babis Xanthopoulos (YC51), Ioannis Galitsios, Nikos Karoulias, Anastasios Mitropoulos, Dinos Kouis (21' Giorgos Kostikos), Evangelos Kousoulakis, Petros Michos, Apostolakis Papaioanou, Nikos Vamvakoulas (80' Christos Ardizoglou), Nikos Anastopoulos. (Coach: Vasilis Archontidis (GRE)).
Goal: Denmark: 1-0 Søren Busk (76').
Referee: Romualdas Yushka (URS)   Attendance: 33.700

27-04-1983   Wembley Stadium, London: England – Hungary   2-0 (1-0)
England: Peter Shilton (C), Kenny Sansom, Phil Neal, Alvin Martin, Gary Mabbutt, Terry Butcher, Sammy Lee, Trevor Francis, Luther Blissett, Peter Withe, Gordon Cowans. (Coach: Robert William (Bobby) Robson (ENG)).
Hungary: Béla Katzirz (C), József Kardos, Gyözö Martos (68' András Töröcsik), József Tóth, József Varga, István Kocsis, Imre Garaba, Tibor Nyilasi, Péter Hannich (YC57), Gyula Hajszán, László Kiss (68' Gyözö Burcsa). (Coach: Kálmán Mészöly (HUN)).
Goals: England: 1-0 Trevor Francis (31'), 2-0 Peter Withe (70').
Referee: Pietro D'Elia (ITA)   Attendance: 50.544

15-05-1983   Népstadion, Budapest: Hungary – Greece   2-3 (1-2)
Hungary: Gábor Zsiborás, József Kardos, Gyözö Martos (40' Karoly Jancsika), József Varga, István Kocsis, Imre Garaba, Tibor Nyilasi, József Póczik (C), Gyula Hajszán, Zoltán Ebedli, Béla Bodonyi (46' László Szokolai). (Coach: Kálmán Mészöly (HUN)).
Greece: Nikos Sarganis, Ioannis Galitsios, Georgios Skartados (75' Stylianos Manolas), Anastasios Mitropoulos, Evangelos Kousoulakis (67' Christos Ardizoglou), Petros Michos, Apostolakis Papaioanou, Nikos Vamvakoulas (YC46), Giorgos Kostikos, Nikos Anastopoulos, Nikos Alavantas. (Coach: Vasilis Archontidis (GRE)).
Goals: Hungary: 1-1 Tibor Nyilasi (24'), 2-3 Gyula Hajszán (88').
Greece: 0-1 Nikos Anastopoulos (15'), 1-2 Giorgos Kostikos (32'), 1-3 Petros Michos (56').
Referee: Edvard Sostatic (YUG)   Attendance: 13.126

01-06-1983   Idrætsparken, Copenhagen: Denmark – Hungary   3-1 (1-1)
Denmark: Ole Kjær, Ivan Nielsen, Jens Jørn Bertelsen, Morten Olsen (C), Ole Madsen, Søren Lerby, Jan Mikkelsen Lauridsen (46' Jesper Olsen), Ole Rasmussen, Klaus Berggreen, Preben Elkjær Larsen (YC59) (75' Kenneth Brylle Larsen), Allan Simonsen. (Coach: Josef Emmanuel Hubertus Piontek (FRG)).
Hungary: Béla Katzirz (C), Gyözö Martos, József Tóth, István Kocsis, Imre Garaba, Tibor Nyilasi, Péter Hannich, József Póczik, Gyula Hajszán (YC80), András Töröcsik (80' József Kardos), László Kiss (65' Lázár Szentes). (Coach: Kálmán Mészöly (HUN)).
Goals: Denmark: 1-0 Preben Elkjær Larsen (3'), 2-1 Jesper Olsen (81'), 3-1 Allan Simonsen (85' penalty).
Hungary: 1-1 Tibor Nyilasi (29').
Referee: Heinz Fahnler (AUT)   Attendance: 44.800

21-09-1983   Wembley Stadium, London: England – Denmark   0-1 (0-1)
England: Peter Shilton, Kenny Sansom, Phil Neal, Russell Osman, Ray Wilkins (C), John Barnes (70' Mark Chamberlain), Sammy Lee (77' Luther Blissett), Terry Butcher, John Gregory, Trevor Francis, Paul Mariner. (Coach: Robert William (Bobby) Robson (ENG)).
Denmark: Ole Kjær, Søren Busk, Ivan Nielsen, Jens Jørn Bertelsen, Morten Olsen (C) (85' Jan Mølby), Søren Lerby (YC87), Jesper Olsen, Michael Laudrup (46' Preben Elkjær Larsen), Ole Rasmussen, Klaus Berggreen, Allan Simonsen. (Coach: Josef Emmanuel Hubertus Piontek (FRG)).
Goal: Denmark: 0-1 Allan Simonsen (36' penalty).
Referee: Alexis Ponnet (BEL)   Attendance: 79.323

12-10-1983   Népstadion, Budapest: Hungary – England   0-3 (0-3)
Hungary: Attila Kovács, József Kardos (YC32), József Varga (YC83), Gyula Csonka, Imre Garaba, Gyözö Burcsa (46' Antal Nagy), Tibor Nyilasi (C), Ferenc Csongrádi, Péter Hannich (64' László Szokolai), Gyula Hajszán (YC56), László Dajka. (Coach: György Mezey (HUN)).
England: Peter Shilton, Kenny Sansom, Alvin Martin, Gary Mabbutt, Bryan Robson (C), Glenn Hoddle, Sammy Lee, Terry Butcher, John Gregory, Paul Mariner (YC71), Luther Blissett (74' Peter Withe). (Coach: Robert William (Bobby) Robson (ENG)).
Goals: England: 0-1 Glenn Hoddle (13'), 0-2 Sammy Lee (19'), 0-3 Paul Mariner (42').
Referee: Bruno Galler (SUI)   Attendance: 19.956

12-10-1983   Idrætsparken, Copenhagen: Denmark – Luxembourg   6-0 (4-0)
Denmark: Ole Kjær, Søren Busk, Ivan Nielsen, Jens Jørn Bertelsen, Morten Olsen (C), Jesper Olsen, Michael Laudrup, Jan Mikkelsen Lauridsen, Klaus Berggreen (84' Per Frimann), Preben Elkjær Larsen (87' Flemming Christensen), Allan Simonsen. (Coach: Josef Emmanuel Hubertus Piontek (FRG)).
Luxembourg: Jean-Paul Defrang, Marcel Bossi, Gilbert Dresch (C), Guy Hellers, Jean-Paul Girres (46' Romain Michaux), Carlo Weis, Nico Wagner, Romain Schreiner (64' Théo Malget), Alain Nurenberg, Jean-Pierre Barboni, Jeannot Reiter. (Coach: Louis Pilot (LUX)).
Goals: Denmark: 1-0 Michael Laudrup (16'), 2-0 Michael Laudrup (23'), 3-0 Preben Elkjær Larsen (37'), 4-0 Allan Simonsen (41'), 5-0 Preben Elkjær Larsen (58'), 6-0 Michael Laudrup (69').
Referee: Kaj Natri (FIN)   Attendance: 44.700

26-10-1983   Népstadion, Budapest: Hungary – Denmark   1-0 (0-0)
Hungary: Attila Kovács, Antal Roth, József Kardos (60' Antal Nagy), József Varga, József Csuhay, Gábor Köhalmi, Ferenc Csongrádi, Péter Hannich, András Töröcsik (YC68) (74' László Dajka), Gábor Pölöskei, Sándor Kiss. (Coach: György Mezey (HUN)).
Denmark: Ole Kjær, Søren Busk, Ivan Nielsen, Jens Jørn Bertelsen, Morten Olsen (C), Søren Lerby, Jesper Olsen, Michael Laudrup, Jan Mikkelsen Lauridsen (60' Preben Elkjær Larsen), Klaus Berggreen, Allan Simonsen. (Coach: Josef Emmanuel Hubertus Piontek (FRG)).
Goal: Hungary: 1-0 Sándor Kiss (57').
Referee: Emilio Carlos Guruceta Muro (ESP)   Attendance: 6.333

16-11-1983   Olympic Stadium, Athens: Greece – Denmark   0-2 (0-1)
Greece: Nikos Sarganis, Nikos Karoulias (YC35), Savas Haralampo Kofidis, Anastasios Mitropoulos (YC65), Giannis Damanakis (38' Dimitrios Saravakos), Petros Michos, Apostolakis Papaioanou, Nikos Vamvakoulas, Giorgos Kostikos (62' Hristos Dimopoulos), Nikos Anastopoulos (C), Nikos Alavantas. (Coach: Vasilis Archontidis (GRE)).
Denmark: Ole Kjær, Søren Busk, Ivan Nielsen, Jens Jørn Bertelsen, Morten Olsen (C), Søren Lerby, Jesper Olsen, Ole Rasmussen (49' Jan Mikkelsen Lauridsen), Klaus Berggreen, Preben Elkjær Larsen, Allan Simonsen (89' Frank Arnesen). (Coach: Josef Emmanuel Hubertus Piontek (FRG)).
Goals: Denmark: 0-1 Preben Elkjær Larsen (16'), 0-2 Allan Simonsen (47').
Referee: Paolo Bergamo (ITA)   Attendance: 19.720

16-11-1983   Stade Municipal, Luxembourg: Luxembourg – England   0-4 (0-2)
Luxembourg: Jean-Paul Defrang, Théo Malget (56' Jean-Paul Girres), Marcel Bossi, Hubert Meunier, Gilbert Dresch (C), Romain Michaux, Guy Hellers, Nico Wagner, Jean-Pierre Barboni (71' Gérard Jeitz), Robert Langers, Jeannot Reiter. (Coach: Louis Pilot (LUX)).
England: Ray Clemence, Kenny Sansom, Alvin Martin, Mike Duxbury, Bryan Robson (C), Glenn Hoddle, Sammy Lee, Terry Butcher, Alan Devonshire, Paul Mariner, Tony Woodcoack (24' John Barnes). (Coach: Robert William (Bobby) Robson (ENG)).
Goals: England: 0-1 Bryan Robson (10'), 0-2 Paul Mariner (38'), 0-3 Terry Butcher (50'), 0-4 Bryan Robson (56').
Referee: Cornelius A. (Cees) Bakker (HOL)   Attendance: 5.418

03-12-1983   Kaftanzoglio Stadium, Thessaloniki: Greece – Hungary   2-2 (1-2)
Greece: Georgios Plitsis, Babis Xanthopoulos, Nikos Karoulias, Anastasios Mitropoulos, Dinos Kouis, Petros Michos, Apostolakis Papaioanou (75' Savas Haralampo Kofidis), Nikos Anastopoulos (C), Giorgos Semertzidis, Hristos Dimopoulos (46' Dimitrios Saravakos), Nikos Alavantas. (Coach: Vasilis Archontidis (GRE)).
Hungary: Attila Kovács, Antal Roth, József Kardos, József Varga (YC65), József Csuhay, Gábor Köhalmi, Ferenc Csongrádi, Péter Hannich (C) (26' Gyula Hajszán), László Dajka (83' Imre Garaba), András Töröcsik, Béla Bodonyi. (Coach: György Mezey (HUN)).
Goals: Greece: 1-0 Nikos Anastopoulos (9'), 2-2 Nikos Anastopoulos (55').
Hungary: 1-1 József Kardos (12'), 1-2 Béla Bodonyi (40').
Referee: Ioan Igna (ROM)   Attendance: 1.500

14-12-1983   Georgios Karaiskakis Stadium, Piraeus: Greece – Luxembourg   1-0 (1-0)
Greece: Nikos Sarganis, Ioannis Galitsios, Nikos Karoulias, Anastasios Mitropoulos, Petros Michos, Apostolakis Papaioanou (88' Savas Haralampo Kofidis), Dimitrios Saravakos, Nikos Anastopoulos (C), Giorgos Semertzidis, Hristos Dimopoulos (68' Konstantinos Batsinilas), Nikos Alavantas. (Coach: Vasilis Archontidis (GRE)).
Luxembourg: Jean-Paul Defrang, Théo Malget, Marcel Bossi, Hubert Meunier (60' Jean Schmitz), Gilbert Dresch (C), Romain Michaux (YC15), Guy Hellers, Jean-Paul Girres, Nico Wagner (46' Serge Jentgen), Jean-Pierre Barboni, Robert Langers. (Coach: Louis Pilot (LUX)).
Goal: Greece: 1-0 Dimitrios Saravakos (18').
Referee: Velitchko Nikolov Tzontchev (BUL)   Attendance: 1.483

GROUP 4

22-09-1982	Swansea	Wales – Norway	1-0 (1-0)
13-10-1982	Oslo	Norway – Yugoslavia	3-1 (1-0)
27-10-1982	Sofia	Bulgaria – Norway	2-2 (1-1)
17-11-1982	Sofia	Bulgaria – Yugoslavia	0-1 (0-1)
15-12-1982	Titograd	Yugoslavia – Wales	4-4 (3-2)
27-04-1983	Wrexham	Wales – Bulgaria	1-0 (0-0)
07-09-1983	Oslo	Norway – Bulgaria	1-2 (1-1)
21-09-1983	Oslo	Norway – Wales	0-0
12-10-1983	Belgrade	Yugoslavia – Norway	2-1 (2-0)
16-11-1983	Sofia	Bulgaria – Wales	1-0 (0-0)
14-12-1983	Cardiff	Wales – Yugoslavia	1-1 (0-0)
21-12-1983	Split	Yugoslavia – Bulgaria	3-2 (1-1)

FINAL STANDING

Pos	Team	Pld	W	D	L	GF	GA	GD	Pts
1	*Yugoslavia*	*6*	*3*	*2*	*1*	*12*	*11*	*+1*	*8*
2	Wales	6	2	3	1	7	6	+1	7
3	Bulgaria	6	2	1	3	7	8	-1	5
4	Norway	6	1	2	3	7	8	-1	4

Yugoslavia qualified for the final tournament in France.

22-09-1982   Vetch Field, Swansea: Wales – Norway   1-0 (1-0)
Wales: Neville Southall, Joey Jones, Paul Price (C), Nigel Stevenson, Brian Flynn (YC61), Mickey Thomas, Robbie James, Chris Marustik, Kenny Jackett, Ian Rush, Alan Curtis (63' Jeremy Charles). (Coach: Harold Michael (Mike) England (WAL)).
Norway: Per Egil Nygård, Åge Hareide, Svein Grøndalen, Bjarne Berntsen, Terje Kojedal, Arne Erlandsen (80' Stein Kollshaugen), Hallvar Thoresen (C) (YC36), Roger Albertsen, Erik Solér, Thomas Lund, Arne Larsen Økland. (Coach: Tor Roste Fossen (NOR)).
Goal: Wales: 1-0 Ian Rush (30').
Referee: Joël Quiniou (FRA)   Attendance: 4.340

13-10-1982   Ullevaal Stadion, Oslo: Norway – Yugoslavia   3-1 (1-0)
Norway: Per Egil Nygård, Åge Hareide (YC47), Svein Grøndalen, Bjarne Berntsen, Terje Kojedal, Hallvar Thoresen, Roger Albertsen, Erik Solér (60' Vidar Davidsen), Thomas Lund, Arne Larsen Økland, Arne Dokken (81' Isak Arne Refvik). (Coach: Tor Roste Fossen (NOR)).
Yugoslavia: Ratko Svilar, Ivan Gudelj, Nenad Stojkovic, Faruk Hadzibegic, Ismet Hadzic, Milan Jovin (46' Nikica Klincarski), Zlatko Krmpotic (YC67), Vladimir Petrovic (YC44), Safet Susic (63' Predrag Pasic), Stjepan Deveric, Dusan Savic. (Coach: Todor Veselinovic (YUG)).
Goals: Norway: 1-0 Thomas Lund (5'), 2-0 Arne Larsen Økland (67'), 3-1 Åge Hareide (88').
Yugoslavia: 2-1 Dusan Savic (74').
Referee: Alojzy Jarguz (POL)   Attendance: 12.264

27-10-1982   Vasil Levski National Stadium, Sofia: Bulgaria – Norway   2-2 (1-1)
Bulgaria: Georgi Velinov, Radoslav Zdravkov (C), Plamen Nikolov, Angel Rangelov, Atanas Marinov (69' Ruzdi Kerimov (YC78)), Georgi Iliev, Stoycho Mladenov, Boycho Velichkov, Georgi Slavkov (59' Spas Dzhevizov), Assen Mihaylov, Zvetan Yontchev. (Coach: Ivan Vutsov (BUL)).
Norway: Per Egil Nygård, Åge Hareide (71' Vidar Davidsen (YC75)), Svein Grøndalen, Bjarne Berntsen, Terje Kojedal, Hallvar Thoresen (C), Kai Erik Herlovsen, Erik Solér, Thomas Lund (YC27), Arne Larsen Økland, Arne Dokken (61' Isak Arne Refvik). (Coach: Tor Roste Fossen (NOR)).
Goals: Bulgaria: 1-0 Boycho Velichkov (13'), 2-2 Plamen Nikolov (68').
Norway: 1-1 Hallvar Thoresen (17' penalty), 1-2 Arne Larsen Økland (66').
Referee: Antonios Vassaras (GRE)   Attendance: 12.746

17-11-1982   Vasil Levski National Stadium, Sofia: Bulgaria – Yugoslavia   0-1 (0-1)
Bulgaria: Georgi Velinov, Radoslav Zdravkov (C), Plamen Nikolov (YC90), Nikolai Grancharov, Georgi Iliev, Vassil Tintchev, Andrey Zhelyaskov, Plamen Markov (71' Stefan Naydenov), Boycho Velichkov, Spas Dzhevizov, Zvetan Yonchev (46' Anio Sadakov). (Coach: Ivan Vutsov (BUL)).
Yugoslavia: Ratko Svilar, Ivan Gudelj (C), Nenad Stojkovic, Faruk Hadzibegic, Miodrag Jesic, Ive Jerolimov, Nijaz Ferhatovic, Aleksandar Trifunovic, Slavoljub Nikolic (YC10) (69' Zvezdan Cvetkovic), Stjepan Deveric (YC62), Zvonko Zivkovic (17' Mitar Mrkela). (Coach: Todor Veselinovic (YUG)).
Goal: Yugoslavia: 0-1 Nenad Stojkovic (36').
Referee: Paolo Casarin (ITA)   Attendance: 8.268

15-12-1982   Gradski Stadion, Titograd: Yugoslavia – Wales   4-4 (3-2)
Yugoslavia: Ratko Svilar, Ivan Gudelj, Nenad Stojkovic (C), Faruk Hadzibegic (YC27), Zvezdan Cvetkovic, Nijaz Ferhatovic (81' Bosko Djurovski), Aleksandar Trifunovic (YC40), Slavoljub Nikolic, Zlatko Kranjcar (58' Miodrag Jesic), Stjepan Deveric, Zvonko Zivkovic. (Coach: Todor Veselinovic (YUG)).
Wales: Dai Davies, Kevin Ratcliffe, Joey Jones (YC1), Paul Price (C), Peter Nicholas (77' Nigel Vaughan), John Mahoney (YC75), Brian Flynn, Mickey Thomas (57' Jeremy Charles), Robbie James, Kenny Jackett, Ian Rush. (Coach: Harold Michael (Mike) England (WAL)).
Goals: Yugoslavia: 1-1 Zvezdan Cvetkovic (14'), 2-1 Zvonko Zivkovic (17'), 3-1 Zlatko Kranjcar (37'), 4-2 Miodrag Jesic (66').
Wales: 0-1 Brian Flynn (6'), 3-2 Ian Rush (39'), 4-3 Joey Jones (70'), 4-4 Robbie James (80').
Referee: Alexis Ponnet (BEL)   Attendance: 12.090

27-04-1983   Racecourse Ground, Wrexham: Wales – Bulgaria   1-0 (0-0)
Wales: Neville Southall, Kevin Ratcliffe, Joey Jones, Paul Price, Peter Nicholas (C), Brian Flynn, Mickey Thomas, Robbie James, Kenny Jackett, Ian Rush (YC69) (69' Jeremy Charles), Gordon Davies. (Coach: Harold Michael (Mike) England (WAL)).
Bulgaria: Georgi Velinov, Nikolai Arabov, Radoslav Zdravkov (C), Petar Petrov, Plamen Nikolov (YC63), Sashko Borisov (YC), Anio Sadakov, Georgi Iordanov (69' Georgi Slavkov), Stoycho Mladenov, Spas Dzhevizov, Zvetan Yonchev (78' Bozhidar Iskrenov). (Coach: Ivan Vutsov (BUL)).
Goal: Wales: 1-0 Jeremy Charles (72').
Referee: Siegfried Kirschen (GDR)   Attendance: 9.006

07-09-1983 Ullevaal Stadion, Oslo: Norway – Bulgaria 1-2 (1-1)
Norway: Tom Risz Jacobsen, Åge Hareide, Svein Grøndalen, Terje Kojedal, Kai Erik Herlovsen (82' Arne Erlandsen), Anders Giske (55' Sverre Brandhaug), Hallvar Thoresen, Roger Albertsen, Erik Solér, Vidar Davidsen, Arne Dokken. (Coach: Tor Roste Fossen (NOR)).
Bulgaria: Borislav Mihaylov, Nikolai Arabov, Georgi Dimitrov (C), Radoslav Zdravkov, Petar Petrov, Nasko Sirakov, Anio Sadakov (YC72), Zhivko Gospodinov, Antim Pehlivanov (87' Georgi Slavkov), Stoycho Mladenov, Roussi Gochev (65' Bozhidar Iskrenov). (Coach: Ivan Vutsov (BUL)).
Goals: Norway: 1-0 Åge Hareide (4').
Bulgaria: 1-1 Stoycho Mladenov (11'), 1-2 Nasko Sirakov (51').
Referee: Heinz Fahnler (AUT)   Attendance: 15.515

21-09-1983 Ullevaal Stadion, Oslo: Norway – Wales 0-0
Norway: Erik Thorstvedt, Åge Hareide, Svein Grøndalen, Terje Kojedal, Svein Fjælberg, Hallvar Thoresen (C), Roger Albertsen, Erik Solér, Vidar Davidsen, Stein Kollshaugen, Arne Dokken. (Coach: Tor Roste Fossen (NOR)).
Wales: Neville Southall, Kevin Ratcliffe, Joey Jones, Paul Price, Jeff Hopkins, Peter Nicholas (C) (YC26), Brian Flynn, Robbie James, Kenny Jackett, Nigel Vaughan, Ian Rush. (Coach: Harold Michael (Mike) England (WAL)).
Referee: Vojtech Christov (TCH)   Attendance: 15.899

12-10-1983 Stadion JNA, Belgrade: Yugoslavia – Norway 2-1 (2-0)
Yugoslavia: Zoran Simovic, Ivan Gudelj, Nenad Stojkovic (50' Mirza Kapetanovic), Luka Peruzovic, Ljubomir Radanovic, Zoran Vujovic, Blaz Sliskovic (88' Dusan Pesic), Zoran Bojovic, Zlatko Vujovic (C), Safet Susic, Sulejman Halilovic. (Coach: Todor Veselinovic (YUG)).
Norway: Tom Risz Jacobsen, Åge Hareide, Svein Grøndalen, Terje Kojedal, Kai Erik Herlovsen, Svein Fjælberg, Svein Mathisen (46' Tom Sundby), Hallvar Thoresen (C), Erik Solér, Vidar Davidsen, Arne Dokken. (Coach: Tor Roste Fossen (NOR)).
Goals: Yugoslavia: 1-0 Zlatko Vujovic (21'), 2-0 Safet Susic (40').
Norway: 2-1 Hallvar Thoresen (89').
Referee: Adolf Prokop (GDR)   Attendance: 9.169

16-11-1983 Vasil Levski National Stadium, Sofia: Bulgaria – Wales 1-0 (0-0)
Bulgaria: Borislav Mihaylov, Nikolai Arabov, Georgi Dimitrov (C) (YC78), Radoslav Zdravkov, Petar Petrov, Nasko Sirakov (YC38), Anio Sadakov, Zhivko Gospodinov (89' Sashko Borisov), Zvetan Danov (46' Roussi Gochev), Bozhidar Iskrenov, Stoycho Mladenov. (Coach: Ivan Vutsov (BUL)).
Wales: Neville Southall, Kevin Ratcliffe, Joey Jones, Paul Price, Jeff Hopkins, Peter Nicholas (YC51) (60' Jeremy Charles), Brian Flynn (C), Mickey Thomas, Robbie James, Nigel Vaughan, Ian Rush. (Coach: Harold Michael (Mike) England (WAL)).
Goal: Bulgaria: 1-0 Roussi Gochev (54').
Referee: Dieter Pauly (FRG)   Attendance: 4.273

14-12-1983 Ninian Park, Cardiff: Wales – Yugoslavia 1-1 (0-0)
Wales: Neville Southall, Kevin Ratcliffe, Joey Jones, Paul Price, Jeff Hopkins, Brian Flynn (C) (82' Jeremy Charles), Mickey Thomas, Robbie James, Kenny Jackett, Nigel Vaughan, Ian Rush. (Coach: Harold Michael (Mike) England (WAL)).
Yugoslavia: Zoran Simovic, Ivan Gudelj, Srecko Katanec, Luka Peruzovic, Ljubomir Radanovic, Zoran Vujovic, Branislav Drobnjak, Mehmed Bazdarevic, Marko Mlinaric (73' Sulejman Halilovic), Zlatko Vujovic (C) (89' Zvezdan Cvetkovic), Safet Susic. (Coach: Todor Veselinovic (YUG)).
Goals: Wales: 1-0 Robbie James (54').
Yugoslavia: 1-1 Mehmed Bazdarevic (81').
Referee: Erik Fredriksson (SWE)   Attendance: 24.902

21-12-1983 Gradski stadion u Poljudu, Split: Yugoslavia – Bulgaria 3-2 (1-1)
Yugoslavia: Zoran Simovic, Ivan Gudelj (70' Sulejman Halilovic), Srecko Katanec, Miodrag Jesic, Luka Peruzovic, Ljubomir Radanovic, Zoran Vujovic, Mehmed Bazdarevic, Marko Mlinaric, Zlatko Vujovic (C) (YC74), Safet Susic. (Coach: Todor Veselinovic (YUG)).
Bulgaria: Borislav Mihaylov, Nikolai Arabov, Georgi Dimitrov (C), Radoslav Zdravkov, Petar Petrov, Nasko Sirakov, Anio Sadakov (81' Sashko Borisov), Zhivko Gospodinov, Bozhidar Iskrenov, Stoycho Mladenov (75' Emil Marinov), Roussi Gochev. (Coach: Ivan Vutsov (BUL)).
Goals: Yugoslavia: 1-1 Safet Susic (31'), 2-1 Safet Susic (53'), 3-2 Ljubomir Radanovic (90'+1').
Bulgaria: 0-1 Bozhidar Iskrenov (28'), 2-2 Georgi Dimitrov (60').
Referee: Augusto Lamo Castillo (ESP)   Attendance: 29.331

GROUP 5

01-05-1982	Hunedoara	Romania – Cyprus	3-1 (2-1)
08-09-1982	Bucharest	Romania – Sweden	2-0 (1-0)
06-10-1982	Bratislava	Czechoslovakia – Sweden	2-2 (0-0)
13-11-1982	Milan	Italy – Czechoslovakia	2-2 (1-1)
13-11-1982	Nicosia	Cyprus – Sweden	0-1 (0-1)
04-12-1982	Florence	Italy – Romania	0-0
12-02-1983	Limassol	Cyprus – Italy	1-1 (0-0)
27-03-1983	Nicosia	Cyprus – Czechoslovakia	1-1 (1-0)
16-04-1983	Prague	Czechoslovakia – Cyprus	6-0 (3-0)
16-04-1983	Bucharest	Romania – Italy	1-0 (1-0)
15-05-1983	Malmö	Sweden – Cyprus	5-0 (0-0)
15-05-1983	Bucharest	Romania – Czechoslovakia	0-1 (0-1)
29-05-1983	Gothenburg	Sweden – Italy	2-0 (1-0)
09-06-1983	Solna	Sweden – Romania	0-1 (0-1)
21-09-1983	Solna	Sweden – Czechoslovakia	1-0 (1-0)
15-10-1983	Naples	Italy – Sweden	0-3 (0-2)
12-11-1983	Limassol	Cyprus – Romania	0-1 (0-0)
16-11-1983	Prague	Czechoslovakia – Italy	2-0 (0-0)
30-11-1983	Bratislava	Czechoslovakia – Romania	1-1 (0-0)
22-12-1983	Perugia	Italy – Cyprus	3-1 (0-0)

FINAL STANDING

Pos	Team	Pld	W	D	L	GF	GA	GD	Pts
1	*Romania*	*8*	*5*	*2*	*1*	*9*	*3*	*+6*	*12*
2	Sweden	8	5	1	2	14	5	+9	11
3	Czechoslovakia	8	3	4	1	15	7	+8	10
4	Italy	8	1	3	4	6	12	-6	5
5	Cyprus	8	0	2	6	4	21	-17	2

Romania qualified for the final tournament in France.

01-05-1982   Stadionul Michael Klein, Hunedoara: Romania – Cyprus   3-1 (2-1)
Romania: Dumitru Moraru, Mircea Rednic, Costica Stefanescu (C), George Iorgulescu, Ion Bogdan (II), Ilie Balaci, László Bölöni, Aurel Ticleanu (46' Ion Petcu), Doru Rodion Camataru, Romulus Gabor, Florea Vaetus (66' Ionel Augustin). (Coach: Mircea Lucescu (ROM)).
Cyprus: Andreas Constantinou (II) (YC25), Nikos Pantziaras, Stephanos Lysandrou (YC66), Stavros Papadopoulos, Nikos Patikis, George Kezos, Kletos Erotocritou, Fivos Vrahimis, Filippos Demetriou (YC58) (76' Chrysanthos Lagos), Nicos Prokopis (16' Yiannakis Yiangoudakis), Fanis Theophanous. (Coach: Vasil Spasov (BUL)).
Goals: Romania: 1-0 Florea Vaetus (16'), 2-0 Doru Rodion Camataru (18'), 3-1 László Bölöni (71').
Cyprus: 2-1 Fivos Vrahimis (29').
Referee: Arsen Hoxha (ALB)   Attendance: 9.103

08-09-1982   23 August Stadium, Bucharest: Romania – Sweden   2-0 (1-0)
Romania: Dumitru Moraru, Ioan Andone, Mircea Rednic, Nicolae Ungureanu, George Iorgulescu, Michael Klein (70' Alexandru Custov), Ilie Balaci, László Bölöni, Aurel Ticleanu (60' Sorin Cartu), Romulus Gabor, Dudu Georgescu. (Coach: Mircea Lucescu (ROM)).
Sweden: Thomas Ravelli, Glenn Hysén (65' Greger Hallén), Hasse Borg, Ingemar Erlandsson (YC70), Stig Fredriksson, Sven Dahlkvist, Peter Nilsson (RC49), Karl-Gunnar Björklund, Michael Andersson (72' Sten-Ove Ramberg), Thomas Larsson, Dan Corneliusson. (Coach: Lars Arnesson (SWE)).
Goals: Romania: 1-0 Ioan Andone (25'), 2-0 Michael Klein (48').
Referee: Edvard Sostaric (YUG)   Attendance: 24.031

06-10-1982   Stadión Tehelné pole, Bratislava: Czechoslovakia – Sweden   2-2 (0-0)
Czechoslovakia: Zdenek Hruska, Ján Fiala, Ladislav Jurkemik, Frantisek Jakubec, Jirí Ondra, Peter Zelensky, Ján Berger, Lubomir Pokluda, Petr Janecka, Vaclav Danek (YC53) (46' Milan Luhovy), Karel Brezík (76' Pavel Chaloupka). (Coach: Frantisek Havranek (TCH)).
Sweden: Thomas Ravelli, Glenn Hysén (YC53), Ingemar Erlandsson, Sven Dahlkvist (YC77), Andreas Ravelli, Glenn Strömberg, Jan Svensson (60' Karl-Gunnar Björklund), Michael Andersson, Tony Persson (YC55) (60' Mats Jingblad), Robert Prytz, Ulf Eriksson. (Coach: Lars Arnesson (SWE)).
Goals: Czechoslovakia: 1-0 Petr Janecka (48'), 2-0 Petr Janecka (53').
Sweden: 2-1 Mats Jingblad (87'), 2-2 Ulf Eriksson (90').
Referee: Robert Bonar (Bob) Valentine (SCO)   Attendance: 14.977

13-11-1982   Stadio Giuseppe Meazza, Milan: Italy – Czechoslovakia 2-2 (1-1)
Italy: Dino Zoff (C), Giuseppe Bergomi, Fulvio Collovati, Claudio Gentile, Gaetano Scirea, Giancarlo Antognoni, Giampiero Marini (YC43), Marco Tardelli (79' Giuseppe Dossena), Bruno Conti, Alessandro Albobelli, Paolo Rossi. (Coach: Vincenzo Bearzot (ITA)).
Czechoslovakia: Ludek Miklosko, Ján Fiala (C), Frantisek Jakubec, Peter Zelensky, Ján Kapko, Zdenek Prokes, Pavel Chaloupka, Jirí Sloup, Jaroslav Nemec, Petr Janecka (70' Ladislav Vízek), Milan Cermák (89' Karel Jarolím). (Coach: Frantisek Havranek (TCH)).
Goals: Italy: 1-0 Alessandro Albobelli (13'), 2-1 Ján Kapko (65' *own goal*).
Czechoslovakia: 1-1 Jirí Sloup (26'), 2-2 Pavel Chaloupka (70').
Referee: Charles George Reinier Corver (HOL)   Attendance: 72.386

13-11-1982   Makareio Stadium, Nicosia: Cyprus – Sweden 0-1 (0-1)
Cyprus: Andreas Constantinou (II), Costas Miamiliotis, Nikos Pantziaras, Nikos Patikis, Lefteris Kouis, Yiannakis Yiangoudakis, Fivos Vrahimis (55' Kyriaskos Vasiliou), Filippos Demetriou, Fanis Theophanous, Andreas Christodoulou, Christakis Omirou "Mavris" (76' Panikos Chatziloizou). (Coach: Vasil Spasov (BUL)).
Sweden: Thomas Ravelli, Glenn Hysén, Ingemar Erlandsson (C), Klas Johansson, Glenn Strömberg (89' Andreas Ravelli), Michael Andersson, Sten-Ove Ramberg, Robert Prytz, Tommy Holmgren (69' Lennart Nilsson), Dan Corneliusson, Håkan Sandberg. (Coach: Lars Arnesson (SWE)).
Goal: Sweden: 0-1 Dan Corneliusson (34').
Referee: Neil Midgley (ENG)   Attendance: 6.155

04-12-1982   Stadio Comunale, Florence: Italy – Romania 0-0
Italy: Dino Zoff (C), Franco Baresi, Fulvio Collovati, Claudio Gentile (YC24), Giancarlo Antognoni, Giampiero Marini, Marco Tardelli, Bruno Conti, Gabriele Oriali, Francesco Graziani (19' Alessandro Albobelli), Paolo Rossi (46' Franco Causio). (Coach: Vincenzo Bearzot (ITA)).
Romania: Silviu Lung, Mircea Rednic, Costica Stefanescu (C), Nicolae Ungureanu, George Iorgulescu (YC11), Michael Klein, Ilie Balaci (YC50), László Bölöni (YC18), Aurel Ticleanu (RC54), Doru Rodion Camataru (86' Ionel Augustin), Romulus Gabor (57' Ioan Andone). (Coach: Mircea Lucescu (ROM)).
Referee: Georges Konrath (FRA)   Attendance: 50.478

12-02-1983   Tsirion Stadium, Limassol: Cyprus – Italy 1-1 (0-0)
Cyprus: Andreas Constantinou (II), Nikos Pantziaras, Nikos Patikis (YC10), George Kezos (YC65), Kletos Erotocritou, Lefteris Kouis (46' Kyriakos Vasiliou), Yiannakis Yiangoudakis, Fanis Theophanous, Andreas Christodoulou (83' Michalakis Karseras), Christakis Omirou "Mavris", Georgios Savvides. (Coach: Vasil Spasov (BUL)).
Italy: Dino Zoff (C), Antonio Cabrini, Fulvio Collovati, Claudio Gentile, Gaetano Scirea, Giancarlo Antognoni, Marco Tardelli, Gabriele Oriali (46' Carlo Ancelotti), Francesco Graziani, Paolo Rossi, Franco Causio. (Coach: Vincenzo Bearzot (ITA)).
Goals: Cyprus: 1-0 Christakis Omirou "Mavris" (47').
Italy: 1-1 Francesco Graziani (58').
Referee: Bogdan Ganev Dochev (BUL)   Attendance: 18.583

27-03-1983   Makario Stadium, Nicosia: Cyprus – Czechoslovakia   1-1 (1-0)
Cyprus: Andreas Constantinou (II), Costas Miamiliotis, Nikos Pantziaras, George Kezos (69'
Andreas Andreou), Kletos Erotocritou, Lefteris Kouis (72' Filippos Demetriou), Yiannakis
Yiangoudakis, Fanis Theophanous, Christakis Omirou "Mavris", Michalakis Karseras,
Georgios Savvides. (Coach: Vasil Spasov (BUL)).
Czechoslovakia: Zdenek Hruska, Ján Fiala (C), Frantisek Jakubec, Peter Zelensky, Zdenek
Prokes, Stanislav Levy, Pavel Chaloupka, Karel Jarolím (81' Zdenek Scasny), Ladislav Vízek,
Vlastimil Petrzela (57' Premysl Bicovsky), Milan Cermák. (Coach: Frantisek Havranek
(TCH)).
Goals: Cyprus: 1-0 Fanis Theophanous (21').
Czechoslovakia: 1-1 Premysl Bicovsky (60').
Referee: Stjepan Glavina (YUG)   Attendance: 6.951

16-04-1983   Stadion Evzena Rosického, Prague: Czechoslovakia – Cyprus   6-0 (3-0)
Czechoslovakia: Zdenek Hruska, Ladislav Jurkemik (C), Frantisek Jakubec, Zdenek Prokes,
Stanislav Levy, Premysl Bicovsky, Pavel Chaloupka, Ladislav Vízek, Vaclav Danek, Milan
Cermák (69' Zdenek Scasny), Zbynek Hotovy. (Coach: Frantisek Havranek (TCH)).
Cyprus: Andreas Constantinou (II) (59' Michalis Pamporis), Costas Miamiliotis, Nikos
Pantziaras, George Kezos, Kletos Erotocritou, Lefteris Kouis, Yiannakis Yiangoudakis,
Filippos Demetriou, Fanis Theophanous (YC30), Christakis Omirou "Mavris" (46' Georgios
Savvides), Pavlos Kounnas. (Coach: Vasil Spasov (BUL)).
Goals: Czechoslovakia: 1-0 Vaclav Danek (4'), 2-0 Ladislav Vízek (29'), 3-0 Zdenek Prokes
(37'), 4-0 Ladislav Vízek (48'), 5-0 Ladislav Jurkemik (57'), 6-0 Vaclav Danek (70').
Referee: Norbert Rolles (LUX)   Attendance: 8.180

16-04-1983   23 August Stadium, Bucharest: Romania – Italy   1-0 (1-0)
Romania: Dumitru Moraru, Mircea Rednic, Costica Stefanescu (C), Nicolae Ungureanu,
George Iorgulescu, Michael Klein, Ilie Balaci, László Bölöni, Ion Geolgau (85' Sorin Cartu),
Doru Rodion Camataru (YC74), Ionel Augustin (YC54) (76' Ioan Andone). (Coach: Mircea
Lucescu (ROM)).
Italy: Dino Zoff (C), Antonio Cabrini, Fulvio Collovati (YC69), Claudio Gentile, Gaetano
Scirea, Giancarlo Antognoni (YC52) (60' Giuseppe Dossena), Giampiero Marini, Marco
Tardelli, Bruno Conti, Paolo Rossi, Roberto Bettega (68' Alessandro Altobelli). (Coach:
Vincenzo Bearzot (ITA)).
Goal: Romania: 1-0 László Bölöni (24').
Referee: Michel Vautrot (FRA)   Attendance: 62.966

15-05-1983   Malmö Stadium, Malmö: Sweden – Cyprus   5-0 (0-0)
Sweden: Thomas Ravelli, Glenn Hysén, Ingemar Erlandsson (C) (35' Andreas Ravelli), Stig
Fredriksson, Sven Dahlkvist, Sten-Ove Ramberg, Robert Prytz, Ulf Eriksson, Tommy
Holmgren, Dan Corneliusson, Håkan Sandberg (79' Björn Nilsson). (Coach: Lars Arnesson
(SWE)).
Cyprus: Michalis Pamporis, Costas Miamiliotis, Nikos Pantziaras (70' Andreas Andreou),
George Kezos, Kletos Erotocritou, Lefteris Kouis, Yiannakis Yiangoudakis, Costas Tserkezos
(YC47), Filippos Demetriou, Georgios Savvides, Fanis Theophanous (67' Pavlos Kounnas).
(Coach: Vasil Spasov (BUL)).
Goals: Sweden: 1-0 Robert Prytz (54'), 2-0 Dan Corneliusson (58'), 3-0 Glenn Hysén (62'),
4-0 Andreas Ravelli (73'), 5-0 Robert Prytz (77').
Referee: Juhani Smolander (FIN)   Attendance: 19.092

15-05-1983   23 August Stadium, Bucharest: Romania – Czechoslovakia   0-1 (0-1)
Romania: Silviu Lung, Mircea Rednic, Costica Stefanescu (C), Nicolae Ungureanu, George Iorgulescu, Michael Klein, Ilie Balaci, László Bölöni, Doru Rodion Camataru (61' Ioan Andone (YC62)), Romulus Gabor (YC40) (46' Ion Geolgau), Ionel Augustin. (Coach: Mircea Lucescu (ROM)).
Czechoslovakia: Zdenek Hruska, Ján Fiala (C) (YC67), Ladislav Jurkemik, Frantisek Jakubec, Peter Zelensky (89' Ludek Kovacík), Zdenek Prokes (YC23), Stanislav Levy (46' Frantisek Stambachr), Premysl Bicovsky, Pavel Chaloupka, Ladislav Vízek, Petr Janecka. (Coach: Frantisek Havranek (TCH)).
Goal: Czechoslovakia: 0-1 Ladislav Vízek (40' penalty).
Referee: Alexis Ponnet (BEL)   Attendance: 30.108

29-05-1983   Nya Ullevi, Gothenburg: Sweden – Italy   2-0 (1-0)
Sweden: Thomas Ravelli, Glenn Hysén, Ingemar Erlandsson (C), Stig Fredriksson, Sven Dahlkvist, Glenn Strömberg, Robert Prytz (YC74) (81' Sten-Ove Ramberg), Ulf Eriksson, Tommy Holmgren, Dan Corneliusson, Håkan Sandberg (85' Björn Nilsson). (Coach: Lars Arnesson (SWE)).
Italy: Dino Zoff (C), Antonio Cabrini, Fulvio Collovati, Claudio Gentile, Gaetano Scirea, Giancarlo Antognoni (46' Giuseppe Dossena), Marco Tardelli (YC32), Bruno Conti, Gabriele Oriali, Francesco Graziani (61' Alessandro Altobelli), Paolo Rossi. (Coach: Vincenzo Bearzot (ITA)).
Goals: Sweden: 1-0 Ulf Eriksson (31'), 2-0 Dan Corneliusson (55').
Referee: Walter Eschweiler (FRG)   Attendance: 32.860

09-06-1983   Råsunda Stadion, Solna: Sweden – Romania   0-1 (0-1)
Sweden: Thomas Ravelli, Glenn Hysén, Ingemar Erlandsson (C), Stig Fredriksson, Sven Dahlkvist, Glenn Strömberg, Robert Prytz (72' Sten-Ove Ramberg (YC82)), Ulf Eriksson, Tommy Holmgren, Dan Corneliusson, Håkan Sandberg (20' Björn Nilsson). (Coach: Lars Arnesson (SWE)).
Romania: Silviu Lung, Ioan Andone (YC53), Mircea Rednic, Costica Stefanescu (C), Nicolae Ungureanu, George Iorgulescu, Michael Klein (YC5), Ilie Balaci (88' Ion Geolgau), László Bölöni, Aurel Ticleanu (72' Ionel Augustin), Doru Rodion Camataru. (Coach: Mircea Lucescu (ROM)).
Goal: Romania: 0-1 Doru Rodion Camataru (30').
Referee: Adolf Prokop (GDR)   Attendance: 31.474

21-09-1983   Råsunda Stadion, Solna: Sweden – Czechoslovakia   1-0 (1-0)
Sweden: Thomas Ravelli, Glenn Hysén, Ingemar Erlandsson (C), Stig Fredriksson, Sven Dahlkvist, Glenn Strömberg (75' Sten-Ove Ramberg), Robert Prytz, Ulf Eriksson (89' Andreas Ravelli), Tommy Holmgren, Dan Corneliusson, Thomas Sunesson. (Coach: Lars Arnesson (SWE)).
Czechoslovakia: Ludek Miklosko, Ján Fiala (C), Ladislav Jurkemik, Frantisek Jakubec, Peter Zelensky, Zdenek Prokes, Premysl Bicovsky, Pavel Chaloupka (65' Frantisek Stambachr), Jirí Sloup (YC84), Ladislav Vízek (80' Ivo Knoflicek), Petr Janecka. (Coach: Frantisek Havranek (TCH)).
Goal: Sweden: 1-0 Dan Corneliusson (17').
Referee: Michel Vautrot (FRA)   Attendance: 20.546

15-10-1983   Stadio San Paolo, Naples: Italy – Sweden   0-3 (0-2)
Italy: Ivano Bordon, Franco Baresi, Giuseppe Bergomi, Antonio Cabrini (C), Pietro Vierchowod, Carlo Ancelotti, Salvatore Bagni, Bruno Conti, Giuseppe Dossena, Paolo Rossi, Bruno Giordano. (Coach: Vincenzo Bearzot (ITA)).
Sweden: Thomas Ravelli, Glenn Hysén (YC30), Ingemar Erlandsson (C) (YC36), Stig Fredriksson, Sven Dahlkvist, Glenn Strömberg, Robert Prytz, Ulf Eriksson, Tommy Holmgren (74' Andreas Ravelli), Dan Corneliusson (84' Mats Jingblad), Thomas Sunesson. (Coach: Lars Arnesson (SWE)).
Goals: Sweden: 0-1 Glenn Strömberg (20'), 0-2 Glenn Strömberg (27'), 0-3 Thomas Sunesson (71').
Referee: José Luis García Carrión (ESP)   Attendance: 60.086

12-11-1983   Tsirion Stadium, Limassol: Cyprus – Romania   0-1 (0-0)
Cyprus: Andreas Constantinou (II), Costas Miamiliotis, Nikos Pantziaras, George Kezos, Kletos Erotocritou, Yiannakis Yiangoudakis, Marios Tsingis, Fanis Theophanous, Pavlos Kounnas (65' Christakis Omirou "Mavris"), Georgios Savvides, Costas Foti (80' Filippos Demetriou). (Coach: Vasil Spasov (BUL)).
Romania: Silviu Lung, Mircea Rednic, Costica Stefanescu (C), Nicolae Ungureanu, Alexandru Nicolae, Michael Klein, László Bölöni (YC24), Aurel Ticleanu, Gheorghe Multescu (46' Gheorghe Hagi), Marcel Coras (73' Romulus Gabor), Doru Rodion Camataru. (Coach: Mircea Lucescu (ROM)).
Goal: Romania: 0-1 László Bölöni (78').
Referee: Ronald Bridges (WAL)   Attendance: 5.277

16-11-1983   Stadion Evzena Rosického, Prague: Czechoslovakia – Italy   2-0 (0-0)
Czechoslovakia: Zdenek Hruska, Ján Fiala (C), Frantisek Jakubec, Peter Zelensky, Zdenek Prokes, Pavel Chaloupka, Frantisek Stambachr, Petr Rada, Ladislav Vízek, Petr Janecka, Vaclav Danek (88' Milan Luhovy). (Coach: Frantisek Havranek (TCH)).
Italy: Ivano Bordon, Giuseppe Bergomi, Antonio Cabrini (C), Pietro Vierchowod, Ubaldo Righetti, Carlo Ancelotti, Salvatore Bagni (77' Giancarlo Antognoni), Marco Tardelli (C) (YC82), Giuseppe Dossena, Paolo Rossi, Bruno Giordano. (Coach: Vincenzo Bearzot (ITA)).
Goals: Czechoslovakia: 1-0 Petr Rada (63'), 2-0 Petr Rada (76').
Referee: George Courtney (ENG)   Attendance: 34.332

30-11-1983   Stadión Tehelné pole, Bratislava: Czechoslovakia – Romania   1-1 (0-0)
Czechoslovakia: Zdenek Hruska, Ján Fiala (C), Frantisek Jakubec, Peter Zelensky (YC25), Zdenek Prokes, Pavel Chaloupka, Frantisek Stambachr (71' Milan Luhovy), Petr Rada (YC64), Ladislav Vízek, Petr Janecka, Vaclav Danek (71' Ladislav Jurkemik). (Coach: Frantisek Havranek (TCH)).
Romania: Silviu Lung (YC33), Mircea Rednic, Costica Stefanescu (C), Nicolae Ungureanu, George Iorgulescu (YC9), Nicolae Negrila, Michael Klein, László Bölöni, Ion Geolgau, Doru Rodion Camataru, Romulus Gabor (YC38) (79' Ionel Augustin, 88' Alexandru Nicolae). (Coach: Mircea Lucescu (ROM)).
Goals: Czechoslovakia: 1-1 Milan Luhovy (85').
Romania: 0-1 Ion Geolgau (82').
Referee: Károly Palotai (HUN)   Attendance: 45.554

22-12-1983 Stadio Renato Curi, Perugia: Italy – Cyprus 3-1 (0-0)
Italy: Giovanni Galli, Franco Baresi (YC39), Giuseppe Bergomi, Antonio Cabrini (C), Pietro Vierchowod (YC84), Ubaldo Righetti (46' Fulvio Collovati), Salvatore Bagni, Bruno Conti (60' Pietro Fanna), Giuseppe Dossena, Alessandro Altobelli, Paolo Rossi. (Coach: Vincenzo Bearzot (ITA)).
Cyprus: Andreas Constantinou (II), Costas Miamiliotis (YC50), Nikos Pantziaras, George Kezos, Kletos Erotocritou, Lefteris Kouis (86' Pavlos Kounnas), Yiannakis Yiangoudakis, Marios Tsingis (YC47), Fanis Theophanous (YC71) (81' Paschalis Christoforou), Koylus Pantziaras, Costas Foti. (Coach: Vasil Spasov (BUL)).
Goals: Italy: 1-0 Alessandro Altobelli (53'), 2-1 Antonio Cabrini (82'), 3-1 Paolo Rossi (86' penalty).
Cyprus: 1-1 Marios Tsingis (68' penalty).
Referee: Thomas Oliver Donnelly (NIR)   Attendance: 20.773

GROUP 6

22-09-1982	Vienna	Austria – Albania	5-0 (2-0)
13-10-1982	Vienna	Austria – Northern Ireland	2-0 (2-0)
27-10-1982	Izmir	Turkey – Albania	1-0 (0-0)
17-11-1982	Vienna	Austria – Turkey	4-0 (3-0)
17-11-1982	Belfast	Northern Ireland – West Germany	1-0 (1-0)
15-12-1982	Tirana	Albania – Northern Ireland	0-0
30-03-1983	Tirana	Albania – West Germany	1-2 (0-0)
30-03-1983	Belfast	Northern Ireland – Turkey	2-1 (2-0)
23-04-1983	Izmir	Turkey – West Duitsland	0-3 (0-2)
27-04-1983	Vienna	Austria – West Germany	0-0
27-04-1983	Belfast	Northern Ireland – Albania	1-0 (0-0)
11-05-1983	Tirana	Albania – Turkey	1-1 (0-1)
08-06-1983	Tirana	Albania – Austria	1-2 (0-1)
21-09-1983	Belfast	Northern Ireland – Austria	3-1 (1-0)
05-10-1983	Gelsenkirchen	West Germany – Austria	3-0 (3-0)
12-10-1983	Ankara	Turkey – Northern Ireland	1-0 (1-0)
26-10-1983	Berlin	West Germany – Turkey	5-1 (1-0)
16-11-1983	Istanbul	Turkey – Austria	3-1 (0-0)
16-11-1983	Hamburg	West Germany – Northern Ireland	0-1 (0-0)
20-11-1983	Saarbrücken	West Germany – Albania	2-1 (1-1)

FINAL STANDING

Pos	Team	Pld	W	D	L	GF	GA	GD	Pts
1	*West Germany*	8	5	1	2	15	5	*+10*	*11*
2	Northern Ireland	8	5	1	2	8	5	+3	11
3	Austria	8	4	1	3	15	10	+5	9
4	Turkey	8	3	1	4	8	16	-8	7
5	Albania	8	0	2	6	4	14	-10	2

West Germany qualified for the final tournament in France.

22-09-1982   Gerhard-Hanappi-Stadium, Vienna: Austria – Albania   5-0 (2-0)
Austria: Friedrich Koncilia, Bernd Krauss, Erich Obermayer (74' Ernst Baumeister), Josef Degeorgi, Heribert Weber, Anton Pichler (25' Karl Brauneder), Herbert Prohaska (C), Felix Gasselich, Walter Schachner, Gernot Jurtin, Maximilian Hagmayr. (Coach: Erich Hof (AUT)).
Albania: Ilir Luarasi (C), Petro Ruci, Muhedin Targaj, Aleko Bregu (RC90), Arjan Hametaj, Luan Vukatana, Haxhi Ballgjini (YC67), Bedri Omuri, Agostin Kola (67' Vasillaq Zëri), Dashnor Bajaziti (75' Shkelqim Muca), Roland Luçi. (Coach: Shyqyri Rreli (ALB)).
Goals: Austria: 1-0 Maximilian Hagmayr (24'), 2-0 Felix Gasselich (40'), 3-0 Agostin Kola (63' *own goal*), 4-0 Maximilian Hagmayr (66'), 5-0 Karl Brauneder (81').
Referee: Yordan Zhezhov (BUL)   Attendance: 9.111

13-10-1982   Praterstadion, Vienna: Austria – Northern Ireland   2-0 (2-0)
Austria: Friedrich Koncilia, Bernd Krauss, Erich Obermayer, Josef Degeorgi, Bruno Pezzey, Heribert Weber, Herbert Prohaska (C), Felix Gasselich, Walter Schachner, Gernot Jurtin (69' Peter Pacult), Maximilian Hagmayr (69' Ernst Baumeister). (Coach: Erich Hof (AUT)).
Northern Ireland: James Platt, Jimmy Nicholl, Mal Donaghy, John O'Neill, Billy Hamilton, John McClelland, David McCreery, Sammy McIlroy (50' Noel Brotherston), Martin O'Neill (C), Ian Stewart (79' Patrick Joseph Healy), Gerry Armstrong. (Coach: William Laurence (Billy) Bingham (NIR)).
Goals: Austria: 1-0 Walter Schachner (3'), 2-0 Walter Schachner (39').
Referee: Valeri Pavlovich Butenko (URS)   Attendance: 9.885

27-10-1982   Izmir Alsancak Stadium, Izmir: Turkey – Albania   1-0 (0-0)
Turkey: Senol Günes, Fatih Terim (C), Muzaffer Badaloglu, Eren Talu, Ali Denizci, Tuna Güneysu (71' Riza Çalimbay), Hakan Kütukcüoglu, Arif Kocabiyik, Senol Çorlu, Erdal Keser (YC81), Selcuk Yula (71' Bilal Yilmaz). (Coach: Coskun Özari (TUR)).
Albania: Perlat Musta, Petro Ruci, Muhedin Targaj (C), Arjan Hametaj, Arjan Bimo, Luan Vukatana, Haxhi Ballgjini, Bedri Omuri, Shkelqim Muça (89' Arben Minga), Agostin Kola, Roland Luçi (YC28). (Coach: Shyqyri Rreli (ALB)).
Goal: Turkey: 1-0 Arif Kocabiyik (86').
Referee: Ioan Igna (ROM)   Attendance: 27.702

17-11-1982   Gerhard-Hanappi-Stadium, Vienna: Austria – Turkey   4-0 (3-0)
Austria: Friedrich Koncilia, Bernd Krauss, Erich Obermayer, Josef Degeorgi (58' Leopold Lainer), Bruno Pezzey (YC80), Heribert Weber (YC42), Herbert Prohaska (C), Felix Gasselich (12' Anton Pichler), Toni Polster, Walter Schachner, Günther Golautschnig. (Coach: Erich Hof (AUT)).
Turkey: Senol Günes, Fatih Terim (C), Muzaffer Badaloglu (YC43), Eren Talu, Ali Denizci (61' Riza Çalimbay), Tuna Güneysu, Hakan Kütukcüoglu, Arif Kocabiyik, Senol Çorlu (61' Hüsnü Özkara), Erdal Keser (YC58), Selcuk Yula. (Coach: Coskun Özari (TUR)).
Goals: Austria: 1-0 Toni Polster (10'), 2-0 Bruno Pezzey (34'), 3-0 Herbert Prohaska (38'), 4-0 Walter Schachner (53').
Referee: Aleksander Suchanek (POL)   Attendance: 9.614

17-11-1982   Windsor Park, Belfast: Northern Ireland – West Germany   1-0 (1-0)
Northern Ireland: James Platt, Jimmy Nicholl, Mal Donaghy, John O'Neill (YC70), John McClelland, Sammy McIlroy, Martin O'Neill (C), Norman Whiteside, Billy Hamilton, Ian Stewart, Noel Brotherston. (Coach: William Laurence (Billy) Bingham (NIR)).
West Germany: Harald Schumacher, Hans-Peter Briegel, Manfred Kaltz, Bernd Förster (YC82), Gerhard Strack, Lothar Matthäus (75' Rudi Völler), Bernd Schuster (75' Stephan Engels), Pierre Littbarski, Uli Stielike, Karl-Heinz Rummenigge (C), Klaus Allofs. (Coach: Josef (Jupp) Derwall (FRG)).
Goal: Northern Ireland: 1-0 Ian Stewart (18').
Referee: Rolf Nyhus (NOR)   Attendance: 20.522

15-12-1982   Stadiumi Qemal Stafa, Tirana: Albania – Northern Ireland   0-0
Albania: Perlat Musta, Petro Ruci, Muhedin Targaj (C), Arjan Hametaj, Arjan Bimo (46' Bedri Omuri), Luan Vukatana, Haxhi Ballgjini, Ferid Rragami (YC38), Agostin Kola, Roland Luçi (80' Shkelqim Muça), Arben Minga. (Coach: Shyqyri Rreli (ALB)).
Northern Ireland: James Platt, Jimmy Nicholl (YC43), Mal Donaghy, John O'Neill, John McClelland, Sammy McIlroy, Martin O'Neill (C), Norman Whiteside, Billy Hamilton, Ian Stewart, Noel Brotherston. (Coach: William Laurence (Billy) Bingham (NIR)).
Referee: André Daina (SUI)   Attendance: 16.898

30-03-1983   Stadiumi Qemal Stafa, Tirana: Albania – West Germany   1-2 (0-0)
Albania: Perlat Musta, Petro Ruci (YC48), Muhedin Targaj (C) (YC40), Arjan Hametaj, Arjan Bimo, Luan Vukatana, Haxhi Ballgjini, Ferid Rragami, Dashnor Bajaziti (29' Ilir Lame), Agostin Kola, Arben Minga. (Coach: Shyqyri Rreli (ALB)).
West Germany: Harald Schumacher, Hans-Peter Briegel, Karlheinz Förster, Bernd Förster, Gerhard Strack, Jonny Otten, Pierre Littbarski, Hansi Müller, Stephan Engels (YC58), Rudi Völler (86' Norbert Meier), Karl-Heinz Rummenigge (C). (Coach: Josef (Jupp) Derwall (FRG)).
Goals: Albania: 1-2 Muhedin Targaj (82' penalty).
West Germany: 0-1 Rudi Völler (53'), 0-2 Karl-Heinz Rummenigge (68' penalty).
Referee: Gianfranco Menegali (ITA)   Attendance: 19.550

30-03-1983   Windsor Park, Belfast: Northern Ireland – Turkey   2-1 (2-0)
Northern Ireland: James Platt, Jimmy Nicholl, Mal Donaghy, John O'Neill, John McClelland, Sammy McIlroy, Martin O'Neill (C), Norman Whiteside, Ian Stewart, Gerry Armstrong, Noel Brotherston. (Coach: William Laurence (Billy) Bingham (NIR)).
Turkey: Eser Özaltindere, Fatih Terim (C), Erdogan Arica (YC27), Eren Talu (81' Arif Kocabiyik), Rasit Çetiner, Hüseyin Çakiroglu, Yusuf Altintas, Hakan Kütukcüoglu, Metin Tekin, Selcuk Yula, Hasan Sengün. (Coach: Coskun Özari (TUR)).
Goals: Northern Ireland: 1-0 Martin O'Neill (5'), 2-0 John McClelland (18').
Turkey: 2-1 Hasan Sengün (55').
Referee: Alain Delmer (FRA)   Attendance: 15.093

23-04-1983	Izmir Alsancak Stadium, Izmir: Turkey – West Germany 0-3 (0-2)
Turkey: Senol Günes, Fatih Terim (C), Erdogan Arica, Rasit Çetiner, Yusuf Altintas, Hakan Kütukcüoglu, Hüseyin Çakiroglu (YC80), Metin Tekin (80' Iskender Günen), Erdal Keser, Selcuk Yula, Hasan Sengün. (Coach: Coskun Özari (TUR)).
West Germany: Harald Schumacher, Hans-Peter Briegel, Karlheinz Förster, Gerhard Strack, Wolfgang Dremmler, Pierre Littbarski (76' Wolfgang Rolff), Hansi Müller, Bernd Schuster, Stephan Engels, Rudi Völler, Karl-Heinz Rummenigge (C). (Coach: Josef (Jupp) Derwall (FRG)).
Goals: West Germany: 0-1 Karl-Heinz Rummenigge (30'), 0-2 Wolfgang Dremmler (36'), 0-3 Karl-Heinz Rummenigge (71').
Referee: Vojtech Christov (TCH)		Attendance: 59.637

27-04-1983	Praterstadion, Vienna: Austria – West Duitsland 0-0
Austria: Friedrich Koncilia, Bernd Krauss, Erich Obermayer (YC19), Josef Degeorgi (YC36), Bruno Pezzey, Heribert Weber (YC86), Herbert Prohaska (C) (86' Leopold Lainer), Felix Gasselich (77' Ernst Baumeister), Reinhard Kienast, Walter Schachner, Hans Krankl. (Coach: Erich Hof (AUT)).
West Germany: Harald Schumacher, Hans-Peter Briegel (39' Bernd Förster), Karlheinz Förster, Gerhard Strack, Wolfgang Dremmler, Pierre Littbarski (YC39), Hansi Müller (YC23) (69' Wolfgang Rolff), Stephan Engels, Bernd Schuster, Rudi Völler, Karl-Heinz Rummenigge (C). (Coach: Josef (Jupp) Derwall (FRG)).
Referee: Brian R.McGinlay (SCO)		Attendance: 50.169

27-04-1983	Windsor Park, Belfast: Northern Ireland – Albania 1-0 (0-0)
Northern Ireland: Pat Jennings, Jimmy Nicholl, Mal Donaghy (YC9), John O'Neill, John McClelland, Sammy McIlroy, Martin O'Neill (C), Billy Hamilton, Ian Stewart, Gerry Armstrong, Noel Brotherston (63' Gerald Mullan). (Coach: William Laurence (Billy) Bingham (NIR)).
Albania: Perlat Musta (YC44), Petro Ruci, Muhedin Targaj, Arjan Hametaj, Sulejman Demollari, Luan Vukatana, Bedri Omuri, Shkelqim Muça, Ilir Lame, Kristaq Eksarko (78' Sulejman Mema), Arben Minga. (Coach: Shyqyri Rreli (ALB)).
Goal: Northern Ireland: 1-0 Ian Stewart (54').
Referee: Ib F.Nielsen (DEN)		Attendance: 10.612

11-05-1983	Stadiumi Qemal Stafa, Tirana: Albania – Turkey 1-1 (0-1)
Albania: Perlat Musta, Petro Ruci, Muhedin Targaj, Arjan Hametaj, Luan Vukatana (46' Arjan Bimo), Haxhi Ballgjini, Bedri Omuri, Shkelqim Muça (46' Pandeli Xhaho), Ilir Lame, Ferid Rragami, Andrea Marko. (Coach: Shyqyri Rreli (ALB)).
Turkey: Adem Ibrahimoglu, Fatih Terim, Alpaslan Eratli, Erdogan Arica, Ismail Demiriz (90' Iskender Günen), Rasit Çetiner, Yusuf Altintas, Hüseyin Çakiroglu (YC67), Metin Tekin (90' Eren Talu), Selcuk Yula, Hasan Sengün. (Coach: Coskun Özari (TUR)).
Goals: Albania: 1-1 Rasit Çetiner (73' *own goal*).
Turkey: 0-1 Metin Tekin (34').
Referee: Mircea-Lucian Salomir (ROM)		Attendance: 15.678

08-06-1983   Stadiumi Qemal Stafa, Tirana: Albania – Austria   1-2 (0-1)
Albania: Perlat Musta, Petro Ruci, Muhedin Targaj (YC69), Arjan Hametaj, Arjan Bimo, Luan Vukatana, Ilir Lame, Ferid Rragami, Pandeli Xhaho (67' Andrea Marko), Arben Minga (53' Milutin Kërçiç), Sefedin Braho. (Coach: Shyqyri Rreli (ALB)).
Austria: Friedrich Koncilia, Bernd Krauss, Erich Obermayer, Anton Pichler, Leopold Lainer, Herbert Prohaska (C), Ernst Baumeister, Felix Gasselich (YC70) (89' Gerald Willfurth), Walter Schachner, Gernot Jurtin, Christian Keglevits (60' Gerhard Steinkogler). (Coach: Erich Hof (AUT)).
Goals: Albania: 1-2 Muhedin Targaj (84').
Austria: 0-1 Walter Schachner (5'), 0-2 Walter Schachner (58').
Referee: László Pádár (HUN)   Attendance: 15.139

21-09-1983   Windsor Park, Belfast: Northern Ireland – Austria   3-1 (1-0)
Northern Ireland: Pat Jennings, Mal Donaghy, Chris Nicholl, John McClelland, Paul Christopher Ramsey, Sammy McIlroy, Martin O'Neill (C), Norman Whiteside, Billy Hamilton, Ian Stewart (YC71), Gerry Armstrong. (Coach: William Laurence (Billy) Bingham (NIR)).
Austria: Friedrich Koncilia, Bernd Krauss, Bruno Pezzey, Heribert Weber, Leopold Lainer, Herbert Prohaska (C), Felix Gasselich, Reinhard Kienast (70' Josef Degeorgi), Martin Gisinger (70' Gerald Willfurth), Walter Schachner, Hans Krankl. (Coach: Erich Hof (AUT)).
Goals: Northern Ireland: 1-0 Billy Hamilton (28'), 2-0 Norman Whiteside (67'), 3-1 Martin O'Neill (89').
Austria: 2-1 Felix Gasselich (83').
Referee: Erik Fredriksson (SWE)   Attendance: 18.013

05-10-1983   Parkstadion, Gelsenkirchen: West Germany – Austria   3-0 (3-0)
West Germany: Harald Schumacher, Hans-Peter Briegel, Karlheinz Förster, Klaus Augenthaler, Gerhard Strack, Wolfgang Dremmler, Wolfgang Rolff, Bernd Schuster (YC76), Norbert Meier (73' Lothar Matthäus), Rudi Völler (73' Herbert Waas), Karl-Heinz Rummenigge (C). (Coach: Josef (Jupp) Derwall (FRG)).
Austria: Friedrich Koncilia, Bernd Krauss (79' Johann Pregesbauer), Josef Degeorgi, Bruno Pezzey, Heribert Weber, Leopold Lainer, Herbert Prohaska (C), Ernst Baumeister (YC82), Gerald Willfurth, Felix Gasselich (46' Gernot Jurtin), Walter Schachner. (Coach: Erich Hof (AUT)).
Goals: West Germany: 1-0 Karl-Heinz Rummenigge (3'), 2-0 Rudi Völler (18'), 3-0 Rudi Völler (20').
Referee: Luigi Agnolin (ITA)   Attendance: 65.496

12-10-1983   19 Mayis Stadium, Ankara: Turkey – Northern Ireland   1-0 (1-0)
Turkey: Adem Ibrahimoglu, Fatih Terim (C), Erdogan Arica, Ismail Demiriz, Rasit Çetiner, Yusuf Altintas, Sedat Özden, Selcuk Yula, Hasan Sengün, Ilyas Tüfekçi, Halil Ibrahim Eren (82' Riza Çalimbay). (Coach: Coskun Özari (TUR)).
Northern Ireland: Pat Jennings, Jimmy Nicholl, Mal Donaghy, Chris Nicholl, John McClelland, Sammy McIlroy, Martin O'Neill (C), Norman Whiteside, Billy Hamilton (64' David McCreery), Ian Stewart, Noel Brotherston (78' James Cleary). (Coach: William Laurence (Billy) Bingham (NIR)).
Goal: Turkey: 1-0 Fatih Terim (17').
Referee: Romualdas Yushka (URS)   Attendance: 21.096

26-10-1983   Olympiastadion, Berlin: West Germany – Turkey   5-1 (1-0)
West Germany: Harald Schumacher, Hans-Peter Briegel (82' Mathias Herget), Klaus Augenthaler, Gerhard Strack, Jonny Otten, Lothar Matthäus, Pierre Littbarski, Uli Stielike, Norbert Meier (82' Michael Rummenigge), Rudi Völler, Karl-Heinz Rummenigge (C). (Coach: Josef (Jupp) Derwall (FRG)).
Turkey: Adem Ibrahimoglu, Fatih Terim (C), Erdogan Arica, Ismail Demiriz, Rasit Çetiner (YC2), Yusuf Altintas, Sedat Özden (70' Cem Pamiroglu), Erdat Keser, Selcuk Yula, Hasan Sengün, Ilyas Tüfekçi. (Coach: Coskun Özari (TUR)).
Goals: West Germany: 1-0 Rudi Völler (44'), 2-1 Karl-Heinz Rummenigge (60'), 3-0 Rudi Völler (65'), 4-0 Uli Stielike (66'), 5-1 Karl-Heinz Rummenigge (74' penalty).
Turkey: 4-1 Hasan Sengün (69').
Referee: Edvard Sostaric (YUG)   Attendance: 30.457

16-11-1983   Ali Sami Yen Stadium, Istanbul: Turkey – Austria   3-1 (0-0)
Turkey: Yasar Duran, Fatih Terim (C), Erdogan Arica, Ismail Demiriz, Rasit Çetiner, Yusuf Altintas, Sedat Özden, Necdet Ergün, Erdat Keser (58' Hasan Sengün), Selcuk Yula, Ilyas Tüfekçi. (Coach: Coskun Özari (TUR)).
Austria: Friedrich Koncilia, Bernd Krauss, Josef Degeorgi (77' Leopold Lainer), Bruno Pezzey (C), Heribert Weber, Gerald Messlender (YC28), Ernst Baumeister, Gerald Willfurth (YC15) (73' Peter Pacult), Heinz Thonhofer, Walter Schachner, Christian Keglevits. (Coach: Erich Hof (AUT)).
Goals: Turkey: 1-0 Ilyas Tüfekçi (62'), 2-0 Selcuk Yula (69'), 3-1 Selcuk Yula (76' penalty).
Austria: 2-1 Ernst Baumeister (71').
Referee: Roger Schoeters (BEL)   Attendance: 21.310

16-11-1983   Volksparkstadion, Hamburg: West Germany – Northern Ireland   0-1 (0-0)
West Germany: Harald Schumacher, Hans-Peter Briegel, Karlheinz Förster, Klaus Augenthaler, Lothar Matthäus, Wolfgang Dremmler, Uli Stielike (84' Gerhard Strack), Wolfgang Rolff, Norbert Meier (69' Pierre Littbarski), Karl-Heinz Rummenigge (C), Herbert Waas. (Coach: Josef (Jupp) Derwall (FRG)).
Northern Ireland: Pat Jennings, Jimmy Nicholl, Mal Donaghy, John McClelland, Paul Christopher Ramsey, Gerald McElhinney, Martin O'Neill (C), Norman Whiteside, Billy Hamilton, Ian Stewart, Gerry Armstrong. (Coach: William Laurence (Billy) Bingham (NIR)).
Goal: Northern Ireland: 0-1 Norman Whiteside (50').
Referee: Károly Palotai (HUN)   Attendance: 61.418

20-11-1983   Ludwigsparkstadion, Saarbrücken: West Germany – Albania   2-1 (1-1)
West Germany: Harald Schumacher, Hans-Peter Briegel (33' Jonny Otten), Karlheinz Förster, Bernd Förster, Gerhard Strack, Lothar Matthäus, Wolfgang Dremmler, Pierre Littbarski (67' Herbert Waas), Norbert Meier, Rudi Völler (YC48), Karl-Heinz Rummenigge (C). (Coach: Josef (Jupp) Derwall (FRG)).
Albania: Perlat Musta (YC58), Petro Ruci, Arjan Hametaj (YC4), Luan Vukatana (YC47) (83' Hasan Lika), Haxhi Ballgjini, Bedri Omuri, Ilir Lame, Ferid Rragami (YC74), Kristaq Eksarko, Genc Tomorri (RC48), Arben Minga. (Coach: Shyqyri Rreli (ALB)).
Goals: West Germany: 1-1 Karl-Heinz Rummenigge (23'), 2-1 Gerhard Strack (79').
Albania: 0-1 Genc Tomorri (22').
Referee: Anders Mattsson (FIN)   Attendance: 37.560

GROUP 7

05-06-1982	Messina	Malta – Iceland	2-1 (1-0)
01-09-1982	Reykjavik	Iceland – Netherlands	1-1 (0-0)
22-09-1982	Rotterdam	Netherlands – Republic of Ireland	2-1 (1-0)
13-10-1982	Dublin	Republic of Ireland – Iceland	2-0 (1-0)
27-10-1982	Málaga	Spain – Iceland	1-0 (0-0)
17-11-1982	Dublin	Republic of Ireland – Spain	3-3 (1-1)
19-12-1982	Aachen	Malta – Netherlands	0-6 (0-4)
16-02-1983	Seville	Spain – Netherlands	1-0 (1-0)
30-03-1983	Ta'Qali	Malta – Republic of Ireland	0-1 (0-0)
27-02-1983	Zaragoza	Spain – Republic of Ireland	2-0 (0-0)
15-05-1983	Ta'Qali	Malta – Spain	2-3 (1-1)
29-05-1983	Reykjavik	Iceland – Spain	0-1 (0-1)
05-06-1983	Reykjavik	Iceland – Malta	1-0 (1-0)
07-09-1983	Groningen	Netherlands – Iceland	3-0 (3-0)
21-09-1983	Reykjavik	Iceland – Republic of Ireland	0-3 (0-2)
12-10-1983	Dublin	Republic of Ireland – Netherlands	2-3 (2-0)
16-11-1983	Rotterdam	Netherlands – Spain	2-1 (1-1)
16-11-1983	Dublin	Republic of Ireland – Malta	8-0 (3-0)
17-12-1983	Rotterdam	Netherlands – Malta	5-0 (2-0)
21-12-1983	Seville	Spain – Malta	12-1 (3-1)

FINAL STANDING

Pos	Team	Pld	W	D	L	GF	GA	GD	Pts
1	*Spain*	*8*	*6*	*1*	*1*	*24*	*8*	*+16*	*13*
2	Netherlands	8	6	1	1	22	6	+16	13
3	Republic of Ireland	8	4	1	3	20	10	+10	9
4	Iceland	8	1	1	6	3	13	-10	3
5	Malta	8	1	0	7	5	37	-32	2

Spain qualified for the final tournament in France.

05-06-1982   Stadio Comunale Giovanni Celeste, Messina (ITA): Malta – Iceland   2-1 (1-0)
Malta: John Bonello, Edwin Farrugia, Costantino Consiglio, Norman Buttigieg, Emanuel Farrugia (65' Mario Farrugia), Carmel Busuttil, John Holland (C), George Xuereb, Emanuel Fabri, Ernest Spiteri-Gonzi, Joseph Xuereb (70' Mario Schembri). (Coach: Victor Scerri (MLT)).
Iceland: Gudmundur Baldursson, Sævar Jónsson, Atli Edvaldsson, Marteinn Geirsson (C), Trausti Haraldsson, Örn Óskarsson (87' Vidar Halldórsson), Pétur Ormslev, Karl Thordarsson, Janus Gudlaugsson (89' Árni Sveinsson), Teitur Thordarson, Lárus Gudmundsson (YC12). (Coach: Jóhannes Atlason (ISL)).
Goals: Malta; 1-0 Ernest Spiteri-Gonzi (44'), 2-0 Emanuel Fabri (48').
Iceland: 2-1 Marteinn Geirsson (51' penalty).
Referee: Pietro D'Elia (ITA)   Attendance: 1.271

01-09-1982 Laugardalsvöllur, Reykjavik: Iceland – Netherlands 1-1 (0-0)
Iceland: Thorsteinn Bjarnason, Sævar Jónsson, Atli Edvaldsson, Marteinn Geirsson (C), Trausti Haraldsson (70' Ómar Torfason), Pétur Ormslev, Karl Thordarsson, Janus Gudlaugsson (13' Gunnar Gíslason), Arnor Gudjohnsen, Lárus Gudmundsson, Vidar Halldórsson. (Coach: Jóhannes Atlason (ISL)).
Netherlands: Hans van Breukelen, Frank Rijkaard, Michel van de Korput, Ben Wijnstekers (C), Edo Ophof, Peter Boeve, Gerald Vanenburg (46' Jurrie Koolhof), Ruud Gullit, Dick Schoenaker, Wim Kieft, Willy van de Kerkhof. (Coach: Cornelis Bernardus (Kees) Rijvers (HOL)).
Goals: Iceland: 1-0 Atli Edvaldsson (49').
Netherlands: 1-1 Dick Schoenaker (51').
Referee: Brian R.McGinlay (SCO) Attendance: 2.862

22-09-1982 Stadion Feijenoord, Rotterdam: Netherlands – Republic of Ireland 2-1 (1-0)
Netherlands: Hans van Breukelen, Michel van de Korput, Ben Wijnstekers (C), Johnny Metgod (46' René van de Kerkhof), Ronald Spelbos, Huub Stevens, Gerald Vanenburg (86' Kees van Kooten), Ruud Gullit, Dick Schoenaker, Willy van de Kerkhof, René van der Gijp. (Coach: Cornelis Bernardus (Kees) Rijvers (HOL)).
Republic of Ireland: Seamus McDonagh, Chris Hughton, David O'Leary, Mark Lawrenson, Tony Galvin (72' Gary Waddock), Michael Martin, Liam Brady (YC45), Gerry Daly (84' Michael Walsh), Tony Grealish (C), Frank Stapleton, Michael Robinson. (Coach: Eoin Kevin Joseph Colin Hand (IRL)).
Goals: Netherlands: 1-0 Dick Schoenaker (1'), 2-0 Ruud Gullit (64').
Republic of Ireland: 2-1 Gerry Daly (80').
Referee: Ivan Grégr (TCH) Attendance: 17.438

13-10-1982 Lansdowne Road, Dublin: Republic of Ireland – Iceland 2-0 (1-0)
Republic of Ireland: Seamus McDonagh, Kevin Moran, David O'Leary, Mark Lawrenson, Ronnie Whelan, Gary Waddock (YC76), Liam Brady (62' Kevin O'Callaghan), Tony Grealish (C), Frank Stapleton, Michael Walsh, Michael Robinson. (Coach: Eoin Kevin Joseph Colin Hand (IRL)).
Iceland: Thorsteinn Bjarnason, Sævar Jónsson, Gunnar Gíslason, Atli Edvaldsson (YC66), Marteinn Geirsson (C), Örn Óskarsson, Pétur Ormslev (39' Ragnar Margeirsson), Arnór Gudjohnsen (YC76), Pétur Pétursson, Lárus Gudmundsson, Vidar Halldórsson. (Coach: Jóhannes Atlason (ISL)).
Goals: Republic of Ireland: 1-0 Frank Stapleton (36'), 2-0 Tony Grealish (75').
Referee: Paul Rion (LUX) Attendance: 23.271

27-10-1982 Estadio La Rosaleda, Málaga: Spain – Iceland 1-0 (0-0)
Spain: Luis Miguel ARCONADA Echarri (C), JOSÉ Antonio CAMACHO Alfaro, Rafael GORDILLO Vázquez (46' FRANCISCO Javier López Alfaro), Francisco "Paco" BONET Serrano, JUAN JOSÉ Jiménez Collar, GERARDO Miranda Concepción, Juan Antonio SEÑOR Gómez, ROBERTO Férnandez Bonillo, Carlos Alonso SANTILLANA, MARCOS Alonso Peña, Juan Carlos PEDRAZA Gómez (81' ENRIQUE MARTÍN Monreal Lizarraga). (Coach: MIGUEL MUÑOZ Mozún (ESP)).
Iceland: Thorsteinn Bjarnason (YC51), Sævar Jónsson, Atli Edvaldsson, Marteinn Geirsson (C), Örn Óskarsson, Ómar Torfason, Sigurdur Grétarsson (75' Gunnar Gíslason), Árni Sveinsson (63' Heimir Karlsson), Arnór Gudjohnsen, Pétur Pétursson, Vidar Halldórsson. (Coach: Jóhannes Atlason (ISL)).
Goal: Spain: 1-0 Juan Carlos PEDRAZA Gómez (60').
Referee: Mario da Silva Luis (POR) Attendance: 15.132

17-11-1982   Lansdowne Raod, Dublin: Republic of Ireland – Spain   3-3 (1-1)
Republic of Ireland: Seamus McDonagh, Chris Hughton, Mark Lawrenson, Ashley Grimes, John Devine, Michael Martin (YC36), Liam Brady, Tony Grealish (C) (61' Michael Walsh), Kevin O'Callaghan, Frank Stapleton, Michael Robinson. (Coach: Eoin Kevin Joseph Colin Hand (IRL)).
Spain: Luis Miguel ARCONADA Echarri (C), JOSÉ Antonio CAMACHO Alfaro, Antonio MACEDA Frances (YC84), Rafael GORDILLO Vázquez, Francisco "Paco" BONET Serrano (YC41), JUAN JOSÉ Jiménez Collar (YC16), VÍCTOR MUÑOZ Manrique, Juan Antonio SEÑOR Gómez, Carlos Alonso SANTILLANA (YC71) (71' ROBERTO Férnandez Bonillo), MARCOS Alonso Peña (YC71), Juan Carlos PEDRAZA Gómez (67' ENRIQUE MARTÍN Monreal Lizarraga (YC86)). (Coach: MIGUEL MUÑOZ Mozún (ESP)).
Goals: Republic of Ireland: 1-0 Ashley Grimes (2'), 2-3 Frank Stapleton (64'), 3-3 Frank Stapleton (76').
Spain: 1-1 Antonio MACEDA Frances (31'), 1-2 Michael Martin (47' *own goal*), 1-3 VÍCTOR MUÑOZ Manrique (60').
Referee: Jan Redelfs (FRG)   Attendance: 35.088

19-12-1982   Tivoli Stadium, Aachen (FRG): Malta – Netherlands   0-6 (0-4)
Malta: John Bonello, Edwin Farrugia, Mario Schembri, Costantino Consiglio (80' Mario Farrugia), Emanuel Farrugia, Joseph Salerno, John Holland (C), George Xuereb, Emanuel Fabri, Raymond Xuereb (32' Michael Degiorgio), Ernest Spiteri-Gonzi. (Coach: Victor Scerri (MLT)).
Netherlands: Piet Schrijvers, Michel van de Korput, Ben Wijnstekers, Hugo Hovenkamp, Edo Ophof, Peter Boeve, Gerald Vanenburg (68' Jurrie Koolhof), Dick Schoenaker, René Hofman (68' Ruud Gullit), Pierre Vermeulen, Kees van Kooten. (Coach: Cornelis Bernardus (Kees) Rijvers (HOL)).
Goals: Netherlands: 0-1 Edo Ophof (22' *penalty*), 0-2 Kees van Kooten (25'), 0-3 Hugo Hovenkamp (34'), 0-4 Dick Schoenaker (39'), 0-5 Dick Schoenaker (51'), 0-6 Kees van Kooten (71').
Referee: Dieter Pauly (FRG)   Attendance: 17.000

16-02-1983   Estadio Ramón Sánchez Pizjuán, Seville: Spain – Netherlands   1-0 (1-0)
Spain: Luis Miguel ARCONADA Echarri (C), JOSÉ Antonio CAMACHO Alfaro, Antonio MACEDA Frances, Rafael GORDILLO Vázquez, JUAN JOSÉ Jiménez Collar, Andoni GOIKOETXEA Olaskoaga, VÍCTOR MUÑOZ Manrique, Juan Antonio SEÑOR Gómez, Francisco José "LOBO" CARRASCO Hidalgo, Manuel SARABIA López (87' Ricardo GALLEGO Redondo), MARCOS Alonso Peña. (Coach: MIGUEL MUÑOZ Mozún (ESP)).
Netherlands: Piet Schrijvers, Ruud Krol, Michel van de Korput, Ben Wijnstekers (C), Hugo Hovenkamp (46' Ruud Gullit), Johnny Metgod (72' Michel Valke), Peter Boeve, Ronald Spelbos, Dick Schoenaker, Jurrie Koolhof, René van der Gijp. (Coach: Cornelis Bernardus (Kees) Rijvers (HOL)).
Goal: Spain: 1-0 Juan Antonio SEÑOR Gómez (44' *penalty*).
Referee: Paolo Bergamo (ITA)   Attendance: 30.499

30-03-1983   Ta'Qali National Stadium, Ta'Qali: Malta – Republic of Ireland   0-1 (0-0)
Malta: John Bonello, Edwin Farrugia, Mario Schembri, Emanuel Farrugia, Michael Degiorgio, John Holland (C), George Xuereb, Emanuel Fabri, Mario Farrugia, Silvio Demanuele, Raymond Xuereb. (Coach: Victor Scerri (MLT)).
Republic of Ireland: Seamus McDonagh, Chris Hughton, Mark Lawrenson, John Devine, Ronnie Whelan, Gary Waddock, Tony Galvin (63' Kevin O'Callaghan), Michael Martin (C), Liam Brady (YC85), Frank Stapleton, Michael Robinson. (Coach: Eoin Kevin Joseph Colin Hand (IRL)).
Goal: Republic of Ireland: 0-1 Frank Stapleton (89').
Referee: Adolf Mathias (AUT)   Attendance: 6.487

27-04-1983   La Romareda, Zaragoza: Spain – Republic of Ireland   2-0 (0-0)
Spain: Luis Miguel ARCONADA Echarri (C), JOSÉ Antonio CAMACHO Alfaro, Antonio MACEDA Frances, Rafael GORDILLO Vázquez, Francisco "Paco" BONET Serrano, JUAN JOSÉ Jiménez Collar, VÍCTOR MUÑOZ Manrique (46' Ricardo GALLEGO Redondo), Juan Antonio SEÑOR Gómez, Francisco José "LOBO" CARRASCO Hidalgo (74' Hipólito "POLI" RINCÓN Povedano), Carlos Alonso SANTILLANA, MARCOS Alonso Peña. (Coach: MIGUEL MUÑOZ Mozún (ESP)).
Republic of Ireland: Seamus McDonagh, Chris Hughton, David O'Leary, Mark Lawrenson, Ashley Grimes (58' Kevin O'Callaghan), Ronnie Whelan (78' Gerry Daly), Gary Waddock, Michael Martin, Tony Grealish (C), Frank Stapleton, Michael Walsh. (Coach: Eoin Kevin Joseph Colin Hand (IRL)).
Goals: Spain: 1-0 Carlos Alonso SANTILLANA (49'), 2-0 Hipólito "POLI" RINCÓN Povedano (89').
Referee: Valeri Pavlovich Butenko (URS)   Attendance: 28.211

15-05-1983   Ta'Qali National Stadium, Ta'Qali: Malta – Spain   2-3 (1-1)
Malta: John Bonello, Edwin Farrugia (YC45), Mario Schembri (C), Norman Buttigieg, Emanuel Farrugia, Joseph Salerno, Carmel Busuttil, Michael Degiorgio (YC56), Emanuel Fabri, Silvio Demanuele, Ernest Spiteri-Gonzi. (Coach: Victor Scerri (MLT)).
Spain: Luis Miguel ARCONADA Echarri (C), JOSÉ Antonio CAMACHO Alfaro, Antonio MACEDA Frances, Rafael GORDILLO Vázquez, Francisco "Paco" BONET Serrano (YC48) (54' Andoni GOIKOETXEA Olaskoaga), VÍCTOR MUÑOZ Manrique, Juan Antonio SEÑOR Gómez, Ricardo GALLEGO Redondo, Francisco José "LOBO" CARRASCO Hidalgo, Carlos Alonso SANTILLANA, MARCOS Alonso Peña (YC45) (46' Hipólito "POLI" RINCÓN Povedano). (Coach: MIGUEL MUÑOZ Mozún (ESP)).
Goals: Malta: 1-1 Carmel Busuttil (30'), 2-1 Carmel Busuttil (47').
Spain: 0-1 Juan Antonio SEÑOR Gómez (21'), 2-2 Francisco José "LOBO" CARRASCO Hidalgo (60'), 2-3 Rafael GORDILLO Vázquez (84').
Referee: Evangelos Gainnakoudakis (GRE)   Attendance: 7.732

29-05-1983   Laugardalsvöllur, Reykjavik: Iceland – Spain   0-1 (0-1)
Iceland: Thorsteinn Bjarnason, Sævar Jónsson, Gunnar Gíslason (50' Árni Sveinsson), Ólafur Björnsson, Sigurdur Lárusson, Janus Gudlaugsson (C), Arnór Gudjohnsen (YC24), Pétur Pétursson (46' Ómar Torfason), Ragnar Margeirsson, Lárus Gudmundsson, Sigurdur Halldórsson. (Coach: Jóhannes Atlason (ISL)).
Spain: Luis Miguel ARCONADA Echarri (C), JOSÉ Antonio CAMACHO Alfaro, Antonio MACEDA Frances, Rafael GORDILLO Vázquez, Andoni GOIKOETXEA Olaskoaga (YC34), VÍCTOR MUÑOZ Manrique (YC29), Juan Antonio SEÑOR Gómez, Ricardo GALLEGO Redondo, Francisco José "LOBO" CARRASCO Hidalgo, Carlos Alonso SANTILLANA (89' Manuel SARABIA López), Hipólito "POLI" RINCÓN Povedano (YC71). (Coach: MIGUEL MUÑOZ Mozún (ESP)).
Goal: Spain: 0-1 Antonio MACEDA Frances (9').
Referee: Ronald Bridges (WAL)   Attendance: 7.055

05-06-1983   Laugardalsvöllur, Reykjavik: Iceland – Malta   1-0 (1-0)
Iceland: Thorsteinn Bjarnason, Sævar Jónsson, Atli Edvaldsson, Ólafur Björnsson, Pétur Ormslev, Árni Sveinsson, Janus Gudlaugsson, Ómar Rafnsson, Pétur Pétursson (46' Sigurdur Jónsson), Lárus Gudmundsson, Vidar Halldórsson. (Coach: Jóhannes Atlason (ISL)).
Malta: John Bonello, Edwin Farrugia, Mario Schembri, Norman Buttigieg, Emanuel Farrugia, Carmel Busuttil, Michael Degiorgio, John Holland (C), Emanuel Fabri (YC57), Silvio Demanuele (46' Ernest Spiteri-Gonzi), Raymond Xuereb. (Coach: Victor Scerri (MLT)).
Goal: Iceland: 1-0 Atli Edvaldsson (43').
Referee: Alex Jacobsen (DEN)   Attendance: 5.718

07-09-1983   Oosterpark Stadion, Groningen: Netherlands – Iceland   3-0 (3-0)
Netherlands: Piet Schrijvers, Ronald Koeman (46' Michel Valke), Ben Wijnstekers (C), Edo Ophof, Peter Boeve, Gerald Vanenburg, Ruud Gullit, Erwin Koeman (69' Bud Brocken), Marco van Basten, Willy van de Kerkhof, Peter Houtman. (Coach: Cornelis Bernardus (Kees) Rijvers (HOL)).
Iceland: Thorsteinn Bjarnason, Sævar Jónsson, Atli Edvaldsson, Jóhannes Edvaldsson, Pétur Ormslev, Ásgeir Sigurvinsson, Ómar Rafnsson, Arnór Gudjohnsen, Pétur Pétursson (69' Sveinbjörn Hákonarson), Lárus Gudmundsson (46' Ásgeir Elíasson), Vidar Halldórsson (C). (Coach: Jóhannes Atlason (ISL)).
Goals: Netherlands: 1-0 Erwin Koeman (17'), 2-0 Ruud Gullit (19'), 3-0 Peter Houtman (21').
Referee: Andrzej Libich (POL)   Attendance: 5.617

21-09-1983   Laugardalsvöllur, Reykjavik: Iceland – Republic of Ireland   0-3 (0-2)
Iceland: Thorsteinn Bjarnason, Sævar Jónsson, Atli Edvaldsson, Jóhannes Edvaldsson, Sigurdur Larusson, Pétur Ormslev (YC54), Janus Gudlaugsson, Arnór Gudjohnsen (52' Ásgeir Elíasson), Pétur Pétursson (82' Sigurdur Grétarsson), Lárus Gudmundsson, Vidar Halldórsson (C). (Coach: Jóhannes Atlason (ISL)).
Republic of Ireland: Seamus McDonagh, Kevin Moran, Chris Hughton, Mark Lawrenson, John Devine, Gary Waddock, Liam Brady, Tony Grealish (C), Kevin O'Callaghan, Frank Stapleton, Michael Robinson (YC24) (76' Michael Walsh). (Coach: Eoin Kevin Joseph Colin Hand (IRL)).
Goals: Republic of Ireland: 0-1 Gary Waddock (16'), 0-2 Michael Robinson (21'), 0-3 Michael Walsh (81').
Referee: Gérard Biguet (FRA)   Attendance: 13.706

12-10-1983   Dalymount Park, Dublin: Republic of Ireland – Netherlands   2-3 (2-0)
Republic of Ireland: Seamus McDonagh, Kevin Moran, Chris Hughton, Mark Lawrenson, John Devine (YC89), Gary Waddock, Liam Brady, Tony Grealish (C) (79' Kevin Sheedy), Kevin O'Callaghan (76' Tony Galvin), Frank Stapleton, Michael Robinson. (Coach: Eoin Kevin Joseph Colin Hand (IRL)).
Netherlands: Piet Schrijvers, Ronald Koeman, Adri van Tiggelen (46' Bud Brocken), Ben Wijnstekers (C), Sonny Silooy (YC24), Edo Ophof, Peter Boeve, Gerald Vanenburg, Ruud Gullit, Marco van Basten, Willy van de Kerkhof. (Coach: Cornelis Bernardus (Kees) Rijvers (HOL)).
Goals: Republic of Ireland: 1-0 Gary Waddock (7'), 2-0 Liam Brady (35' penalty).
Netherlands: 2-1 Ruud Gullit (51'), 2-2 Marco van Basten (66'), 2-3 Ruud Gullit (76').
Referee: André Daina (SUI)   Attendance: 26.406

16-11-1983   Stadion Feijenoord, Rotterdam: Netherlands – Spain   2-1 (1-1)
Netherlands: Piet Schrijvers, Ronald Koeman, Ben Wijnstekers (C), Edo Ophof, Peter Boeve, Gerald Vanenburg, Ruud Gullit, Erwin Koeman, Bud Brocken, Willy van de Kerkhof (YC73), Peter Houtman. (Coach: Cornelis Bernardus (Kees) Rijvers (HOL)).
Spain: Luis Miguel ARCONADA Echarri (C), JOSÉ Antonio CAMACHO Alfaro, Antonio MACEDA Frances, Rafael GORDILLO Vázquez, Andoni GOIKOETXEA Olaskoaga, Juan Antonio SEÑOR Gómez, José Vicente "TENTE" SÁNCHEZ Felip, Ricardo GALLEGO Redondo, Francisco José "LOBO" CARRASCO Hidalgo (83' MARCOS Alonso Peña), Francisco José GÚERRI Ballarín (67' Hipólito "POLI" RINCÓN Povedano (YC70)), Carlos Alonso SANTILLANA. (Coach: MIGUEL MUÑOZ Mozún (ESP)).
Goals: Netherlands: 1-0 Peter Houtman (26'), 2-1 Ruud Gullit (63').
Spain: 1-1 Carlos Alonso SANTILLANA (41').
Referee: Michel Vautrot (FRA)   Attendance: 49.915

16-11-1983   Dalymount Park, Dublin: Republic of Ireland – Malta   8-0 (3-0)
Republic of Ireland: Pat Bonner, Kevin Moran (46' Jacko McDonagh), Chris Hughton, Mark Lawrenson (80' Gary Waddock), Kevin Sheedy, Liam Brady, Gerry Daly, Kevin O'Callaghan, Kieran O'Reagan, Frank Stapleton (C), Michael Walsh. (Coach: Eoin Kevin Joseph Colin Hand (IRL)).
Malta: John Bonello, Alexander Azzopardi, Edwin Farrugia, Costantino Consiglio, Emanuel Farrugia, Carmel Busuttil, John Holland (C), Mario Farrugia (81' Emanuel Fabri), Silvio Demanuele, Noel Attard (68' George Xuereb), Ernest Spiteri-Gonzi. (Coach: Victor Scerri (MLT)).
Goals: Republic of Ireland: 1-0 Mark Lawrenson (25'), 2-0 Frank Stapleton (28'), 3-0 Kevin O'Callaghan (35'), 4-0 Mark Lawrenson (63'), 5-0 Kevin Sheedy (74'), 6-0 Liam Brady (76'), 7-0 Kevin Sheedy (84'), 8-0 Gerry Daly (86').
Referee: Ole Amundsen (DEN)   Attendance: 8.500

17-12-1983   Stadion Feijenoord, Rotterdam: Netherlands – Malta 5-0 (2-0)
Netherlands: Piet Schrijvers, Ronald Koeman, Ben Wijnstekers (C), Edo Ophof, Peter Boeve (71' Michel Valke), Gerald Vanenburg, Ruud Gullit, Erwin Koeman (46' Frank Rijkaard), Bud Brocken, Willy van de Kerkhof, Peter Houtman. (Coach: Cornelis Bernardus (Kees) Rijvers (HOL)).
Malta: John Bonello (YC62), Edwin Farrugia, Simon Tortell (79' Mario Farrugia), Mario Schembri, Norman Buttigieg, Emanuel Farrugia, Michael Degiorgio, John Holland (C), Emanuel Fabri, Silvio Demanuele, Raymond Farrugia (YC65) (87' Alexander Azzopardi). (Coach: Victor Scerri (MLT)).
Goals: Netherlands: 1-0 Bud Brocken (19'), 2-0 Ben Wijnstekers (30'), 3-0 Frank Rijkaard (74'), 4-0 Peter Houtman (79'), 5-0 Frank Rijkaard (90').
Referee: Klaus Peschel (GDR)   Attendance: 58.000

21-12-1983   Estadio Benito Villamarin, Seville: Spain – Malta 12-1 (3-1)
Spain: Francisco "PACO" BUYO Sánchez, JOSÉ Antonio CAMACHO Alfaro, Antonio MACEDA Frances (YC59), Rafael GORDILLO Vázquez (YC34), Andoni GOIKOETXEA Olaskoaga, VÍCTOR MUÑOZ Manrique, Juan Antonio SEÑOR Gómez, Francisco José "LOBO" CARRASCO Hidalgo (C), Manuel SARABIA López, Carlos Alonso SANTILLANA, Hipólito "POLI" RINCÓN Povedano (86' MARCOS Alonso Peña). (Coach: MIGUEL MUÑOZ Mozún (ESP)).
Malta: John Bonello (YC50), Alexander Azzopardi, Simon Tortell (YC23), Norman Buttigieg, Emanuel Farrugia, Michael Degiorgio (YC3,YC76), John Holland (C), Emanuel Fabri (YC34), Silvio Demanuele, Raymond Farrugia (72' Mario Farrugia), Ernest Spiteri-Gonzi. (Coach: Victor Scerri (MLT)).
Goals: Spain: 1-0 Carlos Alonso SANTILLANA (15'), 2-1 Carlos Alonso SANTILLANA (26'), 3-1 Carlos Alonso SANTILLANA (28'), 4-1 Hipólito "POLI" RINCÓN Povedano (46'), 5-1 Hipólito "POLI" RINCÓN Povedano (55'), 6-1 Antonio MACEDA Frances (60'), 7-1 Antonio MACEDA Frances (62'), 8-1 Hipólito "POLI" RINCÓN Povedano (63'), 9-1 Carlos Alonso SANTILLANA (75'), 10-1 Rafael GORDILLO Vázquez (77'), 11-1 Manuel SARABIA López (79'), 12-1 Juan Antonio SEÑOR Gómez (88').
Malta: 1-1 Michael Degiorgio (24').
Referee: Erkan Göksel (TUR)   Attendance: 18.871

FINALS TOURNAMENT IN FRANCE

GROUP STAGE

France qualified automatically as hosts.

GROUP 1

12-06-1984	Paris	France – Denmark	1-0 (0-0)
13-06-1984	Lens	Belgium – Yugoslavia	2-0 (2-0)
16-06-1984	Nantes	France – Belgium	5-0 (3-0)
16-06-1984	Lyon	Denmark – Yugoslavia	5-0 (2-0)
19-06-1984	Saint-Étienne	France – Yugoslavia	3-2 (0-1)
19-06-1984	Strasbourg	Denmark – Belgium	3-2 (1-2)

FINAL STANDING

Pos	Team	Pld	W	D	L	GF	GA	GD	Pts
1	France	3	3	0	0	9	2	+7	6
2	Denmark	3	2	0	1	8	3	+5	4
3	Belgium	3	1	0	2	4	8	-4	2
4	Yugoslavia	3	0	0	3	2	10	-8	0

France and Denmark qualified for the Semi-finals.

12-06-1984   Parc des Princes, Paris: France – Denmark   1-0 (0-0)
France: Joël Bats, Manuel Amoros (C) (RC87), Patrick Battiston, Max Bossis, Yvon Le Roux (60' Jean-François Domergue), Jean Tigana, Alain Giresse, Luis Fernández, Michel Platini, Bernard Lacombe, Bruno Bellone. (Coach: Michel Hidalgo (FRA)).
Denmark: Ole Qvist, Søren Busk, Ivan Nielsen, Jens Jørn Bertelsen, Morten Olsen (C), Frank Arnesen (80' Jesper Olsen), Søren Lerby, Michael Laudrup, Klaus Berggreen, Preben Elkjær Larsen, Allan Simonsen (44' Jan Mikkelsen Lauridsen). (Coach: Josef Emmanuel Hubertus Piontek (FRG)).
Goal: France: 1-0 Michel Platini (78').
Referee: Volker Roth (FRG)   Attendance: 47.570

13-06-1984   Stade Félix-Bollaert, Lens: Belgium – Yugoslavia   2-0 (2-0)
Belgium: Jean-Marie Pfaff, Georges Grün, Lei Clijsters (34' Paul Lambrichts), Michel De Wolf, René Vandereycken, Frank Vercauteren, Walter De Greef, Enzo Scifo, Erwin Vandenbergh, Nico Claesen, Jan Ceulemans (C). (Coach: Guy Jean Léonard Thijs (BEL)).
Yugoslavia: Zoran Simovic, Ivan Gudelj, Velimir Zajec (C), Nenad Stojkovic, Faruk Hadzibegic, Srecko Katanec, Mehmed Bazdarevic (60' Dragan Stojkovic), Zlatko Vujovic (79' Borislav Cvetkovic), Milos Sestic, Safet Susic, Sulejman Halilovic. (Coach: Todor Veselinovic (YUG)).
Goals: Belgium: 1-0 Erwin Vandenbergh (28'), 2-0 Georges Grün (45').
Referee: Erik Fredriksson (SWE)   Attendance: 41.774

16-06-1984   Stade de la Beaujoire, Nantes: France – Belgium   5-0 (3-0)
France: Joël Bats, Patrick Battiston, Max Bossis, Jean-François Domergue, Jean Tigana, Bernard Genghini (79' Thierry Tusseau), Alain Giresse, Luis Fernández, Michel Platini (C), Didier Six, Bernard Lacombe (65' Dominique Rocheteau). (Coach: Michel Hidalgo (FRA)).
Belgium: Jean-Marie Pfaff, Georges Grün, Michel De Wolf, Paul Lambrichts, René Vandereycken, Frank Vercauteren, Walter De Greef, Enzo Scifo (51' René Verheyen), Erwin Vandenbergh (46' Ludo Coeck), Nico Claesen, Jan Ceulemans (C). (Coach: Guy Jean Léonard Thijs (BEL)).
Goals: France: 1-0 Michel Platini (4'), 2-0 Alain Giresse (33'), 3-0 Luis Fernández (43'), 4-0 Michel Platini (74' penalty), 5-0 Michel Platini (89').
Referee: Robert Bonar (Bob) Valentine (SCO)   Attendance: 51.359

16-06-1984   Stade de Gerland, Lyon: Denmark – Yugoslavia   5-0 (2-0)
Denmark: Ole Qvist, Søren Busk, Ivan Nielsen, Jens Jørn Bertelsen, Morten Olsen (C), Frank Arnesen (78' Jan Mikkelsen Lauridsen), Søren Lerby, Michael Laudrup, Ole Rasmussen (61' John Sivebæk), Klaus Berggreen, Preben Elkjær Larsen. (Coach: Josef Emmanuel Hubertus Piontek (FRG)).
Yugoslavia: Tomislav Ivkovic, Ivan Gudelj, Velimir Zajec (C), Nenad Stojkovic, Srecko Katanec (55' Sulejman Halilovic), Branko Miljus, Ljubomir Radanovic, Mehmed Bazdarevic (27' Dragan Stojkovic), Zlatko Vujovic, Safet Susic, Borislav Cvetkovic. (Coach: Todor Veselinovic (YUG)).
Goals: Denmark: 1-0 Frank Arnesen (8'), 2-0 Klaus Berggreen (16'), 3-0 Frank Arnesen (69' penalty), 4-0 Preben Elkjær Larsen (82'), 5-0 Jan Mikkelsen Lauridsen (84').
Referee: Augusto Lamo Castillo (ESP)   Attendance: 34.736

19-06-1984   Stade Geoffroy-Guichard, Saint-Étienne: France – Yugoslavia   3-2 (0-1)
France: Joël Bats, Patrick Battiston, Max Bossis, Jean-François Domergue, Jean Tigana, Jean-Marc Ferreri (77' Daniel Bravo), Alain Giresse, Luis Fernández, Michel Platini (C), Dominique Rocheteau (46' Thierry Tusseau), Didier Six. (Coach: Michel Hidalgo (FRA)).
Yugoslavia: Zoran Simovic, Ivan Gudelj, Velimir Zajec, Nenad Stojkovic, Branko Miljus, Ljubomir Radanovic, Dragan Stojkovic, Mehmed Bazdarevic (85' Srecko Katanec), Zlatko Vujovic (60' Stjepan Deveric), Milos Sestic (C), Safet Susic. (Coach: Todor Veselinovic (YUG)).
Goals: France: 1-1 Michel Platini (59'), 2-1 Michel Platini (62'), 3-1 Michel Platini (77').
Yugoslavia: 0-1 Milos Sestic (32'), 3-2 Dragan Stojkovic (84' penalty).
Referee: André Daina (SUI)   Attendance: 47.589

19-06-1984   Stade de la Meinau, Strasbourg: Denmark – Belgium   3-2 (1-2)
Denmark: Ole Qvist, Søren Busk, Ivan Nielsen, Jens Jørn Bertelsen, Morten Olsen (C), Frank Arnesen (78' John Sivebæk), Søren Lerby, Michael Laudrup, Ole Rasmussen (58' Kenneth Brylle Larsen), Klaus Berggreen, Preben Elkjær Larsen. (Coach: Josef Emmanuel Hubertus Piontek (FRG)).
Belgium: Jean-Marie Pfaff, Georges Grün, Lei Clijsters, Michel De Wolf, René Vandereycken, Frank Vercauteren (62' Eddy Voordeckers), Walter De Greef, Enzo Scifo, Erwin Vandenbergh, Nico Claesen (46' Ludo Coeck), Jan Ceulemans (C). (Coach: Guy Jean Léonard Thijs (BEL)).
Goals: Denmark: 1-2 Frank Arnesen (41' penalty), 2-2 Kenneth Brylle Larsen (60'), 3-2 Preben Elkjær Larsen (84').
Belgium: 0-1 Jan Ceulemans (26'), 0-2 Frank Vercauteren (39').
Referee: Adolf Prokop (GDR)   Attendance: 36.911

GROUP 2

14-06-1984	Strasbourg	West Germany – Portugal	0-0
14-06-1984	Saint-Étienne	Romania – Spain	1-1 (1-1)
17-06-1984	Lens	West Germany – Romania	2-1 (1-0)
17-06-1984	Marseille	Portugal – Spain	1-1 (0-0)
20-06-1984	Paris	West Germany – Spain	0-1 (0-0)
20-06-1984	Nantes	Portugal – Romania	1-0 (0-0)

FINAL STANDING

Pos	Team	Pld	W	D	L	GF	GA	GD	Pts
1	Spain	3	1	2	0	3	2	+1	4
2	Portugal	3	1	2	0	2	1	+1	4
3	West Germany	3	1	1	1	2	2	0	3
4	Romania	3	0	1	2	2	4	-2	1

Spain and Portugal qualified for the Semi-finals.

14-06-1984   Stade de la Meinau, Strabourg: West Germany – Portugal 0-0
West Germany: Harald Schumacher, Andreas Brehme, Guido Buchwald (67' Lothar Matthäus), Hans-Peter Briegel, Karlheinz Förster, Bernd Förster, Uli Stielike, Wolfgang Rolff (67' Rudi Bommer), Rudi Völler, Karl-Heinz Rummenigge (C), Klaus Allofs. (Coach: Josef (Jupp) Derwall (FRG)).
Portugal: Manuel Galrinho BENTO (C), ÁLVARO Monteiro Magalhães, EURICO Monteiro GOMES, JOÃO Domingos da Silva PINTO, António José LIMA PEREIRA, ANTÓNIO Augusto Gomes de SOUSA, CARLOS MANUEL Correia dos Santos, JAIME Moreira PACHECO, Fernando Albino Sousa CHALANA, ANTÓNIO Manuel FRASCO Vieira (79' ANTÓNIO Augusto da Silva VELOSO), Rui Manuel Trindade JORDÃO (85' FERNANDO Mendes Soares GOMES). (Coach: FERNANDO da Silva CABRITA (POR)).
Referee: Romualdas Yushka (URS)   Attendance: 44.707

14-06-1984   Stade Geoffroy-Guichard, Saint-Étienne: Romania – Spain   1-1 (1-1)
Romania: Silviu Lung, Mircea Rednic, Costica Stefanescu (C), Nicolae Ungureanu, George Iorgulescu, Michael Klein, László Bölöni, Marin Dragnea (57' Aurel Ticleanu), Marcel Coras, Doru Rodion Camataru, Romulus Gabor (76' Gheorghe Hagi). (Coach: Mircea Lucescu (ROM)).
Spain: Luis Miguel ARCONADA Echarri (C), JOSÉ Antonio CAMACHO Alfaro, Antonio MACEDA Frances, Rafael GORDILLO Vázquez, Santiago URQUIAGA Pérez Lugar, Andoni GOIKOETXEA Olaskoaga, VÍCTOR MUÑOZ Manrique, Juan Antonio SEÑOR Gómez, Ricardo GALLEGO Redondo (73' JULIO ALBERTO Moreno Casas), Francisco José "LOBO" CARRASCO Hidalgo, Carlos Alonso SANTILLANA. (Coach: MIGUEL MUÑOZ Mozún (ESP)).
Goals: Romania: 1-1 László Bölöni (35').
Spain: 0-1 Francisco José "LOBO" CARRASCO Hidalgo (22' penalty).
Referee: Alexis Ponnet (BEL)   Attendance: 16.972

17-06-1984   Stade Félix-Bollaert, Lens: West Germany – Romania 2-1 (1-0)
West Germany: Harald Schumacher, Andreas Brehme, Hans-Peter Briegel, Karlheinz Förster (80' Guido Buchwald), Bernd Förster, Lothar Matthäus, Uli Stielike, Norbert Meier (65' Pierre Littbarski), Rudi Völler, Karl-Heinz Rummenigge (C), Klaus Allofs. (Coach: Josef (Jupp) Derwall (FRG)).
Romania: Silviu Lung, Ioan Andone, Mircea Rednic, Costica Stefanescu (C), Nicolae Ungureanu, Michael Klein, Gheorghe Hagi (46' Ion Adrian Zare), László Bölöni, Marin Dragnea (62' Aurel Ticleanu), Marcel Coras, Doru Rodion Camataru. (Coach: Mircea Lucescu (ROM)).
Goals: West Germany: 1-0 Rudi Völler (25'), 2-1 Rudi Völler (66').
Romania: 1-1 Marcel Coras (46').
Referee: Johannes Nicolaus Ignacius (Jan) Keizer (HOL)   Attendance: 31.787

17-06-1984   Stade Vélodrome, Marseille: Portugal – Spain 1-1 (0-0)
Portugal: Manuel Galrinho BENTO (C), ÁLVARO Monteiro Magalhães, EURICO Monteiro GOMES, JOÃO Domingos da Silva PINTO, António José LIMA PEREIRA, ANTÓNIO Augusto Gomes de SOUSA, CARLOS MANUEL Correia dos Santos, JAIME Moreira PACHECO, Fernando Albino Sousa CHALANA, ANTÓNIO Manuel FRASCO Vieira (76' Manuel Fernandes Miranda DIAMANTINO), Rui Manuel Trindade JORDÃO. (Coach: FERNANDO da Silva CABRITA (POR)).
Spain: Luis Miguel ARCONADA Echarri (C), JOSÉ Antonio CAMACHO Alfaro, Antonio MACEDA Frances, JULIO ALBERTO Moreno Casas (70' Manuel SARABIA López), Rafael GORDILLO Vázquez, Santiago URQUIAGA Pérez Lugar (79' Juan Antonio SEÑOR Gómez), Andoni GOIKOETXEA Olaskoaga, VÍCTOR MUÑOZ Manrique, Ricardo GALLEGO Redondo, Francisco José "LOBO" CARRASCO Hidalgo, Carlos Alonso SANTILLANA. (Coach: MIGUEL MUÑOZ Mozún (ESP)).
Goals: Portugal: 1-0 ANTÓNIO Augusto Gomes de SOUSA (52').
Spain: 1-1 Carlos Alonso SANTILLANA (73').
Referee: Michel Vautrot (FRA)   Attendance: 24.364

20-06-1984   Parc des Princes, Paris: West Germany – Spain 0-1 (0-0)
West Germany: Harald Schumacher, Andreas Brehme (47' Wolfgang Wolff), Hans-Peter Briegel, Karlheinz Förster, Bernd Förster, Lothar Matthäus, Uli Stielike, Norbert Meier (60' Pierre Littbarski), Rudi Völler, Karl-Heinz Rummenigge (C), Klaus Allofs. (Coach: Josef (Jupp) Derwall (FRG)).
Spain: Luis Miguel ARCONADA Echarri (C), JOSÉ Antonio CAMACHO Alfaro, Antonio MACEDA Frances, JULIO ALBERTO Moreno Casas (76' FRANCISCO Javier López Alfaro), Rafael GORDILLO Vázquez, Andoni GOIKOETXEA Olaskoaga (26' Salvador García Puig "SALVA"), VÍCTOR MUÑOZ Manrique, Juan Antonio SEÑOR Gómez, Ricardo GALLEGO Redondo, Francisco José "LOBO" CARRASCO Hidalgo, Carlos Alonso SANTILLANA. (Coach: MIGUEL MUÑOZ Mozún (ESP)).
Goal: Spain: 0-1 Antonio MACEDA Frances (90').
Referee: Vojtech Christov (TCH)   Attendance: 47.691

20-06-1984   Stade de la Beaujoire, Nantes: Portugal – Romania   1-0 (0-0)
Portugal: Manuel Galrinho BENTO (C), ÁLVARO Monteiro Magalhães, EURICO Monteiro GOMES, JOÃO Domingos da Silva PINTO, António José LIMA PEREIRA, ANTÓNIO Augusto Gomes de SOUSA, CARLOS MANUEL Correia dos Santos (63' Tamagnini Manuel Gomes Batista "NENÉ"), Fernando Albino Sousa CHALANA (15' Manuel Fernandes Miranda DIAMANTINO), ANTÓNIO Manuel FRASCO Vieira, FERNANDO Mendes Soares GOMES, Rui Manuel Trindade JORDÃO. (Coach: FERNANDO da Silva CABRITA (POR)).
Romania: Dumitru Moraru, Mircea Rednic, Costica Stefanescu (C), Nicolae Ungureanu, George Iorgulescu, Nicolae Negrila, Michael Klein, László Bölöni, Mircea Irimescu (59' Romulus Gabor), Marcel Coras, Doru Rodion Camataru (34' Ionel Augustin). (Coach: Mircea Lucescu (ROM)).
Goal: Portugal: 1-0 Tamagnini Manuel Gomes Batista "NENÉ" (81').
Referee: Heinz Fahnler (AUT)   Attendance: 24.464

SEMI-FINALS

23-06-1984   Stade Vélodrome, Marseille: France – Portugal   3-2 (1-0, 1-1) (AET)
France: Joël Bats, Patrick Battiston, Max Bossis, Yvon Le Roux, Jean-François Domergue, Jean Tigana, Alain Giresse, Luis Fernández, Michel Platini (C), Didier Six (104' Bruno Bellone), Bernard Lacombe (66' Jean-Marc Ferreri). (Coach: Michel Hidalgo (FRA)).
Portugal: Manuel Galrinho BENTO (C), ÁLVARO Monteiro Magalhães, EURICO Monteiro GOMES, JOÃO Domingos da Silva PINTO, António José LIMA PEREIRA, ANTÓNIO Augusto Gomes de SOUSA (62' Tamagnini Manuel Gomes Batista "NENÉ"), Manuel Fernandes Miranda DIAMANTINO (46' FERNANDO Mendes Soares GOMES), JAIME Moreira PACHECO, Fernando Albino Sousa CHALANA, ANTÓNIO Manuel FRASCO Vieira, Rui Manuel Trindade JORDÃO. (Coach: FERNANDO da Silva CABRITA (POR)).
Goals: France: 1-0 Jean-François Domergue (24'), 2-2 Jean-François Domergue (114'), 3-2 Michel Platini (119').
Portugal: 1-1 Rui Manuel Trindade JORDÃO (74'), 1-2 Rui Manuel Trindade JORDÃO (98').
Referee: Paolo Bergamo (ITA)   Attendance: 54.848

24-06-1984   Stade de Gerland, Lyon: Denmark – Spain   1-1 (1-0, 1-1) (AET)
Denmark: Ole Qvist, Søren Busk, John Sivebæk, Ivan Nielsen, Jens Jørn Bertelsen, Morten Olsen (C) (113' Kenneth Brylle Larsen), Frank Arnesen (68' Jesper Olsen), Søren Lerby, Michael Laudrup, Klaus Berggreen (RC107), Preben Elkjær Larsen. (Coach: Josef Emmanuel Hubertus Piontek (FRG)).
Spain: Luis Miguel ARCONADA Echarri (C), JOSÉ Antonio CAMACHO Alfaro, Antonio MACEDA Frances, JULIO ALBERTO Moreno Casas (60' Manuel SARABIA López), Rafael GORDILLO Vázquez, Salvador García Puig "SALVA" (102' Santiago URQUIAGA Pérez Lugar), VÍCTOR MUÑOZ Manrique, Juan Antonio SEÑOR Gómez, Ricardo GALLEGO Redondo, Francisco José "LOBO" CARRASCO Hidalgo, Carlos Alonso SANTILLANA. (Coach: MIGUEL MUÑOZ Mozún (ESP)).
Goals: Denmark: 0-1 Søren Lerby (7').
Spain: 1-1 Antonio MACEDA Frances (67').
Referee: George Courtney (ENG)   Attendance: 47.843
Penalties:
1 Kenneth Brylle Larsen   1 Carlos Alonso SANTILLANA
2 Jesper Olsen   2 Juan Antonio SEÑOR Gómez
3 Michael Laudrup   3 Santiago URQUIAGA Pérez Lugar
4 Søren Lerby   4 VÍCTOR MUÑOZ Manrique
* Preben Elkjær Larsen   5 Manuel SARABIA López
(Spain won 5-4 on penalties after extra time)

FINAL

27-06-1984   Parc des Princes, Paris: France – Spain   2-0 (0-0)
France: Joél Bats, Patrick Battiston (73' Manuel Amoros), Max Bossis, Yvon Le Roux (YC54,YC85), Jean-François Domergue, Jean Tigana, Alain Giresse, Luis Férnandez (YC30), Michel Platini (C), Bernard Lacombe (80' Bernard Genghini), Bruno Bellone. (Coach: Michel Hidalgo (FRA)).
Spain: Luis Miguel ARCONADA Echarri (C), JOSÉ Antonio CAMACHO Alfaro, JULIO ALBERTO Moreno Casas (75' Manuel SARABIA López), Santiago URQUIAGA Pérez Lugar, Salvador García Puig "SALVA" (85' ROBERTO Férnandez Bonillo), VÍCTOR MUÑOZ Manrique, FRANCISCO Javier López Alfaro, Juan Antonio SEÑOR Gómez, Ricardo GALLEGO Redondo (YC26), Francisco José "LOBO" CARRASCO Hidalgo, Carlos Alonso SANTILLANA. (Coach: MIGUEL MUÑOZ Mozún (ESP)).
Goals: France: 1-0 Michel Platini (57'), 2-0 Bruno Bellone (90').
Referee: Vojtech Christov (TCH)   Attendance: 47.368

*** France were European Champions ***

GOALSCORERS TOURNAMENT 1982-1984:

Goals	Players
9	Michel Platini (FRA)
7	Carlos Alonso SANTILLANA (ESP), Karl-Heinz Rummenigge (FRG), Rudi Völler (FRG)
6	Preben Elkjær Larsen (DEN), Antonio MACEDA Frances (ESP), Ruud Gullit (HOL)
5	Walter Schachner (AUT), Erwin Vandenbergh (BEL), Nikos Anastopoulos (GRE), Tibor Nyilasi (HUN), Frank Stapleton (IRL)
4	Allan Simonsen (DEN), Hipólito "POLI" RINCÓN Povedano (ESP), Joachim Streich (GDR), Dick Schoenaker (HOL), Rui Manuel Trindade JORDÃO (POR), László Bölöni (ROM), Dan Corneliusson (SWE)
3	François Van Der Elst (BEL), Frank Arnesen (DEN), Michael Laudrup (DEN), Luther Blissett (ENG), Trevor Francis (ENG), Tony Woodcock (ENG), Juan Antonio SEÑOR Gómez (ESP), Peter Houtman (HOL), József Póczik (HUN), Tamagnini Manuel Gomes Batista "NENÉ" (POR), Ladislav Vízek (TCH), Safet Susic (YUG)
2	Muhedin Targaj (ALB), Felix Gasselich (AUT), Maximilian Hagmayr (AUT), Jan Ceulemans (BEL), Ludo Coeck (BEL), Frank Vercauteren (BEL), Klaus Berggreen (DEN), Søren Lerby (DEN), Jesper Olsen (DEN), Glenn Hoddle (ENG), Sammy Lee (ENG), Paul Mariner (ENG), Bryan Robson (ENG), Rafael GORDILLO Vázquez (ESP), Francisco José "LOBO" CARRASCO Hidalgo (ESP), Jean-François Domergue (FRA), Kees van Kooten (HOL), Frank Rijkaard (HOL), Gyula Hajszán (HUN), László Kiss (HUN), Liam Brady (IRL), Gerry Daly (IRL), Mark Lawrenson (IRL), Kevin Sheedy (IRL), Gary Waddock (IRL), Atli Edvaldsson (ISL), Alessandro Altobelli (ITA), Jeannot Reiter (LUX), Carmel Busuttil (MLT), Martin O'Neill (NIR), Ian Stewart (NIR), Norman Whiteside (NIR), Åge

	Hareide (NOR), Arne Larsen Økland (NOR), Hallvar Thoresen (NOR), Wlodzimierz Smolarek (POL), ANTÓNIO Luis Alves Ribeiro de OLIVEIRA (POR), CARLOS MANUEL Correia dos Santos (POR), Doru Rodion Camataru (ROM), Kenny Daglish (SCO), Charlie Nicholas (SCO), John Wark (SCO), Andy Egli (SUI), Ulf Eriksson (SWE), Robert Prytz (SWE), Glenn Strömberg (SWE), Václav Danek (TCH), Petr Janecka (TCH), Petr Rada (TCH), Hasan Sengün (TUR), Selçuk Yula (TUR), Oleg Blokhin (URS), Fyodor Cherenkov (URS), Anatoliy Demyanenko (URS), Robbie James (WAL), Ian Rush (WAL)
1	Genc Tomorri (ALB), Ernst Baumeister (AUT), Karl Brauneder (AUT), Bruno Pezzey (AUT), Toni Polster (AUT), Herbert Prohaska (AUT), Georges Grün (BEL), Georgi Dimitrov (BUL), Roussi Gochev (BUL), Bozhidar Iskrenov (BUL), Stoycho Mladenov (BUL), Plamen Nikolov (BUL), Nasko Sirakov (BUL), Boycho Velichkov (BUL), Christakis Omirou "Mavris" (CYP), Fanis Theophanous (CYP), Marios Tsingis (CYP), Fivos Vrahimis (CYP), Kenneth Brylle Larsen (DEN), Søren Busk (DEN), Allan Hansen (DEN), John Mikkelsen Lauridsen (DEN), Terry Butcher (ENG), Mark Chamberlain (ENG), Steve Coppell (ENG), Phil Neal (ENG), Peter Withe (ENG), Juan Carlos PEDRAZA Gómez (ESP), Manuel SARABIA López (ESP), VÍCTOR MUÑOZ Manrique (ESP), Keijo Kousa (FIN), Ari Valvee (FIN), Bruno Bellone (FRA), Luis Fernández (FRA), Alain Giresse (FRA), Wolfgang Dremmler (FRG), Uli Stielike (FRG), Gerhard Strack (FRG), Rainer Ernst (GDR), Ronald Kreer (GDR), Hans Richter (GDR), Giorgos Kostikos (GRE), Petros Michos (GRE), Dimitrios Saravakos (GRE), Marco van Basten (HOL), Bud Brocken (HOL), Hugo Hovenkamp (HOL), Erwin Koeman (HOL), Edo Ophof (HOL), Ben Wijnstekers (HOL), Béla Bodonyi (HUN), Györö Burcsa (HUN), Péter Hannich (HUN), József Kardos (HUN), Gábor Pölöskei (HUN), Lázár Szentes (HUN), Tony Grealish (IRL), Ashley Grimes (IRL), Kevin O'Callaghan (IRL), Michael Robinson (IRL), Michael Walsh (IRL), Marteinn Geirsson (ISL), Antonio Cabrini (ITA), Francesco Graziani (ITA), Paolo Rossi (ITA), Marcel Di Domenico (LUX), Théo Malget (LUX), Romain Schreiner (LUX), Silvio Demanuele (MLT), Emanuel Fabri (MLT), Ernest Spiteri-Gonzi (MLT), Billy Hamilton (NIR), John McClelland (NIR), Thomas Lund (NOR), Zbigniew Boniek (POL), Dariusz Dziekanowski (POL), Pawel Król (POL), Janusz Kupcewicz (POL), ANTÓNIO Augusto Gomes de SOUSA (POR), FERNANDO Mendes Soares GOMES (POR), JOSÉ LUIS Lopes da Costa e SILVA (POR), Ioan Andone (ROM), Marcel Coras (ROM), Ion Geolgau (ROM), Michael Klein (ROM), Florea Vaetus (ROM), Eamonn Bannon (SCO), Paul Sturrock (SCO), Jean-Paul Brigger (SUI), Alain Geiger (SUI), Heinz Hermann (SUI), Marco Schällibaum (SUI), Claudio Sulser (SUI), Glenn Hysén (SWE), Mats Jingblad (SWE), Andreas Ravelli (SWE), Thomas Sunesson (SWE), Premysl Bicovsky (TCH), Pavel Chaloupka (TCH), Ladislav Jurkemik (TCH), Milan Luhovy (TCH), Zdenek Prokes (TCH), Jirí Sloup (TCH), Arif Kocabiyik (TUR), Metin Tekin (TUR), Fatih Terim (TUR), Ilyas Tüfekçi (TUR), Sergey Andreev (URS), Sergei Baltacha (URS), Nikolay Larionov (URS), Sergey Rodionov (URS), Jeremy Charles (WAL), Brian Flynn (WAL), Joey Jones (WAL), Mehmed Bazdarevic (YUG), Zvezdan Cvetkovic (YUG), Miodrag Jesic (YUG), Zlatko Kranjcar (YUG), Ljubomir Radanovic (YUG), Dusan Savic (YUG), Milos Sestic (YUG), Dejan Stojkovic (YUG), Nenad Stojkovic (YUG), Zlatko Vujovic (YUG), Zvonko Zivkovic (YUG)

| 1 own goal | Agustin Kola (ALB) for Austria, Jukka Ikäläinen (FIN) for Portugal, Michael Martin (IRL) for Spain, Marcel Bossi (LUX) for England, Pawel Janas (POL) for Finland, Roman Wojcicki (POL) for Soviet Union, Heinz Lüdi (SUI) for Belgium, Ján Kapko (TCH) for Italy, Rasit Çetiner (TUR) for Albania |

1988 UEFA European Football Championship

QUALIFYING ROUND

GROUP 1

10-09-1986	Bucharest	Romania – Austria	4-0 (1-0)
15-10-1986	Graz	Austria – Albania	3-0 (1-0)
12-11-1986	Seville	Spain – Romania	1-0 (0-0)
03-12-1986	Tirana	Albania – Spain	1-2 (1-0)
25-03-1987	Bucharest	Romania – Albania	5-1 (3-1)
01-04-1987	Vienna	Austria – Spain	2-3 (1-1)
29-04-1987	Tirana	Albania – Austria	0-1 (0-1)
29-04-1987	Bucharest	Romania – Spain	3-1 (3-0)
14-10-1987	Seville	Spain – Austria	2-0 (0-0)
28-10-1987	Vlorë	Albania – Romania	0-1 (0-0)
18-11-1987	Vienna	Austria – Romania	0-0
18-11-1987	Seville	Spain – Albania	5-0 (3-0)

FINAL STANDING

Pos	Team	Pld	W	D	L	GF	GA	GD	Pts
1	Spain	6	5	0	1	14	6	+8	10
2	Romania	6	4	1	1	13	3	+10	9
3	Austria	6	2	1	3	6	9	-3	5
4	Albania	6	0	0	6	2	17	-15	0

Spain qualified for the final tournament in West Germany.

19-09-1986   Stadionul Steaua, Bucharest: Romania – Austria   4-0 (1-0)
Romania: Dumitru Moraru, Miodrag Belodedici, Mircea Rednic, Stefan Iovan, Adrian Bumbescu, Michael Klein (YC68), Gheorghe Hagi, László Bölöni (C), Victor Piturca (46' Marius Lacatus), Dorin Mateut (72' Ilie Balaci), Doru Rodion Camataru (YC40). (Coach: Mircea Lucescu (ROM)).
Austria: Klaus Lindenberger, Josef Degeorgi, Heribert Weber, Leopold Lainer, Karl Brauneder (65' Peter Pacult), Gerald Messlender (YC40), Ernst Baumeister, Reinhard Kienast (46' Jürgen Werner (I)), Ewald Türmer (YC77), Toni Polster, Walter Schachner (C). (Coach: Branko Elsner (YUG)).
Goals: Romania: 1-0 Stefan Iovan (44'), 2-0 Marius Lacatus (61'), 3-0 Stefan Iovan (64'), 4-0 Gheorghe Hagi (90').
Referee: Gérard Biguet (FRA)   Attendance: 13.611

15-10-1986   Liebenau Stadium, Graz: Austria – Albania   3-0 (1-0)
Austria: Klaus Lindenberger, Heribert Weber (C), Karl Brauneder (YC49), Gerald Messlender, Gerald Piesinger, Manfred Linzmaier, Manfred Zsak, Ernst Baumeister, Jürgen Werner (I), Toni Polster, Andreas Ogris. (Coach: Branko Elsner (YUG)).
Albania: Perlat Musta (YC42), Kreshnik Çipi, Adrian Oçelli (YC65), Rrapo Taho, Alfred Ferko (72' Bedri Omuri), Hysen Zmijani, Mirel Josa (YC57), Sulejman Demollari, Alfred Zijaj, Agostin Kola, Arben Minga (C). (Coach: Agron Sulaj (ALB)).
Goals: Austria: 1-0 Andreas Ogris (18'), 2-0 Toni Polster (66'), 3-0 Manfred Linzmaier (77').
Referee: Klaus Peschel (GDR)   Attendance: 5.456

12-11-1986   Estadio Benito Villamarín, Seville: Spain – Romania   1-0 (0-0)
Spain: Andoni ZUBIZARRETA Urreta, JOSÉ Antonio CAMACHO Alfaro (C), JULIO ALBERTO Moreno Casas, Miguel Porlan Noguera "CHENDO", Manuel SANCHÍS Hontiyuelo, Juan Carlos ARTECHE Gómez, VÍCTOR MUÑOZ Manrique, Ricardo GALLEGO Redondo (77' Juan Antonio SEÑOR Gómez), José Miguel González Martín del Campo "MÍCHEL", Emilio BUTRAGUEÑO Santos, Hipólito "POLI" RINCÓN Povedano (YC74) (85' ELOY José Olaya Prendes). (Coach: MIGUEL MUÑOZ Mozún (ESP)).
Romania: Silviu Lung, Miodrag Belodedici, Nicolae Ungureanu, Stefan Iovan, Adrian Bumbescu, Michael Klein, Gheorghe Hagi, László Bölöni (C), Tudorel Stoica (YC53) (82' Mircea Rednic), Marius Lacatus, Doru Rodion Camataru (80' Pelé Gavrila Balint). (Coaches: Mircea Lucescu (ROM) & Emerich Alexandru Jenei (ROM)).
Goal: Spain: 1-0 José Miguel González Martín del Campo "MÍCHEL" (57').
Referee: Johannes Nicolaus Ignacius (Jan) Keizer (HOL)   Attendance: 41.884

03-12-1986   Stadiumi Qemal Stafa, Tirana: Albania – Spain   1-2 (1-0)
Albania: Perlat Musta, Rrapo Taho, Alfred Ferko (69' Agostin Kola), Hysen Zmijani, Sulejman Demollari, Mirel Josa, Skender Hodja, Bardhyl Jera, Bedri Omuri (YC34), Shkelqim Muça, Arben Minga (C). (Coach: Agron Sulaj (ALB)).
Spain: Andoni ZUBIZARRETA Urreta, JOSÉ Antonio CAMACHO Alfaro (C), Miguel Porlan Noguera "CHENDO", Manuel SANCHÍS Hontiyuelo (YC75), Juan Carlos ARTECHE Gómez (YC34), VÍCTOR MUÑOZ Manrique, Juan Antonio SEÑOR Gómez (46' ELOY José Olaya Prendes), JOAQUÍN Alonso González, José Miguel González Martín del Campo "MÍCHEL", Emilio BUTRAGUEÑO Santos, Hipólito "POLI" RINCÓN Povedano. (Coach: MIGUEL MUÑOZ Mozún (ESP)).
Goals: Albania: 1-0 Shkelqim Muça (27').
Spain: 1-1 Juan Carlos ARTECHE Gómez (67'), 1-2 JOAQUÍN Alonso González (84').
Referee: Antal Huták (HUN)   Attendance: 18.900

25-03-1987   Stadionul Steaua, Bucharest: Romania – Albania   5-1 (3-1)
Romania: Silviu Lung, Miodrag Belodedici, Nicolae Ungureanu, Stefan Iovan, Adrian Bumbescu (YC55), Michael Klein (63' Dorin Mateut), Gheorghe Hagi (67' Mircea Rednic), László Bölöni (C), Tudorel Stoica (YC85), Victor Piturca, Marius Lacatus. (Coach: Emerich Alexandru Jenei (ROM)).
Albania: Perlat Musta, Rrapo Taho, Besnik Bilali (YC26) (41' Bedri Omuri), Hysen Zmijani, Sulejman Demollari, Mirel Josa, Skender Hodja (YC60), Bardhyl Jera, Shkelqim Muça, Sokol Kushta (73' Alfred Ferko), Arben Minga (C). (Coach: Agron Sulaj (ALB)).
Goals: Romania: 1-0 Victor Piturca (2'), 2-1 László Bölöni (42'), 3-1 Gheorghe Hagi (44' penalty), 4-1 Miodrag Belodedici (54'), 5-1 Adrian Bumbescu (70').
Albania: 1-1 Sokol Kushta (35').
Referee: José Rosa dos Santos (POR)   Attendance: 6.154

01-04-1987   Praterstadion, Vienna: Austria – Spain 2-3 (1-1)
Austria: Klaus Lindenberger, Bruno Pezzey (C) (YC1), Gerald Piesinger, Manfred Linzmaier, Manfred Zsak, Ernst Baumeister, Reinhard Kienast, Jürgen Werner (I), Rudolf Weinhofer (72' Alfred Roscher), Toni Polster, Andreas Ogris. (Coach: Branko Elsner (YUG)).
Spain: Andoni ZUBIZARRETA Urreta, JOSÉ Antonio CAMACHO Alfaro (C), Miguel Porlan Noguera "CHENDO" (RC76), Genar ANDRINÚA Cortabarría, VÍCTOR MUÑOZ Manrique, ROBERTO Férnandez Bonillo, Ricardo GALLEGO Redondo, RAMÓN María CALDERÉ del Rey, José Miguel González Martín del Campo "MÍCHEL", Francisco José "LOBO" CARRASCO Hidalgo (YC3), Emilio BUTRAGUEÑO Santos (12' ELOY José Olaya Prendes (YC52), 78' Manuel SANCHÍS Hontiyuelo). (Coach: MIGUEL MUÑOZ Mozún (ESP)).
Goals: Austria: 1-1 Manfred Linzmaier (38'), 2-2 Toni Polster (63').
Spain: 0-1 ELOY José Olaya Prendes (30'), 1-2 ELOY José Olaya Prendes (57'), 2-3 Francisco José "LOBO" CARRASCO Hidalgo (89').
Referee: Bruno Galler (SUI)   Attendance: 31.342

29-04-1987   Qemel Stafa Stadium, Tirana: Albania – Austria 0-1 (0-1)
Albania: Perlat Musta (C), Skender Gega (YC76), Hysen Zmijani, Sulejman Demollari, Skender Hodja, Bardhyl Jera (YC3), Bedri Omuri, Mirel Josa, Shkelqim Muça (68' Sokol Kushta (RC83)), Arben Minga (C), Agim Bubeqi (61' Ledio Pano). (Coach: Agron Sulaj (ALB)).
Austria: Klaus Lindenberger, Bruno Pezzey (C), Karl Brauneder, Gerald Piesinger, Manfred Linzmaier, Manfred Zsak, Ernst Baumeister, Jürgen Werner (I) (YC67), Rudolf Weinhofer (YC41) (46' Robert Frind), Toni Polster (YC74), Andreas Ogris (78' Peter Pacult). (Coach: Branko Elsner (YUG)).
Goal: Austria: 0-1 Toni Polster (8').
Referee: Gerassimos Germanakos (GRE)   Attendance: 17.250

29-04-1987   Stadionul Steaua, Bucharest: Romania – Spain 3-1 (3-0)
Romania: Silviu Lung, Miodrag Belodedici, Nicolae Ungureanu, Stefan Iovan (70' Nicolae Negrila), Adrian Bumbescu (YC15), Michael Klein (88' Pelé Gavrila Balint), Gheorghe Hagi, László Bölöni (C) (YC73), Victor Piturca, Marius Lacatus, Dorin Mateut. (Coach: Emerich Alexandru Jenei (ROM)).
Spain: Andoni ZUBIZARRETA Urreta, JOSÉ Antonio CAMACHO Alfaro (C) (37' MIQUEL SOLER i Sararols), Genar ANDRINÚA Cortabarría, Manuel SANCHÍS Hontiyuelo, Andoni GOIKOETXEA Olaskoaga (20' JOAQUÍN Alonso González (YC61)), VÍCTOR MUÑOZ Manrique, Ricardo GALLEGO Redondo, RAMÓN María CALDERÉ del Rey (YC51), José Miguel González Martín del Campo "MÍCHEL", Emilio BUTRAGUEÑO Santos, ELOY José Olaya Prendes (YC71). (Coach: MIGUEL MUÑOZ Mozún (ESP)).
Goals: Romania: 1-0 Victor Piturca (38'), 2-0 Dorin Mateut (43'), 3-0 Nicolae Ungureanu (45').
Spain: 3-1 RAMÓN María CALDERÉ del Rey (81').
Referee: Alexis Ponnet (BEL)   Attendance: 30.000

14-10-1987　　Estadio Ramón Sánchez Pizjuán, Seville: Spain – Austria　2-0 (0-0)
Spain: Andoni ZUBIZARRETA Urreta, JULIO ALBERTO Moreno Casas, Rafael GORDILLO Vázquez (C), Miguel Porlan Noguera "CHENDO" (YC76), Genar ANDRINÚA Cortabarría, Manuel SANCHÍS Hontiyuelo, VÍCTOR MUÑOZ Manrique, Juan Antonio SEÑOR Gómez, José Miguel González Martín del Campo "MÍCHEL" (78' RAMÓN María CALDERÉ del Rey), Francisco José "LOBO" CARRASCO Hidalgo (71') JOSÉ María BAKERO Escudero, Emilio BUTRAGUEÑO Santos. (Coach: MIGUEL MUÑOZ Mozún (ESP)).
Austria: Klaus Lindenberger, Bruno Pezzey (C), Karl Brauneder, Gerald Messlender, Robert Frind (46' Robert Pecl (YC)), Manfred Zsak (YC9), Ernst Baumeister (65' Manfred Linzmaier), Gerald Willfurth, Reinhard Kienast, Toni Polster, Andreas Ogris. (Coach: Branko Elsner (YUG)).
Goals: Spain: 1-0 José Miguel González Martín del Campo "MÍCHEL" (58' penalty), 2-0 Manuel SANCHÍS Hontiyuelo (64').
Referee: Joël Quiniou (FRA)　　　　　　　　　　Attendance: 57.477

28-10-1987　　Stadiumi Flamurtari, Vlorë: Albania – Romania　0-1 (0-0)
Albania: Artur Shkëlqim Lekbello (II) (60' Sotir Shkurti), Robert Iljadhi, Rrapo Taho, Alfred Ferko, Hysen Zmijani, Sulejman Demollari (46' Alfred Zijai), Mirel Josa, Artur Kristol Lekbello (I), Latif Gjondeda, Shkelqim Muça (C), Agim Bubeqi. (Coach: Agron Sulaj (ALB)).
Romania: Silviu Lung, Miodrag Belodedici, Ioan Andone, Nicolae Ungureanu, Stefan Iovan, Michael Klein, Gheorghe Hagi (81' Mircea Rednic), László Bölöni (C), Marius Lacatus (83' Victor Piturca), Dorin Mateut, Doru Rodion Camataru. (Coach: Emerich Alexandru Jenei (ROM)).
Goal: Romania: 0-1 Michael Klein (58').
Referee: Ignatius W.M.van Swieten (HOL)　　　　Attendance: 8.480

18-11-1987　　Praterstadion, Vienna: Austria – Romania　0-0
Austria: Klaus Lindenberger, Robert Pecl, Bruno Pezzey (C), Karl Brauneder, Robert Frind, Peter Artner, Ernst Baumeister (78' Jürgen Werner (I)), Gerhard Rodax, Gerald Willfurth, Toni Polster, Walter Schachner (81' Andreas Ogris). (Coach: Branko Elsner (YUG)).
Romania: Silviu Lung, Miodrag Belodedici (YC88,RC88), Nicolae Ungureanu (YC87), Stefan Iovan, Adrian Bumbescu, Michael Klein, Gheorghe Hagi, László Bölöni (C), Marius Lacatus (YC31), Dorin Mateut (75' Tudorel Stoica), Doru Rodion Camataru (60' Victor Piturca). (Coach: Emerich Alexandru Jenei (ROM)).
Referee: Rosario Lo Bello (ITA)　　　　　　　　Attendance: 4.120

18-11-1987   Estadio Benito Villamarín, Seville: Spain – Albania   5-0 (3-0)
Spain: Andoni ZUBIZARRETA Urreta, JULIO ALBERTO Moreno Casas (60' Enrique Sánchez Flores "QUIQUE"), Miguel Porlan Noguera "CHENDO", Manuel SANCHÍS Hontiyuelo, Andoni GOIKOETXEA Olaskoaga (YC2), JOSÉ María BAKERO Escudero, VÍCTOR MUÑOZ Manrique (C), Juan Antonio SEÑOR Gómez, RAMÓN María CALDERÉ del Rey (46' Francisco "PACO" LLORENTE Gento), José Miguel González Martín del Campo "MÍCHEL", Emilio BUTRAGUEÑO Santos. (Coach: MIGUEL MUÑOZ Mozún (ESP)).
Albania: Artur Shkëlqim Lekbello (II), Adnan Oçelli (YC4), Robert Iljadhi, Rrapo Taho, Skender Gega, Sulejman Demollari, Artur Kristol Lekbello (I) (YC56) (82' Alfred Zijai), Mirel Josa, Latif Gjondeda (71' Alfred Ferko), Arben Minga (C), Agim Bubeqi. (Coach: Agron Sulaj (ALB)).
Goals: Spain: 1-0 JOSÉ María BAKERO Escudero (6'), 2-0 JOSÉ María BAKERO Escudero (31'), 3-0 José Miguel González Martín del Campo "MÍCHEL" (37' penalty), 4-0 Francisco "PACO" LLORENTE Gento (67'), 5-0 JOSÉ María BAKERO Escudero (74').
Referee: Kurt Röthlisberger (SUI)   Attendance: 45.299

GROUP 2

24-09-1986	Solna	Sweden – Switzerland	2-0 (1-0)
12-10-1986	Lisbon	Portugal – Sweden	1-1 (0-0)
29-10-1986	Bern	Switzerland – Portugal	1-1 (1-0)
15-11-1986	Milan	Italy – Switzerland	3-2 (1-1)
16-11-1986	Ta'Qali	Malta – Sweden	0-5 (0-1)
06-12-1986	Ta'Qali	Malta – Italy	0-2 (0-2)
24-01-1987	Bergamo	Italy – Malta	5-0 (5-0)
14-02-1987	Lisbon	Portugal – Italy	0-1 (0-1)
29-03-1987	Funchal	Portugal – Malta	2-2 (1-1)
15-04-1987	Neuchâtel	Switzerland – Malta	4-1 (3-0)
24-05-1987	Gothenburg	Sweden- Malta	1-0 (1-0)
03-06-1987	Solna	Sweden – Italy	1-0 (1-0)
17-06-1987	Lausanne	Switzerland – Sweden	1-1 (0-0)
23-09-1987	Solna	Sweden – Portugal	0-1 (0-1)
17-10-1987	Bern	Switzerland – Italy	0-0
11-11-1987	Porto	Portugal – Switzerland	0-0
14-11-1987	Naples	Italy – Sweden	2-1 (2-1)
15-11-1987	Ta'Qali	Malta – Switzerland	1-1 (0-1)
05-12-1987	Milan	Italy – Portugal	3-0 (1-0)
20-12-1987	Ta'Qali	Malta – Portugal	0-1 (0-0)

FINAL STANDING

Pos	Team	Pld	W	D	L	GF	GA	GD	Pts
1	*Italy*	8	6	1	1	16	4	+12	13
2	Sweden	8	4	2	2	12	5	+7	10
3	Portugal	8	2	4	2	6	8	-2	8
4	Switzerland	8	1	5	2	9	9	0	7
5	Malta	8	0	2	6	4	21	-17	2

Italy qualified for the final tournament in West Germany.

24-09-1986   Råsunda Stadion, Solna: Sweden – Switzerland   2-0 (1-0)
Sweden: Jan Möller, Roland Nilsson, Peter Larsson, Glenn Hysén, Stig Fredriksson (C), Glenn Strömberg, Robert Prytz, Ulf Eriksson, Björn Nilsson, Anders Palmér (82' Leif Engqvist), Johnny Ekström. (Coach: Olle Nordin (SWE)).
Switzerland: Martin Brunner, Alain Geiger, Andy Egli (C) (YC57), Charly In-Albon, Jürg Wittwer, Claude Ryf, Thomas Bickel (73' Georges Bregy), Heinz Hermann, Erni Maissen, Patrice Mottiez (56' Claudio Sulser), André Halter. (Coach: Daniel Jeandupeux (SUI)).
Goals: Sweden: 1-0 Johnny Ekström (20'), 2-0 Johnny Ekström (80').
Referee: Vojtech Christov (TCH)   Attendance: 27.751

12-10-1986   Estádio Nacional, Lisbon: Portugal – Sweden   1-1 (0-0)
Portugal: José Alberto Teixeira Ferreirinha "ZÉ BETO", ANTÓNIO Augusto da Silva VELOSO, EDUARDO LUÍS Marques Kruss Gomes, FERNANDO Manuel Antunes MENDES, Alberto Gomes JÚNIOR FONSECA, Eduardo José Gomes Camassele Mendes "DITO", ADELINO Carlos Morais NUNES, SHÉU Han (62' JOSÉ Da Silva COELHO), Carlos Manuel Pereira Pinto "ADÃO" (72' MÁRIO JORGE Da Silva Pinto Fernandes), JAIME Jerónimo Das MERCÊS, MANUEL José Tavares FERNANDES (C). (Coach: Rui Seabra (POR)).
Sweden: Jan Möller, Roland Nilsson, Peter Larsson, Glenn Hysén, Stig Fredriksson (C), Glenn Strömberg, Robert Prytz, Ulf Eriksson (80' Leif Engqvist), Björn Nilsson, Anders Palmér (75' Mats Magnusson), Johnny Ekström. (Coach: Olle Nordin (SWE)).
Goals: Portugal: 1-1 JOSÉ Da Silva COELHO (66').
Swedene: 0-1 Glenn Strömberg (52').
Referee: Keith Stuart Hackett (ENG)   Attendance: 19.775

29-10-1986   Wankdorfstadion, Bern: Switzerland – Portugal   1-1 (1-0)
Switzerland: Martin Brunner, Alain Geiger, Andy Egli (C), Claude Ryf, Stefan Marini, Martin Weber, Georges Bregy (YC7), Alain Sutter (77' Dominique Cina), Thomas Bickel (62' Erni Maissen), Heinz Hermann, Beat Sutter. (Coach: Daniel Jeandupeux (SUI)).
Portugal: José Alberto Teixeira Ferreirinha "ZÉ BETO", ANTÓNIO Augusto da Silva VELOSO, EDUARDO LUÍS Marques Kruss Gomes, FERNANDO Manuel Antunes MENDES, Alberto Gomes JÚNIOR FONSECA, Eduardo José Gomes Camassele Mendes "DITO", ADELINO Carlos Morais NUNES (31' MÁRIO JORGE Da Silva Pinto Fernandes), SHÉU Han (22' JOSÉ Da Silva COELHO), Carlos Manuel Pereira Pinto "ADÃO", JAIME Jerónimo Das MERCÊS, MANUEL José Tavares FERNANDES (C) (YC86). (Coach: Rui Seabra (POR)).
Goals: Switzerland: 1-0 Georges Bregy (6').
Portugal: 1-1 MANUEL José Tavares FERNANDES (85').
Referee: Siegfried Kirschen (GDR)   Attendance: 8.500

15-11-1986   Stadio Giuseppe Meazza, Milan: Italy – Switzerland   3-2 (1-1)
Italy: Walter Zenga, Franco Baresi, Giuseppe Bergomi, Antonio Cabrini (C) (10' Giovanni Francini), Dario Bonetti, Roberto Donadoni (41' Aldo Serena), Carlo Ancelotti, Salvatore Bagni (YC65), Giuseppe Dossena, Gianluca Vialli, Alessandro Altobelli. (Coach: Azeglio Vicini (ITA)).
Switzerland: Martin Brunner, Alain Geiger, Jürg Wittwer, Claude Ryf, Martin Weber, Urs Bamert (YC60) (78' Thomas Bickel), Georges Bregy (YC37), Heinz Hermann (C), Beat Sutter, Jean-Paul Brigger, André Halter (68' Dario Zuffi). (Coach: Daniel Jeandupeux (SUI)).
Goals: Italy: 1-0 Roberto Donadoni (1'), 2-1 Alessandro Altobelli (52'), 3-1 Alessandro Altobelli (85' penalty).
Switzerland: 1-1 Jean-Paul Brigger (31'), 3-2 Martin Weber (88').
Referee: Aron Schmidhuber (FRG)   Attendance: 67.422

16-11-1986   Ta'Qali National Stadium, Ta'Qali: Malta – Sweden   0-5 (0-1)
Malta: Raymond Mifsud, Joe Camilleri, Edwin Camilleri, Mario Schembri (70' Dennis Cauchi), Martin Scicluna, Raymond Vella, Kristian Laferla, John Holland (C) (YC29), John Joseph Aquilina (81' Alexander Azzopardi), Dennis Mizzi, Leonard Farrugia. (Coach: Guentcho Dobrev (BUL)).
Sweden: Jan Möller, Peter Larsson, Glenn Hysén, Stig Fredriksson (C), Magnus Andersson, Leif Engqvist, Robert Prytz, Ulf Eriksson, Björn Nilsson (81' Anders Palmér), Mats Magnusson, Johnny Ekström. (Coach: Olle Nordin (SWE)).
Goals: Sweden: 0-1 Glenn Hysén (38'), 0-2 Mats Magnusson (67'), 0-3 Stig Fredriksson (69'), 0-4 Johnny Ekström (82'), 0-5 Johnny Ekström (84').
Referee: Lajos Hartmann (HUN)   Attendance: 8.311

06-12-1986   Ta'Qali National Stadium, Ta'Qali: Malta – Italy   0-2 (0-2)
Malta: John Bonello, John Buttigieg, Martin Scicluna (YC75), William MacKay (33' Alexander Azzopardi), Carmel Busuttil, Raymond Vella, Kristian Laferla, Michael Degiorgio, John Holland (C), Leonard Farrugia, Martin Gregory (83' Carmel Scerri (II)). (Coach: Guentcho Dobrev (BUL)).
Italy: Walter Zenga, Franco Baresi, Giuseppe Bergomi, Riccardo Ferri, Sebastiano Nela, Roberto Donadoni, Giuseppe Giannini, Salvatore Bagni (67' Fernando De Napoli), Giuseppe Dossena (74' Gianfranco Matteoli), Gianluca Vialli, Alessandro Altobelli (C). (Coach: Azeglio Vicini (ITA)).
Goals: Italy: 0-1 Riccardo Ferri (12'), 0-2 Alessandro Altobelli (19').
Referee: Ihsan Türe (TUR)   Attendance: 13.191

24-01-1987   Stadio Atleti Azzurri d'Italia, Bergamo: Italy – Malta   5-0 (5-0)
Italy: Walter Zenga, Franco Baresi, Giuseppe Bergomi, Riccardo Ferri, Antonio Cabrini (C), Roberto Donadoni, Giuseppe Giannini, Salvatore Bagni (56' Fernando De Napoli), Giuseppe Dossena (56' Gianfranco Matteoli), Gianluca Vialli, Alessandro Altobelli (C). (Coach: Azeglio Vicini (ITA)).
Malta: John Bonello, Joseph Galea, John Buttigieg, Martin Scicluna, Carmel Busuttil, Raymond Vella, Kristian Laferla (YC88), Michael Degiorgio (YC14), John Holland (C), Leonard Farrugia (24' Carmel Scerri (II)), Martin Gregory (66' Dennis Cauchi). (Coach: Guentcho Dobrev (BUL)).
Goals: Italy: 1-0 Salvatore Bagni (4'), 2-0 Giuseppe Bergomi (9'), 3-0 Alessandro Altobelli (24'), 5-0 Alessandro Altobelli (35'), 5-0 Gianluca Vialli (45').
Referee: Stefanos Hadjistephanou (CYP)   Attendance: 32.370

14-02-1987   Estádio Nacional, Lisbon: Portugal – Italy   0-1 (0-1)
Portugal: António de JESUS Pereira, ÁLVARO Monteiro Magalhães, ANTÓNIO Augusto da Silva VELOSO, EDUARDO LUÍS Marques Kruss Gomes, Eduardo José Gomes Camassele Mendes "DITO", ANTÓNIO Manuel FRASCO Vieira, Carlos Manuel Pereira Pinto "ADÃO" (30' MÁRIO JORGE Da Silva Pinto Fernandes), JAIME Jerónimo Das MERCÊS, Rui António Da Cruz Ferreira "NASCIMENTO", Joaquim Carvalho de Azevedo "QUIM", MANUEL José Tavares FERNANDES (C) (55' JOSÉ Da Silva COELHO). (Coach: Rui Seabra (POR)).
Italy: Walter Zenga, Franco Baresi, Giuseppe Bergomi, Riccardo Ferri, Antonio Cabrini (C), Roberto Donadoni (82' Fernando De Napoli), Giuseppe Giannini, Salvatore Bagni (YC59), Giuseppe Dossena (76' Gianfranco Matteoli), Gianluca Vialli, Alessandro Altobelli. (Coach: Azeglio Vicini (ITA)).
Goal: Italy: 0-1 Alessandro Altobelli (40').
Referee: Michel Vautrot (FRA)   Attendance: 14.195

29-03-1987   Estádio dos Barreiros, Funchal: Portugal – Malta   2-2 (1-1)
Portugal: António de JESUS Pereira, ÁLVARO Monteiro Magalhães, ANTÓNIO Augusto da Silva VELOSO, EDUARDO LUÍS Marques Kruss Gomes, Eduardo José Gomes Camassele Mendes "DITO", ANTÓNIO Manuel FRASCO Vieira (46' RUI Gil Soares de BARROS), Carlos Manuel Pereira Pinto "ADÃO", JAIME Jerónimo Das MERCÊS, Rui António Da Cruz Ferreira "NASCIMENTO" (81' João Rafael Dos Santos "SKODA"), MANUEL José Tavares FERNANDES (C), JORGE Manuel PLÁCIDO Bravo da Costa. (Coach: Rui Seabra (POR)).
Malta: David Cluett, John Buttigieg, Alexander Azzopardi, Edwin Camilleri, Martin Scicluna, Carmel Scerri (II), Carmel Busuttil (87' Mario Schembri), Raymond Vella, Kristian Laferla, Michael Degiorgio (72' Martin Gregory), Dennis Mizzi. (Coach: Guentcho Dobrev (BUL)).
Goals: Portugal: 1-1 JORGE Manuel PLÁCIDO Bravo da Costa (11'), 2-2 JORGE Manuel PLÁCIDO Bravo da Costa (77').
Malta: 1-1 Dennis Mizzi (23'), 1-2 Carmel Busuttil (68').
Referee: John Kinsella (IRL)   Attendance: 5.000

15-04-1987   Stade de la Maladière, Neuchâtel: Switzerland – Malta   4-1 (3-0)
Switzerland: Martin Brunner, Alain Geiger, Andy Egli (YC43), Claude Ryf, Stefan Marini (81' Philippe Perret), Martin Weber (69' Thomas Bickel), Georges Bregy, Alain Sutter, Heinz Hermann (C), Jean-Paul Brigger, Dominique Cina (RC77). (Coach: Daniel Jeandupeux (SUI)).
Malta: David Cluett, John Buttigieg, Alexander Azzopardi, Edwin Camilleri (46' John Holland), Martin Scicluna, Carmel Scerri (II), Carmel Busuttil, Raymond Vella (C) (YC39), Kristian Laferla (88' Martin Gregory), Michael Degiorgio, Dennis Mizzi (YC87). (Coach: Guentcho Dobrev (BUL)).
Goals: Switzerland: 1-0 Andy Egli (6'), 2-0 Georges Bregy (16'), 3-0 Georges Bregy (38' penalty), 4-1 Georges Bregy (87' penalty).
Malta: 3-1 Carmel Busuttil (71').
Referee: Roger Philippi (LUX)   Attendance: 5.400

24-05-1987   Nya Ullevi, Gothenburg: Sweden – Malta 1-0 (1-0)
Sweden: Thomas Ravelli, Peter Larsson, Glenn Hysén, Stig Fredriksson, Andreas Ravelli, Anders Limpar, Glenn Strömberg, Robert Prytz, Ulf Eriksson (68' Stefan Pettersson), Mats Magnusson, Johnny Ekström (68' Lennart Nilsson). (Coach: Olle Nordin (SWE)).
Malta: David Cluett, John Buttigieg, Alexander Azzopardi, Edwin Camilleri (YC), Martin Scicluna (79' John Holland), Carmel Busuttil, Raymond Vella, Kristian Laferla, Michael Degiorgio (87' Charles Scerri), Dennis Mizzi, Martin Gregory. (Coach: Guentcho Dobrev (BUL)).
Goal: Sweden: 1-0 Johnny Ekström (13').
Referee: Kaj John Natri (FIN)   Attendance: 16.165

03-06-1987   Råsunda Stadion, Solna: Sweden – Italy 1-0 (1-0)
Sweden: Thomas Ravelli, Roland Nilsson, Peter Larsson, Glenn Hysén, Stig Fredriksson, Glenn Strömberg (88' Anders Limpar), Robert Prytz, Ulf Eriksson (80' Andreas Ravelli), Lennart Nilsson, Johnny Ekström, Hans Holmqvist. (Coach: Olle Nordin (SWE)).
Italy: Walter Zenga, Giuseppe Bergomi, Riccardo Ferri (YC71), Giovanni Francini, Roberto Tricella, Fernando De Napoli, Roberto Mancini (46' Luigi De Agostini (YC90)), Giuseppe Giannini, Giuseppe Dossena, Gianluca Vialli, Alessandro Altobelli. (Coach: Azeglio Vicini (ITA)).
Goal: Sweden: 1-0 Peter Larsson (25').
Referee: Dieter Pauly (FRG)   Attendance: 40.070

17-06-1987   Stade Olympique de la Pontaise, Lausanne: Switzerland – Sweden 1-1 (0-0)
Switzerland: Martin Brunner, Alain Geiger, Marcel Koller, Claude Ryf, Stefan Marini, Martin Weber, Georges Bregy (75' Urs Bamert), Heinz Hermann (C), Beat Sutter, Christophe Bonvin (78' Alain Sutter), André Halter (YC64). (Coach: Daniel Jeandupeux (SUI)).
Sweden: Thomas Ravelli, Roland Nilsson, Peter Larsson, Stig Fredriksson (C), Andreas Ravelli, Glenn Strömberg, Robert Prytz, Ulf Eriksson, Lennart Nilsson (78' Mats Magnusson), Johnny Ekström, Hans Holmqvist. (Coach: Olle Nordin (SWE)).
Goals: Switzerland: 1-0 André Halter (57').
Sweden: 1-1 Johnny Ekström (60').
Referee: Gerardus Johannes Maria (Gerard) Geurts (HOL)   Attendance: 7.000

23-09-1987   Råsunda Stadion, Solna: Sweden – Portugal 0-1 (0-1)
Sweden: Thomas Ravelli, Roland Nilsson, Peter Larsson, Glenn Hysén, Stig Fredriksson (C), Torbjörn Persson, Glenn Strömberg, Robert Prytz (74' Andreas Limpar), Björn Nilsson, Mats Magnusson (57' Lennart Nilsson), Johnny Ekström. (Coach: Olle Nordin (SWE)).
Portugal: António de JESUS Pereira, ÁLVARO Monteiro Magalhães, JOÃO Domingos da Silva PINTO, PEDRO Manuel Regareiro VENÂNCIO, MIGUEL Alberto Fernandes MARQUES, António dos Santos Ferreira ANDRÉ (YC60), ANTÓNIO Augusto Gomes de SOUSA, JAIME Fernandes MAGALHÃES, OCEANO Andrade da Cruz (YC18), FERNANDO Mendes Soares GOMES (C) (85' RUI Gil Soares de BARROS), PAULO Jorge FUTRE dos Santos. (Coach: Júlio Cernadas Pereira "JUCA" (POR)).
Goal: Portugal: 0-1 JOÃO Domingos da Silva PINTO (34').
Referee: Valeri Pavlovich Butenko (URS)   Attendance: 28.916

17-10-1987 Wankdorfstadion, Bern: Switzerland – Italy 0-0
Switzerland: Martin Brunner, Alain Geiger, Marcel Koller, Stefan Marini, Martin Weber (YC7), Thomas Bickel (57' Urs Bamert), Marco Schällibaum, Heinz Hermann (C), Beat Sutter, Christophe Bonvin (57' Hans-Peter Zwicker), Jean-Paul Brigger. (Coach: Daniel Jeandupeux (SUI)).
Italy: Walter Zenga, Franco Baresi, Riccardo Ferri, Antonio Cabrini (C), Ciro Ferrara (YC19), Roberto Donadoni, Fernando De Napoli, Giuseppe Giannini, Salvatore Bagni (79' Carlo Ancelotti), Gianluca Vialli (YC65), Alessandro Altobelli (83' Roberto Mancini). (Coach: Azeglio Vicini (ITA)).
Referee: Marcel Van Langenhove (BEL)   Attendance: 29.397

11-11-1987 Estádio das Antas, Porto: Portugal – Switzerland 0-0
Portugal: António de JESUS Pereira, ÁLVARO Monteiro Magalhães, FREDERICO Nobre Rosa, JOÃO Domingos da Silva PINTO (C), MIGUEL Alberto Fernandes MARQUES, António dos Santos Ferreira ANDRÉ, ANTÓNIO Augusto Gomes de SOUSA, ANTÓNIO Manuel FRASCO Vieira (46' CARLOS Alberto Bastos PARENTE), PAULO Jorge FUTRE dos Santos, José RUI Lopes ÁGUAS (74' Carlos Manuel Pereira Pinto "ADÃO"), JOSÉ Da Silva COELHO. (Coach: Júlio Cernadas Pereira "JUCA" (POR)).
Switzerland: Martin Brunner, Alain Geiger, Marcel Koller (81' Philippe Perret), Stefan Marini, Martin Weber, Thomas Bickel, Marco Schällibaum, Heinz Hermann (C), Beat Sutter, Christophe Bonvin, Jean-Paul Brigger (67' Hans-Peter Zwicker). (Coach: Daniel Jeandupeux (SUI)).
Referee: Lajos Németh (HUN)   Attendance: 3.632

14-11-1987 Stadio San Paolo, Naples: Italy – Sweden 2-1 (2-1)
Italy: Walter Zenga, Franco Baresi, Giuseppe Bergomi, Ciro Ferrara, Giovanni Francini (26' Luigi De Agostini), Roberto Donadoni, Fernando De Napoli, Giuseppe Giannini, Salvatore Bagni (89' Carlo Ancelotti), Gianluca Vialli, Alessandro Altobelli (YC55). (Coach: Azeglio Vicini (ITA)).
Sweden: Thomas Ravelli, Roland Nilsson, Peter Larsson, Glenn Hysén, Torbjörn Persson, Jonas Magnus Thern, Glenn Strömberg, Robert Prytz, Björn Nilsson (65' Andreas Limpar), Stefan Pettersson, Johnny Ekström (65' Dan Corneliusson). (Coach: Olle Nordin (SWE)).
Goals: Italy: 1-0 Gianluca Vialli (27'), 2-1 Gianluca Vialli (45'+2').
Sweden: 1-1 Peter Larsson (38').
Referee: Adolf Prokop (GDR)   Attendance: 59.046

15-11-1987 Ta'Qali National Stadium, Ta'Qali: Malta – Switzerland 1-1 (0-1)
Malta: David Cluett, David Carabott (78' Dennis Mizzi), John Buttigieg, Alexander Azzopardi, Edwin Camilleri, Martin Scicluna, Carmel Busuttil, Raymond Vella, Kristian Laferla, Michael Degiorgio, Martin Gregory (58' Carmel Scerri (II)). (Coach: Guentcho Dobrev (BUL)).
Switzerland: Martin Brunner, Alain Geiger, Marcel Koller, Stefan Marini, Martin Weber, Thomas Bickel, Marco Schällibaum, Heinz Hermann, Beat Sutter (75' Christophe Bonvin), Jean-Paul Brigger (87' Patrice Mottiez), Hans-Peter Zwicker (YC83). (Coach: Daniel Jeandupeux (SUI)).
Goals: Malta: 1-1 Carmel Busuttil (89').
Switzerland: 0-1 Hans-Peter Zwicker (2').
Referee: Georgios Koukoulakis (GRE)   Attendance: 7.112

05-12-1987   Stadio Giuseppe Meazza, Milan: Italy – Portugal   3-0 (1-0)
Italy: Walter Zenga, Franco Baresi, Giuseppe Bergomi, Riccardo Ferri, Giovanni Francini, Roberto Donadoni, Fernando De Napoli, Giuseppe Giannini, Salvatore Bagni (61' Luigi De Agostini), Gianluca Vialli, Alessandro Altobelli (C) (68' Roberto Mancini). (Coach: Azeglio Vicini (ITA)).
Portugal: António de JESUS Pereira (68' EDUARDO LÚCIO Esteves Pereira), FREDERICO Nobre Rosa (YC44), Eduardo José Gomes Camassele Mendes "DITO" (C), MIGUEL Alberto Fernandes MARQUES, João Ribeiro da Silva "COSTEADO", HERNÂNI Madruga NEVES, Carlos Manuel Pereira Pinto "ADÃO", Rui António Da Cruz Ferreira "NASCIMENTO" (54' CARLOS Alberto Bastos PARENTE), GILBERTO Dos Santos GOMES, ANTÓNIO José Pereira CARVALHO, JOSÉ Da Silva COELHO (YC12). (Coach: Júlio Cernadas Pereira "JUCA" (POR)).
Goals: Italy: 1-0 Gianluca Vialli (8'), 2-0 Giuseppe Giannini (87'), 3-0 De Agostini (89').
Referee: Johannes Nicolaus Ignacius (Jan) Keizer (HOL)   Attendance: 13.524

20-12-1987   Ta'Qali National Stadium, Ta'Qali: Malta – Portugal   0-1 (0-0)
Malta: David Cluett, David Carabott, John Buttigieg, Joe Camilleri, Alexander Azzopardi, Edwin Camilleri (YC45), Carmel Busuttil, Raymond Vella (C), Kristian Laferla, Dennis Mizzi (65' Michael Degiorgio), Martin Gregory. (Coach: Guentcho Dobrev (BUL)).
Portugal: António de JESUS Pereira, FREDERICO Nobre Rosa, FERNANDO Manuel Antunes MENDES (YC45), Eduardo José Gomes Camassele Mendes "DITO" (C), MIGUEL Alberto Fernandes MARQUES, João Ribeiro da Silva "COSTEADO", RUI Gil Soares de BARROS, Carlos Manuel Pereira Pinto "ADÃO", Rui António Da Cruz Ferreira "NASCIMENTO", GILBERTO Dos Santos GOMES (46' António Aires Dos Santos APARÍCIO), JOSÉ Da Silva COELHO (YC81) (83' ANTÓNIO José Pereira CARVALHO). (Coach: Júlio Cernadas Pereira "JUCA" (POR)).
Goal: Portugal: 0-1 FREDERICO Nobre Rosa (74').
Referee: Hubert Forstinger (AUT)   Attendance: 5.651

GROUP 3

10-09-1986	Reykjavik	Iceland – France	0-0
24-09-1986	Reykjavik	Iceland– Soviet Union	1-1 (1-1)
24-09-1986	Oslo	Norway – East Germany	0-0
11-10-1986	Paris	France – Soviet Union	0-2 (0-0)
29-10-1986	Karl-Marx-Stadt	East Germany – Iceland	2-0 (1-0)
29-10-1986	Simferopol	Soviet Union – Norway	4-0 (3-0)
19-11-1986	Leipzig	East Germany – France	0-0
29-04-1987	Kiev	Soviet Union – East Germany	2-0 (1-0)
29-04-1987	Paris	France – Iceland	2-0 (1-0)
03-06-1987	Oslo	Norway – Soviet Union	0-1 (0-1)
03-06-1987	Reykjavik	Iceland – East Germany	0-6 (0-2)
16-06-1987	Oslo	Norway – France	2-0 (1-0)
09-09-1987	Moscow	Soviet Union – France	1-1 (0-1)
09-09-1987	Reykjavik	Iceland – Norway	2-1 (1-1)
23-09-1987	Oslo	Norway – Iceland	0-2 (0-1)
10-10-1987	East Berlin	East Germany – Soviet Union	1-1 (1-0)
14-10-1987	Paris	France – Norway	1-1 (0-0)
28-10-1987	Magdeburg	East Germany – Norway	3-1 (2-1)
28-10-1987	Simferopol	Soviet Union – Iceland	2-0 (1-0)
18-11-1987	Paris	France – East Germany	0-1 (0-0)

FINAL STANDING

Pos	Team	Pld	W	D	L	GF	GA	GD	Pts
1	*Soviet Union*	8	5	3	0	14	3	+11	13
2	East Germany	8	4	3	1	13	4	+9	11
3	France	8	1	4	3	4	7	-3	6
4	Iceland	8	2	2	4	4	14	-10	6
5	Norway	8	1	2	5	5	12	-7	4

Soviet Union qualified for the final tournament in West Germany.

10-09-1986   Laugardalsvöllur, Reykjavik: Iceland – France   0-0
Iceland: Bjarni Sigurdsson, Sævar Jónsson, Gunnar Gíslason, Atli Edvaldsson (C), Ómar Torfason, Águst Mar Jónsson, Sigurdur Jónsson, Ásgeir Sigurvinsson, Arnor Gudjohnsen, Pétur Pétursson (YC53), Ragnar Margeirsson. (Coach: Sigdried (Siggi) Held (FRG)).
France: Joël Bats, Manuel Amoros (YC88), Patrick Battiston (C), William Ayache (YC55), Basile Boli, Jean Tigana, Bernard Genghini, Philippe Vercruysse (YC65), Luis Fernández, Yannick Stopyra, Stéphane Paille. (Coach: Henri Michel (FRA)).
Referee: Alan Ferguson (SCO)   Attendance: 13.758

24-09-1986   Laugardalsvöllur, Reykjavik: Iceland – Soviet Union   1-1 (1-1)
Iceland: Bjarni Sigurdsson, Sævar Jónsson, Gunnar Gíslason, Atli Edvaldsson (C), Ómar Torfason, Águst Mar Jónsson, Sigurdur Jónsson (YC35), Ásgeir Sigurvinsson, Arnor Gudjohnsen, Pétur Pétursson (YC89), Ragnar Margeirsson. (Coach: Sigdried (Siggi) Held (FRG)).
Soviet Union: Rinat Dasayev, Volodymyr Bezsonov (YC36), Vagiz Khidiyatullin (46' Sergei Rodionov), Oleg Kuznetsov, Anatoliy Demyanenko (C), Nikolai Larionov (80' Gennadiy Litovchenko), Tengiz Sulakvelidze, Vasiliy Rats (YC35), Sergei Aleinikov, Olexandr Zavarov, Oleh Blokhin. (Coach: Valeriy Vasylyovych Lobanovskyi (URS)).
Goals: Iceland: 1-0 Arnor Gudjohnsen (30').
Soviet Union: 1-1 Tengiz Sulakvelidze (44').
Referee: Karl-Josef Assenmacher (FRG)   Attendance: 6.368

24-09-1986   Ullevaal Stadion, Oslo: Norway – East Germany   0-0
Norway: Erik Thorstvedt, Terje Kojedal, Kai Erik Herlovsen, Anders Giske (75' Einar Jan Aas), Svein Fjælberg, Per-Edmund Mordt, Tom Sundby, Jan Berg, Kjetil Osvold, Arne Larsen Økland (C), Sten Glenn Håberg (71' Arve Seland). (Coach: Tor Roste Fossen (NOR)).
East Germany: René Müller (C), Ronald Kreer, Uwe Zötzsche, Frank Rohde, Carsten Sänger, Matthias Liebers, Jörg Stübner, Ulf Kirsten (YC46), Andreas Thom, Rainer Ernst, Frank Pastor. (Coach: Bernd Stange (GDR)).
Referee: Egbert Mulder (HOL)   Attendance: 10.142

11-10-1986   Parc des Princes, Paris: France – Soviet Union   0-2 (0-0)
France: Joël Bats, Manuel Amoros, William Ayache, Basile Boli (YC84) (87' Philippe Vercruysse), Philippe Jeannol, Jean Tigana, Jean-Marc Ferreri, Luis Fernández, Michel Platini (C), Jean-Pierre Papin (70' Bruno Bellone), Yannick Stopyra. (Coach: Henri Michel (FRA)).
Soviet Union: Rinat Dasayev, Volodymyr Bezsonov, Vagiz Khidiyatullin), Oleg Kuznetsov (YC45), Anatoliy Demyanenko (C), Alexandre Chivadze, Vasiliy Rats (YC38), Sergei Aleinikov, Olexandr Zavarov, Pavlo Yakovenko, Ihor Belanov, Sergei Rodionov (81' Oleh Blokhin). (Coach: Valeriy Vasylyovych Lobanovskyi (URS)).
Goals: Soviet Union: 0-1 Ihor Belanov (67'), 0-2 Vasiliy Rats (78').
Referee: Paolo Casarin (ITA)   Attendance: 40.496

29-10-1986   Stadion an der Gellerstraße, Karl-Marx-Stadt:
    East Germany – Iceland   2-0 (1-0)
East Germany: René Müller (C), Frank Rohde, Carsten Sänger (70' Dirk Stahmann), Detlef Schößler, Matthias Döschner, Matthias Liebers (YC64), Jörg Stübner, Ulf Kirsten, Andreas Thom, Rainer Ernst (85' Ralf Minge), Frank Pastor. (Coach: Bernd Stange (GDR)).
Iceland: Bjarni Sigurdsson, Sævar Jónsson (YC84), Gudni Bergsson (78' Gudmundur Torfason), Gunnar Gíslason, Atli Edvaldsson (C), Ómar Torfason, Águst Mar Jónsson (YC79), Pétur Ormslev (YC24), Sigurdur Jónsson, Arnor Gudjohnsen, Ragnar Margeirsson. (Coach: Sigdried (Siggi) Held (FRG)).
Goals: East Germany: 1-0 Andreas Thom (4'), 2-0 Ulf Kirsten (89').
Referee: Zoran Petrovic (YUG)   Attendance: 18.000

29-10-1986   Lokomotiv Stadium, Simferopol: Soviet Union – Norway   4-0 (3-0)
Soviet Union: Rinat Dasayev, Volodymyr Bezsonov, Vagiz Khidiyatullin, Oleg Kuznetsov, Anatoliy Demyanenko (C), Gennadiy Litovchenko (84' Sergei Baltacha), Olexandr Zavarov (20' Oleh Blokhin), Pavlo Yakovenko, Vadim Yevtushenko, Ihor Belanov, Sergei Rodionov. (Coach: Valeriy Vasylyovych Lobanovskyi (URS)).
Norway: Ola By Rise, Rune Bratseth, Einar Jan Aas, Kai Erik Herlovsen, Anders Giske, Per-Edmund Mordt (58' Sten Glenn Håberg), Vidar Davidsen, Tom Sundby, Jan Berg, Kjetil Osvold, Arne Larsen Økland (C) (82' Per Egil Ahlsen). (Coach: Tor Roste Fossen (NOR)).
Goals: Soviet Union: 1-0 Gennadiy Litovchenko (26'), 2-0 Ihor Belanov (28'), 3-0 Oleh Blokhin (33'), 4-0 Vagiz Khidiyatullin (54').
Referee: Howard William King (WAL)   Attendance: 26.314

19-11-1986   Zentralstadion, Leipzig: East Germany – France   0-0
East Germany: René Müller (C), Dirk Stahmann, Frank Rohde, Detlef Schößler, Matthias Döschner, Matthias Liebers, Jörg Stübner, Rico Steinmann (52' Hans Richter), Ulf Kirsten (77' Matthias Sammer), Andreas Thom, Frank Pastor. (Coach: Bernd Stange (GDR)).
France: Joël Bats, Manuel Amoros, Patrick Battiston, William Ayache, Yvon Le Roux, Basile Boli, Jean Tigana, Michel Platini (C), Fabrice Poullain, Jean-Pierre Papin (83' Bruno Bellone), Yannick Stopyra. (Coach: Henri Michel (FRA)).
Referee: George Courtney (ENG)   Attendance: 54.578

29-04-1987   Republican Stadium, Kiev: Soviet Union – East Germany   2-0 (1-0)
Soviet Union: Rinat Dasayev (C), Volodymyr Bezsonov, Vagiz Khidiyatullin, Oleg
Kuznetsov, Anatoliy Demyanenko, Vasiliy Rats, Sergei Aleinikov (86' Oleh Protasov),
Olexandr Zavarov, Oleksiy Mikhaylichenko (72' Pavlo Yakovenko), Ihor Belanov (YC65),
Sergei Rodionov. (Coach: Valeriy Vasylyovych Lobanovskyi (URS)).
East Germany: René Müller (C), Ronald Kreer, Uwe Zötzsche, Frank Rohde, Matthias
Lindner, Matthias Liebers, Jürgen Raab, Jörg Stübner (70' Markus Wuckel), Ulf Kirsten (55'
Heiko Scholz), Andreas Thom, Rainer Ernst. (Coach: Bernd Stange (GDR)).
Goals: Soviet Union: 1-0 Olexandr Zavarov (41'), 2-0 Ihor Belanov (49').
Referee: Erik Fredriksson (SWE)   Attendance: 76.405

29-04-1987   Parc des Princes, Paris: France – Iceland   2-0 (1-0)
France: Joël Bats, Manuel Amoros, Jean-François Domergue, Basile Boli, Jean Christophe
Thouvenel, Luis Fernández, Michel Platini (C), Gérald Passi, Yannick Stopyra (67' Jean-Pierre
Papin), Carmelo Micciche, José Touré. (Coach: Henri Michel (FRA)).
Iceland: Bjarni Sigurdsson, Sævar Jónsson, Gunnar Gíslason, Atli Edvaldsson (C), Ómar
Torfason, Águst Mar Jónsson, Sigurdur Jónsson, Ásgeir Sigurvinsson, Arnor Gudjohnsen,
Pétur Pétursson (69' Sigurdur Grétarsson), Ragnar Margeirsson. (Coach: Sigdried (Siggi) Held
(FRG)).
Goals: France: 1-0 Carmelo Micciche (38'), 2-0 Yannick Stopyra (65').
Referee: Frederick McKnight (NIR)   Attendance: 27.732

03-06-1987   Ullevaal Stadion, Oslo: Norway – Soviet Union   0-1 (0-1)
Norway: Erik Thorstvedt, Rune Bratseth (68' Hans Hermann Henriksen), Terje Kojedal, Kai
Erik Herlovsen, Anders Giske, Per-Edmund Mordt, Per Egil Ahlsen, Hallvar Thoresen (C),
Tom Sundby, Kjetil Osvold (46' Arve Seland), Jörn Andersen. (Coach: Tord Grip (SWE)).
Soviet Union: Rinat Dasayev (C), Vagiz Khidiyatullin, Oleg Kuznetsov, Tengiz Sulakvelidze,
Vasiliy Rats, Sergei Aleinikov, Olexandr Zavarov, Pavlo Yakovenko (68' Anatoliy
Demyanenko), Oleksiy Mikhaylichenko, Ihor Belanov (78' Oleh Protasov), Sergei Rodionov.
(Coach: Valeriy Vasylyovych Lobanovskyi (URS)).
Goal: Soviet Union: 0-1 Olexandr Zavarov (16').
Referee: Marcel Van Langenhove (BEL)   Attendance: 10.473

03-06-1987   Laugardalsvöllur, Reykjavik: Iceland – East Germany   0-6 (0-2)
Iceland: Bjarni Sigurdsson, Sævar Jónsson, Gunnar Gíslason, Atli Edvaldsson (C), Ómar
Torfason, Águst Mar Jónsson (YC82), Sigurdur Jónsson, Ásgeir Sigurvinsson (71' Larus
Gudmundsson), Arnor Gudjohnsen, Pétur Pétursson, Ragnar Margeirsson (77' Pétur
Arnthórsson). (Coach: Sigdried (Siggi) Held (FRG)).
East Germany: René Müller (C), Ronald Kreer, Frank Rohde, Matthias Döschner, Matthias
Lindner, Thomas Doll (77' Heiko Scholz), Jürgen Raab, Rico Steinmann, Andreas Thom,
Rainer Ernst, Ralf Minge (82' Ulf Kirsten). (Coach: Bernd Stange (GDR)).
Goals: East Germany: 0-1 Ralf Minge (15'), 0-2 Andreas Thom (37'), 0-3 Thomas Doll (49'),
0-4 Andreas Thom (67'), 0-5 Matthias Döschner (84'), 0-6 Andreas Thom (89').
Referee: Henning Lund-Sørensen (DEN)   Attendance: 8.758

16-06-1987   Ullevaal Stadion, Oslo: Norway – France   2-0 (0-0)
Norway: Erik Thorstvedt, Terje Kojedal, Anders Giske, Per-Edmund Mordt, Hans Hermann Henriksen, Per Egil Ahlsen, Hallvar Thoresen (C), Tom Sundby, Jan Berg, Jörn Andersen (89' Erik Solér), Arve Seland (63' Kjetil Osvold). (Coach: Tord Grip (SWE)).
France: Joël Bats, Manuel Amoros, Jean-François Domergue, Basile Boli, Jean Christophe Thouvenel, Jean Tigana (C), Jean-Marc Ferreri, Fabrice Poullain (81' Patrick Delamontagne), Gérald Passi, Yannick Stopyra, Carmelo Micciche (75' Philippe Fargeon). (Coach: Henri Michel (FRA)).
Goals: Norway: 1-0 Per-Edmund Mordt (72'), 2-0 Jörn Andersen (80').
Referee: Werner Föckler (FRG)   Attendance: 8.268

09-09-1987   Central Lenin Stadium, Moscow: Soviet Union – France   1-1 (0-1)
Soviet Union: Rinat Dasayev (C), Vagiz Khidiyatullin, Oleg Kuznetsov (YC77), Victor Lossev, Vasiliy Rats, Sergei Aleinikov, Gennadiy Litovchenko, Igor Dobrovolski (69' Oleksiy Mikhaylichenko), Pavlo Yakovenko (YC71), Vadim Tyshchenko (46' Ihor Belanov), Oleh Protasov. (Coach: Valeriy Vasylyovych Lobanovskyi (URS)).
France: Joël Bats, Manuel Amoros, William Ayache, Basile Boli, Rémy Vogel (YC22), Luis Fernández (C) (YC68), Fabrice Poullain, Gérald Passi, Yannick Stopyra, José Touré (74' Yvon Le Roux), Philippe Fargeon (87' Jean-Pierre Papin). (Coach: Henri Michel (FRA)).
Goals: Soviet Union: 1-1 Oleksiy Mikhaylichenko (77').
France: 0-1 José Touré (13').
Referee: Gerassimos Germanakos (GRE)   Attendance: 86.048

09-09-1987   Laugardalsvöllur, Reykjavik: Iceland – Norway   2-1 (1-1)
Iceland: Bjarni Sigurdsson, Sævar Jónsson, Gunnar Gíslason, Atli Edvaldsson (C), Vidar Thorkelsson, Olafur Thordarson, Pétur Ormslev, Gudmundur Torfason, Sigurdur Jónsson (YC37), Pétur Pétursson, Ragnar Margeirsson (78' Pétur Arnthórsson). (Coach: Sigdried (Siggi) Held (FRG)).
Norway: Erik Thorstvedt, Terje Kojedal, Kai Erik Herlovsen (C), Per-Edmund Mordt, Hans Hermann Henriksen, Vegard Skogheim (74' Arne Erlandsen), Erik Solér (77' Jan Kristian Fjærestad), Kjetil Osvold, Trond Sollied, Børre Meinseth, Jörn Andersen. (Coach: Tord Grip (SWE)).
Goals: Iceland: 1-1 Pétur Pétursson (21'), 2-1 Pétur Ormslev (59').
Norway: 0-1 Jörn Andersen (10').
Referee: Wilfred Wallace (IRL)   Attendance: 5.450

23-09-1987   Ullevaal Stadion, Oslo: Norway – Iceland   0-1 (0-1)
Norway: Erik Thorstvedt, Rune Bratseth, Kai Erik Herlovsen, Anders Giske (C), Per-Edmund Mordt, Hans Hermann Henriksen, Vegard Skogheim (46' Ulrich Møller), Erik Solér, Tom Sundby (77' Jan Berg), Kjetil Osvold, Jörn Andersen. (Coach: Tord Grip (SWE)).
Iceland: Bjarni Sigurdsson, Sævar Jónsson, Gudni Bergsson, Gunnar Gíslason, Atli Edvaldsson (C), Vidar Thorkelsson, Olafur Thordarson, Gudmundur Torfason, Pétur Arnthórsson (YC39,YC88), Ragnar Margeirsson, Larus Gudmundsson (86' Halldór Áskelsson). (Coach: Sigdried (Siggi) Held (FRG)).
Goal: Iceland: 0-1 Atli Edvaldsson (31').
Referee: Håkan Lundgren (SWE)   Attendance: 4.561

10-10-1987   Friedrich-Ludwig-Jahn-Sportpark, East Berlin:
East Germany – Soviet Union   1-1 (1-0)
East Germany: René Müller (C), Ronald Kreer, Hans-Uwe Pilz (75' Jörg Stübner), Uwe Zötzsche, Detlef Schößler, Matthias Döschner (YC80), Thomas Doll, Matthias Liebers, Jürgen Raab (84' Ralf Minge), Ulf Kirsten, Andreas Thom. (Coach: Bernd Stange (GDR)).
Soviet Union: Rinat Dasayev (C), Volodymyr Bezsonov, Vagiz Khidiyatullin (72' Vasiliy Rats (YC88)), Oleg Kuznetsov, Anatoliy Demyanenko, Sergei Aleinikov (YC7), Olexandr Zavarov (62' Gennadiy Litovchenko (YC78)), Igor Dobrovolski, Ivan Yaremchuk, Oleksiy Mikhaylichenko (YC55), Oleh Protasov. (Coach: Valeriy Vasylyovych Lobanovskyi (URS)).
Goals: East Germany: 1-1 Ulf Kirsten (44').
Soviet Union: 1-1 Sergei Aleinikov (80').
Referee: Dusan Krchnák (TCH)   Attendance: 18.894

14-10-1987   Parc des Princes, Paris: France – Norway   1-1 (0-0)
France: Bruno Martini, Manuel Amoros, Basile Boli, Luc Sonor, Didier Sènac, Luis Fernández (C), Dominique Bijotat, Eric Cantona, José Touré, Philippe Fargeon, Philippe Anziani (54' Jean-Marc Ferreri). (Coach: Henri Michel (FRA)).
Norway: Erik Thorstvedt, Rune Bratseth, Terje Kojedal, Kai Erik Herlovsen (74' Erik Solér), Anders Giske (C), Per-Edmund Mordt, Hans Hermann Henriksen, Tom Sundby, Jan Berg (78' Vegard Skogheim), Kjetil Osvold (YC40), Børre Meinseth. (Coach: Tord Grip (SWE)).
Goals: France: 1-0 Philippe Fargeon (55').
Norway: 1-1 Tom Sundby (80').
Referee: Joaquin Ramos Marcos (ESP)   Attendance: 11.308

28-10-1987   Ernst-Grube-Stadion, Magdeburg: East Germany – Norway   3-1 (2-1)
East Germany: René Müller (C), Ronald Kreer, Dirk Stahmann, Hans-Uwe Pilz, Detlef Schößler, Matthias Döschner, Thomas Doll, Matthias Liebers, Jürgen Raab, Ulf Kirsten, Andreas Thom. (Coach: Bernd Stange (GDR)).
Norway: Lars Gaute Bø, Rune Bratseth, Terje Kojedal, Anders Giske (C), Per-Edmund Mordt, Arne Erlandsen, Erik Solér (YC71), Tom Sundby, Børre Meinseth, Jan Kristian Fjærestad, Ulrich Möller (62' Jan Berg). (Coach: Tord Grip (SWE)).
Goals: East Germany: 1-0 Ulf Kirsten (14'), 2-1 Andreas Thom (33'), 3-1 Ulf Kirsten (54').
Norway: 1-1 Jan Kristian Fjærestad (32').
Referee: Friedrich Kaupe (AUT)   Attendance: 8.213

28-10-1987   Lokomotiv Stadium, Simferopol: Soviet Union – Iceland   2-0 (1-0)
Soviet Union: Rinat Dasayev (C), Volodymyr Bezsonov, Vagiz Khidiyatullin, Anatoliy Demyanenko, Alexandre Bubnov, Vasiliy Rats (83' Pavlo Yakovenko), Sergei Aleinikov, Gennadiy Litovchenko, Ivan Yaremchuk (65' Oleh Blokhin), Oleh Protasov, Ihor Belanov. (Coach: Valeriy Vasylyovych Lobanovskyi (URS)).
Iceland: Bjarni Sigurdsson, Sævar Jónsson, Gudni Bergsson, Gunnar Gíslason (83' Thorvaldur Örlygsson), Atli Edvaldsson (C), Ómar Torfason (65' Runar Kristinsson), Olafur Thordarson, Gudmundur Torfason, Ragnar Margeirsson, Larus Gudmundsson, Halldór Áskelsson. (Coach: Sigdried (Siggi) Held (FRG)).
Goals: Soviet Union: 1-0 Ihor Belanov (15'), 2-0 Oleh Protasov (52').
Referee: Michal Listkiewicz (POL)   Attendance: 22.136

18-11-1987   Parc des Princes, Paris: France – East Germany   0-1 (0-0)
France: Joël Bats, Manuel Amoros (C), Yvon Le Roux (YC57), Basile Boli (YC74), Sylvain Kastendeuch, Fabrice Poullain, Dominique Bijotat (76' Philippe Fargeon), Bruno Germain, Bruno Bellone, Eric Cantona, Bernard Zénier. (Coach: Henri Michel (FRA)).
East Germany: René Müller (C), Ronald Kreer, Dirk Stahmann (YC16), Hans-Uwe Pilz, Uwe Zötzsche, Matthias Döschner (YC71), Matthias Liebers, Rico Steinmann (YC86), Ulf Kirsten, Andreas Thom, Ralf Minge (63' Rainer Ernst). (Coach: Bernd Stange (GDR)).
Goal: East Germany: 0-1 Rainer Ernst (90').
Referee: Carlos Alberto da Silva Valente (POR)   Attendance: 16.581

GROUP 4

15-10-1986	London	England – Northern Ireland	3-0 (1-0)
29-10-1986	Split	Yugoslavia – Turkey	4-0 (2-0)
12-11-1986	Izmir	Turkey – Northern Ireland	0-0
12-11-1986	London	England – Yugoslavia	2-0 (1-0)
01-04-1987	Belfast	Northern Ireland – England	0-2 (0-2)
29-04-1987	Izmir	Turkey – England	0-0
29-04-1987	Belfast	Northern Ireland – Yugoslavia	1-2 (1-0)
14-10-1987	Sarajevo	Yugoslavia – Northern Ireland	3-0 (2-0)
14-10-1987	London	England – Turkey	8-0 (4-0)
11-11-1987	Belgrade	Yugoslavia – England	1-4 (0-4)
11-11-1987	Belfast	Northern Ireland – Turkey	1-0 (0-0)
16-12-1987	Izmir	Turkey – Yugoslavia	2-3 (0-2)

FINAL STANDING

Pos	Team	Pld	W	D	L	GF	GA	GD	Pts
1	England	6	5	1	0	19	1	+18	11
2	Yugoslavia	6	4	0	2	13	9	+4	8
3	Northern Ireland	6	1	1	4	2	10	-8	3
4	Turkey	6	0	2	4	2	16	-14	2

England qualified for the final tournament in West Germany.

15-10-1986   Wembley Stadium, London: England – Northern Ireland   3-0 (1-0)
England: Peter Shilton, Kenny Sansom, Viv Anderson, Dave Watson, Bryan Robson (C), Glenn Hoddle, Terry Butcher, Chris Waddle, Steve Hodge, Peter Beardsley (83' Tony Cottee), Gary Lineker. (Coach: Robert William (Bobby) Robson (ENG)).
Northern Ireland: Philip Hughes, Mal Donaghy, Alan McDonald, John McClelland (C), Nigel Worthington, Gary Fleming, David Campbell, Colin Clarke, Norman Whiteside (83' Sammy McIlroy), Steve Penney (75' James Quinn), Ian Stewart. (Coach: William Laurence (Billy) Bingham (NIR)).
Goals: England: 1-0 Gary Lineker (33'), 2-0 Chris Waddle (75'), 3-0 Gary Lineker (80').
Referee: Alphonse Costantin (BEL)   Attendance: 35.304

29-10-1986   Gradski stadion u Poljudu, Split: Yugoslavia – Turkey   4-0 (2-0)
Yugoslavia: Mauro Ravnic, Srecko Katanec, Mirsad Baljic, Refik Sabanadzovic, Marko Elsner, Zoran Vujovic, Marko Mlinaric, Milan Jankovic, Haris Skoro (53' Dejan Savicevic), Zlatko Vujovic, Radmilo Mihajlovic (78' Semir Tuce). (Coach: Ivan Osim (YUG)).
Turkey: Fatih Uraz, Erdogan Arica, Ismail Demiriz, Ismail Tavis, Savas Demiral, Ugur Tütüneker, Yusuf Altintas, Senol Çorlu, Tanju Çolak (74' Semih Yuvakuran), Metin Tekin, Erdal Keser (46' Hasan Vezir). (Coach: Coskun Özari (TUR)).
Goals: Yugoslavia: 1-0 Zlatko Vujovic (25'), 2-0 Zlatko Vujovic (33'), 3-0 Dejan Savicevic (73'), 4-0 Zlatko Vujovic (83').
Referee: Carlo Longhi (ITA)   Attendance: 11.270

12-11-1986   Alsancak Stadi, Izmir: Turkey – Northern Ireland   0-0
Turkey: Fatih Uraz, Ismail Demiriz, Ismail Tavis, Savas Demiral, Ugur Tütüneker, Yusuf Altintas (C), Ridvan Dilmen, Senol Çorlu, Kadir Akbulut, Tanju Çolak (10' Orhan Kapucu (YC32)), Metin Tekin. (Coach: Coskun Özari (TUR)).
Northern Ireland: Philip Hughes, Mal Donaghy, Alan McDonald, John McClelland (C), Nigel Worthington, David McCreery, David Campbell (72' Bernard McNally), Danny Wilson, Colin Clarke, Steve Penney, James Quinn (76' Lawrie Sanchez). (Coach: William Laurence (Billy) Bingham (NIR)).
Referee: Stefan Dan Petrescu (ROM)   Attendance: 21.919

12-11-1986   Wembley Stadium, London: England – Yugoslavia   2-0 (1-0)
England: Chris Woods, Kenny Sansom, Mark Wright (YC), Viv Anderson, Gary Mabbutt, Glenn Hoddle, Chris Waddle (80' Trevor Steven), Terry Butcher (C), Steve Hodge (83' Ray Wilkins), Peter Beardsley, Gary Lineker. (Coach: Robert William (Bobby) Robson (ENG)).
Yugoslavia: Mauro Ravnic, Faruk Hadzibegic, Srecko Katanec, Mirsad Baljic (73' Semir Tuce, 75' Predrag Juric), Refik Sabanadzovic, Marko Elsner, Zoran Vujovic, Blaz Sliskovic, Milan Jankovic, Haris Skoro, Zlatko Vujovic (C). (Coach: Ivan Osim (YUG)).
Goals: England: 1-0 Gary Mabbutt (21'), 2-0 Viv Anderson (56').
Referee: Franz Wöhrer (AUT)   Attendance: 60.000

01-04-1987   Windsor Park, Belfast: Northern Ireland – England   0-2 (0-2)
Northern Ireland: George Dunlop, Mal Donaghy, Alan McDonald, John McClelland (C), Nigel Worthington, Gary Fleming, Paul Ramsey, David McCreery, David Campbell (58' Danny Wilson), Norman Whiteside, Kevin Wilson. (Coach: William Laurence (Billy) Bingham (NIR)).
England: Peter Shilton (46' Chris Woods), Kenny Sansom, Mark Wright, Viv Anderson, Gary Mabbutt, Terry Butcher, Bryan Robson (C), Chris Waddle, Steve Hodge, Peter Beardsley, Gary Lineker. (Coach: Robert William (Bobby) Robson (ENG)).
Goals: England: 0-1 Steve Hodge (19'), 0-2 Chris Waddle (42').
Referee: Emilio Sorano Aladrén (ESP)   Attendance: 20.578

29-04-1987   Alsancak Stadi, Izmir: Turkey – England   0-0
Turkey: Fatih Uraz, Erhan Önal (C), Ismail Demiriz, Savas Demiral, Semih Yuvakuran, Ali Çoban (YC78), Ugur Tütüneker, Riza Çalimbay, Iskender Günen (80' Ilyas Tüfekçi), Erdal Keser, Hasan Vezir (88' Feyyaz Uçar). (Coach: Mustafa Denizli (TUR)).
England: Chris Woods, Tony Adams, Kenny Sansom, Viv Anderson, Gary Mabbutt, Bryan Robson (C), Glenn Hoddle, Chris Waddle, Steve Hodge (76' Mark Hateley (YC83)), Gary Lineker, Clive Allen (76' John Barnes). (Coach: Robert William (Bobby) Robson (ENG)).
Referee: Valeri Pavlovich Butenko (URS)   Attendance: 16.017

29-04-1987   Windsor Park, Belfast: Northern Ireland – Yugoslavia   1-2 (1-0)
Northern Ireland: George Dunlop, Mal Donaghy, Alan McDonald, John McClelland (C), Nigel Worthington (YC69), Gary Fleming, David McCreery (46' Paul Ramsey), David Campbell (75' Raymond McCoy), Colin Clarke, Norman Whiteside, Kevin Wilson. (Coach: William Laurence (Billy) Bingham (NIR)).
Yugoslavia: Tomislav Ivkovic, Faruk Hadzibegic (YC38), Srecko Katanec (46' Zoran Vulic), Mirsad Baljic, Marko Elsner, Zoran Vujovic, Aljosa Asanovic (80' Admir Smajic), Dragan Stojkovic (YC82), Milan Jankovic (YC70), Zlatko Vujovic (C) (YC61), Darko Pancev. (Coach: Ivan Osim (YUG)).
Goals: Northern Ireland: 1-0 Colin Clarke (40').
Yugoslavia: 1-1 Dragan Stojkovic (47'), 1-2 Zlatko Vujovic (80').
Referee: Werner Föckler (FRG)   Attendance: 5.482

14-10-1987   Grbavica Stadium, Sarajevo: Yugoslavia – Northern Ireland   3-0 (2-0)
Yugoslavia: Mauro Ravnic, Faruk Hadzibegic, Srecko Katanec, Mirsad Baljic, Ljubomir Radanovic, Zoran Vujovic, Mehmed Bazdarevic, Marko Mlinaric (76' Dragoljub Brnovic), Zlatko Vujovic (C), Borislav Cvetkovic, Fadilj Vokrri (76' Dejan Savicevic). (Coach: Ivan Osim (YUG)).
Northern Ireland: Allen McKnight, Mal Donaghy, Alan McDonald (YC49), Nigel Worthington, Paul Ramsey, David McCreery (C) (YC42), David Campbell (55' Anthony Rogan), Danny Wilson, Bernard McNally, Colin Clarke (48' James Quinn), Kevin Wilson. (Coach: William Laurence (Billy) Bingham (NIR)).
Goals: Yugoslavia: 1-0 Fadilj Vokrri (12'), 2-0 Fadilj Vokrri (34'), 3-0 Faruk Hadzibegic (74').
Referee: Klaus Peschel (GDR)   Attendance: 14.075

14-10-1987   Wembley Stadium, London: England – Turkey   8-0 (4-0)
England: Peter Shilton, Tony Adams, Kenny Sansom, Gary Stevens, Bryan Robson (C), John Barnes, Neil Webb, Trevor Steven (46' Glenn Hoddle), Terry Butcher, Peter Beardsley (71' Cyrille Regis), Gary Lineker. (Coach: Robert William (Bobby) Robson (ENG)).
Turkey: Fatih Uraz, Erhan Önal (C), Semih Yuvakuran, Ali Çoban, Ugur Tütüneker, Riza Çalimbay, Yusuf Altintas, Iskender Günen, Ali Kurtulus Gültiken (35' Savas Demiral), Erdal Keser, Kayhan Kaynak (46' Tanju Çolak). (Coach: Mustafa Denizli (TUR)).
Goals: England: 1-0 John Barnes (1'), 2-0 Gary Lineker (8'), 3-0 John Barnes (28'), 4-0 Gary Lineker (43'), 5-0 Bryan Robson (58'), 6-0 Peter Beardsley (61'), 7-0 Gary Lineker (71'), 8-0 Neil Webb (86').
Referee: Albert Rudolph (Bep) Thomas (HOL)   Attendance: 45.528

11-11-1987   Stadion Crvena Zvezda, Belgrade: Yugoslavia – England   1-4 (0-4)
Yugoslavia: Mauro Ravnic (46' Vladan Radaca), Faruk Hadzibegic, Srecko Katanec, Mirsad Baljic, Marko Elsner (26' Milan Jankovic), Zoran Vujovic, Dragan Stojkovic (YC75), Mehmed Bazdarevic, Marko Mlinaric, Zlatko Vujovic (C), Fadilj Vokrri. (Coach: Ivan Osim (YUG)).
England: Peter Shilton, Tony Adams, Kenny Sansom, Gary Stevens, Bryan Robson (C) (76' Peter Reid), John Barnes, Neil Webb (80' Glenn Hoddle), Trevor Steven, Terry Butcher, Peter Beardsley, Gary Lineker. (Coach: Robert William (Bobby) Robson (ENG)).
Goals: Yugoslavia: 1-4 Srecko Katanec (80').
England: 0-1 Peter Beardsley (3'), 0-2 John Barnes (17'), 0-3 Bryan Robson (20'), 0-4 Tony Adams (25').
Referee: Michel Vautrot (FRA)   Attendance: 49.744

11-11-1987   Windsor Park, Belfast: Northern Ireland – Turkey 1-0 (0-0)
Northern Ireland: Allen McKnight, Mal Donaghy, Alan McDonald, John McClelland (C), Nigel Worthington, Gary Fleming, Danny Wilson (66' David Campbell), Colin Clarke, Norman Whiteside, James Quinn (YC52), Kevin Wilson (66' Lee Doherty). (Coach: William Laurence (Billy) Bingham (NIR)).
Turkey: Okan Gedikali, Ismail Demiriz, Savas Demiral, Semih Yuvakuran (YC65), Gökhan Gedikali, Ugur Tütüneker, Riza Çalimbay, Yusuf Altintas (C), Tanju Çolak (79' Ali Kurtulus Gültiken), Metin Tekin (66' Hami Mandirali), Erdal Keser. (Coach: Mustafa Denizli (TUR)).
Goal: Northern Ireland: 1-0 James Quinn (47').
Referee: Peter Mikkelsen (DEN)   Attendance: 3.931

16-12-1987   Alsancak Stadi, Izmir: Turkey – Yugoslavia 2-3 (0-2)
Turkey: Okan Gedikali, Erhan Önal, Gökhan Gedikali, Ugur Tütüneker (46' Ali Kurtulus Gültiken), Riza Çalimbay, Yusuf Altintas (C), Ünal Karaman, Feyyaz Uçar, Iskender Günen, Tanju Çolak, Erdal Keser (39' Savas Demiral). (Coach: Mustafa Denizli (TUR)).
Yugoslavia: Vladan Radaca, Faruk Hadzibegic, Srecko Katanec (YC69), Ljubomir Radanovic, Admir Smajic (71' Cedomir Janevski), Miodrag Krivokapic, Dejan Savicevic, Dragoljub Brnovic (YC33), Mehmed Bazdarevic (C), Haris Skoro (77' Predrag Juric), Dragan Jakovljevic. (Coach: Ivan Osim (YUG)).
Goals: Turkey: 1-3 Yusuf Altintas (68'), 2-3 Feyyaz Uçar (71').
Yugoslavia: 0-1 Ljubomir Radanovic (6'), 0-2 Srecko Katanec (40'), 0-3 Faruk Hadzibegic (54' penalty).
Referee: Bruno Galler (SUI)   Attendance: 4.657

GROUP 5

15-10-1986	Poznan	Poland – Greece	2-1 (2-1)
15-10-1986	Budapest	Hungary – Netherlands	0-1 (0-0)
12-11-1986	Athens	Greece – Hungary	2-1 (1-0)
19-11-1986	Amsterdam	Netherlands – Poland	0-0
03-12-1986	Nicosia	Cyprus – Greece	2-4 (2-1)
21-12-1986	Limassol	Cyprus – Netherlands	0-2 (0-1)
14-01-1987	Athens	Greece – Cyprus	3-1 (0-0)
08-02-1987	Nicosia	Cyprus – Hungary	0-1 (0-0)
25-03-1987	Rotterdam	Netherlands – Greece	1-1 (0-1)
12-04-1987	Gdansk	Poland – Cyprus	0-0
29-04-1987	Athens	Greece – Poland	1-0 (0-0)
29-04-1987	Rotterdam	Netherlands – Hungary	2-0 (2-0)
17-05-1987	Budapest	Hungary – Poland	5-3 (1-1)
23-09-1987	Warsaw	Poland – Hungary	3-2 (1-1)
14-10-1987	Zabrze	Poland – Netherlands	0-2 (0-2)
14-10-1987	Budapest	Hungary – Greece	3-0 (3-0)
28-10-1987	*Rotterdam*	*Netherlands – Cyprus*	*8-0 (4-0)*
11-11-1987	Limassol	Cyprus – Poland	0-1 (0-0)
02-12-1987	Budapest	Hungary – Cyprus	1-0 (0-0)
09-12-1987	Amsterdam	Netherlands – Cyprus	4-0 (2-0)
16-12-1987	Rhodes	Greece – Netherlands	0-3 (0-1)

Netherlands vs Cyprus played on 28th October 1987 was marred by crowd violence and the result was annulled. The match was replayed behind closed doors on 9th December 1987.

FINAL STANDING

Pos	Team	Pld	W	D	L	GF	GA	GD	Pts
1	*Netherlands*	*8*	*6*	*2*	*0*	*15*	*1*	*+14*	*14*
2	Greece	8	4	1	3	12	13	-1	9
3	Hungary	8	4	0	4	13	11	+2	8
4	Poland	8	3	2	3	9	11	-2	8
5	Cyprus	8	0	1	7	3	16	-13	1

Netherlands qualified for the final tournament in West Germany.

15-10-1986   Stadion Miejski, Poznan: Poland – Greece   2-1 (2-1)
Poland: Jacek Kazimierski, Marek Ostrowski, Krzysztof Pawlak, Pawel Król, Waldemar Matysik, Jan Karás (YC78), Ryszard Tarasiewicz, Waldemar Prusik, Wlodimierz Smolarek (64' Krzysztof Baran), Dariusz Dziekanowski (46' Jan Urban), Marek Lesniak. (Coach: Wojciech Lazarek (POL)).
Greece: Antonios Minou, Stylianos Manolas (YC75), Georgios Skartados (82' Efstratios Apostolakis), Petros Xanthopoulos, Savas Haralampo Kofidis, Konstantinos Antoniou, Petros Michos, Konstantinos Mavridis (74' Konstantinos Batsinilas), Dimitrios Saravakos, Nikos Anastopoulos, Nikos Alavantas. (Coach: Miltos Papapostolou (GRE)).
Goals: Poland: 1-0 Dariusz Dziekanowski (4'), 2-1 Dariusz Dziekanowski (39').
Greece: 1-1 Nikos Anastopoulos (12').
Referee: Emilio Soriano Aladrén (ESP)   Attendance: 23.000

15-10-1986   Népstadion, Budapest: Hungary – Netherlands   0-1 (0-0)
Hungary: József Szendrei, Sándor Sallai, Antal Róth (46' József Keller), József Kardos, Attila Pintér (YC49), Tamás Preszeller, Imre Garaba (C), Lajos Détári, Márton Esterházy, Kálmán Kovács, Imre Boda (65' József Szekeres). (Coach: Imre Komora (HUN)).
Netherlands: Hans van Breukelen, Frank Rijkaard, Ronald Koeman, Adri van Tiggelen, Sonny Silooy, Ronald Spelbos (YC13), Jan Wouters, Ruud Gullit (C), Simon Tahamata (88' Wilbert Suvrijn), Marco van Basten, John van 't Schip (YC22). (Coach: Marinus Jacobus Hendricus (Rinus) Michels (HOL)).
Goal: Netherlands: 0-1 Marco van Basten (67').
Referee: Bruno Galler (SUI)   Attendance: 14.000

12-11-1986   Olympic Stadium, Athens: Greece – Hungary   2-1 (1-0)
Greece: Antonios Minou, Efstratios Apostolakis, Stylianos Manolas, Savas Haralampo Kofidis, Anastasios Mitropoulos (78' Petros Xanthopoulos), Konstantinos Antoniou, Petros Michos, Apostolakis Papaioanou (64' Georgios Skartados), Nikolaos Vamvakoulas, Dimitrios Saravakos, Nikos Anastopoulos (C). (Coach: Miltos Papapostolou (GRE)).
Hungary: József Szendrei, Sándor Sallai, Antal Róth, Antal Nagy (C), Gyula Csonka, Tamás Preszeller, Imre Garaba, Lajos Détári, Györö Burcsa (46' Imre Boda), Márton Esterházy, Ferenc Mészáros (69' Károly Csapó). (Coach: Imre Komora (HUN)).
Goals: Greece: 1-0 Anastasios Mitropoulos (38'), 2-0 Nikos Anastopoulos (65').
Hungary: 2-1 Imre Boda (73').
Referee: Velodi Miminoshvili (URS)   Attendance: 16.666

19-11-1986   Olympisch Stadion, Amsterdam: Netherlands – Poland   0-0
Netherlands: Hans van Breukelen, Frank Rijkaard, Ronald Koeman (46' John Bosman), Adri van Tiggelen, Sonny Silooy, Ronald Spelbos, Jan Wouters, Ruud Gullit (C), Simon Tahamata (72' René van der Gijp), Marco van Basten, John van 't Schip. (Coach: Marinus Jacobus Hendricus (Rinus) Michels (HOL)).
Poland: Jacek Kazimierski, Roman Wójcicki, Krzysztof Pawlak, Pawel Król (YC), Dariusz Wdowczyk, Jan Karás (C), Waldemar Prusik, Andrzej Rudy (46' Ryszard Tarasiewicz), Wlodimierz Smolarek, Zbigniew Boniek, Dariusz Dziekanowski (65' Jan Urban). (Coach: Wojciech Lazarek (POL)).
Referee: Joël Quiniou (FRA)   Attendance: 52.750

03-12-1986   Makario Stadium, Nicosia: Cyprus – Greece   2-4 (2-1)
Cyprus: Andreas Haritou, Costas Miamiliotis, Evagoras Christofi (YC), Nikos Pantziaras (C), Demetris Misos, Antonis "Antrellis" Elias (67' Stavros Papadopoulos), Yiannakis Yiangoudakis, Floros Nicolaou (78' Andreas Kantilos), Panayiotis Marangos, Georgios Savvides, Ioannis Ioannou. (Coach: Panikos Iacovou (CYP)).
Greece: Antonios Minou, Efstratios Apostolakis, Stylianos Manolas, Savas Haralampo Kofidis, Anastasios Mitropoulos (YC) (73' Athanasios Anastasiadis), Konstantinos Antoniou, Petros Michos, Apostolakis Papaioanou, Nikolaos Vamvakoulas, Dimitrios Saravakos (46' Konstantinos Batsinilas), Nikos Anastopoulos (C). (Coach: Miltos Papapostolou (GRE)).
Goals: Cyprus: 1-1 Evagoras Christofi (28'), 2-1 Georgios Savvides (41').
Greece: 0-1 Konstantinos Antoniou (14'), 2-2 Apostolakis Papaioanou (48'), 2-3 Konstantinos Batsinilas (73'), 2-4 Nikos Anastopoulos (85').
Referee: Velitchko Nikolov Tzontchev (BUL)   Attendance: 9.583

21-12-1986   Tsirion Stadium, Limassol: Cyprus – Netherlands   0-2 (0-1)
Cyprus: Andreas Haritou, Costas Miamiliotis, Avraam Socratous, Evagoras Christofi, Demetris Misos, Christakis Tsikkos, Yiannakis Yiangoudakis (C), Pavlos Savva, Panayiotis Marangos (81' Floros Nicolaou), Georgios Savvides, Ioannis Ioannou (46' Loizos Mavroudis). (Coach: Panikos Iacovou (CYP)).
Netherlands: Hans van Breukelen, Frank Rijkaard (64' Gerald Vanenburg), Adri van Tiggelen, Sonny Silooy, Ronald Spelbos, Jan Wouters, Ruud Gullit (C), Arnold Mühren, Simon Tahamata, John Bosman, René van der Gijp. (Coach: Marinus Jacobus Hendricus (Rinus) Michels (HOL)).
Goals: Netherlands: 0-1 Ruud Gullit (19'), 0-2 John Bosman (72').
Referee: Ioan Igna (ROM)   Attendance: 7.483

14-01-1987   Olympic Stadium, Athens: Greece – Cyprus   3-1 (0-0)
Greece: Theolokis Papadopoulos, Efstratios Apostolakis, Stylianos Manolas, Savas Haralampo Kofidis (46' Konstantinos Batsinilas), Konstantinos Antoniou, Petros Michos, Apostolakis Papaioanou (72' Anastasios Mitropoulos), Nikolaos Vamvakoulas, Andreas Bonovas, Dimitrios Saravakos, Nikos Anastopoulos (C). (Coach: Miltos Papapostolou (GRE)).
Cyprus: Andreas Haritou, Costas Miamiliotis, Charalambos Pittas, Evagoras Christofi, Nikos Pantziaras (C), Demetris Misos, Yiannakis Yiangoudakis, Pavlos Savva (YC76), Loizos Mavroudis (86' Christakis Georgiou), Panayiotis Marangos (83' Floros Nicolaou), Georgios Savvides. (Coach: Panikos Iacovou (CYP)).
Goals: Greece: 1-0 Nikos Anastopoulos (54'), 2-1 Andreas Bonovas (63'), 3-1 Nikos Anastopoulos (66').
Cyprus: 1-1 Pavlos Savva (60').
Referee: Helmut Kohl (AUT)   Attendance: 41.076

08-02-1987   Makario Stadium, Nicosia: Cyprus – Hungary   0-1 (0-0)
Cyprus: Andreas Haritou, Avraam Socratous, Charalambos Pittas, Evagoras Christofi (YC55), Demetris Misos, Yiannakis Yiangoudakis (C), Pavlos Savva, Panayiotis Marangos (75' Floros Nicolaou), Giorgos Lemesios, Georgios Savvides, Loizas Mavroudis (50' Panayiotis Xiourouppas). (Coach: Panikos Iacovou (CYP)).
Hungary: József Szendrei (C), Sándor Sallai, Antal Róth (YC53), József Kardos, Tamás Preszeller, Gábor Híres (YC78), György Bognár (80' Imre Garaba), Péter Hannich, István Varga, Kálmán Kovács, Imre Boda. (Coach: József Verebes (HUN)).
Goal: Hungary: 0-1 Imre Boda (49').
Referee: Dragisa Komadinic (YUG)   Attendance: 4.195

25-03-1987   Stadion Feijenoord, Rotterdam: Netherlands – Greece   1-1 (0-1)
Netherlands: Hans van Breukelen, Frank Rijkaard, Ronald Koeman (70' John Bosman), Sonny Silooy, Ronald Spelbos, Jan Wouters, Ruud Gullit (C), Arnold Mühren, Marco van Basten (YC), John van 't Schip, René van der Gijp (82' Aron Winter). (Coach: Marinus Jacobus Hendricus (Rinus) Michels (HOL)).
Greece: Theolokis Papadopoulos, Efstratios Apostolakis (70' Petros Xanthopoulos), Stylianos Manolas, Savas Haralampo Kofidis, Anastasios Mitropoulos (YC), Konstantinos Antoniou, Petros Michos, Nikolaos Vamvakoulas, Andreas Bonovas (82' Georgios Skartados), Dimitrios Saravakos, Nikos Anastopoulos (C). (Coach: Miltos Papapostolou (GRE)).
Goals: Netherlands: 1-1 Marco van Basten (56').
Greece: 0-1 Dimitrios Saravakos (5').
Referee: Carlo Longhi (ITA)   Attendance: 43.841

12-04-1987   Stadion Lechii, Gdansk: Poland – Cyprus   0-0
Poland: Jacek Kazimierski, Pawel Król, Dariusz Wdowczyk, Jan Karás (C), Waldemar Prusik, Jerzy Wijas, Wlodimierz Smolarek, Dariusz Dziekanowski (66' Leszek Iwanicki), Jan Furtok (46' Jacek Bayer), Jan Urban, Miroslaw Okonski. (Coach: Wojciech Lazarek (POL)).
Cyprus: Andreas Haritou, Costas Miamiliotis, Charalambos Pittas, Nikos Pantziaras (C) (YC44), Demetris Misos, Yiannakis Yiangoudakis, Pavlos Savva, Floros Nicolaou, Marios Tsingis (86' Kyriakos Pantziaras), Panayiotis Marangos, Georgios Savvides. (Coach: Panikos Iacovou (CYP)).
Referee: Simo Ruokonen (FIN)   Attendance: 23.500

29-04-1987   Olympic Stadium, Athens: Greece – Poland   1-0 (0-0)
Greece: Theolokis Papadopoulos, Stylianos Manolas, Georgios Skartados (73' Petros Xanthopoulos), Savas Haralampo Kofidis, Konstantinos Antoniou, Petros Michos, Nikolaos Vamvakoulas, Andreas Bonovas, Dimitrios Saravakos (88' Apostolakis Papaioanou), Nikos Anastopoulos (C), Nikos Alavantas. (Coach: Miltos Papapostolou (GRE)).
Poland: Jacek Kazimierski, Marek Ostrowski (59' Waldemar Prusik), Roman Wojcicki, Krzysztof Pawlak, Pawel Król, Dariusz Wdowczyk, Waldemar Matysik (C), Ryszard Tarasiewicz, Wlodimierz Smolarek, Dariusz Dziekanowski, Jan Furtok (67' Marek Lésniak). (Coach: Wojciech Lazarek (POL)).
Goal: Greece: 1-0 Dimitrios Saravakos (57').
Referee: Zoran Petrovic (YUG)   Attendance: 68.324

29-04-1987   Stadion Feijenoord, Rotterdam: Netherlands – Hungary   2-0 (2-0)
Netherlands: Joop Hiele, Frank Rijkaard, Ronald Koeman, Adri van Tiggelen, Sonny Silooy, Jan Wouters, Gerald Vanenburg, Ruud Gullit (C), Arnold Mühren, Marco van Basten, John van 't Schip (19' René van der Gijp). (Coach: Marinus Jacobus Hendricus (Rinus) Michels (HOL)).
Hungary: József Szendrei (C), Sándor Sallai (39' Tibor Végh), József Kardos, Zoltán Péter (69' Györö Burcsa), Tamás Preszeller, Gábor Híres, Imre Garaba, József Kiprich, Lajos Détári, Péter Hannich, Kálmán Kovács. (Coach: József Verebes (HUN)).
Goals: Netherlands: 1-0 Ruud Gullit (36'), 2-0 Arnold Mühren (39').
Referee: George Courtney (ENG)   Attendance: 53.035

17-05-1987   Népstadion, Budapest: Hungary – Poland   5-3 (1-1)
Hungary: József Gáspár, Zoltán Péter (65' Tamás Preszeller (YC79)), Gábor Híres, Tibor Farkas (YC33), Attila Szalai, Imre Garaba (C) (YC86), József Kiprich, Lajos Détári, József Szekeres, Sándor Rostás (46' Rezsö Kékesi (YC82)), István Vincze. (Coach: József Verebes (HUN)).
Poland: Józef Wandzik, Roman Wójcicki, Krzysztof Pawlak, Pawel Król, Dariusz Wdowczyk, Waldemar Matysik, Ryszard Tarasiewicz (46' Marek Lésniak), Waldemar Prusik, Wlodimierz Smolarek, Jan Urban (65' Kazimierz Przybys), Dariusz Marciniak (YC82). (Coach: Wojciech Lazarek (POL)).
Goals: Hungary: 1-1 István Vincze (38'), 2-2 Lajos Détári (62' penalty), 3-2 Zoltán Péter (65'), 4-2 Lajos Détári (75'), 5-3 Tamás Preszeller (88').
Poland: 0-1 Dariusz Marciniak (26'), 1-2 Wlodimierz Smolarek (58'), 4-3 Roman Wójcicki (80').
Referee: Adolf Prokop (GDR)   Attendance: 5.900

23-09-1987   Polish Army Stadium, Warsaw: Poland – Hungary   3-2 (1-1)
Poland: Józef Wandzik, Pawel Król, Jacek Grembocki, Jozef Dankowski (46' Jaroslaw Araszkiewicz), Andrzej Iwan, Ryszard Tarasiewicz, Waldemar Prusik, Wieslaw Cisek (YC63) (66' Czeslaw Jakolcewicz), Dariusz Dziekanowski, Jan Urban, Marek Lésniak. (Coach: Wojciech Lazarek (POL)).
Hungary: Péter Disztl, Sándor Sallai, Zoltán Péter (YC26), Ervin Kovács, Arpad Toma, Attila Herédi (YC23), Imre Garaba (C), Lajos Détári, György Bognár (81' József Fitos), József Szekeres (81' György Handel), Ferenc Mészáros. (Coach: József Garama (HUN)).
Goals: Poland: 1-0 Dariusz Dziekanowski (6'), 2-1 Ryszard Tarasiewicz (58'), 3-1 Marek Lésniak (62').
Hungary: 1-1 György Bognár (10'), 3-2 Ferenc Mészáros (64').
Referee: Ihsan Türe (TUR)   Attendance: 12.000

14-10-1987   Górnik Stadium, Zabrze: Poland – Netherlands   0-2 (0-2)
Poland: Marek Szczech, Kazimierz Przybys, Pawel Król, Marek Kostrzewa, Andrzej Iwan, Jan Karás (46' Czeslaw Jakolcewicz), Ryszard Tarasiewicz, Waldemar Prusik (C), Jaroslaw Araszkiewicz (67' Ryszard Robakiewicz), Dariusz Dziekanowski, Jan Urban. (Coach: Wojciech Lazarek (POL)).
Netherlands: Hans van Breukelen, Ronald Koeman, Berry van Aerle, Adri van Tiggelen, Sonny Silooy, Ronald Spelbos, Gerald Vanenburg, Ruud Gullit (C), Arnold Mühren, Marco van Basten (78' Aron Winter), John van 't Schip. (Coach: Marinus Jacobus Hendricus (Rinus) Michels (HOL)).
Goals: Netherlands: 0-1 Ruud Gullit (31'), 0-2 Ruud Gullit (39').
Referee: Robert Bonar (Bob) Valentine (SCO)   Attendance: 17.500

14-10-1987   Népstadion, Budapest: Hungary – Greece   3-0 (3-0)
Hungary: Péter Disztl, Sándor Sallai, Zoltán Péter, Arpad Toma, Attila Herédi (YC30), Imre Garaba, József Kiprich, Lajos Détári, György Bognár, Gyula Hajszán (80' Kálmán Kovács), Ferenc Mészáros. (Coach: József Garama (HUN)).
Greece: Theolokis Papadopoulos, Stylianos Manolas (YC37), Petros Xanthopoulos (80' Efstratios Apostolakis), Savas Haralampo Kofidis, Anastasios Mitropoulos (YC8,YC40), Konstantinos Antoniou (46' Konstantinos Mavridis), Petros Michos, Nikolaos Vamvakoulas, Andreas Bonovas, Dimitrios Saravakos, Nikos Anastopoulos. (Coach: Miltos Papapostolou (GRE)).
Goals: Hungary: 1-0 Lajos Détári (4'), 2-0 György Bognár (11'), 3-0 Ferenc Mészáros (15').
Referee: Dieter Pauly (FRG)   Attendance: 8.000

28-10-1987   Stadion Feijenoord, Rotterdam: Netherlands – Cyprus   8-0 (4-0)
Netherlands: Hans van Breukelen, Ronald Koeman, Berry van Aerle, Adri van Tiggelen, Sonny Silooy, Ronald Spelbos, Gerald Vanenburg, Ruud Gullit (C) (85' Hans Gillhaus), Arnold Mühren, John Bosman, John van 't Schip. (Coach: Marinus Jacobus Hendricus (Rinus) Michels (HOL)).
Cyprus: Andreas Haritou (4' Antonis Kleftis), Avraam Socratous, Costas Miamiliotis (72' Kyriakos Pantziaras), Charalambos Pittas, Evagoras Christofi, Demetris Misos, Yiannakis Yiangoudakis (C), Pavlos Savva, Christos Christoforou, Loizos Mavroudis, Georgios Savvides. (Coach: Panikos Iacovou (CYP)).
Goals: Netherlands: 1-0 John Bosman (1'), 2-0 Ruud Gullit (20'), 3-0 John Bosman (39'), 4-0 Ronald Spelbos (40'), 5-0 John van 't Schip (47'), 6-0 John Bosman (53'), 7-0 John Bosman (61'), 8-0 John Bosman (67').
Referee: Roger Philippi (LUX)   Attendance: 49.670
The match was marred by crowd violence and the result was annulled. The match was replayed behind closed doors on 9th December 1987.

11-11-1987   Tsirion Stadium, Limassol: Cyprus – Poland   0-1 (0-0)
Cyprus: Andreas Haritou, Costas Miamiliotis, Avraam Socratous, Charalambos Pittas, Christakis Christoforou, Yiannakis Yiangoudakis (C), Pavlos Savva, Floros Nicolaou (74' Marios Tsingis), Loizos Mavroudis, Panayiotis Xiourouppas (60' George Mavroudis), Georgios Savvides. (Coach: Takis Charalambous (CYP)).
Poland: József Wandzik, Pawel Król, Witold Wenclewski, Dariusz Wdowczyk, Ryszard Tarasiewicz, Waldemar Prusik (C), Jaroslaw Araszkiewicz (46' Robert Warzycha), Andrzej Rudy, Dariusz Dziekanowski, Jan Urban (58' Krzysztof Warzycha), Marek Lésniak. (Coach: Wojciech Lazarek (POL)).
Goal: Poland: 0-1 Marek Lésniak (74').
Referee: Dimitar Charlatchki (BUL)   Attendance: 2.497

02-12-1987   Népstadion, Budapest: Hungary – Cyprus   1-0 (0-0)
Hungary: Péter Disztl, Sándor Sallai (C) (YC90+3), Ervin Kovács (YC55), Arpad Toma, József Fitos, József Kiprich (YC87), Lajos Détári (75' István Vincze), György Bognár, József Keller, Kálmán Kovács, Ferenc Mészáros (46' Gyula Hajszán). (Coach: József Garama (HUN)).
Cyprus: George Pantziaras, Costas Miamiliotis (YC23), Avraam Socratous (YC40), Charalambos Pittas, Demetris Misos (YC71), Yiannakis Yiangoudakis (C), Pavlos Savva, Floros Nicolaou, Loizos Mavroudis (85' Christakis Christoforou), Marios Tsingis, Panayiotis Xiourouppas (69' George Mavroudis). (Coach: Takis Charalambous (CYP)).
Goal: Hungary: 1-0 József Kiprich (88').
Referee: Stefan Dan Petrescu (ROM)   Attendance: 2.300

09-12-1987   De Meer Stadium, Amsterdam: Netherlands – Cyprus   4-0 (2-0)
Netherlands: Hans van Breukelen, Ronald Koeman, Berry van Aerle, Adri van Tiggelen, Sonny Silooy, Aron Winter, Gerald Vanenburg, Ruud Gullit (C), Arnold Mühren, John van 't Schip, John Bosman (YC73). (Coach: Marinus Jacobus Hendricus (Rinus) Michels (HOL)).
Cyprus: George Pantziaras (YC63), George Christodoulou, Avraam Socratous, Charalambos Pittas, Demetris Misos, Antonis "Antrellis" Elias, Yiannakis Yiangoudakis (C) (58' Ara Petrosian), Pavlos Savva, Floros Nicolaou, Loizos Mavroudis (YC63), Marios Tsingis (88' George Savva). (Coach: Takis Charalambous (CYP)).
Goals: Netherlands: 1-0 John Bosman (34'), 2-0 John Bosman (43'), 3-0 Ronald Koeman (63'), 4-0 John Bosman (66').
Referee: Ivan Gregr (TCH)   Attendance: 300
This match was played behind closed doors.

16-12-1987   Diagoras Stadium, Rhodes: Greece – Netherlands   0-3 (0-1)
Greece: Christos Michail, Ioannis Kalitzakis (30' Theodoros Pachatouridis), Pavlos Papaioannou (13' Sotirios Mavrommatis), Iakovos Hatziathanassiou, Lyssandros Georgamlis, Georgios Mitsibonas (C), Pagonis Vakalopoulos, Evangelos Vlachos, Mihalis Ziogas, Athanasios Kanaras, Ioannis Samaras. (Coach: Miltos Papapostolou (GRE)).
Netherlands: Hans van Breukelen, Ronald Koeman (C), Berry van Aerle (63' John de Wolf), Adri van Tiggelen, Sjaak Troost (63' Hans Gillhaus), Joop Lankjaar, Aron Winter, Gerald Vanenburg, Hendrie Krüzen, John van 't Schip, John Bosman. (Coach: Marinus Jacobus Hendricus (Rinus) Michels (HOL)).
Goals: Netherlands: 0-1 Ronald Koeman (18'), 0-2 Joop Lankjaar (76'), 0-3 Hans Gillhaus (81').
Referee: Keith Stuart Hackett (ENG)   Attendance: 3.432

GROUP 6

10-09-1986	Helsinki	Finland – Wales	1-1 (1-0)
15-10-1986	Brno	Czechoslovakia – Finland	3-0 (2-0)
29-10-1986	Copenhagen	Denmark – Finland	1-0 (0-0)
12-11-1986	Bratislava	Czechoslovakia – Denmark	0-0
01-04-1987	Wrexham	Wales – Finland	4-0 (2-0)
29-04-1987	Helsinki	Finland – Denmark	0-1 (0-0)
29-04-1987	Wrexham	Wales – Czechoslovakia	1-1 (0-0)
03-06-1987	Copenhagen	Denmark – Czechoslovakia	1-1 (1-0)
09-09-1987	Helsinki	Finland – Czechoslovakia	3-0 (1-0)
09-09-1987	Cardiff	Wales – Denmark	1-0 (1-0)
14-10-1987	Copenhagen	Denmark – Wales	1-0 (0-0)
11-11-1987	Prague	Czechoslovakia – Wales	2-0 (1-0)

FINAL STANDING

Pos	Team	Pld	W	D	L	GF	GA	GD	Pts
1	*Denmark*	*6*	*3*	*2*	*1*	*4*	*2*	*+2*	*8*
2	Czechoslovakia	6	2	3	1	7	5	+2	7
3	Wales	6	2	2	2	7	5	+2	6
4	Finland	6	1	1	4	4	10	-6	3

Denmark qualified for the final tournament in West Germany.

10-09-1986   Olympic Stadium, Helsinki: Finland – Wales   1-1 (1-0)
Finland: Kari Laukkanen, Erkka Petäjä, Jari Europaeus, Esa Pekonen, Ari Hjelm, Kari Ukkonen, Jukka Ikäläinen (C), Markus Törnvall, Pasi Tauriainen, Mika Lipponen (76' Ari Valvee), Jari Rantanen. (Coach: Martti Kuusela (FIN)).
Wales: Martin Thomas, Clayton Blackmore (80' Steve Lowndes), Mark Aizlewood, Kevin Ratcliffe (C), Peter Nicholas, Robbie James, Kenny Jackett, David Williams (51' Neil Slatter), Ian Rush, Dean Saunders, Jeremy Charles. (Coach: Harold Michael (Mike) England (WAL)).
Goals: Finland: 1-0 Ari Hjelm (10').
Wales: 1-1 Neil Slatter (66').
Referee: Gerald Losert (AUT)   Attendance: 9.840

15-10-1986   Stadion Za Luzánkami, Brno: Czechoslovakia – Finland   3-0 (2-0)
Czechoslovakia: Ludek Miklosko, Frantisek Straka (YC87), Lubos Kubík (77' Jirí Ondra), Ján Fiala (C), Stanislav Levy (YC25), Ivan Hasek, Karel Kula (YC36), Tomás Skuhravy (81' Stanislav Griga), Ivo Knoflícek, Petr Janecka, Jozef Chovanec. (Coach: Josef Masopust (TCH)).
Finland: Kari Laukkanen, Erkka Petäjä, Jari Europaeus, Esa Pekonen, Ari Hjelm (3' Petri Juha Tiainen), Kari Ukkonen (YC66), Jukka Ikäläinen (C), Markus Törnvall, Pasi Tauriainen (33' Ari Valvee (RC39)), Mika Lipponen, Jari Rantanen (YC33). (Coach: Martti Kuusela (FIN)).
Goals: Czechoslovakia: 1-0 Petr Janecka (37'), 2-0 Ivo Knoflícek (43'), 3-0 Karel Kula (67').
Referee: Gerassimos Germanakos (GRE)   Attendance: 26.351

29-10-1986   Idrætsparken, Copenhagen: Denmark – Finland   1-0 (0-0)
Denmark: Troels Rasmussen, Søren Busk, John Sivebæk, Ivan Nielsen, Jens Jørn Bertelsen, Morten Olsen (C), Frank Arnesen (77' Henrik Andersen), Jan Mølby, Søren Lerby, John Eriksen, Claus Illemann Nielsen (80' Steen Thychosen). (Coach: Josef Emmanuel Hubertus Piontek (FRG)).
Finland: Kari Laukkanen, Erkka Petäjä, Jari Europaeus, Esa Pekonen (YC), Ari Hjelm, Kari Ukkonen (YC), Petri Juha Tiainen, Jukka Ikäläinen (C), Markus Törnvall (69' Pasi Tauriainen), Mika Lipponen (77' Ari Jalasvaara), Jari Rantanen. (Coach: Martti Kuusela (FIN)).
Goal: Denmark: 1-0 Jens Jørn Bertelsen (67').
Referee: Thomas Oliver Donnelly (NIR)   Attendance: 40.300

12-11-1986   Stadión Tehelné pole, Bratislava: Czechoslovakia – Denmark   0-0
Czechoslovakia: Ludek Miklosko, Frantisek Straka, Lubos Kubík (75' Jirí Ondra), Ján Fiala, Stanislav Levy (YC), Ivan Hasek, Karel Kula, Tomás Skuhravy (80' Stanislav Griga), Ivo Knoflícek, Petr Janecka, Jozef Chovanec. (Coach: Josef Masopust (TCH)).
Denmark: Troels Rasmussen, Søren Busk, Ivan Nielsen, Jens Jørn Bertelsen, Morten Olsen, Frank Arnesen, Jan Mølby (46' Henrik Andersen), Søren Lerby (YC), Michael Laudrup (88' Jesper Olsen), Klaus Berggreen (YC), Preben Elkjær Larsen. (Coach: Josef Emmanuel Hubertus Piontek (FRG)).
Referee: Alexis Ponnet (BEL)   Attendance: 47.042

01-04-1987   Racecourse Ground, Wrexham: Wales – Finland   4-0 (2-0)
Wales: Neville Southall, Clayton Blackmore, Kevin Ratcliffe (C), Pat van den Hauwe (13' Mark Aizlewood), Peter Nicholas, David Phillips, Glyn Hodges, Robbie James, Kenny Jackett, Ian Rush, Andy Jones. (Coach: Harold Michael (Mike) England (WAL)).
Finland: Kari Laukkanen, Erkka Petäjä, Jari Europaeus, Erik Holmgren, Hannu Turunen (70' Ismo Lius), Esa Pekonen, Ari Hjelm, Petri Juha Tiainen (62' Mika Lipponen), Jukka Ikäläinen (C), Pasi Tauriainen, Jari Rantanen. (Coach: Martti Kuusela (FIN)).
Goals: Wales: 1-0 Ian Rush (7'), 2-0 Glyn Hodges (28'), 3-0 David Phillips (63'), 4-0 Andy Jones (86').
Referee: Ignatius W.M.van Swieten (HOL)   Attendance: 7.696

29-04-1987   Olympic Stadium, Helsinki: Finland – Denmark   0-1 (0-0)
Finland: Kari Laukkanen, Erkka Petäjä, Jari Europaeus, Aki Lahtinen, Esa Pekonen, Kari Ukkonen, Petri Juha Tiainen (65' Ari Valvee), Jukka Ikäläinen (C), Mika Lipponen (65' Ari Hjelm), Jari Rantanen, Ismo Lius. (Coach: Martti Kuusela (FIN)).
Denmark: Troels Rasmussen, Jan Heintze, Søren Busk, Ivan Nielsen, Jens Jørn Bertelsen, Morten Olsen (C), Frank Arnesen, Jan Mølby (YC), Søren Lerby (41' Lars Lunde), Klaus Berggreen (77' John Sivebæk), John Eriksen. (Coach: Josef Emmanuel Hubertus Piontek (FRG)).
Goal: Denmark: 0-1 Jan Mølby (53').
Referee: Dimitar Dobromirov Dimitrov (BUL)   Attendance: 29.197

29-04-1987   Racecourse Ground, Wrexham: Wales – Czechoslovakia   1-1 (0-0)
Wales: Neville Southall, Clayton Blackmore, Kevin Ratcliffe (C), Neil Slatter, Pat van den Hauwe, Mark Hughes, Peter Nicholas, David Phillips, Glyn Hodges (78' Andy Jones), Robbie James, Ian Rush. (Coach: Harold Michael (Mike) England (WAL)).
Czechoslovakia: Ludek Miklosko, Frantisek Straka, Lubos Kubík (YC), Ján Fiala (C), Josef Novák, Ivan Hasek, Karel Kula, Tomás Skuhravy (82' Miroslav Kadlec), Ivo Knoflícek, Petr Janecka (87' Milan Luhovy), Jozef Chovanec. (Coach: Josef Masopust (TCH)).
Goals: Wales: 1-1 Ian Rush (82').
Czechoslovakia: 0-1 Ivo Knoflícek (74').
Referee: Krzysztof Czemarmazowicz (POL)   Attendance: 14.150

03-06-1987   Idrætsparken, Copenhagen: Denmark – Czechoslovakia   1-1 (1-0)
Denmark: Troels Rasmussen, Søren Busk, John Sivebæk, Ivan Nielsen, Jens Jørn Bertelsen, Morten Olsen (C), Frank Arnesen, Jan Mølby, Søren Lerby, Preben Elkjær Larsen (YC83) (86' John Eriksen), Flemming Povlsen (66' Jesper Olsen). (Coach: Josef Emmanuel Hubertus Piontek (FRG)).
Czechoslovakia: Ludek Miklosko, Frantisek Straka, Lubos Kubík, Ján Fiala (C), Josef Novák, Ivan Hasek, Karel Kula (81' Julius Bielik), Tomás Skuhravy (46' Karel Jarolím), Ivo Knoflícek, Petr Janecka, Jozef Chovanec. (Coach: Josef Masopust (TCH)).
Goals: Denmark: 1-0 Jan Mølby (16').
Czechoslovakia: 1-1 Ivan Hasek (48').
Referee: Claudio Pieri (ITA)   Attendance: 46.300

09-09-1987   Olympic Stadium, Helsinki: Finland – Czechoslovakia   3-0 (1-0)
Finland: Kari Laukkanen, Erkka Petäjä, Jari Europaeus, Erik Holmgren, Aki Lahtinen, Ari Hjelm, Petri Juha Tiainen, Pasi Rautiainen (63' Markku Kanerva), Jukka Ikäläinen (C), Jari Rantanen, Ismo Lius. (Coach: Jukka Keijo Olavi Vakkila (FIN)).
Czechoslovakia: Ludek Miklosko, Frantisek Straka, Lubos Kubík (63' Ivan Hasek), Ján Fiala, Josef Novák, Karel Jarolím, Karel Kula (75' Pavel Chaloupka), Tomás Skuhravy, Ivo Knoflícek, Petr Janecka, Jozef Chovanec (C). (Coach: Josef Masopust (TCH)).
Goals: Finland: 1-0 Ari Hjelm (29'), 2-0 Ismo Lius (71'), 3-0 Petri Juha Tiainen (82').
Referee: Neil Midgley (ENG)   Attendance: 6.430

09-09-1987   Ninian Park, Cardiff: Wales – Denmark   1-0 (1-0)
Wales: Neville Southall, Clayton Blackmore, Kevin Ratcliffe (C), Neil Slatter, Pat van den Hauwe, Mark Hughes, Peter Nicholas, David Phillips (YC51), Glyn Hodges (70' Mark Aizlewood), Robbie James (YC18) (88' Barry Horne), Andy Jones. (Coach: Harold Michael (Mike) England (WAL)).
Denmark: Troels Rasmussen, John Sivebæk, Ivan Nielsen, Jens Jørn Bertelsen, Morten Olsen (C), Kent Nielsen, Søren Lerby, Michael Laudrup (46' John Faxe Jensen), Klaus Berggreen, Preben Elkjær Larsen, Flemming Povlsen (65' Claus Illemann Nielsen). (Coach: Josef Emmanuel Hubertus Piontek (FRG)).
Goal: Wales: 1-0 Mark Hughes (19').
Referee: Siegfried Kirschen (GDR)   Attendance: 20.535

14-10-1987   Idrætsparken, Copenhagen: Denmark – Wales   1-0 (0-0)
Denmark: Troels Rasmussen, Jan Heintze (46' Flemming Povlsen), John Sivebæk, Ivan Nielsen, Morten Olsen (C), Søren Lerby, Jesper Olsen, Michael Laudrup (85' Lars Olsen), John Faxe Jensen, Per Frimann, Preben Elkjær Larsen. (Coach: Josef Emmanuel Hubertus Piontek (FRG)).
Wales: Eddie Niedzwiecki, Clayton Blackmore, Kevin Ratcliffe (C), Neil Slatter, Pat van den Hauwe, Mark Hughes (YC), Peter Nicholas, David Phillips, Robbie James (YC) (72' Andy Jones), Kenny Jackett (65' Glyn Hodges), Ian Rush. (Coach: Harold Michael (Mike) England (WAL)).
Goal: Denmark: 1-0 Preben Elkjær Larsen (50').
Referee: Ioan Igna (ROM)   Attendance: 44.500

11-11-1987   Letna Stadium, Prague: Czechoslovakia – Wales   2-0 (1-0)
Czechoslovakia: Ludek Miklosko, Miroslav Katlec, Frantisek Straka, Stanislav Levy, Josef Novák (YC45), Ivan Hasek, Lubomír Moravcik (70' Karel Kula), Michal Bílek, Tomás Skuhravy, Ivo Knoflícek, Jozef Chovanec. (Coach: Josef Masopust (TCH)).
Wales: Neville Southall, Clayton Blackmore (66' Glyn Hodges), Kevin Ratcliffe (C), Neil Slatter (46' Andy Jones), Pat van den Hauwe, Mark Hughes, Peter Nicholas, David Phillips, Geraint Williams, Kenny Jackett, Ian Rush. (Coach: Harold Michael (Mike) England (WAL)).
Goals: Czechoslovakia: 1-0 Ivo Knoflícek (32'), 2-0 Michal Bílek (89').
Referee: Erik Fredriksson (SWE)   Attendance: 6.443

GROUP 7

10-09-1986	Brussels	Belgium – Republic of Ireland	2-2 (1-1)
10-09-1986	Glasgow	Scotland – Bulgaria	0-0
14-10-1986	Luxembourg	Luxembourg – Belgium	0-6 (0-3)
15-10-1986	Dublin	Republic of Ireland – Scotland	0-0
12-11-1986	Glasgow	Scotland – Luxembourg	4-0 (2-0)
19-11-1986	Brussels	Belgium – Bulgaria	1-1 (0-0)
18-02-1987	Glasgow	Scotland – Republic of Ireland	0-1 (0-1)
01-04-1987	Sofia	Bulgaria – Republic of Ireland	2-1 (1-0)
01-04-1987	Anderlecht	Belgium – Scotland	4-1 (1-1)
29-04-1987	Dublin	Republic of Ireland – Belgium	0-0
30-04-1987	Luxembourg	Luxembourg – Bulgaria	1-4 (0-0)
20-05-1987	Sofia	Bulgaria – Luxembourg	3-0 (2-0)
28-05-1987	Luxembourg	Luxembourg – Republic of Ireland	0-2 (0-1)
09-09-1987	Dublin	Republic of Ireland – Luxembourg	2-1 (1-1)
23-09-1987	Sofia	Bulgaria – Belgium	2-0 (1-0)
14-10-1987	Dublin	Republic of Ireland – Bulgaria	2-0 (0-0)
14-10-1987	Glasgow	Scotland – Belgium	2-0 (1-0)
11-11-1987	Brussels	Belgium – Luxembourg	3-0 (1-0)
11-11-1987	Sofia	Bulgaria – Scotland	0-1 (0-0)
20-12-1987	Esch-sur-Alzette	Luxembourg – Scotland	0-0

FINAL STANDING

Pos	Team	Pld	W	D	L	GF	GA	GD	Pts
1	*Republic of Ireland*	8	4	3	1	10	5	+5	*11*
2	Bulgaria	8	4	2	2	12	6	+6	10
3	Belgium	8	3	3	2	16	8	+8	9
4	Scotland	8	3	3	2	7	5	+2	9
5	Luxembourg	8	0	1	7	2	23	-21	1

Republic of Ireland qualified for the final tournament in West Germany.

10-09-1986   Stade du Heysel, Brussels: Belgium – Republic of Ireland   2-2 (1-1)
Belgium: Jean-Marie Pfaff, Georges Grün, Lei Clijsters, Philippe Desmet, Patrick Vervoort, Stéphane Demol, Frank Vercauteren, Franky Van Der Elst, Enzo Scifo (YC43), Nico Claesen, Jan Ceulemans. (Coach: Guy Jean Léonard Thijs (BEL)).
Republic of Ireland: Pat Bonner, Paul McGrath, Kevin Moran, Chris Hughton (82' Jim Beglin), Mark Lawrenson, David Langan, Ray Houghton, Tony Galvin (YC38) (80' Ronnie Whelan), Liam Brady, John Aldridge, Frank Stapleton. (Coach: John (Jack) Charlton (ENG)).
Goals: Belgium: 1-0 Nico Claesen (14'), 2-1 Enzo Scifo (69').
Republic of Ireland: 1-1 Frank Stapleton (18'), 2-2 Liam Brady (90').
Referee: Ioan Igna (ROM)   Attendance: 22.212

10-09-1986   Hampden Park, Glasgow: Scotland – Bulgaria   0-0
Scotland: Jim Leighton, Richard Gough, Maurice Malpas, David Narey, Willie Miller (C), Roy Aitken, Paul McStay, Gordon Strachan, Davie Cooper, Charlie Nicholas (53' Kenny Dalglish), Mo Johnston. (Coach: Andrew (Andy) Roxburgh (ENG)).
Bulgaria: Borislav Mihaylov, Georgi Dimitrov (C), Petar Petrov, Nikolai Iliev, Plamen Nikolov (YC), Nasko Sirakov, Anio Sadakov, Hristo Kolev, Plamen Simeonov (78' Georgi Karushev), Ilia Voinov, Petar Alexandrov (88' Latchezar Tanev). (Coach: Hristo Stefanov Mladenov (BUL)).
Referee: Erik Fredriksson (SWE)   Attendance: 35.070

14-10-1986   Stade Municipal, Luxembourg: Luxembourg – Belgium   0-6 (0-3)
Luxembourg: John Van Rijswijck, Théo Malget, Marcel Bossi, Hubert Meunier (C), Laurent Schonckert, Jeff Saibene (73' Marc Thomé), Jean-Paul Girres, Carlo Weis, Jean-Pierre Barboni, Robert Langers, Jeannot Reiter (58' Théo Scholten). (Coach: Paul Philipp (LUX)).
Belgium: Jacques Munaron, Lei Clijsters, Eric Gerets, Philippe Desmet, Patrick Vervoort, Stéphane Demol (52' Georges Grün), Frank Vercauteren, Enzo Scifo (57' Léo Van Der Elst), Erwin Vandenbergh, Nico Claesen, Jan Ceulemans (C). (Coach: Guy Jean Léonard Thijs (BEL)).
Goals: Belgium: 0-1 Eric Gerets (6'), 0-2 Nico Claesen (9'), 0-3 Frank Vercauteren (41'), 0-4 Nico Claesen (54'), 0-5 Jan Ceulemans (87'), 0-6 Nico Claesen (89').
Referee: Krzysztof Czemarmazowicz (POL)   Attendance: 9.534

15-10-1986   Lansdowne Road, Dublin: Republic of Ireland – Scotland   0-0
Republic of Ireland: Pat Bonner, Paul McGrath, Micky McCarthy, Kevin Moran (72' Gerry Daly (YC)), David Langan, Jim Beglin, Ray Houghton, Kevin Sheedy, Liam Brady, John Aldridge, Frank Stapleton. (Coach: John (Jack) Charlton (ENG)).
Scotland: Jim Leighton, Richard Gough, Alan Hansen, David Narey, Ray Stewart, Roy Aitken, Paul McStay, Murdo MacLeod, Gordon Strachan, Graeme Sharp, Mo Johnston. (Coach: Andrew (Andy) Roxburgh (ENG)).
Referee: Einar Halle (NOR)   Attendance: 48.000

12-11-1986   Hampden Park, Glasgow: Scotland – Luxembourg   3-0 (2-0)
Scotland: Jim Leighton, Richard Gough, Alan Hansen (73' Paul McStay), Ray Stewart, Roy Aitken (C), Murdo MacLeod (65' Ally McCoist), Davie Cooper, Pat Nevin, Brian McClair, Kenny Dalglish, Mo Johnston. (Coach: Andrew (Andy) Roxburgh (ENG)).
Luxembourg: John Van Rijswijck, Théo Malget (80' Gérard Jeitz), Marcel Bossi, Hubert Meunier (C), Laurent Schonckert (YC), Gianni Di Pentima, Guy Hellers, Carlo Weis, Théo Scholten (89' Jeff Saibene), Jean-Pierre Barboni, Robert Langers. (Coach: Paul Philipp (LUX)).
Goals: Scotland: 1-0 Davie Cooper (24' penalty), 2-0 Davie Cooper (38'), 3-0 Mo Johnston (66').
Referee: Eysteinn Gudmunsson (ISL)   Attendance: 35.078

19-11-1986   Stade du Heysel, Brussels: Belgium – Bulgaria   1-1 (0-0)
Belgium: Jean-Marie Pfaff, Lei Clijsters (46' Michel Renquin), Eric Gerets, Philippe Desmet (56' Georges Grün), Patrick Vervoort, Stéphane Demol, Frank Vercauteren, Enzo Scifo, Pierre Janssen, Nico Claesen (YC44), Jan Ceulemans (C). (Coach: Guy Jean Léonard Thijs (BEL)).
Bulgaria: Borislav Mihaylov, Georgi Dimitrov (C), Petar Petrov, Nikolai Iliev, Plamen Nikolov, Nasko Sirakov, Anio Sadakov (YC42), Hristo Kolev, Plamen Simeonov, Bojidar Iskrenov (87' Ilia Voinov), Petar Alexandrov (57' Latchezar Tanev). (Coach: Hristo Stefanov Mladenov (BUL)).
Goals: Belgium: 1-0 Pierre Janssen (48').
Bulgaria: 1-1 Latchezar Tanev (62').
Referee: Victoriano Sánchez Arminio (ESP)   Attendance: 22.780

18-02-1987   Hampden Park, Glasgow: Scotland – Republic of Ireland   0-1 (0-1)
Scotland: Jim Leighton, Richard Gough, Maurice Malpas (68' Ally McCoist), Alan Hansen, Ray Stewart, Roy Aitken (C), Gordon Strachan, Davie Cooper (46' Paul McStay), Pat Nevin, Brian McClair, Mo Johnston. (Coach: Andrew (Andy) Roxburgh (ENG)).
Republic of Ireland: Pat Bonner, Paul McGrath, Micky McCarthy (YC26), Kevin Moran (YC14), Mark Lawrenson (YC38), Ray Houghton, Ronnie Whelan, Tony Galvin, Liam Brady (61' John Byrne), John Aldridge, Frank Stapleton (C). (Coach: John (Jack) Charlton (ENG)).
Goal: Republic of Ireland: 0-1 Mark Lawrenson (7').
Referee: Henrik Johan (Henk) van Ettekoven (HOL)   Attendance: 45.081

01-04-1987   Vasil Levski National Stadium, Sofia: Bulgaria – Republic of Ireland   2-1 (1-0)
Bulgaria: Borislav Mihaylov, Georgi Dimitrov (C), Nikolai Iliev, Plamen Nikolov, Krassimir Bezinski, Nasko Sirakov, Anio Sadakov, Hristo Kolev, Plamen Simeonov (65' Ilia Voinov (YC)), Bojidar Iskrenov (61' Petar Alexandrov), Latchezar Tanev, (Coach: Hristo Stefanov Mladenov (BUL)).
Republic of Ireland: Pat Bonner, Paul McGrath (YC), Micky McCarthy, Kevin Moran, Chris Hughton, John Anderson, Ronnie Whelan, Tony Galvin, Liam Brady (YC), John Aldridge (YC), Frank Stapleton (C) (87' Niall Quinn). (Coach: John (Jack) Charlton (ENG)).
Goals: Bulgaria: 1-0 Latchezar Tanev (41'), 2-1 Latchezar Tanev (82' penalty).
Republic of Ireland: 1-1 Frank Stapleton (53').
Referee: Carlos Alberto da Silva Valente (POR)   Attendance: 35.247

01-04-1987   Constant Vanden Stock Stadium, Anderlecht: Belgium – Scotland   4-1 (1-1)
Belgium: Jean-Marie Pfaff, Georges Grün, Lei Clijsters, Philippe Desmet (YC90), Patrick Vervoort, Stéphane Demol, Frank Vercauteren, Franky Van Der Elst (89' Guy Vandersmissen), Enzo Scifo (72' Léo Van Der Elst), Erwin Vandenbergh, Nico Claesen. (Coach: Guy Jean Léonard Thijs (BEL)).
Scotland: Jim Leighton, Richard Gough (YC), Maurice Malpas, David Narey, Alex McLeish, Roy Aitken, Paul McStay, Jim Bett (81' Pat Nevin), Jim McInally, Paul Sturrock, Ally McCoist. (Coach: Andrew (Andy) Roxburgh (ENG)).
Goals: Belgium: 1-0 Nico Claesen (10'), 2-1 Nico Claesen (55'), 3-1 Frank Vercauteren (75'), 4-1 Nico Claesen (86').
Scotland: 1-1 Paul McStay (14').
Referee: Michel Vautrot (FRA)   Attendance: 26.650

29-04-1987 Lansdowne Road, Dublin: Republic of Ireland – Belgium   0-0
Republic of Ireland: Pat Bonner, Paul McGrath, Micky McCarthy, Kevin Moran, John Anderson, Ray Houghton, Ronnie Whelan, Tony Galvin, Liam Brady (77' John Byrne), John Aldridge, Frank Stapleton (C). (Coach: John (Jack) Charlton (ENG)).
Belgium: Jean-Marie Pfaff, Georges Grün, Philippe Albert (66' Pierre Janssen), Lei Clijsters, Eric Gerets, Philippe Desmet, Patrick Vervoort, Frank Vercauteren (YC), Enzo Scifo, Nico Claesen, Jan Ceulemans (C). (Coach: Guy Jean Léonard Thijs (BEL)).
Referee: Heinz Holzmann (AUT)   Attendance: 44.629

30-04-1987   Stade Municipal, Luxembourg: Luxembourg – Bulgaria   1-4 (0-0)
Luxembourg: John Van Rijswijck, Théo Malget, Marcel Bossi, Gilbert Dresch (72' Gérard Jeitz), Laurent Schonckert, Guy Hellers, Jean-Paul Girres (86' Patrick Juchem), Carlo Weis (C), Jean-Pierre Barboni, Robert Langers, Jeannot Reiter. (Coach: Paul Philipp (LUX)).
Bulgaria: Borislav Mihaylov, Georgi Dimitrov (C), Petar Petrov, Nikolai Iliev, Plamen Nikolov, Nasko Sirakov, Anio Sadakov, Hristo Kolev, Plamen Simeonov (46' Petar Alexandrov), Bojidar Iskrenov (61' Georgi Iordanov), Latchezar Tanev. (Coach: Hristo Stefanov Mladenov (BUL)).
Goals: Luxembourg: 1-2 Robert Langers (59').
Bulgaria: 0-1 Anio Sadakov (49'), 0-2 Nasko Sirakov (55'), 1-3 Latchezar Tanev (62'), 1-4 Hristo Kolev (82').
Referee: Gudmundur Haraldsson (ISL)   Attendance: 1.920

20-05-1987   Vasil Levski National Stadium, Sofia: Bulgaria – Luxembourg   3-0 (2-0)
Bulgaria: Borislav Mihaylov, Georgi Dimitrov (C), Petar Petrov, Nikolai Iliev, Plamen Nikolov, Nasko Sirakov, Anio Sadakov (11' Ilia Voinov), Georgi Iordanov, Hristo Kolev, Luboslav Penev (63' Petar Alexandrov), Latchezar Tanev. (Coach: Hristo Stefanov Mladenov (BUL)).
Luxembourg: John Van Rijswijck, Théo Malget, Marcel Bossi, Hubert Meunier (C), Laurent Schonckert, Guy Hellers (YC), Jean-Paul Girres, Carlo Weis (YC), Jean-Pierre Barboni (71' Gérard Jeitz), Robert Langers, Jeannot Reiter (YC) (86' Marc Thomé). (Coach: Paul Philipp (LUX)).
Goals: Bulgaria: 1-0 Nasko Sirakov (32'), 2-0 Georgi Iordanov (39'), 3-0 Hristo Kolev (56').
Referee: Ion Craciunescu (ROM)   Attendance: 14.756

28-05-1987   Stade Municipal, Luxembourg: Luxembourg – Republic of Ireland   0-2 (0-1)
Luxembourg: John Van Rijswijck, Théo Malget, Marcel Bossi, Hubert Meunier (C), Laurent Schonckert, Guy Hellers, Jean-Paul Girres (82' Marc Thomé), Carlo Weis, Jean-Pierre Barboni, Robert Langers (69' Gérard Jeitz), Jeannot Reiter. (Coach: Paul Philipp (LUX)).
Republic of Ireland: Pat Bonner, Paul McGrath, Micky McCarthy, Kevin Moran (46' John Byrne), John Anderson (52' David Langan), Ray Houghton, Ronnie Whelan, Tony Galvin, Liam Brady, John Aldridge (YC), Frank Stapleton. (Coach: John (Jack) Charlton (ENG)).
Goals: Republic of Ireland: 0-1 Tony Galvin (44'), 0-2 Ronnie Whelan (63').
Referee: Renzo Peduzzi (SUI)   Attendance: 4.965

09-09-1987   Lansdowne Road, Dublin: Republic of Ireland – Luxembourg   2-1 (1-1)
Republic of Ireland: Gerry Peyton, Paul McGrath, Kevin Moran, Ashley Grimes, David Langan, Ray Houghton, Ronnie Whelan, Tony Galvin (56' Niall Quinn (YC)), Liam Brady, Frank Stapleton, John Byrne. (Coach: John (Jack) Charlton (ENG)).
Luxembourg: John Van Rijswijck, Théo Malget (YC), Marcel Bossi, Hubert Meunier, Laurent Schonckert, Guy Hellers (YC), Carlo Weis, Théo Scholten (65' Gilbert Dresch), Jean-Pierre Barboni (YC) (79' Gérard Jeitz), Robert Langers, Armin Krings. (Coach: Paul Philipp (LUX)).
Goals: Republic of Ireland: 1-1 Frank Stapleton (31'), 2-1 Paul McGrath (75').
Luxembourg: 0-1 Armin Krings (28').
Referee: Keith Cooper (WAL)   Attendance: 18.000

23-09-1987   Vasil Levski National Stadium, Sofia: Bulgaria – Belgium   2-0 (1-0)
Bulgaria: Borislav Mihaylov, Georgi Dimitrov (C), Petar Petrov, Nikolai Iliev (YC55), Plamen Nikolov, Nasko Sirakov, Anio Sadakov, Plamen Simeonov, Hristo Stoichkov (66' Georgi Iordanov), Bojidar Iskrenov (YC52) (81' Ilia Voinov), Latchezar Tanev. (Coach: Hristo Stefanov Mladenov (BUL)).
Belgium: Jean-Marie Pfaff (C), Georges Grün, Lei Clijsters (YC65), Eric Gerets, Michel Renquin (YC1), Philippe Desmet (YC60), Patrick Vervoort (YC10), Franky Van Der Elst (60' Daniel Veyt), Enzo Scifo (70' Guy Vandersmissen), Marc Degryse, Nico Claesen. (Coach: Guy Jean Léonard Thijs (BEL)).
Goals: Bulgaria: 1-0 Nasko Sirakov (19'), 2-0 Latchezar Tanev (70').
Referee: Karl-Heinz Tritschler (FRG)   Attendance: 51.000

14-10-1987   Lansdowne Road, Dublin: Republic of Ireland – Bulgaria   2-0 (0-0)
Republic of Ireland: Pat Bonner, Paul McGrath, Micky McCarthy, Kevin Moran, Mark Lawrenson, Ray Houghton, Ronnie Whelan, Tony Galvin (75' Niall Quinn), Liam Brady (RC84), John Aldridge (YC10) (75' John Byrne), Frank Stapleton. (Coach: John (Jack) Charlton (ENG)).
Bulgaria: Antonio Ananiev (54' Ilia Valov), Georgi Dimitrov, Petar Petrov, Nikolai Iliev, Plamen Nikolov (YC), Nasko Sirakov, Anio Sadakov, Plamen Simeonov, Ilia Voinov (64' Petar Alexandrov), Hristo Stoichkov, Bojidar Iskrenov. (Coach: Hristo Stefanov Mladenov (BUL)).
Goals: Republic of Ireland: 1-0 Paul McGrath (52'), 2-0 Kevin Moran (83').
Referee: Johannes Nicolaus Ignacius (Jan) Keizer (HOL)   Attendance: 22.000

14-10-1987   Hampden Park, Glasgow: Scotland – Belgium   2-0 (1-0)
Scotland: Jim Leighton, Maurice Malpas (54' Derek Whyte), Alex McLeish, Steve Clarke, Roy Aitken (C), Paul McStay, Gary Gillespie, Ian Durrant, Ian Wilson, Ally McCoist (YC20), Mo Johnston (72' Graeme Sharp). (Coach: Andrew (Andy) Roxburgh (ENG)).
Belgium: Michel Preud'homme, Georges Grün, Lei Clijsters, Eric Gerets, Patrick Vervoort, Frank Vercauteren, Franky Van Der Elst, Luc Beyens (YC50) (55' Philippe Desmet), Marc Degryse, Nico Claesen, Jan Ceulemans. (Coach: Guy Jean Léonard Thijs (BEL)).
Goals: Scotland: 1-0 Ally McCoist (13'), 2-0 Paul McStay (79').
Referee: Paolo Casarin (ITA)   Attendance: 16.052

11-11-1987 Stade du Heysel, Brussels: Belgium – Luxembourg 3-0 (1-0)
Belgium: Michel Preud'homme, Georges Grün, Lei Clijsters, Paul De Mesmaecker, Pascal Plovie (46' Frank Dekenne), Raymond Mommens, Luc Beyens (71' Peter Crève), Marc Degryse, Nico Claesen, Marc Van Der Linden, Jan Ceulemans (C). (Coach: Guy Jean Léonard Thijs (BEL)).
Luxembourg: John Van Rijswijck, Marcel Bossi, Pierre Petry, Laurent Schonckert (YC) (65' Hubert Meunier), Guy Hellers (YC), Carlo Weis (C), Gérard Jeitz (YC), Théo Scholten (46' Jean-Paul Girres), Jean-Pierre Barboni, Robert Langers, Jeannot Reiter. (Coach: Paul Philipp (LUX)).
Goals: Belgium: 1-0 Jan Ceulemans (18'), 2-0 Marc Degryse (55'), 3-0 Peter Crève (81').
Referee: Egil Nervik (NOR) Attendance: 2.504

11-11-1987 Vasil Levski National Stadium, Sofia: Bulgaria – Scotland 0-1 (0-0)
Bulgaria: Borislav Mihaylov, Petar Petrov, Nikolai Iliev, Plamen Nikolov (YC50), Krassimir Bezinksi, Nasko Sirakov (C), Anio Sadakov, Plamen Simeonov, Hristo Stoichkov, Bojidar Iskrenov, Petar Alexandrov (44' Ilia Voinov). (Coach: Hristo Stefanov Mladenov (BUL)).
Scotland: Jim Leighton, Maurice Malpas, Alex McLeish, Steve Nicol, Steve Clarke (YC51), Roy Aitken (C), Paul McStay (46' Gary MacKay), Gary Gillespie, Brian McClair, Ian Wilson, Graeme Sharp (79' Gordon Durie). (Coach: Andrew (Andy) Roxburgh (ENG)).
Goal: Scotland: 0-1 Gary MacKay (86').
Referee: Helmut Kohl (AUT) Attendance: 49.976

02-12-1987 Stade de la Frontière, Esch-sur-Alzette: Luxembourg – Scotland 0-0
Luxembourg: John Van Rijswijck, Marcel Bossi, Pierre Petry, Hubert Meunier (C), Jean-Paul Girres (87' Jeff Saibene), Carlo Weis, Gérard Jeitz, Théo Scholten, Jean-Pierre Barboni, Robert Langers, Jeannot Reiter (53' Armin Krings). (Coach: Paul Philipp (LUX)).
Scotland: Jim Leighton, Maurice Malpas, Willie Miller, Alex McLeish (C), Derek Whyte (62' Eric Black), Roy Aitken (YC80), Paul McStay, Pat Nevin (62' Gary MacKay), Ian Wilson, Graeme Sharp, Mo Johnston. (Coach: Andrew (Andy) Roxburgh (ENG)).
Referee: Manfred Neuner (FRG) Attendance: 1.999

FINAL TOURNAMENT IN WEST GERMANY

GROUP STAGE

West Germany automatically qualified as hosts.

GROUP 1

10-06-1988	Düsseldorf	West Germany – Italy	1-1 (0-0)
11-06-1988	Hanover	Denmark – Spain	2-3 (1-1)
14-06-1988	Gelsenkirchen	West Germany – Denmark	2-0 (1-0)
14-06-1988	Frankfurt	Italy – Spain	1-0 (0-0)
17-06-1988	Munich	West Germany – Spain	2-0 (1-0)
17-06-1988	Cologne	Italy – Denmark	2-0 (0-0)

FINAL STANDING

Pos	Team	Pld	W	D	L	GF	GA	GD	Pts
1	West Germany	3	2	1	0	5	1	+4	5
2	Italy	3	2	1	0	4	1	+3	5
3	Spain	3	1	0	2	3	5	-2	2
4	Denmark	3	0	0	3	2	7	-5	0

West Germany and Italy qualified for the Semi-Finals.

10-06-1988 Rheinstadion, Düsseldorf: West Germany – Italy 1-1 (0-0)
West Germany: Eike Immel, Andreas Brehme (76' Ulrich Borowka), Jürgen Kohler, Thomas Berthold, Olaf Thon, Guido Buchwald, Mathias Herget, Lothar Matthäus (C), Pierre Littbarski, Rudi Völler (81' Dieter Eckstein), Jürgen Klinsmann. (Coach: Franz Beckenbauer (FRG)).
Italy: Walter Zenga, Paolo Maldini (YC6), Franco Baresi, Giuseppe Bergomi (C), Riccardo Ferri, Roberto Donadoni, Carlo Ancelotti (YC57), Fernando De Napoli (86' Luigi De Agostini), Giuseppe Giannini, Roberto Mancini, Gianluca Vialli (89' Alessandro Altobelli). (Coach: Azeglio Vicini (ITA)).
Goals: West Germany: 1-1 Andreas Brehme (55').
Italy: 0-1 Roberto Mancini (52').
Referee: Keith Stuart Hackett (ENG) Attendance: 62.552

11-06-1988   Niedersachsenstadion, Hanover: Denmark – Spain   2-3 (1-1)
Denmark: Troels Rasmussen, Jan Heintze, Søren Busk, John Sivebæk, Ivan Nielsen, Morten Olsen (C) (74' Lars Olsen), Søren Lerby, Michael Laudrup, John Dulle Helt (46' John Faxe Jensen), Preben Elkjær Larsen, Flemming Povlsen. (Coach: Josef Emmanuel Hubertus Piontek (FRG)).
Spain: Andoni ZUBIZARRETA Urreta, Pedro TOMÁS REÑONES Crego (YC69), JOSÉ Antonio CAMACHO Alfaro (C) (YC45) (46' MIQUEL SOLER i Sararols), Rafael GORDILLO Vázquez (81' Rafael MARTÍN VÁZQUEZ), Genar ANDRINÚA Cortabarría, Manuel SANCHÍS Hontiyuelo, JOSÉ María BAKERO Escudero, VÍCTOR MUÑOZ Manrique (YC48), Ricardo GALLEGO Redondo, José Miguel González Martín del Campo "MÍCHEL", Emilio BUTRAGUEÑO Santos. (Coach: MIGUEL MUÑOZ Mozún (ESP)).
Goals: Denmark: 1-1 Michael Laudrup (24'), 2-3 Flemming Povlsen (82').
Spain: 0-1 José Miguel González Martín del Campo "MÍCHEL" (5'), 1-2 Emilio BUTRAGUEÑO Santos (53'), 1-3 Rafael GORDILLO Vázquez (66').
Referee: Albert Rudolph (Bep) Thomas (HOL)   Attendance: 55.707

14-06-1988   Parkstadion, Gelsenkirchen: West Germany – Denmark   2-0 (1-0)
West Germany: Eike Immel, Andreas Brehme, Jürgen Kohler, Olaf Thon, Guido Buchwald (33' Ulrich Borowka), Mathias Herget, Lothar Matthäus (C), Pierre Littbarski, Wolfgang Rolff (YC81), Rudi Völler (74' Frank Mill), Jürgen Klinsmann. (Coach: Franz Beckenbauer (FRG)).
Denmark: Peter Schmeichel, Jan Heintze, John Sivebæk, Ivan Nielsen, Morten Olsen (C), Lars Olsen, Søren Lerby, Michael Laudrup (62' John Eriksen), Kim Vilfort (73' Klaus Berggreen), Preben Elkjær Larsen (YC37), Flemming Povlsen (YC84). (Coach: Josef Emmanuel Hubertus Piontek (FRG)).
Goals: West Germany: 1-0 Jürgen Klinsmann (10'), 2-0 Olaf Thon (85').
Referee: Robert Bonar (Bob) Valentine (SCO)   Attendance: 64.812

14-06-1988   Waldstadion, Frankfurt: Italy – Spain   1-0 (0-0)
Italy: Walter Zenga, Paolo Maldini, Franco Baresi, Giuseppe Bergomi (C), Riccardo Ferri (YC34), Roberto Donadoni, Carlo Ancelotti, Fernando De Napoli, Giuseppe Giannini, Roberto Mancini (69' Alessandro Altobelli), Gianluca Vialli (88' Luigi De Agostini). (Coach: Azeglio Vicini (ITA)).
Spain: Andoni ZUBIZARRETA Urreta, Pedro TOMÁS REÑONES Crego, Rafael GORDILLO Vázquez (C), Genar ANDRINÚA Cortabarría, Manuel SANCHÍS Hontiyuelo, MIQUEL SOLER i Sararols, JOSÉ María BAKERO Escudero, VÍCTOR MUÑOZ Manrique, Ricardo GALLEGO Redondo (68' Rafael MARTÍN VÁZQUEZ), José Miguel González Martín del Campo "MÍCHEL" (73' Aitor BEGUIRISTÁIN Mújica), Emilio BUTRAGUEÑO Santos. (Coach: MIGUEL MUÑOZ Mozún (ESP)).
Goal: Italy: 1-0 Gianluca Vialli (73').
Referee: Erik Fredriksson (SWE)   Attendance: 47.506

17-06-1988   Olympiastadion, Munich: West Germany – Spain   2-0 (1-0)
West Germany: Eike Immel, Andreas Brehme, Jürgen Kohler, Olaf Thon (YC47), Mathias Herget (YC75), Ulrich Borowka, Lothar Matthäus (C), Pierre Littbarski (62' Wolfram Wuttke), Wolfgang Rolff, Rudi Völler, Jürgen Klinsmann (83' Frank Mill). (Coach: Franz Beckenbauer (FRG)).
Spain: Andoni ZUBIZARRETA Urreta, Pedro TOMÁS REÑONES Crego, JOSÉ Antonio CAMACHO Alfaro (C), Rafael GORDILLO Vázquez (C) (YC88), Genar ANDRINÚA Cortabarría, Manuel SANCHÍS Hontiyuelo (YC80), JOSÉ María BAKERO Escudero, VÍCTOR MUÑOZ Manrique, Rafael MARTÍN VÁZQUEZ (YC34), José Miguel González Martín del Campo "MÍCHEL", Emilio BUTRAGUEÑO Santos (51' JULIO SALINAS Fernández). (Coach: MIGUEL MUÑOZ Mozún (ESP)).
Goals: West Germany: 1-0 Rudi Völler (29'), 2-0 Rudi Völler (51').
Referee: Michel Vautrot (FRA)   Attendance: 63.802

17-06-1988   Müngersdorfer Stadion, Cologne: Italy – Denmark   2-0 (0-0)
Italy: Walter Zenga, Paolo Maldini, Franco Baresi, Giuseppe Bergomi (C), Riccardo Ferri, Roberto Donadoni (85' Luigi De Agostini), Carlo Ancelotti, Fernando De Napoli, Giuseppe Giannini, Roberto Mancini (66' Alessandro Altobelli), Gianluca Vialli. (Coach: Azeglio Vicini (ITA)).
Denmark: Peter Schmeichel, Jan Heintze, Ivan Nielsen, Morten Olsen (C) (67' Klaus Berggreen), Lars Olsen, Bjørn Kristensen (YC71), Michael Laudrup (YC22), John Faxe Jensen, Per Frimann (58' Kim Vilfort), John Eriksen, Flemming Povlsen. (Coach: Josef Emmanuel Hubertus Piontek (FRG)).
Goals: Italy: 1-0 Alessandro Altobelli (67'), 2-0 Luigi De Agostini (87').
Referee: Bruno Galler (SUI)   Attendance: 53.951

GROUP 2

12-06-1988	Stuttgart	England – Republic of Ireland	0-1 (0-1)
12-06-1988	Cologne	Netherlands – Soviet Union	0-1 (0-0)
15-06-1988	Düsseldorf	England – Netherlands	1-3 (0-1)
15-06-1988	Hanover	Republic of Ireland – Soviet Union	1-1 (1-0)
18-06-1988	Frankfurt	England – Soviet Union	1-3 (1-2)
18-06-1988	Gelsenkirchen	Republic of Ireland – Netherlands	0-1 (0-0)

FINAL STANDING

Pos	Team	Pld	W	D	L	GF	GA	GD	Pts
1	*Soviet Union*	3	2	1	0	5	2	+3	5
2	*Netherlands*	3	2	0	1	4	2	+2	4
3	Republic of Ireland	3	1	1	1	2	2	0	3
4	England	3	0	0	3	2	7	-5	0

Soviet Union and Netherlands qualified for the Semi-finals.

12-06-1988   Neckarstadion, Stuttgart: England – Republic of Ireland   0-1 (0-1)
England: Peter Shilton, Tony Adams, Kenny Sansom, Gary Stevens, Mark Wright, Bryan Robson (C), Chris Waddle, John Barnes, Neil Webb (60' Glenn Hoddle), Peter Beardsley (82' Mark Hateley), Gary Lineker. (Coach: Robert William (Bobby) Robson (ENG)).
Republic of Ireland: Pat Bonner, Paul McGrath, Chris Morris, Micky McCarthy, Kevin Moran, Chris Hughton, Ray Houghton, Ronnie Whelan, Tony Galvin (77' Kevin Sheedy), John Aldridge, Frank Stapleton (C) (62' Niall Quinn). (Coach: John (Jack) Charlton (ENG)).
Goal: Republic of Ireland: 0-1 Ray Houghton (6').
Referee: Siegfried Kirschen (GDR)   Attendance: 51.373

12-06-1988   Müngersdorfer Stadion, Cologne: Netherlands – Soviet Union   0-1 (0-0)
Netherlands: Hans van Breukelen, Frank Rijkaard, Ronald Koeman, Berry van Aerle, Adri van Tiggelen, Jan Wouters, Gerald Vanenburg (59' Marco van Basten), Ruud Gullit (C), Arnold Mühren, John van 't Schip, John Bosman. (Coach: Marinus Jacobus Hendricus (Rinus) Michels (HOL)).
Soviet Union: Rinat Dasayev (C), Volodymyr Bezsonov, Vagiz Khidiyatullin (YC40), Oleh Kuznetsov, Anatoliy Demyanenko, Vasiliy Rats, Gennadiy Litovchenko (YC21), Olexander Zavarov (90' Tengiz Sulakvelidze), Oleksiy Mikhaylichenko, Oleh Protasov, Ihor Belanov (82' Sergei Aleinikov). (Coach: Valeriy Vasylyovych Lobanovskyi (URS)).
Goal: Soviet Union: 0-1 Vasiliy Rats (52').
Referee: Dieter Pauly (FRG)   Attendance: 54.336

15-06-1988   Rheinstadion, Düsseldorf: England – Netherlands   1-3 (0-1)
England: Peter Shilton, Tony Adams, Kenny Sansom, Gary Stevens, Mark Wright, Bryan Robson (C), Glenn Hoddle, John Barnes, Trevor Steven (68' Chris Waddle), Peter Beardsley (72' Mark Hateley), Gary Lineker. (Coach: Robert William (Bobby) Robson (ENG)).
Netherlands: Hans van Breukelen, Frank Rijkaard, Ronald Koeman, Berry van Aerle, Adri van Tiggelen, Jan Wouters, Gerald Vanenburg (60' Wim Kieft), Erwin Koeman, Ruud Gullit (C), Arnold Mühren, Marco van Basten (87' Wilbert Suvrijn). (Coach: Marinus Jacobus Hendricus (Rinus) Michels (HOL)).
Goals: England: 1-1 Bryan Robson (53').
Netherlands: 0-1 Marco van Basten (44'), 1-2 Marco van Basten (71'), 1-3 Marco van Basten (75').
Referee: Paolo Casarin (ITA)   Attendance: 63.940

15-06-1988   Niedersachsenstadion, Hanover: Republic of Ireland – Soviet Union   1-1 (1-0)
Republic of Ireland: Pat Bonner, Chris Morris, Micky McCarthy, Kevin Moran, Chris Hughton, Ray Houghton, Kevin Sheedy, Ronnie Whelan, Tony Galvin, John Aldridge, Frank Stapleton (C) (80' Tony Cascarino). (Coach: John (Jack) Charlton (ENG)).
Soviet Union: Rinat Dasayev (68' Viktor Chanov), Vagiz Khidiyatullin, Oleh Kuznetsov, Anatoliy Demyanenko (C), Tengiz Sulakvelidze (46' Sergei Gotsmanov), Vasiliy Rats, Sergei Aleinikov, Olexander Zavarov, Oleksiy Mikhaylichenko, Oleh Protasov, Ihor Belanov. (Coach: Valeriy Vasylyovych Lobanovskyi (URS)).
Goals: Republic of Ireland: 1-0 Ronnie Whelan (38').
Soviet Union: 1-1 Oleh Protasov (74').
Referee: Emilio Soriano Aladrén (ESP)   Attendance: 38.308

18-06-1988   Waldstadion, Frankfurt: England – Soviet Union   1-3 (1-2)
England: Chris Woods, Tony Adams, Kenny Sansom, Gary Stevens, Dave Watson, Bryan Robson (C), Glenn Hoddle, John Barnes, Steve McMahon (54' Neil Webb), Trevor Steven, Gary Lineker (69' Mark Hateley). (Coach: Robert William (Bobby) Robson (ENG)).
Soviet Union: Rinat Dasayev (C), Volodymyr Bezsonov, Vagiz Khidiyatullin, Oleh Kuznetsov, Vasiliy Rats, Sergei Aleinikov, Gennadiy Litovchenko, Olexander Zavarov (85' Sergei Gotsmanov), Oleksiy Mikhaylichenko, Oleh Protasov (YC42), Ihor Belanov (44' Viktor Pasulko). (Coach: Valeriy Vasylyovych Lobanovskyi (URS)).
Goals: England: 1-1 Tony Adams (16').
Soviet Union: 0-1 Sergei Aleinikov (3'), 1-2 Oleksiy Mikhaylichenko (28'), 1-3 Viktor Pasulko (73').
Referee: José Rosa dos Santos (POR)   Attendance: 48.335

18-06-1988   Parkstadion, Gelsenkirchen: Republic of Ireland – Netherlands   0-1 (0-0)
Republic of Ireland: Pat Bonner, Pat McGrath, Chris Morris (46' Kevin Sheedy), Micky McCarthy, Kevin Moran, Chris Hughton, Ray Houghton, Ronnie Whelan, Tony Galvin, John Aldridge, Frank Stapleton (C) (83' Tony Cascarino). (Coach: John (Jack) Charlton (ENG)).
Netherlands: Hans van Breukelen, Frank Rijkaard, Ronald Koeman, Berry van Aerle, Adri van Tiggelen, Jan Wouters (YC60), Gerald Vanenburg, Erwin Koeman (51' Wim Kieft), Ruud Gullit (C), Arnold Mühren (79' John Bosman), Marco van Basten. (Coach: Marinus Jacobus Hendricus (Rinus) Michels (HOL)).
Goal: Netherlands: 0-1 Wim Kieft (82').
Referee: Horst Brummeier (AUT)   Attendance: 64.731

SEMI-FINALS

21-06-1988   Volksparkstadion, Hamburg: West Germany – Netherlands   1-2 (0-0)
West Germany: Eike Immel, Andreas Brehme, Jürgen Kohler, Olaf Thon, Mathias Herget (44' Hans Pflügler), Ulrich Borowka, Lothar Matthäus (C), Wolfgang Rolff, Rudi Völler, Jürgen Klinsmann, Frank Mill (79' Pierre Littbarski). (Coach: Franz Beckenbauer (FRG)).
Netherlands: Hans van Breukelen (YC60), Frank Rijkaard, Ronald Koeman, Berry van Aerle, Adri van Tiggelen, Jan Wouters, Gerald Vanenburg, Ruud Gullit (C), Erwin Koeman (89' Wilbert Suvrijn), Arnold Mühren (58' Wim Kieft), Marco van Basten. (Coach: Marinus Jacobus Hendricus (Rinus) Michels (HOL)).
Goals: West Germany: 1-0 Lothar Matthäus (55' penalty).
Netherlands: 1-1 Ronald Koeman (74' penalty), 1-2 Marco van Basten (88').
Referee: Ioan Igna (ROM)   Attendance: 56.115

22-06-1988   Neckarstadion, Stuttgart: Soviet Union – Italy   2-0 (0-0)
Soviet Union: Rinat Dasayev (C), Volodymyr Bezsonov (YC32) (36' Anatoliy Demyanenko), Vagiz Khidiyatullin, Oleh Kuznetsov (YC2), Vasiliy Rats, Sergei Aleinikov, Gennadiy Litovchenko, Olexander Zavarov, Oleksiy Mikhaylichenko, Sergei Gotsmanov (YC44), Oleh Protasov. (Coach: Valeriy Vasylyovych Lobanovskyi (URS)).
Italy: Walter Zenga, Paolo Maldini (65' Luigi De Agostini), Franco Baresi (YC33), Giuseppe Bergomi (C), Riccardo Ferri (YC85), Roberto Donadoni, Carlo Ancelotti, Fernando De Napoli (YC78), Giuseppe Giannini, Roberto Mancini (46' Alessandro Altobelli), Gianluca Vialli. (Coach: Azeglio Vicini (ITA)).
Goals: Soviet Union: 1-0 Gennadiy Litovchenko (58'), 2-0 Oleh Protasov (62').
Referee: Alexis Ponnet (BEL)   Attendance: 61.606

FINAL

25-06-1988 Olympiastadion, Munich: Soviet Union – Netherlands 0-2 (0-1)
Soviet Union: Rinat Dasayev (C), Vagiz Khidiyatullin (YC42), Anatoliy Demyanenko (YC31), Vasiliy Rats, Sergei Aleinikov, Gennadiy Litovchenko (YC33), Olexander Zavarov, Oleksiy Mikhaylichenko, Sergei Gotsmanov (68' Sergei Baltacha), Oleh Protasov (71' Viktor Pasulko), Ihor Belanov. (Coach: Valeriy Vasylyovych Lobanovskyi (URS)).
Netherlands: Hans van Breukelen, Frank Rijkaard, Ronald Koeman, Berry van Aerle (YC50), Adri van Tiggelen, Jan Wouters (YC37), Gerald Vanenburg, Ruud Gullit (C), Erwin Koeman, Arnold Mühren, Marco van Basten. (Coach: Marinus Jacobus Hendricus (Rinus) Michels (HOL)).
Goals: Netherlands: 0-1 Ruud Gullit (32'), 0-2 Marco van Basten (54').
Referee: Michel Vautrot (FRA)   Attendance: 62.770

*** Netherlands were European Champions ***

GOALSCORERS TOURNAMENT 1986-1988:

Goals	Players
7	Nico Claesen (BEL), Marco van Basten (HOL), Alessandro Altobelli (ITA)
6	Johnny Ekström (SWE)
5	Latchezar Tanev (BUL), Gary Lineker (ENG), Andreas Thom (GDR), Nikos Anastopoulos (GRE), Ruud Gullit (HOL), Gianluca Vialli (ITA)
4	José Miguel González Martín del Campo "MÍCHEL" (ESP), Ulf Kirsten (GDR), John Bosman (HOL), Georges Bregy (SUI), Ihor Belanov (URS), Zlatko Vujovic (YUG)
3	Toni Polster (AUT), Nasko Sirakov (BUL), John Barnes (ENG), Bryan Robson (ENG), JOSÉ María BAKERO Escudero (ESP), Ronald Koeman (HOL), Lajos Détári (HUN), Frank Stapleton (IRL), Carmel Busuttil (MLT), Dariusz Dziekanowski (POL), Ivo Knoflícek (TCH), Oleh Protasov (URS)
2	Manfred Linzmaier (AUT), Jan Ceulemans (BEL), Frank Vercauteren (BEL), Hristo Kolev (BUL), Jan Mølby (DEN), Tony Adams (ENG), Peter Beardsley (ENG), Chris Waddle (ENG), ELOY José Olaya Prendes (ESP), Ari Hjelm (FIN), Rudi Völler (FRG), Dimitrios Saravakos (GRE), Imre Boda (HUN), György Bognár (HUN), Ferenc Mészáros (HUN), Paul McGrath (IRL), Ronnie Whelan (IRL), Luigi De Agostini (ITA), Jörn Andersen (NOR), Marek Leśniak (POL), JORGE Manuel PLÁCIDO Bravo da Costa (POR), Gheorghe Hagi (ROM), Stefan Iovan (ROM), Victor Piturca (ROM), Davie Cooper (SCO), Paul McStay (SCO), Peter Larsson (SWE), Sergei Aleinikov (URS), Gennadiy Litovchenko (URS), Oleksiy Mikhaylichenko (URS), Vasiliy Rats (URS), Olexandr Zavarov (URS), Ian Rush (WAL), Faruk Hadzibegic (YUG), Srecko Katanec (YUG), Fadilj Vokrri (YUG)

| 1 | Sokol Kushta (ALB), Shkelqim Muça (ALB), Andreas Ogris (AUT), Peter Crève (BEL), Marc Degryse (BEL), Eric Gerets (BEL), Pierre Janssen (BEL), Enzo Scifo (BEL), Georgi Iordanov (BUL), Anio Sadakov (BUL), Evagoras Christofi (CYP), Pavlos Savva (CYP), Georgios Savvides (CYP), Jens Jørn Bertelsen (DEN), Preben Elkjær Larsen (DEN), Michael Laudrup (DEN), Flemming Povlsen (DEN), Viv Anderson (ENG), Steve Hodge (ENG), Gary Mabbutt (ENG), Neil Webb (ENG), Juan Carlos ARTECHE Gómez (ESP), Emilio BUTRAGUEÑO Santos (ESP), Rafael GORDILLO Vázquez (ESP), JOAQUÍN Alonso González (ESP), Francisco José "LOBO" CARRASCO Hidalgo (ESP), Francisco "PACO" LLORENTE Gento (ESP), RAMÓN María CALDERÉ del Rey (ESP), Manuel SANCHÍS Hontiyuelo (ESP), Ismo Lius (FIN), Petri Juha Tiainen (FIN), Philippe Fargeon (FRA), Carmelo Micciche (FRA), Yannick Stopyra (FRA), José Touré (FRA), Andreas Brehme (FRG), Jürgen Klinsmann (FRG), Lothar Matthäus (FRG), Olaf Thon (FRG), Thomas Doll (GDR), Matthias Döschner (GDR), Rainer Ernst (GDR), Ralf Minge (GDR), Konstantinos Antoniou (GRE), Konstantinos Batsinilas (GRE), Andreas Bonovas (GRE), Anastasios Mitropoulos (GRE), Apostolakis Papaioanou (GRE), Hans Gillhaus (HOL), Wim Kieft (HOL), Joop Lankjaar (HOL), Arnold Mühren (HOL), József Kiprich (HUN), Zoltán Péter (HUN), Tamás Preszeller (HUN), István Vincze (HUN), Liam Brady (IRL), Tony Galvin (IRL), Ray Houghton (IRL), Mark Lawrenson (IRL), Kevin Moran (IRL), Atli Edvaldsson (ISL), Arnor Gudjohnsen (ISL), Pétur Ormslev (ISL), Pétur Pétursson (ISL), Salvatore Bagni (ITA), Giuseppe Bergomi (ITA), Roberto Donadoni (ITA), Riccardo Ferri (ITA), Giuseppe Giannini (ITA), Roberto Mancini (ITA), Armin Krings (LUX), Robert Langers (LUX), Dennis Mizzi (MLT), Colin Clarke (NIR), James Quinn (NIR), Jan Kristian Fjærestad (NOR), Per-Edmund Mordt (NOR), Tom Sundby (NOR), Dariusz Marciniak (POL), Wlodimierz Smolarek (POL), Ryszard Tarasiewicz (POL), Roman Wójcicki (POL), FREDERICO Nobre Rosa (POR), JOÃO Domingos da Silva PINTO (POR), JOSÉ Da Silva COELHO (POR), MANUEL José Tavares FERNANDES (POR), Miodrag Belodedici (ROM), László Bölöni (ROM), Adrian Bumbescu (ROM), Michael Klein (ROM), Marius Lacatus (ROM), Dorin Mateut (ROM), Nicolae Ungureanu (ROM), Mo Johnston (SCO), Gary MacKay (SCO), Ally McCoist (SCO), Jean-Paul Brigger (SUI), Andy Egli (SUI), André Halter (SUI), Martin Weber (SUI), Hans-Peter Zwicker (SUI), Stig Fredriksson (SWE), Glenn Hysén (SWE), Mats Magnusson (SWE), Glenn Strömberg (SWE), Michal Bílek (TCH), Ivan Hasek (TCH), Petr Janecka (TCH), Karel Kula (TCH), Yusuf Altintas (TUR), Feyyaz Uçar (TUR), Oleh Blokhin (URS), Vagiz Khidiyatullin (URS), Viktor Pasulko (URS), Tengiz Sulakvelidze (URS), Glyn Hodges (WAL), Mark Hughes (WAL), Andy Jones (WAL), David Phillips (WAL), Neil Slatter (WAL), Ljubomir Radanovic (YUG), Dejan Savicevic (YUG), Dragan Stojkovic (YUG) |

1992 UEFA European Football Championship

QUALIFYING ROUND

GROUP 1

30-05-1990	Reykjavik	Iceland – Albania	2-0 (1-0)
05-09-1990	Reykjavik	Iceland – France	1-2 (0-1)
26-09-1990	Kosice	Czechoslovakia – Iceland	1-0 (1-0)
10-10-1990	Seville	Spain – Iceland	2-1 (1-0)
13-10-1990	Paris	France – Czechoslovakia	2-1 (0-0)
14-11-1990	Prague	Czechoslavakia – Spain	3-2 (1-1)
17-11-1990	Tirana	Albania – France	0-1 (0-1)
19-12-1990	Seville	Spain – Albania	9-0 (4-0)
20-02-1991	Paris	France – Spain	3-1 (1-1)
30-03-1991	Paris	France – Albania	5-0 (4-0)
01-05-1991	Tirana	Albania – Czechoslovakia	0-2 (0-0)
26-05-1991	Tirana	Albania – Iceland	1-0 (0-0)
05-06-1991	Reykjavik	Iceland – Czechoslovakia	0-1 (0-1)
03-09-1991	Bratislava	Czechoslovakia – France	1-2 (1-0)
25-09-1991	Reykjavik	Iceland – Spain	2-0 (0-0)
12-10-1991	Seville	Spain – France	1-2 (1-2)
16-10-1991	Olomouc	Czechoslovakia – Albania	2-1 (2-0)
13-11-1991	Seville	Spain – Czechoslovakia	2-1 (1-0)
20-11-1991	Paris	France – Iceland	3-1 (1-0)
18-12-1991	*Tirana*	*Albania – Spain*	*cancelled*

FINAL STANDING

Pos	Team	Pld	W	D	L	GF	GA	GD	Pts
1	*France*	*8*	*8*	*0*	*0*	*20*	*6*	*+14*	*16*
2	Czechoslovakia	8	5	0	3	12	9	+3	10
3	Spain	7	3	0	4	17	12	+5	6
4	Iceland	8	2	0	6	7	10	-3	4
5	Albania	7	1	0	6	2	21	-19	2

France qualified for the final tournament in Sweden.

30-05-1990   Laugardalsvöllur, Reykjavik: Iceland – Albania   2-0 (1-0)
Iceland: Birkir Kristinsson, Sævar Jónsson, Gudni Bergsson, Atli Edvaldsson (C), Thorvaldur Örlygsson (46' Kristian Jónsson), Olafur Thordarson, Pétur Ormslev, Sigurdur Grétarsson, Gudmundur Torfason (66' Ormarr Örlygsson), Arnor Gudjohnsen, Pétur Pétursson. (Coach: Bo (Bosse) Johansson (SWE)).
Albania: Fotaq (Foto) Strakosha, Edmond (Eduard) Abazi, Rudi Vata, Pjerin Noga (79' Roland Iljadhi), Naum Kove, Sulejman Demollari (C) (YC51), Artur Tushe Lekbello (II), Mirel Josa (YC52), Lefter Millo, Fatbardh Jera, Ylli Shehu (46' Pjerin Arberi). (Coach: Bejkush Birçe (ALB)).
Goals: Iceland: 1-0 Arnor Gudjohnsen (41'), 2-0 Atli Edvaldsson (82').
Referee: Frederick McKnight (NIR)   Attendance: 5.250

05-09-1990   Laugardalsvöllur, Reykjavik: Iceland – France   1-2 (0-1)
Iceland: Bjarni Sigurdsson, Sævar Jónsson, Gudni Bergsson, Thorgrimur Thráinsson, Atli Edvaldsson, Thorvaldur Örlygsson (63' Runar Kristinsson), Olafur Thordarson, Pétur Ormslev (63' Ragnar Margeirsson), Sigurdur Grétarsson, Arnor Gudjohnsen, Pétur Pétursson. (Coach: Bo (Bosse) Johansson (SWE)).
France: Bruno Martini, Laurent Blanc (76' Jean-Philippe Durand), Manuel Amoros, Basile Boli, Didier Deschamps, Bernard Casoni, Franck Sauzée, Bernard Pardo, Jean-Pierre Papin, Eric Cantona (83' Luis Fernández), Christian Perez. (Coach: Michel Platini (FRA)).
Goals: Iceland: 1-2 Atli Edvaldsson (85').
France: 0-1 Jean-Pierre Papin (12'), 0-2 Eric Cantona (74').
Referee: David F.T.Syme (SCO)   Attendance: 8.388

26-09-1990   Vsesportovy Areál Stadium, Kosice: Czechoslovakia – Iceland   1-0 (1-0)
Czechoslovakia: Ján Stejskal, Michal Hipp, Miroslav Kadlec, Lubos Kubík (YC71), Dusan Tittel, Ivan Hasek (C), Ján Kocian, Lubomír Moravcík, Michal Bílek (75' Vladimir Weiss), Karel Kula, Vaclav Danek. (Coach: Milan Mácala (TCH)).
Iceland: Bjarni Sigurdsson, Sævar Jónsson, Gudni Bergsson, Thorgrimur Thráinsson, Atli Edvaldsson (C) (YC65), Runar Kristinsson (61' Kristian Jónsson), Olafur Thordarson, Sigurdur Grétarsson, Sigurdur Jónsson (YC17), Arnor Gudjohnsen (YC69), Ragnar Margeirsson (80' Pétur Ormslev). (Coach: Bo (Bosse) Johansson (SWE)).
Goal: Czechoslovakia: 1-0 Vaclav Danek (43').
Referee: Todor Kolev (BUL)   Attendance: 35.247

10-10-1990   Estadio Benito Villamarín, Seville: Spain – Iceland   2-1 (1-0)
Spain: Andoni ZUBIZARRETA Urreta, Manuel SANCHÍS Hontiyuelo, Fernando Muñoz García "NANDO" (YC34), Ricardo Jesús SERNA Orozco, Andoni GOIKOETXEA Olaskoaga (YC69), Rafael MARTÍN VÁZQUEZ, Rafael "RAFA" PAZ Marin (62' Aitor BEGUIRISTÁIN Mújica), FERNANDO Gómez Colomer, José Miguel González Martín del Campo "MÍCHEL", Emilio BUTRAGUEÑO Santos, CARLOS Antonio Muñoz Cobo (71' Ernesto VALVERDE Tejero). (Coach: LUIS SUÁREZ Miramontes (ESP)).
Iceland: Bjarni Sigurdsson, Sævar Jónsson (YC69), Gudni Bergsson, Kristian Jónsson (YC68) (79' Anthony Gregory), Thorgrimur Thráinsson, Atli Edvaldsson (YC88), Olafur Thordarson, Sigurdur Grétarsson, Sigurdur Jónsson (YC12) (71' Pétur Ormslev), Arnor Gudjohnsen, Ragnar Margeirsson. (Coach: Bo (Bosse) Johansson (SWE)).
Goals: Spain: 1-0 Emilio BUTRAGUEÑO Santos (44'), 2-0 CARLOS Antonio Muñoz Cobo (63').
Iceland: 2-1 Sigurdur Jónsson (66').
Referee: Victor Mintoff (MLT)   Attendance: 18.399

13-10-1990   Parc des Princes, Paris: France – Czechoslovakia   2-1 (0-0)
France: Bruno Martini, Laurent Blanc, Basile Boli, Jocelyn Angloma (52' Luis Fernández), Didier Deschamps, Bernard Casoni, Franck Sauzée (C), Pascal Vahirua (84' Franck Silvestre), Jean-Philippe Durand, Jean-Pierre Papin, Eric Cantona. (Coach: Michel Platini (FRA)).
Czechoslovakia: Ján Stejskal, Michal Hipp, Miroslav Kadlec, Lubos Kubík (YC51) (84' Dusan Tittel), Ján Kocian (C), Michal Bílek (82' Ladislav Pecko), Karel Kula (YC10), Ivo Knoflícek, Jozef Chovanec, Tomás Skuhravy, Lubomír Moravcík (YC62). (Coach: Milan Mácala (TCH)).
Goals: France: 1-0 Jean-Pierre Papin (60'), 2-0 Jean-Pierre Papin (83').
Czechoslovakia: 2-1 Tomás Skuhravy (89').
Referee: George Courtney (ENG)   Attendance: 38.249

14-11-1990   Evzena Rosického Stadium, Prague: Czechoslovakia – Spain   3-2 (1-1)
Czechoslovakia: Ludek Miklosko, Ivan Hasek (C), Michal Hipp (YC19), Ján Kocian, Miroslav Kadlec, Lubomír Moravcík, Dusan Tittel (YC73), Karel Kula, Michal Bílek (84' Milos Belak), Vaclav Danek (89' Pavel Kuka), Tomás Skuhravy. (Coach: Milan Mácala (TCH)).
Spain: Andoni ZUBIZARRETA Urreta (YC9), Manuel SANCHÍS Hontiyuelo, Fernando Muñoz García "NANDO", Enrique Sánchez Flores "QUIQUE", Ricardo Jesús SERNA Orozco, Andoni GOIKOETXEA Olaskoaga, Rafael MARTÍN VÁZQUEZ (YC58), ROBERTO Férnandez Bonillo, José Miguel González Martín del Campo "MÍCHEL" (85' Guillermo AMOR Martinez), Emilio BUTRAGUEÑO Santos (C), CARLOS Antonio Muñoz Cobo (61' JOSÉ María BAKERO Escudero). (Coach: LUIS SUÁREZ Miramontes (ESP)).
Goals: Czechoslovakia: 1-0 Vaclav Danek (16'), 2-2 Vaclav Danek (67'), 3-2 Lubomír Moravcík (77').
Spain: 1-1 ROBERTO Férnandez Bonillo (30'), 1-2 CARLOS Antonio Muñoz Cobo (54').
Referee: Karl-Heinz Tritschler (FRG)   Attendance: 17.773

17-11-1990   Stadiumi Qemal Stafa, Tirana: Albania – France   0-1 (0-1)
Albania: Anesti Arapi, Genc Ibro (YC51), Lorenc Leskaj (46' Alfred Ferko), Arian Stafa (YC56), Hysen Zmijani (YC48), Sulejman Demollari (C), Artur Tushe Lekbello (II), Skender Hodja, Sokol Kushta, Mirel Josa, Kujtim Majaçi (56' Edward Kaçaçi). (Coach: Agron Sulaj (ALB)).
France: Bruno Martini, Laurent Blanc, Basile Boli, Didier Deschamps (YC63), Jean-Marc Ferreri, Bernard Casoni, Franck Sauzée (C), Pascal Vahirua (80' Jocelyn Angloma), Bernard Pardo, Christian Perez, Philippe Tibeuf (65' David Ginola). (Coach: Michel Platini (FRA)).
Goal: France: 0-1 Basile Boli (25').
Referee: Bruno Galler (SUI)   Attendance: 12.972

19-12-1990   Estadio Benito Villamarín, Seville: Spain – Albania   9-0 (4-0)
Spain: Andoni ZUBIZARRETA Urreta, Fernando Ruiz HIERRO, Rafael ALKORTA Martínez, Manuel SANCHÍS Hontiyuelo, Guillermo AMOR Martinez, Andoni GOIKOETXEA Olaskoaga (75' JOSÉ María BAKERO Escudero), Rafael MARTÍN VÁZQUEZ, José Miguel González Martín del Campo "MÍCHEL" (62' Enrique Sánchez Flores "QUIQUE"), Emilio BUTRAGUEÑO Santos (C), Manuel Sánchez Delgado "MANOLO", CARLOS Antonio Muñoz Cobo. (Coach: LUIS SUÁREZ Miramontes (ESP)).
Albania: Anesti Arapi, Genc Ibro, Arian Stafa, Alfred Ferko (YC3) (55' Mirel Josa), Gjergji Dema, Hysen Zmijani (C), Artur Tushe Lekbello (II), Bledar Kola (37' Sulejman Demollari), Lefter Millo, Sokol Kushta, Ermal Tahiri. (Coach: Agron Sulaj (ALB)).
Goals: Spain: 1-0 Guillermo AMOR Martinez (21'), 2-0 CARLOS Antonio Muñoz Cobo (24'), 3-0 Emilio BUTRAGUEÑO Santos (31'), 4-0 Fernando Ruiz HIERRO (40'), 5-0 Emilio BUTRAGUEÑO Santos (57'), 6-0 CARLOS Antonio Muñoz Cobo (65'), 7-0 Emilio BUTRAGUEÑO Santos (68'), 8-0 JOSÉ María BAKERO Escudero (76), 9-0 Emilio BUTRAGUEÑO Santos (88').
Referee: Alphonse Costantin (BEL)   Attendance: 12.625

20-02-1991   Parc des Princes, Paris: France – Spain   3-1 (1-1)
France: Bruno Martini, Laurent Blanc, Manuel Amoros (C), Basile Boli, Bernard Casoni (YC16), Franck Sauzée, Pascal Vahirua (82' Didier Deschamps), Jean-Philippe Durand, Bernard Pardo (YC40) (51' Luis Fernández), Jean-Pierre Papin, Eric Cantona. (Coach: Michel Platini (FRA)).
Spain: Andoni ZUBIZARRETA Urreta, Manuel SANCHÍS Hontiyuelo, Fernando Muñoz García "NANDO", Enrique Sánchez Flores "QUIQUE", Juan Francisco Rodríguez Herrera "JUANITO", Guillermo AMOR Martinez, Andoni GOIKOETXEA Olaskoaga, JOSÉ María BAKERO Escudero, José Miguel González Martín del Campo "MÍCHEL", Juan VIZCAÍNO Morcillo (YC44) (60' MIQUEL SOLER i Sararols), Emilio BUTRAGUEÑO Santos (C) (74' Manuel Sánchez Delgado "MANOLO"). (Coach: LUIS SUÁREZ Miramontes (ESP)).
Goals: France: 1-1 Franck Sauzée (14'), 2-1 Jean-Pierre Papin (58'), 3-1 Laurent Blanc (76').
Spain: 0-1 JOSÉ María BAKERO Escudero (10').
Referee: Tullio Lanese (ITA)   Attendance: 41.474

30-03-1991   Parc des Prince, Paris: France – Albania   5-0 (4-0)
France: Bruno Martini, Laurent Blanc, Manuel Amoros (C), Basile Boli, Luis Fernández, Franck Sauzée, Pascal Vahirua (56' Pascal Baills), Christophe Cocard, Jean-Philippe Durand, Jean-Pierre Papin (72' Didier Deschamps), Eric Cantona. (Coach: Michel Platini (FRA)).
Albania: Blendi Nallbani (YC82), Rudi Vata, Adnan Oçelli, Josif Gjergji, Hysen Zmijani, Sulejman Demollari (C), Artur Tushe Lekbello (II), Dashnor Dume, Agim Canaj (YC80), Ermal Tahiri, Jlir Kepa. (Coach: Bejkush Birçe (ALB)).
Goals: France: 1-0 Franck Sauzée (1'), 2-0 Franck Sauzée (9'), 3-0 Jean-Pierre Papin (33' penalty), 4-0 Jean-Pierre Papin (42'), 5-0 Hysen Zmijani (81' *own goal*).
Referee: Einar Halle (NOR)   Attendance: 24.181

01-05-1991   Stadiumi Qemal Stafa, Tirana: Albania – Czechoslovakia 0-2 (0-0)
Albania: Blendi Nallbani, Adnan Oçelli, Fatos Daja, Gjergji Dema (YC49), Zamir Shpuza (YC77), Hysen Zmijani (C), Adrian Barbullushi (64' Edmond Dosti), Dashnor Dume (73' Bledar Kola), Arben Milori, Eqerem Memushi, Sokol Kushta. (Coach: Bejkush Birçe (ALB)).
Czechoslovakia: Ludek Miklosko, Miroslav Kadlec, Lubos Kubík (YC65), Dusan Tittel, Ivan Hasek (C) (20' Pavel Hapal), Lubomír Moravcík (YC68), Jirí Nemec, Alois Grussmann, Karel Kula, Pavel Kuka, Roman Kukleta (85' Radomir Chylek). (Coach: Milan Mácala (TCH)).
Goals: Czechoslovakia: 0-1 Lubos Kubík (47'), 0-2 Karel Kula (66').
Referee: Carlo Longhi (ITA)   Attendance: 4.205

26-05-1991   Stadiumi Qemal Stafa, Tirana: Albania – Iceland 1-0 (0-0)
Albania: Blendi Nallbani, Edmond (Eduard) Abazi (YC64), Adnan Oçelli (YC21), Fatos Daja, Zamir Shpuza, Sulejman Demollari (C) (RC77), Artur Tushe Lekbello (II), Lefter Millo, Arben Milori, Eqerem Memushi (17' Mirel Josa), Sokol Kushta. (Coach: Bejkush Birçe (ALB)).
Iceland: Bjarni Sigurdsson, Ólafur Kristjánsson, Sævar Jónsson (C), Gudni Bergsson, Gunnar Gíslason (YC77), Runar Kristinsson (69' Hlynur Stéfansson), Thorvaldur Örlygsson, Olafur Thordarson (YC72), Sigurdur Grétarsson, Eyjölfur Sverrisson, Anthony Gregory (77' Andri Marteinsson). (Coach: Bo (Bosse) Johansson (SWE)).
Goal: Albania: 1-0 Edmond (Eduard) Abazi (65').
Referee: Sándor Varga (HUN)   Attendance: 2.349

05-06-1991   Laugardalsvöllur, Reykjavik: Iceland – Czechoslavakia 0-1 (0-1)
Iceland: Bjarni Sigurdsson, Sævar Jónsson (C), Gudni Bergsson, Gunnar Gíslason, Atli Edvaldsson (C), Runar Kristinsson, Thorvaldur Örlygsson, Olafur Thordarson, Sigurdur Jónsson, Arnor Gudjohnsen (YC46), Eyjölfur Sverrisson (70' Hlynur Stéfansson). (Coach: Bo (Bosse) Johansson (SWE)).
Czechoslovakia: Ludek Miklosko, Lubos Kubík (YC60), Dusan Tittel, Ivan Hasek (C), Ján Kocian, Jirí Nemec, Alois Grussmann, Karel Kula, Pavel Hapal, Tomás Skuhravy (41' Pavel Kuka), Vaclav Danek (YC83) (87' Ladislav Pecko). (Coach: Milan Mácala (TCH)).
Goal: Czechoslovakia: 0-1 Ivan Hasek (15').
Referee: John Spillane (IRL)   Attendance: 5.102

04-09-1991   Stadión Tehelné pole, Bratislava: Czechoslovakia – France 1-2 (1-0)
Czechoslovakia: Ludek Miklosko, Jirí Novotny, Dusan Tittel, Lubomír Moravcík, Václav Nemecek (YC36), Martin Frydek (72' Ondrej Kristofik), Ján Kocian (C), Ladislav Pecko, Jirí Nemec, Pavel Hapal (78' Ivo Knoflícek), Pavel Kuka. (Coach: Milan Mácala (TCH)).
France: Bruno Martini, Laurent Blanc, Manuel Amoros (C), Basile Boli, Jocelyn Angloma (76' Jean-Philippe Durand), Didier Deschamps, Bernard Casoni, Franck Sauzée, Pascal Vahirua, Christophe Cocard (46' Christian Perez), Jean-Pierre Papin (YC43). (Coach: Michel Platini (FRA)).
Goals: Czechoslovakia: 1-0 Václav Nemecek (19').
France: 1-1 Jean-Pierre Papin (53'), 1-2 Jean-Pierre Papin (89').
Referee: Peter Mikkelsen (DEN)   Attendance: 44.884

25-09-1991   Laugardalsvöllur, Reykjavik: Iceland – Spain   2-0 (0-0)
Iceland: Birkir Kristinsson, Gudni Bergsson, Kristian Jónsson, Thorvaldur Örlygsson, Olafur Thordarson, Pétur Ormslev, Sigurdur Grétarsson (C), Sigurdur Jónsson (YC13), Valur Valsson (46' Andri Marteinsson), Eyjölfur Sverrisson, Baldur Bjarnason (74' Hördur Magnússon). (Coach: Ásgeir Elíasson (ISL)).
Spain: Andoni ZUBIZARRETA Urreta, Manuel SANCHÍS Hontiyuelo, Roberto SOLOZÁBAL Villanueva, ABELARDO Fernández Antuña, Andoni GOIKOETXEA Olaskoaga, Rafael MARTÍN VÁZQUEZ (YC42) (68' Fernando Ruiz HIERRO), José Miguel González Martín del Campo "MÍCHEL", EUSEBIO SACRISTÁN Mena, Juan VIZCAÍNO Morcillo, Emilio BUTRAGUEÑO Santos (C), Manuel Sánchez Delgado "MANOLO". (Coach: VICENTE MIERA Campos (ESP)).
Goals: Iceland: 1-0 Thorvaldur Örlygsson (71'), 2-0 Eyjölfur Sverrisson (79').
Referee: Cornelius A. (Cees) Bakker (HOL)   Attendance: 3.848

12-10-1991   Estadio Benito Villamarín, Seville: Spain – France   1-2 (1-2)
Spain: Andoni ZUBIZARRETA Urreta, Fernando Ruiz HIERRO, Manuel SANCHÍS Hontiyuelo (YC38), Roberto SOLOZÁBAL Villanueva (46' EUSEBIO SACRISTÁN Mena), CRISTÓBAL Parralo Aguilera, ABELARDO Fernández Antuña, Rafael MARTÍN VÁZQUEZ (74' ÁLVARO Cervera Díaz), Juan VIZCAÍNO Morcillo, Ricardo González BANGO (YC40), Emilio BUTRAGUEÑO Santos (C), Manuel Sánchez Delgado "MANOLO". (Coach: VICENTE MIERA Campos (ESP)).
France: Bruno Martini, Laurent Blanc, Manuel Amoros (C) (YC21), Basile Boli, Jocelyn Angloma, Didier Deschamps, Bernard Casoni, Luis Fernández (82' Jean-Philippe Durand), Jean-Pierre Papin (YC2), Eric Cantona, Christian Perez (YC11) (62' Remi Garde). (Coach: Michel Platini (FRA)).
Goals: Spain: 1-2 ABELARDO Fernández Antuña (33').
France: 0-1 Luis Fernández (12'), 0-2 Jean-Pierre Papin (15').
Referee: Hubert Forstinger (AUT)   Attendance: 9.399

16-10-1991   Andruv Stadium, Olomouc: Czechoslavakia – Albania   2-1 (2-0)
Czechoslovakia: Ludek Miklosko (C), Dusan Tittel, Ludovit Lancz (46' Roman Sedlácek), Lubomír Moravcík (YC52), Václav Nemecek, Martin Frydek, Bartolomej Jurasko, Karel Kula, Pavel Hapal, Pavel Kuka (YC71), Vaclav Danek (72' Ladislav Pecko). (Coach: Milan Mácala (TCH)).
Albania: Fotaq (Foto) Strakosha, Edmond (Eduard) Abazi (YC32), Kreshnik Çipi, Salvador Kaçaj, Hysen Zmijani (C), Artur Tushe Lekbello (II), Adrian Barbullushi, Latif Gjondeda, Mirel Josa, Arben Milori (RC63), Agostin Kola (51' Fatos Daja). (Coach: Bejkush Birçe (ALB)).
Goals: Czechoslavakia: 1-0 Karel Kula (35'), 2-0 Ludovit Lancz (39').
Albania: 2-1 Hysen Zmijani (60').
Referee: Michal Listkiewicz (POL)   Attendance: 2.366

13-11-1991 Estadio Ramón Sánchez Pizjuán, Seville: Spain – Czechoslovakia 2-1 (1-0)
Spain: Andoni ZUBIZARRETA Urreta, Fernando Ruiz HIERRO, Manuel SANCHÍS Hontiyuelo, MIQUEL SOLER i Sararols, Roberto SOLOZÁBAL Villanueva, ABELARDO Fernández Antuña, Rafael MARTÍN VÁZQUEZ (46' Miguel Ángel NADAL Homar), José Miguel González Martín del Campo "MÍCHEL", Juan VIZCAÍNO Morcillo, Emilio BUTRAGUEÑO Santos (C), Gabriel MOYA Sanz (60' Ignacio CONTE Crespo). (Coach: VICENTE MIERA Campos (ESP)).
Czechoslovakia: Ján Stejskal, Jiri Novotny, Jan Suchopárek, Lubomir Vlk (61' Alois Grussmann), Milos Glonek (YC40), Václav Nemecek, Ladislav Pecko, Jirí Nemec, Karel Kula, Ondrej Kristofík, Peter Dubovsky (80' Radoslav Látal). (Coach: Milan Mácala (TCH)).
Goals: Spain: 1-0 ABELARDO Fernández Antuña (10'), 2-1 José Miguel González Martín del Campo "MÍCHEL" (78' penalty).
Czechoslovakia: 1-1 Václav Nemecek (60').
Referee: Kurt Röthlisberger (SUI) Attendance: 8.691

20-11-1991 Parc des Princes, Paris: France – Iceland 3-1 (1-0)
France: Bruno Martini, Laurent Blanc, Manuel Amoros (C), Jocelyn Anglerma, Didier Deschamps (67' Jean-Philippe Durand), Bernard Casoni (46' Basile Boli), Luis Fernández, Pascal Vahirua, Eric Cantona, Christian Perez, Amara Simba. (Coach: Michel Platini (FRA)).
Iceland: Birkir Kristinsson, Gudni Bergsson (80' Sævar Jónsson), Kristian Jónsson, Thorvaldur Örlygsson, Pétur Ormslev, Sigurdur Grétarsson (C) (YC63), Gudmundur Torfason (56' Eyjölfur Sverrisson), Kristinn Rúnar Jónsson, Valur Valsson, Arnor Gudjohnsen, Baldur Bjarnason. (Coach: Ásgeir Elíasson (ISL)).
Goals: France: 1-0 Amara Simba (41'), 2-0 Eric Cantona (59'), 3-0 Eric Cantona (67').
Iceland: 3-1 Eyjölfur Sverrisson (70').
Referee: Erik Fredriksson (SWE) Attendance: 27.393

18-12-1991 Stadiumi Qemal Stafa, Tirana: Albania – Spain cancelled
At the request of the Spanish Football Federation, the game was cancelled by UEFA two days before the scheduled date due to the social unrest in Albania.

GROUP 2

12-09-1990	Geneva	Switzerland – Bulgaria	2-0 (1-0)
12-09-1990	Glasgow	Scotland – Romania	2-1 (1-1)
17-10-1990	Bucharest	Romania – Bulgaria	0-3 (0-1)
17-10-1990	Glasgow	Scotland – Switzerland	2-1 (1-0)
14-11-1990	Sofia	Bulgaria – Scotland	1-1 (0-1)
14-11-1990	Serravalle	San Marino – Switzerland	0-4 (0-3)
05-12-1990	Bucharest	Romania – San Marino	6-0 (3-0)
27-03-1991	Glasgow	Scotland – Bulgaria	1-1 (0-0)
27-03-1991	Serravalle	San Marino – Romania	1-3 (1-2)
03-04-1991	Neuchâtel	Switzerland – Romania	0-0
01-05-1991	Sofia	Bulgaria – Switzerland	2-3 (2-0)
01-05-1991	Serravalle	San Marino – Scotland	0-2 (0-0)
22-05-1991	Serravalle	San Marino – Bulgaria	0-3 (0-2)
05-06-1991	St.Gallen	Switzerland – San Marino	7-0 (3-0)
11-09-1991	Bern	Switzerland – Scotland	2-2 (2-0)
16-10-1991	Sofia	Bulgaria – San Marino	4-0 (3-0)

16-10-1991	Bucharest	Romania – Scotland	1-0 (0-0)
13-11-1991	Glasgow	Scotland – San Marino	4-0 (3-0)
13-11-1991	Bucharest	Romania – Switzerland	1-0 (0-0)
20-11-1991	Sofia	Bulgaria – Romania	1-1 (0-1)

FINAL STANDING

Pos	Team	Pld	W	D	L	GF	GA	GD	Pts
1	*Scotland*	*8*	*4*	*3*	*1*	*14*	*7*	*+7*	*11*
2	Switzerland	8	4	2	2	19	7	+12	10
3	Romania	8	4	2	2	13	7	+6	10
4	Bulgaria	8	3	3	2	15	8	+7	9
5	San Marino	8	0	0	8	1	33	-32	0

Scotland qualified for the final tournament in Sweden.

12-09-1990   Stade des Charmilles, Geneva: Switzerland – Bulgaria   2-0 (1-0)
Switzerland: Philipp Walker, Marc Hottiger (YC55), Dominique Herr, Alain Geiger, Marcel Koller, Peter Schepull, Alain Sutter (88' Blaise Piffaretti), Thomas Bickel, Heinz Hermann (C), Adrian Knup (YC50) (60' Stéphane Chapuisat), Kübilay Türkyilmaz. (Coach: Ulrich (Uli) Stielike (FRG)).
Bulgaria: Ilia Valov, Trifon Ivanov, Nasko Zhelev, Dimitar Vasev (13' Kalin Bankov), Nikolai Iliev (YC86), Pavel Dotchev (YC34), Krasimir Balakov (64' Nikolai Todorov), Georgi Iordanov, Kostadin Yanchev, Hristo Stoichkov (C), Emil Kostadinov (YC22). (Coach: Ivan Vutsov (BUL)).
Goals: Switzerland: 1-0 Marc Hottiger (19'), 2-0 Thomas Bickel (63').
Referee: Guy Goethals (BEL)   Attendance: 9.088

12-09-1990   Hampden Park, Glasgow: Scotland – Romania   2-1 (1-1)
Scotland: Andy Goram, Maurice Malpas, Stewart McKimmie, Alex McLeish, Brian Irvine, Paul McStay, Murdo MacLeod (YC55), Gary McAllister (72' Pat Nevin), Bobby Connor (58' Tom Boyd), Ally McCoist, John Robertson. (Coach: Andrew (Andy) Roxburgh (ENG)).
Romania: Silviu Lung, Dan Petrescu, Emil Sandoi, Ioan Lupescu, Gheorghe Popescu, Michael Klein (C), Iosif Rotariu, Gheorghe Hagi, Marius Lacatus, Dorin Mateut (70' Ioan Sabau), Doru Rodion Camataru (72' Florin Raducioiu). (Coach: Gheorghe Constantin (ROM)).
Goals: Scotland: 1-1 John Robertson (37'), 2-1 Ally McCoist (76').
Romania: 0-1 Doru Rodion Camataru (13').
Referee: Ildefonso Urizar Azpitarte (ESP)   Attendance: 12.801

17-10-1990   Stadionul Steaua, Bucharest: Romania – Bulgaria   0-3 (0-1)
Romania: Bogdan Stelea, Dan Petrescu, Ioan Andone, Ioan Lupescu, Gheorghe Popescu, Michael Klein (YC8) (46' Dorin Mateut), Iosif Rotariu, Ioan Sabau, Gheorghe Hagi (C), Florin Raducioiu (46' Emil Sandoi), Marius Lacatus. (Coach: Gheorghe Constantin (ROM)).
Bulgaria: Borislav Mihaylov (YC65), Trifon Ivanov (YC34), Dimitar Vasev, Nikolai Iliev (C) (YC28), Pavel Dotchev, Zlatko Yankov, Nasko Sirakov (76' Emil Kostadinov), Krasimir Balakov, Georgi Iordanov (46' Nikolai Todorov), Kostadin Yanchev, Hristo Stoichkov (YC8). (Coach: Ivan Vutsov (BUL)).
Goals: Bulgaria: 0-1 Nasko Sirakov (28'), 0-2 Nikolai Todorov (48'), 0-3 Nikolai Todorov (76').
Referee: José Rosa dos Santos (POR)   Attendance: 15.350

17-10-1990 Hampden Park, Glasgow: Scotland – Switzerland 2-1 (1-0)
Scotland: Andy Goram, Tom Boyd (68' Gordon Durie), Dave McPherson, Stewart McKimmie, Alex McLeish (C), Steve Nicol, Murdo MacLeod (YC77), Stuart McCall, Gary McAllister (77' John Collins (YC88)), Ally McCoist, John Robertson. (Coach: Andrew (Andy) Roxburgh (ENG)).
Switzerland: Philipp Walker, Dominique Herr, Peter Schepull (63' Frédéric Chassot), Andy Egli (RC89), Alain Sutter, Thomas Bickel (YC78), Heinz Hermann (C), Blaise Piffaretti (78' Beat Sutter), Stéphane Chapuisat, Adrian Knup, Kübilay Türkyilmaz. (Coach: Ulrich (Uli) Stielike (FRG)).
Goals: Scotland: 1-0 John Robertson (34' penalty), 2-0 Gary McAllister (53').
Switzerland: 2-1 Adrian Knup (65' penalty).
Referee: Esa Antero Palsi (FIN)   Attendance: 20.740

14-11-1990 Vasil Levski National Stadium, Sofia: Bulgaria – Scotland 1-1 (0-1)
Bulgaria: Borislav Mihaylov, Pavel Dotchev, Kalin Bankov (YC75), Zlatko Yankov, Nasko Sirakov, Georgi Iordanov, Kostadin Yanchev (70' Nikolai Todorov), Dimitar Mladenov, Krasimir Balakov (75' Emil Kostadinov), Hristo Stoichkov (C) (YC64), Luboslav Penev. (Coach: Ivan Vutsov (BUL)).
Scotland: Andy Goram, Tom Boyd, Maurice Malpas (C) (YC61), Dave McPherson, Stewart McKimmie (YC81), Gary Gillespie, Gary McAllister, Jim McInally, Brian McClair, Gordon Durie (YC34) (72' Pat Nevin), Ally McCoist. (Coach: Andrew (Andy) Roxburgh (ENG)).
Goals: Bulgaria: 1-1 Nikolai Todorov (74').
Scotland: 0-1 Ally McCoist (9').
Referee: Friedrich Kaupe (AUT)   Attendance: 31.462

14-11-1990 Stadio Olimpico, Serravalle: San Marino – Switzerland 0-4 (0-3)
San Marino: Pier-Luigi Benedettini, Marco Montironi (YC81), Bruno Muccioli (46' Ivan Matteoni), Loris Zanotti (YC70), Luca Gobbi, William Guerra, Fabio Francini, Massimo Ceccoli, Massimo Bonini (46' Ivan Toccaceli), Valdes Pasolini, Marco Macina. (Coach: Giorgio Leoni (SMR)).
Switzerland: Philipp Walker, Marc Hottiger, Dominique Herr, Alain Geiger, Alain Sutter, Thomas Bickel (59' Blaise Piffaretti), Heinz Hermann, Beat Sutter, Stéphane Chapuisat, Adrian Knup, Kübilay Türkyilmaz (46' Frédéric Chassot). (Coach: Ulrich (Uli) Stielike (FRG)).
Goals: Switzerland: 0-1 Alain Sutter (7'), 0-2 Stéphane Chapuisat (27'), 0-3 Adrian Knup (43'), 0-4 Frédéric Chassot (87').
Referee: Costas Kapsos (CYP)   Attendance: 931

05-12-1990 Stadionul Steaua, Bucharest: Romania – San Marino 6-0 (3-0)
Romania: Florian Prunea, Dan Petrescu, Mircea Rednic, Stefan Iovan, Ioan Lupescu (57' Constantin Stanici (YC84)), Gheorghe Popescu, Ilie Dumitrescu (46' Pavel Badea), Ioan Sabau, Florin Raducioiu, Marius Lacatus (C), Dorin Mateut. (Coach: Mircea Radulescu (ROM)).
San Marino: Pier-Luigi Benedettini, Marco Montironi (RC53), Loris Zanotti, William Guerra (C), Ivan Matteoni, Ivan Toccaceli, Fabio Francini, Massimo Ceccoli, Valdes Pasolini (85' Paolo Zanotti), Marco Macina (46' Gian Carlo Bacciocchi), Paolo Conti. (Coach: Giorgio Leoni (SMR)).
Goals: Romania: 1-0 Ioan Sabau (2'), 2-0 Dorin Mateut (18'), 3-0 Florin Raducioiu (43'), 4-0 Ioan Lupescu (56'), 5-0 Pavel Badea (77'), 6-0 Dan Petrescu (85').
Referee: Manfred Roßner (GDR)   Attendance: 6.380

27-03-1991   Hampden Park, Glasgow: Scotland – Bulgaria   1-1 (0-0)
Scotland: Andy Goram, Richard Gough, Maurice Malpas, Dave McPherson, Alex McLeish (C), Paul McStay, Gordon Strachan (82' John Robertson), Jim McInally, Brian McClair, Gordon Durie (82' John Collins), Ally McCoist. (Coach: Andrew (Andy) Roxburgh (ENG)).
Bulgaria: Borislav Mihaylov (C), Trifon Ivanov, Nikolai Iliev, Pavel Dotchev, Zlatko Yankov, Nasko Sirakov (YC39) (87' Latchezar Tanev (YC88)), Ilyan Kiryakov, Georgi Iordanov, Krasimir Balakov (YC35) (87' Petar Alexandrov), Emil Kostadinov, Luboslav Penev. (Coach: Ivan Vutsov (BUL)).
Goals: Scotland: 1-0 John Collins (83').
Bulgaria: 1-1 Emil Kostadinov (89').
Referee: Erik Fredriksson (SWE)   Attendance: 33.119

27-03-1991   Stadio Olimpico, Serravalle: San Marino – Romania   1-3 (1-2)
San Marino: Pier-Luigi Benedettini, Bruno Muccioli, Luca Gobbi, William Guerra (C) (YC90), Ivan Matteoni, Claudio Canti (YC42), Fabio Francini, Massimo Ceccoli (67' Luca Riccardi), Valdes Pasolini (89' Marco Mularoni), Marco Mazza, Paolo Mazza (YC44). (Coach: Giorgio Leoni (SMR)).
Romania: Florian Prunea, Dan Petrescu, Emil Sandoi, (46' Daniel Timofte), Ioan Lupescu (73' Pavel Badea), Gheorghe Popescu, Michael Klein, Ioan Sabau, Gheorghe Hagi, Florin Raducioiu, Marius Lacatus (C), Dorin Mateut. (Coach: Mircea Radulescu (ROM)).
Goals: San Marino: 1-1 Valdes Pasolini (30' penalty).
Romania: 0-1 Gheorghe Hagi (18' penalty), 1-2 Florin Raducioiu (45'), 1-3 Ivan Matteoni (83' *own goal*).
Referee: Roger Philippi (LUX)   Attendance: 745

03-04-1991   Stde de la Maladière, Neuchâtel: Switzerland – Romania   0-0
Switzerland: Stefan Huber, Marc Hottiger, Dominique Herr, Alain Geiger, Marcel Koller, Christophe Ohrel, Jean-Michel Aeby, Heinz Hermann (C), Adrian Knup, Kübilay Türkyilmaz (75' Beat Sutter), Christophe Bonvin (30' Thomas Bickel). (Coach: Ulrich (Uli) Stielike (FRG)).
Romania: Florian Prunea, Dan Petrescu, Emil Sandoi, Ioan Lupescu, Gheorghe Popescu (YC43), Michael Klein, Ioan Sabau, Daniel Timofte, Gheorghe Hagi (80' Dorin Mateut), Florin Raducioiu (85' Ion Timofte), Marius Lacatus (C) (YC80). (Coach: Mircea Radulescu (ROM)).
Referee: Gérard Biguet (FRA)   Attendance: 9.262

01-05-1991   Vasil Levski National Stadium, Sofia: Bulgaria – Switzerland   2-3 (2-0)
Bulgaria: Borislav Mihaylov (C), Trifon Ivanov, Nikolai Iliev, Pavel Dotchev (75' Nikolai Todorov), Zlatko Yankov, Nasko Sirakov (65' Latchezar Tanev), Ilyan Kiryakov, Georgi Iordanov, Krasimir Balakov (YC52), Emil Kostadinov, Luboslav Penev (YC68). (Coach: Ivan Vutsov (BUL)).
Switzerland: Stefan Huber, Marc Hottiger, Dominique Herr (46' Stéphane Chapuisat), Marcel Koller, Andy Egli, Christophe Ohrel (YC9), Heinz Hermann (C), Beat Sutter, Adrian Knup (88' Peter Schepull), Kübilay Türkyilmaz, Christophe Bonvin. (Coach: Ulrich (Uli) Stielike (FRG)).
Goals: Bulgaria: 1-0 Emil Kostadinov (12'), 2-0 Nasko Sirakov (27').
Switzerland: 2-1 Adrian Knup (59'), 2-2 Adrian Knup (85'), 2-3 Kübilay Türkyilmaz (90').
Referee: Karl-Josef Assenmacher (FRG)   Attendance: 35.142

01-05-1991   Stadio Olimpico, Serravalle: San Marino – Scotland   0-2 (0-0)
San Marino: Pier-Luigi Benedettini, Bruno Muccioli (YC55), Loris Zanotti (YC12) (60' Ivan Toccaceli), Luca Gobbi, William Guerra (C), Claudio Canti, Fabio Francini, Massimo Ceccoli, Valdes Pasolini (77' Ivan Matteoni), Marco Mazza, Paolo Mazza. (Coach: Giorgio Leoni (SMR)).
Scotland: Andy Goram, Maurice Malpas, Dave McPherson, Stewart McKimmie, Steve Nicol (74' John Robertson), Gordon Strachan (C), Stuart McCall, Gary McAllister, Brian McClair (57' Pat Nevin), Kevin Gallacher (YC65), Gordon Durie. (Coach: Andrew (Andy) Roxburgh (ENG)).
Goals: Scotland: 0-1 Gordon Strachan (63' penalty), 0-2 Gordon Durie (67').
Referee: Besnik Kaimi (ALB)   Attendance: 3.512

22-05-1991   Stadio Olimpico, Serravalle: San Marino – Bulgaria   0-3 (0-2)
San Marino: Pier-Luigi Benedettini, Marco Montironi, Bruno Muccioli (YC32), Luca Gobbi, William Guerra (C), Claudio Canti, Fabio Francini, Massimo Ceccoli (82' Ivan Matteoni), Valdes Pasolini (62' Nicola Bacciocchi), Marco Mazza, Paolo Mazza (YC34). (Coach: Giorgio Leoni (SMR)).
Bulgaria: Borislav Mihaylov, Trifon Ivanov (YC35), Emil Dimitrov, Sasho Angelov, Zlatko Yankov (76' Nikolai Todorov), Nasko Sirakov, Ilyan Kiryakov, Georgi Georgiev (YC66), Emil Kostadinov, Luboslav Penev, Velko Yotov (56' Kiril Metkov). (Coach: Krasimir Borisov Georgiev (BUL)).
Goals: Bulgaria: 0-1 Trifon Ivanov (13'), 0-2 Nasko Sirakov (20'), 0-3 Luboslav Penev (70').
Referee: Victor Mintoff (MLT)   Attendance: 612

05-06-1991   Espenmoos Stadium, St.Gallen: Switzerland – San Marino   7-0 (3-0)
Switzerland: Stefan Huber, Marc Hottiger (74' Peter Schepull), Dominique Herr, Marcel Koller, Andy Egli (74' Christophe Ohrel), Alain Sutter, Heinz Hermann (C) (YC18), Beat Sutter (YC80), Stéphane Chapuisat, Adrian Knup, Kübilay Türkyilmaz. (Coach: Ulrich (Uli) Stielike (FRG)).
San Marino: Pier-Luigi Benedettini, Marco Montironi, Loris Zanotti (YC3), Luca Gobbi, William Guerra (C), Ivan Matteoni (46' Mauro Valentini), Claudio Canti, Fabio Francini, Valdes Pasolini, Marco Mazza (YC80), Nicola Bacciocchi (69' Marco Mularoni). (Coach: Giorgio Leoni (SMR)).
Goals: Switzerland: 1-0 Adrian Knup (3'), 2-0 Marc Hottiger (13'), 3-0 Beat Sutter (29'), 4-0 Heinz Hermann (55'), 5-0 Christophe Ohrel (78'), 6-0 Adrian Knup (87'), 7-0 Kübilay Türkyilmaz (90').
Referee: Erman Totoglu (TUR)   Attendance: 6.982

11-09-1991   Wankdorfstadion, Bern: Switzerland – Scotland   2-2 (2-0)
Switzerland: Stefan Huber, Marc Hottiger, Dominique Herr (YC55), Alain Sutter (60' Thomas Bickel), Christophe Ohrel, Ciriaco Sforza, Heinz Hermann (C) (YC15), Marcel Heldmann (68' Beat Sutter), Stéphane Chapuisat (YC74), Adrian Knup, Kübilay Türkyilmaz. (Coach: Ulrich (Uli) Stielike (FRG)).
Scotland: Andy Goram, Tom Boyd, Maurice Malpas, Dave McPherson, Stewart McKimmie (70' Brian McClair), Steve Nicol, Gordon Strachan (C), Stuart McCall (YC86), Gordon Durie, Ally McCoist, Mo Johnston (41' Gary McAllister). (Coach: Andrew (Andy) Roxburgh (ENG)).
Goals: Switzerland: 1-0 Stéphane Chapuisat (30'), 2-0 Heinz Hermann (38').
Scotland: 2-1 Gordon Durie (47'), 2-2 Ally McCoist (83').
Referee: Tullio Lanese (ITA)   Attendance: 42.012

16-10-1991   Balgarka Armia Stadium, Sofia: Bulgaria – San Marino   4-0 (3-0)
Bulgaria: Borislav Mihaylov (C), Nikolai Iliev, Zaprian Rakov, Radoslav Vidov (YC35), Zlatko Yankov, Ilyan Kiryakov, Hristo Kolev (64' Ivaylo Yordanov), Hristo Stoichkov (68' Yordan Letchkov), Krasimir Balakov, Emil Kostadinov, Luboslav Penev. (Coach: Dimitar Penev (BUL)).
San Marino: Pier-Luigi Benedettini, Luca Gobbi, William Guerra (C), Ivan Matteoni, Ivan Toccaceli, Mauro Valentini, Fabio Francini, Valdes Pasolini (YC43), Pier-Angelo Manzaroli (78' Nicola Bacciocchi), Pier-Domenico Della Valle, Paolo Mazza (74' Marco Mularoni). (Coach: Giorgio Leoni (SMR)).
Goals: Bulgaria: 1-0 Luboslav Penev (18'), 2-0 Hristo Stoichkov (31' penalty), 3-0 Zlatko Yankov (38'), 4-0 Nikolai Iliev (84').
Referee: Jirí Ulrich (TCH)   Attendance: 7.352

16-10-1991   Stadionul Steaua, Bucharest: Romania – Scotland   1-0 (0-0)
Romania: Silviu Lung, Dan Petrescu, Emil Sandoi, Ioan Lupescu, Gheorghe Popescu, Michael Klein, Daniel Timofte (59' Ion Timofte), Dorinel Munteanu, Gheorghe Hagi (C), Florin Raducioiu (74' Ilie Dumitrescu), Marius Lacatus. (Coach: Mircea Radulescu (ROM)).
Scotland: Andy Goram, Tom Boyd (58' Kevin Gallacher), Maurice Malpas (YC79), Dave McPherson, Stewart McKimmie, Craig Levein, Gordon Strachan (C), Stuart McCall, Brian McClair, Mike Galloway (70' Roy Aitken), Gordon Durie (YC74). (Coach: Andrew (Andy) Roxburgh (ENG)).
Goal: Romania: 1-0 Gheorghe Hagi (75' penalty).
Referee: Aron Schmidhuber (FRG)   Attendance: 15.850

13-11-1991   Hampden Park, Glasgow: Scotland – San Marino   4-0 (3-0)
Scotland: Andy Goram, Richard Gough, Maurice Malpas, Dave McPherson (46' Mo Johnston), Paul McStay, Craig Levein (60' Kevin Gallacher), Stuart McCall, Gary McAllister, Gordon Durie, Ally McCoist, John Robertson. (Coach: Andrew (Andy) Roxburgh (ENG)).
San Marino: Pier-Luigi Benedettini, Bruno Muccioli (YC30), Loris Zanotti, Luca Gobbi (46' Marco Montironi), William Guerra, Claudio Canti, Fabio Francini (YC85), Massimo Bonini, Valdes Pasolini (67' Pier-Angelo Manzaroli), Marco Mazza, Paolo Mazza. (Coach: Giorgio Leoni (SMR)).
Goals: Scotland: 1-0 Paul McStay (10'), 2-0 Richard Gough (31'), 3-0 Gordon Durie (38'), 4-0 Ally McCoist (62').
Referee: Rune Pedersen (NOR)   Attendance: 35.170

13-11-1991   Stadionul Steaua, Bucharest: Romania – Switzerland   1-0 (0-0)
Romania: Silviu Lung, Emil Sandoi, Mihai Adrian Popescu, Ioan Lupescu, Gheorghe Popescu, Michael Klein (2' Dorinel Munteanu), Daniel Timofte (46' Ioan Sabau), Gheorghe Hagi, Florin Raducioiu, Marius Lacatus (YC12), Dorin Mateut. (Coach: Mircea Radulescu (ROM)).
Switzerland: Stefan Huber, Marc Hottiger, Dominique Herr, Peter Schepull, Alain Sutter, Christophe Ohrel, Ciriaco Sforza (YC38), Heinz Hermann (77' Thomas Bickel), Beat Sutter (65' Christophe Bonvin), Stéphane Chapuisat, Kübilay Türkyilmaz (YC9). (Coach: Ulrich (Uli) Stielike (FRG)).
Goal: Romania: 1-0 Dorin Mateut (69').
Referee: John Blankenstein (HOL)   Attendance: 23.000

20-11-1991   Vasil Levski National Stadium, Sofia: Bulgaria – Romania   1-1 (0-1)
Bulgaria: Borislav Mihaylov (C), Petar Hubtchev, Nikolai Iliev (55' Dimitar Mladenov), Zaprian Rakov (YC38), Zlatko Yankov, Nasko Sirakov, Ilyan Kiryakov, Hristo Stoichkov, Emil Kostadinov (70' Georgi Iordanov (YC89)), Krasimir Balakov, Luboslav Penev. (Coach: Dimitar Penev (BUL)).
Romania: Silviu Lung, Emil Sandoi (69' Ion Timofte), Mihai Adrian Popescu, Ioan Lupescu, Gheorghe Popescu, Ioan Sabau, Dorinel Munteanu (YC88), Gheorghe Hagi (C), Florin Raducioiu, Marius Lacatus (61' Ilie Dumitrescu), Dorin Mateut. (Coach: Mircea Radulescu (ROM)).
Goals: Bulgaria: 1-1 Nasko Sirakov (55').
Romania: 0-1 Mihai Adrian Popescu (31').
Referee: Peter Mikkelsen (DEN)   Attendance: 27.744

GROUP 3

12-09-1990	Moscow	Soviet Union – Norway	2-0 (1-0)
10-10-1990	Bergen	Norway – Hungary	0-0
17-10-1990	Budapest	Hungary – Italy	1-1 (1-0)
31-10-1990	Budapest	Hungary – Cyprus	4-2 (3-1)
03-11-1990	Rome	Italy – Soviet Union	0-0
14-11-1990	Nicosia	Cyprus – Norway	0-3 (0-1)
22-12-1990	Limassol	Cyprus – Italy	0-4 (0-3)
03-04-1991	Limassol	Cyprus – Hungary	0-2 (0-2)
17-04-1991	Budapest	Hungary – Soviet Union	0-1 (0-1)
01-05-1991	Oslo	Norway – Cyprus	3-0 (0-0)
01-05-1991	Salerno	Italy – Hungary	3-1 (2-0)
29-05-1991	Moscow	Soviet Union – Cyprus	4-0 (1-0)
05-06-1991	Oslo	Norway – Italy	2-1 (2-0)
28-08-1991	Oslo	Norway – Soviet Union	0-1 (0-0)
25-09-1991	Moscow	Soviet Union – Hungary	2-2 (1-1)
12-10-1991	Moscow	Soviet Union – Italy	0-0
30-10-1991	Szombathely	Hungary – Norway	0-0
13-11-1991	Genoa	Italy – Norway	1-1 (0-0)
13-11-1991	Limassol	Cyprus – Soviet Union	0-3 (0-1)
21-12-1991	Foggia	Italy – Cyprus	2-0 (1-0)

FINAL STANDING

Pos	Team	Pld	W	D	L	GF	GA	GD	Pts
1	*Soviet Union*	*8*	*5*	*3*	*0*	*13*	*2*	*+11*	*13*
2	Italy	8	3	4	1	12	5	+7	10
3	Norway	8	3	3	2	9	5	+4	9
4	Hungary	8	2	4	2	10	9	+1	8
5	Cyprus	8	0	0	8	2	25	-23	0

Soviet Union qualified for the final tournament in Sweden.

The Soviet Union team were replaced by the CIS (= Commonwealth of Independent States) in the final tournament following the dissolution of the Soviet Union just after the end of the qualifying stages.

12-09-1990   Central Lenin Stadium, Moscow: Soviet Union – Norway 2-0 (1-0)
Soviet Union: Aleksandr Uvarov, Sergei Gorlukovich, Oleh Kuznetsov, Andrei Chernyshov, Igor Dobrovolski, Igor Shalimov, Oleksiy Mikhaylichenko (C), Andrei Kanchelskis, Vadim Tyshchenko (79' Vassili Kulkov), Oleh Protasov, Ivan Hetsko (71' Igor Kolyvanov). (Coach: Anatoliy Fyodorovich Byshovets (URS)).
Norway: Erik Thorstvedt, Rune Bratseth (C), Gunnar Halle, Pål Lydersen, Tore André Pedersen, Jahn Ivar Mini Jakobsen, Ørjan Berg (62' Erik Pedersen), Per Egil Ahlsen, Tom Gulbrandsen, Jan Åge Fjørtoft (66' Tore André Dahlum), Jörn Andersen (YC15). (Coach: Ingvar Stadheim (NOR)).
Goals: Soviet Union: 1-0 Andrei Kanchelskis (22'), 2-0 Oleh Kuznetsov (60').
Referee: Hubert Forstinger (AUT)   Attendance: 23.000

10-10-1990   Brann Stadion, Bergen: Norway – Hungary 0-0
Norway: Erik Thorstvedt, Rune Bratseth (C), Gunnar Halle, Pål Lydersen, Tore André Pedersen, Jahn Ivar Mini Jakobsen (71' Jörn Andersen), Per Egil Ahlsen, Erik Pedersen, Sverre Brandhaug, Jan Åge Fjørtoft (82' Tore André Dahlum), Gøran Sørloth. (Coach: Ingvar Stadheim (NOR)).
Hungary: Zsolt Petry, Attila Pintér, József Szalma, Ervin Kovács, Zsolt Limperger, Emil Lörincz, József Kiprich (87' Imre Fodor), György Bognar (C), Tamás Mónos, István Kozma, Kálmán Kovács. (Coach: Kálmán Mészöly (HUN)).
Referee: John Spillane (IRL)   Attendance: 6.304

17-10-1990   Népstadion, Budapest; Hungary – Italy 1-1 (1-0)
Hungary: Zsolt Petry, József Szalma, Zsolt Limperger, Emil Lörincz, László Disztl, Imre Garaba (C) (YC37) (60' Imre Fodor), József Kiprich, György Bognar, Tamás Mónos, István Kozma (87' István Urbányi), Kálmán Kovács (YC47). (Coach: Kálmán Mészöly (HUN)).
Italy: Walter Zenga, Franco Baresi, Giuseppe Bergomi (C), Riccardo Ferri, Roberto Donadoni, Fernando De Napoli, Giuseppe Giannini (YC51) (87' Nicola Berti), Luigi De Agostini, Giancarlo Marocchi, Roberto Baggio (YC54), Salvatore Schillaci (81' Aldo Serena). (Coach: Azeglio Vicini (ITA)).
Goals: Hungary: 1-0 László Disztl (16').
Italy: 1-1 Roberto Baggio (54' penalty).
Referee: Bo Karlsson (SWE)   Attendance: 24.431

31-10-1990   Népstadion, Budapest; Hungary – Cyprus 4-2 (3-1)
Hungary: Zsolt Petry, József Szalma, Zsolt Limperger, Emil Lörincz, László Disztl, Imre Garaba (C), József Kiprich (75' Vendel Rugovics), György Bognar, Tamás Mónos, István Kozma (55' Pál Fischer), Kálmán Kovács. (Coach: Kálmán Mészöly (HUN)).
Cyprus: Marios Onisiforou, Yiannis Kalotheou, George Christodoulou, Costas Miamiliotis, Avraam Socratous, Kostakis Konstantinou (76' Panayiotis Orfanidis), Yiannakis Yiangoudakis (C), Pavlos Savva, Spyros Kastanas, Andreas Kantilos (58' Angelos Tsolakis), Panayiotis Xiourouppas (YC69). (Coach: Panikos Iacovou (CYP)).
Goals: Hungary: 1-0 Emil Lörincz (1'), 2-1 George Christodoulou (18' *own goal*), 3-1 József Kiprich (19' penalty), 4-1 József Kiprich (67' penalty).
Cyprus: 1-1 Panayiotis Xiourouppas (13'), 4-2 Angelos Tsolakis (89').
Referee: Plarent Kotherja (ALB)   Attendance: 2.204

03-11-1990   Stadio Olimpico, Rome: Italy – Soviet Union   0-0
Italy: Walter Zenga, Paolo Maldini, Franco Baresi (C), Riccardo Ferri, Ciro Ferrara, Fernando De Napoli, Luigi De Agostini, Massimo Crippa, Roberto Mancini, Roberto Baggio, Salvatore Schillaci (67' Aldo Serena). (Coach: Azeglio Vicini (ITA)).
Soviet Union: Aleksandr Uvarov, Akhrik Tsveiba (YC76), Andrei Chernyshov, Vassili Kulkov, Aleksandr Mostovoi (86' Vladimir Tatarchuk), Sergei Aleinikov, Igor Dobrovolski (YC51), Igor Shalimov, Oleksiy Mikhaylichenko (C), Andrei Kanchelskis, Ivan Hetsko (67' Oleh Protasov). (Coach: Anatoliy Fyodorovich Byshovets (URS)).
Referee: Marcel Van Langenhove (BEL)   Attendance: 52.208

14-11-1990   Makario Stadium, Nicosia: Cyprus – Norway   0-3 (0-1)
Cyprus: Andreas Haritou, Yiannis Kalotheou (YC23) (50' Andreas Kantilos), George Christodoulou, Costas Miamiliotis, Avraam Socratous, Yiannakis Yiangoudakis (C), Pavlos Savva, Spyros Kastanas, Floros Nicolaou, Angelos Tsolakis (75' Kostakis Konstantinou), Panayiotis Xiourouppas. (Coach: Panikos Iacovou (CYP)).
Norway: Erik Thorstvedt, Rune Bratseth (C), Gunnar Halle, Pål Lydersen, Tore André Pedersen, Karl-Petter Løken (66' Erik Pedersen), Øyvind Leonhardsen, Lars Roar Bohinen, Sverre Brandhaug, Gøran Sørloth, Tore André Dahlum (79' Jan Åge Fjørtoft). (Coach: Egil Olsen (NOR)).
Goals: Norway: 0-1 Gøran Sørloth (39'), 0-2 Lars Roar Bohinen (50'), 0-3 Sverre Brandhaug (64').
Referee: Zoran Petrovic (YUG)   Attendance: 2.133

22-12-1990   Tsirion Stadium, Limassol: Cyprus – Italy   0-4 (0-3)
Cyprus: Marios Onisiforou, Yiannis Kalotheou, George Christodoulou, Costas Miamiliotis, Avraam Socratous, Nikodemos Papavasiliou (57' Panayiotis Xiourouppas), Yiannakis Yiangoudakis (C), Pavlos Savva (65' Georgios Konstantinou), Floros Nicolaou, Panayiotis Pounnas, Angelos Tsolakis. (Coach: Panikos Iacovou (CYP)).
Italy: Walter Zenga, Giuseppe Bergomi (C), Pietro Vierchowod (YC5), Ciro Ferrara, Nicolas Berti, Massimo Crippa (YC55), Stefano Eranio, Giancarlo Marocchi, Attilio Lombardo, Salvatore Schillaci, Aldo Serena. (Coach: Azeglio Vicini (ITA)).
Goals: Italy: 0-1 Pietro Vierchowod (15'), 0-2 Aldo Serena (22'), 0-3 Attilio Lombardo (44'), 0-4 Aldo Serena (50').
Referee: Ivan Gregr (TCH)   Attendance: 9.185

03-04-1991   Tsirion Stadium, Limassol: Cyprus – Hungary   0-2 (0-2)
Cyprus: Socrates Marangos, Georgios Konstantinou, Demetris Ioannou, Kostakis Konstantinou, Charalambos Pittas (74' Christakis Kasianos), Yiannakis Yiangoudakis (C), Pavlos Savva (81' Andreas Sotiriou), Floros Nicolaou, Charalambos Christophi, Angelos Tsolakis (YC80), Georgios Savvides. (Coach: Andreas Michaelides (CYP)).
Hungary: Zsolt Petry, József Szalma, Zsolt Limperger, Emil Lörincz, László Disztl, Tibor Nagy, József Kiprich (YC88), György Bognar (C), Tamás Mónos, Kálmán Kovács, Pál Fischer (71' János Marozsán). (Coach: Kálmán Mészöly (HUN)).
Goals: Hungary: 0-1 Tamás Mónos (15'), 0-2 József Kiprich (40').
Refereee: Gerhard Kapl (AUT)   Attendance: 1.844

17-04-1991   Népstadion, Budapest: Hungary – Soviet Union   0-1 (0-1)
Hungary: Zsolt Petry, József Szalma, Zsolt Limperger (YC89), Emil Lörincz, László Disztl, Imre Garaba (C), József Kiprich, György Bognar (69' Istvan Vincze), Tamás Mónos, István Kozma (63' Lajos Détári), Kálmán Kovács. (Coach: Kálmán Mészöly (HUN)).
Soviet Union: Aleksandr Uvarov, Dmitri Galyamin, Akhrik Tsveiba, Andrei Chernyshov (YC22), Vassili Kulkov, Sergei Aleinikov (YC19), Igor Shalimov, Oleksiy Mikhaylichenko (C) (YC58), Andrei Kanchelskis, Sergei Yuran (85' Dmitri Kuznetsov), Igor Kolyvanov. (Coach: Anatoliy Fyodorovich Byshovets (URS)).
Goal: Soviet Union: 0-1 Oleksiy Mikhaylichenko (30').
Referee: Aron Schmidhuber (FRG)   Attendance: 43.221

01-05-1990   Ullevaal Stadion, Oslo: Norway – Cyprus   3-0 (0-0)
Norway: Erik Thorstvedt, Stig Inge Bjørnebye, Rune Bratseth (C) (46' Kåre Ingebrigtsen), Gunnar Halle (75' Erik Pedersen), Pål Lydersen, Tore André Pedersen, Øyvind Leonhardsen, Per Egil Ahlsen, Sverre Brandhaug, Gøran Sørloth, Tore André Dahlum. (Coach: Egil Olsen (NOR)).
Cyprus: Andreas Haritou, Yiannis Kalotheou (83' Georgios Konstantinou), Kostakis Konstantinou, Demetris Ioannou (YC82), Charalambos Pittas, Yiannakis Yiangoudakis (C) (YC55), Floros Nicolaou, Charalambos Christophi, Kostas Kosta, Panayiotis Xiourouppas (90' Andreas Sotiriou), Georgios Savvides. (Coach: Andreas Michaelides (CYP)).
Goals: Norway: 1-0 Pål Lydersen (49' penalty), 2-0 Tore André Dahlum (65'), 3-0 Gøran Sørloth (90').
Referee: Kaj John Natri (FIN)   Attendance: 5.825

01-05-1991   Stadio Arechi, Salerno: Italy – Hungary   3-1 (2-0)
Italy: Walter Zenga, Paolo Maldini, Franco Baresi (C), Riccardo Ferri, Ciro Ferrara (72' Pietro Vierchowod), Roberto Donadoni (37' Stefano Eranio), Fernando De Napoli, Giuseppe Giannini (YC37), Massimo Crippa, Gianluca Vialli, Roberto Mancini. (Coach: Azeglio Vicini (ITA)).
Hungary: Zsolt Petry, Zsolt Limperger, Emil Lörincz, László Disztl, János Palaczky (33' István Kozma), Imre Garaba (C) (YC42), József Kiprich (46' József Gregor), Lajos Détári, György Bognar, Tamás Mónos, Kálmán Kovács. (Coach: Kálmán Mészöly (HUN)).
Goals: Italy: 1-0 Roberto Donadoni (4'), 2-0 Roberto Donadoni (16'), 3-0 Gianluca Vialli (56').
Hungary: 3-1 György Bognar (65' penalty).
Referee: Joseph Betram (Joe) Worrall (ENG)   Attendance: 37.602

29-05-1991   Central Lenin Stadium, Moscow: Soviet Union – Cyprus   4-0 (1-0)
Soviet Union: Aleksandr Uvarov, Dmitri Galyamin, Andrei Chernyshov, Vassili Kulkov, Aleksandr Mostovoi (74' Dmitri Kuznetsov), Sergei Aleinikov, Igor Shalimov, Oleksiy Mikhaylichenko (C), Andrei Kanchelskis, Sergei Yuran (46' Igor Korneev), Igor Kolyvanov. (Coach: Anatoliy Fyodorovich Byshovets (URS)).
Cyprus: Andreas Haritou, Yiannis Kalotheou, George Christodoulou (YC54) (89' Pavlos Savva), Demetris Ioannou, Charalambos Pittas, Yiannakis Yiangoudakis (C), Floros Nicolaou, Charalambos Christophi, Kostas Kosta, Panayiotis Xiourouppas (YC20) (87' Kostakis Konstantinou), Georgios Savvides. (Coach: Andreas Michaelides (CYP)).
Goals: Soviet Union: 1-0 Aleksandr Mostovoi (10'), 2-0 Oleksiy Mikhaylichenko (51'), 3-0 Igor Korneev (87'), 4-0 Sergei Aleinikov (89').
Referee: Stefan Dan Petrescu (ROM)   Attendance: 14.200

05-06-1991   Ullevaal Stadion, Oslo: Norway – Italy   2-1 (2-0)
Norway: Erik Thorstvedt, Rune Bratseth, Pål Lydersen, Tore André Pedersen (YC11), Karl-Petter Løken, Jahn Ivar Mini Jakobsen, Lars Roar Bohinen (YC84), Per Egil Ahlsen, Kåre Ingebrigtsen, Gøran Sørloth (YC89), Tore André Dahlum (46' Erik Pedersen). (Coach: Egil Olsen (NOR)).
Italy: Walter Zenga, Paolo Maldini, Franco Baresi, Riccardo Ferri (88' Giuseppe Bergomi (RC89)), Ciro Ferrara (YC30), Fernando De Napoli (53' Salvatore Schillaci), Massimo Crippa, Stefano Eranio, Attilio Lombardo, Gianluca Vialli, Roberto Mancini (YC16). (Coach: Azeglio Vicini (ITA)).
Goals: Norway: 1-0 Tore André Dahlum (4'), 2-0 Lars Roar Bohinen (25').
Italy: 2-1 Salvatore Schillaci (77').
Referee: Mario van der Ende (HOL)   Attendance: 24.346

28-08-1991   Ullevaal Stadion, Oslo: Norway – Soviet Union   0-1 (0-0)
Norway: Erik Thorstvedt, Rune Bratseth, Gunnar Halle, Pål Lydersen, Tore André Pedersen, Karl-Petter Løken, Roger Nilsen (66' Dag Riisnæs), Øyvind Leonhardsen, Jahn Ivar Mini Jakobsen (80' Bent Skammelsrud), Jan Åge Fjørtoft (YC89), Gøran Sørloth. (Coach: Egil Olsen (NOR)).
Soviet Union: Stanislav Cherchesov, Oleh Kuznetsov, Akhrik Tsveiba, Andrei Chernyshov, Vassili Kulkov, Sergei Aleinikov, Igor Shalimov, Oleksiy Mikhaylichenko, Andrei Kanchelskis (72' Igor Korneev), Sergei Yuran (46' Aleksandr Mostovoi), Igor Kolyvanov. (Coach: Anatoliy Fyodorovich Byshovets (URS)).
Goal: Soviet Union: 0-1 Aleksandr Mostovoi (74').
Referee: Howard William King (WAL)   Attendance: 24.383

25-09-1991   Central Lenin Stadium, Moscow: Soviet Union – Hungary   2-2 (1-1)
Soviet Union: Stanislav Cherchesov, Dmitri Galyamin, Akhrik Tsveiba (23' Oleh Kuznetsov), Andrei Chernyshov, Vassili Kulkov (YC52), Aleksandr Mostovoi (68' Sergei Yuran), Sergei Aleinikov, Igor Shalimov, Oleksiy Mikhaylichenko (C), Andrei Kanchelskis, Igor Kolyvanov. (Coach: Anatoliy Fyodorovich Byshovets (URS)).
Hungary: Zsolt Petry, József Szalma, Zsolt Limperger (YC75), Emil Lörincz, László Disztl, József Kiprich, Lajos Détári, Tamás Mónos (42' József Duró), István Kozma (68' Pál Fischer), Péter Lipcsei (YC33), Kálmán Kovács. (Coach: Kálmán Mészöly (HUN)).
Goals: Soviet Union: 1-1 Igor Shalimov (37' penalty), 2-1 Andrei Kanchelskis (50').
Hungary: 0-1 József Kiprich (16'), 2-2 József Kiprich (84').
Referee: Zoran Petrovic (YUG)   Attendance: 34.973

12-10-1991   Central Lenin Stadium, Moscow: Soviet Union – Italy   0-0
Soviet Union: Stanislav Cherchesov, Dmitri Galyamin, Oleh Kuznetsov (46' Akhrik Tsveiba), Andrei Chernyshov, Vassili Kulkov, Sergei Aleinikov (YC39), Igor Shalimov, Oleksiy Mikhaylichenko (C), Andrei Kanchelskis, Oleh Protasov (70' Dmitri Kuznetsov), Igor Kolyvanov. (Coach: Anatoliy Fyodorovich Byshovets (URS)).
Italy: Walter Zenga, Paolo Maldini, Franco Baresi (C), Pietro Vierchowod (YC79), Ciro Ferrara, Fernando De Napoli, Giuseppe Giannini (70' Roberto Mancini), Massimo Crippa, Gianluigi Lentini (68' Attilio Lombardo), Gianluca Vialli, Ruggiero Rizzitelli. (Coach: Azeglio Vicini (ITA)).
Referee: Bruno Galler (SUI)   Attendance: 86.486

30-10-1991   Rohonci úti stadion, Szombathely: Hungary – Norway   0-0
Hungary: Zsolt Petry, Attila Pintér, Emil Lörincz, Tibor Nagy, Lajos Détári, József Duró, Flórián Urbán, István Pisont (83' Denes Eszenyi), Péter Lipcsei (71' Béla Illés), Kálmán Kovács, Pál Fischer. (Coach: Róbert Glázer (HUN)).
Norway: Frode Grodås, Stig Inge Bjørnebye, Rune Bratseth, Tore André Pedersen, Karl-Petter Løken, Øyvind Leonhardsen (78' Kåre Ingebrigtsen), Kjetil Rekdal, Jahn Ivar Mini Jakobsen, Lars Roar Bohinen, Per Egil Ahlsen, Gøran Sørloth (46' Jan Åge Fjørtoft). (Coach: Egil Olsen (NOR)).
Referee: Gérard Biguet (FRA)   Attendance: 4.609

13-11-1991   Stadio Comunale Luigi Ferraris, Genoa: Italy – Norway   1-1 (0-0)
Italy: Gianluca Pagliuca, Paolo Maldini, Alessandro Costacurta (YC17), Franco Baresi (C), Riccardo Ferri, Nicola Berti (72' Fernando De Napoli), Carlo Ancelotti (YC81), Stefano Eranio, Gianluca Vialli, Gianfranco Zola, Francesco Baiano (58' Ruggiero Rizzitelli). (Coach: Arrigo Sacchi (ITA)).
Norway: Erik Thorstvedt, Ronny Johnsen (46' Jan Pedersen), Rune Bratseth (C), Pål Lydersen, Karl-Petter Løken, Kjetil Rekdal, Jahn Ivar Mini Jakobsen, Per Egil Ahlsen, Kåre Ingebrigtsen (84' Ørjan Berg (YC87)), Jan Åge Fjørtoft (YC15), Gøran Sørloth (YC60). (Coach: Egil Olsen (NOR)).
Goals: Italy: 1-1 Ruggiero Rizzitelli (83').
Norway: 0-1 Jahn Ivar Mini Jakobsen (60').
Referee: Karl-Josef Assenmacher (FRG)   Attendance: 21.372

13-11-1991   Tsirion Stadium, Limassol: Cyprus – Soviet Union   0-3 (0-1)
Cyprus: Andreas Haritou, Avraam Socratous, Kostakis Konstantinou, Charalambos Pittas, Marios Charalambous, Neophytos Larkou, Pavlos Savva, Kostas Kosta, Christakis Koliantris (74' Loukas Hadjiloukas), Georgios Savvides (46' Andreas Sotiriou), Yiannos Ioannou. (Coach: Andreas Michaelides (CYP)).
Soviet Union: Dmitri Kharin, Dmitri Galyamin, Oleh Kuznetsov, Akhrik Tsveiba, Andrei Chernyshov (YC71), Vassili Kulkov, Igor Shalimov, Oleksiy Mykhaylichenko, Andrei Kanchelskis, Oleh Protasov (69' Aleksandr Mostovoi), Igor Kolyvanov (46' Sergei Yuran (YC64)). (Coach: Anatoliy Fyodorovich Byshovets (URS)).
Goals: Soviet Union: 0-1 Oleh Protasov (26'), 0-2 Sergei Yuran (78'), 0-3 Andrei Kanchelskis (81').
Referee: Andrew Wilson Waddell (SCO)   Attendance: 3.379

21-12-1991   Stadio Comunale Pino Zaccheria, Foggia: Italy – Cyprus   2-0 (1-0)
Italy: Walter Zenga, Paolo Maldini, Alessandro Costacurta, Franco Baresi (C), Demetrio Albertini, Dino Baggio, Nicola Berti (YC45), Alberico Evani, Roberto Baggio (69' Pierluigi Casiraghi), Gianluca Vialli (69' Francesco Baiano), Gianfranco Zola. (Coach: Arrigo Sacchi (ITA)).
Cyprus: Michalis Christofi, Kostakis Konstantinou, Georgios Konstantinou, Charalambos Pittas, Marios Charalambous, Pavlos Savva, Floros Nicolaou (C), Christakis Koliantris, Vasos Tsaggaris (63' Andreas Kantilos), Andreas Sotiriou, Yiannos Ioannou (78' Neophytos Larkou). (Coach: Andreas Michaelides (CYP)).
Goals: Italy: 1-0 Gianluca Vialli (28'), 2-0 Roberto Baggio (56').
Referee: Joaquin Ramos Marcos (ESP)   Attendance: 17.732

GROUP 4

12-09-1990	Landskrona	Faroe Islands – Austria	1-0 (0-0)
12-09-1990	Belfast	Northern Ireland – Yugoslavia	0-2 (0-1)
10-10-1990	Copenhagen	Denmark – Faroe Islands	4-1 (2-1)
17-10-1990	Belfast	Northern Ireland – Denmark	1-1 (0-1)
31-10-1990	Belgrade	Yugoslavia – Austria	4-1 (2-1)
14-11-1990	Copenhagen	Denmark – Yugoslavia	0-2 (0-0)
14-11-1990	Vienna	Austria – Northern Ireland	0-0
27-03-1991	Belgrade	Yugoslavia – Northern Ireland	4-1 (1-1)
01-05-1991	Belgrade	Yugoslavia – Denmark	1-2 (0-1)
01-05-1991	Belfast	Northern Ireland – Faroe Islands	1-1 (1-0)
16-05-1991	Belgrade	Yugoslavia – Faroe Islands	7-0 (2-0)
22-05-1991	Salzburg	Austria – Faroe Islands	3-0 (1-0)
05-06-1991	Odensen	Denmark – Austria	2-1 (2-0)
11-09-1991	Landskrona	Faroe Islands – Northern Ireland	0-5 (0-3)
25-09-1991	Landskrona	Faroe Islands – Denmark	0-4 (0-2)
09-10-1991	Vienna	Austria – Denmark	0-3 (0-3)
16-10-1991	Landskrona	Faroe Islands – Yugoslavia	0-2 (0-1)
16-10-1991	Belfast	Northern Ireland – Austria	2-1 (2-1)
13-11-1991	Odense	Denmark – Northern Ireland	2-1 (2-0)
13-11-1991	Vienna	Austria – Yugoslavia	0-2 (0-2)

FINAL STANDING

Pos	Team	Pld	W	D	L	GF	GA	GD	Pts
1	Yugoslavia	8	7	0	1	24	4	+20	14
2	*Denmark*	*8*	*6*	*1*	*1*	*18*	*7*	*+11*	*13*
3	Northern Ireland	8	2	3	3	11	11	0	7
4	Austria	8	1	1	6	6	14	-8	3
5	Faroe Islands	8	1	1	6	3	26	-23	3

Yugoslavia won the group, but were banned from the final tournament in Sweden.

Yugoslavia were placed under sanctions on 30th May 1992 by United Nations Security Council Resolution 757 following the outbreak of the Yugoslav Wars. FIFA therefore immediately suspended the Yugoslav football team from competitive football, meaning they could not participate in the final tournament. Group runners-up Denmark were invited to take their place in the finals.

12-09-1990   Landskrona IP, Landskrona (SWE): Fareo Islands – Austria   1-0 (0-0)
Faroe Islands: Jens Knudsen, Allan Mørkøre (YC44), Jóannes Jakobsen (C), Tummas Eli Hansen, Mikkjal Danielsen, Jan Dam, Julian Hansen, Torkil Nielsen, Abraham Hansen, Kári Reynheim (YC87), Kurt Mørkøre (YC8). (Coach: Páll Gudlaugsson (ISL)).
Austria: Michael Konsel, Robert Pecl, Kurt Russ, Michael Streiter (YC58), Heinz Peischl, Andreas Herzog (62' Gerald Willfurth), Manfred Linzmaier, Gerhard Rodax, Andreas Reisinger (62' Peter Pacult), Jürgen Hartmann, Toni Polster. (Coach: Josef Hickersberger (AUT)).
Goal: Faroe Islands: 1-0 Torkil Nielsen (61').
Referee: Egil Nervik (NOR)   Attendance: 1.157

12-09-1990   Windsor Park, Belfast: Northern Ireland – Yugoslavia   0-2 (0-1)
Northern Ireland: Paul Kee, Mal Donaghy, Alan McDonald (C), Nigel Worthington, Gerry Taggart, Anthony Rogan, Robert Dennison (65' Colin Clarke), Danny Wilson, Kingsley Black, Iain Dowie (YC68), Kevin Wilson. (Coach: William Laurence (Billy) Bingham (NIR)).
Yugoslavia: Tomislav Ivkovic (YC52), Predrag Spasic, Faruk Hadzibegic (C), Zoran Vulic, Ilija Najdoski, Dragan Stojkovic, Dejan Savicevic, Davor Jozic, Robert Prosinecki, Darko Pancev (85' Zeljko Petrovic), Dragisa Binic (88' Vlada Stosic). (Coach: Ivan Osim (YUG)).
Goals: Yugoslavia: 0-1 Darko Pancev (36'), 0-2 Robert Prosinecki (86').
Referee: Jacobus H. (Jaap) Uilenberg (HOL)   Attendance: 9.008

10-10-1990   Idrætsparken, Copenhagen: Denmark – Faroe Islands   4-1 (2-1)
Denmark: Peter Schmeichel (YC), Jan Heintze, John Sivebæk, Kent Nielsen, Lars Olsen (C), Michael Laudrup, Kim Vilfort, Jan Bartram, Brian Laudrup, Flemming Povlsen, Lars Elstrup (73' Erik Rasmussen). (Coach: Richard Møller Nielsen (DEN)).
Faroe Islands: Jens Knudsen (YC), Allan Mørkøre (89' Magni Jarnskor), Jóannes Jakobsen (C), Tummas Eli Hansen, Mikkjal Danielsen, Jan Dam (YC), Julian Hansen, Torkil Nielsen, Abraham Hansen, Kári Reynheim, Kurt Mørkøre (76' Gunnar Mohr). (Coach: Páll Gudlaugsson (ISL)).
Goals: Denmark: 1-0 Michael Laudrup (8'), 2-1 Lars Elstrup (37'), 3-1 Michael Laudrup (48'), 4-1 Flemming Povlsen (89').
Faroe Islands: 1-1 Allan Mørkøre (21').
Referee: Gudmundur Haraldsson (ISL)   Attendance: 38.563

17-10-1990   Windsor Park, Belfast: Northern Ireland – Denmark   1-1 (0-1)
Northern Ireland: Paul Kee, Mal Donaghy, Alan McDonald (C), Nigel Worthington, Gerry Taggart, Anthony Rogan, Danny Wilson, Kingsley Black, Colin O'Neill (71' Stephen McBride), Colin Clarke, Iain Dowie. (Coach: William Laurence (Billy) Bingham (NIR)).
Denmark: Peter Schmeichel, Jan Heintze, John Sivebæk, Kent Nielsen, Lars Olsen, John Larsen, Michael Laudrup (80' John Dulle Helt), Kim Vilfort, Jan Bartram, Brian Laudrup (70' Lars Elstrup), Flemming Povlsen. (Coach: Richard Møller Nielsen (DEN)).
Goals: Northern Ireland: 1-1 Colin Clarke (58').
Denmark: 0-1 Jan Bartram (11' penalty).
Referee: Roger Philippi (LUX)   Attendance: 9.079

31-10-1990   Stadion Crvena Zvezda, Belgrade: Yugoslavia – Austria   4-1 (2-1)
Yugoslavia: Tomislav Ivkovic, Predrag Spasic (YC12), Faruk Hadzibegic, Srecko Katanec (46' Robert Jarni), Zoran Vulic, Davor Jozic, Mehmed Bazdarevic, Robert Prosinecki, Zlatko Vujovic (C), Darko Pancev, Safet Susic (63' Zvonimir Boban). (Coach: Ivan Osim (YUG)).
Austria: Michael Konsel, Ernst Aigner, Robert Pecl (YC24), Michael Streiter (YC63), Peter Schöttel, Andreas Herzog (46' Manfred Linzmaier), Peter Artner, Alfred Hörtnagl, Andreas Reisinger, Toni Polster (C), Andreas Ogris (52' Peter Pacult). (Coach: Alfred Riedl (AUT)).
Goals: Yugoslavia: 1-1 Darko Pancev (32'), 2-1 Srecko Katanec (43'), 3-1 Darko Pancev (52'), 4-1 Darko Pancev (85').
Austria: 0-1 Andreas Ogris (15').
Referee: Aron Schmidhuber (FRG)   Attendance: 11.422

14-11-1990   Idrætsparken, Copenhagen: Denmark – Yugoslavia   0-2 (0-0)
Denmark: Peter Schmeichel, Jan Heintze, John Sivebæk, Kent Nielsen, Lars Olsen (C), Jan Mølby (72' Lars Elstrup), Michael Laudrup, Kim Vilfort (YC13), Jan Bartram, Brian Laudrup, Flemming Povlsen (46' John Faxe Jensen). (Coach: Richard Møller Nielsen (DEN)).
Yugoslavia: Tomislav Ivkovic, Predrag Spasic, Faruk Hadzibegic, Srecko Katanec, Zoran Vulic (YC6), Davor Jozic, Mehmed Bazdarevic, Robert Jarni, Zlatko Vujovic (C) (YC39) (88' Ilija Najdoski), Darko Pancev (11' Zvonimir Boban), Safet Susic. (Coach: Ivan Osim (YUG)).
Goals: Yugoslavia: 0-1 Mehmed Bazdarevic (77'), 0-2 Robert Jarni (84').
Referee: Neil Midgley (ENG)   Attendance: 39.700

14-11-1990   Praterstadion, Vienna: Austria – Northern Ireland   0-0
Austria: Michael Konsel, Robert Pecl, Peter Schöttel (YC70), Heinz Peischl, Andreas Poiger, Peter Artner, Manfred Linzmaier, Alfred Hörtnagl, Gerald Willfurth (YC29), Toni Polster (C) (67' Peter Pacult), Andreas Ogris. (Coach: Alfred Riedl (AUT)).
Northern Ireland: Paul Kee, Mal Donaghy, Alan McDonald (C), Nigel Worthington, Gerry Taggart, Anthony Rogan, Robert Dennison, Danny Wilson, Kingsley Black (82' Stephen Morrow), Colin Clarke (YC61) (63' Iain Dowie), Kevin Wilson. (Coach: William Laurence (Billy) Bingham (NIR)).
Referee: Gérard Biguet (FRA)   Attendance: 6.753

27-03-1991   Stadion Crvena Zvezda, Belgrade: Yugoslavia – Northern Ireland   4-1 (1-1)
Yugoslavia: Tomislav Ivkovic, Predrag Spasic, Faruk Hadzibegic, Zoran Vulic (84' Ilija Najdoski), Dejan Savicevic, Davor Jozic, Mehmed Bazdarevic, Robert Jarni, Robert Prosinecki, Darko Pancev, Dragisa Binic. (Coach: Ivan Osim (YUG)).
Northern Ireland: Paul Kee, Mal Donaghy, Anthony Rogan (YC67), Colin Hill, Stephen Morrow, Gary Fleming, Robert Dennison (78' James Quinn), Kingsley Black, Jim Magilton, Iain Dowie, Kevin Wilson (53' Colin Clarke). (Coach: William Laurence (Billy) Bingham (NIR)).
Goals: Yugoslavia: 1-0 Dragisa Binic (35'), 2-1 Darko Pancev (47'), 3-1 Darko Pancev (60'), 4-1 Darko Pancev (62').
Northern Ireland: 1-1 Colin Hill (44').
Referee: Yusuf Namoglu (TUR)   Attendance: 5.086

01-05-1991   Stadion Crvena Zvezda, Belgrade: Yugoslavia – Denmark   1-2 (0-1)
Yugoslavia: Tomislav Ivkovic, Predrag Spasic, Faruk Hadzibegic (C), Zoran Vulic, Dejan Savicevic, Davor Jozic (YC66), Mehmed Bazdarevic, Robert Jarni (85' Ilija Najdoski), Robert Prosinecki, Darko Pancev (YC53), Dragisa Binic. (Coach: Ivan Osim (YUG)).
Denmark: Peter Schmeichel, John Sivebæk (55' Henrik Larsen (YC82)), Kent Nielsen, Lars Olsen (C), Bjørn Kristensen, Kim Christofte, John Faxe Jensen (83' Bjarne Goldbæk), Kim Vilfort, Jan Bartram, Flemming Povlsen, Bent Christensen Arensøe. (Coach: Richard Møller Nielsen (DEN)).
Goals: Yugoslavia: 1-1 Darko Pancev (50').
Denmark: 0-1 Bent Christensen Arensøe (31'), 1-2 Bent Christensen Arensøe (63').
Referee: Joël Quiniou (FRA)   Attendance: 16.477

01-05-1991   Windsor Park, Belfast: Northern Ireland – Faroe Islands   1-1 (1-0)
Northern Ireland: Paul Kee, Mal Donaghy, Alan McDonald, Nigel Worthington, Garry Taggart, Danny Wilson (82' Robert Dennison), Kingsley Black, Jim Magilton, Colin Clarke, Iain Dowie (82' Paul Williams), Kevin Wilson. (Coach: William Laurence (Billy) Bingham (NIR)).
Faroe Islands: Jens Knudsen, Allan Mørkøre, Jóannes Jakobsen (C), Tummas Eli Hansen, Mikkjal Danielsen, Jan Dam, Torkil Nielsen, Abraham Hansen, Kári Reynheim (73' Albert Ari Thomassen), Kurt Mørkøre (88' Jens Erik Rasmussen), Jan Allan Müller. (Coach: Páll Gudlaugsson (ISL)).
Goals: Northern Ireland: 1-0 Colin Clarke (45').
Faroe Islands: 1-1 Kári Reynheim (63').
Referee: Michel Piraux (BEL)   Attendance: 7.253

16-05-1991   Stadion Crvena Zvezda, Belgrade: Yugoslavia – Faroe Islands   7-0 (2-0)
Yugoslavia: Tomislav Ivkovic (C) (77' Drazen Ladic), Predrag Spasic, Vujadin Stanojkovic, Sinisa Mihajlovic, Zoran Vulic, Ilija Najdoski, Zvonimir Boban, Dejan Savicevic, Robert Jarni (65' Davor Suker), Robert Prosinecki, Darko Pancev. (Coach: Ivan Osim (YUG)).
Faroe Islands: Jens Knudsen, Allan Mørkøre, Jóannes Jakobsen (C), Tummas Eli Hansen, Mikkjal Danielsen, Jan Dam, Torkil Nielsen, Abraham Hansen, Magni Jarnskor (57' Jákup Símun Simonsen), Kári Reynheim, Kurt Mørkøre (49' Jan Allan Müller). (Coach: Páll Gudlaugsson (ISL)).
Goals: Yugoslavia: 1-0 Ilija Najdoski (21'), 2-0 Robert Prosinecki (24'), 3-0 Darko Pancev (51'), 4-0 Zoran Vulic (65'), 5-0 Zvonimir Boban (68'), 6-0 Darko Pancev (72'), 7-0 Davor Suker (85').
Referee: Vassilios Nikakis (GRE)   Attendance: 6.745

22-05-1991   Lehener Stadion, Salzburg: Austria – Faroe Islands   3-0 (1-0)
Austria: Michael Konsel (86' Franz Wohlfahrt), Kurt Russ, Michael Streiter, Peter Schöttel, Andreas Herzog, Arnold Wetl, Michael Baur, Peter Stöger, Jürgen Hartmann, Andreas Ogris (C), Heimo Pfeifenberger (24' Alfred Hörtnagl). (Coach: Alfred Riedl (AUT)).
Faroe Islands: Jens Knudsen, Allan Mørkøre, Jóannes Jakobsen (C), Tummas Eli Hansen, Mikkjal Danielsen, Jan Dam (70' Albert Ari Thomassen), Jens Erik Rasmussen (YC53) (83' Gunnar Mohr), Torkil Nielsen, Abraham Hansen (YC13), Jákup Símun Simonsen (YC68), Kári Reynheim. (Coach: Páll Gudlaugsson (ISL)).
Goals: Austria: 1-0 Heimo Pfeifenberger (13'), 2-0 Michael Streiter (48'), 3-0 Arnold Wetl (69').
Referee: Loizos Loizou (CYP)   Attendance: 11.757

05-06-1991   Odense Stadium, Odense: Denmark – Austria 2-1 (2-0)
Denmark: Peter Schmeichel, Kent Nielsen, Lars Olsen (C), Morten Bruun, Brian Steen Nielsen, Kim Vilfort, Henrik Larsen, Johnny Anker Hansen, Flemming Povlsen (78' Erik Rasmussen), Bent Christensen Arensøe, Claus Illeman Nielsen (46' Bjarne Goldbæk). (Coach: Richard Møller Nielsen (DEN)).
Austria: Otto Konrad, Kurt Russ (72' Christian Prosenik), Michael Streiter (YC49), Peter Schöttel (68' Alfred Hörtnagl), Michael Baur, Andreas Herzog (C), Peter Stöger, Jürgen Hartmann, Andreas Ogris, Heimo Pfeifenberger (YC36), Christoph Westerthaler. (Coach: Alfred Riedl (AUT)).
Goals: Denmark: 1-0 Bent Christensen Arensøe (2'), 2-0 Bent Christensen Arensøe (33').
Austria: 2-1 Andreas Ogris (83').
Referee: Michal Listkiewicz (POL)   Attendance: 12.521

11-09-1991   Landskrona IP, Landskrona (SWE): Faroe Islands – Northern Ireland   0-5 (0-3)
Faroe Islands: Jens Knudsen, Allan Mørkøre (YC57,RC68), Jóannes Jakobsen (81' Kurt Mørkøre), Tummas Eli Hansen, Mikkjal Danielsen, Jan Dam, Torkil Nielsen, Abraham Hansen, Albert Ari Thomassen (YC46) (53' Jan Allan Müller), Todi Jónsson, Kári Reynheim. (Coach: Páll Gudlaugsson (ISL)).
Northern Ireland: Tommy Wright, Mal Donaghy, Alan McDonald, Garry Taggart, Stephen Morrow, Robert Dennison, Kingsley Black (73' Stephen McBride), Jim Magilton, Colin Clarke, Iain Dowie, Kevin Wilson (73' Michael O'Neill). (Coach: William Laurence (Billy) Bingham (NIR)).
Goals: Northern Ireland: 0-1 Kevin Wilson (8'), 0-2 Colin Clarke (12'), 0-3 Alan McDonald (14'), 0-4 Colin Clarke (51'), 0-5 Colin Clarke (68' penalty).
Referee: Simo Ruokonen (FIN)   Attendance: 1.623

25-09-1991   Landskrona IP, Landskrona (SWE): Faroe Islands – Denmark   0-4 (0-2)
Faroe Islands: Jens Knudsen (46' Kaj Leo Johannesen), Jóannes Jakobsen (C), Tummas Eli Hansen, Mikkjal Danielsen, Jan Dam (YC66), Abraham Hansen (YC27), Magni Jarnskor, Todi Jónsson (83' Eydfinn Davidsen), Kári Reynheim (YC36), Kurt Mørkøre, Jan Allan Müller. (Coach: Páll Gudlaugsson (ISL)).
Denmark: Peter Schmeichel, John Sivebæk, Kent Nielsen, Lars Olsen (C), Kim Christofte (60' Johnny Mølby), John Faxe Jensen (YC40), Kim Vilfort, Henrik Larsen, Flemming Povlsen, Bent Christensen Arensøe, Lars Elstrup (69' Frank Pingel). (Coach: Richard Møller Nielsen (DEN)).
Goals: Denmark: 0-1 Kim Christofte (2' penalty), 0-2 Bent Christensen Arensøe (6'), 0-3 Frank Pingel (70'), 0-4 Kim Vilfort (75').
Referee: James (Jim) McCluskey (SCO)   Attendance: 2.589

09-10-1991   Praterstadion, Vienna: Austria – Denmark   0-3 (0-3)
Austria: Otto Konrad, Walter Kogler, Peter Schöttel (46' Harald Gschnaidtner), Franz Resch, Andreas Herzog, Peter Stöger, Peter Artner, Christian Prosenik, Michael Baur, Andreas Ogris (C), Peter Pacult. (Coach: Alfred Riedl (AUT)).
Denmark: Peter Schmeichel, John Sivebæk, Kent Nielsen, Lars Olsen (C), Kim Christofte (59' Johnny Mølby), John Faxe Jensen, Kim Vilfort, Henrik Larsen (81' Brian Jensen), Flemming Povlsen, Bent Christensen Arensøe, Lars Elstrup. (Coach: Richard Møller Nielsen (DEN)).
Goals: Denmark: 0-1 Peter Artner (9' *own goal*), 0-2 Flemming Povlsen (15'), 0-3 Bent Christensen Arensøe (37').
Referee: Frans Van Den Wijngaert (BEL)   Attendance: 7.453

16-10-1991   Landskrona IP, Landskrona (SWE): Faroe Islands – Yugoslavia 0-2 (0-1)
Faroe Islands: Jens Knudsen, Allan Mørkøre (YC76), Jóannes Jakobsen (C), Tummas Eli
Hansen, Mikkjal Danielsen, Jan Dam, Abraham Hansen, Todi Jónsson (89' Magni Jarnskor),
Kári Reynheim, Kurt Mørkøre, Jan Allan Müller (88' Eydfinn Davidsen). (Coach: Páll
Gudlaugsson (ISL)).
Yugoslavia: Fahrudin Omerovic, Predrag Spasic, Faruk Hadzibegic (C), Sinisa Mihajlovic (64'
Predrag Mijatovic), Ilija Najdoski, Branko Brnovic, Vladimir Jugovic, Dejan Savicevic,
Mehmed Bazdarevic, Slavisa Jokanovic, Vladan Lukic (80' Mario Stanic). (Coach: Ivan Osim
(YUG)).
Goals: Yugoslavia: 0-1 Vladimir Jugovic (13'), 0-2 Dejan Savicevic (80').
Referee: Günther Habermann (GDR)   Attendance: 2.485

16-10-1991   Windsor Park, Belfast: Northern Ireland – Austria 2-1 (2-1)
Northern Ireland: Tommy Wright, Mal Donaghy, Nigel Worthington, Garry Taggart, Colin
Hill, Robert Dennison, Kingsley Black, Jim Magilton, Colin Clarke (46' Danny Wilson), Iain
Dowie, Kevin Wilson. (Coach: William Laurence (Billy) Bingham (NIR)).
Austria: Wolfgang Knaller, Walter Kogler, Leopold Lainer, Herbert Gager, Peter Stöger (61'
Christoph Westerthaler), Peter Artner, Manfred Zsak, Jürgen Hartmann, Leopold Rotter,
Andreas Ogris, Christian Keglevits (61' Andreas Herzog). (Coach: Dietmar Constantini
(AUT)).
Goals: Northern Ireland: 1-0 Iain Dowie (18'), 2-0 Kingsley Black (42').
Austria: 2-1 Leopold Lainer (44').
Referee: Leif Sundell (SWE)   Attendance: 6.854

13-11-1991   Odense Stadium, Odense: Denmark – Northern Ireland 2-1 (2-0)
Denmark: Peter Schmeichel, John Sivebæk, Kent Nielsen, Lars Olsen (C) (51' Frank Pingel),
Kim Christofte, Torben Piechnik, Johnny Mølby, Kim Vilfort, Henrik Larsen, Flemming
Povlsen, Lars Elstrup. (Coach: Richard Møller Nielsen (DEN)).
Northern Ireland: Alan Fettis, Mal Donaghy, Nigel Worthington, Garry Taggart, Colin Hill,
Michael Hughes, Kingsley Black (82' Robert Dennison), Jim Magilton, Colin Clarke (66' Iain
Dowie), Kevin Wilson, Stephen McBride. (Coach: William Laurence (Billy) Bingham (NIR)).
Goals: Denmark: 1-0 Flemming Povlsen (22'), 2-0 Flemming Povlsen (36').
Northern Ireland: 2-1 Garry Taggart (71').
Referee: Alexey Nikolayevich Spirin (URS)   Attendance: 10.881

13-11-1991   Praterstadion, Vienna: Austria – Yugoslavia 0-2 (0-2)
Austria: Wolfgang Knaller, Walter Kogler (YC77), Kurt Garger, Leopold Lainer, Herbert
Gager, Andreas Herzog, Peter Stöger (YC4) (66' Christian Keglevits), Peter Artner, Manfred
Zsak, Andreas Ogris (C), Christoph Westerthaler (75' Michael Baur). (Coach: Dietmar
Constantini (AUT)).
Yugoslavia: Fahrudin Omerovic, Faruk Hadzibegic (C), Sinisa Mihajlovic, Darko Milanic
(YC58), Budimir Vujacic (YC11), Dzoni Novak (70' Branko Brnovic), Dejan Savicevic,
Mehmed Bazdarevic, Slavisa Jokanovic, Darko Pancev, Vladan Lukic (46' Predrag Mijatovic).
(Coach: Ivan Osim (YUG)).
Goals: Yugoslavia: 0-1 Vladan Lukic (18'), 0-2 Dejan Savicevic (38').
Referee: Pietro D'Elia (ITA)   Attendance: 6.212

GROUP 5

12-09-1990	Anderlecht	Belgium – East Germany	0-2 (0-0)
17-10-1990	Cardiff	Wales – Belgium	3-1 (1-1)
31-10-1990	Luxembourg	Luxembourg – Germany	2-3 (0-2)
14-11-1990	Luxembourg	Luxembourg – Wales	0-1 (0-1)
27-02-1991	Anderlecht	Belgium – Luxembourg	3-0 (3-0)
27-03-1991	Anderlecht	Belgium – Wales	1-1 (0-0)
01-05-1991	Hanover	Germany – Belgium	1-0 (1-0)
05-06-1991	Cardiff	Wales – Germany	1-0 (0-0)
11-09-1991	Luxembourg	Luxembourg – Belgium	0-2 (0-1)
16-10-1991	Nuremberg	Germany – Wales	4-1 (3-0)
13-11-1991	Cardiff	Wales – Luxembourg	1-0 (0-0)
20-11-1991	Anderlecht	Belgium – Germany	0-1 (0-1)
18-12-1991	Leverkusen	Germany – Luxembourg	4-0 (2-0)

FINAL STANDING

Pos	Team	Pld	W	D	L	GF	GA	GD	Pts
1	Germany	6	5	0	1	13	4	+9	10
2	Wales	6	4	1	1	8	6	+2	9
3	Belgium	6	2	1	3	7	6	+1	5
4	Luxembourg	6	0	0	6	2	14	-12	0

Germany qualified for the final tournament in Sweden.

At the time of the draw on 2nd February 1990, Group 5 had contained a fifth team, East Germany. As the reunification of Germany was confirmed with effect on 3rd October 1990, East Germany's game on 12th September in Belgium was duly re-classed as a friendly. This was East Germany's last ever internationl match, which it won 2-0. All other games involving East Germany were cancelled as they withdrew to join the German DFB.

12-09-1990 *Constant Vanden Stock Stadium, Anderlecht:*
Belgium – East Germany 0-2 (0-0)
<u>Belgium</u>: Michel Preud'homme, Lorenzo Staelens, Stéphane Demol (46' Philippe Albert), Pascal Plovie, Michel De Wolf, Geert Broeckaert, Enzo Scifo (46' Marc Degryse), Franky Van Der Elst, Bruno Versavel (69' Danny Boffin), Erwin Vandenbergh, Jan Ceulemans (C) (46' Marc Wilmots). (Coach: Guy Jean Léonard Thijs (BEL)).
<u>East Germany</u>: Jens Schmidt (90' Jens Adler), Heiko Peschke, Jörg Schwanke, Andreas Wagenhaus, Detlef Schößler, Matthias Sammer (C), Jörg Stübner (25' Stefan Böger), Dariusz Wosz, Heiko Bonan, Heiko Scholz (85' Torsten Kracht), Uwe Rösler. (Coach: Eduard Geyer (GDR)).
<u>Goals</u>: East Germany: 0-1 Matthias Sammer (74'), 0-2 Matthias Sammer (89').
<u>Referee</u>: John Blankenstein (HOL)   <u>Attendance</u>: 5.194

17-10-1990   Cardiff Arms Park, Cardiff: Wales – Belgium   3-1 (1-1)
Wales: Neville Southall, Clayton Blackmore (YC6), Mark Aizlewood, Eric Young, Kevin Ratcliffe (C), Paul John Bodin, Mark Hughes, Barry Horne, Peter Nicholas (YC71), Ian Rush, Dean Saunders. (Coach: Terence Charles (Terry) Yorath (WAL)).
Belgium: Michel Preud'homme, Georges Grün, Bruno Versavel, Eric Gerets, Michel De Wolf, Marc Emmers, Stéphane Demol, Franky Van Der Elst, Enzo Scifo, Luc Nilis (73' Marc Wilmots), Jan Ceulemans (C). (Coach: Guy Jean Léonard Thijs (BEL)).
Goals: Wales: 1-1 Ian Rush (29'), 2-1 Dean Saunders (86'), 3-1 Mark Hughes (88').
Belgium: 0-1 Bruno Versavel (24').
Referee: Kurt Röthlisberger (SUI)   Attendance: 14.274

31-10-1990   Stade Municipal, Luxembourg: Luxembourg – Germany   2-3 (0-2)
Luxembourg: John Van Rijswijck, Théo Malget, Marcel Bossi, Pierre Petry, Marc Birsens, Jeff Saibene (85' Gérard Jeitz), Joël Groff, Guy Hellers (YC48), Jean-Paul Girres, Carlo Weis (C), Robert Langers. (Coach: Paul Philipp (LUX)).
Germany: Bodo Illgner, Andreas Brehme, Jürgen Kohler, Thomas Berthold, Manfred Binz, Lothar Matthäus (C), Thomas Häßler, Thomas Strunz, Uwe Bein (73' Knut Reinhardt), Rudi Völler, Jürgen Klinsmann. (Coach: Hans-Hubert (Berti) Vogts (GER)).
Goals: Luxembourg: 1-2 Jean-Paul Girres (57'), 2-3 Robert Langers (65').
Germany: 0-1 Jürgen Klinsmann (16'), 0-2 Uwe Bein (30'), 0-3 Rudi Völler (49').
Referee: Kim Milton Nielsen (DEN)   Attendance: 9.512

14-11-1990   Stade Municipal, Luxembourg: Luxembourg – Wales   0-1 (0-1)
Luxembourg: John Van Rijswijck, Théo Malget, Marcel Bossi (YC10), Pierre Petry, Marc Birsens, Jeff Saibene, Guy Hellers, Jean-Paul Girres, Carlo Weis (C) (YC48), Robert Langers (YC11), Patrick Morocutti (58' Armin Krings). (Coach: Paul Philipp (LUX)).
Wales: Neville Southall (YC46), Clayton Blackmore (RC11), Mark Aizlewood, Eric Young, Kevin Ratcliffe (C) (YC89), Paul John Bodin, Mark Hughes, Barry Horne, Peter Nicholas, Ian Rush (83' Gary Speed), Dean Saunders (90' Malcolm Allen). (Coach: Terence Charles (Terry) Yorath (WAL)).
Goal: Wales: 0-1 Ian Rush (15').
Referee: Jiří Ulrich (TCH)   Attendance: 6.703

27-02-1991   Constant Vanden Stock Stadium, Anderlecht:
              Belgium – Luxembourg   3-0 (3-0)
Belgium: Michel Preud'homme, Georges Grün, Philippe Albert (YC36), Bruno Versavel, Frank Dauwen, Marc Emmers, Enzo Scifo, Marc Wilmots, Marc Degryse, Erwin Vandenbergh, Jan Ceulemans (C). (Coach: Guy Jean Léonard Thijs (BEL)).
Luxembourg: Paul Koch, Théo Malget (46' Gérard Jeitz), Marcel Bossi, Pierre Petry, Marc Birsens, Jeff Saibene (YC80), Joël Groff (77' Denis Scuto), Guy Hellers, Jean-Paul Girres, Carlo Weis (YC33), Armin Krings. (Coach: Paul Philipp (LUX)).
Goals: Belgium: 1-0 Erwin Vandenbergh (7'), 2-0 Jan Ceulemans (16'), 3-0 Enzo Scifo (35').
Referee: Loizos Loizou (CYP)   Attendance: 11.105

27-03-1991   Constant Vanden Stock Stadium, Anderlecht: Belgium – Wales   1-1 (0-0)
Belgium: Michel Preud'homme, Georges Grün, Philippe Albert, Lei Clijsters (YC61), Bruno Versavel (YC86), Eric Gerets, Franky Van Der Elst, Enzo Scifo, Marc Wilmots, Marc Degryse, Erwin Vandenbergh. (Coach: Guy Jean Léonard Thijs (BEL)).
Wales: Neville Southall, Mark Aizlewood, Eric Young, Kevin Ratcliffe, Paul John Bodin, Mark Hughes (YC86), Barry Horne (YC78), Peter Nicholas, David Phillips, Ian Rush, Dean Saunders. (Coach: Terence Charles (Terry) Yorath (WAL)).
Goals: Belgium: 1-0 Marc Degryse (48').
Wales: 1-1 Dean Saunders (60').
Referee: Emilio Soriano Aladrén (ESP)   Attendance: 18.591

01-05-1991   Niedersachsenstadion, Hanover: Germany – Belgium   1-0 (1-0)
Germany: Bodo Illgner, Andreas Brehme, Thomas Berthold, Stefan Reuter, Dietmar Beiersdorfer, Lothar Matthäus (C), Thomas Häßler, Matthias Sammer, Thomas Doll, Rudi Völler (87' Karl-Heinz Riedle), Jürgen Klinsmann (77' Thomas Helmer). (Coach: Hans-Hubert (Berti) Vogts (GER)).
Belgium: Michel Preud'homme, Bertrand Crasson, Georges Grün (C), Philippe Albert (YC25), Bruno Versavel, Marc Emmers, Patrick Vervoort, Franky Van Der Elst, Enzo Scifo, Marc Wilmots (77' Luc Nilis), Marc Degryse. (Coach: Guy Jean Léonard Thijs (BEL)).
Goal: Germany: 1-0 Lothar Matthäus (3').
Referee: Zoran Petrovic (YUG)   Attendance: 52.363

05-06-1991   Cardiff Arms Park, Cardiff: Wales – Germany   1-0 (0-0)
Wales: Neville Southall, Andy Melville, Mark Aizlewood, Kevin Ratcliffe, Paul John Bodin, Mark Hughes, Barry Horne, Peter Nicholas (YC33), David Phillips, Ian Rush, Dean Saunders (88' Gary Speed). (Coach: Terence Charles (Terry) Yorath (WAL)).
Germany: Bodo Illgner, Andreas Brehme, Jürgen Kohler, Thomas Berthold (RC60), Stefan Reuter, Guido Buchwald, Thomas Helmer, Lothar Matthäus (46' Thomas Doll), Matthias Sammer (76' Stefan Effenberg), Rudi Völler, Jürgen Klinsmann. (Coach: Hans-Hubert (Berti) Vogts (GER)).
Goal: Wales: 1-0 Ian Rush (66').
Referee: Bo Karlsson (SWE)   Attendance: 34.603

11-09-1991   Stade Municipal, Luxembourg: Luxembourg – Belgium   0-2 (0-1)
Luxembourg: John Van Rijswijck, Marcel Bossi (C), Pierre Petry, Marc Birsens, Thomas Wolf, Joël Groff, Guy Hellers, Jean-Paul Girres, Gérard Jeitz (YC26), Robert Langers (YC34) (67' Marc Thomé), Patrick Morocutti (77' Armin Krings). (Coach: Paul Philipp (LUX)).
Belgium: Michel Preud'homme, Georges Grün (C) (75' Dirk Medved), Vital Borkelmans, Marc Emmers, Patrick Vervoort, Lorenzo Staelens, Stéphane Demol (80' Frank Dauwen), Franky Van Der Elst, Enzo Scifo, Luc Nilis, Marc Degryse. (Coach: Paul Van Himst (BEL)).
Goals: Belgium: 0-1 Enzo Scifo (25'), 0-2 Marc Degryse (49').
Referee: Rémi Harrel (FRA)   Attendance: 6.872

16-10-1991   Frankenstadion, Nuremberg: Germany – Wales 4-1 (3-0)
Germany: Bodo Illgner, Andreas Brehme (YC16), Jürgen Kohler (YC84), Stefan Reuter, Guido Buchwald, Manfred Binz, Lothar Matthäus (C), Andreas Möller, Thomas Doll (79' Stefan Effenberg), Karl-Heinz Riedle (75' Thomas Häßler), Rudi Völler. (Coach: Hans-Hubert (Berti) Vogts (GER)).
Wales: Neville Southall, Andy Melville, Eric Young (85' Ryan Giggs), Kevin Ratcliffe (C), Paul John Bodin, Mark Bowen, Gavin Maguire (YC15) (46' Gary Speed), Mark Hughes, Barry Horne (YC50), Ian Rush, Dean Saunders (RC51). (Coach: Terence Charles (Terry) Yorath (WAL)).
Goals: Germany: 1-0 Andreas Möller (34'), 2-0 Rudi Völler (39'), 3-0 Karl-Heinz Riedle (45'), 4-0 Thomas Doll (73').
Wales: 4-1 Paul John Bodin (84' penalty).
Referee: Joël Quiniou (FRA)   Attendance: 46.491

13-11-1991   Cardiff Arms Park, Cardiff: Wales – Luxembourg 1-0 (0-0)
Wales: Neville Southall, Andy Melville (63' Ryan Giggs), Mark Aizlewood, Eric Young, Mark Bowen (70' Paul John Bodin), Gary Speed, Mark Hughes, Barry Horne, Peter Nicholas, David Phillips, Ian Rush. (Coach: Terence Charles (Terry) Yorath (WAL)).
Luxembourg: John Van Rijswijck, Théo Malget (YC77), Marcel Bossi (YC27), Pierre Petry (YC65), Marc Birsens, Thomas Wolf (YC76), Joël Groff, Guy Hellers (YC50), Jean-Paul Girres (87' Gérard Jeitz), Carlo Weis, Robert Langers (67' Armin Krings). (Coach: Paul Philipp (LUX)).
Goal: Wales: 1-0 Paul John Bodin (77' penalty).
Referee: Sándor Puhl (HUN)   Attendance: 19.813

20-11-1991   Constant Vanden Stock Stadium, Anderlecht: Belgium – Germany 0-1 (0-1)
Belgium: Michel Preud'homme, Georges Grün (C), Philippe Albert (YC78), Vital Borkelmans, Danny Boffin, Marc Emmers, Stéphane Demol (46' Dirk Medved), Enzo Scifo, Marc Wilmots (71' Luc Nilis), Johan Walem, Marc Degryse. (Coach: Paul Van Himst (BEL)).
Germany: Bodo Illgner, Andreas Brehme, Jürgen Kohler, Stefan Reuter, Guido Buchwald (YC64), Manfred Binz, Lothar Matthäus (C) (YC52), Andreas Möller (81' Stefan Effenberg), Thomas Doll, Karl-Heinz Riedle (YC43), Rudi Völler. (Coach: Hans-Hubert (Berti) Vogts (GER)).
Goal: Germany: 0-1 Rudi Völler (16').
Referee: Tullio Lanese (ITA)   Attendance: 16.138

18-12-1991   Ulrich Haberland Stadium, Leverkusen: Germany – Luxembourg 4-0 (2-0)
Germany: Bodo Illgner, Andreas Brehme, Jürgen Kohler, Stefan Reuter, Guido Buchwald, Manfred Binz, Lothar Matthäus (C), Andreas Möller (70' Uwe Bein), Thomas Doll (46' Thomas Häßler), Karl-Heinz Riedle, Rudi Völler. (Coach: Hans-Hubert (Berti) Vogts (GER)).
Luxembourg: John Van Rijswijck, Théo Malget, Marcel Bossi, Pierre Petry, Marc Birsens, Thomas Wolf, Joël Groff (79' Luc Holtz), Guy Hellers, Jean-Paul Girres (83' Gérard Jeitz), Carlo Weis (C), Robert Langers. (Coach: Paul Philipp (LUX)).
Goals: Germany: 1-0 Lothar Matthäus (15' penalty), 2-0 Guido Buchwald (44'), 3-0 Karl-Heinz Riedle (51'), 4-0 Thomas Häßler (62').
Referee: Zbigview Przesmycki (POL)   Attendance: 20.395

GROUP 6

12-09-1990	Helsinki	Finland – Portugal	0-0
17-10-1990	Porto	Portugal – Netherlands	1-0 (0-0)
31-10-1990	Athens	Greece – Malta	4-0 (2-0)
21-11-1990	Rotterdam	Netherlands – Greece	2-0 (2-0)
25-11-1990	Ta'Qali	Malta – Finland	1-1 (1-0)
19-12-1990	Ta'Qali	Malta – Netherlands	0-8 (0-3)
23-01-1991	Athens	Greece – Portugal	3-2 (1-1)
09-02-1991	Ta'Qali	Malta – Portugal	0-1 (0-1)
20-02-1991	Porto	Portugal – Malta	5-0 (3-0)
13-03-1991	Rotterdam	Netherlands – Malta	1-0 (1-0)
17-02-1991	Rotterdam	Netherlands – Finland	2-0 (1-0)
16-05-1991	Helsinki	Finland – Malta	2-0 (0-0)
05-06-1991	Helsinki	Finland – Netherlands	1-1 (0-0)
11-09-1991	Porto	Portugal – Finland	1-0 (1-0)
09-10-1991	Helsinki	Finland – Greece	1-1 (0-0)
16-10-1991	Rotterdam	Netherlands – Portugal	1-0 (1-0)
30-10-1991	Athens	Greece – Finland	2-0 (0-0)
20-11-1991	Lisbon	Portugal – Greece	1-0 (1-0)
04-12-1991	Thessaloniki	Greece – Netherlands	0-2 (0-1)
22-12-1991	Ta'Qali	Malta – Greece	1-1 (1-0)

FINAL STANDING

Pos	Team	Pld	W	D	L	GF	GA	GD	Pts
1	*Netherlands*	8	6	1	1	17	2	+15	*13*
2	Portugal	8	5	1	2	11	4	+7	11
3	Greece	8	3	2	3	11	9	+2	8
4	Finland	8	1	4	3	5	8	-3	6
5	Malta	8	0	2	6	2	23	-21	2

Netherlands qualified for the final tournament in Sweden.

12-09-1990   Olympic Stadium, Helsinki: Finland – Portugal   0-0
Finland: Olavi Huttunen, Erkka Petäjä, Ari Heikkinen, Jari Europaeus (C), Erik Holmgren, Jari Rinne, Ari Hjelm, Petri Järvinen (84' Marko Myyry), Jari Litmanen, Mixu Paatelainen, Kimmo Juhani Tarkkio (73' Tommi Paavola). (Coach: Jukka Vakkila (FIN)).
Portugal: SILVINO de Almeida LOURO, JOÃO Domingos da Silva PINTO (C) (YC35), ANTÓNIO Augusto da Silva VELOSO, JORGE da Costa FERREIRA, PEDRO Manuel Regateiro VENÂNCIO, ANTÓNIO Manuel Tavares FONSECA (65' António Manuel PACHECO DOMINGOS), António dos Santos Ferreira ANDRÉ, JAIME Moreira PACHECO, VÍTOR Manuel da Costa Araújo PANEIRA, RUI Gil Soares de BARROS, José RUI Lopes ÁGUAS (46' JORGE Paulo CADETE Santos Reis). (Coach: CARLOS Manuel Brito Leal QUEIRÓZ (POR)).
Referee: Jozef Marko (TCH)   Attendance: 10.242

17-10-1990 Estádio das Antas, Porto: Portugal – Netherlands 1-0 (0-0)
Portugal: SILVINO de Almeida LOURO, JOÃO Domingos da Silva PINTO (C), ANTÓNIO Augusto da Silva VELOSO, PEDRO Manuel Regateiro VENÂNCIO, JOSÉ Martins LEAL, VÍTOR Manuel da Costa Araújo PANEIRA (YC78), OCEANO Andrade da Cruz, Manuel António COUTO GUIMARÃES (88' PEDRO Alexandre Marques Caldas XAVIER), JOSÉ Orlando SEMEDO (90' JORGE da Costa FERREIRA), José RUI Lopes ÁGUAS, JORGE Paulo CADETE Santos Reis. (Coach: CARLOS Manuel Brito Leal QUEIRÓZ (POR)).
Netherlands: Hans van Breukelen, Frank de Boer (75' Hans Gillhaus), Stan Valckx, Adri van Tiggelen (YC23) (60' John van 't Schip), Graeme Rutjes, Danny Blind, Richard Witschge, Gerald Vanenburg, Ruud Gullit (C), Marco van Basten, Dennis Bergkamp. (Coach: Marinus Jacobus Hendricus (Rinus) Michels (HOL)).
Goal: Portugal: 1-0 José RUI Lopes ÁGUAS (54').
Referee: Siegfried Kirschen (GDR)   Attendance: 17.198

31-10-1990   Olympic Stadium, Athens: Greece – Malta 4-0 (2-0)
Greece: Theolokis Papadopoulos, Efstratios Apostolakis, Stylianos Manolas, Ioannis Kalitzakis (YC35), Georgios Papadopoulos, Panagiotis Tsalouchidis, Nikolaos Tsiantakis, Savas Haralampo Kofidis, Vassilios Karapialis, Dimitrios Saravakos (C), Vasilios Dimitriadis (33' Stefanos Borbokis). (Coach: Antonis Georgiadis (GRE)).
Malta: Reginald Cini, David Carabott, Joseph Galea (YC13), John Buttigieg, Silvio Vella, Carmel Scerri (II), Carmel Busuttil, Raymond Vella, Kristian Laferla, Jesmond Zerafa, Hubert Suda (46' Michael Degiorgio). (Coach: Horst Heese (GER)).
Goals: Greece: 1-0 Nikolaos Tsiantakis (37'), 2-0 Vassilios Karapialis (40'), 3-0 Dimitrios Saravakos (59'), 4-0 Stefanos Borbokis (88').
Referee: Ion Craciunescu (ROM)   Attenedance: 7.768

21-11-1990   Stadion Feijenoord, Rotterdam: Netherlands – Greece 2-0 (2-0)
Netherlands: Hans van Breukelen, Graeme Rutjes, Danny Blind, Jerry de Jong, Jan Wouters (YC32), Richard Witschge, Gerald Vanenburg, Marco van Basten (C), Dennis Bergkamp (81' Aron Winter), Bryan Roy, John van 't Schip. (Coach: Marinus Jacobus Hendricus (Rinus) Michels (HOL)).
Greece: Theolokis Papadopoulos, Efstratios Apostolakis, Stylianos Manolas (YC9), Ioannis Kalitzakis, Georgios Papadopoulos, Panagiotis Tsalouchidis, Nikolaos Tsiantakis, Savas Haralampo Kofidis (53' Nikolaos Karageorgiou), Vassilios Karapialis, Dimitrios Saravakos (C), Stefanos Borbokis. (Coach: Antonis Georgiadis (GRE)).
Goals: Netherlands: 1-0 Dennis Bergkamp (7'), 2-0 Marco van Basten (18').
Referee: Lajos Nemeth (HUN)   Attendance: 20.233

25-11-1990   Ta'Qali National Stadium, Ta'Qali: Malta – Finland 1-1 (1-0)
Malta: David Cluett, David Carabott, Joseph Galea, John Buttigieg (YC77), Silvio Vella, Carmel Scerri (II), Carmel Busuttil, Raymond Vella (C), Kristian Laferla, Michael Degiorgio (YC6), Joseph Zarb (71' Hubert Suda). (Coach: Horst Heese (GER)).
Finland: Olavi Huttunen, Ari Heikkinen, Jari Europaeus (C), Erik Holmgren, Jari Rinne (YC6) (46' Erkka Petajä), Ari Hjelm, Marko Myyry, Jari Litmanen, Mixu Paatelainen, Kimmo Juhani Tarkkio (79' Ari Tegelberg), Pasi Tauriainen. (Coach: Jukka Vakkila (FIN)).
Goals: Malta: 1-0 Hubert Suda (37').
Finland: 1-1 Erik Holmgren (87').
Referee: Sadik Deda (TUR)   Attendance: 8.667

19-12-1990   Ta'Qali National Stadium, Ta'Qali: Malta – Netherlands   0-8 (0-3)
Malta: David Cluett, David Carabott, Joseph Galea, Joe Camilleri, Edwin Camilleri (46' Hubert Suda), Silvio Vella, Carmel Scerri (II) (YC8) (72' Jesmond Zerafa), Carmel Busuttil, Raymond Vella (C), Kristian Laferla, Michael Degiorgio. (Coach: Horst Heese (GER)).
Netherlands: Hans van Breukelen, Frank de Boer, Danny Blind, Jerry de Jong, Jan Wouters, Ruud Gullit (C) (68' John van den Brom), Erwin Koeman (46' Aron Winter), Marco van Basten, Dennis Bergkamp, Bryan Roy, John van 't Schip. (Coach: Marinus Jacobus Hendricus (Rinus) Michels (HOL)).
Goals: Netherlands: 0-1 Marco van Basten (9'), 0-2 Marco van Basten (20'), 0-3 Marco van Basten (23'), 0-4 Aron Winter (53'), 0-5 Dennis Bergkamp (60'), 0-6 Marco van Basten (64'), 0-7 Dennis Bergkamp (66'), 0-8 Marco van Basten (80' penalty).
Referee: Rolf Blattmann (SUI)   Attendance: 10.254

23-01-1991   Olympic Stadium, Athens: Greece – Portugal   3-2 (1-1)
Greece: Nikos Sarganis, Efstratios Apostolakis, Stylianos Manolas (RC90), Ioannis Kalitzakis, Georgios Papadopoulos, Panagiotis Tsalouchidis, Nikolaos Tsiantakis, Savas Haralampo Kofidis (70' Daniel Ioannis Papadopoulos), Georgios Toursounidis, Dimitrios Saravakos (C), Stefanos Borbokis (68' Vasilios Dimitriadis). (Coach: Antonis Georgiadis (GRE)).
Portugal: VÍTOR Manuel Martins BAÍA, JOÃO Domingos da Silva PINTO (C), ANTÓNIO Augusto da Silva VELOSO, PEDRO Manuel Regateiro VENÂNCIO, JOSÉ Martins LEAL, PAULO Manuel Carvalho de SOUSA (71' JORGE Paulo CADETE Santos Reis), VÍTOR Manuel da Costa Araújo PANEIRA, OCEANO Andrade da Cruz (YC48), RUI Gil Soares de BARROS (71' ADELINO Carlos Morais NUNES), PAULO Jorge FUTRE dos Santos, José RUI Lopes ÁGUAS. (Coach: CARLOS Manuel Brito Leal QUEIRÓZ (POR)).
Goals: Greece: 1-0 Stefanos Borbokis (7'), 2-2 Stylianos Manolas (68'), 3-2 Panagiotis Tsalouchidis (85').
Portugal: 1-1 José RUI Lopes ÁGUAS (18'), 1-2 PAULO Jorge FUTRE dos Santos (62').
Referee: Carlo Longhi (ITA)   Attendance: 8.553

09-02-1991   Ta'Qali National Stadium, Ta'Qali: Malta – Portugal   0-1 (0-1)
Malta: David Cluett, Joseph Galea (RC89), John Buttigieg, Alexander Azzopardi, Silvio Vella, Carmel Busuttil, Raymond Vella (C), Kristian Laferla, Michael Degiorgio, Jesmond Zerafa, Hubert Suda. (Coach: Horst Heese (GER)).
Portugal: VÍTOR Manuel Martins BAÍA, JOÃO Domingos da Silva PINTO (C), ANTÓNIO Augusto da Silva VELOSO (YC61), PEDRO Manuel Regateiro VENÂNCIO, JOSÉ Martins LEAL, VÍTOR Manuel da Costa Araújo PANEIRA, OCEANO Andrade da Cruz, RUI Gil Soares de BARROS (67' JORGE Paulo CADETE Santos Reis), JOSÉ Orlando SEMEDO, PAULO Jorge FUTRE dos Santos (82' PAULO Manuel Carvalho de SOUSA), José RUI Lopes ÁGUAS. (Coach: CARLOS Manuel Brito Leal QUEIRÓZ (POR)).
Goal: Portugal: 0-1 PAULO Jorge FUTRE dos Santos (27').
Referee: Manfred Neuner (GER)   Attendance: 3.264

20-02-1991	Estádio das Antas, Porto: Portugal – Malta 5-0 (3-0)
Portugal: VÍTOR Manuel Martins BAÍA, JOÃO Domingos da Silva PINTO (C) (46' JORGE Paulo CADETE Santos), ANTÓNIO Augusto da Silva VELOSO, PEDRO Manuel Regateiro VENÂNCIO (YC28) (67' PAULO Sérgio Braga MADEIRA), JOSÉ Martins LEAL, PAULO Manuel Carvalho de SOUSA, VÍTOR Manuel da Costa Araújo PANEIRA (YC72), OCEANO Andrade da Cruz, JOSÉ Orlando SEMEDO, PAULO Jorge FUTRE dos Santos, José RUI Lopes ÁGUAS. (Coach: CARLOS Manuel Brito Leal QUEIRÓZ (POR)).
Malta: David Cluett (YC34), John Buttigieg (YC51), Joe Camilleri (38' Carmel Scerri (II)), Alexander Azzopardi, Silvio Vella, Carmel Busuttil, Raymond Vella (C), Kristian Laferla, Michael Degiorgio, Jesmond Zerafa, Hubert Suda (50' David Carabott). (Coach: Horst Heese (GER)).
Goals: Portugal: 1-0 José RUI Lopes ÁGUAS (5'), 2-0 JOSÉ Martins LEAL (34'), 3-0 VÍTOR Manuel da Costa Araújo PANEIRA (41' penalty), 4-0 PAULO Jorge FUTRE dos Santos (48'), 5-0 JORGE Paulo CADETE Santos Reis (81').
Referee: John Spillane (IRL)	Attendance: 5.303

13-03-1991	Stadion Feijenoord, Rotterdam: Netherlands – Malta 1-0 (1-0)
Netherlands: Hans van Breukelen, Frank de Boer (46' Wim Kieft), Danny Blind, Jan Wouters, Ruud Gullit (C), Richard Witschge, Marciano Vink, Marco van Basten, Dennis Bergkamp, Bryan Roy (68' Gerald Vanenburg), John van 't Schip. (Coach: Marinus Jacobus Hendricus (Rinus) Michels (HOL)).
Malta: Reginald Cini, Joe Camilleri, Alexander Azzopardi (89' Nicholas Saliba), Edwin Camilleri, Silvio Vella, Carmel Scerri (II), Raymond Vella (C), Kristian Laferla, Michael Degiorgio, Joe Brincat (84' Hubert Suda), Jesmond Zerafa. (Coach: Horst Heese (GER)).
Goal: Netherlands: 1-0 Marco van Basten (31' penalty).
Referee: Dusan Krchnák (TCH)	Attendance: 36.383

17-04-1991	Stadion Feijenoord, Rotterdam: Netherlands – Finland 2-0 (1-0)
Netherlands: Hans van Breukelen, Danny Blind, Jerry de Jong, Jan Wouters, Ruud Gullit (C), Richard Witschge, Marciano Vink, Marco van Basten (76' Graeme Rutjes), Dennis Bergkamp (72' Wim Kieft), John van 't Schip (YC53), Pieter Huistra. (Coach: Marinus Jacobus Hendricus (Rinus) Michels (HOL)).
Finland: Olavi Huttunen, Markku Kanerva, Erkka Petäjä, Ari Heikkinen, Jari Europaeus (C), Erik Holmgren, Marko Myyry, Kari Ukkonen, Jari Litmanen (46' Ari Tegelberg), Mixu Paatelainen (83' Harri Nyyssönen), Pasi Tauriainen. (Coach: Jukka Vakkila (FIN)).
Goals: Netherlands: 1-0 Marco van Basten (9'), 2-0 Ruud Gullit (76').
Referee: Jan Damgaard (DEN)	Attendance: 21.426

16-05-1991	Olympic Stadion, Helsinki: Finland – Malta 2-0 (0-0)
Finland: Olavi Huttunen, Markku Kanerva, Erkka Petäjä (C), Ari Heikkinen, Erik Holmgren, Petri Järvinen, Marko Myyry, Kari Ukkonen, Jari Litmanen, Mixu Paatelainen (YC67) (74' Tommi Paavola), Kimmo Juhani Tarkkio (89' Pasi Tauriainen). (Coach: Jukka Vakkila (FIN)).
Malta: Reginald Cini, John Buttigieg, Edwin Camilleri (YC25), Silvio Vella, Carmel Scerri (II), Carmel Busuttil, Raymond Vella (C), Kristian Laferla, Michael Degiorgio, Joe Brincat (YC31) (71' Jesmond Zerafa), Hubert Suda. (Coach: Horst Heese (GER)).
Goals: Finland: 1-0 Petri Järvinen (51'), 2-0 Jari Litmanen (87').
Referee: Rune Pedersen (NOR)	Attendance: 5.150

05-06-1991   Olympic Stadium, Helsinki: Finland – Netherlands   1-1 (0-0)
Finland: Olavi Huttunen, Erkka Petäjä (C), Ari Heikkinen, Erik Holmgren, Petri Järvinen, Marko Myyry, Kari Ukkonen (82' Ari Hjelm), Jari Litmanen, Mixu Paatelainen (67' Ari Tegelberg), Kimmo Juhani Tarkkio, Tommi Paavola. (Coach: Jukka Vakkila (FIN)).
Netherlands: Joop Hiele, Frank de Boer, Ronald Koeman, Graeme Rutjes, Danny Blind, Aron Winter, Jan Wouters, Richard Witschge, Marco van Basten (C), John van 't Schip, Pieter Huistra (76' Wim Kieft). (Coach: Marinus Jacobus Hendricus (Rinus) Michels (HOL)).
Goals: Finland: 1-1 Erik Holmgren (77').
Netherlands: 0-1 Frank de Boer (60').
Referee: Brian R.McGinlay (SCO)   Attendance: 21.207

11-09-1991   Estádio das Antas, Porto: Portugal – Finland   1-0 (1-0)
Portugal: VÍTOR Manuel Martins BAÍA, FERNANDO Manuel Silva COUTO, JOÃO Domingos da Silva PINTO (C), ANTÓNIO Augusto da Silva VELOSO, JOSÉ Martins LEAL, SAMUEL Silva QUINA, RUI Gil Soares de BARROS, Manuel António COUTO GUIMARÃES, PAULO Jorge FUTRE dos Santos, José RUI Lopes ÁGUAS (58' OCEANO Andrade da Cruz), Duarte CÉSAR Gonçalves de BRITO (81' JORGE Paulo CADETE Santos). (Coach: CARLOS Manuel Brito Leal QUEIRÓZ (POR)).
Finland: Olavi Huttunen, Erkka Petäjä (C), Ari Heikkinen, Erik Holmgren, Petri Järvinen, Marko Myyry, Kari Ukkonen (73' Jari Litmanen), Mixu Paatelainen, Kimmo Juhani Tarkkio, Tommi Paavola, Pasi Tauriainen (60' Jouko Antero Vuorela). (Coach: Jukka Vakkila (FIN)).
Goal: Portugal: 1-0 Duarte CÉSAR Gonçalves de BRITO (22').
Referee: Arturo Martino (SUI)   Attendance: 7.236

09-10-1991   Olympic Stadium, Helsinki: Finland – Greece   1-1 (0-0)
Finland: Olavi Huttunen, Erkka Petäjä (C), Ari Heikkinen, Erik Holmgren (63' Mixu Paatelainen), Jouko Antero Vuorela, Ari Hjelm, Petri Järvinen (71' Ari Tegelberg), Marko Myyry, Kari Ukkonen, Jari Litmanen, Kimmo Juhani Tarkkio. (Coach: Jukka Vakkila (FIN)).
Greece: Nikos Sarganis, Efstratios Apostolakis, Ioannis Kalitzakis, Nikolaos Karageorgiou, Pavlos Papaioannou, Panagiotis Tsalouchidis, Nikolaos Tsiantakis, Dimitrios Saravakos (C), Vassilios Karapialis (83' Georgios Toursounidis), Georgios Mitsibonas, Stefanos Borbokis (68' Georgios Athanasiadis). (Coach: Antonis Georgiadis (GRE)).
Goals: Finland: 1-0 Kari Ukkonen (50').
Greece: 1-1 Panagiotis Tsalouchidis (74').
Referee: Sergei Grigorievich Khusainov (URS)   Attendance: 5.255

16-10-1991   Stadion Feijenoord, Rotterdam: Netherlands – Portugal   1-0 (1-0)
Netherlands: Hans van Breukelen, Frank Rijkaard (74' Aron Winter), Ronald Koeman, Adri van Tiggelen (YC52), Danny Blind, Jan Wouters, Ruud Gullit (C), Richard Witschge (87' John van 't Schip), Erwin Koeman, Marco van Basten, Dennis Bergkamp. (Coach: Marinus Jacobus Hendricus (Rinus) Michels (HOL)).
Portugal: VÍTOR Manuel Martins BAÍA, FERNANDO Manuel Silva COUTO, JOÃO Domingos da Silva PINTO (C), PEDRO Manuel Regateiro VENÂNCIO, JOSÉ Martins LEAL, OCEANO Andrade da Cruz (YC12), RUI Gil Soares de BARROS, Manuel António COUTO GUIMARÃES (56' LUÍS Filipe Madeira Caeiro FIGO), EMÍLIO Manuel Delgado PEIXE (YC74) (80' Duarte CÉSAR Gonçalves de BRITO), PAULO Jorge FUTRE dos Santos, JORGE Paulo CADETE Santos. (Coach: CARLOS Manuel Brito Leal QUEIRÓZ (POR)).
Goal: Netherlands: 1-0 Richard Witschge (20').
Referee: George Courtney (ENG)   Attendance: 40.057

30-10-1991   Olympic Stadium, Athens: Greece – Finland   2-0 (0-0)
Greece: Nikos Sarganis, Efstratios Apostolakis, Ioannis Kalitzakis, Nikolaos Karageorgiou, Pavlos Papaioannou, Panagiotis Tsalouchidis, Nikolaos Tsiantakis, Vassilios Karapialis (73' Georgios Toursounidis), Georgios Mitsibonas, Georgios Athanasiadis (YC44) (46' Stefanos Borbokis), Dimitrios Saravakos (C). (Coach: Antonis Georgiadis (GRE)).
Finland: Olavi Huttunen, Erkka Petäjä (C) (YC30), Ari Heikkinen, Erik Holmgren, Jouko Antero Vuorela (56' Mixu Paatelainen), Ari Hjelm, Petri Järvinen, Kari Ukkonen (YC70), Jyrki Tapio Huhtamäki (83' Ari Tegelberg), Jari Litmanen, Kimmo Juhani Tarkkio. (Coach: Jukka Vakkila (FIN)).
Goals: Greece: 1-0 Dimitrios Saravakos (49'), 2-0 Stefanos Borbokis (51').
Referee: Gerhard Kapl (AUT)   Attendance: 9.036

20-11-1991   Estádio da Luz, Lisbon: Portugal – Greece   1-0 (1-0)
Portugal: VÍTOR Manuel Martins BAÍA, FERNANDO Manuel Silva COUTO, RUI Fernando da Silva Calapez Pereira BENTO, JOÃO Domingos da Silva PINTO (C), JOSÉ Martins LEAL, VÍTOR Manuel da Costa Araújo PANEIRA (46' OCEANO Andrade da Cruz), RUI Gil Soares de BARROS, JOSÉ Orlando SEMEDO (15' LUÍS Filipe Madeira Caeiro FIGO), EMÍLIO Manuel Delgado PEIXE, JOÃO Manuel Vieira PINTO, José RUI Lopes ÁGUAS. (Coach: CARLOS Manuel Brito Leal QUEIRÓZ (POR)).
Greece: Nikos Sarganis, Efstratios Apostolakis, Ioannis Kalitzakis, Nikolaos Karageorgiou, Pavlos Papaioannou (59' Georgios Athanasiadis), Panagiotis Tsalouchidis, Nikolaos Tsiantakis (YC9), Vassilios Karapialis (YC20), Georgios Mitsibonas, Dimitrios Saravakos (C) (YC20), Stefanos Borbokis (69' Vasilios Dimitriadis). (Coach: Antonis Georgiadis (GRE)).
Goal: Portugal: 1-0 JOÃO Manuel Vieira PINTO (17').
Referee: Alphonse Costantin (BEL)   Attendance: 25.052

04-12-1991   Kaftanzoglio Stadium, Thessaloniki: Greece – Netherlands   0-2 (0-1)
Greece: Nikos Sarganis, Ioannis Kalitzakis, Georgios Papadopoulos, Pavlos Papaioannou (46' Nikolaos Karageorgiou), Panagiotis Tsalouchidis, Nikolaos Nioplias, Nikolaos Tsiantakis, Vassilios Karapialis (62' Georgios Toursounidis), Georgios Mitsibonas, Konstantinos Lagonidis, Dimitrios Saravakos. (Coach: Antonis Georgiadis (GRE)).
Netherlands: Hans van Breukelen, Frank Rijkaard (61' Aron Winter), Ronald Koeman, Adri van Tiggelen, Danny Blind, Jan Wouters, Richard Witschge, Erwin Koeman, Marco van Basten, Dennis Bergkamp, Wim Kieft (83' Peter Bosz). (Coach: Marinus Jacobus Hendricus (Rinus) Michels (HOL)).
Goals: Netherlands: 0-1 Dennis Bergkamp (37'), 0-2 Danny Blind (87').
Referee: Bo Karlsson (SWE)   Attendance: 25.053

22-12-1991   Ta'Qali National Stadium, Ta'Qali: Malta – Greece   1-1 (1-0)
Malta: David Cluett, Joseph Galea, Silvio Vella (YC54), Carmel Scerri (II) (34' Stefan Sultana), Carmel Busuttil, Raymond Vella (C) (73' Joe Camilleri), Kristian Laferla, Michael Degiorgio, Joe Brincat, Nicholas Saliba, Martin Gregory. (Coach: Philip (Pippo) Psaila (MLT)).
Greece: Georgios Plitsis, Ioannis Kalitzakis, Pavlos Papaioannou, Georgios Kapouranis, Panagiotis Tsalouchidis (C), Nikolaos Nioplias, Nikolaos Tsiantakis, Spyridon Marangos (55' Petros Marinakis), Georgios Mitsibonas (YC62), Vasilios Dimitriadis, Georgios Donis (57' Asterios Giotsas). (Coach: Antonis Georgiadis (GRE)).
Goals: Malta: 1-0 Stefan Sultana (42').
Greece: 1-1 Petros Marinakis (67').
Referee: Michel Girard (FRA)   Attendance: 6.690

GROUP 7

17-10-1990	Dublin	Republic of Ireland – Turkey	5-0 (2-0)
17-10-1990	London	England – Poland	2-0 (1-0)
14-11-1990	Dublin	Republic of Ireland – England	1-1 (0-0)
14-11-1990	Istanbul	Turkey – Poland	0-1 (0-1)
27-03-1991	London	England – Republic of Ireland	1-1 (1-1)
17-04-1991	Warsaw	Poland – Turkey	3-0 (0-0)
01-05-1991	Dublin	Republic of Ireland – Poland	0-0
01-05-1991	Izmir	Turkey – England	0-1 (0-1)
16-11-1991	Poznan	Poland – Republic of Ireland	3-3 (0-1)
16-10-1991	London	England – Turkey	1-0 (1-0)
13-11-1991	Poznan	Poland – England	1-1 (1-0)
13-11-1991	Istanbul	Turkey – Republic of Ireland	1-3 (1-1)

FINAL STANDING

Pos	Team	Pld	W	D	L	GF	GA	GD	Pts
1	*England*	*6*	*3*	*3*	*0*	*7*	*3*	*+4*	*9*
2	Republic of Ireland	6	2	4	0	13	6	+7	8
3	Poland	6	2	3	1	8	6	+2	7
4	Turkey	6	0	0	6	1	14	-13	0

England qualified for the final tournament in Sweden.

17-10-1990   Lansdowne Road, Dublin: Republic of Ireland – Turkey 5-0 (2-0)
Republic of Ireland: Pat Bonner, Steve Staunton, Denis Irwin, Micky McCarthy (C), Chris Hughton, David O'Leary, Andy Townsend (YC60) (75' Kevin Moran), Ray Houghton, John Sheridan, John Aldridge, Niall Quinn (68' Tony Cascarino (YC89)). (Coach: John (Jack) Charlton (ENG)).
Turkey: Engin Ipekoglu (YC73), Bülent Korkmaz (YC5), Kemal Serdar, Gökhan Keskin, Ercan Kol (46' Metin Tekin), Tugay Kerimoglu, Mehmet Özdilek, Oguz Çetin, Riza Çalimbay (C) (YC73), Hami Mandirali, Sercan Görgülü (46' Tanju Çolak). (Coach: Josef Emmanuel Hubertus Piontek (GER)).
Goals: Republic of Ireland: 1-0 John Aldridge (15'), 2-0 David O'Leary (40'), 3-0 John Aldridge (58'), 4-0 Niall Quinn (66'), 5-0 John Aldridge (73').
Referee: Erik Fredriksson (SWE)   Attendance: 42.603

17-10-1990   Wembley Stadium, London: England – Poland 2-0 (1-0)
England: Chris Woods, Stuart Pearce, Des Walker, Paul Parker, Mark Wright, Lee Dixon, John Barnes, Paul Gascoigne, David Platt, Gary Lineker (C) (57' Chris Waddle), Steve Bull (57' Peter Beardsley). (Coach: Graham Taylor (ENG)).
Poland: József Wandzik, Roman Szewczyk, Janusz Nawrocki, Dariusz Wdowczyk, Ryszard Tarasiewicz, Zbigniew Kaczmarek (C), Piotr Czachowski, Robert Warzycha, Roman Kosecki (85' Dariusz Kubicki), Jacek Ziober, Jan Furtok (75' Krzysztof Warzycha). (Coach: Andrzej Strejlau (POL)).
Goals: England: 1-0 Gary Lineker (39' penalty), 2-0 Peter Beardsley (89').
Referee: Tullio Lanese (ITA)   Attendance: 69.353

14-11-1990   Lansdowne Road, Dublin: Republic of Ireland – England   1-1 (0-0)
Republic of Ireland: Pat Bonner, Steve Staunton, Paul McGrath, Chris Morris, Micky McCarthy (C), David O'Leary (YC28), Andy Townsend, Ray Houghton, Ronnie Whelan (YC30) (74' Alan McLoughlin), John Aldridge, Niall Quinn (61' Tony Cascarino). (Coach: John (Jack) Charlton (ENG)).
England: Chris Woods, Tony Adams, Stuart Pearce, Des Walker, Mark Wright, Lee Dixon, Steve McMahon, David Platt, Gordon Cowans, Peter Beardsley (YC25), Gary Lineker (C). (Coach: Graham Taylor (ENG)).
Goals: Republic of Ireland: 1-1 Tony Cascarino (79').
England: 0-1 David Platt (67').
Referee: Pietro D'Elia (ITA)   Attendance: 45.494

14-11-1990   BJK İnönü Stadium, Istanbul: Turkey – Poland   0-1 (0-1)
Turkey: Engin Ipekoglu, Bülent Korkmaz, Gökhan Keskin (YC81), Ülken Durak (67' Mehmet Özdilek), Oguz Çetin, Riza Çalimbay (C), Muhammet Riza Altintas (67' Sercan Görgülü), Yusuf Altintas, Ünal Karaman, Hami Mandirali, Tanju Çolak. (Coach: Josef Emmanuel Hubertus Piontek (GER)).
Poland: Józef Wandzik, Janusz Nawrocki, Dariusz Kubicki, Dariusz Wdowczyk, Ryszard Tarasiewicz, Zbigniew Kaczmarek (C), Roman Kosecki, Waldemar Prusik, Robert Warzycha (YC40), Dariusz Dziekanowski (74' Jacek Ziober), Krzysztof Warzycha. (Coach: Andrzej Strejlau (POL)).
Goal: Poland: 0-1 Dariusz Dziekanowski (37').
Referee: Alexey Nikolayevich Spirin (URS)   Attendance: 24.868

27-03-1991   Wembley Stadium, London: England – Republic of Ireland   1-1 (1-1)
England: David Seaman, Tony Adams (46' Lee Sharpe), Stuart Pearce, Des Walker, Mark Wright, Lee Dixon, Bryan Robson (C), John Barnes, David Platt, Peter Beardsley, Gary Lineker (75' Ian Wright). (Coach: Graham Taylor (ENG)).
Republic of Ireland: Pat Bonner, Steve Staunton, Denis Irwin, Paul McGrath (YC27), Kevin Moran (C), David O'Leary, Andy Townsend, Ray Houghton, Kevin Sheedy, John Aldridge (72' Tony Cascarino), Niall Quinn. (Coach: John (Jack) Charlton (ENG)).
Goals: England: 1-0 Lee Dixon (10').
Republic of Ireland: 1-1 Niall Quinn (29').
Referee: Kurt Röthlisberger (SUI)   Attendance: 77.753

17-04-1991   Polish Army Stadium, Warsaw: Poland – Turkey   3-0 (0-0)
Poland: Józef Wandzik, Czeslaw Jakolcewicz, Dariusz Kubicki, Dariusz Wdowczyk, Ryszard Tarasiewicz, Zbigniew Kaczmarek (C) (63' Piotr Czachowski), Roman Kosecki, Jacek Ziober (76' Piotr Soczynski), Robert Warzycha, Jan Urban, Krzysztof Warzycha. (Coach: Andrzej Strejlau (POL)).
Turkey: Engin Ipekoglu, Bülent Korkmaz (YC81), Kemal Serdar, Gökhan Keskin, Tayfun Hut, Mehmet Özdilek, Riza Çalimbay (C), Muhammet Riza Altintas, Feyyaz Uçar (69' Faruk Yigit), Tanju Çolak (YC43), Abdullah Duran (78' Osman Yildirim). (Coach: Josef Emmanuel Hubertus Piontek (GER)).
Goals: Poland: 1-0 Ryszard Tarasiewicz (72'), 2-0 Ryszard Tarasiewicz (80'), 3-0 Roman Kosecki (87').
Referee: Mircea-Lucian Salomir (ROM)   Attendance: 10.610

01-05-1991   Lansdowne Road, Dublin: Republic of Ireland – Poland   0-0
Republic of Ireland: Pat Bonner, Steve Staunton, Denis Irwin, Paul McGrath, Kevin Moran (C), David O'Leary, Andy Townsend, Ray Houghton, Kevin Sheedy, John Aldridge (56' Bernard Slaven), Niall Quinn (69' Tony Cascarino). (Coach: John (Jack) Charlton (ENG)).
Poland: Józef Wandzik, Piotr Soczynski (YC48), Roman Szewczyk, Czeslaw Jakolcewicz, Dariusz Kubicki, Dariusz Wdowczyk, Ryszard Tarasiewicz (C) (YC58), Piotr Czachowski, Robert Warzycha (YC81), Jan Furtok (88' Roman Kosecki), Jan Urban (86' Krzysztof Warzycha). (Coach: Andrzej Strejlau (POL)).
Referee: John Blankenstein (HOL)   Attendance: 45.795

01-05-1991   Atatürk Stadium, Izmir: Turkey – England   0-1 (0-1)
Turkey: Hayrettin Demirbas, Recep Çetin, Ogün Temizkanoglu, Gökhan Keskin, Mehmet Özdilek, Riza Çalimbay (C), Muhammet Riza Altintas, Ünal Karaman, Ridvan Dilmen, Tanju Çolak, Ali Kurtulus Gültiken (72' Feyyaz Uçar). (Coach: Josef Emmanuel Hubertus Piontek (GER)).
England: David Seaman, Stuart Pearce, Des Walker, Lee Dixon, Gary Pallister, John Barnes, David Platt, Dennis Wise, Geoff Thomas (46' Steve Hodge), Gary Lineker (C), Alan Smith. (Coach: Graham Taylor (ENG)).
Goal: England: 0-1 Dennis Wise (32').
Referee: Wolf-Günter Wiesel (GER)   Attendance: 12.316

16-10-1991   Stadion Miejski, Poznan: Poland – Republic of Ireland   3-3 (0-1)
Poland: Józef Wandzik, Piotr Soczynski, Janusz Nawrocki (79' Dariusz Skrzypczak), Dariusz Kubicki (32' Andrzej Lesiak), Dariusz Wdowczyk, Ryszard Tarasiewicz (C), Piotr Czachowski, Roman Kosecki, Jacek Ziober, Jan Furtok (YC70), Jan Urban. (Coach: Andrzej Strejlau (POL)).
Republic of Ireland: Pat Bonner, Steve Staunton (YC52) (59' Terry Phelan), Denis Irwin, Paul McGrath, Chris Morris, Kevin Moran (C), David O'Leary, Andy Townsend, Kevin Sheedy, Roy Keane, Tony Cascarino. (Coach: John (Jack) Charlton (ENG)).
Goals: Poland: 1-1 Piotr Czachowski (59'), 2-3 Jan Furtok (77'), 3-3 Jan Urban (86').
Republic of Ireland: 0-1 Paul McGrath (12'), 1-2 Andy Townsend (64'), 1-3 Tony Cascarino (68').
Referee: Guy Goethals (BEL)   Attendance: 11.400

16-10-1991   Wembley Stadiu, London: England – Turkey   1-0 (1-0)
England: Chris Woods, Stuart Pearce, Des Walker, Lee Dixon, Gary Mabbutt, David Batty (YC58), Bryan Robson, Chris Waddle, David Platt, Gary Lineker (C), Alan Smith. (Coach: Graham Taylor (ENG)).
Turkey: Hayrettin Demirbas, Recep Çetin, Ogün Temizkanoglu, Gökhan Keskin (YC3), Tugay Kerimoglu, Oguz Çetin, Orhan Çikirikçi, Riza Çalimbay (C), Ünal Karaman, Feyyaz Uçar (76' Hami Mandirali), Turhan Sofuoglu. (Coach: Josef Emmanuel Hubertus Piontek (GER)).
Goal: England: 1-0 Alan Smith (21').
Referee: Antonio Martín Navarrete (ESP)   Attendance: 50.896

13-11-1991   Stadion Miejski, Pozan: Poland – England   1-1 (1-0)
Poland: Jaroslaw Bako, Tomasz Waldoch, Piotr Soczynski, Roman Szewczyk (77' Adam Fedoruk), Piotr Czachowski, Roman Kosecki (YC75), Dariusz Skrzypczak (80' Wojciech Kowalczyk), Robert Warzycha (YC61), Jacek Ziober, Jan Furtok, Jan Urban (C). (Coach: Andrzej Strejlau (POL)).
England: Chris Woods, Stuart Pearce, Des Walker, Lee Dixon, Gary Mabbutt, David Platt, Andy Sinton (70' Tony Daley), Geoff Thomas, Andy Gray (46' Alan Smith), David Rocastle (YC61), Gary Lineker (C). (Coach: Graham Taylor (ENG)).
Goals: Poland: 1-0 Roman Szewczyk (32').
England: 1-1 Gary Lineker (77').
Referee: Hubert Forstinger (AUT)   Attendance: 10.300

13-11-1991   BJK Inönü Stadium, Istanbul: Turkey – Republic of Ireland   1-3 (1-1)
Turkey: Hayrettin Demirbas, Recep Çetin (YC50) (68' Bülent Korkmaz), Ogün Temizkanoglu, Gökhan Keskin, Tugay Kerimoglu, Oguz Çetin, Orhan Çikirikçi, Riza Çalimbay (C), Feyyaz Uçar (46' Ridvan Dilmen), Turhan Sofuoglu, Hami Mandirali. (Coach: Josef Emmanuel Hubertus Piontek (GER)).
Republic of Ireland: Pat Bonner, Steve Staunton (YC30), Terry Phelan, Paul McGrath, Micky McCarthy (C), Chris Hughton, David O'Leary, Kevin Sheedy, John Aldridge, Tony Cascarino, John Byrne. (Coach: John (Jack) Charlton (ENG)).
Goals: Turkey: 1-1 Riza Çalimbay (13' penalty).
Republic of Ireland: 0-1 John Byrne (8'), 1-2 Tony Cascarino (55'), 1-3 John Byrne (58').
Referee: Zoran Petrovic (YUG)   Attendance: 33.061

FINAL TOURNAMENT IN SWEDEN

GROUP STAGE

Sweden automatically qualified as hosts.

GROUP 1

10-06-1992	Solna	Sweden – France	1-1 (1-0)
11-06-1992	Malmö	Denmark – England	0-0
14-06-1992	Malmö	France – England	0-0
14-06-1992	Solna	Sweden – Denmark	1-0 (0-0)
17-06-1992	Solna	Sweden – England	2-1 (0-1)
17-06-1992	Malmö	France – Denmark	1-2 (0-1)

FINAL STANDING

Pos	Team	Pld	W	D	L	GF	GA	GD	Pts
1	*Sweden*	*3*	*2*	*1*	*0*	*4*	*2*	*+2*	*5*
2	Denmark	3	1	1	1	2	2	+3	3
3	France	3	0	2	1	2	3	-1	2
4	England	3	0	2	1	1	2	-1	2

Sweden and Denmark qualified for the Semi-finals.

10-06-1992   Råsunda Stadion, Solna: Sweden – France   1-1 (1-0)
Sweden: Thomas Ravelli, Roland Nilsson, Jan Eriksson, Patrick Andersson, Joachim Björklund, Klas Ingesson, Jonas Thern (C) (YC87), Stefan Schwarz (YC39), Anders Limpar, Tomas Brolin, Kennet Andersson (74' Martin Dahlin). (Coach: Leif Tommy Svensson (SWE)).
France: Bruno Martini, Manuel Amoros (C), Laurent Blanc, Bernard Casoni, Basile Boli, Jocelyn Angloma (YC35) (66' Luis Fernández), Didier Deschamps, Franck Sauzée, Pascal Vahirua (46' Christian Perez), Jean-Pierre Papin, Eric Cantona (YC53). (Coach: Michel Platini (FRA)).
Goals: Sweden: 1-0 Jan Eriksson (24').
France: 1-1 Jean-Pierre Papin (58').
Referee: Alexey Nikolayevich Spirin (URS)   Attendance: 29.860

11-06-1992   Malmö Stadion, Malmö: Denmark – England   0-0
Denmark: Peter Schmeichel, John Sivebæk (YC83), Kent Nielsen, Lars Olsen (C), Henrik Andersen, Kim Christofte, John Jensen, Kim Vilfort, Brian Laudrup, Flemming Povlsen, Bent Christensen Arensøe. (Coach: Richard Møller Nielsen (DEN)).
England: Chris Woods, Keith Curie (YC9) (62' Tony Daley (YC67)), Martin Keown (YC7), Des Walker, Stuart Pearce, Trevor Steven, David Platt, Carlton Palmer, Paul Merson (71' Neil Webb), Gary Lineker (C), Alan Smith. (Coach: Graham Taylor (ENG)).
Referee: John Blankenstein (HOL)   Attendance: 26.385

14-06-1992   Malmö Stadion, Malmö: France – England   0-0
France: Bruno Martini, Manuel Amoros (C), Basile Boli, Laurent Blanc, Bernard Casoni, Jean-Philippe Durand, Didier Deschamps, Franck Sauzée (46' Jocelyn Angloma), Luis Fernández (YC31) (75' Christian Perez), Jean-Pierre Papin, Eric Cantona. (Coach: Michel Platini (FRA)).
England: Chris Woods, Carlton Palmer, Martin Keown, Des Walker, Stuart Pearce, Trevor Steven, David Batty (YC69), David Platt, Andy Sinton, Gary Lineker (C), Alan Shearer. (Coach: Graham Taylor (ENG)).
Referee: Sánder Puhl (HUN)   Attendance: 26.535

14-06-1992   Råsunda Stadion, Solna: Sweden – Denmark   1-0 (0-0)
Sweden: Thomas Ravelli, Roland Nilsson, Jan Eriksson, Patrick Andersson (YC40), Joachim Björklund, Klas Ingesson, Jonas Thern (C), Stefan Schwarz, Anders Limpar (90' Magnus Erlingmark), Tomas Brolin, Martin Dahlin (77' Johnny Ekström). (Coach: Leif Tommy Svensson (SWE)).
Denmark: Peter Schmeichel, John Sivebæk, Kent Nielsen, Lars Olsen (C), Henrik Andersen (YC14), Kim Christofte, John Jensen (63' Henrik Larsen), Kim Vilfort, Brian Laudrup, Flemming Povlsen, Bent Christensen Arensøe (51' Torben Frank). (Coach: Richard Møller Nielsen (DEN)).
Goal: Sweden: 1-0 Tomas Brolin (58').
Referee: Aron Schmidhuber (GER)   Attendance: 29.902

17-06-1992   Råsunda Stadion, Solna: Sweden – England   2-1 (0-1)
Sweden: Thomas Ravelli, Roland Nilsson, Jan Eriksson, Patrick Andersson (YC43), Joachim Björklund (YC70), Klas Ingesson, Jonas Thern (C), Stefan Schwarz (YC69), Anders Limpar (46' Johnny Ekström), Tomas Brolin, Martin Dahlin. (Coach: Leif Tommy Svensson (SWE)).
England: Chris Woods, David Batty, Martin Keown, Des Walker, Stuart Pearce, Tony Daley (YC10), Neil Webb (YC81), Carlton Palmer, David Platt, Andy Sinton (76' Paul Merson), Gary Lineker (C) (62' Alan Smith). (Coach: Graham Taylor (ENG)).
Goals: Sweden: 1-1 Jan Eriksson (51'), 2-1 Tomas Brolin (82').
England: 0-1 David Platt (4').
Referee: José Rosa dos Santos (POR)   Attendance: 30.126

17-06-1992   Malmö Stadion, Malmö: France – Denmark   1-2 (0-1)
France: Bruno Martini, Manuel Amoros (C), Basile Boli (YC38), Laurent Blanc, Bernard Casoni (YC15), Didier Deschamps (YC73), Christian Perez (YC32) (79' Christophe Cocard), Jean-Philippe Durand, Pascal Vahirua (46' Luis Fernández), Jean-Pierre Papin, Eric Cantona. (Coach: Michel Platini (FRA)).
Denmark: Peter Schmeichel, John Sivebæk, Kent Nielsen (61' Torben Piechnik), Lars Olsen (C), Henrik Andersen, Kim Christofte, John Jensen, Henrik Larsen, Brian Laudrup, Torben Frank (YC45) (66' Lars Elstrup), Flemming Povlsen (YC14). (Coach: Richard Møller Nielsen (DEN)).
Goals: France: 1-1 Jean-Pierre Papin (60').
Denmark: 0-1 Henrik Larsen (8'), 1-2 Lars Elstrup (78').
Referee: Hubert Forstinger (AUT)   Attendance: 25.673

GROUP 2

12-06-1992	Gothenburg	Netherlands – Scotland	1-0 (0-0)
12-06-1992	Norrköping	CIS – Germany	1-1 (0-0)
15-06-1992	Norrköping	Scotland – Germany	0-2 (0-1)
15-06-1992	Gothenburg	Netherlands – CIS	0-0
18-06-1992	Gothenburg	Netherlands – Germany	3-1 (2-0)
18-06-1992	Norrköping	Scotland – CIS	3-0 (2-0)

FINAL STANDING

Pos	Team	Pld	W	D	L	GF	GA	GD	Pts
1	*Netherlands*	3	2	1	0	4	1	+3	5
2	*Germany*	3	1	1	1	4	4	0	3
3	Scotland	3	1	0	2	3	3	0	2
4	CIS	3	0	2	1	1	4	-3	2

Netherlands and Germany qualified for the Semi-finals.

12-06-1992   Nya Ullevi, Gothenburg: Netherlands – Scotland   1-0 (0-0)
Netherlands: Hans van Breukelen, Berry van Aerle, Ronald Koeman, Adri van Tiggelen, Frank Rijkaard, Jan Wouters (54' Wim Jonk), Bryan Roy, Rob Witschge (YC25), Ruud Gullit (C), Dennis Bergkamp (84' Aron Winter), Marco van Basten. (Coach: Marinus Jacobus Hendricus (Rinus) Michels (HOL)).
Scotland: Andy Goram, Richard Gough (C), Maurice Malpas, Dave McPherson, Stewart McKimmie, Gordon Durie, Paul McStay, Stuart McCall, Gary McAllister, Brian McClair (78' Duncan Ferguson), Ally McCoist (73' Kevin Gallacher). (Coach: Andrew (Andy) Roxburgh (ENG)).
Goal: Netherlands: 1-0 Dennis Bergkamp (75').
Referee: Bo Karlsson (SWE)   Attendance: 35.720

12-06-1992   Idrottsparken, Norrköping: CIS – Germany   1-1 (0-0)
CIS: Dmitri Kharin (YC75), Andrei Chernyshov, Oleh Kuznetsov, Akhrik Tsveiba (YC88), Andrei Kanchelskis, Igor Shalimov (84' Viktor Onopko), Igor Dobrovolski (YC70), Oleksiy Mikhaylichenko (C), Volodymyr Lyutyi (54' Andrei Ivanov), Dmitri Kuznetsov, Igor Kolyvanov. (Coach: Anatoliy Fyodorovich Byshovets (URS)).
Germany: Bodo Illgner, Stefan Reuter (65' Jürgen Klinsmann), Jürgen Kohler, Manfred Binz, Guido Buchwald, Andreas Brehme, Stefan Effenberg, Thomas Häßler, Thomas Doll, Rudi Völler (C) (46' Andreas Möller), Karl-Heinz Riedle. (Coach: Hans-Hubert (Berti) Vogts (GER)).
Goals: CIS: 1-0 Igor Dobrovolski (64' penalty).
Germany: 1-1 Thomas Häßler (90').
Referee: Gérard Biguet (FRA)   Attendance: 17.410

15-06-1992   Idrottsparken, Norrköping: Scotland – Germany   0-2 (0-1)
Scotland: Andy Goram, Richard Gough (C), Maurice Malpas, Dave McPherson, Stewart McKimmie, Paul McStay, Stuart McCall (YC90), Gary McAllister, Brian McClair, Gordon Durie (55' Pat Nevin), Ally McCoist (68' Kevin Gallacher). (Coach: Andrew (Andy) Roxburgh (ENG)).
Germany: Bodo Illgner, Manfred Binz, Matthias Sammer, Jürgen Kohler, Guido Buchwald, Andreas Brehme (C), Stefan Effenberg, Andreas Möller, Thomas Häßler (YC87), Jürgen Klinsmann, Karl-Heinz Riedle (67' Stefan Reuter, 75' Michael Schulz). (Coach: Hans-Hubert (Berti) Vogts (GER)).
Goals: Germany: 0-1 Karl-Heinz Riedle (29'), 0-2 Stefan Effenberg (47').
Referee: Guy Goethals (BEL)   Attendance: 17.638

15-06-1992   Nya Ullevi, Gothenburg: Netherlands – CIS   0-0
Netherlands: Hans van Breukelen, Berry van Aerle, Ronald Koeman (YC26), Adri van Tiggelen, Frank Rijkaard, Jan Wouters (YC68), Bryan Roy, Rob Witschge, Ruud Gullit (C) (72' John van 't Schip), Dennis Bergkamp (80' Eric Viscaal), Marco van Basten. (Coach: Marinus Jacobus Hendricus (Rinus) Michels (HOL)).
CIS: Dmitri Kharin, Andrei Chernyshov, Oleh Kuznetsov, Akhrik Tsveiba (YC22), Andrei Kanchelskis, Sergei Aleinikov (57' Dmitri Kuznetsov), Oleksiy Mikhaylichenko (C), Viktor Onopko, Igor Kolyvanov, Igor Dobrovolski, Sergei Yuran (65' Sergei Kiryakov). (Coach: Anatoliy Fyodorovich Byshovets (URS)).
Referee: Peter Mikkelsen (DEN)   Attendance: 34.400

18-06-1992   Nya Ullevi, Gothenburg: Netherlands – Germany   3-1 (2-0)
Netherlands: Hans van Breukelen, Adri van Tiggelen, Ronald Koeman, Frank de Boer (61'
Aron Winter), Frank Rijkaard, Jan Wouters, Rob Witschge, Dennis Bergkamp (87' Peter
Bosz), Ruud Gullit (C), Marco van Basten, Bryan Roy. (Coach: Marinus Jacobus Hendricus
(Rinus) Michels (HOL)).
Germany: Bodo Illgner, Manfred Binz (46' Matthias Sammer), Michael Frontzeck, Thomas
Helmer, Jürgen Kohler (YC50), Andreas Brehme (C), Stefan Effenberg, Andreas Möller,
Thomas Häßler, Karl-Heinz Riedle (76' Thomas Doll), Jürgen Klinsmann. (Coach: Hans-
Hubert (Berti) Vogts (GER)).
Goals: Netherlands: 1-0 Frank Rijkaard (4'), 2-0 Rob Witschge (15'), 3-1 Dennis Bergkamp
(72').
Germany: 2-1 Jürgen Klinsmann (52').
Referee: Pierluigi Pairetto (ITA)   Attendance: 37.725

18-06-1992   Idrottsparken, Norrköping: Scotland – CIS   3-0 (2-0)
Scotland: Andy Goram, Richard Gough (C), Tom Boyd, Dave McPherson, Stewart
McKimmie, Paul McStay, Gary McAllister, Stuart McCall (YC67), Brian McClair (65' Jim
McInally), Ally McCoist, Kevin Gallacher (79' Pat Nevin). (Coach: Andrew (Andy) Roxburgh
(ENG)).
CIS: Dmitri Kharin, Andrei Chernyshov (YC52), Kahaber Tskhadadze, Oleh Kuznetsov,
Oleksiy Mikhaylichenko (C) (YC85), Sergei Aleinikov (46' Dmitri Kuznetsov (YC84)), Viktor
Onopko, Andrei Kanchelskis, Igor Dobrovolski, Sergei Yuran, Sergei Kiryakov (46' Igor
Korneev). (Coach: Anatoliy Fyodorovich Byshovets (URS)).
Goals: Scotland: 1-0 Paul McStay (7'), 2-0 Brian McClair (16'), 3-0 Gary McAllister (84'
penalty).
Referee: Kurt Röthlisberger (SUI)   Attendance: 14.660

SEMI-FINALS

21-06-1992   Råsunda Stadion, Solna: Sweden – Germany   2-3 (0-1)
Sweden: Thomas Ravelli, Roland Nilsson, Jan Eriksson, Joachim Björklund, Roger Lung
(YC14), Kennet Andersson, Klas Ingesson, Jonas Thern (C), Joakim Nilsson (58' Anders
Limpar), Tomas Brolin, Martin Dahlin (YC72) (73' Johnny Ekström). (Coach: Leif Tommy
Svensson (SWE)).
Germany: Bodo Illgner, Thomas Helmer, Jürgen Kohler, Guido Buchwald (YC35), Stefan
Reuter (YC43), Andreas Brehme (C), Matthias Sammer, Stefan Effenberg (YC3), Thomas
Häßler, Karl-Heinz Riedle (YC29), Jürgen Klinsmann (89' Thomas Doll). (Coach: Hans-
Hubert (Berti) Vogts (GER)).
Goals: Sweden: 1-2 Tomas Brolin (64' penalty), 2-3 Kennet Andersson (89').
Germany: 0-1 Thomas Häßler (11'), 0-2 Karl-Heinz Riedle (59'), 1-3 Karl-Heinz Riedle (88').
Referee: Tullio Lanese (ITA)   Attendance: 28.827

22-06-1992   Nya Ullevi, Gothenburg: Netherlands – Denmark   2-2 (1-2, 2-2) (AET)
Netherlands: Hans van Breukelen, Adri van Tiggelen, Ronald Koeman, Frank de Boer (46'
Wim Kieft), Frank Rijkaard (YC42), Jan Wouters, Rob Witschge, Dennis Bergkamp, Ruud
Gullit (C), Marco van Basten, Bryan Roy (115' John van 't Schip). (Coach: Marinus Jacobus
Hendricus (Rinus) Michels (HOL)).
Denmark: Peter Schmeichel, John Sivebæk, Torben Piechnik, Lars Olsen (C), Henrik Andersen
(YC15) (70' Claus Christiansen), Kim Christofte, John Jensen, Kim Vilfort, Henrik Larsen,
Brian Laudrup (57' Lars Elstrup), Flemming Povlsen. (Coach: Richard Møller Nielsen (DEN)).
Goals: Netherlands: 1-1 Dennis Bergkamp (23'), 2-2 Frank Rijkaard (86').
Denmark: 0-1 Henrik Larsen (5'), 1-2 Henrik Larsen (33').
Referee: Emilio Soriano Aladrén (ESP)   Attendance: 37.450
Penalties: 1 Ronald Koeman   1 Henrik Larsen
                 * Marco van Basten   2 Flemming Povlsen
                 2 Dennis Bergkamp   3 Lars Elstrup
                 3 Frank Rijkaard   4 Kim Vilfort
                 4 Rob Witschge   5 Kim Christofte
(After extra time Denmark win 5-4 on penalties)

FINAL

26-06-1992   Nya Ullevi, Gothenburg: Denmark – Germany   2-0 (1-0)
Denmark: Peter Schmeichel, John Sivebæk (66' Claus Christiansen), Kent Nielsen, Torben
Piechnik (YC32), Lars Olsen (C), Kim Christofte, John Jensen, Kim Vilfort, Henrik Larsen,
Brian Laudrup, Flemming Povlsen. (Coach: Richard Møller Nielsen (DEN)).
Germany: Bodo Illgner, Thomas Helmer, Jürgen Kohler, Guido Buchwald, Stefan Reuter
(YC55), Andreas Brehme (C), Matthias Sammer (46' Thomas Doll (YC83)), Stefan Effenberg
(YC35) (80' Andreas Thom), Thomas Häßler (YC39), Karl-Heinz Riedle, Jürgen Klinsmann
(YC88). (Coach: Hans-Hubert (Berti) Vogts (GER)).
Goals: Denmark: 1-0 John Jensen (18'), 2-0 Kim Vilfort (78').
Referee: Bruno Galler (SUI)   Attendance: 37.800

*** **Denmark were European Champions** ***

GOALSCORERS TOURNAMENT 1990-1992:

Goals	Players
11	Jean-Pierre Papin (FRA)
10	Darko Pancev (YUG)
8	Marco van Basten (HOL)
7	Dennis Bergkamp (HOL)
6	Bent Christensen Arensøe (DEN), Adrian Knup (SUI)
5	Emilio BUTRAGUEÑO Santos (ESP), Karl-Heinz Riedle (GER), József Kiprich (HUN), Colin Clarke (NIR)
4	Nasko Sirakov (BUL), Flemming Povlsen (DEN), CARLOS Antonio Muñoz Cobo (ESP), Ally McCoist (SCO)

3	Nikolai Todorov (BUL), Henrik Larsen (DEN), Eric Cantona (FRA), Franck Sauzée (FRA), Thomas Häßler (GER), Rudi Völler (GER), Stefanos Borbokis (GRE), John Aldridge (IRL), Tony Cascarino (IRL), PAULO Jorge FUTRE dos Santos (POR), José RUI Lopes ÁGUAS (POR), Gordon Durie (SCO), Tomas Brolin (SWE), Vaclav Danek (TCH), Andrei Kanchelskis (URS), Ian Rush (WAL)
2	Andreas Ogris (AUT), Marc Degryse (BEL), Enzo Scifo (BEL), Emil Kostadinov (BUL), Luboslav Penev (BUL), Lars Elstrup (DEN), Michael Laudrup (DEN), Kim Vilfort (DEN), Gary Lineker (ENG), David Platt (ENG), ABELARDO Fernández Antuña (ESP), JOSÉ María BAKERO Escudero (ESP), Erik Holmgren (FIN), Jürgen Klinsmann (GER), Lothar Matthäus (GER), Dimitrios Saravakos (GRE), Panagiotis Tsalouchidis (GRE), Frank Rijkaard (HOL), John Byrne (IRL), Naill Quinn (IRL), Atli Edvaldsson (ISL), Eyjölfur Sverrisson (ISL), Roberto Baggio (ITA), Roberto Donadoni (ITA), Aldo Serena (ITA), Gianluca Vialli (ITA), Lars Roar Bohinen (NOR), Tore André Dahlum (NOR), Gøran Sørloth (NOR), Ryszard Tarasiewicz (POL), Gheorghe Hagi (ROM), Dorin Mateut (ROM), Florin Raducioiu (ROM), Gary McAllister (SCO), Paul McStay (SCO), John Robertson (SCO), Stéphane Chapuisat (SUI), Heinz Hermann (SUI), Marc Hottiger (SUI), Kübilay Türkyilmaz (SUI), Jan Eriksson (SWE), Karel Kula (TCH), Václav Nemecek (TCH), Oleksiy Mikhaylichenko (URS), Aleksandr Mostovoi (URS), Paul John Bodin (WAL), Dean Saunders (WAL), Robert Prosinecki (YUG), Dejan Savicevic (YUG)
1	Edmond (Eduard) Abazi (ALB), Hysen Zmijani (ALB), Leopold Lainer (AUT), Heimo Pfeifenberger (AUT), Michael Streiter (AUT), Arnold Wetl (AUT), Jan Ceulemans (BEL), Erwin Vandenbergh (BEL), Bruno Versavel (BEL), Nikolai Iliev (BUL), Trifon Ivanov (BUL), Hristo Stoichkov (BUL), Zlatko Yankov (BUL), Angelos Tsolakis (CYP), Panayiotis Xiourouppas (CYP), Jan Bartram (DEN), Kim Christofte (DEN), John Jensen (DEN), Frank Pingel (DEN), Peter Beardsley (ENG), Lee Dixon (ENG), Alan Smith (ENG), Dennis Wise (ENG), Guillermo AMOR Martinez (ESP), Fernando Ruiz HIERRO (ESP), José Miguel González Martín del Campo "MÍCHEL" (ESP), ROBERTO Férnandez Bonillo (ESP), Allan Mørkøre (FAR), Torkil Nielsen (FAR), Kári Reynheim (FAR), Petri Järvinen (FIN), Jari Litmanen (FIN), Kari Ukkonen (FIN), Laurent Blanc (FRA), Basile Boli (FRA), Luis Fernández (FRA), Amara Simba (FRA), Uwe Bein (GER), Guido Buchwald (GER), Thomas Doll (GER), Stefan Effenberg (GER), Andreas Möller (GER), Vassilios Karapialis (GRE), Stylianos Manolas (GRE), Petros Marinakis (GRE), Nikolaos Tsiantakis (GRE), Danny Blind (HOL), Frank de Boer (HOL), Ruud Gullit (HOL), Aron Winter (HOL), Richard Witschge (HOL), Rob Witschge (HOL), György Bognar (HUN), László Disztl (HUN), Emil Lörincz (HUN), Tamás Mónos (HUN), Paul McGrath (IRL), David O'Leary (IRL), Andy Townsend (IRL), Arnor Gudjohnsen (ISL), Sigurdur Jónsson (ISL), Thorvaldur Örlygsson (ISL), Attilio Lombardo (ITA), Ruggiero Rizzitelli (ITA), Salvatore Schillaci (ITA), Pietro Vierchowod (ITA), Jean-Paul Girres (LUX), Robert Langers (LUX), Hubert Suda (LUX), Stefan Sultana (MLT), Kingsley Black (NIR), Iain Dowie (NIR), Colin Hill (NIR), Alan McDonald (NIR), Garry Taggart (NIR), Kevin Wilson (NIR), Sverre Brandhaug (NOR), Jahn Ivar Mini Jakobsen (NOR), Pål Lydersen (NOR), Piotr Czachowski (POL), Dariusz Dziekanowski (POL), Jan Furtok (POL), Roman Kosecki (POL), Roman Szewczyk (POL), Jan Urban (POL), Duarte CÉSAR Gonçalves de BRITO

	(POR), JOÃO Manuel Vieira PINTO (POR), JORGE Paulo CADETE Santos Reis (POR), JOSÉ Martins LEAL (POR), VÍTOR Manuel da Costa Araújo PANEIRA (POR), Pavel Badea (ROM), Doru Rodion Camataru (ROM), Ioan Lupescu (ROM), Dan Petrescu (ROM), Mihai Adrian Popescu (ROM), Ioan Sabau (ROM), John Collins (SCO), Richard Gough (SCO), Brian McClair (SCO), Gordon Strachan (SCO), Valdes Pasolini (SMR), Thomas Bickel (SUI), Frédéric Chassot (SUI), Christophe Ohrel (SUI), Alain Sutter (SUI), Beat Sutter (SUI), Kennet Andersson (SWE), Ivan Hasek (TCH), Lubos Kubík (TCH), Ludovit Lancz (TCH), Lubomír Moravcík (TCH), Tomás Skuhravy (TCH), Riza Çalimbay (TUR), Sergei Aleinikov (URS), Igor Dobrovolski (CIS/URS), Igor Korneev (URS), Oleh Kuznetsov (URS), Oleh Protasov (URS), Igor Shalimov (URS), Sergei Yuran (URS), Mark Hughes (WAL), Mehmed Bazdarevic (YUG), Dragisa Binic (YUG), Zvonimir Boban (YUG), Robert Jarni (YUG), Vladimir Jugovic (YUG), Srecko Katanec (YUG), Vladan Lukic (YUG), Ilija Najdoski (YUG), Davor Suker (YUG), Zoran Vulic (YUG)
1 own goal	Hysen Zmijani (ALB) for France, Peter Artner (AUT) for Denmark, George Christodoulou (CYP) for Hungary, Ivan Matteoni (SMR) for Romania

1996 UEFA European Football Championship

QUALIFYING ROUND – GROUP 1

04-09-1994	Ramat Gan	Israel – Poland	2-1 (1-0)
07-09-1994	Bratislava	Slovakia – France	0-0
07-09-1994	Bucharest	Romania – Azerbaijan	3-0 (1-0)
08-10-1994	Saint-Étienne	France – Romania	0-0
12-10-1994	Ramat Gan	Israel – Slovakia	2-2 (2-2)
12-10-1994	Mielec	Poland – Azerbaijan	1-0 (1-0)
12-11-1994	Bucharest	Romania – Slovakia	3-2 (1-0)
16-11-1994	Zabrze	Poland – France	0-0
16-11-1994	Trabzon	Azerbaijan – Israel	0-2 (0-1)
13-12-1994	Trabzon	Azerbaijan – France	0-2 (0-1)
14-12-1994	Ramat Gan	Israel – Romania	1-1 (0-0)
29-03-1995	Bucharest	Romania – Poland	2-1 (1-1)
29-03-1995	Kosice	Slovakia – Azerbaijan	4-1 (4-0)
29-03-1995	Ramat Gan	Israel – France	0-0
25-04-1995	Zabrze	Poland – Israel	4-3 (1-2)
26-04-1995	Trabzon	Azerbaijan – Romania	1-4 (1-2)
26-04-1995	Nantes	France – Slovakia	4-0 (2-0)
07-06-1995	Zabrze	Poland – Slovakia	5-0 (1-0)
07-06-1995	Bucharest	Romania – Israel	2-1 (1-0)
16-08-1995	Trabzon	Azerbaijan – Slovakia	0-1 (0-0)
16-08-1995	Paris	France – Poland	1-1 (0-1)
06-09-1995	Auxerre	France – Azerbaijan	10-0 (3-0)
06-09-1995	Zabrze	Poland – Romania	0-0
06-09-1995	Kosice	Slovakia – Israel	1-0 (0-0)
11-10-1995	Bucharest	Romania – France	1-3 (0-2)
11-10-1995	Bratislava	Slovakia – Poland	4-1 (1-1)
11-10-1995	Tel Aviv	Israel – Azerbaijan	2-0 (1-0)
15-11-1995	Caen	France – Israel	2-0 (0-0)
15-11-1995	Kosice	Slovakia – Romania	0-2 (0-0)
15-11-1995	Trabzon	Azerbaijan – Poland	0-0

FINAL STANDING

Pos	Team	Pld	W	D	L	GF	GA	GD	Pts
1	Romania	10	6	3	1	18	9	+9	21
2	France	10	5	5	0	22	2	+20	20
3	Slovakia	10	4	2	4	14	18	-4	14
4	Poland	10	3	4	3	14	12	+2	13
5	Israel	10	3	3	4	13	13	0	12
6	Azerbaijan	10	0	1	9	2	29	-27	1

Romania and France qualified for the final tournament in England.

04-09-1994   National Stadium, Ramat Gan: Israel – Poland   2-1 (1-0)
Israel: Ben Zion Ginzburg, Alon Harazi, Marko Balbul (YC17), Moshe Glam, Nir Klinger (C), Tal Banin (YC6), Haim Revivo, Alon Hazan, Eyal Berkovic (85' Ronny Levy), Ronen Harazi, Ronny Rosenthal (89' Reuven Atar). (Coach: Shlomo Scharf (ISR)).
Poland: Józef Wandzik, Jacek Bak, Tomasz Waldoch, Roman Szewczyk, Tomasz Lapinski (YC85), Krzysztof Maciejewski, Marcin Jalocha (47' Ryszard Czerwiec), Roman Kosecki (C), Jerzy Brzeczek (YC25), Wojciech Kowalczyk, Gregorz Mielcarski (58' Dariusz Gesior). (Coach: Henryk Apostel (POL)).
Goals: Israel: 1-0 Ronen Harazi (43'), 2-0 Ronen Harazi (58').
Poland: 2-1 Roman Kosecki (80').
Referee: Frans Van Den Wijngaert (BEL)   Attendance: 3.500

07-09-1994   Stadión Tehelné pole, Bratislava: Slovakia – France   0-0
Slovakia: Ladislav Molnár, Dusan Tittel (YC67), Milos Glonek, Tomás Stúpala, Marián Zeman, Vladimír Kinder, Lubomír Moravcik (C), Robert Tomaschek, Ondrej Kristofík, Vladislav Zvara (64' Marek Penska), Stefan Rusnák (80' Vladimir Weiss). (Coach: Jozef Venglos (SVK)).
France: Bernard Lama, Laurent Blanc, Éric Di Meco, Alain Roche, Jocelyn Angloma, Didier Dechamps, Paul Le Guen, Reynald Pedros (64' Christophe Dugarry), Youri Djorkaeff (81' Bixente Lizarazu), Eric Cantona (C), David Ginola. (Coach: Aimé Jacquet (FRA)).
Referee: Peter Mikkelsen (DEN)   Attendance: 14.329

07-09-1994   Stadionul Steaua, Bucharest: Romania – Azerbaijan   3-0 (1-0)
Romania: Bogdan Stelea (87' Dumitru Stangaciu), Dan Petrescu, Daniel Prodan, Miodrag Belodedici, Tibor Selymes (84' Florin Carstea), Ioan Lupescu (76' Daniel Timofte), Gheorghe Popescu (C), Ilie Dumitrescu, Dorinel Munteanu, Florin Raducioiu, Marius Lacatus. (Coach: Anghel Iordanescu (ROM)).
Azerbaijan: Aleksandr Zhidkov (YC41), Arif Asadov (YC60), Fuzuli Allahverdiyev, Gennadi Drozdov, Tarlan Akhmedov, Rasim Abusev (YC58), Shakhin Diniyev, Vali Gasimov, Nazim Süleymanov (C) (59' Vidadi Rzayev), Samir Alekberov, Yunis Hüseynov (82' Emin Agayev). (Coach: Agaselim Mirjavadov (AZE)).
Goals: Romania: 1-0 Miodrag Belodedici (44'), 2-0 Dan Petrescu (59'), 3-0 Florin Raducioiu (88').
Referee: Robert Sedlacek (AUT)   Attendance: 7.000

08-10-1994   Stade Geoffroy-Guichard, Saint-Étienne: France – Romania   0-0
France: Bernard Lama, Bixente Lizarazu, Marcel Desailly, Laurent Blanc, Alain Roche, Jocelyn Angloma, Christian Karembeu, Reynald Pedros, Eric Cantona (C), Patrice Loko (83' Christophe Dugarry), Nicolas Ouédec (72' Zinédine Zidane). (Coach: Aimé Jacquet (FRA)).
Romania: Bogdan Stelea, Dan Petrescu, Daniel Prodan, Miodrag Belodedici, Tibor Selymes, Ioan Lupescu, Gheorghe Popescu, Ilie Dumitrescu (YC58), Daniel Timofte (YC6) (72' Marius Lacatus), Gheorghe Hagi (C), Florin Raducioiu (79' Basarab Nica Panduru). (Coach: Anghel Iordanescu (ROM)).
Referee: Leif Sundell (SWE)   Attendance: 31.144

12-10-1994 National Stadium, Ramat Gan: Israel – Slovakia 2-2 (2-2)
Israel: Ben Zion Ginzburg, Alon Harazi, Marko Balbul, Moshe Glam, Nir Klinger (C) (65' Amir Shelach), Tal Banin (58' Avi Nimni), Haim Revivo, Alon Hazan, Eyal Berkovic (YC73), Ronen Harazi (YC12), Ronny Rosenthal. (Coach: Shlomo Scharf (ISR)).
Slovakia: Ladislav Molnár, Dusan Tittel, Milos Glonek (YC2), Tomás Stúpala, Marián Zeman (RC30), Vladimír Kinder, Lubomír Moravcik (C), Vladimir Weiss (74' Ivan Kozák), Ondrej Kristofík, Peter Dubovsky, Stefan Rusnák (75' Vladislav Zvara). (Coach: Jozef Venglos (SVK)).
Goals: Israel: 1-2 Ronen Harazi (23'), 2-2 Tal Banin (32' penalty).
Slovakia: 0-1 Stefan Rusnák (6'), 0-2 Lubomír Moravcik (14').
Referee: John Blankenstein (HOL)   Attendance: 7.500

12-10-1994   Stadion Stali Mielec, Mielec: Poland – Azerbaijan 1-0 (1-0)
Poland: Józef Wandzik, Tomasz Waldoch, Waldemar Jaskulski, Tomasz Lapinski (79' Krzysztof Maciejewski), Piotr Swierczewski, Marek Kozminski (69' Adam Fedoruk), Roman Kosecki (C), Sylwester Czerzewski, Jerzy Brzeczek, Krzysztof Warzycha, Andrzej Juskowiak. (Coach: Henryk Apostel (POL)).
Azerbaijan: Aleksandr Zhidkov, Arif Asadov, Fuzuli Allahverdiyev (YC58), Tarlan Akhmedov (YC75), Aslan Kerimov, Rasim Abusev (YC12) (89' Makhmud Gurganov), Shakhin Diniyev (C), Khalig Mardanov, Vali Gasimov, Samir Alekberov, Yunis Hüseynov. (Coach: Agaselim Mirjavadov (AZE)).
Goal: Poland: 1-0 Andrzej Juskowiak (44').
Referee: Ilkka Koho (FIN)   Attendance: 4.600

12-11-1994   Stadionul Steaua, Bucharest: Romania – Slovakia 3-2 (1-0)
Romania: Bogdan Stelea, Dan Petrescu, Daniel Prodan, Miodrag Belodedici, Ioan Lupescu, Gheorghe Popescu, Ilie Dumitrescu, Dorinel Munteanu, Gheorghe Hagi (C), Florin Raducioiu (85' Ion Vladoiu), Marius Lacatus (75' Daniel Timofte). (Coach: Anghel Iordanescu (ROM)).
Slovakia: Ladislav Molnár, Dusan Tittel, Milos Glonek, Tomás Stúpala, Vladimír Kinder, Miroslav Chvíla (YC90), Marek Penska (46' Jaroslav Timko), Lubomír Moravcik (C) (YC88), Robert Tomaschek, Ondrej Kristofík, Peter Dubovsky. (Coach: Jozef Venglos (SVK)).
Goals: Romania: 1-0 Gheorghe Popescu (6'), 2-0 Gheorghe Hagi (47'), 3-2 Daniel Prodan (81').
Slovakia: 2-1 Peter Dubovsky (56'), 2-2 Miroslav Chvíla (78').
Referee: Vadim Zhuk (BLS)   Attendance: 10.283

16-11-1994   Górnik Zabrze Stadium, Zabrze: Poland – France 0-0
Poland: Józef Wandzik, Tomasz Waldoch, Waldemar Jaskulski, Piotr Swierczewski, Marek Kozminski (29' Jacek Bak), Roman Kosecki (C), Sylwester Czerzewski, Marek Swierczewski, Krzysztof Warzycha, Andrzej Juskowiak, Henryk Baluszynski (83' Dariusz Gesior). (Coach: Henryk Apostel (POL)).
France: Bernard Lama, Marcel Desailly, Laurent Blanc, Éric Di Meco, Alain Roche, Jocelyn Angloma (YC37), Christian Karembeu (RC50), Paul Le Guen, Reynald Pedros (28' Youri Djorkaeff), Eric Cantona (C), Nicolas Ouédec (78' Christophe Dugarry). (Coach: Aimé Jacquet (FRA)).
Referee: Angelo Amendolia (ITA)   Attendance: 15.400

16-11-1994   Hüseyin Avni Aker Stadium, Trabzon: Azerbaijan – Israel   0-2 (0-1)
Azerbaijan: Aleksandr Zhidkov, Arif Asadov, Fuzuli Allahverdiyev, Tarlan Akhmedov (RC88), Fayk Dzhabarov, Shakhin Diniyev (C), Lev Mayorov (46' Emin Agayev), Vali Gasimov, Nazim Suleymanov (C), Samir Alekberov, Yunis Hüseynov (77' Vidadi Rzayev). (Coach: Agaselim Mirjavadov (AZE)).
Israel: Ben Zion Ginzburg, Alon Harazi, Marko Balbul, Moshe Glam, Nir Klinger (C), Tal Banin (YC23), Haim Revivo, Alon Hazan, Eyal Berkovic (66' Avi Nimni), Ronen Harazi (83' Amir Shelach), Ronny Rosenthal. (Coach: Shlomo Scharf (ISR)).
Goals: Israel: 0-1 Ronen Harazi (29'), 0-2 Ronny Rosenthal (51').
Referee: László Vágner (HUN)   Attendance: 2.863

13-12-1994   Hüseyin Avni Aker Stadium, Trabzon: Azerbaijan – France   0-2 (0-1)
Azerbaijan: Aleksandr Zhidkov (41' Elkhan Hasanov), Emin Agayev, Arif Asadov (79' Vladislav Kadyrov), Fuzuli Allahverdiyev, Fayk Dzhabarov (YC55), Yashar Vagabzade, Rasim Abusev, Shakhin Diniyev (C), Vali Gasimov (79' Vidadi Rzayev), Samir Alekberov, Yunis Hüseynov. (Coach: Agaselim Mirjavadov (AZE)).
France: Bernard Lama, Marcel Desailly (71' Jean-Michel Ferri), Laurent Blanc, Éric Di Meco (YC68), Alain Roche, Jocelyn Angloma, Paul Le Guen, Reynald Pedros (76' Corentin Martins), Jean-Pierre Papin, Eric Cantona (C), Patrice Loko. (Coach: Aimé Jacquet (FRA)).
Goals: France: 0-1 Jean-Pierre Papin (24'), 0-2 Patrice Loko (56').
Referee: Rune Pedersen (NOR)   Attendance: 533

14-12-1994   National Stadium, Ramat Gan: Israel – Romania   1-1 (0-0)
Israel: Ben Zion Ginzburg, Alon Harazi, Marko Balbul (YC12), Moshe Glam, Nir Klinger (C), Haim Revivo, Alon Hazan, Eyal Berkovic, Ronny Levy (YC73) (76' Itzhak Zohar), Ronen Harazi (88' Amir Shelach), Ronny Rosenthal. (Coach: Shlomo Scharf (ISR)).
Romania: Bogdan Stelea, Dan Petrescu, Daniel Prodan, Miodrag Belodedici, Tibor Selymes, Ioan Lupescu, Gheorghe Popescu (YC64), Ilie Dumitrescu (73' Ovidiu Stinga), Dorinel Munteanu (52' Ion Vladoiu), Gheorghe Hagi (C), Marius Lacatus. (Coach: Anghel Iordanescu (ROM)).
Goals: Israel: 1-1 Ronny Rosenthal (83').
Romania: 0-1 Marius Lacatus (69').
Referee: Antonio Martín Navarrete (ESP)   Attendance: 38.000

29-03-1995   Stadionul Steaua, Bucharest: Romania – Poland   2-1 (1-1)
Romania: Bogdan Stelea, Dan Petrescu, Daniel Prodan, Miodrag Belodedici, Tibor Selymes, Gheorghe Popescu, Ilie Dumitrescu, Dorinel Munteanu, Gheorghe Hagi (C) (87' Ion Vladoiu), Florin Raducioui, Marius Lacatus (46' Danut Lupu (YC67)). (Coach: Anghel Iordanescu (ROM)).
Poland: József Wandzik, Tomasz Waldoch, Waldemar Jaskulski (RC71), Piotr Swierczewski, Roman Kosecki (C) (YC62), Sylwester Czereszewski (71' Tomasz Sokolowski (I)), Marek Swierczewski, Piotr Nowak (56' Tomasz Wieszczycki), Krzysztof Warzycha, Andrzej Juskowiak, Henryk Baluszynski. (Coach: Henryk Apostel (POL)).
Goals: Romania: 1-1 Florin Raducioui (45'), 2-1 Florin Raducioui (54').
Poland: 0-1 Andrzej Juskowiak (41' penalty).
Referee: Kurt Röthlisberger (SUI)   Attendance: 13.480

29-03-1995   Vsesportovy areál, Kosice: Slovakia – Azerbaijan   4-1 (3-0)
Slovakia: Ladislav Molnár, Dusan Tittel, Milos Glonek, Tomás Stúpala, Marián Zeman, Vladimír Kinder, Marek Penska, Lubomír Moravcik (C) (73' Karol Prazenica), Ondrej Kristofík, Peter Dubovsky, Jaroslav Timko. (Coach: Jozef Venglos (SVK)).
Azerbaijan: Elkhan Hasanov, Emin Agayev (YC13), Arif Asadov, Sakit Aliyev (75' Vladislav Kadyrov), Fayk Dzhabarov, Yashar Vagabzade, Rasim Abusev, Shakhin Diniyev (YC37), Vali Gasimov (68' Samir Alekberov), Nazim Suleymanov (C), Yunis Hüseynov. (Coach: Agaselim Mirjavadov (AZE)).
Goals: Slovakia: 1-0 Dusan Tittel (33'), 2-0 Jaroslav Timko (39'), 3-0 Peter Dubovsky (45' penalty), 4-0 Jaroslav Timko (51').
Azerbaijan: 4-1 Nazim Suleymanov (79' penalty).
Referee: Vassilios Nikakis (GRE)   Attendance: 12.450

29-03-1995   National Stadium, Ramat Gan: Israel – France   0-0
Israel: Ben Zion Ginzburg, Alon Harazi, Moshe Glam (YC39), Nir Klinger (C), Felix Halfon, Tal Banin, Haim Revivo, Alon Hazan, Eyal Berkovic (64' Itzhak Zohar), Ronen Harazi, Ronny Rosenthal. (Coach: Shlomo Scharf (ISR)).
France: Bernard Lama, Marcel Desailly, Laurent Blanc, Éric Di Meco, Alain Roche, Jocelyn Angloma, Paul Le Guen (C), Reynald Pedros, Corentin Martins (78' Youri Djorkaeff), Patrice Loko, Nicolas Ouédec (YC55) (65' David Ginola). (Coach: Aimé Jacquet (FRA)).
Referee: James (Jim) McCluskey (SCO)   Attendance: 39.000

25-04-1995   Górnik Zabrze Stadium, Zabrze: Poland – Israel   4-3 (1-2)
Poland: Józef Wandzik, Tomasz Waldoch, Tomasz Lapinski (YC33), Piotr Swierczewski, Marek Kozminski, Roman Kosecki (C), Marek Swierczewski, Piotr Nowak (46' Tomasz Wieszczycki (YC89)), Wojciech Kowalczyk (YC40), Andrzej Juskowiak, Henryk Baluszynski (46' Krzysztof Bukalski). (Coach: Henryk Apostel (POL)).
Israel: Ben Zion Ginzburg, Alon Harazi (YC88), Moshe Glam (YC38), Nir Klinger (C), Felix Halfon (YC61), Tal Banin, Haim Revivo (YC23), Alon Hazan (YC13), Eyal Berkovic, Ronny Rosenthal, Ofer Mizrahi (73' Itzhak Zohar). (Coach: Shlomo Scharf (ISR)).
Goals: Poland: 1-0 Piotr Nowak (1'), 2-2 Andrzej Juskowiak (50'), 3-2 Wojciech Kowalczyk (55'), 4-2 Roman Kosecki (62').
Israel: 1-1 Ronny Rosenthal (37'), 1-2 Haim Revivo (43'), 4-3 Itzhak Zohar (79').
Referee: Anders Frisk (SWE)   Attendance: 5.500

26-04-1995   Hüseyin Avni Aker Stadium, Trabzon: Azerbaijan – Romania   1-4 (1-2)
Azerbaijan: Elkhan Hasanov, Arif Asadov, Igor Getman, Tarlan Akhmedov (21' Yashar Vagabzade), Fayk Dzhabarov (75' Vladislav Kadyrov), Rasim Abusev, Shakhin Diniyev, Vyacheslav Lychkin, Nazim Suleymanov (C), Samir Alekberov, Yunis Hüseynov. (Coach: Agaselim Mirjavadov (AZE)).
Romania: Bogdan Stelea (85' Florian Prunea), Dan Petrescu, Daniel Prodan, Miodrag Belodedici, Tibor Selymes, Ioan Lupescu, Gheorghe Popescu (C) (YC76) (82' Daniel Timofte), Ilie Dumitrescu, Dorinel Munteanu, Florin Raducioui, Marius Lacatus (74' Danut Lupu). (Coach: Anghel Iordanescu (ROM)).
Goals: Azerbaijan: 1-1 Nazim Suleymanov (33').
Romania: 0-1 Florin Raducioui (1' penalty), 1-2 Ilie Dumitrescu (39'), 1-3 Florin Raducioui (74'), 1-4 Florin Raducioui (77').
Referee: Dimitar Ivanov (Dimo) Momirov (BUL)   Attendance: 372

26-04-1995   Stade de la Beaujoire, Nantes: France – Slovakia 4-0 (2-0)
France: Bernard Lama, Marcel Desailly, Laurent Blanc, Éric Di Meco (YC53), Alain Roche, Zinédine Zidane (74' Youri Djorkaeff), Jocelyn Anglomaa, Didier Deschamps (C), Vincent Guérin, Patrice Loko, David Ginola. (Coach: Aimé Jacquet (FRA)).
Slovakia: Ladislav Molnár, Dusan Tittel (YC33), Milos Glonek, Tomás Stúpala, Marián Zeman, Vladimír Kinder, Marek Penska (74' Stefan Maixner), Lubomír Moravcik (C), Robert Tomaschek (46' Jaroslav Timko), Ondrej Kristofík, Peter Dubovsky (YC25). (Coach: Jozef Venglos (SVK)).
Goals: France: 1-0 Ondrej Kristofík (27' own goal), 2-0 David Ginola (42'), 3-0 Laurent Blanc (58'), 4-0 Vincent Guérin (63').
Referee: Bernd Heynemann (GER)   Attendance: 23.910

07-06-1995   Górnik Zbrze Stadium, Zabrze: Poland – Slovakia 5-0 (1-0)
Poland: Maciej Szczesny (YC37), Tomasz Waldoch, Jacek Zielinksi, Waldemar Jaskulski (YC54) (70' Sylwester Czereszewski), Krzysztof Bukalski, Piotr Swierczewski, Marek Kozminski (YC62), Roman Kosecki (C), Piotr Nowak, Wojciech Kowalczyk (46' Tomasz Wieszczycki (YC63)), Andrzej Juskowiak. (Coach: Henryk Apostel (POL)).
Slovakia: Alexander Vencel, Milos Glonek (YC61), Marián Zeman, Ivan Kozák (58' Marek Penska), Lubomír Moravcik (C), Robert Tomaschek (YC25), Ondrej Kristofík (68' Vladimir Weiss), Peter Dubovsky, Karol Prazenica, Jan Solar, Jaroslav Timko (YC87). (Coach: Jozef Venglos (SVK)).
Goals: Poland: 1-0 Andrzej Juskowiak (10'), 2-0 Tomasz Wieszczycki (58'), 3-0 Roman Kosecki (64'), 4-0 Piotr Nowak (68'), 5-0 Andrzej Juskowiak (72').
Referee: Robert Sedlacek (AUT)   Attendance: 9.515

07-06-1995   Stadionul Steaua, Bucharest: Romania – Israel 2-1 (1-0)
Romania: Bogdan Stelea, Dan Petrescu, Daniel Prodan (YC29), Miodrag Belodedici, Tibor Selymes, Ioan Lupescu (C), Ilie Dumitrescu (YC44) (61' Ion Vladoiu (YC89)), Danut Lupu (YC56) (88' Nica Panduru), Dorinel Munteanu, Florin Raducioui (RC67), Marius Lacatus. (Coach: Anghel Iordanescu (ROM)).
Israel: Refael Cohen, David Amsalem, Nir Klinger (C), Felix Halfon (46' Marko Balbul, 74' Itzhak Zohar), Gadi Brumer, Tal Banin, Alon Hazan, Eyal Berkovic, Amir Shelach, Ofer Mizrahi (YC14), Eliezer Drieks (YC57). (Coach: Shlomo Scharf (ISR)).
Goals: Romania: 1-0 Marius Lacatus (16'), 2-1 Dorinel Munteanu (65').
Israel: 1-1 Eyal Berkovic (60').
Referee: Rune Pedersen (NOR)   Attendance: 18.575

16-08-1995   Hüseyin Avni Aker Stadium, Trabzon: Azerbaijan – Slovakia 0-1 (0-0)
Azerbaijan: Nizami Sadykov, Igor Getman (YC71), Emin Agayev (71' Arif Asadov), Tarlan Akhmedov, Vladyslav Nosenko (RC90+1), Rasim Abusev, Shakhin Diniyev (C) (46' Makhmud Gurbanov), Vladislav Kadyrov, Vyacheslav Lychkin, Samir Alekberov (YC23), Yunis Hüseynov. (Coach: Agaselim Mirjavadov (AZE)).
Slovakia: Ladislav Molnár, Dusan Tittel, Vladimír Kinder, Igor Balis (90' Karol Prazenica), Milos Sobona (YC11), Lubomír Moravcik (C) (74' Lubomir Faktor), Ladislav Pecko (YC48), Robert Tomaschek (RC81), Peter Dubovsky, Julius Simon, Stefan Rusnák (56' Tibor Jancula). (Coach: Jozef Jankech (SVK)).
Goal: Slovakia: 0-1 Tibor Jancula (59').
Referee: Alain Hamer (LUX)   Attendance: 200

16-08-1995   Parc des Princes, Paris: France – Poland   1-1 (0-1)
France: Bernard Lama, Lilian Thuram, Bixente Lizarazu, Marcel Desailly, Frank Leboeuf (69'
Youri Djorkaeff), Zinédine Zidane (YC88), Jocelyn Angloma (65' Christian Karembeu),
Didier Deschamps (C), Vincent Guérin (YC33), Christophe Dugarry, David Ginola (63'
Reynald Pedros). (Coach: Aimé Jacquet (FRA)).
Poland: Andrzej Wozniak, Tomasz Waldoch, Jacek Zielinksi (YC17), Tomasz Lapinski
(RC55), Piotr Swierczewski, Marek Kozminski, Roman Kosecki (C) (71' Pawel Wojtala),
Piotr Nowak (56' Ryszard Czerwiec), Tomasz Iwan (YC38), Wojciech Kowalczyk (60'
Krzysztof Bukalski), Andrzej Juskowiak. (Coach: Henryk Apostel (POL)).
Goals: France: 1-1 Youri Djorkaeff (86').
Poland: 0-1 Andrzej Juskowiak (34').
Referee: Manuel Díaz Vega (ESP)   Attendance: 40.426

06-09-1995   Stade de l'Abbé-Deschamps, Auxerre: France – Azerbaijan   10-0 (3-0)
France: Bernard Lama, Bixente Lizarazu, Marcel Desailly (C), Frank Leboeuf, Zinédine
Zidane, Jocelyn Angloma (57' Lilian Thuram), Didier Deschamps, Vincent Guérin, Reynald
Pedros (65' David Ginola), Youri Djorkaeff, Christophe Dugarry (69' Christophe Cocard).
(Coach: Aimé Jacquet (FRA)).
Azerbaijan: Elkhan Hasanov (36' Nizami Sadykov), Emin Agayev, Arif Asadov, Igor Getman
(YC49), Tarlan Akhmedov, Makhmud Gurbanov (46' Samir Alekberov), Rasim Abusev,
Shakhin Diniyev (C), Vladislav Kadyrov (74' Mushvig Huseynov), Vyacheslav Lychkin,
Yunis Hüseynov. (Coach: Agaselim Mirjavadov (AZE)).
Goals: France: 1-0 Marcel Desailly (13'), 2-0 Youri Djorkaeff (17'), 3-0 Vincent Guérin (32'),
4-0 Reynald Pedros (48'), 5-0 Frank Leboeuf (53'), 6-0 Christophe Dugarry (66'), 7-0
Zinédine Zidane (71'), 8-0 Frank Leboeuf (74'), 9-0 Youri Djorkaeff (77'), 10-0 Christophe
Cocard (90').
Referee: Alfred Micallef (MLT)   Attendance: 13.479

06-09-1995   Górnik Zabrze Stadium, Zabrze: Poland – Romania   0-0
Poland: Andrzej Wozniak, Tomasz Waldoch, Jacek Zielinksi, Waldemar Jaskulski, Jacek
Bednarz (62' Krzysztof Bukalski (YC88)), Piotr Swierczewski (YC37), Marek Kozminski,
Roman Kosecki (C), Tomasz Wieszczycki (70' Jerzy Podbrozny), Tomasz Iwan (71' Ryszard
Czerwiec), Andrzej Juskowiak. (Coach: Henryk Apostel (POL)).
Romania: Bogdan Stelea, Dan Petrescu, Daniel Prodan, Gheorghe Mihali (YC32), Tibor
Selymes, Ioan Lupescu, Gheorghe Popescu (C), Ioan Sabau (YC12), Dorinel Munteanu (75'
Constantin Galca (YC82)), Ion Vladoiu (64' Nica Panduru), Marius Lacatus (YC25) (84' Ion
Timofte). (Coach: Anghel Iordanescu (ROM)).
Referee: Dermot J.Gallagher (ENG)   Attendance: 18.000

06-09-1995   Vsesportovy areál, Kosice: Slovakia – Israel   1-0 (0-0)
Slovakia: Ladislav Molnár, Dusan Tittel, Vladimír Kinder, Igor Balis (89' Rastislav Kostka),
Miroslav Karhan, Lubomír Moravcik (C), Ladislav Pecko (YC58), Peter Dubovsky, Jozef
Juriga, Julius Simon (80' Lubomir Faktor), Tibor Jancula (66' Stefan Rusnák). (Coach: Jozef
Jankech (SVK)).
Israel: Refael Cohen, Alon Harazi, Moshe Glam, Nir Klinger (C) (46' Ronny Rosenthal), Gadi
Brumer, Tal Banin (YC43), Haim Revivo, Alon Hazan, Eyal Berkovic (66' Eliezer Drieks),
Amir Shelach, Ofer Mizrahi. (Coach: Shlomo Scharf (ISR)).
Goal: Slovakia: 1-0 Tibor Jancula (54').
Referee: Marnix Sandra (BEL)   Attendance: 7.810

11-10-1995   Stadionul Steaua, Bucharest: Romania – France   1-3 (0-2)
Romania: Bogdan Stelea, Dan Petrescu, Daniel Prodan, Gheorghe Mihali (46' Danut Lupu), Tibor Selymes, Ioan Lupescu, Gheorghe Popescu, Ilie Dumitrescu (46' Ion Vladoiu (YC80)), Dorinel Munteanu, Gheorghe Hagi (C) (63' Nica Panduru), Marius Lacatus. (Coach: Anghel Iordanescu (ROM)).
France: Fabien Barthez (YC68), Marcel Desailly, Frank Leboeuf (YC17), Éric Di Meco (C), Zinédine Zidane (86' Lilian Thuram), Jocelyn Angloma, Didier Deschamps, Christian Karembeu, Vincent Guérin, Youri Djorkaeff (71' Bixente Lizarazu (YC83)), Christophe Dugarry (63' Mickaël Madar). (Coach: Aimé Jacquet (FRA)).
Goals: Romania: 1-2 Marius Lacatus (52').
France: 0-1 Christian Karembeu (27'), 0-2 Youri Djorkaeff (41'), 1-3 Zinédine Zidane (78').
Referee: Pierluigi Pairetto (ITA)   Attendance: 23.200

11-10-1995   Stadión Tehelné pole, Bratislava: Slovakia – Poland   4-1 (1-1)
Slovakia: Ladislav Molnár, Dusan Tittel (YC63), Marián Zeman, Vladimír Kinder (YC81), Igor Balis (YC33), Miroslav Karhan, Lubomír Moravcik (C), Peter Dubovsky, Jozef Juriga (65' Marek Ujlaky), Julius Simon, Tibor Jancula (86' Marian Bochnovic). (Coach: Jozef Jankech (SVK)).
Poland: Andrzej Wozniak, Tomasz Waldoch, Jacek Zielinksi, Tomasz Lapinski (YC28), Krzysztof Bukalski, Piotr Swierczewski (RC75), Marek Kozminski (76' Jacek Bednarz), Roman Kosecki (C) (RC65), Tomasz Iwan, Andrzej Juskowiak, Henryk Baluszynski (80' Sylwester Czerzewski). (Coach: Henryk Apostel (POL)).
Goals: Slovakia: 1-1 Peter Dubovsky (31' penalty), 2-1 Tibor Jancula (68'), 3-1 Marek Ujlaky (78'), 4-1 Julius Simon (82').
Poland: 0-1 Andrzej Juskowiak (19').
Referee: Jorge Emanuel Monteiro Coroado (POR)   Attendance: 11.653

11-10-1995   Bloomfield Stadium, Tel Aviv: Israel – Azerbaijan   2-0 (1-0)
Israel: Ben Zion Ginzburg, David Amsalem, Felix Halfon, Gadi Brumer, Tal Banin (C), Haim Revivo (88' Nir Klinger), Alon Hazan, Eyal Berkovic (72' Itzhat Zohar), Amir Shelach, Ronen Harazi (81' Reuven Atar), Ronny Rosenthal. (Coach: Shlomo Scharf (ISR)).
Azerbaijan: Aleksandr Zhidkov, Arif Asadov (YC20), Tarlan Akhmedov, Yashar Vagabzade, Samir Khairov (58' Emin Agayev), Rasim Abusev, Vidadi Rzayev (YC2) (70' Gurban Gurbanov), Vyacheslav Lychkin (79' Ilham Mammadov), Vali Gasimov, Nazim Suleymanov (C), Vladislav Kadyrov. (Coach: Kazbek Tuayev (AZE)).
Goals: Israel: 1-0 Ronen Harazi (31'), 2-0 Ronen Harazi (51').
Referee: Claude Détruche (SUI)   Attendance: 7.000

15-11-1995   Stade Michel d'Ornano, Caen: France – Israel   2-0 (0-0)
France: Bernard Lama, Marcel Desailly, Frank Leboeuf, Éric Di Meco (63' Bixente Lizarazu), Zinédine Zidane, Jocelyn Angloma, Didier Deschamps (YC21), Christian Karembeu (90' Marc Keller), Vincent Guérin (C), Youri Djorkaeff, Mickaël Madar (63' Patrice Loko). (Coach: Aimé Jacquet (FRA)).
Israel: Refael Cohen, Moshe Glam, Nir Klinger (79' Itzhat Zohar), Felix Halfon, Gadi Brumer, Tal Banin (YC74), Alon Hazan (YC81), Eyal Berkovic (70' Reuven Atar), Amir Shelach, Ronen Harazi (85' Ofer Mizrahi), Ronny Rosenthal. (Coach: Shlomo Scharf (ISR)).
Goals: France: 1-0 Youri Djorkaeff (69'), 2-0 Bixente Lizarazu (89').
Referee: Gerd Grabher (AUT)   Attendance: 20.822

15-11-1995　Vsesportovy areál, Kosice: Slovakia – Romania　0-2 (0-0)
Slovakia: Ladislav Molnár, Dusan Tittel, Vladimír Kinder, Igor Balis, Miroslav Karhan, Lubomír Moravcik (C), Ladislav Pecko (46' Jozef Juriga), Robert Tomaschek (YC7), Peter Dubovsky (YC84), Julius Simon (76' Robert Semeník), Tibor Jancula (68' Marek Ujlaky). (Coach: Jozef Jankech (SVK)).
Romania: Bogdan Stelea, Dan Petrescu, Daniel Prodan (YC56), Tibor Selymes, Anton Dobos, Ioan Lupescu, Gheorghe Popescu, Dorinel Munteanu, Gheorghe Hagi (C) (84' Nica Panduru), Viorel Moldovan (87' Ion Timofte), Marius Lacatus (72' Ilie Dumitrescu). (Coach: Anghel Iordanescu (ROM)).
Goals: Romania: 0-1 Gheorghe Hagi (67'), 0-2 Dorinel Munteanu (80').
Referee: Jacobus H. (Jaap) Uilenberg (HOL)　　Attendance: 9.676

15-11-1995　Hüseyin Avni Aker Stadium, Trabzon: Azerbaijan – Poland　0-0
Azerbaijan: Aleksandr Zhidkov, Igor Getman, Emin Agayev, Tarlan Akhmedov, Yashar Vagabzade, Deni Gaysumov (YC87), Rasim Abusev, Vidadi Rzayev (69' Gurban Gurbanov), Vali Gasimov, Nazim Suleymanov (C) (86' Vyacheslav Lychkin), Vladislav Kadyrov (65' Makhmud Gurbanov). (Coach: Kazbek Tuayev (AZE)).
Poland: Andrzej Wozniak, Tomasz Waldoch (C), Waldemar Jaskulski, Pawel Wojtala, Krzysztof Bukalski (70' Tomasz Lenart), Sylwester Czereszewski, Marek Swierczewski, Ryszard Czerwiec, Tomasz Sokolowski (I), Henryk Baluszynski (64' Marcin Kuzba), Slawomir Majak (46' Rafal Siadaczka). (Coach: Henryk Apostel (POL)).
Referee: Leslie William Mottram (SCO)　　Attendance: 200

GROUP 2

07-09-1994	Brussels	Belgium – Armenia	2-0 (1-0)
07-09-1994	Limassol	Cyprus – Spain	1-2 (1-2)
07-09-1994	Skopje	Macedonia – Denmark	1-1 (1-0)
08-10-1994	Yerevan	Armenia – Cyprus	0-0
12-10-1994	Copenhagen	Denmark – Belgium	3-1 (1-1)
12-10-1994	Skopje	Macedonia – Spain	0-2 (0-2)
16-11-1994	Brussels	Belgium – Macedonia	1-1 (1-0)
16-11-1994	Limassol	Cyprus – Armenia	2-0 (1-0)
16-11-1994	Seville	Spain – Denmark	3-0 (1-0)
17-12-1994	Skopje	Macedonia – Cyprus	3-0 (2-0)
17-12-1994	Brussels	Belgium – Spain	1-4 (1-1)
29-03-1995	Seville	Spain – Belgium	1-1 (1-1)
29-03-1995	Limassol	Cyprus – Denmark	1-1 (1-1)
26-04-1995	Yerevan	Armenia – Spain	0-2 (0-0)
26-04-1995	Copenhagen	Denmark – Macedonia	1-0 (0-0)
26-04-1995	Brussels	Denmark – Cyprus	2-0 (1-0)
10-05-1995	Yerevan	Armenia – Macedonia	2-2 (1-0)
07-06-1995	Copenhagen	Denmark – Cyprus	4-0 (1-0)
07-06-1995	Seville	Spain – Armenia	1-0 (0-0)
07-06-1995	Skopje	Macedonia – Belgium	0-5 (0-4)
16-08-1995	Yerevan	Armenia – Denmark	0-2 (0-1)
06-09-1995	Brussels	Belgium – Denmark	1-3 (1-2)
06-09-1995	Skopje	Macedonia – Armenia	1-2 (0-0)
06-09-1995	Granada	Spain – Cyprus	6-0 (1-0)

07-10-1995	Yerevan	Armenia – Belgium	0-2 (0-2)
11-10-1995	Copenhagen	Denmark – Spain	1-1 (0-1)
11-10-1995	Limassol	Cyprus – Macedonia	1-1 (0-1)
15-11-1995	Elche	Spain – Macedonia	3-0 (1-0)
15-11-1995	Copenhagen	Denmark – Armenia	3-1 (2-0)
15-11-1995	Limassol	Cyprus – Belgium	1-1 (1-0)

FINAL STANDING

Pos	Team	Pld	W	D	L	GF	GA	GD	Pts
1	*Spain*	*10*	*8*	*2*	*0*	*25*	*4*	*+21*	*26*
2	*Denmark*	*10*	*6*	*3*	*1*	*19*	*9*	*+10*	*21*
3	Belgium	10	4	3	3	17	13	+4	15
4	Macedonia	10	1	4	5	9	18	-9	7
5	Cyprus	10	1	4	5	6	20	-14	7
6	Armenia	10	1	2	7	5	17	-12	5

Spain and Denmark qualified for the final tournament in England.

07-09-1994   Constant Vanden Stock Stadium, Brussels: Belgium – Armenia 2-0 (1-0)
Belgium: Michel Preud'homme, Rudi Smidts (YC74), Philippe Albert, Michel De Wolf (YC50), Régis Genaux, Lorenzo Staelens (76' Marc Emmers), Franky Van Der Elst (C), Stéphane Van Der Heyden (67' Danny Boffin), Luís Oliveira, Marc Degryse, Josip Weber. (Coach: Paul Van Himst (BEL)).
Armenia: Armenak Petrosyan, Sargis Hovsepyan, Yervand Sukiasyan, Yervand Krbashyan, Ashot Khachatryan, Sargis Hovhannisyan, Aramais Tonoyan, Arton Petrosyan, Razmik Grigoryan, Armen Shahgeldyan (46' Arsen Avetisyan), Hamlet Apetnakovich Mkhitaryan. (Coach: Eduard Markarov (ARM)).
Goals: Belgium: 1-0 Yervand Krbashyan (3' *own goal*), 2-0 Marc Degryse (73').
Referee: John Ferry (NIR)   Attendance: 6.140

07-09-1994   Tsirion Stadium, Limassol: Cyprus – Spain 1-2 (1-2)
Cyprus: Nicos Panayiotou, Kostakis Konstantinou, Demetris Ioannou, Charalambos Pittas (C), Marios Charalambous (YC87), Evagoras Christofi, Kostas Kosta (YC50), Kostakis Fasouliotis (62' Kostakis Malekkos), Georgios Savvides (77' Charalambos Andreou), Andreas Sotiriou, Sinisa Gogic. (Coach: Andreas Michaelides (CYP)).
Spain: Andoni ZUBIZARRETA Urreta (C), Fernando Ruiz HIERRO, Miguel Ángel NADAL Homar, Francisco José CAMARASA Castellar, Salvador González Marco "VORO", SERGI BARJUÁN i Esclusa, JULEN GUERRERO López, Jon Andoni GOIKOETXEA Lasa, Josep GUARDIOLA i Sala (63' José Luis Pérez CAMINERO), José Emilio AMAVISCA Gárate (80' José Ángel "CUCO" ZIGANDA Lucunza), Francisco HIGUERA Fernández. (Coach: JAVIER CLEMENTE Lázaro (ESP)).
Goals: Cyprus 1-2 Andreas Sotiriou (36').
Spain: 0-1 Francisco HIGUERA Fernández (17'), 0-2 Marios Charalambous (26' *own goal*).
Referee: Marc Batta (FRA)   Attendance: 5.024

07-09-1994   Gradski Stadion, Skopje: Macedonia – Denmark   1-1 (1-0)
Macedonia: Kire Trajcev, Vujadin Stanojkovic, Ilija Najdoski, Mitko Stojkovski, Ljupco Markovski, Bosko Djurovski, Boban Babunski (YC46) (67' Dragan Kanatlarovski), Zoran Jovanovski, Toni Micevski, Darko Pancev (C) (RC47), Zoran Boskovski (YC11) (82' Zarko Serafimovski). (Coach: Andon Doncevski (MCD)).
Denmark: Peter Schmeichel, Thomas Helveg (YC28), Marc Rieper, Lars Olsen (C), Jakob Friis-Hansen, Brian Steen Nielsen, Michael Laudrup, John Faxe Jensen (67' Henrik Larsen), Kim Vilfort (52' Flemming Povlsen), Brian Laudrup (YC26), Bent Christensen Arensøe. (Coach: Richard Møller Nielsen (DEN)).
Goals: Macedonia: 1-0 Mitko Stojkovski (4').
Denmark: 1-1 Flemming Povlsen (87').
Referee: Mario van der Ende (HOL)   Attendance: 22.000

08-10-1994   Hrazdan Stadium, Yerevan: Armenia – Cyprus   0-0
Armenia: Harutyun Abrahamyan, Yervand Sukiasyan, Sargis Hovhannisyan, Aramais Tonoyan (C), Vardan Khachatryan, Harutyun Vardanyan, Artur Petrosyan, Razmik Grigoryan (YC54), Ardaches Adamyan, Arsen Avetisyan, Hamlet Apetnakovich Mkhitaryan (80' Varazdat Avetisyan). (Coach: Eduard Markarov (ARM)).
Cyprus: Michalis Christofi, Yiannis Kalotheou, Demetris Ioannou, Charalambos Pittas (C), Marios Charalambous (YC4), Loizos Stefani, Kostakis Fasouliotis (70' Kostakis Malekkos), Andonis Zembashis, Georgios Savvides, Andreas Sotiriou, Sinisa Gogic. (Coach: Andreas Michaelides (CYP)).
Referee: Zbigniew Przesmycki (POL)   Attendance: 3.600

12-10-1994   Parken Stadium, Copenhagen: Denmark – Belgium   3-1 (1-1)
Denmark: Peter Schmeichel, Thomas Helveg, Marc Rieper, Lars Olsen (C), Jens Risager (79' Jakob Kjeldbjerg), Jakob Friis-Hansen, Brian Steen Nielsen, Michael Laudrup, Kim Vilfort (70' John Faxe Jensen), Brian Laudrup, Mark Strudal. (Coach: Richard Møller Nielsen (DEN)).
Belgium: Gilbert Bodart, Eric Van Meir, Rudi Smidts, Philippe Albert, Vital Borkelmans (76' Luís Oliveira), Régis Genaux (YC79), Gert Verheyen, Franky Van Der Elst (C) (YC40), Lorenzo Staelens, Marc Degryse, Josip Weber. (Coach: Paul Van Himst (BEL)).
Goals: Denmark: 1-1 Kim Vilfort (35'), 2-1 John Faxe Jensen (72'), 3-1 Mark Strudal (86').
Belgium: 0-1 Marc Degryse (31').
Referee: Pierlugi Pairetto (ITA)   Attendance: 40.075

12-10-1994   Gradski Stadion, Skopje: Macedonia – Spain   0-2 (0-2)
Macedonia: Kire Trajcev (51' Danco Celesky), Vujadin Stanojkovic, Ilija Najdoski (C) (YC24), Mitko Stojkovski, Bosko Djurovski, Boban Babunski (39' Ljupco Markovski (YC82)), Zoran Jovanovski, Toni Micevski, Toni Savevski, Zoran Boskovski, Milko Djurovski (71' Zarko Serafimovski). (Coach: Andon Doncevski (MCD)).
Spain: Andoni ZUBIZARRETA Urreta (C), Fernando Ruiz HIERRO, Miguel Ángel NADAL Homar, Rafael ALKORTA Martínez (YC49), ALBERT FERRER i Llopis (YC12), SERGI BARJUÁN i Esclusa, ABELARDO Fernández Antuña, LUIS ENRIQUE Martínez García, José Luis Pérez CAMINERO, Francisco HIGUERA Fernández (YC60) (76' José Emilio AMAVISCA Gárate), JULIO SALINAS Fernández (63' PIER Luigi Cherubino Loggi). (Coach: JAVIER CLEMENTE Lázaro (ESP)).
Goals: Spain: 0-1 JULIO SALINAS Fernández (15'), 0-2 JULIO SALINAS Fernández (24').
Referee: Gerd Grabher (AUT)   Attendance: 21.000

16-11-1994   Constant Vanden Stock Stadium, Brussels: Belgium – Macedonia   1-1 (1-0)
Belgium: Michel Preud'homme, Bertrand Crasson, Rudi Smidts, Régis Genaux, Gert Verheyen, Danny Boffin, Lorenzo Staelens, Franky Van Der Elst (C), Johan Walem (69' Gilles De Bilde), Luc Nilis, Marc Degryse. (Coach: Paul Van Himst (BEL)).
Macedonia: Danco Celesky (YC88), Vujadin Stanojkovic, Cedomir Janevski, Ilija Najdoski (C), Mitko Stojkovski, Ljupco Markovski, Bosko Djurovski (YC47), Zoran Jovanovski, Toni Micevski, Zoran Boskovski (87' Dragan Kanatlarovski), Milko Djurovski (80' Zarko Serafimovski). (Coach: Andon Doncevski (MCD)).
Goals: Belgium: 1-0 Gert Verheyen (31').
Macedonia: 1-1 Zoran Boskovski (50').
Referee: Sergei Grigorievich Khusainov (URS)   Attendance: 18.934

16-11-1994   Tsirion Stadium, Limassol: Cyprus – Armenia   2-0 (1-0)
Cyprus: Michalis Christofi, Demetris Ioannou, Charalambos Pittas (C), Evagoras Christofi, Loizos Stefani (YC65), Andonis Zembashis (86' Georgios Elia), Andreas Andreou, Georgios Savvides, Andreas Sotiriou, Sinisa Gogic, Kostakis Malekkos (68' Kostakis Fasouliotis). (Coach: Andreas Michaelides (CYP)).
Armenia: Harutyun Abrahamyan, Sargis Hovsepyan, Yervand Sukiasyan, Yervand Krbashyan, Sargis Hovhannisyan, Aramais Tonoyan (C), Tigram Gspeyan (68' Arsen Avetisyan), Harutyun Vardanyan (YC19), Artur Petrosyan, Razmik Grigoryan, Hamlet Vladimirovich Mkhitaryan (83' Varazdat Avetisyan). (Coach: Eduard Markarov (ARM)).
Goals: Cyprus: 1-0 Andreas Sotiriou (6'), 2-0 Kostakis Fasouliotis (85').
Referee: Gerald R.Ashby (ENG)   Attendance: 3.254

16-11-1994   Estadio Ramón Sánchez Pizjuán, Seville: Spain – Denmark   3-0 (1-0)
Spain: Andoni ZUBIZARRETA Urreta (C), Miguel Ángel NADAL Homar, Rafael ALKORTA Martínez, ALBERT FERRER i Llopis, ALBERTO BELSUÉ Arias, SERGI BARJUÁN i Esclusa, ABELARDO Fernández Antuña, LUIS ENRIQUE Martínez García (YC39), José Luis Pérez CAMINERO (71' JOSÉ María BAKERO Escudero), DONATO Gama da Silva, JULIO SALINAS Fernández (56' Francisco HIGUERA Fernández). (Coach: JAVIER CLEMENTE Lázaro (ESP)).
Denmark: Peter Schmeichel, Thomas Helveg, Marc Rieper, Lars Olsen (C), Jens Risager, Jakob Friis-Hansen (YC42) (64' Bent Christensen Arensøe), Brian Steen Nielsen, Michael Laudrup, Kim Vilfort, Brian Laudrup, Mark Strudal (46' John Faxe Jensen). (Coach: Richard Møller Nielsen (DEN)).
Goals: Spain: 1-0 Miguel Ángel NADAL Homar (41'), 2-0 DONATO Gama da Silva (56'), 3-0 LUIS ENRIQUE Martínez García (87').
Referee: James (Jim) McCluskey (SCO)   Attendance: 26.428

17-12-1994   Gradski Stadion, Skopje: Macedonia – Cyprus   3-0 (2-0)
Macedonia: Danco Celesky, Vujadin Stanojkovic, Cedomir Janevski (RC85), Ilija Najdoski (C), Mitko Stojkovski, Ljupco Markovski, Bosko Djurovski, Boban Babunski (YC55) (70' Zoran Jovanovski), Toni Micevski, Zoran Boskovski (85' Zarko Serafimovski), Milko Djurovski. (Coach: Andon Doncevski (MCD)).
Cyprus: Michalis Christofi, Yiannis Kalotheou, Demetris Ioannou, Marios Charalambous (YC17), Evagoras Christofi (C), Loizos Stefani, Zacharias Charalambous (YC67), Kostakis Fasouliotis, Georgios Savvides (65' Kostakis Malekkos), Andreas Sotiriou (78' Charalambos Andreou), Sinisa Gogic. (Coach: Andreas Michaelides (CYP)).
Goals: Macedonia: 1-0 Bosko Djurovski (14'), 2-0 Bosko Djurovski (25'), 3-0 Bosko Djurovski (90').
Referee: Hartmut Strampe (GER)   Attendance: 7.000

Following crowd trouble during the home match on 17th December 1994 against Cyprus, Macedonia were ordered by UEFA to play their next two home games – on 7th June 1995 against Belgium and on 6th September 1995 against Armenia – behind closed doors.

17-12-1994   Constant Vander Stock Stadium, Brussels: Belgium – Spain   1-4 (1-1)
Belgium: Michel Preud'homme (YC46), Bertrand Crasson, Rudi Smidts, Philippe Albert (YC48), Régis Genaux, Lorenzo Staelens, Danny Boffin, Franky Van Der Elst (C), Alain Bettagno (46' Gert Verheyen), Marc Degryse, Gilles De Bilde. (Coach: Paul Van Himst (BEL)).
Spain: Andoni ZUBIZARRETA Urreta (C), Fernando Ruiz HIERRO, Miguel Ángel NADAL Homar, Rafael ALKORTA Martínez (YC66), ALBERTO BELSUÉ Arias, SERGI BARJUÁN i Esclusa, ABELARDO Fernández Antuña (YC45), LUIS ENRIQUE Martínez García, JULEN GUERRERO López (67' Salvador González Marco "VORO" (YC69)), DONATO Gama da Silva, JULIO SALINAS Fernández (70' Jon Andoni GOIKOETXEA Lasa). (Coach: JAVIER CLEMENTE Lázaro (ESP)).
Goals: Belgium: 1-0 Marc Degryse (6').
Spain: 1-1 Fernando Ruiz HIERRO (28'), 1-2 DONATO Gama da Silva (56'), 1-3 JULIO SALINAS Fernández (68'), 1-4 LUIS ENRIQUE Martínez García (89').
Referee: Ahmet Çakar (TUR)   Attendance: 15.074

29-03-1995   Estadio Ramón Sánchez Pizjuán, Seville: Spain – Belgium   1-1 (1-1)
Spain: Andoni ZUBIZARRETA Urreta (C), Fernando Ruiz HIERRO, Miguel Ángel NADAL Homar (YC41), ALBERTO BELSUÉ Arias, SERGI BARJUÁN i Esclusa, ABELARDO Fernández Antuña (YC60), LUIS ENRIQUE Martínez García, JULEN GUERRERO López (35' Francisco HIGUERA Fernández), DONATO Gama da Silva, José Emilio AMAVISCA Gárate, JULIO SALINAS Fernández (YC36) (63' Juan Antonio PIZZI Torroja). (Coach: JAVIER CLEMENTE Lázaro (ESP)).
Belgium: Gilbert Bodart, Rudi Smidts, Dirk Medved, Régis Genaux (YC20), Pascal Renier, Emmanuel Karagiannis (84' Bertrand Crasson), Günther Schepens, Lorenzo Staelens, Johan Walem (69' Gert Verheyen), Marc Degryse (C), Gilles De Bilde. (Coach: Paul Van Himst (BEL)).
Goals: Spain: 1-0 JULEN GUERRERO López (25').
Belgium: 1-1 Marc Degryse (27').
Referee: Rémi Harrel (FRA)   Attendance: 27.000

29-03-1995   Tsirion Stadium, Limassol: Cyprus – Denmark   1-1 (1-1)
Cyprus: Nicos Panayiotou, George Christodoulou, Demetris Ioannou (YC2), Charalambos Pittas (C), Marios Charalambous, Panayiotis Engomitis, Kostas Kosta (YC75), Loucas Hadjiloucas (87' Kostakis Konstantinou), Andreas Andreou, Sinisa Gogic, Marios Agathocleous. (Coach: Andreas Michaelides (CYP)).
Denmark: Peter Schmeichel, Michael Schjønberg, Marc Rieper, Jes Høgh, Jacob Laursen, Jakob Friis-Hansen (46' Thomas Helveg), Brian Steen Nielsen, Michael Laudrup (C), Peter Nielsen (YC71), Brian Laudrup, Peter Rasmussen. (Coach: Richard Møller Nielsen (DEN)).
Goals: Cyprus: 1-1 Marios Agathocleous (45').
Denmark: 0-1 Michael Schjønberg (3').
Referee: Brendan Shorte (IRL)   Attendance: 7.261

26-04-1995 Hrazdan Stadium, Yerevan: Armenia – Spain 0-2 (0-0)
Armenia: Harutyun Abrahamyan, Sargis Hovsepyan, Yervand Sukiasyan (YC35), Sargis Hovhannisyan, Aramais Tonoyan (C), Harutyun Vardanyan, Artur Petrosyan, Razmik Grigoryan (64' Hovhannes Tahmazyan), Ardaches Adamyan (46' Arsen Avetisyan), Armen Shahgeldyan, Hamlet Apetnakovich Mkhitaryan. (Coach: Samvel Darbinyan (ARM)).
Spain: Andoni ZUBIZARRETA Urreta (C), Miguel Ángel NADAL Homar, Rafael ALKORTA Martínez, ALBERTO BELSUÉ Arias, Aitor KARANKA de la Hoz, LUIS ENRIQUE Martínez García, Jon Andoni GOIKOETXEA Lasa, Jorge OTERO Bouzos, DONATO Gama da Silva (68' Francisco José CAMARASA Castellar), José Emilio AMAVISCA Gárate, Juan Antonio PIZZI Torroja (58' JULIO SALINAS Fernández). (Coach: JAVIER CLEMENTE Lázaro (ESP)).
Goals: Spain: 0-1 José Emilio AMAVISCA Gárate (48'), 0-1 Jon Andoni GOIKOETXEA Lasa (62').
Referee: Adrian Porumboiu (ROM)	Attendance: 35.000

26-04-1995 Parken Stadium, Copenhagen: Denmark – Macedonia 1-0 (0-0)
Denmark: Peter Schmeichel, Michael Schjønberg, Marc Rieper, Jes Høgh, Jacob Laursen, Claus Thomsen, Brian Steen Nielsen, Michael Laudrup (C), Peter Nielsen (78' Thomas Helveg (YC83)), Brian Laudrup, Peter Rasmussen (46' Erik Bo Andersen). (Coach: Richard Møller Nielsen (DEN)).
Macedonia: Danco Celesky, Vujadin Stanojkovic, Ilija Najdoski, Mitko Stojkovski, Ljupco Markovski (26' Nedzmedin Memedi), Bosko Djurovski (YC82), Zoran Jovanovski, Toni Micevski, Zarko Serafimovski (YC38) (77' Marijanco Stojkovski), Darco Pancev (C), Zoran Boskovski (YC37). (Coach: Andon Doncevski (MCD)).
Goal: Denmark: 1-0 Peter Nielsen (71').
Referee: Karol Ihring (SVK)	Attendance: 38.888

26-04-1995 Constant Vander Stock Stadium, Brussels: Belgium – Cyprus 2-0 (1-0)
Belgium: Gilbert Bodart, Rudi Smidts, Georges Grün (C), Dirk Medved, Pascal Renier, Emmanuel Karagiannis (YC61), Günther Schepens, Lorenzo Staelens, Luc Nilis, Marc Degryse, Gilles De Bilde (76' Michaël Goossens). (Coach: Paul Van Himst (BEL)).
Cyprus: Nicos Panayiotou, Yiannis Kalotheou, George Christodoulou, Demetris Ioannou (YC20), Charalambos Pittas (C), Marios Charalambous, Panayiotis Engomitis (YC37), Nikodemos Papavasiliou (YC17) (72' Andreas Sotiriou), Andreas Andreou (YC76), Sinisa Gogic, Marios Agathocleous (YC50) (61' Neophytos Larkou). (Coach: Andreas Michaelides (CYP)).
Goals: Belgium: 1-0 Gilles De Bilde (20'), 2-0 Günther Schepens (46').
Referee: David Roland Elleray (ENG)	Attendance: 17.703

10-05-1995 Hrazdan Stadium, Yerevan: Armenia – Macedonia 2-2 (1-0)
Armenia: Harutyun Abrahamyan, Sargis Hovsepyan, Yervand Sukiasyan, Sargis Hovhannisyan, Aramais Tonoyan (C), Harutyun Vardanyan (79' Tigran Gspeyan), Artur Petrosyan, Razmik Grigoryan (YC3), Hamlet Vladimirovich Mkhitaryan (69' Hovhannes Tahmazyan), Arsen Avetisyan, Armen Shahgeldyan. (Coach: Samvel Darbinyan (ARM)).
Macedonia: Danco Celesky, Vujadin Stanojkovic, Cedomir Janevski (59' Nedzmedin Memedi), Ilija Najdoski, Mitko Stojkovski, Ljupco Markovski (YC47), Boban Babunski, Toni Micevski (69' Dragan Kanatlarovski), Zarko Serafimovski, Georgi Hristov, Darco Pancev. (Coach: Andon Doncevski (MCD)).
Goals: Armenia: 1-0 Razmik Grigoryan (21'), 2-0 Armen Shahgeldyan (49').
Macedonia: 2-1 Georgi Hristov (59'), 2-2 Ljupco Markovski (69').
Referee: Christer Fällström (SWE)	Attendance: 5.000

07-06-1995   Parken Stadium, Copenhagen: Denmark – Cyprus   4-0 (1-0)
Denmark: Peter Schmeichel, Michael Schjønberg, Marc Rieper, Jes Høgh, Jacob Laursen (YC39), Brian Steen Nielsen (46' Peter Rasmussen), Michael Laudrup (C), John Faxe Jensen, Kim Vilfort (88' Erik Bo Andersen), Brian Laudrup, Mikkel Beck. (Coach: Richard Møller Nielsen (DEN)).
Cyprus: Andreas Petridis (YC57), George Christodoulou, Charalambos Pittas (C), Marios Charalambous, Panayiotis Engomitis (YC10), Neophytos Larkou, Kostas Kosta, Loucas Hadjiloucas (60' Kostakis Fasouliotis), Andreas Andreou (RC13), Andreas Sotiriou (YC15) (68' Charalambos Andreou), Sinisa Gogic (YC78). (Coach: Andreas Michaelides (CYP)).
Goals: Denmark: 1-0 Kim Vilfort (45'), 2-0 Kim Vilfort (51'), 3-0 Brian Laudrup (59'), 4-0 Michael Laudrup (76').
Referee: Werner Müller (SUI)   Attendance: 40.199

07-06-1995   Estadio Benito Villamarín, Seville: Spain – Armenia   1-0 (0-0)
Spain: Andoni ZUBIZARRETA Urreta (C), Agustín ARANZÁBAL Alkorta, Fernando Ruiz HIERRO, Miguel Ángel NADAL Homar, Rafael ALKORTA Martínez, ALBERTO BELSUÉ Arias, ABELARDO Fernández Antuña, LUIS ENRIQUE Martínez García, JULEN GUERRERO López (78' José Luis Pérez CAMINERO), Jon Andoni GOIKOETXEA Lasa (46' JULIO SALINAS Fernández), José Emilio AMAVISCA Gárate. (Coach: JAVIER CLEMENTE Lázaro (ESP)).
Armenia: Harutyun Abrahamyan, Sargis Hovsepyan, Hovhannes Tahmazyan, Yervand Sukiasyan, Aramais Tonoyan (C) (YC76), Harutyun Vardanyan (RC63), Artur Petrosyan (76' Varazdat Avetisyan), Hamlet Vladimirovich Mkhitaryan, Aram Nigoyan (62' Hakob Ter-Petrosyan), Arsen Avetisyan, Armen Shahgeldyan. (Coach: Samvel Darbinyan (ARM)).
Goal: Spain: 1-0 Fernando Ruiz HIERRO (63' penalty).
Referee: Roger Philippi (LUX)   Attendance: 12.000

07-06-1995   Grdski Stadion, Skopje: Macedonia – Belgium   0-5 (0-4)
Macedonia: Danco Celesky, Vujadin Stanojkovic, Cedomir Janevski, Ilija Najdoski (YC45), Mitko Stojkovski, Bosko Djurovski (61' Georgi Hristov), Boban Babunski, Toni Micevski, Zarko Serafimovski (35' Nedzmedin Memedi), Darco Pancev (C), Zoran Boskovski. (Coach: Andon Doncevski (MCD)).
Belgium: Gilbert Bodart, Rudi Smidts, Georges Grün (C), Bruno Versavel, Régis Genaux, Pascal Renier, Emmanuel Karagiannis, Günther Schepens (82' Philippe Léonard), Lorenzo Staelens, Enzo Scifo, Gilles De Bilde. (Coach: Paul Van Himst (BEL)).
Goals: Belgium: 0-1 Georges Grün (14'), 0-2 Enzo Scifo (18'), 0-3 Günther Schepens (28'), 0-4 Bruno Versavel (43'), 0-5 Enzo Scifo (58').
Referee: Ryszard Wójcik (POL)   Attendance: behind closed doors

16-08-1995   Hrazdan Stadium, Yerevan: Armenia – Denmark   0-2 (0-1)
Armenia: Armenak Petrosyan, Sargis Hovsepyan, Hovhannes Tahmazyan (41' Hakob Ter-Petrosyan), Ashot Khachatryan (YC45), Sargis Hovhannisyan, Aramais Tonoyan (C), Vardan Khachatryan, Artur Petrosyan, Razmik Grigoryan, Arsen Avetisyan (79' Varazdat Avetisyan), Armen Shahgeldyan. (Coach: Samvel Darbinyan (ARM)).
Denmark: Peter Schmeichel, Marc Rieper, Jes Høgh, Jacob Laursen, Claus Thomsen, Jens Risager (85' Michael Schjønberg), Brian Steen Nielsen, Michael Laudrup (C), John Faxe Jensen (YC30) (46' Allan Nielsen), Mikkel Beck, Peter Rasmussen. (Coach: Richard Møller Nielsen (DEN)).
Goals: Denmark: 0-1 Michael Laudrup (33'), 0-2 Allan Nielsen (46').
Referee: Georg Dardenne (GER)   Attendance: 22.000

312

06-09-1995   King Baudouin Stadium, Brussels: Belgium – Denmark   1-3 (1-2)
Belgium: Gilbert Bodart, Rudi Smidts (76' Pascal Renier), Georges Grün (C) (YC68), Dirk Medved, Régis Genaux (YC26), Emmanuel Karagiannis, Günther Schepens (55' Ronald Foguenne), Lorenzo Staelens (12' Luc Nilis), Enzo Scifo, Marc Degryse, Gilles De Bilde. (Coach: Paul Van Himst (BEL)).
Denmark: Peter Schmeichel, Marc Rieper, Jes Høgh, Jacob Laursen, Claus Thomsen, Jens Risager, Brian Steen Nielsen, Michael Laudrup (C), Kim Vilfort, Brian Laudrup (75' Erik Bo Andersen), Mikkel Beck (68' Peter Rasmussen (YC75)). (Coach: Richard Møller Nielsen (DEN)).
Goals: Belgium: 1-2 Georges Grün (25').
Denmark: 0-1 Michael Laudrup (19'), 0-2 Mikkel Beck (21'), 1-3 Kim Vilfort (65').
Referee: Vadim Zhuk (BLS)   Attendance: 39.627

06-09-1995   Gradski Stadion, Skopje: Macedonia – Armenia   1-2 (0-0)
Macedonia: Danco Celesky, Mitko Stojkovski, Ljupco Markovski (C), Boban Babunski, Igor Nikolovski, Zoran Jovanovski (YC49), Toni Micevski, Zarko Serafimovski (46' Saso Ivan Karadzov), Nedzmedin Memedi (YC61) (65' Dragan Veselinovski), Toni Savevski, Georgi Hristov. (Coach: Andon Doncevski (MCD)).
Armenia: Armenak Petrosyan, Sargis Hovsepyan, Sargis Hovhannisyan (C) (YC65), Vardan Khachatryan, Tigran Gspeyan, Harutyun Vardanyan, Artur Petrosyan (85' Ashot Khachatryan), Razmik Grigoryan (68' Varazdat Avetisyan), Hamlet Vladimirovich Mkhitaryan, Levon Stepanyan (74' Hakob Ter-Petrosyan), Armen Shahgeldyan (YC88). (Coach: Samvel Darbinyan (ARM)).
Goals: Macedonia: 1-0 Toni Micevski (56').
Armenia: 1-1 Razmik Grigoryan (61'), 1-2 Armen Shahgeldyan (78').
Referee: Vítor Manuel Melo Pereira (POR)   Attendance: behind closed doors

06-09-1995   Estadio Nuevo Los Cármenes, Granada: Spain – Cyprus   6-0 (1-0)
Spain: Andoni ZUBIZARRETA Urreta (C), Agustín ARANZÁBAL Alkorta, Fernando Ruiz HIERRO, Miguel Ángel NADAL Homar, Rafael ALKORTA Martínez, ALBERTO BELSUÉ Arias, LUIS ENRIQUE Martínez García, JULEN GUERRERO López (78' Javier MANJARÍN Pereda), José Luis Pérez CAMINERO, José Emilio AMAVISCA Gárate (52' Francisco Javier González Pérez "FRAN"), ALFONSO Pérez Muñóz (62' Juan Antonio PIZZI Torroja). (Coach: JAVIER CLEMENTE Lázaro (ESP)).
Cyprus: Nicos Panayiotou, George Christodoulou (YC52), Giorgos Panayi (YC58), Charalambos Pittas (C), Sozos Andreou, Loucas Hadjiloucas (67' Yiannis Ioannou), Nicos Charalambous (YC53), Sinisa Gogic, Kostakis Malekkos (57' Andreas Sotiriou), Dimitris Assiotis, Antonis Antoniou (81' Charalambos Andreou). (Coach: Andreas Michaelides (CYP)).
Goals: Spain: 1-0 JULEN GUERRERO López (44'), 2-0 ALFONSO Pérez Muñóz (49'), 3-0 Juan Antonio PIZZI Torroja (75'), 4-0 Fernando Ruiz HIERRO (78'), 5-0 Juan Antonio PIZZI Torroja (79'), 6-0 José Luis Pérez CAMINERO (83').
Referee: Dirk Zier Gerardus (Dick) Jol (HOL)   Attendance: 16.150

07-10-1995   Hrazdan Stadium, Yerevan: Armenia – Belgium   0-2 (0-2)
Armenia: Harutyun Abrahamyan, Sargis Hovsepyan, Yervand Sukiasyan, Ashot Khachatryan (C), Vardan Khachatryan (YC87), Tigran Gspeyan, Artur Petrosyan, Razmik Grigoryan (46' Varazdat Avetisyan), Arsen Avetisyan, Armen Shahgeldyan, Hamlet Apetnakovich Mkhitaryan (71' Hayk Markaryan). (Coach: Samvel Darbinyan (ARM)).
Belgium: Filip De Wilde, Bertrand Crasson, Rudi Smidts, Glen De Boeck, Régis Genaux, Emmanuel Karagiannis (80' Sven Vermant), Lorenzo Staelens, Günther Schepens, Enzo Scifo (C), Luc Nilis, Gilles De Bilde (63' Michaël Goossens). (Coach: Paul Van Himst (BEL)).
Goals: Belgium: 0-1 Luc Nilis (28'), 0-2 Luc Nilis (38').
Referee: Mitko Emilov Mitrev (BUL)   Attendance: 8.000

11-10-1995   Parken Stadium, Copenhagen: Denmark – Spain   1-1 (0-1)
Denmark: Peter Schmeichel (YC45), Marc Rieper, Jes Høgh, Jacob Laursen (YC17), Torben Piechnik, Jens Risager, Brian Steen Nielsen (67' Morten Weighorst), Michael Laudrup (C), Kim Vilfort, Mikkel Beck, Peter Rasmussen. (Coach: Richard Møller Nielsen (DEN)).
Spain: Andoni ZUBIZARRETA Urreta (C), Fernando Ruiz HIERRO, Miguel Ángel NADAL Homar, Rafael ALKORTA Martínez (YC55), ALBERTO BELSUÉ Arias, SERGI BARJUÁN i Esclusa, ABELARDO Fernández Antuña (YC37), LUIS ENRIQUE Martínez García (YC45), José Luis Pérez CAMINERO (30' Francisco Javier González Pérez "FRAN"), Juan Antonio PIZZI Torroja (YC22) (46' ALFONSO Pérez Muñóz), Javier MANJARÍN Pereda (63' DONATO Gama da Silva). (Coach: JAVIER CLEMENTE Lázaro (ESP)).
Goals: Denmark: 1-1 Kim Vilfort (47').
Spain: 0-1 Fernando Ruiz HIERRO (18' penalty).
Referee: Václav Krondl (CZE)   Attendance: 40.262

11-10-1995   Tsirion Stadium, Limassol: Cyprus – Macedonia   1-1 (0-1)
Cyprus: Andreas Petridis, Yiannis Kalotheou (63' Marios Agathocleous), George Christodoulou, Charalambos Pittas (C), Marios Charalambous, Panayiotis Engomitis (46' Nikodemos Papavasiliou), Kostas Kosta, Georgios Savvides, Andreas Sotiriou (79' Neophytos Larkou), Sinisa Gogic, Kostakis Malekkos. (Coach: Andreas Michaelides (CYP)).
Macedonia: Danco Celesky, Borce Jovanovski, Ljupco Markovski (C), Igor Nikolovski, Saso Ivan Karadzov, Zoran Jovanovski, Zarko Serafimovski (77' Rade Karanfilovski), Nedzmedin Memedi, Toni Savevski, Dragan Veselinovski (84' Georgi Hristov), Sasa Ciric. (Coach: Andon Doncevski (MCD)).
Goals: Cyprus: 1-1 Marios Agathocleous (90').
Macedonia: 0-1 Borce Jovanovski (34').
Referee: Leslie John R.Irvine (NIR)   Attendance: 4.513

15-11-1995   Estadio Martínez Valero, Elche: Spain – Macedonia   3-0 (1-0)
Spain: Andoni ZUBIZARRETA Urreta, Miguel Ángel NADAL Homar (RC38), Rafael ALKORTA Martínez, ALBERTO BELSUÉ Arias, SERGI BARJUÁN i Esclusa, José Luis Pérez CAMINERO, DONATO Gama da Silva, José Emilio AMAVISCA Gárate (46' ALBERT FERRER i Llopis), Francisco Narvaez Machon "KIKO" (75' Jon Andoni GOIKOETXEA Lasa), Juan Antonio PIZZI Torroja (46' ALFONSO Pérez Muñóz), Javier MANJARÍN Pereda. (Coach: JAVIER CLEMENTE Lázaro (ESP)).
Macedonia: Danco Celesky (C), Borce Jovanovski (YC27), Mitko Stojkovski, Boban Babunski, Saso Ivan Karadzov, Zoran Jovanovski (73' Igor Nikolovski), Toni Micevski, Zarko Serafimovski (57' Dragan Veselinovski, 78' Georgi Hristov), Nedzmedin Memedi (YC36), Zoran Boskovski, Sasa Ciric. (Coach: Andon Doncevski (MCD)).
Goals: Spain: 1-0 Francisco Narvaez Machon "KIKO" (9'), 2-0 Javier MANJARÍN Pereda (72'), 3-0 José Luis Pérez CAMINERO (78').
Referee: Edgar Steinborn (GER)   Attendance: 21.350

15-11-1995   Parken Stadium, Copenhagen: Denmark – Armenia   3-1 (2-0)
Denmark: Peter Schmeichel, Thomas Helveg, Michael Schjønberg, Marc Rieper, Jes Høgh, Jens Risager, Brian Steen Nielsen, Michael Laudrup (C), Kim Vilfort, Mikkel Beck, Peter Rasmussen. (Coach: Richard Møller Nielsen (DEN)).
Armenia: Harutyun Abrahamyan, Sargis Hovsepyan, Vardan Khachatryan (C), Tigran Gspeyan (79' Yervand Krbashyan), Harutyun Vardanyan, Hakob Artoyan, Artur Petrosyan, Hamlet Vladimirovich Mkhitaryan, Arsen Avetisyan, Varazdat Avetisyan (72' Hayk Margaryan), Samvel Nikolyan. (Coach: Samvel Darbinyan (ARM)).
Goals: Denmark: 1-0 Michael Schjønberg (20'), 2-0 Mikkel Beck (35'), 3-1 Michael Laudrup (58').
Armenia: 2-1 Artur Petrosyan (47').
Referee: Gilles Veissière (FRA)   Attendance: 40.208

15-11-1995   Tsirion Stadium, Limassol: Cyprus – Belgium   1-1 (1-0)
Cyprus: Nicos Panayiotou, George Christodoulou, Charalambos Pittas (C), Marios Charalambous (RC23), Panayiotis Engomitis, Nikodemos Papavasiliou, Kostas Kosta (YC37), Andreas Andreou, Sinisa Gogic (87' Georgios Elia (YC90)), Kostakis Malekkos (YC31) (50' Neophytos Larkou), Marios Agathocleous (74' Andonis Zembashis). (Coach: Andreas Michaelides (CYP)).
Belgium: Filip De Wilde, Rudi Smidts (77' Günther Schepens), Georges Grün (C), Glen De Boeck (YC36), Régis Genaux, Danny Boffin (YC32) (58' Dirk Huysmans), Emmanuel Karagiannis (46' Michaël Goossens), Lorenzo Staelens, Luc Nilis, Marc Degryse, Gilles De Bilde. (Coach: Paul Van Himst (BEL)).
Goals: Cyprus: 1-0 Marios Agathocleous (20').
Belgium: 1-1 Gilles De Bilde (65').
Referee: Graziano Cesari (ITA)   Attendance: 2.021

GROUP 3

07-09-1994	Reykjavik	Iceland – Sweden	0-1 (0-1)
07-09-1994	Budapest	Hungary – Turkey	2-2 (2-0)
12-10-1994	Istanbul	Turkey – Iceland	5-0 (3-0)
12-10-1994	Bern	Switzerland – Sweden	4-2 (1-1)
16-11-1994	Solna	Sweden – Hungary	2-0 (1-0)
16-11-1994	Lausanne	Switzerland – Iceland	1-0 (1-0)
14-12-1994	Istanbul	Turkey – Switzerland	1-2 (1-2)
29-03-1995	Budapest	Hungary – Switzerland	2-2 (0-0)
29-03-1995	Istanbul	Turkey – Sweden	2-1 (0-1)
26-04-1995	Budapest	Hungary – Sweden	1-0 (1-0)
26-04-1995	Bern	Switzerland – Turkey	1-2 (1-1)
01-06-1995	Stockholm	Sweden – Iceland	1-1 (1-1)
11-06-1995	Reykjavik	Iceland – Hungary	2-1 (0-1)
16-08-1995	Reykjavik	Iceland – Switzerland	0-2 (0-2)
06-09-1995	Gothenburg	Sweden – Switzerland	0-0
06-09-1995	Istanbul	Turkey – Hungary	2-0 (2-0)
11-10-1995	Zurich	Switzerland – Hungary	3-0 (1-0)
11-10-1995	Reykjavik	Iceland – Turkey	0-0
11-11-1995	Budapest	Hungary – Iceland	1-0 (0-0)
15-11-1995	Stockholm	Sweden – Turkey	2-2 (1-0)

FINAL STANDING

Pos	Team	Pld	W	D	L	GF	GA	GD	Pts
1	Switzerland	8	5	2	1	15	7	+8	17
2	Turkey	8	4	3	1	16	8	+8	15
3	Sweden	8	2	3	3	9	10	-1	9
4	Hungary	8	2	2	4	7	13	-6	8
5	Iceland	8	1	2	5	3	12	-9	5

Switzerland and Turkey qualified for the final tournament in England.

07-09-1994   Laugardalsvöllur, Reykjavik: Iceland – Sweden   0-1 (0-1)
Iceland: Birkir Kristinsson, Gudni Bergsson (C), Kristian Jónsson, Sigursteinn Gíslason, Runar Kristinsson, Thorvaldur Örlygsson (YC24) (60' Bjarki Gunnlaugsson), Hlynur Stefánsson, Sigurdur Jónsson (YC44), Arnar Gunnlaugsson, Arnor Gudjohnsen, Eyjölfur Sverrisson. (Coach: Ásgeir Elíasson (ISL)).
Sweden: Thomas Ravelli, Roland Nilsson (C), Patrik Andersson, Joachim Björklund (YC49), Roger Ljung (YC9), Stefan Schwarz, Tomas Brolin (YC14), Håkan Mild, Klas Ingesson, Martin Dahlin (68' Henrik Larsson), Kennet Andersson. (Coach: Leif Tommy Svensson (SWE)).
Goal: Sweden: 0-1 Klas Ingesson (36').
Referee: Leslie William Mottram (SCO)   Attendance: 14.361

07-09-1994   Népstadion, Budapest: Hungary – Turkey   2-2 (2-0)
Hungary: Zsolt Petry, Géza Mészöly, András Telek, József Kiprich (66' László Wukovics), Lajos Détári (C), Gábor Halmai, István Kozma, József Duró (61' János Bánfi), Flórián Urbán (YC72), Péter Lipcsei (YC68), Kálmán Kovács. (Coach: Kálmán Mészöly (HUN)).
Turkey: Engin Ipekoglu, Bülent Korkmaz, Recep Çetin, Ogün Temizkanoglu (YC38), Gökhan Keskin (46' Arif Erdem), Ilker Yagcioclu, Tugay Kerimoglu (YC37), Oguz Çetin (C), Orhan Çikirikçi, Hakan Sükür, Ertugrul Saglam (YC58) (87' Abdullah Ercan). (Coach: Fatih Terim (TUR)).
Goals: Hungary: 1-0 József Kiprich (4'), 2-0 Gábor Halmai (43').
Turkey: 2-1 Hakan Sükür (67'), 2-2 Bülent Korkmaz (72').
Referee: Pierluigi Pairetto (ITA)   Attendance: 10.000

12-10-1994   Ali Sami Yen Stadium, Istanbul: Turkey – Iceland   5-0 (3-0)
Turkey: Engin Ipekoglu (86' Rüstü Reçber), Bülent Korkmaz, Recep Çetin, Ogün Temizkanoglu, Gökhan Keskin, Abdullah Ercan, Oguz Çetin (C), Orhan Çikirikçi (5' Mutlu Topçu), Hakan Sükür (63' Sergen Yalçin), Arif Erdem, Saffet Sancakli. (Coach: Fatih Terim (TUR)).
Iceland: Birkir Kristinsson (3' Kristján Finnbogason), Gudni Bergsson (C), Kristian Jónsson, Sigursteinn Gíslason, Runar Kristinsson, Thorvaldur Örlygsson, Hlynur Stefánsson (85' Bjarki Gunnlaugsson), Sigurdur Jónsson (YC49), Arnar Gunnlaugsson (73' Arnar Gretarsson), Arnor Gudjohnsen, Eyjölfur Sverrisson. (Coach: Ásgeir Elíasson (ISL)).
Goals: Turkey: 1-0 Saffet Sancakli (8'), 2-0 Saffet Sancakli (26'), 3-0 Hakan Sükür (27'), 4-0 Hakan Sükür (61'), 5-0 Sergen Yalçin (66').
Referee: Nikolai Vladislavovich Levnikov (RUS)   Attendance: 11.280

12-10-1994   Wankdorfstadion, Bern: Switzerland – Sweden   4-2 (1-1)
Switzerland: Marco Pascolo, Marc Hottiger, Dominique Herr, Alain Geiger (C), Pascal Thüler, Murat Yakin (YC79) (84' Stéphane Henchoz), Alain Sutter, Christophe Ohrel, Ciriaco Sforza, Stéphane Chapuisat, Marco Grassi (68' Kübilay Türkyilmaz). (Coach: Roy Hodgson (ENG)).
Sweden: Thomas Ravelli, Roland Nilsson, Patrik Andersson, Joachim Björklund (YC49), Pontus Kåmark, Jesper Blomqvist (YC22) (81' Henrik Larsson), Stefan Schwarz, Jonas Magnus Thern (C) (49' Håkan Mild), Tomas Brolin, Martin Dahlin (YC51), Kennet Andersson. (Coach: Leif Tommy Svensson (SWE)).
Goals: Swtzerland: 1-1 Christophe Ohrel (36'), 2-2 Jesper Blomqvist (63' *own goal*), 3-2 Ciriaco Sforza (78'), 4-2 Kübilay Türkyilmaz (82').
Sweden: 0-1 Kennet Andersson (6'), 1-2 Martin Dahlin (61').
Referee: David Roland Elleray (ENG)   Attendance: 24.000

16-11-1994   Råsunda Stadion, Solna: Sweden – Hungary   2-0 (1-0)
Sweden: Thomas Ravelli, Roland Nilsson, Patrik Andersson, Joachim Björklund, Pontus Kåmark, Stefan Schwarz, Jonas Magnus Thern (C), Tomas Brolin (72' Stefan Rehn), Martin Dahlin, Kennet Andersson, Henrik Larsson. (Coach: Leif Tommy Svensson (SWE)).
Hungary: Zsolt Petry, Géza Mészöly (YC38), Emil Lörincz, János Bánfi, József Kiprich, Lajos Détári (C), István Kozma, József Duró (75' Kálmán Kovács), Flórián Urbán (YC49), Péter Lipcsei (YC52) (58' Gábor Halmai), László Klausz. (Coach: Kálmán Mészöly (HUN)).
Goals: Sweden: 1-0 Tomas Brolin (42'), 2-0 Martin Dahlin (69').
Referee: Mario van der Ende (HOL)   Attendance: 27.571

16-11-1994   Stade Olympique de la Pontaise, Lausanne: Switzerland – Iceland   1-0 (1-0)
Switzerland: Marco Pascolo, Stéphane Henchoz, Marc Hottiger, Alain Geiger (C), Pascal Thüler, Alain Sutter, Christophe Ohrel, Thomas Bickel, Ciriaco Sforza, Stéphane Chapuisat, Marco Grassi (67' Kübilay Türkyilmaz). (Coach: Roy Hodgson (ENG)).
Iceland: Birkir Kristinsson, Gudni Bergsson (C), Kristian Jónsson, Sigursteinn Gíslason (83' Haraldur Ingólfsson), Dadi Izudin Dervic, Arnar Gretarsson (63' Bjarki Gunnlaugsson), Runar Kristinsson, Thorvaldur Örlygsson, Hlynur Stefánsson, Arnar Gunnlaugsson, Eyjölfur Sverrisson. (Coach: Ásgeir Elíasson (ISL)).
Goal: Switzerland: 1-0 Thomas Bickel (44').
Referee: Patrick Kelly (IRL)   Attendance: 15.800

14-12-1994   Ali Sami Yen Stadium, Istanbul: Turkey – Switzerland   1-2 (1-2)
Turkey: Rüstü Reçber (YC71), Bülent Korkmaz, Recep Çetin (YC62), Ogün Temizkanoglu (YC55), Gökhan Keskin, Abdullah Ercan (YC38), Oguz Çetin (C), Cengiz Atila (46' Iker Yagcioglu), Hakan Sükür, Arif Erdem (75' Sergen Yalçin), Saffet Sancakli. (Coach: Fatih Terim (TUR)).
Switzerland: Marco Pascolo, Marc Hottiger (YC83), Dominique Herr, Alain Geiger (C), Marcel Koller, Pascal Thüler, Alain Sutter, Christophe Ohrel, Thomas Bickel (YC44) (65' Christophe Bonvin), Ciriaco Sforza, Nestor Subiat (77' Marco Grassi). (Coach: Roy Hodgson (ENG)).
Goals: Turkey: 1-2 Recep Çetin (41').
Switzerland: 0-1 Marcel Koller (6'), 0-2 Thomas Bickel (16').
Referee: Ion Craciunescu (ROM)   Attendance: 22.516

29-03-1995   Népstadion, Budapest: Hungary – Switzerland   2-2 (0-0)
Hungary: Zsolt Petry (YC79), Géza Mészöly, Ervin Kovács, Emil Lörincz, József Kiprich (76' Gábor Márton), Gábor Halmai, Béla Illés, István Kozma (C) (YC78), Mihály Mracskó (YC29), István Sallói, István Vincze (81' László Klausz). (Coach: Kálmán Mészöly (HUN)).
Switzerland: Marco Pascolo, Marc Hottiger, Dominique Herr, Alain Geiger (C), Marcel Koller, Walter Fernandez, Alain Sutter, Christophe Ohrel, Thomas Bickel (67' Marco Grassi), Ciriaco Sforza, Nestor Subiat (YC79) (88' Stéphane Henchoz). (Coach: Roy Hodgson (ENG)).
Goals: Hungary: 1-0 József Kiprich (52'), 2-0 Béla Illés (76').
Switzerland: 2-1 Nestor Subiat (78'), 2-2 Nestor Subiat (84').
Referee: Alfred Wieser (AUT)   Attendance: 13.000

29-03-1995   BJK Inönü Stadium, Istanbul: Turkey – Sweden   2-1 (0-1)
Turkey: Engin Ipekoglu, Emre Asik, Alpay Özalan, Bülent Korkmaz, Tolunay Kafkas, Recep Çetin, Sergen Yalçin (75' Mutlu Topçu), Abdullah Ercan, Hakan Sükür (YC79), Ertugrul Saglam (46' Oguz Çetin), Metin Tekin. (Coach: Fatih Terim (TUR)).
Sweden: Thomas Ravelli, Roland Nilsson, Patrik Andersson, Joachim Björklund (RC78), Roger Ljung, Stefan Schwarz, Jonas Magnus Thern (C), Pär Zetterberg (78' Stefan Rehn), Martin Dahlin (YC25), Kennet Andersson, Henrik Larsson (75' Jesper Blomqvist). (Coach: Leif Tommy Svensson (SWE)).
Goals: Turkey: 1-1 Emre Asik (63'), 2-1 Sergen Yalçin (73').
Sweden: 0-1 Kennet Andersson (23' penalty).
Referee: Alfredo Trentalange (ITA)   Attendance: 12.526

26-04-1995   Népstadion, Budapest: Hungary – Sweden   1-0 (1-0)
Hungary: Zoltán Vegh, Géza Mészöly, József Csábi, Gábor Halmai, Béla Illés, István Kozma (C), Mihály Mracskó, István Sallói (YC89), Péter Lipcsei, István Vincze (YC39) (68' Flórián Urbán (YC80)), Aurél Csertöi (88' Zoltán Szlezák). (Coach: Kálmán Mészöly (HUN)).
Sweden: Thomas Ravelli, Roland Nilsson (C), Patrik Andersson, Roger Ljung, Pontus Kåmark, Niclas Alexandersson (82' Niklas Gudmundsson), Stefan Schwarz (YC87), Håkan Mild (YC15) (62' Robert Andersson), Pär Zetterberg, Klas Ingesson, Kennet Andersson (YC34). (Coach: Leif Tommy Svensson (SWE)).
Goal: Hungary: 1-0 Gábor Halmai (2').
Referee: Antonio Jesús López Nieto (ESP)   Attendance: 8.300

26-04-1995   Wankdorfstadion, Bern: Switzerland – Turkey   1-2 (1-1)
Switzerland: Marco Pascolo, Marc Hottiger, Dominique Herr, Alain Geiger (C), Walter Fernandez (75' Marco Walker), Alain Sutter, Christophe Ohrel, Thomas Bickel, Ciriaco Sforza, Marco Grassi, Christophe Bonvin (69' Dario Zuffi). (Coach: Roy Hodgson (ENG)).
Turkey: Engin Ipekoglu, Emre Asik (YC24), Alpay Özalan, Bülent Korkmaz (YC78), Tolunay Kafkas (YC85), Recep Çetin, Oguz Temizkanoglu, Sergen Yalçin (79' Suat Kaya), Abdullah Ercan, Oguz Çetin (C) (83' Ertugrul Saglam), Hakan Sükür. (Coach: Fatih Terim (TUR)).
Goals: Switzerland: 1-1 Marc Hottiger (37').
Turkey: 0-1 Hakan Sükür (17'), 1-2 Ogün Temizkanoglu (56').
Referee: Frans Van Den Wijngaert (BEL)   Attendance: 24.000

01-06-1995   Råsunda Stadion, Solna: Sweden – Iceland   1-1 (1-1)
Sweden: Thomas Ravelli, Patrik Andersson, Pontus Kåmark, Gary Sundgren, Jesper Mattsson, Stefan Schwarz, Jonas Magnus Thern (C), Tomas Brolin, Anders Limpar (50' Henrik Larsson), Martin Dahlin, Kennet Andersson. (Coach: Leif Tommy Svensson (SWE)).
Iceland: Birkir Kristinsson, Gudni Bergsson (C) (YC17), Kristian Jónsson, Olafur Adolfsson, Runar Kristinsson, Thorvaldur Örlygsson (YC34), Hlynur Stefánsson, Sigurdur Jónsson, Arnar Gunnlaugsson (75' Bjarki Gunnlaugsson), Arnor Gudjohnsen (89' Olafur Thordarson), Eyjölfur Sverrisson. (Coach: Ásgeir Elíasson (ISL)).
Goals: Sweden: 1-1 Tomas Brolin (16' penalty).
Iceland: 0-1 Arnar Gunnlaugsson (3').
Referee: Atanas Uzunov (BUL)   Attendance: 25.676

11-06-1995   Laugardarsvöllur, Reykjavik: Iceland – Hungary   2-1 (0-1)
Iceland: Birkir Kristinsson, Gudni Bergsson (C), Kristian Jónsson (YC53), Olafur Adolfsson, Arnar Gretarsson, Runar Kristinsson, Olafur Thordarson (66' Bjarki Gunnlaugsson), Sigurdur Jónsson, Arnar Gunnlaugsson, Arnor Gudjohnsen (YC48), Eyjölfur Sverrisson. (Coach: Ásgeir Elíasson (ISL)).
Hungary: Zsolt Petry, Géza Mészöly, József Csábi, Gábor Halmai (YC35), Béla Illés (66' Gábor Márton), István Kozma (C), Mihály Mracskó (YC22), István Sallói, Péter Lipcsei, István Vincze (68' István Hamar), Aurél Csertöi (YC49). (Coach: Kálmán Mészöly (HUN)).
Goals: Iceland: 1-1 Gudni Bergsson (61'), 2-1 Sigurdur Jónsson (68').
Hungary: 0-1 István Vincze (20').
Referee: Alain Sars (FRA)   Attendance: 4.474

16-08-1995   Laugardalsvöllur, Reykjavik: Iceland – Switzerland   0-2 (0-2)
Iceland: Birkir Kristinsson, Gudni Bergsson (C), Kristian Jónsson (88' Dadi Izudin Dervic), Olafur Adolfsson, Runar Kristinsson, Thorvaldur Örlygsson, Olafur Thordarson, Sigurdur Jónsson, Arnar Gunnlaugsson, Bjarki Gunnlaugsson, Eyjölfur Sverrisson (65' Haraldur Ingólfsson). (Coach: Ásgeir Elíasson (ISL)).
Switzerland: Marco Pascolo, Stéphane Henchoz, Marc Hottiger, Yvan Quentin, Alain Geiger (C), Alain Sutter (74' Thomas Bickel), Christophe Ohrel, Ciriaco Sforza, Sébastien Fournier, Adrian Knup, Kübilay Türkyilmaz (82' Christophe Bonvin). (Coach: Roy Hodgson (ENG)).
Goals: Switzerland: 0-1 Christophe Ohrel (4'), 0-2 Kübilay Türkyilmaz (18').
Referee: Ryszard Wójcik (POL)   Attendance: 8.387

06-09-1995   Nya Ullevi, Gothenburg: Sweden – Switzerland   0-0
Sweden: Bengt Andersson, Patrik Andersson, Joachim Björklund (YC9), Pontus Kåmark, Michael Nilsson, Niclas Alexandersson, Stefan Schwarz (87' Magnus Erlingmark), Jonas Magnus Thern (C), Tomas Brolin (75' Henrik Larsson), Martin Dahlin (YC87), Kennet Andersson. (Coach: Leif Tommy Svensson (SWE)).
Switzerland: Marco Pascolo, Stéphane Henchoz, Marc Hottiger, Yvan Quentin, Alain Geiger (C), Alain Sutter (46' Dominique Herr), Christophe Ohrel, Ciriaco Sforza, Sébastien Fournier, Adrian Knup, Kübilay Türkyilmaz (YC84) (88' Marco Grassi). (Coach: Roy Hodgson (ENG)).
Referee: Piero Ceccarini (ITA)   Attendance: 40.505

06-09-1995   BJK Inönü Stadium, Istanbul: Turkey – Hungary   2-0 (2-0)
Turkey: Rüstü Reçber, Alpay Özalan, Recep Çetin, Ogün Temizkanoglu, Osman Özköylü, Tugay Kerimoglu, Sergen Yalçin (46' Tolunay Kafkas), Abdullah Ercan, Oguz Çetin (C), Hakan Sükür (YC31) (87' Bülent Uygun), Hami Mandirali (YC53) (84' Bülent Korkmaz). (Coach: Fatih Terim (TUR)).
Hungary: Zsolt Petry, Géza Mészöly (YC20), András Telek, Norbert Nagy (46' László Klausz), József Kiprich (YC84), Gábor Halmai, Béla Illés (46' István Sallói), István Kozma (C), László Arany, László Farkasházy, Péter Lipcsei. (Coach: Kálmán Mészöly (HUN)).
Goals: Turkey: 1-0 Hakan Sükür (9'), 2-0 Hakan Sükür (31').
Referee: Václav Krondl (CZE)   Attendance: 25.358

11-10-1995   Hardturm Stadion, Zürich: Switzerland – Hungary   3-0 (1-0)
Switzerland: Marco Pascolo, Stéphane Henchoz, Marc Hottiger (YC32), Yvan Quentin, Alain Geiger (C), Christophe Ohrel, Ciriaco Sforza (YC58), Sébastien Fournier (82' Thomas Bickel), Murat Yakin, Adrian Knup (89' Christophe Bonvin), Kübilay Türkyilmaz (85' Alain Sutter). (Coach: Roy Hodgson (ENG)).
Hungary: Attila Hajdú, András Telek, Tibor Simon (YC21) (25' Zoltán Jagodics), Gábor Halmai, Béla Illés (C) (64' Tamás Mónos), Flórián Urbán, Mihály Mracskó, Elek Nyilas (64' László Arany), Péter Lipcsei (YC8), István Vincze, Robert Jován. (Coach: Kálmán Mészöly (HUN)).
Goals: Switzerland: 1-0 Kübilay Türkyilmaz (23'), 2-0 Ciriaco Sforza (56'), 3-0 Christophe Ohrel (88').
Referee: Charles Agius (MLT)   Attendance: 21.000

11-10-1995   Laugardalsvöllur, Reykjavik: Iceland – Turkey   0-0
Iceland: Birkir Kristinsson, Gudni Bergsson (C), Sigursteinn Gíslason (YC45), Olafur Adolfsson, Runar Kristinsson, Thorvaldur Örlygsson, Sigurdur Jónsson (44' Arnar Gretarsson), Haraldur Ingólfsson (71' Hlynur Stefánsson), Arnar Gunnlaugsson, Arnor Gudjohnsen, Eyjölfur Sverrisson (82' Bjarki Gunnlaugsson). (Coach: Ásgeir Elíasson (ISL)).
Turkey: Rüstü Reçber, Alpay Özalan, Recep Çetin (YC63), Ogün Temizkanoglu (YC32), Osman Özköylü (YC40), Tugay Kerimoglu, Sergen Yalçin (75' Tolunay Kafkas), Abdullah Ercan (YC60), Oguz Çetin (C), Ertugrul Saglam, Hami Mandirali. (Coach: Fatih Terim (TUR)).
Referee: Hartmut Strampe (GER)   Attendance: 2.308

11-11-1995   Stadion Rudolf Illovszky, Budapest: Hungary – Iceland   1-0 (0-0)
Hungary: Attila Hajdú, János Bánfi, József Csábi, Zoltán Szlezák (YC60), Béla Illés (C) (YC77) (88' András Zombori), Tamás Mónos, József Duró, Elek Nyilas, Zoltán Bükszegi, István Vincze (86' Tamás Nagy), Ferenc Orosz (74' László Farkasházy). (Coach: Kálmán Mészöly (HUN)).
Iceland: Birkir Kristinsson, Gudni Bergsson (C), Kristian Jónsson, Sigursteinn Gíslason, Olafur Adolfsson, Arnar Gretarsson (80' Hlynur Stefánsson), Runar Kristinsson (YC39) (83' Einar Daníelsson), Thorvaldur Örlygsson (YC44), Arnar Gunnlaugsson, Arnor Gudjohnsen, Eyjölfur Sverrisson. (Coach: Ásgeir Elíasson (ISL)).
Goal: Hungary: 1-0 Béla Illés (55').
Referee: Georgios Bikas (GRE)   Attendance: 1.139

15-11-1995   Råsunda Stadion, Solna: Sweden – Turkey   2-2 (1-0)
Sweden: Bengt Andersson, Teddy Lucic, Patrik Andersson (C), Joachim Björklund, Niclas Alexandersson, Stefan Schwarz, Tomas Brolin (72' Pär Zetterberg), Håkan Mild, Christer Fursth (YC29), Jörgen Pettersson (82' Dan Sahlin), Martin Dahlin. (Coach: Leif Tommy Svensson (SWE)).
Turkey: Rüstü Reçber, Alpay Özalan, Tolunay Kafkas, Ogün Temizkanoglu (46' Arif Erdem), Halil Ibrahim Kara, Osman Özköylü, Tugay Kerimoglu, Oguz Çetin (C) (69' Ertugrul Saglam), Tayfun Korkut, Hakan Sükür, Oktay Derelioglu (46' Kemalettin Sentürk). (Coach: Fatih Terim (TUR)).
Goals: Sweden: 1-0 Niclas Alexandersson (25'), 2-1 Jörgen Pettersson (64').
Turkey: 1-1 Hakan Sükür (63'), 2-2 Patrik Andersson (72' *own goal*).
Referee: Ryszard Wójcik (POL)   Attendance: 16.238

GROUP 4

04-09-1994	Tallinn	Estonia – Croatia	0-2 (0-1)
07-09-1994	Maribor	Slovenia – Italy	1-1 (1-1)
07-09-1994	Kiev	Ukraine – Lithuania	0-2 (0-0)
08-10-1994	Tallinn	Estonia – Italy	0-2 (0-1)
09-10-1994	Zagreb	Croatia – Lithuania	2-0 (0-0)
12-10-1994	Kiev	Ukraine – Slovenia	0-0
13-11-1994	Kiev	Ukraine – Estonia	3-0 (2-0)
16-11-1994	Palermo	Italy – Croatia	1-2 (0-1)
16-11-1994	Maribor	Slovenia – Lithuania	1-2 (0-0)
25-03-1995	Zagreb	Croatia – Ukraine	4-0 (2-0)
25-03-1995	Salerno	Italy – Estonia	4-1 (1-0)
29-03-1995	Vilnius	Lithuania – Croatia	0-0
29-03-1995	Kiev	Ukraine – Italy	0-2 (0-2)
29-03-1995	Maribor	Slovenia – Estonia	3-0 (1-0)
26-04-1995	Tallinn	Estonia – Ukraine	0-1 (0-1)
26-04-1995	Vilnius	Lithuania – Italy	0-1 (0-1)
26-04-1995	Zagreb	Croatia – Slovenia	2-0 (1-0)
07-06-1995	Vilnius	Lithuania – Slovenia	2-1 (0-0)
11-06-1995	Tallinn	Estonia – Slovenia	1-3 (1-1)
11-06-1995	Kiev	Ukraine – Croatia	1-0 (1-0)
16-08-1995	Tallinn	Estonia – Lithuania	0-1 (0-0)
03-09-1995	Zagreb	Croatia – Estonia	7-1 (4-1)
06-09-1995	Udine	Italy – Slovenia	1-0 (1-0)
06-09-1995	Vilnius	Lithuania – Ukraine	1-3 (1-0)
08-10-1995	Split	Croatia – Italy	1-1 (0-1)
11-10-1995	Vilnius	Lithuania – Estonia	5-0 (4-0)
11-10-1995	Ljubljana	Slovenia – Ukraine	3-2 (0-2)
11-11-1995	Bari	Italy – Ukraine	3-1 (1-1)
15-11-1995	Ljubljana	Slovenia – Croatia	1-2 (1-1)
15-11-1995	Emilia	Italy – Lithuania	4-0 (0-0)

FINAL STANDING

Pos	Team	Pld	W	D	L	GF	GA	GD	Pts
1	*Croatia*	*10*	*7*	*2*	*1*	*22*	*5*	*+17*	*23*
2	*Italy*	*10*	*7*	*2*	*1*	*20*	*6*	*+14*	*23*
3	Lithuania	10	5	1	4	13	12	+1	16
4	Ukraine	10	4	1	5	11	15	-4	13
5	Slovenia	10	3	2	5	13	13	0	11
6	Estonia	10	0	0	10	3	31	-28	0

Croatia and Italy qualified for the final tournament in England.

04-09-1994   Kadrioru Stadium, Tallinn: Estonia – Croatia   0-2 (0-1)
Estonia: Mart Poom (C), Marek Lemsalu, Igor Prins, Urmas Kaljend, Viktor Alonen (YC37), Urmas Kirs (75' Toomas Kröm), Indro Olumets, Toomas Kallaste, Dzintar Klavan, Marko Kristal, Tarmo Linnumäe. (Coach: Roman Ubakivi (EST)).
Croatia: Drazen Ladic, Slaven Bilic, Nikola Jerkan, Aljosa Asanovic (88' Igor Cvitanovic), Zvonimir Boban, Robert Jarni, Robert Prosinecki, Dzevad Turkovic, Igor Stimac (YC69), Davor Suker (C), Alen Boksic. (Coach: Miroslav Blazevic (CRO)).
Goals: Croatia: 0-1 Davor Suker (44'), 0-2 Davor Suker (69').
Referee: Václav Krondl (CZE)   Attendance: 1.215

07-09-1994   Ljudski vrt, Maribor: Slovenia – Italy   1-1 (1-1)
Slovenia: Marko Simeunovic, Marinko Galic, Srecko Katanec (C) (57' Peter Binkovski), Darko Milanic (YC60), Robert Englaro, Dzoni Novak, Ales Ceh, Alfred Jermanis, Gregor Zidan (88' Ales Krizan), Saso Udovic, Primoz Gliha. (Coach: Dr. Zdenko Verdenik (SLO)).
Italy: Gianluca Pagliuca, Alessandro Costacurta, Christian Panucci (YC5), Franco Baresi (C), Roberto Mussi, Demetrio Albertini (YC35), Dino Baggio (55' Alberico Evani), Roberto Donadoni, Giuseppe Signori, Pierluigi Casiraghi, Gianfranco Zola (55' Nicola Berti). (Coach: Arrigo Sacchi (ITA)).
Goals: Slovenia: 1-0 Saso Udovic (14').
Italy: 1-1 Alessandro Costacurta (16').
Referee: Bernd Heynemann (GER)   Attendance: 5.200

07-09-1994   Republikan Stadium, Kiev: Ukraine – Lithuania   0-2 (0-0)
Ukraine: Dmytro Tyapushkin, Viktor Skrypnyk, Yuriy Sak (8' Serhiy Kovalets), Oleksandr Yevtushok, Serhiy Popov, Igor Petrov (C), Yuriy Maksymov, Serhiy Konovalov, Yevhen Pokhlebayev (59' Serhiy Nahornyak), Oleh Protasov, Borys Finkel. (Coach: Oleh Bazylevych (UKR)).
Lithuania: Gintaras Stauce (C), Aurelius Skarbalius, Viaceslavas Sukristovas, Tomas Ziukas, Andrejus Tereskinas, Raimondas Vainoras, Nerijus Gudaitis, Rolandas Vaineikis (79' Ramunas Stonkus), Valdas Ivanauskas, Irmantas Stumbrys, Arūnas Suika (54' Audrius Zuta). (Coach: Algimantas Liubinskas (LIT)).
Goals: Lithuania: 0-1 Valdas Ivanauskas (52'), 0-2 Aurelius Skarbalius (60').
Referee: Bo Karlsson (SWE)   Attendance: 25.000

08-10-1994 Kadrioru Stadium, Tallinn: Estonia – Italy 0-2 (0-1)
Estonia: Mart Poom (C), Marek Lemsalu, Urmas Kaljend (YC51), Viktor Alonen, Urmas Kirs, Martin Reim, Toomas Kallaste, Dzintar Klavan (75' Risto Kallaste), Marko Kristal, Tarmo Linnumäe (YC46), Toomas Krõm (67' Indro Olumets (YC81)). (Coach: Roman Ubakivi (EST)).
Italy: Gianluca Pagliuca, Paolo Maldini (C), Alessandro Costacurta, Giuseppe Favalli (87' Luigi Apolloni), Christian Panucci, Dino Baggio, Roberto Rambaudi, Alberico Evani (83' Demetrio Albertini), Giuseppe Signori, Pierluigi Casiraghi, Gianfranco Zola. (Coach: Arrigo Sacchi (ITA)).
Goals: Italy: 0-1 Christian Panucci (20'), 0-2 Pierluigi Casiraghi (78').
Referee: Werner Müller (SUI) Attendance: 3.850

09-10-1994 Stadion Maksimir, Zagreb: Croatia – Lithuania 2-0 (0-0)
Croatia: Drazen Ladic, Slaven Bilic, Nikola Jerkan (YC12), Aljosa Asanovic, Zvonimir Boban (C), Robert Jarni, Mladen Mladenovic (YC32), Igor Stimac (90' Elvis Brajkovic), Davor Suker, Alen Boksic (78' Ardian Kozniku), Nikola Jurcevic (YC20). (Coach: Miroslav Blazevic (CRO)).
Lithuania: Gintaras Stauce (C) (YC42), Aurelius Skarbalius, Viaceslavas Sukristovas (YC55), Tomas Ziukas, Andrejus Tereskinas, Raimondas Vainoras, Nerijus Gudaitis, Romas Mazeikis, Rolandas Vaineikis (60' Arvymas Korsakovas), Irmantas Stumbrys, Audrius Zuta (YC3) (75' Eimantas Poderis). (Coach: Algimantas Liubinskas (LIT)).
Goals: Croatia: 1-0 Nikola Jerkan (56'), 2-0 Ardian Kozniku (80').
Referee: Alfred Wieser (AUT) Attendance: 7.515

12-10-1994 Republikan Stadium, Kiev: Ukraine – Slovenia 0-0
Ukraine: Dmytro Tyapushkin, Oleh Kuznetsov, Oleh Luzhny (C), Serhiy Diryavka (YC81), Serhiy Shmatovalenko, Serhiy Lezhentsev, Oleksiy Mikhaylichenko (77' Igor Petrov), Serhiy Konovalov (65' Tymerlan Huseynov), Serhiy Kovalets (YC73), Dmytro Mykhaylenko, Victor Leonenko. (Coach: József Sabo (UKR)).
Slovenia: Bosko Boskovic, Marinko Galic, Darko Milanic (C), Ales Krizan, Dzoni Novak (79' Vladimir Kokol), Ales Ceh (YC87), Alfred Jermanis, Gregor Zidan (YC85), Igor Benedejcic, Saso Udovic (63' Primoz Gliha), Matjaz Florijancic. (Coach: Dr. Zdenko Verdenik (SLO)).
Referee: Atanas Uzunov (BUL) Attendance: 8.500

13-11-1994 Republikan Stadium, Kiev: Ukraine – Estonia 3-0 (2-0)
Ukraine: Oleksandr Shovkovsky (81' Oleh Suslov), Oleh Kuznetsov, Oleh Luzhny, Sergiy Popov, Serhiy Lezhentsev, Serhiy Bezhenar (YC32), Gennadiy Litovchenko (C), Serhiy Konovalov, Serhiy Kovalets (71' Igor Petrov), Gennadiy Orbu, Serhiy Skachenko (46' Tymerlan Huseynov). (Coach: József Sabo (UKR)).
Estonia: Rain Vessenberg, Marek Lemsalu, Viktor Alonen, Urmas Kirs, Risto Kallaste (C), Indro Olumets, Marko Kristal (YC75), Tarmo Linnumäe, Meelis Lindmaa, Mati Pari, Indrek Zelinksi. (Coach: Roman Ubakivi (EST)).
Goals: Ukraine: 1-0 Serhiy Konovalov (30'), 2-0 Urmas Kirs (44' *own goal*), 3-0 Tymerlan Huseynov (72').
Referee: Léon Schellings (BEL) Attendance: 4.000

16-11-1994   Stadio Della Favorita, Palermo: Italy – Croatia   1-2 (0-1)
Italy: Gianluca Pagliuca, Paolo Maldini (C), Alessandro Costacurta (YC67), Christian Panucci, Paolo Negro, Demetrio Albertini (54' Roberto Di Matteo), Dino Baggio, Roberto Rambaudi (46' Roberto Donadoni), Attilio Lombardo, Roberto Baggio, Pierluigi Casiraghi. (Coach: Arrigo Sacchi (ITA)).
Croatia: Drazen Ladic, Slaven Bilic, Nikola Jerkan, Elvis Brajkovic, Aljosa Asanovic, Zvonimir Boban (C) (YC66), Robert Jarni (YC1), Roberto Prosinecki (57' Mladen Mladenovic), Igor Stimac (YC81), Davor Suker, Nikola Jurcevic (89' Ardian Kozniku). (Coach: Miroslav Blazevic (CRO)).
Goals: Italy: 1-2 Dino Baggio (89').
Croatia: 0-1 Davor Suker (32'), 0-2 Davor Suker (57').
Referee: Joël Quiniou (FRA)   Attendance: 33.570

16-11-1994   Ljudski vrt, Maribor: Slovenia – Lithuania   1-2 (0-0)
Slovenia: Bosko Boskovic, Marinko Galic, Robert Englaro, Ales Krizan (46' Andrej Poljsak), Ales Ceh, Zlatko Zahovic, Alfred Jermanis, Gregor Zidan, Igor Benedejcic (YC19) (46' Peter Binkovski), Primoz Gliha, Matjaz Florijancic. (Coach: Dr. Zdenko Verdenik (SLO)).
Lithuania: Gintaras Stauce (C), Viaceslavas Sukristovas, Andrejus Tereskinas, Raimondas Vainoras, Nerijus Gudaitis, Romas Mazeikis, Irmantas Stumbrys, Arūnas Suika (70' Audrius Zuta), Valdas Ivanauskas, Vytautas Apanavicius (RC88), Arminas Narbekovas. (Coach: Algimantas Liubinskas (LIT)).
Goals: Slovenia: 1-0 Zlatko Zahovic (55').
Lithuania: 1-1 Viaceslavas Sukristovas (64'), 1-2 Audrius Zuta (87').
Referee: Karol Ihring (SVK)   Attendance: 4.000

25-03-1995   Stadion Maksimir, Zagreb: Croatia – Ukraine   4-0 (2-0)
Croatia: Drazen Ladic, Slaven Bilic, Nikola Jerkan (YC51), Dubravko Pavlicic, Aljosa Asanovic, Zvonimir Boban (C), Robert Jarni, Roberto Prosinecki, Davor Suker, Alen Boksic (74' Dzevad Turkovic), Nikola Jurcevic (YC65) (80' Goran Vlaovic). (Coach: Miroslav Blazevic (CRO)).
Ukraine: Dmytro Tyapushkin (YC70), Oleh Luzhny (C), Serhiy Smatovalenko, Yuriy Bukel, Andriy Telesnenko (YC40), Yuriy Kalitvintsev, Serhiy Konovalov, Serhiy Mizin, Andriy Shevchenko, Victor Leonenko, Yuriy Martynov (46' Yuriy Sak). (Coach: Anatoli Konkov (UKR)).
Goals: Croatia: 1-0 Zvonimir Boban (13'), 2-0 Davor Suker (21'), 3-0 Roberto Prosinecki (71'), 4-0 Davor Suker (79').
Referee: Hans-Jürgen Weber (GER)   Attendance: 11.156

25-03-1995   Stadio Arechi, Salerno: Italy – Estonia   4-1 (1-0)
Italy: Angelo Peruzzi, Paolo Maldini (C), Paolo Negro (YC43), Amedeo Carboni, Lorenzo Minotti, Demetrio Albertini, Dino Baggio, Stefano Eranio (58' Attilio Lombardo), Alessandro Del Piero (69' Nicola Berti), Gianfranco Zola, Fabrizio Ravanelli. (Coach: Arrigo Sacchi (ITA)).
Estonia: Mart Poom, Marek Lemsalu (C), Urmas Kirs, Risto Kallaste (YC70), Alari Lell (76' Mati Pari), Indro Olumets, Toomas Kallaste, Marko Kristal (YC19), Tarmo Linnumäe, Meelis Lindmaa, Toomas Krõm (YC44) (68' Martin Reim). (Coach: Roman Ubakivi (EST)).
Goals: Italy: 1-0 Gianfranco Zola (44'), 2-0 Demetrio Albertini (59'), 3-0 Gianfranco Zola (65'), 4-1 Fabrizio Ravanelli (84').
Estonia: 3-1 Martin Reim (72').
Referee: Roger Philippi (LUX)   Attendance: 38.000

29-03-1995   Zalgiris Stadium, Vilnius: Lithuania – Croatia   0-0
Lithuania: Gintaras Stauce (C), Aurelius Skarbalius, Viaceslavas Sukristovas, Tomas Ziukas, Raimondas Vainoras, Nerijus Gudaitis, Ramunas Stonkus, Ricardas Zdancius (69' Audrius Zuta), Arūnas Suika (YC31), Valdas Ivanauskas, Arminas Narbekovas (24' Remigijus Pocius). (Coach: Benjaminas Zelkevicius (LIT)).
Croatia: Drazen Ladic, Slaven Bilic, Dubravko Pavlicic (YC27) (45' Mladen Mladenovic), Elvis Brajkovic, Zvonimir Soldo, Aljosa Asanovic (YC45), Robert Jarni, Roberto Prosinecki (YC12), Igor Stimac, Davor Suker (C), Alen Boksic. (Coach: Miroslav Blazevic (CRO)).
Referee: Walter Keith Burge (WAL)   Attendance: 9.500

29-03-1995   Republikan Stadium, Kiev: Ukraine – Italy   0-2 (0-2)
Ukraine: Dmytro Tyapushkin, Oleh Luzhny (C) (56' Yuriy Bukel), Oleksandr Yevtushok, Andriy Khomyn (YC16), Andriy Telesnenko, Yuriy Kalitvintsev, Serhiy Konovalov (74' Yevhen Pokhlebayev), Hennadiy Orbu, Serhiy Mizin, Andriy Shevchenko, Victor Leonenko. (Coach: Anatoli Konkov (UKR)).
Italy: Angelo Peruzzi, Paolo Maldini (C), Antonio Benarrivo, Luigi Apolloni, Lorenzo Minotti, Demetrio Albertini, Roberto Di Matteo (YC83), Nicola Berti, Attilio Lombardo (73' Antonio Conte), Pierluigi Casiraghi (62' Fabrizio Ravanelli), Gianfranco Zola. (Coach: Arrigo Sacchi (ITA)).
Goals: Italy: 0-1 Attilio Lombardo (12'), 0-2 Gianfranco Zola (38').
Referee: Sándor Puhl (HUN)   Attendance: 10.000

29-03-1995   Ljudski vrt, Maribor: Slovenia – Estonia   3-0 (1-0)
Slovenia: Bosko Boskovic, Marinko Galic, Darko Milanic (C), Robert Englaro, Dzoni Novak, Ales Ceh (YC41), Zlatko Zahovic (66' Vladimir Kokol), Alfred Jermanis (70' Stefan Skaper), Gregor Zidan, Primoz Gliha, Matjaz Florijancic. (Coach: Dr. Zdenko Verdenik (SLO)).
Estonia: Mart Poom (YC28), Urmas Kirs, Risto Kallaste, Gert Olesk, Martin Reim (C), Indro Olumets, Toomas Kallaste, Tarmo Linnumäe (YC10), Meelis Lindmaa, Marko Lepik, Arjo Arbeiter (78' Alari Lell). (Coach: Roman Ubakivi (EST)).
Goals: Slovenia: 1-0 Zlatko Zahovic (40'), 2-0 Primoz Gliha (52'), 3-0 Vladimir Kokol (90').
Referee: José João Mendes Pratas (POR)   Attendance: 1.850

26-04-1995   Kadrioru Stadium, Tallinn: Estonia – Ukraine   0-1 (0-1)
Estonia: Mart Poom, Marek Lemsalu (C), Viktor Alonen, Urmas Kirs, Risto Kallaste (YC67), Alari Lell, Martin Reim (66' Mati Pari), Indro Olumets, Toomas Kallaste, Marko Kristal, Toomas Krõm (46' Martin Lepa). (Coach: Roman Ubakivi (EST)).
Ukraine: Oleh Suslov, Oleh Luzhny (C), Igor Zhabchenko, Serhiy Diryavka, Sergiy Smatovalenko, Oleksandr Holovko, Yuriy Maksymov, Hennadiy Orbu, Oleh Naduda (YC69) (85' Oleksandr Yevtushok), Sergiy Nahornyak (46' Sergiy Konovalov (YC86)), Tymerlan Huseynov. (Coach: Anatoli Konkov (UKR)).
Goal: Ukraine: 0-1 Tymerlan Huseynov (17').
Referee: Tore Hollung (NOR)   Attendance: 1.100

26-04-1995   Zalgiris Stadium, Vilnius: Lithuania – Italy   0-1 (0-1)
Lithuania: Gintaras Stauce (C), Aurelius Skarbalius, Viaceslavas Sukristovas, Tomas Ziukas, Andrejus Tereskinas, Raimondas Vainoras, Nerijus Gudaitis (70' Eimantas Poderis), Arūnas Suika, Valdas Ivanauskas, Vytautas Apanavicius (46' Aidas Preiksaitis), Vaidotas Slekys. (Coach: Benjaminas Zelkevicius (LIT)).
Italy: Gianluca Pagliuca, Paolo Maldini (C), Alessandro Costacurta, Antonio Benarrivo, Lorenzo Minotti, Roberto Di Matteo, Antonio Conte (22' Dino Baggio), Massimo Crippa (YC72) (84' Nicola Berti), Attilio Lombardo, Pierluigi Casiraghi, Gianfranco Zola. (Coach: Arrigo Sacchi (ITA)).
Goal: Italy: 0-1 Gianfranco Zola (11').
Referee: James (Jim) McCluskey (SCO)   Attendance: 15.000

26-04-1995   Stadion Maksimir, Zagreb: Croatia – Slovenia   2-0 (1-0)
Croatia: Drazen Ladic (RC11), Slaven Bilic, Nikola Jerkan, Aljosa Asanovic, Zvonimir Boban (C), Robert Jarni, Roberto Prosinecki (YC80), Igor Stimac (YC19), Davor Suker (YC66) (88' Dubravko Pavlicic), Alen Boksic, Nikola Jurcevic (11' Tonci Gabric *goalkeeper*). (Coach: Miroslav Blazevic (CRO)).
Slovenia: Bosko Boskovic, Marinko Galic, Darko Milanic (C) (80' Stefan Skaper), Robert Englaro (YC13), Dzoni Novak, Zlatko Zahovic (65' Vladimir Kokol), Alfred Jermanis, Gregor Zidan (RC79), Peter Binkovski, Primoz Gliha, Matjaz Florijancic. (Coach: Dr. Zdenko Verdenik (SLO)).
Goals: Croatia: 1-0 Roberto Prosinecki (15'), 2-0 Davor Suker (85').
Referee: Oguz Sarvan (TUR)   Attendance: 14.059

07-06-1995   Zalgiris Stadium, Vilnius: Lithuania – Slovenia   2-1 (0-0)
Lithuania: Gintaras Stauce (C), Aurelius Skarbalius, Viaceslavas Sukristovas, Tomas Ziukas, Andrejus Tereskinas, Raimondas Vainoras, Ramunas Stonkus, Darius Maciulevicius (74' Virginijus Baltusnikas), Valdas Ivanauskas (YC73), Vaidotas Slekys, Aidas Preiksaitis (68' Arūnas Suika). (Coach: Benjaminas Zelkevicius (LIT)).
Slovenia: Bosko Boskovic, Marinko Galic (77' Ales Krizan), Darko Milanic (C), Robert Englaro, Dzoni Novak (59' Stefan Skaper), Ales Ceh, Zlatko Zahovic, Alfred Jermanis, Vladimir Kokol, Primoz Gliha, Matjaz Florijancic (YC42). (Coach: Dr. Zdenko Verdenik (SLO)).
Goals: Lithuania: 1-0 Ramunas Stonkus (47'), 2-0 Arūnas Suika (70').
Slovenia: 2-1 Primoz Gliha (83').
Referee: László Vágner (HUN)   Attendance: 2.600

11-06-1995   Kadrioru Stadium, Tallinn: Estonia – Slovenia   1-3 (1-1)
Estonia: Mart Poom, Viktor Alonen, Urmas Kirs, Martin Lepa (46' Dzintar Klavan), Martin Reim (C), Indro Olumets, Toomas Kallaste, Marko Kristal, Tarmo Linnumäe, Mati Pari, Arjo Arbeiter (60' Lembit Rajala (YC72)). (Coach: Roman Ubakivi (EST)).
Slovenia: Bosko Boskovic, Marinko Galic, Darko Milanic (C), Robert Englaro (YC68), Dzoni Novak, Ales Ceh, Zlatko Zahovic, Alfred Jermanis (65' Matjaz Cviki), Vladimir Kokol (46' Ales Krizan), Primoz Gliha, Matjaz Florijancic (YC8). (Coach: Dr. Zdenko Verdenik (SLO)).
Goals: Estonia: 1-0 Martin Reim (26').
Slovenia: 1-1 Dzoni Novak (38'), 1-2 Dzoni Novak (69'), 1-3 Zlatko Zahovic (79').
Referee: Paul Anthony Durkin (ENG)   Attendance: 1.100

11-06-1995   Republikan Stadium, Kiev: Ukraine – Croatia 1-0 (1-0)
Ukraine: Oleh Suslov, Viktor Skrypnyk, Igor Zhabchenko, Volodymyr Horilyi (YC74), Oleksandr Holovko, Yuriy Kalitvintsev, Yuriy Maksymov (C), Hennadiy Orbu, Yevhen Pokhlebayev (YC45), Tymerlan Huseynov (46' Pavlo Shkapenko), Oleksandr Palyanytsya (76' Sergiy Nahornyak). (Coach: Anatoli Konkov (UKR)).
Croatia: Tonci Gabric (RC28), Slaven Bilic, Nikola Jerkan, Dubravko Pavlicic (YC18) (29' Marijan Mrmic *goalkeeper*), Zvonimir Soldo, Aljosa Asanovic (49' Nenad Pralija), Zvonimir Boban (C) (39' Darko Butorovic), Robert Jarni, Mladen Mladenovic, Davor Suker, Alen Boksic. (Coach: Miroslav Blazevic (CRO)).
Goal: Ukraine: 1-0 Yuriy Kalitvintsev (13').
Referee: Kurt Röthlisberger (SUI)   Attendance: 8.500

16-08-1995   Kadrioru Stadium, Tallinn: Estonia – Lithuania 0-1 (0-0)
Estonia: Mart Poom, Marek Lemsalu (C) (YC33), Urmas Kirs, Risto Kallaste, Alari Lell, Janek Kiisman (46' Arvo Kraam), Martin Lepa, Martin Reim, Ivan O'Konnel-Bronin (73' Gert Olesk), Marko Kristal, Meelis Lindmaa. (Coach: Roman Ubakivi (EST)).
Lithuania: Gintaras Stauce (C), Aurelius Skarbalius (76' Tomas Kancelskis), Viaceslavas Sukristovas, Tomas Ziukas, Andrejus Tereskinas, Raimondas Vainoras, Ramunas Stonkus, Darius Maciulevicius, Valdas Ivanauskas, Arūnas Suika, Vaidotas Slekys (YC37) (66' Audrius Zuta). (Coach: Benjaminas Zelkevicius (LIT)).
Goal: Lithuania: 0-1 Darius Maciulevicius (48').
Referee: Karl-Erik Nilsson (SWE)   Attendance: 900

03-09-1995   Stadion Maksimir, Zagreb: Croatia – Estonia 7-1 (4-1)
Croatia: Drazen Ladic (29' Marijan Mrmic), Slaven Bilic (74' Nemad Pralija), Nikola Jerkan, Mario Stanic, Zvonimir Boban (C), Robert Jarni (YC81), Robert Prosinecki, Mladen Mladenovic, Igor Stimac (83' Dzevad Turkovic), Davor Suker, Alen Boksic. (Coach: Miroslav Blazevic (CRO)).
Estonia: Mart Poom, Marek Lemsalu (C), Urmas Kirs, Risto Kallaste, Janek Kiisman (43' Alari Lell), Martin Lepa (46' Tarmo Linnumäe), Martin Reim, Toomas Kallaste, Marko Kristal (YC18), Meelis Lindmaa (76' Indro Olumets (YC65)), Lembit Rajala. (Coach: Roman Ubakivi (EST)).
Goals: Croatia: 1-0 Mladen Mladenovic (3'), 2-1 Davor Suker (19' penalty), 3-1 Alen Boksic (29'), 4-1 Zvonimir Boban (41'), 5-1 Davor Suker (58'), 6-1 Igor Stimac (80'), 7-1 Davor Suker (88').
Estonia: 1-1 Martin Reim (16').
Referee: Aron Huzu (ROM)   Attendance: 8.653

06-09-1995   Stadio Friui, Udine: Italy – Slovenia 1-0 (1-0)
Italy: Angelo Peruzzi, Alessandro Costacurta (C), Ciro Ferrara, Amedeo Carboni, Alessio Tachinardi (YC8), Demetrio Albertini, Angelo Di Livio, Roberto Di Matteo, Alessandro Del Piero (46' Giuseppe Signori), Gianfranco Zola (YC32) (60' Roberto Baggio), Fabrizio Ravanelli (81' Dino Baggio). (Coach: Arrigo Sacchi (ITA)).
Slovenia: Branko Zupan, Marinko Galic, Darko Milanic (C), Andrej Poljsak (YC30), Ales Ceh, Zlatko Zahovic (58' Vili Becaj), Alfred Jermanis (YC6), Vladimir Kokol (46' Peter Binkovski (YC75)), Saso Udovic, Primoz Gliha, Matjaz Cviki (78' Sandi Valentincic). (Coach: Dr. Zdenko Verdenik (SLO)).
Goal: Italy: 1-0 Fabrizio Ravanelli (13').
Referee: Ladislav Gadosi (SVK)   Attendance: 18.532

06-09-1995   Zalgiris Stadium, Vilnius: Lithuania – Ukraine 1-3 (1-0)
Lithuania: Gintaras Stauce (C), Aurelius Skarbalius (78' Rimantas Zvingilas), Viaceslavas Sukristovas (YC10), Tomas Ziukas, Andrejus Tereskinas (69' Aidas Preiksaitis), Raimondas Vainoras, Ramunas Stonkus, Darius Maciulevicius, Valdas Ivanauskas, Arūnas Suika, Vaidotas Slekys. (Coach: Benjaminas Zelkevicius (LIT)).
Ukraine: Oleh Suslov, Oleh Luzhny (C), Viktor Skrypnyk, Igor Zhabchenko (66' Yevhen Pokhlebayev), Serhiy Bezhenar, Volodymyr Horilyi (YC53), Oleksandr Holovko (YC81), Andriy Husin, Yuriy Kalitvintsev (YC4), Hennadiy Orbu, Tymerlan Huseynov (87' Oleksandr Yevtushok). (Coach: Anatoli Konkov (UKR)).
Goals: Lithuania: 1-0 Darius Maciulevicius (14').
Ukraine: 1-1 Tymerlan Huseynov (66'), 1-2 Tymerlan Huseynov (70'), 1-3 Andriy Husin (83').
Referee: Brendan Shorte (IRL)   Attendance: 6.000

08-10-1995   Stadion Poljud, Split: Croatia – Italy 1-1 (0-1)
Croatia: Drazen Ladic, Nikola Jerkan, Dubravko Pavlicic (YC66), Mario Stanic, Aljosa Asanovic (YC16), Zvonimir Boban (C) (YC73), Mladen Mladenovic, Igor Stimac (YC19), Davor Suker, Alen Boksic, Nikolas Jurcevic (YC3) (46' Ardian Kozniku). (Coach: Miroslav Blazevic (CRO)).
Italy: Luca Bucci (RC9), Paolo Maldini (C) (YC37), Alessandro Costacurta, Luigi Apolloni, Ciro Ferrara (83' Antonio Benarrivo), Demetrio Albertini, Angelo Di Livio, Roberto Di Matteo, Alessandro Del Piero (85' Massimo Crippa), Gianfranco Zola (9' Francesco Toldo (YC47) goal keeper), Fabrizio Ravanelli. (Coach: Arrigo Sacchi (ITA)).
Goals: Croatia: 1-1 Davor Suker (48' penalty).
Italy: 0-1 Demetrio Albertini (29').
Referee: Jacobus H. (Jaap) Uilenberg (HOL)   Attendance: 30.255

11-10-1995   Zalgiris Stadium, Vilnius: Lithuania – Estonia 5-0 (4-0)
Lithuania: Gintaras Stauce (C) (46' Valdemaras Martinkenas), Tomas Kancelskis, Raimondas Vainoras, Ramunas Stonkus, Virginijus Baltusnikas, Darius Maciulevicius, Arūnas Suika (72' Rimantas Zvingilas), Donatas Vencevicius, Valdas Ivanauskas, Vaidotas Slekys (46' Edgaras Jankauskas), Gintaras Rimkus (YC3). (Coach: Benjaminas Zelkevicius (LIT)).
Estonia: Mart Poom (C), Risto Kallaste (YC32), Alari Lell (46' Marko Kristal, 79' Toomas Kröm), Gert Olesk (YC40), Martin Lepa (46' Martin Reim (YC47)), Toomas Kallaste, Tarmo Linnumäe, Meelis Lindmaa, Andres Oper, Indrek Zelinski (YC52), Lembit Rajala. (Coach: Roman Ubakivi (EST)).
Goals: Lithuania: 1-0 Darius Maciulevicius (8'), 2-0 Arūnas Suika (13'), 3-0 Arūnas Suika (38'), 4-0 Vaidotas Slekys (44'), 5-0 Valdas Ivanauskas (60').
Referee: Didier Pauchard (FRA)   Attendance: 2.500

11-10-1995   Centralni Stadion Bezigrad, Ljubljana: Slovenia – Ukraine 3-2 (0-2)
Slovenia: Branko Zupan, Marinko Galic (YC74), Darko Milanic (C) (YC48), Robert Englaro, Dzoni Novak, Ales Ceh, Zlatko Zahovic, Mladen Rudonja, Saso Udovic (YC73), Primoz Gliha, Matjaz Florijancic (70' Matjaz Cviki). (Coach: Dr. Zdenko Verdenik (SLO)).
Ukraine: Oleh Suslov, Oleh Luzhny (C), Viktor Skrypnyk (YC21), Ihor Zhabchenko (YC16), Serhiy Smatovalenko (81' Andriy Polunin), Serhiy Bezhenar, Oleksandr Holovko (YC45), Andriy Husin (46' Serhiy Nahornyak (YC80)), Yuriy Kalitvintsev (78' Oleksandr Yevtushok), Hennadiy Orbu, Tymerlan Huseynov. (Coach: Anatoli Konkov (UKR)).
Goals: Slovenia: 1-2 Saso Udovic (50'), 2-2 Zlatko Zahovic (73'), 3-2 Saso Udovic (90').
Ukraine: 0-1 Viktor Skrypnyk (23'), 0-2 Tymerlan Huseynov (44').
Referee: Alain Hamer (LUX)   Attendance: 2.750

11-11-1995   Stadio San Nicola, Bari: Italy – Ukraine 3-1 (1-1)
Italy: Angelo Peruzzi, Paolo Maldini (C), Alessandro Costacurta, Antonio Benarrivo, Ciro Ferrara, Demetrio Albertini, Dino Baggio (YC32) (46' Massimo Crippa (YC70)), Roberto Di Matteo, Alessandro Del Piero (87' Amedeo Carboni), Gianfranco Zola (65' Marco Simone), Fabrizio Ravanelli. (Coach: Arrigo Sacchi (ITA)).
Ukraine: Oleh Suslov, Oleh Luzhny (C) (YC57), Viktor Skrypnyk, Serhiy Bezhenar (YC11), Volodymyr Horilyi (14' Oleksandr Yevtushok), Yuriy Kalitvintsev, Andriy Polunin, Hennadiy Orbu, Volodymyr Sharan (51' Serhiy Popov), Serhiy Nahornyak (72' Yevhen Pokhlebayev), Tymerlan Huseynov. (Coach: Anatoli Konkov (UKR)).
Goals: Italy: 1-1 Fabrizio Ravanelli (22'), 2-1 Fabrizio Ravanelli (49'), 3-1 Paolo Maldini (54').
Ukraine: 0-1 Andriy Polunin (19').
Referee: Serge Muhmenthaler (SUI)   Attendance: 43.999

15-11-1995   Centralni Stadion Bezigrad, Ljubljana: Slovenia – Croatia 1-2 (1-1)
Slovenia: Branko Zupan, Marinko Galic, Robert Englaro (YC65), Ales Krizan, Samir Zulic (61' Matjaz Cviki), Dzoni Novak (C), Ales Ceh, Alfred Jermanis, Saso Udovic (YC50), Primoz Gliha, Matjaz Florijancic (61' Mladen Rudonja). (Coach: Dr. Zdenko Verdenik (SLO)).
Croatia: Drazen Ladic, Slaven Bilic, Nikola Jerkan, Zvonimir Soldo, Mario Stanic (YC52), Robert Jarni, Robert Prosinecki, Nenad Pralija (YC63) (63' Mladen Mladenovic), Ivica Mornar, Davor Suker (C), Nikolas Jurcevic. (Coach: Miroslav Blazevic (CRO)).
Goals: Slovenia: 1-0 Primoz Gliha (36').
Croatia: 1-1 Davor Suker (40' penalty), 1-2 Nikolas Jurcevic (54').
Referee: Guy Goethals (BEL)   Attendance: 6.800

15-11-1995   Stadio Giglio, Reggio Emilia: Italy – Lithuania 4-0 (0-0)
Italy: Angelo Peruzzi, Paolo Maldini (C) (72' Amedeo Carboni), Alessandro Costacurta, Roberto Mussi, Ciro Ferrara, Demetrio Albertini, Roberto Di Matteo, Francesco Statuto (46' Fabrizio Ravanelli), Alessandro Del Piero, Pierluigi Casiraghi (46' Gianfranco Zola), Marco Simone (YC62). (Coach: Arrigo Sacchi (ITA)).
Lithuania: Gintaras Stauce (C), Aurelius Skarbalius, Tomas Ziukas, Andrejus Tereskinas (YC20), Raimondas Vainoras (YC32), Ramunas Stonkus, Darius Maciulevicius (46' Rimantas Zvingilas), Arūnas Suika (78' Donatas Vencevicius), Valdas Ivanauskas (YC25) (59' Raimondas Zutautas), Aidas Preiksaitis, Gintaras Rimkus. (Coach: Benjaminas Zelkevicius (LIT)).
Goals: Italy: 1-0 Alessandro Del Piero (51'), 2-0 Gianfranco Zola (66'), 3-0 Gianfranco Zola (81'), 4-0 Gianfranco Zola (83').
Referee: Manuel Díaz Vega (ESP)   Attendance: 22.272

GROUP 5

06-09-1994	Ostrava	Czech Republic – Malta	6-1 (3-0)
07-09-1994	Luxembourg	Luxembourg – Netherlands	0-4 (0-1)
07-09-1994	Oslo	Norway – Belarus	1-0 (0-0)
12-10-1994	Ta'Qali	Malta – Czech Republic	0-0
12-10-1994	Oslo	Norway – Netherlands	1-1 (0-1)
12-10-1994	Minsk	Belarus – Luxembourg	2-0 (0-0)
16-11-1994	Minsk	Belarus – Norway	0-4 (0-2)
16-11-1994	Rotterdam	Netherlands – Czech Republic	0-0

14-12-1994	Rotterdam	Netherlands – Luxembourg	5-0 (3-0)
14-12-1994	Ta'Qali	Malta – Norway	0-1 (0-1)
22-02-1995	Ta'Qali	Malta – Luxembourg	0-1 (0-0)
29-03-1995	Luxembourg	Luxembourg – Norway	0-2 (0-1)
29-03-1995	Rotterdam	Netherlands – Malta	4-0 (1-0)
29-03-1995	Ostrava	Czech Republic – Belarus	4-2 (2-1)
26-04-1995	Minsk	Belarus – Malta	1-1 (0-0)
26-04-1995	Prague	Czech Republic – Netherlands	3-1 (0-1)
26-04-1995	Oslo	Norway – Luxembourg	5-0 (3-0)
07-06-1995	Luxembourg	Luxembourg – Czech Republic	1-0 (0-0)
07-06-1995	Oslo	Norway – Malta	2-0 (1-0)
07-06-1995	Minsk	Belarus – Netherlands	1-0 (1-0)
16-08-1995	Oslo	Norway – Czech Republic	1-1 (1-0)
06-09-1995	Prague	Czech Republic – Norway	2-0 (1-0)
06-09-1995	Rotterdam	Netherlands – Belarus	1-0 (0-0)
06-09-1995	Luxembourg	Luxembourg – Malta	1-0 (1-0)
07-10-1995	Minsk	Belarus – Czech Republic	0-2 (0-1)
11-10-1995	Ta'Qali	Malta – Netherlands	0-4 (0-0)
11-10-1995	Luxembourg	Luxembourg – Belarus	0-0
12-11-1995	Ta'Qali	Malta – Belarus	0-2 (0-0)
15-11-1995	Prague	Czech Republic – Luxembourg	3-0 (1-0)
15-11-1995	Rotterdam	Netherlands – Norway	3-0 (0-0)

FINAL STANDING

Pos	Team	Pld	W	D	L	GF	GA	GD	Pts
1	*Czech Republic*	*10*	*6*	*3*	*1*	*21*	*6*	*+15*	*21*
2	*Netherlands*	*10*	*6*	*2*	*2*	*23*	*5*	*+18*	*20*
3	Norway	10	6	2	2	17	7	+10	20
4	Belarus	10	3	2	5	8	13	-5	11
5	Luxembourg	10	3	1	6	3	21	-18	10
6	Malta	10	0	2	8	2	22	-20	2

Czech Republic qualified for the final tournament in England.
Netherlands advanced to the qualifying play-off.

06-09-1994 Bazaly, Ostrava: Czech Republic – Malta 6-1 (3-0)
Czech Republic: Petr Kouba, Jiri Novotny, Lubos Kubík, Jan Suchopárek, Radoslav Látal (87' Petr Vesely), Václav Nemecek (C) (YC28), Jirí Nemec, Daniel Smejkal, Martin Frydek (83' Patrik Berger), Pavel Kuka, Horst Siegl. (Coach: Dusan Uhrin (CZE)).
Malta: David Cluett, Joseph Galea, John Buttigieg, Joe Camilleri, Richard Buhagiar (YC20), Silvio Vella (YC46), Carmel Busuttil (C), Kristian Laferla, Joe Brincat, Nicholas Saliba, Martin Gregory (83' Edwin Camilleri). (Coach: Pietro Ghedin (ITA)).
Goals: Czech Republic: 1-0 Daniel Smejkal (5' penalty), 2-0 Lubos Kubík (32'), 3-0 Horst Siegl (34'), 4-0 Joe Camilleri (60' *own goal*), 5-1 Horst Siegl (77'), 6-1 Patrik Berger (86').
Malta: 4-1 Kristian Laferla (73').
Referee: Loizos Loizou (CYP) Attendance: 10.226

07-09-1994   Stade Josy Barthel, Luxembourg: Luxembourg – Netherlands   0-4 (0-1)
Luxembourg: Paul Koch (YC60), Marc Birsens, Thomas Wolf, Ralph Ferron, Jeff Strasser (YC20), Manuel Cardoni (75' Patrick Morocutti), Jeff Saibene, Joël Groff, Carlo Weis (C), Luc Holtz, Robert Langers (86' Daniel Theis). (Coach: Paul Philipp (LUX)).
Netherlands: Ed de Goey, Frank de Boer, Stan Valckx, Danny Blind (C) (YC41), Ronald de Boer, Aron Winter, Wim Jonk, Rob Witschge (YC44), Marc Overmars, Bryan Roy (72' Peter van Vossen), John Bosman. (Coach: Dirk Nicolaas (Dick) Advocaat (HOL)).
Goals: Netherlands: 0-1 Bryan Roy (22'), 0-2 Ronald de Boer (64'), 0-3 Ronald de Boer (67'), 0-4 Wim Jonk (90').
Referee: Alan Snoddy (NIR)   Attendance: 8.120

07-09-1994   Ullevaal Stadion, Oslo: Norway – Belarus   1-0 (0-0)
Norway: Frode Grodås, Henning Berg, Stig Inge Bjørnebye, Pål Lydersen, Tore André Pedersen, Erik Mykland, Kjetil Rekdal, Jostein Flo (69' Geir Frigård), Jahn Ivar Mini Jakobsen, Lars Roar Bohinen (46' Øyvind Leonhardsen), Jan Åge Fjørtoft (C). (Coach: Egil Roger Olsen (NOR)).
Belarus: Valeri Shantalosov, Sergei Gurenko, Andrei Sosnitski, Alexandre Metlitskiy, Erik Yakhimovich, Andrei Zygmantovich (C), Yuri Antonovich (YC85), Sergey Kulanin (46' Petr Kachuro), Aleksandr Khatskevich, Sergei Gerasimets (YC72), Mikhail Markhel. (Coach: Sergey Borovskiy (BLS)).
Goal: Norway: 1-0 Geir Frigård (87').
Referee: Guy Goethals (BEL)   Attendance: 16.739

12-10-1994   Ta'Qali National Stadium, Ta'Qali: Malta – Czech Republic   0-0
Malta: David Cluett, David Carabott (YC62) (86' Edwin Camilleri), Joseph Galea (RC80), John Buttigieg (YC45), Joe Camilleri, Silvio Vella, Carmel Busuttil (C), Kristian Laferla, Joe Brincat (YC35), Nicholas Saliba (75' Joseph Sant-Fournier), Martin Gregory (YC67). (Coach: Pietro Ghedin (ITA)).
Czech Republic: Pavel Srníček, Jiri Novotny (RC58), Lubos Kubík (YC29), Jan Suchopárek (YC66), Radoslav Látal, Ivan Hasek, Václav Nemecek (C) (44' Miroslav Kadlec), Jiří Nemec, Daniel Smejkal (70' Martin Frydek), Tomás Skuhravy, Pavel Kuka. (Coach: Dusan Uhrin (CZE)).
Referee: Jorge Emanuel Monteiro Coroado (POR)   Attendance: 3.088

12-10-1994   Ullevaal Stadion, Oslo: Norway – Netherlands   1-1 (0-1)
Norway: Erik Thorstvedt (C), Henning Berg, Stig Inge Bjørnebye, Pål Lydersen, Tore André Pedersen, Øyvind Leonhardsen, Erik Mykland, Kjetil Rekdal, Lars Roar Bohinen, Sigurd Rushfeldt (63' Jostein Flo), Jan Åge Fjørtoft (C) (77' Geir Frigård). (Coach: Egil Roger Olsen (NOR)).
Netherlands: Ed de Goey, Michael Reiziger (77' Ulrich van Gobbel), Frank de Boer (YC48), Stan Valckx (YC42), Danny Blind (C), Aron Winter, Wim Jonk, Rob Witschge, Marc Overmars, Dennis Bergkamp (70' Ronald de Boer), Bryan Roy. (Coach: Dirk Nicolaas (Dick) Advocaat (HOL)).
Goals: Norway: 1-1 Kjetil Rekdal (51' penalty).
Netherlands: 0-1 Bryan Roy (21').
Referee: James (Jim) McCluskey (SCO)   Attendance: 22.293

12-10-1994   Dinamo Stadium, Minsk: Belarus – Luxembourg   2-0 (0-0)
Belarus: Valeri Shantalosov, Sergei Gurenko (RC68), Alexandre Metlitskiy (YC82), Erik Yakhimovich, Pavel Rodnionok (80' Andrei Sosnitski), Sergei Aleinikov, Andrei Zygmantovich (C), Miroslav Romashchenko, Sergei Gerasimets, Yuri Shukanov, Mikhail Markhel (65' Yuri Antonovich). (Coach: Sergey Borovskiy (BLS)).
Luxembourg: Paul Koch, Marc Birsens (YC66), Thomas Wolf, Ralph Ferron (YC37) (82' Jean Vanek), Jeff Strasser, Manuel Cardoni (YC50), Jeff Saibene, Guy Hellers, Carlo Weis (C), Luc Holtz (57' Patrick Morocutti), Stefano Fanelli. (Coach: Paul Philipp (LUX)).
Goals: Belarus: 1-0 Miroslav Romashchenko (67'), 2-0 Sergei Gerasimets (76').
Referee: Richard O'Hanlon (IRL)   Attendance: 6.549

16-11-1994   Dinamo Stadium, Minsk: Belarus – Norway   0-4 (0-2)
Belarus: Valeri Shantalosov, Alexandre Metlitskiy, Erik Yakhimovich, Pavel Rodnionok, Sergei Yaskovich, Andrei Zygmantovich (C), Yuri Antonovich, Miroslav Romashchenko (82' Igor Gurinovich), Sergei Gerasimets, Yuri Shukanov, Mikhail Markhel (46' Andrei Yusipets). (Coach: Sergey Borovskiy (BLS)).
Norway: Frode Grodås, Ronny Johnsen, Henning Berg, Stig Inge Bjørnebye (43' Pål Lydersen), Gunnar Halle, Øyvind Leonhardsen (YC60), Erik Mykland, Kjetil Rekdal, Lars Roar Bohinen, Sigurd Rushfeldt (77' Jahn Ivar Mini Jakobsen), Jan Åge Fjørtoft (C) (YC51). (Coach: Egil Roger Olsen (NOR)).
Goals: Norway: 0-1 Henning Berg (36'), 0-2 Øyvind Leonhardsen (39'), 0-3 Lars Roar Bohinen (52'), 0-4 Kjetil Rekdal (83' penalty).
Referee: Lube Spassov (BUL)   Attendance: 5.711

16-11-1994   Stadion Feijenoord, Rotterdam: Netherlands – Czech Republic   0-0
Netherlands: Ed de Goey, Frank de Boer, Stan Valckx, Danny Blind (C), Aron Winter, Wim Jonk, Rob Witschge (79' Arthur Numan), Bryan Roy (YC32), Gaston Taument, Peter van Vossen, Youri Mulder (70' Patrick Kluivert). (Coach: Dirk Nicolaas (Dick) Advocaat (HOL)).
Czech Republic: Pavel Srnícek, Miroslav Kadlec, Lubos Kubík (C) (YC29), Jan Suchopárek (YC58), Radoslav Látal, Karel Poborsky (75' Patrik Berger), Michal Bílek, Jirí Nemec, Pavel Hapal, Pavel Kuka (90' Petr Samec), Horst Siegl. (Coach: Dusan Uhrin (CZE)).
Referee: Sándor Puhl (HUN)   Attendance: 41.195

14-12-1994   Stadion Feijenoord, Rotterdam: Netherlands – Luxembourg   5-0 (3-0)
Netherlands: Ed de Goey, Frank de Boer, Arthur Numan, Stan Valckx, Danny Blind (C), Ronald de Boer, Aron Winter (75' Pierre van Hooijdonk), Wim Jonk, Marc Overmars, Bryan Roy, Youri Mulder (46' Clarence Seedorf). (Coach: Dirk Nicolaas (Dick) Advocaat (HOL)).
Luxembourg: Paul Koch, Marc Birsens, Thomas Wolf, Ralph Ferron, Jeff Strasser (YC19), Manuel Cardoni, Joël Groff, Guy Hellers, Carlo Weis (C) (YC69), Luc Holtz, Robert Langers (62' Daniel Theis). (Coach: Paul Philipp (LUX)).
Goals: Netherlands: 1-0 Youri Mulder (7'), 2-0 Bryan Roy (16'), 3-0 Wim Jonk (39'), 4-0 Ronald de Boer (52'), 5-0 Clarence Seedorf (90').
Referee: Daniel Roduit (SUI)   Attendance: 26.000

14-12-1994   Ta'Qali National Stadium, Ta'Qali: Malta – Norway   0-1 (0-1)
Malta: David Cluett, David Carabott (62' Richard Buhagiar), John Buttigieg, Joe Camilleri, Silvio Vella, Carmel Busuttil (C), Kristian Laferla, Joe Brincat, Nicholas Saliba (86' Carmel Scerri (II)), Michael Woods, Martin Gregory. (Coach: Pietro Ghedin (ITA)).
Norway: Frode Grodås, Ronny Johnsen, Henning Berg, Stig Inge Bjørnebye, Gunnar Halle (YC17), Erik Mykland (YC88), Kjetil Rekdal, Jostein Flo, Lars Roar Bohinen (73' Ståle Solbakken), Sigurd Rushfeldt (85' Jahn Ivar Mini Jakobsen), Jan Åge Fjørtoft (C). (Coach: Egil Roger Olsen (NOR)).
Goal: Norway: 0-1 Jan Åge Fjørtoft (10').
Referee: Gianni Beschin (ITA)   Attendance: 5.717

22-02-1995   Ta'Qali National Stadium, Ta'Qali: Malta – Luxembourg   0-1 (0-0)
Malta: David Cluett, David Carabott (YC26) (77' Nicholas Saliba), John Buttigieg (YC52), Joe Camilleri (YC70), Richard Buhagiar, Silvio Vella, Carmel Busuttil (C), Kristian Laferla, Joe Brincat, Hubert Suda (58' Charles Sciberras), Martin Gregory. (Coach: Pietro Ghedin (ITA)).
Luxembourg: Paul Koch, Marc Birsens, Thomas Wolf (C), Jean Vanek, Manuel Cardoni (83' Luc Holtz), Jeff Saibene (YC62), Joël Groff, Guy Hellers (YC31), Carlo Weis, Frank Deville, Robert Langers (88' Sacha Schneider). (Coach: Paul Philipp (LUX)).
Goal: Luxembourg: 0-1 Manuel Cardoni (55').
Referee: Mateo Beusan (CRO)   Attendance: 7.327

29-03-1995   Stade Josy Barthel, Luxembourg: Luxembourg – Norway   0-2 (0-1)
Luxembourg: Serge Rohmann, Marc Birsens (84' Sacha Schneider), Ralph Ferron (RC71), Jean Vanek, Jeff Strasser, Manuel Cardoni, Jeff Saibene (77' Patrick Feyder), Joël Groff, Carlo Weis (C) (YC74), Frank Deville, Robert Langers. (Coach: Paul Philipp (LUX)).
Norway: Erik Thorstvedt (C), Ronny Johnsen, Henning Berg, Stig Inge Bjørnebye, Alf Inge Håland, Øyvind Leonhardsen, Kjetil Rekdal (YC20) (84' Ståle Solbakken), Jostein Flo (YC16) (46' Gunnar Aase), Jahn Ivar Mini Jakobsen, Lars Roar Bohinen, Jan Åge Fjørtoft. (Coach: Egil Roger Olsen (NOR)).
Goals: Norway: 0-1 Øyvind Leonhardsen (35'), 0-2 Gunnar Aase (77').
Referee: Nikolai Vladislavovich Levnikov (RUS)   Attendance: 3.031

29-03-1995   Stadion Feijenoord, Rotterdam: Netherlands – Malta   4-0 (1-0)
Netherlands: Ed de Goey, Frank de Boer, Stan Valckx, Danny Blind (C), Clarence Seedorf, Ronald de Boer (76' Patrick Kluivert), Aron Winter, Wim Jonk, Marc Overmars, Dennis Bergkamp, Bryan Roy (59' Eric van der Luer). (Coach: Guus Hiddink (HOL)).
Malta: David Cluett, Joseph Galea (YC25), Joe Camilleri, Edwin Camilleri (YC79), Richard Buhagiar (YC61), Silvio Vella (87' Martin Gregory), Carmel Busuttil (86' Gilbert Agius), Kristian Laferla (C) (YC86), Nicholas Saliba, Joseph Sant-Fournier, Michael Woods (YC65). (Coach: Pietro Ghedin (ITA)).
Goals: Netherlands: 1-0 Clarence Seedorf (38'), 2-0 Dennis Bergkamp (74' penalty), 3-0 Aron Winter (77'), 4-0 Patrick Kluivert (82').
Referee: Gylfi Thór Orrason (ISL)   Attendance: 30.288

29-03-1995   Bazaly, Ostrava: Czech Republic – Belarus   4-2 (2-1)
Czech Republic: Pavel Srnícek, Tomás Repka (YC76), Miroslav Kadlec, Radoslav Látal, Patrik Berger, Václav Nemecek (C), Pavel Hapal, Daniel Smejkal, Martin Frydek (86' Michal Bílek), Pavel Kuka, Horst Siegl (88' Petr Samec). (Coach: Dusan Uhrin (CZE)).
Belarus: Valeri Shantalosov, Sergei Gurenko, Andrei Sosnitski, Alexandre Metlitskiy, Erik Yakhimovich (77' Pavel Rodnionok), Vladimir Zhuravel (81' Yevhen Kashentsev), Alexandre Taykov (YC53), Andrei Zygmantovich (C) (YC52), Sergei Gerasimets, Andrei Yusipets, Igor Gurinovich. (Coach: Sergey Borovskiy (BLS)).
Goals: Czech Republic: 1-0 Miroslav Kadlec (5'), 2-0 Patrik Berger (17'), 3-1 Patrik Berger (63'), 4-1 Pavel Kuka (69').
Belarus: 2-1 Sergei Gerasimets (44' penalty), 4-2 Igor Gurinovich (88').
Referee: Gilles Veissière (FRA)   Attendance: 5.549

26-04-1995   Dinamo Stadium, Minsk: Belarus – Malta   1-1 (0-0)
Belarus: Andrei Satsunkevich, Sergei Gurenko, Alexandre Metlitskiy (YC63) (70' Pavel Rodnionok), Vladimir Zhuravel, Alexandre Taykov, Andrei Zygmantovich (C), Yuri Antonovich, Sergei Gerasimets, Andrei Yusipets (76' Petr Kachuro), Yuri Shukanov, Igor Gurinovich. (Coach: Sergey Borovskiy (BLS)).
Malta: David Cluett, David Carabott, John Buttigieg, Edwin Camilleri, Silvio Vella, Carmel Busuttil (89' Lawrence Attard (YC90)), Kristian Laferla (C), Nicholas Saliba, Joseph Sant-Fournier, Michael Woods, Martin Gregory (25' Gilbert Agius). (Coach: Pietro Ghedin (ITA)).
Goals: Belarus: 1-0 Alexandre Taykov (57').
Malta: 1-1 David Carabott (71').
Referee: Ladislav Gadosi (SVK)   Attendance: 6.915

26-04-1995   Letná Stadium, Prague: Czech Republic – Netherlands   3-1 (0-1)
Czech Republic: Petr Kouba, Tomás Repka, Miroslav Kadlec, Jan Suchopárek, Patrik Berger, Václav Nemecek (C), Jirí Nemec, Pavel Hapal (YC14), Martin Frydek (46' Radoslav Látal), Tomás Skuhravy, Pavel Kuka (90' Horst Siegl). (Coach: Dusan Uhrin (CZE)).
Netherlands: Ed de Goey, Frank de Boer (YC56), Arthur Numan (YC32), Stan Valckx, Danny Blind (C), Clarence Seedorf, Ronald de Boer, Aron Winter (64' Patrick Kluivert), Wim Jonk, Marc Overmars, Peter van Vossen (46' Peter Bosz). (Coach: Guus Hiddink (HOL)).
Goals: Czech Republic: 1-1 Tomás Skuhravy (49'), 2-1 Václav Nemecek (56'), 3-1 Patrik Berger (63').
Nehterlands: 0-1 Wim Jonk (7').
Referee: Helmut Krug (GER)   Attendance: 17.463

26-04-1995   Ullevaal Stadion, Oslo: Norway – Luxembourg   5-0 (3-0)
Norway: Frode Grodås, Ronny Johnsen, Henning Berg (63' Alf Inge Håland), Gunnar Halle, Roger Nilsen, Øyvind Leonhardsen (YC15), Kjetil Rekdal, Jahn Ivar Mini Jakobsen, Lars Roar Bohinen (33' Ståle Solbakken), Jan Åge Fjørtoft (C), Harald Brattbakk. (Coach: Egil Roger Olsen (NOR)).
Luxembourg: Paul Koch, Jean Vanek, Patrick Feyder, Jeff Strasser (YC60), Manuel Cardoni, Jeff Saibene (73' Marc Lamborelle), Joël Groff (YC79), Guy Hellers, Luc Holtz (55' Daniel Theis), Frank Deville (YC66), Robert Langers (C). (Coach: Paul Philipp (LUX)).
Goals: Norway: 1-0 Jahn Ivar Mini Jakobsen (9'), 2-0 Jan Åge Fjørtoft (10'), 3-0 Harald Brattbakk (23'), 4-0 Henning Berg (46'), 5-0 Kjetil Rekdal (49').
Referee: John Ferry (NIR)   Attendance: 15.124

07-06-1995 Stade Josy Barthel, Luxembourg: Luxembourg – Czech Republic 1-0 (0-0)
Luxembourg: Paul Koch, Marc Birsens, Jean Vanek, Jeff Strasser, Joël Groff, Guy Hellers, Carlo Weis (C) (YC10), Daniel Theis (73' Jeff Saibene), Frank Deville, Claude Ganser (86' Manuel Cardoni), Robert Langers. (Coach: Paul Philipp (LUX)).
Czech Republic: Petr Kouba, Tomás Repka (68' Martin Frydek), Miroslav Kadlec, Jan Suchopárek, Radoslav Látal, Patrik Berger, Václav Nemecek (C) (YC44), Jirí Nemec, Pavel Hapal, Tomás Skuhravy (59' Radek Drulák), Pavel Kuka. (Coach: Dusan Uhrin (CZE)).
Goal: Luxembourg: 1-0 Guy Hellers (89').
Referee: John Ashman (WAL) Attendance: 1.630

07-06-1995 Ullevaal Stadion, Oslo: Norway – Malta 2-0 (1-0)
Norway: Erik Thorstvedt (C), Ronny Johnsen, Henning Berg, Alf Inge Håland, Roger Nilsen (69' Harald Brattbakk), Erik Mykland, Kjetil Rekdal (82' Kåre Ingebrigtsen), Jorstein Flo, Jahn Ivar Mini Jakobsen, Ståle Solbakken, Jan Åge Fjørtoft. (Coach: Egil Roger Olsen (NOR)).
Malta: David Cluett, David Carabott, John Buttigieg (27' Nicholas Saliba), Richard Buhagiar (YC54) (75' Edwin Camilleri), Silvio Vella, Carmel Busuttil, Kristian Laferla (C), Joseph Sant-Fournier, Michael Woods, Lawrence Attard, Gilbert Agius. (Coach: Pietro Ghedin (ITA)).
Goals: Norway: 1-0 Jan Åge Fjørtoft (42'), 2-0 Jorstein Flo (88').
Referee: Zbigniew Przesmycki (POL) Attendance: 15.180

07-06-1995 Dinamo Stadium, Minsk: Belarus – Netherlands 1-0 (1-0)
Belarus: Valeri Shantalosov, Sergei Gurenko, Pavel Rodnionok, Vladimir Zhuravel, Alexandre Taykov, Andrei Zygmantovich (C), Andrei Dovnar (86' Yevhen Kashentsev), Miroslav Romashchenko (54' Yuri Antonovich (YC87)), Sergei Gerasimets, Petr Kachuro, Andrei Yusipets. (Coach: Sergey Borovskiy (BLS)).
Netherlands: Edwin van der Sar, Stan Valckx (64' Arthur Numan), Danny Blind (C) (70' Aron Winter), Johan de Kock (YC62), Clarence Seedorf, Ronald de Boer, Wim Jonk (YC87), Edgar Davids, Patrick Kluivert (YC53), Marc Overmars, John van 't Schip. (Coach: Guus Hiddink (HOL)).
Goal: Belarus: 1-0 Sergei Gerasimets (27').
Referee: Adrian Porumboiu (ROM) Attendance: 22.000

16-08-1995 Ullevaal Stadion, Oslo: Norway – Czech Republic 1-1 (1-0)
Norway: Erik Thorstvedt (C), Ronny Johnsen, Henning Berg, Alf Inge Håland, Karl-Petter Løken, Øyvind Leonhardsen, Jorstein Flo, Jahn Ivar Mini Jakobsen (68' Geirmund Brendesæter), Lars Roar Bohinen, Ståle Solbakken, Jan Åge Fjørtoft (80' Harald Brattbakk). (Coach: Egil Roger Olsen (NOR)).
Czech Republic: Petr Kouba, Tomás Repka, Miroslav Kadlec (C), Jan Suchopárek (YC70), Radoslav Látal (77' Karel Poborsky), Patrik Berger (46' Pavel Nedved), Jirí Nemec (YC21), Pavel Hapal (YC3), Martin Frydek, Pavel Kuka, Radek Drulák (77' Petr Samec). (Coach: Dusan Uhrin (CZE)).
Goals: Norway: 1-0 Henning Berg (27').
Czech Republic: 1-1 Jan Suchopárek (80').
Referee: Sergei Grigorievich Khusainov (RUS) Attendance: 22.054

335

06-09-1995   Letná Stadium, Prague: Czech Republic – Norway   2-0 (1-0)
Czech Republic: Petr Kouba, Tomás Repka, Miroslav Kadlec, Jan Suchopárek, Radoslav Látal (YC31), Pavel Nedved, Václav Nemecek (C), Jirí Nemec, Martin Frydek (70' Karel Poborsky), Tomás Skuhravy (80' Vratislav Lokvenc), Pavel Kuka (18' Radek Drulák). (Coach: Dusan Uhrin (CZE)).
Norway: Erik Thorstvedt (C), Ronny Johnsen, Henning Berg, Erland Johnsen, Karl-Petter Løken (YC2), Øyvind Leonhardsen, Jorstein Flo (YC69), Jahn Ivar Mini Jakobsen (YC55), Lars Roar Bohinen (75' Kjetil Rekdal), Ståle Solbakken (YC30), Jan Åge Fjørtoft (69' Harald Brattbakk). (Coach: Egil Roger Olsen (NOR)).
Goals: Czech Republic: 1-0 Tomás Skuhravy (6' penalty), 2-0 Radek Drulák (87').
Referee: Kurt Röthlisberger (SUI)   Attendance: 19.522

06-09-1995   Stadion Feijenoord, Rotterdam: Netherlands – Belarus   1-0 (0-0)
Netherlands: Edwin van der Sar, Michael Reiziger (71' Orlando Trustfull (YC80)), Frank de Boer (YC28), Danny Blind (C), Johan de Kock, Ronald de Boer, Aron Winter (RC76), Richard Witschge (86' Arthur Numan), Marc Overmars, Dennis Bergkamp, René Eijkelkamp (64' Youri Mulder). (Coach: Guus Hiddink (HOL)).
Belarus: Andrei Satsunkevich (YC17), Sergei Gurenko, Pavel Rodnionok, Vladimir Zhuravel (89' Sergei Vekhtev), Alexandre Taykov, Andrei Zygmantovich (C) (YC16), Andrei Dovnar, Miroslav Romashchenko (85' Yuri Vergeychyk), Sergei Gerasimets, Petr Kachuro, Andrei Yusipets (68' Yevhen Kashentsev). (Coach: Sergey Borovskiy (BLS)).
Goal: Netherlands: 1-0 Youri Mulder (83').
Referee: Robert Sedlacek (AUT)   Attendance: 18.830

06-09-1995   Stade Josy Barthel, Luxembourg: Luxembourg – Malta   1-0 (1-0)
Luxembourg: Paul Koch, Marc Birsens, Jean Vanek, Jeff Strasser, Jeff Saibene, Joël Groff (YC43) (67' Daniel Theis), Guy Hellers, Carlo Weis (C), Luc Holtz (85' Manuel Cardoni), Frank Deville, Robert Langers. (Coach: Paul Philipp (LUX)).
Malta: David Cluett, David Carabott (46' Lawrence Attard), Joseph Galea (YC78), John Buttigieg (RC42), Richard Buhagiar, Desmond Delia (28' Gilbert Agius, 89' Martin Gregory), Carmel Busuttil (C) (YC28), Kristian Laferla, Nicholas Saliba, Joseph Sant-Fournier, Michael Woods. (Coach: Pietro Ghedin (ITA)).
Goal: Luxembourg: 1-0 Luc Holtz (44').
Referee: Algirdas Dubinskas (LIT)   Attendance: 4.809

07-11-1995   Dinamo Stadium, Minsk: Belarus – Czech Republic   0-2 (0-1)
Belarus: Valeri Shantalosov, Sergei Gurenko, Pavel Rodnionok, Vladimir Zhuravel (C), Alexandre Taykov, Valentin Belkevich, Andrei Dovnar, Sergei Gerasimets (YC27), Petr Kachuro, Andrei Yusipets (74' Vasili Baranov), Yevhen Kashentsev. (Coach: Sergey Borovskiy (BLS)).
Czech Republic: Petr Kouba, Tomás Repka, Miroslav Kadlec, Radoslav Látal, Pavel Nedved (YC70) (73' Patrik Berger), Václav Nemecek (C) (15' Michal Hornák), Jirí Nemec (YC44), Pavel Hapal, Martin Frydek (88' Karel Poborsky), Pavel Kuka, Radek Drulák. (Coach: Dusan Uhrin (CZE)).
Goals: Czech Republic: 0-1 Martin Frydek (25'), 0-2 Patrik Berger (84').
Referee: Anders Frisk (SWE)   Attendance: 9.500

11-10-1995   Ta'Qali National Stadium, Ta'Qali: Malta – Netherlands   0-4 (0-0)
Malta: David Cluett, David Carabott, Ivan Zammit, Richard Buhagiar, Carmel Busuttil (C), Kristian Laferla, Joe Brincat, Nicholas Saliba, Michael Woods, Lawrence Attard (70' Joseph Galea), Gilbert Agius (6' Joseph Sant-Fournier (YC14)). (Coach: Pietro Ghedin (ITA)).
Netherlands: Edwin van der Sar, Michael Reiziger, Frank de Boer, Arthur Numan, Danny Blind (C) (80' Orlando Trustfull), Clarence Seedorf, Ronald de Boer, Richard Witschge, Patrick Kluivert (YC58), Marc Overmars, Youri Mulder (65' Glenn Helder). (Coach: Guus Hiddink (HOL)).
Goals: Netherlands: 0-1 Marc Overmars (52'), 0-2 Marc Overmars (61'), 0-3 Marc Overmars (66'), 0-4 Clarence Seedorf (81').
Referee: Kim Milton Nielsen (DEN)   Attendance: 10.502

11-10-1995   Stade Josy Barthel, Luxembourg: Luxembourg – Belarus   0-0
Luxembourg: Paul Koch, Marc Birsens (YC47), Jean Vanek, Jeff Strasser, Jeff Saibene, Guy Hellers, Carlo Weis (C), Luc Holtz (89' Marc Lamborelle), Frank Deville, Robert Langers (80' Daniel Theis), Patrick Morocutti (72' Manuel Cardoni). (Coach: Paul Philipp (LUX)).
Belarus: Valeri Shantalosov, Sergei Gurenko, Pavel Rodnionok, Vladimir Zhuravel (C), Alexandre Taykov, Valentin Belkevich, Andrei Dovnar (YC36), Sergei Gerasimets, Petr Kachuro, Andrei Yusipets, Yevhen Kashentsev (88' Yuri Vergeychyk). (Coach: Sergey Borovskiy (BLS)).
Referee: Paul Anthony Durkin (ENG)   Attendance: 4.272

12-11-1995   Ta'Qali National Stadium, Ta'Qali: Malta – Belarus   0-2 (0-0)
Malta: David Cluett, Ivan Zammit, Richard Buhagiar, Silvio Vella (YC43), Carmel Busuttil (C) (YC75), Kristian Laferla, Joe Brincat (50' Joseph Sant-Fournier), Nicholas Saliba, Michael Woods, Lawrence Attard, Gilbert Agius (63' David Carabott). (Coach: Pietro Ghedin (ITA)).
Belarus: Valeri Shantalosov, Sergei Gurenko, Alexandre Metlitskiy (YC44), Alexandre Taykov, Andrei Zygmantovich (C) (60' Andrei Yusipets), Andrei Dovnar, Oleg Khmelnitskiy (42' Valentin Belkevich), Vasili Baranov, Yuri Maleev (75' Vladimir Makovkiy), Sergei Gerasimets, Petr Kachuro. (Coach: Sergey Borovskiy (BLS)).
Goals: Belarus: 0-1 Sergei Gerasimets (78'), 0-2 Sergei Gerasimets (82').
Referee: Tokat Metin (TUR)   Attendance: 3.025

15-11-1995   Letná Stadium, Prague: Czech Republic – Luxembourg   3-0 (1-0)
Czech Republic: Petr Kouba, Miroslav Kadlec, Jan Suchopárek, Radoslav Látal, Pavel Nedved, Patrik Berger (82' Vladimir Smicer), Václav Nemecek (C) (70' Karel Poborsky), Pavel Hapal, Martin Frydek (YC4), Pavel Kuka (YC85) (85' Vratislav Lokvenc), Radek Drulák. (Coach: Dusan Uhrin (CZE)).
Luxembourg: Paul Koch (YC24), Ralph Ferron, Jean Vanek, Jeff Strasser, Jeff Saibene (89' Manuel Cardoni), Joël Groff, Guy Hellers (YC14), Carlo Weis (C) (YC59), Luc Holtz (77' Claude Ganser), Frank Deville (YC31) (60' Daniel Theis), Robert Langers. (Coach: Paul Philipp (LUX)).
Goals: Czech Republic: 1-0 Radek Drulák (37'), 2-0 Radek Drulák (46'), 3-0 Patrik Berger (59').
Referee: Alfred Wieser (AUT)   Attendance: 20.239

15-11-1995 Stadion Feijenoord, Rotterdam: Netherlands – Norway 3-0 (0-0)
Netherlands: Edwin van der Sar, Michael Reiziger, Frank de Boer (YC13), Arthur Numan, Danny Blind (C), Clarence Seedorf (YC51), Ronald de Boer (78' Youri Mulder), Richard Witschge (56' Edgar Davids), Glenn Helder (85' Johan de Kock), Marc Overmars, Dennis Bergkamp. (Coach: Guus Hiddink (HOL)).
Norway: Frode Grodås, Henning Berg, Stig Inge Bjørnebye, Erland Johnsen, Karl-Petter Løken (62' Alf Inge Håland), Erik Mykland (59' Øyvind Leonhardsen), Kjetil Rekdal (YC31), Jahn Ivar Mini Jakobsen, Lars Roar Bohinen (80' Ståle Solbakken), Tore André Flo, Jan Åge Fjørtoft (C). (Coach: Egil Roger Olsen (NOR)).
Goals: Netherlands: 1-0 Clarence Seedorf (48'), 2-0 Youri Mulder (88'), 3-0 Marc Overmars (89').
Referee: Dermot J.Gallagher (ENG)   Attendance: 42.325

GROUP 6

20-04-1994	Belfast	Northern Ireland – Liechtenstein	4-1 (3-0)
07-09-1994	Riga	Latvia – Republic of Ireland	0-3 (0-2)
07-09-1994	Eschen	Liechtenstein – Austria	0-4 (0-3)
07-09-1994	Belfast	Northern Ireland – Portugal	1-2 (0-1)
09-10-1994	Riga	Latvia – Portugal	1-3 (0-1)
12-10-1994	Vienna	Austria – Northern Ireland	1-2 (1-2)
12-10-1994	Dublin	Republic of Ireland – Liechtenstein	4-0 (3-0)
13-11-1994	Lisbon	Portugal – Austria	1-0 (1-0)
15-11-1994	Eschen	Liechtenstein – Latvia	0-1 (0-1)
16-11-1994	Belfast	Northern Ireland – Republic of Ireland	0-4 (0-3)
18-12-1994	Lisbon	Portugal – Liechtenstein	8-0 (3-0)
29-03-1995	Dublin	Republic of Ireland – Northern Ireland	1-1 (0-0)
29-03-1995	Salzburg	Austria – Latvia	5-0 (2-0)
26-04-1995	Riga	Latvia – Northern Ireland	0-1 (0-0)
26-04-1995	Salzburg	Austria – Liechtenstein	7-0 (3-0)
26-04-1995	Dublin	Republic of Ireland – Portugal	1-0 (1-0)
03-06-1995	Porto	Portugal – Latvia	3-2 (3-0)
03-06-1995	Eschen	Liechtenstein – Republic of Ireland	0-0
07-06-1995	Belfast	Northern Ireland – Latvia	1-2 (1-0)
11-06-1995	Dublin	Republic of Ireland – Austria	1-3 (0-0)
15-08-1995	Eschen	Liechtenstein – Portugal	0-7 (0-3)
16-08-1995	Riga	Latvia – Austria	3-2 (1-0)
03-09-1995	Porto	Portugal – Northern Ireland	1-1 (0-0)
06-09-1995	Vienna	Austria – Republic of Ireland	3-1 (1-0)
06-09-1995	Riga	Latvia – Liechtenstein	1-0 (0-0)
11-10-1995	Vienna	Austria – Portugal	1-1 (1-0)
11-10-1995	Dublin	Republic of Ireland – Latvia	2-1 (0-0)
11-10-1995	Eschen	Liechtenstein – Northern Ireland	0-4 (0-1)
15-11-1995	Lisbon	Portugal – Republic of Ireland	3-0 (0-0)
15-11-1995	Belfast	Northern Ireland – Austria	5-3 (2-0)

FINAL STANDING

Pos	Team	Pld	W	D	L	GF	GA	GD	Pts
1	*Portugal*	*10*	*7*	*2*	*1*	*29*	*7*	*+22*	*23*
2	*Republic of Ireland*	*10*	*5*	*2*	*3*	*17*	*11*	*+6*	*17*
3	Northern Ireland	10	5	2	3	20	15	+5	17
4	Austria	10	5	1	4	29	14	+15	16
5	Latvia	10	4	0	6	11	20	-9	12
6	Liechtenstein	10	0	1	9	1	40	-39	1

Portugal qualified for the final tournament in England.
Republic of Ireland advanced to the qualifying play-off.

20-04-1994   Windsor Park, Belfast: Northern Ireland – Liechtenstein 4-1 (3-0)
Northern Ireland: Tommy Wright, Mal Donaghy (C), Nigel Worthington, Gerry Taggart, Gary Fleming, Steve Lomas (80' Michael O'Neill), Michael Hughes, Jim Magilton, James Quinn, Iain Dowie (77' Phillip Gray), Kevin Wilson. (Coach: Bryan Hamilton (NIR)).
Liechtenstein: Martin Oehri, Mario Frick, Daniel Telser, Haral Zech (YC59), Heinrich Stocker (68' Daniel Hasler), Wolfgang Ospelt, Roland Moser (C), Alex Quaderer, Jürg Ritter, Christoph Frick, Christian Matt (64' Thomas Hanselmann). (Coach: Dietrich Weise (GER)).
Goals: Northern Ireland: 1-0 James Quinn (4'), 2-0 Steve Lomas (25'), 3-0 James Quinn (32'), 4-0 Iain Dowie (48').
Liechtenstein: 4-1 Daniel Hasler (82').
Referee: Roelof Luinge (HOL)   Attendance: 7.150

07-09-1994   Daugava Stadium, Riga: Latvia – Republic of Ireland 0-3 (0-2)
Latvia: Olegs Karavajevs, Mihails Zemlinskis, Igors Troickis, Juris Sevlakovs (C), Vitalijs Astafjevs, Valentins Lobanovs, Vladimirs Babicevs, Aleksejs Sarando, Vadims Mikuckis (63' Aleksandrs Jelisejevs), Jevgenijs Milevskis (46' Igors Vladimirovich Stepanovs (YC78)), Rolands Bulders. (Coach: Janis Gilis (LAT)).
Republic of Ireland: Alan Kelly, Steve Staunton, Gary Kelly, Denis Irwin, Paul McGrath, Phil Babb, Jason McAteer (81' Eddie McGoldrick), Andy Townsend (C), John Sheridan, John Aldridge, Niall Quinn (72' Tony Cascarino). (Coach: John (Jack) Charlton (ENG)).
Goals: Republic of Ireland: 0-1 John Aldridge (16'), 0-2 John Sheridan (29'), 0-3 John Aldridge (75' penalty).
Referee: Anders Frisk (SWE)   Attendance: 3.226

07-09-1994   Sportpark, Eschen: Liechtenstein – Austria 0-4 (0-3)
Liechtenstein: Martin Heeb, Mario Frick, Daniel Hasler, Patrick Hefti, Daniel Telser, Harald Zech (69' Christian Matt), Jürgen Ospelt, Wolfgang Ospelt (28' Thomas Hanselmann), Roland Moser (C), Alex Quaderer, Peter Klaunzer. (Coach: Dietrich Weise (GER)).
Austria: Franz Wohlfahrt, Wolfgang Feiersinger, Peter Schöttel, Jürgen Werner-Klausriegler (YC53), Peter Stöger, Christian Prosenik, Johann Kogler, Franz Aigner, Toni Polster (C), Andreas Ogris (63' Harald Cerny), Heimo Pfeifenberger (YC20) (75' Thomas Flögel). (Coach: Herbert Prohaska (AUT)).
Goals: Austria: 0-1 Toni Polster (18'), 0-2 Franz Aigner (22'), 0-3 Toni Polster (45'), 0-4 Toni Polster (79').
Referee: Wieland Ziller (GER)   Attendance: 5.800

07-09-1994   Windsor Park, Belfast: Northern Ireland – Portugal   1-2 (0-1)
Northern Ireland: Alan Fettis, Alan McDonald (C) (YC62) (83' Gerry Taggart), Nigel Worthington, Stephen Morrow, Gary Fleming (YC83), Keith Gillespie (83' George O'Boyle), Steve Lomas (YC16), Michael Hughes, Jim Magilton, James Quinn, Phillip Gray. (Coach: Bryan Hamilton (NIR)).
Portugal: VÍTOR Manuel Martins BAÍA, JOÃO Domingos da Silva PINTO (C), HÉLDER Marino Rodrigues Cristóvão, PAULO Sérgio Braga MADEIRA, LUÍS Filipe Madeira Caeiro FIGO, RUI Manuel César COSTA, PAULO Manuel Carvalho de SOUSA (YC60), VÍTOR Manuel da Costa Araújo PANEIRA (63' ANTÓNIO José dos Santos FOLHA), João Paulo Maio dos "PAULINHO" SANTOS, JOSÉ Fernando Gomes TAVARES, Ricardo Manuel Andrade Silva SÁ PINTO (YC55) (80' DOMINGOS José Paciência DE OLIVEIRA). (Coach: ANTÓNIO Luis Alves Ribeiro OLIVEIRA (POR)).
Goals: Northern Ireland: 1-1 James Quinn (58' penalty).
Portugal: 0-1 RUI Manuel César COSTA (8'), 1-2 DOMINGOS José Paciência DE OLIVEIRA (81').
Referee: Rune Pedersen (NOR)   Attendance: 6.301

09-10-1994   Daugava Stadium, Riga: Latvia – Portugal   1-3 (0-1)
Latvia: Olegs Karavajevs, Mihails Zemlinskis, Igors Troickis, Juris Sevlakovs (C), Dzintars Sprogis (65' Boris Monjaks), Valerijs Ivanovs, Vitalijs Astafjevs, Vladimirs Babicevs (YC44), Igors Vladimirovich Stepanovs (YC36), Aleksandrs Glazovs (46' Jevgenijs Milevskis), Aleksejs Semjonovs. (Coach: Janis Gilis (LAT)).
Portugal: VÍTOR Manuel Martins BAÍA, JOÃO Domingos da Silva PINTO (C), HÉLDER Marino Rodrigues Cristóvão, PAULO Sérgio Braga MADEIRA, LUÍS Filipe Madeira Caeiro FIGO (81' JOSÉ Fernando Gomes TAVARES), RUI Manuel César COSTA, PAULO Manuel Carvalho de SOUSA, VÍTOR Manuel da Costa Araújo PANEIRA (60' PAULO Lourenço Martins ALVES), Manuel António COUTO GUIMARÃES, JOÃO Manuel Vieira PINTO, DOMINGOS José Paciência DE OLIVEIRA. (Coach: ANTÓNIO Luis Alves Ribeiro OLIVEIRA (POR)).
Goals: Latvia: 1-3 Jevgenijs Milevskis (87').
Portugal: 0-1 JOÃO Manuel Vieira PINTO (31'), 0-2 JOÃO Manuel Vieira PINTO (69'), 0-3 LUÍS Filipe Madeira Caeiro FIGO (70').
Referee: Eric Blareau (BEL)   Attendance: 1.200

12-10-1994   Ernst-Happel-Stadion, Vienna: Austria – Northern Ireland   1-2 (1-2)
Austria: Franz Wohlfahrt, Wolfgang Feiersinger, Peter Schöttel (YC40), Jürgen Werner-Klausriegler, Peter Stöger, Peter Artner (YC38), Adolf Hütter, Christian Prosenik (66' Heimo Pfeifenberger), Johann Kogler, Toni Polster (C), Andreas Ogris (46' Ralf Hasenhüttl). (Coach: Herbert Prohaska (AUT)).
Northern Ireland: Paul Kee, Alan McDonald (C) (YC9), Nigel Worthington (YC58), Gerry Taggart, Gary Fleming, Keith Gillespie (56' Michael O'Neill), Steve Lomas (YC70), Michael Hughes, Jim Magilton, Iain Dowie (73' James Quinn), Phillip Gray. (Coach: Bryan Hamilton (NIR)).
Goals: Austria: 1-1 Toni Polster (24' penalty).
Northern Ireland: 0-1 Keith Gillespie (2'), 1-2 Phillip Gray (36').
Referee: Antonio Jesús López Nieto (ESP)   Attendance: 19.742

12-10-1994 Lansdowne Road, Dublin: Republic of Ireland – Liechtenstein 4-0 (3-0)
Republic of Ireland: Pat Bonner (C), Steve Staunton, Gary Kelly, Denis Irwin (46' Alain McLoughlin), Phil Babb, Alan Kernaghan, Jason McAteer, John Sheridan, Eddie McGoldrick, Tommy Coyne, Niall Quinn. (Coach: John (Jack) Charlton (ENG)).
Liechtenstein: Martin Heeb, Mario Frick (YC67), Patrick Hefti, Daniel Telser, Harald Zech, Thomas Hanselmann, Wolfgang Ospelt, Roland Moser (C) (YC67), Jürg Ritter (YC54), Modestus Haas (YC74) (78' Peter Klaunzer), Armin Heidegger (72' Christian Matt). (Coach: Dietrich Weise (GER)).
Goals: Republic of Ireland: 1-0 Tommy Coyne (3'), 2-0 Tommy Coyne (5'), 3-0 Niall Quinn (31'), 4-0 Niall Quinn (82').
Referee: Bragi Bergmann (ISL)   Attendance: 32.980

13-11-1994 Estádio da Luz, Lisbon: Portugal – Austria 1-0 (1-0)
Portugal: VÍTOR Manuel Martins BAÍA, JOÃO Domingos da Silva PINTO (C), HÉLDER Marino Rodrigues Cristóvão, PAULO Sérgio Braga MADEIRA, LUÍS Filipe Madeira Caeiro FIGO (YC79), RUI Manuel César COSTA (85' DOMINGOS José Paciência DE OLIVEIRA), PAULO Manuel Carvalho de SOUSA, OCEANO Andrade da Cruz, João Paulo Maio dos "PAULINHO" SANTOS, JOÃO Manuel Vieira PINTO (YC79), Ricardo Manuel Andrade Silva SÁ PINTO (YC50) (71' VÍTOR Manuel da Costa Araújo PANEIRA). (Coach: ANTÓNIO Luis Alves Ribeiro OLIVEIRA (POR)).
Austria: Otto Konrad, Thomas Winklhofer (YC80), Wolfgang Feiersinger (YC6), Peter Schöttel (YC16), Christian Fürstaller, Dietmar Kühbauer (YC33) (46' Christian Prosenik), Harald Cerny (71' Adolf Hütter), Peter Stöger (RC82), Peter Artner, Johann Kogler (YC77), Toni Polster (C). (Coach: Herbert Prohaska (AUT)).
Goal: Portugal: 1-0 LUÍS Filipe Madeira Caeiro FIGO (37').
Referee: Peter Mikkelsen (DEN)   Attendance: 22.273

15-11-1994 Sportpark, Eschen: Liechtenstein – Latvia 0-1 (0-1)
Liechtenstein: Martin Heeb, Mario Frick, Daniel Hasler, Patrick Hefti, Daniel Telser, Harald Zech (59' Peter Klaunzer), Roland Hilti, Wolfgang Ospelt, Roland Moser (C), Jürg Ritter, Armin Heidegger (58' Rolf Oehri). (Coach: Dietrich Weise (GER)).
Latvia: Olegs Karavajevs, Mihails Zemlinskis, Igors Troickis, Juris Sevlakovs (C), Dzintars Sprogis, Valerijs Ivanovs, Olegs Blagonadezdins (46' Vadims Mikuckis), Vitalijs Astafjevs (YC70), Vladimirs Babicevs (72' Aleksejs Sarando), Aleksejs Semjonovs, Jevgenijs Milevskis. (Coach: Janis Gilis (LAT)).
Goal: Latvia: 0-1 Vladimirs Babicevs (14').
Referee: Piotr Werner (POL)   Attendance: 1.300

16-11-1994 Windsor Park, Belfast: Northern Ireland – Republic of Ireland 0-4 (0-3)
Northern Ireland: Paul Kee, Nigel Worthington, Gerry Taggart, Stephen Morrow (C), Gary Fleming, Keith Gillespie (62' Kevin Wilson), Michael Hughes, Michael O'Neill (46' Darren Patterson), Jim Magilton (YC14), Iain Dowie, Phillip Gray. (Coach: Bryan Hamilton (NIR)).
Republic of Ireland: Alan Kelly, Steve Staunton, Gary Kelly, Denis Irwin, Paul McGrath, Phil Babb, Andy Townsend (C), John Sheridan (80' Tommy Coyne), Roy Keane (44' Jason McAteer), John Aldridge, Niall Quinn. (Coach: John (Jack) Charlton (ENG)).
Goals: Republic of Ireland: 0-1 John Sheridan (6'), 0-2 Roy Keane (11'), 0-3 John Aldridge (38'), 0-4 Andy Townsend (54').
Referee: Serge Muhmenthaler (SUI)   Attendance: 10.336

18-12-1994   Estádio da Luz, Lisbon: Portugal – Liechtenstein   8-0 (3-0)
Portugal: VÍTOR Manuel Martins BAÍA, FERNANDO Manuel Silva COUTO, JOÃO Domingos da Silva PINTO (C), LUÍS Filipe Madeira Caeiro FIGO, RUI Manuel César COSTA, VÍTOR Manuel da Costa Araújo PANEIRA (57' PAULO Lourenço Martins ALVES), OCEANO Andrade da Cruz, João Paulo Maio dos "PAULINHO" SANTOS, ANTÓNIO José dos Santos FOLHA, JOÃO Manuel Vieira PINTO (70' CARLOS Alberto de Oliveira SECRETÁRIO), DOMINGOS José Paciência DE OLIVEIRA. (Coach: ANTÓNIO Luis Alves Ribeiro OLIVEIRA (POR)).
Liechtenstein: Martin Heeb, Mario Frick, Daniel Hasler (59' Christian Matt), Patrick Hefti, Daniel Telser, Harald Zech, Roland Hilti, Wolfgang Ospelt (46' Rolf Oehri (YC62)), Roland Moser (C), Jürg Ritter, Armin Heidegger. (Coach: Dietrich Weise (GER)).
Goals: Portugal: 1-0 DOMINGOS José Paciência DE OLIVEIRA (3'), 2-0 DOMINGOS José Paciência DE OLIVEIRA (12'), 3-0 OCEANO Andrade da Cruz (45'), 4-0 JOÃO Manuel Vieira PINTO (57'), 5-0 FERNANDO Manuel Silva COUTO (73'), 6-0 ANTÓNIO José dos Santos FOLHA (74'), 7-0 PAULO Lourenço Martins ALVES (75'), 8-0 PAULO Lourenço Martins ALVES (79').
Referee: Lubomír Pucek (CZE)   Attendance: 22.800

29-03-1995   Lansdowne Road, Dublin: Republic of Ireland – Northern Ireland   1-1 (0-0)
Republic of Ireland: Alan Kelly, Steve Staunton, Gary Kelly, Denis Irwin, Paul McGrath, Phil Babb, Andy Townsend (C), John Sheridan (YC80), Roy Keane, Niall Quinn (82' Tony Cascarino), David Kelly (YC9) (74' Jason McAteer). (Coach: John (Jack) Charlton (ENG)).
Northern Ireland: Alan Fettis, Alan McDonald (C) (YC8), Nigel Worthington, Gerry Taggart, Colin Hill, Stephen Morrow, Darren Patterson, Keith Gillespie, Michael Hughes, Jim Magilton, Iain Dowie. (Coach: Bryan Hamilton (NIR)).
Goals: Republic of Ireland: 1-0 Niall Quinn (47').
Northern Ireland: 1-1 Iain Dowie (73').
Referee: Mario van der Ende (HOL)   Attendance: 32.200

29-03-1995   Lehener Stadion, Salzburg: Austria – Latvia   5-0 (2-0)
Austria: Otto Konrad, Wolfgang Feiersinger, Christian Fürstaller, Dietmar Kühbauer, Andreas Herzog, Peter Artner (75' Adolf Hütter), Johann Kogler, Stephan Marasek, Toni Polster (C), Andreas Ogris (YC24) (46' Dieter Ramusch), Heimo Peifenberger. (Coach: Herbert Prohaska (AUT)).
Latvia: Raimonds Laizans, Mihails Zemlinskis (YC40) (67' Vadims Mikuckis), Igors Troickis (YC24), Juris Sevlakovs (C), Dzintars Sprogis (YC7), Boris Monjaks, Olegs Blagonadezdins, Vitalijs Astafjevs, Valentins Lobanovs (RC69), Vladimirs Babicevs (73' Andrejs Stolcers), Vitalijs Teplovs. (Coach: Janis Gilis (LAT)).
Goals: Austria: 1-0 Andreas Herzog (17'), 2-0 Heimo Peifenberger (40'), 3-0 Andreas Herzog (59'), 4-0 Toni Polster (69' penalty), 5-0 Toni Polster (90+1').
Referee: Charles Agius (MLT)   Attendance: 5.262

26-04-1995   Daugava Stadium, Riga: Latvia – Northern Ireland   0-1 (0-0)
Latvia: Raimonds Laizans, Igors Stepanovs, Mihails Zemlinskis, Igors Troickis, Juris Sevlakovs (C), Dzintars Sprogis, Olegs Blagonadezdins (29' Rihards Butkus, 71' Boris Monjaks), Vitalijs Astafjevs, Vladimirs Babicevs, Aleksandrs Jelisejevs, Vitalijs Teplovs (YC54). (Coach: Janis Gilis (LAT)).
Northern Ireland: Alan Fettis, Alan McDonald (C), Nigel Worthington, Colin Hill, Darren Patterson, Barry Hunter, Keith Gillespie (YC65) (78' George O'Boyle), Michael Hughes (YC90), Kevin Horlock, Iain Dowie (80' James Quinn), Kevin Wilson. (Coach: Bryan Hamilton (NIR)).
Goal: Northern Ireland: 0-1 Iain Dowie (70' penalty).
Referee: Finn Lambeck (DEN)   Attendance: 1.560

26-04-1995   Lehener Stadion, Salzburg: Austria – Liechtenstein   7-0 (3-0)
Austria: Otto Konrad, Wolfgang Feiersinger, Christian Fürstaller (71' Adolf Hütter), Dieter Ramusch, Dietmar Kühbauer, Andreas Herzog, Peter Artner, Johann Kogler, Stephan Marasek, Toni Polster (C), Herfried Sabitzer (69' Markus Pürk). (Coach: Herbert Prohaska (AUT)).
Liechtenstein: Martin Oehri, Daniel Hasler, Daniel Telser, Harald Zech, Heinrich Stocker, Roland Hilti (YC49), Jürgen Ospelt, Roland Moser (C) (YC53), Rolf Oehri (46' Patrik Marxer (YC88)), Jürg Ritter (65' Christian Matt), Alex Burgmeier. (Coach: Dietrich Weise (GER)).
Goals: Austria: 1-0 Dietmar Kühbauer (8'), 2-0 Toni Polster (11'), 3-0 Herfried Sabitzer (17'), 4-0 Toni Polster (54' penalty), 5-0 Markus Pürk (84'), 6-0 Adolf Hütter (87'), 7-0 Adolf Hütter (89').
Referee: Vasyl Hryhorovych Melnychuk (UKR)   Attendance: 5.700

26-04-1995   Lansdowne Road, Dublin: Republic of Ireland – Portugal   1-0 (1-0)
Republic of Ireland: Alan Kelly, Steve Staunton, Gary Kelly, Denis Irwin, Paul McGrath, Phil Babb, Andy Townsend (C), Ray Houghton (85' Alan Kernaghan), John Sheridan, John Aldridge (85' Jeff Kenna), Niall Quinn. (Coach: John (Jack) Charlton (ENG)).
Portugal: VÍTOR Manuel Martins BAÍA, FERNANDO Manuel Silva COUTO, JORGE Paulo COSTA Almeida, JOÃO Domingos da Silva PINTO (C), HÉLDER Marino Rodrigues Cristóvão (64' ANTÓNIO José dos Santos FOLHA), LUÍS Filipe Madeira Caeiro FIGO (76' PEDRO Alexandre dos Santos BARBOSA), RUI Manuel César COSTA, PAULO Manuel Carvalho de SOUSA, João Paulo Maio dos "PAULINHO" SANTOS, JOÃO Manuel Vieira PINTO, DOMINGOS José Paciência DE OLIVEIRA. (Coach: ANTÓNIO Luis Alves Ribeiro OLIVEIRA (POR)).
Goal: Republic of Ireland: 1-0 Steve Staunton (44').
Referee: Christer Fällström (SWE)   Attendance: 33.500

03-06-1995 Estádio das Antas, Porto: Portugal – Latvia 3-2 (3-0)
Portugal: VÍTOR Manuel Martins BAÍA (C), FERNANDO Manuel Silva COUTO, JORGE Paulo COSTA Almeida, CARLOS Alberto de Oliveira SECRETÁRIO, FERNANDO Jesus Vieira Alves NÉLSON (80' PEDRO Alexandre dos Santos BARBOSA), LUÍS Filipe Madeira Caeiro FIGO, RUI Manuel César COSTA, PAULO Manuel Carvalho de SOUSA (YC34) (46' PAULO Jorge FUTRE dos Santos), João Paulo Maio dos "PAULINHO" SANTOS, ANTÓNIO José dos Santos FOLHA, DOMINGOS José Paciência DE OLIVEIRA. (Coach: ANTÓNIO Luis Alves Ribeiro OLIVEIRA (POR)).
Latvia: Raimonds Laizans, Mihails Zemlinskis (YC52), Igors Troickis, Juris Sevlakovs (C), Valerijs Ivanovs, Boris Monjaks, Vitalijs Astafjevs, Imants Bleidelis (38' Vladimirs Babicevs), Armands Zeiberlins, Vits Rimkus, Vitalijs Teplovs (60' Dzintars Sprogis). (Coach: Janis Gilis (LAT)).
Goals: Portugal: 1-0 LUÍS Filipe Madeira Caeiro FIGO (5'), 2-0 CARLOS Alberto de Oliveira SECRETÁRIO (19'), 3-0 DOMINGOS José Paciência DE OLIVEIRA (20').
Latvia: 3-1 Vits Rimkus (51'), 3-2 Vits Rimkus (82').
Referee: Zoran Petrovic (YUG)   Attendance: 26.619

03-06-1995 Sportpark, Eschen: Liechtenstein – Republic of Ireland 0-0
Liechtenstein: Martin Heeb, Mario Frick, Daniel Hasler, Daniel Telser, Harald Zech, Thomas Hanselmann, Roland Hilti, Jürgen Ospelt (33' Jürgen Zech), Wolfgang Ospelt (C) (YC37) (62' Patrik Marxer), Jürg Ritter, Alex Burgmeier. (Coach: Dietrich Weise (GER)).
Republic of Ireland: Alan Kelly, Steve Staunton, Gary Kelly, Denis Irwin, Paul McGrath, Phil Babb, Jason McAteer (71' Jeff Kenna), John Sheridan, Ronnie Whelan (C) (YC45), John Aldridge (YC67), Niall Quinn (59' Tony Cascarino). (Coach: John (Jack) Charlton (ENG)).
Referee: Charles Agius (MLT)   Attendance: 4.500

07-06-1995 Windsor Park, Belfast: Northern Ireland – Latvia 1-2 (1-0)
Northern Ireland: Alan Fettis, Alan McDonald (C) (YC49), Nigel Worthington, Gerry Taggart, Stephen Morrow, Keith Rowland (63' Keith Gillespie), Patrick McGibbon (46' Darren Patterson), Michael Hughes, Gerard McMahon, Jim Magilton, Iain Dowie (YC67). (Coach: Bryan Hamilton (NIR)).
Latvia: Raimonds Laizans (YC84), Artūrs Zakresevskis (YC48), Igors Troickis (C), Dzintars Sprogis, Valerijs Ivanovs, Boris Monjaks (YC44), Vitalijs Astafjevs, Imants Bleidelis (YC70), Vladimirs Babicevs (82' Vitalijs Teplovs), Armands Zeiberlins, Vits Rimkus (69' Aleksandrs Jelisejevs). (Coach: Janis Gilis (LAT)).
Goals: Northern Ireland: 1-0 Iain Dowie (44').
Latvia: 1-1 Armands Zeiberlins (57'), 1-2 Vitalijs Astafjevs (61').
Referee: Juan Ansuátegui Roca (ESP)   Attendance: 6.935

11-06-1995 Lansdowne Road, Dublin: Republic of Ireland – Austria 1-3 (0-0)
Republic of Ireland: Alan Kelly, Steve Staunton (46' Jeff Kenna), Gary Kelly, Denis Irwin, Paul McGrath, Phil Babb, Ray Houghton, John Sheridan, Ronnie Whelan (C) (YC74), Tommy Coyne, Niall Quinn (57' Tony Cascarino). (Coach: John (Jack) Charlton (ENG)).
Austria: Michael Konsel, Anton Pfeffer, Peter Schöttel, Christian Fürstaller, Dieter Ramusch (71' Andreas Ogris), Dietmar Kühbauer (YC78), Christian Prosenik, Johann Kogler, Stephan Marasek, Toni Polster (C) (YC57), Heimo Pfeifenberger (82' Adolf Hütter). (Coach: Herbert Prohaska (AUT)).
Goals: Republic of Ireland: 1-0 Ray Houghton (67').
Austria: 1-1 Toni Polster (69'), 1-2 Andreas Ogris (74'), 1-3 Toni Polster (78').
Referee: Markus Merk (GER)   Attendnce: 33.000

15-08-1995   Sportpark, Eschen: Liechtenstein – Portugal   0-7 (0-3)
Liechtenstein: Martin Heeb, Mario Frick, Daniel Hasler, Daniel Telser (66' Rolf Oehri), Harald Zech (YC8), Thomas Hanselmann, Heinrich Stocker (46' Christoph Frick), Roland Hilti, Jürgen Zech, Roland Moser (C), Peter Klaunzer (46' Patrik Marxer). (Coach: Dietrich Weise (GER)).
Portugal: ALFREDO da Silva Castro (82' RUI MANUEL dion Silva Correia), FERNANDO Manuel Silva COUTO, JORGE Paulo COSTA Almeida (YC78), CARLOS Alberto de Oliveira SECRETÁRIO, DIMAS Manuel Marques Teixeira (55' PAULO Lourenço Martins ALVES), RUI Manuel César COSTA, OCEANO Andrade da Cruz (C) (46' Ricardo Manuel Andrade Silva SÁ PINTO (YC84)), João Paulo Maio dos "PAULINHO" SANTOS, ANTÓNIO José dos Santos FOLHA, RUI Gil Soares de BARROS, DOMINGOS José Paciência DE OLIVEIRA. (Coach: ANTÓNIO Luis Alves Ribeiro OLIVEIRA (POR)).
Goals: Portugal: 0-1 DOMINGOS José Paciência DE OLIVEIRA (25'), 0-2 João Paulo Maio dos "PAULINHO" SANTOS (33'), 0-3 RUI Manuel César COSTA (41'), 0-4 PAULO Lourenço Martins ALVES (66'), 0-5 RUI Manuel César COSTA (70' penalty), 0-5 PAULO Lourenço Martins ALVES (73'), 0-7 PAULO Lourenço Martins ALVES (90').
Referee: Dragutin Karlo Poljak (CRO)   Attendance: 3.500

16-08-1995   Daugava Stadium, Riga: Latvia – Austria   3-2 (1-0)
Latvia: Raimonds Laizans, Artūrs Zakresevskis (82' Boris Monjaks), Mihails Zemlinskis, Igors Troickis, Juris Sevjakovs (C), Valerijs Ivanovs, Vitalijs Astafjevs, Imants Bleidelis, Vladimirs Babicevs (76' Aleksandrs Jelisejevs), Armands Zeiberlins (YC24), Vits Rimkus. (Coach: Janis Gilis (LAT)).
Austria: Otto Konrad, Anton Pfeffer, Wolfgang Feiersinger (YC81), Walter Kogler, Peter Schöttel, Christian Prosenik (YC44) (64' Dieter Ramusch), Johann Kogler (46' Markus Schopp), Stephan Marasek, Toni Polster (C), Andreas Ogris (64' Peter Stöger), Heimo Pfeifenberger. (Coach: Herbert Prohaska (AUT)).
Goals: Latvia: 1-0 Vits Rimkus (12'), 2-0 Vits Rimkus (59'), 3-2 Armands Zeiberlins (88').
Austria: 2-1 Toni Polster (69'), 2-2 Dieter Ramusch (78').
Referee: Ilkka Koho (FIN)   Attendance: 2.600

03-09-1995   Estádio das Antas, Porto: Portugal – Northern Ireland   1-1 (0-0)
Portugal: VÍTOR Manuel Martins BAÍA (C), FERNANDO Manuel Silva COUTO, JORGE Paulo COSTA Almeida (73' RUI Gil Soares de BARROS), CARLOS Alberto de Oliveira SECRETÁRIO, LUÍS Filipe Madeira Caeiro FIGO (YC22), RUI Manuel César COSTA (82' PAULO Lourenço Martins ALVES), PAULO Manuel Carvalho de SOUSA, OCEANO Andrade da Cruz, João Paulo Maio dos "PAULINHO" SANTOS (YC60), ANTÓNIO José dos Santos FOLHA, DOMINGOS José Paciência DE OLIVEIRA. (Coach: ANTÓNIO Luis Alves Ribeiro OLIVEIRA (POR)).
Northern Ireland: Alan Fettis, Nigel Worthington (C), Colin Hill, Stephen Morrow, Barry Hunter, Keith Gillespie (YC60), Steve Lomas, Michael Hughes, Neil Lennon, Jim Magilton (78' Keith Rowland), Iain Dowie (YC34) (76' Phillip Gray). (Coach: Bryan Hamilton (NIR)).
Goals: Portugal: 1-0 DOMINGOS José Paciência DE OLIVEIRA (47').
Northern Ireland: 1-1 Michael Hughes (66').
Referee: Rémi Harrel (FRA)   Attendance: 26.780

06-09-1995   Ernst-Happel-Stadion, Vienna: Austria – Republic of Ireland   3-1 (1-0)
Austria: Michael Konsel, Anton Pfeffer, Peter Schöttel (YC45), Christian Fürstaller, Markus Schopp, Dietmar Kühbauer, Andreas Herzog, Peter Stöger, Stephan Marasek, Toni Polster (C) (79' Harald Cerny), Heimo Pfeifenberger. (Coach: Herbert Prohaska (AUT)).
Republic of Ireland: Alan Kelly, Gary Kelly, Denis Irwin, Paul McGrath, Alan Kernaghan, Mark Kennedy (YC61), Andy Townsend (C) (YC26), Ray Houghton (67' Tony Cascarino), John Sheridan, Roy Keane (YC81), Niall Quinn. (Coach: John (Jack) Charlton (ENG)).
Goals: Austria: 1-0 Peter Stöger (3'), 2-0 Peter Stöger (64'), 3-1 Peter Stöger (77').
Republic of Ireland: 2-1 Paul McGrath (74').
Referee: Ahmet Çakar (TUR)   Attendance: 24.000

06-09-1995   Daugava Stadium, Riga: Latvia – Liechtenstein   1-0 (0-0)
Latvia: Olegs Karavajevs, Mihails Zemlinskis, Igors Troickis, Juris Sevjakovs (C), Valerijs Ivanovs, Boris Monjaks, Vitalijs Astafjevs, Imants Bleidelis (31' Rolands Bulders), Vladimirs Babicevs (74' Juris Karasauskas), Armands Zeiberlins, Vits Rimkus. (Coach: Janis Gilis (LAT)).
Liechtenstein: Martin Heeb, Mario Frick (C) (YC51), Daniel Hasler, Daniel Telser, Heinrich Stocker (88' Peter Klaunzer), Roland Hilti, Jürgen Zech, Rolf Oehri (62' Herbert Bicker), Patrik Marxer (72' Daniel Frick), Christoph Frick, Harry Schädler. (Coach: Dietrich Weise (GER)).
Goal: Latvia: 1-0 Armands Zeiberlins (83').
Referee: Tom Henning Øvrebø (NOR)   Attendance: 3.800

11-10-1995   Ernst-Happel-Stadion, Vienna: Austria – Portugal   1-1 (1-0)
Austria: Michael Konsel, Anton Pfeffer, Wolfgang Feiersinger, Peter Schöttel (YC10), Markus Schopp, Dietmar Kühbauer, Andreas Herzog, Peter Stöger, Stephan Marasek, Toni Polster (C) (82' Harald Cerny), Heimo Pfeifenberger. (Coach: Herbert Prohaska (AUT)).
Portugal: VÍTOR Manuel Martins BAÍA (C), JORGE Paulo COSTA Almeida (YC78), CARLOS Alberto de Oliveira SECRETÁRIO (58' Ricardo Manuel Andrade Silva SÁ PINTO (YC69)), HÉLDER Marino Rodrigues Cristóvão, FERNANDO Jesus Vieira Alves NÉLSON, RUI Manuel César COSTA, PAULO Manuel Carvalho de SOUSA, OCEANO Andrade da Cruz, João Paulo Maio dos "PAULINHO" SANTOS, JOÃO Manuel Vieira PINTO (46' ANTÓNIO José dos Santos FOLHA), DOMINGOS José Paciência DE OLIVEIRA (71' JOSÉ Manuel Martins DOMINGUEZ). (Coach: ANTÓNIO Luis Alves Ribeiro OLIVEIRA (POR)).
Goals: Austria: 1-0 Peter Stöger (21').
Portugal: 1-1 João Paulo Maio dos "PAULINHO" SANTOS (49').
Referee: Nikolai Vladislavovich Levnikov (RUS)   Attendance: 44.000

11-10-1995   Lansdowne Road, Dublin: Republic of Ireland – Latvia   2-1 (0-0)
Republic of Ireland: Alan Kelly, Jeff Kenna, Steve Staunton, Gary Kelly, Terry Phelan, Paul McGrath (YC41), Phil Babb, Jason McAteer, Andy Townsend (C), John Aldridge (79' David Kelly, 84' Mark Kennedy), Niall Quinn (YC68). (Coach: John (Jack) Charlton (ENG)).
Latvia: Olegs Karavajevs, Igors Stepanovs, Artūrs Zakresevskis, Mihails Zemlinskis, Igors Troickis, Juris Sevjakovs (C), Valerijs Ivanovs, Vitalijs Astafjevs (YC26), Vladimirs Babicevs (71' Aleksandrs Jelisejevs), Armands Zeiberlins, Vits Rimkus. (Coach: Janis Gilis (LAT)).
Goals: Republic of Ireland: 1-0 John Aldridge (61' penalty), 2-0 John Aldridge (64').
Latvia: 2-1 Vits Rimkus (78').
Referee: Juan Antonio Fernández Marín (ESP)   Attendance: 33.500

11-10-1995   Sportpark, Eschen: Liechtenstein – Northern Ireland   0-4 (0-1)
Liechtenstein: Martin Oehri (C), Daniel Hasler, Patrick Hefti, Daniel Telser, Harald Zech, Heinrich Stocker (46' Rolf Sele), Roland Hilti (66' Jürgen Ospelt), Peter Klaunzer, Rolf Oehri, Christoph Frick (78' Thomas Hanselmann), Franz Schädler. (Coach: Dietrich Weise (GER)).
Northern Ireland: Alan Fettis (76' Trevor Wood), Nigel Worthington (C), Colin Hill, Barry Hunter, Steve Lomas, Michael Hughes (90' Keith Rowland), Gerard McMahon (81' Patrick McGibbon), Neil Lennon, Michael O'Neill, James Quinn, Phillip Gray. (Coach: Bryan Hamilton (NIR)).
Goals: Northern Ireland: 0-1 Michael O'Neill (36'), 0-2 Gerard McMahon (49'), 0-3 James Quinn (55'), 0-4 Phillip Gray (71').
Referee: Lubos Michel (SVK)   Attendance: 1.100

15-11-1995   Estádio da Luz, Lisbon: Portugal – Republic of Ireland   3-0 (0-0)
Portugal: VÍTOR Manuel Martins BAÍA (C) (85' Adelino Augusto Barbosa BARROS "NENO"), FERNANDO Manuel Silva COUTO, CARLOS Alberto de Oliveira SECRETÁRIO, HÉLDER Marino Rodrigues Cristóvão, LUÍS Filipe Madeira Caeiro FIGO, RUI Manuel César COSTA (YC60), PAULO Manuel Carvalho de SOUSA, OCEANO Andrade da Cruz, João Paulo Maio dos "PAULINHO" SANTOS, JOÃO Manuel Vieira PINTO (71' JORGE Paulo CADETE Santos Reis), DOMINGOS José Paciência DE OLIVEIRA (71' ANTÓNIO José dos Santos FOLHA). (Coach: ANTÓNIO Luis Alves Ribeiro OLIVEIRA (POR)).
Republic of Ireland: Alan Kelly, Jeff Kenna, Steve Staunton (C) (78' Alan Kernaghan), Gary Kelly, Denis Irwin, Paul McGrath, Phil Babb (YC34), Mark Kennedy (75' Tony Cascarino), Jason McAteer, John Aldridge, Niall Quinn (YC55). (Coach: John (Jack) Charlton (ENG)).
Goals: Portugal: 1-0 RUI Manuel César COSTA (59'), 2-0 HÉLDER Marino Rodrigues Cristóvão (74'), 3-0 JORGE Paulo CADETE Santos Reis (89').
Referee: Piero Ceccarini (ITA)   Attendance: 71.766

15-11-1995   Windsor Park, Belfast: Northern Ireland – Austria   5-3 (2-0)
Northern Ireland: Alan Fettis, Nigel Worthington (C), Colin Hill, Barry Hunter, Keith Gillespie (YC88), Steve Lomas, Michael Hughes, Neil Lennon, Michael O'Neill, Iain Dowie (79' James Quinn), Phillip Gray (76' Alan McDonald). (Coach: Bryan Hamilton (NIR)).
Austria: Michael Konsel, Anton Pfeffer, Wolfgang Feiersinger, Walter Kogler, Markus Schopp (YC89), Dietmar Kühbauer (46' Christian Stumpf), Andreas Herzog (46' Arnold Wetl), Peter Stöger, Stephan Marasek, Toni Polster (C), Heimo Pfeifenberger. (Coach: Herbert Prohaska (AUT)).
Goals: Northern Ireland: 1-0 Michael O'Neill (27'), 2-0 Iain Dowie (32' penalty), 3-0 Barry Hunter (53'), 4-1 Phillip Gray (64'), 5-2 Michael O'Neill (76').
Austria: 3-1 Markus Schopp (56'), 4-2 Christian Stumpf (70'), 5-3 Arnold Wetl (81').
Referee: Leif Sundell (SWE)   Attendance: 8.451

GROUP 7

07-09-1994	Tbilisi	Georgia – Moldova	0-1 (0-1)
07-09-1994	Cardiff	Wales – Albania	2-0 (1-0)
12-10-1994	Chisinau	Moldova – Wales	3-2 (2-1)
12-10-1994	Sofia	Bulgaria – Georgia	2-0 (0-0)
16-11-1994	Tirana	Albania – Germany	1-2 (1-1)
16-11-1994	Sofia	Bulgaria – Moldova	4-1 (1-0)
16-11-1994	Tbilisi	Georgia – Wales	5-0 (2-0)

14-12-1994	Chisinau	Moldova – Germany	0-3 (0-2)
14-12-1994	Cardiff	Wales – Bulgaria	0-3 (0-2)
14-12-1994	Tirana	Albania – Georgia	0-1 (0-1)
18-12-1994	Kaiserslautern	Germany – Albania	2-1 (2-0)
29-03-1995	Tbilisi	Georgia – Germany	0-2 (0-2)
29-03-1995	Sofia	Bulgaria – Wales	3-1 (1-0)
29-03-1995	Tirana	Albania – Moldova	3-0 (2-0)
26-04-1995	Tbilisi	Georgia – Albania	2-0 (2-0)
26-04-1995	Chisinau	Moldova – Bulgaria	0-3 (0-1)
26-04-1995	Düsseldorf	Germany – Wales	1-1 (1-1)
07-06-1995	Sofia	Bulgaria – Germany	3-2 (0-2)
07-06-1995	Cardiff	Wales – Georgia	0-1 (0-0)
07-06-1995	Chisinau	Moldova – Albania	2-3 (2-2)
06-09-1995	Tiranan	Albania – Bulgaria	1-1 (1-1)
06-09-1995	Nuremberg	Germany – Georgia	4-1 (1-1)
06-09-1995	Cardiff	Wales – Moldova	1-0 (0-0)
07-10-1995	Sofia	Bulgaria – Albania	3-0 (1-0)
08-10-1995	Leverkusen	Germany – Moldova	6-1 (3-0)
11-10-1995	Tbilisi	Georgia – Bulgaria	2-1 (1-0)
11-10-1995	Cardiff	Wales – Germany	1-2 (0-0)
15-11-1995	Berlin	Germany – Bulgaria	3-1 (0-0)
15-11-1995	Tirana	Albania – Wales	1-1 (1-1)
15-11-1995	Chisinau	Moldova – Georgia	3-2 (2-0)

FINAL STANDING

Pos	Team	Pld	W	D	L	GF	GA	GD	Pts
1	Germany	10	8	1	1	27	10	+17	25
2	Bulgaria	10	7	1	2	24	10	+14	22
3	Georgia	10	5	0	5	14	13	+1	15
4	Moldova	10	3	0	7	11	27	-16	9
5	Wales	10	2	2	6	9	19	-10	8
6	Albania	10	2	2	6	10	16	-6	8

Germany and Bulgaria qualified for the final tournament in England.

07-09-1994   Boris Paichadze Stadium, Tbilisi: Georgia – Moldova 0-1 (0-1)
Georgia: Irakli Zoidze, Kakhaber Tskhadadze (C), Murtaz Shelia, Georgi Nemsadze (YC81), Mikheil Kavelashvili, Revaz Arveladze (69' Zaza Revishvili), Archil Arveladze, Gocha Jamarauli, Giorgi Kinkladze, Shota Arveladze, Guia Guruli (YC22) (46' Gela Inalishvili). (Coach: Alexandr Chivadze (GEO)).
Moldova: Vasile Coselev (YC47), Serghei Stroenco, Sergiu Secu (YC17), Valerii Pogorelov, Alexandr Curtianu, Serghei Belous, Andrei Stroenco (YC49) (54' Radu Rebeja), Igor Oprea, Alexandru Spiridon (C) (81' Volodymyr Cosse), Serghei Nani, Serghei Clescenco. (Coach: Ion Caras (MOL)).
Goals: Moldova: 0-1 Igor Oprea (40').
Referee: Ahmet Çakar (TUR)   Attendance: 62.000

07-09-1994   Cardiff Arms Park, Cardiff: Wales – Albania   2-0 (1-0)
Wales: Neville Southall, Adrian Williams, Andy Melville, Chris Coleman, Paul Bodin (YC90), Gary Speed, Ryan Giggs, David Phillips, Jeremy Goss (75' Mark Pembridge), Nathan Blake (80' Iwan Roberts), Ian Rush (C). (Coach: Michael John (Mike) Smith (ENG)).
Albania: Fotaq (Foto) Strakosha, Rudi Vata (Foto) Strakosha, Rudi Vata (YC67), Salvador Kaçaj, Ilir Shulku (YC70), Arian Xhumba, Sulejman Demollari (C), Bledar Kola, Arian Bellaj, Agostin Kola (53' Indrit Fortuzi), Ylli Shehu (80' Edmond Dosti), Ledio Pano. (Coach: Neptun Bajko (ALB)).
Goals: Wales: 1-0 Chris Coleman (6'), 2-0 Ryan Giggs (67').
Referee: Gianni Beschin (ITA)   Attendance: 15.791

12-10-1994   Stadionul Republican, Chisinau: Moldova – Wales   3-2 (2-1)
Moldova: Vasile Coselev, Serghei Stroenco, Sergiu Secu, Valerii Pogorelov, Radu Rebeja (YC54), Alexandr Curtianu, Serghei Belous (85' Emilian Caras), Igor Oprea, Alexandru Spiridon (C) (YC81), Serghei Nani, Iurii Miterev (46' Volodymyr Cosse). (Coach: Ion Caras (MOL)).
Wales: Neville Southall, Adrian Williams, Chris Coleman (YC34), Mark Bowen, Kit Symons, Gary Speed, Mark Pembridge, Barry Horne (C), David Phillips, Nathan Blake (85' Andy Melville), Iwan Roberts (YC54). (Coach: Michael John (Mike) Smith (ENG)).
Goals: Moldova: 1-1 Radu Rebeja (8'), 2-1 Sergiu Secu (28'), 3-2 Valerii Pogorelov (80').
Wales: 0-1 Gary Speed (6'), 2-2 Nathan Blake (70').
Referee: István Vad (HUN)   Attendance: 12.000

12-10-1994   Vasil Levski National Stadium, Sofia: Bulgaria – Georgia   2-0 (0-0)
Bulgaria: Dimitar Popov, Trifon Ivanov, Tsanko Tsvetanov, Petar Hubchev, Daniel Borimirov (54' Emil Kostadinov), Zlatko Yankov (YC73), Yordan Lechkov, Nasko Sirakov (69' Luboslav Penev), Ilyan Kiryakov, Hristo Stoichkov (C), Krasimir Balakov. (Coach: Dimitar Penev (BUL)).
Georgia: Akaki Devadze, Kakhaber Tskhadadze (C) (YC31), Murtaz Shelia, Zaza Revishvili, George Chikhradze, Georgi Nemsadze (71' Gela Inalishvili), Giorgi Kinkladze, Kakha Gogichaishvili, Dimitri Kudinovi (YC6), Temur Ketsbaia, Shota Arveladze (77' Guia Guruli). (Coach: Alexandr Chivadze (GEO)).
Goals: Bulgaria: 1-0 Emil Kostadinov (55'), 2-0 Emil Kostadinov (62').
Referee: Ladislav Gadosi (SVK)   Attendance: 48.000

16-11-1994   Qemal Stafa Stadium, Tirana: Albania – Germany   1-2 (1-1)
Albania: Fotaq (Foto) Strakosha, Rudi Vata, Salvador Kaçaj (YC22), Arian Xhumba, Hysen Zmijani (66' Ledio Pano (YC82)), Sulejman Demollari (C) (56' Bledar Kola), Artur Tushe Lekbello (II), Lefter Millo, Arian Bellaj (YC80), Sokol Kushta, Altin Rraklli. (Coach: Neptun Bajko (ALB)).
Germany: Andreas Köpke, Jürgen Kohler, Thomas Berthold, Stefan Reuter, Lothar Matthäus (C), Andreas Möller, Matthias Sammer (46' Thomas Strunz (YC88)), Dieter Eilts, Ralf Weber (82' Dirk Schuster), Ulf Kirsten, Jürgen Klinsmann. (Coach: Hans-Hubert (Berti) Vogts (GER)).
Goals: Albania: 1-1 Hysen Zmijani (33').
Germany: 0-1 Jürgen Klinsmann (18'), 1-2 Ulf Kirsten (46').
Referee: Vasyl Hryhorovych Melnychuk (UKR)   Attendance: 18.500

16-11-1994 Vasil Levski National Stadium, Sofia: Bulgaria – Moldova 4-1 (1-0)
Bulgaria: Borislav Mihaylov (C), Trifon Ivanov, Tsanko Tsvetanov, Petar Hubchev, Ivaylo Yordanov, Yordan Lechkov (86' Stanimir Stoilov), Ilyan Kiryakov, Hristo Stoichkov, Emil Kostadinov, Luboslav Penev (79' Nasko Sirakov), Krasimir Balakov. (Coach: Dimitar Penev (BUL)).
Moldova: Vasile Coselev, Serghei Stroenco (YC27), Sergiu Secu, Valerii Pogorelov, Radu Rebeja, Alexandr Curtianu (80' Volodymyr Cosse), Serghei Belous, Igor Oprea, Alexandru Spiridon (C), Serghei Nani, Serghei Clescenco. (Coach: Ion Caras (MOL)).
Goals: Bulgaria: 1-0 Hristo Stoichkov (44'), 2-1 Krasimir Balakov (64'), 3-1 Hristo Stoichkov (84'), 4-1 Emil Kostadinov (87').
Moldova: 1-1 Serghei Clescenco (61').
Referee: Denis McArdle (IRL)   Attendance: 36.048

16-11-1994 Boris Paicahdze Stadium, Tbilisi: Georgia – Wales 5-0 (2-0)
Georgia: Akaki Devadze, Kakhaber Tskhadadze (C) (YC33), Murtaz Shelia, Zaza Revishvili, George Chikhradze, Georgi Nemsadze (42' Gela Inalishvili), Giorgi Kinkladze, Kakha Gogichaishvili, Temur Ketsbaia (74' Mikheil Kavelashvili), Shota Arveladze, Gocha Gogrichiani. (Coach: Alexandr Chivadze (GEO)).
Wales: Neville Southall, Andy Melville, Chris Coleman, Mark Bowen, Alan Neilson (46' Kit Symons), Gary Speed (YC42), Mark Hughes (YC44), Barry Horne (C), David Phillips, Ian Rush, Dean Saunders. (Coach: Michael John (Mike) Smith (ENG)).
Goals: Georgia: 1-0 Temur Ketsbaia (29'), 2-0 Giorgi Kinkladze (39'), 3-0 Temur Ketsbaia (48'), 4-0 Gocha Gogrichiani (58'), 5-0 Shota Arveladze (65').
Referee: Alain Sars (FRA)   Attendance: 45.000

14-12-1994 Stadionul Republican, Chisinau: Moldova – Germany 0-3 (0-2)
Moldova: Vasile Coselev, Serghei Stroenco, Sergiu Secu, Valerii Pogorelov, Radu Rebeja (80' Ion Testemitanu), Alexandr Curtianu, Serghei Belous, Igor Oprea (57' Vladimir Gaidamasciuc), Alexandru Spiridon (C), Serghei Nani, Serghei Clescenco. (Coach: Ion Caras (MOL)).
Germany: Andreas Köpke, Thomas Berthold (YC47), Stefan Reuter, Thomas Helmer, Lothar Matthäus (C), Andreas Möller (YC56) (78' Stefan Kuntz), Thomas Häßler, Matthias Sammer (YC31), Ralf Weber, Ulf Kirsten (68' Thomas Strunz), Jürgen Klinsmann. (Coach: Hans-Hubert (Berti) Vogts (GER)).
Goals: Germany: 0-1 Ulf Kirsten (6'), 0-2 Jürgen Klinsmann (38'), 0-3 Lothar Matthäus (71').
Referee: Jef L.F.van Vliet (HOL)   Attendance: 26.000

14-12-1994 Cardiff Arms Park, Cardiff: Wales – Bulgaria 0-3 (0-2)
Wales: Neville Southall, Andy Melville (YC69), Chris Coleman, Mark Aizlewood, Mark Bowen, Gary Speed, Mark Hughes (YC80), David Phillips, Vinnie Jones, Ian Rush (C) (YC67), Dean Saunders. (Coach: Michael John (Mike) Smith (ENG)).
Bulgaria: Borislav Mihaylov (C), Trifon Ivanov, Emil Kremenliev, Tsanko Tsvetanov, Ivaylo Yordanov, Zlatko Yankov, Yordan Lechkov, Hristo Stoichkov, Emil Kostadinov (YC21) (74' Nasko Sirakov), Luboslav Penev (74' Ilyan Kiryakov), Krasimir Balakov. (Coach: Dimitar Penev (BUL)).
Goals: Bulgaria: 0-1 Trifon Ivanov (5'), 0-2 Emil Kostadinov (16'), 0-3 Hristo Stoichkov (51').
Referee: Leif Sundell (SWE)   Attendance: 23.206

14-12-1994   Qemal Stafa Stadium, Tirana: Albania – Georgia   0-1 (0-1)
Albania: Fotaq (Foto) Strakosha, Rudi Vata (30' Ilir Shulku), Gjergji Dema, Salvador Kaçaj, Arian Xhumba, Sulejman Demollari (C), Artur Tushe Lekbello (II) (46' Sajmir Malko (YC53)), Bledar Kola, Arian Bellaj, Indrit Fortuzi, Altin Rraklli. (Coach: Neptun Bajko (ALB)).
Georgia: Akaki Devadze, Murtaz Shelia (C), Zaza Revishvili, George Chikhradze, Giorgi Kinkladze (YC45), Gela Inalishvili, Kakha Gogichaishvili (63' Mikhail Jishkariani), Dimitri Kudinovi, Temur Ketsbaia (YC53), Shota Arveladze (72' Gocha Jamarauli), Gocha Gogrichiani. (Coach: Alexandr Chivadze (GEO)).
Goal: Georgia: 0-1 Shota Arveladze (18').
Referee: László Molnár (HUN)   Attendance: 9.700

18-12-1994   Fritz-Walter-Stadion, Kaiserslautern: Germany – Albania   2-1 (2-0)
Germany: Andreas Köpke, Thomas Berthold, Stefan Reuter, Thomas Helmer, Lothar Matthäus (C), Andreas Möller, Thomas Häßler (78' Thomas Strunz), Matthias Sammer, Ralf Weber, Ulf Kirsten (58' Stefan Kuntz), Jürgen Klinsmann. (Coach: Hans-Hubert (Berti) Vogts (GER)).
Albania: Fotaq (Foto) Strakosha, Gjergji Dema, Salvador Kaçaj, Ilir Shulku, Arian Xhumba, Sajmir Malko, Hysen Zmijani, Sulejman Demollari (C), Bledar Kola (60' Alvaro Zalla), Arian Bellaj, Altin Rraklli. (Coach: Neptun Bajko (ALB)).
Goals: Germany: 1-0 Lothar Matthäus (8'), 2-0 Jürgen Klinsmann (17').
Albania: 2-1 Altin Rraklli (58').
Referee: Svend Erik Christensen (DEN)   Attendance: 20.310

29-03-1995   Boris Paicahdze Stadium, Tbilisi: Georgia – Germany   0-2 (0-2)
Georgia: Akaki Devadze, Kakhaber Tskhadadze (C), Murtaz Shelia, Zaza Revishvili, George Chikhradze, Revaz Arveladze (77' Mikheil Kavelashvili), Gocha Jamarauli (62' Gocha Gogrichiani), Giorgi Kinkladze, Kakha Gogichaishvili, Dimitri Kudinovi, Shota Arveladze. (Coach: Alexandr Chivadze (GEO)).
Germany: Andreas Köpke, Jürgen Kohler (YC80), Stefan Reuter (YC28), Thomas Helmer, Markus Babbel (YC52), Andreas Möller, Mario Basler, Dieter Eilts, Ralf Weber (YC29) (46' Steffen Freund (YC65)), Jürgen Klinsmann (C), Heiko Herrlich. (Coach: Hans-Hubert (Berti) Vogts (GER)).
Goals: Germany: 0-1 Jürgen Klinsmann (24'), 0-2 Jürgen Klinsmann (45').
Referee: Martin John Dale Bodenham (ENG)   Attendance: 75.000

29-03-1995   Vasil Levski National Stadium, Sofia: Bulgaria – Wales   3-1 (1-0)
Bulgaria: Borislav Mihaylov (C), Trifon Ivanov, Emil Kremenliev, Tsanko Tsvetanov (65' Ilyan Kiryakov), Petar Hubchev, Zlatko Yankov, Yordan Lechkov, Hristo Stoichkov, Emil Kostadinov, Luboslav Penev (YC82), Krasimir Balakov. (Coach: Dimitar Penev (BUL)).
Wales: Neville Southall, Chris Coleman, Mark Bowen, Kyt Symons, Gary Speed, Ryan Giggs, Barry Horne (C) (YC44), David Phillips, Vinnie Jones (78' John Cornforth (YC85)), John Hartson (YC8), Dean Saunders. (Coach: Michael John (Mike) Smith (ENG)).
Goals: Bulgaria: 1-0 Krasimir Balakov (37'), 2-0 Luboslav Penev (70'), 3-0 Luboslav Penev (80').
Wales: 3-1 Dean Saunders (81').
Referee: Michel Piraux (BEL)   Attendance: 60.000

29-03-1995   Qemal Stafa Stadium, Tirana: Albania – Moldova   3-0 (2-0)
Albania: Fotaq (Foto) Strakosha (82' Blendi Nallbani), Eduard Abazi, Rudi Vata, Salvador Kaçaj, Ilir Shulku (YC90), Arian Xhumba (69' Indrit Fortuzi), Sajmir Malko, Sulejman Demollari (C), Arian Bellaj, Sokol Kushta (88' Edmond Dalipaj), Altin Rraklli. (Coach: Neptun Bajko (ALB)).
Moldova: Vasile Coselev, Serghei Stroenco (YC42), Sergiu Secu, Valerii Pogorelov, Alexandr Curtianu (73' Emilian Caras), Serghei Belous, Igor Oprea, Alexandru Spiridon (C), Serghei Nani, Vladimir Gaidamasciuc (69' Andrei Stroenco), Serghei Clescenco. (Coach: Ion Caras (MOL)).
Goals: Albania: 1-0 Sokol Kushta (32'), 2-0 Salvador Kaçaj (43'), 3-0 Sokol Kushta (78').
Referee: Urs Meier (SUI)   Attendance: 8.500

26-04-1995   Boris Paichadze Stadium, Tbilisi: Georgia – Albania   2-0 (2-0)
Georgia: Akaki Devadze, Murtaz Shelia (C) (75' Nugzar Lobzhanidze), George Chikhradze, Gocha Jamarauli, Gela Inalishvili, Kakha Gogichaishvili, Dimitri Kudinovi, Georgi Ghudushauri, Temur Ketsbaia, Shota Arveladze, David Kizilashvili (60' Archil Arveladze). (Coach: Alexandr Chivadze (GEO)).
Albania: Fotaq (Foto) Strakosha, Rudi Vata, Salvador Kaçaj, Arian Xhumba (YC44), Sajmir Malko, Sulejman Demollari (C), Ardian Mema, Indrit Fortuzi (57' Sokol Prenga), Sokol Kushta (83' Edmond Dosti), Altin Rraklli, Edmond Dalipaj. (Coach: Neptun Bajko (ALB)).
Goals: Georgia: 1-0 Shota Arveladze (2'), 2-0 Temur Ketsbaia (41').
Referee: Roelof Luinge (HOL)   Attendance: 20.000

26-04-1995   Stadionul Republican, Chisinau: Moldova – Bulgaria   0-3 (0-1)
Moldova: Vasile Coselev, Oleg Fistican, Sergiu Secu, Emilian Caras (63' Vladimir Gaidamasciuc), Valerii Pogorelov, Radu Rebeja, Alexandr Curtianu (C), Serghei Belous, Igor Oprea (80' Boris Cebotari), Serghei Nani, Serghei Clescenco. (Coach: Ion Caras (MOL)).
Bulgaria: Borislav Mihaylov (C), Trifon Ivanov, Emil Kremenliev (YC62) (81' Ilyan Kiryakov), Tsanko Tsvetanov, Petar Hubchev, Ivaylo Yordanov, Zlatko Yankov, Yordan Lechkov, Hristo Stoichkov (76' Petar Mihtarski), Lyuboslav Penev, Krasimir Balakov. (Coach: Dimitar Penev (BUL)).
Goals: Bulgaria: 0-1 Krasimir Balakov (29'), 0-2 Hristo Stoichkov (54'), 0-3 Hristo Stoichkov (67').
Referee: Jiří Ulrich (CZE)   Attendance: 16.000

26-04-1995   Rheinstadion, Düsseldorf: Germany – Wales   1-1 (1-1)
Germany: Andreas Köpke, Stefan Reuter, Markus Babbel, Christian Ziege (85' Stefan Kuntz), Thomas Häßler, Mario Basler (75' Mehmet Scholl), Steffen Freund, Dieter Eilts, Ralf Weber, Jürgen Klinsmann (C), Heiko Herrlich. (Coach: Hans-Hubert (Berti) Vogts (GER)).
Wales: Neville Southall, Chris Coleman (46' Adrian Williams), Mark Bowen, Kyt Symons, Gary Speed, Mark Hughes (89' John Hartson), Barry Horne (C), David Phillips, Vinnie Jones (YC69), Ian Rush, Dean Saunders. (Coach: Michael John (Mike) Smith (ENG)).
Goals: Germany: 1-1 Heiko Herrlich (41').
Wales: 0-1 Dean Saunders (7').
Referee: José-María García-Aranda Encinar (ESP)   Attendance: 43.461

07-06-1995   Vasil Levski National Stadium, Sofia: Bulgaria – Germany   3-2 (0-2)
Bulgaria: Borislav Mihaylov (C), Trifon Ivanov (YC46), Emil Kremenliev, Tsanko Tsvetanov, Petar Hubchev, Ivaylo Yordanov (62' Emil Kostadinov), Zlatko Yankov, Yordan Lechkov (80' Nasko Sirakov), Hristo Stoichkov, Luboslav Penev, Krasimir Balakov. (Coach: Dimitar Penev (BUL)).
Germany: Andreas Köpke, Stefan Reuter (YC27), Thomas Helmer, Markus Babbel, Thomas Häßler, Matthias Sammer (YC90), Thomas Strunz (90' Ulf Kirsten), Mario Basler (80' Andreas Möller), Dieter Eilts, Jürgen Klinsmann (C) (YC78), Heiko Herrlich (YC2). (Coach: Hans-Hubert (Berti) Vogts (GER)).
Goals: Bulgaria: 1-2 Hristo Stoichkov (46' penalty), 2-2 Hristo Stoichkov (66' penalty), 3-2 Emil Kostadinov (69').
Germany: 0-1 Jürgen Klinsmann (17'), 0-2 Thomas Strunz (43').
Referee: Pierluigi Pairetto (ITA)   Attendance: 44.208

07-06-1995   Cardiff Arms Park, Cardiff: Wales – Georgia   0-1 (0-0)
Wales: Neville Southall, Adrian Williams, Mark Bowen, Kyt Symons, Mark Hughes (84' Mark Pembridge), Barry Horne (C), David Phillips, John Cornforth, Vinnie Jones (RC28), Ian Rush, Dean Saunders (84' John Hartson). (Coach: Michael John (Mike) Smith (ENG)).
Georgia: Akaki Devadze (YC89), Kakhaber Tskhadadze (C), Murtaz Shelia, George Chikhradze (YC70), Besiki Beradze, Mikheil Kavelashvili (73' Levan Tskitishvili), Giorgi Kinkladze, Gela Inalishvili, Kakha Gogichaishvili, Temur Ketsbaia, Shota Arveladze (87' Giorgi Kilasonia). (Coach: Alexandr Chivadze (GEO)).
Goal: Georgia: 0-1 Giorgi Kinkladze (73').
Referee: Ilkka Koho (FIN)   Attendance: 8.241

07-06-1995   Stadionul Republican, Chisinau: Moldova – Albania   2-3 (2-2)
Moldova: Eugen Ivanov, Serghei Stroenco (C), Oleg Fistican, Sergiu Secu (YC23), Valerii Pogorelov, Radu Rebeja (73' Volodymyr Cosse), Alexandr Curtianu (C), Serghei Belous (55' Iurii Miterev), Andrei Stroenco, Serghei Nani, Serghei Clescenco. (Coach: Ion Caras (MOL)).
Albania: Fotaq (Foto) Strakosha, Rudi Vata, Salvador Kaçaj, Ilir Shulku, Sajmir Malko (YC58), Artan Bano (YC63), Sulejman Demollari (C) (78' Ledio Pano), Bledar Kola, Arian Bellaj, Sokol Kushta, Altin Rraklli (86' Sokol Prenga). (Coach: Neptun Bajko (ALB)).
Goals: Moldova: 1-1 Alexandr Curtianu (10'), 2-1 Serghei Clescenco (15').
Albania: 0-1 Sokol Kushta (8'), 2-2 Arian Bellaj (25'), 2-3 Rudi Vata (71').
Referee: Léon Schellings (BEL)   Attendance: 7.000

06-09-1995   Qemal Stafa Stadium, Tirana: Albania – Bulgaria   1-1 (1-1)
Albania: Fotaq (Foto) Strakosha, Eduard Abazi, Rudi Vata (YC20), Ilir Shulku, Arian Xhumba, Artur Tushe Lekbello (II), Bledar Kola (65' Ylli Shehu, 89' Ledio Pano), Arian Bellaj, Sokol Kushta (C) (YC40), Altin Rraklli, Kliton Bozgo (86' Sulejman Demollari). (Coach: Neptun Bajko (ALB)).
Bulgaria: Borislav Mihaylov (C), Trifon Ivanov, Emil Kremenliev, Tsanko Tsvetanov, Petar Hubchev (RC37), Daniel Borimirov (YC22), Yordan Lechkov (76' Krassimir Chomakov), Hristo Stoichkov, Emil Kostadinov, Luboslav Penev (76' Nasko Sirakov), Krasimir Balakov. (Coach: Dimitar Penev (BUL)).
Goals: Albania: 1-1 Altin Rraklli (10').
Bulgaria: 0-1 Hristo Stoichkov (8').
Referee: Charles Agius (MLT)   Attendance: 6.050

06-09-1995   Frankenstadion, Nuremburg: Germany – Georgia   4-1 (1-1)
Germany: Oliver Kahn, Jürgen Kohler, Thomas Helmer, Markus Babbel, Christian Ziege (YC62), Andreas Möller, Thomas Häßler, Thomas Strunz, Steffen Freund, Ulf Kirsten, Jürgen Klinsmann (C). (Coach: Hans-Hubert (Berti) Vogts (GER)).
Georgia: Akaki Devadze, Murtaz Shelia (C) (YC57), George Chikhradze, Gocha Gudzhabidze, Georgi Nemsadze, Mikheil Kavelashvili (46' Giorgi Kilasonia), Giorgi Kinkladze, Kakha Gogichaishvili (66' Archil Arveladze), Dimitri Kudinovi, Temur Ketsbaia, Shota Arveladze. (Coach: Alexandr Chivadze (GEO)).
Goals: Germany: 1-1 Andreas Möller (38'), 2-1 Christian Ziege (56'), 3-1 Ulf Kirsten (61'), 4-1 Markus Babbel (72').
Georgia: 0-1 Temur Ketsbaia (28').
Referee: James (Jim) McCluskey (SCO)   Attendance: 40.750

06-09-1995   Cardiff Arms Park, Cardiff: Wales – Moldova   1-0 (0-0)
Wales: Neville Southall, Adrian Williams, Chris Coleman (YC76), Mark Bowen, Kyt Symons, Gary Speed, Mark Hughes, Mark Pembridge, Barry Horne (C), Ian Rush (67' John Hartson), Lee Nogan (46' David Phillips). (Coach: Robert Anthony (Bobby) Gould (ENG)).
Moldova: Eugen Ivanov, Serghei Stroenco (C), Oleg Fistican (RC90), Ion Testemitanu, Vitali Culibaba, Radu Rebeja (80' Vladislav Gavriliuc), Boris Cebotari, Serghei Belous, Igor Oprea, Serghei Nani (76' Alexandru Suharev), Serghei Clescenco. (Coach: Ion Caras (MOL)).
Goal: Wales: 1-0 Gary Speed (55').
Referee: Gylfi Thór Orrason (ISL)   Attendance: 6.721

07-10-1995   Vasil Levski National Stadium, Sofia: Bulgaria – Albania   3-0 (1-0)
Bulgaria: Borislav Mihaylov (C), Trifon Ivanov, Emil Kremenliev (YC84), Tsanko Tsvetanov, Zlatko Yankov, Yordan Lechkov, Ilyan Kiryakov (87' Daniel Borimirov), Hristo Stoichkov, Emil Kostadinov (85' Nasko Sirakov), Luboslav Penev, Krasimir Balakov. (Coach: Dimitar Penev (BUL)).
Albania: Fotaq (Foto) Strakosha, Eduard Abazi (85' Sulejman Demollari), Gjergji Dema (YC39), Ilir Shulku, Arian Xhumba, Sajmir Malko, Hysen Zmijani, Bledar Kola, Arian Bellaj, Sokol Kushta (C), Altin Rraklli. (Coach: Neptun Bajko (ALB)).
Goals: Bulgaria: 1-0 Yordan Lechkov (14'), 2-0 Emil Kostadinov (80'), 3-0 Emil Kostadinov (82').
Referee: Juha Hirviniemi (FIN)   Attendance: 25.000

08-10-1995   Ulrich Haberland Stadion, Leverkusen: Germany – Moldova   6-1 (3-0)
Germany: Andreas Köpke, Thomas Helmer, Markus Babbel, Christian Ziege, Andreas Möller (77' Mehmet Scholl), Thomas Häßler, Matthias Sammer (83' Christian Wörns), Steffen Freund, Dieter Eilts, Jürgen Klinsmann (C), Heiko Herrlich (63' Fredi Bobic). (Coach: Hans-Hubert (Berti) Vogts (GER)).
Moldova: Eugen Ivanov (YC85), Serghei Stroenco (C), Ion Testemitanu, Sergiu Secu, Vitali Culibaba, Radu Rebeja, Alexandr Curtianu, Serghei Belous, Igor Oprea (86' Vladislav Gavriliuc), Serghei Nani (59' Iurii Miterev), Serghei Clescenco. (Coach: Ion Caras (MOL)).
Goals: Germany: 1-0 Serghei Stroenco (15' own goal), 2-0 Thomas Helmer (18'), 3-0 Matthias Sammer (23'), 4-0 Andreas Möller (47'), 5-0 Andreas Möller (61'), 6-0 Matthias Sammer (71').
Moldova: 6-1 Radu Rebeja (81').
Referee: Zygmunt Ziober (POL)   Attendance: 18.400

11-10-1995   Boris Paichadze Stadium, Tbilisi: Georgia – Bulgaria   2-1 (1-0)
Georgia: Irakli Zoidze, Murtaz Shelia (C) (YC61), George Chikhradze, Georgi Nemsadze (YC27), Archil Arveladze (46' Mikheil Kavelashvili), Gocha Jamarauli (75' Giorgi Kilasonia), Giorgi Kinkladze, Kakha Gogichaishvili (YC44), Dimitri Kudinovi, Georgi Ghudushauri (83' Bediki Beradze), Shota Arveladze. (Coach: Alexandr Chivadze (GEO)).
Bulgaria: Borislav Mihaylov (C) (YC47), Trifon Ivanov (57' Krassimir Chomakov), Tsanko Tsvetanov, Zlatko Yankov, Yordan Lechkov, Nasko Sirakov (51' Daniel Borimirov), Ilyan Kiryakov, Hristo Stoichkov, Emil Kostadinov, Luboslav Penev, Krasimir Balakov. (Coach: Dimitar Penev (BUL)).
Goals: Georgia: 1-0 Shota Arveladze (1'), 2-0 Giorgi Kinkladze (48' penalty).
Bulgaria: 2-1 Hristo Stoichkov (87').
Referee: Urs Meier (SUI)   Attendance: 45.000

11-10-1995   Cardiff Arms Park, Cardiff: Wales – Germany   1-2 (0-0)
Wales: Neville Southall (YC3), Steve Jenkins (75' Paul Mardon), Andy Melville, Mark Bowen, Kyt Symons, Gary Speed, Ryan Giggs, Mark Pembridge (YC23) (84' David Williams), Barry Horne (C), Nathan Blake (YC40) (84' Glyn Hodges), Dean Saunders. (Coach: Robert Anthony (Bobby) Gould (ENG)).
Germany: Andreas Köpke, Thomas Helmer, Markus Babbel (46' Christian Wörns), Christian Ziege (YC76), Andreas Möller, Thomas Häßler, Matthias Sammer (YC82), Steffen Freund, Dieter Eilts, Jürgen Klinsmann (C), Heiko Herrlich (72' Stefan Kuntz). (Coach: Hans-Hubert (Berti) Vogts (GER)).
Goals: Wales: 1-1 Thomas Helmer (78' *own goal*).
Germany: 0-1 Kyt Symons (74' *own goal*), 1-2 Jürgen Klinsmann (84').
Referee: Ion Craciunescu (ROM)   Attendance: 27.000

15-11-1995   Olympiastadion, Berlin: Germany – Bulgaria   3-1 (0-0)
Germany: Andreas Köpke, Jürgen Kohler (46' Thomas Strunz), Thomas Helmer, Markus Babbel, Thomas Häßler (87' Stefan Reuter), Matthias Sammer, Mario Basler, Steffen Freund (YC67), Dieter Eilts, Stefan Kuntz (82' Fredi Bobic), Jürgen Klinsmann (C) (YC35). (Coach: Hans-Hubert (Berti) Vogts (GER)).
Bulgaria: Dimitar Popov (YC75), Emil Kremenliev, Tsanko Tsvetanov, Gosho Ginchev, Valentin Dartilov (YC55), Zlatko Yankov, Yordan Lechkov (61' Ilyan Kiryakov), Hristo Stoichkov (C), Emil Kostadinov, Luboslav Penev (78' Nasko Sirakov), Krasimir Balakov (YC36) (82' Daniel Borimirov). (Coach: Dimitar Penev (BUL)).
Goals: Germany: 1-1 Jürgen Klinsmann (50'), 2-1 Thomas Häßler (56'), 3-1 Jürgen Klinsmann (76' penalty).
Bulgaria: 0-1 Hristo Stoichkov (47').
Referee: Vassilios Nikakis (GRE)   Attendance: 75.841

15-11-1995   Qemal Stafa Stadium, Tirana: Albania – Wales   1-1 (1-1)
Albania: Fotaq (Foto) Strakosha, Rudi Vata, Gjergji Dema (84' Arben Milori), Ilir Shulku, Sajmir Malko, Hysen Zmijani, Artur Tushe Lekbello (II) (YC70), Sokol Kushta (C) (57' Alban Bushi), Ledio Pano, Altin Rraklli, Kliton Bozgo (78' Alvaro Zalla). (Coach: Neptun Bajko (ALB)).
Wales: Neville Southall, Steve Jenkins, Andy Melville, Eric Young, Mark Bowen (YC21), Ryan Giggs, Mark Pembridge (YC38), David Phillips, Ceri Hughes (63' Robbie Savage), Gareth Taylor (YC62) (84' John Robinson), Dean Saunders. (Coach: Robert Anthony (Bobby) Gould (ENG)).
Goals: Albania: 1-0 Sokol Kushta (4' penalty).
Wales: 1-1 Mark Pembridge (42').
Referee: David Suheil (ISR)   Attendance: 2.100

15-11-1995 Stadionul Republican, Chisinau: Moldova – Georgia 3-2 (2-0)
Moldova: Vasile Coselev, Ion Testemitanu, Serghei Secu, Vitali Culibaba, Alexandr Curtianu (C) (76' Boris Cebotari), Serghei Belous, Igor Oprea (YC13) (53' Alexandru Suharev), Serghei Nani, Iurii Miterev, Serghei Chirilov (80' Vladislav Gavriliuc), Serghei Clescenco (YC30).
(Coach: Ion Caras (MOL)).
Georgia: Irakli Zoidze, George Chikhradze (RC40), Besiki Beradze, Levan Tskitishvili, Gocha Jamarauli (62' Mamuka Machavariani), Giorgi Kinkladze, Kakha Gogichaishvili, Dimitri Kudinovi, Georgi Ghudushauri (58' David Janashia), Temur Ketsbaia, Shota Arveladze.
(Coach: Alexandr Chivadze (GEO)).
Goals: Moldova: 1-0 Ion Testemitanu (5' penalty), 2-0 Iurii Miterev (18'), 3-1 Iurii Miterev (73').
Georgia: 2-1 David Janashia (68'), 3-2 Vitali Culibaba (81' *own goal*).
Referee: Mario van der Ende (HOL)   Attendance: 6.000

GROUP 8

07-09-1994	Toftir	Faroe Islands – Greece	1-5 (0-2)
07-09-1994	Helsinki	Finland – Scotland	0-2 (0-1)
12-10-1994	Glasgow	Scotland – Faroe Islands	5-1 (3-0)
12-10-1994	Thessaloniki	Greece – Finland	4-0 (1-0)
12-10-1994	Moscow	Russia – San Marino	4-0 (1-0)
16-11-1994	Athens	Greece – San Marino	2-0 (1-0)
16-11-1994	Helsinki	Finland – Faroe Islands	5-0 (1-0)
16-11-1994	Glasgow	Scotland – Russia	1-1 (1-1)
14-12-1994	Helsinki	Finland – San Marino	4-1 (2-1)
18-12-1994	Athens	Greece – Scotland	1-0 (1-0)
29-03-1995	Moscow	Russia – Scotland	0-0
29-03-1995	Serravalle	San Marino – Finland	0-2 (0-1)
26-04-1995	Serravalle	San Marino – Scotland	0-2 (0-1)
26-04-1995	Thessaloniki	Greece – Russia	0-3 (0-1)
26-04-1995	Toftir	Faroe Islands – Finland	0-4 (0-0)
06-05-1995	Moscow	Russia – Faroe Islands	3-0 (0-0)
25-05-1995	Toftir	Faroe Islands – San Marino	3-0 (2-0)
07-06-1995	Serravalle	San Marino – Russia	0-7 (0-2)
07-06-1995	Toftir	Faroe Islands – Scotland	0-2 (0-2)
11-06-1995	Helsinki	Finland – Greece	2-1 (1-1)
16-08-1995	Helsinki	Finland – Russia	0-6 (0-3)
16-08-1995	Glasgow	Scotland – Greece	1-0 (0-0)
06-09-1995	Glasgow	Scotland – Finland	1-0 (1-0)
06-09-1995	Toftir	Faroe Islands – Russia	2-5 (1-1)
06-09-1995	Serravalle	San Marino – Greece	0-4 (0-2)
11-10-1995	Moscow	Russia – Greece	2-1 (1-0)
11-10-1995	Serravalle	San Marino – Faroe Islands	1-3 (0-2)
15-11-1995	Glasgow	Scotland – San Marino	5-0 (2-0)
15-11-1995	Moscow	Russia – Finland	3-1 (1-1)
15-11-1995	Heraklion	Greece – Faroe Islands	5-0 (0-0)

FINAL STANDING

Pos	Team	Pld	W	D	L	GF	GA	GD	Pts
1	*Russia*	*10*	*8*	*2*	*0*	*34*	*5*	*+29*	*26*
2	*Scotland*	*10*	*7*	*2*	*1*	*19*	*3*	*+16*	*23*
3	Greece	10	6	0	4	23	9	+14	18
4	Finland	10	5	0	5	18	18	0	15
5	Faroe Islands	10	2	0	8	10	35	-25	6
6	San Marino	10	0	0	10	2	36	-34	0

Russia and Scotland qualified for the final tournament in England.

07-09-1994 Svangaskard, Toftir: Faroe Islands – Greece 1-5 (0-2)
Faroe Islands: Jens Knudsen, Øssur Hansen (55' Henning Jarnskor), Óli Johannesen, Allan Mørkøre (85' Jens Erik Rasmussen), Tummas Eli Hansen, Jan Dam, Jens Kristian Hansen, Abraham Hansen (C), Magni Jarnskor, Todi Jónsson, Jan Allan Müller (YC73). (Coach: Allan Simonsen (DEN)).
Greece: Christos Athana Karkamanis, Efstratios Apostolakis, Ioannis Kalitzakis, Kyriakos Karataidis (RC71), Konstantinos Pavlopoulos, Panagiotis Tsalouchidis (YC5), Minas Hantzidis (82' Theodoros Zagorakis), Alexis Alexandris, Vasilis Tsiartas, Dimitrios Saravakos (C), Christos Kostis (77' Dimitrios Markos). (Coach: Konstantinos Polychroniou (GRE)).
Goals: Faroe Islands: 1-5 Jan Allan Müller (88').
Greece: 0-1 Dimitrios Saravakos (11'), 0-2 Panagiotis Tsalouchidis (17'), 0-3 Alexis Alexandris (54'), 0-4 Alexis Alexandris (61'), 0-5 Panagiotis Tsalouchidis (86').
Referee: Michel Piraux (BEL)   Attendance: 2.412

07-09-1994 Olympic Stadium, Helsinki: Finland – Scotland 0-2 (0-1)
Finland: Petri Antero Jakonen, Markku Kanerva, Janne Mäkelä, Aki Hyryläinen, Antti Heinola (30' Erik Holmgren (YC53)), Ari Hjelm (C), Kim Suominen, Rami Rantanen (41' Petri Järvinen), Janne Lindberg, Jari Litmanen, Mixu Paatelainen. (Coach: Tommy Lindholm (FIN)).
Scotland: Andy Goram, Tom Boyd, Colin Hendry, Stewart McKimmie, Alan McLaren, John Collins (YC9), Paul McStay, Craig Levein (78' Stuart McCall), Gary McAllister (C), Andy Walker (64' Eoin Jess), Duncan Shearer. (Coach: James Craig Brown (SCO)).
Goals: Scotland: 0-1 Duncan Shearer (29'), 0-2 John Collins (65').
Referee: Ryszard Wójcik (POL)   Attendance: 12.845

12-10-1994 Hampden Park, Glasgow: Scotland – Faroe Islands 5-1 (3-0)
Scotland: Andy Goram, Tom Boyd, Colin Hendry (58' Billy McKinlay), Stewart McKimmie, Alan McLaren, John Collins, Paul McStay (C), Craig Levein, Pat Nevin, Scott Booth (69' Andy Walker), John McGinlay. (Coach: James Craig Brown (SCO)).
Faroe Islands: Jens Knudsen, Øssur Hansen, Óli Johannesen, Tummas Eli Hansen, Jan Dam (54' Djóni Nolsøe Joensen), Jens Kristian Hansen, Magni Jarnskor (C) (YC44), Henning Jarnskor, Todi Jónsson, Kurt Mørkøre (72' Janus Rasmussen), Jan Allan Müller. (Coach: Allan Simonsen (DEN)).
Goals: Scotland: 1-0 John McGinlay (5'), 2-0 Scott Booth (34'), 3-0 John Collins (41'), 4-0 Billy McKinlay (61'), 5-0 John Collins (72').
Faroe Islands: 5-1 Jan Allan Müller (75').
Referee: Terje Hauge (NOR)   Attendance: 19.885

12-10-1994   Kaftanzoglio Stadium, Thessaloniki: Greece – Finland   4-0 (1-0)
Greece: Elias Atmatsidis, Nikos Dabizas, Efstratios Apostolakis, Ioannis Kalitzakis, Dimitrios Markos (63' Georgios Toursounidis), Panagiotis Tsalouchidis (C) (YC35), Theodoros Zagorakis (YC44), Vasilis Tsiartas, Mihalis Kasapis, Zisis Vryzas (42' Daniel Batista Lima), Nikos Machlas. (Coach: Konstantinos Polychroniou (GRE)).
Finland: Petri Antero Jakonen, Markku Kanerva (YC12), Janne Mäkelä, Aki Hyryläinen (YC18), Antti Heinola (22' Erik Holmgren (YC35)), Ari Hjelm (C), Petri Järvinen (73' Antti Sumiala), Kim Suominen, Janne Lindberg, Jari Litmanen, Mixu Paatelainen (YC2). (Coach: Tommy Lindholm (FIN)).
Goals: Greece: 1-0 Dimitrios Markos (22'), 2-0 Daniel Batista Lima (69'), 3-0 Nikos Machlas (76'), 4-0 Nikos Machlas (89').
Referee: Philippe Leduc (FRA)   Attendance: 7.704

12-10-1994   Luzhniki Stadium, Moscow: Russia – San Marino   4-0 (1-0)
Russia: Stanislav Cherchesov, Yuri Nikiforov, Viktor Onopko (C), Vassili Kulkov (61' Omari Tetradze), Andrei Pyatnitskiy, Valeri Karpin, Ilya Tsymbalar (55' Igor Kolyvanov), Igor Shalimov, Andrei Kanchelskis, Dmitri Radchenko, Sergei Kiryakov. (Coach: Oleg Romantsev (RUS)).
San Marino: Pier-Luigi Benedettini, Mirko Gennari, Luca Gobbi, William Guerra (21' Pier-Domenico Della Valle (YC78)), Ivan Matteoni, Mauro Valentini (YC31), Fabio Francini (67' Claudio Canti), Massimo Bonini (C), Marco Mazza (YC82), Nicola Bacciocchi, Pier-Angelo Manzaroli. (Coach: Giorgio Leoni (SMR)).
Goals: Russia: 1-0 Valeri Karpin (43'), 2-0 Igor Kolyvanov (63'), 3-0 Yuri Nikiforov (64'), 4-0 Dmitri Radchenko (67').
Referee: Alain Hamer (LUX)   Attendance: 5.500

16-11-1994   Spiros Louis Stadium, Athens: Greece – San Marino   2-0 (1-0)
Greece: Elias Atmatsidis, Nikos Dabizas, Efstratios Apostolakis, Ioannis Kalitzakis, Spyridon Marangos (46' Konstantinos Frantzeskos), Theodoros Zagorakis, Vasilis Tsiartas, Georgios Toursounidis, Mihalis Kasapis, Zisis Vryzas (71' Daniel Batista Lima), Nikos Machlas. (Coach: Konstantinos Polychroniou (GRE)).
San Marino: Pier-Luigi Benedettini, Mirko Gennari (46' Claudio Canti), Luca Gobbi, William Guerra, Mauro Valentini (YC36), Fabio Francini, Massimo Bonini (C) (YC57), Nicola Bacciocchi, Pier-Angelo Manzaroli, Pier-Domenico Della Valle (75' Brian Gasperoni), Davide Gualtieri. (Coach: Giorgio Leoni (SMR)).
Goals: Greece: 1-0 Nikos Machlas (21'), 2-0 Konstantinos Frantzeskos (84').
Referee: Haim Lipkovitz (ISR)   Attendance: 2.859

16-11-1994   Olympic Stadium, Helsinki: Finland – Faroe Islands   5-0 (1-0)
Finland: Kari Laukkanen, Markku Kanerva, Janne Mäkelä, Anders Eriksson, Petri Helin, Ari Hjelm (C), Kari Ukkonen, Janne Lindberg (78' Marko Rajamäki), Jari Litmanen, Antti Sumiala (90' Jukka Ruhanen), Mixu Paatelainen. (Coach: Tommy Lindholm (FIN)).
Faroe Islands: Jens Knudsen, Øssur Hansen (79' Jens Erik Rasmussen), Óli Johannesen, Tummas Eli Hansen (RC51), Magni Jarnskor (C), Henning Jarnskor, Djóni Nolsøe Joensen, Janus Rasmussen, Todi Jónsson, Kurt Mørkøre (YC67), Jan Allan Müller. (Coach: Allan Simonsen (DEN)).
Goals: Finland: 1-0 Antti Sumiala (36'), 2-0 Jari Litmanen (52'), 3-0 Jari Litmanen (71'), 4-0 Mixu Paatelainen (74'), 5-0 Mixu Paatelainen (83').
Referee: Gylfi Thór Orrason (ISL)   Attendance: 2.420

16-11-1994 Hampden Park, Glasgow: Scotland – Russia 1-1 (1-1)
Scotland: Andy Goram, Tom Boyd, Stewart McKimmie, Alan McLaren, John Collins, Billy McKinlay (83' Pat Nevin), Craig Levein, Stuart McCall, Gary McAllister (C), Scott Booth, John McGinlay (63' John Spencer). (Coach: James Craig Brown (SCO)).
Russia: Stanislav Cherchesov, Sergei Gorlukovich, Yuri Nikiforov, Viktor Onopko (C), Vassili Kulkov, Vladislav Radimov, Andrei Pyatnitskiy (71' Omari Tetradze), Valeri Karpin, Igor Shalimov, Andrei Kanchelskis, Dmitri Radchenko. (Coach: Oleg Romantsev (RUS)).
Goals: Scotland: 1-0 Scott Booth (18').
Russia: 1-1 Dmitri Radchenko (24').
Referee: Bo Karlsson (SWE) Attendance: 31.254

14-12-1994 Olympic Stadium, Helsinki: Finland – San Marino 4-1 (2-1)
Finland: Kari Laukkanen, Markku Kanerva, Janne Mäkelä, Anders Eriksson, Petri Helin (74' Marko Myyry), Ari Hjelm (C), Kari Ukkonen, Janne Lindberg, Jari Litmanen, Antti Sumiala, Mixu Paatelainen (YC82). (Coach: Tommy Lindholm (FIN)).
San Marino: Pier-Luigi Benedettini, Mirko Gennari, Luca Gobbi, William Guerra, Claudio Canti, Brian Gasperoni (YC80), Massimo Bonini (C), Nicola Bacciocchi (89' Claudio Peverani), Pier-Angelo Manzaroli, Pier-Domenico Della Valle, Marco Mularoni (60' Davide Gualtieri). (Coach: Giorgio Leoni (SMR)).
Goals: Finland: 1-0 Mixu Paatelainen (24'), 2-0 Mixu Paatelainen (30'), 3-1 Mixu Paatelainen (86'), 4-1 Mixu Paatelainen (90').
San Marino: 2-1 Pier-Domenico Della Valle (34').
Referee: Hermann Albrecht (GER) Attendance: 3.140

18-12-1994 Spiros Louis Stadium, Athens: Greece – Scotland 1-0 (1-0)
Greece: Elias Atmatsidis, Efstratios Apostolakis (C), Ioannis Kalitzakis, Michalis Vlachos, Panagiotis Tsalouchidis, Nikolaos Nioplias (YC44) (86' Theofilos Karasavvidis), Alexis Alexandris (71' Spyridon Marangos), Theodoros Zagorakis, Georgios Toursounidis, Mihalis Kasapis, Nikos Machlas. (Coach: Konstantinos Polychroniou (GRE)).
Scotland: Andy Goram (76' Jim Leighton), Tom Boyd, Colin Hendry (YC76), Stewart McKimmie (YC50), Alan McLaren, John Collins, Billy McKinlay (YC12) (46' John Spencer), Stuart McCall (YC41), Gary McAllister (C), Duncan Ferguson, John McGinlay. (Coach: James Craig Brown (SCO)).
Goals: Greece: 1-0 Efstratios Apostolakis (16' penalty).
Referee: John Blankenstein (HOL) Attendance: 7.976

29-03-1995 Luzhniki Stadium, Moscow: Russia – Scotland 0-0
Russia: Dmitri Kharin, Yuri Nikiforov, Dmitri Khlestov, Viktor Onopko (C), Yuri Kovtun, Valeri Karpin, Igor Dobrovolskiy (YC61), Igor Shalimov (70' Vladislav Radimov), Andrei Kanchelskis, Dmitri Radchenko (57' Nikolay Pisarev), Sergei Kiryakov (YC36). (Coach: Oleg Romantsev (RUS)).
Scotland: Jim Leighton, Tom Boyd, Colin Calderwood, Colin Hendry, Stewart McKimmie, Alan McLaren, John Collins, Paul McStay, Gary McAllister (C), Darren Jackson (77' Duncan Shearer), John McGinlay (YC29) (83' Billy McKinlay). (Coach: James Craig Brown (SCO)).
Referee: Hartmut Strampe (GER) Attendance: 13.939

29-03-1995   Stadio Olimpico, Serravalle: San Marino – Finland   0-2 (0-1)
San Marino: Pier-Luigi Benedettini, Mirko Gennari (YC55), Luca Gobbi, William Guerra, Mauro Valentini, Fabio Francini, Massimo Bonini (C), Marco Mazza (70' Ivan Matteoni), Pier-Angelo Manzaroli, Paolo Montagna (75' Davide Gualtieri), Marco Mularoni. (Coach: Giorgio Leoni (SMR)).
Finland: Kari Laukkanen, Janne Mäkelä, Anders Eriksson, Petri Helin, Ari Hjelm (C), Petri Järvinen (76' Marko Rajamäki), Marko Myyry (83' Sami Hyypiä), Kari Ukkonen, Janne Lindberg, Jari Litmanen, Antti Sumiala. (Coach: Jukka Ikäläinen (FIN)).
Goals: Finland: 0-1 Jari Litmanen (45'), 0-2 Antti Sumiala (66').
Referee: David Suheil (ISR)   Attendance: 824

26-04-1995   Stadio Olimpico, Serravalle: San Marino – Scotland   0-2 (0-1)
San Marino: Pier-Luigi Benedettini (YC20), Mirko Gennari, Luca Gobbi, William Guerra, Claudio Canti, Massimo Bonini (C) (46' Ivan Matteoni), Marco Mazza (YC24), Nicola Bacciocchi, Pier-Angelo Manzaroli, Pier-Domenico Della Valle, Marco Mularoni (YC37) (72' Davide Gualtieri). (Coach: Giorgio Leoni (SMR)).
Scotland: Jim Leighton, Tom Boyd, Colin Calderwood, Colin Hendry, Alan McLaren, John Collins, Gary McAllister (C), Pat Nevin (79' Billy McKinlay), Darren Jackson, Duncan Shearer (68' John Spencer), John McGinlay. (Coach: James Craig Brown (SCO)).
Goals: Scotland: 0-1 John Collins (19'), 0-2 Colin Calderwood (86').
Referee: Loizos Loizou (CYP)   Attendance: 1.484

26-04-1995   Kaftanzoglio Stadium, Thessaloniki: Greece – Russia   0-3 (0-1)
Greece: Elias Atmatsidis, Nikos Dabizas (YC63), Efstratios Apostolakis (C), Ioannis Kalitzakis (RC26), Panagiotis Tsalouchidis, Nikolaos Nioplias (46' Vasilis Tsiartas), Theodoros Zagorakis, Georgios Toursounidis, Mihalis Kasapis, Nikos Machlas (58' Demis Nikolaidis), Georgios Donis. (Coach: Konstantinos Polychroniou (GRE)).
Russia: Dmitri Kharin, Yuri Nikiforov (YC14), Dmitri Khlestov, Viktor Onopko (C) (YC69), Yuri Kovtun (YC12), Vassili Kulkov, Andrei Pyatnitskiy (46' Sergei Kiryakov (YC65)), Valeri Karpin, Igor Dobrovolskiy, Dmitri Radchenko (77' Aleksandr Mostovoy), Vladimir Beschastnikh. (Coach: Oleg Romantsev (RUS)).
Goals: Russia: 0-1 Yuri Nikiforov (37'), 0-2 Theodoros Zagorakis (78' *own goal*), 0-3 Vladimir Beschastnikh (79').
Referee: Loris Stafoggia (ITA)   Attendance: 29.616

26-04-1995   Svangaskard, Toftir: Faroe Islands – Finland   0-4 (0-0)
Faroe Islands: Jens Knudsen, Øssur Hansen, Óli Johannesen, Allan Mørkøre, Jens Kristian Hansen, Allan Joensen, Magni Jarnskor (C) (79' Henning Jarnskor), Janus Rasmussen, Julian Schantz Johnsson, Todi Jónsson, Kurt Mørkøre. (Coach: Allan Simonsen (DEN)).
Finland: Kari Laukkanen, Sami Hyypiä, Janne Mäkelä, Anders Eriksson (YC17), Petri Helin, Ari Hjelm (C), Kari Ukkonen (YC15), Janne Lindberg (81' Kim Suominen), Jari Litmanen, Antti Sumiala (80' Joonas Kolkka (YC65)), Mixu Paatelainen. (Coach: Jukka Ikäläinen (FIN)).
Goals: Finland: 0-1 Ari Hjelm (54'), 0-2 Mixu Paatelainen (74'), 0-3 Janne Lindberg (77'), 0-4 Petri Helin (82').
Referee: Alan Christopher Howells (WAL)   Attendance: 1.338

06-05-1995   Luzhniki Stadium, Moscow: Russia – Faroe Islands   3-0 (0-0)
Russia: Stanislav Cherchesov, Yuri Nikiforov, Dmitri Khlestov, Viktor Onopko (C), Yuri Kovtun, Andrei Pyatnitskiy (18' Vladimir Lebed), Omari Tetradze, Dmitri Cheryshev, Valeri Kechinov, Nikolay Pisarev, Mukhsin Mukhamadiev. (Coach: Oleg Romantsev (RUS)).
Faroe Islands: Jens Knudsen, Øssur Hansen (C), Óli Johannesen, Jens Kristian Hansen, Allan Joensen, Jens Erik Rasmussen, Magni Jarnskor, Henning Jarnskor (68' Djóni Nolsøe Joensen), Janus Rasmussen, Todi Jónsson, Kurt Mørkøre. (Coach: Allan Simonsen (DEN)).
Goals: Russia: 1-0 Valeri Kechinov (62'), 2-0 Nikolay Pisarev (71'), 3-0 Mukhsin Mukhamadiev (78').
Referee: Sergo Kvaratskhelia (GEO)   Attendance: 5.024

25-05-1995   Svangaskard, Toftir: Faroe Islands – San Marino   3-0 (2-0)
Faroe Islands: Jens Knudsen, Øssur Hansen, Óli Johannesen, Jens Kristian Hansen, Jens Erik Rasmussen, Magni Jarnskor (C), Henning Jarnskor, Janus Rasmussen, Julian Schantz Johnsson, Todi Jónsson, Kurt Mørkøre. (Coach: Allan Simonsen (DEN)).
San Marino: Pier-Luigi Benedettini, Mirko Gennari, Luca Gobbi, Claudio Canti, Mauro Valentini (YC45), Brian Gasperoni, Fabio Francini (YC49), Massimo Bonini (C) (60' Andrea Ugolini), Nicola Bacciocchi, Pier-Angelo Manzaroli, Marco Mularoni (YC20). (Coach: Giorgio Leoni (SMR)).
Goals: Faroe Islands: 1-0 Jens Kristian Hansen (5'), 2-0 Jens Erik Rasmussen (8'), 3-0 Julian Schantz Johnsson (62').
Referee: Brendan Shorte (IRL)   Attendance: 3.450

07-06-1995   Stadio Olimpico, Serravalle: San Marino – Russia   0-7 (0-2)
San Marino: Pier-Luigi Benedettini, Mirko Gennari, Luca Gobbi, William Guerra (C), Mauro Valentini (YC34), Fabio Francini, Marco Mazza, Nicola Bacciocchi, Pier-Angelo Manzaroli (YC9), Pier-Domenico Della Valle (63' Claudio Canti), Paolo Montagna (78' Massimo Bonini). (Coach: Giorgio Leoni (SMR)).
Russia: Stanislav Cherchesov, Viktor Onopko (C), Yuri Kovtun, Vassili Kulkov, Valeri Karpin, Igor Dobrovolskiy (60' Dmitri Radchenko), Igor Shalimov, Omari Tetradze, Vladimir Beschastnikh, Sergei Kiryakov (87' Dmitri Cheryshev), Igor Kolyvanov. (Coach: Oleg Romantsev (RUS)).
Goals: Russia: 0-1 Igor Dobrovolskiy (22' penalty), 0-2 Vassili Kulkov (38'), 0-3 Sergei Kiryakov (49'), 0-4 Igor Shalimov (50'), 0-5 Vladimir Beschastnikh (59'), 0-6 Igor Kolyvanov (64'), 0-7 Dmitri Cheryshev (89').
Referee: Karel Bohunek (CZE)   Attendance: 1.367

07-06-1995   Svangaskard, Toftir: Faroe Islands – Scotland   0-2 (0-2)
Faroe Islands: Jens Knudsen, Øssur Hansen, Óli Johannesen, Tummas Eli Hansen, Jens Kristian Hansen, Jens Erik Rasmussen (75' Jan Allan Müller), Magni Jarnskor (C) (56' Allan Joensen), Henning Jarnskor, Janus Rasmussen, Julian Schantz Johnsson, Todi Jónsson. (Coach: Allan Simonsen (DEN)).
Scotland: Jim Leighton, Colin Calderwood (YC20), Stewart McKimmie, Alan McLaren, Rab McKinnon (YC73), Craig Burley, John Collins, Billy McKinlay, Darren Jackson, Duncan Shearer (86' John Robertson), John McGinlay (76' Scot Gemmill). (Coach: James Craig Brown (SCO)).
Goals: Scotland: 0-1 Billy McKinlay (20'), 0-2 John McGinlay (29').
Referee: Vladimír Hrinák (SVK)   Attendance: 3.881

11-06-1995   Olympic Stadium, Helsinki: Finland – Greece 2-1 (1-1)
Finland: Kari Laukkanen, Erik Holmgren, Janne Mäkelä (YC70), Petri Helin (YC48), Marko Tuomela, Ari Hjelm (C), Marko Myyry, Janne Lindberg, Jari Litmanen, Antti Sumiala (63' Petri Järvinen), Mixu Paatelainen (YC82) (86' Petri Juha Tiainen). (Coach: Jukka Ikäläinen (FIN)).
Greece: Nikolaos Michopoulos, Nikos Dabizas, Efstratios Apostolakis (C), Dimitrios Markos (58' Daniel Batista Lima), Panagiotis Tsalouchidis (YC26), Alexandros Alexiou, Theodoros Zagorakis, Vasilis Tsiartas (71' Nikos Machlas), Mihalis Kasapis, Georgios Donis, Demis Nikolaidis (YC61). (Coach: Konstantinos Polychroniou (GRE)).
Goals: Finland: 1-1 Jari Litmanen (45+1' penalty), 2-1 Ari Hjelm (54').
Greece: 0-1 Demis Nikolaidis (6').
Referee: Helmut Krug (GER)   Attendance: 10.518

16-08-1995   Olympic Stadium, Helsinki: Finland – Russia 0-6 (0-3)
Finland: Kari Laukkanen, Markku Kanerva, Erik Holmgren, Janne Mäkelä (YC8) (46' Petri Järvinen), Rami Nieminen, Ari Hjelm (C), Rami Rantanen (65' Tommi Grönlund), Janne Lindberg, Petri Juha Tiainen, Antti Sumiala (YC72), Mixu Paatelainen (46' Kim Suominen (YC49)). (Coach: Jukka Ikäläinen (FIN)).
Russia: Dmitri Kharin (72' Stanislav Cherchesov), Yuri Nikiforov, Dmitri Khlestov, Viktor Onopko (C), Yuri Kovtun, Vassili Kulkov, Valeri Karpin (YC52) (60' Andrei Kanchelskis), Ilya Tsymbalar, Aleksandr Mostovoy, Dmitri Radchenko (66' Sergei Kiryakov), Igor Kolyvanov (YC34). (Coach: Oleg Romantsev (RUS)).
Goals: Russia: 0-1 Vassili Kulkov (32'), 0-2 Valeri Karpin (41'), 0-3 Aleksandr Mostovoy (42'), 0-4 Vassili Kulkov (49'), 0-5 Igor Kolyvanov (66'), 0-6 Igor Kolyvanov (69').
Referee: Sándor Puhl (HUN)   Attendance: 14.210

16-08-1995   Hampden Park, Glasgow: Scotland – Greece 1-0 (0-0)
Scotland: Jim Leighton, Tom Boyd, Colin Calderwood, Tosh McKinlay, Stewart McKimmie, Craig Burley (YC9), John Collins, Stuart McCall, Gary McAllister (C), Darren Jackson (70' John Robertson), Duncan Shearer (70' Ally McCoist). (Coach: James Craig Brown (SCO)).
Greece: Elias Atmatsidis, Nikos Dabizas, Efstratios Apostolakis (C), Ioannis Kalitzakis (YC77), Kyriakos Karataidis, Panagiotis Tsalouchidis, Theodoros Zagorakis (77' Giorgos Georgiadis), Vasilis Tsiartas, Mihalis Kasapis, Zisis Vryzas (29' Nikos Machlas), Daniel Batista Lima (51' Alexis Alexandris). (Coach: Konstantinos Polychroniou (GRE)).
Goal: Scotland: 1-0 Ally McCoist (71').
Referee: Peter Mikkelsen (DEN)   Attendance: 33.910

06-09-1995   Hampden Park, Glasgow: Scotland – Finland 1-0 (1-0)
Scotland: Jim Leighton, Tom Boyd, Colin Calderwood, Colin Hendry, Tosh McKinlay, Stewart McKimmie (89' Billy McKinlay), Alan McLaren, John Collins, Gary McAllister (C), Scott Booth (82' Darren Jackson), John Spencer (70' Ally McCoist). (Coach: James Craig Brown (SCO)).
Finland: Kari Laukkanen, Markku Kanerva (YC33), Erik Holmgren, Rami Nieminen (64' Tommi Grönlund), Kari Rissanen (YC30), Ari Hjelm (C), Petri Järvinen, Marko Myyry, Kim Suominen, Janne Lindberg, Jari Litmanen. (Coach: Jukka Ikäläinen (FIN)).
Goal: Scotland: 1-0 Scott Booth (11').
Referee: Vasyl Hryhorovych Melnychuk (UKR)   Attendance: 35.018

06-09-1995   Svangaskard, Toftir: Faroe Islands – Russia   2-5 (1-1)
Faroe Islands: Jens Knudsen, Øssur Hansen, Óli Johannesen, Tummas Eli Hansen (C) (YC78) (81' Allan Joensen), Jens Kristian Hansen, Henning Jarnskor, Janus Rasmussen, Julian Schantz Johnsson, Todi Jónsson, Kurt Mørkøre (YC19), Jan Allan Müller (72' Jens Erik Rasmussen). (Coach: Allan Simonsen (DEN)).
Russia: Stanislav Cherchesov, Yuri Nikiforov, Viktor Onopko (C), Yuri Kovtun, Vassili Kulkov (64' Ramiz Mamedov), Ilya Tsymbalar (YC76), Aleksandr Mostovoy, Igor Shalimov, Andrei Kanchelskis (57' Vladimir Beschastnikh), Dmitri Radchenko (46' Sergei Kiryakov), Igor Kolyvanov. (Coach: Oleg Romantsev (RUS)).
Goals: Faroe Islands: 1-1 Henning Jarnskor (11'), 2-1 Todi Jónsson (55').
Russia: 0-1 Aleksandr Mostovoy (9' penalty), 2-2 Sergei Kiryakov (61'), 2-3 Igor Kolyvanov (65'), 2-4 Ilya Tsymbalar (83'), 2-5 Igor Shalimov (86').
Referee: Alan Snoddy (NIR)   Attendance: 1.792

06-09-1995   Stadio Olimpico, Serravalle: San Marino – Greece   0-4 (0-2)
San Marino: Stefano Muccioli, Mirko Gennari, Luca Gobbi, William Guerra (C), Ivan Matteoni, Fabio Francini (77' Claudio Canti), Marco Mazza (YC57), Nicola Bacciocchi, Pier-Angelo Manzaroli, Pier-Domenico Della Valle (YC70) (88' Claudio Peverani), Marco Mularoni (35' Paolo Montagna). (Coach: Giorgio Leoni (SMR)).
Greece: Elias Atmatsidis (YC43), Nikos Dabizas, Efstratios Apostolakis (C), Kyriakos Karataidis, Marinos Ouzounidis, Panagiotis Tsalouchidis, Theodoros Zagorakis, Giorgos Georgiadis (58' Grigoris Georgatos), Nikos Machlas (78' Daniel Batista Lima), Georgios Donis, Demis Nikolaidis (46' Alexis Alexandris). (Coach: Konstantinos Polychroniou (GRE)).
Goals: Greece: 0-1 Panagiotis Tsalouchidis (6'), 0-2 Giorgos Georgiadis (32'), 0-3 Alexis Alexandris (59'), 0-4 Georgios Donis (81').
Referee: Milan Mitrovic (SLO)   Attendance: 886

11-10-1995   Luzhniki Stadium, Moscow: Russia – Greece   2-1 (1-0)
Russia: Dmitri Kharin, Yuri Nikiforov, Dmitri Khlestov, Viktor Onopko (C), Yuri Kovtun (YC62), Vassili Kulkov, Valeri Karpin (75' Igor Shalimov), Ilya Tsymbalar (68' Dmitri Radchenko), Aleksandr Mostovoy, Sergei Yuran (46' Sergei Kiryakov), Igor Kolyvanov (YC8). (Coach: Oleg Romantsev (RUS)).
Greece: Nikolaos Michopoulos, Efstratios Apostolakis (C), Ioannis Kalitzakis (46' Nikos Dabizas), Marinos Ouzounidis, Panagiotis Tsalouchidis, Alexis Alexandris, Theodoros Zagorakis, Vasilis Tsiartas (46' Grigoris Georgatos), Mihalis Kasapis (YC33), Georgios Donis, Daniel Batista Lima (69' Nikos Machlas). (Coach: Konstantinos Polychroniou (GRE)).
Goals: Russia: 1-0 Yuri Kovtun (36'), 2-1 Viktor Onopko (71').
Greece: 1-1 Panagiotis Tsalouchidis (63').
Referee: Gerd Grabher (AUT)   Attendance: 19.190

11-10-1995   Stadio Olimpico, Serravalle: San Marino – Faroe Islands   1-3 (0-2)
San Marino: Stefano Muccioli, Vittorio Valentini, Mirko Gennari, William Guerra (C), Ivan Matteoni (73' Claudio Peverani), Mauro Valentini, Fabio Francini, Marco Mazza (59' Marco Mularoni), Nicola Bacciocchi, Pier-Angelo Manzaroli, Paolo Montagna (83' Brian Gasperoni). (Coach: Giorgio Leoni (SMR)).
Faroe Islands: Jens Knudsen, Øssur Hansen (83' Kári Reynheim), Allan Mørkøre, Jan Dam, Jens Kristian Hansen, Andreas Falkvard Hansen (YC73), Magni Jarnskor (C), Henning Jarnskor (90' Harley Bertholdsen), Janus Rasmussen, Todi Jónsson (76' John Petersen), Jan Allan Müller. (Coach: Allan Simonsen (DEN)).
Goals: San Marino: 1-2 Mauro Valentini (55').
Faroe Islands: 0-1 Todi Jónsson (42'), 0-2 Todi Jónsson (45'), 1-3 Todi Jónsson (61').
Referee: Roland Beck (LIE)   Attendance: 928

15-11-1995   Hampden Park, Glasgow: Scotland – San Marino   5-0 (2-0)
Scotland: Jim Leighton, Tom Boyd, Colin Calderwood, Colin Hendry, Alan McLaren, John Collins (59' Billy McKinlay), Gary McAllister (C) (48' Ally McCoist), Pat Nevin, Scot Gemmill, Eoin Jess, Scott Booth (63' Darren Jackson). (Coach: James Craig Brown (SCO)).
San Marino: Stefano Muccioli, Federico Moroni (YC40), Mirko Gennari, William Guerra (C) (71' Paolo Montagna), Ivan Matteoni, Mauro Valentini, Fabio Francini, Marco Mazza (YC33) (82' Pier-Domenico Della Valle), Nicola Bacciocchi, Pier-Angelo Manzaroli, Marco Mularoni (YC27) (50' Claudio Canti). (Coach: Giorgio Leoni (SMR)).
Goals: Scotland: 1-0 Eoin Jess (31'), 2-0 Scott Booth (45'), 3-0 Ally McCoist (49'), 4-0 Pat Nevin (71'), 5-0 Fabio Francini (90' *own goal*).
Referee: Karel Bohunek (CZE)   Attendance: 29.492

15-11-1995   Luzhniki Stadium, Moscow: Russia – Finland   3-1 (1-1)
Russia: Stanislav Cherchesov, Yuri Nikiforov (YC84), Dmitri Khlestov, Viktor Onopko (C), Vassili Kulkov, Ramiz Mamedov (46' Igor Dobrovolskiy), Valeri Karpin (75' Andrei Kanchelskis), Ilya Tsymbalar, Aleksandr Mostovoy, Dmitri Radchenko (62' Sergei Kiryakov), Sergei Yuran (YC47). (Coach: Oleg Romantsev (RUS)).
Finland: Antti Niemi, Jussi Nuorela (YC9), Aki Hyryläinen, Rami Nieminen, Kari Rissanen, Ari Hjelm (C), Marko Myyry, Kim Suominen (88' Harri Ylönen), Janne Lindberg, Tommi Grönlund (70' Jukka Koskinen (YC70)), Antti Sumiala. (Coach: Jukka Ikäläinen (FIN)).
Goals: Russia: 1-0 Dmitri Radchenko (40'), 2-1 Vassili Kulkov (55'), 3-1 Sergei Kiryakov (70').
Finland: 1-1 Kim Suominen (44').
Referee: Markus Merk (GER)   Attendance: 6.000

15-11-1995   Theodoros Vardinogiannis Stadium, Heraklion:
              Greece – Faroe Islands   5-0 (0-0)
Greece: Elias Atmatsidis, Nikos Dabizas, Efstratios Apostolakis (C), Marinos Ouzounidis, Panagiotis Tsalouchidis (46' Demis Nikolaidis), Alexis Alexandris (76' Grigoris Georgatos), Theodoros Zagorakis (YC57) (71' Konstantinos Konstantinidis), Vasilis Tsiartas, Mihalis Kasapis, Nikos Machlas, Georgios Donis. (Coach: Konstantinos Polychroniou (GRE)).
Faroe Islands: Jákub Mikkelsen, Øssur Hansen (89' Harley Bertholdsen), Óli Johannesen, Allan Mørkøre (YC44), Tummas Eli Hansen, Jan Dam, Jens Kristian Hansen, Magni Jarnskor (C), Henning Jarnskor, Kári Reynheim (55' Julian Schantz Johnsson), Jan Allan Müller (83' John Petersen). (Coach: Allan Simonsen (DEN)).
Goals: Greece: 1-0 Alexis Alexandris (59'), 2-0 Demis Nikolaidis (62'), 3-0 Nikos Machlas (66'), 4-0 Georgios Donis (76'), 5-0 Vasilis Tsiartas (80').
Referee: Mitko Emilov Mitrev (BUL)   Attendance: 9.088

QUALIFYING PLAY-OFF

13-12-1995   Anfield, Liverpool: Republic of Ireland – Netherlands   0-2 (0-1)
Republic of Ireland: Alan Kelly, Gary Kelly, Paul McGrath, Phil Babb, Denis Irwin, Jeff Kenna, Andy Townsend (C) (51' Jason McAteer), John Sheridan, Terry Phelan, John Aldridge (72' Alan Kernaghan (YC85)), Tony Cascarino. (Coach: John (Jack) Charlton (ENG)).
Netherlands: Edwin van der Sar, Michael Reiziger, Danny Blind (C) (YC79), Clarence Seedorf, Winston Bogarde, Ronald de Boer, Dennis Bergkamp (58' Johan de Kock), Edgar Davids, Marc Overmars, Patrick Kluivert, Glenn Helder (79' Aron Winter). (Coach: Guus Hiddink (HOL)).
Goals: Netherlands: 0-1 Patrick Kluivert (29'), 0-2 Patrick Kluivert (88').
Referee: Vadim Zhuk (BLS)   Attendance: 40.050

FINAL TOURNAMENT IN ENGLAND

GROUP STAGE

England automatically qualified as hosts.

GROUP A

08-06-1996	London	England – Switzerland	1-1 (1-0)
10-06-1996	Birmingham	Netherlands – Scotland	0-0
13-06-1996	Birmingham	Switzerland – Netherlands	0-2 (0-0)
15-06-1996	London	Scotland – England	0-2 (0-0)
18-06-1996	Birmingham	Scotland – Switzerland	1-0 (1-0)
18-06-1996	London	Netherlands – England	1-4 (0-1)

FINAL STANDING

Pos	Team	Pld	W	D	L	GF	GA	GD	Pts
1	England	3	2	1	0	7	2	+5	7
2	Netherlands	3	1	1	1	3	4	-1	4
3	Scotland	3	1	1	1	1	2	-1	4
4	Switzerland	3	0	1	2	1	4	-3	1

England and Netherlands qualified for the Quarter-finals.

08-06-1996   Wembley Stadium, London: England – Switzerland   1-1 (1-0)
England: David Seaman, Gary Neville (YC26), Tony Adams (C) (YC80), Gareth Southgate, Stuart Pearce, Darren Anderton, Paul Ince, Paul Gascoigne (77' David Platt), Steve McManaman (70' Steve Stone), Teddy Sheringham (70' Nick Barmby), Alan Shearer. (Coach: Terry Venables (ENG)).
Switzerland: Marco Pascolo, Sébastien Jeanneret, Stéphane Henchoz, Ramon Vega (YC89), Yvan Quentin (YC43), Johann Vogel (YC28), Alain Geiger (C) (71' Marcel Koller), Ciriaco Sforza, Christophe Bonvin (67' Stéphane Chapuisat), Marco Grassi (YC84), Kübilay Türkyilmaz. (Coach: Artur Jorge Braga Melo Teixeira (POR)).
Goals: England: 1-0 Alan Shearer (23').
Switzerland: 1-1 Kübilay Türkyilmaz (83' penalty).
Referee: Manuel Díaz Vega (ESP)   Attendance: 76.567

10-06-1996 Villa Park, Birmingham: Netherlands – Scotland 0-0
Netherlands: Edwin van der Sar, Michael Reiziger, Johan de Kock, Winston Bogarde, Ronald de Boer (C) (68' Aron Winter), Clarence Seedorf, Edgar Davids, Richard Witschge (YC26) (78' Philip Cocu), Gaston Taument (YC28) (63' Patrick Kluivert), Dennis Bergkamp, Jordi Cruyff. (Coach: Guus Hiddink (HOL)).
Scotland: Andy Goram, Stewart McKimmie (85' Craig Burley), Colin Calderwood, Colin Hendry, Tom Boyd (YC4), Stuart McCall, Gary McAllister (C), John Collins, Gordon Durie, Kevin Gallacher (YC32) (56' Billy McKinlay), Scott Booth (46' John Spencer). (Coach: James Craig Brown (SCO)).
Referee: Leif Sundell (SWE)   Attendance: 34.363

13-06-1996 Villa Park, Birmingham: Switzerland – Netherlands 0-2 (0-0)
Switzerland: Marco Pascolo, Marc Hottiger, Ramon Vega, Stéphane Henchoz, Sébastien Jeanneret (YC32) (69' Alexandre Comisetti), Yvan Quentin, Johann Vogel, Ciriaco Sforza (C), Marco Grassi (YC72), Stéphane Chapuisat (YC40), Külibay Türkyilmaz (YC62). (Coach: Artur Jorge Braga Melo Teixeira (POR)).
Netherlands: Edwin van der Sar, Michael Reiziger, Danny Blind (C), Winston Bogarde, Ronald de Boer (80' Edgar Davids), Aron Winter, Clarence Seedorf (YC14) (26' Johan de Kock), Richard Witschge, Jordi Cruyff (84' Patrick Kluivert), Dennis Bergkamp, Peter Hoekstra. (Coach: Guus Hiddink (HOL)).
Goals: Netherlands: 0-1 Jordi Cruyff (66'), 0-2 Dennis Bergkamp (79').
Referee: Atanas Uzunov (BUL)   Attendance: 36.800

15-06-1996 Wembley Stadium, London: Scotland – England 0-2 (0-0)
Scotland: Andy Goram, Stewart McKimmie, Colin Calderwood, Colin Hendry (YC70), Tom Boyd, Tosh McKinlay (82' Craig Burley), Stuart McCall, Gary McAllister (C), John Collins (29'), John Spencer (YC38) (67' Ally McCoist), Gordon Durie (87' Eoin Jess). (Coach: James Craig Brown (SCO)).
England: David Seaman, Gary Neville, Tony Adams (C), Gareth Southgate, Stuart Pearce (46' Jamie Redkanpp, 85' Sol Campbell), Darren Anderton, Paul Ince (YC68) (80' Steve Stone), Paul Gascoigne, Steve McManaman, Teddy Sheringham, Alan Shearer (YC75). (Coach: Terry Venables (ENG)).
Goals: England: 0-1 Alan Shearer (53'), 0-2 Paul Gascoigne (79').
Referee: Pierluigi Pairetto (ITA)   Attendance: 76.864

18-06-1996 Villa Park, Birmingham: Scotland – Switzerland 1-0 (1-0)
Scotland: Andy Goram, Tosh McKinlay (60' Scott Booth), Colin Calderwood (YC23), Colin Hendry, Tom Boyd, Craig Burley, Stuart McCall (YC28), Gary McAllister (C), John Collins (YC42), Gordon Durie, Ally McCoist (84' John Spencer). (Coach: James Craig Brown (SCO)).
Switzerland: Marco Pascolo, Marc Hottiger, Stéphane Henchoz, Ramon Vega (YC23), Yvan Quentin (81' Alexandre Comisetti), Marcel Koller (46' Raphael Wicky (YC55)), Ciriaco Sforza (C), Johann Vogel (YC53), Christophe Bonvin, Stéphane Chapuisat (46' Sébastien Fournier (YC63)), Külibay Türkyilmaz. (Coach: Artur Jorge Braga Melo Teixeira (POR)).
Goal: Scotland: 1-0 Ally McCoist (36').
Referee: Václav Krondl (CZE)   Attendance: 34.946

18-06-1996   Wembley Stadium, London: Netherlands – England   1-4 (0-1)
Netherlands: Edwin van der Sar, Michael Reiziger, Danny Blind (C) (YC23), Winston Bogarde, Ronald de Boer (73' Philip Cocu), Clarence Seedorf, Aron Winter (YC18), Richard Witschge (46' Johan de Kock), Jordi Cruyff, Dennis Bergkamp (YC67), Peter Hoekstra (72' Patrick Kluivert). (Coach: Guus Hiddink (HOL)).
England: David Seaman, Gary Neville, Tony Adams (C), Gareth Southgate (YC90), Stuart Pearce, Darren Anderton, Paul Ince (YC43) (68' David Platt), Paul Gascoigne, Steve McManaman, Teddy Sheringham (YC41) (77' Robbie Fowler), Alan Shearer (76' Nick Barmby). (Coach: Terry Venables (ENG)).
Goals: Netherlands: 1-4 Patrick Kluivert (78').
England: 0-1 Alan Shearer (23' penalty), 0-2 Teddy Sheringham (51'), 0-3 Alan Shearer (57'), 0-4 Teddy Sheringham (62').
Referee: Gerd Grabher (AUT)   Attendance: 76.798

GROUP B

09-06-1996	Leeds	Spain – Bulgaria	1-1 (0-0)
10-06-1996	Newcastle upon Tyne	Romania – France	0-1 (0-1)
13-06-1996	Newcastle upon Tyne	Bulgaria – Romania	1-0 (1-0)
15-06-1996	Leeds	France – Spain	1-1 (0-0)
18-06-1996	Newcastle upon Tyne	France – Bulgaria	3-1 (1-0)
18-06-1996	Leeds	Romania – Spain	1-2 (1-1)

FINAL STANDING

Pos	Team	Pld	W	D	L	GF	GA	GD	Pts
1	France	3	2	1	0	5	2	+3	7
2	Spain	3	1	2	0	4	3	+1	5
3	Bulgaria	3	1	1	1	3	4	-1	4
4	Romania	3	0	0	3	1	4	-3	0

France and Spain qualified for the Quarter-finals.

09-06-1996   Elland Road, Leeds: Spain – Bulgaria   1-1 (0-0)
Spain: Andoni ZUBIZARRETA Urreta, ALBERTO BELSUÉ Arias, Rafael ALKORTA Martínez, ABELARDO Fernández Antuña (YC90), SERGI BARJUÁN i Esclusa (YC39), Fernando Ruiz HIERRO, José Luis Pérez CAMINERO (YC27) (82' DONATO Gama da Silva), Guillermo AMOR Martinez (YC42) (70' ALFONSO Pérez Muñóz), JULEN GUERRERO López (51' José Emilio AMAVISCA Gárate), LUIS ENRIQUE Martínez García, Juan Antonio PIZZI Torroja (RC75). (Coach: JAVIER CLEMENTE Lázaro (ESP)).
Bulgaria: Borislav Mihaylov (C), Petar Hubchev (RC72), Radostin Kishishev (YC55), Trifon Ivanov, Ilyan Kiryakov (72' Tsanko Tsvetanov), Zlatko Yankov (YC77), Emil Kostadinov (73' Ivaylo Yordanov), Yordan Lechkov, Krasimir Balakov, Hristo Stoichkov (YC29), Luboslav Penev (78' Daniel Borimirov). (Coach: Dimitar Penev (BUL)).
Goals: Spain: 1-1 ALFONSO Pérez Muñóz (74').
Bulgaria: 0-1 Hristo Stoichkov (65' penalty).
Referee: Piero Ceccarini (ITA)   Attendance: 24.006

10-06-1996   St James'Park, Newcastle upon Tyne: Romania – France   0-1 (0-1)
Romania: Bogdan Stelea, Gheorghe Popescu, Miodrag Belodedici, Gheorghe Mihali (YC49), Dan Petrescu (78' Iulian Filipescu), Tibor Selymes (YC71), Ioan Lupescu, Dorinel Munteanu, Gheorghe Hagi (C), Marius Lacatus (56' Adrian Ilie (YC90)), Florin Raduciou (46' Viorel Moldovan). (Coach: Anghel Iordanescu (ROM)).
France: Bernard Lama, Lilian Thuram, Marcel Desailly, Laurent Blanc, Éric Di Meco (YC20) (68' Bixente Lizarazu), Didier Deschamps (C), Vincent Guérin, Christian Karembeu, Zinédine Zidane (80' Alain Roche), Youri Djorkaeff, Christophe Dugarry (68' Patrice Loko). (Coach: Aimé Jacquet (FRA)).
Goal: France: 0-1 Christophe Dugarry (25').
Referee: Helmut Krug (GER)   Attendance: 26.323

13-06-1996   St James'Park, Newcastle upon Tyne: Bulgaria – Romania   1-0 (1-0)
Bulgaria: Borislav Mihaylov (C), Radostin Kishishev (YC48), Trifon Ivanov, Tsanko Tsvetanov, Zlatko Yankov, Emil Kostadinov (32' Daniel Borimirov (YC64)), Yordan Lechkov (90' Boncho Genchev), Ivaylo Yordanov, Krasimir Balakov, Hristo Stoichkov, Luboslav Penev (72' Nasko Sirakov). (Coach: Dimitar Penev (BUL)).
Romania: Bogdan Stelea, Gheorghe Popescu (78' Adrian Ilie), Daniel Prodan, Miodrag Belodedici, Dan Petrescu, Tibor Selymes, Ioan Lupescu (46' Constantin Galca), Dorinel Munteanu, Gheorghe Hagi (C), Marius Lacatus (29' Viorel Moldovan), Florin Raduciou. (Coach: Anghel Iordanescu (ROM)).
Goal: Bulgaria: 1-0 Hristo Stoichkov (3').
Referee: Peter Mikkelsen (DEN)   Attendance: 19.107

15-06-1996   Elland Road, Leeds: France – Spain   1-1 (0-0)
France: Bernard Lama, Jocelyn Angloma (65' Alain Roche), Marcel Desailly, Laurent Blanc (YC43), Bixente Lizarazu, Didier Deschamps (C), Vincent Guérin (81' Lilian Thuram), Christian Karembeu (YC60), Zinédine Zidane, Youri Djorkaeff (YC63), Patrice Loko (74' Christophe Dugarry). (Coach: Aimé Jacquet (FRA)).
Spain: Andoni ZUBIZARRETA Urreta, Juan Manuel "JUANMA" López Martinez, Rafael ALKORTA Martínez, ABELARDO Fernández Antuña, Jorge OTERO Bouzos (YC56) (59' Francisco Narvaez Machon "KIKO"), SERGI BARJUÁN i Esclusa, Fernando Ruiz HIERRO, José Luis Pérez CAMINERO, LUIS ENRIQUE Martínez García (YC12) (55' Javier MANJARÍN Pereda), José Emilio AMAVISCA Gárate (YC53), ALFONSO Pérez Muñóz (83' JULIO SALINAS Fernández). (Coach: JAVIER CLEMENTE Lázaro (ESP)).
Goals: France: 1-0 Youri Djorkaeff (48').
Spain: 1-1 José Luis Pérez CAMINERO (85').
Referee: Vadim Zhuk (BLS)   Attendance: 35.626

18-06-1996   St James' Park, Newcastle upon Tyne: France – Bulgaria   3-1 (1-0)
France: Bernard Lama, Lilian Thuram, Marcel Desailly (YC3), Laurent Blanc, Bixente Lizarazu, Didier Deschamps (C), Vincent Guérin, Christian Karembeu, Zinédine Zidane (62' Reynald Pedros), Youri Djorkaeff, Christophe Dugarry (YC36) (70' Patrice Loko). (Coach: Aimé Jacquet (FRA)).
Bulgaria: Borislav Mihaylov (C), Petar Hubchev, Emil Kremenliev (YC14), Trifon Ivanov (YC8), Tsanko Tsvetanov, Zlatko Yankov (79' Daniel Borimirov), Ivaylo Yordanov, Yordan Lechkov, Krasimir Balakov (82' Georgi Donkov), Hristo Stoichkov, Luboslav Penev. (Coach: Dimitar Penev (BUL)).
Goals: France: 1-0 Laurent Blanc (21'), 2-0 Luboslav Penev (63' *own goal*), 3-1 Patrice Loko (90').
Bulgaria: 2-1 Hristo Stoichkov (69').
Referee: Dermot J.Gallagher (ENG) (28' Paul Anthony Durkin (ENG))
Attendance: 26.976

18-06-1996   Elland Road, Leeds: Romania – Spain   1-2 (1-1)
Romania: Florian Prunea, Gheorghe Popescu, Anton Dobos, Daniel Prodan (86' Ioan Lupescu), Dan Petrescu, Tibor Selymes, Ovidiu Stinga, Constantin Galca (YC77), Gheorghe Hagi (C) (YC21), Adrian Ilie (YC47) (66' Dorinel Munteanu), Florin Raduciou (77' Ion Vladoiu). (Coach: Anghel Iordanescu (ROM)).
Spain: Andoni ZUBIZARRETA Urreta (C), Juan Manuel "JUANMA" López Martinez, Rafael ALKORTA Martínez, ABELARDO Fernández Antuña (64' Guillermo AMOR Martinez), SERGI BARJUÁN i Esclusa, Miguel Ángel NADAL Homar (YC59), Fernando Ruiz HIERRO, Javier MANJARÍN Pereda, José Emilio AMAVISCA Gárate (72' JULEN GUERRERO López, Francisco Narvaez Machon "KIKO" (YC36), Juan Antonio PIZZI Torroja (57' ALFONSO Pérez Muñóz). (Coach: JAVIER CLEMENTE Lázaro (ESP)).
Goals: Romania: 1-1 Florin Raduciou (29').
Spain: 0-1 Javier MANJARÍN Pereda (11'), 1-2 Guillermo AMOR Martinez (84').
Referee: Ahmet Çakar (TUR)   Attendance: 32.719

GROUP C

09-06-1996	Manchester	Germany – Czech Republic	2-0 (2-0)
11-06-1996	Liverpool	Italy – Russia	2-1 (1-1)
14-06-1996	Liverpool	Czech Republic – Italy	2-1 (2-1)
16-06-1996	Manchester	Russia – Germany	0-3 (0-0)
19-06-1996	Liverpool	Russia – Czech Republic	3-3 (0-2)
19-06-1996	Manchester	Italy – Germany	0-0

FINAL STANDING

Pos	Team	Pld	W	D	L	GF	GA	GD	Pts
1	*Germany*	*3*	*2*	*1*	*0*	*5*	*0*	*+5*	*7*
2	*Czech Republic*	*3*	*1*	*1*	*1*	*5*	*6*	*-1*	*4*
3	Italy	3	1	1	1	3	3	0	4
4	Russia	3	0	1	2	4	8	-4	1

Germany and Czech Republic qualified for the Quarter-finals.

09-06-1996   Old Trafford, Manchester: Germany – Czech Republic   2-0 (2-0)
Germany: Andreas Köpke, Matthias Sammer, Thomas Helmer, Jürgen Kohler (C) (14' Markus Babbel (YC59)), Stefan Reuter (YC69), Christian Ziege (YC28), Dieter Eilts, Thomas Häßler (YC77), Andreas Möller (YC58), Fredi Bobic (65' Thomas Strunz), Stefan Kuntz (YC52) (83' Oliver Bierhoff). (Coach: Hans-Hubert (Berti) Vogts (GER)).
Czech Republic: Petr Kouba, Michal Hornák (78'), Miroslav Kadlec (C) (YC67), Jan Suchopárek, Radoslav Látal, Jirí Nemec, Radek Bejbl (YC19), Pavel Nedved (YC45), Martin Frydek (46' Patrik Berger), Karel Poborsky (46' Radek Drulák (YC67)), Pavel Kuka. (Coach: Dusan Uhrin (CZE)).
Goals: Germany: 1-0 Christian Ziege (26'), 2-0 Andreas Möller (32').
Referee: David Roland Elleray (ENG)   Attendance: 37.300

11-06-1996   Anfield, Liverpool: Italy – Russia   2-1 (1-1)
Italy: Angelo Peruzzi, Roberto Mussi, Alessandro Costacurta, Luigi Apolloni, Paolo Maldini (C), Angelo Di Livio (62' Diego Fuser), Roberto Di Matteo, Demetrio Albertini (YC14), Alessandro Del Piero (46' Roberto Donadoni (YC83)), Gianfranco Zola, Pierluigi Casiraghi (80' Fabrizio Ravanelli). (Coach: Arrigo Sacchi (ITA)).
Russia: Stanislav Cherchesov, Omari Tetradze, Viktor Onopko (C) (YC8), Yuri Kovtun (YC82), Yevgeni Bushmanov (46' Igor Yanovski), Andrei Kanchelskis, Valeri Karpin (63' Sergei Kiryakov), Vladimir Radimov, Ilya Tsymbalar (71' Igor Dobrovolskiy), Aleksandr Mostovoy, Igor Kolyvanov (YC31). (Coach: Oleg Romantsev (RUS)).
Goals: Italy: 1-0 Pierluigi Casiraghi (5'), 2-1 Pierluigi Casiraghi (52').
Russia: 1-1 Ilya Tsymbalar (21').
Referee: Leslie William Mottram (SCO)   Attendance: 35.120

14-06-1996   Anfield, Liverpool: Czech Republic – Italy   2-1 (2-1)
Czech Republic: Petr Kouba, Jan Suchopárek (YC20), Miroslav Kadlec (C) (YC90), Michal Hornák, Radoslav Látal (YC50) (88' Václav Nemecek), Radek Bejbl, Jirí Nemec, Pavel Nedved, Karel Poborsky, Patrik Berger (64' Vladimir Smicer), Pavel Kuka (YC59). (Coach: Dusan Uhrin (CZE)).
Italy: Angelo Peruzzi, Roberto Mussi, Alessandro Costacurta, Luigi Apolloni (RC29), Paolo Maldini (C), Diego Fuser (YC90), Dino Baggio (39' Amedeo Carboni), Demetrio Albertini, Roberto Donadoni, Fabrizio Ravanelli (58' Pierluigi Casiraghi), Enrico Chiesa (78' Gianfranco Zola). (Coach: Arrigo Sacchi (ITA)).
Goals: Czech Republic: 1-0 Pavel Nedved (4'), 2-1 Radek Bejbl (35').
Italy: 1-1 Enrico Chiesa (18').
Referee: Antonio Jesús López Nieto (ESP)   Attendance: 37.320

16-06-1996   Old Trafford, Manchester: Russia – Germany   0-3 (0-0)
Russia: Dmitri Kharin, Omari Tetradze, Viktor Onopko (C) (YC30), Yuri Nikiforov, Yuri Kovtun (RC70), Andrei Kanchelskis (YC13), Vladislav Radimov (46' Valeri Karpin), Dmitri Khokhlov (66' Igor Simutenkov), Ilya Tsymbalar, Aleksandr Mostovoy, Igor Kolyvanov. (Coach: Oleg Romantsev (RUS)).
Germany: Andreas Köpke, Matthias Sammer, Markus Babbel (YC16), Thomas Helmer, Stefan Reuter, Christian Ziege, Dieter Eilts, Thomas Häßler (67' Steffen Freund), Andreas Möller (87' Thomas Strunz), Jürgen Klinsmann (C), Oliver Bierhoff (YC31) (85' Stefan Kuntz). (Coach: Hans-Hubert (Berti) Vogts (GER)).
Goals: Germany: 0-1 Matthias Sammer (56'), 0-2 Jürgen Klinsmann (77'), 0-3 Jürgen Klinsmann (90').
Referee: Kim Milton Nielsen (DEN)   Attendance: 50.760

19-06-1996   Anfield, Liverpool: Russia – Czech Republic   3-3 (0-2)
Russia: Stanislav Cherchesov, Omari Tetradze, Yuri Nikiforov (YC5), Sergei Gorlukovich, Igor Yanovski (YC61), Valeri Karpin (C), Dmitri Khokhlov, Vladislav Radimov (YC26), Ilya Tsymbalar (YC28) (67' Igor Shalimov), Igor Kolyvanov (46' Aleksandr Mostovoy), Igor Simutenkov (46' Vladimir Beschastnikh). (Coach: Oleg Romantsev (RUS)).
Czech Republic: Petr Kouba, Michal Hornák, Lubos Kubík (C), Jan Suchopárek, Radoslav Látal, Radek Bejbl, Jirí Nemec (YC77), Pavel Nedved (YC60), Karel Poborsky, Patrik Berger (90' Václav Nemecek), Pavel Kuka (69' Vladimir Smicer). (Coach: Dusan Uhrin (CZE)).
Goals: Russia: 1-2 Aleksandr Mostovoy (49'), 2-2 Omari Tetradze (54'), 3-2 Vladimir Beschastnikh (85').
Czech Republic: 0-1 Jan Suchopárek (5'), 0-2 Pavel Kuka (19'), 3-3 Vladimir Smicer (88').
Referee: Anders Frisk (SWE)   Attendance: 21.128

19-06-1996   Old Trafford, Manchester: Italy – Germany   0-0
Italy: Angelo Peruzzi, Roberto Mussi, Alessandro Costacurta, Paolo Maldini (C), Amedeo Carboni (76' Moreno Torricelli), Diego Fuser (81' Angelo Di Livio), Roberto Di Matteo (67' Enrico Chiesa), Demetrio Albertini, Roberto Donadoni, Pierluigi Casiraghi (YC18), Gianfranco Zola. (Coach: Arrigo Sacchi (ITA)).
Germany: Andreas Köpke, Matthias Sammer, Steffen Freund, Thomas Helmer, Thomas Strunz (RC59), Christian Ziege, Dieter Eilts, Thomas Häßler, Andreas Möller (89' Marco Bode), Jürgen Klinsmann (C), Fredi Bobic. (Coach: Hans-Hubert (Berti) Vogts (GER)).
Referee: Guy Goethals (BEL)   Attendance: 53.740

GROUP D

09-06-1996	Sheffield	Denmark – Portugal	1-1 (1-0)
11-06-1996	Nottingham	Turkey – Croatia	0-1 (0-0)
14-06-1996	Nottingham	Portugal – Turkey	1-0 (0-0)
16-06-1996	Sheffield	Croatia – Denmark	3-0 (0-0)
19-06-1996	Nottingham	Croatia – Portugal	0-3 (0-2)
19-06-1996	Sheffield	Turkey – Denmark	0-3 (0-0)

FINAL STANDING

Pos	Team	Pld	W	D	L	GF	GA	GD	Pts
1	*Portugal*	3	2	1	0	5	1	+4	7
2	*Croatia*	3	2	0	1	4	3	+1	6
3	Denmark	3	1	1	1	4	4	0	4
4	Turkey	3	0	0	3	0	5	-5	0

Portugal and Croatia qualified for the Quarter-finals.

09-06-1996   Hillsborough, Sheffield: Denmark – Portugal   1-1 (1-0)
Denmark: Peter Schmeichel, Thomas Helveg (YC30), Marc Rieper, Jes Høgh, Jens Risager (YC14), Brian Steen Nielsen, Claus Thomsen (83' Torben Piechnik), Henrik Larsen (90' Kim Vilfort), Michael Laudrup (C), Mikkel Beck, Brian Laudrup. (Coach: Richard Møller Nielsen (DEN)).
Portugal: VÍTOR Manuel Martins BAÍA (C), João Paulo Maio dos "PAULINHO" SANTOS (YC9), HÉLDER Marino Rodrigues Cristóvão, FERNANDO Manuel Silva COUTO, DIMAS Manuel Marques Teixeira, OCEANO Andrade da Cruz (YC24) (37' ANTÓNIO José dos Santos FOLHA), RUI Manuel César COSTA, PAULO Manuel Carvalho de SOUSA (YC58) (79' JOSÉ Fernando Gomes TAVARES), LUÍS Filipe Madeira Caeiro FIGO (62' DOMINGOS José Paciência DE OLIVEIRA), JOÃO Manuel Vieira PINTO (YC73), Ricardo Manuel Andrade Silva SÁ PINTO (YC41). (Coach: ANTÓNIO Luis Alves Ribeiro OLIVEIRA (POR)).
Goals: Denmark: 1-0 Brian Laudrup (22').
Portugal: 1-1 Ricardo Manuel Andrade Silva SÁ PINTO (53').
Referee: Mario van der Ende (HOL)   Attendance: 34.993

11-06-1996   City Ground, Nottingham: Turkey – Croatia   0-1 (0-0)
Turkey: Rüstü Reçber, Vedat Inceefe, Rahim Zafer, Ogün Temizkanoglu (C), Alpay Özalan, Tolunay Kafkas (YC31) (89' Saffet Sancakli), Arif Erdem (82' Hami Mandirali), Tugay Kerimoglu, Abdullah Ercan, Sergen Yalçin, Hakan Sükür. (Coach: Fatih Terim (TUR)).
Croatia: Drazen Ladic, Nikola Jerkan, Slaven Bilic, Igor Stimac, Mario Stanic, Robert Jarni, Zvonimir Boban (C) (YC55) (57' Zvonimir Soldo), Robert Prosinecki, Aljosa Asanovic (YC40), Alen Boksic (73' Goran Vlaovic), Davor Suker (90' Dubravko Pavlicic). (Coach: Miroslav Blazevic (CRO)).
Goal: Croatia: 0-1 Goran Vlaovic (86').
Referee: Serge Muhmenthaler (SUI)   Attendance: 22.406

14-06-1996   City Ground, Nottingham: Portugal – Turkey   1-0 (0-0)
Portugal: VÍTOR Manuel Martins BAÍA (C), João Paulo Maio dos "PAULINHO" SANTOS (YC2), HÉLDER Marino Rodrigues Cristóvão, FERNANDO Manuel Silva COUTO, DIMAS Manuel Marques Teixeira, PAULO Manuel Carvalho de SOUSA, ANTÓNIO José dos Santos FOLHA (46' JOSÉ Fernando Gomes TAVARES (YC72)), RUI Manuel César COSTA, LUÍS Filipe Madeira Caeiro FIGO (YC58), JOÃO Manuel Vieira PINTO (77' HUGO Cardoso PORFIRIO), Ricardo Manuel Andrade Silva SÁ PINTO (65' JORGE Paulo CADETE Santos Reis). (Coach: ANTÓNIO Luis Alves Ribeiro OLIVEIRA (POR)).
Turkey: Rüstü Reçber, Vedat Inceefe (YC65), Ogün Temizkanoglu (46' Rahim Zafer (YC73)), Alpay Özalan, Recep Çetin, Oguz Çetin (C) (69' Arif Erdem), Tugay Kerimoglu, Abdullah Ercan (YC43), Sergen Yalçin, Saffet Sancakli (63' Tolunay Kafkas (YC76)), Hakan Sükür. (Coach: Fatih Terim (TUR)).
Goal: Portugal: 1-0 FERNANDO Manuel Silva COUTO (66').
Referee: Sándor Puhl (HUN)   Attendance: 22.670

16-06-1996   Hillsborough, Sheffield: Croatia – Denmark   3-0 (0-0)
Croatia: Drazen Ladic, Nikola Jerkan, Slaven Bilic, Igor Stimac, Mario Stanic (YC20), Robert Jarni, Robert Prosinecki (YC23) (88' Mladen Mladenovic), Zvonimir Boban (C) (82' Nikola Jurcevic), Aljosa Asanovic, Davor Suker, Goran Vlaovic (YC39) (82' Zvonimir Soldo). (Coach: Miroslav Blazevic (CRO)).
Denmark: Peter Schmeichel, Thomas Helveg (46' Jacob Laursen), Marc Rieper, Jes Høgh, Michael Schjønberg, Brian Steen Nielsen, Claus Thomsen, Henrik Larsen (69' Stig Tøfting), Michael Laudrup (C), Kim Vilfort (59' Mikkel Beck), Brian Laudrup. (Coach: Richard Møller Nielsen (DEN)).
Goals: Croatia: 1-0 Davor Suker (53' penalty), 2-0 Zvonimir Boban (81'), 3-0 Davor Suker (90').
Referee: Marc Batta (FRA)   Attendance: 33.671

19-06-1996   City Ground, Nottingham: Croatia – Portugal   0-3 (0-2)
Croatia: Marijan Mrmic, Dubravko Pavlicic (YC36), Slaven Bilic, Zvonimir Soldo, Dario Simic, Robert Jarni (C) (YC30), Mladen Mladenovic (46' Zvonimir Boban), Nikola Jurcevic, Robert Prosinecki (46' Aljosa Asanovic, Igor Pamic (YC10) (46' Davor Suker), Goran Vlaovic. (Coach: Miroslav Blazevic (CRO)).
Portugal: VÍTOR Manuel Martins BAÍA (C), CARLOS Alberto de Oliveira SECRETÁRIO, FERNANDO Manuel Silva COUTO, HÉLDER Marino Rodrigues Cristóvão, DIMAS Manuel Marques Teixeira, OCEANO Andrade da Cruz, PAULO Manuel Carvalho de SOUSA (70' JOSÉ Fernando Gomes TAVARES), RUI Manuel César COSTA (61' PEDRO Alexandre dos Santos BARBOSA), LUÍS Filipe Madeira Caeiro FIGO, Ricardo Manuel Andrade Silva SÁ PINTO (46' DOMINGOS José Paciência DE OLIVEIRA), JOÃO Manuel Vieira PINTO. (Coach: ANTÓNIO Luis Alves Ribeiro OLIVEIRA (POR)).
Goals: Portugal: 0-1 LUÍS Filipe Madeira Caeiro FIGO (4'), 0-2 JOÃO Manuel Vieira PINTO (33'), 0-3 DOMINGOS José Paciência DE OLIVEIRA (82').
Referee: Bernd Heynemann (GER)   Attendance: 20.484

19-06-1996   Hillsborough, Sheffield: Turkey – Denmark   0-3 (0-0)
Turkey: Rüstü Reçber (YC89), Vedat Inceefe, Ogün Temizkanoglu, Alpay Özalan, Recep Çetin (C) (68' Bülent Korkmaz), Tugay Kerimoglu (YC44), Hami Mandirali, Tayfun Korkut (YC61), Abdullah Ercan, Orhan Çikirikçi (68' Saffet Sancakli), Hakan Sükür (46' Arif Erdem). (Coach: Fatih Terim (TUR)).
Denmark: Peter Schmeichel, Thomas Helveg (YC57), Jes Høgh, Marc Rieper, Michael Schjønberg (46' Henrik Larsen (YC81)), Brian Steen Nielsen, Claus Thomsen, Allan Nielsen, Michael Laudrup (C), Erik Bo Andersen (88' Søren Andersen), Brian Laudrup. (Coach: Richard Møller Nielsen (DEN)).
Goals: Denmark: 0-1 Brian Laudrup (50'), 0-2 Allan Nielsen (69'), 0-3 Brian Laudrup (84').
Referee: Nikolai Vladislavovich Levnikov (RUS)   Attendance: 28.671

QUARTER-FINALS

22-06-1996   Wembley Stadium, London: Spain – England   0-0 (AET)
Spain: Andoni ZUBIZARRETA Urreta (C), Miguel Ángel NADAL Homar, Rafael ALKORTA Martínez (72'), ABELARDO Fernández Antuña (YC1), ALBERTO BELSUÉ Arias (YC40), Fernando Ruiz HIERRO, Guillermo AMOR Martinez, Javier MANJARÍN Pereda (46' José Luis Pérez CAMINERO), SERGI BARJUÁN i Esclusa, Francisco Narvaez Machon "KIKO", JULIO SALINAS Fernández (46' ALFONSO Pérez Muñóz (YC50)). (Coach: JAVIER CLEMENTE Lázaro (ESP)).
England: David Seaman, Gary Neville (YC47), Tony Adams (C), Gareth Southgate, Stuart Pearce, Steve McManaman (109' Nick Barmby), David Platt, Paul Gascoigne, Darren Anderton (109' Steve Stone), Alan Shearer, Teddy Sheringham (109' Robbie Fowler). (Coach: Terry Venables (ENG)).
Referee: Marc Batta (FRA)   Attendance: 75.440
Penalties: 1 Alan Shearer   * Fernando Ruiz HIERRO
                2 David Platt   1 Guillermo AMOR Martinez
                3 Stuart Pearce   2 ALBERTO BELSUÉ Arias
                4 Paul Gascoigne   * Miguel Ángel NADAL Homar
(After extra time England win 4-2 on penalties)

22-06-1996   Anfield, Liverpool: France – Netherlands   0-0 (AET)
France: Bernard Lama, Lilian Thuram, Laurent Blanc, Marcel Desailly, Bixente Lizarazu, Christian Karembeu (YC48), Didier Deschamps (C) (YC7), Vincent Guérin, Zinédine Zidane, Youri Djorkaeff, Patrice Loko (61' Christophe Dugarry, 80' Reynald Pedros). (Coach: Aimé Jacquet (FRA)).
Netherlands: Edwin van der Sar, Michael Reiziger, Johan de Kock (YC68), Winston Bogarde (YC90), Danny Blind (C), Ronald de Boer, Richard Witschge (80' Youri Mulder), Dennis Bergkamp (60' Clarence Seedorf), Jordi Cruyff (69' Aron Winter), Philip Cocu, Patrick Kluivert (YC89). (Coach: Guus Hiddink (HOL)).
Referee: Antonio Jesús López Nieto (ESP)   Attendance: 37.465
Penalties: 1 Johan de Kock   1 Zinédine Zidane
                2 Ronald de Boer   2 Youri Djorkaeff
                3 Patrick Kluivert   3 Bixente Lizarazu
                * Clarence Seedorf   4 Vincent Guérin
                4 Danny Blind   5 Laurent Blanc
(After extra time France win 5-4 on penalties)

23-06-1996   Old Trafford, Manchester: Germany – Croatia   2-1 (1-0)
Germany: Andreas Köpke, Matthias Sammer (YC5), Markus Babbel, Thomas Helmer, Stefan Reuter, Christian Ziege, Dieter Eilts, Andreas Möller, Mehmet Scholl (88' Thomas Häßler), Fredi Bobic (46' Stefan Kuntz), Jürgen Klinsmann (C) (YC7) (39' Steffen Freund). (Coach: Hans-Hubert (Berti) Vogts (GER)).
Croatia: Drazen Ladic, Nikola Jerkan, Slaven Bilic, Igor Stimac (RC56), Mario Stanic, Robert Jarni, Nikola Jurcevic (78' Mladen Mladenovic), Zvonimir Boban (C), Aljosa Asanovic, Davor Suker, Goran Vlaovic. (Coach: Miroslav Blazevic (CRO)).
Goals: Germany: 1-0 Jürgen Klinsmann (20' penalty), 2-1 Matthias Sammer (59').
Croatia: 1-1 Davor Suker (51').
Referee: Leif Sundell (SWE)   Attendance: 43.412

23-06-1996   Villa Park, Birmingham: Czech Republic – Portugal   1-0 (0-0)
Czech Republic: Petr Kouba, Jan Suchopárek (YC1), Miroslav Kadlec, Michal Hornák, Radoslav Látal (RC82), Jirí Nemec, Václav Nemecek (C) (90' Patrik Berger), Radek Bejbl, Karel Poborsky, Vladimir Smicer (46' Lubos Kubík), Pavel Kuka. (Coach: Dusan Uhrin (CZE)).
Portugal: VÍTOR Manuel Martins BAÍA (C), CARLOS Alberto de Oliveira SECRETÁRIO (YC59), FERNANDO Manuel Silva COUTO, HÉLDER Marino Rodrigues Cristóvão (YC10), DIMAS Manuel Marques Teixeira, OCEANO Andrade da Cruz (65' ANTÓNIO José dos Santos FOLHA), PAULO Manuel Carvalho de SOUSA, RUI Manuel César COSTA, LUÍS Filipe Madeira Caeiro FIGO (82' JORGE Paulo CADETE Santos Reis), JOÃO Manuel Vieira PINTO (YC90), Ricardo Manuel Andrade Silva SÁ PINTO (YC40) (46' DOMINGOS José Paciência DE OLIVEIRA). (Coach: ANTÓNIO Luis Alves Ribeiro OLIVEIRA (POR)).
Goal: Czech Republic: 1-0 Karel Poborsky (53').
Referee: Helmut Krug (GER)   Attendance: 26.832

SEMI-FINALS

26-06-1996   Old Trafford, Manchester: France – Czech Republic   0-0 (AET)
France: Bernard Lama, Lilian Thuram (YC43) (83' Jocelyn Angloma), Laurent Blanc (C), Alain Roche (YC50), Bixente Lizarazu (YC64), Marcel Desailly, Sabri Lamouchi (62' Reynald Pedros), Vincent Guérin, Zinédine Zidane, Youri Djorkaeff, Patrice Loko. (Coach: Aimé Jacquet (FRA)).
Czech Republic: Petr Kouba, Michal Hornák, Miroslav Kadlec, Karel Rada, Pavel Nedved (YC77), Václav Nemecek (C) (YC83), Jirí Nemec (84' Lubos Kubík (YC97)), Pavel Novotny, Karel Poborsky, Vladimir Smicer (46' Patrik Berger), Radek Drulák (70' Martin Kotulek). (Coach: Dusan Uhrin (CZE)).
Referee: Leslie William Mottram (SCO)   Attendance: 43.877
Penalties: 1 Zinédine Zidane   1 Lubos Kubík
              2 Youri Djorkaeff   2 Pavel Nedved
              3 Bixente Lizarazu   3 Patrik Berger
              4 Vincent Guérin   4 Karel Poborsky
              5 Laurent Blanc   5 Karel Rada
              * Reynald Pedros   6 Miroslav Kadlec
(After extra time Czech Republic win 6-5 on penalties)

26-06-1996   Wembley Stadium, London: Germany – England   1-1 (1-1, 1-1) (AET)
Germany: Andreas Köpke, Matthias Sammer, Thomas Helmer (110' Marco Bode), Markus Babbel, Stefan Reuter (YC46), Christian Ziege, Dieter Eilts, Steffen Freund (118' Thomas Strunz), Andreas Möller (C) (YC80), Mehmet Scholl (77' Thomas Häßler), Stefan Kuntz. (Coach: Hans-Hubert (Berti) Vogts (GER)).
England: David Seaman, Gareth Southgate, Tony Adams (C), Stuart Pearce, Darren Anderton, Steve McManaman, David Platt, Paul Ince, Paul Gascoigne (YC73), Alan Shearer, Teddy Sheringham. (Coach: Terry Venables (ENG)).
Goals: Germany: 1-1 Stefan Kuntz (16').
England: 0-1 Alan Shearer (3').
Referee: Sándor Puhl (HUN)   Attendance: 75.862
Penalties: 1 Alan Shearer   1 Thomas Häßler
             2 David Platt   2 Thomas Strunz
             3 Stuart Pearce   3 Stefan Reuter
             4 Paul Gascoigne   4 Christian Ziege
             5 Teddy Sheringham   5 Stefan Kuntz
             * Gareth Southgate   6 Andreas Möller
(After extra time Germany win 6-5 on penalties)

FINAL

30-06-1996   Wembley Stadium, London: Czech Republic – Germany   1-2 (0-0, 1-1) (AET)
Czech Republic: Petr Kouba, Jan Suchopárek, Miroslav Kadlec (C), Michal Hornák (YC47), Karel Rada, Pavel Nedved, Jirí Nemec, Radek Bejbl, Patrik Berger, Karel Poborsky (88' Vladimir Smicer), Pavel Kuka. (Coach: Dusan Uhrin (CZE)).
Germany: Andreas Köpke, Matthias Sammer (YC69), Thomas Helmer (YC63), Dieter Eilts (46' Marco Bode), Markus Babbel, Christian Ziege (YC91), Thomas Häßler, Thomas Strunz, Mehmet Scholl (69' Oliver Bierhoff), Stefan Kuntz Jürgen Klinsmann (C). (Coach: Hans-Hubert (Berti) Vogts (GER)).
Goals: Czech Republic: 1-0 Patrik Berger (59' penalty).
Germany: 1-1 Oliver Bierhoff (73'), 1-2 Oliver Bierhoff (95').
Referee: Pierluigi Pairetto (ITA)   Attendance: 73.611

*** **Germany were European Champions** ***

GOALSCORERS TOURNAMENT 1994-1996:

Goals	Players
15	Davor Suker (CRO)
13	Hristo Stoichkov (BUL)
12	Jürgen Klinsmann (GER)
11	Toni Polster (AUT)
7	Emil Kostadinov (BUL), Patrik Berger (CZE), Mixu Paatelainen (FIN), Gianfranco Zola (ITA), Andrzej Juskowiak (POL), DOMINGOS José Paciência DE OLIVEIRA (POR), Florin Raducioiu (ROM), Hakan Sükür (TUR)

6	Youri Djorkaeff (FRA), Ronen Harazi (ISR)
5	Sergei Gerasimets (BLS), Kim Vilfort (DEN), Alan Shearer (ENG), John Aldridge (IRL), Vits Rimkus (LAT), Iain Dowie (NIR), PAULO Lourenço Martins ALVES (POR), Igor Kolyvanov (RUS), Tymerlan Huseynov (UKR)
4	Sokol Kushta (ALB), Peter Stöger (AUT), Marc Degryse (BEL), Brian Laudrup (DEN), Michael Laudrup (DEN), Fernando Ruiz HIERRO (ESP), Todi Jónsson (FAR), Jari Litmanen (FIN), Shota Arveladze (GEO), Temur Ketsbaia (GEO), Andreas Möller (GER), Matthias Sammer (GER), Alexis Alexandris (GRE), Nikos Machlas (GRE), Panagiotis Tsalouchidis (GRE), Patrick Kluivert (HOL), Marc Overmars (HOL), Clarence Seedorf (HOL), Fabrizio Ravanelli (ITA), James Quinn (NIR), JOÃO Manuel Vieira PINTO (POR), LUÍS Filipe Madeira Caeiro FIGO (POR), RUI Manuel César COSTA (POR), Vassili Kulkov (RUS), Scott Booth (SCO), John Collins (SCO), Zlatko Zahovic (SLO), Kübilay Türkyilmaz (SUI)
3	Krasimir Balakov (BUL), Zvonimir Boban (CRO), Marios Agathocleous (CYP), Radek Drulák (CZE), José Luis Pérez CAMINERO (ESP), JULIO SALINAS Fernández (ESP), Martin Reim (EST), Giorgi Kinkladze (GEO), Ulf Kirsten (GER), Ronald de Boer (HOL), Wim Jonk (HOL), Youri Mulder (HOL), Bryan Roy (HOL), Niall Quinn (IRL), Ronny Rosenthal (ISR), Pierluigi Casiraghi (ITA), Armands Zeiberlins (LAT), Darius Maciulevicius (LIT), Arūnas Suika (LIT), Bosko Djurovski (MCD), Phillip Gray (NIR), Michael O'Neill (NIR), Henning Berg (NOR), Jan Åge Fjørtoft (NOR), Kjetil Rekdal (NOR), Roman Kosecki (POL), Marius Lacatus (ROM), Vladimir Beschastnikh (RUS), Sergei Kiryakov (RUS), Aleksandr Mostovoy (RUS), Dmitri Radchenko (RUS), Ally McCoist (SCO), Primoz Gliha (SLO), Saso Udovic (SLO), Christophe Ohrel (SUI), Peter Dubovsky (SVK), Tibor Jancula (SVK)
2	Altin Rraklli (ALB), Razmik Grigoryan (ARM), Armen Shahgeldyan (ARM), Andreas Herzog (AUT), Adolf Hütter (AUT), Nazim Suleymanov (AZE), Gilles De Bilde (BEL), Georges Grün (BEL), Luc Nilis (BEL), Günther Schepens (BEL), Enzo Scifo (BEL), Luboslav Penev (BUL), Roberto Prosinecki (CRO), Andreas Sotiriou (CYP), Pavel Kuka (CZE), Horst Siegl (CZE), Tomás Skuhravy (CZE), Jan Suchopárek (CZE), Mikkel Beck (DEN), Allan Nielsen (DEN), Michael Schjønberg (DEN), Teddy Sheringham (ENG), ALFONSO Pérez Muñóz (ESP), DONATO Gama da Silva (ESP), JULEN GUERRERO López (ESP), LUIS ENRIQUE Martínez García (ESP), Javier MANJARÍN Pereda (ESP), Juan Antonio PIZZI Torroja (ESP), Jan Allan Müller (FAR), Ari Hjelm (FIN), Antti Sumiala (FIN), Laurent Blanc (FRA), Christophe Dugarry (FRA), Vincent Guérin (FRA), Frank Leboeuf (FRA), Patrice Loko (FRA), Zinédine Zidane (FRA), Oliver Bierhoff (GER), Lothar Matthäus (GER), Christian Ziege (GER), Georgios Donis (GRE), Demis Nikolaidis (GRE), Dennis Bergkamp (HOL), Gábor Halmai (HUN), Béla Illés (HUN), József Kiprich (HUN), Tommy Coyne (IRL), John Sheridan (IRL), Demetrio Albertini (ITA), Valdas Ivanauskas (LIT), Serghei Clescenco (MOL), Iurii Miterev (MOL), Radu Rebeja (MOL), Øyvind Leonhardsen (NOR), Piotr Nowak (POL), FERNANDO Manuel Silva COUTO (POR), João Paulo Maio dos FERNANDO Maio dos "PAULINHO" SANTOS (POR), Gheorghe Hagi (ROM), Dorinel Munteanu (ROM), Valeri Karpin (RUS), Yuri Nikiforov (RUS), Igor Shalimov (RUS), Ilya Tsymbalar (RUS), John McGinlay (SCO), Billy McKinlay (SCO), Dzoni Novak (SLO), Thomas Bickel (SUI), Ciriaco Sforza (SUI), Nestor

	Subiat (SUI), Jaroslav Timko (SVK), Kennet Andersson (SWE), Tomas Brolin (SWE), Martin Dahlin (SWE), Saffet Sancakli (TUR), Sergen Yalçin (TUR), Dean Saunders (WAL), Gary Speed (WAL)
1	Arian Bellaj (ALB), Salvador Kaçaj (ALB), Rudi Vata (ALB), Hysen Zmijani (ALB), Artur Petrosyan (ARM), Franz Aigner (AUT), Dietmar Kühbauer (AUT), Andreas Ogris (AUT), Heimo Peifenberger (AUT), Markus Pürk (AUT), Dieter Ramusch (AUT), Herfried Sabitzer (AUT), Markus Schopp (AUT), Christian Stumpf (AUT), Arnold Wetl (AUT), Gert Verheyen (BEL), Bruno Versavel (BEL), Igor Gurinovich (BLS), Miroslav Romashchenko (BLS), Alexandre Taykov (BLS), Trifon Ivanov (BUL), Yordan Lechkov (BUL), Alen Boksic (CRO), Nikola Jerkan (CRO), Nikolas Jurcevic (CRO), Ardian Kozniku (CRO), Mladen Mladenovic (CRO), Igor Stimac (CRO), Goran Vlaovic (CRO), Kostakis Fasouliotis (CYP), Radek Bejbl (CZE), Martin Frydek (CZE), Miroslav Kadlec (CZE), Lubos Kubík (CZE), Pavel Nedved (CZE), Václav Nemecek (CZE), Karel Poborsky (CZE), Daniel Smejkal (CZE), Vladimir Smicer (CZE), John Faxe Jensen (DEN), Peter Nielsen (DEN), Flemming Povlsen (DEN), Mark Strudal (DEN), Paul Gascoigne (ENG), José Emilio AMAVISCA Gárate (ESP), Guillermo AMOR Martinez (ESP), Jon Andoni GOIKOETXEA Lasa (ESP), Francisco HIGUERA Fernández (ESP), Francisco Narvaez Machon "KIKO" (ESP), Miguel Angel NADAL Homar (ESP), Jens Kristian Hansen (FAR), Henning Jarnskor (FAR), Julian Schantz Johnsson (FAR), Jens Erik Rasmussen (FAR), Petri Helin (FIN), Janne Lindberg (FIN), Kim Suominen (FIN), Christophe Cocard (FRA), Marcel Desailly (FRA), David Ginola (FRA), Christian Karembeu (FRA), Bixente Lizarazu (FRA), Jean-Pierre Papin (FRA), Reynald Pedros (FRA), Gocha Gogrichiani (GEO), David Janashia (GEO), Markus Babbel (GER), Thomas Häßler (GER), Thomas Helmer (GER), Heiko Herrlich (GER), Stefan Kuntz (GER), Thomas Strunz (GER), Efstratios Apostolakis (GRE), Daniel Batista Lima (GRE), Konstantinos Frantzeskos (GRE), Giorgos Georgiadis (GRE), Dimitrios Markos (GRE), Dimitrios Saravakos (GRE), Vasilis Tsiartas (GRE), Jordi Cruyff (HOL), Aron Winter (HOL), István Vincze (HUN), Ray Houghton (IRL), Roy Keane (IRL), Paul McGrath (IRL), Steve Staunton (IRL), Andy Townsend (IRL), Gudni Bergsson (ISL), Arnar Gunnlaugsson (ISL), Sigurdur Jónsson (ISL), Tal Banin (ISR), Eyal Berkovic (ISR), Haim Revivo (ISR), Itzhak Zohar (ISR), Dino Baggio (ITA), Enrico Chiesa (ITA), Alessandro Costacurta (ITA), Alessandro Del Piero (ITA), Attilio Lombardo (ITA), Paolo Maldini (ITA), Christian Panucci (ITA), Vitalijs Astafjevs (LAT), Vladimirs Babicevs (LAT), Jevgenijs Milevskis (LAT), Daniel Hasler (LIE), Aurelius Skarbalius (LIT), Vaidotas Slekys (LIT), Ramunas Stonkus (LIT), Viaceslavas Sukristovas (LIT), Audrius Zuta (LIT), Manuel Cardoni (LUX), Guy Hellers (LUX), Luc Holtz (LUX), Zoran Boskovski (MCD), Georgi Hristov (MCD), Borce Jovanovski (MCD), Ljupco Markovski (MCD), Toni Micevski (MCD), Mitko Stojkovski (MCD), David Carabott (MLT), Kristian Laferla (MLT), Alexandr Curtianu (MOL), Igor Oprea (MOL), Valerii Pogorelov (MOL), Sergiu Secu (MOL), Ion Testemitanu (MOL), Keith Gillespie (NIR), Michael Hughes (NIR), Barry Hunter (NIR), Steve Lomas (NIR), Gerard McMahon (NIR), Gunnar Aase (NOR), Lars Roar Bohinen (NOR), Harald Brattbakk (NOR), Jorstein Flo (NOR), Geir Frigård (NOR), Jahn Ivar Mini Jakobsen (NOR), Wojciech Kowalczyk (POL), Tomasz Wieszczycki (POL), ANTÓNIO José dos Santos FOLHA (POR), CARLOS Alberto de Oliveira

	SECRETÁRIO (POR), HÉLDER Marino Rodrigues Cristóvão (POR), JORGE Paulo CADETE Santos Reis (POR), OCEANO Andrade da Cruz (POR), Ricardo Manuel Andrade Silva SÁ PINTO (POR), Miodrag Belodedici (ROM), Ilie Dumitrescu (ROM), Dan Petrescu (ROM), Gheorghe Popescu (ROM), Daniel Prodan (ROM), Dmitri Cheryshev (RUS), Igor Dobrovolskiy (RUS), Valeri Kechinov (RUS), Yuri Kovtun (RUS), Mukhsin Mukhamadiev (RUS), Viktor Onopko (RUS), Nikolay Pisarev (RUS), Omari Tetradze (RUS), Colin Calderwood (SCO), Eoin Jess (SCO), Pat Nevin (SCO), Duncan Shearer (SCO), Vladimir Kokol (SLO), Pier-Domenico Della Valle (SMR), Mauro Valentini (SMR), Marc Hottiger (SUI), Marcel Koller (SUI), Miroslav Chvíla (SVK), Lubomír Moravcik (SVK), Stefan Rusnák (SVK), Julius Simon (SVK), Dusan Tittel (SVK), Marek Ujlaky (SVK), Niclas Alexandersson (SWE), Klas Ingesson (SWE), Jörgen Pettersson (SWE), Emre Asik (TUR), Recep Çetin (TUR), Bülent Korkmaz (TUR), Ogün Temizkanoglu (TUR), Andriy Husin (UKR), Yuriy Kalitvintsev (UKR), Serhiy Konovalov (UKR), Andriy Polunin (UKR), Viktor Skrypnyk (UKR), Nathan Blake (WAL), Chris Coleman (WAL), Ryan Giggs (WAL), Mark Pembridge (WAL)
1 own goal	Yervand Krbashyan (ARM) for Belgium, Luboslav Penev (BUL) for France, Marios Charalambous (CYP) for Spain, Urmas Kirs (EST) for Ukraine, Thomas Helmer (GER) for Wales, Theodoros Zagorakis (GRE) for Russia, Joe Camilleri (MLT) for Czech Republic, Vitali Culibaba (MOL) for Georgia, Serghei Stroenco (MOL) for Germany, Fabio Francini (SMR) for Scotland, Ondrej Kristofík (SVK) for France, Patrik Andersson (SWE) for Turkey, Jesper Blomqvist (SWE) for Switzerland, Kyt Symons (WAL) for Germany

2000 UEFA European Football Championship

QUALIFYING ROUND

GROUP 1

05-09-1998	Minsk	Belarus – Denmark	0-0
05-09-1998	Liverpool	Wales – Italy	0-2 (0-1)
10-10-1998	Udine	Italy – Switzerland	2-0 (1-0)
10-10-1998	Copenhagen	Denmark – Wales	1-2 (0-0)
14-10-1998	Cardiff	Wales – Belarus	3-2 (1-1)
14-10-1998	Zürich	Switzerland – Denmark	1-1 (0-0)
27-03-1999	Minsk	Belarus – Switzerland	0-1 (0-0)
27-03-1999	Copenhagen	Denmark – Italy	1-2 (0-1)
31-03-1999	Ancona	Italy – Belarus	1-1 (1-1)
31-03-1999	Zürich	Switzerland – Wales	2-0 (1-0)
05-06-1999	Copenhagen	Denmark – Belarus	1-0 (1-0)
05-06-1999	Bologna	Italy – Wales	4-0 (3-0)
09-06-1999	Lausanne	Switzerland – Italy	0-0
09-06-1999	Liverpool	Wales – Denmark	0-2 (0-0)
04-09-1999	Copenhagen	Denmark – Switzerland	2-1 (0-0)
04-09-1999	Minsk	Belarus – Wales	1-2 (1-1)
08-09-1999	Napoli	Italy – Denmark	2-3 (2-1)
08-09-1999	Lausanne	Switzerland – Belarus	2-0 (0-0)
09-10-1999	Minsk	Belarus – Italy	0-0
09-10-1999	Wrexham	Wales – Switzerland	0-2 (0-1)

FINAL STANDING

Pos	Team	Pld	W	D	L	GF	GA	GD	Pts
1	*Italy*	8	4	3	1	13	5	+8	15
2	*Denmark*	8	4	2	2	11	8	+3	14
3	Switzerland	8	4	2	2	9	5	+4	14
4	Wales	8	3	0	5	7	16	-9	9
5	Belarus	8	0	3	5	4	10	-6	3

Italy qualified for the final tournament in Belgium/Netherlands.

Denmark qualified for the second round play-offs.

05-09-1998   Dinamo Stadium, Minsk: Belarus – Denmark   0-0
Belarus: Andrei Satsunkevich, Erik Yakhimovich, Andrei Ostrovsky, Sergei Shtanyuk, Miroslav Romashchenko (39' Vyacheslav Gerashchenko), Sergei Gurenko (C), Aleksandr Khatskevich, Vasili Baranov, Valentin Belkevich, Vladimir Makovskiy (89' Maksim Romashchenko), Andrei Lavrik. (Coach: Mikhail Vergeenko (BLS)).
Denmark: Peter Schmeichel (C), Ole Tobiasen, Marc Rieper, Jes Høgh, Jan Heintze, Thomas Helveg, Allan Nielsen, Claus Thomsen, Martin Jørgensen (67' Thomas Gravesen), Jon Dahl Tomasson (81' Søren Frederiksen), Peter Møller (67' Søren Andersen). (Coach: Bo (Bosse) Johansson (SWE)).
Referee: Georg Dardenne (GER)   Attendance: 32.000

05-09-1998   Anfield, Liverpool: Wales – Italy   0-2 (0-1)
Wales: Paul Jones, John Robinson, Adrian Williams, Kit Symons, Chris Coleman, Darren Barnard, Andy Johnson, Ryan Giggs, Gary Speed (C) (YC72), Nathan Blake (YC11) (65' Dean Saunders), Mark Hughes (76' Robbie Savage). (Coach: Robert Anthony (Bobby) Gould (ENG)).
Italy: Angelo Peruzzi, Christian Panucci, Mark Iuliano, Fabio Cannavaro, Gianluca Pessotto, Diego Fuser, Dino Baggio, Demetrio Albertini (C) (67' Luigi Di Biagio), Eusebio Di Francesco (85' Michele Serena), Christian Vieri, Alessandro Del Piero (75' Roberto Baggio). (Coach: Dino Zoff (ITA)).
Goals: Italy: 0-1 Diego Fuser (19'), 0-2 Christian Vieri (77').
Referee: Terje Hauge (NOR)   Attendance: 23.160
(The match was played in Liverpool due to the lack of suitable stadium in Wales).

10-10-1998   Stadio del Friuli, Udine: Italy – Switzerland   2-0 (1-0)
Italy: Gianluigi Buffon, Christian Panucci, Fabio Cannavaro (YC87), Paolo Maldini (C), Moreno Torricelli, Diego Fuser, Dino Baggio, Demetrio Albertini, Eusebio Di Francesco (62' Jonathan Bachini), Filippo Inzaghi, Alessandro Del Piero (70' Francesco Totti). (Coach: Dino Zoff (ITA)).
Switzerland: Andreas Hilfiker, Stefan Wolf (59' Frédéric Chassot), Stéphane Henchoz, Ramon Vega, Patrick Müller, Johann Vogel, Régis Rothenbühler, Raphael Wicky (72' Fabio Celestini), Ciriaco Sforza (C), David Sesa, Stéphane Chapuisat. (Coach: Gilbert Gress (FRA)).
Goals: Italy: 1-0 Alessandro Del Piero (18'), 2-0 Alessandro Del Piero (62').
Referee: Alain Sars (FRA)   Attendance: 35.247

10-10-1998   Parken Stadium, Copenhagen: Denmark – Wales   1-2 (0-0)
Denmark: Mogens Krogh, Ole Tobiasen, Marc Rieper, Jes Høgh (C), Jan Heintze, Thomas Helveg, Brian Steen Nielsen, Per Frandsen (76' Thomas Gravesen), Søren Frederiksen, Martin Jørgensen, Mikkel Beck (65' Ebbe Sand). (Coach: Bo (Bosse) Johansson (SWE)).
Wales: Paul Jones, Chris Coleman, Adrian Williams, Kit Symons, Darren Barnard, Andy Johnson (62' Mark Pembridge), Robbie Savage (YC24), Dean Saunders (81' John Robinson), Gary Speed (C) (YC43), Mark Hughes, Nathan Blake (69' Craig Bellamy). (Coach: Robert Anthony (Bobby) Gould (ENG)).
Goals: Denmark: 1-0 Søren Frederiksen (57').
Wales: 1-1 Adrian Williams (58'), 1-2 Craig Bellamy (87').
Referee: Sándor Piller (HUN)   Attendance: 36.009

14-10-1998   Ninian Park, Cardiff: Wales – Belarus 3-2 (1-1)
Wales: Paul Jones, Kit Symons, Chris Coleman, John Robinson, Robbie Savage, Andy Johnson, Darren Barnard (YC63), Mark Pembridge, Dean Saunders, Mark Hughes (C), Nathan Blake. (Coach: Robert Anthony (Bobby) Gould (ENG)).
Belarus: Andrei Satsunkevich, Erik Yakhimovich, Sergei Shtanyuk, Andrei Ostrovsky, Vyacheslav Gerashchenko (YC66) (88' Maksim Romashchenko), Aleksandr Khatskevich (YC56), Vasili Baranov (71' Sergei Gerasimets), Sergei Gurenko (C) (YC40), Valentin Belkevich, Andrei Lavrik, Vladimir Makovskiy (74' Petr Kachuro). (Coach: Mikhail Vergeenko (BLS)).
Goals: Wales: 1-0 John Robinson (15'), 2-2 Chris Coleman (55'), 3-2 Kit Symons (80').
Belarus: 1-1 Sergei Gurenko (22'), 1-2 Valentin Belkevich (50').
Referee: Lawrence Sammut (MLT)   Attendance: 7.813

14-10-1998   Hardturm Stadion, Zürich: Switzerland – Denmark 1-1 (0-0)
Switzerland: Andreas Hilfiker, Sébastien Jeanneret (76' Régis Rothenbühler), Stéphane Henchoz, Patrick Müller (77' Francesco Di Jorio), Ciriaco Sforza (C) (YC34), Johann Vogel, Raphael Wicky, Sébastien Fournier, Fabio Celestini, David Sesa (90' Bernt Haas), Stéphane Chapuisat (YC40). (Coach: Gilbert Gress (FRA)).
Denmark: Mogens Krogh, Ole Tobiasen (YC5), Marc Rieper, Jes Høgh (C), Jan Heintze, Thomas Helveg, Brian Steen Nielsen (YC34), Per Frandsen (50' Søren Colding), Søren Frederiksen (51' Ebbe Sand), Martin Jørgensen, Jon Dahl Tomasson (77' Mikkel Beck). (Coach: Bo (Bosse) Johansson (SWE)).
Goals: Switzerland: 1-0 Stéphane Chapuisat (58').
Denmark: 1-1 Ole Tobiasen (88').
Referee: Miroslav Radoman (YUG)   Attendance: 12.500

27-03-1999   Dinamo Stadium, Minsk: Belarus – Switzerland 0-1 (0-0)
Belarus: Gennadi Tumilovich, Erik Yakhimovich (YC76), Aleksandr Lukhvich, Vyacheslav Gerashchenko (YC83) (85' Vadim Skripchenko), Sergei Gurenko (C), Aleksandr Khatskevich (YC54), Maksim Romashchenko, Valentin Belkevich, Vasili Baranov (58' Aleksandr Chayka), Andrei Lavrik, Vladimir Makovskiy (86' Andrei Ostrovsky). (Coach: Mikhail Vergeenko (BLS)).
Switzerland: Martin Brunner, Marc Hodel, Stéphane Henchoz (YC82), Sébastien Jeanneret (YC38), Johann Vogel, Sébastien Fournier, Ciriaco Sforza (C), Raphael Wicky (YC58) (65' Patrick Müller), Alexandre Comisetti, David Sesa (73' Patrick De Napoli), Stéphane Chapuisat. (Coach: Gilbert Gress (FRA)).
Goal: Switzerland: 0-1 Sébastien Fournier (72').
Referee: Oguz Sarvan (TUR)   Attendance: 35.000

27-03-1999   Parken Stadium, Copenhagen: Denmark – Italy 1-2 (0-1)
Denmark: Peter Schmeichel (C), René Henriksen, Jes Høgh, Jan Heintze, Thomas Helveg, Bjarne Goldbæk (83' Søren Colding), Allan Nielsen (YC56) (77' Stig Tøfting), Claus Thomsen, Martin Jørgensen, Jesper Grønkjær (53' Miklos Molnar), Ebbe Sand. (Coach: Bo (Bosse) Johansson (SWE)).
Italy: Gianluigi Buffon, Christian Panucci, Paolo Maldini (C), Fabio Cannavaro, Alessandro Nesta (YC31), Luigi Di Biagio, Diego Fuser (YC36) (46' Antonio Conte), Dino Baggio, Eusebio Di Francesco, Filippo Inzaghi, Enrico Chiesa (63' Francesco Totti). (Coach: Dino Zoff (ITA)).
Goals: Denmark: 1-1 Ebbe Sand (56').
Italy: 0-1 Filippo Inzaghi (1'), 1-2 Antonio Conte (68').
Referee: Antonio Jesús López Nieto (ESP)   Attendance: 41.429

31-03-1999 Stadio del Conero, Ancona: Italy – Belarus 1-1 (1-1)
Italy: Gianluigi Buffon, Christian Panucci, Paolo Maldini (C), Fabio Cannavaro, Alessandro Nesta, Dino Baggio, Luigi Di Biagio (46' Giuliano Giannichedda), Antonio Conte, Francesco Totti (46' Eusebio Di Francesco (YC73)), Filippo Inzaghi, Enrico Chiesa (63' Roberto Baggio). (Coach: Dino Zoff (ITA)).
Belarus: Gennadi Tumilovich (YC35), Erik Yakhimovich, Aleksandr Lukhvich, Andrei Ostrovsky, Sergei Gurenko (C), Radislav Orlovskiy, Maksim Romashchenko, Valentin Belkevich, Vasili Baranov, Andrei Lavrik, Vladimir Makovskiy. (Coach: Mikhail Vergeenko (BLS)).
Goals: Italy: 1-1 Filippo Inzaghi (32' penalty).
Belarus: 0-1 Valentin Belkevich (25').
Referee: Michel Piraux (BEL)   Attendance: 20.735

31-03-1999 Letzigrund Stadion, Zürich: Switzerland – Wales 2-0 (1-0)
Switzerland: Martin Brunner, Stéphane Henchoz, Sébastien Jeanneret, Stefan Wolf, Patrick Müller, Raphael Wicky, Sébastien Fournier, Ciriaco Sforza (C), Johann Vogel (YC48), Alexandre Comisetti (68' Patrick Bühlmann), Stéphane Chapuisat. (Coach: Gilbert Gress (FRA)).
Wales: Paul Jones (26' Mark Crossley), John Robinson, Kit Symons, Chris Coleman, Mark Pembridge, Robbie Savage (YC58), Andy Johnson, Dean Saunders, Gary Speed (C), Nathan Blake (64' John Hartson), Mark Hughes (YC37) (72' Craig Bellamy). (Coach: Robert Anthony (Bobby) Gould (ENG)).
Goals: Switzerland: 1-0 Stéphane Chapuisat (4'), 2-0 Stéphane Chapuisat (70').
Referee: Miroslav Liba (CZE)   Attendance: 13.500

05-06-1999 Parken Stadium, Copenhagen: Denmark – Belarus 1-0 (1-0)
Denmark: Peter Schmeichel (C), Søren Colding, René Henriksen, Jes Høgh, Jan Heintze, Bjarne Goldbæk, Allan Nielsen, Stig Tøfting (66' Brian Steen Nielsen), Martin Jørgensen, Jesper Grønkjær, Ebbe Sand (77' Miklos Molnar (YC90+1)). (Coach: Bo (Bosse) Johansson (SWE)).
Belarus: Gennadi Tumilovich, Erik Yakhimovich (YC43), Aleksandr Lukhvich (YC56), Andrei Ostrovsky (46' Maksim Romashchenko), Sergei Gurenko (C), Aleksandr Khatskevich (69' Aleksandr Kulchiy), Radislav Orlovskiy, Valentin Belkevich, Vasili Baranov, Andrei Lavrik, Vladimir Makovskiy (85' Nikolai Ryndyuk). (Coach: Mikhail Vergeenko (BLS)).
Goal: Denmark: 1-0 Jan Heintze (22').
Referee: Lucílio Cardoso Cortez Batista (POR)   Attendance: 24.876

05-06-1999 Stadio Renato Dall'Ara, Bologna: Italy – Wales 4-0 (3-0)
Italy: Gianluigi Buffon, Christian Panucci, Paolo Maldini (C), Fabio Cannavaro, Paolo Negro, Demetrio Albertini, Diego Fuser (74' Angelo Di Livio), Antonio Conte, Eusebio Di Francesco, Filippo Inzaghi (58' Enrico Chiesa), Christian Vieri (46' Vincenzo Montella). (Coach: Dino Zoff (ITA)).
Wales: Paul Jones, John Robinson (59' Steve Jenkins), Rob Page, Andy Melville, Adrian Williams, Darren Barnard, Craig Bellamy (78' Mark Pembridge), Dean Saunders (46' John Hartson), Ryan Giggs, Gary Speed (C), Mark Hughes. (Coach: Robert Anthony (Bobby) Gould (ENG)).
Goals: Italy: 1-0 Christian Vieri (7'), 2-0 Filippo Inzaghi (37'), 3-0 Paolo Maldini (40'), 4-0 Enrico Chiesa (89').
Referee: Edgar Steinborn (GER)   Attendance: 12.392

09-06-1999   Stade Olympique de la Pontaise, Lausanne: Switzerland – Italy 0-0
Switzerland: Stefan Huber, Patrick Müller, Marc Hodel, Sébastien Jeanneret (76' Francesco Di Jorio), Raphael Wicky (69' Bernt Haas), Johann Vogel, Ciriaco Sforza (C), Régis Rothenbühler, Alexandre Comisetti (55' Fabio Celestini), David Sesa, Stéphane Chapuisat. (Coach: Gilbert Gress (FRA)).
Italy: Gianluigi Buffon, Christian Panucci (69' Giuseppe Pancaro), Paolo Maldini (C), Fabio Cannavaro, Paolo Negro (YC52), Demetrio Albertini, Diego Fuser (60' Angelo Di Livio), Antonio Conte, Eusebio Di Francesco, Filippo Inzaghi, Christian Vieri (60' Enrico Chiesa). (Coach: Dino Zoff (ITA)).
Referee: Graham Poll (ENG)   Attendance: 13.124

09-06-1999   Anfield, Liverpool: Wales – Denmark 0-2 (0-0)
Wales: Paul Jones, Steve Jenkins, John Robinson (85' Mark Pembridge), Andy Melville, Chris Coleman, Darren Barnard (90' Andy Legg), Gary Speed (C), Dean Saunders, John Hartson (YC30) (87' Craig Bellamy), Ryan Giggs, Mark Hughes. (Coach: Mark Hughes (WAL)).
Denmark: Peter Schmeichel (C), Søren Colding, René Henriksen, Jes Høgh, Jan Heintze, Bjarne Goldbæk, Allan Nielsen (81' Stig Tøfting), Martin Jørgensen (89' Per Frandsen), Jesper Grønkjær, Miklos Molnar (70' Jon Dahl Tomasson), Ebbe Sand. (Coach: Bo (Bosse) Johansson (SWE)).
Goals: Denmark: 0-1 Jon Dahl Tomasson (84'), 0-2 Stig Tøfting (89' penalty).
Referee: Armand Ancion (BEL)   Attendance: 10.956
(The match was played in Liverpool due to the lack of suitable stadium in Wales).

04-09-1999   Parken Stadium, Copenhagen: Denmark – Switzerland 2-1 (0-0)
Denmark: Peter Schmeichel (C), René Henriksen, Jes Høgh, Jan Heintze, Thomas Helveg (YC39), Bjarne Goldbæk (51' Søren Colding), Allan Nielsen (80' Brian Steen Nielsen), Stig Tøfting, Martin Jørgensen, Jon Dahl Tomasson (87' Morten Wieghorst), Ebbe Sand. (Coach: Bo (Bosse) Johansson (SWE)).
Switzerland: Stefan Huber, Patrick Müller, Marc Hodel, Sébastien Jeanneret (YC13), Raphael Wicky (89' Thomas Wyss), Johann Vogel, Ciriaco Sforza (C), Francesco Di Jorio (59' Kübilay Türkyilmaz), David Sesa (78' Sascha Müller), Stéphane Chapuisat, Patrick Bühlmann. (Coach: Gilbert Gress (FRA)).
Goals: Denmark: 1-0 Allan Nielsen (54'), 2-1 Jon Dahl Tomasson (81').
Switzerland: 1-1 Kübilay Türkyilmaz (79').
Referee: Ryszard Wójcik (POL)   Attendance: 41.667

04-09-1999   Dinamo Stadium, Minsk: Belarus – Wales 1-2 (1-1)
Belarus: Gennadi Tumilovich (YC40), Igor Tarlovski, Aleksandr Lukhvich, Andrei Ostrovsky, Sergei Gurenko (C), Vasili Baranov, Aleksandr Chayka (YC24), Aleksandr Kulchiy, Radislav Orlovskiy (59' Maksim Romashchenko), Andrei Lavrik (YC57), Vladimir Makovskiy. (Coach: Mikhail Vergeenko (BLS)).
Wales: Paul Jones, Rob Page, Andy Melville, Chris Coleman, John Robinson, Darren Barnard, Mark Pembridge (YC66) (81' Carl Robinson), Dean Saunders, Gary Speed (C), Ryan Giggs, Nathan Blake. (Coach: Mark Hughes (WAL)).
Goals: Belarus: 1-0 Vasili Baranov (29').
Wales: 1-1 Dean Saunders (42'), 1-2 Ryan Giggs (86').
Referee: Tom Henning Øvrebø (NOR)   Attendance: 20.400

08-09-1999   Stadio San Paolo, Napoli: Italy – Denmark   2-3 (2-1)
Italy: Gianluigi Buffon, Christian Panucci (YC45), Fabio Cannavaro, Alessandro Nesta, Giuseppe Pancaro (YC48), Diego Fuser (YC43), Eusebio Di Francesco (70' Antonio Conte), Demetrio Albertini (C), Dino Baggio (46' Giuliano Giannichedda (RC87)), Christian Vieri (78' Francesco Totti), Filippo Inzaghi. (Coach: Dino Zoff (ITA)).
Denmark: Peter Schmeichel (C) (YC60), Jan Heintze, René Henriksen, Jes Høgh, Thomas Helveg (52' Bjarne Goldbæk), Søren Colding (YC44), Martin Jørgensen, Stig Tøfting (YC22) (52' Morten Wieghorst (YC78,YC80)), Allan Nielsen, Jon Dahl Tomasson (86' Michael Schjønberg), Ebbe Sand. (Coach: Bo (Bosse) Johansson (SWE)).
Goals: Italy: 1-0 Diego Fuser (10'), 2-0 Christian Vieri (34').
Denmark: 2-1 Martin Jørgensen (39' penalty), 2-2 Morten Wieghorst (58'), 2-3 Jon Dahl Tomasson (64').
Referee: Dirk Zier Gerardus (Dick) Jol (HOL)   Attendance: 48.919

08-09-1999   Stade Olympique de la Pontaise, Lausanne: Switzerland – Belarus   2-0 (0-0)
Switzerland: Stefan Huber, Marc Hodel, Patrick Müller (78' Stefan Wolf), Stéphane Henchoz, Raphael Wicky, Johann Vogel, Ciriaco Sforza (C), Francesco Di Jorio, Patrick Bühlmann (70' David Sesa), Kübilay Türkyilmaz (YC26), Stéphane Chapuisat (63' Alexandre Comisetti). (Coach: Gilbert Gress (FRA)).
Belarus: Yuri Afanasenko (YC85), Erik Yakhimovich, Aleksandr Lukhvich, Andrei Ostrovsky, Igor Tarlovski, Sergei Gurenko (C), Vasili Baranov, Aleksandr Chayka, Aleksandr Kulchiy (55' Petr Kachuro), Andrei Lavrik (YC22), Vladimir Makovskiy (69' Maksim Romashchenko). (Coach: Mikhail Vergeenko (BLS)).
Goals: Switzerland: 1-0 Kübilay Türkyilmaz (68'), 2-0 Kübilay Türkyilmaz (86' penalty).
Referee: Leslie John R.Irvine (NIR)   Attendance: 12.500

09-10-1999   Dinamo Stadium, Minsk: Belarus – Italy   0-0
Belarus: Valeri Shantalosov, Erik Yakhimovich, Igor Tarlovski, Aleksandr Lukhvich, Andrei Ostrovsky, Sergei Gurenko (C), Vasili Baranov, Radislav Orlovskiy, Aleksandr Chayka, Maksim Romashchenko (46' Vladimir Makovskiy (YC84)), Sergei Gerasimets (79' Aleksandr Kulchiy). (Coach: Sergey Borovskiy (BLS)).
Italy: Gianluigi Buffon, Christian Panucci, Paolo Maldini (C), Fabio Cannavaro, Alessandro Nesta, Gianluca Zambrotta, Luigi Di Biagio (YC59), Francesco Moriero, Antonio Conte (YC73), Filippo Inzaghi, Christian Vieri (81' Alessandro Del Piero). (Coach: Dino Zoff (ITA)).
Referee: Claude Colombo (FRA)   Attendance: 32.000

09-10-1999   Racecourse Ground, Wrexham: Wales – Switzerland   0-2 (0-1)
Wales: Paul Jones, Mark Delaney, Rob Page, Chris Coleman (YC67), John Robinson, Darren Barnard (YC88), Robbie Savage, Dean Saunders (67' John Hartson), Gary Speed (C), Nathan Blake (78' Matthew Jones), John Oster (78' Neil Roberts). (Coach: Mark Hughes (WAL)).
Switzerland: Pascal Zuberbühler (YC50), Stéphane Henchoz, Bernt Haas, Christophe Jaquet (71' Thomas Wyss), Marc Hodel, Sébastien Jeanneret (YC89), Francesco Di Jorio, Johann Vogel (C), David Sesa, Alexandre Rey (67' Alexandre Comisetti), Patrick Bühlmann. (Coach: Gilbert Gress (FRA)).
Goals: Switzerland: 0-1 Alexandre Rey (16'), 0-2 Patrick Bühlmann (60').
Referee: Spiridon Papadakos (GRE)   Attendance: 5.064

GROUP 2

05-09-1998	Tbilisi	Georgia – Albania	1-0 (0-0)
06-09-1998	Athens	Greece – Slovenia	2-2 (0-1)
06-09-1998	Oslo	Norway – Latvia	1-3 (1-1)
10-10-1998	Riga	Latvia – Georgia	1-0 (1-0)
10-10-1998	Ljubljana	Slovenia – Norway	1-2 (1-1)
14-10-1998	Athens	Greece – Georgia	3-0 (3-0)
14-10-1998	Oslo	Norway – Albania	2-2 (0-1)
14-10-1998	Maribor	Slovenia – Latvia	1-0 (0-0)
18-11-1998	Tirana	Albania – Greece	0-0
27-03-1999	Tbilisi	Georgia – Slovenia	1-1 (1-0)
27-03-1999	Athens	Greece – Norway	0-2 (0-1)
31-03-1999	Riga	Latvia – Greece	0-0
28-04-1999	Riga	Latvia – Albania	0-0
28-04-1999	Tbilisi	Georgia – Norway	1-4 (0-4)
30-05-1999	Oslo	Norway – Georgia	1-0 (1-0)
05-06-1999	Tbilisi	Georgia – Greece	1-2 (0-0)
05-06-1999	Tirana	Albania – Norway	1-2 (1-1)
05-06-1999	Riga	Latvia – Slovenia	1-2 (1-2)
09-06-1999	Tirana	Albania – Slovenia	0-1 (0-1)
09-06-1999	Athens	Greece – Latvia	1-2 (1-1)
18-08-1999	Ljubljana	Slovenia – Albania	2-0 (0-0)
04-09-1999	Tirana	Albania – Latvia	3-3 (1-1)
04-09-1999	Oslo	Norway – Greece	1-0 (1-0)
04-09-1999	Ljubljana	Slovenia – Georgia	2-1 (0-0)
08-09-1999	Tbilisi	Georgia – Latvia	2-2 (1-0)
08-09-1999	Oslo	Norway – Slovenia	4-0 (3-0)
06-10-1999	Athens	Greece – Albania	2-0 (1-0)
09-10-1999	Tirana	Albania – Georgia	2-1 (2-0)
09-10-1999	Riga	Latvia – Norway	1-2 (0-0)
09-10-1999	Maribor	Slovenia – Greece	0-3 (0-2)

FINAL STANDING

Pos	Team	Pld	W	D	L	GF	GA	GD	Pts
1	*Norway*	*10*	*8*	*1*	*1*	*21*	*9*	*+12*	*25*
2	*Slovenia*	*10*	*5*	*2*	*3*	*12*	*14*	*-2*	*17*
3	Greece	10	4	3	3	13	8	+5	15
4	Latvia	10	3	4	3	13	12	+1	13
5	Albania	10	1	4	5	8	14	-6	7
6	Georgia	10	1	2	7	8	18	-10	5

Norway qualified for the final tournament in Belgium/Netherlands.

Slovenia qualified for the second round play-offs.

05-09-1998   Boris Paichadze Stadium, Tbilisi: Georgia – Albania 1-0 (0-0)
Georgia: David Gvaramadze, Levan Kobiashvili (YC7), Kakha Kaladze, Levan Silagadze (44' Georgi Kiknadze (YC83)), Mamuka Tsereteli (YC23), Levan Tskitishvili, Georgi Nemsadze (C), Gocha Jamarauli, Giorgi Kinkladze, Aleksandre Iashvili (62' Archil Arveladze), Temur Ketsbaia (54' Zaza Janashia (YC70,YC80)). (Coach: Vladimir Gutsaev (GEO)).
Albania: Fotaq (Foto) Strakosha, Luan Pinari (RC71), Rudi Vata (C), Ilir Shulku, Arian Xhumba, Altin Lala (YC52), Altin Haxhi, Bledar Kola (YC67), Igli Tare (68' Arian Peço, 87' Artur Maxhuni), Altin Rraklli, Alban Bushi (YC62) (74' Alpin Gallo). (Coach: Astrit Hafizi (ALB)).
Goal: Georgia: 1-0 Archil Arveladze (66').
Referee: Claude Détruche (SUI)   Attendance: 25.000

06-09-1998   Spiros Louis Stadium, Athens: Greece – Slovenia   2-2 (0-1)
Greece: Elias Atmatsidis, Nikos Dabizas, Ioannis Kalitzakis, Dimitrios Markos, Marinos Ouzounidis, Vassilios Borbokis (YC21) (83' Nikos Liberopoulos), Theodoros Zagorakis (YC12), Vasilis Tsiartas (46' Konstantinos Frantzeskos), Mihalis Kasapis (78' Grigoris Georgatos), Nikos Machlas, Demis Nikolaidis (C). (Coach: Anghel Iordanescu (ROM)).
Slovenia: Marko Simeunovic, Marinko Galic (YC87), Aleksander Knavs, Darko Milanic, Miran Pavlin, Dzoni Novak, Ales Ceh (YC46), Zlatko Zahovic (YC4), Milan Osterc (YC47) (68' Ermin Siljak, 71' Milenko Acimovic), Mladen Rudonja, Saso Udovic (46' Robert Englaro). (Coach: Srecko Katanec (SLO)).
Goals: Greece: 1-1 Nikos Machlas (55' penalty), 2-1 Konstantinos Frantzeskos (58').
Slovenia: 0-1 Zlatko Zahovic (18'), 2-2 Zlatko Zahovic (72').
Referee: Alfredo Trentalange (ITA)   Attendance: 28.908

06-09-1998   Ullevaal Stadion, Oslo: Norway – Latvia 1-3 (1-1)
Norway: Per Espen Baardsen, Ronny Johnsen (YC84), Stig Inge Bjørnebye, Vegard Heggem (60' Henning Berg), Erik Hoftun, Petter Rudi (78' Håvard Flo), Kjetil Rekdal (C), Ståle Solbakken, Tore André Flo, Ole Gunnar Solskjær (63' Jostein Flo), Frank Strandli. (Coach: Nils Johan Semb (NOR)).
Latvia: Olegs Karavajevs (YC80), Artūrs Zakresevskis, Mihails Zemlinskis, Valerijs Ivanovs, Juris Laizans (51' Viktors Lukasevics), Andrejs Stolcers, Imants Bleidelis, Valentins Lobanovs, Vladimirs Babicevs (C), Aleksejs Sarando (73' Rolands Bulders), Marians Pahars (80' Aleksandrs Isakovs). (Coach: Revaz Mikhaylovich Dzodzuashvili (GEO)).
Goals: Norway: 1-1 Ståle Solbakken (18').
Latvia: 0-1 Marians Pahars (11'), 1-2 Andrejs Stolcers (53'), 1-3 Mihails Zemlinskis (63' penalty).
Referee: Sergei Shmolik (BLS)   Attendance: 11.031

10-10-1998   Daugava Stadium, Riga: Latvia – Georgia 1-0 (1-0)
Latvia: Olegs Karavajevs, Mihails Zemlinskis, Valerijs Ivanovs, Viktors Lukasevics, Andrejs Stolcers, Vitalijs Astafjevs (75' Aleksandrs Isakovs), Imants Bleidelis (51' Juris Laizans), Valentins Lobanovs, Vladimirs Babicevs (C), Aleksejs Sarando, Marians Pahars (86' Rolands Bulders). (Coach: Revaz Mikhaylovich Dzodzuashvili (GEO)).
Georgia: David Gvaramadze, Levan Kobiashvili, Kakha Kaladze, Gela Shekiladze, Georgi Gakhokidze (60' Georgi Demetradze), Georgi Nemsadze (C) (YC55), Mikheil Kavelashvili (YC55), Gocha Jamarauli, Giorgi Kinkladze, Temur Ketsbaia, Shota Arveladze. (Coach: Vladimir Gutsaev (GEO)).
Goal: Latvia: 1-0 Andrejs Stolcers (3').
Referee: Constantin Dan Zotta (ROM)   Attendance: 1.900

10-10-1998   Bezigrad Stadium, Ljubljana: Slovenia – Norway   1-2 (1-1)
Slovenia: Marko Simeunovic, Marinko Galic, Aleksander Knavs, Darko Milanic (C) (YC60), Miran Pavlin, Dzoni Novak, Ales Ceh (YC15), Zlatko Zahovic, Milan Osterc (46' Robert Englaro), Mladen Rudonja, Saso Udovic (64' Milenko Acimovic). (Coach: Srecko Katanec (SLO)).
Norway: Frode Grodås (C), Henning Berg, Stig Inge Bjørnebye, Alf Inge Håland, Vegard Heggem (85' Vidar Riseth), Erik Hoftun (YC34), Roar Strand (77' Daniel Hestad), Kjetil Rekdal, Jostein Flo, Ståle Solbakken, Tore André Flo (90' Sigurd Rushfeldt). (Coach: Nils Johan Semb (NOR)).
Goals: Slovenia: 1-0 Zlatko Zahovic (24').
Norway: 1-1 Tore André Flo (45'), 1-2 Kjetil Rekdal (80').
Referee: Andreas Schluchter (SUI)   Attendance: 6.200

14-10-1998   Spiros Louis Stadium, Athens: Greece – Georgia   3-0 (3-0)
Greece: Elias Atmatsidis, Nikos Dabizas, Ioannis Kalitzakis, Dimitrios Markos (YC81), Marinos Ouzounidis, Elias Poursanidis, Theodoros Zagorakis, Konstantinos Frantzeskos (75' Vasilis Tsiartas), Grigoris Georgatos, Nikos Liberopoulos (68' Stelios Giannakopoulos), Nikos Machlas (84' Dimitrios Mavrogenidis). (Coach: Anghel Iordanescu (ROM)).
Georgia: Nikoloz Togonidze, Levan Kobiashvili, Kakha Kaladze (YC29), Murtaz Shelia, Gela Shekiladze, Georgi Nemsadze (C), Mikheil Kavelashvili (58' Georgi Gakhokidze), Gocha Jamarauli, Giorgi Kinkladze, Temur Ketsbaia (YC51), Shota Arveladze. (Coach: Vladimir Gutsaev (GEO)).
Goals: Greece: 1-0 Nikos Machlas (12'), 2-0 Nikos Liberopoulos (15'), 3-0 Marinos Ouzounidis (36').
Referee: Atanas Uzunov (BUL)   Attendance: 12.681

14-10-1998   Ullevaal Stadion, Oslo: Norway – Albania   2-2 (0-1)
Norway: Frode Grodås (C), Henning Berg, Stig Inge Bjørnebye, Alf Inge Håland (56' Steffen Iversen), Vegard Heggem, Erik Hoftun, Roar Strand, Kjetil Rekdal, Jostein Flo (YC22) (56' Ole Gunnar Solskjær), Ståle Solbakken (89' Sigurd Rushfeldt), Tore André Flo. (Coach: Nils Johan Semb (NOR)).
Albania: Fotaq (Foto) Strakosha, Rudi Vata (C), Ilir Shulku, Arian Xhumba, Ervin Fakaj, Altin Lala (YC80), Altin Haxhi, Bledar Kola (89' Edmond Dalipaj), Igli Tare, Altin Rraklli (YC46), Alban Bushi (83' Mahir Halili). (Coach: Astrit Hafizi (ALB)).
Goals: Norway: 1-2 Kjetil Rekdal (81'), 2-2 Henning Berg (87').
Albania: 0-1 Alban Bushi (37'), 0-2 Igli Tare (52').
Referee: Gerd Grabher (AUT)   Attendance: 17.770

14-10-1998   Ljudski vrt, Maribor: Slovenia – Latvia   1-0 (0-0)
Slovenia: Marko Simeunovic, Marinko Galic (YC1), Aleksander Knavs (46' Primoz Gliha), Darko Milanic (C), Robert Englaro, Miran Pavlin, Dzoni Novak, Zlatko Zahovic, Rudi Istenic (YC22) (65' Milenko Acimovic), Mladen Rudonja, Saso Udovic (89' Zeljko Milinovic). (Coach: Srecko Katanec (SLO)).
Latvia: Olegs Karavajevs, Aleksandrs Isakovs, Mihails Zemlinskis, Valerijs Ivanovs (88' Vits Rimkus), Viktors Lukasevics, Andrejs Stolcers, Vitalijs Astafjevs (C) (YC75) (79' Rolands Bulders), Imants Bleidelis (52' Mihails Miholaps), Valentins Lobanovs, Aleksejs Sarando, Marians Pahars. (Coach: Revaz Mikhaylovich Dzodzuashvili (GEO)).
Goal: Slovenia: 1-0 Saso Udovic (86').
Referee: Karen Nalbandyan (ARM)   Attendance: 3.292

18-11-1998   Qemal Stafa Stadium, Tirana: Albania – Greece   0-0
Albania: Fotaq (Foto) Strakosha, Rudi Vata (C), Ilir Shulku, Arian Xhumba (YC28), Ervin Fakaj (YC78), Altin Haxhi (YC75), Bledar Kola, Igli Tare (YC64), Altin Rraklli, Edmond Dalipaj (51' Mahir Halili), Alban Bushi. (Coach: Astrit Hafizi (ALB)).
Greece: Elias Atmatsidis, Nikos Dabizas (YC64) (89' Leonidas Vokolos), Ioannis Kalitzakis, Dimitrios Markos, Marinos Ouzounidis (YC36), Elias Poursanidis (YC54), Theodoros Zagorakis, Konstantinos Frantzeskos (46' Nikos Liberopoulos (YC68)), Grigoris Georgatos, Nikos Machlas, Demis Nikolaidis (C) (68' Konstantinos Konstantinidis (YC75)). (Coach: Anghel Iordanescu (ROM)).
Referee: Victor José Esquinas Torres (ESP)   Attendance: 18.670

27-03-1999   Boris Paichadze Stadium, Tbilisi: Georgia – Slovenia   1-1 (1-0)
Georgia: Soso Grishikashvili, Levan Kobiashvili, Kakha Kaladze, Mamuka Tsereteli, George Balashvili (YC20), Gia Chkhaidze, Georgi Nemsadze (C), Gocha Jamarauli (84' Georgi Daraselia), Rati Aleksidze (46' Giorgi Kinkladze), Georgi Demetradze (73' Mikheil Kavelashvili), Zaza Janashia. (Coach: Vladimir Gutsaev (GEO)).
Slovenia: Marko Simeunovic, Spasoje Bulajic, Amir Karic, Zeljko Milinovic (YC38), Aleksander Knavs, Darko Milanic (C) (YC6), Miran Pavlin (YC45) (77' Rudi Istenic), Ales Ceh, Zlatko Zahovic, Mladen Rudonja (YC65) (90' Zeljko Mitrakovic), Saso Udovic (60' Milenko Acimovic). (Coach: Srecko Katanec (SLO)).
Goals: Georgia: 1-0 Zaza Janashia (43').
Slovenia: 1-1 Aleksander Knavs (52').
Referee: Alain Hamer (LUX)   Attendance: 12.000

27-03-1999   Spiros Louis Stadium, Athens: Greece – Norway   0-2 (0-1)
Greece: Elias Atmatsidis, Nikos Dabizas, Georgios Anatolakis, Dimitrios Markos (54' Nikos Machlas), Marinos Ouzounidis, Stelios Giannakopoulos, Elias Poursanidis, Theodoros Zagorakis (46' Dimitrios Mavrogenidis), Grigoris Georgatos, Nikos Liberopoulos (75' Konstantinos Frantzeskos), Demis Nikolaidis (C). (Coach: Anghel Iordanescu (ROM)).
Norway: Thomas Myhre, Ronny Johnsen, André Bergdølmo (65' Gunnar Halle), Henning Berg (C), Vegard Heggem, Roar Strand (59' Lars Roar Bohinen), Petter Rudi, Erik Mykland, Ståle Solbakken, Steffen Iversen, Ole Gunnar Solskjær (88' John Carew). (Coach: Nils Johan Semb (NOR)).
Goals: Norway: 0-1 Ole Gunnar Solskjær (37'), 0-2 Ole Gunnar Solskjær (87').
Referee: Leslie John R.Irvine (NIR)   Attendance: 42.566

31-03-1999   Daugava Stadiu, Riga: Latvia – Greece   0-0
Latvia: Olegs Karavajevs, Mihails Zemlinskis, Valerijs Ivanovs (28' Aleksandrs Isakovs), Viktors Lukasevics, Olegs Blagonadezdins, Andrejs Stolcers, Vitalijs Astafjevs (C), Valentins Lobanovs, Aleksejs Sarando (62' Igors Stepanovs), Marians Pahars, Mihails Miholaps (46' Rolands Bulders). (Coach: Revaz Mikhaylovich Dzodzuashvili (GEO)).
Greece: Elias Atmatsidis, Nikos Dabizas (YC77), Dimitrios Mavrogenidis, Marinos Ouzounidis, Stelios Giannakopoulos (74' Theodoros Zagorakis), Elias Poursanidis, Mihalis Kasapis, Grigoris Georgatos (74' Konstantinos Frantzeskos), Nikos Liberopoulos, Nikos Machlas (79' Yannis Anastasiou), Demis Nikolaidis (C). (Coach: Vasilios Daniel (GRE)).
Referee: Knud Erik Fisker (DEN)   Attendance: 4.300

28-04-1999   Daugava Stadiu, Riga: Latvia – Albania   0-0
Latvia: Olegs Karavajevs, Igors Stepanovs (YC80) (84' Aleksejs Sarando), Aleksandrs Isakovs, Valerijs Ivanovs, Viktors Lukasevics, Olegs Blagonadezdins, Andrejs Rubins, Andrejs Stolcers (C) (60' Juris Laizans), Valentins Lobanovs, Mihails Miholaps (69' Viktors Dobrecovs), Rolands Bulders. (Coach: Revaz Mikhaylovich Dzodzuashvili (GEO)).
Albania: Fotaq (Foto) Strakosha, Rudi Vata (C) (78' Redi Jupi), Ilir Shulku, Arian Xhumba, Ervin Fakaj, Altin Lala, Altin Haxhi, Bledar Kola, Igli Tare, Altin Rraklli (81' Edmond Dalipaj), Alban Bushi (86' Mahir Halili). (Coach: Astrit Hafizi (ALB)).
Referee: Eric Romain (BEL)   Attendance: 2.700

28-04-1999   Boris Paichadze Stadium, Tbilisi: Georgia – Norway   1-4 (0-4)
Georgia: Nikoloz Togonidze, Levan Kobiashvili, Kakha Kaladze, Mamuka Tsereteli, Gela Shekiladze (46' Zurab Popkhadze), Aleksandr Rekhviashvili (82' Georgi Kiknadze), Givi Didava, Georgi Nemsadze (C), Gocha Jamarauli, Temur Ketsbaia (46' Georgi Demetradze), Zaza Janashia. (Coach: Vladimir Gutsaev (GEO)).
Norway: Thomas Myhre, André Bergdølmo, Alf Inge Håland, Tore André Pedersen, Erik Hoftun, Petter Rudi (83' Vidar Riseth), Erik Mykland, Ståle Solbakken (C), Steffen Iversen, Tore André Flo (87' John Carew), Ole Gunnar Solskjær (46' Roar Strand). (Coach: Nils Johan Semb (NOR)).
Goals: Georgia: 1-4 Zaza Janashia (58').
Norway: 0-1 Gela Shekiladze (16' *own goal*), 0-2 Tore André Flo (27'), 0-3 Ole Gunnar Solskjær (35'), 0-4 Tore André Flo (38').
Referee: Sándor Puhl (HUN)   Attendance: 14.000

30-05-1999   Ullevaal Stadion, Oslo: Norway – Georgia   1-0 (1-0)
Norway: Frode Olsen, Vidar Riseth (70' Kjetil Rekdal), André Bergdølmo, Vegard Heggem, Tore André Pedersen (YC71), Erik Hoftun, Øyvind Leonhardsen (46' Petter Rudi), Erik Mykland, Ståle Solbakken (C), Steffen Iversen (84' Tore André Dahlum), Tore André Flo. (Coach: Nils Johan Semb (NOR)).
Georgia: David Gvaramadze, Kakha Kaladze (YC30), Mamuka Tsereteli, Levan Tskitishvili, Givi Didava (46' Zurab Popkhadze), Walter Guchua (52' David Chichveishvili), Georgi Nemsadze (C), Mikheil Kavelashvili (YC65), Gocha Jamarauli, Georgi Demetradze (76' Mikheil Ashvetia), Temur Ketsbaia. (Coach: Johan (Jan) Boskmap (HOL)).
Goal: Norway: 1-0 Steffen Iversen (3').
Referee: Luc Huyghe (BEL)   Attendance: 18.236

05-06-1999   Boris Paichadze Stadium, Tbilisi: Georgia – Greece   1-2 (0-0)
Georgia: David Gvaramadze, Levan Kobiashvili, Otar Khizaneishvili, David Chichveishvili (9' Givi Didava (YC21)), Mamuka Tsereteli (YC4), Badri Akhvlediani (65' Zurab Khizanishvili), Levan Tskitishvili (56' Ratu Aleksidze), Georgi Nemsadze (C) (YC52), Gocha Jamarauli, Mikheil Ashvetia, Temur Ketsbaia. (Coach: Johan (Jan) Boskmap (HOL)).
Greece: Elias Atmatsidis, Georgios Anatolakis, Dimitrios Mavrogenidis, Marinos Ouzounidis, Konstantinos Konstantinidis (YC33) (46' Nikolaos Frousos (YC74)), Elias Poursanidis (YC77), Theodoros Zagorakis (80' Konstantinos Frantzeskos), Mihalis Kasapis (YC32), Grigoris Georgatos (61' Yannis Anastasiou), Andreas Niniadis, Nikos Machlas (C). (Coach: Vasilios Daniel (GRE)).
Goals: Georgia: 1-0 Temur Ketsbaia (54').
Greece: 1-1 Konstantinos Frantzeskos (86'), 1-2 Nikos Machlas (90').
Referee: William Smith Geates Young (SCO)   Attendance: 7.400

05-06-1999   Qemal Stafa Stadium, Tirana: Albania – Norway 1-2 (1-1)
Albania: Fotaq (Foto) Strakosha, Rudi Vata (C), Ilir Shulku (YC49), Arian Xhumba, Ervin Fakaj (63' Arian Bellaj), Altin Lala, Altin Haxhi (YC89), Bledar Kola (70' Albert Duro), Igli Tare, Altin Rraklli (81' Erjon Bogdani), Alban Bushi. (Coach: Astrit Hafizi (ALB)).
Norway: Frode Olsen, André Bergdølmo, Alf Inge Håland, Tore André Pedersen (YC47) (63' Bjørn Otto Bragstad), Erik Hoftun, Petter Rudi (79' Tore André Dahlum), Erik Mykland (YC84), Kjetil Rekdal (C), Ståle Solbakken (90' Vidar Riseth), Steffen Iversen, Tore André Flo. (Coach: Nils Johan Semb (NOR)).
Goals: Albania: 1-1 Igli Tare (16').
Norway: 0-1 Steffen Iversen (3'), 1-2 Tore André Flo (83').
Referee: Livio Bazzoli (ITA)   Attendance: 13.000

05-06-1999   Daugava Stadium, Riga: Latvia – Slovenia 1-2 (1-2)
Latvia: Aleksandrs Kolinko, Mihalis Zemlinskis (YC38), Viktors Lukasevics, Juris Laizans, Andrejs Stolcers, Vitalijs Astafjevs (43' Andrejs Rubins), Valentins Lobanovs (46' Igors Korablovs), Vladimirs Babicevs (C), Aleksejs Sarando (59' Imants Bleidelis), Marians Pahars (YC77), Mihails Miholaps (YC48). (Coach: Revaz Mikhaylovich Dzodzuashvili (GEO)).
Slovenia: Marko Simeunovic, Marinko Galic (YC74), Amir Karic (YC17), Zeljko Milinovic, Aleksander Knavs, Miran Pavlin (78' Rudi Istenic), Dzoni Novak, Ales Ceh (C), Zlatko Zahovic, Mladen Rudonja (YC55) (88' Milan Osterc), Saso Udovic (65' Milenko Acimovic). (Coach: Srecko Katanec (SLO)).
Goals: Latvia: 1-0 Marians Pahars (17').
Slovenia: 1-1 Zlatko Zahovic (26'), 1-2 Zlatko Zahovic (42' penalty).
Referee: Juan Manuel Brito Arceo (ESP)   Attendance: 2.800

09-06-1999   Qemal Stafa Stadium, Tirana: Albania – Slovenia 0-1 (0-1)
Albania: Fotaq (Foto) Strakosha, Rudi Vata (C), Ilir Shulku, Arian Xhumba, Albert Duro, Altin Lala, Arian Bellaj, Igli Tare, Erjon Bogdani (73' Edmond Dalipaj), Altin Rraklli (46' Mahir Halili), Alban Bushi (YC20). (Coach: Astrit Hafizi (ALB)).
Slovenia: Marko Simeunovic, Marinko Galic, Amir Karic, Zeljko Milinovic, Aleksander Knavs, Miran Pavlin, Dzoni Novak, Ales Ceh (C), Zlatko Zahovic, Milan Osterc (82' Rudi Istenic), Saso Udovic (65' Milenko Acimovic). (Coach: Srecko Katanec (SLO)).
Goal: Slovenia: 0-1 Zlatko Zahovic (25' penalty).
Referee: Adrian Stoica (ROM)   Attendance: 5.100

09-06-1999   Spiros Louis Stadium, Athens: Greece – Latvia 1-2 (1-1)
Greece: Elias Atmatsidis, Georgios Anatolakis (YC90), Dimitrios Mavrogenidis, Marinos Ouzounidis, Akis Zikos, Theodoros Zagorakis, Mihalis Kasapis, Konstantinos Frantzeskos (61' Yannis Anastasiou), Grigoris Georgatos (YC39) (72' Dimitrios Markos), Andreas Niniadis (80' Nikolaos Frousos), Nikos Machlas (C). (Coach: Vasilios Daniel (GRE)).
Latvia: Aleksandrs Kolinko (YC39), Igors Korablovs, Mihalis Zemlinskis, Viktors Lukasevics (YC84), Juris Laizans, Andrejs Rubins (64' Aleksandrs Zizmanovs), Vitalijs Astafjevs (54' Imants Bleidelis), Valentins Lobanovs, Vladimirs Babicevs (C), Maris Verpakovskis (46' Mihails Miholaps), Marians Pahars (YC38). (Coach: Revaz Mikhaylovich Dzodzuashvili (GEO)).
Goals: Greece: 1-1 Andreas Niniadis (39' penalty).
Latvia: 0-1 Maris Verpakovskis (24'), 1-2 Mihails Zemlinskis (90' penalty).
Referee: Lubomír Pucek (CZE)   Attendance: 15.135

18-08-1999   Bezigrad Stadium, Ljubljana: Slovenia – Albania   2-0 (0-0)
Slovenia: Mladen Dabanovic, Marinko Galic, Aleksander Knavs, Darko Milanic (C) (61' Zeljko Milinovic), Miran Pavlin, Dzoni Novak (90' Rudi Istenic), Ales Ceh (YC26), Zlatko Zahovic, Milan Osterc, Mladen Rudonja, Saso Udovic (46' Milenko Acimovic). (Coach: Srecko Katanec (SLO)).
Albania: Fotaq (Foto) Strakosha, Luan Pinari, Rudi Vata (C), Ilir Shulku, Arian Xhumba, Altin Haxhi (YC20), Bledar Kola (YC68), Edvin Murati (59' Mahir Halili), Arian Bellaj (YC26), Igli Tare, Altin Rraklli (YC58) (60' Erjon Bogdani). (Coach: Astrit Hafizi (ALB)).
Goals: Slovenia: 1-0 Zlatko Zahovic (49'), 2-0 Milan Osterc (80').
Referee: Joaquim Paulo Gomes Ferreira Paraty da Silva (POR)   Attendance: 6.900

04-09-1999   Qemal Stafa Stadium, Tirana: Albania – Latvia   3-3 (1-1)
Albania: Fotaq (Foto) Strakosha, Rudi Vata (C), Ilir Shulku (YC60), Arian Xhumba, Ervin Fakaj (73' Erjon Bogdani), Altin Lala, Altin Haxhi, Edvin Murati (46' Edmond Dalipaj), Arian Bellaj, Igli Tare (77' Devis Mukaj), Alban Bushi (YC80). (Coach: Astrit Hafizi (ALB)).
Latvia: Aleksandrs Kolinko, Igors Stepanovs, Mihalis Zemlinskis, Valerijs Ivanovs (61' Olegs Blagonadezdins), Viktors Lukasevics (YC54,YC86), Andrejs Rubins, Andrejs Stolcers (84' Rolands Bulders), Vitalijs Astafjevs (C) (YC53) (81' Vladimirs Babicevs), Imants Bleidelis, Valentins Lobanovs (YC50), Mihails Miholaps. (Coach: Garry Stephen Johnson (ENG)).
Goals: Albania: 1-1 Alban Bushi (29'), 2-3 Alban Bushi (79'), 3-3 Devis Mukaj (90').
Latvia: 0-1 Vitalijs Astafjevs (20'), 1-2 Vitalijs Astafjevs (63'), 1-3 Andrejs Stolcers (70').
Referee: Alain Hamer (LUX)   Attendance: 4.000

04-09-1999   Ullevaal Stadion, Oslo: Norway – Greece   1-0 (1-0)
Norway: Frode Olsen, André Bergdølmo, Henning Berg (C) (YC90), Vegard Heggem, Erik Hoftun, Øyvind Leonhardsen (74' Vidar Riseth), Erik Mykland, Bent Skammelsrud, Steffen Iversen, Tore André Flo, Ole Gunnar Solskjær (YC22) (69' Petter Rudi). (Coach: Nils Johan Semb (NOR)).
Greece: Elias Atmatsidis (YC90), Nikos Dabizas, Dimitrios Mavrogenidis, Marinos Ouzounidis, Elias Poursanidis, Theodoros Zagorakis (C) (50' Nikos Machlas), Mihalis Kasapis, Grigoris Georgatos, Andreas Niniadis (46' Stelios Giannakopoulos (YC76)), Nikos Liberopoulos (YC28), Demis Nikolaidis. (Coach: Vasilios Daniel (GRE)).
Goal: Norway: 1-0 Øyvind Leonhardsen (35').
Referee: Markus Merk (GER)   Attendance: 24.133

04-09-1999   Bezigrad Stadium, Ljubljana: Slovenia – Georgia   2-1 (0-0)
Slovenia: Marko Simeunovic, Marinko Galic (YC26), Zeljko Milinovic, Aleksander Knavs, Miran Pavlin, Dzoni Novak, Ales Ceh (C), Zlatko Zahovic (88' Rudi Istenic), Milan Osterc (46' Milenko Acimovic), Mladen Rudonja, Saso Udovic (77' Amir Karic). (Coach: Srecko Katanec (SLO)).
Georgia: David Gvaramadze, Levan Kobiashvili, Kakha Kaladze (C), Badri Akhvlediani (YC3) (46' Gela Shekiladze), Levan Tskitishvili (YC52), Givi Didava, Mikheil Kavelashvili, Archil Arveladze, Tengiz Sitchinava, Shota Arveladze, Mikheil Potskhveria. (Coach: Johan (Jan) Boskmap (HOL)).
Goals: Slovenia: 1-0 Milenko Acimovic (48'), 2-1 Zlatko Zahovic (80').
Georgia: 1-1 Shota Arveladze (55').
Referee: Jan Willem Wegereef (HOL)   Attendance: 7.000

08-09-1999   Boris Paichadze Stadium, Tbilisi: Georgia – Latvia   2-2 (1-0)
Georgia: David Gvaramadze, Levan Kobiashvili, Kakha Kaladze, Mamuka Tsereteli (YC10,YC80), Gela Shekiladze, Levan Tskitishvili (69' Tengiz Sitchinava), Givi Didava, Georgi Nemsadze (C) (YC34), Mikheil Kavelashvili (74' Archil Arveladze), Gocha Jamarauli (YC52), Shota Arveladze (71' Georgi Demetradze). (Coach: Johan (Jan) Boskmap (HOL)).
Latvia: Aleksandrs Kolinko, Igors Stepanovs, Aleksandrs Isakovs (58' Vladimirs Babicevs), Mihalis Zemlinskis (C), Valerijs Ivanovs, Juris Laizans (82' Rolands Bulders), Andrejs Rubins, Andrejs Stolcers (75' Aleksejs Sarando), Imants Bleidelis, Valentins Lobanovs, Marians Pahars (YC36). (Coach: Garry Stephen Johnson (ENG)).
Goals: Georgia: 1-0 Shota Arveladze (29'), 2-0 Mikheil Kavelashvili (51').
Latvia: 2-1 Imants Bleidelis (61'), 2-2 Igors Stepanovs (90').
Referee: Miroslav Radoman (YUG)   Attendance: 4.500

08-09-1999   Ullevaal Stadion, Oslo: Norway – Slovenia   4-0 (3-0)
Norway: Frode Olsen, André Bergdølmo, Henning Berg (C), Vegard Heggem, Erik Hoftun, Øyvind Leonhardsen (YC57), Erik Mykland, Bent Skammelsrud (77' Vidar Riseth), Steffen Iversen, Tore André Flo (87' Andreas Lund), Ole Gunnar Solskjær (77' Jan Sørensen). (Coach: Nils Johan Semb (NOR)).
Slovenia: Marko Simeunovic (46' Mladen Davanovic), Zeljko Milinovic (YC21), Aleksander Knavs (YC26), Miran Pavlin (YC44), Dzoni Novak (YC3), Ales Ceh (C), Zlatko Zahovic (YC3), Rudi Istenic (RC56), Milan Osterc (82' Milenko Acimovic), Mladen Rudonja, Saso Udovic (41' Amir Karic). (Coach: Srecko Katanec (SLO)).
Goals: Norway: 1-0 Erik Hoftun (16'), 2-0 Steffen Iversen (18'), 3-0 Ole Gunnar Solskjær (29'), 4-0 Øyvind Leonhardsen (68').
Referee: Gilles Veissière (FRA)   Attendance: 24.288

06-10-1999   Spiros Louis Stadium, Athens: Greece – Albania   2-0 (1-0)
Greece: Elias Atmatsidis, Nikos Dabizas, Marinos Ouzounidis (YC55), Giorgios Amanatidis, Akis Zikos, Elias Poursanidis, Theodoros Zagorakis (46' Giorgos Georgiadis), Vasilis Tsiartas (75' Andreas Niniadis (YC89)), Grigoris Georgatos (67' Konstantinos Konstantinidis, Nikos Machlas, Demis Nikolaidis. (Coach: Vasilios Daniel (GRE)).
Albania: Fotaq (Foto) Strakosha, Rudi Vata (C), Arian Xhumba, Altin Lala, Altin Haxhi (YC25), Bledar Kola, Edvin Murati (54' Albert Duro), Arian Bellaj (YC83) (84' Erjon Bogdani), Igli Tare (68' Devis Mukaj), Altin Rraklli, Alban Bushi. (Coach: Astrit Hafizi (ALB)).
Goals: Greece: 1-0 Vasilis Tsiartas (1'), 2-0 Giorgos Georgiadis (88').
Referee: Valentin Valentinovich Ivanov (RUS)   Attendance: 11.384

09-10-1999   Qemal Stafa Stadium, Tirana: Albania – Georgia   2-1 (2-0)
Albania: Arjan Beqaj, Rudi Vata (C), Ilir Shulku, Arian Xhumba, Ervin Fakaj, Albert Duro, Altin Lala, Bledar Kola, Igli Tare (90' Erjon Bogdani), Altin Rraklli (72' Devis Mukaj), Alban Bushi (YC44) (56' Edvin Murati (YC90+3)). (Coach: Astrit Hafizi (ALB)).
Georgia: Grigol Chanturia, Levan Kobiashvili, Kakha Kaladze (YC65), David Chichveishvili (YC5), Gela Shekiladze (YC90+2), Georgi Gakhokidze, Givi Didava, Georgi Nemsadze (C), Archil Arveladze (80' David Janashia), Gocha Jamarauli, Shota Arveladze. (Coach: Johan (Jan) Boskmap (HOL)).
Goals: Albania: 1-0 Altin Rraklli (30'), 2-0 Bledar Kola (36').
Georgia: 2-1 Shota Arveladze (53').
Referee: Alfred Micallef (MLT)   Attendance: 650

09-10-1999   Daugava Stadium, Riga: Latvia – Norway   1-2 (0-0)
Latvia: Aleksandrs Kolinko, Mihalis Zemlinskis, Valerijs Ivanovs, Viktors Lukasevics (81' Juris Laizans), Olegs Blagonadezdins, Andrejs Rubins, Andrejs Stolcers, Vitalijs Astafjevs (C), Imants Bleidelis, Valentins Lobanovs, Marians Pahars. (Coach: Garry Stephen Johnson (ENG)).
Norway: Frode Olsen, André Bergdølmo, Henning Berg (C), Vegard Heggem, Erik Hoftun (YC71), Øyvind Leonhardsen, Erik Mykland (81' Ståle Solbakken), Bent Skammelsrud, Steffen Iversen (46' Andreas Lund), Tore André Flo, Ole Gunnar Solskjær (89' Vidar Riseth). (Coach: Nils Johan Semb (NOR)).
Goals: Latvia: 1-1 Marians Pahars (54').
Norway: 0-1 Ole Gunnar Solskjær (53'), 1-2 Tore André Flo (87').
Referee: Dietmar Drabek (AUT)   Attendance: 2.500

09-10-1999   Ljudski vrt, Maribor: Slovenia – Greece   0-3 (0-2)
Slovenia: Marko Simeunovic, Marinko Galic (YC53), Muamer Vugdalic (83' Robert Englaro), Edi Bajrektarevic, Milenko Acimovic (YC79), Simon Seslar, Dzoni Novak, Ales Ceh (C), Mladen Rudonja, Ante Simundza (60' Milan Osterc), Saso Udovic (46' Amir Karic). (Coach: Srecko Katanec (SLO)).
Greece: Elias Atmatsidis (C), Nikos Dabizas, Paraskevas Antzas (70' Theodoros Zagorakis), Konstantinos Konstantinidis, Giorgios Amanatidis, Akis Zikos, Elias Poursanidis, Vasilis Tsiartas (65' Andreas Niniadis), Giorgos Georgiadis, Nikos Liberopoulos, Demis Nikolaidis (80' Nikos Machlas). (Coach: Vasilios Daniel (GRE)).
Goals: Greece: 0-1 Vasilis Tsiartas (39'), 0-2 Giorgos Georgiadis (42'), 0-3 Demis Nikolaidis (80').
Referee: Gamal Mahmoud Ahmed El-Ghandour (EGY)   Attendance: 2.500
(Gamal Mahmoud Ahmed El-Ghandour was the first African referee to referee a match in the UEFA European Football Championship)

GROUP 3

05-09-1998	Helsinki	Finland – Moldova	3-2 (2-2)
05-09-1998	Istanbul	Turkey – Northern Ireland	3-0 (1-0)
10-10-1998	Belfast	Northern Ireland – Finland	1-0 (1-0)
10-10-1998	Bursa	Turkey – Germany	1-0 (0-0)
14-10-1998	Chisinau	Moldova – Germany	1-3 (1-3)
14-10-1998	Istanbul	Turkey – Finland	1-3 (0-1)
18-11-1998	Belfast	Northern Ireland – Moldova	2-2 (0-1)
27-03-1999	Belfast	Northern Ireland – Germany	0-3 (0-2)
27-03-1999	Istanbul	Turkey – Moldova	2-0 (1-0)
31-03-1999	Nuremberg	Germany – Finland	2-0 (2-0)
31-03-1999	Chisinau	Moldova – Northern Ireland	0-0
04-06-1999	Leverkusen	Germany – Moldova	6-1 (3-0)
05-06-1999	Helsinki	Finland – Turkey	2-4 (2-2)
09-06-1999	Chisinau	Moldova – Finland	0-0
04-09-1999	Helsinki	Finland – Germany	1-2 (0-2)
04-09-1999	Belfast	Northern Ireland – Turkey	0-3 (0-1)
08-09-1999	Dortmund	Germany – Northern Ireland	4-0 (4-0)
08-09-1999	Chisinau	Moldova – Turkey	1-1 (1-0)
09-10-1999	Munich	Germany – Turkey	0-0
09-10-1999	Helsinki	Finland – Northern Ireland	4-1 (1-0)

FINAL STANDING

Pos	Team	Pld	W	D	L	GF	GA	GD	Pts
1	Germany	8	6	1	1	20	4	+16	19
2	Turkey	8	5	2	1	15	6	+9	17
3	Finland	8	3	1	4	13	13	0	10
4	Northern Ireland	8	1	2	5	4	19	-15	5
5	Moldova	8	0	4	4	7	17	-10	4

Germany qualified for the final tournament in Belgium/Netherlands.
Turkey qualified for the second round play-offs.

05-09-1998   Olympic Stadium, Helsinki: Finland – Moldova   3-2 (2-2)
Finland: Antti Niemi, Sami Hyypiä, Harri Ylönen (YC61), Marko Tuomela, Joonas Kolkka (72' Sami Mahlio), Jarkko Wiss, Tommi Tapani Kautonen, Aarno Turpeinen (46' Juha Reini), Jari Litmanen (C) (YC76), Jonathan Johansson (80' Antti Sumiala), Mixu Paatelainen (YC28). (Coach: Richard Møller Nielsen (DEN)).
Moldova: Vasile Coselev, Serghei Stroenco, Oleg Fistican (75' Ivan Tabanov (YC90)), Ion Testemitanu (YC53), Alexandru Guzun, Radu Rebeja (46' Ghenadie Pusca (YC85,YC89)), Serghei Epureanu (71' Alexandru Suharev), Alexandr Curtianu (C) (YC88), Igor Oprea (YC66), Vladimir Gaidamasciuc, Serghei Clescenco. (Coach: Ivan Daniliants (AUT)).
Goals: Finland: 1-0 Joonas Kolkka (8'), 2-2 Jonathan Johansson (44'), 3-2 Mixu Paatelainen (63').
Moldova: 1-1 Igor Oprea (10'), 1-2 Igor Oprea (12').
Referee: Graham Peter Barber (ENG)   Attendance: 18.717

05-09-1998   Ali Sami Yen Stadium, Istanbul: Turkey – Northern Ireland   3-0 (1-0)
Turkey: Rüstü Reçber, Mert Korkmaz, Alpay Özalan, Saffet Akbas, Tugay Kerimoglu (C) (77' Oguz Çetin), Okan Buruk (87' Arif Erdem), Tayfur Havutçu, Sergen Yalçin, Abdullah Ercan, Hakan Sükür, Oktay Derelioglu (82' Hami Mandirali). (Coach: Mustafa Denizli (TUR)).
Northern Ireland: Alan Fettis, Aaron Hughes, Colin Hill, Stephen Morrow, Keith Rowland (46' James Quinn), Keith Gillespie (73' James Whitley), Michael Hughes, Kevin Horlock, Philip Mulryne, Neil Lennon (YC25), Iain Dowie (C). (Coach: Lawrence (Lawrie) McMenemy (ENG)).
Goals: Turkey: 1-0 Oktay Derelioglu (18'), 2-0 Tayfur Havutçu (50' penalty), 3-0 Oktay Derelioglu (58').
Referee: Ryszard Wójcik (POL)   Attendance: 19.840

10-10-1998   Windsor Park, Belfast: Northern Ireland – Finland   1-0 (1-0)
Northern Ireland: Alan Fettis, Aaron Hughes, Stephen Morrow, Keith Rowland (88' James Quinn), Darren Patterson, Keith Gillespie (75' Jon McCarthy), Michael Hughes, Kevin Horlock, Philip Mulryne, Neil Lennon, Iain Dowie (C) (82' George O'Boyle). (Coach: Lawrence (Lawrie) McMenemy (ENG)).
Finland: Antti Niemi, Sami Hyypiä, Harri Ylönen, Juha Reini, Joonas Kolkka, Jari Ilola, Simo Valakari, Aki Riihilahti (76' Jari Litmanen), Tommi Tapani Kautonen, Jonathan Johansson, Mixu Paatelainen (C). (Coach: Richard Møller Nielsen (DEN)).
Goal: Northern Ireland: 1-0 Keith Rowland (36').
Referee: Zoran Arsic (YUG)   Attendance: 10.002

10-10-1998   Atatürk Stadium, Bursa: Turkey – Germany   1-0 (0-0)
Turkey: Rüstü Reçber, Mert Korkmaz, Alpay Özalan, Fatih Akyel, Ogün Temizkanoglu (C) (88' Hakan Ünsal), Tugay Kerimoglu (60' Oktay Derelioglu), Tayfur Havutçu, Sergen Yalçin (80' Saffet Akbas), Abdullah Ercan, Tayfun Korkut (YC29,YC71), Hakan Sükür. (Coach: Mustafa Denizli (TUR)).
Germany: Oliver Kahn, Marko Rehmer (YC33), Jörg Heinrich (75' Oliver Neuville), Jens Nowotny, Markus Babbel (YC10), Carsten Ramelow, Lars Ricken (80' Marco Bode), Stefan Beinlich, Jens Jeremies (YC89), Oliver Bierhoff (C), Ulf Kirsten. (Coach: Erich Ribbeck (GER)).
Goal: Turkey: 1-0 Hakan Sükür (70').
Referee: Hugh Dallas (SCO)   Attendance: 17.505

14-10-1998   Stadionul Republican, Chisinau: Moldova – Germany   1-3 (1-3)
Moldova: Vasile Coselev, Serghei Stroenco, Oleg Fistican, Ion Testemitanu, Alexandru Guzun (YC43), Radu Rebeja, Serghei Epureanu, Alexandr Curtianu (C) (52' Alexandru Suharev), Igor Oprea (YC4,YC84), Vladimir Gaidamasciuc, Serghei Clescenco (YC11). (Coach: Ivan Daniliants (AUT)).
Germany: Oliver Kahn, Michael Tarnat, Marko Rehmer, Jens Nowotny, Markus Babbel, Carsten Ramelow (YC87), Lars Ricken (52' Oliver Neuville), Stefan Beinlich (YC18) (83' Dariusz Wosz), Christian Nerlinger (YC52), Oliver Bierhoff (C), Ulf Kirsten (73' Carsten Jancker). (Coach: Erich Ribbeck (GER)).
Goals: Moldova: 1-0 Alexandru Guzun (6').
Germany: 1-1 Ulf Kirsten (19'), 1-2 Ulf Kirsten (35'), 1-3 Oliver Bierhoff (38').
Referee: Juan Antonio Fernández Marín (ESP)   Attendance: 5.400

14-10-1998   Ali Sami Yen Stadium, Istanbul: Turkey – Finland   1-3 (0-1)
Turkey: Rüstü Reçber, Alpay Özalan, Fatih Akyel, Ogün Temizkanoglu (C), Tugay Kerimoglu (46' Hami Mandirali), Okan Buruk (46' Mert Korkmaz), Tayfur Havutçu (YC41), Sergen Yalçin (83' Hasan Sas), Abdullah Ercan (YC44), Hakan Sükür (YC32), Oktay Derelioglu. (Coach: Mustafa Denizli (TUR)).
Finland: Antti Niemi, Sami Hyypiä, Harri Ylönen, Marko Tuomela (YC90+3), Juha Reini, Jari Ilola, Aki Riihilahti (76' Simo Valakari), Tommi Tapani Kautonen (YC27), Jari Litmanen (C), Jonathan Johansson (90' Jarmo Saastoimenen), Mixu Paatelainen (46' Joonas Kolkka (YC73)). (Coach: Richard Møller Nielsen (DEN)).
Goals: Turkey: 1-2 Ogün Temizkanoglu (74').
Finland: 0-1 Mixu Paatelainen (5'), 0-2 Jonathan Johansson (51'), 1-3 Jari Litmanen (90+6').
Referee: Václav Krondl (CZE)   Attendance: 20.420

18-11-1998   Windsor Park, Belfast: Northern Ireland – Moldova   2-2 (0-1)
Northern Ireland: Alan Fettis, Danny Griffin, Stephen Morrow, Keith Rowland (78' Phillip Gray), Darren Patterson, Peter Kennedy (YC87), Keith Gillespie (YC44) (88' Jon McCarthy), Steve Lomas (C), Michael Hughes, Neil Lennon, Iain Dowie. (Coach: Lawrence (Lawrie) McMenemy (ENG)).
Moldova: Serghei Dinov (YC75), Serghei Stroenco (YC60), Oleg Fistican, Ion Testemitanu (85' Vitali Maevici), Alexandru Guzun (68' Ghenadie Pusca), Radu Rebeja (YC44), Serghei Epureanu, Alexandr Curtianu (C) (YC35,YC65), Vladimir Gaidamasciuc, Gheorghe Stratulat (YC23) (62' Alexandru Suharev), Serghei Clescenco. (Coach: Ivan Daniliants (AUT)).
Goals: Northern Ireland: 1-1 Iain Dowie (49'), 2-2 Neil Lennon (63').
Moldova: 0-1 Vladimir Gaidamasciuc (22'), 1-2 Ion Testemitanu (56').
Referee: Vladimír Hrinák (SVK)   Attendance: 11.142

27-03-1999   Windsor Park, Belfast: Northern Ireland – Germany   0-3 (0-2)
Northern Ireland: Maik Taylor, Stephen Morrow, Keith Rowland (67' Danny Sonner), Darren Patterson (YC83), Mark Williams, Keith Gillespie (83' Jon McCarthy), Steve Lomas (C), Michael Hughes, Kevin Horlock, Neil Lennon (67' Peter Kennedy), Iain Dowie. (Coach: Lawrence (Lawrie) McMenemy (ENG)).
Germany: Oliver Kahn, Christian Wörns (YC53), Jörg Heinrich, Markus Babbel, Dietmar Hamann, Jens Jeremies, Lothar Matthäus (46' Jens Nowotny), Thomas Strunz, Marco Bode (YC10) (78' Michael Preetz), Oliver Neuville (67' Carsten Jancker), Oliver Bierhoff (C). (Coach: Erich Ribbeck (GER)).
Goals: Germany: 0-1 Marco Bode (19'), 0-1 Marco Bode (43'), 0-3 Dietmar Hamann (62').
Referee: Graziano Cesari (ITA)   Attendance: 14.270

27-03-1999   Ali Sami Yen Stadium, Istanbul: Turkey – Moldova   2-0 (1-0)
Turkey: Rüstü Reçber, Alpay Özalan, Fatih Akyel, Ogün Temizkanoglu (C), Tugay Kerimoglu (86' Ayhan Akman), Okan Buruk, Tayfur Havutçu, Sergen Yalçin, Abdullah Ercan, Hakan Sükür, Oktay Derelioglu (9' Hami Mandirali, 75' Arif Erdem). (Coach: Mustafa Denizli (TUR)).
Moldova: Serghei Dinov, Serghei Stroenco (C), Oleg Fistican, Alexandru Guzun, Ivan Tabanov (YC20), Radu Rebeja, Serghei Epureanu, Oleg Sischin (YC44,YC60), Vladimir Gaidamasciuc (YC33), Gheorghe Stratulat, Serghei Clescenco (81' Alexandru Suharev). (Coach: Ivan Daniliants (AUT)).
Goals: Turkey: 1-0 Hakan Sükür (35'), 2-0 Sergen Yalçin (90+5').
Referee: Konrad Plautz (AUT)   Attendance: 19.454

31-03-1999   Frankenstadion, Nuremburg: Germany – Finland   2-0 (2-0)
Germany: Oliver Kahn, Christian Wörns (YC16), Jörg Heinrich, Markus Babbel, Dietmar Hamann (70' Jens Nowotny), Jens Jeremies, Lothar Matthäus, Thomas Strunz, Marco Bode (76' Carsten Jancker), Oliver Neuville (64' Ulf Kirsten), Oliver Bierhoff (C). (Coach: Erich Ribbeck (GER)).
Finland: Antti Niemi, Sami Hyypiä, Harri Ylönen, Juha Reini (YC39) (88' Mika Lehkosuo), Tomi Kinnunen, Jari Ilola, Aki Riihilahti, Tommi Tapani Kautonen (70' Joonas Kolkka), Jari Litmanen (C), Jonathan Johansson, Mixu Paatelainen (46' Jarmo Saastoimenen). (Coach: Richard Møller Nielsen (DEN)).
Goals: Germany: 1-0 Jens Jeremies (31'), 2-0 Oliver Neuville (36').
Referee: Sergei Grigorievich Khusainov (RUS)   Attendance: 40.758

31-03-1999   Stadionul Republican, Chisinau: Moldova – Northern Ireland   0-0
Moldova: Serghei Dinov, Adrian Sosnovschi, Serghei Stroenco (C), Oleg Fistican, Alexandru Guzun, Radu Rebeja, Serghei Epureanu, Igor Oprea (89' Gheorghe Stratulat), Vladimir Gaidamasciuc, Alexandru Suharev, Serghei Clescenco. (Coach: Ivan Daniliants (AUT)).
Northern Ireland: Maik Taylor, Stephen Morrow, Darren Patterson (64' Aaron Hughes), Mark Williams, Keith Gillespie, Steve Lomas (C), Michael Hughes (YC13), Kevin Horlock (YC61), Stephen Robinson, Neil Lennon, Iain Dowie (YC22). (Coach: Lawrence (Lawrie) McMenemy (ENG)).
Referee: Edo Trivkovic (CRO)   Attendance: 9.237

04-06-1999   BayArena, Leverkusen: Germany – Moldova 6-1 (3-0)
Germany: Oliver Kahn, Jörg Heinrich, Jens Nowotny, Dietmar Hamann, Jens Jeremies (44'
Mehmet Scholl), Lothar Matthäus (74' Markus Babbel), Thomas Strunz, Marco Bode, Oliver
Neuville, Oliver Bierhoff (C), Ulf Kirsten (53' Carsten Ramelow). (Coach: Erich Ribbeck
(GER)).
Moldova: Serghei Dinov, Serghei Stroenco, Oleg Fistican, Alexandru Guzun, Vitali Maevici
(54' Oleg Sischin), Radu Rebeja, Serghei Epureanu, Alexandr Curtianu (C), Igor Oprea
(YC82), Vladimir Gaidamasciuc (74' Gheorghe Stratulat), Serghei Clescenco (YC29) (82'
Alexandru Suharev). (Coach: Ivan Daniliants (AUT)).
Goals: Germany: 1-0 Oliver Bierhoff (2'), 2-0 Ulf Kirsten (26'), 3-0 Marco Bode (37'), 4-0
Oliver Bierhoff (56'), 5-0 Mehmet Scholl (70'), 6-1 Oliver Bierhoff (82').
Moldova: 5-1 Oleg Sischin (75').
Referee: Jorge Emanuel Monteiro Coroado (POR)   Attendance: 21.000

05-06-1999   Olympic Stadium, Helsinki: Finland – Turkey 2-4 (2-2)
Finland: Antti Niemi, Sami Hyypiä, Toni Kuivasto, Hannu Tihinen, Harri Ylönen, Joonas
Kolkka, Simo Valakari (YC73), Aki Riihilahti, Jari Litmanen (C), Jonathan Johansson, Mixu
Paatelainen. (Coach: Richard Møller Nielsen (DEN)).
Turkey: Rüştü Reçber, Ali Beserter, Alpay Özalan, Fatih Akyel (YC63), Saffet Akbas, Ayhan
Akman (YC57) (74' Tugay Kerimoglu), Tayfur Havutçu, Sergen Yalçin (89' Ümit Davala),
Abdullah Ercan (90' Hakan Ünsal), Tayfun Korkut, Hakan Sükür (C). (Coach: Mustafa Denizli
(TUR)).
Goals: Finland: 1-0 Hannu Tihinen (10'), 2-0 Mixu Paatelainen (14').
Turkey: 2-1 Tayfur Havutçu (25'), 2-2 Hakan Sükür (34'), 2-3 Tayfur Havutçu (84'), 2-4
Hakan Sükür (87').
Referee: Dirk Zier Gerardus (Dick) Jol (HOL)   Attendance: 36.042

09-06-1999   Stadionul Republican, Chisinau: Moldova – Finland 0-0
Moldova: Serghei Dinov, Serghei Stroenco, Oleg Fistican (YC50), Alexandru Guzun, Radu
Rebeja, Serghei Epureanu, Oleg Sischin (74' Serghei Belous), Alexandr Curtianu (C), Igor
Oprea (79' Vladimir Gaidamasciuc), Gheorghe Stratulat, Alexandru Suharev (88' Serghei
Chirilov). (Coach: Ivan Daniliants (AUT)).
Finland: Antti Niemi, Sami Hyypiä, Hannu Tihinen (46' Tommi Tapani Kautonen), Harri
Ylönen, Juha Reini (86' Mika Lehkosuo), Joonas Kolkka (YC54), Jari Ilola, Simo Valakari,
Aki Riihilahti, Jonathan Johansson (60' Mikael Forssell), Mixu Paatelainen (C). (Coach:
Richard Møller Nielsen (DEN)).
Referee: Florenzo Treossi (ITA)   Attendance: 6.100

04-09-1999   Olympic Stadium, Helsinki: Finland – Germany 1-2 (0-2)
Finland: Antti Niemi (46' Pasi Laaksonen), Sami Hyypiä (C), Toni Kuivasto, Harri Ylönen
(YC44) (46' Shefki Kuqi), Janne Salli, Jarmo Saastamoinen, Teemu Tainio (YC74), Jarkko
Wiss, Aki Riihilahti, Jonathan Johansson, Mika Kottila. (Coach: Richard Møller Nielsen
(DEN)).
Germany: Jens Lehmann, Thomas Linke, Jens Nowotny, Markus Babbel, Mehmet Scholl (78'
Christian Nerlinger), Christian Ziege, Jens Jeremies, Lothar Matthäus, Oliver Neuville (89'
Thomas Strunz), Oliver Bierhoff (C), Ulf Kirsten (32' Bernd Schneider). (Coach: Erich
Ribbeck (GER)).
Goals: Finland: 1-2 Janne Salli (63').
Germany: 0-1 Oliver Bierhoff (2'), 0-2 Oliver Bierhoff (16').
Referee: Antonio Jesús López Nieto (ESP)   Attendance: 20.184

04-09-1999   Windsor Park, Belfast: Northern Ireland – Turkey   0-3 (0-1)
Northern Ireland: Maik Taylor, Aaron Hughes, Barry Hunter, Peter Kennedy, Mark Williams (YC31), Steve Lomas (C) (YC55), Michael Hughes, Kevin Horlock, Neil Lennon, Jon McCarthy (63' Keith Gillespie), Iain Dowie (76' James Quinn). (Coach: Lawrence (Lawrie) McMenemy (ENG)).
Turkey: Rüstü Reçber, Ali Beserter, Alpay Özalan, Ogün Temizkanoglu (C), Tugay Kerimoglu, Tayfur Havutçu, Sergen Yalçin (90' Ümit Karan), Abdullah Ercan (YC66) (75' Hakan Ünsal), Tayfun Korkut, Hakan Sükür (C), Arif Erdem (78' Okan Buruk). (Coach: Mustafa Denizli (TUR)).
Goals: Turkey: 0-1 Arif Erdem (44'), 0-2 Arif Erdem (46'), 0-3 Arif Erdem (48').
Referee: Alain Sars (FRA)   Attendance: 7.270

08-09-1999   Westfalenstadion, Dortmund: Germany – Northern Ireland   4-0 (4-0)
Germany: Jens Lehmann, Thomas Linke (YC69), Jens Nowotny (46' Christian Wörns), Markus Babbel (30' Thomas Strunz (YC77)), Mehmet Scholl, Christian Ziege (YC42), Jens Jeremies, Lothar Matthäus, Marco Bode, Oliver Neuville (66' Bernd Schneider), Oliver Bierhoff (C). (Coach: Erich Ribbeck (GER)).
Northern Ireland: Maik Taylor, Stephen Morrow, Peter Kennedy, Mark Williams, Ian Nolan, Steve Lomas (YC58), Michael Hughes (C), Kevin Horlock (YC34), Neil Lennon (46' Keith Gillespie), Jon McCarthy, Iain Dowie (46' James Quinn (YC57)). (Coach: Lawrence (Lawrie) McMenemy (ENG)).
Goals: Germany: 1-0 Oliver Bierhoff (2'), 2-0 Christian Ziege (15'), 3-0 Christian Ziege (35'), 4-0 Christian Ziege (45').
Referee: Georgios Bikas (GRE)   Attendance: 41.000

08-09-1999   Stadionul Republican, Chisinau: Moldova – Turkey   1-1 (1-0)
Moldova: Serghei Dinov, Serghei Stroenco (C), Oleg Fistican, Alexandru Guzun, Radu Rebeja (YC49), Vadim Boret, Serghei Epureanu, Iurie Osipenco, Igor Oprea (YC73), Vladimir Gaidamasciuc (46' Gheorghe Stratulat (YC63)), Serghei Clescenco (82' Serghei Chirilov). (Coach: Ivan Daniliants (AUT)).
Turkey: Rüstü Reçber, Ali Beserter, Alpay Özalan, Fatih Akyel (46' Ayhan Akman), Hakan Ünsal, Ogün Temizkanoglu (C), Okan Buruk (46' Tugay Kerimoglu), Tayfur Havutçu, Sergen Yalçin (87' Ümit Davala), Hakan Sükür, Arif Erdem (YC60). (Coach: Mustafa Denizli (TUR)).
Goals: Moldova: 1-0 Serghei Epureanu (3').
Turkey: 1-1 Tayfur Havutçu (76').
Referee: Andreas Schluchter (SUI)   Attendance: 4.500

09-10-1999   Olympiastadion, Munich: Germany – Turkey   0-0
Germany: Oliver Kahn, Thomas Linke, Markus Babbel, Bernd Schneider (87' Mustafa Dogan), Mehmet Scholl (YC32), Dietmar Hamann (46' Christian Nerlinger (YC77)), Christian Ziege (75' Marco Bode), Jens Jeremies, Lothar Matthäus, Oliver Neuville, Oliver Bierhoff (C). (Coach: Erich Ribbeck (GER)).
Turkey: Rüstü Reçber, Ali Beserter, Alpay Özalan, Fatih Akyel, Ogün Temizkanoglu (C), Okan Buruk (YC69) (71' Arif Erdem), Tayfur Havutçu (84' Oktay Derelioglu), Sergen Yalçin (YC82), Abdullah Ercan (YC54) (68' Ergün Penbe), Tayfun Korkut, Hakan Sükür. (Coach: Mustafa Denizli (TUR)).
Referee: Pierluigi Collina (ITA)   Attendance: 63.572

09-10-1999   Olympic Stadium, Helsinki: Finland – Northern Ireland 4-1 (1-0)
Finland: Jani Viander, Sami Hyypiä, Toni Kuivasto, Hannu Tihinen, Joonas Kolkka, Jarkko Wiss (86' Sami Ylä-Jussila), Aki Riihilahti (86' Simo Valakari), Mika Lehkosuo, Jari Litmanen (C), Jonathan Johansson, Mixu Paatelainen. (Coach: Richard Møller Nielsen (DEN)).
Northern Ireland: Maik Taylor, Stephen Morrow, Peter Kennedy, Mark Williams, Ian Nolan, Iain Jenkins (79' James Whitley), Michael Hughes (75' Damien Johnson), Jeff Whitley, Neil Lennon (C), Jon McCarthy, James Quinn (YC64) (67' Adrian Coote). (Coach: Lawrence (Lawrie) McMenemy (ENG)).
Goals: Finland: 1-0 Jonathan Johansson (9'), 2-1 Sami Hyypiä (63'), 3-1 Joonas Kolkka (72'), 4-1 Joonas Kolkka (82').
Northern Ireland: 1-1 Jeff Whitley (59').
Referee: Armand Ancion (BEL)   Attendance: 8.217

GROUP 4

05-09-1998	Yerevan	Armenia – Andorra	3-1 (1-0)
05-09-1998	Reykjavik	Iceland – France	1-1 (1-1)
05-09-1998	Kiev	Ukraine – Russia	3-2 (2-0)
10-10-1998	Aixovall	Andorra – Ukraine	0-2 (0-2)
10-10-1998	Yerevan	Armenia – Iceland	0-0
10-10-1998	Moscow	Russia – France	2-3 (1-2)
14-10-1998	Paris	France – Andorra	2-0 (0-0)
14-10-1998	Reykjavik	Iceland – Russia	1-0 (0-0)
14-10-1998	Kiev	Ukraine – Armenia	2-0 (1-0)
27-03-1999	Aixovall	Andorra – Iceland	0-2 (0-0)
27-03-1999	Yerevan	Armenia – Russia	0-3 (0-1)
27-03-1999	Paris	France – Ukraine	0-0
31-03-1999	Paris	France – Armenia	2-0 (2-0)
31-03-1999	Moscow	Russia – Andorra	6-1 (3-0)
31-03-1999	Kiev	Ukraine – Iceland	1-1 (0-0)
05-06-1999	Paris	France – Russia	2-3 (0-1)
05-06-1999	Reykjavik	Iceland – Armenia	2-0 (1-0)
05-06-1999	Kiev	Ukraine – Andorra	4-0 (2-0)
09-06-1999	Barcelona	Andorra – France	0-1 (0-0)
09-06-1999	Yerevan	Armenia – Ukraine	0-0
09-06-1999	Moscow	Russia – Iceland	1-0 (1-0)
04-09-1999	Reykjavik	Iceland – Andorra	3-0 (2-0)
04-09-1999	Moscow	Russia – Armenia	2-0 (1-0)
04-09-1999	Kiev	Ukraine – France	0-0
08-09-1999	Aixovall	Andorra – Russia	1-2 (1-1)
08-09-1999	Reykjavik	Iceland – Ukraine	0-1 (0-1)
08-09-1999	Yerevan	Armenia – France	2-3 (1-1)
09-10-1999	Aixovall	Andorra – Armenia	0-3 (0-1)
09-10-1999	Paris	France – Iceland	3-2 (2-0)
09-10-1999	Moscow	Russia – Ukraine	1-1 (0-0)

FINAL STANDING

Pos	Team	Pld	W	D	L	GF	GA	GD	Pts
1	France	10	6	3	1	17	10	+7	21
2	Ukraine	10	5	5	0	14	4	+10	20
3	Russia	10	6	1	3	22	12	+10	19
4	Iceland	10	4	3	3	12	7	+5	15
5	Armenia	10	2	2	6	8	15	-7	8
6	Andorra	10	0	0	10	3	28	-25	0

France qualified for the final tournament in Belgium/Netherlands.

Ukraine qualified for the second round play-offs.

05-09-1998   Hrazdan Stadium, Yerevan: Armenia – Andorra   3-1 (1-0)
Armenia: Roman Berezovskiy, Sargis Hovsepyan, Yervand Sukiasyan, Yervand Krbashyan, Harutyun Vardanyan (C), Albert Sarkisyan (YC52), Armen Adamyan (YC44), Ardaches Adamyan (86' Tigran Gspeyan), Tigran Hovhannisyan (83' Feliks Khojoyan), Armen Shahgeldyan, Garnik Avalyan (69' Tigran Yesayan). (Coach: Suren Barseghyan (ARM)).
Andorra: Jesús Luis Álvarez de Eulate "KOLDO", ÓSCAR SONEJEE Masand, ANTONI (Toni) LIMA Solà, JORDI ESCURA Aixas, José Manuel "TXEMA" GARCÍA Luena, FRANCESC Xavier RAMÍREZ, GENÍS GARCÍA Iscza, JESÚS Julián LUCENDO Heredia (C), ÁNGEL MARTÍN García, JULIÀ SÁNCHEZ Soto (YC54), JUSTO Ruiz GONZALEZ. (Coach: MANOEL MILUIR Macedo Cunha (BRA)).
Goals: Armenia; 1-0 Garnik Avalyan (40'), 2-0 Tigran Yesayan (72'), 3-1 Tigran Yesayan (90').
Andorra: 2-1 JESÚS Julián LUCENDO Heredia (85').
Referee: Richard O'Hanlon (IRL)   Attendance: 2.000

05-09-1998   Laugardalsvöllur, Reykjavik: Iceland – France   1-1 (1-1)
Iceland: Birkir Kristinsson (YC72), Pétur Marteinsson, Audun Helgason, Larus Sigurdsson (YC12), Hermann Hreidarsson, Runar Kristinsson, Helgi Kolvidsson, Thordur Gudjónsson, Arnar Gunnlaugsson (69' Stefán Thor Thórdarson), Eyjölfur Sverrisson (C), Rikhardur Dadason. (Coach: Gudjón Thórdarsson (ISL)).
France: Fabien Barthez, Lilian Thuram, Bixente Lizarazu, Frank Leboeuf, Zinédine Zidane, Robert Pirès, Didier Deschamps (C), Christian Karembeu (YC17), Lilian Laslandes, Youri Djorkaeff, Christophe Dugarry (67' Thierry Henry). (Coach: Roger Lemerre (FRA)).
Goals: Iceland: 1-0 Rikhardur Dadason (32').
France: 1-1 Christophe Dugarry (35').
Referee: Eric Blareau (BEL)   Attendance: 10.382

05-09-1998   Olimpiysky NSC, Kiev: Ukraine – Russia   3-2 (2-0)
Ukraine: Oleksandr Shovkovsky, Vladyslav Vaschuk, Serhiy Popov, Volodymyr Mykytin, Yuriy Dmytrulin, Oleksandr Holovko (C), Andriy Gusin, Serhiy Kovalov (YC3) (87' Valeriy Kryventsov), Serhiy Rebrov, Andriy Shevchenko, Serhiy Skachenko (46' Yuriy Kalitvintsev). (Coach: József Sabo (UKR)).
Russia: Dmitri Kharin (RC72), Viktor Onopko, Yuri Kovtun (YC49), Igor Chugainov, Igor Yanovski (YC13), Valery Minko, Yevgeniy Varlamov, Sergei Semak (73' Stas Cherchesov *goalkeeper*), Andrei Kanchelskis (71' Valeri Karpin), Dmitri Alenichev (64' Aleksandr Mostovoy), Igor Kolyvanov (C). (Coach: Anatoliy Fyodorovich Byshovets (URS)).
Goals: Ukraine: 1-0 Serhiy Popov (14'), 2-0 Serhiy Skachenko (24'), 3-1 Serhiy Rebrov (74' penalty).
Russia: 2-1 Yevgeniy Varlamov (67'), 3-2 Viktor Onopko (88').
Referee: Markus Merk (GER)   Attendance: 82.100

10-10-1998   Camp d'Esports d'Aixovall, Aixovall: Andorra – Ukraine   0-2 (0-2)
Andorra: Jesús Luis Álvarez de Eulate "KOLDO", ILDEFONS LIMA Solá, ÓSCAR SONEJEE Masand, ANTONI (Toni) LIMA Solà (C), José Manuel "TXEMA" GARCÍA Luena, FRANCESC Xavier RAMÍREZ, ÁNGEL MARTÍN García, AGUSTI POL Pérez, JULIÀ SÁNCHEZ Soto (88' Manolo "MANEL" JIMÉNEZ Soria), JUSTO Ruiz GONZALEZ, EMILIANO GONZÁLEZ Arquez. (Coach: MANOEL MILUIR Macedo Cunha (BRA)).
Ukraine: Oleksandr Shovkovsky, Vladyslav Vaschuk, Oleg Luzhny (C), Serhiy Popov (YC53), Volodymyr Mykytin (46' Serhiy Kovalov), Oleksandr Holovko, Andriy Gusin, Yuriy Maksymov (YC50) (52' Valeriy Kryventsov), Vitaliy Kosovskyi, Serhiy Rebrov, Andriy Shevchenko (70' Dmytro Mykhaylenko). (Coach: József Sabo (UKR)).
Goals: Ukraine: 0-1 Vitaliy Kosovskyi (31'), 0-2 Serhiy Rebrov (44').
Referee: Anton Guetzov (BUL)   Attendance: 850

10-10-1998   Hrazdan Stadium, Yerevan: Armenia – Iceland   0-0
Armenia: Roman Berezovskiy, Sargis Hovsepyan, Yervand Sukiasyan, Vardan Khachatryan (C) (YC45), Harutyun Vardanyan, Albert Sarkisyan (YC12), Artur Petrosyan (82' Tigran Hovhannisyan), Ardaches Adamyan, Armen Shahgeldyan, Karapet Mikaelyan, Éric Assadourian (62' Tigran Yesayan). (Coach: Suren Barseghyan (ARM)).
Iceland: Birkir Kristinsson, Audun Helgason, Larus Sigurdsson, Steinar Adolfsson, Hermann Hreidarsson, Runar Kristinsson, Sigurdur Jónsson (C) (YC58), Helgi Kolvidsson (YC67), Thordur Gudjónsson, Arnar Gunnlaugsson, Rikhardur Dadason. (Coach: Gudjón Thórdarsson (ISL)).
Referee: Morgan Norman (SWE)   Attendance: 2.000

10-10-1998   Luzhniki Stadium, Moscow: Russia – France   2-3 (1-2)
Russia: Sergei Ovchinnikov (YC90), Dmitri Khlestov (YC90), Viktor Onopko (C), Igor Yanovski, Yevgeniy Varlamov, Yegor Titov, Andrei Tikhonov, Valeri Karpin, Aleksandr Mostovoy, Dmitri Alenichev (70' Sergei Semak), Vladimir Beschastnikh (60' Alexey Gerasimenko). (Coach: Anatoliy Fyodorovich Byshovets (URS)).
France: Bernard Lama, Lilian Thuram (YC85), Bixente Lizarazu, Marcel Desailly, Laurent Blanc, Zinédine Zidane, Robert Pirès, Emmanuel Petit (46' Alain Boghossian), Didier Deschamps (C), Nicolas Anelka (86' Tony Vairelles), Youri Djorkaeff (YC51) (54' Patrick Vieira). (Coach: Roger Lemerre (FRA)).
Goals: Russia: 1-2 Igor Yanovski (45'), 2-2 Aleksandr Mostovoy (55').
France: 0-1 Nicolas Anelka (13'), 0-2 Robert Pirès (28'), 2-3 Alain Boghossian (81').
Referee: Piero Ceccarini (ITA)   Attendance: 20.989

14-10-1998   Stade de France, Paris: France – Andorra   2-0 (0-0)
France: Bernard Lama, Vincent Candela, Bixente Lizarazu (YC83), Frank Leboeuf, Laurent Blanc, Zinédine Zidane, Didier Deschamps (C), David Trézéguet (67' Nicolas Anelka), Tony Vairelles (YC67), Youri Djorkaeff (81' Alain Boghossian), Christophe Dugarry (67' Robert Pirès). (Coach: Roger Lemerre (FRA)).
Andorra: Jesús Luis Álvarez de Eulate "KOLDO", ILDEFONS LIMA Solá, ÓSCAR SONEJEE Masand, ANTONI (Toni) LIMA Solà (YC26), José Manuel "TXEMA" GARCÍA Luena, FRANCESC Xavier RAMÍREZ (YC51) (80' JULIÀ SÁNCHEZ Soto), JESÚS Julián LUCENDO Heredia (C) (85' Manolo "MANEL" JIMÉNEZ Soria), ÁNGEL MARTÍN García, AGUSTI POL Pérez, JUSTO Ruiz GONZALEZ, EMILIANO GONZÁLEZ Arquez. (Coach: MANOEL MILUIR Macedo Cunha (BRA)).
Goals: France: 1-0 Vincent Candela (54'), 2-0 Youri Djorkaeff (59').
Referee: Dani Koren (ISR)   Attendance: 75.416

14-10-1998   Laugardalsvöllur, Reykjavik: Iceland – Russia   1-0 (0-0)
Iceland: Birkir Kristinsson, Audun Helgason, Larus Sigurdsson, Steinar Adolfsson, Hermann Hreidarsson, Runar Kristinsson, Sigurdur Jónsson (C), Helgi Kolvidsson (85' Stefán Thor Thórdarson), Thordur Gudjónsson (6' Helgi Sigurdsson), Arnar Gunnlaugsson, Rikhardur Dadason. (Coach: Gudjón Thórdarsson (ISL)).
Russia: Stas Cherchesov, Viktor Onopko (C), Yuri Kovtun, Igor Yanovski, Yevgeniy Varlamov, Yegor Titov, Aleksei Smertin (YC,YC75), Andrei Tikhonov (13' Aleksei Igonin), Valeri Karpin (59' Dmitri Khokhlov), Aleksandr Mostovoy (YC85), Igor Shalimov. (Coach: Anatoliy Fyodorovich Byshovets (URS)).
Goal: Iceland: 1-0 Yuri Kovtun (87' own goal).
Referee: René H.J.Temmink (HOL)   Attendance: 3.345

14-10-1998   Olimpiysky NSC, Kiev: Ukraine – Armenia   2-0 (1-0)
Ukraine: Oleksandr Shovkovsky, Vladyslav Vaschuk, Oleg Luzhny (C), Serhiy Popov (75' Yuriy Maksymov), Yuriy Dmytrulin, Oleksandr Holovko, Andriy Gusin, Vitaliy Kosovskyi, Serhiy Rebrov, Andriy Shevchenko (78' Valeriy Kryventsov), Serhiy Skachenko (59' Serhiy Kovalov). (Coach: József Sabo (UKR)).
Armenia: Roman Berezovskiy, Sargis Hovsepyan (YC23), Yervand Sukiasyan (YC30), Yervand Krbashyan (83' Tigran Hovhannisyan), Vardan Khachatryan (C), Harutyun Vardanyan, Artur Petrosyan, Ardaches Adamyan, Armen Shahgeldyan, Karapet Mikaelyan (65' Garnik Avalyan), Éric Assadourian (71' Tigran Yesayan). (Coach: Suren Barseghyan (ARM)).
Goals: Ukraine: 1-0 Serhiy Skachenko (31'), 2-0 Andriy Gusin (80').
Referee: Marcel Lica (ROM)   Attendance: 14.850

27-03-1999   Camp d'Esports d'Aixovall, Aixovall: Andorra – Iceland   0-2 (0-0)
Andorra: Jesús Luis Álvarez de Eulate "KOLDO", ILDEFONS LIMA Solá, ÓSCAR SONEJEE Masand, ANTONI (Toni) LIMA Solà, José Manuel "TXEMA" GARCÍA Luena, FRANCESC Xavier RAMÍREZ (YC48) (77' EMILIANO GONZÁLEZ Arquez), Manolo "MANEL" JIMÉNEZ Soria (63' JULIÀ SÁNCHEZ Soto), JESÚS Julián LUCENDO Heredia (C), ÁNGEL MARTÍN García (YC43), AGUSTI POL Pérez, JUSTO Ruiz GONZALEZ (82' RICARD IMBERNON Rios (YC85)). (Coach: MANOEL MILUIR Macedo Cunha (BRA)).
Iceland: Birkir Kristinsson, Audun Helgason, Steinar Adolfsson, Brynjar Gunnarsson (YC49) (71' Hermann Hreidarsson (YC89)), Runar Kristinsson (YC45), Sigurdur Jónsson (C), Thordur Gudjónsson, Arnar Gunnlaugsson (81' Tryggvi Gudmundsson), Helgi Sigurdsson, Stefán Thor Thórdarson, Eyjölfur Sverrisson (60' Arnar Gretarsson). (Coach: Gudjón Thórdarsson (ISL)).
Goals: Iceland: 0-1 Eyjölfur Sverrisson (58'), 0-2 Steinar Adolfsson (66').
Referee: Charles Agius (MLT)   Attendance: 900

27-03-1999   Hrazdan Stadium, Yerevan: Armenia – Russia   0-3 (0-1)
Armenia: Roman Berezovskiy, Sargis Hovsepyan, Yervand Krbashyan (64' Hayk Harutyunyan), Sargis Hovhannisyan (YC35), Harutyun Vardanyan (C), Artur Mkrtchyan (YC15), Albert Sarkisyan, Artur Petrosyan, Artur Voskanyan (78' Manuk Kakosyan), Armen Shahgeldyan, Karapet Mikaelyan (82' Tigran Yesayan). (Coach: Suren Barseghyan (ARM)).
Russia: Aleksandr Filimonov, Dmitri Khlestov, Viktor Onopko (C), Igor Yanovski (YC73), Yuri Drozdov, Yegor Titov (YC52), Valeri Karpin, Ilya Tsymbalar, Dmitri Alenichev (64' Andrei Tikhonov), Sergei Yuran (86' Dmitri Khokhlov), Aleksandr Panov (46' Vladimir Beschastnikh). (Coach: Oleg Ivanovich Romantsev (URS)).
Goals: Russia: 0-1 Valeri Karpin (7'), 0-2 Valeri Karpin (63' penalty), 0-3 Vladimir Beschastnikh (89').
Referee: Terje Hauge (NOR)   Attendance: 10.000

27-03-1999   Stade de France, Paris: France – Ukraine   0-0
France: Fabien Barthez, Lilian Thuram, Bixente Lizarazu, Marcel Desailly, Laurent Blanc, Robert Pirès (84' Vikash Dhorasoo), Emmanuel Petit (78' Alain Boghossian), Didier Deschamps (C), Nicolas Anelka, Youri Djorkaeff, Christophe Dugarry (69' Sylvain Wiltord). (Coach: Roger Lemerre (FRA)).
Ukraine: Oleksandr Shovkovsky, Vladyslav Vaschuk, Oleg Luzhny (C), Serhiy Popov, Volodymyr Mykytin (YC44), Oleksandr Holovko, Andriy Gusin (YC62) (86' Viktor Skrypnyk), Serhiy Kovalov (55' Vitaliy Kosovskyi), Serhiy Rebrov, Andriy Shevchenko, Serhiy Skachenko (69' Yuriy Maksymov). (Coach: József Sabo (UKR)).
Referee: Günter Benkö (AUT)   Attendance: 78.519

31-03-1999   Stade de France, Paris: France – Armenia   2-0 (2-0)
France: Fabien Barthez, Lilian Thuram, Marcel Desailly, Laurent Blanc, Didier Deschamps (C), Alain Boghossian, Patrick Vieira (YC76), Sylvain Wiltord, Nicolas Anelka, Youri Djorkaeff (69' Robert Pirès), Christophe Dugarry (46' David Trézéguet). (Coach: Roger Lemerre (FRA)).
Armenia: Roman Berezovskiy, Sargis Hovsepyan, Yervand Sukiasyan (C), Sargis Hovhannisyan, Harutyun Vardanyan, Artur Mkrtchyan (39' Vardan Khachatryan), Albert Sarkisyan, Artur Petrosyan, Artur Voskanyan (YC75), Armen Shahgeldyan (53' Tigran Yesayan), Karapet Mikaelyan. (Coach: Suren Barseghyan (ARM)).
Goals: France: 1-0 Sylvain Wiltord (2'), 2-0 Christophe Dugarry (45').
Referee: Georgios Bikas (GRE)   Attendance: 78.852

31-03-1999 Central Stadium Lokomotiv, Moscow: Russia – Andorra 6-1 (3-0)
Russia: Aleksandr Filimonov, Vadim Evseev (46' Andrei Tikhonov), Dmitri Khlestov, Viktor Onopko (C), Yegor Titov, Aleksei Smertin, Valeri Karpin, Ilya Tsymbalar, Dmitri Alenichev, Aleksandr Shirko, Vladimir Beschastnikh. (Coach: Oleg Ivanovich Romantsev (URS)).
Andorra: Jesús Luis Álvarez de Eulate "KOLDO", ILDEFONS LIMA Solá (YC59), ÓSCAR SONEJEE Masand, ANTONI (Toni) LIMA Solà, José Manuel "TXEMA" GARCÍA Luena, ROBERTO JONÁS Alonso Martínez (58' EMILIANO GONZÁLEZ Arquez), Manolo "MANEL" JIMÉNEZ Soria, JESÚS Julián LUCENDO Heredia (C) (67' JULIÀ SÁNCHEZ Soto), ÁNGEL MARTÍN García, AGUSTI POL Pérez, JUSTO Ruiz GONZALEZ. (Coach: MANOEL MILUIR Macedo Cunha (BRA)).
Goals: Russia: 1-0 Yegor Titov (8'), 2-0 Vladimir Beschastnikh (13'), 3-0 Viktor Onopko (43'), 4-0 Ilya Tsymbalar (50'), 5-0 Vladimir Beschastnikh (63'), 6-1 Dmitri Alenichev (89').
Andorra: 5-1 EMILIANO GONZÁLEZ Arquez (73').
Referee: Mikko Vuorela (FIN)   Attendance: 10.333

31-03-1999 Olimpiysky NSC, Kiev: Ukraine – Iceland 1-1 (0-0)
Ukraine: Oleksandr Shovkovsky, Vladyslav Vaschuk, Oleg Luzhny (C), Serhiy Popov (75' Yuriy Kalitvintsev), Volodymyr Mykytin, Oleksandr Holovko, Andriy Gusin, Vitaliy Kosovskyi, Serhiy Rebrov, Andriy Shevchenko, Serhiy Skachenko (46' Yuriy Maksymov). (Coach: József Sabo (UKR)).
Iceland: Birkir Kristinsson, Audun Helgason, Larus Sigurdsson, Steinar Adolfsson, Hermann Hreidarsson, Brynjar Gunnarsson, Runar Kristinsson (78' Helgi Kolvidsson), Sigurdur Jónsson (C), Thordur Gudjónsson, Helgi Sigurdsson (84' Sverrir Sverrisson), Eyjölfur Sverrisson. (Coach: Gudjón Thórdarsson (ISL)).
Goals: Ukraine: 1-0 Vladyslav Vaschuk (59').
Iceland: 1-1 Larus Sigurdsson (66').
Referee: Dani Koren (ISR)   Attendance: 40.000

05-06-1999 Stade de France, Paris: France – Russia 2-3 (0-1)
France: Fabien Barthez (YC52), Lilian Thuram, Vincent Candela (88' Robert Pirès), Marcel Desailly, Laurent Blanc, Emmanuel Petit, Didier Deschamps (C) (YC9), Sylvain Wiltord, Nicolas Anelka, Youri Djorkaeff (90' Alain Boghossian), Christophe Dugarry (57' Patrick Vieira). (Coach: Roger Lemerre (FRA)).
Russia: Aleksandr Filimonov, Dmitri Khlestov, Viktor Onopko (C), Yevgeniy Varlamov (YC47), Yegor Titov (YC1), Aleksei Smertin, Sergei Semak (59' Vladimir Beschastnikh), Andrei Tikhonov (71' Ilya Tsymbalar), Valeri Karpin, Aleksandr Mostovoy (YC15) (25' Dmitri Khokhlov), Aleksandr Panov. (Coach: Oleg Ivanovich Romantsev (URS)).
Goals: France: 1-1 Emmanuel Petit (47'), 2-1 Sylvain Wiltord (53').
Russia: 0-1 Aleksandr Panov (37'), 2-2 Aleksandr Panov (74'), 2-3 Valeri Karpin (86').
Referee: Paul Anthony Durkin (ENG)   Attendance: 78.228

05-06-1999   Laugardalsvöllur, Reykjavik: Iceland – Armenia   2-0 (1-0)
Iceland: Birkir Kristinsson, Pétur Marteinsson, Audun Helgason (73' Helgi Kolvidsson), Hermann Hreidarsson, Brynjar Gunnarsson, Runar Kristinsson, Sigurdur Jónsson (C), Thordur Gudjónsson, Helgi Sigurdsson (83' Einar Daníelsson) Eyjölfur Sverrisson, Rikhardur Dadason (71' Heidar Helguson). (Coach: Gudjón Thórdarsson (ISL)).
Armenia: Roman Berezovskiy, Sargis Hovsepyan, Yervand Sukiasyan (YC62) (66' Artur Mkrtchyan), Vardan Khachatryan (C), Harutyun Vardanyan (YC59), Hayk Harutyunyan (YC42), Albert Sarkisyan (YC79), Artur Petrosyan (YC17) (77' Aram Hayrapetyan), Artur Voskanyan (87' Karen Grigoryan), Armen Shahgeldyan, Karapet Mikaelyan. (Coach: Suren Barseghyan (ARM)).
Goals: Iceland: 1-0 Rikhardur Dadason (31'), 2-0 Runar Kristinsson (46').
Referee: Mikko Vuorela (FIN)   Attendance: 5.565

05-06-1999   Olimpiysky NSC, Kiev: Ukraine – Andorra   4-0 (2-0)
Ukraine: Valeriy Vorobyov, Vladyslav Vaschuk, Oleg Luzhny (C), Serhiy Popov, Volodymyr Mykytin (71' Serhiy Mizin), Yuriy Dmytrulin (78' Roman Maksymyuk (YC84)), Oleksandr Holovko, Andriy Gusin, Eduard Tsykhmeystruk, Serhiy Rebrov, Andriy Shevchenko (67' Serhiy Skachenko). (Coach: József Sabo (UKR)).
Andorra: Jesús Luis Álvarez de Eulate "KOLDO", ILDEFONS LIMA Solá, ÓSCAR SONEJEE Masand, ANTONI (Toni) LIMA Solà (C), José Manuel "TXEMA" GARCÍA Luena, FRANCESC Xavier RAMÍREZ, ÁNGEL MARTÍN García (52' JESÚS Julián LUCENDO Heredia), AGUSTI POL Pérez, JULIÀ SÁNCHEZ Soto (YC73), JUSTO Ruiz GONZALEZ (YC81), EMILIANO GONZÁLEZ Arquez. (Coach: DAVID RODRIGO Lo (ESP)).
Goals: Ukraine: 1-0 Serhiy Popov (36'), 2-0 Serhiy Rebrov (41'), 3-0 Yuriy Dmytrulin (56'), 4-0 Andriy Gusin (87').
Referee: Andreas Georgiou (CYP)   Attendance: 49.000

09-06-1999   Estadi Olímpic de Montjuïc, Barcelona (ESP): Andorra – France   0-1 (0-0)
Andorra: Jesús Luis Álvarez de Eulate "KOLDO", ILDEFONS LIMA Solá (YC71), ÓSCAR SONEJEE Masand, ANTONI (Toni) LIMA Solà (C) (YC58,RC86), José Manuel "TXEMA" GARCÍA Luena (70' ROBERTO JONÁS Alonso Martínez), FRANCESC Xavier RAMÍREZ, Manolo "MANEL" JIMÉNEZ Soria (YC76) (89' GENÍS GARCÍA Iscza), JESÚS Julián LUCENDO Heredia (C) (77' ÁNGEL MARTÍN García), AGUSTI POL Pérez, JUSTO Ruiz GONZALEZ (YC28), EMILIANO GONZÁLEZ Arquez. (Coach: DAVID RODRIGO Lo (ESP)).
France: Ulrich Ramé, Vincent Candela, Marcel Desailly (C), Frank Leboeuf (YC63), Vikash Dhorasoo (61' Robert Pirès), Emmanuel Petit (56' Patrick Vieira), Alain Boghossian, Christian Karembeu, Sylvain Wiltord, Nicolas Anelka, Christophe Dugarry (RC24). (Coach: Roger Lemerre (FRA)).
Goal: France: 0-1 Frank Leboeuf (85' penalty).
Referee: Michael Thomas Ross (NIR)   Attendance: 7.600

09-06-1999   Hrazdan Stadium, Yerevan: Armenia – Ukraine   0-0
Armenia: Roman Berezovskiy, Sargis Hovsepyan (46' Artur Mkrtchyan), Sargis Hovhannisyan, Vardan Khachatryan (C), Harutyun Vardanyan, Tigran Petrosyan (63' Karen Grigoryan), Albert Sarkisyan (YC80), Artur Petrosyan, Artur Voskanyan, Armen Shahgeldyan, Karapet Mikaelyan (46' Hayk Harutyunyan). (Coach: Suren Barseghyan (ARM)).
Ukraine: Valeriy Vorobyov, Vladyslav Vaschuk (YC18), Oleg Luzhny (C), Serhiy Popov (36' Serhiy Kovalov), Volodymyr Mykytin, Yuriy Dmytrulin, Oleksandr Holovko, Andriy Gusin, Eduard Tsykhmeystruk, Serhiy Rebrov (70' Serhiy Skachenko), Andriy Shevchenko (80' Vasyl Kardash). (Coach: József Sabo (UKR)).
Referee: Roberto Anthony Boggi (ITA)   Attendance: 6.000

09-06-1999   Dynamo Stadium, Moscow: Russia – Iceland   1-0 (1-0)
Russia: Aleksandr Filimonov, Dmitri Khlestov, Viktor Onopko (C), Yevgeniy Varlamov (55' Igor Yanovski), Aleksei Smertin, Sergei Semak (46' Viktor Bulatov), Andrei Tikhonov, Valeri Karpin (YC44), Vladimir Beschastnikh (70' Ilya Tsymbalar), Dmitri Khokhlov, Aleksandr Panov. (Coach: Oleg Ivanovich Romantsev (URS)).
Iceland: Birkir Kristinsson, Pétur Marteinsson, Audun Helgason, Larus Sigurdsson, Hermann Hreidarsson (59' Steinar Adolfsson), Brynjar Gunnarsson (80' Heidar Helguson), Runar Kristinsson, Sigurdur Jónsson (46' Helgi Kolvidsson), Thordur Gudjónsson, Eyjölfur Sverrisson, Rikhardur Dadason. (Coach: Gudjón Thórdarsson (ISL)).
Goal: Russia: 1-0 Valeri Karpin (44').
Referee: Metin Tokat (TUR)   Attendance: 33.900

04-09-1999   Laugardalsvöllur, Reykjavik: Iceland – Andorra   3-0 (2-0)
Iceland: Birkir Kristinsson, Audun Helgason, Larus Sigurdsson (28' Arnar Vidarsson), Hermann Hreidarsson, Brynjar Gunnarsson, Bjarni Gudjónsson, Sigurdur Jónsson (C), Thordur Gudjónsson, Tryggvi Gudmundsson, Helgi Sigurdsson (58' Heidar Helguson), Rikhardur Dadason (78' Eidur Gudjohnsen). (Coach: Gudjón Thórdarsson (ISL)).
Andorra: Jesús Luis Álvarez de Eulate "KOLDO" (C), ÓSCAR SONEJEE Masand, JORDI ESCURA Aixas, José Manuel "TXEMA" GARCÍA Luena, FRANCESC Xavier RAMÍREZ, Manolo "MANEL" JIMÉNEZ Soria, Alexandre "ALEX" GODOY (67' GENÍS GARCÍA Iscza), ÁNGEL MARTÍN García (61' Armando ARMAND" GODOY Venturi (YC88)), AGUSTI POL Pérez (90' DAVID BUXO Escabros), JULIÀ SÁNCHEZ Soto, EMILIANO GONZÁLEZ Arquez. (Coach: DAVID RODRIGO Lo (ESP)).
Goals: Iceland: 1-0 Thordur Gudjónsson (27'), 2-0 Hermann Hreidarsson (32'), 3-0 Eidur Gudjohnsen (90').
Referee: Miroslav Liba (CZE)   Attendance: 5.210

04-09-1999   Luzhniki Stadium, Moscow: Russia – Armenia   2-0 (1-0)
Russia: Aleksandr Filimonov, Dmitri Khlestov, Viktor Onopko (C), Yegor Titov (80' Sergei Semak), Aleksei Smertin, Dmitri Khokhlov, Andrei Tikhonov (73' Igor Yanovski), Valeri Karpin, Dmitri Alenichev, Vladimir Beschastnikh, Aleksandr Panov (79' Aleksandr Shirko). (Coach: Oleg Ivanovich Romantsev (URS)).
Armenia: Roman Berezovskiy, Sargis Hovsepyan, Sargis Hovhannisyan (YC51), Vardan Khachatryan (C), Harutyun Vardanyan (YC28), Artur Mkrtchyan, Hayk Harutyunyan (55' Manuk Kakosyan), Romik Khachatryan (85' Tigran Petrosyan), Artur Voskanyan (YC83), Armen Shahgeldyan (79' Marcelo Alejandro Devani), Karapet Mikaelyan. (Coach: Suren Barseghyan (ARM)).
Goals: Russia: 1-0 Vladimir Beschastnikh (8' penalty), 2-0 Valeri Karpin (70').
Referee: Charles Agius (MLT)   Attendance: 36.000

04-09-1999   Olimpiysky NSC, Kiev: Ukraine – France   0-0
Ukraine: Oleksandr Shovkovsky, Vladyslav Vaschuk, Oleg Luzhny (C), Serhiy Popov, Yuriy Dmytrulin (46' Volodymyr Mykytin), Oleksandr Holovko, Andriy Gusin (YC6) (81' Eduard Tsykhmeystruk), Yuriy Maksymov (67' Serhiy Konovalov), Vitaliy Kosovskyi, Serhiy Rebrov, Andriy Shevchenko. (Coach: József Sabo (UKR)).
France: Fabien Barthez, Lilian Thuram, Bixente Lizarazu, Marcel Desailly, Laurent Blanc, Zinédine Zidane, Didier Deschamps (C), Christian Karembeu, Patrick Vieira, Nicolas Anelka (52' Lilian Laslandes), Youri Djorkaeff (68' Robert Pirès). (Coach: Roger Lemerre (FRA)).
Referee: Hugh Dallas (SCO)   Attendance: 78.000

08-09-1999   Camp d'Esports d'Aixovall, Aixovall: Andorra – Russia   1-2 (1-1)
Andorra: Jesús Luis Álvarez de Eulate "KOLDO", ILDEFONS LIMA Solá, ÓSCAR SONEJEE Masand (58' DAVID BUXO Escabros), JORDI ESCURA Aixas, José Manuel "TXEMA" GARCÍA Luena, FRANCESC Xavier RAMÍREZ (YC78), Manolo "MANEL" JIMÉNEZ Soria, Alexandre "ALEX" GODOY, JULIÀ SÁNCHEZ Soto (89' Armando ARMAND" GODOY Venturi), JUSTO Ruiz GONZALEZ (C), EMILIANO GONZÁLEZ Arquez. (Coach: DAVID RODRIGO Lo (ESP)).
Russia: Aleksandr Filimonov, Dmitri Khlestov, Viktor Onopko (C), Yegor Titov, Aleksei Smertin (YC39), Andrei Tikhonov, Dmitri Khokhlov (56' Artem Bezrodnyi), Valeri Karpin (60' Yuri Drozdov), Dmitri Alenichev, Aleksandr Shirko, Vladimir Beschastnikh (46' Aleksandr Panov). (Coach: Oleg Ivanovich Romantsev (URS)).
Goals: Andorra: 1-1 JUSTO Ruiz GONZALEZ (39' penalty).
Russia: 0-1 Viktor Onopko (23'), 1-2 Viktor Onopko (57').
Referee: Jørn West Larsen (DEN)   Attendance: 1.000

08-09-1999   Laugardalsvöllur, Reykjavik: Iceland – Ukraine   0-1 (0-1)
Iceland: Birkir Kristinsson, Pétur Marteinsson, Audun Helgason, Larus Sigurdsson, Hermann Hreidarsson, Brynjar Gunnarsson, Runar Kristinsson, Sigurdur Jónsson (C) (YC42) (85' Arnar Vidarsson), Helgi Kolvidsson (58' Heidar Helguson), Thordur Gudjónsson, Rikhardur Dadason (YC37) (72' Eidur Gudjohnsen). (Coach: Gudjón Thórdarsson (ISL)).
Ukraine: Oleksandr Shovkovsky, Vladyslav Vaschuk, Oleg Luzhny (C) (YC73) (79' Volodymyr Mykytin), Serhiy Popov (YC9), Yuriy Dmytrulin, Oleksandr Holovko (YC37), Yuriy Maksymov, Serhiy Konovalov (YC46) (66' Eduard Tsykhmeystruk), Vitaliy Kosovskyi, Serhiy Rebrov, Andriy Shevchenko. (Coach: József Sabo (UKR)).
Goal: Ukraine: 0-1 Serhiy Rebrov (43' penalty).
Referee: Vítor Manuel Melo Pereira (POR)   Attendance: 7.072

08-09-1999   Hrazdan Stadium, Yerevan: Armenia – France   2-3 (1-1)
Armenia: Roman Berezovskiy (YC66), Sargis Hovsepyan, Vardan Khachatryan (C) (YC44), Artur Mkrtchyan, Hayk Harutyunyan (64' Razmik Grigoryan), Tigran Petrosyan, Romik Khachatryan (YC41) (74' Artur Kocharyan), Albert Sarkisyan, Armen Shahgeldyan, Tigran Yesayan, Karapet Mikaelyan (67' Marcelo Alejandro Devani). (Coach: Suren Barseghyan (ARM)).
France: Fabien Barthez (YC90), Lilian Thuram, Bixente Lizarazu, Marcel Desailly (YC45), Laurent Blanc (YC55), Zinédine Zidane (72' Frédéric Déhu (YC,YC89)), Didier Deschamps (C), Christian Karembeu, Sylvain Wiltord (62' Laurent Robert), Lilian Laslandes, Youri Djorkaeff. (Coach: Roger Lemerre (FRA)).
Goals: Armenia: 1-0 Karapet Mikaelyan (6'), 2-3 Armen Shahgeldyan (90' penalty).
France: 1-1 Youri Djorkaeff (44' penalty), 1-2 Zinédine Zidane (66'), 1-3 Lilian Laslandes (74').
Referee: Atanas Uzunov (BUL)   Attendance: 14.500

09-10-1999   Camp d'Esports d'Aixovall, Aixovall: Andorra – Armenia   0-3 (0-1)
Andorra: Jesús Luis Álvarez de Eulate "KOLDO", ILDEFONS LIMA Solá, ÓSCAR
SONEJEE Masand (YC29), JORDI ESCURA Aixas, José Manuel "TXEMA" GARCÍA Luena
(58' ROBERTO JONÁS Alonso Martínez), FRANCESC Xavier RAMÍREZ (YC81), Manolo
"MANEL" JIMÉNEZ Soria, Alexandre "ALEX" GODOY (46' AGUSTI POL Pérez), JULIÀ
SÁNCHEZ Soto, JUSTO Ruiz GONZALEZ (C), EMILIANO GONZÁLEZ Arquez (62'
Francisco XAVIER SORIA Gómez). (Coach: DAVID RODRIGO Lo (ESP)).
Armenia: Harutyun Abrahamyan, Yervand Sukiasyan (C), Harutyun Vardanyan (YC40), Artur
Mkrtchyan, Artur Petrosyan (80' Ara Hakobyan), Romik Khachatryan, Albert Sarkisyan
(RC31), Tigran Petrosyan (82' Artur Kocharyan), Artur Voskanyan (YC23), Armen
Shahgeldyan (YC38) (79' Artur S.Minasyan), Tigran Yesayan. (Coach: Suren Barseghyan
(ARM)).
Goals: Armenia: 0-1 Artur Petrosyan (26'), 0-2 Tigran Yesayan (59'), 0-3 Shahgeldyan (62').
Referee: Peter Jones (ENG)   Attendance: 700

09-10-1999   Stade de France, Paris: France – Iceland   3-2 (2-0)
France: Bernard Lama, Lilian Thuram, Bixente Lizarazu, Marcel Desailly, Laurent Blanc,
Zinédine Zidane, Didier Deschamps (C), Alain Boghossian (90' Patrick Vieira), Sylvain
Wiltord (83' Tony Vairelles), Lilian Laslandes (64' David Trézéguet), Youri Djorkaeff.
(Coach: Roger Lemerre (FRA)).
Iceland: Birkir Kristinsson, Pétur Marteinsson (81' Helgi Kolvidsson), Audun Helgason, Larus
Sigurdsson, Hermann Hreidarsson, Brynjar Gunnarsson, Runar Kristinsson (YC29), Thordur
Gudjónsson, Helgi Sigurdsson (YC40) (65' Heidar Helguson (YC90)), Eyjölfur Sverrisson (C),
Rikhardur Dadason (53' Eidur Gudjohnsen). (Coach: Gudjón Thórdarsson (ISL)).
Goals: France: 1-0 Rikhardur Dadason (18' *own goal*), 2-0 Youri Djorkaeff (38'), 3-2 David
Trézéguet (71').
Iceland: 2-1 Eyjölfur Sverrisson (48'), 2-2 Brynjar Gunnarsson (56').
Referee: Bernd Heynemann (GER)   Attendance: 78.391

09-10-1999   Luzhniki Stadium, Moscow: Russia – Ukraine   1-1 (0-0)
Russia: Aleksandr Filimonov, Dmitri Khlestov (YC48), Viktor Onopko (C), Yuri Drozdov,
Yegor Titov, Aleksei Smertin, Andrei Tikhonov (61' Vladimir Beschastnikh), Valeri Karpin,
Dmitri Khokhlov, Dmitri Alenichev, Aleksandr Panov (79' Sergei Semak). (Coach: Oleg
Ivanovich Romantsev (URS)).
Ukraine: Oleksandr Shovkovsky, Vladyslav Vaschuk, Oleg Luzhny (C), Yuriy Dmytrulin (75'
Serhiy Kovalov), Oleksandr Holovko, Andriy Gusin, Yuriy Maksymov (77' Gennadiy Moroz),
Serhiy Mizin, Serhiy Rebrov, Andriy Shevchenko, Serhiy Skachenko (41' Volodymyr
Mykytin). (Coach: József Sabo (UKR)).
Goals: Russia: 1-0 Valeri Karpin (75').
Ukraine: 1-1 Andriy Shevchenko (87').
Referee: David Roland Elleray (ENG)   Attendance: 78.600

GROUP 5

05-09-1998	Solna	Sweden – England	2-1 (2-1)
06-09-1998	Burgas	Bulgaria – Poland	0-3 (0-2)
10-10-1998	London	England – Bulgaria	0-0
10-10-1998	Warsaw	Poland – Luxembourg	3-0 (2-0)
14-10-1998	Burgas	Bulgaria – Sweden	0-1 (0-0)
14-10-1998	Luxembourg	Luxembourg – England	0-3 (0-2)
27-03-1999	London	England – Poland	3-1 (2-1)

27-03-1999	Gothenburg	Sweden – Luxembourg	2-0 (1-0)
31-03-1999	Luxembourg	Luxembourg – Bulgaria	0-2 (0-2)
31-03-1999	Chorzow	Poland – Sweden	0-1 (0-1)
04-06-1999	Warsaw	Poland – Bulgaria	2-0 (1-0)
05-06-1999	London	England – Sweden	0-0
09-06-1999	Sofia	Bulgaria – England	1-1 (1-1)
09-06-1999	Luxembourg	Luxembourg – Poland	2-3 (0-2)
04-09-1999	London	England – Luxembourg	6-0 (5-0)
04-09-1999	Solna	Sweden – Bulgaria	1-0 (0-0)
08-09-1999	Luxembourg	Luxembourg – Sweden	0-1 (0-1)
08-09-1999	Warsaw	Poland – England	0-0
09-10-1999	Solna	Sweden – Poland	2-0 (0-0)
10-10-1999	Sofia	Bulgaria – Luxembourg	3-0 (1-0)

FINAL STANDING

Pos	Team	Pld	W	D	L	GF	GA	GD	Pts
1	*Sweden*	*8*	*7*	*1*	*0*	*10*	*1*	*+9*	*22*
2	*England*	*8*	*3*	*4*	*1*	*14*	*4*	*+10*	*13*
3	Poland	8	4	1	3	12	8	+4	13
4	Bulgaria	8	2	2	4	6	8	-2	8
5	Luxembourg	8	0	0	8	2	23	-21	0

Sweden qualified for the final tournament in Belgium/Netherlands.
England qualified for the second round play-offs.

05-09-1998   Råsunda Stadion, Solna: Sweden – England   2-1 (2-1)
Sweden: Magnus Hedman, Roland Nilsson, Patrik Andersson (C), Joachim Björklund, Pontus Kåmark (82' Teddy Lucic), Johan Mjällby, Fredrik Ljungberg, Stefan Schwarz (YC24), Jörgen Pettersson, Andreas Andersson (90' Daniel Andersson), Henrik Larsson. (Coaches: Lars Lagerbäck & Tommy Söderberg (SWE)).
England: David Seaman, Sol Campbell (75' Paul Merson), Graeme Le Saux, Tony Adams, Gareth Southgate, Paul Scholes (86' Teddy Sheringham), Darren Anderton (42' Rob Lee), Paul Ince (YC67,YC67), Jamie Redknapp (YC82), Michael Owen (YC7), Alan Shearer (C). (Coach: Glenn Hoddle (ENG)).
Goals: Sweden: 1-1 Andreas Andersson (30'), 2-1 Johan Mjällby (32').
England: 0-1 Alan Shearer (1').
Referee: Pierluigi Collina (ITA)   Attendance: 35.394

05-09-1998   Neftochimik Stadium, Burgas: Bulgaria – Poland   0-3 (0-2)
Bulgaria: Zdravko Zdravkov, Zahari Sirakov, Gosho Ginchev, Zlatomir Zagorcic (YC9) (50' Ivaylo Petkov), Radostin Kishishev (YC72), Daniel Borimitov (46' Mitko Ivanov Trendafilov), Milen Petkov (46' Iliya Gruev), Ivaylo Yordanov, Hristo Stoichkov (C), Doncho Donev, Georgi Bachev. (Coach: Hristo Atanasov Bonev-Zuma (BUL)).
Poland: Kazimierz Sidorczuk, Jacek Bak (YC7), Jacek Zielinski, Tomasz Lapinski, Rafal Siadaczka, Tomasz Hajto (YC28) (68' Tomasz Klos), Piotr Swierczewski (YC11) (77' Radoslav Michalski), Sylwester Czereszewski, Tomasz Iwan (YC40), Jerzy Brzeczek (C) (YC25), Miroslaw Trzeciak (84' Andrzej Juskowiak). (Coach: Janusz Wójcik (POL)).
Goals: Poland: 0-1 Tomasz Hajto (19'), 0-2 Piotr Swierczewski (44'), 0-3 Tomasz Iwan (48').
Referee: Marc Batta (FRA)   Attendance: 17.100

10-10-1998   Wembley Stadium, London: England – Bulgaria   0-0
England: David Seaman, Sol Campbell, Gary Neville, Gareth Southgate, Andy Hinchcliffe (34' Graeme Le Saux), Paul Scholes (76' Teddy Sheringham), Darren Anderton (YC56) (66' David Batty), Rob Lee, Jamie Redknapp (YC81), Michael Owen, Alan Shearer (C). (Coach: Glenn Hoddle (ENG)).
Bulgaria: Zdravko Zdravkov, Rosen Kirilov, Zlatomir Zagorcic, Valentin Naydenov, Mariyan Hristov (89' Georgi Ivanov), Radostin Kishishev (YC65), Milen Petkov, Ivaylo Yordanov, Zlatko Yankov, Hristo Stoichkov (C) (59' Georgi Bachev), Ilian Iliev (62' Iliya Gruev). (Coach: Dimitar Petrov Dimitrov (BUL)).
Referee: László Vágner (HUN)   Attendance: 72.974

10-10-1998   Polish Army Stadium, Warsaw: Poland – Luxembourg   3-0 (2-0)
Poland: Adam Matysek, Krzysztof Ratajczyk (69' Rafal Siadaczka), Jacek Zielinski (YC88), Tomasz Lapinski, Piotr Swierczewski, Sylwester Czereszewski (75' Jacek Bak), Tomasz Hajto (61' Slawomir Majak), Tomasz Iwan, Jerzy Brzeczek (C), Andrzej Juskowiak, Miroslaw Trzeciak. (Coach: Janusz Wójcik (POL)).
Luxembourg: Paul Koch, Marc Birsens (C) (RC30), Ralph Ferron (YC39), Nico Funck, Laurent Deville (YC15), Jeff Strasser, Manuel Cardoni, Jeff Saibene, Luc Holtz (70' Eugene Afrika), Daniel Theis (46' Frank Deville), Marcel Christophe (63' Serge Thill). (Coach: Paul Philipp (LUX)).
Goals: Poland: 1-0 Jerzy Brzeczek (18'), 2-0 Andrzej Juskowiak (33'), 3-0 Miroslaw Trzeciak (65').
Referee: Bujar Pregja (ALB)   Attendance: 8.300

14-10-1998   Neftochimik Stadium, Burgas: Bulgaria – Sweden   0-1 (0-0)
Bulgaria: Zdravko Zdravkov, Rosen Kirilov (17' Velian Mitev Parushev (YC22)), Zlatomir Zagorcic (YC53), Valentin Naydenov (69' Georgi Ivanov), Mariyan Hristov, Ivaylo Petkov, Milen Petkov, Ivaylo Yordanov, Zlatko Yankov, Stoytcho Stoilov (C), Ilian Iliev (60' Georgi Bachev). (Coach: Dimitar Petrov Dimitrov (BUL)).
Sweden: Magnus Hedman, Teddy Lucic (YC16) (76' Gary Sundgren), Roland Nilsson, Patrik Andersson (C), Joachim Björklund, Johan Mjällby, Fredrik Ljungberg, Martin Åslund (YC17) (71' Jesper Blomqvist), Stefan Schwarz, Håkan Mild, Henrik Larsson (87' Magnus Erlingmark). (Coaches: Lars Lagerbäck & Tommy Söderberg (SWE)).
Goal: Sweden: 0-1 Henrik Larsson (62').
Referee: Bernd Heynemann (GER)   Attendance: 12.000

14-10-1998   Stade Josy Barthel, Luxembourg: Luxembourg – England   0-3 (0-2)
Luxembourg: Paul Koch, Ralph Ferron, Nico Funck, Laurent Deville, Jeff Strasser, Manuel Cardoni (YC38), Jeff Saibene (C), Daniel Theis (61' Luc Holtz), Frank Deville (85' Christian Alverdi), Patrick Posing, Marcel Christophe (78' Paolo Amodio). (Coach: Paul Philipp (LUX)).
England: David Seaman, Sol Campbell, Rio Ferdinand, Gareth Southgate, David Beckham (YC21), Phil Neville, Paul Scholes (77' Ian Wright), Darren Anderton (63' Rob Lee), David Batty, Michael Owen, Alan Shearer (C). (Coach: Glenn Hoddle (ENG)).
Goals: England: 0-1 Michael Owen (18'), 0-2 Alan Shearer (38' penalty), 0-3 Gareth Southgate (88').
Referee: Sotirios Vorgias (GRE)   Attendance: 8.054

27-03-1999   Wembley Stadium, London: England – Poland   3-1 (2-1)
England: David Seaman, Sol Campbell, Gary Neville, Graeme Le Saux, Martin Keown, David Beckham (78' Phil Neville), Paul Scholes (YC27) (84' Jamie Redknapp), Steve McManaman (69' Ray Parlour), Tim Sherwood (YC54), Andy Cole, Alan Shearer (C). (Coach: Kevin Keegan (ENG)).
Poland: Adam Matysek, Jacek Bak, Krzysztof Ratajczyk (YC13), Jacek Zielinski, Tomasz Lapinski, Tomasz Hajto (YC19), Rafal Siadaczka (67' Wojciech Kowalczyk), Piotr Swierczewski (46' Tomasz Klos), Tomasz Iwan, Jerzy Brzeczek (C), Miroslaw Trzeciak (84' Andrzej Juskowiak). (Coach: Janusz Wójcik (POL)).
Goals: England: 1-0 Paul Scholes (12'), 2-0 Paul Scholes (22'), 3-1 Paul Scholes (70').
Poland: 2-1 Jerzy Brzeczek (28').
Referee: Vítor Manuel Melo Pereira (POR)   Attendance: 73.836

27-03-1999   Nya Ullevi, Gothenburg: Sweden – Luxembourg   2-0 (1-0)
Sweden: Magnus Hedman, Patrik Andersson (C), Joachim Björklund, Pontus Kåmark (62' Teddy Lucic), Johan Mjällby, Gary Sundgren, Fredrik Ljungberg (79' Daniel Andersson), Niclas Alexandersson, Stefan Schwarz, Kennet Andersson, Henrik Larsson. (Coaches: Lars Lagerbäck & Tommy Söderberg (SWE)).
Luxembourg: Philippe Felgen, Marc Birsens (C), Ralph Ferron, Jean Vanek, Nico Funck, Laurent Deville, Jeff Strasser, Manuel Cardoni, Jeff Saibene (89' Frank Deville), Daniel Theis (69' Luc Holtz), Marcel Christophe (81' Mikhail Zaritskiy). (Coach: Paul Philipp (LUX)).
Goals: Sweden: 1-0 Johan Mjällby (34'), 2-0 Henrik Larsson (86').
Referee: Vasyl Hryhorovych Melnychuk (UKR)   Attendance: 37.728

31-03-1999   Stade Josy Barthel, Luxembourg: Luxembourg – Bulgaria   0-2 (0-2)
Luxembourg: Philippe Felgen, Marc Birsens (C), Ralph Ferron (75' Luc Holtz), Jean Vanek, Laurent Deville, Jeff Strasser (YC70), Manuel Cardoni, Jeff Saibene (YC63), Daniel Theis (89' Frank Deville), Patrick Posing (46' Mikhail Zaritskiy), Marcel Christophe. (Coach: Paul Philipp (LUX)).
Bulgaria: Zdravko Zdravkov, Ilian Stoyanov (46' Ivaylo Petkov (YC75)), Georgi Markov, Stiliyan Petrov, Radostin Kishishev, Milen Petkov, Hristo Yovov (80' Georgi Ivanov), Ivaylo Yordanov, Zlatko Yankov, Hristo Stoichkov (C) (72' Svetoslav Todorov), Ilian Iliev. (Coach: Dimitar Petrov Dimitrov (BUL)).
Goals: Bulgaria: 0-1 Hristo Stoichkov (17'), 0-2 Ivaylo Yordanov (38').
Referee: Milan Mitrovic (SLO)   Attendance: 3.004

31-03-1999   National Stadium, Chorzow: Poland – Sweden   0-1 (0-1)
Poland: Kazimierz Sidorczuk, Tomasz Waldoch, Jacek Zielinski, Tomasz Lapinski, Rafal Siadaczka (83' Dariusz Adamczuk (YC84)), Tomasz Iwan, Radoslav Michalski (YC64) (88' Jacek Bak), Jerzy Brzeczek (C), Andrzej Juskowiak, Slawomir Majak (69' Wojciech Kowalczyk), Miroslaw Trzeciak. (Coach: Janusz Wójcik (POL)).
Sweden: Magnus Hedman, Teddy Lucic, Patrik Andersson (C), Joachim Björklund (YC78), Pontus Kåmark, Johan Mjällby, Fredrik Ljungberg, Stefan Schwarz, Håkan Mild (73' Niclas Alexandersson), Kennet Andersson, Henrik Larsson (90' Jörgen Pettersson). (Coaches: Lars Lagerbäck & Tommy Söderberg (SWE)).
Goal: Sweden: 0-1 Fredrik Ljungberg (36').
Referee: Markus Merk (GER)   Attendance: 28.860

04-06-1999   Polish Army Stadium, Warsaw: Poland – Bulgaria   2-0 (1-0)
Poland: Adam Matysek, Tomasz Waldoch, Jacek Zielinski (YC52), Tomasz Lapinski (C), Rafal Siadaczka, Tomasz Hajto (80' Slawomir Majak), Tomasz Iwan, Radoslav Michalski, Krzysztof Nowak (73' Jerzy Brzeczek), Artur Wichniarek (58' Tomasz Frankowski), Miroslaw Trzeciak. (Coach: Janusz Wójcik (POL)).
Bulgaria: Dimitar Ivankov, Georgi Markov, Rosen Kirilov, Zlatomir Zagorcic, Stiliyan Petrov, Radostin Kishishev, Ivaylo Petkov (80' Ilian Iliev), Milen Petkov, Hristo Yovov (YC32) (46' Georgi Bachev), Stanimir Stoilov, Hristo Stoichkov (C) (63' Georgi Ivanov). (Coach: Dimitar Petrov Dimitrov (BUL)).
Goals: Poland: 1-0 Tomasz Hajto (15'), 2-0 Tomasz Iwan (61').
Referee: Stefano Braschi (ITA)   Attendance: 6.266

05-06-1999   Wembley Stadium, London: England – Sweden   0-0
England: David Seaman, Sol Campbell, Graeme Le Saux (46' Michael Gray), Martin Keown (35' Rio Ferdinand), David Beckham (75' Ray Parlour), Phil Neville, Paul Scholes (YC27,YC51), David Batty (YC58), Tim Sherwood, Andy Cole (YC33), Alan Shearer (C) (YC78). (Coach: Kevin Keegan (ENG)).
Sweden: Magnus Hedman (YC39), Roland Nilsson, Patrik Andersson (C), Joachim Björklund, Pontus Kåmark, Johan Mjällby (82' Daniel Andersson), Fredrik Ljungberg, Stefan Schwarz (YC49), Håkan Mild (69' Niclas Alexandersson), Kennet Andersson (YC90), Henrik Larsson (6' Magnus Svensson). (Coaches: Lars Lagerbäck & Tommy Söderberg (SWE)).
Referee: José-María García-Aranda Encinar (ESP)   Attendance: 75.824

09-06-1999   Bulgarian Army Stadium, Sofia: Bulgaria – England   1-1 (1-1)
Bulgaria: Dimitar Ivankov, Georgi Markov, Rosen Kirilov, Zlatomir Zagorcic, Stiliyan Petrov, Radostin Kishishev, Milen Petkov, Hristo Yovov (46' Martin Petrov (YC53,YC59)), Stanimir Stoilov, Hristo Stoichkov (C) (73' Georgi Bachev), Ilian Iliev (YC49) (60' Daniel Borimirov). (Coach: Dimitar Petrov Dimitrov (BUL)).
England: David Seaman, Sol Campbell (YC52), Michael Gray, Jonathan Woodgate (64' Ray Parlour), Gareth Southgate (YC19), Phil Neville, David Batty, Jamie Redknapp, Teddy Sheringham (YC31), Robbie Fowler (YC3) (81' Emile Heskey), Alan Shearer (C). (Coach: Kevin Keegan (ENG)).
Goals: Bulgaria: 1-1 Georgi Markov (17').
England: 0-1 Alan Shearer (14').
Referee: Mario van der Ende (HOL)   Attendance: 19.500

09-06-1999   Stade Josy Barthel, Luxembourg: Luxembourg – Poland   2-3 (0-2)
Luxembourg: Philippe Felgen, Marc Birsens (C), Jean Vanek, Nico Funck, Jeff Strasser (YC90), Manuel Cardoni (YC27), Jeff Saibene (85' Christian Alverdi), Daniel Theis (46' Sacha Schneider), Frank Deville (YC46), Marcel Christophe, Mikhail Zaritskiy (66' Patrick Posing). (Coach: Paul Philipp (LUX)).
Poland: Adam Matysek, Tomasz Klos (YC89), Tomasz Waldoch, Tomasz Lapinski (C), Rafal Siadaczka, Tomasz Hajto (66' Jerzy Brzeczek), Tomasz Iwan, Radoslav Michalski, Krzysztof Nowak, Artur Wichniarek (YC34) (87' Slawomir Majak), Miroslaw Trzeciak. (Coach: Janusz Wójcik (POL)).
Goals: Luxembourg: 1-3 Marc Birsens (76'), 2-3 Jean Vanek (82').
Poland: 0-1 Rafal Siadaczka (22'), 0-2 Artur Wichniarek (45'), 0-3 Tomasz Iwan (68').
Referee: Valentin Valentinovich Ivanov (RUS)   Attendance: 2.806

04-09-1999   Wembley Stadium, London: England – Luxembourg   6-0 (5-0)
England: Nigel Martyn, Tony Adams (64' Phil Neville), Stuart Pearce (YC71), Martin Keown, David Beckham (64' Michael Owen), Ray Parlour, Kieron Dyer (46' Gary Neville), David Batty, Steve McManaman, Robbie Fowler, Alan Shearer (C). (Coach: Kevin Keegan (ENG)).
Luxembourg: Philippe Felgen, Manou Schauls, Marc Birsens (C), Ralph Ferron, Jean Vanek, Nico Funck (YC54), Jeff Saibene, Daniel Theis, Sacha Schneider (46' Christian Alverdi), Patrick Posing (82' Frank Deville), Marcel Christophe (61' Mikhail Zaritskiy). (Coach: Paul Philipp (LUX)).
Goals: England: 1-0 Alan Shearer (10' penalty), 2-0 Alan Shearer (27'), 3-0 Steve McManaman (30'), 4-0 Alan Shearer (34'), 5-0 Steve McManaman (44'), 6-0 Michael Owen (90').
Referee: Sergei Shmolik (BLS)   Attendance: 68.772

04-09-1999   Råsunda Stadion, Solna: Sweden – Bulgaria   1-0 (0-0)
Sweden: Magnus Hedman, Daniel Andersson (YC38), Roland Nilsson, Patrik Andersson (C), Joachim Björklund, Pontus Kåmark, Johan Mjällby, Fredrik Ljungberg (63' Niclas Alexandersson), Håkan Mild (82' Magnus Svensson), Kennet Andersson, Henrik Larsson. (Coaches: Lars Lagerbäck & Tommy Söderberg (SWE)).
Bulgaria: Dimitar Ivankov, Georgi Markov, Rosen Kirilov (YC57), Zlatomir Zagorcic (26' Zlatko Yankov), Stiliyan Petrov, Mariyan Hristov (YC66), Daniel Borimirov, Ivaylo Petkov, Milen Petkov (RC59), Stanimir Stoilov (C) (89' Iliya Gruev), Svetoslav Todorov (YC29) (46' Hristo Yovov). (Coach: Dimitar Petrov Dimitrov (BUL)).
Goal: Sweden: 1-0 Niclas Alexandersson (65').
Referee: Dani Koren (ISR)   Attendance: 35.640

08-09-1999   Stade Josy Barthel, Luxembourg: Luxembourg – Sweden   0-1 (0-1)
Luxembourg: Philippe Felgen, Manou Schauls, Marc Birsens (C), Jean Vanek, Nico Funck (YC84), Christian Alverdi (72' Daniel Theis), Jeff Strasser, Jeff Saibene (87' Luc Holtz), Sacha Schneider (46' Mikhail Zaritskiy), Patrick Posing, Marcel Christophe. (Coach: Paul Philipp (LUX)).
Sweden: Magnus Hedman, Teddy Lucic, Roland Nilsson, Patrik Andersson (C), Johan Mjällby, Niclas Alexandersson, Stefan Schwarz (YC41) (78' Daniel Andersson), Håkan Mild, Magnus Svensson (46' Pär Zetterberg), Kennet Andersson, Henrik Larsson. (Coaches: Lars Lagerbäck & Tommy Söderberg (SWE)).
Goal: Sweden: 0-1 Niclas Alexandersson (39').
Referee: Attila Hanácsek (HUN)   Attendance: 4.228

08-09-1999   Polish Army Stadium, Warsaw: Poland – England   0-0
Poland: Adam Matysek (YC36), Tomasz Klos (89' Jacek Bak), Tomasz Waldoch (C), Jacek Zielinksi, Rafal Siadaczka (YC57), Tomasz Hajto (YC55), Tomasz Iwan (YC74), Radoslav Michalski, Krzysztof Nowak, Radoslaw Gilewicz (63' Andrzej Juskowiak), Miroslaw Trzeciak (59' Piotr Swierczewski). (Coach: Janusz Wójcik (POL)).
England: Nigel Martyn, Gary Neville (13' Phil Neville), Tony Adams, Stuart Pearce, Martin Keown (YC12), David Beckham, Paul Scholes, David Batty (RC84), Steve McManaman (70' Kieron Dyer), Robbie Fowler (66' Michael Owen), Alan Shearer (C). (Coach: Kevin Keegan (ENG)).
Referee: Günter Benkö (AUT)   Attendance: 14.025

09-10-1999   Råsunda Stadion, Solna: Sweden – Poland   2-0 (0-0)
Sweden: Magnus Hedman, Roland Nilsson (46' Gary Sundgren (YC84)), Patrik Andersson (C), Joachim Björklund, Pontus Kåmark, Johan Mjällby, Fredrik Ljungberg (83' Håkan Mild), Niclas Alexandersson, Stefan Schwarz, Kennet Andersson, Henrik Larsson. (Coaches: Lars Lagerbäck & Tommy Söderberg (SWE)).
Poland: Adam Matysek, Tomasz Klos (YC23), Tomasz Waldoch (C) (YC18), Jacek Zielinksi, Rafal Siadaczka, Tomasz Hajto (YC57), Piotr Swierczewski (88' Artur Wichniarek), Sylwester Czereszewski (73' Krzysztof Nowak), Radoslav Michalski, Andrzej Juskowiak (81' Pawel Kryszalowicz), Miroslaw Trzeciak (YC49). (Coach: Janusz Wójcik (POL)).
Goals: Sweden: 1-0 Kennet Andersson (54'), 2-0 Henrik Larsson (90').
Referee: Urs Meier (SUI)   Attendance: 35.037

10-10-1999   Bulgarian Army Stadium, Sofia: Bulgaria – Luxembourg   3-0 (1-0)
Bulgaria: Zdravko Zdravkov, Georgi Markov, Zlatomir Zagorcic (YC14) (83' Biser Ivanov), Stiliyan Petrov, Mariyan Hristov (63' Svetoslav Todorov), Daniel Borimirov, Ivaylo Petkov, Aleksandar Aleksandrov, Ivaylo Yordanov (C), Stanimir Stoilov, Georgi Bachev (60' Rumen Hristov). (Coach: Dimitar Petrov Dimitrov (BUL)).
Luxembourg: Philippe Felgen, Manou Schauls, Marc Birsens (C), Jean Vanek, Christian Alverdi (69' Daniel Theis), Jeff Strasser, Manuel Cardoni (86' Luc Holtz), Jeff Saibene, Patrick Posing (57' Frank Deville), Marcel Christophe, Mikhail Zaritskiy. (Coach: Paul Philipp (LUX)).
Goals: Bulgaria: 1-0 Daniel Borimirov (40'), 2-0 Ivaylo Petkov (67'), 3-0 Rumen Hristov (77').
Referee: Ladislav Gadosi (SVK)   Attendance: 2.000

GROUP 6

05-09-1998	Vienna	Austria – Israel	1-1 (1-0)
05-09-1998	Larnaca	Cyprus – Spain	3-2 (1-0)
10-10-1998	Larnaca	Cyprus – Austria	0-3 (0-0)
10-10-1998	Serravalle	San Marino – Israel	0-5 (0-3)
14-10-1998	Ramat Gan	Israel – Spain	1-2 (0-0)
14-10-1998	Serravalle	San Marino – Austria	1-4 (0-0)
18-11-1998	Serravalle	San Marino – Cyprus	0-1 (0-1)
10-02-1999	Limassol	Cyprus – San Marino	4-0 (3-0)
27-03-1999	Valencia	Spain – Austria	9-0 (5-0)
28-03-1999	Ramat Gan	Israel – Cyprus	3-0 (1-0)
31-03-1999	Serravalle	San Marino – Spain	0-6 (0-2)
28-04-1999	Graz	Austria – San Marino	7-0 (3-0)
05-06-1999	Villarreal	Spain – San Marino	9-0 (4-0)
06-06-1999	Ramat Gan	Israel – Austria	5-0 (2-0)
04-09-1999	Vienna	Austria – Spain	1-3 (0-1)
05-09-1999	Limassol	Cyprus – Israel	3-2 (1-1)
08-09-1999	Ramat Gan	Israel – San Marino	8-0 (3-0)
08-09-1999	Badajoz	Spain – Cyprus	8-0 (5-0)
09-10-1999	Vienna	Austria – Cyprus	3-1 (2-0)
10-10-1999	Albacete	Spain – Israel	3-0 (2-0)

FINAL STANDING

Pos	Team	Pld	W	D	L	GF	GA	GD	Pts
1	Spain	8	7	0	1	42	5	+37	21
2	Israel	8	4	1	3	25	9	+16	13
3	Austria	8	4	1	3	19	20	-1	13
4	Cyprus	8	4	0	4	12	21	-9	12
5	San Marino	8	0	0	8	1	44	-43	0

Spain qualified for the final tournament in Belgium/Netherlands.

Israel qualified for the second round play-offs.

05-09-1998 Ernst-Happel-Stadion, Vienna: Austria – Israel 1-1 (1-0)
Austria: Franz Wohlfahrt, Anton Pfeffer, Wolfgang Feiersinger, Peter Schöttel (C) (YC57) (72' Martin Hiden), Dietmar Kühbauer (YC61), Harald Cerny (74' Peter Stöger), Roman Mählich (YC61), Hannes Reinmayr, Martin Amerhauser, Iviva Vastic (YC49), Mario Haas (71' Christian Mayrleb). (Coach: Herbert Prohaska (AUT)).
Israel: Refael Cohen, David Amsalem (RC61), Arik Benado, Alon Harazi (YC55), Ran Ben Shimon, Walid Badir (YC44), Haim Revivo, Eyal Berkovic, Amir Shelach (C) (46' Avi Nimni), Yosef Abukasis (46' Alon Mizrahi), Ronen Harazi (61' Najwan Ghrayib). (Coach: Shlomo Scharf (ISR)).
Goals: Austria: 1-0 Hannes Reinmayr (7').
Israel: 1-1 Avi Nimni (68' penalty).
Referee: Anders Frisk (SWE)   Attendance: 20.000

05-09-1998 Antonis Papadopoulos Stadium, Larnaca: Cyprus – Spain 3-2 (1-0)
Cyprus: Nikos Panayiotou, Demetris Ioannou (81' Akis Ioakim), Charalambos Pittas (C), Marios Charalambous, Panayiotis Engomitis, Kostas Kosta (YC39), Vassos Melanarkitis, Milenko Spoljaric, Marios Christodoulou, Sinisa Gogic (62' Marios Agathocleous (YC81)), Kostakis Malekkos (56' Panayiotis Pounnas). (Coach: Panikos Georgiou (CYP)).
Spain: José Santiago CAÑIZARES Ruíz, MÍCHEL SALGADO Fernández, Fernando Ruiz HIERRO (C), Miguel Angel NADAL Homar (66' Guillermo AMOR Martinez), Rafael ALKORTA Martínez, SERGI BARJUÁN i Esclusa (YC30), LUIS ENRIQUE Martínez García, RAÚL González Blanco, Fernando MORIENTES Sánchez, JOSEBA Andoni ETXEBERRIA Lizardi (60' SANTIAGO EZQUERRO Marín), ALFONSO Pérez Muñóz (39' Francisco Narvaez Machon "KIKO"). (Coach: JAVIER CLEMENTE Lázaro (ESP)).
Goals: Cyprus: 1-0 Panayiotis Engomitis (43'), 2-0 Sinisa Gogic (49'), 3-1 Milenko Spoljaric (77').
Spain: 2-1 RAÚL González Blanco (73'), 3-2 Fernando MORIENTES Sánchez (80').
Referee: Sergei Grigorievich Khusainov (RUS)   Attendance: 1.876

10-10-1998   Antonis Papadopoulos Stadium, Larnaca: Cyprus – Austria 0-3 (0-0)
Cyprus: Nikos Panayiotou, Demetris Ioannou (RC33), Charalambos Pittas (C) (67' Ioannis Okkas (YC78)), Marios Charalambous (YC25), Panayiotis Engomitis, Kostas Kosta (YC4), Vassos Melanarkitis (67' Nicolaos Georgiou), Milenko Spoljaric (YC58), Marios Agathocleous (46' Panayiotis Pounnas), Sinisa Gogic, Marios Christodoulou. (Coach: Panikos Georgiou (CYP)).
Austria: Franz Wohlfahrt, Martin Hiden, Anton Pfeffer (YC23), Peter Schöttel (C), Dietmar Kühbauer, Harald Cerny, Arnold Wetl (YC10), Roman Mählich (YC70), Hannes Reinmayr (80' Peter Stöger), Ivica Vastic (84' Edi Glieder), Mario Haas (80' Christian Mayrleb). (Coach: Herbert Prohaska (AUT)).
Goals: Austria: 0-1 Harald Cerny (55'), 0-2 Harald Cerny (61'), 0-3 Hannes Reinmayr (74').
Referee: Fernand Meese (BEL)   Attendance: 5.679

10-10-1998   Stadio Olimpico, Serravalle: San Marino – Israel 0-5 (0-3)
San Marino: Federico Gasperoni, Simone Bacciocchi (YC50) (56' Vittorio Valentini), Mirko Gennari, William Guerra (C), Ivan Matteoni (YC36), Mauro Valentini, Mauro Marani, Riccardo Muccioli, Pier-Domenico Della-Valle (67' Fabio Francini), Andy Selva, Paolo Montagna (80' Davide Gualtieri). (Coach: Giampaolo Mazza (ITA)).
Israel: Refael Cohen, Alon Harazi, Najwan Ghrayib, Arik Benado (69' Amir Shelach), Ran Ben Shimon, Jan Talesnikov, Walid Badir, Haim Revivo (C), Eyal Berkovic (72' Offer Shitrit), Avi Nimni (61' Tal Banin), Alon Mizrahi. (Coach: Shlomo Scharf (ISR)).
Goals: Israel: 0-1 Haim Revivo (16'), 0-2 Avi Nimni (18'), 0-3 Alon Mizrahi (32'), 0-4 Mauro Valentini (58' *own goal*), 0-5 Najwan Ghrayib (83').
Referee: Asim Khudiev (AZE)   Attendance: 872

14-10-1998   National Stadium, Ramat Gan: Israel – Spain 1-2 (0-0)
Israel: Refael Cohen, Alon Harazi, Najwan Ghrayib, Arik Benado, Ran Ben Shimon, Jan Talesnikov (58' Alon Mizrahi (YC78)), Haim Revivo (C), Walid Badir, Alon Hazan (YC49) (75' Tal Banin), Eyal Berkovic, Avi Nimni. (Coach: Shlomo Scharf (ISR)).
Spain: José Santiago CAÑIZARES Ruíz, MÍCHEL SALGADO Fernández, Agustín ARANZÁBAL Alkorta, Fernando Ruiz HIERRO (C) (YC11), Rafael ALKORTA Martínez, Francisco Javier "JAVI" DE PEDRO Falque (YC18) (73' JOSEBA Andoni ETXEBERRIA Lizardi), LUIS ENRIQUE Martínez García, Vicente ENGONGA Maté (YC5), BITTOR ALKIZA Fernández, RAÚL González Blanco (89' MARCOS VALES Illanes), Francisco Narvaez Machon "KIKO" (YC88) (88' Ismael URZÁIZ Aranda). (Coach: JOSÉ Antonio CAMACHO Alfaro (ESP)).
Goals: Israel: 1-0 Alon Hazan (64').
Spain: 1-1 Fernando Ruiz HIERRO (65'), 1-2 JOSEBA Andoni ETXEBERRIA Lizardi (78').
Referee: David Roland Elleray (ENG)   Attendance: 37.000

14-10-1998   Stadio Olimpico, Serravalle: San Marino – Austria 1-4 (0-0)
San Marino: Federico Gasperoni, Simone Bacciocchi, Mirko Gennari, William Guerra (C), Ivan Matteoni, Mauro Valentini (YC66) (80' Pier-Domenico Della-Valle), Mauro Marani, Riccardo Muccioli, Fabio Francini (69' Vittorio Valentini), Andy Selva, Andrea Ugolini (YC34) (61' Paolo Montagna). (Coach: Giampaolo Mazza (ITA)).
Austria: Franz Wohlfahrt, Martin Hiden, Anton Pfeffer, Peter Schöttel (C), Dietmar Kühbauer, Harald Cerny, Arnold Wetl, Hannes Reinmayr (46' Christian Mayrleb), Andreas Heraf (YC13), Ivica Vastic (YC65) (70' Peter Stöger), Mario Haas (68' Edi Glieder). (Coach: Herbert Prohaska (AUT)).
Goals: San Marino: 1-4 Andy Selva (81' penalty).
Austria: 0-1 Ivica Vastic (58'), 0-2 Christian Mayrleb (64'), 0-3 Martin Hiden (69'), 0-4 Edi Glieder (76').
Referee: Valery Onufer (UKR)   Attendance: 1.218

18-11-1998   Stadio Olimpico, Serravalle: San Marino – Cyprus 0-1 (0-1)
San Marino: Federico Gasperoni, Vittorio Valentini, Mirko Gennari, William Guerra (C) (YC54), Ivan Matteoni (75' Fabio Francini), Mauro Valentini (YC13), Brian Gasperoni (YC44), Mauro Marani (YC60), Riccardo Muccioli (YC58) (83' Luciano Mularoni), Paolo Montagna (66' Nicola Bacciocchi), Andrea Ugolini. (Coach: Giampaolo Mazza (ITA)).
Cyprus: Nikos Panayiotou, Charalambos Pittas (C), Marios Charalambous, Panayiotis Panayiotou, Andreas Sofocleous, Panayiotis Engomitis, Vassos Melanarkitis, Milenko Spoljaric, Sinisa Gogic (YC32) (85' Ioannis Okkas), Kostakis Malekkos (73' Michalis Konstantinou), Marios Agathocleous (73' Yiannos Ioannou (YC89)). (Coach: Panikos Georgiou (CYP)).
Goal: Cyprus: 0-1 Milenko Spoljaric (40').
Referee: John McDermott (IRL)   Attendance: 510

10-02-1999   Tsirion Stadium, Limassol: Cyprus – San Marino 4-0 (3-0)
Cyprus: Nikos Panayiotou, Georgios Theodotou, Charalambos Pittas (C), Marios Charalambous, Akis Ioakim (YC90+4), Vassos Melanarkitis, Milenko Spoljaric, Marios Christodoulou, Michalis Konstantinou (83' Ioannis Okkas), Sinisa Gogic (YC23) (83' Yiannos Ioannou), Kostakis Malekkos (90' Aristos Aristocleous). (Coach: Panikos Georgiou (CYP)).
San Marino: Federico Gasperoni, Vittorio Valentini (YC75), Mirko Gennari, Luca Gobbi, William Guerra (C) (YC19), Ermanno Zonzini, Mauro Marani (86' Damiano Vannucci), Pier-Domenico Della Valle (YC50) (72' Pier-Angelo Manzaroli), Luciano Mularoni, Andy Selva, Andrea Ugolini (48' Nicola Bacciocchi). (Coach: Giampaolo Mazza (ITA)).
Goals: Cyprus: 1-0 Vassos Melanarkitis (18'), 2-0 Michalis Konstantinou (32'), 3-0 Michalis Konstantinou (45+2'), 4-0 Marios Christodoulou (90').
Referee: Roland Beck (LIE)   Attendance: 3.000

27-03-1999   Mestalla Stadium, Valencia: Spain – Austria   9-0 (5-0)
Spain: José Santiago CAÑIZARES Ruíz (YC40), MÍCHEL SALGADO Fernández, Fernando Ruiz HIERRO (C) (YC82), MARCELINO Elena Sierra, SERGI BARJUÁN i Esclusa, Juan Carlos VALERÓN Santana (72' GAIZKA MENDIETA Zabala), Josep GUARDIOLA i Sala, Francesco Javier González Pérez "FRAN", RAÚL González Blanco, JOSEBA Andoni ETXEBERRIA Lizardi (83' Daniel "DANI" GARCÍA Lara), Ismael URZÁIZ Aranda (60' Pedro MUNITIS Álvarez). (Coach: JOSÉ Antonio CAMACHO Alfaro (ESP)).
Austria: Franz Wohlfahrt, Anton Pfeffer (YC61), Wolfgang Feiersinger (53' Walter Kogler), Peter Schöttel (YC64), Günther Neukirchner, Andreas Herzog (C), Harald Cerny, Arnold Wetl, Roman Mählich, Christian Prosenik (YC17) (58' Hannes Reinmayr), Mario Haas (70' Christian Mayrleb). (Coach: Herbert Prohaska (AUT)).
Goals: Spain: 1-0 RAÚL González Blanco (6'), 2-0 RAÚL González Blanco (17'), 3-0 Ismael URZÁIZ Aranda (30'), 4-0 Fernando Ruiz HIERRO (35' penalty), 5-0 Ismael URZÁIZ Aranda (44'), 6-0 RAÚL González Blanco (48'), 7-0 RAÚL González Blanco (74'), 8-0 Arnold Wetl (77' *own goal*), 9-0 Francesco Javier González Pérez "FRAN" (84').
Referee: Gilles Veissière (FRA)   Attendance: 35.500

28-03-1999   National Stadium, Ramat Gan: Israel – Cyprus   3-0 (1-0)
Israel: Nir Davidovitch, Arik Benado (YC33), Alon Harazi, Najwan Ghrayib, Walid Badir (YC39) (46' Alon Mizrahi), Tal Banin (C), Haim Revivo (85' Avraham Tikva), Eyal Berkovic, Amir Shelach, Avi Nimni, Ronen Harazi (46' Ofer Talkar). (Coach: Shlomo Scharf (ISR)).
Cyprus: Nikos Panayiotou, Georgios Theodotou, Demetris Ioannou, Charalambos Pittas (C), Marios Charalambous, Andreas Sofocleous, Vassos Melanarkitis (YC60), Milenko Spoljaric (79' Marios Agathocleous), Marios Christodoulou, Michalis Konstantinou (66' Ioannis Okkas), Kostakis Malekkos (YC44) (46' Charis Nicolaou). (Coach: Panikos Georgiou (CYP)).
Goals: Israel: 1-0 Tal Banin (11'), 2-0 Alon Mizrahi (48'), 3-0 Alon Mizrahi (52').
Referee: Marcel Lica (ROM)   Attendance: 30.000

31-03-1999   Stadio Olimpico, Serravalle: San Marino – Spain   0-6 (0-2)
San Marino: Federico Gasperoni, Vittorio Valentini (YC15), Mirko Gennari, Luca Gobbi (C) (51' Simone Della Balda), Mauro Valentini, Ermanno Zonzini, Brian Gasperoni (76' Riccardo Muccioli), Mauro Marani, Pier-Angelo Manzaroli, Andy Selva (YC51), Paolo Montagna (59' Davide Gualtieri). (Coach: Giampaolo Mazza (ITA)).
Spain: José Santiago CAÑIZARES Ruíz, MÍCHEL SALGADO Fernández, Francisco "PACO" Jémez Martín, MARCELINO Elena Sierra, SERGI BARJUÁN i Esclusa (C) (YC72), Juan Carlos VALERÓN Santana (YC48) (78' IVÁN HELGUERA Bujía), Josep GUARDIOLA i Sala (70' Vicente ENGONGA Maté), Francesco Javier González Pérez "FRAN", RAÚL González Blanco, JOSEBA Andoni ETXEBERRIA Lizardi, Ismael URZÁIZ Aranda (62' Daniel "DANI" GARCÍA Lara). (Coach: JOSÉ Antonio CAMACHO Alfaro (ESP)).
Goals: Spain: 0-1 Francesco Javier González Pérez "FRAN" (21'), 0-2 RAÚL González Blanco (45'), 0-3 Ismael URZÁIZ Aranda (49'), 0-4 RAÚL González Blanco (58'), 0-5 RAÚL González Blanco (67'), 0-6 JOSEBA Andoni ETXEBERRIA Lizardi (74').
Referee: Goran Maric (CRO)   Attendance: 2.020

28-04-1999 Arnold Schwarzenegger Stadion, Graz: Austria – San Marino 7-0 (3-0)
Austria: Franz Wohlfahrt, Thomas Winklhofer (78' Klaus Rohseano), Wolfgang Feiersinger, Günther Neukirchner, Markus Schopp (70' Richard Kitzbichler), Andreas Herzog (C), Harald Cerny (70' Edi Glieder), Martin Amerhauser, Christian Prosenik, Ivica Vastic, Christian Mayrleb. (Coach: Otto Baric (SRB)).
San Marino: Federico Gasperoni, Mirko Gennari (46' Simone Bacciocchi (YC81)), Luca Gobbi (YC85), William Guerra (C), Ermanno Zonzini, Brian Gasperoni (15' Pier-Angelo Manzaroli), Riccardo Muccioli, Damiano Vannucci, Simone Della Balda (YC75), Andy Selva, Paolo Montagna (79' Nicola Bacciocchi). (Coach: Giampaolo Mazza (ITA)).
Goals: Austria: 1-0 Christian Mayrleb (24'), 2-0 Ivica Vastic (41'), 3-0 Ivica Vastic (44'), 4-0 Christian Mayrleb (53'), 5-0 Martin Amerhauser (70'), 6-0 Andreas Herzog (81' penalty), 7-0 Ivica Vastic (84').
Referee: Kyros Vassaras (GRE) Attendance: 15.400

05-06-1999 Estadio El Madrigal, Villarreal: Spain – San Marino 9-0 (4-0)
Spain: José Santiago CAÑIZARES Ruíz, MÍCHEL SALGADO Fernández (62' Pedro MUNITIS Álvarez), Agustín ARANZÁBAL Alkorta, Fernando Ruiz HIERRO (C), MARCELINO Elena Sierra, LUIS ENRIQUE Martínez García, JULEN GUERRERO López (74' GAIZKA MENDIETA Zabala), Josep GUARDIOLA i Sala, RAÚL González Blanco (62' Ismael URZÁIZ Aranda), Fernando MORIENTES Sánchez, JOSEBA Andoni ETXEBERRIA Lizardi. (Coach: JOSÉ Antonio CAMACHO Alfaro (ESP)).
San Marino: Federico Gasperoni, Mirko Gennari (89' Damiano Vannucci), Luca Gobbi (YC82), William Guerra (C), Ermanno Zonzini, Mauro Marani (YC37), Nicola Bacciocchi, Pier-Angelo Manzaroli (74' Vittorio Valentini), Pier-Domenico Della Valle, Simone Della Balda, Paolo Montagna (56' Andrea Ugolini). (Coach: Giampaolo Mazza (ITA)).
Goals: Spain: 1-0 Fernando Ruiz HIERRO (8' penalty), 2-0 LUIS ENRIQUE Martínez García (22'), 3-0 JOSEBA Andoni ETXEBERRIA Lizardi (25'), 4-0 JOSEBA Andoni ETXEBERRIA Lizardi (45'), 5-0 RAÚL González Blanco (56'), 6-0 LUIS ENRIQUE Martínez García (68'), 7-0 LUIS ENRIQUE Martínez García (70'), 8-0 Mirko Gennari (87' *own goal*), 9-0 GAIZKA MENDIETA Zabala (89').
Referee: Gerard Perry (IRL) Attendance: 16.150

06-06-1999 National Stadium, Ramat Gan: Israel – Austria 5-0 (2-0)
Israel: Nir Davidovitch, Arik Benado, Alon Harazi, Najwan Ghrayib, Tal Banin (C) (YC17), Haim Revivo, Alon Hazan, Eyal Berkovic (77' Avraham Tikva), Amir Shelach (YC83), Yosef Abukasis (82' Idan Tal), Alon Mizrahi (75' Nir Sivilia). (Coach: Shlomo Scharf (ISR)).
Austria: Franz Wohlfahrt, Thomas Winklhofer, Walter Kogler, Günther Neukirchner, Zoran Barisic, Andreas Herzog (C) (YC32), Harald Cerny, Roman Mählich (YC12), Martin Amerhauser (46' Christian Prosenik), Ivica Vastic (YC42) (56' Edi Glieder), Christian Mayrleb (68' Mario Haas). (Coach: Otto Baric (SRB)).
Goals: Israel: 1-0 Eyal Berkovic (26'), 2-0 Haim Revivo (45'), 3-0 Eyal Berkovic (47'), 4-0 Alon Mizrahi (53'), 5-0 Najwan Ghrayib (74').
Referee: Lubos Michel (SVK) Attendance: 42.000

04-09-1999   Ernst-Happel-Stadion, Vienna: Austria – Spain 1-3 (0-1)
Austria: Alexander Manninger, Thomas Winklhofer (YC50), Michael Streiter, Michael Hatz (YC40), Robert Ibertsberger, Roland Kirchler (YC19) (67' Markus Weissenberger), Dietmar Kühbauer, Harald Cerny, Roman Mählich (60' Markus Schopp), Ivica Vastic (C), Christian Mayrleb. (Coach: Otto Baric (SRB)).
Spain: José Santiago CAÑIZARES Ruíz, MÍCHEL SALGADO Fernández, Fernando Ruiz HIERRO (C), Francisco "PACO" Jémez Martín, SERGI BARJUÁN i Esclusa, Juan Carlos VALERÓN Santana (72' Vicente ENGONGA Maté (YC86)), LUIS ENRIQUE Martínez García, Josep GUARDIOLA i Sala (YC51), RAÚL González Blanco, Fernando MORIENTES Sánchez (87' JULEN GUERRERO López), JOSEBA Andoni ETXEBERRIA Lizardi (80' GAIZKA MENDIETA Zabala). (Coach: JOSÉ Antonio CAMACHO Alfaro (ESP)).
Goals: Austria: 1-1 Fernando Ruiz HIERRO (49' *own goal*).
Spain: 0-1 RAÚL González Blanco (22'), 1-2 Fernando Ruiz HIERRO (55'), 1-3 LUIS ENRIQUE Martínez García (88').
Referee: Michel Piraux (BEL)   Attendance: 27.000

05-09-1999   Tsirion Stadium, Limassol: Cyprus – Israel 3-2 (1-1)
Cyprus: Nikos Panayiotou, Charalambos Pittas (C), Marios Charalambous (YC41), Panayiotis Engomitis (YC29), Kostas Kaiafas (80' Aristos Aristocleous), Nikodemos Papavasiliou (64' Marios Christodoulou), Kostas Kosta, Vassos Melanarkitis, Milenko Spoljaric (YC31), Ioannis Okkas, Sinisa Gogic (71' Michalis Konstantinou). (Coach: Stavros Papadopoulos (CYP)).
Israel: Nir Davidovitch (YC87), Arik Benado, Alon Harazi, Najwan Ghrayib (YC14), Tal Banin (C) (YC52), Haim Revivo (YC66), Alon Hazan, Eyal Berkovic (16' Walid Badir (YC31)), Amir Shelach (64' Nir Sivilia), Yosef Abukasis (YC11) (55' Yossi Benayoun), Alon Mizrahi. (Coach: Shlomo Scharf (ISR)).
Goals: Cyprus: 1-0 Panayiotis Engomitis (27'), 2-1 Milenko Spoljaric (53'), 3-2 Milenko Spoljaric (87' penalty).
Israel: 1-1 Walid Badir (30'), 2-2 Yossi Benayoun (81').
Referee: Graham Peter Barber (ENG)   Attendance: 12.000

08-09-1999   National Stadium, Ramat Gan: Israel – San Marino 8-0 (3-0)
Israel: Nir Davidovitch, David Amsalem, Arik Benado (65' Alon Halfon), Alon Harazi (YC48), Ofer Talker, Yossi Benayoun, Haim Revivo (C), Alon Hazan, Jan Talesnikov, Avraham Tikva (62' Yosef Abukasis (46' Nir Sivilia). (Coach: Shlomo Scharf (ISR)).
San Marino: Federico Gasperoni, Fabrizio Pellicioni, Simone Bacciocchi, Mirko Gennari, Marko Tomassoni, Ermanno Zonzini (74' Pier-Domenico Della Valle), Brian Gasperoni, Nicola Bacciocchi (C) (58' Roberto Selva), Simone Della Balda, Andy Selva (YC,YC75), Paolo Montagna (80' Marco De Luigi). (Coach: Giampaolo Mazza (ITA)).
Goals: Israel: 1-0 Yossi Benayoun (24'), 2-0 Alon Mizrahi (37'), 3-0 Haim Revivo (40'), 4-0 Yossi Benayoun (46'), 5-0 Haim Revivo (68'), 6-0 Yossi Benayoun (71'), 7-0 Nir Sivilia (83'), 8-0 Yosef Abukasis (89').
Referee: Ilhami Kaplan (TUR)   Attendance: 25.078

08-09-1999   Estadio Nuevo Vivero, Badajoz: Spain – Cyprus   8-0 (5-0)
Spain: José Santiago CAÑIZARES Ruíz (78' ANTONIO JIMÉNEZ Sistachs), MÍCHEL SALGADO Fernández, Agustín ARANZÁBAL Alkorta, CÉSAR MARTÍN Villar, Fernando Ruiz HIERRO (C), LUIS ENRIQUE Martínez García (61' GAIZKA MENDIETA Zabala), JULEN GUERRERO López, Josep GUARDIOLA i Sala, RAÚL González Blanco, JOSEBA Andoni ETXEBERRIA Lizardi (46' Pedro MUNITIS Álvarez), Ismael URZÁIZ Aranda. (Coach: JOSÉ Antonio CAMACHO Alfaro (ESP)).
Cyprus: Nikos Panayiotou, Loukas Louka, Charalambos Pittas (46' Georgios Theodotou), Panayiotis Engomitis, Charis Nicolaou (46' Aristos Aristocleous), Nikodemos Papavasiliou, Kostas Kosta, Vassos Melanarkitis, Marios Christodoulou (YC90), Ioannis Okkas, Sinisa Gogic (88' Yiasemakis Yiasoumi). (Coach: Stavros Papadoupoulos (CYP)).
Goals: Spain: 1-0 Ismael URZÁIZ Aranda (19'), 2-0 Ismael URZÁIZ Aranda (25'), 3-0 JULEN GUERRERO López (34'), 4-0 Ismael URZÁIZ Aranda (38'), 5-0 JULEN GUERRERO López (42'), 6-0 JULEN GUERRERO López (56'), 7-0 CÉSAR MARTÍN Villar (81'), 8-0 Fernando Ruiz HIERRO (89').
Referee: Alfredo Trentalange (ITA)   Attendance: 13.700

09-10-1999   Ernst-Happel-Stadion, Vienna: Austria – Cyprus   3-1 (2-0)
Austria: Alexander Manninger, Thomas Winklhofer, Günther Neukirchner (46' Andreas Herzog), Robert Ibertsberger (RC75), Markus Weissenberger (83' Gerd Wimmer), Roland Kirchler, Dietmar Kühbauer (YC25), Harald Cerny (74' Jürgen Kauz), Ivica Vastic (C) (YC27), Christian Mayrleb, Edi Glieder. (Coach: Otto Baric (SRB)).
Cyprus: Nikos Panayiotou, Marios Charalambous, Klimis Alexandrou, Panayiotis Engomitis, Kostas Kaiafas (RC29), Kostas Kosta, Vassos Melanarkitis (81' Marios Dimitriou), Milenko Spoljaric (YC30,YC45), Marios Christodoulou, Ioannis Okkas (46' Georgios Theodotou), Sinisa Gogic (25' Marios Agathocleous). (Coach: Stavros Papadoupoulos (CYP)).
Goals: Austria: 1-0 Edi Glieder (5'), 2-0 Ivica Vastic (22'), 3-1 Andreas Herzog (81').
Cyprus: 2-1 Kostas Kosta (62').
Referee: Livio Bazzoli (ITA)   Attendance: 10.100

10-10-1999   Estadio Carlos Belmonte, Albacete: Spain – Israel   3-0 (2-0)
Spain: ANTONIO JIMÉNEZ Sistachs, MÍCHEL SALGADO Fernández (YC83), Fernando Ruiz HIERRO (C) (24' CÉSAR MARTÍN Villar), Francisco "PACO" Jémez Martín, SERGI BARJUÁN i Esclusa, LUIS ENRIQUE Martínez García, JULEN GUERRERO López (70' GAIZKA MENDIETA Zabala), Josep GUARDIOLA i Sala, RAÚL González Blanco, Fernando MORIENTES Sánchez (78' Ismael URZÁIZ Aranda), JOSEBA Andoni ETXEBERRIA Lizardi. (Coach: JOSÉ Antonio CAMACHO Alfaro (ESP)).
Israel: Dudu Aouate, David Amsalem, Arik Benado (50' Alon Halfon), Shimon Gershon, Idan Tal, Tal Banin (C), Haim Revivo, Alon Hazan (82' Jan Talesnikov), Eyal Berkovic (68' Yossi Benayoun), Amir Shelach (YC22), Amir Turgeman. (Coach: Shlomo Scharf (ISR)).
Goals: Spain: 1-0 Fernando MORIENTES Sánchez (30'), 2-0 CÉSAR MARTÍN Villar (38'), 3-0 RAÚL González Blanco (52').
Referee: Helmut Krug (GER)   Attendance: 16.100

GROUP 7

02-09-1998	Bucharest	Romania – Liechtenstein	7-0 (4-0)
05-09-1998	Kosice	Slovakia – Azerbaijan	3-0 (3-0)
06-09-1998	Budapest	Hungary – Portugal	1-3 (1-0)
10-10-1998	Baku	Azerbaijan – Hungary	0-4 (0-0)
10-10-1998	Vaduz	Liechtenstein – Slovakia	0-4 (0-3)
10-10-1998	Porto	Portugal – Romania	0-1 (0-0)
14-10-1998	Vaduz	Liechtenstein – Azerbaijan	2-1 (0-0)
14-10-1998	Budapest	Hungary – Romania	1-1 (0-0)
14-10-1998	Bratislava	Slovakia – Portugal	0-3 (0-2)
26-03-1999	Guimarães	Portugal – Azerbaijan	7-0 (2-0)
27-03-1999	Budapest	Hungary – Liechtenstein	5-0 (3-0)
27-03-1999	Bucharest	Romania – Slovakia	0-0
31-03-1999	Baku	Azerbaijan – Romania	0-1 (0-0)
31-03-1999	Bratislava	Slovakia – Hungary	0-0
31-03-1999	Vaduz	Liechtenstein – Portugal	0-5 (0-1)
05-06-1999	Baku	Azerbaijan – Liechtenstein	4-0 (2-0)
05-06-1999	Bucharest	Romania – Hungary	2-0 (2-0)
05-06-1999	Lisbon	Portugal – Slovakia	1-0 (0-0)
09-06-1999	Bucharest	Romania – Azerbaijan	4-0 (2-0)
09-06-1999	Györ	Hungary – Slovakia	0-1 (0-0)
09-06-1999	Coimbra	Portugal – Liechenstein	8-0 (3-0)
04-09-1999	Baku	Azerbaijan – Portugal	1-1 (0-0)
04-09-1999	Vaduz	Liechtenstein – Hungary	0-0
04-09-1999	Bratislava	Slovakia – Romania	1-5 (1-2)
08-09-1999	Dubnica nad Váhom	Slovakia - Liechtenstein	2-0 (1-0)
08-09-1999	Bucharest	Romania – Portugal	1-1 (1-1)
08-09-1999	Budapest	Hungary – Azerbaijan	3-0 (1-0)
09-10-1999	Baku	Azerbaijan – Slovakia	0-1 (0-0)
09-10-1999	Vaduz	Liechtenstein – Romania	0-3 (0-1)
09-10-1999	Lisbon	Portugal – Hungary	3-0 (2-0)

FINAL STANDING

Pos	Team	Pld	W	D	L	GF	GA	GD	Pts
1	Romania	10	7	3	0	25	3	+22	24
2	Portugal	10	7	2	1	32	4	+28	23
3	Slovakia	10	5	2	3	12	9	+3	17
4	Hungary	10	3	3	4	14	10	+4	12
5	Azerbaijan	10	1	1	8	6	26	-20	4
6	Liechtenstein	10	1	1	8	2	39	-37	4

Romania and Portugal qualified for the final tournament in Belgium/Netherlands.

02-09-1998   Stadionul Steaua, Bucharest: Romania – Liechtenstein   7-0 (4-0)
Romania: Bogdan Stelea (82' Bogdan Lobont), Dan Petrescu, Florin Batranu, Catalin Munteanu (76' Ioan Sabau), Florentin Petre, Gheorghe Popescu (C), Constantin Galca, Dorinel Munteanu, Cosmin Contra, Viorel Moldovan, Adrian Ilie (70' Dumitru Mihalcea). (Coach: Victor Piturca (ROM)).
Liechtenstein: Martin Oehri, Michael Stocklasa (62' Marco Büchel), Christof Ritter, Patrick Hefti, Daniel Telser (89' Marco Ender), Harald Zech (C), Thomas Hanselmann (YC84), Hansjörg Lingg, Rolf Oehri, Matthias Beck, Modestus Haas (YC27) (63' Martin Stocklasa). (Coach: Ralf Loose (GER)).
Goals: Romania: 1-0 Gheorghe Popescu (18'), 2-0 Catalin Munteanu (30'), 3-0 Adrian Ilie (32'), 4-0 Adrian Ilie (45'), 5-0 Adrian Ilie (53'), 6-0 Viorel Moldovan (56'), 7-0 Modestus Haas (60' *own goal*).
Referee: Salem Prolic (BOS)   Attendance: 2.830

05-09-1998   Lokomotiva Stadium, Kosice: Slovakia – Azerbaijan   3-0 (3-0)
Slovakia: Alexander Vencel, Stanislav Varga, Marek Spilár, Dusan Tittel, Vladimír Kinder (YC18), Lubomír Moravcik (C), Robert Tomaschek, Peter Dubovsky (62' Vladislav Zvara), Miroslav Sovic, Martin Fabus (62' Tibor Jancula), Jozef Majoros (81' Marek Ujlaky). (Coach: Jozef Jankech (SVK)).
Azerbaijan: Dmitriy Kramarenko (YC25), Emin Agayev (YC32), Arif Asadov, Faig Jabbarov, Deni Gaysumov, Rasim Abusov, Vyacheslav Lychkin (65' Vidadi Rzayev), Veli Gasimov (78' Yunis Hüseynov), Nazim Suleymanov (C) (46' Rufat Guliyev), Gurban Gurbanov, Narvik Sirkhayev. (Coach: Vagif Sadykov (AZE)).
Goals: Slovakia: 1-0 Martin Fabus (17'), 2-0 Peter Dubovsky (26' penalty), 3-0 Lubomír Moravcik (37').
Referee: Alan Snoddy (NIR)   Attendance: 3.243

06-09-1998   Népstadion, Budapest: Hungary – Portugal   1-3 (1-0)
Hungary: Gábor Király, János Mátyus, János Hrutka, Pál Lakos, Csaba Fehér (79' Zoltán Kovács), Tibor Dombi (79' György Korsós), Krisztián Lisztes (46' Pál Dárdai), Gábor Halmai, Béla Illés (C), István Hamar, Ferenc Horváth. (Coach: Bertalan Bicskei (HUN)).
Portugal: VÍTOR Manuel Martins BAÍA (C), JORGE Paulo COSTA Almeida, CARLOS Alberto de Oliveira SECRETÁRIO (YC19), DIMAS Manuel Marques Teixeira, PAULO Sérgio Braga MADEIRA, LUÍS Filipe Madeira Caeiro FIGO, RUI Manuel César COSTA (YC53), PAULO Jorge Gomes BENTO (YC29), João Paulo Maio dos "PAULINHO" SANTOS, JOÃO Manuel Vieira PINTO, Ricardo Manuel Andrade Silva SÁ PINTO. (Coach: HUMBERTO Manuel de Jesus COELHO (POR)).
Goals: Hungary: 1-0 Ferenc Horváth (32').
Portugal: 1-1 Ricardo Manuel Andrade Silva SÁ PINTO (56'), 1-2 Ricardo Manuel Andrade Silva SÁ PINTO (77'), 1-3 RUI Manuel César COSTA (85').
Referee: Urs Meier (SUI)   Attendance: 46.500

10-10-1998   Tofiq Bahramov Stadium, Baku: Azerbaijan – Hungary   0-4 (0-0)
Azerbaijan: Dmitriy Kramarenko (59' Aleksandr Zhidkov), Emin Agayev, Arif Asadov (50' Ilkham Mammadov), Deni Gaysumov, Aslan Kerimov, Rasim Abusov (C), Vidadi Rzayev, Vyacheslav Lychkin (YC58,YC60), Elshan Gambarov (55' Veli Gasimov), Gurban Gurbanov, Narvik Sirkhayev. (Coach: Vagif Sadykov (AZE)).
Hungary: Gábor Király, János Mátyus, János Hrutka (YC77), Pál Dárdai, Csaba Fehér (YC29), Krisztián Lisztes (74' Tibor Dombi (YC76)), Béla Illés, István Pisont, István Hamar, József Sebök (C) (64' György Korsós), Ferenc Horváth (5' Miklós Fehér). (Coach: Bertalan Bicskei (HUN)).
Goals: Hungary: 0-1 Pál Dárdai (58'), 0-2 Béla Illés (85' penalty), 0-3 István Pisont (87'), 0-4 Miklós Fehér (90').
Referee: Stéphane Bré (FRA)   Attendance: 11.400

10-10-1998   Rheinpark Stadion, Vaduz: Liechtenstein – Slovakia   0-4 (0-3)
Liechtenstein: Martin Oehri, Mario Frick (C) (YC35), Daniel Hasler, Michael Stocklasa, Martin Telser, Christof Ritter, Patrick Hefti (YC75) (77' Hansjörg Lingg), Harald Zech, Thomas Hanselmann, Rolf Oehri (46' Jürgen Ospelt), Modestus Haas (33' Martin Stocklasa). (Coach: Ralf Loose (GER)).
Slovakia: Alexander Vencel, Stanislav Varga (65' Milan Timko), Marek Spilár, Dusan Tittel, Vladimír Kinder (31' Ivan Kozák), Lubomír Moravcik (C), Robert Tomaschek, Peter Dubovsky, Miroslav Sovic, Martin Fabus (61' Tibor Jancula), Jozef Majoros. (Coach: Jozef Jankech (SVK)).
Goals: Slovakia: 0-1 Miroslav Sovic (3'), 0-2 Peter Dubovsky (13'), 0-3 Robert Tomaschek (36'), 0-4 Robert Tomaschek (61').
Referee: Vladimir Antonov (MOL)   Attendance: 1.850

10-10-1998   Estádio das Antas, Porto: Portugal – Romania   0-1 (0-0)
Portugal: VÍTOR Manuel Martins BAÍA (C), FERNANDO Manuel Silva COUTO (YC90), JORGE Paulo COSTA Almeida (YC90), DIMAS Manuel Marques Teixeira, ABEL Luís da Silva Costa XAVIER (85' Daniel da Cruz Carvalho "DANI"), LUÍS Filipe Madeira Caeiro FIGO, RUI Manuel César COSTA, PAULO Jorge Gomes BENTO (70' SÉRGIO Paulo Marceneiro CONCEIÇÃO), João Paulo Maio dos "PAULINHO" SANTOS, JOÃO Manuel Vieira PINTO (77' NUNO "GOMES" Miguel Soares Pereira Ribeiro), Ricardo Manuel Andrade Silva SÁ PINTO. (Coach: HUMBERTO Manuel de Jesus COELHO (POR)).
Romania: Bogdan Stelea, Iulian Filipescu, Dan Petrescu (83' Cosmin Contra), Liviu Ciobotariu, Catalin Munteanu (62' Ioan Lupescu), Florentin Petre, Gheorghe Popescu (C), Constantin Galca, Dorinel Munteanu (YC60), Laurentiu Rosu (YC,YC65), Viorel Moldovan (89' Dumitru Mihalcea). (Coach: Victor Piturca (ROM)).
Goal: Romania: 0-1 Dorinel Munteanu (90').
Referee: Helmut Krug (GER)   Attendance: 37.354

14-10-1998   Rheinpark Stadion, Vaduz: Liechtenstein – Azerbaijan   2-1 (0-0)
Liechtenstein: Peter Jehle, Mario Frick (C), Martin Stocklasa, Daniel Hasler, Michael Stocklasa, Martin Telser, Christof Ritter, Harald Zech, Hansjörg Lingg, Herbert Bicker (67' Jürgen Ospelt), Thomas Beck (74' Ronny Büchel). (Coach: Ralf Loose (GER)).
Azerbaijan: Aleksandr Zhidkov (YC44), Emin Agayev, Ilham Yadullayev (YC47), Deni Gaysumov, Makhmud Gurbanov (25' Nazim Suleymanov), Aslan Kerimov, Rasim Abusov (C) (YC72) (76' Rufat Guliyev), Vidadi Rzayev, Elshan Gambarov (50' Ilkham Mammadov), Gurban Gurbanov, Narvik Sirkhayev. (Coach: Vagif Sadykov (AZE)).
Goals: Liechtenstein: 1-0 Mario Frick (47'), 2-0 Martin Telser (49').
Azerbaijan: 2-1 Gurban Gurbanov (59').
Referee: Herbert Barr (NIR)   Attendance: 1.450

14 10 1998   Népstadion, Budapest: Hungary – Romania   1-1 (0-0)
Hungary: Gábor Király, Vilmos Sebök (YC49), János Mátyus, János Hrutka, Pál Dárdai (YC89), Csaba Fehér, Béla Illés (C), István Pisont, István Hamar (89' Norbert Tóth), Gábor Egressy (78' Krisztián Lisztes), Miklós Fehér (75' Ferenc Hámori (YC87,YC87)). (Coach: Bertalan Bicskei (HUN)).
Romania: Bogdan Stelea, Iulian Filipescu (YC59,YC90), Dan Petrescu, Liviu Ciobotariu, Florentin Petre (69' Denis Serban), Ioan Lupescu, Gheorghe Popescu (C) (YC87), Constantin Galca, Dorinel Munteanu, Viorel Moldovan (85' Dumitru Mihalcea), Gheorghe Craioveanu (75' Catalin Munteanu). (Coach: Victor Piturca (ROM)).
Goals: Hungary: 1-1 János Hrutka (82').
Romania: 0-1 Viorel Moldovan (50').
Referee: Kim Milton Nielsen (DEN)   Attendance: 25.000

14-10-1998   Stadión Tehelné pole, Bratislava: Slovakia – Portugal   0-3 (0-2)
Slovakia: Alexander Vencel, Stanislav Varga (YC48), Marek Spilár, Dusan Tittel (YC54), Vladimír Kinder (46' Ivan Kozák), Lubomír Moravcik (C) (YC60), Robert Tomaschek (YC78), Peter Dubovsky, Miroslav Sovic (YC33) (81' Attila Pinte), Martin Fabus (57' Szilárd Németh), Jozef Majoros. (Coach: Jozef Jankech (SVK)).
Portugal: VÍTOR Manuel Martins BAÍA (C), FERNANDO Manuel Silva COUTO, JORGE Paulo COSTA Almeida (YC82), DIMAS Manuel Marques Teixeira, ABEL Luís da Silva Costa XAVIER, LUÍS Filipe Madeira Caeiro FIGO (89' NUNO "CAPUCHO" Fernando Gonçalves Rocha), RUI Manuel César COSTA (67' Francisco José Rodrigues da Costa "COSTINHA"), PAULO Jorge Gomes BENTO, João Paulo Maio dos "PAULINHO" SANTOS, JOÃO Manuel Vieira PINTO (46' SÉRGIO Paulo Marceneiro CONCEIÇÃO), Ricardo Manuel Andrade Silva SÁ PINTO. (Coach: HUMBERTO Manuel de Jesus COELHO (POR)).
Goals: Portugal: 0-1 JOÃO Manuel Vieira PINTO (17'), 0-2 JOÃO Manuel Vieira PINTO (30'), 0-3 ABEL Luís da Silva Costa XAVIER (70').
Referee: Oguz Sarvan (TUR)   Attendance: 22.059

26-03-1999   Estádio Dom Afonso Henriques, Guimarães: Portugal – Azerbaijan   7-0 (2-0)
Portugal: VÍTOR Manuel Martins BAÍA (C) (77' PEDRO Manuel ESPINHA Ferreira), FERNANDO Manuel Silva COUTO, CARLOS Alberto de Oliveira SECRETÁRIO, DIMAS Manuel Marques Teixeira, PAULO Sérgio Braga MADEIRA, LUÍS Filipe Madeira Caeiro FIGO (72' Pedro Miguel Carreiro Resendes "PAULETA"), RUI Manuel César COSTA (82' PEDRO Alexandre dos Santos BARBOSA), PAULO Manuel Carvalho de SOUSA, SÉRGIO Paulo Marceneiro CONCEIÇÃO, JOÃO Manuel Vieira PINTO, Ricardo Manuel Andrade Silva SÁ PINTO. (Coach: HUMBERTO Manuel de Jesus COELHO (POR)).
Azerbaijan: Dmitriy Kramarenko (YC41), Emin Agayev, Arif Asadov (YC9), Tarlan Akhmedov (C) (YC30), Aleksey Stukas, Rasim Abusov (YC,YC67), Bakhtiyar Musayev (62' Vidadi Rzayev), Vyacheslav Lychkin, Elshan Gambarov (71' Vadim Vasilyev), Gurban Gurbanov, Narvik Sirkhayev. (Coach: Ahmad Latifovich Alasgarov (AZE)).
Goals: Portugal: 1-0 Ricardo Manuel Andrade Silva SÁ PINTO (28'), 2-0 JOÃO Manuel Vieira PINTO (37'), 3-0 PAULO Sérgio Braga MADEIRA (68'), 4-0 JOÃO Manuel Vieira PINTO (71'), 5-0 SÉRGIO Paulo Marceneiro CONCEIÇÃO (75'), 6-0 Pedro Miguel Carreiro Resendes "PAULETA" (82'), 7-0 Pedro Miguel Carreiro Resendes "PAULETA" (84').
Referee: Jacek Granat (POL)   Attendance: 14.650

27-03-1999   Üllöi úti Stadion, Budapest: Hungary – Liechtenstein   5-0 (3-0)
Hungary: Gábor Király, Vilmos Sebők, János Mátyus, János Hrutka (77' József Somogyi), Norbert Tóth (75' István Hamar), György Korsós, Gábor Halmai, Béla Illés (C) (YC66), István Pisont, József Sebők (70' Tibor Dombi), Miklós Fehér. (Coach: Bertalan Bicskei (HUN)).
Liechtenstein: Peter Jehle (YC88), Mario Frick (C), Martin Stocklasa (YC40), Daniel Hasler (YC50), Michael Stocklasa, Martin Telser, Christof Ritter, Thomas Hanselmann (46' Patrick Hefti), Hansjörg Lingg (YC41) (74' Patrick Burgmeier), Albert Wohlwend, Matthias Beck (76' Jürgen Ospelt). (Coach: Ralf Loose (GER)).
Goals: Hungary: 1-0 József Sebők (16'), 2-0 Vilmos Sebők (33'), 3-0 Vilmos Sebők (41'), 4-0 Béla Illés (73'), 5-0 Vilmos Sebők (85' penalty).
Referee: Costas Kapitanis (CYP)   Attendance: 9.534

27-03-1999   Stadionul National, Bucharest: Romania – Slovakia   0-0
Romania: Bogdan Stelea, Dan Petrescu, Florin Batranu (YC28), Catalin Munteanu (68' Ioan Lupescu), Florentin Petre, Gheorghe Popescu (C), Constantin Galca (YC12), Dorinel Munteanu, Laurentiu Rosa, Viorel Moldovan (72' Gheorghe Craioveanu), Adrian Ilie (YC50). (Coach: Victor Piturca (ROM)).
Slovakia: Miroslav König, Stanislav Varga, Roman Kratochvil, Vladimír Labant (YC38,YC80), Marián Zeman, Igor Balis, Tibor Zátek (76' Peter Dzúrik), Miroslav Karhan, Robert Tomaschek (C), Peter Dubovsky (86' Marián Suchancok), Jozef Majoros (70' Peter Slicho). (Coach: Jozef Adamec (SVK)).
Referee: Graham Peter Barber (ENG)   Attendance: 9.750

31-03-1999   Tofiq Bahramov Stadium, Baku: Azerbaijan – Romania   0-1 (0-0)
Azerbaijan: Huseyn Mahammadov, Emin Agayev (77' Rufat Guliyev), Arif Asadov, Tarlan Akhmedov (C), Vladimir Poshekhontsev, Zaur Tagizade (68' Elshan Gambarov), Makhmud Gurbanov (65' Vidadi Rzayev), Aslan Kerimov, Vyacheslav Lychkin, Gurban Gurbanov, Narvik Sirkhayev. (Coach: Ahmad Latifovich Alasgarov (AZE)).
Romania: Bogdan Lobont, Iulian Filipescu (YC79), Liviu Ciobotariu, Florentin Petre, Ioan Lupescu (C), Constantin Galca, Dorinel Munteanu, Cosmin Contra, Laurentiu Rosa (74' Daniel Florea), Viorel Moldovan, Gheorghe Craioveanu (89' Dumitru Mihalcea). (Coach: Victor Piturca (ROM)).
Goal: Romania: 0-1 Florentin Petre (49').
Referee: Roelof Luinge (HOL)   Attendance: 30.000

31-03-1999   Stadión Tehelné pole, Bratislava: Slovakia – Hungary   0-0
Slovakia: Miroslav König, Stanislav Varga, Roman Kratochvil, Marián Zeman (13' Peter Dzúrik (YC57)), Igor Balis, Tibor Zátek (79' Norbert Hrncár), Miroslav Karhan (YC52), Robert Tomaschek (C), Peter Dubovsky, Attila Pinte (82' Peter Slicho), Jozef Majoros. (Coach: Jozef Adamec (SVK)).
Hungary: Gábor Király, Vilmos Sebök, János Mátyus, János Hrutka, Norbert Tóth (YC90), György Korsós, Gábor Halmai, Béla Illés (C), István Pisont, József Sebök (YC19) (55' Tibor Dombi (YC82)), Miklós Fehér (63' István Hamar). (Coach: Bertalan Bicskei (HUN)).
Referee: Claude Colombo (FRA)   Attendance: 19.452

31-03-1999   Rheinpark Stadion, Vaduz: Liechtenstein – Portugal   0-5 (0-1)
Liechtenstein: Peter Jehle, Mario Frick (C), Daniel Hasler, Michael Stocklasa (64' Matthias Beck), Martin Telser, Christof Ritter (YC26) (83' Jürgen Ospelt), Patrick Hefti, Harald Zech, Hansjörg Lingg, Christoph Frick, Albert Wohlwend (82' Patrick Burgmeier). (Coach: Ralf Loose (GER)).
Portugal: VÍTOR Manuel Martins BAÍA (C), FERNANDO Manuel Silva COUTO, CARLOS Alberto de Oliveira SECRETÁRIO, DIMAS Manuel Marques Teixeira, PAULO Sérgio Braga MADEIRA, LUÍS Filipe Madeira Caeiro FIGO, RUI Manuel César COSTA, PAULO Manuel Carvalho de SOUSA, SÉRGIO Paulo Marceneiro CONCEIÇÃO (89' NUNO "CAPUCHO" Fernando Gonçalves Rocha), JOÃO Manuel Vieira PINTO (75' NUNO "GOMES" Miguel Soares Pereira Ribeiro), Ricardo Manuel Andrade Silva SÁ PINTO (60' Pedro Miguel Carreiro Resendes "PAULETA"). (Coach: HUMBERTO Manuel de Jesus COELHO (POR)).
Goals: Portugal: 0-1 RUI Manuel César COSTA (16' penalty), 0-2 LUÍS Filipe Madeira Caeiro FIGO (49'), 0-3 PAULO Sérgio Braga MADEIRA (53'), 0-4 PAULO Sérgio Braga MADEIRA (59'), 0-5 RUI Manuel César COSTA (78').
Referee: Gylfi Thór Orrason (ISL)   Attendance: 3.548

05-06-1999   Tofiq Bahramov Stadium, Baku: Azerbaijan – Liechtenstein   4-0 (2-0)
Azerbaijan: Dmitriy Kramarenko, Emin Agayev, Ilham Yadullayev, Tarlan Akhmedov (C), Zaur Tagizade (YC19) (67' Mirbaghir Isayev), Makhmud Gurbanov, Aslan Kerimov, Vyacheslav Lychkin (74' Aleksey Stukas), Gurban Gurbanov, Narvik Sirkhayev, Vadim Vasilyev (60' Elmir Khankishiyev). (Coach: Ahmad Latifovich Alasgarov (AZE)).
Liechtenstein: Peter Jehle, Martin Stocklasa (YC86), Daniel Hasler (C), Michael Stocklasa (73' Albert Wohlwend), Martin Telser, Christof Ritter, Harald Zech, Hansjörg Lingg, Christoph Frick (YC42), Herbert Bicker (58' Matthias Beck), Harald Benz (46' Thomas Beck). (Coach: Ralf Loose (GER)).
Goals: Azerbaijan: 1-0 Gurban Gurbanov (15'), 2-0 Vyacheslav Lychkin (41'), 3-0 Zaur Tagizade (60'), 4-0 Mirbaghir Isayev (73').
Referee: Knud Stadsgaard (DEN)   Attendance: 8.500

05-06-1999   Stadionul Steaua, Bucharest: Romania – Hungary   2-0 (2-0)
Romania: Bogdan Lobont, Iulian Filipescu, Dan Petrescu, Stefan Nanu, Florentin Petre, Gheorghe Popescu, Constantin Galca, Dorinel Munteanu, Gheorghe Hagi (C) (46' Ioan Lupescu), Viorel Moldovan (61' Ioan Ganea), Adrian Ilie (YC55) (88' Gheorghe Craioveanu). (Coach: Victor Piturca (ROM)).
Hungary: Gábor Király, Vilmos Sebök, János Mátyus, János Hrutka, Pál Dárdai, György Korsós, Gábor Halmai (YC45), Béla Illés (C) (82' Sándor Preisinger), Gábor Egressy, József Sebök (76' Miklós Herczeg), Miklós Fehér (46' István Pisont). (Coach: Bertalan Bicskei (HUN)).
Goals: Romania: 1-0 Adrian Ilie (2'), 2-0 Dorinel Munteanu (15').
Referee: Rune Pedersen (NOR)   Attendance: 23.000

05-06-1999   Estádio José de Alvalade, Lisbon: Portugal – Slovakia   1-0 (0-0)
Portugal: VÍTOR Manuel Martins BAÍA (C), FERNANDO Manuel Silva COUTO, DIMAS Manuel Marques Teixeira, PAULO Sérgio Braga MADEIRA, ABEL Luís da Silva Costa XAVIER (32' SÉRGIO Paulo Marceneiro CONCEIÇÃO), LUÍS Filipe Madeira Caeiro FIGO (90' PEDRO Alexandre dos Santos BARBOSA), RUI Manuel César COSTA, PAULO Jorge Gomes BENTO, PAULO Manuel Carvalho de SOUSA, JOÃO Manuel Vieira PINTO (60' NUNO "CAPUCHO" Fernando Gonçalves Rocha), Ricardo Manuel Andrade Silva SÁ PINTO (YC89). (Coach: HUMBERTO Manuel de Jesus COELHO (POR)).
Slovakia: Miroslav König, Stanislav Varga, Roman Kratochvil, Vladimír Labant, Milan Timko (YC41), Miroslav Karhan, Robert Tomaschek (C) (YC72), Peter Dubovsky, Vladislav Zvara (31' Jozef Valachovic), Attila Pinte (64' Peter Slicho), Jozef Majoros (83' Vladimír Kozuch). (Coach: Jozef Adamec (SVK)).
Goal: Portugal: 1-0 NUNO "CAPUCHO" Fernando Gonçalves Rocha (62').
Referee: Claus Bo Larsen (DEN)   Attendance: 20.300

09-06-1999   Stadionul Steaua, Bucharest: Romania – Azerbaijan   4-0 (2-0)
Romania: Bogdan Lobont, Iulian Filipescu, Dan Petrescu, Stefan Nanu, Florentin Petre (67' Viorel Moldovan), Ioan Lupescu, Gheorghe Popescu (C), Constantin Galca, Dorinel Munteanu, Ioan Ganea (61' Gheorghe Craioveanu), Ion Vladoiu (YC54) (79' Laurentiu Rosu). (Coach: Victor Piturca (ROM)).
Azerbaijan: Dmitriy Kramarenko (YC69), Emin Agayev (70' Igor Getman), Ilham Yadullayev (YC44), Tarlan Akhmedov (C), Vladimir Poshekhontsev, Zaur Tagizade, Makhmud Gurbanov (61' Bakhtiyar Musayev), Aslan Kerimov, Vyacheslav Lychkin (81' Vadim Vasilyev), Gurban Gurbanov, Narvik Sirkhayev (YC29). (Coach: Ahmad Latifovich Alasgarov (AZE)).
Goals: Romania: 1-0 Ioan Ganea (36'), 2-0 Dorinel Munteanu (44' penalty), 3-0 Ion Vladoiu (49'), 4-0 Laurentiu Rosu (89').
Referee: Zeljko Siric (CRO)   Attendance: 5.200

09-06-1999   ETO Park, Györ: Hungary – Slovakia   0-1 (0-0)
Hungary: Gábor Király, Vilmos Sebök, János Mátyus (YC29), János Hrutka (YC37), Pál Dárdai, György Korsós, Gábor Halmai (73' István Pisont), Béla Illés (C), Gábor Egressy (60' Tibor Dombi), József Somogyi (78' Sándor Preisinger), József Sebök (YC65). (Coach: Bertalan Bicskei (HUN)).
Slovakia: Miroslav König, Stanislav Varga (C), Roman Kratochvil, Jozef Valachovic, Vladimír Labant, Milan Timko, Miroslav Karhan, Péter Németh (YC71), Vladislav Zvara (81' Peter Dzúrik), Attila Pinte, Martin Fabus. (Coach: Jozef Adamec (SVK)).
Goal: Slovakia: 0-1 Martin Fabus (53').
Referee: Manuel Díaz Vega (ESP)   Attendance: 18.300

09-06-1999   Estádio Municipal de Coimbra, Coimbra: Portugal – Liechtenstein 8-0 (3-0)
Portugal: VÍTOR Manuel Martins BAÍA (C), FERNANDO Manuel Silva COUTO, CARLOS Alberto de Oliveira SECRETÁRIO (16' NUNO "CAPUCHO" Fernando Gonçalves Rocha), DIMAS Manuel Marques Teixeira, PAULO Sérgio Braga MADEIRA, LUÍS Filipe Madeira Caeiro FIGO, RUI Manuel César COSTA, PAULO Manuel Carvalho de SOUSA (63' PEDRO Alexandre dos Santos BARBOSA), SÉRGIO Paulo Marceneiro CONCEIÇÃO, JOÃO Manuel Vieira PINTO, Ricardo Manuel Andrade Silva SÁ PINTO. (Coach: HUMBERTO Manuel de Jesus COELHO (POR)).
Liechtenstein: Peter Jehle, Daniel Hasler (C), Michael Stocklasa (66' Patrick Burgmeier), Martin Telser (75' Ronny Büchel), Christof Ritter, Daniel Telser (53' Hansjörg Lingg), Harald Zech, Jürgen Ospelt, Herbert Bicker, Albert Wohlwend, Thomas Beck. (Coach: Ralf Loose (GER)).
Goals: Portugal: 1-0 Ricardo Manuel Andrade Silva SÁ PINTO (29'), 2-0 JOÃO Manuel Vieira PINTO (41'), 3-0 Ricardo Manuel Andrade Silva SÁ PINTO (45'), 4-0 Ricardo Manuel Andrade Silva SÁ PINTO (52'), 5-0 JOÃO Manuel Vieira PINTO (60'), 6-0 JOÃO Manuel Vieira PINTO (68'), 7-0 RUI Manuel César COSTA (81'), 8-0 RUI Manuel César COSTA (90' penalty).
Referee: Dietmar Drabek (AUT)   Attendance: 14.020

04-09-1999   Tofiq Bahramov Stadium, Baku: Azerbaijan – Portugal 1-1 (0-0)
Azerbaijan: Dmitriy Kramarenko (YC86), Emin Agayev (YC36), Kamal Guliyev (YC58), Adaim Niftaliyev, Tarlan Akhmedov (C), Vladimir Poshekhontsev, Zaur Tagizade (YC84,YC84), Bakhtiyar Musayev (YC12) (58' Makhmud Gurbanov), Vyacheslav Lychkin (87' Aleksey Stukas), Igor Getman, Vadim Vasilyev (YC26) (55' Elshan Gambarov). (Coach: Ahmad Latifovich Alasgarov (AZE)).
Portugal: VÍTOR Manuel Martins BAÍA (C), FERNANDO Manuel Silva COUTO, CARLOS Alberto de Oliveira SECRETÁRIO (YC83), DIMAS Manuel Marques Teixeira (YC42), PAULO Sérgio Braga MADEIRA, LUÍS Filipe Madeira Caeiro FIGO, RUI Manuel César COSTA, PAULO Jorge Gomes BENTO (29' Pedro Miguel Carreiro Resendes "PAULETA"), PAULO Manuel Carvalho de SOUSA (68' NUNO "CAPUCHO" Fernando Gonçalves Rocha (YC71)), JOÃO Manuel Vieira PINTO, Ricardo Manuel Andrade Silva SÁ PINTO (46' SÉRGIO Paulo Marceneiro CONCEIÇÃO). (Coach: HUMBERTO Manuel de Jesus COELHO (POR)).
Goals: Azerbaijan: 1-0 Zaur Tagizade (51').
Portugal: 1-1 LUÍS Filipe Madeira Caeiro FIGO (90').
Referee: Dermot J.Gallagher (ENG)   Attendance: 8.000
(The match was originally played on 3rd September 1999 but was abandoned following floodlight failure)

04-09-1999   Rheinpark Stadion, Vaduz: Liechtenstein – Hungary 0-0
Liechtenstein: Peter Jehle, Mario Frick (C) (90' Matthias Beck), Martin Stocklasa, Daniel Hasler, Michael Stocklasa, Martin Telser (66' Christof Ritter), Patrick Hefti (YC73), Harald Zech, Jürgen Ospelt, Frédéric Gigon, Thomas Beck (82' Herbert Bicker). (Coach: Ralf Loose (GER)).
Hungary: Gábor Király, Vilmos Sebök, János Mátyus, Pál Dárdai, Tibor Dombi (60' Thomas Sowunmi (YC74)), György Korsós, Gábor Halmai, Béla Illés (C), Gábor Egressy, Miklós Fehér (46' Miklós Lendvai), Ferenc Horváth (75' Miklós Herczeg). (Coach: Bertalan Bicskei (HUN)).
Referee: Sten Kaldma (EST)   Attendance: 1.650

04-09-1999   Stadión Tehelné pole, Bratislava: Slovakia – Romania   1-5 (1-2)
Slovakia: Miroslav König, Stanislav Varga (C), Roman Kratochvil (73' Jaroslav Hrabal), Jozef Valachovic, Vladimír Labant, Igor Balis (67' Tibor Jancula), Miroslav Karhan, Vladimír Janocko, Péter Németh, Szilárd Németh, Martin Fabus (80' Marek Ujlaky). (Coach: Jozef Adamec (SVK)).
Romania: Bogdan Stelea, Iulian Filipescu, Dan Petrescu, Liviu Ciobotariu, Gheorghe Popescu, Constantin Galca, Ioan Sabau (82' Ovidiu Stinga), Dorinel Munteanu, Gheorghe Hagi (C) (75' Ioan Lupescu), Ioan Ganea (57' Viorel Moldovan), Adrian Ilie. (Coach: Victor Piturca (ROM)).
Goals: Slovakia: 1-1 Vladimír Labant (21' penalty).
Romania: 0-1 Adrian Ilie (6'), 1-2 Gheorghe Hagi (29'), 1-3 Liviu Ciobotariu (65'), 1-4 Viorel Moldovan (87'), 1-5 Viorel Moldovan (90').
Referee: Graziano Cesari (ITA)   Attendance: 8.143

08-09-1999   Mestsky stadión, Dubnica nad Váhom: Slovakia – Liechtenstein   2-0 (1-0)
Slovakia: Kamil Susko, Stanislav Varga (C), Jozef Valachovic (YC16,RC37), Vladimír Labant, Igor Balis (YC81), Miroslav Karhan, Marek Ujlaky, Vladimír Janocko (40' Jaroslav Hrabal), Peter Dzúrik (YC17), Szilárd Németh (75' Vladimír Kozuch), Martin Fabus (60' Péter Németh). (Coach: Jozef Adamec (SVK)).
Liechtenstein: Peter Jehle, Mario Frick (C) (11' Marco Büchel, 55' Albert Wohlwend), Martin Stocklasa (YC40), Daniel Hasler (YC40), Michael Stocklasa, Martin Telser (YC74), Christof Ritter, Harald Zech, Jürgen Ospelt (YC24), Frédéric Gigon (YC44) (55' Matthias Beck), Thomas Beck. (Coach: Ralf Loose (GER)).
Goals: Slovakia: 1-0 Szilárd Németh (4'), 2-0 Miroslav Karhan (55').
Referee: Andreas Georgiou (CYP)   Attendance: 3.052

08-09-1999   Stadionul Steaua, Bucharest: Romania – Portugal   1-1 (1-1)
Romania: Bogdan Stelea, Iulian Filipescu (YC40), Dan Petrescu (YC45) (46' Stefan Nanu (YC76)), Liviu Ciobotariu, Gheorghe Popescu, Constantin Galca, Ioan Sabau, Dorinel Munteanu (YC21), Gheorghe Hagi (C) (YC25), Viorel Moldovan (68' Ioan Lupescu), Adrian Ilie (YC86) (86' Ioan Ganea). (Coach: Victor Piturca (ROM)).
Portugal: VÍTOR Manuel Martins BAÍA (C), FERNANDO Manuel Silva COUTO (YC53), RUI Fernando da Silva Calapez Pereira BENTO, DIMAS Manuel Marques Teixeira, PAULO Sérgio Braga MADEIRA, LUÍS Filipe Madeira Caeiro FIGO, RUI Manuel César COSTA, PAULO Jorge Gomes BENTO, PAULO Manuel Carvalho de SOUSA (68' SÉRGIO Paulo Marceneiro CONCEIÇÃO), JOÃO Manuel Vieira PINTO (YC4) (81' Pedro Miguel Carreiro Resendes "PAULETA"), Ricardo Manuel Andrade Silva SÁ PINTO. (Coach: HUMBERTO Manuel de Jesus COELHO (POR)).
Goals: Romania: 1-0 Gheorghe Hagi (37').
Portugal: 1-1 LUÍS Filipe Madeira Caeiro FIGO (45').
Referee: Hartmut Strampe (GER)   Attendance: 23.000

08-09-1999   Üllöi úti Stadion, Budapest: Hungary – Azerbaijan   3-0 (1-0)
Hungary: Gábor Király, Vilmos Sebök (YC49), János Mátyus, János Hrutka, György Korsós (YC90), Gábor Halmai, Béla Illés (C) (YC19), Miklós Lendvai, Gábor Egressy, Thomas Sowunmi (88' Ákos Füzi), Miklós Herczeg (73' Ferenc Horváth). (Coach: Bertalan Bicskei (HUN)).
Azerbaijan: Jahangir Hasanzade, Ilham Yadullayev, Kamal Guliyev (YC49), Arif Asadov, Adaim Niftaliyev, Vladimir Poshekhontsev, Igor Getman, Aslan Kerimov (59' Elshan Gambarov), Bakhtiyar Musayev (C), Vyacheslav Lychkin (67' Aleksey Stukas), Vadim Vasilyev (90' Farrukh Ismayilov). (Coach: Ahmad Latifovich Alasgarov (AZE)).
Goals: Hungary: 1-0 Vilmos Sebök (28'), 2-0 Gábor Egressy (51'), 3-0 Thomas Sowunmi (54').
Referee: Saso Lazarevski (MCD)   Attendance: 2.910

09-10-1999   Tofiq Bahramov Stadium, Baku: Azerbaijan – Slovakia   0-1 (0-0)
Azerbaijan: Dmitriy Kramarenko, Emin Agayev (79' Aslan Kerimov), Ilham Yadullayev, Adaim Niftaliyev, Mirbaghir Isayev (56' Farrukh Ismayilov), Tarlan Akhmedov (C), Vladimir Poshekhontsev (YC73), Igor Getman, Bakhtiyar Musayev, Elshan Gambarov (46' Vyacheslav Lychkin (YC90)), Vadim Vasilyev. (Coach: Ahmad Latifovich Alasgarov (AZE)).
Slovakia: Kamil Susko, Stanislav Varga (C) (YC77), Roman Kratochvil, Vladimír Labant (84' Attila Pinte), Milan Timko, Ivan Kozák, Marián Suchancok, Miroslav Karhan (86' Marián Zeman), Vladimír Janocko (90' Vladimír Kozuch), Péter Németh (YC46), Martin Fabus. (Coach: Jozef Adamec (SVK)).
Goal: Slovakia: 0-1 Vladimír Labant (71').
Referee: Kyros Vassaras (GRE)   Attendance: 6.000

09-10-1999   Rheinpark Stadion, Vaduz: Liechtenstein – Romania   0-3 (0-1)
Liechtenstein: Peter Jehle, Mario Frick (C) (YC53) (89' Matthias Beck), Martin Stocklasa (YC68), Martin Telser (75' Herbert Bicker), Christof Ritter, Patrick Hefti (YC90), Harald Zech, Jürgen Ospelt, Christoph Frick (YC42) (88' Albert Wohlwend), Frédéric Gigon, Thomas Beck (RC53). (Coach: Ralf Loose (GER)).
Romania: Bogdan Stelea, Dan Petrescu, Liviu Ciobotariu, Stefan Nanu, Florentin Petre, Gheorghe Popescu, Constantin Galca (75' Ioan Lupescu), Gheorghe Hagi (C) (77' Ovidiu Stinga), Laurentiu Rosu, Viorel Moldovan (YC59) (62' Ioan Ganea), Adrian Ilie. (Coach: Victor Piturca (ROM)).
Goals: Romania: 0-1 Laurentiu Rosu (26'), 0-2 Ioan Ganea (65'), 0-3 Ioan Ganea (75').
Referee: Andrei Butenko (RUS)   Attendance: 2.200

09-10-1999   Estádio da Luz, Lisbon: Portugal – Hungary   3-0 (2-0)
Portugal: VÍTOR Manuel Martins BAÍA (C), JORGE Paulo COSTA Almeida, CARLOS Alberto de Oliveira SECRETÁRIO (46' ABEL Luís da Silva Costa XAVIER), DIMAS Manuel Marques Teixeira, PAULO Sérgio Braga MADEIRA, LUÍS Filipe Madeira Caeiro FIGO, RUI Manuel César COSTA (82' PAULO Jorge Gomes BENTO), PAULO Manuel Carvalho de SOUSA, SÉRGIO Paulo Marceneiro CONCEIÇÃO, Pedro Miguel Carreiro Resendes "PAULETA" (YC25,YC42), JOÃO Manuel Vieira PINTO (89' Ricardo Manuel Andrade Silva SÁ PINTO). (Coach: HUMBERTO Manuel de Jesus COELHO (POR)).
Hungary: Gábor Király, Attila Dragóner (YC74), János Mátyus, Pál Lakos, György Korsós, Gábor Halmai (C), Miklós Lendvai, István Pisont (25' Pál Dárdai), Gábor Egressy, Thomas Sowunmi (82' Zoltán Kovács), Ferenc Horváth (75' Miklós Herczeg (YC88)). (Coach: Bertalan Bicskei (HUN)).
Goals: Portugal: 1-0 RUI Manuel César COSTA (15' penalty), 2-0 JOÃO Manuel Vieira PINTO (17'), 3-0 ABEL Luís da Silva Costa XAVIER (58').
Referee: Kim Milton Nielsen (DEN)   Attendance: 56.000

GROUP 8

05-09-1998	Dublin	Republic of Ireland – Croatia	2-0 (2-0)
06-09-1998	Skopje	Macedonia – Malta	4-0 (1-0)
10-10-1998	Ta'Qali	Malta – Croatia	1-4 (1-0)
14-10-1998	Zagreb	Croatia – Macedonia	3-2 (2-1)
14-10-1998	Dublin	Republic of Ireland – Malta	5-0 (2-0)
18-11-1998	Ta'Qali	Malta – Macedonia	1-2 (0-0)
18-11-1998	Belgrade	Yugoslavia – Republic of Ireland	1-0 (0-0)
10-02-1999	Ta'Qali	Malta – Yugoslavia	0-3 (0-1)
05-06-1999	Skopje	Macedonia – Croatia	1-1 (0-1)
08-06-1999	Thessaloniki	Yugoslavia – Malta	4-1 (1-1)
09-06-1999	Dublin	Republic of Ireland – Macedonia	1-0 (0-0)
18-08-1999	Belgrade	Yugoslavia – Croatia	0-0
21-08-1999	Zagreb	Croatia – Malta	2-1 (1-0)
01-09-1999	Dublin	Republic of Ireland – Yugoslavia	2-1 (0-0)
04-09-1999	Zagreb	Croatia – Republic of Ireland	1-0 (0-0)
05-09-1999	Belgrade	Yugoslavia – Macedonia	3-1 (1-0)
08-09-1999	Skopje	Macedonia – Yugoslavia	2-4 (0-4)
08-09-1999	Ta'Qali	Malta – Republic of Ireland	2-3 (0-2)
09-10-1999	Zagreb	Croatia – Yugoslavia	2-2 (1-2)
09-10-1999	Skopje	Macedonia – Republic of Ireland	1-1 (0-1)

FINAL STANDING

Pos	Team	Pld	W	D	L	GF	GA	GD	Pts
1	*Yugoslavia*	8	5	2	1	18	8	+10	17
2	*Republic of Ireland*	8	5	1	2	14	6	+8	16
3	Croatia	8	4	3	1	13	9	+4	15
4	Macedonia	8	2	2	4	13	14	-1	8
5	Malta	8	0	0	8	6	27	-21	0

Yugoslavia qualified for the final tournament in Belgium/Netherlands.
Republic of Ireland qualified for the second round play-offs.

05-09-1998 Lansdowne Road, Dublin: Republic of Ireland – Croatia 2-0 (2-0)
Republic of Ireland: Shay Given, Steve Staunton, Denis Irwin, Phil Babb, Kenny Cunningham, Damian Duff (46' Jeff Kenna), Jason McAteer, Mark Kinsella (YC35), Roy Keane (C), Keith O'Neill (9' Tony Cascarino), Robbie Keane (YC33) (62' Lee Carsley). (Coach: Michael Joseph (Mike) McCarthy (IRL)).
Croatia: Drazen Ladic, Dario Simic, Igor Tudor (YC32) (62' Petar Krpan), Zvonimir Soldo (77' Mario Tokic), Mario Stanic (YC65,YC70), Aljosa Asanovic, Zvonimir Boban (C), Krunoslav Jurcic (RC71), Silvio Maric (46' Igor Pamic (YC73)), Robert Jarni, Igor Stimac. (Coach: Miroslav Blazevic (CRO)).
Goals: Republic of Ireland: 1-0 Denis Irwin (4' penalty), 2-0 Roy Keane (15').
Referee: Vítor Manuel Melo Pereira (POR) Attendance: 34.000

433

06-09-1998   Gradski stadion, Skopje: Macedonia – Malta   4-0 (1-0)
Macedonia: Petar Milosevski, Goce Sedloski, Mitko Stojkovski (C) (76' Vlatko Gosev), Igor Nikolovski (72' Dzevded Sainovski), Goran Stavrevski, Milan Stojanoski (YC64) (69' Artim Shakiri), Srdjan Zaharievski, Toni Micevski (YC60), Goran Lazarevski, Viktor Trenevski, Risto Bozinov. (Coach: Gjoko Hadzhievski (MCD)).
Malta: Mario Muscat, Brian Said, Jeffrey Chetcuti (YC53), Darren Debono, David Camilleri (YC32), Antoine Zahra (74' David Carabott), Noel Turner, Carmel Busuttil (C), Joe Brincat, Jonathan Magri Overend, Gilbert Agius (67' Hubert Suda). (Coach: Josif Ilic (SRB)).
Goals: Macedonia: 1-0 Risto Bozinov (20'), 2-0 Risto Bozinov (47'), 3-0 Artim Shakiri (70'), 4-0 Artim Shakiri (76').
Referee: Jan Willem Wegereef (HOL)   Attendance: 4.000

10-10-1998   Ta'Qali National Stadium, Ta'Qali: Malta – Croatia   1-4 (1-0)
Malta: Mario Muscat, Jeffrey Chetcuti, John Buttigieg, Darren Debono, Michael Spiteri (YC90), David Camilleri, Antoine Zahra (77' Paul Sixsmith), Carmel Busuttil (C), Joe Brincat, Gilbert Agius (54' Ivan Zammit), Hubert Suda (57' Noel Turner). (Coach: Josif Ilic (SRB)).
Croatia: Drazen Ladic, Dario Simic (83' Mario Tokic), Igor Tudor, Zvonimir Soldo (YC28), Daniel Saric, Aljosa Asanovic, Zvonimir Boban (C), Silvio Maric, Robert Jarni (88' Mario Cvitanovic), Davor Suker (YC10), Jurica Vucko (16' Davor Vugrinec). (Coach: Miroslav Blazevic (CRO)).
Goals: Malta: 1-0 Hubert Suda (29' penalty).
Croatia: 1-1 Dario Simic (54'), 1-2 Davor Vugrinec (68'), 1-3 Davor Vugrinec (74'), 1-4 Davor Suker (81').
Referee: Bohdan Benedik (SVK)   Attendance: 1.573

14-10-1998   Stadion Maksimir, Zagreb: Croatia – Macedonia   3-2 (2-1)
Croatia: Drazen Ladic, Dario Simic, Igor Tudor (YC58), Zvonimir Soldo, Mario Stanic, Aljosa Asanovic (YC44) (62' Daniel Saric (YC76)), Zvonimir Boban (C), Silvio Maric, Robert Jarni, Igor Stimac (YC33) (81' Krunoslav Jurcic (YC82)), Davor Suker. (Coach: Miroslav Blazevic (CRO)).
Macedonia: Petar Milosevski, Goce Sedloski, Igor Nikolovski (78' Milan Stojanoski), Goran Stavrevski, Artim Shakiri, Srdjan Zaharievski (YC68), Toni Micevski (C) (46' Vlatko Gosev), Goran Lazarevski (YC27) (58' Risto Bozinov), Viktor Trenevski, Dzevded Sainovski, Sasa Ciric. (Coach: Gjoko Hadzhievski (MCD)).
Goals: Croatia: 1-1 Davor Suker (16'), 2-1 Zvonimir Boban (45'), 3-2 Zvonimir Boban (70').
Macedonia: 0-1 Sasa Ciric (2'), 2-2 Dzevded Sainovski (55').
Referee: Nikolai Vladislavovich Levnikov (RUS)   Attendance: 8.541

14-10-1998   Lansdowne Road, Dublin: Republic of Ireland – Malta   5-0 (2-0)
Republic of Ireland: Shay Given, Jeff Kenna, Gary Breen, Steve Staunton, Kenny Cunningham, Damian Duff, Jason McAteer (85' Mark Kennedy), Mark Kinsella, Roy Keane (C), Robbie Keane (82' Lee Carsley), Niall Quinn (73' Tony Cascarino). (Coach: Michael Joseph (Mike) McCarthy (IRL)).
Malta: Reginald Cini, Jeffrey Chetcuti, David Carabott, John Buttigieg, Darren Debono (YC81), Paul Sixsmith (77' David Camilleri), Michael Spiteri, Antoine Zahra (70' Ivan Zammit), Noel Turner, Joe Brincat (C), Hubert Suda (66' Gilbert Agius). (Coach: Josif Ilic (SRB)).
Goals: Republic of Ireland: 1-0 Robbie Keane (17'), 2-0 Robbie Keane (19'), 3-0 Roy Keane (54'), 4-0 Niall Quinn (62'), 5-0 Gary Breen (82').
Referee: Roy Helge Olsen (NOR)   Attendance: 34.500

18-11-1998   Ta'Qali National Stadium, Ta'Qali: Malta – Macedonia   1-2 (0-0)
Malta: Mario Muscat, John Buttigieg, Darren Debono (YC48), Paul Sixsmith, Michael Spiteri, David Camilleri, Carmel Busuttil (C), Joe Brincat, Nicholas Saliba (68' Noel Turner), Michael Cutajar (60' Gilbert Agius), Chucks Nwoko (56' David Carabott). (Coach: Josif Ilic (SRB)).
Macedonia: Petar Milosevski (YC87), Goce Sedloski, Boban Babunski, Igor Nikolovski (80' Vlatko Gosev (YC84)), Goran Stavrevski (YC34), Artim Shakiri, Srdjan Zaharievski, Toni Micevski (C), Dragan Veselinovski, Dzevded Sainovski (90' Vanco Trajcev (YC89)), Risto Bozinov (65' Goran Stankovski). (Coach: Gjoko Hadzhievski (MCD)).
Goals: Malta: 1-2 Paul Sixsmith (69').
Macedonia: 0-1 Igor Nikolovski (49'), 0-2 Srdjan Zaharievski (63').
Referee: Sergei Shmolik (BLS)   Attendance: 1.295

18-11-1998   Crvena Zvezda Stadium, Belgrade: Yugoslavia – Republic of Ireland   1-0 (0-0)
Yugoslavia: Ivica Kralj, Goran Djorovic, Sinisa Mihajlovic, Miroslav Djukic (YC44), Dejan Stankovic, Vladimir Jugovic (85' Nenad Grozdic), Dragan Stojkovic (C) (46' Darko Kovacevic), Jovan Stankovic, Slavisa Jokanovic (YC48), Savo Milosevic (75' Ljubinko Drulovic), Predrag Mijatovic. (Coach: Milan Zivadinovic (SRB)).
Republic of Ireland: Shay Given, Gary Breen, Steve Staunton, Denis Irwin, Kenny Cunningham, Damian Duff, Jason McAteer (83' Keith O'Neill), Mark Kinsella, Alan McLoughlin (72' Tony Cascarino), Roy Keane (C), Niall Quinn (72' David Connolly). (Coach: Michael Joseph (Mike) McCarthy (IRL)).
Goal: Yugoslavia: 1-0 Predrag Mijatovic (64').
Referee: Karl-Erik Nilsson (SWE)   Attendance: 28.250

10-02-1999   Ta'Qali National Stadium, Ta'Qali: Malta – Yugoslavia   0-3 (0-1)
Malta: Ernest Barry, Brian Said, David Carabott, John Buttigieg (YC39), Michael Spiteri, David Camilleri (73' Paul Sixsmith), Noel Turner, Carmel Busuttil (C), Nicholas Saliba, Gilbert Agius (59' Graham Bencini), Chucks Nwoko (82' Michael Cutajar). (Coach: Josif Ilic (SRB)).
Yugoslavia: Ivica Kralj, Zoran Mirkovic (YC37), Goran Djorovic, Sinisa Mihajlovic, Miroslav Djukic, Albert Nadj, Dejan Stankovic (87' Nenad Grozdic), Jovan Stankovic (75' Djordje Tomic), Slavisa Jokanovic, Darko Kovacevic (70' Savo Milosevic), Predrag Mijatovic (C). (Coach: Milan Zivadinovic (SRB)).
Goals: Yugoslavia: 0-1 Albert Nadj (22'), 0-2 Albert Nadj (55'), 0-3 Savo Milosevic (90+1').
Referee: Pascal Garibian (FRA)   Attendance: 1.781

05-06-1999   Gradski stadion, Skopje: Macedonia – Croatia   1-1 (0-1)
Macedonia: Petar Milosevski, Boban Babunski (YC54) (61' Srdjan Zaharievski), Igor Nikolovski, Goran Stavrevski, Milan Stojanoski, Artim Shakiri (YC44), Toni Micevski (C), Viktor Trenevski (YC3) (46' Risto Bozinov), Vanco Trajcev (80' Georgi Hristov), Dzevded Sainovski, Sasa Ciric. (Coach: Gjoko Hadzhievski (MCD)).
Croatia: Drazen Ladic, Dario Simic, Goran Juric, Zvonimir Soldo, Daniel Saric (YC28), Aljosa Asanovic (87' Igor Biscan), Zvonimir Boban (C), Robert Jarni (YC85), Davor Vugrinec (64' Goran Vlaovic), Davor Suker, Alen Boksic (19' Milan Rapaic). (Coach: Miroslav Blazevic (CRO)).
Goals: Macedonia: 1-1 Georgi Hristov (81').
Croatia: 0-1 Davor Suker (19').
Referee: Hugh Dallas (SCO)   Attendance: 10.000

08-06-1999   Toumba Stadium, Thessaloniki (GRE): Yugoslavia – Malta   4-1 (1-1)
Yugoslavia: Ivica Kralj, Zoran Mirkovic, Goran Djorovic, Nisa Saveljic (YC17), Miroslav Djukic, Albert Nadj (46' Savo Milosevic), Dejan Stankovic (64' Nenad Grozdic), Dragan Stojkovic (C) (78' Ljubinko Drulovic), Slavisa Jokanovic, Darko Kovacevic, Predrag Mijatovic. (Coach: Milan Zivadinovic (SRB)).
Malta: Ernest Barry, Brian Said, Jeffrey Chetcuti (YC17), David Carabott, John Buttigieg (YC86), Richard Buhagiar (81' Michael Cutajar), Darren Debono, David Camilleri (64' Joe Brincat), Carmel Busuttil (C) (YC60), Nicholas Saliba, Chucks Nwoko (84' Stefan Sultana). (Coach: Josif Ilic (SRB)).
Goals: Yugoslavia: 1-1 Predrag Mijatovic (34'), 2-1 Savo Milosevic (49'), 3-1 Darko Kovacevic (75'), 4-1 Savo Milosevic (90').
Malta: 0-1 Nicholas Saliba (8').
Referee: Morgan Norman (SWE)   Attendance: 2.000

09-06-1999   Lansdowne Road, Dublin: Republic of Ireland – Macedonia   1-0 (0-0)
Republic of Ireland: Alan Kelly, Stephen Carr, Gary Breen, Denis Irwin, Kenny Cunningham (C), Damian Duff (62' Kevin Kilbane), Mark Kennedy, Mark Kinsella, Lee Carsley, Robbie Keane (67' Tony Cascarino), Niall Quinn (81' David Connolly). (Coach: Michael Joseph (Mike) McCarthy (IRL)).
Macedonia: Petar Milosevski, Boban Babunski, Igor Nikolovski, Goran Stavrevski, Milan Stojanoski, Artim Shakiri, Toni Micevski (C), Viktor Trenevski (77' Georgi Hristov (YC85)), Vanco Trajcev (46' Nedzmedin Memedi), Dzevded Sainovski (71' Goce Sedloski), Sasa Ciric. (Coach: Gjoko Hadzhievski (MCD)).
Goal: Republic of Ireland: 1-0 Niall Quinn (65').
Referee: Urs Meier (SUI)   Attendance: 28.108

18-08-1999   Crvena Zvezda Stadium, Belgrade, Belgrade: Yugoslavia – Croatia   0-0
Yugoslavia: Aleksandar Kocic, Zoran Mirkovic (YC21), Goran Djorovic (46' Ljubinko Drulovic), Sinisa Mihajlovic, Miroslav Djukic, Albert Nadj, Dejan Stankovic, Jovan Stankovic, Slavisa Jokanovic (YC58), Darko Kovacevic (59' Savo Milosevic), Predrag Mijatovic (C). (Coach: Vujadin Boskov (SRB)).
Croatia: Drazen Ladic, Dario Simic, Robert Kovac, Zvonimir Soldo, Mario Stanic (46' Milan Rapaic), Aljosa Asanovic, Zvonimir Boban (C) (YC3) (79' Igor Biscan), Krunoslav Jurcic (YC78), Robert Jarni (YC9), Igor Stimac, Davor Suker. (Coach: Miroslav Blazevic (CRO)).
Referee: Kim Milton Nielsen (DEN)   Attendance: 48.282

21-08-1999   Stadion Maksimir, Zagreb: Croatia – Malta   2-1 (1-0)
Croatia: Marijan Mrmic, Dario Simic, Igor Biscan (YC7), Milan Rapaic, Zvonimir Soldo, Mario Stanic (46' Goran Vlaovic (YC74)), Aljosa Asanovic, Zvonimir Boban (C) (16' Daniel Saric), Igor Stimac, Davor Suker, Josip Simic (46' Alen Boksic). (Coach: Miroslav Blazevic (CRO)).
Malta: Ernest Barry, Brian Said (YC15), David Carabott, Darren Debono, Silvio Vella, David Camilleri, Carmel Busuttil (C) (72' Ifeanyi Okonkwo), Joe Brincat (YC31), Nicholas Saliba (YC5), Gilbert Agius (83' Stefan Sultana), Chucks Nwoko (YC42) (90' Adrian Mifsud). (Coach: Josif Ilic (SRB)).
Goals: Croatia: 1-0 Mario Stanic (34'), 2-0 Zvonimir Soldo (55').
Malta: 2-1 David Carabott (60').
Referee: Atanas Uzunov (BUL)   Attendance: 20.000

01-09-1999   Lansdowne Road, Dublin: Republic of Ireland – Yugoslavia 2-1 (0-0)
Republic of Ireland: Alan Kelly, Gary Breen, Steve Staunton, Denis Irwin (65' Stephen Carr), Kenny Cunningham, Kevin Kilbane, Mark Kennedy, Mark Kinsella, Roy Keane (C) (69' Lee Carsley), Robbie Keane, Niall Quinn (78' Tony Cascarino). (Coach: Michael Joseph (Mike) McCarthy (IRL)).
Yugoslavia: Aleksandar Kocic, Drazen Bolic, Slobodan Komljenovic, Sinisa Mihajlovic (67' Nisa Saveljic), Miroslav Djukic, Albert Nadj (74' Darko Kovacevic), Dejan Stankovic, Dejan Govedarica, Dejan Savicevic (C) (52' Ljubinko Drulovic), Savo Milosevic, Predrag Mijatovic. (Coach: Vujadin Boskov (SRB)).
Goals: Republic of Ireland: 1-0 Robbie Keane (53'), 2-1 Mark Kennedy (69').
Yugoslavia: 1-1 Dejan Stankovic (59').
Referee: Pierlugi Collina (ITA)   Attendance: 31.400

04-09-1999   Stadion Maksimir, Zagreb: Croatia – Republic of Ireland 1-0 (0-0)
Croatia: Drazen Ladic, Dario Simic, Slaven Bilic (46' Tomislav Rukavina), Robert Kovac, Milan Rapaic, Zvonimir Soldo, Mario Stanic (85' Josip Simic), Aljosa Asanovic, Robert Jarni, Igor Stimac (YC86), Davor Suker (C). (Coach: Miroslav Blazevic (CRO)).
Republic of Ireland: Alan Kelly, Stephen Carr, Gary Breen, Steve Staunton (C) (YC44), Gary Kelly (73' Ian Harte), Kenny Cunningham, Damien Duff (57' Kevin Kilbane (YC66)), Mark Kinsella, Alan McLoughlin (YC51), Lee Carsley (YC37), Tony Cascarino (83' Niall Quinn). (Coach: Michael Joseph (Mike) McCarthy (IRL)).
Goal: Croatia: 1-0 Davor Suker (90+1').
Referee: Manuel Díaz Vega (ESP)   Attendance: 21.032

05-09-1999   Partizan Stadium, Belgrade: Yugoslavia – Macedonia 3-1 (1-0)
Yugoslavia: Ivica Kralj, Mladen Krstajic, Zoran Mirkovic, Nisa Saveljic (YC25), Miroslav Djukic, Dejan Stankovic (74' Dejan Govedarica), Dragan Stojkovic (66' Dejan Savicevic), Ljubinko Drulovic, Slavisa Jokanovic, Savo Milosevic (83' Darko Kovacevic (YC90)), Predrag Mijatovic. (Coach: Vujadin Boskov (SRB)).
Macedonia: Petar Milosevski, Boban Babunski, Goran Stavrevski, Zoran Jovanoski (58' Zarko Serafimovski (YC68)), Artim Shakiri, Toni Micevski (C) (52' Marjan Gerasimovski), Toni Savevski, Dragan Veselinovski, Goran Lazarevski, Georgi Hristov, Sasa Ciric (76' Nedzmedin Memedi). (Coach: Dragan Kanatlarovski (MCD)).
Goals: Yugoslavia: 1-0 Dragan Stojkovic (36'), 2-0 Dragan Stojkovic (54'), 3-1 Dejan Savicevic (77').
Macedonia: 2-1 Sasa Ciric (64' penalty).
Referee: Anders Frisk (SWE)   Attendance: 20.320

08-09-1999   Gradski stadion, Skopje: Macedonia – Yugoslavia 2-4 (0-4)
Macedonia: Petar Milosevski, Boban Babunski, Goran Stavrevski, Zoran Jovanoski (YC52), Artim Shakiri (YC53), Toni Micevski (C) (40' Zarko Serafimovski), Toni Savevski (46' Marjan Gerasimovski), Dragan Veselinovski (40' Dzevded Sainovski), Goran Lazarevski, Georgi Hristov, Sasa Ciric. (Coach: Dragan Kanatlarovski (MCD)).
Yugoslavia: Ivica Kralj, Mladen Krstajic, Zoran Mirkovic (40' Slobodan Komljenovic (YC67)), Sinisa Mihajlovic, Miroslav Djukic, Dejan Stankovic, Dragan Stojkovic (C) (46' Dejan Savicevic), Ljubinko Drulovic, Slavisa Jokanovic, Savo Milosevic (83' Darko Kovacevic), Predrag Mijatovic. (Coach: Vujadin Boskov (SRB)).
Goals: Macedonia: 1-4 Artim Shakiri (59'), 2-4 Sasa Ciric (88').
Yugoslavia: 0-1 Savo Milosevic (1'), 0-2 Boban Babunski (4' *own goal*), 0-3 Dejan Stankovic (16'), 0-4 Ljubinko Drulovic (36').
Referee: Lubos Michel (SVK)   Attendance: 13.000

08-09-1999   Ta'Qali National Stadium, Ta'Qali: Malta – Republic of Ireland   2-3 (0-2)
Malta: Ernest Barry, Brian Said (YC15), Jeffrey Chetcuti (23' Richard Buhagiar), David Carabott, John Buttigieg (30' Silvio Vella), Darren Debono, David Camilleri, Carmel Busuttil (C), Nicholas Saliba, Gilbert Agius (67' Daniel Theuma), Chucks Nwoko. (Coach: Josif Ilic (SRB)).
Republic of Ireland: Alan Kelly, Stephen Carr, Gary Breen (75' Ian Harte), Steve Staunton (C), Kenny Cunningham, Kevin Kilbane (66' Damien Duff), Mark Kennedy (54' Alan McLoughlin), Mark Kinsella, Lee Carsley, Robbie Keane, Niall Quinn. (Coach: Michael Joseph (Mike) McCarthy (IRL)).
Goals: Malta: 1-2 Brian Said (62'), 2-2 David Carabott (68' penalty).
Republic of Ireland: 0-1 Robbie Keane (13'), 0-2 Gary Breen (20'), 2-3 Steve Staunton (72').
Referee: Sorin Corpodean (ROM)   Attendance: 4.018

09-10-1999   Stadion Maksimir, Zagreb: Croatia – Yugoslavia   2-2 (1-2)
Croatia: Drazen Ladic, Igor Tudor (YC48) (82' Milan Rapaic), Goran Juric (YC87), Robert Kovac (61' Igor Biscan), Zvonimir Soldo (YC29), Mario Stanic (YC37), Aljosa Asanovic, Robert Jarni, Tomislav Rukavina, Davor Suker (C), Alen Boksic (76' Josip Simic). (Coach: Miroslav Blazevic (CRO)).
Yugoslavia: Ivica Kralj, Zoran Mirkovic (RC41), Goran Djorovic, Sinisa Mihajlovic (YC32), Miroslav Djukic, Albert Nadj (57' Ljubinko Drulovic), Dejan Stankovic, Dragan Stojkovic (C) (54' Drazen Bolic), Slavisa Jokanovic (YC36), Savo Milosevic, Predrag Mijatovic (75' Dejan Savicevic). (Coach: Vujadin Boskov (SRB)).
Goals: Croatia: 1-0 Aljosa Asanovic (20'), 2-2 Mario Stanic (47').
Yugoslavia: 1-1 Predrag Mijatovic (25'), 1-2 Dejan Stankovic (31').
Referee: José María García- Aranda Encinar (ESP)   Attendance: 38.743

09-10-1999   Gradski stadion, Skopje: Macedonia – Republic of Ireland   1-1 (0-1)
Macedonia: Antonio Filevski, Goce Sedloski, Goran Stanic (70' Srdjan Zaharievski), Boban Babunski (C), Goran Stavrevski (YC68), Milan Stojanoski (56' Argend Beqiri (YC87)), Marjan Gerasimovski, Zoran Jovanoski (78' Nedzmedin Memedi), Toni Savevski, Dzevded Sainovski (YC28), Georgi Hristov (YC89). (Coach: Dragan Kanatlarovski (MCD)).
Republic of Ireland: Alan Kelly, Gary Breen, Steve Staunton (C), Gary Kelly, Denis Irwin, Kenny Cunningham, Mark Kennedy (85' Matt Holland), Mark Kinsella (YC60), Alan McLoughlin, Robbie Keane (66' Keith O'Neill), Niall Quinn (78' Tony Cascarino). (Coach: Michael Joseph (Mike) McCarthy (IRL)).
Goals: Macedonia: 1-1 Goran Stavrevski (90').
Republic of Ireland: 0-1 Niall Quinn (18').
Referee: Juan Antonio Fernández Marín (ESP)   Attendance: 4.500

GROUP 9

04-06-1998	Tallinn	Estonia – Faroe Islands	5-0 (2-0)
19-08-1998	Sarjevo	Bosnia and Herzegovina – Faroe Islands	1-0 (0-0)
05-09-1998	Vilnius	Lithuania – Scotland	0-0
06-09-1998	Sarajevo	Bosnia and Herzegovina – Estonia	1-1 (0-1)
06-09-1998	Toftir	Faroe Islands – Czech Republic	0-1 (0-0)
10-10-1998	Sarajevo	Bosnia and Herzegovina – Czech Republic	1-3 (0-1)
10-10-1998	Vilnius	Lithuania – Faroe Islands	0-0
10-10-1998	Edinburgh	Scotland – Estonia	3-2 (0-1)
14-10-1998	Teplice	Czech Republic – Estonia	4-1 (4-0)

438

14-10-1998	Vilnius	Lithuania – Bosnia and Herzegovina	4-2 (1-1)
14-10-1998	Aberdeen	Scotland – Faroe Islands	2-1 (2-0)
27-03-1999	Teplice	Czech Republic – Lithuania	2-0 (1-0)
31-03-1999	Vilnius	Lithuania – Estonia	1-2 (0-0)
31-03-1999	Glasgow	Scotland – Czech Republic	1-2 (0-2)
05-06-1999	Sarajevo	Bosnia and Herzegovina – Lithuania	2-0 (1-0)
05-06-1999	Tallinn	Estonia – Czech Republic	0-2 (0-1)
05-06-1999	Toftir	Faroe Islands – Scotland	1-1 (0-1)
09-06-1999	Prague	Czech Republic – Scotland	3-2 (0-1)
09-06-1999	Tallinn	Estonia – Lithuania	1-2 (1-0)
09-06-1999	Toftir	Faroe Islands – Bosnia and Herzegovina	2-2 (1-1)
04-09-1999	Sarajevo	Bosnia and Heregovina – Scotland	1-2 (1-2)
04-09-1999	Tórshavn	Faroe Islands – Estonia	0-2 (0-0)
04-09-1999	Vilnius	Lithuania – Czech Republic	0-4 (0-0)
08-09-1999	Teplice	Czech Republic – Bosnia and Herzegovina	3-0 (1-0)
08-09-1999	Tallinn	Estonia – Scotland	0-0
08-09-1999	Tórshavn	Faroe Islands – Lithuania	0-1 (0-0)
05-10-1999	Glasgow	Scotland – Bosnia and Herzegovina	1-0 (1-0)
09-10-1999	Prague	Czech Republic – Faroe Islands	2-0 (1-0)
09-10-1999	Tallinn	Estonia – Bosnia and Herzegovina	1-4 (1-1)
09-10-1999	Glasgow	Scotland – Lithuania	3-0 (0-0)

FINAL STANDING

Pos	Team	Pld	W	D	L	GF	GA	GD	Pts
1	*Czech Republic*	*10*	*10*	*0*	*0*	*26*	*5*	*+21*	*30*
2	*Scotland*	*10*	*5*	*3*	*2*	*15*	*10*	*+5*	*18*
3	Bosnia and Herzegovina	10	3	2	5	14	17	-3	11
4	Lithuania	10	3	2	5	8	16	-8	11
5	Estonia	10	3	2	5	15	17	-2	11
6	Faroe Islands	10	0	3	7	4	17	-13	3

Chech Republic qualified for the final tournament in Belgium/Netherlands.
Scotland qualified for the second round play-offs.

04-06-1998   Kadrioru Stadium, Tallinn: Estonia – Faroe Islands   5-0 (2-0)
Estonia: Mart Poom, Marek Lemsalu, Kristen Viikmäe (79' Ivan O'Konnel-Bronin), Urmas Kirs (YC52), Sergei Hohlov-Simson, Martin Reim (C), Sergei Terehhov, Marko Kristal, Janek Meet, Andres Oper, Indrek Zelinski (YC30). (Coach: Teitur Thordarson (ISL)).
Faroe Islands: Jens Knudsen (RC40), Øssur Hansen (83' Henning Jarnskor), Allan Mørkøre, Jan Dam (C), Jens Kristian Hansen, Pól Thorsteinsson, Sámal Joensen, Julian Schantz Johnsson, John Petersen, Todi Jónsson (83' Uni Arge), Jan Allan Müller (40' Jákup Mikkelsen *goalkeeper*). (Coach: Allan Simonsen (DEN)).
Goals: Estonia: 1-0 Kristen Viikmäe (12'), 2-0 Martin Reim (40'), 3-0 Sergei Terehhov (75'), 4-0 Andres Oper (86'), 5-0 Urmas Kirs (90').
Referee: Martin Ingvarsson (SWE)   Attendance: 2.500

19-08-1998   Kosevo Stadium, Sarajevo: Bosnia and Herzegovina – Faroe Islands   1-0 (0-0)
Bosnia and Herzegovina: Mirsad Dedic, Mirsad Hibic, Muhamed Konjic, Sead Kapetanovic, Mirza Varesanovic, Hasan Salihamidzic (80' Nermin Sabic), Sejad Halilovic (YC58), Sergej Barbarez (74' Jasmin Mujdza), Elvir Baljic, Elvir Bolic (65' Edin Mujcin), Mehmed Kodro (C). (Coach: Dzemaludin Musovic (BOS)).
Faroe Islands: Jákup Mikkelsen, Óli Johannesen, Allan Mørkøre, Jens Kristian Hansen (C), Pól Thorsteinsson, Hans Frodi Hansen, Sámal Joensen (YC65), Henning Jarnskor, Julian Schantz Johnsson (YC12), John Petersen (YC73), Uni Arge (77' Jákup á Borg). (Coach: Allan Simonsen (DEN)).
Goal: Bosnia and Herzegovina: 1-0 Elvir Baljic (65').
Referee: Tomasz Mikulski (POL)   Attendance: 28.000

05-09-1998   Zalgiris Stadium, Vilnius: Lithuania – Scotland   0-0
Lithuania: Gintaras Stauce, Tomas Zvirgzdauskas, Andrius Skerla, Aurelius Skarbalius (YC54), Virginijus Baltusnikas, Deividas Semberas (YC4), Aidas Preiksaitis, Raimondas Zutautas, Gediminas Sugzda (62' Orestas Buitkus), Edgaras Jankauskas, Grazvydas Mikulenas (88' Vaidotas Slekys). (Coach: Kestutis Latoza (LIT)).
Scotland: Jim Leighton, Christian Dailly, Tom Boyd, Colin Calderwood (71' Callum Davidson (YC75)), Colin Hendry (C), Matt Elliott, John Collins, Paul Lambert, Kevin Gallacher (YC50), Darren Jackson (57' Barry Ferguson), Ally McCoist (83' Neil McCann). (Coach: James Craig Brown (SCO)).
Referee: Constantin Dan Zotta (ROM)   Attendance: 4.500

06-09-1998   Kosevo Stadium, Sarajevo: Bosnia and Herzegovina – Estonia   1-1 (0-1)
Bosnia and Herzegovina: Mirsad Dedic, Mirsad Hibic, Muhamed Konjic (C), Sead Kapetanovic (YC35), Mirza Varesanovic (YC61), Suvad Katana (55' Edin Mujcin), Hasan Salihamidzic, Sejad Halilovic (77' Elvir Bolic), Jasmin Mujdza (65' Nermin Sabic), Sergej Barbarez, Elvir Baljic. (Coach: Dzemaludin Musovic (BOS)).
Estonia: Mart Poom, Urmas Rooba (80' Janek Meet), Viktor Alonen, Urmas Kirs, Sergei Hohlov-Simson, Martin Reim (C), Sergei Terehhov, Maksim Smirnov (YC69), Marko Kristal, Andres Oper, Indrek Zelinski (80' Kristen Viikmäe). (Coach: Teitur Thordarson (ISL)).
Goals: Bosnia and Herzegovina: 1-1 Sergej Barbarez (74' penalty).
Estonia: 0-1 Mirsad Hibic (29' *own goal*).
Referee: Charles Agius (MLT)   Attendance: 14.750

06-09-1998   Svangaskard, Toftir: Faroe Islands – Czech Republic   0-1 (0-0)
Faroe Islands: Jákup Mikkelsen, Óli Johannesen, Allan Mørkøre (YC30), Jens Kristian Hansen (C), Pól Thorsteinsson, Hans Frodi Hansen, Henning Jarnskor (YC32), Julian Schantz Johnsson, John Petersen, Todi Jónsson, Uni Arge (76' Magni Jarnskor). (Coach: Allan Simonsen (DEN)).
Czech Republic: Tomás Postulka, Radek Bejbl (80' Radoslav Látal), Karel Rada, Jan Suchopárek, Tomás Votava, Pavel Nedved (YC,YC86), Karel Poborsky (80' Radek Sloncík (YC81)), Vladimír Smicer, Jirí Nemec (C), Martin Cízek (55' Patrik Berger), Vratislav Lokvenc. (Coach: Jozef Chovanec (CZE)).
Goal: Czech Republic: 0-1 Vladimír Smicer (87').
Referee: Juha Hirviniemi (FIN)   Attendance: 2.589

10-10-1998   Kosevo Stadium, Sarajevo:
Bosnia and Herzegovina – Czech Republic   1-3 (0-1)
Bosnia and Herzegovina: Mirsad Dedic, Mirsad Hibic (YC81), Muhamed Konjic (C), Sead Kapetanovic, Mirza Varesanovic, Suvad Katana, Hasan Salihamidzic (64' Enes Demirovic (YC78)), Edin Mujcin (62' Marko Topic), Sejad Halilovic, Sergej Barbarez (YC13), Elvir Baljic (69' Bakir Besirevic). (Coach: Dzemaludin Musovic (BOS)).
Czech Republic: Tomás Postulka, Radek Bejbl, Tomás Repka (YC3), Jan Suchopárek, Radoslav Látal, Tomás Votava, Vladimír Smicer (85' Radek Sloncík), Patrik Berger, Miroslav Baranek (YC20) (69' Karel Rada), Jirí Nemec (C) (YC36), Vratislav Lokvenc (78' Pavel Kuka). (Coach: Jozef Chovanec (CZE)).
Goals: Bosnia and Herzegovina: 1-2 Marko Topic (87').
Czech Republic: 0-1 Miroslav Baranek (12'), 0-2 Vladimír Smicer (58'), 1-3 Pavel Kuka (90').
Referee: Domenico Messina (ITA)   Attendance: 22.000

10-10-1998   Zalgiris Stadium, Vilnius: Lithuania – Faroe Islands   0-0
Lithuania: Gintaras Stauce (C), Tomas Zvirgzdauskas, Andrius Skerla (YC82), Aurelius Skarbalius, Virginijus Baltusnikas, Aidas Preiksaitis, Raimondas Zutautas (YC54), Saulius Mikalajūnas (72' Rimantas Zvingilas), Edgaras Jankauskas, Grazvydas Mikulenas (46' Orestas Buitkus), Valdas Ivanauskas (YC75). (Coach: Kestutis Latoza (LIT)).
Faroe Islands: Jákup Mikkelsen, Óli Johannesen, Jens Kristian Hansen (C) (YC81), Pól Thorsteinsson, Hans Frodi Hansen, Sámal Joensen, Henning Jarnskor, Julian Schantz Johnsson, John Petersen, Todi Jónsson, Uni Arge (86' Jákup á Borg). (Coach: Allan Simonsen (DEN)).
Referee: Charles Schaack (LUX)   Attendance: 800

10-10-1998   Tynecastle Park, Edinburgh: Scotland – Estonia   3-2 (0-1)
Scotland: Jim Leighton, David Weir (YC89), Callum Davidson, Tom Boyd, Colin Calderwood (56' Simon Thomas Donnelly (YC86)), Colin Hendry (C), Allan Johnston, Billy McKinlay, Ian Durrant, Kevin Gallacher (17' Darren Jackson (YC62)), Ally McCoist (68' Billy Dodds (YC80)). (Coach: James Craig Brown (SCO)).
Estonia: Mart Poom, Urmas Rooba (YC77), Viktor Alonen (YC43), Urmas Kirs (YC60), Sergei Hohlov-Simson, Martin Reim (C), Sergei Terehhov, Maksim Smirnov, Marko Kristal (YC,YC83), Andres Oper, Indrek Zelinski (88' Kristen Viikmäe). (Coach: Teitur Thordarson (ISL)).
Goals: Scotland: 1-1 Billy Dodds (70'), 2-2 Sergei Hohlov-Simson (79' *own goal*), 3-2 Billy Dodds (85').
Estonia: 0-1 Sergei Hohlov-Simson (35'), 1-2 Maksim Smirnov (75').
Referee: Joaquim José Bento Marques (POR)   Attendance: 16.930

14-10-1998   Na Stínadlech, Teplice: Czech Republic – Estonia   4-1 (4-0)
Czech Republic: Tomás Postulka, Radek Bejbl (79' Martin Cízek), Tomás Repka, Jan Suchopárek (YC66), Radoslav Látal, Tomás Votava (YC30) (52' Karel Rada), Pavel Nedved, Vladimír Smicer, Patrik Berger, Jirí Nemec (C), Vratislav Lokvenc (60' Pavel Kuka). (Coach: Jozef Chovanec (CZE)).
Estonia: Mart Poom, Urmas Rooba, Kristen Viikmäe (46' Arjo Arbeiter (YC50)), Viktor Alonen, Sergei Hohlov-Simson (YC20), Martin Reim (C), Sergei Terehhov (62' Ivan O'Konnel-Bronin), Maksim Smirnov (46' Raivo Nõmmik), Janek Meet, Andres Oper (YC47), Indrek Zelinski. (Coach: Teitur Thordarson (ISL)).
Goals: Czech Republic: 1-0 Pavel Nedved (8'), 2-0 Patrik Berger (20'), 3-0 Patrik Berger (38'), 4-0 Janek Meet (45' *own goal*).
Estonia: 4-1 Arjo Arbeiter (90+1').
Referee: Eyjólfur Ólafsson (ISL)   Attendance: 13.123

14-10-1998   Zalgiris Stadium, Vilnius: Lithuania – Bosnia and Herzegovina   4-2 (1-1)
Lithuania: Gintaras Stauce (C), Tomas Zvirgzdauskas, Andrius Skerla, Dainius Gleveckas, Aurelius Skarbalius (64' Rimantas Zvingilas), Deividas Semberas, Aidas Preiksaitis, Raimondas Zutautas (YC57), Saulius Mikalajūnas (88' Virginijus Baltusnikas), Valdas Ivanauskas, Edgaras Jankauskas (YC9) (80' Tomas Danilevicius). (Coach: Kestutis Latoza (LIT)).
Bosnia and Herzegovina: Mirsad Dedic, Muhamed Konjic (C), Sead Kapetanovic (82' Jasmin Mujdza), Mirza Varesanovic, Suvad Katana (76' Marko Topic), Hasan Salihamidzic (YC46), Edin Mujcin (YC10) (80' Bakir Besirevic), Sejad Halilovic, Edin Ramcic, Sergej Barbarez (YC81), Elvir Baljic (RC70). (Coach: Dzemaludin Musovic (BOS)).
Goals: Lithuania: 1-1 Valdas Ivanauskas (11'), 2-1 Valdas Ivanauskas (67'), 3-2 Valdas Ivanauskas (77'), 4-2 Virginijus Baltusnikas (90+3').
Bosnia and Herzegovina: 0-1 Muhamed Konjic (5'), 2-2 Elvir Baljic (68').
Referee: Manfred Schüttengruber (AUT)   Attendance: 1.000

14-10-1998   Pittodrie Stadium, Aberdeen: Scotland – Faroe Islands   2-1 (2-0)
Scotland: Neil Sullivan, David Weir, Callum Davidson, Tom Boyd, Colin Hendry (C), Matt Elliott (YC49), Allan Johnston (81' Stephen Glass), Simon Thomas Donnelly, Craig Burley, Billy McKinlay (46' Ian Durrant), Billy Dodds (YC83). (Coach: James Craig Brown (SCO)).
Faroe Islands: Jákup Mikkelsen, Óli Johannesen, Jens Kristian Hansen (C), Pól Thorsteinsson, Hans Frodi Hansen (YC39), Sámal Joensen, Henning Jarnskor (YC48) (81' John Hansen), Julian Schantz Johnsson, John Petersen, Todi Jónsson, Uni Arge (YC59) (61' Jákup á Borg). (Coach: Allan Simonsen (DEN)).
Goals: Scotland: 1-0 Craig Burley (21'), 2-0 Billy Dodds (44').
Faroe Islands: 2-1 John Petersen (85' penalty).
Referee: Costas Kapitanis (CYP)   Attendance: 18.517

27-03-1999   Na Stínadlech, Teplice: Czech Republic – Lithuania   2-0 (1-0)
Czech Republic: Pavel Srnícek, Tomás Repka (YC3), Michal Horňák, Jan Suchopárek, Pavel Nedved, Karel Poborsky (53' Pavel Kuka), Vladimír Smicer (80' Miroslav Baranek), Patrik Berger, Jirí Nemec (C), Martin Hasek, Vratislav Lokvenc (70' Jan Koller). (Coach: Jozef Chovanec (CZE)).
Lithuania: Gintaras Stauce (C), Tomas Zvirgzdauskas, Andrius Skerla, Darius Zutautas, Aurelius Skarbalius, Raimondas Vainoras, Deividas Semberas, Aidas Preiksaitis, Saulius Mikalajūnas (78' Grazvydas Mikulenas), Valdas Ivanauskas (82' Orestas Buitkus), Edgaras Jankauskas (YC28) (67' Rimantas Zvingilas). (Coach: Kestutis Latoza (LIT)).
Goals: Czech Republic: 1-0 Michal Horňák (10'), 2-0 Patrik Berger (74' penalty).
Referee: Attila Juhos (HUN)   Attendance: 14.658

31-03-1999   Zalgiris Stadium, Vilnius: Lithuania – Estonia   1-2 (0-0)
Lithuania: Gintaras Stauce (C), Tomas Zvirgzdauskas, Andrius Skerla, Aurelius Skarbalius (36' Dainius Gleveckas, 53' Orestas Buitkus), Raimondas Vainoras, Deividas Semberas, Darius Maciulevicius, Aidas Preiksaitis, Raimondas Zutautas, Saulius Mikalajūnas, Grazvydas Mikulenas (YC38) (46' Arturas Fomenka). (Coach: Kestutis Latoza (LIT)).
Estonia: Mart Poom (YC53), Marek Lemsalu, Kristen Viikmäe, Erko Saviauk, Urmas Kirs (YC51), Sergei Hohlov-Simson, Martin Reim (C), Sergei Terehhov, Maksim Smirnov (90' Viktor Alonen), Mark Svets (YC45) (62' Marko Kristal), Andres Oper (66' Indrek Zelinski (YC84). (Coach: Teitur Thordarson (ISL)).
Goals: Lithuania: 1-2 Arturas Fomenka (83').
Estonia: 0-1 Sergei Terehhov (48'), 0-2 Sergei Terehhov (77').
Referee: Alfredo Trentalange (ITA)   Attendance: 2.000

31-03-1999   Celtic Park, Glasgow: Scotland – Czech Republic   1-2 (0-2)
Scotland: Neil Sullivan, David Weir, Callum Davidson (52' Allan Johnston), Tom Boyd, Matt Elliott, Craig Burley, Paul Lambert, Gary McAllister (C) (64' Don Hutchison), Eoin Jess, David Hopkin (YC53), Neil McCann. (Coach: James Craig Brown (SCO)).
Czech Republic: Pavel Srnícek, Michal Hornák, Jan Suchopárek, Tomás Votava, Pavel Nedved, Karel Poborsky (76' Karel Rada), Vladimír Smicer (84' Miroslav Baranek (YC90)), Patrik Berger, Jirí Nemec (C), Martin Hasek, Vratislav Lokvenc (70' Pavel Kuka). (Coach: Jozef Chovanec (CZE)).
Goals: Scotland: 1-2 Eoin Jess (68').
Czech Republic: 0-1 Jan Suchopárek (27'), 0-2 Vladimír Smicer (35').
Referee: Kim Milton Nielsen (DEN)   Attendance: 44.513

05-06-1999   Kosevo Stadium, Sarajevo: Bosnia and Herzegovina – Lithuania   2-0 (1-0)
Bosnia and Herzegovina: Mirsad Dedic, Mirsad Hibic, Sead Kapetanovic (YC49), Mirza Varesanovic, Hasan Salihamidzic (RC67), Nermin Sabic (YC9), Senad Repuh (85' Elvir Bolic), Bakir Besirevic, Edin Smajic, Marko Topic (86' Almir Turkovic), Mehmed Kodro (C) (79' Edin Mujcin). (Coach: Faruk Hadzibegic (BOS)).
Lithuania: Pavel Leus, Tomas Zvirgzdauskas, Tomas Kancelskis (YC84), Andrius Skerla, Marius Skinderis (YC15), Darius Gvildys (YC,YC81), Deividas Semberas (64' Grazvydas Mikulenas (YC66)), Darius Maciulevicius (46' Arturas Fomenka), Aidas Preiksaitis, Saulius Mikalajūnas (YC85), Valdas Ivanauskas (C). (Coach: Kestutis Latoza (LIT)).
Goals: Bosnia and Herzegovina: 1-0 Mehmed Kodro (26' penalty), 2-0 Elvir Bolic (89').
Referee: Arturo Daudén Ibáñez (ESP)   Attendance: 6.100

05-06-1999   Kadrioru Stadium, Tallinn: Estonia – Czech Republic   0-2 (0-1)
Estonia: Mart Poom, Marek Lemsalu, Kristen Viikmäe, Erko Saviauk, Urmas Kirs, Sergei Hohlov-Simson (YC45), Martin Reim (C), Sergei Terehhov (80' Mark Svets), Viktor Alonen (65' Maksim Smirnov, 74' Ivan O'Konnel-Bronin), Andres Oper, Marko Kristal. (Coach: Teitur Thordarson (ISL)).
Czech Republic: Pavel Srnícek, Michal Hornák, Jan Suchopárek, Tomás Repka, Pavel Nedved (85' Tomás Galásek), Karel Poborsky, Martin Hasek, Jirí Nemec (C), Patrik Berger, Vladimír Smicer (65' Pavel Kuka), Vratislav Lokvenc (70' Jan Koller). (Coach: Jozef Chovanec (CZE)).
Goals: Czech Republic: 0-1 Patrik Berger (44'), 0-2 Jan Koller (88').
Referee: Juan Ansuátegui Roca (ESP)   Attendance: 2.925

05-09-1999   Svangaskard, Toftir: Faroe Islands – Scotland   1-1 (0-1)
Faroe Islands: Jákup Mikkelsen, Øssur Hansen (86' John Hansen), Óli Johannesen, Allan Mørkøre, Pól Thorsteinsson, Hans Frodi Hansen, Jóhannis Sámal Joensen (69' Jákup á Borg (YC80)), Sámal Joensen, Julian Schantz Johnsson, John Petersen (79' Uni Arge), Todi Jónsson (C). (Coach: Allan Simonsen (DEN)).
Scotland: Neil Sullivan, David Weir, Callum Davidson, Tom Boyd (C), Colin Calderwood, Matt Elliott (RC44), Allan Johnston (YC77) (86' Scot Gemmill), Paul Lambert, Ian Durrant (46' Colin Cameron), Kevin Gallacher (88' Eoin Jess), Billy Dodds. (Coach: James Craig Brown (SCO)).
Goals: Faroe Islands: 1-1 Hans Frodi Hansen (87').
Scotland: 0-1 Allan Johnston (38').
Referee: Philippe Kalt (FRA)   Attendance: 4.100

09-06-1999   Letensky Stadion, Prague: Czech Republic – Scotland   3-2 (0-1)
Czech Republic: Pavel Srnícek, Tomás Repka, Michal Hornák, Jan Suchopárek (YC42), Pavel Nedved, Karel Poborsky (YC53) (69' Pavel Kuka), Vladimír Smicer (YC61), Patrik Berger, Jirí Nemec (C), Martin Hasek (60' Miroslav Baranek), Vratislav Lokvenc (69' Jan Koller). (Coach: Jozef Chovanec (CZE)).
Scotland: Neil Sullivan, David Weir, Callum Davidson (YC33), Paul Ritchie (YC76), Tom Boyd (C), Colin Calderwood, Allan Johnston, Paul Lambert, Ian Durrant (71' Eoin Jess), Kevin Gallacher, Billy Dodds (YC77). (Coach: James Craig Brown (SCO)).
Goals: Czech Republic: 1-2 Tomás Repka (65'), 2-2 Pavel Kuka (75'), 3-2 Jan Koller (87').
Scotland: 0-1 Paul Ritchie (30'), 0-2 Allan Johnston (62').
Referee: Helmut Krug (GER)   Attendance: 21.149

09-06-1999   Kadrioru Stadium, Tallinn: Estonia – Lithuania   1-2 (1-0)
Estonia: Mart Poom, Marek Lemsalu, Kristen Viikmäe, Viktor Alonen, Urmas Kirs, Urmas Kaal, Martin Reim (C), Sergei Terehhov (75' Ivan O'Konnel-Bronin), Marko Kristal (80' Mark Svets), Andres Oper (YC86), Indrek Zelinski. (Coach: Teitur Thordarson (ISL)).
Lithuania: Pavel Leus, Tomas Zvirgzdauskas, Andrius Skerla, Marius Skinderis (YC84), Darius Zutautas (46' Darius Maciulevicius (YC81)), Aurelius Skarbalius, Tomas Razanauskas, Raimondas Zutautas, Saulius Mikalajūnas, Tomas Ramelis, Valdas Ivanauskas (C) (88' Aidas Preiksaitis). (Coach: Kestutis Latoza (LIT)).
Goals: Estonia: 1-0 Andres Oper (8').
Lithuania: 1-1 Tomas Ramelis (51'), 1-2 Darius Maciulevicius (56').
Referee: Hermann Albrecht (GER)   Attendance: 1.500

09-06-1999   Svangaskard, Toftir: Faroe Islands – Bosnia and Herzegovina   2-2 (1-1)
Faroe Islands: Jákup Mikkelsen, Øssur Hansen (69' Henning Jarnskor), Óli Johannesen (YC17), Allan Mørkøre, Pól Thorsteinsson, Hans Frodi Hansen, Sámal Joensen, Julian Schantz Johnsson, John Petersen, Todi Jónsson (C), Uni Arge (88' Jóhannis Sámal Joensen). (Coach: Allan Simonsen (DEN)).
Bosnia and Herzegovina: Mirsad Dedic, Mirsad Hibic, Mirza Varesanovic (YC45), Nermin Sabic (YC24), Edin Mujcin, Senad Repuh (79' Adnan Osmanhodzic), Bakir Besirevic, Edin Smajic, Marko Topic (88' Samir Muratovic), Elvir Bolic (C) (YC51), Almir Turkovic (64' Omer Joldic). (Coach: Faruk Hadzibegic (BOS)).
Goals: Faroe Islands: 1-1 Uni Arge (36'), 2-1 Uni Arge (47').
Bosnia and Herzegovina: 0-1 Elvir Bolic (13'), 2-2 Elvir Bolic (49').
Referee: Peter Jones (ENG)   Attendance: 4.800

04-09-1999   Kosevo Stadium, Sarajevo: Bosnia and Herzegovina – Scotland   1-2 (1-2)
Bosnia and Herzegovina: Mirsad Dedic, Mirsad Hibic, Muhamed Konjic (C), Omer Joldic (77' Senad Repuh), Sejad Halilovic (YC35) (61' Edin Mujcin (YC79)), Jasmin Mujdza (77' Enes Demirovic), Bakir Besirevic, Sergej Barbarez, Marko Topic, Elvir Bolic, Mehmed Kodro. (Coach: Faruk Hadzibegic (BOS)).
Scotland: Neil Sullivan (YC51), David Weir, Colin Calderwood (46' Christian Dailly), Colin Hendry (C), Barry Ferguson (69' Ian Durrant), Don Hutchison (YC19), Craig Burley, John Collins, David Hopkin, Neil McCann (74' Kevin Gallacher), Billy Dodds. (Coach: James Craig Brown (SCO)).
Goals: Bosnia and Herzegovina: 1-1 Elvir Bolic (23').
Scotland: 0-1 Don Hutchison (13'), 1-2 Billy Dodds (45').
Referee: Nikolai Vladislavovich Levnikov (RUS)   Attendance: 15.600

04-09-1999   Tórsvøllur, Tórshavn: Faroe Islands – Estonia   0-2 (0-0)
Faroe Islands: Jákup Mikkelsen, Óli Johannesen, Allan Mørkøre, Jens Kristian Hansen (C), Pól Thorsteinsson (75' Øssur Hansen), Hans Frodi Hansen, Sámal Joensen (YC42) (87' Jákup á Borg), Julian Schantz Johnsson, John Petersen (YC19), Todi Jónsson, Uni Arge (87' Henning Jarnskor). (Coach: Allan Simonsen (DEN)).
Estonia: Mart Poom, Raio Piiroja, Erko Saviauk (80' Marek Lemsalu), Aivar Anniste (66' Ivan O'Konnel-Bronin), Viktor Alonen (YC44), Urmas Kirs, Sergei Hohlov-Simson (C), Martin Reim, Sergei Terehhov (YC45), Marko Kristal, Indrek Zelinski (75' Dmitri Ustritski). (Coach: Teitur Thordarson (ISL)).
Goals: Estonia: 0-1 Martin Reim (85'), 0-2 Raio Piiroja (90').
Referee: Edo Trivkovic (CRO)   Attendance: 2.300

04-09-1999   Zalgiris Stadium, Vilnius: Lithuania – Czech Republic   0-4 (0-0)
Lithuania: Gintaras Stauce (C), Tomas Zvirgzdauskas, Darius Zutautas, Andrejus Tereskinas, Deividas Semberas (55' Andrius Skerla), Tomas Razanauskas, Donatas Vencevicius (YC67), Aidas Preiksaitis (81' Tomas Danilevicius), Saulius Mikalajūnas, Edgaras Jankauskas (RC20), Valdas Ivanauskas (38' Tomas Ramelis). (Coach: Kestutis Latoza (LIT)).
Czech Republic: Pavel Srnícek, Marek Niki, Radek Bejbl, Karel Rada, Tomás Repka, Pavel Nedved (YC39) (77' Miroslav Baranek), Karel Poborsky (74' Radek Sloncík), Patrik Berger, Jirí Nemec (C) (71' Pavel Horváth), Jan Koller, Pavel Kuka (YC44). (Coach: Jozef Chovanec (CZE)).
Goals: Czech Republic: 0-1 Pavel Nedved (60'), 0-2 Pavel Nedved (62'), 0-3 Jan Koller (64'), 0-4 Jan Koller (90+3').
Referee: Jacek Granat (POL)   Attendance: 2.000

08-09-1999   Na Stínadlech, Teplice: Czech Republic – Bosnia and Herzegovina   3-0 (1-0)
Czech Republic: Pavel Srnícek, Marek Niki, Radek Bejbl, Tomás Repka, Jan Suchopárek, Pavel Nedved (85' Martin Hasek), Karel Poborsky, Patrik Berger, Jirí Nemec (C), Jan Koller (59' Vratislav Lokvenc), Pavel Kuka (81' Miroslav Baranek). (Coach: Jozef Chovanec (CZE)).
Bosnia and Herzegovina: Mirsad Dedic, Mirsad Hibic, Muhamed Konjic (C) (YC11), Mirza Varesanovic, Nermin Sabic (YC39), Faruk Ihtijarevic (72' Enes Demirovic), Omer Joldic (72' Senad Repuh), Bakir Besirevic, Sergej Barbarez (YC62), Marko Topic (72' Elvir Bolic), Mehmed Kodro. (Coach: Faruk Hadzibegic (BOS)).
Goals: Czech Republic: 1-0 Jan Koller (25'), 2-0 Patrik Berger (60' penalty), 3-0 Karel Poborsky (68').
Referee: Karl-Erik Nilsson (SWE)   Attendance: 10.112

08-09-1999   Kadrioru Stadium, Tallinn: Estonia – Scotland   0-0
Estonia: Mart Poom, Raio Piiroja, Erko Saviauk, Aivar Anniste, Urmas Kirs, Sergei Hohlov-Simson (C), Martin Reim, Sergei Terehhov, Ivan O'Konnel-Bronin (46' Indrek Zelinski), Marko Kristal, Andres Oper. (Coach: Teitur Thordarson (ISL)).
Scotland: Neil Sullivan, Christian Dailly, David Weir, Callum Davidson, Colin Hendry (C), Allan Johnston (54' Neil McCann), Don Hutchison (YC89), Craig Burley, John Collins, Ian Durrant (66' Barry Ferguson), Billy Dodds. (Coach: James Craig Brown (SCO)).
Referee: Fritz Stuchlik (AUT)   Attendance: 4.500

08-09-1999   Tórsvøllur, Tórshavn: Faroe Islands – Lithuania   0-1 (0-0)
Faroe Islands: Jákup Mikkelsen, Øssur Hansen, Óli Johannesen, Allan Mørkøre, Jens Kristian Hansen (C), Pól Thorsteinsson (YC87), Hans Frodi Hansen, Henning Jarnskor (86' Hedin á Lakjuni), Julian Schantz Johnsson (65' Fródi Benjaminsen), Todi Jónsson, Uni Arge (46' Jákup á Borg). (Coach: Allan Simonsen (DEN)).
Lithuania: Gintaras Stauce (C) (81' Gytis Padimanskas), Tomas Zvirgzdauskas, Marius Skinderis, Darius Zutautas, Andrejus Tereskinas, Deividas Semberas (YC37), Tomas Razanauskas (75' Andrius Skerla), Donatas Vencevicius, Aidas Preiksaitis, Saulius Mikalajūnas, Tomas Ramelis. (Coach: Kestutis Latoza (LIT)).
Goal: Lithuania: 0-1 Tomas Ramelis (53').
Referee: Eric Romain (BEL)   Attendance: 680

05-10-1999   Ibrox Stadium, Glasgow: Scotland – Bosnia and Herzegovina   1-0 (1-0)
Scotland: Neil Sullivan, Christian Dailly, David Weir, Callum Davidson, Colin Hendry (C) (37' Colin Calderwood), Craig Burley, John Collins, Paul Lambert, David Hopkin (YC86), Kevin Gallacher (79' Mark Burchill), Billy Dodds (89' Gary McSwegan). (Coach: James Craig Brown (SCO)).
Bosnia and Herzegovina: Adnan Guso, Sead Kapetanovic, Mirza Varesanovic, Faruk Hudjurovic, Nermin Sabic, Faruk Ihtijarevic (76' Marko Topic), Edin Mujcin (83' Alen Avdic), Bakir Besirevic, Sergej Barbarez (YC25), Elvir Baljic, Elvir Bolic (C). (Coach: Faruk Hadzibegic (BOS)).
Goal: Scotland: 1-0 John Collins (25' penalty).
Referee: Leif Sundell (SWE)   Attendance: 30.574

09-10-1999   Letensky Stadion, Prague: Czech Republic – Faroe Islands   2-0 (1-0)
Czech Republic: Pavel Srnícek, Radek Bejbl (66' Pavel Horváth), Karel Rada, Tomás Repka, Jan Suchopárek (YC32) (74' Pavel Verbír), Karel Poborsky, Vladimír Smicer, Patrik Berger (RC60), Miroslav Baranek (59' Michal Hornák), Jirí Nemec (C), Jan Koller. (Coach: Jozef Chovanec (CZE)).
Faroe Islands: Jens Knudsen (YC60), Óli Johannesen (YC41), Allan Mørkøre, Jens Kristian Hansen (C), Pól Thorsteinsson (RC60), Hans Frodi Hansen, Sámal Joensen, Henning Jarnskor (YC8) (88' Øssur Hansen), Julian Schantz Johnsson, John Petersen (71' Rógvi Jacobsen), Todi Jónsson. (Coach: Allan Simonsen (DEN)).
Goals: Czech Republic: 1-0 Jan Koller (11'), 2-0 Pavel Verbír (80').
Referee: Marcel Lica (ROM)   Attendance: 21.362

09-10-1999   Kadrioru Stadium, Tallinn: Estonia – Bosnia and Herzegovina   1-4 (1-1)
Estonia: Martin Kaalma, Raio Piiroja (YC34), Aivar Anniste (61' Erko Saviauk), Viktor Alonen, Urmas Kirs, Sergei Hohlov-Simson (C) (YC72), Martin Reim, Sergei Terehhov (73' Ivan O'Konnel-Bronin), Marko Kristal, Andres Oper, Indrek Zelinski (39' Kristen Viikmäe). (Coach: Teitur Thordarson (ISL)).
Bosnia and Herzegovina: Adnan Guso, Sead Kapetanovic, Mirza Varesanovic (YC38), Faruk Hudjurovic, Nermin Sabic (60' Samir Duro), Faruk Ihtijarevic, Omer Joldic, Bakir Besirevic, Marko Topic, Elvir Baljic (88' Alen Avdic), Elvir Bolic (C) (80' Edin Mujcin). (Coach: Faruk Hadzibegic (BOS)).
Goals: Estonia: 1-0 Andres Oper (3').
Bosnia and Herzegovina: 1-1 Elvir Baljic (41'), 1-2 Elvir Baljic (57'), 1-3 Elvir Baljic (66'), 1-4 Elvir Baljic (86').
Referee: Roelof Luinge (HOL)   Attendance: 800

09-10-1999   Hampden Park, Glasgow: Scotland – Lithuania   3-0 (0-0)
Scotland: Jonathan Gould, Christian Dailly, David Weir, Callum Davidson, Paul Ritchie, Don Hutchison, Craig Burley (46' Colin Cameron), Paul Lambert (C), Brian O'Neill, Mark Burchill (79' Billy Dodds), Gary McSwegan (82' Kevin Gallacher). (Coach: James Craig Brown (SCO))
Lithuania: Pavel Leus, Tomas Zvirgzdauskas, Andrius Skerla, Marius Skinderis, Darius Zutautas, Andrejus Tereskinas (YC47) (82' Arturas Fomenko), Tomas Razanauskas, Irmantas Stumbrys (YC44) (55' Donatas Vencevicius), Saulius Mikalajūnas, Grazvydas Mikulenas, Vidas Dancenko (55' Darius Maciulevicius). (Coach: Robertas Tautkus (LIT)).
Goals: Scotland: 1-0 Don Hutchison (48'), 2-0 Gary McSwegan (50'), 3-0 Colin Cameron (89').
Referee: Stéphane Bré (FRA)   Attendance: 22.059

SECOND ROUND PLAY-OFFS

13-11-1999   Hampden Park, Glasgow: Scotland – England   0-2 (0-2)
Scotland: Neil Sullivan, Christian Dailly (YC24), David Weir, Paul Ritchie, Colin Hendry (C) (YC5), Barry Ferguson (YC40), Don Hutchison (YC88), Craig Burley, John Collins, Kevin Gallacher (YC16) (82' Mark Burchill), Billy Dodds. (Coach: James Craig Brown (SCO)).
England: David Seaman, Sol Campbell, Tony Adams (YC75), Martin Keown, David Beckham, Phil Neville (YC50), Paul Scholes (YC21), Paul Ince (YC76), Jamie Redknapp (YC60), Michael Owen (67' Andy Cole), Alan Shearer (C). (Coach: Kevin Keegan (ENG)).
Goals: England: 0-1 Paul Scholes (21'), 0-2 Paul Scholes (42').
Referee: Manuel Díaz Vega (ESP)   Attendance: 50.132

13-11-1999   Bezigrad Stadium, Ljubljana: Slovenia – Ukraine   2-1 (0-1)
Slovenia: Mladen Dabanovic, Amir Karic, Zeljko Milinovic (YC65), Aleksander Knavs (YC26), Darko Milanic (C) (73' Milan Osterc), Miran Pavlin (YC37), Dzoni Novak, Ales Ceh, Zlatko Zahovic, Mladen Rudonja (YC86), Saso Udovic (46' Milenko Acimovic). (Coach: Srecko Katanec (SLO)).
Ukraine: Oleksandr Shovkovsky, Vladyslav Vaschuk, Dmytro Parfyonov (YC52,YC60), Serhiy Popov, Yuriy Dmytrulin, Oleksandr Holovko (C), Andriy Gusin (YC87,YC88), Vitaliy Kosovskyi, Serhiy Kandaurov (YC50) (56' Vasyl Kardash), Serhiy Rebrov, Andriy Shevchenko. (Coach: József Sabo (UKR)).
Goals: Slovenia: 1-1 Zlatko Zahovic (53'), 2-1 Milenko Acimovic (84').
Ukraine: 0-1 Andriy Shevchenko (33').
Referee: Urs Meier (SUI)   Attendance: 17.000

13-11-1999   National Stadium, Ramat Gan: Israel – Denmark   0-5 (0-2)
Israel: Dudu Aouate, David Amsalem, Arik Benado (YC68), Alon Harazi (YC55), Ran Ben Shimon (38' Idan Tal (YC66)), Tal Banin (C) (YC53) (79' Jan Talesnikov), Haim Revivo (RC57), Alon Hazan, Eyal Berkovic, Josef Abukasis (38' Yossi Benayoun), Amir Turgeman. (Coach: Shlomo Scharf (ISR)).
Denmark: Peter Schmeichel (C), Thomas Helveg, René Henriksen, Jan Heintze, Jes Høgh, Martin Jørgensen (86' Michael Schjønberg), Jesper Grønkjær (YC12), Stig Tøfting (79' Bjarne Goldbæk), Brian Steen Nielsen, Jon Dahl Tomasson (79' Søren Andersen), Ebbe Sand. (Coach: Bo (Bosse) Johansson (SWE)).
Goals: Denmark: 0-1 Jon Dahl Tomasson (2'), 0-2 Jon Dahl Tomasson (34'), 0-3 Stig Tøfting (66'), 0-4 Martin Jørgensen (69'), 0-5 Brian Steen Nielsen (72').
Referee: David Roland Elleray (ENG)   Attendance: 42.000

13-11-1999   Lansdowne Road, Dublin: Republic of Ireland – Turkey   1-1 (0-0)
Republic of Ireland: Alan Kelly (61' Dean Kiely), Stephen Carr, Gary Breen, Denis Irwin, Kenny Cunningham, Kevin Kilbane, Rory Delap (53' Damien Duff), Roy Keane (C), Lee Carsley, Robbie Keane (YC86), Tony Cascarino (75' David Connolly). (Coach: Michael Joseph (Mike) McCarthy (IRL)).
Turkey: Rüstü Reçber, Ali Beserter, Alpay Özalan, Hakan Ünsal (67' Tugay Kerimoglu), Ogün Temizkanoglu (C), Ümit Davala (46' Arif Erdem), Tayfur Havutçu, Sergen Yalçin (85' Mert Korkmaz), Abdullah Ercan, Tayfun Korkut, Hakan Sükür. (Coach: Mustafa Denizli (TUR)).
Goals: Republic of Ireland: 1-0 Robbie Keane (79').
Turkey: 1-1 Tayfur Havutçu (83' penalty).
Referee: Anders Frisk (SWE)   Attendance: 33.610

17-11-1999   Olympic Stadium, Kiev: Ukraine – Slovenia   1-1 (0-0)
Ukraine: Oleksandr Shovkovsky, Serhiy Fedorov, Vladyslav Vaschuk, Oleg Luzhny (C), Yuriy Dmytrulin (YC75), Oleksandr Holovko, Vitaliy Kosovskyi (74' Serhiy Popov), Serhiy Kandaurov (46' Serhiy Kovalov), Serhiy Rebrov, Andriy Shevchenko, Serhiy Skachenko (58' Gennadiy Moroz). (Coach: József Sabo (UKR)).
Slovenia: Mladen Dabanovic, Marinko Galic, Amir Karic (74' Milan Osterc), Zeljko Milinovic, Darko Milanic (C) (YC14), Miran Pavlin (YC10), Dzoni Novak, Ales Ceh, Zlatko Zahovic (YC9), Mladen Rudonja, Saso Udovic (58' Milenko Acimovic (YC86)). (Coach: Srecko Katanec (SLO)).
Goals: Ukraine: 1-0 Serhiy Rebrov (68').
Slovenia: 1-1 Miran Pavlin (78').
Referee: Bernd Heynemann (GER)   Attendance: 52.800

17-11-1999   Bursa Atatürk Stadium, Bursa: Turkey – Republic of Ireland   0-0
Turkey: Rüstü Reçber (38' Engin Ipekoglu), Ali Beserter, Alpay Özalan, Ogün Temizkanoglu (C), Okan Buruk, Tayfur Havutçu, Sergen Yalçin, Abdullah Ercan, Tayfun Korkut (46' Fatih Akyel), Hakan Sükür, Arif Erdem (83' Ümit Davala). (Coach: Mustafa Denizli (TUR)).
Republic of Ireland: Dean Kiely, Stephen Carr (6' Jeff Kenna, 80' Tony Cascarino), Gary Breen, Denis Irwin, Kenny Cunningham, Kevin Kilbane, Rory Delap, Mark Kinsella, Roy Keane (C), David Connolly (69' Damien Duff), Niall Quinn. (Coach: Michael Joseph (Mike) McCarthy (IRL)).
Referee: Gilles Veissière (FRA)   Attendance: 19.900
(Turkey 1-1 Republic of Ireland on aggregate. Turkey qualified on the away goals rule)

17-11-1999   Parken Stadium, Copenhagen: Denmark – Israel   3-0 (2-0)
Denmark: Peter Schmeichel (C) (18' Thomas Sørensen), Thomas Helveg (70' Jacob Laursen), René Henriksen, Jan Heintze, Jes Høgh, Martin Jørgensen, Jesper Grønkjær (83' Michael Schjønberg), Stig Tøfting, Brian Steen Nielsen, Jon Dahl Tomasson, Ebbe Sand. (Coach: Bo (Bosse) Johansson (SWE)).
Israel: Shavit Elimelech, David Amsalem (43' Walid Badir), Alon Harazi, Ofer Talkar, Idan Tal (28' Jan Talesnikov), Yossi Benayoun (72' Shimon Gershon (YC85)), Tal Banin (C), Alon Hazan, Eyal Berkovic (YC19), Amir Shelach, Amir Turgeman. (Coach: Shlomo Scharf (ISR)).
Goals: Denmark: 1-0 Ebbe Sand (4'), 2-0 Brian Steen Nielsen (14'), 3-0 Jon Dahl Tomasson (64').
Referee: Vítor Manuel Melo Pereira (POR)   Attendance: 41.186

17-11-1999   Wembley Stadium, London: England – Scotland   0-1 (0-1)
England: David Seaman, Sol Campbell, Tony Adams, Gareth Southgate, David Beckham, Phil Neville, Paul Scholes (90' Ray Parlour), Paul Ince (YC43), Jamie Redknapp (YC66), Michael Owen (63' Emile Heskey), Alan Shearer (C). (Coach: Kevin Keegan (ENG)).
Scotland: Neil Sullivan, Christian Dailly (YC60), David Weir, Callum Davidson (YC51), Colin Hendry (C), Barry Ferguson, Don Hutchison, Craig Burley, John Collins, Neil McCann (74' Mark Burchill), Billy Dodds. (Coach: James Craig Brown (SCO)).
Goal: Scotland: 0-1 Don Hutchison (38').
Referee: Pierluigi Collina (ITA)   Attendance: 75.848

FINAL TOURNAMENT IN BELGIUM/NETHERLANDS

GROUP STAGE

Belgium and Netherlands automatically qualified as hosts.

GROUP A

12-06-2000	Liège	Germany – Romania	1-1 (1-1)
12-06-2000	Eindhoven	Portugal – England	3-2 (2-2)
17-06-2000	Arnhem	Romania – Portugal	0-1 (0-0)
17-06-2000	Charleroi	England – Germany	1-0 (0-0)
20-06-2000	Charleroi	England – Romania	2-3 (2-1)
20-06-2000	Rotterdam	Portugal – Germany	3-0 (1-0)

FINAL STANDING

Pos	Team	Pld	W	D	L	GF	GA	GD	Pts
1	Portugal	3	3	0	0	7	2	+5	9
2	Romania	3	1	1	1	4	4	0	4
3	England	3	1	0	2	5	6	-1	3
4	Germany	3	0	1	2	1	5	-4	1

Portugal and Romania qualified for the Quarter-finals.

12-06-2000   Stade Maurice Dufrasne, Liège: Germany – Romania   1-1 (1-1)
Germany: Oliver Kahn, Lothar Matthäus (78' Sebastian Deisler), Thomas Linke (46' Marko Rehmer), Jens Nowotny, Markus Babbel, Christian Ziege, Jens Jeremies, Mehmet Scholl, Thomas Häßler (73' Dietmar Hamann), Oliver Bierhoff (C), Paulo Rink. (Coach: Erich Ribbeck (GER)).
Romania: Bogdan Stelea, Gheorghe Popescu, Dan Petrescu (69' Cosmin Contra), Liviu Ciobotariu, Iulian Filipescu, Cristian Chivu, Dorinel Munteanu, Constantin Galca, Gheorghe Hagi (C) (YC49) (73' Adrian Mutu), Viorel Moldovan (85' Ioan Lupescu), Adrian Ilie (YC49). (Coach: Emerich Jenei (ROM)).
Goals: Germany: 1-1 Mehmet Scholl (28').
Romania: 0-1 Viorel Moldovan (5').
Referee: Kim Milton Nielsen (DEN)   Attendance: 28.500

12-06-2000   Philips Stadion, Eindhoven: Portugal – England   3-2 (2-2)
Portugal: VÍTOR Manuel Martins BAÍA (C) (YC89), ABEL Luís da Silva Costa XAVIER, JORGE Paulo COSTA Almeida, FERNANDO Manuel Silva COUTO, DIMAS Manuel Marques Teixeira, PAULO Jorge Gomes BENTO, José Luís da Cruz VIDIGAL, RUI Manuel César COSTA (85' Roberto Luis Gaspar de Deus Severo "BETO"), LUÍS Filipe Madeira Caeiro FIGO, NUNO "GOMES" Miguel Soares Pereira Ribeiro (89' NUNO "CAPUCHO" Fernando Gonçalves Rocha), JOÃO Manuel Vieira PINTO (75' SÉRGIO Paulo Marceneiro CONCEIÇÃO). (Coach: HUMBERTO Manuel de Jesus COELHO (POR)).
England: David Seaman, Gary Neville, Tony Adams (82' Martin Keown), Sol Campbell, Phil Neville, David Beckham, Paul Scholes, Paul Ince (YC44), Steve McManaman (58' Dennis Wise), Michael Owen (46' Emile Heskey), Alan Shearer (C). (Coach: Kevin Keegan (ENG)).
Goals: Portugal: 1-2 LUÍS Filipe Madeira Caeiro FIGO (22'), 2-2 JOÃO Manuel Vieira PINTO (37'), 3-2 NUNO "GOMES" Miguel Soares Pereira Ribeiro (59').
England: 0-1 Paul Scholes (3'), 0-2 Steve McManaman (18').
Referee: Anders Frisk (SWE)   Attendance: 31.500

17-06-2000   GelreDome, Arnhem: Romania – Portugal   0-1 (0-0)
Romania: Bogdan Stelea, Cosmin Contra (YC27), Iulian Filipescu, Gheorghe Popescu, Cristian Chivu, Constantin Galca, Dan Petrescu (YC22) (64' Florentin Petre), Dorinel Munteanu, Gheorghe Hagi (C) (YC16), Viorel Moldovan (69' Ionel Ganea), Adrian Ilie (78' Laurentiu Rosu). (Coach: Emerich Jenei (ROM)).
Portugal: VÍTOR Manuel Martins BAÍA (C), CARLOS Alberto de Oliveira SECRETÁRIO, JORGE Paulo COSTA Almeida, FERNANDO Manuel Silva COUTO, DIMAS Manuel Marques Teixeira, PAULO Jorge Gomes BENTO, José Luís da Cruz VIDIGAL, RUI Manuel César COSTA (87' Francisco José Rodrigues da Costa "COSTINHA"), LUÍS Filipe Madeira Caeiro FIGO (YC30), NUNO "GOMES" Miguel Soares Pereira Ribeiro (56' Ricardo Manuel Andrade Silva SÁ PINTO), JOÃO Manuel Vieira PINTO (56' SÉRGIO Paulo Marceneiro CONCEIÇÃO). (Coach: HUMBERTO Manuel de Jesus COELHO (POR)).
Goal: Portugal: 0-1 Francisco José Rodrigues da Costa "COSTINHA" (90+4').
Referee: Gilles Veissière (FRA)   Attendance: 28.400

17-06-2000   Stade du Pays de Charleroi, Charleroi: England – Germany   1-0 (0-0)
England: David Seaman, Gary Neville, Sol Campbell, Martin Keown, Phil Neville, David Beckham (YC41), Paul Scholes (71' Nick Barmby), Paul Ince, Dennis Wise, Michael Owen (61' Steven Gerrard), Alan Shearer (C). (Coach: Kevin Keegan (ENG)).
Germany: Oliver Kahn (C), Lothar Matthäus, Markus Babbel, Jens Nowotny, Sebastian Deisler (72' Michael Ballack), Christian Ziege, Dietmar Hamann, Jens Jeremies (YC43) (78' Marco Bode), Mehmet Scholl, Carsten Jancker, Ulf Kirsten (70' Paulo Rink). (Coach: Erich Ribbeck (GER)).
Goal: England: 1-0 Alan Shearer (53').
Referee: Pierluigi Collina (ITA)   Attendance: 27.700

20-06-2000   Stade du Pays de Charleroi, Charleroi: England – Romania 2-3 (2-1)
England: Nigel Martyn, Gary Neville, Sol Campbell, Martin Keown, Phil Neville, David Beckham, Paul Scholes (81' Gareth Southgate), Paul Ince, Dennis Wise (75' Nick Barmby), Michael Owen (66' Emile Heskey), Alan Shearer (C) (YC64). (Coach: Kevin Keegan (ENG)).
Romania: Bogdan Stelea, Cosmin Contra (YC44), Iulian Filipescu (YC71), Gheorghe Popescu (C) (32' Miodrag Belodedici), Cristian Chivu (YC18), Dan Petrescu (YC40), Constantin Galca (68' Laurentiu Rosu), Dorinel Munteanu, Adrian Ilie (YC45) (74' Ionel Ganea), Viorel Moldovan, Adrian Mutu. (Coach: Emerich Jenei (ROM)).
Goals: England: 1-1 Alan Shearer (41' penalty), 2-1 Michael Owen (45').
Romania: 0-1 Cristian Chivu (22'), 2-2 Dorinel Munteanu (48'), 2-3 Ionel Ganea (89' penalty).
Referee: Urs Meier (SUI)   Attendance: 27.000

20-06-2000   Stadion Feijenoord, Rotterdam: Portugal – Germany 3-0 (1-0)
Portugal: PEDRO Manuel ESPINHA Ferreira (90' Joaquim Manuel Sampaio Silva "QUIM"), Roberto Luis Gaspar de Deus Severo "BETO" (YC27), JORGE Paulo COSTA Almeida, FERNANDO Manuel Silva COUTO (C), RUI JORGE Sousa Dias Macedo Oliveira, SÉRGIO Paulo Marceneiro CONCEIÇÃO, PAULO Manuel Carvalho de SOUSA (72' José Luís da Cruz VIDIGAL), Francisco José Rodrigues da Costa "COSTINHA", NUNO "CAPUCHO" Fernando Gonçalves Rocha, Ricardo Manuel Andrade Silva SÁ PINTO, Pedro Miguel Carreiro Resendes "PAULETA" (67' NUNO "GOMES" Miguel Soares Pereira Ribeiro). (Coach: HUMBERTO Manuel de Jesus COELHO (POR)).
Germany: Oliver Kahn (C), Lothar Matthäus, Marko Rehmer, Thomas Linke, Jens Nowotny, Sebastian Deisler (YC27), Michael Ballack (YC25) (46' Paulo Rink (YC90)), Mehmet Scholl (60' Thomas Häßler), Dietmar Hamann, Marco Bode, Carsten Jancker (YC26) (69' Ulf Kirsten). (Coach: Erich Ribbeck (GER)).
Goals: Portugal: 1-0 SÉRGIO Paulo Marceneiro CONCEIÇÃO (35'), 2-0 SÉRGIO Paulo Marceneiro CONCEIÇÃO (54'), 3-0 SÉRGIO Paulo Marceneiro CONCEIÇÃO (71').
Referee: Dirk Zier Gerardus (Dick) Jol (HOL)   Attendance: 51.504

GROUP B

10-06-2000	Brussels	Belgium – Sweden	2-1 (1-0)
11-06-2000	Arnhem	Turkey – Italy	1-2 (0-0)
14-06-2000	Brussels	Italy – Belgium	2-0 (1-0)
15-06-2000	Eindhoven	Sweden – Turkey	0-0
19-06-2000	Brussels	Turkey – Belgium	2-0 (1-0)
19-06-2000	Eindhoven	Italy – Sweden	2-1 (1-0)

FINAL STANDING

Pos	Team	Pld	W	D	L	GF	GA	GD	Pts
1	*Italy*	3	3	0	0	6	2	+4	9
2	*Turkey*	3	1	1	1	3	2	+1	4
3	Belgium	3	1	0	2	2	5	-3	3
4	Sweden	3	0	1	2	2	4	-2	1

Italy and Turkey qualified for the Quarter-finals.

10-06-2000   King Baudouin Stadium, Brussels: Belgium – Sweden   2-1 (1-0)
Belgium: Filip De Wilde, Lorenzo Staelens (C), Eric Deflandre, Joos Valgaeren, Philippe Léonard (72' Nico Van Kerckhoven (YC90)), Yves Vanderhaeghe, Gert Verheyen (YC65) (88' Jacky Peeters), Bart Goor, Marc Wilmots, Émile Mpenza, Branko Strupar (69' Luc Nilis (YC77)). (Coach: Robert Waseige (BEL)).
Sweden: Magnus Hedman, Olof Mellberg, Patrik Andersson (C) (YC45,YC81), Joachim Björklund, Roland Nilsson (46' Teddy Lucic), Johan Mjällby, Niclas Alexandersson, Daniel Andersson (70' Yksel Osmanovski), Fredrik Ljungberg, Kennet Andersson, Jörgen Petterson (50' Henrik Larsson). (Coaches: Lars Lagerbäck & Tommy Söderberg (SWE)).
Goals: Belgium: 1-0 Bart Goor (43'), 2-0 Émile Mpenza (46').
Sweden: 2-1 Johan Mjällby (53').
Referee: Markus Merk (GER)   Attendance: 46.700

11-06-2000   GelreDome, Arnhem: Turkey – Italy   1-2 (0-0)
Turkey: Rüstü Reçber, Ogün Temizkanoglu (C), Fatih Akyel, Alpay Özalan, Tayfur Havutçu, Ümit Davala (76' Tugay Kerimoglu), Okan Buruk (88' Ergün Penbe), Tayfun Korkut, Abdullah Ercan, Sergen Yalçin (81' Arif Erdem), Hakan Sükür. (Coach: Mustafa Denizli (TUR)).
Italy: Francesco Toldo, Fabio Cannavaro, Alessandro Nesta, Paolo Maldini (C), Gianluca Zambrotta, Gianluca Pessotto (62' Mark Iuliano), Demetrio Albertini, Antonio Conte, Stefano Fiore (75' Alessandro Del Piero), Francesco Totti (83' Angelo Di Livio), Filippo Inzaghi. (Coach: Dino Zoff (ITA)).
Goals: Turkey: 1-1 Okan Buruk (62').
Italy: 0-1 Antonio Conte (52'), 1-2 Filippo Inzaghi (70' penalty).
Referee: Hugh Dallas (SCO)   Attendance: 22.500

14-06-2000   King Baudouin Stadium, Brussels: Italy – Belgium   2-0 (1-0)
Italy: Francesco Toldo, Fabio Cannavaro, Alessandro Nesta, Mark Iuliano, Gianluca Zambrotta (YC47), Paolo Maldini (C), Demetrio Albertini, Antonio Conte (YC44), Stefano Fiore (83' Massimo Ambrosini), Francesco Totti (63' Alessandro Del Piero), Filippo Inzaghi (77' Marco Delvecchio). (Coach: Dino Zoff (ITA)).
Belgium: Filip De Wilde, Lorenzo Staelens (C), Eric Deflandre, Joos Valgaeren, Nico Van Kerckhoven (46' Marc Hendrikx), Yves Vanderhaeghe, Gert Verheyen (67' Mbo Mpenza), Bart Goor, Marc Wilmots (YC70), Émile Mpenza, Branko Strupar (58' Luc Nilis). (Coach: Robert Waseige (BEL)).
Goals: Italy: 1-0 Francesco Totti (6'), 2-0 Stefano Fiore (66').
Referee: José María García- Aranda Encinar (ESP)   Attendance: 44.500

15-06-2000   Philips Stadion, Eindhoven: Sweden – Turkey   0-0
Sweden: Magnus Hedman, Gary Sundgren, Joachim Björklund, Olof Mellberg, Teddy Lucic, Johan Mjällby (C) (YC68), Niclas Alexandersson (63' Anders Andersson), Fredrik Ljungberg, Håkan Mild, Kennet Andersson (46' Jörgen Petterson), Henrik Larsson (78' Magnus Svensson). (Coaches: Lars Lagerbäck & Tommy Söderberg (SWE)).
Turkey: Rüstü Reçber, Ümit Davala (45' Tayfun Korkut), Ogün Temizkanoglu (C) (59' Tugay Kerimoglu), Fatih Akyel, Alpay Özalan, Hakan Ünsal, Suat Kaya (YC5), Okan Buruk, Mustafa Izzet (58' Sergen Yalçin), Arif Erdem, Hakan Sükür. (Coach: Mustafa Denizli (TUR)).
Referee: Dirk Zier Gerardus (Dick) Jol (HOL)   Attendance: 28.560

19-06-2000   King Baudouin Stadium, Brussels: Turkey – Belgium   2-0 (1-0)
Turkey: Rüstü Reçber, Alpay Özalan, Ogün Temizkanoglu (C), Fatih Akyel, Suat Kaya, Tayfun Korkut (YC50), Abdullah Ercan, Okan Buruk (77' Ergün Penbe), Tugay Kerimoglu (37' Tayfur Havutçu), Arif Erdem (87' Osman Özköylü (YC88)), Hakan Sükür. (Coach: Mustafa Denizli (TUR)).
Belgium: Filip De Wilde (RC84), Lorenzo Staelens (C), Eric Deflandre, Joos Valgaeren, Nico Van Kerckhoven, Yves Vanderhaeghe (YC44), Gert Verheyen (63' Branko Strupar), Bart Goor (59' Marc Hendrikx), Marc Wilmots, Émile Mpenza (YC63), Luc Nilis (79' Gilles De Bilde). (Coach: Robert Waseige (BEL)).
Goals: Turkey: 1-0 Hakan Sükür (45'), 2-0 Hakan Sükür (70').
Referee: Kim Milton Nielsen (DEN) (42' Günter Benkö (AUT))   Attendance: 43.000
(Following the red card for Filip De Wilde, the right-back Eric Deflandre took over in goal).

19-06-2000   Philips Stadion, Eindhoven: Italy – Sweden   2-1 (1-0)
Italy: Francesco Toldo, Ciro Ferrara, Paolo Negro, Mark Iuliano (46' Fabio Cannavaro), Gianluca Pessotto, Paolo Maldini (C) (42' Alessandro Nesta), Angelo Di Livio (64' Stefano Fiore), Luigi Di Biagio, Massimo Ambrosini, Alessandro Del Piero, Vincenzo Montella. (Coach: Dino Zoff (ITA)).
Sweden: Magnus Hedman, Olof Mellberg, Patrik Andersson (C), Joachim Björklund, Tomas Gustafsson-Antonelius (75' Kennet Andersson), Johan Mjällby (56' Daniel Andersson), Magnus Svensson (52' Niclas Alexandersson), Håkan Mild, Fredrik Ljungberg, Yksel Osmanovski, Henrik Larsson. (Coaches: Lars Lagerbäck & Tommy Söderberg (SWE)).
Goals: Italy: 1-0 Luigi Di Biagio (39'), 2-1 Alessandro Del Piero (88').
Sweden: 1-1 Henrik Larsson (77').
Referee: Vítor Manuel Melo Pereira (POR)   Attendance: 29.500

GROUP C

13-06-2000	Rotterdam	Spain – Norway	0-1 (0-0)
13-06-2000	Charleroi	Yugoslavia – Slovenia	3-3 (0-1)
18-06-2000	Amsterdam	Slovenia – Spain	1-2 (0-1)
18-06-2000	Liège	Norway – Yugoslavia	0-1 (0-1)
21-06-2000	Bruges	Yugoslavia – Spain	3-4 (1-1)
21-06-2000	Arnhem	Slovenia – Norway	0-0

FINAL STANDING

Pos	Team	Pld	W	D	L	GF	GA	GD	Pts
1	Spain	3	2	0	1	6	5	+1	6
2	Yugoslavia	3	1	1	1	7	7	0	4
3	Norway	3	1	1	1	1	1	0	4
4	Slovenia	3	0	2	1	4	5	-1	2

Spain and Yugoslavia qualified for the Quarter-finals.

13-06-2000   Stadion Feijenoord, Rotterdam: Spain – Norway   0-1 (0-0)
Spain: JOSÉ Francisco MOLINA Jiménez, MÍCHEL SALGADO Fernández (YC69), Fernando Ruiz HIERRO (C), Francisco "PACO" Jémez Martín, Agustín ARANZÁBAL Alkorta, JOSEBA Andoni ETXEBERRIA Lizardi (YC17) (72' GAIZKA MENDIETA Zabala), Josep GUARDIOLA i Sala, Juan Carlos VALERÓN Santana (80' IVÁN HELGUERA Bujía), Francisco Javier González Pérez "FRAN" (72' ALFONSO Pérez Muñóz), RAÚL González Blanco, Ismael URZÁIZ Aranda. (Coach: JOSÉ Antonio CAMACHO Alfaro (ESP)).
Norway: Thomas Myhre, Vegard Heggem, Henning Berg (C) (59' Dan Eggen), Bjørn Otto Bragstad, André Bergdølmo (YC32), Eirik Bakke, Bent Skammelsrud, Erik Mykland, Steffen Iversen (89' Vidar Riseth), Tore André Flo (71' John Carew), Ole Gunnar Solskjær. (Coach: Nils Johan Semb (NOR)).
Goal: Norway: 0-1 Steffen Iversen (65').
Referee: Gamal Mahmoud Ahmed El-Ghandour (EGY)   Attendance: 41.500

13-06-2000   Stade du Pays de Charleroi, Charleroi: Yugoslavia – Slovenia   3-3 (0-1)
Yugoslavia: Ivica Kralj, Ivan Dudic, Miroslav Djukic, Sinisa Mihajlovic (YC54,YC60), Albert Nadj, Dejan Stankovic (36' Dragan Stojkovic), Vladimir Jugovic, Slavisa Jokanovic, Ljubinko Drulovic, Predrag Mijatovic (C) (82' Mateja Kezman), Darko Kovacevic (52' Savo Milosevic). (Coach: Vujadin Boskov (SRB)).
Slovenia: Mladen Dabanovic, Zeljko Milinovic, Marinko Galic, Darko Milanic (C) (YC32), Dzoni Novak, Ales Ceh, Miran Pavlin (74' Zoran Pavlovic), Amir Karic (78' Milan Osterc), Zlatko Zahovic, Mladen Rudonja, Saso Udovic (64' Milenko Acimovic). (Coach: Srecko Katanec (SLO)).
Goals: Yugoslavia: 1-3 Savo Milosevic (67'), 2-3 Ljubinko Drulovic (70'), 3-3 Savo Milosevic (73').
Slovenia: 0-1 Zlatko Zahovic (23'), 0-2 Miran Pavlin (52'), 0-3 Zlatko Zahovic (57').
Referee: Vítor Manuel Melo Pereira (POR)   Attendance: 16.478

18-06-2000   Amsterdam ArenA, Amsterdam: Slovenia – Spain   1-2 (0-1)
Slovenia: Mladen Dabanovic, Zeljko Milinovic, Darko Milanic (C) (YC24) (68' Aleksander Knavs), Dzoni Novak (YC53), Ales Ceh, Miran Pavlin (YC11) (82' Milenko Acimovic), Amir Karic (YC85), Zlatko Zahovic, Mladen Rudonja, Saso Udovic (46' Milan Osterc). (Coach: Srecko Katanec (SLO)).
Spain: José Santiago CAÑIZARES Ruíz, MÍCHEL SALGADO Fernández, Fernando Ruiz HIERRO (C), ABELARDO Fernández Antuña, Agustín ARANZÁBAL Alkorta (YC62), JOSEBA Andoni ETXEBERRIA Lizardi, Josep GUARDIOLA i Sala (81' IVÁN HELGUERA Bujía (YC82)), Juan Carlos VALERÓN Santana (89' Vicente ENGONGA Maté), GAIZKA MENDIETA Zabala, RAÚL González Blanco, ALFONSO Pérez Muñóz (71' Ismael URZÁIZ Aranda). (Coach: JOSÉ Antonio CAMACHO Alfaro (ESP)).
Goals: Slovenia: 1-1 Zlatko Zahovic (59').
Spain: 0-1 RAÚL González Blanco (4'), 1-2 JOSEBA Andoni ETXEBERRIA Lizardi (60').
Referee: Markus Merk (GER)   Attendance: 51.300

18-06-2000   Stade Maurice Dufrasne, Liège: Norway – Yugoslavia   0-1 (0-1)
Norway: Thomas Myhre, Vegard Heggem (35' Stig Inge Bjørnebye), Dan Eggen, Bjørn Otto Bragstad, André Bergdølmo, Eirik Bakke (YC66) (76' Roar Strand), Bent Skammelsrud (C), Erik Mykland (YC31), Steffen Iversen (71' John Carew), Tore André Flo, Ole Gunnar Solskjær. (Coach: Nils Johan Semb (NOR)).
Yugoslavia: Ivica Kralj, Slobodan Komljenovic, Miroslav Djukic, Nisa Saveljic, Goran Djorovic, Dragan Stojkovic (C) (84' Albert Nadj), Vladimir Jugovic (YC81), Slavisa Jokanovic (YC28) (89' Dejan Govedarica (YC90+2)), Ljubinko Drulovic (YC81), Predrag Mijatovic (87' Mateja Kezman (RC88)), Savo Milosevic. (Coach: Vujadin Boskov (SRB)).
Goal: Yugoslavia: 0-1 Savo Milosevic (8').
Referee: Hugh Dallas (SCO)   Attendance: 27.250

21-06-2000   Jan Breydel Stadion, Bruges: Yugoslavia – Spain   3-4 (1-1)
Yugoslavia: Ivica Kralj, Slobodan Komljenovic (YC27), Miroslav Djukic, Sinisa Mihajlovic, Goran Djorovic (12' Jovan Stankovic (YC45)), Dragan Stojkovic (C) (YC56) (68' Nisa Saveljic (YC87)), Vladimir Jugovic (46' Dejan Govedarica), Slavisa Jokanovic (YC37,YC63), Ljubinko Drulovic, Predrag Mijatovic, Savo Milosevic. (Coach: Vujadin Boskov (SRB)).
Spain: José Santiago CAÑIZARES Ruíz, MÍCHEL SALGADO Fernández (46' Pedro MUNITIS Álvarez), ABELARDO Fernández Antuña (C), Francisco "PACO" Jémez Martín (64' Ismael URZÁIZ Aranda), SERGI BARJUÁN i Esclusa (YC62), GAIZKA MENDIETA Zabala, Josep GUARDIOLA i Sala, IVÁN HELGUERA Bujía, Francisco Javier González Pérez "FRAN" (22' JOSEBA Andoni ETXEBERRIA Lizardi), RAÚL González Blanco, ALFONSO Pérez Muñóz. (Coach: JOSÉ Antonio CAMACHO Alfaro (ESP)).
Goals: Yugoslavia: 1-0 Savo Milosevic (30'), 2-1 Dejan Govedarica (50'), 3-2 Slobodan Komljenovic (75').
Spain: 1-1 ALFONSO Pérez Muñóz (38'), 2-2 Pedro MUNITIS Álvarez (51'), 3-3 GAIZKA MENDIETA Zabala (90+4' penalty), 3-4 ALFONSO Pérez Muñóz (90+5').
Referee: Gilles Veissière (FRA)   Attendance: 26.611

21-06-2000   GelreDome, Arnhem: Slovenia – Norway   0-0
Slovenia: Mladen Dabanovic, Zeljko Milinovic, Marinko Galic (83' Milenko Acimovic), Aleksander Knavs, Dzoni Novak, Ales Ceh (C), Miran Pavlin (YC44), Amir Karic, Zlatko Zahovic, Mladen Rudonja, Ermin Siljak (86' Milan Osterc). (Coach: Srecko Katanec (SLO)).
Norway: Thomas Myhre, André Bergdølmo, Dan Eggen, Bjørn Otto Bragstad, Stig Inge Bjørnebye, Steffen Iversen, Erik Mykland (YC24), Ståle Solbakken (C), Ole Gunnar Solskjær (YC59), John Carew (61' Eirik Bakke, 82' Roar Strand), Tore André Flo. (Coach: Nils Johan Semb (NOR)).
Referee: Graham Poll (ENG)   Attendance: 21.000

GROUP D

11-06-2000	Bruges	France – Denmark	3-0 (1-0)
11-06-2000	Amsterdam	Netherlands – Czech Republic	1-0 (0-0)
16-06-2000	Bruges	Czech Republic – France	1-2 (1-1)
16-06-2000	Rotterdam	Denmark – Netherlands	0-3 (0-0)
21-06-2000	Liège	Denmark – Czech Republic	0-2 (0-0)
21-06-2000	Amsterdam	France – Netherlands	2-3 (2-1)

455

FINAL STANDING

Pos	Team	Pld	W	D	L	GF	GA	GD	Pts
1	Netherlands	3	3	0	0	7	2	+5	9
2	France	3	2	0	1	7	4	+3	6
3	Czech Republic	3	1	0	2	3	3	0	3
4	Denmark	3	0	0	3	0	8	-8	0

Netherlands and France qualified for the Quarter-finals.

11-06-2000   Jan Breydel Stadium, Bruges: France – Denmark   3-0 (1-0)
France: Fabien Barthez, Lilian Thuram, Marcel Desailly, Laurent Blanc, Bixente Lizarazu, Didier Deschamps (C), Emmanuel Petit, Zinédine Zidane, Youri Djorkaeff (58' Patrick Vieira), Nicolas Anelka (82' Sylvain Wiltord), Thierry Henry. (Coach: Roger Lemerre (FRA)).
Denmark: Peter Schmeichel (C), Søren Colding, René Henriksen, Michael Schjønberg (YC90), Jan Heintze, Morten Bisgaard (72' Thomas Gravesen), Stig Tøfting (72' Martin Jørgensen), Allan Nielsen, Jesper Grønkjær, Jon Dahl Tomasson (79' Mikkel Beck), Ebbe Sand. (Coach: Bo (Bosse) Johansson (SWE)).
Goals: France: 1-0 Laurent Blanc (16'), 2-0 Thierry Henry (64'), 3-0 Sylvain Wiltord (90+2').
Referee: Günter Benkö (AUT)   Attendance: 28.100

11-06-2000   Amsterdam ArenA, Amsterdam: Netherlands – Czech Republic   1-0 (0-0)
Netherlands: Edwin van der Sar, Michael Reiziger, Jaap Stam (75' Bert Konterman), Frank de Boer (C) (YC36), Giovanni van Bronckhorst (YC89), Clarence Seedorf (57' Ronald de Boer), Phillip Cocu, Edgar Davids, Boudewijn Zenden (78' Marc Overmars), Dennis Bergkamp, Patrick Kluivert. (Coach: Frank Rijkaard (HOL)).
Czech Republic: Pavel Srnícek, Tomás Repka (YC66), Karel Rada, Petr Gabriel, Radoslav Látal (RC90) (70' Radek Bejbl), Karel Poborsky (YC48), Tomás Rosicky, Pavel Nedved (YC22) (89' Vratislav Lokvenc), Jirí Nemec (C), Vladimír Smicer (83' Pavel Kuka), Jan Koller. (Coach: Jozef Chovanec (CZE)).
Goal: Netherlands: 1-0 Frank de Boer (89' penalty).
Referee: Pierluigi Collina (ITA)   Attendance: 50.833

16-06-2000   Jan Breydel Stadium, Bruges: Czech Republic – France   1-2 (1-1)
Czech Republic: Pavel Srnícek, Tomás Repka, Karel Rada, Petr Gabriel (YC14) (46' Milan Fukal), Radek Bejbl (49' Vratislav Lokvenc), Karel Poborsky, Tomás Rosicky (62' Marek Jankulovski (YC69)), Pavel Nedved, Jirí Nemec (C) (YC67), Vladimír Smicer, Jan Koller. (Coach: Jozef Chovanec (CZE)).
France: Fabien Barthez, Lilian Thuram (YC62), Marcel Desailly, Laurent Blanc, Vincent Candela, Didier Deschamps (C), Patrick Vieira, Emmanuel Petit (46' Youri Djorkaeff), Zinédine Zidane, Nicolas Anelka (55' Christophe Dugarry), Thierry Henry (89' Sylvain Wiltord). (Coach: Roger Lemerre (FRA)).
Goals: Czech Republic: 1-1 Karel Poborsky (35' penalty).
France: 0-1 Thierry Henry (7'), 1-2 Youri Djorkaeff (60').
Referee: Graham Poll (ENG)   Attendance: 27.243

16-06-2000   Stadion Feijenoord, Rotterdam: Denmark – Netherlands   0-3 (0-0)
Denmark: Peter Schmeichel (C), Søren Colding, René Henriksen, Michael Schjønberg (82' Thomas Helveg), Jan Heintze, Morten Bisgaard, Thomas Gravesen (67' Brian Steen Nielsen), Allan Nielsen (YC50) (61' Stig Tøfting), Jesper Grønkjær, Jon Dahl Tomasson, Ebbe Sand. (Coach: Bo (Bosse) Johansson (SWE)).
Netherlands: Edwin van der Sar (YC80) (89' Sander Westerveld), Michael Reiziger (YC10), Bert Konterman (YC56), Frank de Boer (C), Giovanni van Bronckhorst (YC4), Boudewijn Zenden, Phillip Cocu, Edgar Davids, Marc Overmars (62' Ronald de Boer), Dennis Bergkamp (76' Aron Winter), Patrick Kluivert. (Coach: Frank Rijkaard (HOL)).
Goals: Netherlands: 0-1 Patrick Kluivert (57'), 0-2 Ronald de Boer (66'), 0-3 Boudewijn Zenden (77').
Referee: Urs Meier (SUI)   Attendance: 51.117

21-06-2000   Stade Maurice Dufrasne, Liège: Denmark – Czech Republic   0-2 (0-0)
Denmark: Peter Schmeichel (C), Thomas Helveg, René Henriksen, Michael Schjønberg, Jan Heintze (68' Søren Colding), Bjarne Goldbæk, Brian Steen Nielsen, Stig Tøfting (YC56), Jesper Grønkjær (YC52), Jon Dahl Tomasson, Mikkel Beck (74' Miklos Molnar (YC85)). (Coach: Bo (Bosse) Johansson (SWE)).
Czech Republic: Pavel Srnícek, Milan Fukal (YC62), Karel Rada (YC69), Tomás Repka, Radek Bejbl (62' Marek Jankulovski), Karel Poborsky (YC52), Pavel Nedved, Jirí Nemec (C), Patrik Berger, Vladimír Smicer (79' Vratislav Lokvenc), Jan Koller (74' Pavel Kuka). (Coach: Jozef Chovanec (CZE)).
Goals: Czech Republic: 0-1 Vladimír Smicer (64'), 0-2 Vladimír Smicer (67').
Referee: Gamal Mahmoud Ahmed El-Ghandour (EGY)   Attendance: 18.000

21-06-2000   Amsterdam ArenA, Amsterdam: France – Netherlands   2-3 (2-1)
France: Bernard Lama, Christian Karembeu, Marcel Desailly (C) (YC75), Frank Leboeuf, Vincent Candela, Robert Pirès, Patrick Vieira (YC90) (90' Didier Deschamps), Johan Micoud, Christophe Dugarry (YC45) (67' Youri Djorkaeff), David Trézéguet, Sylvain Wiltord (80' Nicolas Anelka). (Coach: Roger Lemerre (FRA)).
Netherlands: Sander Westerveld, Paul Bosvelt, Jaap Stam, Frank de Boer (C), Arthur Numan, Marc Overmars (90' Peter van Vossen), Phillip Cocu (YC85), Edgar Davids (YC81), Boudewijn Zenden, Dennis Bergkamp (78' Aron Winter), Patrick Kluivert (60' Roy Makaay). (Coach: Frank Rijkaard (HOL)).
Goals: France: 1-0 Christophe Dugarry (8'), 2-1 David Trézéguet (31').
Netherlands: 1-1 Patrick Kluivert (14'), 2-2 Frank de Boer (51'), 2-3 Boudewijn Zenden (59').
Referee: Anders Frisk (SWE)   Attendance: 51.000

QUARTER-FINALS

24-06-2000   Amsterdam ArenA, Amsterdam: Turkey – Portugal   0-2 (0-1)
Turkey: Rüstü Reçber, Fatih Akyel, Ogün Temizkanoglu (C) (YC82) (84' Sergen Yalçin), Alpay Özalan (RC30), Tayfun Korkut, Ergün Penbe, Tayfur Havutçu, Okan Buruk (YC32) (62' Suat Kaya), Hakan Ünsal (YC56), Arif Erdem (62' Oktay Derelioglu), Hakan Sükür. (Coach: Mustafa Denizli (TUR)).
Portugal: VÍTOR Manuel Martins BAÍA (C), JORGE Paulo COSTA Almeida, FERNANDO Manuel Silva COUTO (YC37), DIMAS Manuel Marques Teixeira, Francisco José Rodrigues da Costa "COSTINHA" (YC41) (46' PAULO Manuel Carvalho de SOUSA (YC60)), PAULO Jorge Gomes BENTO, SÉRGIO Paulo Marceneiro CONCEIÇÃO, RUI Manuel César COSTA (YC39) (87' NUNO "CAPUCHO" Fernando Gonçalves Rocha), LUÍS Filipe Madeira Caeiro FIGO, JOÃO Manuel Vieira PINTO (YC29), NUNO "GOMES" Miguel Soares Pereira Ribeiro (75' Ricardo Manuel Andrade Silva SÁ PINTO). (Coach: HUMBERTO Manuel de Jesus COELHO (POR)).
Goals: Portugal: 0-1 NUNO "GOMES" Miguel Soares Pereira Ribeiro (44'), 0-2 NUNO "GOMES" Miguel Soares Pereira Ribeiro (56').
Referee: Dirk Zier Gerardus (Dick) Jol (HOL)   Attendance: 42.000

24-06-2000   King Baudouin Stadium, Brussels: Italy – Romania   2-0 (2-0)
Italy: Francesco Toldo, Fabio Cannavaro, Alessandro Nesta, Mark Iuliano, Gianluca Zambrotta, Paolo Maldini (C) (46' Gianluca Pessotto), Stefano Fiore, Demetrio Albertini (YC38), Antonio Conte (55' Luigi Di Biagio), Filippo Inzaghi, Francesco Totti (75' Alessandro Del Piero). (Coach: Dino Zoff (ITA)).
Romania: Bogdan Stelea, Iulian Filipescu, Miodrag Belodedici, Liviu Ciobotariu, Cristian Chivu, Florentin Petre, Constantin Galca (68' Ioan Lupescu), Gheorghe Hagi (C) (YC38,YC59), Dorinel Munteanu, Viorel Moldovan (54' Ionel Ganea), Adrian Mutu. (Coach: Emerich Jenei (ROM)).
Goals: Italy: 1-0 Francesco Totti (33'), 2-0 Filippo Inzaghi (43').
Referee: Vítor Manuel Melo Pereira (POR)   Attendance: 41.000

25-06-2000   Stadion Feijenoord, Rotterdam: Netherlands – Yugoslavia   6-1 (2-0)
Netherlands: Edwin van der Sar (65' Sander Westerveld), Paul Bosvelt (YC48), Jaap Stam, Frank de Boer (C), Arthur Numan, Marc Overmars, Phillip Cocu, Edgar Davids, Boudewijn Zenden (86' Ronald de Boer), Patrick Kluivert (60' Roy Makaay), Dennis Bergkamp. (Coach: Frank Rijkaard (HOL)).
Yugoslavia: Ivica Kralj, Slobodan Komljenovic, Miroslav Djukic, Sinisa Mihajlovic, Nisa Saveljic (56' Jovan Stankovic), Dragan Stojkovic (C) (52' Dejan Stankovic), Dejan Govedarica, Vladimir Jugovic, Ljubinko Drulovic (70' Darko Kovacevic), Predrag Mijatovic, Savo Milosevic. (Coach: Vujadin Boskov (SRB)).
Goals: Netherlands: 1-0 Patrick Kluivert (24'), 2-0 Patrick Kluivert (38'), 3-0 Dejan Govedarica (51' *own goal*), 4-0 Patrick Kluivert (54'), 5-0 Marc Overmars (78'), 6-0 Marc Overmars (90+1').
Yugoslavia: 6-1 Savo Milosevic (90+2').
Referee: José María García- Aranda Encinar (ESP)   Attendance: 47.700

25-06-2000   Jan Breydel Stadion, Bruges: Spain – France   1-2 (1-2)
Spain: José Santiago CAÑIZARES Ruíz, MÍCHEL SALGADO Fernández (YC64), ABELARDO Fernández Antuña (C), Francisco "PACO" Jémez Martín (YC71), Agustín ARANZÁBAL Alkorta, GAIZKA MENDIETA Zabala (57' Ismael URZÁIZ Aranda), Josep GUARDIOLA i Sala (YC61), IVÁN HELGUERA Bujía (77' GÉRARD López Segú), Pedro MUNITIS Álvarez (73' JOSEBA Andoni ETXEBERRIA Lizardi), ALFONSO Pérez Muñóz (YC55), RAÚL González Blanco. (Coach: JOSÉ Antonio CAMACHO Alfaro (ESP)).
France: Fabien Barthez, Lilian Thuram, Marcel Desailly, Laurent Blanc, Bixente Lizarazu, Patrick Vieira, Didier Deschamps (C) (YC60), Youri Djorkaeff, Zinédine Zidane, Thierry Henry (81' Nicolas Anelka), Christophe Dugarry. (Coach: Roger Lemerre (FRA)).
Goals: Spain: 1-1 GAIZKA MENDIETA Zabala (38' penalty).
France: 0-1 Zinédine Zidane (32'), 1-2 Youri Djorkaeff (44').
Referee: Pierluigi Collina (ITA)   Attendance: 26.614

SEMI-FINALS

28-06-2000   King Baudouin Stadium, Brussels: France – Portugal   2-1 (0-1, 1-1) (AET)
France: Fabien Barthez, Lilian Thuram, Marcel Desailly (YC39), Laurent Blanc, Bixente Lizarazu, Patrick Vieira (YC23), Didier Deschamps (C), Emmanuel Petit (87' Robert Pirès), Zinédine Zidane, Nicolas Anelka (72' Sylvain Wiltord), Thierry Henry (105' David Trézéguet). (Coach: Roger Lemerre (FRA)).
Portugal: VÍTOR Manuel Martins BAÍA (C), ABEL Luís da Silva Costa XAVIER, FERNANDO Manuel Silva COUTO, JORGE Paulo COSTA Almeida (YC55), DIMAS Manuel Marques Teixeira (YC62) (91' RUI JORGE Sousa Dias Macedo Oliveira), Francisco José Rodrigues da Costa "COSTINHA", José Luís da Cruz VIDIGAL (YC44) (61' PAULO Jorge Gomes BENTO), SÉRGIO Paulo Marceneiro CONCEIÇÃO, RUI Manuel César COSTA (78' JOÃO Manuel Vieira PINTO (YC117)), LUÍS Filipe Madeira Caeiro FIGO (YC54), NUNO "GOMES" Miguel Soares Pereira Ribeiro (RC116). (Coach: HUMBERTO Manuel de Jesus COELHO (POR)).
Goals: France: 1-1 Thierry Henry (51'), 2-1 Zinédine Zidane (117' penalty).
Portugal: 0-1 NUNO "GOMES" Miguel Soares Pereira Ribeiro (19').
Referee: Günter Benkö (AUT)   Attendance: 48.000
(France won the match with Zinédine Zidane's Golden Goal)

29-06-2000   Amsterdam ArenA, Amsterdam: Italy – Netherlands   0-0 (AET)
Italy: Francesco Toldo (YC38), Gianluca Zambrotta (YC15,YC34), Fabio Cannavaro, Alessandro Nesta, Mark Iuliano (YC16), Paolo Maldini (C) (YC45), Luigi Di Biagio (YC87), Demetrio Albertini (77' Gianluca Pessotto), Stefano Fiore (83' Francesco Totti), Alessandro Del Piero, Filippo Inzaghi (67' Marco Delvecchio). (Coach: Dino Zoff (ITA)).
Netherlands: Edwin van der Sar, Paul Bosvelt, Jaap Stam (YC93), Frank de Boer (C), Giovanni van Bronckhorst (YC75), Marc Overmars, Phillip Cocu (95' Aron Winter), Edgar Davids (YC50), Boudewijn Zenden (YC28) (77' Peter van Vossen), Patrick Kluivert, Dennis Bergkamp (86' Clarence Seedorf). (Coach: Frank Rijkaard (HOL)).
Referee: Markus Merk (GER)   Attendance: 51.300
Penalties: 1 Luigi Di Biagio   * Frank de Boer
              2 Gianluca Pessotto   * Jaap Stam
              3 Francesco Totti   1 Patrick Kluivert
              * Paolo Maldini   * Paul Bosvelt
(After extra time Italy won 3-1 on penalties)

FINAL

02-07-2000   Stadion Feijenoord, Rotterdam: France – Italy   2-1 (0-0, 1-1) (AET)
France: Fabien Barthez, Lilian Thuram (YC58), Marcel Desailly, Laurent Blanc, Bixente Lizarazu (86' Robert Pirès), Patrick Vieira, Didier Deschamps (C), Youri Djorkaeff (76' David Trézéguet), Zinédine Zidane, Thierry Henry, Christophe Dugarry (58' Sylvain Wiltord).
(Coach: Roger Lemerre (FRA)).
Italy: Francesco Toldo, Fabio Cannavaro (YC42), Alessandro Nesta, Mark Iuliano, Gianluca Pessotto, Paolo Maldini (C), Demetrio Albertini, Luigi Di Biagio (YC31) (66' Massimo Ambrosini), Stefano Fiore (53' Alessandro Del Piero), Francesco Totti (YC90), Marco Delvecchio (86' Vincenzo Montella). (Coach: Dino Zoff (ITA)).
Goals: France: 1-1 Sylvain Wiltord (90+3'), 2-1 David Trézéguet (103').
Italy: 0-1 Marco Delvecchio (55').
Referee: Anders Frisk (SWE)   Attendance: 48.200
(France won the match with David Trézéguet's Golden Goal)

*** France were European Champions ***

GOALSCORERS TOURNAMENT 1998-2000:

Goals	Players
12	RAÚL González Blanco (ESP), Zlatko Zahovic (SLO)
9	JOÃO Manuel Vieira PINTO (POR), Savo Milosevic (YUG)
8	Alan Shearer (ENG)
7	Oliver Bierhoff (GER)
6	Elvir Baljic (BOS), Jan Koller (CZE), Jon Dahl Tomasson (DEN), Paul Scholes (ENG), Ismael URZÁIZ Aranda (ESP), RUI Manuel César COSTA (POR), Ricardo Manuel Andrade Silva SÁ PINTO (POR), Valeri Karpin (RUS), Hakan Sükür (TUR)
5	Ivica Vastic (AUT), Patrik Berger (CZE), Vladimír Smicer (CZE), Fernando Ruiz HIERRO (ESP), JOSEBA Andoni ETXEBERRIA Lizardi (ESP), Youri Djorkaeff (FRA), Patrick Kluivert (HOL), Robbie Keane (IRL), Alon Mizrahi (ISR), Filippo Inzaghi (ITA), Tore André Flo (NOR), Ole Gunnar Solskjær (NOR), Adrian Ilie (ROM), Viorel Moldovan (ROM), Tayfur Havutçu (TUR), Serhiy Rebrov (UKR)
4	Elvir Bolic (BOS), Davor Suker (CRO), Milenko Spoljaric (CYP), LUIS ENRIQUE Martínez García (ESP), Sylvain Wiltord (FRA), Vilmos Sebök (HUN), Yossi Benayoun (ISR), Haim Revivo (ISR), Steffen Iversen (NOR), LUÍS Filipe Madeira Caeiro FIGO (POR), NUNO "GOMES" Miguel Soares Pereira Ribeiro (POR), SÉRGIO Paulo Marceneiro CONCEIÇÃO (POR), Ioan Ganea (ROM), Dorinel Munteanu (ROM), Vladimir Beschastnikh (RUS), Viktor Onopko (RUS), Billy Dodds (SCO), Henrik Larsson (SWE)

3	Alban Bushi (ALB), Tigran Yesayan (ARM), Christian Mayrleb (AUT), Pavel Nedved (CZE), Steve McManaman (ENG), Michael Owen (ENG), GAIZKA MENDIETA Zabala (ESP), JULEN GUERRERO López (ESP), Andres Oper (EST), Sergei Terehhov (EST), Jonathan Johansson (FIN), Joonas Kolkka (FIN), Mixu Paatelainen (FIN), Christophe Dugarry (FRA), Thierry Henry (FRA), David Trézéguet (FRA), Zinédine Zidane (FRA), Shota Arveladze (GEO), Marco Bode (GER), Ulf Kirsten (GER), Christian Ziege (GER), Nikos Machlas (GRE), Niall Quinn (IRL), Alessandro Del Piero (ITA), Christian Vieri (ITA), Marians Pahars (LAT), Andrejs Stolcers (LAT), Valdas Ivanauskas (LIT), Sasa Ciric (MCD), Artim Shakiri (MCD), Tomasz Iwan (POL), PAULO Sérgio Braga MADEIRA (POR), Don Hutchison (SCO), Stéphane Chapuisat (SUI), Kübilay Türkyilmaz (SUI), Johan Mjällby (SWE), Arif Erdem (TUR), Predrag Mijatovic (YUG)
2	Igli Tare (ALB), Armen Shahgeldyan (ARM), Harald Cerny (AUT), Edi Glieder (AUT), Andreas Herzog (AUT), Hannes Reinmayr (AUT), Gurban Gurbanov (AZE), Zaur Tagizade (AZE), Valentin Belkevich (BLS), Zvonimir Boban (CRO), Mario Stanic (CRO), Davor Vugrinec (CRO), Panayiotis Engomitis (CYP), Michalis Konstantinou (CYP), Pavel Kuka (CZE), Karel Poborsky (CZE), Martin Jørgensen (DEN), Brian Steen Nielsen (DEN), Ebbe Sand (DEN), Stig Tøfting (DEN), ALFONSO Pérez Muñóz (ESP), CÉSAR MARTÍN Villar (ESP), Francesco Javier González Pérez "FRAN" (ESP), Fernando MORIENTES Sánchez (ESP), Martin Reim (EST), Uni Arge (FAR), Zaza Janashia (GEO), Mehmet Scholl (GER), Konstantinos Frantzeskos (GRE), Giorgos Georgiadis (GRE), Vasilis Tsiartas (GRE), Frank de Boer (HOL), Marc Overmars (HOL), Boudewijn Zenden (HOL), Béla Illés (HUN), Gary Breen (IRL), Roy Keane (IRL), Rikhardur Dadason (ISL), Eyjölfur Sverrisson (ISL), Eyal Berkovic (ISR), Najwan Ghrayib (ISR), Avi Nimni (ISR), Antonio Conte (ITA), Diego Fuser (ITA), Francesco Totti (ITA), Vitalijs Astafjevs (LAT), Mihails Zemlinskis (LAT), Tomas Ramelis (LIT), Risto Bozinov (MCD), David Carabott (MLT), Igor Oprea (MOL), Øyvind Leonhardsen (NOR), Kjetil Rekdal (NOR), Jerzy Brzeczek (POL), Tomasz Hajto (POL), ABEL Luís da Silva Costa XAVIER (POR), Pedro Miguel Carreiro Resendes "PAULETA" (POR), Gheorghe Hagi (ROM), Laurentiu Rosu (ROM), Aleksandr Panov (RUS), Allan Johnston (SCO), Milenko Acimovic (SLO), Miran Pavlin (SLO), Peter Dubovsky (SVK), Martin Fabus (SVK), Vladimír Labant (SVK), Robert Tomaschek (SVK), Niclas Alexandersson (SWE), Oktay Derelioglu (TUR), Andriy Gusin (UKR), Serhiy Popov (UKR), Andriy Shevchenko (UKR), Serhiy Skachenko (UKR), Ljubinko Drulovic (YUG), Albert Nadj (YUG), Dejan Savicevic (YUG), Dejan Stankovic (YUG), Dragan Stojkovic (YUG)
1	Bledar Kola (ALB), Devis Mukaj (ALB), Altin Rraklli (ALB), EMILIANO GONZÁLEZ Arquez (AND), JESÚS Julián LUCENDO Heredia (AND), JUSTO Ruiz GONZALEZ (AND), Garnik Avalyan (ARM), Karapet Mikaelyan (ARM), Artur Petrosyan (ARM), Martin Amerhauser (AUT), Martin Hiden (AUT), Mirbaghir Isayev (AZE), Vyacheslav Lychkin (AZE), Vasili Baranov (BLS), Sergei Gurenko (BLS), Bart Goor (BEL), Émile Mpenza (BEL), Sergej Barbarez (BOS), Mehmed Kodro (BOS), Muhamed Konjic (BOS), Marko Topic (BOS), Daniel Borimirov (BUL), Rumen Hristov (BUL), Georgi Markov (BUL), Ivaylo Petkov (BUL), Hristo Stoichkov (BUL), Ivaylo Yordanov (BUL), Aljosa Asanovic (CRO), Dario Simic (CRO), Zvonimir Soldo (CRO), Marios Christodoulou (CYP), Sinisa

Gogic (CYP), Kostas Kosta (CYP), Vassos Melanarkitis (CYP), Miroslav
Baranek (CZE), Michal Hornák (CZE), Tomás Repka (CZE), Jan
Suchopárek (CZE), Pavel Verbír (CZE), Søren Frederiksen (DEN), Jan
Heintze (DEN), Allan Nielsen (DEN), Ole Tobiasen (DEN), Morten
Wieghorst (DEN), Gareth Southgate (ENG), Pedro MUNITIS Álvarez
(ESP), Arjo Arbeiter (EST), Sergei Hohlov-Simson (EST), Urmas Kirs
(EST), Raio Piiroja (EST), Maksim Smirnov (EST), Kristen Viikmäe (EST),
Hans Frodi Hansen (FAR), John Petersen (FAR), Sami Hyypiä (FIN), Jari
Litmanen (FIN), Janne Salli (FIN), Hannu Tihinen (FIN), Nicolas Anelka
(FRA), Laurent Blanc (FRA), Alain Boghossian (FRA), Vincent Candela
(FRA), Lilian Laslandes (FRA), Frank Leboeuf (FRA), Emmanuel Petit
(FRA), Robert Pirès (FRA), Archil Arveladze (GEO), Mikheil Kavelashvili
(GEO), Temur Ketsbaia (GEO), Dietmar Hamann (GER), Jens Jeremies
(GER), Oliver Neuville (GER), Nikos Liberopoulos (GRE), Demis
Nikolaidis (GRE), Andreas Niniadis (GRE), Marinos Ouzounidis (GRE),
Ronald de Boer (HOL), Pál Dárdai (HUN), Gábor Egressy (HUN), Miklós
Fehér (HUN), Ferenc Horváth (HUN), János Hrutka (HUN), István Pisont
(HUN), József Sebök (HUN), Thomas Sowunmi (HUN), Denis Irwin (IRL),
Mark Kennedy (IRL), Steve Staunton (IRL), Steinar Adolfsson (ISL), Eidur
Gudjohnsen (ISL), Thordur Gudjónsson (ISL), Brynjar Gunnarsson (ISL),
Hermann Hreidarsson (ISL), Runar Kristinsson (ISL), Larus Sigurdsson
(ISL), Yosef Abukasis (ISR), Walid Badir (ISR), Tal Banin (ISR), Alon
Hazan (ISR), Nir Sivilia (ISR), Enrico Chiesa (ITA), Marco Delvecchio
(ITA), Luigi Di Biagio (ITA), Stefano Fiore (ITA), Paolo Maldini (ITA),
Imants Bleidelis (LAT), Igors Stepanovs (LAT), Maris Verpakovskis
(LAT), Mario Frick (LIE), Martin Telser (LIE), Virginijus Baltusnikas
(LIT), Arturas Fomenka (LIT), Darius Maciulevicius (LIT), Marc Birsens
(LUX), Jean Vanek (LUX), Georgi Hristov (MCD), Igor Nikolovski
(MCD), Dzevded Sainovski (MCD), Goran Stavrevski (MCD), Srdjan
Zaharievski (MCD), Brian Said (MLT), Nicholas Saliba (MLT), Paul
Sixsmith (MLT), Hubert Suda (MLT), Serghei Epureanu (MOL), Vladimir
Gaidamasciuc (MOL), Alexandru Guzun (MOL), Oleg Sischin (MOL), Ion
Testemitanu (MOL), Iain Dowie (NIR), Neil Lennon (NIR), Keith Rowland
(NIR), Jeff Whitley (NIR), Henning Berg (NOR), Erik Hoftun (NOR), Ståle
Solbakken (NOR), Andrzej Juskowiak (POL), Rafal Siadaczka (POL), Piotr
Swierczewski (POL), Miroslaw Trzeciak (POL), Artur Wichniarek (POL),
Francisco José Rodrigues da Costa "COSTINHA" (POR), NUNO
"CAPUCHO" Fernando Gonçalves Rocha (POR), Cristian Chivu (ROM),
Liviu Ciobotariu (ROM), Catalin Munteanu (ROM), Florentin Petre (ROM),
Gheorghe Popescu (ROM), Ion Vladoiu (ROM), Dmitri Alenichev (RUS),
Aleksandr Mostovoy (RUS), Ilya Tsymbalar (RUS), Yegor Titov (RUS),
Yevgeniy Varlamov (RUS), Igor Yanovski (RUS), Craig Burley (SCO),
Colin Cameron (SCO), John Collins (SCO), Eoin Jess (SCO), Gary
McSwegan (SCO), Paul Ritchie (SCO), Aleksander Knavs (SLO), Milan
Osterc (SLO), Saso Udovic (SLO), Andy Selva (SMR), Patrick Bühlmann
(SUI), Sébastien Fournier (SUI), Alexandre Rey (SUI), Miroslav Karhan
(SVK), Lubomír Moravcik (SVK), Szilárd Németh (SVK), Miroslav Sovic
(SVK), Andreas Andersson (SWE), Kennet Andersson (SWE), Fredrik
Ljungberg (SWE), Okan Buruk (TUR), Ogün Temizkanoglu (TUR), Sergen
Yalçin (TUR), Yuriy Dmytrulin (UKR), Vitaliy Kosovskyi (UKR),
Vladyslav Vaschuk (UKR), Craig Bellamy (WAL), Chris Coleman (WAL),
Ryan Giggs (WAL), John Robinson (WAL), Dean Saunders (WAL), Kit

	Symons (WAL), Adrian Williams (WAL), Dejan Govedarica (YUG), Slobodan Komljenovic (YUG), Darko Kovacevic (YUG)
1 own goal	Arnold Wetl (AUT) for Spain, Mirsad Hibic (BOS) for Estonia, Fernando Ruiz HIERRO (ESP) for Austria, Sergei Hohlov-Simson (EST) for Scotland, Janek Meet (EST) for Czech Republic, Gela Shekiladze (GEO) for Norway, Rikhardur Dadason (ISL) for France, Modestus Haas (LIE) for Romania, Boban Babunski (MCD) for Yugoslavia, Yuri Kovtun (RUS) for Iceland, Mirko Gennari (SMR) for Spain, Mauro Valentini (SMR) for Israel, Dejan Govedarica (YUG) for Netherlands